THE COMPLETE GUIDE TO CARIBBEAN CRUISES

Portions of this book appear in *Fodor's Caribbean*.

Fodor's THE COMPLETE GUIDE TO CARIBBEAN CRUISES

Publisher: Amanda D'Acierno, *Senior Vice President*

Editorial: Arabella Bowen, *Executive Editorial Director*; Linda Cabasin, *Editorial Director*

Design: Fabrizio La Rocca, *Vice President, Creative Director*; Tina Malaney, *Associate Art Director*; Chie Ushio, *Senior Designer*; Ann McBride, *Production Designer*

Photography: Melanie Marin, *Associate Director of Photography*; Jessica Parkhill and Jennifer Romains, *Researchers*

Maps: Rebecca Baer, *Senior Map Editor*; David Lindroth; Mark Stroud, Moon Street Cartography, *Cartographers*

Production: Linda Schmidt, *Managing Editor*; Evangelos Vasilakis, *Associate Managing Editor*; Angela L. McLean, *Senior Production Manager*

Sales: Jacqueline Lebow, *Sales Director*

Marketing & Publicity: Heather Dalton, *Marketing Director*; Katherine Fleming, *Senior Publicist*

Business & Operations: Susan Livingston, *Vice President, Strategic Business Planning*; Sue Daulton, *Vice President, Operations*

Fodors.com: Megan Bell, *Executive Director, Revenue & Business Development*; Yasmin Marinaro, *Senior Director, Marketing & Partnerships*

Editorial Contributors: Carol M. Bareuther, Robyn Bardgett, Kate Bradshaw, David Dudenhoefer, Jessica Dupuy, Anna Evans, Kristin Finan, Kinsey Gidick, Marlise Kast-Myers, Lynda Lohr, Catherine MacGillivray, Jill Martin, Marie Elena Martinez, Steve Master, Elise Meyer, Amy Peniston, Todd Price, Vernon O'Reilly Ramesar, Patrick Rodgers, Laura Rodini, Heather Rodino, Paul Rubio, Ramona Settle, Jordan Simon, Summer Teal Simpson, Lan Sluder, Eileen Robinson Smith, Roberta Sotonoff, Jeffrey Van Fleet, Rob Young, Jane E. Zarem

Writer: Linda Coffman

Editor: Douglas Stallings

Production Editor: Carrie Parker

Fodor's is a registered trademark of Random House LLC. All rights reserved. Published in the United States by Fodor's Travel, a division of Random House LLC, New York, a Penguin Random House Company, and in Canada by Random House of Canada Limited, Toronto. No maps, illustrations, or other portions of this book may be reproduced in any form without written permission from the publisher.

5th Edition

ISBN 978-0-8041-4167-3

ISSN 1558-819X

SPECIAL SALES

This book is available at special discounts for bulk purchases for sales promotions or premiums. For more information, e-mail specialmarkets@randomhouse.com

PRINTED IN THE UNITED STATES OF AMERICA

10 9 8 7 6 5 4 3 2 1

CONTENTS

MAPS

ABOUT
THIS GUIDE

Fodor's Recommendations

Everything in this guide is worth doing—we don't cover what isn't—but exceptional sights, hotels, and restaurants are recognized with additional accolades. **Fodor's**Choice★ indicates our top recommendations; and **Best Bets** call attention to notable hotels and restaurants in various categories. Care to nominate a new place? Visit Fodors.com/contact-us.

Trip Costs

We list prices wherever possible to help you budget well. Hotel and restaurant price categories from **$** to **$$$$** are noted alongside each recommendation. For hotels, we include the lowest cost of a standard double room in high season. For restaurants, we cite the average price of a main course at dinner or, if dinner isn't served, at lunch. For attractions, we always list adult admission fees; discounts are usually available for children, students, and senior citizens.

Hotels

Our local writers vet every hotel to recommend the best overnights in each price category, from budget to expensive. Unless otherwise specified, you can expect private bath, phone, and TV in your room. For expanded hotel reviews, facilities, and deals visit Fodors.com.

Restaurants

Unless we state otherwise, restaurants are open for lunch and dinner daily. We mention dress code only when there's a specific requirement and reservations only when they're essential or not accepted. To make restaurant reservations, visit Fodors.com.

Credit Cards

The hotels and restaurants in this guide typically accept credit cards. If not, we'll say so.

Top Picks
★ **Fodor's**Choice

Listings
- ⊠ Address
- ⊠ Branch address
- ☎ Telephone
- 🖷 Fax
- ⊕ Website
- ✉ E-mail
- 🖼 Admission fee
- ☉ Open/closed times
- Ⓜ Subway
- ✛ Directions or Map coordinates

Hotels &
Restaurants
- 🏨 Hotel
- ⬎ Number of rooms
- ⵜⵓⵍ Meal plans
- ✕ Restaurant
- ⌕ Reservations
- 👔 Dress code
- ▭ No credit cards
- Ⓢ Price

Other
- ⇨ See also
- ☞ Take note
- 🏌 Golf facilities

BEST OF CRUISING

Best Cruise Line: Mainstream

- **Carnival Cruise Lines.** With its adults-only Serenity area, water park–style slides, and Vegas-style entertainment (not to mention all the other activities), the line's ships are designed to appeal to the widest range of travelers.

- **Norwegian Cruise Line.** Noted for their family-friendly accommodations, specialty dining, and outstanding entertainment, the line gets high marks from passengers of all ages.

- **Royal Caribbean International.** The line appeals to families with its high-energy entertainment, extensive sports facilities, youth programs, and even nurseries for toddlers and babies.

Best Cruise Line: Premium

- **Princess Cruises.** Sophisticated styling includes piazza-style atriums, many different specialty restaurants, quiet enclaves, and fast-paced dance clubs. Spas are noted for their facilities and service.

- **Holland America Line.** Traditional cruise enthusiasts find that HAL hits the right note with gracious, art-filled ships that also include all the latest high-tech gadgets.

- **Celebrity Cruises.** For sheer beauty and excellent cuisine, Celebrity ships deliver a quality experience in modern surroundings.

Best Cruise Line: Luxury

- **Compagnie du Ponant.** Expect an exceptional, intimate experience aboard luxurious, all-inclusive yacht cruises to inaccessible worldwide locations and remote ports of call.

- **Crystal Cruises.** Luxurious appointments and a high level of service are hallmarks of the ultra-luxe line's nearly all-inclusive ships.

- **SeaDream Yacht Club.** Luxury-minded small ships cater to guests' every wish as they sail to ports of call that the big ships can't visit.

- **Seabourn Cruise Line.** Divine dining options, posh suite accommodations, and personalized service set these ships apart.

- **Silversea Cruises.** Butlers assigned to every suite add an extra level of pampering on luxuriously appointed vessels.

- **Regent Seven Seas Cruises.** In the luxury segment Regent offers the most all-inclusive cruises, even including all shore excursions in the fare.

Best Cruise Ship: Large

- ***Crystal Serenity,* Crystal Cruises.** With overnight calls in many ports and some of the best enrichment programs at sea, *Crystal Serenity* offers an upscale experience on a larger scale than other luxury lines.

- ***Celebrity Reflection,* Celebrity Cruises.** *Celebrity Reflection* offers a dozen places to dine, with half of them included in the fare, and a serene atmosphere for total relaxation.

- ***MSC Divina,* MSC Cruises.** *MSC Divina* offers a thoroughly international cruise that appeals to a wide range of passengers, both American and European.

Best Cruise Ship: Medium

- ***Azamara Quest,* Azamara Club Cruises.** Destination-oriented and totally refurbished in 2013, *Azamara Quest* is noteworthy for offering fine dining and a complimentary destination event on every sailing.

- ***Oceania Riviera,* Oceania Cruises.** The newest ship in the fleet, *Riviera* is the choice of foodies and destination collectors.

- *Seven Seas Navigator,* **Regent Seven Seas Cruises.** With complimentary gourmet specialty restaurants and shore excursions, *Seven Seas Navigator* is a stylish choice for discerning travelers.

- *Oceania Regatta,* **Oceania Cruises.** With only 684 passengers onboard, *Regatta* scores high marks for its country-club-casual ambiance in intimate spaces with beautifully appointed accommodations, unobtrusive service, and fine dining.

Best Cruise Ship: Small

- *Seabourn Sojourn,* **Seabourn Cruise Line.** The 450-passenger ship evokes a club-like atmosphere, scoring high points for impeccable service, elegant suites, and excellent recreational facilities.

- *Silver Spirit,* **Silversea Cruises.** The largest ship in the Silversea fleet has more space for high-end specialty restaurants, expansive decks and lounges, and a theater for superior entertainment.

- *SeaDream I,* **SeaDream Yacht Club.** *SeaDream I* offers casual luxury on a truly yacht-like vessel with superb food and service.

Best Nontraditional Ships

- *Tere Moana,* **Paul Gauguin Cruises.** The newest addition to the fleet carries the cruise line's hospitable spirit of Polynesia into the Caribbean. Literally "Ocean Traveler," *Tere Moana* emphasizes unique itineraries that larger ships cannot offer by exploring hidden ports throughout the Caribbean.

- *Royal Clipper,* **Star Clippers.** As unlike a traditional cruise ship as possible, *Royal Clipper* sails from Barbados on voyages to off-the-beaten track destinations in the Grenadines and Windward Islands. In addition to the daily raising of the sails, a highlight of every cruise occurs when engines are turned off and passage is made under full sail.

- *Wind Surf,* **Windstar Cruises.** While the sails overhead only give the illusion of actual "sailing," they add to the ambiance of voyages to unspoiled regions of the Caribbean where barbeques are held on pristine beaches and voyages usually include an overnight port call.

Best Regular Outside Cabins

- *MSC Divina,* **MSC Cruises.** Consistently spacious and offering plenty of storage space, MSC's standard cabins are ideal for two and surprisingly roomy for families.

- *Noordam,* **Holland America Line.** Comfort is key, and all cabins have DVD players, flat-screen televisions, lighted magnifying makeup mirrors, and comfortable bedding.

- *Wind Surf,* **Windstar Cruises.** The nautical feel and efficiency of Windstar cabins get our nod for "ship-y" and ultimately ship-shape quarters.

Best Inside Cabins

- *Eurodam,* **Holland American Line.** The large inside cabin category measures in at a whopping 284 square feet—some of the largest such accommodations at sea.

- *Norwegian Epic,* **Norwegian Cruise Line.** Studio cabins for solo travelers aboard *Norwegian Epic* are the ideal accommodations for singles who don't have to pay a supplement to sail.

- *Disney Fantasy,* **Disney Cruise Line.** Designed with families in mind, *Disney Fantasy*'s inside cabins have all the space needed for a comfortable cruise and "virtual" portholes for a view of the sea.

Best Suites

■ *Queen Mary 2,* **Cunard Line.** Two Grand Duplex apartments with butler service each cover 2,250 square feet on two levels connected by a gently curving staircase.

■ *Norwegian Epic,* **Norwegian Cruise Line.** High atop *Norwegian Epic,* suites in The Haven are idyllic retreats with an entire private deck, restaurant, and lounge.

■ *Riviera,* **Oceania Cruises.** Spanning the width of the ship, Owner's Suites are decorated in furnishings by Ralph Lauren Home and have a private fitness room and two whirlpool tubs to relax in.

■ *Silver Spirit,* **Silversea Cruises.** Owner's Suites are the largest on board and have an ideal midship location, stylish furnishings, and plenty of room to entertain guests.

■ *MSC Divina,* **MSC Cruises.** The Yacht Club suites occupy a private enclave served by butlers and a concierge with an exclusive lounge, pool, restaurant, and bar area. Wines and liquor are complimentary.

Best Beds

■ **Holland America Line.** The Mariner's Dream bed on every Holland America ship is a Sealy 9-inch innerspring mattress with a pillow top and additional plush-foam comfort layers.

■ **Oceania Cruises.** Oceania has outfitted its entire fleet with high-quality Euro-top mattresses, 350-thread-count Egyptian cotton linens, silk-cut duvets, and goosedown pillows.

■ **Royal Caribbean Line.** A 9-inch spring mattress with pillow top sets the stage for 220-thread-count cotton blend sheets and cushy microfiber pillows on most ships in the fleet.

Best Bathrooms

■ **Regent Seven Seas Cruises.** The marble bathrooms with separate shower and full-size tub on *Seven Seas Navigator* are totally pampering.

■ **Seabourn Cruises.** Seabourn's bath amenities are ultradeluxe. Just ask, and your attendant will draw your bath using luxury products of your choice.

■ **Silversea Cruises.** Double vanities, marble-clad showers, separate tubs, and fluffy, oversized towels are luxurious appointments, even in standard suites. Top suites add whirlpool tubs.

Best Regular Dining Room Cuisine

■ **Holland America Line.** Under the leadership of Master Chef Rudi Sodamin, the culinary staff of Holland America Line creates dishes high in quality and taste.

■ **Regent Seven Seas Cruises.** Creative dishes and wines chosen to complement all menus are a hallmark of Regent Seven Seas. Service is attentive, but not hovering or intrusive.

■ **SeaDream Yacht Club.** A true gourmet meal is hard to come by on land, let alone at sea, but SeaDream chefs accomplish just such a feat. With only 112 passengers on board, every meal is individually prepared.

Best Specialty Restaurants

■ **Lawn Club Grill, Celebrity Cruises.** Celebrity's newest ships house six specialty restaurants and cafés, including the interactive Lawn Club Grill where you can prepare your own pizza or grilled steak under the chef's watchful eye.

■ **Silk Road, Crystal Cruises.** Silk Road receives consistently rave reviews for the beautifully prepared dishes, including ultrafresh sushi. Presentation is as beautiful as the food.

■ **Todd English, Cunard Line.** Aboard *Queen Mary 2,* cuisine in this restaurant, named for the award-winning chef and restaurateur, is as otherworldly as the exotic Moroccan surroundings in which it is served.

Best Ships for Romantics

■ *Silver Spirit,* **Silversea Cruises.** In the care of the conscientious staff, including a butler, guests want for nothing—leaving couples all the time they need to concentrate on one another.

■ *SeaDream I & II,* **SeaDream Yacht Club.** Luxurious, intimate settings include snug alcoves for private dining alfresco and suite bathrooms have a to-die-for shower large enough for two with multijet massaging showerheads.

■ *Wind Surf,* **Windstar Cruises.** For sheer enchantment, you can't beat billowing white sails overhead and the thrill of skimming across the sea. Cozy and inviting, with warm, unobtrusive service, the ship has a coed sauna.

Best Ships for Families

■ *Norwegian Epic,* **Norwegian Cruise Line.** Facilities for teens and tots have to be seen to be believed. Pools, playrooms, and discos are elaborate, and even picky kids should find the active programs enticing.

■ *Independence of the Seas,* **Royal Caribbean International.** Well-conceived areas for children and teens, plus sports facilities that invite family members to play together, are bonuses for parents who want to spend quality family time with the kids.

■ *Disney Fantasy,* **Disney Cruise Line.** Designed from the keel up with family fun in mind, Disney Fantasy delivers all the entertainment and age-appropriate activities and facilities.

Best Ships for Spa Lovers

■ *Celebrity Reflection,* **Celebrity Cruise Line.** Attractive, tranquil decor and a full complement of wraps, massages, and deluxe treatments are features of the AquaSpa. The expansive Persian Garden thermal suite includes cold and hot rooms as well as a Turkish hammam.

■ *Norwegian Epic,* **Norwegian Cruise Line.** Massages and facials take a back seat to the elaborate pleasures of a soothing whirlpool and indoor relaxation areas worthy of a fine European spa resort.

■ *Queen Mary 2,* **Cunard Line.** Canyon Ranch operates the utterly decadent spa on this ship. In addition to offering a wide range of massages and spa treatments, the Aqua Therapy Center facilities are the finest afloat.

Best Ships for Fitness Fanatics

■ *MSC Divina,* **MSC Cruises.** Gyms afford a view of the sea from nearly every stair-stepper, treadmill, and exercise cycle.

■ *Ruby Princess,* **Princess Cruises.** Stationary bicycles, treadmills, and other machines are positioned for wide-open views of sea and sky. Laps in the swim-against-the-current pool also provide a stimulating workout.

■ *Independence of the Seas,* **Royal Caribbean.** Huge and well-equipped gyms and exercise classes almost take a backseat to full-size outdoor basketball courts, rock-climbing walls, and the unique experience of ice-skating at sea.

Best Ships for Entertainment

■ *Norwegian Epic,* Norwegian Cruise Line. NCL's largest ship offers some of the most elaborate and unique entertainment afloat, including Blue Man Group, a dueling-piano bar, and a Cirque du Soleil–style dinner show.

■ *Oasis & Allure of the Seas,* **Royal Caribbean Cruise Line.** In addition to Broadway musicals and guest entertainers, Royal Caribbean's megasize ship offers Aqua Theater performances featuring dancers, divers, and acrobats in a 137-gallon specially designed pool.

Best Ships for Travelers with Disabilities

■ *Celebrity Reflection,* **Celebrity Cruises.** Although accommodations designed for accessibility are some of the best at sea, equally as desirable are the line's "easy" shore excursion options.

■ *Nieuw Amsterdam,* **Holland America Line.** At the forefront of accessible cruise travel, the ship has a variety of services for passengers with mobility, sight, and breathing impairments. All shore tenders are equipped with wheelchair-accessible platforms.

■ *Royal Princess,* **Princess Cruises.** Not only are accessible staterooms and suites available in a wide range of categories but there is also shore-side wheelchair access to appropriate tours on vehicles equipped with lifts.

Best Ships for Shoppers

■ *Celebrity Reflection,* **Celebrity Cruises.** With more than a dozen shops and boutiques to browse, *Celebrity Reflection* provides the most extensive retail therapy at sea. There's little you won't find.

■ *Crystal Serenity,* **Crystal Cruises.** Signature apparel, sportswear, formal wear, and luxury cosmetics are all available in thousands of square feet of exclusive boutiques.

■ *Emerald Princess,* **Princess Cruise Line.** Should your luggage be lost or delayed, you're in luck. These shipboard boutiques are stocked with nearly everything you need to carry on in style.

Best Ships for Service

■ *Eurodam,* **Holland America Line.** Holland America Line's Filipino and Indonesian stewards and servers go out of their way to provide gracious service with a sincere smile and genuine warmth.

■ *SeaDream I,* **SeaDream Yacht Club.** A Corona with no lime, extra juice in your rum punch: whatever your preference, it will be remembered by all servers on board. They seem to network behind the scenes to ensure perfection.

■ *Seven Seas Navigator,* **Regent Seven Seas Cruises.** Staff efforts almost go unnoticed, yet even out-of-the-ordinary requests are handled with ease. Butlers provide personalized service to guests in the top-category suites.

■ *Silver Spirit,* **Silversea Cruises.** The mostly European staff don't seem to understand the word no. Every attempt is made to satisfy even the most unusual request by butlers assigned to every suite.

Best Enrichment Programs

■ **Crystal Cruises.** Discover your inner artist by learning to play piano in the Creative Learning Institute. Expert instruction and lectures can be found in the areas of arts and entertainment, business and technology, lifestyle and wellness, and wine and food.

■ **Cunard Line.** After a trip through the heavens in the only planetarium at sea, on board *Queen Mary 2* you can attend lectures presented by guest speakers on wide-ranging topics or delve into classes ranging from computer instruction to wine appreciation.

■ **Holland America Line.** Guest lecturers cover a wide range of topics and the

Culinary Arts Center offers hands-on cooking classes, gourmet food presentations, and tasting events.

Best Ports for Strolling

- **Grand Cayman, Cayman Islands.** If you aren't interested in a trip to Stingray City, the shops of George Town are just a short stroll from the dock.

- **Key West, Florida.** If you're lucky enough to dock at Mallory Square or Pier B, Old Town's major attractions are all within easy walking distance.

- **Nassau, Bahamas.** Those who don't want to head to the beach or Atlantis can stroll around or shop in historic Nassau, which is readily accessible by foot from the cruise terminal.

Best Daylong Excursions

- **Antigua Safari, Antigua.** A 4x4 adventure in an open-air Land Rover explores the most beautiful parts of the island, where regular bus excursions cannot go. The off-road expedition passes through Antigua's rainforest with its lush tropical plants and proceeds along the breathtaking coast before arriving at a stunning beach for a refreshing swim. Drivers act as guides, and refreshing rum punch is included.

- **Mayan Ruins at Chacchoben, Costa Maya.** If your ship calls at Costa Maya, the ruins are about a one- hour bus ride to the border of Belize. The first sight is a fully excavated pyramid-shaped temple rising out of the jungle. After a walk through the rainforest, the path to two more temples requires climbing rock steps carved into the hillside. At the top, not only do you get close to the temples, but there is also a treetop view of the rainforest.

- **Rainforest Aerial Tram, Puerto Limón.** If you're lucky enough to call in Puerto Limón, Costa Rica, hightail it out of the less than charming port to experience the lush rainforest canopy upclose. A daylong excursion will include the tram, lunch, and a hike.

Best Ports for Shoppers

- **Charlotte Amalie, St. Thomas, USVI.** The bargains aren't as plentiful here as they used to be, but the selection of merchandise is staggering, from electronics to delicately embroidered linens. Buy cigarettes and liquor here for the lowest prices in the Caribbean.

- **Philipsburg, St. Maarten.** The length of Front Street is a shopper's haven with jewelry, clothing, and artworks being the best buys—all at duty-free prices. A special treat is Guavaberry Liqueur, the locally made folk liqueur of St. Maarten, available only on the island.

- **Road Town, Tortola, BVI.** Though not known for deals—goods are not duty-free—shops here offer a great variety of art by local and Caribbean artists, island wear, beach bags, and hand-crafted jewelry. Foodies can spice up their cuisine at Sunny Caribbee, where a wide selection of spices, rubs, and sauces are available.

Best Ports for History Lovers

- **Key West, Florida.** Among the historic sites in the southernmost port in the United States are Audubon House, where many of naturalist John James Audubon's engravings are displayed; The Little White House, vacation home of President Harry Truman; and Ernest Hemingway's home and studio, where he wrote some of his famous works.

- **San Juan, Puerto Rico.** Old San Juan is packed with churches, fortresses, historic homes, and museums. And it's all served by a free bus that hits the major sights, stopping a few short blocks from the main cruise pier.

■ **Willemstad, Curaçao.** Museum Kurá Hulanda contains a rich collection of artifacts and exhibits that follow the heritage of islanders from Africa to the Caribbean. One in particular that touches visitors is a life-size reconstruction of a slave ship's hold.

Best Ports for Beach Lovers

■ **Antigua.** Antiguans boast that their homeland has a beach for every day of the year. While this may be an exaggeration, the sugary, white-sand beaches are lovely, and all are open to the public. Half Moon Bay and Runaway Beach are popular for swimming and sunning; Morris Bay is a desirable snorkeling spot; and Dickensen Bay Beach north of St. John's has watersports concessions, beach chair rentals, and beach bars.

■ **St. John, USVI.** Trunk Bay is so popular that it's likely to be crowded, but it's gorgeous and the underwater trail near the shore is perfect for snorkeling. Caneel Bay is known for attracting the rich and famous its seven distinct beach areas. Hawksnest Beach is another popular public beach.

■ **Virgin Gorda, BVI.** The pools around The Baths are excellent for swimming and snorkeling, and there are full facilities there. A trail from The Baths leads to Devil's Bay National Park, where a 15-minute trek through boulders and coastal vegetation ends at a secluded coral beach.

Best Ports for Active Excursions

■ **Dominica.** A 40-minute drive through Dominica's lush rainforest on twisting mountain roads passes waterfalls, banana plantations, and fields of pineapple and bright tropical flowers, ending at the launch point of the river tubing adventure at Layou River Gorge. After floating down the river in wooden-bottomed tubes past rapids and rocks, trays of coconut, mango, and pineapple and a potent punch made with local rum and freshly squeezed native fruits awaits.

■ **Belize.** River-tubing trips explore isolated caves where the ancient Maya were said to have conducted religious ceremonies. The current moves your inner tube as you leisurely drift along the waterways connecting jungle caverns.

■ **St. Maarten.** One of the Caribbean's most popular cruise activities is the America's Club 12-Meter Regatta. Not only is it a thrill to sail on one of these super-fast yachts, but you can join in to crew the vessel for a real America's Cup–style race. This one should definitely be booked on board as it is always sold out once you go ashore.

Best Ports for Food Lovers

■ **Grand Cayman, Cayman Islands.** A short stroll from the dock where cruise-ship tenders dock puts you in George Town, where there are any number of excellent restaurants.

■ **St. Barth.** Though by no means an inexpensive endeavor, lunch in one of the island's many picturesque outdoor cafés is a joy and may make you feel as if you are in the French Riviera instead of the Caribbean.

■ **St. Maarten.** Grand Case is one of the Caribbean's culinary capitals, offering a host of excellent waterside restaurants serving French and Caribbean cuisine. Those on a budget can simply visit the *lolos,* stands set up to serve excellent local food.

Best Ports for Rum Lovers

■ **St. Croix, USVI.** The Virgin Islands are the home of Cruzan Rum, one of the finest in the Caribbean. In St. Croix you can tour the factory, drink samples, and bring home a bottle or three.

■ **San Juan, Puerto Rico.** It goes without saying that Bacardí is one of the world's best known and most popular rums. Tour the factory during a port call in San Juan, and sample some unique cocktails created by their mixologists. You can reach it independently by a cheap ferry service followed by a short shared taxi ride.

■ **Barbados.** Mount Gay is one of the Caribbean's oldest rums, having been distilled in Barbados since 1703. You can tour the company's visitors center and have a tasting (and even lunch if you wish).

Best Ports for Budget Cruisers

■ **Grand Turk.** You only need to step off the cruise pier to enjoy a beautiful beach or a purpose-built cruise port with shops and a giant Margaritaville restaurant. Or you can hop in a taxi for the short drive into Cockburn Town, where you can stroll the quaint capital of the Turks & Caicos Islands.

■ **Curaçao.** Nearly everything of interest in Willemstad is within walking distance from the port, and there is no charge for crossing from one side of town to the other on the ferry or on the Queen Emma Bridge, which swings open to allow ships to pass.

■ **Panama Canal Zone.** The experience of passing through the locks from the Caribbean to Gatun Lake takes place entirely on board your ship. If you're just doing a stop in Panama City, a cheap taxi can take you to the Miraflores Locks.

Best Ports to Take a Day Sail

■ **St. Barth.** With its excellent coral reef, St. Barth is an ideal island to take a catamaran sail and anchor in a sheltered cove for snorkeling and swimming.

■ **Tortola, BVI.** You can hop on a sailboat and reach any number of excellent snorkeling spots in just a few hours of sailing, one reason the British Virgin Islands is one of the world's top sailing destinations.

■ **St. Lucia, USVI.** Most ships dock in Castries, so to see the Pitons—the island's twin-mountain symbol—a sail along the coastline to Soufrière is the way to go for the best views and photo opps.

CRUISING:
THE BASICS

The words *value* and *cruise* may not sound like they belong in the same sentence, let alone the same conversation, but if you haven't considered a cruise vacation lately, you might be surprised. A cruise can be less expensive than staying home and a lot more relaxing. Mundane, everyday chores are forgotten as crewmembers take care of everything from cleaning your cabin to washing the dishes. Breakfast in bed? Just ask and it's yours. A cruise sounds too good to be true, but it isn't. And sailing away on your ship of dreams is more affordable—and enjoyable—than ever.

Over lunch at the Lido buffet on our first cruise, I scanned the ship's daily newsletter and found myself in seagoing heaven before I'd even gone out to sea. Not only would I not be cooking or cleaning, but I had my choice of fun and exciting ways to spend the days and evenings on board. Morning walks on the promenade deck led to aerobics before breakfast. After lunch there were lectures and trivia games. Every night was like Saturday night—dressing for dinner, seeing a show, and dancing until the wee hours. My husband Mel's agenda was a bit different. His sea days were spent lounging at the pool. Clearly, he enjoyed relaxing while the captain did the driving.

We found ourselves attended to by an excellent service staff in first-class surroundings and fed multiple-course meals, all for a single, affordable fare. Our only obligation was to enjoy ourselves as the luxurious cruise ship sped from one port of call to the next. Once ashore, we took in the sights, shopped, and discovered a variety of Caribbean cultures. Instead of uncomfortable island-hopping by plane—been there, done that—we visited several destinations while our needs were catered to in high style.

Mel and I enjoy meeting new people, and we made friends for life on our first cruise. Many more years—and cruises—have followed, and

CARIBBEAN CRUISING MILESTONES

1966	1972	1975
Norwegian Caribbean Line (now Norwegian Cruise Line) begins offering seven-night cruises from then-obscure Port of Miami.	**Carnival Cruise Lines'** "Fun Ship" fleet is launched with a single converted ocean liner that runs aground off Miami's Dodge Island during its inaugural voyage.	*The Love Boat* television series, starring Princess Cruises' *Pacific Princess*, introduces the idea of cruise vacations to millions of weekly fans.

we've met more people along the way. We still receive holiday greetings from a newlywed couple who conceived their first child during a rather fateful honeymoon cruise. Over the years, I have met hundreds of other passengers through Internet websites I have hosted, and it's always a pleasure to answer their questions and possibly see them on a cruise ship. My love of cruises has forever changed my travel habits. All clichés aside, there is nothing like a cruise.

WHAT IS CRUISING?

Ocean travel in the early decades of the 20th century was just another means of getting to a destination. Ships were the only practical way of traveling from one continent to another. Even so, venerable ocean liners such as the *Normandie* offered an occasional round-trip pleasure cruise to exotic locales like Brazil for the pre-Lenten Carnaval.

However, early cruisers didn't have the comforts of today as they steamed toward the unfamiliar. As on *Normandie,* it was common to find air-conditioned comfort only in ships' first-class dining rooms. However, they could at least find relief from Rio's heat in one of that era's few outdoor swimming pools at sea. (At that time, if an ocean liner had a permanent swimming pool at all, it was often indoors and deep in the hull.)

Carnival Cruise Line executives like to reminisce about the tiny gyms on their early ships, which were converted ocean liners, and then point to how far ship designs have evolved. I remember those ships well. It was even difficult to find the casino on Carnival's first Fun Ship, the *Mardi Gras,* let alone the indoor swimming pool. You won't find claustrophobic natatoriums or ill-equipped, windowless gyms on today's modern cruise ships. Designed for contemporary travelers and tastes, these vessels carry passengers amid conveniences unheard of in the heyday of the North Atlantic ocean liner or even on board the earliest ships permanently dedicated to cruising.

There's much to like on cruise ships these days. Nearly everything about cruises has changed, from the presence of air-conditioning and roomier cabins to the ever longer list of activities. In the old days, entertainment was staid, and there was no cruise director to lead the merriment. In

---

1978 After sailing for less than a decade, **Royal Caribbean** "stretches" *Song of Norway*—cutting it in half and inserting a new middle section.

1979 In an unprecedented move, **Norwegian Cruise Line** purchases the SS *France* and rechristens it SS *Norway,* the largest cruise liner to sail from Miami at the time.

1988 **Holland America Line,** one of the most revered names in passenger shipping, is purchased by Carnival Corporation.

truth, passengers were usually required to entertain themselves, with after-dinner cigars, brandy, and cards for the gentlemen in a smoking room, conversation for the ladies in a separate drawing room.

As cruising evolved, swimming pools and pool games became common, and the position of cruise director grew to be the most visible in the hierarchy of shipboard staff. These days, as the average age of cruise passengers drops, more attention is focused on keeping people active. Gyms and spas have grown in size, with today's emphasis on healthy living. Menus now offer lighter fare as well as vegetarian dishes.

By night, lavish production shows, cabaret acts, comedy shows, and classical concerts are staged for your enjoyment. Discos and dance clubs rock into the early morning hours. And on most ships there's no cover charge or ticket to purchase—all are included in your fare. No one dresses to dine every night anymore, and even traditional formal dinners can be skipped if the casual dining option is more to your liking.

If you ask six couples what they enjoyed most about their Caribbean cruise vacation, you are likely to get a dozen different responses. Nearly everyone raves about the meals, an opportunity to sample unfamiliar dishes with the assurance that if you don't like something, you can get something else simply by asking. The gracious, nonstop service and attention to detail often come as a surprise to first-time cruisers, who may not be used to a server taking their tray at the end of the buffet line and showing them to a table. Many cruisers appreciate the ease of unpacking only once and settling into accommodations that visit a variety of destinations.

As you might have guessed, it's the unique social atmosphere that appeals most to me. I rarely encounter the same level of sociability at resorts Mel and I visit, where we typically live out of a suitcase and seldom meet fellow travelers.

Today's cruise ships are lively and luxurious floating resorts that offer something to satisfy the expectations of almost everyone, but each cruise line and cruise ship is different. Most people find that selecting the right cruise is a bit more complicated than booking a land-based resort vacation.

CARIBBEAN CRUISING MILESTONES (CONT.)

| 1990 | With a refitted vessel from its budget Fantasy Cruises line, the Chandris family of Greek shipping prominence launches **Celebrity Cruises**, a premium cruising option. | 1991 | A boyhood dream for Michael Krafft becomes a cruise line reality when **Star Clippers** sails onto the scene with the tallest clipper ships ever built. | 1998 | The *Magic* and *Wonder* of Walt Disney's beloved resort vacations go to sea with the launch of **Disney Cruise Line**. |

1

The more you know about cruise travel, the better prepared you will be when the time comes to make your choices. Unfortunately, although cruises have come a long way from the days when ships were viewed as the travel pick of well-heeled, newlywed, or nearly dead passengers, misconceptions still abound. Most disappointments—and the inevitable complaints—are the result of misunderstandings that stem from unmet expectations. Having the right information debunks the most persistent myths.

My goal is to help you make the right decisions so the cruise you select will be the best fit for you. If you're taking the family, you don't want to sail on a ship without a good children's program. Nor would you be happiest on a ship without a casino if your favorite vacation spot up to now has been Las Vegas. You need the tools to select the proper wardrobe and desirable accommodations. In this book, we'll do our comparison shopping together. We'll give you the dimensions of every cabin category and outline the amenities of every ship plying Caribbean waters so you can pick the cruise ship that fits your needs. Planning to sail away is fun, and I want you to enjoy cruises as much as I do.

Now, let's get started.

WHAT'S ON THE SHIP?

Some people fear they won't know the ropes and will stand out as a first-timer. Although some passengers are certain to be repeat cruisers, the majority are in the same boat, so to speak, and will be cruising for the first time. Keep in mind that most of today's larger cruise ships have the same basic arrangement. Once on board, you will encounter a reception area and shore excursion desk, very likely centrally located in a multideck atrium or lobby. Explore a bit farther, and you will discover lounges, a main restaurant, buffet restaurant, showroom, Internet–business center, boutiques, photo shop, library, spa, and a gym. Cabins are lined up along quiet passageways. And that is just inside.

Out on open decks there are swimming pools, hot tubs, bars, and a plethora of deck chairs. You're likely to find a deck dedicated to sports with courts for volleyball and basketball. Some ships take the facilities up a notch and include waterslides, miniature golf, in-line skating

2001	As a testament to their 20-year appeal, the diminutive Sea Goddess ships are rebuilt in luxurious fashion for the **SeaDream Yacht Club**.	2003	Carnival Corporation acquires **Princess Cruises**, foiling an attempt by Royal Caribbean to become the world's largest cruise company.	2009	**Royal Caribbean** launches the world's largest purpose-built cruise ship, *Oasis of the Seas*. Its sister ship, *Allure of the Seas*, made its debut in 2010.

tracks, rock-climbing walls, and even a surf simulator or bowling alley. For joggers there's the outdoor promenade deck or a designated track for running and walking. Children and teens have their own playrooms, swimming pools, video arcades, and, in some cases, lounges and party rooms. The hottest trend at sea is an adults-only retreat complete with spa-style amenities. Deck plans and signage point the way to all the features. Still, it may take a couple of hours—or possibly even a couple of days—to get your bearings.

WHAT A CRUISE COSTS

More than 16 million people embarked on cruises in 2012, and most of them sailed on ships that were designed and launched in the previous decade. A massive shipbuilding program commenced in the early 1990s, and with so many new ships—more than 100 new ships were introduced between 2000 and the end of 2012—cruise lines had many berths to fill and did so by pricing their cruises attractively. Fares in recent years, which could be found as low as $50 per person, per night, are reminiscent of those offered in the 1980s. Even factoring in inflation, you can see that cruises are actually selling for less today than they did 25 years ago, even as the ships and amenities are far superior.

It's no secret that the entire travel industry has suffered tremendously during the recent global recession. With flights more expensive and with fewer seats, more Americans take to the highways on domestic road trips. Cruise lines are in an enviable position compared to resorts, to which travelers might have to fly; if passengers can't fly to traditional embarkation ports, ships can be moved to where passengers are able to reach them by car, and in the past decade, the cruise industry has done exactly that. Continuing low cruise fares, new ships, and accessible home ports have combined to make cruises more popular than ever.

But—and there's always a but—the economic downturn that began in late 2008 also put a damper on cruise travel, which has resulted in continuing low fares, particularly on many Caribbean routes. New, more feature-filled ships, including Royal Caribbean's massive *Oasis of the Seas* and *Allure of the Seas* and Norwegian Cruise Line's *Norwegian Breakaway* have been able to capture higher fares, which has been good for the cruise industry. But the good news for cruise consumers is that deals are still out there—even on some of the newest ships, which continue to be priced less than they were in 1990, especially in the Caribbean. As you will see, when you crunch the numbers to compare the total cost of a cruise to that of a traditional resort vacation, a cruise compares favorably.

ADD-ONS

Most cruises are *not* all-inclusive and have never been. Although low fares have brought cruise vacations within the realm of reality for many people who could only fantasize about them in the past, those same rock-bottom fares can cause consternation to passengers on tight budgets when they factor in the extras. Increasingly, cruise lines devise creative ways to entice passengers to spend additional money once on board their dream ships. In the industry, it's called "onboard revenue enhancement," and *charge, charge, charge* is the mantra; if you heed it, you can see the cost of your cruise vacation rising faster than a helicopter over a Caribbean island volcano.

Although your cruise ticket price includes a lot—accommodations, food, entertainment, taxes, and port charges are covered in the ticket price—there are also many add-ons. Air fare, tips, shore excursions, travel insurance, passports, cocktails, soft drinks, and even bottled water can increase the bottom line. Some of these add-ons (spa visits, alcoholic drinks, specialty restaurants) are purely optional and can be easily avoided; others (tips, travel to the port, and passports) cannot. Holding down the add-on expenses is not easy; after all, the cruise is your vacation, which you deserve, and you want it to be special. But there are ways to minimize those costs. To get the true picture of what you can expect before your budget floats out of sight, you must consider those extras.

In addition to transportation to your port of embarkation, which is usually not included in the cruise fare these days, there are a few costs that are often overlooked but that add to your overall cruise costs. Before leaving home, consider the cost of passports or passport cards (now required for some travel to the Caribbean) and travel insurance (optional, but highly recommended).

ADDING UP THE COST OF THE EXTRAS

The majority of onboard extras are strictly discretionary. For instance, whether to purchase alcoholic beverages or cappuccino is your choice, and no one will blink an eye if you shy away from the casino or spa. However, it's unlikely you will be able to avoid all extras. Bottled water seems to be an unavoidable expense these days, and tipping isn't optional. Although the extras greatly enhance the overall experience of a cruise, they can quickly add up and exceed your initial budget if you're not careful. Even if you're frugal, you should expect to pay at least $100 (and often much more) beyond the cost of your cruise for tips and incidentals.

Cruise passengers often find themselves in something of a catch-22 situation: you must either pay a higher fare up front for a more-luxurious cruise or pay for nonincluded items later. Just as you may compare the cost of a cruise vacation to a resort vacation, consider the cost of a less-inclusive mainstream cruise versus the cost of a more-inclusive luxury cruise. In addition to the added comfort, you may decide—by determining and budgeting for your personal priorities in advance—that there's not so much difference between the cost of a truly all-inclusive luxury cruise and a less-inclusive mainstream cruise, particularly if you prefer suite accommodations. Of course, it all depends on the cabin category you book and your individual spending habits. Read the fine print in your chosen cruise line's literature (either a brochure or website), and you should face no spending bombshells once you are on board.

What Things Cost On Board

Here's a list of what some of the most popular extras cost on board a ship.

Alcoholic coffee drinks: $6–$8

Alternative restaurants: $4–$75 per person

Beer: $5–$6

Bingo: $5–$10 per card for multiple games in each session

Bottled water: $2.50–$4

Casino gambling: 1¢–$10 for slot machines; $5 and up for table games

Cell phone calls: $2.50–$5 per minute

Cocktails: $6–$10

Dry cleaning: $7–$11 per piece (50% of these prices for pressing)

Gratuities: $11–$15 per person, per day

Internet access: 35¢–$1 per minute

Laundry: $1–$10 per piece

Medical treatment: $75 and up, depending on treatment

Personal training: $75–$90 per hour

Photographs: $9–$25 each

Salon services: $30–$100

Shore excursions: $25–$110

Sodas: $2–$2.50

Spa treatments: $125–$199

Special exercise classes: $10–$12 per class

Specialty ice cream and coffee: $4–$6

Video arcade games: $1–$2 per game

Wine by the glass: $7–$9

CUTTING YOUR BAR TAB DOWN TO SIZE

Bar drinks and wine typically cost about what you would expect to pay at a nice lounge or restaurant in a resort or big city in the United States. Unless you really want a souvenir glass to take home, order tropical umbrella drinks in regular glasses—the keepsake glasses cost extra. Wine by the bottle is a more economical choice at dinner than ordering it by the glass, and any wine you don't finish will be kept for you and served the next night. Gifts of wine or champagne ordered from the cruise line (either by you, a friend, or your travel agent) can be taken to the dining room. Wine from any other source will incur a corkage fee that can run up to $25 per bottle.

Whether to BYOB is a hotly debated issue. Many cruise lines look the other way at soft drinks and bottled water toted aboard by arriving passengers, but most lines do not allow passengers to bring alcoholic beverages on board. Duty-free liquor purchased ashore will be collected when you return to the ship and held until the last night aboard, when it's delivered to your cabin. Similarly, liquor purchases from the ship's own duty-free store will be held until the last night. You may be allowed to bring aboard a bottle of wine or champagne for a special occasion in your carry-on when you initially board the ship, but do not even think of carting on a case of beer.

1

Tap water is always plentiful and free. Why not bring along a powdered drink mix for a flavorful and refreshing change? An insulated cup or mug makes it easy to prepare and keep chilled—cabin stewards fill ice buckets in passenger staterooms at least twice a day. You can also order up a pitcher of fruit juice with your room service breakfast and keep what's left for later; juices are a healthy choice and complimentary with meals (there's usually a charge for juice if you order it at the bar).

In lounges, request the less-expensive bar-brand mixed drinks or the reduced-price drink of the day. On some ships discounted beverage cards for unlimited fountain soft drinks are available for approximately $5 a day for children and $6.50 a day for adults. Be sure to attend the Captain's Welcome Aboard Party, where complimentary drinks are often served. If you're a repeat passenger, do not miss the repeaters' get-together for the same reason.

SHIP SIZES

Although all ships share certain similarities, there's one distinct difference that can be as important as any other single factor in whether you enjoy your cruise: ship size. Choosing the right ship is quite possibly the most important decision you can make when booking your cruise, and your lifestyle and expectations should be major considerations when making this choice. This is one time when size matters and can make or break your vacation.

The size of the ship affects every other aspect of the cruise: entertainment and dining options, the kind of activities you'll be offered, and even the ports of call you can visit. It stands to reason that the larger the ship, the more room there is for features like alternative dining venues, huge show lounges and casinos, elaborate swimming pools, and expansive spa and fitness facilities. This has to be balanced by the fact that there are intriguing ports of call that only smaller ships can visit because of docking or tendering considerations. Keep your priorities in mind while you're examining cruise line brochures.

Large ships start at approximately 70,000 tons and go up in size from there. These are the ships that have more than 1,800 passengers and often carry as many as 3,600-plus cruisers. They are the megaships that include the bells and whistles modern passengers have come to associate with a cruise. Larger ships offer nonstop activities designed for all interests; they have high-energy Las Vegas– or Broadway-style music revues; a wider variety of restaurants and lounges; dance clubs and discos; well-rounded children's programs; and more. Royal Caribbean's extra-large megaship vessels even include rock-climbing walls, ice-skating rinks, miniature golf courses, and surfing simulators. Carnival's megaships have some of the largest casinos and most lavish spas and exercise facilities afloat.

Midsize ships range from approximately 25,000 to 70,000 tons and carry between 400 and 1,700 passengers. There's no lack of entertainment and features on these ships, but they tend not to have some of the more extravagant facilities. Alternative dining is generally an

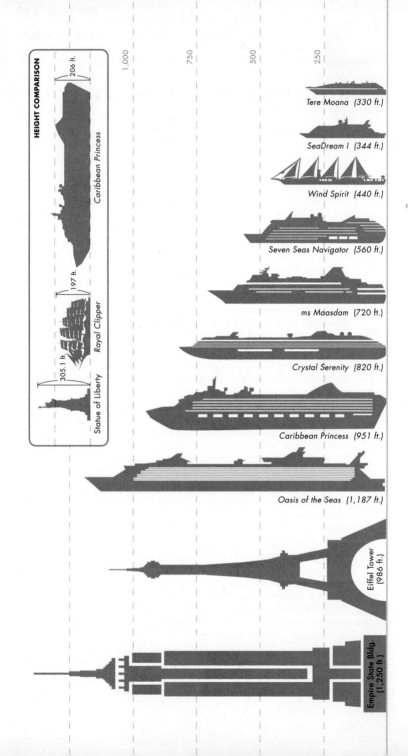

HEIGHT COMPARISON

206 ft.

Caribbean Princess

197 ft.

Royal Clipper

305.1 ft.

Statue of Liberty

1,000

750

500

250

Tere Moana (330 ft.)

SeaDream I (344 ft.)

Wind Spirit (440 ft.)

Seven Seas Navigator (560 ft.)

ms Maasdam (720 ft.)

Crystal Serenity (820 ft.)

Caribbean Princess (951 ft.)

Oasis of the Seas (1,187 ft.)

Eiffel Tower (986 ft.)

Empire State Bldg. (1,250 ft.)

1

option, and in addition to the traditional daytime activities, there will be ample nightlife, a casino, shows, and a spa. By necessity, they are usually on a smaller scale but no less satisfying. Although there are more ships this size in premium and luxury fleets, some older Carnival ships also fall within this range. The most upscale midsize ships have a higher passenger-space ratio, meaning there's more room per person than on a larger ship. It's usually not difficult to find a deck chair by the pool on a sunny day. Smack in the middle of this range is Regent Seven Seas Cruise's *Seven Seas Voyager,* which has one of the highest passenger-space ratios on the seas; if you cruise on this ship, you may wonder where everyone is.

Small ships range from megayachts and sailing vessels of less than 5,000 tons to ships of about 25,000 tons. These ships may have as few as 70 passengers or as many as 350. On smaller vessels, passengers tend to entertain themselves rather than be entertained. Lounges on small ships are more intimate, and the only entertainment is usually done cabaret-style. Intriguing itineraries are more often the focus of the voyage and often include some ports of call such as St. Barth or Bequia, which are not suited for larger ships. Restaurants often accommodate all guests in a single open seating. On board luxurious small ships, gracious service and fine dining are paramount, and your table is likely to be set with signature china, European crystal, and heavy silver, and covered with Belgian linens. Good things do come in small packages; a well-kept secret is that Windstar Cruises' superyacht *Wind Surf* has one of the largest spas at sea relative to her size.

TYPES OF CRUISE LINES

Just as cruise ships differ by size and style, so do the cruise lines themselves, and finding a cruise line that matches your personality is as important as finding the right ship. Some cruise lines cater to families, others to couples, active singles, and even food and wine aficionados. Each cruise line has a unique personality that will appeal to different lifestyles. Selecting the right one can mean the difference between struggling with unmet expectations and enjoying the vacation of a lifetime.

Some of the differences are subtle, but today's cruise lines still fall into three basic categories: Mainstream, Premium, and Luxury.

MAINSTREAM LINES

What you'll find. Mainstream cruise lines usually have a little something for everyone:

■ Ships tend to be the big, bigger, and biggest at sea, carrying the highest number of passengers per available space.

■ Ship decor runs the gamut from glitz and glitter to nautical kitsch.

■ Staterooms range from inside cabins for three and four to a variety of outside cabin configurations with or without balconies. Top-notch suites may or may not come with numerous extra amenities.

■ Schedules include enough activities to keep even the most hyperactive passenger content. Expect to find deck sports and pool games, team

CRUISING FAMILY TREE

CARNIVAL CORPORATION

Carnival Cruise Lines: Founded in 1972 by Israeli-born Ted Arison, who got his feet wet at Norwegian Caribbean Line, Carnival's "Fun Ship" fleet of 21 ships is now the largest afloat.

Costa Cruises: Costa's name first appeared in 1854, when Italian founder Giacomo Costa began trading olive oil by sea, and grew to include passenger ships in 1947. Carnival completed a buy-out of the cruise line in 2000.

Cunard Line: Samuel Cunard founded the venerable line in 1839 to carry mail and passengers between Great Britain and North America. After a succession of owners, the company's stability was assured when Carnival bought it in 1998.

Holland America Line: Since 1873, the Dutch company has roamed the globe, carrying passengers and goods worldwide and operating its first vacation cruise in 1895. In 1989 the premium line was purchased by Carnival.

Princess Cruises: Founded by Stanley McDonald in 1965 to carry cruisers from California to Mexico, Princess burst into prominence in 1977 as star of television's *The Love Boat*. In 2003 Princess joined the list of Carnival-owned cruise lines.

The Yachts of Seabourn: Norwegian industrialist and luxury cruise pioneer Atle Brynestad founded Seabourn in 1987. Partially owned by Carnival since 1991, the line was acquired in full by Carnival in 1999.

DISNEY CORPORATION

Disney Cruise Line: When Disney launched their first ship in 1998, the cruise line had an instant winner with family fun and entertainment for all ages. Even Walt Disney's most beloved character, Mickey Mouse, sails on every cruise.

ROYAL CARIBBEAN CRUISES, LTD.

Azamara Club Cruises: Launched in 2007, Azamara is a deluxe premium line with two mid-size ships that are ideal for discerning travelers who want a cruise experience that approaches luxury without the price of luxury.

Celebrity Cruises: Greek shipping tycoon John D. Chandris founded premium Celebrity Cruises in 1989, in essence replacing a previous budget venture, Chandris-Fantasy Cruises. Celebrity was acquired by Royal Caribbean Cruises, Ltd. in 1997.

Royal Caribbean International: In 1969 a partnership of three Norwegian shipping firms made Wisconsin native Edwin Stephan's dream a reality, and a cruise line composed of modern, purpose-built ships was formed.

STAR CRUISES/APOLLO MANAGEMENT

Norwegian Cruise Line: Established in 1966 by Norwegian Knut Kloster, the former Norwegian Caribbean Line introduced regularly scheduled Caribbean cruises from Miami. Co-owned by Star Cruises and Apollo Management, NCL continues to be an industry innovator.

NIPPON YUSEN KAISHA (NYK)

Crystal Cruises: Founded in 1988 by NYK, one of the world's largest shipping companies, Crystal Cruises strives to offer its passengers the best large, luxury cruise-ship experience in the world.

MEDITERRANEAN SHIPPING COMPANY

MSC Cruises: Established in Naples in 1995, MSC is the family-run cruise division of the world's second-largest container shipping operator. Old hands in the industry, the company began operating the Starlauro line in the 1980s.

PRESTIGE CRUISE HOLDINGS

Regent Seven Seas Cruises: RSSC was formed in 1994 when Diamond Cruises merged with Seven Seas Cruises. Previously operating just one ship each, the resulting company has grown to be one of the world's largest luxury cruise lines.

Oceania Cruises: Founded by cruise industry veterans Joe Watters and Frank Del Rio in 2003, Oceania's fleet is made up of mid-size premium vessels that offer sailings to worldwide destinations in comfortable style.

INDIVIDUALLY OWNED

Compagnie du Ponant: Founded in 1988 by Jean-Emmanuel Sauvée, this French cruise line operates four small, luxurious, yachtlike vessels that offer destination-intensive cruises all over the world.

Paul Gauguin Cruises: Pacific Beachcomber SC, the largest luxury hotel and cruise company in French Polynesia, purchased the beloved *Paul Gauguin* from Regent Seven Seas Cruises in 2010 and launched a second ship, *Tere Moana*, in 2012.

SeaDream Yacht Club: Seabourn founder Atle Brynestad teamed up with former Seabourn President & CEO Larry Pimentel to establish SeaDream in 2001. The mega-yachts formerly sailed under the Sea Goddess name.

Silversea Cruises: The former owners of Sitmar Cruises, the Lefebvre family of Rome, launched Silversea in 1994 to deliver the most luxurious cruises on the highest-quality ships at sea.

Star Clippers: In 1990, Swedish entrepreneur Mikael Krafft realized his boyhood dream by founding Star Clippers, a modern cruise line that re-creates the golden age of sail with meticulously detailed tall sailing ships.

Windstar Cruises: Created in 1984 to offer an alternative to traditional big-ship cruises, Windstar first sailed in 1986. The unique line was acquired in 2011 by Xanterra Holding Corp., which has operated in the hospitality and leisure industry for more than 100 years.

trivia and scavenger-hunt contests, bingo, golf lessons, karaoke, fitness classes, a high-tech gym, and full-service spa.

■ Entertainment tends to be high-energy, Las Vegas–style production shows; you can always find a variety of lounges and dance clubs; and in the liveliest piano bars everyone might be encouraged to sing along.

■ Large spas accompany fully equipped gyms; jogging tracks are common, as are multiple swimming pools and hot tubs. Adults-only retreats and accommodations with spa amenities are a growing trend.

■ Some lines still offer traditional dining, with two assigned seatings in the main restaurant for dinner. But increasingly, most mainstream cruise lines have introduced variations of open seating dining and alternative restaurant options that allow passengers to dine when and with whom they please. Choice is the keyword on these ships, and you can always find something to eat, either from 24-hour room service or a variety of locations. One thing is typical, though: although generous in quantity, food is often likened to banquet-style fare.

■ Service is friendly but not necessarily polished.

■ Ideal for families, these cruise lines offer some of the most extensive programs for children and teens.

What won't you find? As a rule, sodas and bottled water are not complimentary.

Who's on board? First-timers, repeat passengers, young and old alike. Mainstream cruise lines are ideal for anyone who is looking for a fun and exhilarating vacation.

PREMIUM LINES

What you'll find. Premium lines usually offer a more subdued atmosphere and refined style:

■ Ships tend to be newer midsize to large vessels that carry fewer passengers than mainstream ships and have a more spacious feel.

■ Decor is usually more glamorous and subtle, with toned-down colors and extensive original art.

■ Staterooms range from inside cabins for three or four to outside cabins with or without balconies to suites with numerous amenities, including butlers on some lines.

■ In addition to traditional cruise activities, on-board lectures are common. Port talks often include history and cultural topics, in addition to the usual shopping advice.

■ Production shows are somewhat more sophisticated, and gentlemen hosts on some sailings keep single ladies dancing the night away.

■ An exercise or beauty regimen is a pleasure in the fully outfitted gyms and spas. Adults-only retreats and accommodations with spa amenities are a growing trend.

■ Most ships offer both two traditional assigned seatings for dinner as well as variations of open seating dining and alternative restaurant options. High marks are afforded the quality cuisine and presentation. Many ships have upscale bistros or specialty restaurants, which typically require reservations and command an additional charge. But nowadays, there's also usually a more casual dining option available.

■ Attentive service is polished and unobtrusive.

■ Programs for children and teens are well run but not as comprehensive as those found on mainstream ships because there aren't usually as many children on board.

What won't you find? The cruise staff won't bombard you with noise—announcements are kept to a minimum.

Who's on board? First-timers and experienced passengers who enjoy a more upscale experience in lower-key surroundings. Premium lines attract families, singles, and groups; however, expect the passengers to be older on average, particularly on sailings longer than 7 to 10 days.

LUXURY LINES

What you'll find. The air on these deluxe vessels is as rarified as the champagne and caviar:

■ Ships range from megayachts for only a hundred or so privileged guests to midsize vessels, which are considered large for this category. Space is so abundant that you might wonder where the other passengers are hiding.

■ Tasteful and elegant surroundings often include such touches as authentic antiques and priceless art collections.

■ Spacious staterooms are frequently all suites. On the newest ships, all cabins feature an ocean view or balcony, not to mention a high-tech entertainment center with CD or MP3 players and TVs with a DVD. Expect designer bath toiletries, fine linens, and fresh-cut flowers. Some lines include complimentary in-suite bar setups for all categories; butlers attend to the needs of guests in exclusive top-category suites.

■ Enrichment programs with celebrity and scholarly guest speakers and culinary classes taught by famous chefs augment traditional shipboard activities. Libraries are well stocked with books, music, and movies to borrow.

■ Evening entertainment varies by ship size, from cabaret to stylish production shows to none at all. Luxury-minded passengers tend to entertain themselves.

■ Health clubs and spas are fully equipped and staffed with professionals who bring new meaning to indulgence. After jogging or a serious workout, guests can wind down with a swim or savor a relaxing soak in generously sized hot tubs.

■ Open seating is the norm, and guests dine where and with whom they please during dinner hours. Top international chefs are tapped for their culinary expertise in designing menus to please the palate. Meals are prepared to order with the freshest high-quality ingredients and are presented with flair, just like in a top restaurant at home. Complimentary wines accompany meals on most high-end lines.

■ At this level, the service staffs anticipate their guests' desires, and it's rare that a special request goes unfulfilled.

■ Small, adult-oriented luxury cruise ships are usually inappropriate for children and teens. The lack of organized activities makes these ships undesirable for young families.

What won't you find? No one will be groveling for gratuities. If they're not already included in the fare, they are oh-so-discreetly suggested.

Who's on board? Well-off couples and singles accustomed to the best travel accommodations and service. Small groups and families gravitate to the larger vessels in this category. Traveling in style to collect exotic destinations is highly desirable to luxury-minded passengers.

CABINS

In years gone by, cabins were almost an afterthought. The general attitude of both passengers and the cruise lines used to be that a cabin is a cabin and is used only for changing clothes and sleeping. That's why the cabins on most older cruise ships are skimpy in size and short on amenities.

Until you actually get on board you may not realize that nearly every cabin on your ship is identical. How'd they do that? It's simple, really. Cruise ships are built in sections and, except for some luxury suites, the cabins are prefabricated and dropped into place with everything all ready to hook up, even the plumbing. There are some variations in size, but the main difference between cabins in the myriad price categories is location: on a higher or lower deck, forward or aft, inside or outside.

Cabins high on the ship with a commanding view fetch higher fares. But you should also know that they are also more susceptible to side-to-side movement; in rough seas you could find yourself tossed right out of bed. On lower decks, you'll pay less and find more stability, particularly in the middle of the ship.

Forward cabins have a tendency to be oddly shaped, as they follow the contour of the bow, and they may have portholes instead of picture windows. They are also likely to be noisy; when the ship's anchor drops, you won't need a wake-up call. In rough seas, you can feel the ship's pitch (its upward and downward motion) more in the front.

Should you go for the stern location instead? You're more likely to hear engine and machinery noise there, as well as feel the pitch and possibly some vibration. However, many passengers feel the view of the ship's wake (the ripples it leaves behind as its massive engines move it forward) is worth any noise or vibration they might encounter there.

No location is perfect, but midship on a lower deck is almost always preferable to the extremes—either far forward or aft.

Above all, don't be confused by all the categories listed in cruise line brochures—the categories more accurately reflect price levels based on location than any physical differences in the cabins themselves (keep repeating: prefabricated). Shipboard accommodations fall into four basic configurations: inside cabins, outside cabins, balcony cabins, and suites.

INSIDE CABINS

An inside cabin is just that: a stateroom that's located inside the ship with no window or porthole. These are always the least expensive cabins and are ideal for passengers who would rather spend their vacation funds on excursions or other incidentals than on upgraded accommodations. Inside cabins are generally just as spacious as outside cabins, and decor and amenities are similar. On the newest vessels, you may even find small refrigerators and a cozy sitting area.

To give the illusion of more space, inside cabins may have a mock window (complete with curtain) or, in the case of *Disney Dream* and *Disney Fantasy*, a monitor with the appearance of a porthole that streams a real-time video view from outside the ship. Many also rely on the generous use of mirrors for an open feeling. On NCL's *Norwegian Epic*, inside single cabins have windows onto the corridor. On *Queen Mary 2* and Royal Caribbean's largest vessels, some inside cabins feature windows overlooking the grand lobby or promenade. Although they don't offer a sea view, these cabins do provide a prime spot for watching Royal Caribbean's nighttime parades on the "street" below.

Many ships locate triple and quad cabins (accommodating three or more passengers) on the inside. Essentially, they look just like a standard double cabin but have bunk beds that either fold down from the wall or disappear into the ceiling. Parents sometimes book an inside cabin for their older children and teens, while their own cabin is an outside across the hall with a window or balcony.

For passengers who want a very dark room for sleeping, an inside cabin is ideal. Use a bit of creativity, and even your inside cabin can have a window on the sea if your ship has a television channel that features a continuous view from the bridge. Tune in that channel before you retire and turn off the sound—it will be dark all night and you will awaken with sunshine and a seascape.

OUTSIDE CABINS

A standard outside cabin has either a picture window or porthole. To give the illusion of more space, these cabins might also rely on the generous use of mirrors for an even airier feeling. In addition to the usual amenities, outside staterooms often have a small refrigerator and a sitting area.

Two twin beds can be joined together to create one large bed, the equivalent of a queen- or king-size bed. Going one step further, standard and larger outside staterooms on modern ships are often outfitted with a small sofa or love seat with a cocktail table or small side table. Some of those tables can be raised for dining. The sofas usually contain fold-out beds and can accommodate a third person. Disney Cruise Line's cabins for five even incorporate a clever Murphy bed that drops down from the wall. Floor-to-ceiling curtains that can be drawn from wall to wall to create a private sleeping space are a nice touch in some outside cabins with sitting areas. Cabins that are termed larger may have a combination bathtub-shower instead of just a shower.

CABIN FEVER: Typical Cabin Features

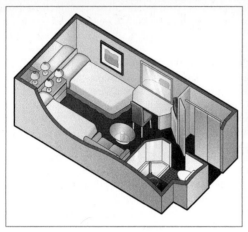

Standard Staterooms

■ There are three standard cabin types: Inside, Outside, and Balcony.

■ The average size of a standard cabin is 175—180 square feet (including the interior space devoted to bathrooms and closets).

■ Strategically placed mirrors as well as clever lighting and furniture placement give the illusion of more space.

■ Beds are usually two twins that can be combined to form a single queen (some also have a sofa bed or fold-down upper berths).

■ Furnishings typically include bedside tables and reading lamps, a combination desk–vanity table and chair or stool, and possibly a small sitting area with either a chair or love seat and coffee table.

■ Hanging closets and drawers and/or shelves are built-in for storage; you may even find unexpected storage beneath the sofa cushions as well as under the beds. Nearly all cabins have a TV and telephone (some with voice mail), an ice bucket and glassware, and many also have a small refrigerator (some are minibars).

■ Bathrooms feature open or enclosed shelves and a shower. Shampoo, lotion, and soaps or shower gel are usually provided, often in dispensers rather than individual packages.

■ A balcony is one of the most popular stateroom amenities and adds an additional dimension to a cruise—personal space with fresh air and sea breezes.

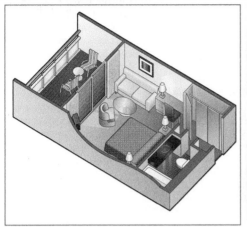

Suites

■ A suite is usually at least 300 square feet.

■ The sleeping area is separated from the living area, but often by a curtain rather than a wall.

■ Some suites have queen- or king-size beds, but often they're two twins that can be combined.

■ Furnishings include everything that's in a standard cabin, but some suites have separate dining alcoves and a butler's pantry. There's often a DVD, VCR, or CD player.

■ Minibars are usually stocked, but the contents are not always complimentary.

■ Storage is generally abundant and many suites have walk-in closets.

■ Bathrooms also contain generous storage and usually a bathtub with shower or a separate shower.

■ Some bathrooms have twin sinks or jetted tubs.

■ A guest powder room is not uncommon in top-of-the-line suites.

■ Toiletries may carry designer labels and include a variety of shampoo,

■ conditioner, shower gel, mouthwash, and soaps.

■ Bathrobes are almost always furnished for use during the cruise.

■ Most suites have balconies; some offer access to a concierge lounge.

BALCONY CABINS

A balcony—or veranda—cabin is an outside cabin with floor-to-ceiling glass doors that open onto a private deck. Although the cabin may have large expanses of glass, the balcony is sometimes cut out of the cabin's square footage (depending on the ship).

Balconies are usually furnished with two chairs and a table for lounging and casual dining outdoors. However, you should be aware that balconies are not always completely private. Dividers might be opaque and may not extend all the way from ceiling to floor or from the ship's hull to the railing. On some ships, including those with aft-facing balconies, the balconies are stepped like a layer cake; this means that certain balconies are visible from the decks above.

The furnishings and amenities of balcony cabins are otherwise much like those in standard outside cabins. Like outside staterooms, most balcony staterooms have a separate sitting area outfitted with a small sofa or love seat and small table. Some balcony cabins may even have a combination bathtub-shower instead of just a shower.

> **WORD OF MOUTH**
>
> "A cruise is a way for us to kick back and relax and have some time together without any cell phones, pagers, or radios beeping at us. We book ships that offer an elegant experience rather than casual or high-energy atmosphere. Also, for the Caribbean, we tend to book for the ship and stateroom rather than the ports. We spend much of the time in the cabin and on the veranda so for us booking a suite makes sense."
> —Sue C.

SUITES

Suites are the most lavish accommodations afloat, and although they are always larger than regular cabins, they do not always have separate rooms for sleeping. Some luxury ships designate all accommodations as suites, and they can range in size from about 250 to 1,500 square feet. The most expansive (and expensive) have large living rooms and separate bedrooms and may also have huge private outdoor sundecks equipped with hot tubs, changing rooms, and dining areas.

Even smaller suites (often termed minisuites) and penthouses are generous in size, and the largest villa suites on certain Norwegian Cruise Line ships are more like apartments at sea that measure an extraordinary 5,350 square feet.

Suites almost always have amenities that standard cabins do not have. True suites have separate living and sleeping areas. Depending on the cruise line, you may find a small refrigerator or minibar stocked with complimentary soft drinks, bottled water, and the alcoholic beverages of your choice. A bottle of champagne on ice almost always awaits you upon embarkation. Little extras might include afternoon tea and evening canapés delivered to you and served by a white-gloved butler.

Top-drawer suites on some ships include the luxurious touch of complimentary laundry service, in-cabin Internet connections, and complex entertainment centers with big-screen plasma TVs, DVD players, and CD stereo systems.

Back-to-Back Sailings

CLOSE UP

One week at sea might not be enough, so go ahead and book two. Ships with alternating itineraries—Eastern Caribbean one week and Western Caribbean the next—recycle the menus and entertainment weekly but won't repeat any (or many) ports of call.

Between the time the first cruise ends and the second begins, there are a few things to take into account depending on the cruise line, the port,

and customs procedures. Sometimes you're issued a new key–charge card by the purser and invited to relax on board the ship; other times you might have to go into the terminal and check back in. You might even need to get off the ship, go through customs, and then complete the normal boarding process. You'll be informed a day or two before the turnaround, but in any case you do not have to pack up your belongings unless you're changing cabins.

Expect roomy closets, abundant storage, and deluxe imported soaps and toiletries in the bathroom. The bathroom may even be outfitted with a jetted tub and separate shower. Butlers' pantries and guest powder rooms are often featured in top suite categories.

Suite balconies are usually furnished with at least two chairs and a small table for outdoor lounging. Depending on the ship and balcony size, you may also find a table and chairs for alfresco dining and reclining chaise longues for sunbathing. These balconies do not always offer 100% privacy. Dividers might be opaque or might not extend all the way from ceiling to floor or from the ship's hull to the railing.

An added bonus to the suite life is the extra level of services many ships offer. At the least you should expect priority boarding and disembarkation, concierge service during the cruise, and top consideration when making restaurant and spa reservations. Even space on sold-out shore excursions may be available to you, or you might be bumped to the top of the waiting list. Some suites come with butler service; the butler can handle tasks from valet services and unpacking your suitcases to daily delivery of tea and hors d'oeuvres. Your butler will make all your reservations for you.

Buyer beware: Most so-called minisuites are usually little more than slightly larger versions of standard balcony cabins and don't often include extra services you can get in regular suites. Sometimes you don't even get more elaborate amenities. They're still generally a good value for the price if space matters.

ITINERARIES

It's a common misperception that Caribbean islands and itineraries are pretty much the same. Each island has its own personality and style, some derived from their colonial culture, others from their geography. Most are home to friendly residents and offer pleasant diversions and enough shopping for even the most addicted shopaholic. It's quite

SHIPS BY ITINERARY AND HOME PORT

SHIP	HOME PORT	CRUISE LENGTH	ITINERARY
Azamara Cruises			
Azamara Quest	Miami, FL	8, 10, 11, or 12 nights	Eastern or Southern Caribbean
Carnival Cruise Lines			
Carnival Breeze	Miami, FL	6 nights	Western Caribbean
		8 nights	Eastern or Southern Caribbean
Carnival Conquest	Miami, FL	7 nights	Eastern or Western Caribbean
Carnival Dream	Port Canaveral, FL	6, 7, or 8 nights	Eastern, Western, or Southern Caribbean
Carnival Ecstasy	Miami, FL	4 or 5 nights	Bahamas and Key West or Western Caribbean
Carnival Elation	New Orleans, LA	4 or 5 nights	Western Caribbean
Carnival Fantasy	Charleston, SC	5 nights	Bahamas
		7 nights	Eastern Caribbean
Carnival Fascination	Jacksonville, FL	4 or 5 nights	Bahamas
Carnival Freedom	Fort Lauderdale, FL	8 nights	Eastern or Western Caribbean
		6 nights	Western Caribbean
Carnival Glory	Miami, FL	7 nights	Eastern or Western Caribbean
Carnival Imagination	Miami, FL	4 nights	Western Caribbean
		3 nights	Bahamas
Carnival Legend	Tampa, FL	7 nights	Western Caribbean
Carnival Liberty	Miami, FL	7 nights	Eastern or Western Caribbean
Carnival Magic	Galveston, TX	7 nights	Eastern or Western Caribbean
Carnival Paradise	Tampa, FL	4 or 5 nights	Western Caribbean
Carnival Pride	Baltimore, MD	7 nights	Bahamas or Eastern Caribbean
Carnival Sensation	Port Canaveral, FL	3 or 4 nights	Bahamas
Carnival Splendor	New York, NY	8 nights	Bahamas or Eastern Caribbean
Carnival Sunshine	New Orleans, LA	7 nights	Eastern or Western Caribbean
Carnival Triumph	Galveston, TX	4 or 5 nights	Western Caribbean

SHIP	HOME PORT	CRUISE LENGTH	ITINERARY
Carnival Valor	San Juan, PR	6 nights	Southern Caribbean
Carnival Victory	Miami, FL	4 or 5 nights	Eastern or Western Caribbean
Celebrity Cruises			
Celebrity Constellation	Fort Lauderdale, FL	3, 4, or 5 nights	Bahamas or Western Caribbean
Celebrity Eclipse	Miami, FL	14 nights	Southern Caribbean
Celebrity Equinox	Fort Lauderdale, FL	10 or 11 nights	Western or Southern Caribbean
Celebrity Reflection	Miami, FL	7 nights	Eastern Caribbean
Celebrity Silhouette	Fort Lauderdale, FL	7 nights	Eastern or Western Caribbean
Celebrity Summit	San Juan, PR	7 nights	Southern Caribbean
Costa Cruises			
Costa Luminosa	Miami, FL	10 nights	Western Caribbean
Costa Magica	Guadeloupe	7 nights	Eastern Caribbean
Costa Mediterreanea	Guadeloupe	7 nights	Eastern or Southern Caribbean
Crystal Cruises			
Crystal Serenity	Miami, FL	10, 11, or 14 nights	Western, Southern Caribbean, and Panama Canal
Cunard Line			
Queen Mary 2	New York, NY	12 or 19 nights	Eastern Caribbean
Disney Cruise Line			
Disney Dream	Port Canaveral, FL	3, 4, or 5 nights	Bahamas
Disney Fantasy	Port Canaveral, FL	7 nights	Eastern or Western Caribbean
Disney Magic	San Juan, PR	7 nights	Southern Caribbean
	Port Canaveral, FL	7 nights	Eastern or Western Caribbean
Disney Wonder	Miami, FL	5 nights	Western Caribbean
Holland America Line			
Eurodam	Fort Lauderdale, FL	7 nights	Eastern or Western Caribbean
Maasdam	Fort Lauderdale, FL	10 nights	Eastern Caribbean
	Fort Lauderdale, FL	11 nights	Southern Caribbean
	Fort Lauderdale, FL	14 nights	Southern Caribbean or Panama Canal

SHIP	HOME PORT	CRUISE LENGTH	ITINERARY
Nieuw Amsterdam	Fort Lauderdale, FL	7 nights	Eastern or Western Caribbean
Noordam	Fort Lauderdale, FL	10 or 11 nights	Southern Caribbean
Ryndam	Tampa, FL	7 nights	Western Caribbean
		14 nights	Southern Caribbean
Veendam	Fort Lauderdale, FL	7 nights	Eastern Caribbean
Westerdam	Fort Lauderdale, FL	7 nights	Eastern Caribbean
Zuiderdam	Fort Lauderdale, FL	10 or 11 nights	Southern Caribbean and Panama Canal
MSC Cruises			
MSC Divina	Miami, FL	7 nights	Eastern or Western Caribbean
Norwegian Cruise Line			
Norwegian Breakaway	New York, NY	7 nights	Bahamas
	New York, NY	12 nights	Southern Caribbean
Norwegian Dawn	Tampa, FL	7 nights	Western Caribbean
	New Orleans, LA	7 nights	Western Caribbean
Norwegian Epic	Miami, FL	7 nights	Eastern or Western Caribbean
Norwegian Gem	New York, NY	9 nights	Eastern Caribbean
Norwegian Getaway	Miami, FL	7 nights	Eastern Caribbean
Norwegian Jewel	New Orleans, LA	7 nights	Western Caribbean
	Houston, TX	7 nights	Western Caribbean
Norwegian Pearl	Miami, FL	7 nights	Western Caribbean
	Miami, FL	10 nights	Eastern Caribbean
	Miami, FL	11 nights	Southern Caribbean
Norwegian Sky	Miami, FL	3 or 4 nights	Bahamas
Norwegian Sun	Tampa, FL	7 nights	Western Caribbean
	Miami, FL	11 nights	Southern Caribbean
Oceania Cruises			
Insignia	San Juan, PR	7 nights	Southern Caribbean
Regatta	Miami, FL	10 nights	Eastern and Southern Caribbean
	Miami, FL	7 nights	Western Caribbean
Riviera	Miami, FL	10 to 14 nights	Eastern and Southern Caribbean

SHIP	HOME PORT	CRUISE LENGTH	ITINERARY
Paul Gauguin Cruises			
Tere Moana	Phillipsburg, St. Maarten	7 nights	Southern Caribbean and Panama Canal
Princess Cruises			
Caribbean Princess	Fort Lauderdale, FL	4 or 5 nights	Eastern or Western Caribbean
Coral Princess	Fort Lauderdale, FL	10 or 11 nights	Southern Caribbean and Panama Canal
Emerald Princess	Houston, TX	7 nights	Western Caribbean
Island Princess	Fort Lauderdale, FL	10 or 11 nights	Southern Caribbean and Panama Canal
Regal Princess	Fort Lauderdale, FL	7 nights	Eastern Caribbean
Royal Princess	Fort Lauderdale, FL	10 nights	Eastern or Southern Caribbean
Ruby Princess	Fort Lauderdale, FL	7 nights	Eastern or Western Caribbean
Regent Seven Seas Cruises			
Seven Seas Navigator	Miami, FL	7 or 10 nights	Eastern or Western Caribbean
Royal Caribbean International			
Adventure of the Seas	San Juan, PR	7 nights	Southern Caribbean
	Miami, FL	4 nights	Bahamas
	Miami, FL	7 nights	Eastern Caribbean
Allure of the Seas	Fort Lauderdale, FL	7 nights	Eastern or Western Caribbean
Brilliance of the Seas	Tampa, FL	4 or 5 nights	Western Caribbean
Enchantment of the Seas	Port Canaveral, FL	3 or 4 nights	Bahamas
Explorer of the Seas	Cape Liberty, NJ	7 nights	Bahamas
	Cape Liberty, NJ	9 nights	Eastern Caribbean
Freedom of the Seas	Port Canaveral, FL	7 nights	Eastern or Western Caribbean
Grandeur of the Seas	Baltimore, MD	7 or 8 nights	Bahamas
	Baltimore, MD	10 nights	Eastern Caribbean
Independence of the Seas	Fort Lauderdale, FL	6 nights	Western Caribbean
	Fort Lauderdale, FL	8 nights	Eastern Caribbean
Jewel of the Seas	San Juan, PR	7 nights	Southern Caribbean
Legend of the Seas	Fort Lauderdale, FL	10 or 11 nights	Southern Caribbean

SHIP	HOME PORT	CRUISE LENGTH	ITINERARY
Liberty of the Seas	Fort Lauderdale, FL	5 nights	Western Caribbean
Majesty of the Seas	Miami, FL	3 nights	Bahamas
	Miami, FL	4 nights	Bahamas and Key West
Navigator of the Seas	Galveston, TX	7 nights	Western Caribbean
Oasis of the Seas	Fort Lauderdale, FL	7 nights	Eastern or Western Caribbean
Serenade of the Seas	New Orleans, LA	7 nights	Western Caribbean
Vision of the Seas	Colon, Panama	7 nights	Southern Caribbean
Seabourn Cruise Line			
Seabourn Pride	Phillipsburg, St. Maarten	7 to 14 nights	Southern Caribbean
	Oranjestad, Aruba	7 to 14 nights	Southern Caribbean
Seabourn Sojourn	Fort Lauderdale, FL	10 nights	Southern Caribbean
Seabourn Spirit	Phillipsburg, St. Maarten	7 to 14 nights	Southern Caribbean
	Bridgetown, Barbados	7 to 14 nights	Southern Caribbean
SeaDream Yacht Club			
SeaDream I	San Juan, PR	7 nights	Southern Caribbean
	St. Thomas, USVI	7 nights	Southern Caribbean
	Marigot, St. Martin	7 nights	Southern Caribbean
	Bridgetown, Barbados	7 nights	Southern Caribbean
Silversea Cruise Line			
Silver Cloud	Fort Lauderdale, FL	10 to 14 nights	Southern Caribbean
	San Juan, PR	7 nights	Southern Caribbean
Silver Spirit	San Juan, PR	7 nights	Southern Caribbean
	Fort Lauderdale, FL	7 to 15 nights	Southern Caribbean
Silver Whisper	Fort Lauderdale, FL	8 to 15 nights	Southern Caribbean
Star Clippers			
Royal Clipper	Bridgetown, Barbados	7 nights	Southern Caribbean
Star Clipper	Phillipsburg, St. Maarten	7 nights	Southern Caribbean
Windstar Cruises			
Wind Spirit	Bridgetown, Barbados	7 nights	Southern Caribbean
Wind Surf	Phillipsburg, St. Maarten	7 nights	Southern Caribbean

possible to take as many as four or five Caribbean cruises and repeat very few islands.

One-week Caribbean cruises come in three distinct flavors: Eastern, Western, and Southern. Longer cruises of 10 and 11 nights are frequently called something like Caribbean Circle or Exotic Caribbean. Short cruises of less than a week generally include ports in the Bahamas and sometimes Key West, Florida.

The Eastern Caribbean is often the choice of first-time cruisers and those veterans who relish more at-sea days. Three, sometimes four, ports of call generally include St. Thomas, St. Maarten, San Juan, and, possibly, a stop at the cruise line's private island for a beach party.

For passengers who consider snorkeling and scuba diving a high priority, the Western Caribbean offers the best options. Typical Western Caribbean ports include Key West, Jamaica, Grand Cayman, Cozumel, Roatan (Honduras), and sometimes a private island.

Southern Caribbean cruises afford the choice of more island destinations—usually as many as five. Often embarking in San Juan, ships on Southern Caribbean itineraries may call on Antigua, Aruba, Barbados, Tortola, Virgin Gorda, Curaçao, Grenada, Martinique, St. Barths, St. Kitts, St. Lucia, and sometimes St. Thomas or St. Maarten. When sailing from a Florida port of embarkation, a Southern Caribbean cruise is generally longer, often 10 to 12 nights.

Abundant sunny days and balmy nights make the Caribbean an ideal vacation destination any time of year. Even brief late afternoon tropical showers simply sweeten the air without overly dampening spirits. However, experienced cruisers know that storms can crop up at the most inopportune times. Passengers numbering in the hundreds of thousands embark on cruises during the official hurricane season, from June 1 through November 30, without a thought about storms on land or at sea. For some, it's the only time of year they can schedule a family vacation. Others just don't give it a second thought. After all, the official hurricane season consumes a full six months of the year.

Although it's something to ponder in terms of comfort and convenience, most travelers do not let hurricane season stand in the way of scheduling a cruise during that time frame. Chances are, you'll never encounter a problem, and a ship at sea is not necessarily the worst place to be when a hurricane is looming over the horizon. Modern cruise ships are equipped with sophisticated communications gear and receive regular weather bulletins and storm advisories. Your ship will have the equipment necessary to ensure your safety.

When a hurricane is imminent, your major concern should be your embarkation port. When a hurricane barrels down on your embarkation city, flights in and out are certain to be delayed or cancelled by airport closures. Assuming you made it to the ship and have sailed, the itinerary will often be modified as necessary to avoid storms. If a hurricane has a tryst with one of your Caribbean port stops, you will alter course to a different (and possibly more interesting) port. In

CLOSE UP

Taking Your Toddler to Sea

Cruise ships are wonderful places for family vacations, but you must understand the rules before promising your littlest sailors unlimited playtime, either in the kid's program or the swimming pool. Nothing is sadder than the face of a toddler who isn't allowed in the ship's pool—even the kiddie pool—because he or she isn't potty-trained. Even swim diapers won't pass muster in most cases.

Cruise ships must comply with the Center for Disease Control's (CDC) Vessel Sanitation Program (VSP) regulations. Charged with the prevention of pool contamination and the resulting spread of bacteria that can cause illness after "accidents" in pools and water parks at sea, the VSP provides health and safety requirements to cruise lines, including the ban on *any* diapers in the pools.

The straight poop is that swim diapers are not completely leak-proof. They can prevent solids from escaping,

but cannot contain urine or diarrhea completely, nor do they stop seepage of infection-causing germs.

However, not all cruise ships entirely ban water play for youngsters who are not potty-trained. Special wading pools approved by VSP standards have their own separate water and disinfection systems and heavy-duty filtration units that can be "flushed out" when diaper accidents occur. Such splash zones are found on all Disney Cruise Line ships and on Royal Caribbean's *Freedom of the Seas, Liberty of the Seas,* and *Independence of the Seas.*

About those kids' programs: Check the Cruise Line Profiles for age limits— some are as low as two years of age, but most will accept only children three and older. Although being toilet trained isn't always a prerequisite for participation, only the counselors on Disney Cruise Line, Carnival Cruise Lines, and Royal Caribbean ships with nurseries will change diapers.

the extreme, you could end up in the Western Caribbean when your planned itinerary is the Eastern Caribbean. The ship will go where the captain and crew feel it is safest. Your very life depends on their judgment, and they take that responsibility seriously. It's a big ocean out there; happily, there's a lot of room for your ship to maneuver safely.

KEEPING IN TOUCH

No longer do passengers have to depend on the Marconi operator in the radio room to send telegraphed ship-to-shore messages. Technology has gone to sea in a big way, and connecting with your family or business from a modern cruise ship is as close as the direct-dial telephone in your cabin. However, because rates vary from a low of $1.99 to as much as $15 *per minute*, most passengers agree that it's best to reserve their cabin telephone for emergency use only.

The ability to use your own mobile phone from the high seas is a communication alternative that is gaining popularity. It's also cheaper than using a cabin phone if your ship offers the service. Rates from your ship at sea may range from $2.50 to $5 per minute, or more. And this is true even if your own mobile phone company provides the roaming service aboard your ship. When in port, depending on the agreements your home mobile service provider has established, you may be able to connect to local networks.

Email is likely to be the least expensive way to stay in touch, even though charges on board can be expensive. Cruise ship computer systems vary widely, and the speed can be maddeningly slow at times. Most ships have a dedicated Internet center where you can go online using the ship's computers; some ships have in-cabin broadband data ports or wireless systems that allow you to use your own laptop or one you can rent on board in your cabin or in public "hot spots." Packages that include a flat rate for a block of time are usually available and reduce the per-minute cost.

A few ships still don't have these high-tech communication options, but you won't be cut off totally even then. Some ships offer only a simple email service and charge per email message sent and received. Once on shore, you can find Internet cafés with high-speed connections, often located near the cruise ship pier; almost any crew member can point the way to them.

PLANNING YOUR CRUISE

With something for everyone and the option to do nothing at all, cruises are truly the best of all vacation styles for travel companions with different interests. On board, you may do as much or as little as you please. Off the ship, there's always a new destination over the horizon to tempt you to explore. You only have to unpack once, and the most important item on your list of things to do is getting back to the ship on time after a day in port.

So you know you want to take a cruise, yet the choices you face seem endless. Whether you give it much thought, you probably realize every vacation is about more than money. In addition to spending your hard-earned cash, you're spending your time, and that can be priceless. You could be disappointed if you don't plan wisely. By making informed choices you're less likely to waste your money and precious vacation time.

DOING RESEARCH

Years before the Internet became a savvy traveler's primary information resource, brochures, obtained either from travel agencies or ordered directly from cruise lines, were often the first glimpse of what potential passengers might expect on cruise vacations. In some cases, they still are.

Open any cruise brochure and you're sure to find a dizzying display of information and photographs. What you want are simple facts, organized in an informative manner. What are you likely to find?

First of all, you have to select the right brochure. Although some cruise lines feature their entire fleet and all itineraries in one volume, others publish brochures for specific destinations. Brochures are enticing books, and, fortunately, most contain a table of contents, listing such topics as staterooms, dining options, onboard facilities, activities, entertainment, and children's programs up front.

What more do potential passengers want to know? They want simple facts in language they can follow. Can you bring a bottle of champagne to celebrate a special occasion? Or will one be provided free for the asking? What should you pack to be appropriately dressed? What do the staterooms look like? What is included in the fare (and what is not)? And, most important, what happens if you must cancel in case of an emergency? For answers to those questions and more, begin reading in the *back* of the brochure.

You probably would not start reading a mystery novel on the last page, but if you immediately turn to the last few pages of a cruise brochure you will find the so-called fine print, which everyone needs to know or at least should want to find out. The section may be titled "Things to know before you go," "What you need to know," "Important policies," or even "Terms and conditions." Read it! Read it closely. Also look toward the back of the brochure for details about Air & Sea transportation programs, insurance, and amenity packages to enhance your cruise. Answers to frequently asked questions can be found simply by thumbing through the brochure from back to front.

After absorbing the facts, go back to the front pages of the brochure and take a good look at the illustrations. Would you be happy to share a cruise with the people pictured? Although they are more likely than not models, those people *could* be your shipmates. A brochure that features children in a majority of photos is giving you a solid hint that the cruise line caters to families. Similarly, representations of stylish middle-aged or older couples hint at a particular demographic the line is recruiting.

And here's another thing about those pictures: As a rule, accommodations look exactly like the brochure illustrations and are perfectly adequate for the average passenger; however, most people find their staterooms are somewhat smaller than what they expected. Wide-angle lenses help photographers capture the small space on film, but they also make the cabin appear larger than it is in reality.

Location, location, location. Think of a deck plan as a map of a ship, which, unlike a road map, can give a fairly precise idea of what features the neighborhood will hold, particularly when it's time to select a cabin.

A brief description of ports of call and shore excursions is a practicality covered in most brochures. Ports and itineraries are an important factor in most travelers' cruise selections. The brochures of port-intensive cruise lines tend to provide a tad more insight into the destinations and have more shore-excursion descriptions than their contemporary fun-in-the-sun cousins.

Cruise line websites are also excellent resources for decision making and planning. Websites often display even more current information than brochures, which are printed far in advance. In addition, detailed ports of call and shore excursion information is often more extensive online than in brochures.

Still, for the latest information and answers to your questions, a trusted travel agent is a cruise passenger's best friend.

PLANNING FOR YOUR SPECIAL NEEDS

Who takes cruises these days? Some passengers arrive with more in mind than getting a suntan. Couples not only honeymoon on cruises, but they get married on ships or in ports of call. People with disabilities are drawn to the ease of travel by ship, and singles find the atmosphere conducive to making friends. Same-sex couples can blend into the mix just as easily as large groups and multigeneration families. But if you have a special interest or need, you may want to consider some specific things to make your cruise a satisfying experience.

CRUISE LINES AT A GLANCE

Before you narrow your search to a few specific ships, you want the assurance that you aren't looking for it in the wrong cruise line. To help you decide which cruise line might be most appropriate for you, we have rated several areas important to most passengers on a scale of 5 (most suitable) to 0 (no options). A lower number doesn't necessarily indicate an inferior product, however. For example, a cruise line that offers structured programs for children only seasonally will have a lower Family Friendly rating. Although it might have wonderful playrooms with well-planned activities, it will probably be less appealing to parents with children than a highly rated cruise line that caters to families year-round.

Even within a single cruise line's fleet, individual ship facilities can vary widely. The newest vessels often have more dining and entertainment choices and the latest in high-tech gadgetry and gizmos. Look for a general overview here before exploring the details outlined in our Cruise Line Profiles and Cruise Ship Reviews in Chapter 5.

Short cruises are defined as fewer than seven nights. They are great getaways for busy people as well as a way to sample cruising before committing to a full week, or even longer, at sea.

Although fares are usually quoted per person for an entire cruise, pricing is ultimately based on double occupancy per cabin. For that reason—and also because cruises vary in length—we have simplified our cost ranges to reflect the realistic price of a cabin per night for two passengers. Even fares within a cabin type (inside or outside) vary depending on location, and you may find the category you select is at the high end of a price range even if entry-level fares fall in the lower end.

CRUISE LINE	Cost–Inside Cabin	Cost–Outside Cabin
Azamara Club Cruises	$$	$$
Carnival Cruise Lines	$	$$
Celebrity Cruises	$$	$$
Compagnie du Ponant		$$$$
Costa Cruises	$	$$
Crystal Cruises		$$$$
Cunard Line	$$	$$$
Disney Cruise Line	$$	$$$
Holland America Line	$$	$$$
MSC Cruises	$	$$
Norwegian Cruise Line	$	$$
Oceania Cruises	$$	$$$
Paul Gauguin Cruies		$$$$
Princess Cruises	$	$$
Regent Seven Seas Cruises		$$$$$
Royal Caribbean International	$	$$
Seabourn Cruise Line		$$$$$
SeaDream Yacht Club		$$$$$
Silversea Cruises		$$$$$
Star Clippers	$$$	$$$$
Windstar Cruises		$$$$

Key to Costs:

$$$$$	Over $600
$$$$	$450–$600
$$$	$300–$450
$$	$200–$300
$	$125–$200

Short Cruises	Fine Dining	Service	Lectures/ Enrichment Programs	Entertainment/ Shows	Family-Friendly	Accessible	Spa	Sports Facilities
	▲▲▲▲	▲▲▲▲	▲▲▲▲	▲▲		▲▲▲	▲▲▲▲	▲▲
x	▲▲▲▲	▲▲▲		▲▲▲▲▲	▲▲▲▲▲	▲▲▲	▲▲▲▲	▲▲▲▲▲
x	▲▲▲▲	▲▲▲▲	▲▲▲	▲▲▲	▲▲▲	▲▲▲	▲▲▲▲	▲▲▲
	▲▲▲▲▲	▲▲▲▲	▲▲▲	▲▲	▲▲▲	▲	▲	▲▲
	▲▲	▲▲	▲▲	▲▲▲	▲▲	▲▲▲	▲▲▲	▲▲
	▲▲▲▲▲	▲▲▲▲▲	▲▲▲▲▲	▲▲▲	▲▲	▲▲▲▲	▲▲▲▲	▲▲▲
	▲▲▲▲	▲▲▲▲	▲▲▲▲▲	▲▲▲	▲▲▲	▲▲▲▲	▲▲▲▲▲	▲▲▲
x	▲▲▲▲	▲▲▲▲	▲▲▲	▲▲▲▲▲	▲▲▲▲▲	▲▲▲▲	▲▲▲▲▲	▲▲▲▲
	▲▲▲▲	▲▲▲▲	▲▲▲	▲▲▲	▲▲▲	▲▲▲	▲▲▲▲	▲▲▲▲
	▲▲	▲▲▲	▲▲▲	▲▲▲	▲▲	▲▲	▲▲▲	▲▲▲
	▲▲▲	▲▲▲		▲▲▲▲▲	▲▲▲▲▲	▲▲▲	▲▲▲▲	▲▲▲▲▲
	▲▲▲▲	▲▲▲▲	▲▲▲	▲▲		▲▲▲	▲▲▲	▲▲
	▲▲▲▲▲	▲▲▲▲▲	▲▲▲▲	▲▲	▲▲	▲	▲▲▲	▲▲▲
	▲▲▲▲	▲▲▲	▲▲▲▲	▲▲▲	▲▲▲▲	▲▲▲▲▲	▲▲▲▲	▲▲▲▲
x	▲▲▲▲▲	▲▲▲▲▲	▲▲▲▲	▲▲▲		▲▲▲▲	▲▲▲▲▲	▲▲▲
x	▲▲▲	▲▲▲		▲▲▲▲▲	▲▲▲▲▲	▲▲▲▲	▲▲▲▲	▲▲▲▲▲
	▲▲▲▲▲	▲▲▲▲▲	▲▲▲▲▲	▲▲		▲▲	▲▲▲▲	▲▲▲▲
	▲▲▲▲▲	▲▲▲▲▲	▲▲	▲▲		▲	▲▲▲▲	▲▲▲
x	▲▲▲▲▲	▲▲▲▲▲	▲▲▲▲	▲▲▲		▲▲▲	▲▲▲▲	▲▲▲
	▲▲▲▲	▲▲▲▲					▲▲▲	
	▲▲▲▲	▲▲▲▲▲		▲▲▲			▲▲	▲▲▲

CLOSE UP

Cruise Line Contacts

You can obtain cruise brochures from your travel agent or directly from the cruise lines that still publish them—some, like Carnival Cruise Lines, have done away with printed brochures in favor of sharing detailed information online. Here are the phone numbers and websites for all the cruise lines covered in this book:

Azamara Club Cruises (☎ 877/999–9553 ⊕ www.azamaraclubcruises.com)

Carnival Cruise Lines (☎ 800/227–6482 ⊕ www.carnival.com)

Celebrity Cruises (☎ 800/437–3111 ⊕ www.celebrity.com)

Costa Cruises (☎ 800/462–6782 ⊕ www.costacruise.com)

Crystal Cruises (☎ 888/799–4625 ⊕ www.crystalcruises.com)

Cunard Line (☎ 800/728–6273 ⊕ www.cunard.com)

Disney Cruise Line (☎ 888/325–2500 ⊕ www.disneycruise.com)

Holland America Line (☎ 800/577–1728 ⊕ www.hollandamerica.com)

MSC Cruises (☎ 800/666–9333 ⊕ www.msccruisesusa.com)

Norwegian Cruise Line (☎ 800/327–7030 ⊕ www.ncl.com)

Oceania Cruises (☎ 800/531–5658 ⊕ www.oceaniacruises.com)

Paul Gauguin Cruises (☎ 800/848–6172 ⊕ www.pgcruises.com)

Princess Cruises (☎ 800/774–6237 ⊕ www.princess.com)

Regent Seven Seas Cruises (☎ 877/505–5370 ⊕ www.rssc.com)

Royal Caribbean International (☎ 800/327–6700 ⊕ www.royalcaribbean.com)

Seabourn Cruise Line (☎ 800/929–9391 ⊕ www.seabourn.com)

SeaDream Yacht Club (☎ 800/707–4911 ⊕ www.seadreamyachtclub.com)

Silversea Cruises (☎ 800/722–9955 ⊕ www.silversea.com)

Star Clippers (☎ 800/442–0551 ⊕ www.starclippers.com)

Windstar Cruises (☎ 877/827–7245 ⊕ www.windstarcruises.com)

HONEYMOONS AND ANNIVERSARIES

With a little careful planning, any cruise can be turned into a special event—a heavenly honeymoon, a renewal of your commitment to each other, or a celebration of a special anniversary.

Cruise lines are certainly aware of the magical effects their vessels have on couples. Nearly all offer options in the way of romance or anniversary packages that can be arranged ahead of time through your travel agent. Packages may include goodies such as a bottle of champagne in your stateroom, logo robes to keep, his-and-hers spa treatments, formal portraits in elegant frames, or breakfast in bed on the morning of your choice. Renewals of vows are sometimes performed privately by the captain on arrangement or in a festive group setting, followed by a champagne toast to your commitment.

CLOSE UP

2

Brochure Speak

Some armchair brochure browsers become enraptured with such descriptions as "crystalline waters" and "historic wonders." These are just some of the buzz words employed to entice you to set sail. But other phrases hint at more practical considerations, and it's helpful to know how to decode the brochure's language:

■ A port of embarkation that is close by—or relatively close to home—means you can drive to your cruise or at least find a convenient, and possibly cheap, airline flight. Look for "homeland cruises" and "convenient departure ports" described in the brochures.

■ The term "all-inclusive" is a misnomer that is rarely, if ever, found in a cruise brochure and only found in practice on some luxury lines. Think *somewhat* all-inclusive and be sure to reread the fine print.

■ "Floating resorts" are cruise ships that offer everything from rock-climbing walls and miniature golf courses to facilities and activities that appeal to a wide range of age groups. These are usually the biggest and most modern vessels at sea. Other ships may be a bit older, but that does not mean they are less well equipped to offer the expected amenities, activities, and entertainment.

■ "Choices" are substantially hyped, especially when it comes to dining. It's your vacation, and you should be able to choose where to eat and what to wear, within reason. On days when you have been ashore, are tired, or just do not feel like dressing up, it's nice to have the choice of casual dining versus the more prim-and-proper directive to either dress up for a meal in the restaurant or stay in your room.

■ "Gourmet dining" is a bit too wishful for what you'll normally get on a mainstream cruise. Unless the cruise is on a smaller, extremely exclusive (and expensive) ship, meals are more likely to resemble very good, high-quality banquet food than the made-to-order meals of shoreside gourmet establishments. There's definitely true gourmet dining at sea, but not on every ship.

■ "Fine dining" is something you can often find on a mainstream cruise, but it usually comes with an additional price tag. Some alternative restaurants carry cover charges ranging from nominal to hefty.

■ "Spacious" is in the eye of the beholder. Only the top-category accommodations on many ships afford the spaciousness of an average hotel room. Look for stateroom diagrams and the square footage of your chosen stateroom category, which may or may not be indicated in the brochure.

■ "Elegance" and "luxury" are, again, in the eye of the beholder. A typical Las Vegas resort is not the same as a Miami Beach art deco–era hotel, although each has its own appeal for different tastes. Determine your priorities and make your ship selection carefully.

■ "Rack rate" fares are never the bottom line. Don't expire from sticker shock—you can expect to pay much less than brochure rate, often as much as half off the published price, depending on when you book your cruise. Exceptions are fares published on cruise lines' own websites, which are closer to what you will pay. However, your travel agent may be able to do better.

CLOSE UP

Planning the Perfect Wedding

Andrea and her fiancé were on a Carnival cruise when she caught a very brief glimpse of a bride and was smitten with the idea of being married on a cruise ship. "Carnival was the first place I called for details," she said. "It was a pleasant surprise to find out they had a whole wedding department. I did no comparison shopping because I knew this was the way I had to do it." Andrea's friends who were also planning weddings spent nearly twice as much on their nuptials as her dream cruise ship ceremony. First she dealt with the cruise line's wedding department: "Carnival assigns you to a wedding coordinator at a company called A Wedding For You. I worked with two women from there. My travel agent did some planning also."

There were 100 wedding guests on board for Andrea's big day, and 57 of them sailed with the newlyweds. Andrea was thrilled: "What a great time!! It was more like a four-day reception! You are allowed as many sailing guests as you want; however,

only 50 people can come aboard to just see the wedding. As soon as the ship was cleared, everyone was allowed to board. We were on the ship by 11:30 and the wedding was at 1. Because the guests boarded so early, we were able to schedule a cocktail hour in the lounge. It worked out nicely. The only drawback was that I wish the actual reception afterward was longer. It was only an hour and a half."

Andrea took advantage of ordering her bouquet and the men's boutonnieres through Carnival and was delighted but said, "It would have cost a fortune to get bouquets for all seven bridesmaids as well, so we did that on our own. You need to keep in mind that you are not allowed to bring fresh flowers on board the ship—they must be silk. Another snag was the ship only had one videographer, and another wedding on the ship that day booked before we did, so they got his services. Your best bet is to book early!"

Your very own balcony is the ideal setting for spending time alone together; why not also share a room service meal surrounded by sea sounds? Princess Cruises adds a twist to make the occasion even more memorable—Ultimate Balcony Dining. You choose either a champagne breakfast ($32 per couple) or a multicourse dinner ($100 per couple) and prepare to be pampered as your own waiter serves it to you on your private balcony.

WEDDINGS

Every couple dreams of a perfect wedding, closely followed by the ideal honeymoon. For many brides and grooms, destination weddings—exchanging vows in an exotic location—are the height of perfection. Tying the knot on a cruise ship offers the best of both worlds: a wedding and honeymoon wrapped into a package that takes the worry out of planning and combines pampering with privacy for newlyweds. Cruise line wedding coordinators take the anxiety out of seemingly insurmountable tasks such as arranging for a marriage license and finding a clergyman—undertakings that assume even more importance in unfamiliar surroundings. Brides-to-be should take note that cruise weddings are increasingly popular. To avoid disappointment, start planning as soon as you've announced your engagement and set a date.

Nearly every cruise line can assist with a ceremony on the ship prior to sailing or while docked in a port of call. Wedding options vary from a simple private ceremony in an intimate ship's chapel to elaborate nuptials and a reception attended by family and friends, who might even sail with the happy couple after sharing their special day. Brides and grooms merely decide what type of wedding they want—aboard ship or ashore in a Caribbean port—and what amenities fit their budgets. The cruise line and wedding coordinator take care of the rest.

Services differ between cruise lines, so you should investigate your options before you book your cruise. Packages can include not only the ceremony but also flowers, photographs, a video recording, champagne, wedding cake, and music. Although a number of newer ships—notably those of Carnival, Costa, Norwegian Cruise Line, Princess, and Royal Caribbean—have dedicated wedding chapels, only Princess Cruises, Azamara Cruises, Cunard, Line, and Celebrity Cruises can offer the romance of a wedding at sea with the captain officiating on certain ships. Bridal couples marrying on Princess ships can even invite friends and family at home to attend the ceremony virtually by tuning into the line's Wedding Cam on the Internet.

Contacts The Wedding Experience (☎ 877/580–3556 ⊕ www. theweddingexperience.com) is the exclusive wedding service provider for Royal Caribbean International, Celebrity Cruises, Costa Cruises, Princess Cruises, Carnival Cruise Lines, Norwegian Cruise Line, Windstar Cruises, and Azamara Club Cruises.

SOLO TRAVEL

When you're watching your fellow cruisers walking up the gangway two-by-two, you may think you're cruising on Noah's Ark rather than the Love Boat. But it doesn't take long to find other singles on almost any cruise. They may be sailing on their own or in small groups or with family. However, you need not rely solely on singles' get-togethers organized by the ship's social staff to meet your fellow cruisers: head to the gym, the hot tub, or the computer center, where striking up a conversation and forming friendships is less forced. Because families generally opt for the early dinner seating, request late seating and ask to be assigned to a large table to increase your opportunity to meet others. You are likely to find the maître d' has arranged tables so that passengers who appear to be traveling by themselves are seated together.

Shipboard hours are easily filled with lectures, shows, and activities where singles are urged to join in and where you can find like-minded fellow passengers. Single women may be delighted to discover the cruise line has arranged to have courtly dance hosts on board to make sure they won't be left out of the dancing and other social activities.

On port days, shore excursions are the most effortless way to see the sights, but don't discount teaming up with newly made friends to explore together independently. If you've been to a port previously, offer to lead a walking tour. Single travelers are eager to share their experiences with one another, and an informal group increases everyone's comfort level when in a new environment.

There are distinct advantages to traveling solo on a cruise ship. The desolation of hotel homesickness is unlikely to strike; plus, there's the luxury of having a stateroom with storage and amenities designed for two. There's also a major drawback: cruising single in a couple's world is pricey. With the exception of Norwegian Cruise Line's *Norwegian Epic, Norwegian Breakaway,* and *Norwegian Getaway,* most modern cruise ships do not have single cabins, and nearly all fares are based on double occupancy. Supplements for sailing solo can range from an additional 25% to 100% of the cost of the basic cruise fare, depending on cabin category and cruise line.

For certain cruises and/or cabin categories, the upscale lines Crystal, Regent Seven Seas, Seabourn, and Silversea charge a relatively low supplement to the solo cruiser's fare for occupying a double cabin. For instance, Seabourn's Run of Ship Single Savings allows guaranteed single occupancy in a Category A or higher suite at 150% or 175% of the double-occupancy fare. If you don't mind relinquishing privacy, some lines, such as Holland America Line, will match you with a roommate. In that case, you pay the lower double-occupancy rate and, if there's no one to pair you up with, you get a cabin to yourself for no additional charge. A singles roommate Match Program is also offered by Princess Cruises for occasional hosted singles cruises. Special offers waiving the single supplement are also available from various cruise lines from time to time.

Contacts Cruise Mates (⊕ *www.cruisemates.com/articles/single*) is an Internet-only cruise magazine and community with feature articles and a singles message board. **SinglesCruise.com** (☎ *800/393–5000* ⊕ *www.singlescruise.com*), a member company of Carlson Travel Group, hosts singles group cruises and will match solo cruise passengers with a roommate of the same sex and smoking preference. **Singles Cruise Resource** (☎ *888/724–5123 or 303/690–8937* ⊕ *www.solocruiseresource.com*), an affiliate agency of CruiseOne, a division of the world's largest seller of cruises, caters to the needs of singles by finding affordable cruises and reduced single-supplement fares for solo travelers.

FAMILIES

Cruising can be a rewarding family travel experience. Most parents report that their children have such a great time that they barely see them after boarding. Couples who wish to share adult time on their family cruise vacation no longer find it necessary to engage a nanny or bring along a family member to watch over their little ones. Mom can savor some well-earned beauty rest while Dad heads for a solitary jog on the deck, secure in the knowledge that the children are happy and well cared for in the youth center.

Baby on Board

Not all moms on board have checked their little ones into cruise camp—some of their babies haven't arrived yet. After baby is born, mothers do the pampering 24/7, so a cruise is the ideal prestork vacation for mothers-to-be to rest up and get pampered themselves.

Expectant moms should be aware of certain time constraints when planning a cruise. Although the stated terms and conditions vary, as a general rule cruise lines will not allow you to sail if you are from 24 to 28 weeks into your pregnancy (or will be before the cruise ends). A statement from your attending physician that establishes your due date might also be required prior to sailing. Also consider, if you're prone to seasickness, combining it with morning sickness might be a mistake.

Even after baby arrives, parents should check with the cruise line for age restrictions—most cruise lines will not allow infants younger than six months old to sail. Exceptions include certain Royal Caribbean ships that have nurseries for babies as young as six months and Disney Cruise Line, which accepts babies that are at least 12 weeks old and also offers nursery facilities for them (hourly fees are charged for nursery drop-off).

Youth programs on today's large cruise ships are staffed by counselors who have been carefully screened and chosen for their ability to relate to children; most have a background in education or early-childhood development. Their function is to provide a safe environment for age-appropriate play and learning, a day camp at sea. Activities vary by cruise line, but the emphasis is on enjoyable pursuits that can offer an educational bonus. Science and astronomy programs, arts and crafts projects, history and geography of the ports of call, and even training in social graces and dance are only a few of the planned pursuits. The basic complimentary programs usually last all day and, after a late afternoon break, resume in the evening; however, there's usually an hourly charge for late-night babysitting. A notable exception is Cunard Line, which provides complimentary babysitting on their ocean liners.

Not all youth programs are equally comprehensive. Most mainstream and premium cruise lines, including Carnival, Costa, Disney, Holland America, Norwegian, Princess, and Royal Caribbean, operate their programs all day on sea days, but hours may be limited on port days. Upscale lines that feature seasonal children's programs might close entirely on port days, while others offer little more than babysitting for an additional charge. The best programs schedule escorted educational shore excursions for older children and teens; both Carnival and Disney offer kid-oriented excursions in some ports of call. Disney even has regularly scheduled shoreside activities and excursions for all ages at its own private Bahamian island, Castaway Cay.

Most children's programs are divided by age group, but infants or toddlers who aren't toilet trained generally will not be accepted. Even on ships with nurseries, counselors will rarely change diapers or assist children with their bathroom needs, due to health and legal constraints. The exceptions are Disney Cruise Line, Carnival Cruise Lines, and certain Royal Caribbean ships that have nurseries. On some ships, parents are issued a beeper to summon them in case of a problem.

Possibly the pickiest passengers on any ship are those in the 13 to 17 age group. Usually the biggest hurdle with teenagers is convincing them that any family vacation can be fun. Teens are not always keen to join group activities. However, there are probably an equal number who enjoy hanging out with others at the teen center. Unlike younger children, teens are generally free to come and go as they please in a less-structured environment. Facilities vary, but most ships have at least a video game area and computers. The newest ships have discreetly chaperoned activity centers and discos designed specifically for teens, yet with an adult flavor; vessels without them usually allow teens to dance in the adult disco until about 11 pm.

Most major cruise lines, including Royal Caribbean, Carnival, Disney, Norwegian, Princess, and Holland America, have invested substantially since the late 1990s in their teen programs. Their facilities and programs give teens a place to go to relieve the boredom that used to result in mischievous pranks (think punching elevator buttons to stop on every floor and mixing up the breakfast order tags hung outside stateroom doors late at night). For teens, there can be a lot of freedom on a ship, but there are also rules. During group activities, they are not allowed to smoke, curse, or consume alcoholic beverages. Security will step in if any vandalism or violent behavior is observed. The same is true for younger children enrolled in the ship's youth programs. Children are subject to disciplinary procedures for unacceptable actions. After a warning, a time-out may be issued, and suspension or dismissal from the program is the ultimate punishment for continued unsuitable behavior. Entire families can be put off the ship at the next port for serious infractions.

In case of an emergency, cruise line counselors are trained to institute YEP, the Youth Evacuation Program. All children under the age of 13 are issued an ID bracelet that must be worn at all times when they register with a shipboard youth program. On hearing the ship's emergency signal, parents are instructed to go to their muster stations, stand in the front row, and await the arrival of their children. All children are outfitted with a life jacket, escorted to their assigned muster station, and supervised until they are reunited with their parents.

The number of children on board any cruise depends a lot on the time of year: peak periods for family cruises are during school holidays and summer vacations. Be sure to attend the youth program orientation with your children and enroll them on the first day of the cruise. Prepaid soft-drink cards that allow children to order an unlimited number of fountain drinks anywhere on the ship cost about $5 a day, plus gratuity, and can be real money-savers.

Families can often save money with special discounted fares for young children occupying the same stateroom as their parents. Although infants sail free on some cruise lines, port charges are usually assessed regardless of your child's age. Holland America Line goes the extra distance for young families, providing not only high chairs, booster chairs, and cribs, but even baby food, with at least 30 days' advance notice. Families preparing to sail on Disney or Royal Caribbean with tiny travelers have access to online services that allow them to order baby supplies in advance of their cruise and have them delivered to their stateroom rather than packing them from home. Make sure you or your travel agent requests what you need, and don't forget to reserve a crib for your little one no matter what cruise line you choose.

Disney Cruise Line's staterooms were designed to be particularly family-friendly; nearly all have a split bathroom configuration with one room containing a sink and bathtub with shower and the other a sink and toilet. Norwegian Cruise Line's newest vessels have many interconnecting cabins, often several in a row—a big advantage for large families who want additional bathrooms as well as space. Even luxury line Crystal is courting families by adding connecting doors between more staterooms aboard Crystal Symphony to create family-friendly accommodations. Several cabin categories have sofa beds that offer an additional berth to accommodate parents with more than two children.

TRAVELERS WITH DISABILITIES

As recently as the early 1990s, accessibility on a cruise ship meant little more than a few inside staterooms set aside for passengers with mobility impairments. Most public restrooms and nearly all en suite bathrooms had a step-over entryway—even passengers without mobility issues often tripped until they became accustomed to them. Even so, the overall conveniences and relative safety associated with a cruise vacation have always appealed to passengers with disabilities.

In the wake of the Americans with Disabilities Act (ADA), the cruise industry began demonstrating voluntary ADA compliance by designing new ships from the keel up with expanded accessibility in mind; now that compliance with the ADA has been declared mandatory, you can expect further measures to make cruising easier for passengers with many kinds of disabilities. Auxiliary aids, such as flashers for the hearing impaired and buzzers for visually impaired passengers, are often available on request. All ship elevators have raised Braille signage, and even some passageway handrails feature directions in Braille at regular intervals.

When evaluating a cruise, passengers with disabilities (ranging from use of a cane or walker to complete dependence on a wheelchair or reliance on a service animal) should pay particular attention not only to the facilities on board their chosen vessel but also to the conditions they are likely to find in ports of call and on shore excursions. More than the usual amount of planning is necessary for smooth sailing. To the extent possible, cruise lines attempt to accommodate guests with a wide range of disabilities. However, they cannot provide personal care and should not be expected to.

Beginning with embarkation, every effort is made to accommodate passengers who require assistance. Even so, certain ship transfer operations may not be fully accessible to wheelchairs or scooters. When a ship is unable to dock, passengers are taken ashore on tenders that are sometimes hard to negotiate even for those without mobility or sensory impairments. Some people with limited mobility may even find it difficult to embark or debark the ship when docked due to the steep angle of gangways caused by high or low tide.

PASSENGERS WHO USE SERVICE ANIMALS

Cruise lines welcome service animals aboard their fleets, and crew members often go the extra distance to provide for their comfort. However, itineraries may include ports of call that have very specific and strict rules about the importation of animals, and it will be your responsibility to find out what special requirements must be met before your service animal will be allowed off the ship.

The Caribbean islands that are the most open to allowing entry to service animals are Aruba, the Bahamas, the Cayman Islands, Curaçao, St. Maarten, Martinique, Guadeloupe, and Puerto Rico, and the Caribbean coastal areas of Venezuela, Colombia, and Mexico. Island nations that have animal quarantine regulations modeled on the British system include Antigua, Barbados, Grenada, Jamaica, St. Lucia, and Trinidad and Tobago. Although it does not have a quarantine procedure, the Dominican Republic's entry policy is in flux at this writing. The best places to obtain specific information on required documentation and immunizations are the U.S. State Department (International Travel Information), local customs offices in the specific ports, personal veterinarians, and the Seeing Eye, Inc. If your service animal does not have the proper proof of vaccinations, or if there are local quarantine requirements, it can be denied the right to leave the ship, and you'll be required to stay on board as well.

Contacts **The Seeing Eye, Inc.** (☎ 973/539–4425 ⊕ www.seeingeye.org). **U.S. Department of State, Bureau of Consular Affairs** (☎ 888/407–4747 ⊕ travel. state.gov/index.html).

PASSENGERS IN WHEELCHAIRS

All cruise lines offer a limited number of staterooms designed to be wheelchair- and/or scooter-accessible. Booking a newer vessel will generally assure more choice for passengers with disabilities, including more available cabins in a larger variety of categories, some even with private verandas. Public rooms in these newer ships are more accessible, with ramps and fewer raised thresholds. Nevertheless, physical barriers in both cabins and public rooms remain in many older ships.

For persons incapable of walking, a wheelchair is generally their primary mobility aid for getting on and off the ship. In those instances, crew-member squads may offer assistance that involves carrying passengers. Situations sometimes occur when mobility-impaired passengers may not be able to go ashore at the time they prefer. Or, they may be unable to go ashore at all in certain private islands or ports such as Grand Cayman, where there's no pier and all passengers are tendered ashore. For the safety of all concerned, the ship's captain will make the final determination regarding whether it's possible to carry mobility-impaired passengers and their mobility assistance devices ashore (wheelchair, scooter, walker, etc.). The captain will take into account all

Family Radios

The kids are in the youth center, and you have a beeper in case the counselor feels you're needed. But where's your husband? Don't laugh . . . it happens to me all the time. We're strolling along the Lido deck, and I ask a question. No response. No surprise. My husband has wandered off. Again. Locating him on a ship with 13 passenger decks can mean a lot of walking.

Enter the solution: a simple pair of two-way radios. By and large, they work beautifully on even the largest ships, although interior steel may stop the signal in a few spots. They're worth their weight in gold for keeping track of older children and teens. Some ships have sets for rent, and they are sold in almost any electron-

ics or computer superstore. When shopping for radios, look for:

■ **Rugged construction:** You want them to be sturdy and capable of standing up to wear and tear and dropping. Water resistance is important on a ship as well.

■ **Subchannels:** These little gems are popular, and the main channels get a lot of use. You want to tune them in to a subchannel to avoid other passengers' chatter.

■ **Rechargeable batteries:** It goes without saying that batteries don't last long, even when they're on standby.

Apply common sense when using your radios. There's no need to shout, "Can you hear me?" into your handset or tune the volume to an ear-splitting decibel.

---

appropriate conditions, including weather, the ship's location, weight of the guest, and so on.

Third-party transfer vehicles and shore excursion facilities may not be fully accessible to those with disabilities. Cruise lines attempt to deal only with companies that comply with legal requirements. However, they cannot guarantee that all those companies, particularly those contracted in foreign countries, are able to provide accessible facilities to people with disabilities.

If you need a wheelchair for mobility, bring your own; while most ships carry a limited number of wheelchairs, they generally aren't allowed off the ship and are used only during embarkation, debarkation, and in emergencies. If you need a wheelchair or scooter for mobility but aren't able to travel with it, you can rent one for the duration of your cruise.

PASSENGERS WHO REQUIRE OXYGEN

Passengers who need continuous oxygen for chronic conditions must make their own arrangements prior to travel. Cruise lines do permit oxygen to be brought on board ships for personal use, but passengers are required to provide their own oxygen in these circumstances. There are companies that regularly provide supplemental oxygen and/or oxygen equipment for cruise ship passengers. Be sure to bring the service company's address and any local contacts in your ports of call.

Contacts **Advanced Aeromedical** (☎ *800/346-3556 or 757/481-1590* ⊕ *www.aeromedic.com*) rents oxygen equipment to cruise ship passengers. **Care Vacations/Cruise Ship Assist** (☎ *877/478-7827 or 780/986-6404* ⊕ *www. cruiseshipassist.com*) is a Canada-based company that rents mobility equipment, including powered and unpowered wheelchairs and scooters, as well as oxygen and oxygen equipment, and provides airport and hotel transfers to passengers with disabilities. The company services most major ports of embarkation in the United States and Canada and also some ports elsewhere in the world. **Scootaround** (☎ *888/441-7575 or 204/982-0657* ⊕ *www.scootaround.com*) rents scooters and powered and regular wheelchairs to cruise ship passengers. The company delivers them to your cruise ship in most North American ports of embarkation.

GAY AND LESBIAN CRUISES

Gay cruises have become a big business in recent years. Several companies now charter entire ships several times a year for all-gay cruises, featuring such extras as special entertainment, activities, and parties tailored to their clients' unique tastes. Atlantis Events markets primarily to gay men and also owns RSVP Vacations; the cruises are different, especially because RSVP makes more of an effort to appeal to both gay men and lesbians, while Atlantis cruises are really geared solely to gay men. Olivia Cruises specializes in all-lesbian trips. R Family Vacations specializes in family trips for gay parents and their kids. Other companies simply book blocks of cabins for gay and lesbian groups and operate as any other affinity group aboard a cruise ship.

Contacts **Atlantis Events** (☎ *310/859-8800, 800/628-5268 for reservations* ⊕ *www.atlantisevents.com*). **Olivia Cruises & Resorts** (☎ *800/631-6277 or 415/962-5700* ⊕ *www.olivia.com*). **R Family Vacations** (☎ *917/522-0985* ⊕ *www.rfamilyvacations.com*). **RSVP Vacations** (☎ *800/328-7787* ⊕ *www. rsvpvacations.com*).

NUDIST CRUISES

Nudist travel has been growing for several decades. For obvious reasons, all-nude cruises aren't permitted unless a group can charter the entire ship. Bare Necessities Tour & Travel is the only company that offers these cruises, usually several times a year on small- to medium-size ships. For those who are curious: yes, nude passengers must have something to sit on in public areas—a towel or, for the more discerning, an elegant silk scarf.

Contacts **Bare Necessities Tour & Travel** (☎ *800/743-0405 or 512/499-0405* ⊕ *www.cruisenude.com*).

GROUP TRAVEL

Enterprising travel agents have long known that organizing a group is a great way to provide a reduced fare to their clients as well as earn enough free tour-conductor berths for themselves to accompany the group. However, anyone who wants to coordinate a family reunion or simply arrange a carefree vacation for friends to travel together can book a group cruise and receive a discounted rate and free berths. To qualify as a group, your party must usually include a minimum of 16 passengers in at least eight cabins (third and fourth passengers in a cabin do not count), although fewer are required on some upscale cruise lines.

As the number of cabins booked increases, the number of free berths rises proportionally. For large groups, there's also the possibility that the cruise line will kick in a few perks, such as a complimentary cocktail party. Before taking on the responsibilities involved in organizing a group cruise, you should be aware that tour conductor berths are not totally free—port charges and taxes are not included. Be sure group members know the arrangement up front and are in agreement. Some groups feel it's more equitable to split the proceeds from the tour conductor berth in order to reduce everyone's cost.

If family and friends are uninterested and your travel agent has no group cruises planned, there are other ways to reap the benefits of a group cruise fare. College alumni organizations sometimes offer group travel opportunities, as do music and sports clubs, museums, civic and church groups, and even cruise-travel websites. Look around for like-minded individuals and you're likely to discover that some of them have cruise plans.

Contacts **Countryside Travel** (☎ 800/603–5755 ⊕ www.cruisemaster.com) specializes in groups and honeymoon cruises. **Cruise Mates** (☎ 602/279–4356 ⊕ www.cruisemates.com/articles/CMcruise) is an Internet cruise magazine and community that hosts several group cruises a year for online users. Bookings are handled by highly qualified independent travel agents. **CruisePlanning.net** (☎ 800/561–0802 or 570/323–0112 ⊕ www.cruiseplanning.net) is a member of the Cruise Planners network that specializes in group cruises. **Entertainment Cruise Productions LLC** (☎ 888/852–9987 ⊕ www.jazzcruises-ecp.com) specializes in full-ship charters focused on jazz and popular music. **Sixthman** (☎ 877/749–8462 ⊕ www.sixthman.net) specializes in full-ship charters with an emphasis on celebrating music and fan communities. **Skyscraper Tours, Inc.** (☎ 877/442–5659 ⊕ www.skyscrapertours.com) offers several annual hosted group cruises. **Whet Travel Inc.** (☎ 877/438–9438 ⊕ www.whettravel.com) specializes in large affinity groups interested in music and dance.

PAYING FOR YOUR TRIP

When shopping for a cruise, don't overlook strategies to save money. Watch the travel section of your Sunday newspaper for cruise line promotions, and get quotes from several sources, such as local and Internet travel agencies, for comparison.

Take advantage of your buying power as well. Senior citizens often qualify for discounts, as do airline employees, who are eligible for low rates from interline agents that serve the airline industry. Residents of certain states (particularly those that have cruise ports) are often able to obtain discounted fares during advertised promotions. Some credit card companies reward their users with travel point programs that can be used for substantial fare reductions or even free cruises. If you're

CLOSE UP

What Impacts Your Fare

You think airline fares are confusing? Cruise fares rise and fall like waves during a tropical storm and can seem equally contrary. On a single day it's possible to get as many as a half dozen different price quotes directly from many cruise lines because fares fluctuate. You and your shipmates paid for the same cruise, but you may not have paid the same fare.

One thing never changes—do not ever, under any circumstances, pay brochure rate. You can do better, often as much as half off those inflated fares. These factors can enter the mix when pricing cruises:

■ **The date of your cruise:** Fares are seasonal, with the lowest from about the second week of September until the week before Thanksgiving and the highest in summer and during holiday periods.

■ **When you book:** Early booking discounts are nearly always offered; last-minute discounts might be available as well.

■ **Popularity of the ship:** Some ships are stars and fill quickly, while others are wallflowers and just don't book up as fast.

■ **Itinerary:** Certain itineraries hold higher appeal, especially those considered unique or exotic.

■ **Age:** No, not the ship's age. Fare discounts may be available for senior citizens, and children sometimes sail free with their parents.

■ **Where you live:** Regional discounts may be available, particularly if a cruise line is trying to introduce a ship into a port near where you live.

■ **Group pricing:** Even if you're not a member of a group, travel agents may have access to lower group fares.

■ **Who your travel agent is:** Top-performing agencies can pass along lower fares to their clients.

■ **You're a repeat passenger:** Discounts and other goodies are often available to loyal passengers.

■ **The accommodations you choose:** Advertisements for low fares inevitably include the word "from . . ." and the figure that follows is going to get you on board in the lowest category; if you want a better cabin, you'll pay more for the space and location you prefer.

on active military duty, retired from military service, a first responder (police officer, firefighter, paramedic), or educator, you may qualify for discounts with some cruise lines. Discounts and promotions have a limited lifetime and might be capacity controlled, but you won't get them if you don't ask. You'll also be required to prove your eligibility.

Many travel agents who specialize in booking cruises belong to consortiums that book blocks of cabins on a number of ships, thus enabling them to pass along group savings to individuals who don't want the hassle of putting together a group of their own but who want the advantage of the lower group fare. Just because a travel agency is small doesn't mean it can't get you the bargains offered by bigger name-brand agencies. Don't be afraid to ask if there are any such deals available.

Timing and flexibility can also save you money. An affordable one-week cruise in May can cost you hundreds of dollars less per person than the same ship and itinerary in travel-heavy June.

Here's one thing that nearly everyone agrees on: It's a great feeling to have the majority of your vacation expenses paid before leaving home. This includes cruises.

The first step in actually booking a cruise is paying a deposit to reserve a cabin. The amount varies by cruise line and the length of the cruise, but it's generally about $250 per person for a one-week sailing. The balance of your fare is usually due from 60 to 75 days prior to the sailing date.

Always pay your cruise fare with a credit card. Though it rarely happens, travel agencies can suffer financial difficulties, or unscrupulous travel sellers can prey on unsuspecting victims and disappear with their money. Credit card companies will support you with a refund in the case of fraud or other unforeseen difficulties. Be sure to check your billing statements to ascertain that the charges are credited to the cruise line and not the travel agent.

Many people balk at the idea of putting such large charges on their credit card. However, by saving a set amount every week until your final cruise payment is due, you can pay the entire balance when your next credit card statement arrives.

In the unfortunate event that you must cancel your trip, most cruise deposits are fully refundable before the final payment date. After that, cancellation fees will apply, and these range from the amount of your deposit to 100% of the entire fare, depending on how long you wait before canceling your cruise.

Be aware that many travel agencies now charge a "service fee" for booking your cruise that can range from $15 to $50 or higher and is generally nonrefundable if you cancel at any time. Ask about service fees up front—some agencies tack on additional fees for any changes you make in your booking, such as switching your cabin or dining preference, a name change on the reservation, and even in the event that you request a price reduction if the cruise line lowers the fare for your sailing.

WHEN TO BOOK YOUR CRUISE

You will certainly save money if you can book your cruise far in advance. In addition to having a better choice of desirable staterooms, significantly discounted prices are available to those who place a deposit on a cruise from six months to a year in advance of sailing. Just as department stores schedule first-of-the-year white sales on linens, the cruise industry has its January through March Wave Season, when it books a large number of passengers for the year. Availability is often the best during this period, and some of the year's choice bargains can be booked during the cruise lines' annual sales push.

Should the price drop before your final payment is due, some cruise lines will extend the reduced fare to early bookings; however, that practice is less common than in the past. If you book early, it will be up to you to discover the fare reduction and request the lesser amount. Acting on your behalf, a good travel agent will monitor fare fluctuations and do that for you. Keep in mind that the lower fare may stipulate that it applies only to new bookings—in that case you could be offered an upgraded cabin or an onboard credit as a courtesy instead of a refund to match the lower fare. The availability of those perks may, however, depend on whether you took advantage of an early-saver or nonrefundable fare pricing.

A wrinkle in cruise pricing is the last-minute discount offered to new bookings after the final payment is due, usually within 60 days of sailing. Cruise lines do not want to sail with empty cabins and will sometimes offer unsold space at deeply reduced fares in specific geographic regions—often through agencies within driving distance of the port of embarkation. Although these discounts can be substantial, your choice of cabins and locations is limited to whatever is left over. Top suites and the lowest-category inside staterooms almost always sell out early. A last-minute reservation could mean your cabin is in a noisy location over the show lounge or under the galley. Although demand for cruises is high, cruise industry insiders advise that you should never assume the date you want is sold out—always check with a travel agent.

If you booked early and cannot take advantage of the last-minute savings, take heart. Ask your travel agent to check into the lower fare for you anyway: some cruise lines will honor it or may give you an upgraded stateroom or, better still, an onboard credit.

BOOKING YOUR CRUISE

Charting your cruising course doesn't have to be difficult, but it isn't as simple as booking airplane seats or reserving a hotel room. Even after you've settled on a cruise line and cruise ship that's right for you, there will still be many questions to answer and details to get right. First-time cruisers who may want and need some additional insight and advice, may wish to stick to a traditional travel agent who is close at hand. Of course, if you've taken numerous cruises and are more concerned with the price—and if you're willing to go to bat for yourself if something goes wrong—a Web-based agency might be the way to go.

USING A TRAVEL AGENT

Whether it is your 1st or 50th sailing, your best friend in booking a cruise is a knowledgeable travel agent. The last thing you want when considering a costly cruise vacation is an agent who has never been on a cruise, calls a cruise ship "the boat," or—worse still—quotes brochure rates. The most important steps in cruise travel planning are research, research, and more research; your partner in this process is an experienced travel agent. Booking a cruise is a complex process, and it's seldom wise to try to go it alone, particularly the first time. But how do you find a cruise travel agent you can trust?

First off, look for signs indicating you're dealing with an agency affiliated with Cruise Lines International Association (CLIA). Preferably,

10 Questions to Answer Before Visiting a Travel Agent

If you've decided to use a travel agent, congratulations. You'll have someone on your side to make your booking and to intercede if something goes wrong. Ask yourself these 10 simple questions, and you'll be better prepared to help the agent do his or her job:

1. Who will be going on the cruise?

2. What can you afford to spend for the entire trip?

3. Where would you like to go?

4. How much vacation time do you have?

5. When can you get away?

6. What are your interests?

7. Do you prefer a casual or a structured vacation?

8. What kind of accommodations do you want?

9. What are your dining preferences?

10. How will you get to the embarkation port?

2

your agent should be certified as an Accredited Cruise Counselor (ACC), Master Cruise Counselor (MCC), or Elite Cruise Counselor (ECC) by CLIA. Those agents have completed demanding training programs, including touring or sailing on a specific number of ships. They make it their business to know all they can to serve their clients' needs.

Make sure the travel agency you've chosen belongs to a professional trade organization. In North America, membership in the American Society of Travel Agents (ASTA) indicates an agency has pledged to follow the code of ethics set forth by the world's largest association for travel professionals. In the best of all worlds, your travel agent is affiliated with both ASTA and CLIA. Additionally, many agencies and home-based travel agents belong to such brand-name travel-agent networks as American Express Travel and Uniglobe, which puts the power and support of international corporations in their corner. If you're dealing with a local travel agency, look around the office when you arrive. Racks containing a wide variety of cruise line brochures and the presence of trade magazines and newspapers are good signs. The agent who makes it a point to read industry publications is an informed agent, one who is likely to keep up with the latest trends and who can provide you with up-to-the-minute data.

Some agencies have preferred-supplier relationships with specific cruise lines and prominently display only their products. If you have done your homework and know what cruise line sounds most appealing to you, be alert if an agent tries to change your mind without specific reasons.

When you've found a jewel of an agent, then what? Ask many questions. Whether you do that in person, over the phone, or by email is up to you. However, it's important that you get to know your agent and that your agent gets to know you. Above all else, be honest about your expectations and budget. Seldom can a travel agent who doesn't know you well guess what your interests are and how much you can afford to spend. Don't be shy. If you have champagne taste and a beer budget, say so. Do not hesitate to interview prospective agents and be wary if they do not interview you right back.

Contrary to what conventional wisdom might suggest, cutting out the travel agent and booking directly with a cruise line won't necessarily get you the lowest price. Nearly three-quarters of all cruise bookings are still handled through travel agents, and many are able to secure group fares or other discounts not offered directly by cruise lines. In fact, cruise line reservation systems simply are not capable of dealing with tens of thousands of direct calls from potential passengers. They will take your reservation and often ask if you would like to assign it to a travel agent. Without an agent working on your behalf, you're on your own. A good travel agent is your advocate.

When you use a travel agent to book a cruise, most cruise line customer service departments are reluctant to respond to your questions over the telephone. Instead, they refer you to your travel agent, who is expected to make queries on your behalf. This is the time a knowledgeable and dedicated travel agent can come in handy. Do not rely on Internet message boards for authoritative responses to your questions—that is a service more accurately provided by your travel agent.

Cruise Line Organizations Cruise Lines International Association (*CLIA* ☎ 754/224-2200 ⊕ *www.cruising.org*).

Recommended Travel Agents AAA (☎ *800/222-6953* ⊕ *www.aaa.com*) isn't just for car travel. The company has a searchable database to locate member agencies by zip code.

American Express Travel (☎ *800/335-3342* ⊕ *www.americanexpressvacations. com*) offers options for online booking.

Avoya Travel (☎ *800/490-2921* ⊕ *www.avoyatravel.com*) in business since the 1960s (formerly known as America's Vacation Center), is a family-owned agency with hundreds of professional Personal Vacation Planners worldwide.

Countryside Travel (☎ *800/603-5755* ⊕ *www.cruisemaster.com*) specializes in groups and honeymoons.

Cruise Brothers (☎ *800/827-7779 or 401/941-3999* ⊕ *www.cruisebrothers. com*), in business since the mid-1970s, is one of the largest family-owned, cruises-only agencies in the United States.

Cruise Connections Canada (☎ *800/661-9283* ⊕ *www.cruise-connections. com*) is Canada's leading cruise retailer and one of the largest cruise retailers in North America.

Cruise One (☎ *800/278-4731* ⊕ *www.cruiseone.com*) is owned by World Travel Holdings, the world's largest cruise retailer, and offers a satisfaction guarantee. The company has more than 400 member agencies nationwide, and its website has a searchable database of member cruise specialists.

Cruise Planners, Inc. (☎ *800/683-0206* ⊕ *www.cruiseplanners.com*) is a network of home-based agent franchises. The website offers a searchable database to locate member agencies.

Cruises Inc. (☎ *888/282–1249 or 800/854–0500* ⊕ *www.cruisesinc.com*) is owned by World Travel Holdings, the world's largest cruise retailer, and offers a satisfaction guarantee. The company has more than 450 member agencies nationwide, and its website has a searchable database of member cruise specialists.

Cruises Only (☎ *800/278–4737* ⊕ *www.cruisesonly.com*) is owned by World Travel Holdings, the world's largest cruise retailer, and offers a lowest-price guarantee as well as a money-back satisfaction guarantee. Agents are available to assist clients around the clock.

Ensemble Travel (☎ *800/442–6871* ⊕ *www.ensembletravel.com*) is an international network of 1,100 expert travel agencies. Call to be connected to the nearest member agency.

Hartford Holidays (☎ *800/828–4813 or 516/746–6670* ⊕ *www.hartfordholidays.com*) has been family-owned and -operated for 30 years.

Lighthouse Travel (☎ *800/719–9917 or 805/566–3905* ⊕ *www.lighthousetravel.com*) specializes in cruises.

Northstar Cruises (☎ *800/249–9360 or 973/228–5005* ⊕ *www.northstarcruises.com*) is a top producer for most major cruise lines.

Skyscraper Tours, Inc. (☎ *877/442–5659* ⊕ *www.skyscrapertours.com*) offers several annual hosted group cruises.

Uniglobe International (⊕ *www.uniglobetravel.com*) has more than 700 franchise locations worldwide; the Internet website has a searchable database of member cruise agencies.

Vacation.com (☎ *800/843–0733* ⊕ *www.vacation.com*), a subsidiary of Amadeus Global Travel Distribution, is a network of thousands of travel agencies across the United States and Canada.

Virtuoso (☎ *866/401–7974 or 817/870–0300* ⊕ *www.virtuoso.com*) is the world's most exclusive association of upscale travel agencies. Call to locate members specializing in cruises.

Travel Agent Professional Organizations American Society of Travel Agents (*ASTA* ☎ *703/739–2782, 800/965–2782 for 24-hr hotline* ⊕ *www.travelsense.org*). **Association of British Travel Agents** (☎ *020/7637–2444* ⊕ *www.abta.com*). **Association of Canadian Travel Agencies** (☎ *866/725–2282 or 613/237–3657* ⊕ *www.acta.ca*). **Australian Federation of Travel Agents** (☎ *02/9264–3299 or 1300/363–416* ⊕ *www.afta.com.au*). **Travel Agents Association of New Zealand** (☎ *04/496–4898* ⊕ *www.taanz.org.nz*).

BOOKING YOUR CRUISE ONLINE

In addition to local travel agencies, there are many hardworking, dedicated travel professionals working for websites. Both big-name travel sellers and mom-and-pop agencies compete for the attention of cyber-savvy clients, and it never hurts to compare prices from a variety of these sources. Some cruise lines even allow you to book directly with them through their websites.

As a rule, Web-based and toll-free brokers will do a decent job for you. They often offer discounted fares, though not always the lowest, so it pays to check around. If you know precisely what you want and how much you should pay to get a real bargain—and you don't mind dealing with an anonymous voice on the phone—by all means make your reservations when the price is right. Just don't expect the personal service you get from an agent you know. Also, be prepared to spend a lot of time and effort on the phone if something goes wrong.

Online Agencies Cruise.com (⊕ *www.cruise.com* ☎ *888/333–3116*) lays claim to being the largest website specializing in discounted cruises on the Internet and offers a lowest-price guarantee.

Cruise Compete (☎ *800/764–4410* ⊕ *www.cruisecompete.com*) allows you to get competing bids from top travel agencies, who respond to your request for bids with their best rates for your trip.

Cruise Direct (☎ *888/407–2784* ⊕ *www.cruisedirect.com*) allows customers to book their own travel arrangements through the website and a toll-free number.

Cruise411.com (☎ *800/553–7090* ⊕ *www.cruise411.com*) has a booking engine online that allows you to book directly or temporarily hold most cruise reservations without deposit or payment if you prefer to call in your booking.

Expedia (☎ *800/397–3342* ⊕ *www.expedia.com*) is a full-service online travel seller that books cruises, too.

iCruise.com (☎ *800/427–8473* ⊕ *www.icruise.com*) charges a hefty cancellation fee, so be sure you know what you want before using their booking engine.

jetBlue (☎ *800/538–2583* ⊕ *www.jetblue.com*) now allows you to book cruises on its website.

Moment's Notice (☎ *888/241–3366* ⊕ *www.moments-notice.com*) offers a searchable database for last-minute deals; call toll-free for reservations.

Orbitz (☎ *888/656–4546* ⊕ *www.orbitz.com*) is a full-service online travel seller that books cruises.

7 Blue Seas (☎ *800/242–1781* ⊕ *www.7blueseas.com*) offers a comprehensive online cruise information website; bookings are made through the toll-free call center.

Travelocity (☎ *888/872–8356* ⊕ *www.travelocity.com*) is a full-service online travel seller with a 24-hour help desk for service issues.

CONSUMER PROTECTION

Before you actually book your cruise and make your deposit, it's well worth the effort to check with the Better Business Bureau for complaints against the agent you have decided to use. Always pay by credit card, and make sure the correct amount appears on your statement as a charge by the cruise line, not the travel agency. If you've paid by credit card, you can cancel payment or get reimbursed if there's a problem (and you can provide documentation). Check to see what kind of complaints (if any) have been filed against the agency you've chosen to work with and whether they were resolved. Finally, always consider travel insurance that includes default coverage for your travel agency and cruise line.

Contacts Canadian Council of Better Business Bureaus (☎ *416/644–4936* ⊕ *www.bbb.org/canada*). **Council of Better Business Bureaus** (☎ *703/276–0100* ⊕ *www.bbb.org*).

2

INSURANCE

When you book your cruise, your travel agent should ask you if you want to purchase travel insurance. Travel insurance plans cover trip cancellation and interruption, supplier default, and international medical care—or various combinations of these. If the agent doesn't ask you, you should ask for the information.

Comprehensive travel policies typically cover trip cancellation and interruption, letting you cancel or cut your trip short because of a personal emergency, illness, or, in some cases, acts of terrorism in your destination. Such policies also cover evacuation and medical care. Some also cover you for trip delays because of bad weather or mechanical problems, as well as for lost or delayed baggage. Another type of coverage to look for is financial default—that is, when your trip is disrupted because a tour operator, airline, or cruise line goes out of business. Generally you must buy this when you book your trip or shortly thereafter, and it's only available to you if your operator isn't on a list of excluded companies.

If you're going on a cruise (or any trip abroad for that matter), consider buying medical-only coverage at the very least. Neither Medicare nor some private insurers cover medical expenses anywhere outside the United States besides Mexico and Canada (including time aboard a cruise ship, even if it leaves from a U.S. port). Medical-only policies typically reimburse you for medical care (excluding that related to preexisting conditions) and hospitalization abroad and provide for evacuation. You still have to pay the bills and await reimbursement from the insurer, though.

Expect comprehensive travel insurance policies to cost about 4% to 7% of the total price of your trip (it's more like 12% if you're over age 70). A medical-only policy may or may not be cheaper than a comprehensive policy. Always read the fine print of your policy to make sure that you are covered for the risks that are of most concern to you. Compare several policies to make sure you're getting the best price and range of coverage available.

Comprehensive Travel Insurers Allianz Global Assistance (☎ *866/884–3556* ⊕ *www.allianztravelinsurance.com*). **CSA Travel Protection** (☎ *800/711–1197* ⊕ *www.csatravelprotection.com*). **HTH Worldwide** (☎ *610/254–8700 or 888/243–2358* ⊕ *www.hthworldwide.com*). **Travelex Insurance** (☎ *800/228–9792* ⊕ *www.travelex-insurance.com*). **Travel Guard International** (☎ *715/345–0505 or 800/826–4919* ⊕ *www.travelguard.com*). **Travel Insured International** (☎ *800/243–3174* ⊕ *www.travelinsured.com*).

Insurance Comparison Sites InsureMyTrip.com (☎ *800/487–4722* ⊕ *www.insuremytrip.com).* SquareMouth.com (☎ *800/240–0369* ⊕ *www. quotetravelinsurance.com).*

CRUISE LINE INSURANCE POLICIES

Nearly all cruise lines offer their own line of insurance. Most policies are underwritten by major insurers and typically include trip cancellation-interruption protection, travel delay protection, baggage loss or delay protection, emergency medical and/or dental benefits, emergency medical evacuation and transportation to the nearest medical facility, repatriation of remains in case of death, and other worldwide emergency assistance. All policies contain coverage limitations and terms and conditions that you should read carefully. Policies purchased through the cruise lines are generally based on the total price of the trip booked with them despite age and are often the most cost-effective coverage for senior citizens. However, they may not cover certain add-on elements such as airfare and the cost of a precruise hotel that you paid for independently. Compare the coverage and rates with similar polices from third-party insurers to determine which is best for you.

Some cruise lines, including Holland America Line, Silversea, and Princess Cruises, offer upgraded levels of cruise insurance that include considerably more liberal cancellation policies. They allow you to cancel up to 24 hours prior to departure for any reason whatsoever and receive either a cash refund or cruise credit of 75% to 100% of your fare. Seabourn goes a step further and covers your cruise payment if you must cancel due to a preexisting condition that is denied by insurance—the cruise line will issue a future travel credit equal to the cancellation penalties imposed.

Keep in mind that insurance purchased from an independent carrier is more likely to include coverage if the cruise line goes out of business before or during your cruise. Although it's a rare and unlikely occurrence, you do want to be insured in the event that it happens.

MEDICAL-ONLY PLANS

It's wise to sign up with a medical-assistance company even if you don't purchase other kinds of general travel insurance. Members get doctor referrals, emergency evacuation or repatriation, hotlines for medical consultation, cash for emergencies, and other assistance. Most general travel insurance policies include medical coverage and evacuation.

Medical-Only Insurers International Medical Group (☎ *800/628–4664* ⊕ *www.imglobal.com).* International SOS (☎ *215/942–8000 or 713/521–7611* ⊕ *www.internationalsos.com).* Wallach & Company (☎ *800/237–6615 or 504/687–3166* ⊕ *www.wallach.com).*

MAKING DECISIONS ABOUT YOUR CRUISE

Once you've settled on a specific ship of a particular cruise line, you'll have numerous decisions to make before your travel agent actually completes your booking. You need to settle on your dining arrangements, pick your stateroom, decide how you'll get to the port of embarkation,

What to Do When There's Trouble at Sea

You've booked your cruise, but your mother is sick and you must cancel. What then? Look at the cruise line's cancellation policy. If your final payment has not been made, you should qualify for a deposit refund. Otherwise, you may have to pay a cancellation penalty depending on how close it is to your time of departure. Is there any way you can avoid this kind of loss? Well, the obvious answer is to buy travel insurance.

Situations that would be covered by travel insurance are never the responsibility of cruise lines when you fail to purchase it. Although anyone with a heart will sympathize if your spouse dies a week before your sailing, cruise lines are businesses, and they don't "owe" you a refund. You might be able to get your credit card company or a consumer advocate to intercede on your behalf—and sometimes that works—but don't count on it.

But not all cruise disasters happen before you leave. Things can go just as wrong at sea as they do on land. When a major disaster strikes, such as a fire on a ship that leaves it dead in the water with no power or working toilets, you should expect more than a sincere apology from the cruise line. Historically, when an instance of that magnitude occurs, the least you can expect is a fare refund. When Carnival Cruise Lines' *Carnival Triumph* experienced such a break down in 2013, passengers were refunded their fare as well as what they had spent on board during the cruise. The line also provided them with transportation home once the ship finally docked as well as a check for $500 for the inconvenience of being stuck at sea for days.

Compensation varies by cruise line, but the least you can expect is a full or partial fare refund and monetary assistance for transportation costs to get home if, for instance, your vessel breaks down in a port of call and you must disembark before the cruise is scheduled to end.

When a cruise line cancels or delays a sailing, the result can vary depending on when the cancellation occurs. If a ship is unexpectedly chartered, cruise lines will cancel individual reservations. That usually occurs far enough in advance that you may be offered alternate sailing dates with no change of fare. If you decide not to sail, then your deposit will be refunded and (possibly) any change fees for airfare you have purchased on your own. These situations are generally handled on a case-by-case basis.

When a cruise is canceled for other reasons closer to sailing date, you should be offered the same conditions for an alternate date, and might be reimbursed for any airfare change costs you may incur. If a sailing is delayed at the last minute, you should expect some compensation for the days your cruise was shortened, and if you were already at the embarkation port when notified, you should request reimbursement for expenses incurred before boarding.

When negotiating compensation, one of the least successful things to do is state that if the cruise line doesn't do as you wish, you "will never sail with them again" or, worse, threaten to sue. At that point they will wait to hear from your lawyer.

2

whether you want to arrive at the port of embarkation early or stay a few days after your cruise, and lay out any special requests or requirements you may have.

MAKING DINING ARRANGEMENTS

Your travel agent will ask you to make a number of decisions before he or she books your cruise. When you're sailing on a traditional cruise with assigned dinner seating, your seating selection can set the tone for your entire trip. Which is best? Early dinner seating is generally scheduled between 6 and 6:30, while late seating can begin from 8 to 8:30. The best seating depends on you, your lifestyle, and your personal preferences.

You may wish to choose early seating if:

- You have small children accustomed to an early meal and bedtime.
- Your personal routine calls for meals at an earlier hour.
- You retire earlier in the evening and are an early riser.
- You do not want to experience that full feeling at bedtime.
- You want to attend the early shows, enjoy the casino and other activities, and take in the midnight buffet.

Late seating may be better if:

- You're a night owl and do not mind finishing dinner after 10.
- Your itinerary is port intensive, and you don't want to rush to get ready for dinner after a day of touring.
- You like to indulge in a late-afternoon nap.
- You do not care about midnight snacks and like to sleep late.
- Your personal habit is to dine late.
- You enjoy leisurely dining and lingering over coffee at the end of the meal.

Cruise lines understand that strict schedules do not satisfy the desires of all modern cruise passengers. Most cruise lines now include alternatives to the set schedules in the dining room, including casual versions of their dinner menus in their Lido buffets, where more flexibility is allowed in dress and mealtimes. Specialty à la carte restaurants are showing up on more ships, although a surcharge or gratuity is usually required.

Open seating, an amenity primarily associated with more upscale cruise lines, allows passengers the flexibility of dining any time during restaurant hours and being seated with whomever they please.

Led by Norwegian Cruise Line's Freestyle Cruising concept, other mainstream and premium cruise lines have explored adaptations of open seating to add variety and a more personalized experience for their passengers. Princess Cruises offers Anytime Dining; Holland America Line's option is called As You Wish dining; Royal Caribbean calls their version of open seating My Time Dining; Celebrity Cruises offers Celebrity Select Dining; and Carnival Cruise Lines has Your Time Dining fleetwide.

SPECIALTY RESTAURANTS

CRUISE LINE	SHIP	CUISINE TYPE	CHARGE (PER PERSON)
Azamara Club Cruises	Azamara Journey and Quest	Steakhouse	$25 (comp. for suite occupants)
		Mediterranean	$25 (comp. for suite occupants)
Carnival	Spirit-, Conquest-, Dream-class, and Carnival Sunshine	Steaks and seafood	$35
	Carnival Magic, Breeze, and Sunshine	Italian	$12 dinner, lunch free
	Carnival Breeze and Sunshine	Sushi	À la carte
	Carnival Sunshine	Asian	$12 dinner, lunch free
	All ships	International with champagne reception	$75
	Carnival Magic	Italian	$10
Celebrity	All ships	Continental	$45
	Solstice-class and Constellation	Italian	$35
	Solstice- and Millennium-class	Crêperie	$5
	Solstice and Equinox	Asian	$30
	Eclipse, Silhouette, Infinity, Reflection, Millennium, and Summit	American	$45
	Silhouette and Reflection	Grill	$40
Costa	Costa Atlantica	Italian-Tuscan steakhouse	À la carte (comp. dinner for two for suite occupants)
Crystal	All ships	Italian, Asian, Sushi	No charge
		International with wine pairings	$210
Cunard	Queen Mary 2	Mediterranean	À la carte lunch or dinner
Disney	All ships	Northern Italian	$20 dinner, $20 brunch
	Disney Dream and Fantasy	French	$75
Holland America	All ships	Steaks and seafood	$25 dinner, $10 lunch
		Italian	$10
	Signature-class	Asian	$15 dinner, lunch no charge

SPECIALTY RESTAURANTS

CRUISE LINE	SHIP	CUISINE TYPE	CHARGE (PER PERSON)
	All ships	International	$39 dinner, $89 with wine pairing
	Rotterdam	Dutch	$69 with wine pairing
MSC	MSC Divina	Mexican	À la carte
Norwegian	All ships	French	$20
	All ships	Steakhouse	$30
	All	Italian	$15
	All ships, except Sky	Sushi	À la carte
		Teppanyaki	$25
	All ships, except Sky and Sun	Asian	$15
	Norwegian Epic	Chinese noodle bar	À la carte
	All ships except Sky, Spirit, and Pride of America	Brazilian Churrascaria	$20
	Breakaway and Getaway	Seafood	$49
Oceania	All ships	Italian	No charge
		Steakhouse	No charge
	Marina and Riviera	French	No charge
		Asian	No charge
		International	$95–$165, with wine pairings
Princess	Sun- and Coral-class, Pacific and Ocean Princess	Steakhouse	$20
	All ships, except Sun-class	Italian	$25
	Grand-class, Caribbean, Crown, Emerald, Ruby, Royal, and Regal Princess	Steaks and seafood	$25
	All ships	International	$95 with wine pairings
Regent Seven Seas	All ships	Steaks and seafood	No charge
.		Italian	No charge
	Mariner, Voyager	French	No charge
Royal Caribbean	Oasis-, Freedom-, Radiance-class and Enchantment, Mariner, and Navigator of the Seas	Steakhouse	$30

SPECIALTY RESTAURANTS

CRUISE LINE	SHIP	CUISINE TYPE	CHARGE (PER PERSON)
	Oasis-, Freedom-, Radiance-class, and Voyager-class and Rhapsody, Brilliance, and Grandeur of the Seas	Italian	$15 lunch, $20 dinner
	Allure and Radiance of the Seas	Brazilian Churrascaria	$30
	All ships	Johnny Rockets diner	$4.95
	Oasis-class	American	$40
		Spa cuisine	$20 dinner, breakfast and lunch no charge
	Oasis-class, and Radiance, Brilliance, Serenade, and Splendour of the Seas	Seafood (Oasis), Mexican (Allure, Radiance, Brilliance, Serenade, Splendour)	À la carte plus $3 cover charge for lunch or dinner
	All ships except Majesty, Jewel, and Enchantment of the Seas	Asian	À la carte plus $3 cover charge for lunch, $5 for dinner
	All ships except Majesty of the Seas	International with wine pairings	$95
Seabourn	All ships	International	No charge
Silversea	All ships	International	$30
		International with wine pairings	$30, plus cost of wines
		Italian	No charge
	Silver Spirit	Asian	$30
Windstar	Wind Surf	French	No charge

Some cruise lines will warn you that, while dining preferences may be requested by your travel agent, no requests are guaranteed. And it's true that table assignments are generally not confirmed until embarkation, but the lines do try to satisfy all their guests. If you are unhappy with your dinner seating, see the maître d' during the first day of your cruise for assistance. Changes after the first evening are generally discouraged; there will even be a designated place to meet with dining room staff and iron out seating problems on embarkation day. Check the daily program for the time and location.

SELECTING YOUR STATEROOM

Your choice of stateroom or cabin is likely to be a major factor in how you enjoy your cruise. If it truly doesn't matter where you sleep, go ahead and book the least-expensive category guarantee you can find. The cheapest cabin on a ship is typically an inside stateroom on a lower

DECIPHER YOUR DECK PLAN

LIDO DECK

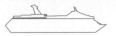

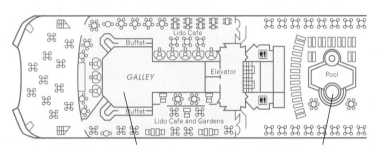

The Lido Deck is a potential source of noise—deck chairs are set out early in the morning and put away late at night; the sound of chairs scraping on the floor of the Lido buffet can be an annoyance.

Music performances by poolside bands can often be heard on upper-deck balconies located immediately below.

UPPER DECK AFT

Take note of where lifeboats are located—views from some outside cabins can be partially, or entirely, obstructed by the boats.

Upper-deck cabins, as well as those far forward and far aft, are usually more susceptible to motion than those in the middle of the ship on a low deck.

Cabins near elevators or stairs are a double-edged sword. Being close by is a convenience; however, although the elevators aren't necessarily noisy, the traffic they attract can be.

Balcony cabins are indicated by a rectangle split into two sections. The small box is the balcony.

MAIN PUBLIC DECK

Cabins immediately below restaurants and dining rooms can be noisy. Late sleepers might be bothered by early breakfast noise, early sleepers by late diners.

Theaters and dining rooms are often located on middle or lower decks.

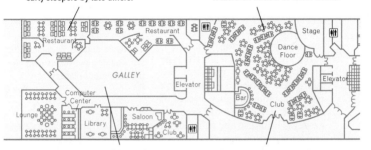

The ship's galley isn't usually labeled on deck plans, but you can figure out where it is by locating a large blank space near the dining room. Cabins beneath it can be very noisy.

Locate the ship's show lounge, disco, children's playroom, and teen center and avoid booking a cabin directly above or below them for obvious reasons.

LOWER DECK AFT

Cabins designated for passengers with disabilities are often situated near elevators.

Interior cabins have no windows and are the least expensive on board.

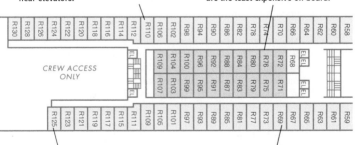

Lower-deck cabins, particularly those far aft, can be plagued by mechanical noises and vibration.

Ocean-view cabins are generally located on lower decks.

deck. Although ship designers do all they can to make these inside cabins feel less claustrophobic, there's no getting around the fact that you won't have any kind of view to the outside world. There's sometimes a curtain where the porthole or window would typically be in an outside cabin, but it will be covering nothing but blank wall space.

There are a few simple ways you can get a bit more for your money. Fares are determined by the type of accommodation reserved, and guarantee bookings—when you reserve a cabin category instead of a specific stateroom—can save you money. The cruise line will assign you a cabin within the fare category you book, or you may even be upgraded to a higher category. Be aware that you could end up at the very front or back of the ship or—much worse—below the disco.

> **WORD OF MOUTH**
>
> "We love to cruise and early on found out that we preferred saving money by booking an inside room. This cruise we booked an inside with no assignment. We were told that we would probably get an upgrade and we got a higher deck. It is easy enough to run up or down stairs to see whatever is of interest outside. By running the stairs all day we can also eat all the sumptuous dinners!"
>
> —Bev G

On the other hand, if you view your cabin as your sanctuary, you will want a bit more than standard inside for your home away from home. For an inside cabin with a view of the inside action, Royal Caribbean's Voyager-, Freedom-, and Oasis-class ships and Cunard Line's *Queen Mary 2* offer accommodations with windows overlooking interior lobbies and, in the case of Royal Caribbean's Oasis-class ships, balconies facing courtyards open to the sky. Obstructed-view outside locations offer natural light, but there might be a lifeboat outside your window instead of an ocean view. Moving up a few categories may cost less than you imagine and result in a more comfortable space with a large window or even a balcony. High-end suites should include perks that justify their cost.

Although cruise ship cabins are not all created equal, they are all designed for comfort, convenience, and practicality. Standard cabins on modern cruise vessels haven't quite achieved parity with land-based resort accommodations in terms of size, but cruise lines recognize that small touches (and more spacious quarters) go a long way toward overall passenger contentment. You're likely to find your cabin equipped with amenities such as a personal safe, robes for use on board, a hair dryer, and bathroom toiletries—the added niceties that hotels have long provided for their guests.

Aside from the little details that vary from cruise line to cruise line, staterooms are furnished for functionality. At the very least, a cabin contains beds (often twin beds that can be combined to form a queen- or king-size bed), a dressing table–writing desk, a chair, drawers or shelf storage, a closet, and a bathroom with shower. There's almost always a television and telephone. Cabins on newer ships often have sitting areas with a sofa or love seat and a coffee table.

The cabin dressing table–writing desk will almost always have two different electric receptacles—one will accept standard U.S.-style plugs (110-volt), and the other is for European-style plugs (220-volt). To plug in more than one gadget at a time, you'll need a power strip, or, for dual voltage appliances, a plug adapter. You'll have to bring along your own adapter—the kind that allows U.S.-style plugs with flat prongs to be inserted into European-style round receptacles. I had always packed a short power strip in order to use more than one appliance until my husband pointed out I could recharge my cell phone while using the computer simply by utilizing the second receptacle with a flat-to-round prong adapter attached. Cabin bathrooms generally feature a dual-voltage plug receptacle suitable for electric shavers only. The hair dryers provided are usually built into the wall or tucked away in a drawer.

GETTING TO THE CRUISE PORT

For the convenience of one-stop shopping, all cruise lines have a so-called Air & Sea program that allows you to purchase your airline ticket to the port of embarkation and your cruise ticket at the same time; you'll also get airport transfers. An added bonus is that by bundling all your air, land, and sea transportation together, you can have a cruise vacation that's much more worry-free. On the other hand, forward-thinking cruisers who buy discounted airline tickets in advance can often save a bundle—or at least enough to cover the cost of a precruise overnight hotel. Comparison shopping makes sense if you have the time and inclination to do it.

The main drawback of an Air & Sea program is an obvious one: you can't choose the time you fly. The cruise lines buy the number of seats they need, but the airlines themselves pick the flights. Although all flights should be scheduled to give you enough time to make your embarkation, you might find yourself with an inconvenient flight time, and there's not much you can do about that. Even if your preferred air carrier has nonstop service from your gateway airport directly to your port of embarkation, you might be scheduled with an extremely early departure or with multiple stops along the way.

Flights assigned to cruise passengers aren't always the most desirable because cruise lines pay low contractual fares and because independent travelers tend to book the most desirable flights. Basically, that means you're getting what the airlines have open when the time comes to assign flights. If you want to be assured you'll fly on a particular airline at a particular time, request an "air deviation." For a fee—plus any associated airline charges—the cruise line will attempt to book your preference. There's no guarantee you'll get what you want, but they will try.

Your airline tickets are usually issued 30 days before sailing, and the cruise line cannot confirm specific seat assignments. This is where booking through a travel agent will help you. Most cruise specialists are savvy enough to secure flight numbers 30 days out and nail down seat assignments. Make sure yours does.

A Cruising Bill of Rights

In 2013, after a string of mishaps on large cruise ships, the Cruise Lines International Association (CLIA), adopted a so-called Bill of Rights for cruise passengers that outlines what a passenger is entitled to when booking a cruise on a member line. Most of the major cruise lines in the world are members of CLIA. Some critics of this bill say that it actually limits what a cruise line will do for passengers when something goes wrong, while others feel that it helps clarify the responsibilities of cruise lines for the benefit of passengers.

Here is the full "bill of rights."

1. The right to disembark a docked ship if essential provisions such as food, water, restroom facilities, and access to medical care cannot adequately be provided onboard, subject only to the Master's concern for passenger safety and security, customs, and immigration requirements of the port.

2. The right to a full refund for a trip that is canceled due to mechanical failures, or a partial refund for voyages that are terminated early due to those failures.

3. The right to have available on board ships operating beyond rivers or coastal waters full-time, professional emergency medical attention, as needed until shoreside medical care becomes available.

4. The right to timely information updates as to any adjustments in the itinerary of the ship in the event of a mechanical failure or emergency, as well as timely updates of the status of efforts to address mechanical failures.

5. The right to a ship crew that is properly trained in emergency and evacuation procedures.

6. The right to an emergency power source in the case of a main generator failure.

7. The right to transportation to the ship's scheduled port of disembarkation or the passenger's home city in the event a cruise is terminated early due to mechanical failures.

8. The right to lodging if disembarkation and an overnight stay in an unscheduled port are required when a cruise is terminated early due to mechanical failures.

9. The right to have included on each cruise line's website a toll-free phone line that can be used for questions or information concerning any aspect of shipboard operations.

10. The right to have this Cruise Line Passenger Bill of Rights published on each line's website.

There are distinct advantages to using a cruise line's Air & Sea program. When major holidays draw near, an Air & Sea program may be the only way to secure any airline reservation, let alone an affordable one. And when you're taking a one-way cruise you'll have to purchase two one-way tickets, which is often more expensive than a round-trip, unless you purchase the cruise line's budget-friendly air add-on.

These programs have perks other than price. For example, there's comfort in knowing someone is looking out for you and your luggage as well as providing ground transportation to the ship. Uniformed cruise line agents meet incoming passengers to smooth their way from airport to pier.

Even with Air & Sea flight arrangements, lengthy airline delays can result in literally missing the boat. However, it's a common misconception that when you use a cruise line's Air & Sea program, the cruise line is responsible for getting you to your ship. On the contrary, the responsibility is with the airline. When cruise lines contract with airlines for tickets, the airline is responsible for getting you to the next port of call if a flight is cancelled; they should even put you on a different airline's flight to ensure that you don't miss the ship if that is possible. However, cruise line personnel will help you make alternate arrangements. You'll be given an emergency telephone number to call in case your flight is delayed, and the line will help you find alternate flights. They can also assist with hotel arrangements and transfers (sometimes the airline will pay for these if they are at fault).

If you must fly to port the same day your ship sails, it's wise to request the first flight of the day from your departure city. Delays in later flights can snowball, creating air-scheduling havoc and scarce seats as flyers scramble to get on board later flights.

You should also consider your flight home as well. Although your itinerary may state that the ship docks back in its home port at 7 am, passengers are unlikely to begin leaving the vessel much earlier than 9 am. Prior to disembarkation, the ship must be cleared by Customs and Immigration. On leaving the ship all passengers must be cleared through Customs and Immigration as well. This is normally done in the terminal, either before or after retrieving your luggage. In any event, cruise lines normally warn you not to schedule your flight home before noon or even 1 pm, depending on the port location. In New York City, the suggested time is no earlier than midafternoon.

Suppose you don't want to fly. After 9/11, cruise lines realized that the traveling public wanted more alternatives, and the solution was surprisingly simple. If passengers couldn't get to the ports easily, bring the ports to them. In addition to the busiest embarkation ports of Miami, Fort Lauderdale, Port Canaveral, and New York, other port cities are also capable of handling passenger ships. Some ships cruise from New Orleans, Tampa, Jacksonville, Charleston, Houston, or Baltimore. By 2005, relative newcomer Galveston, Texas, ranked as the fifth-busiest cruise port in the United States, thanks largely to a substantial drive-to market. Secure parking is always available, either within the port itself or nearby. Off-site parking is almost always less expensive than parking within the port and often includes a free shuttle to and from the port.

Missing the Boat

The first port of call on your itinerary might be Key West, but don't hurry there to board the ship if you missed its initial sailing. By trying to do so you'll violate the Passenger Services Act of 1886 (PSA), which was enacted to protect American passenger shipping interests.

The relevant part of the PSA reads as follows: "No foreign vessel shall transport passengers between ports or places in the United States, either directly or by way of a foreign port, under a penalty of $300 for each passenger so transported and landed." An exception was made for cruise ships:

"Foreign-flagged cruise ships may carry passengers from a U.S. port as long as they return them to the same port (a 'cruise to nowhere'). Foreign vessels may also call at intermediate U.S. ports as long as no passenger permanently leaves the vessel at those ports and the vessel makes at least one call at a foreign port."

Even outdated U.S. laws die hard—or hardly ever die—so the PSA still rules the high seas. Yes, a few exceptions exist. And, no, officials won't allow you to pay the fine and board in just any U.S. port.

ARRIVING EARLY AT THE EMBARKATION PORT

The possibility of flight delays and cancellations is the best reason to pad your vacation with a precruise day of relaxation. Arrive early and unwind—an especially wise move if your home is in the snowbelt and your cruise is in January. The extra expense is well worth the peace of mind.

Pre- and postcruise packages, which can include hotel accommodations and ground transportation, are offered by most cruise lines. Like airfare, the convenience of a package is often offset by a higher price tag.

With a bit of research, you can make your own independent arrangements at considerable savings. Many hotels near major ports of embarkation have their own packages and offers, which may include transportation to the cruise port. Some hotels offer free or reduced rate parking for the duration of your cruise, a handy addition if you are driving.

GETTING READY

Once your ideal cruise is booked, it's time to start getting yourself and your family prepared for the trip. Some of the steps you can take are merely for your convenience while others are really important. But it's critical that you prepare in advance for your cruise; don't wait until the last minute, when even a minor oversight could ruin your vacation. As your sailing date approaches, do not hesitate to ask your travel agent if you have any questions.

Many cruise passengers claim that planning is half the fun, and they really throw themselves into the process. That makes sense when you consider you may be out of touch with your home, family, and business when your cruise ship is at sea. Depending on the itinerary, that could be for many hours, even days, at a time.

You'll sleep better if you think ahead. Some of the things you'll need to do before your cruise take time—for instance, obtaining the proper documents. Other details may seem relatively simple but can expand in significance if you leave them all for the last minute. By breaking your preparation down into manageable chunks, you'll have plenty of time to get ready and won't be frazzled in the last week before your cruise. The last thing you want is to leave something important undone because you were in a rush. It's easier to leave your worries behind on the dock when you plan with care.

DOCUMENTS

It's every passenger's responsibility to have proper identification. If you arrive at port without the travel documents you need, you will not be allowed to board your cruise ship and the cruise line will not issue you a refund. Most travel agents know the requirements and can guide you to the proper agencies to obtain the documents you need if you don't already have them.

PASSPORTS

Cruises to the Bahamas, Mexico, and the Caribbean require proof of citizenship for all passengers. As of June 1, 2009, all American citizens are required to present a passport or other approved document denoting citizenship and identity for all land *and* sea travel into the United States. However, the rules can still be confusing:

If you are a U.S. citizen traveling to the Caribbean on a cruise that begins and ends in the same U.S. port, then you will still be permitted to depart from or enter the United States with proof of identity (a government-issued photo ID such as a driver's license), along with proof of citizenship (a government-issued birth certificate with official seal). A U.S.-issued Enhanced Driver's License (EDL), which denotes identity and citizenship, is also an acceptable alternative to a passport for reentry into the United States.

■ You can also use one of the new U.S. passport cards, which are less expensive than a full passport but aren't good for international air travel (flights to Puerto Rico, St. Thomas, and St. Croix from U.S. airports are *not* considered international travel).

■ You may still be required to present a U.S. passport when you dock in a foreign port, depending on the islands or countries that your cruise ship is visiting. Foreign policies differ.

■ If your cruise begins in one U.S. port and ends in a different port, then you will be required to have a valid passport or passport card.

■ If your cruise begins or ends in Puerto Rico or St. Thomas, then you do not need a valid passport; flights to Puerto Rico are considered regular domestic flights, though flights to St. Thomas are slightly different (no passport is required, but you must show proof of citizenship in the form of a photo ID plus an official birth certificate).

■ If your cruise begins in a foreign port (Barbados, the Dominican Republic, or some other Caribbean island), then you must have a valid passport; a passport card will not do in such a case because you will need the passport to fly back to the United States.

■ Canadian citizens must have a valid passport to enter or leave the United States.

■ Resident aliens of the United States need a valid passport from their home country as well as their Alien Resident Receipt Card (form I-551), commonly known as a green card.

■ Citizens of all other foreign countries—if they aren't permanent residents of the United States—must carry a valid passport and a visa waiver or multiple-entry visa for the United States.

■TIP➜ Even if you are taking a cruise that begins and ends in the same U.S. port, you may still want to travel with a valid passport that will enable you to fly from the United States to meet your ship at the first port should you miss the scheduled embarkation; a valid passport will also allow you to leave the ship without significant delays and complications before the cruise ends if you must fly back to the United States due to an emergency.

GETTING OR RENEWING A PASSPORT

Because more people will now require passports to travel, you should apply for a passport as far in advance of your cruise as possible if you don't have one or need to renew your current passport. The process usually takes at least six weeks and can take longer during very busy periods. The best time to apply for a passport or to renew is in fall and winter. Before any trip, check your passport's expiration date, and, if necessary, renew it as soon as possible.

You can expedite your passport application if you're traveling within two weeks by paying a fee of $60 (in addition to the regular passport fee) and appearing in person at a regional passport office. Also, several passport expediting services will handle your application for you (for a hefty fee, of course) and can get you a passport even sooner. For

FODOR'S CRUISE PREPARATION TIME LINE

3 TO 4 MONTHS BEFORE SAILING

■ Check with your travel agent or the State Department for the identification required for your cruise.

■ Gather the necessary identification you need. If you need to replace a lost birth certificate, apply for a new passport, or renew one that's about to expire, start the paperwork now. Doing it at the last minute is stressful and often costly.

60 TO 75 DAYS BEFORE SAILING

■ Make the final payment on your cruise fare. Though the dates vary, your travel agent should remind you when the payment date draws near. Failure to submit the balance on time can result in the cancellation of your reservation.

■ Make a packing list for each person you'll be packing for.

■ Begin your wardrobe planning now. Try things on to make sure they fit and are in good repair (it's amazing how stains can magically appear months after something has been dry cleaned). Set things aside.

■ If you need to shop, get started so you have time to find just the right thing (and perhaps to return or exchange just the right thing). You may also need to allow time for alterations.

■ Make kennel reservations for your pets. (If you're traveling during a holiday period, you may need to do this even earlier.)

■ Arrange for a house sitter.

■ If you're cruising, but your kids are staying home:

■ Make child care arrangements.

■ Go over children's schedules to make sure they'll have everything they need while you're gone (gift for a birthday party, supplies for a school project, permission slip for a field trip).

■ If you have small children, you may want to put together a small bag of treats for them to open while you're gone—make a tape of yourself reading a favorite bedtime story or singing a lullaby (as long as it's you, it will sound fantastic to them).

30 DAYS BEFORE SAILING

■ If you purchased an Air & Sea package, call your travel agent for the details of your airline schedule. Request seat assignments.

■ If your children are sailing with you, check their wardrobes now (do it too early and the really little kids may actually grow out of garments).

■ Make appointments for any personal services you wish to have prior to your cruise. For example, a haircut or manicure.

■ Get out your luggage and check the locks and zippers. Check for anything that might have spilled inside on a previous trip.

■ If you need new luggage or want an extra piece to bring home souvenirs, purchase it now.

2 TO 4 WEEKS BEFORE SAILING

■ Receive your cruise documents through the travel agent, or download them online.

■ Examine the documents for accuracy (correct cabin number, sailing date, and dining arrangements); make sure names are spelled correctly. If there's something you do not understand, ask now.

■ Read all the literature in your document package for suggestions specific to your cruise. Most cruise lines include helpful information.

■ Pay any routine bills that may be due while you're gone.

■ Go over your personalized packing list again. Finish shopping.

3

1 WEEK BEFORE SAILING
■ Finalize your packing list and continue organizing everything in one area.

■ Buy film or digital media and check the batteries in your camera.

■ Refill prescription medications with an adequate supply.

■ Make two photocopies of your passport or ID and credit cards. Leave one copy with a friend and carry the other copy separately from the originals.

■ Get cash and/or traveler's checks at the bank. If you use traveler's checks, keep a separate record of the serial numbers. Get a supply of one-dollar bills for tipping baggage handlers (at the airport, hotel, pier, etc.).

■ You may also want to put valuables and jewelry that you won't be taking with you in the safety deposit box while you're at the bank.

■ Arrange to have your mail held at the post office or ask a neighbor to pick it up.

■ Stop newspaper delivery or ask a neighbor to bring it in for you.

■ Arrange for lawn and houseplant care or snow removal during your absence (if necessary).

■ Leave your itinerary, the ship's telephone number (plus the name of your ship and your stateroom number), and a house key with a relative or friend.

■ If traveling with young children, purchase small games or toys to keep them occupied while en route to your embarkation port.

3 DAYS BEFORE SAILING
■ Confirm your airline flights; departure times are sometimes subject to change.

■ Put a card with your name, address, telephone number, and itinerary inside each suitcase.

■ Fill out the luggage tags that came with your document packet and follow the instructions regarding when and how to attach them.

■ If you haven't already done it online, complete any other paperwork that the cruise line included with your documents (foreign customs and immigration forms, onboard charge application, etc.). Do not wait until you're standing in the pier check-in line to fill them in!

■ Do last-minute laundry and tidy up the house.

■ Pull out the luggage and begin packing.

THE DAY BEFORE SAILING
■ Take pets to the kennel.

■ Water houseplants and lawn (if necessary).

■ Dispose of any perishable food in the refrigerator.

■ Mail any last-minute bills.

■ Set timers for indoor lights.

■ Reorganize your wallet. Remove anything you will not need (department store or gas credit cards, etc.), put them in an envelope.

■ Finish packing and lock your suitcases.

DEPARTURE DAY
■ Adjust the thermostat and double-check the door locks.

■ Turn off the water if there's danger of frozen pipes while you're away.

■ Arrange to be at the airport a minimum of two hours before your departure time (follow the airline's instructions).

■ Have photo ID and/or passport ready for airport check-in.

■ Slip your car keys, parking claim checks, and airline tickets in your carry-on luggage. Never pack these items in checked luggage.

U.S. citizens, a passport costs $135 if you're 16 or older, $105 if you are under 16. It's valid for 10 years if you're 16 or older, 5 years if you are under 16. A cheaper alternative is a passport card, which costs $55 for an adult, $40 for a minor under 16 (though this card is *not* valid for international air travel, only for border crossings by land and sea). You can usually renew a passport by mail as long as you can send in your current passport and are over 16 years old. If you're applying for a passport for the first time, you'll have to appear in person to make

> ### ONLINE CRUISE PREP
>
> To expedite your preboarding paperwork, some cruise lines have convenient forms on their websites. As long as you have your reservation (or booking) number, you can provide the required immigration information, reserve shore excursions, and even indicate any special requests from the comfort of your home. Be sure to print a copy of the form to present at the pier.

your application, but most cities and towns large and small have some office that processes passport applications—usually a post office or courthouse. Some public libraries or county or state courthouses even process applications.

U.S. Passport Information **National Passport Information Center** (☎ *877/487–2778, 888/874–7793 TDD/TTY ⊕ travel.state.gov).*

PERMISSION LETTERS

But you may need even more documentation than that. Often, single parents or grandparents want to take their children or grandchildren on a cruise; it's also not uncommon for parents to invite their teenager's friend to sail along. An often-overlooked requirement is a notarized letter of permission, which is usually required anytime a child under 18 travels to a foreign country with anyone other than both of his or her parents. The absent or noncustodial parent (or parents) must usually give explicit written permission for their children to travel outside the United States.

Airlines, cruise lines, and immigration agents can—and usually will—deny minor children initial boarding or entry to foreign countries without proper proof of identification and citizenship *and* a permission letter from absent or noncustodial parents. This requirement would apply to any single (divorced, widowed, or simply married-but-solo) parents, grandparents, or family friends taking children on a cruise. Many cruises have been spoiled because groups arrived at the dock or the airport with the kids but without a letter of permission. (Or at the very least, there's been a lot of anxiety waiting for faxed letters to arrive at the last minute.)

There's a good reason for why this letter is now a requirement. According to Department of State Publication 10542: "With the number of international child custody cases on the rise, several countries have instituted passport requirements to help prevent child abductions. For example, Mexico has a law that requires a child traveling alone, or with only one parent, or in someone else's custody, to carry written,

SAMPLE PERMISSION LETTER

Here's the text you might use for a typical letter of permission. You should type this up yourself, putting in all the specific details of your trip in place of the blanks.

CONSENT FOR MINOR CHILDREN TO TRAVEL

Date: _____

I (we): _____

authorize my/our minor child(ren): _____

to travel to: _____ on _____

aboard Airline/Flight Number: _____

and/or Cruise Ship: _____

with _____.

Their expected date of return is: _____.

In addition, I (we) authorize: _____ to consent to any necessary routine or emergency medical treatment during the aforementioned trip.

Signed: _____(Parent)

Signed: _____(Parent)

Address: _____

_____

_____

Telephone:_____

Sworn to and signed before me, a Notary Public,

this _____ day of _____, 20_____

_____

Notary Public Signature and Seal

notarized consent from the absent parent or parents. No authorization is needed if the child travels alone and is in possession of a U.S. passport. A child traveling alone with a birth certificate requires written, notarized authorization from both parents."

Proof of identity and citizenship is rather straightforward: you need either a certified copy of a birth certificate or a passport for your child. The permission letter is a bit more vexing because most people aren't aware of the necessity to have it, let alone what it should include. An attorney could prepare a formal affidavit, but a simple letter-style document is adequate as long as it's signed before an authorized notary. To be acceptable, it should include specific details about the trip, the custodial adult(s), and the child(ren). Although no one wants to think about medical emergencies while on vacation, it's also wise to include consent for the custodial adult to authorize emergency treatment for the child in case the need should arise.

Some parents, particularly mothers who do not share the same last name as their children, should take no chances and also carry a copy of their divorce decree or, in the case of widows, a death certificate for their spouse.

After going to all the trouble to secure proper documentation, it could turn out that no one even asks for it. Why did you bother? Because if you had not, the possibility existed that your cruise ship may have sailed without you and your very disappointed family. You may even find that it's easier to enter a port of call than to leave it with your own child.

> **WORD OF MOUTH**
>
> "Try not to resent the men who wear a navy blue blazer, gray slacks, and the same black shoes for almost every dressy occasion and look just fine. It may be boring, but it's easy to pack!"
> —Janet N.

PICKING A CRUISE WARDROBE

So your closet is not full of designer outfits and matching shoes? Not to worry, neither are the closets of most cruise ship passengers. The reality is that you do not need to overextend a credit card and fill your suitcases with new cruise duds. Despite any fashion anxiety, you probably have almost everything you need.

Cruise wear falls into three categories: casual, informal, and formal. Cruise documents should include information indicating how many evenings fall into each of those categories. You'll know when to wear what by reading your ship's daily newsletter, where each evening's dress code will be prominently announced. Dress codes are primarily directed toward adults, so children's wardrobes can be planned based on what their parents are wearing and the activities they are participating in.

CASUAL WEAR

First and foremost, there's casual wear. This is exactly what it implies: clothing to be comfortable in. Your plans for the day will dictate what you should wear. For warm-weather cruises, you'll typically need swimwear, a cover-up, and sandals for pool and beach. Time spent ashore touring and shopping calls for shorts topped with T-shirts or polo-style shirts and comfy walking shoes. Conservative is the rule to live by, and mix-and-match will save room in your suitcase. If you intend to purchase souvenir T-shirts, plan to make them a part of your cruise wardrobe and pack fewer tops.

Evening casual does not mean shorts. For men it's khaki-type slacks and a nice polo or sport shirt. Ladies' evening-casual outfits might consist of sporty dresses, skirts and tops, or pants outfits. By sticking to two colors and a few accessories, you can mix up tops and bottoms for a different look every night.

The first and last nights on board are always casual for obvious reasons—you may not have your luggage before dinner that first night, and you've already packed for home on the last night. Many people consider denim jeans casual wear. Some cruise lines discourage them in the dining room. Use your own judgment, and keep in mind that denim is hot—you might want to wear lighter fabrics in the Caribbean heat.

INFORMAL WEAR

Informal dress is a little trickier because it applies only to evening wear and can mean different things depending on the cruise line. Informal for women is a dressier dress or pants outfit; for men it almost always includes a sport coat and often a tie. Check your documents carefully for a specific definition of "informal."

FORMAL WEAR

It has been said that Formal Night is fantasyland for women and torture for men—from the sounds of male grumbling, that is. If you like to dress up, this is your night to shine. You'll see women in everything from simple cocktail dresses to elaborate, glittering gowns. Tuxedos (either all black or with a white dinner jacket) or dark suits are required for gentlemen, but a quick review of the dining room will show you that on most mainstream cruises, dark suits prevail. If you have been a mother of the bride lately, chances are your outfit for the wedding is just perfect for formal night. For children, Sunday-best is entirely appropriate.

If a man decides to go all out, then he must decide whether to buy or rent a tuxedo, which is ultimately a point of individual preference. As a rule of thumb, if you're going to wear a tuxedo more than two or three times, it makes economic sense to purchase one. Most cruise lines make it easy to rent the entire outfit, though—and if you do so, it will be waiting for you when you board. Be sure to make these arrangements well before your cruise; your travel agent can get the details from the cruise line.

If yours is a rental, try it on immediately so alterations can be made if necessary.

Even if you're renting a tuxedo, by all means buy your own studs. You don't have to spend a fortune on them; just get some that look classy. Why? A sure-fire way to spot a rented tuxedo is by the inexpensive studs that come with them. A few words about vests: Many men with a little girth consider them more comfortable than cummerbunds.

Which formal night is most formal? Every woman wants to know the answer to that question because we all have a dress we think is more stylish, or maybe we just feel more beautiful wearing it. Unless you eat like a bird or never gain an ounce, save your roomiest formal outfit for the second formal night.

How glittery can you get without being mistaken for a showgirl? Totally sequined and beaded dresses are not as fashionable as they once were, and you may want to avoid the temptation of borrowing your daughter's frou-frou prom dress as well—neither makes a good fashion statement. When selecting formal outfits, think simple. There's nothing more elegant than a well-cut, simple, black dress. But there's nothing more fun than a flashy or sexy dress that turns heads. It's totally up to you. One of the most practical and useful garments any woman can own is a pair of black, silky cocktail pants. They take up no room at all in the suitcase and don't wrinkle. Best of all, with two dressy tops you have two different formal outfits with a minimum of fuss. Even better, they usually have comfortable elastic waistbands.

If formal is just not a part of your vocabulary or lifestyle, consider booking on one of the cruise lines that have modified it or done away with it altogether. On some cruise lines every night is country-club casual.

OTHER CRUISE WARDROBE TIPS

For versatility and to stretch your options, coordinate your wardrobe by selecting garments in one or two basic colors to mix and match. No one really notices whether you recycle outfits, so don't be afraid to wear the same things more than once. Create different looks with accessories, either from home or purchased in port. To pack small, take only two pairs of shoes; comfortable all-purpose shoes for day and dressier ones for evening. If you must have your big, clunky athletic shoes, wear them on the plane and pack the others.

An absolute essential for women is a shawl or light sweater. Aggressive air-conditioning can make public rooms uncomfortable, particularly if you're sunburned from a day at the beach.

Expenses for cruise ship laundry, pressing, and dry-cleaning services can add up fast, especially laundry, as charges are per item and the rates are similar to those charged in hotels. Happily, some ships have a low-cost or free self-serve laundry room (the room usually has an iron and ironing board in addition to washers and dryers). You can make laundry less important when shopping if you look for clothing made of lightweight microfiber. Besides taking up less suitcase space, microfiber sheds wrinkles and dries quickly. In terms of comfort, these fabrics wick moisture away from the body, keeping you cool in the tropics and necessitating fewer clothing changes. Tuck a small bottle of laundry liquid and clothespins in your suitcase and, in a pinch, you can wash smaller items in your bathroom sink and hang them to dry in the shower. A hair dryer speeds the process along in record time.

After all this obsessing about clothing, consider the unthinkable: What if your luggage is delayed? What if it doesn't show up until the end of the cruise? Unfortunately, this happens. And if it happens to you, do not stress out. Shop here and there and pick up what you need until the next stop—your luggage could appear in the next port. Avoid some of the anxiety lost luggage can cause by carrying on your essentials when you board. Consider using a garment bag or rollaboard containing formal clothing, a bathing suit, and at least one casual outfit just in case.

And here's one last thought about cruise wear: Be considerate by adhering to each evening's dress code and do not rush back to your cabin to change into shorts immediately after dinner.

PICKING LUGGAGE

It just so happens that the best luggage for your cruise is also suitable for many other purposes. Airport and pier baggage handlers are notoriously rough with suitcases, so a top consideration is sturdiness. Your suitcase does not have to be top-of-the-line, but it should be built well enough to withstand the rigors of conveyors and sorting machines, not to mention being stacked, dropped, and thrown through the air.

Luggage can be a significant investment, so the right choice in terms of design and durability is important. Brand-name luggage that comes with a good warranty is always desirable, but no-name or private label brands can also stand the test of time.

Hard-sided luggage is usually the longest wearing of all. In addition to being the most rugged, the built-in locks also make these suitcases the most secure and watertight. For frequent flyers who want the greatest mileage, it makes sense to look at hard-sided luggage. Improved composition materials have made their shells lighter; however, even when empty they can be heavy.

If casual observations at airport conveyors are any indication, soft-sided suitcases are by far the most popular choice. They're lighter in weight, their zippers can be secured pretty easily, almost all have wheels, and some are expandable for additional packing volume.

What should you look for in a suitcase? Hard-sided suitcases should have metal piano hinges and solid hardware. Combination locks are great, but look for those that also have key locks. Unless a clasp is locked, it could snap open. Wheels (preferably in-line skate type) should turn smoothly and be set wide for stability. Retractable handle assemblies should be strong and adjustable for maximum comfort and ease of maneuverability. Padded interiors with pockets and garment tie-downs are fairly standard.

The soft-sided suitcases you're considering should be covered in a tightly woven ballistic nylon for the greatest durability; other fabrics can snag, pill, and tear more easily. None of these fabrics is indestructible, but ballistic nylon is usually judged to be the best, especially when it's also Teflon® coated. Frame construction is also an important factor in the ultimate stability of the suitcase; it should be strong enough that it does not flex out of shape when the suitcase is fully packed. Corners should be reinforced with rubber bumpers hefty enough to prevent abrasion, which all too often occurs in these vulnerable areas. Wheels and handle assemblies should have the same properties as hard-sided cases; a solid skid plate between the wheels is beneficial to protect the suitcase fabric from damage when inevitable encounters with curbs and escalators occur. Look for self-healing, industrial-grade zippers that move smoothly and have large-enough zipper pulls for ease of use. Interiors can include a variety of wet bags, pockets, and other organizers, particularly in the lid door.

All suitcases should be well balanced with adequate feet so they do not fall over when you're waiting in a check-in line. In addition, many of the newest models include removable garment bags or suiters for wrinkle-free packing.

Even some of the smallest 22-inch suitcases are outfitted with suiters—those fold-up panels that accommodate hanging garments. These are great wrinkle-proof organizers that tuck formal clothing neatly into the suitcase. The handiest are the ones that are removable for times that you don't need them.

Business travelers have long favored garment bags for carry-on ease and quick, wrinkle-free packing. Their bulky favorites are being replaced these days by garment bags on wheels that are virtually rolling closets with multiple pockets and organizers for folded items, shoes, and even toiletries. Look for the same construction qualities as any soft-sided suitcase. These bags hold a lot but are not sized as carry-ons.

You know the days of massive steamer trunks are history, but is there a maximum amount of luggage that you can bring on a cruise ship? Yes, there really is a limit of sorts. Although some cruise lines state that each passenger is allowed 200 pounds of personal luggage, you're unlikely to see anyone's bags actually being weighed. However, it's not the cruise line restrictions that passengers need to worry about. Cruisers arriving at their embarkation port by air should be aware of airline restrictions. Most major airlines enforce suitcase size and weight policies, resulting in a rude (and expensive) surprise to some travelers with large, heavy suitcases.

Unfortunately, many 29- to 30-inch suitcases now exceed the maximum size limitation of 62 linear inches (a combination of length, width, depth) for airline checked luggage and are often subject to additional charges. Then there's the matter of suitcase wheel assemblies and whether they're included in the measurements or not. That depends on who you ask, and responses are all over the map. It seems the ultimate arbiter of oversize dimensions is the agent checking in passengers at the airport.

Those 29- to 30-inch suitcases are likely to incur excess weight charges, as well. As many travelers discover, they hold so much that they are prone to be overly heavy. Depending on their size, rolling garment bags might also fall into the category of too big to be checked free of charge. These days, you'll usually be charged extra for anything over 50 pounds; on a few airlines the limit is still 70 pounds, but on a few it's even as low as 40 pounds.

Don't even think of expanding a suitcase in the 29- to 30-inch size range to accommodate the addition of souvenirs for the trip home—the additional size and weight just will not fly these days without adding

Drugs: What You Can't Pack

It goes without saying that you shouldn't purchase illegal drugs in the islands and try to bring them into the United States at the end of your cruise. In an odd twist, a group of hapless cruisers attempted to actually board a cruise ship in Florida with stashes they planned to consume on board. They were met in the terminal by U.S. Customs, a drug-sniffing dog, and local law enforcement agents who took the unusual step of examining passengers leaving the United States. It seems the excited group shared their packing lists with one another on the Internet and tipped off the authorities. The most common hiding place for their drugs wasn't very original—inside their underwear—and when they realized the search was on it caused quite a melee.

Moral of this story? Other than exercising discretion when sharing your plans openly in a chat room, just say no to buying drugs in foreign ports unless your vacation strategy includes spending time in the brig—or worse, in a Caribbean jail.

a fee as robust as the bag. Take a folding tote bag for purchases, and carry it on the plane home.

Remember that two suitcases in the 24- to 26-inch size range will hold as much (or more) than a single larger suitcase and are kinder to your back when you have to lift them. Most airlines charge for checked bags these days, so check with your airline and budget for anything you wish to check. The charges are quite high for excess baggage; don't be caught by surprise at the airport check-in counter.

Whether you buy new bags or carry your trusty old ones, take the following steps before you leave for the airport:

■ Ascertain the exact baggage regulations of the airline(s) you're most likely to fly with and strictly adhere to them.

■ For ease of moving through check-in lines, buy luggage pieces that can piggyback on one another.

■ Measure suitcases for size and include the wheels just in case.

■ Weigh packed suitcases on the bathroom scale.

PACKING

You may find that packing less is more if you follow this experienced travelers' adage: "Pack your suitcases and remove half the contents. Then take twice as much money!" I have a confession. I'm a packaholic. I was hopelessly addicted to overburdening my husband with bulging garment bags and suitcases that barely closed. The overflow from my tote bag got stashed in his pockets. Practicality has forced me to change my ways.

I became a confirmed packing list maker following my very first cruise on the SS *Norway*. I overlooked one little grooming essential that I really needed: tweezers. One of my tablemates forgot to pack her hair dryer. And it dawned on us that a cruise is unlike a resort vacation in one important way: there's no local supermarket or drugstore to pop into when you need something. Although many ships stock a variety of sundries, they may not have just what you need and, if they do, the cost can be considerably more than comparable items at home. My tablemate and I were both able to find suitable replacements ashore for our forgotten items, but we spent two days at sea before arriving in our first port of call where we could shop for them.

Aha! A light went on in my brain. If I had checklists, I would be less likely to leave something out of my suitcase. What simplicity. Why hadn't anyone thought of it before? While planning my second cruise, I began by creating basic packing lists for my husband and myself. Over the years I've added and deleted items—for instance, I prefer my own brand of shampoo to the products provided by most hotels and cruise lines. On the other hand, it's seldom necessary to pack a hair dryer these days, although some ships' accommodations don't provide them in all categories. I've welcomed suggestions from users of my website, CruiseDiva.com, as well. The packing list for babies was compiled entirely from my readers' input.

I begin with personal essentials and a day-by-day schedule of wardrobe requirements. This has worked fine to rein in my packing excesses. Now, mind you, the following checklists contain just about everything anyone would need on a cruise. As a result, there are many items you can just cross off. How much of each clothing item to pack (such as shirts, shorts, and underwear) is determined by the length of your cruise and your planned activities. A good rule of thumb is to pack one daytime outfit for every two days of travel. However, you may need more shirts and shorts if your plans include adventurous excursions. Clothing tends to get soiled and sweaty under some conditions and you'll want to change more frequently.

Instead of strappy sandals, you may need hiking boots and bug spray, or water shoes and no formal wear. Customize these lists to work for you based on where you're going, what you intend to do, and which cruise line you're traveling with.

PACKING FOR CHILDREN AND TEENS

About the only difference between the wardrobes of parents and younger family members is that children's clothing is smaller and takes up less space in a suitcase. Their requirements will mimic the adult versions of the bathing suits, shorts, T-shirts, shoes, and so on, which are outlined in the packing lists. If your plans include dining every night as a family, the children should be suitably attired to conform to the cruise line's dress code, although comfort is more important for their happiness than being overly formal, particularly when it comes to younger children.

Make the planning and packing stage of cruise preparation a family affair by enlisting everyone's help. To make things easy, make stacks of clothing for each child for every day of the cruise, including underwear and socks. Put each day's stack in a zipper-top plastic bag and label them Monday, Tuesday, and so on. Once on board the ship, each child can easily unpack his or her own suitcase and slip the plastic bags into drawers. Every morning they will know what to wear.

Teenagers can be quite independent creatures with definite ideas about what they prefer to wear. They're likely to insist on making their own clothing selections. Parents, you might want to keep an eye on what they've chosen to oversee the appropriateness of their wardrobes.

A TRAVEL FIRST-AID KIT

In addition to clothing, consider packing some indispensable first-aid and emergency items. Not all scrapes happen within close proximity of the ship's medical center, and some minor accidents or illnesses do not require treatment. Be prepared at all times, both on board and ashore, with basic items for first aid such as a few adhesive bandages and a small bottle of waterless antibacterial hand sanitizer, which can also be used to clean small cuts.

For all-around care, these items should be sufficient:

- adhesive bandages
- first-aid antibacterial cream
- waterless antibacterial hand sanitizer
- aspirin or nonaspirin pain reliever
- antinausea medication
- antidiarrheal medication
- antacid tablets
- antihistamine
- seasickness remedy
- zipper-top plastic bags or ice bag
- dental adhesive
- prescription medications

Even people without dentures may have several capped teeth or fillings. It's rare that a shipboard medical center features a resident dentist, so a small container of dental adhesive or special dental repair kit is handy. A temporary repair can mean the difference between discomfort and relief from sensitivity to hot and cold until a dentist is available in port.

A problem to consider when traveling is edema, the accumulation of excess fluid in body tissues. It's a common condition, particularly after long airplane flights and while cruising in hot, humid climates. Swollen ankles and feet are regular complaints, but you can take some preventative measures. During precruise flights drink plenty of water but avoid caffeine and alcoholic beverages, walk around the plane every hour, and wear special compression stockings. Should swelling still develop, raise

PACKING LISTS FOR THE FAMILY

CLOTHING FOR WOMEN
- gowns or cocktail dresses
- dress shoes and hosiery
- skirts, blouses, or pant outfits
- accessories (scarves, pins, etc.)
- shawl or sweater
- casual shoes
- T-shirts or polo shirts
- shorts or slacks
- bathing suit
- tennis shoes and socks
- undergarments
- sleepwear

CLOTHING FOR MEN
- tuxedo and accessories (studs, formal shirts, tie, cummerbund, belt), or dark business suit with shirts and ties
- dress shoes and black socks
- sport coat
- slacks and belt
- polo or golf shirts
- khaki pants
- casual shoes
- T-shirts
- shorts
- bathing suit
- tennis shoes and socks
- undergarments
- sleepwear

PACKING FOR BABY
Mothers accustomed to carrying diaper bags chock-full of gear know their babies and toddlers have as many essentials as most infantry divisions in the field. Your own physician should be your guide, but consider these suggestions from a pediatrician and experienced moms when packing for small passengers' general travel needs:

- Children's Benadryl (seasickness or restlessness)
- PediaCare decongestant
- sunblock
- adhesive bandages
- Children's Tylenol
- diaper rash ointment
- hat
- disinfectant ointment
- water shoes
- diapers
- bottles and sippy cups
- disposable bibs
- diaper wipes
- hand and face wipes
- cotton swabs
- nail clippers
- poolside robe
- bathing suit
- sunglasses
- bottled water
- juice boxes
- favorite blanket or toy
- pacifiers
- thermometer

For flights, the pediatrician suggests giving little ones a sippy cup during airplane take-offs and landings. Also consider bringing an umbrella stroller for walks around the ship and in port with your baby. The stroller is especially handy at airports.

ESSENTIALS FOR YOUR CARRY-ON

Your carry-on is your hedge against lost luggage. In addition to the toiletries, valuables, and medicines you can't do without, you should consider putting a basic change of clothing and fresh undergarments in it as well. In case your luggage is delayed, those items should help you make it through the time it takes for your suitcases to catch up with you.

As of this writing, heightened security measures have restricted the amounts of liquids, gels, and aerosols that can be carried onto airplanes. However, solid cosmetics and personal hygiene items such as lipstick, lip balm, and similar solids are permitted in carry-on bags without restriction. For carry-on liquids and gels, each container must be three ounces or smaller, and all the containers must be placed inside a single, quart-size, zippered, clear plastic bag. One, and only one, plastic bag is allowed per passenger. Exceptions to the size restrictions are made for prescription and over-the-counter medicines, as well as baby formula and breast milk, all of which must be declared before inspection. For the latest regulations on what's allowed and what isn't, check with the Transportation Security Administration (⊕ *www.tsa.gov*).

- passport, money, documents, and keys
- camera, film or memory cards, and extra batteries
- extra glasses
- reading glasses (if you use them)
- contact lens supplies
- toothbrush and toothpaste
- mouthwash and dental floss
- deodorant
- shampoo and conditioner (if you want your own brand)
- sunglasses
- shaving kit
- jewelry
- hat or cap
- travel clock
- small flashlight and nightlight
- perfume
- body and hand lotions
- talcum powder
- sun screen
- cosmetics
- brushes, combs, and hair spray
- hair dryer (if your cruise ship doesn't provide them)
- curling iron
- shower cap
- feminine hygiene products
- short, multiplug extension cord
- notebook and pen
- duct tape
- cable ties
- liquid laundry soap
- folding tote bag or waist pack
- binoculars

Post-9/11 airline regulations still prohibit sharp objects in carry-on bags, so pack your Swiss Army knife, larger tools (more than 7 inches in length), and razor-type implements (like box cutters, utility knives, and razor blades not in a cartridge) in your checked luggage. Your safety razor, a cigarette lighter, and one book of safety (non–strike anywhere) matches may be taken onto the airplane in carry-on baggage. When in doubt about whether an item is allowed in your carry-on, check the current list on the TSA website (⊕ *www.tsa.gov*).

3

Tips for Checked Luggage

The following tips apply whether you're checking your luggage at the airport or the cruise terminal:

■ Arrive at the airport in plenty of time, preferably two hours or more before departure. One of the leading causes of lost luggage is late arrivals—baggage handlers just do not have time to scan your bags and then to get them to the plane.

■ Avoid airport curbside check-in. A whopping 87% of lost or stolen luggage originates at those curbside stations.

■ One of the most common causes of misrouted bags is gate agent error. Know the three-letter code of your destination airport and verify it on the luggage tag before your bag is put on the conveyor belt.

■ Avoid connecting flights whenever possible.

■ Make sure the connection times are adequate. Do not accept anything less than an hour between flights. You might make the plane, but your luggage may not.

■ Secure your bags. Check the locking devices when you arrive at your destination, and report any damage or missing items to the airline or cruise line immediately.

■ Label luggage on the inside and outside with your name, phone number, and address (preferably a business address). Include a copy of your itinerary on the inside of your bags so you can be traced more easily.

■ Remove any old claim checks from the bags.

■ When tagging suitcases for check-in on your ship, use all the tags you receive. Put two tags on each checked bag just in case one is damaged or falls off.

your feet and apply an ice-filled zipper-top plastic bag for relief. Sleeping with elevated feet can help as well—try putting a folded blanket or life vest under the mattress.

All medications and first-aid supplies should be in their original containers and should be hand carried—do not pack them in checked luggage. Always have enough prescription medicine on hand for a couple of extra days in case of travel delays when returning home. Contact lens and eyeglasses wearers should consider packing an extra pair.

PACKING STRATEGIES

Once your major wardrobe selections are complete and the suitcases are ready, devise a streamlined packing strategy. Here are my suggestions:

■ Personalize the packing list and stick with it. Assemble everything on the list before starting to pack, and check items off when they're folded and placed in the suitcase.

■ Resist the urge to toss in something "just in case"—that's the item you surely won't need.

■ Pack small. When they're compressed, undergarments and knits take only a third of the suitcase space they normally occupy. Simply fill a large zippered storage bag with these articles and force all the air out before zipping it shut. Keep in mind that when you use zippered storage bags to compress clothing, you'll save room and get more in your luggage, but the suitcases could end up heavier because they hold more.

■ Plan ahead and shop for sample- or small-size containers of favorite toiletries.

■ Don't forget that you can carry onto your flight only small containers of liquids and gels (whatever will fit in a single, quart-size zippered storage bag); larger sizes will have to go in your checked bags.

■ To help keep garments wrinkle-free, leave them on their hangers, cover them with dry-cleaning bags, and fold over once before placing them in the suitcase. Unpacking is a snap; just open your suitcase and start hanging things in the closet.

■ Do not bring along a travel iron to touch up wrinkled garments. Irons are a fire hazard, and their use in passenger cabins is prohibited. Instead, pack a clothing steamer.

■ T-shirts can serve as a swimsuit cover-up or a nightshirt. Knit sport shirts can do double duty as well; a shirt worn a short time at dinner can easily be donned the next day for touring or lounging on the ship.

■ If the ship has self-service laundry facilities, you can pack lighter and wash clothes midway through the cruise. Remember, other passengers have the same idea, so you might encounter long lines and surly tempers. Use the ship's laundry service instead. It's pricier, but who wants to spend valuable cruise time washing clothes?

■ Use every bit of luggage space. Women's shoes will often fit inside men's. Stuff socks and other small items inside larger space-wasters. A tote bag that folds into its own zippered pocket is handy as a shopping or beach bag and invaluable when it's time to pack the souvenirs that are preventing your suitcase from closing.

■ Cross-pack your luggage with your travel companion. Chances are if a suitcase is missing, it'll turn up eventually. In the meantime, you'll both have fresh clothing until it does.

■ Valuables should never be packed in your checked luggage. Jewelry, medicine, cameras, travel documents, and a change of underclothes belong in your carry-on. For safety and peace of mind, carry traveler's checks, cash, and copies of your passport and credit cards in a money pouch under your clothing.

■ Tuck copies of your packing lists in with your travel documents. If your luggage is waylaid, you'll have a handy record of the contents.

A caveat: Unfortunately, some garments defy the dry cleaning–bag packing method. Clothing that is slightly creased or wrinkled can often be freshened up by steaming. If you don't have a clothing steamer, just hang those items in the bathroom while taking a hot, steamy shower, and often the wrinkles will fall right out. If all else fails, many ships have ironing stations in their self-service passenger launderettes or, for maximum convenience, send the offending garments to the ship's laundry for pressing.

Duct Tape—the Essential Travel Tool

So, your bags are packed and you're ready to cruise? Not quite yet if you skipped the duct tape. Don't leave your home port without one of a traveler's handiest necessities. Duct tape no longer belongs only in the garage. Some of its more mundane uses are luggage repair (fix a broken hinge with ease) and security (baggage handlers won't tamper with duct tape, it's too much trouble). Wrapped in duct tape, your luggage is easy to spot in terminals as well. For individuality, duct tape comes in colors, as well as the traditional silver. For even higher suitcase visibility, there are snazzy neon colors. It's water resistant (an important feature for ocean travelers) and can serve as an indestructible luggage tag as well as a strap—just write your name and address on the tape. Best of all, duct tape is easy to tear by hand and you don't need scissors to cut it.

There are literally thousands of uses for duct tape. Every homeowner knows that when something is supposed to stick together and it doesn't, nothing holds like duct tape. What about at sea? Is the bottom ready to fall out of your cabin's vanity drawer? Tape it until the carpenter arrives. You're a late sleeper and the drapes don't quite close? Keep the sun at bay by taping them together. Everyone has had the stitching in a hem unravel at the last minute. Duct tape to the rescue! There are bottle lids to secure, rattles to silence, drawers that won't stay shut when the ship is rolling, and other little things that happen when you least expect them.

Frequent travelers have all noticed that soft-sided luggage often becomes unzipped for one reason or another during baggage handling, either at the airport or cruise terminal. Lock the zippers together with inexpensive cable ties, which can usually be found with electrical supplies in home improvement centers. If your luggage requires hand-screening, you'll find a note inside the suitcase indicating that the contents were examined. If you use a traditional combination or keyed lock, it will be cut off and discarded. Inspectors in foreign countries can't always open the TSA-approved locks.

Once they're attached, cable ties must be removed with scissors or nail clippers. When flying to your embarkation port, never put scissors in your carry-on. Instead, place them in an unlocked outside suitcase pocket or simply pack nail clippers in your carry-on to cut the plastic ties. To keep sticky-fingered baggage handlers from riffling through your things, always secure luggage before checking in at the cruise terminal, and remember to take extra cable ties for the trip home.

4

ENJOYING
YOUR CRUISE

Visit Fodors.com for advice, updates, and bookings

With the planning, packing, and anticipation behind them, veteran cruisers sometimes view embarkation day as anticlimactic. However, for first-time cruise passengers, embarking on your first ship can be more than exhilarating—it can be downright intimidating.

Take a deep breath. You've come this far, and your ship is within sight. That first glimpse could well be an "oh my gosh" moment if you've booked a megaship. They're huge and dwarf nearly everything in their vicinity. Sit back and savor the moment because soon you'll be busy. There will be a lot happening around you, and it will all be new. Procedures may differ slightly from cruise line to cruise line, but don't worry: once you understand the process and know what to expect, you can go with the flow.

Above all, don't stress. There can be advantages to waiting in line when you reach the terminal: your luggage may beat you to your cabin, and you could meet some interesting people. After the check-in and boarding process is behind you, the fun and relaxation begin.

Think of the ship as your first destination, a movable port of call. Plan to enjoy your time on board as much as you can. Repeat after me: "They won't run out of food."

BOARDING

What exactly can you expect? First of all, keep in mind that your embarkation day cannot officially begin until the ship is clear of departing passengers and their luggage. The disembarkation process can seem as drawn-out as a divorce. While the previous weeks' passengers make their way reluctantly down the gangway, the staff and crew are busy readying the ship for the next sailing. By the time the last straggler departs, trucks are already arriving at the dock with provisions, and a lot of heavy work is going on behind the scenes. Staterooms and public lounges are thoroughly cleaned and readied, and a steady stream of supplies and luggage is brought aboard. There can even be an exchange of crew members, with some leaving and others arriving. The vessel's entire turnaround procedure is as carefully choreographed as the most intricate ballet.

WHAT TO EXPECT

CHECKING IN

Whether you take a bus transfer or taxi from the airport or a hotel, the first people you encounter at the cruise terminal are baggage handlers. They're not cruise line employees, and they do expect a tip—$2 per suitcase is sufficient. Be sure your ship's luggage tags are securely fastened to your locked suitcases before you hand them over. If you booked a guarantee and haven't received your cabin assignment, your luggage tags may be marked TBA (to be announced), or there may be a blank space where the cabin number should be written in. The baggage handlers will have a copy of the ship's manifest and can give you the proper cabin number.

Cruise line shoreside staff are milling about to point you in the right direction, and they're easily recognizable in official-looking uniforms with name tags and, often, a clipboard. Once inside the terminal, you might encounter a check-in line. Actual boarding time is often scheduled for noon, but some cruise lines will process early arrivals and then direct them to a holding area. During check-in, you'll be asked to produce your documents and any forms you were sent to complete ahead of time—or a printed copy of those you filled in online—plus proof of citizenship and a credit card (to cover charges on board). You're issued a boarding card that usually also doubles as your stateroom key and shipboard charge card. At some point—usually before you enter the check-in area—you and your hand luggage will pass through a security procedure similar to those at airports.

Although the gangway is generally not removed until 30 minutes before sailing, U.S. government security regulations require cruise lines to submit certain passenger information to law enforcement authorities at least 60 minutes prior to departure. To meet that requirement, they must have the necessary information in their computers at least 90 minutes before departure. If you arrive too late and your information is not in the system before the deadline, you run the risk being denied boarding even though the ship won't be sailing for more than an hour.

Everyone is eager to get on board and begin their vacation, but this is not the time to get cranky if you have to wait. Keep in mind that you cannot board until the ship is ready for you. Once boarding begins, you'll inevitably have your first experience with the ship's photographer and will be asked to pose for an embarkation picture. It only takes a second, so smile. You're under no obligation to purchase any photos taken of you during the cruise, but they're a nice souvenir if you do decide to buy them.

PAYING FOR THINGS ON BOARD

Let's step back a moment and take a look at what happened when you checked in at the pier. Because a cashless society prevails on cruise ships, an imprint was made of your credit card or you had to place a cash deposit for use against your onboard charges. Then you were issued a boarding/charge card that usually doubles as your stateroom key. An itemized bill is provided at the end of the voyage listing your purchases. Most onboard expenditures are charged to your shipboard account, with the exception of casino gaming (though some machines now accept your ship charge card as well as coins and paper money).

To avoid surprises at the end of your cruise, it's a good idea to set aside your charge slips and request an interim printout of your bill from the purser to ensure accuracy. Should you change your mind about charging onboard purchases, you can always inform the purser and pay in cash or traveler's checks instead. If your cash deposit was more than you spent, you'll receive a refund; if you charge more than the deposit, you'll be asked to put more on your account.

SETTLING IN

Congratulations! Once you cross the gangway, your cruise has begun. The actual boarding procedures can vary; however, you'll have to produce your boarding card for the security officer who will take your digital image to enter into the ship's

> **CAUTION**
>
> If your luggage doesn't appear when and where it should (either at the airport or cruise terminal), report the problem immediately before leaving the building and insist on a local phone number so you can follow up.

security system, if that step wasn't already taken during check-in. When leaving and reboarding the ship in port, your boarding pass is scanned and your image will appear on a screen for verification.

After you're greeted by the staff members awaiting your arrival, you'll be directed to your cabin, or, depending on the cruise line, a steward will relieve you of your carry-on luggage and accompany you. Stewards on high-end cruise lines such as Seabourn, Regent Seven Seas, SeaDream, and Silversea not only show you the way but also hand you a glass of champagne as a welcome-aboard gesture. Although a tip isn't necessarily expected by the steward who shows you to your cabin, a couple of dollars is usually appreciated by those on mainstream and premium cruise lines. On some luxury lines, gratuities are included in the fare and not expected. Your offer of a tip will be graciously refused.

Some cruise lines restrict access to cabins until a specified time and will direct you to a buffet or restaurant to enjoy lunch while you wait. Once you're in your cabin, make sure that everything is in order. Try the plumbing and set the air-conditioning—your cabin may feel warm while docked, but will cool off quickly when the ship is under way. You should find a copy of the ship's daily schedule in the cabin. Take a few moments to look it over; you'll want to know what time the muster drill takes place (a placard on the back of your cabin door will indicate directions to your emergency station), as well as meal hours and the schedule for various activities and entertainments.

Rented tuxedos are either hanging in the closet or will be delivered sometime during the afternoon, and bon voyage gifts sent by your friends or travel agent usually appear as well. Be patient if you're expecting deliveries, particularly on megaships. Cabin stewards participate in the ship's turnaround and are extremely busy, although yours will no doubt introduce himself at the first available opportunity. It will also be a while before your checked luggage arrives, so, if you haven't had lunch already, your initial order of business is usually the welcome-aboard buffet. Bring along the daily schedule to read more closely while you eat.

While making your way to the Lido buffet, no doubt you'll notice bar waiters offering trays of colorful tropical drinks, often in souvenir glasses that you can keep. Beware: They are not complimentary! If you choose one, you'll be asked to sign for it. Again, as with the photos, you're under no obligation to purchase; however, the glasses are fun souvenirs.

Do your plans for the cruise include booking shore excursions and indulging in spa treatments and salon services? The most popular tours sometimes sell out, spas can be busy during sea days, and salons are particularly busy before formal nights, so your next stops should be the Shore Excursion Desk to book tours and the spa and salon to make appointments.

Dining room seating arrangements are another matter for consideration. Some people like to check the main dining room to determine the location of their table. If it's not to your liking—or if you requested a large table and find yourself assigned to a small one—you'll want to see the headwaiter. He'll be stationed in a lounge with his charts handy to make changes; the daily schedule will indicate where and when to meet with him. If you plan to dine in the ship's specialty restaurants, you'll want to make those reservations as soon as possible.

Do not get in the habit of referring to your cruise ship as a "boat." A boat is often carried on a ship, and if you're in a boat, you're either headed for a day ashore or your ship is sinking! Even more confusing to many passengers are the directional terms *port* and *starboard*. An easy way to associate them is by remembering that *port* and *left* each contain four letters.

By late afternoon or early evening, luggage should arrive outside the cabin door, and you can unpack, settle into your cabin, and prepare for dinner. Just in case your luggage does not arrive before dinner, as sometimes happens when you're dining at the early seating, it's a good idea to have toiletries and appropriate attire in your carry-on so you can freshen up and change. Dress codes are always casual on the first evening of cruises.

For the rest of the afternoon and into the night you may find other introductory activities scheduled, such as tours of the spa and fitness center, port and shopping talks, and casino gaming lessons. Of course, there will be the compulsory muster drill, held prior to sailing or—in some unusual circumstances—within at least the first 24 hours of every cruise. No matter what terminology is used to describe it—Muster Station, Lifeboat Drill, General Emergency Stations, Compulsory Coast Guard Drill—this exercise is mandatory and required by law.

THE LIFEBOAT DRILL

Unpleasant and unlikely as it may seem, emergencies do happen. That's why one of the first things you may notice in your stateroom are the bright orange personal flotation devices (PFD), or life jackets, that are sometimes prominently displayed on the beds or stored in a closet with a small placard on the door to indicate their location. When you're checking your stateroom's features, take a moment to study the emergency card on the back of the door. The cards differ, ship by ship, but usually indicate "you are here"—the location of your cabin—and the direction you should go in case of an emergency. Your muster station will be indicated, usually by number or letter.

Common Nautical Terms

Before acquainting yourself with your ship, you should add a few nautical terms to your vocabulary:

Berth. Sleeping space on a ship (literally refers to your bed).

Bow. The pointy end of the ship, also known as *forward*. Yes, it's also the front of the ship.

Bridge. The navigational control center (where the captain drives the ship).

Bulkhead. A wall or upright partition separating a ship's compartments.

Cabin. Your accommodation on a ship (used interchangeably with *stateroom*).

Course. Measured in degrees, the direction in which a ship is headed.

Debark. To leave a ship (also known as *disembarkation*).

Draft. The depth of water needed to float a ship; the measurement from a ship's waterline to the lowest point of its keel.

Embark. To go on board a ship (also known as *embarkation*).

Galley. The ship's kitchen.

Gangway. The stairway or ramp used to access the ship from the dock.

Hatch. An opening or door on a ship, either vertical or horizontal.

Head. A bathroom aboard a ship.

Helm. The apparatus for steering a ship.

Muster. To assemble the passengers and/or crew on a ship.

Pitch. Plunging in a longitudinal direction; the up-and-down motion of a ship (a major cause of seasickness).

Port. The left side of the ship when you're facing forward.

Promenade. Usually outside, a deck that fully or partially encircles the ship, popular for walking and jogging.

Roll. Side-to-side movement of the ship (another seasickness culprit).

Stabilizers. Retractable finlike devices below the waterline that extend from a ship's hull to reduce roll and provide stability. (They're your best friend if you're prone to motion sickness.)

Starboard. The right side of the ship when you're facing forward.

Stern. The rounded end of the ship, also called *aft*. It's the back end.

Tender. A boat carried on a ship that's used to take passengers ashore when it's not possible to tie up at a dock.

Thrusters. Fanlike propulsion devices under the waterline that move a ship sideways.

Wake. The ripples left on the water's surface by a moving ship.

Cruise lines take the safety of their guests and vessels very seriously, so shortly before sailing an announcement will be made that the lifeboat drill begins when the alarm bells are sounded—seven short blasts, followed by one longer blast. Be prepared with your PFD in hand, if you are required to bring it, and proceed to your muster station. Carry the life jacket unless you are instructed to wear it, and be sure the ties don't trail on the floor; it's easy to get tripped up on them as you ascend or descend stairs. Crew members will be stationed at the stairwells on each deck to give directions. Procedures vary—on some cruise lines you'll muster in a public room to receive instructions and then continue to the lifeboat station; on others you'll immediately go to the muster station on an open deck; on some ships you are no longer required to bring your PFD to the drill.

In all cases, crew members will be on hand to check your stateroom number off their list and show you how to properly put on your PFD. You'll notice it has two important features: a light that is activated in water and a whistle. An officer assigned to your boat will instruct the group on the procedures to follow if it becomes necessary to actually lower and enter the lifeboats or to jump into the water. Should you have the urge to blow the whistle attached to the PFD, restrain yourself—you should use the whistle only in a real emergency. Stewards check the cabins to make sure that everyone attends the muster drill, so don't even think about hiding out and not participating. In an emergency situation, your survival could depend on it. Afterward, stow your life jackets back in the cabin and prepare for sail-away festivities on the pool deck.

THE FIRST EVENING

A highlight of embarkation day is the first dinner in the main restaurant, where you'll meet your waitstaff and tablemates. Order whatever you like from the menu of appetizers, salads, soups, and entrées, but save room for dessert! Other than iced tea, coffee, hot tea, and tap water, beverages in the dining room are not complimentary on most mainstream and premium ships.

After dinner you'll find the entire ship alive with action. The casino, shops, and lounges will be open to greet guests, and the cruise director usually introduces his staff at a welcome-aboard show in the main theater (shows are scheduled to coordinate with dinner seatings).

Back in your cabin for the night, you'll find that the steward has left the next day's schedule of activities, straightened things up during your absence, filled the ice bucket, provided fresh linens in the bathroom, turned down the bed, and possibly placed a chocolate on your pillow. On mainstream cruise ships you may even find a towel animal—a whimsical creature fashioned from towels—on the bed. Some stewards demonstrate a creative streak, leaving a different one every night.

TIPPING

You don't have to go overboard with extras, but one area not to skimp on is gratuities. Tipping aboard a cruise ship is possibly one of the most delicate—yet frequently debated—topics of conversation among cruise passengers. Whom should you tip? How much should you tip? What is customary and recommended? Should parents tip the full amount for children or is half adequate? Why do you have to tip at all?

Like their land-bound contemporaries, cruise ship service personnel depend on gratuities for a major portion of their compensation. Educate yourself about gratuities by reading your cruise line brochure, where suggested tipping levels are usually listed in the back with the rest of

CLOSE UP

Recommended Tips by Cruise Line

Each cruise line has a different tipping policy. Some allow you to add tips to your shipboard account; others expect you to dole out the dollars in cash on the last night of the cruise. Here are the suggested tipping amounts for each line covered in this book. Gratuity recommendations are often higher if you're staying in a suite with extra services, such as a butler. *The ship profiles in Chapter 5 give you the details:*

Azamara Club Cruises: No tipping expected

Carnival Cruise Line: $11.50 per person per day

Celebrity Cruises: $12–$15.50 per person per day

Costa Cruises: $11 per person per day

Crystal Cruises: No tipping expected

Cunard Line: $11.50–$13.50 per person per day

Disney Cruise Line: $12 per person per day

Holland American Line: $11.50–$12 per person per day

MSC Cruises: $12 per person per day

Norwegian Cruise Line: $12 per person per day

Oceania Cruises: $15–$22 per person per day

Paul Gauguin Cruises: No tipping expected

Princess Cruises: $11.50–$12 per person per day

Regent Seven Seas Cruises: No tipping expected

Royal Caribbean: $12–$14.25 per person per day

Seabourn Cruises: No tipping expected

SeaDream Yacht Club: No tipping expected

Silversea Cruises: No tipping expected

Star Clippers: €8 per person per day

Windstar Cruises: $12 per person per day

the fine print. Then read over the small booklet that comes with your cruise documents for up-to-the-minute information.

BEFORE YOU BOARD

The whom-to-tip decision is easy. It's up to your discretion to tip anyone who provides a service you would like to recognize. This begins as early as your airport check-in. Porters carrying your bags in airports expect a tip, as do the agents at curbside check-in (even if they charge a fee). Depending on your city, $1 to $2 a bag will do. The same rule applies when you retrieve your suitcases at the baggage claim area at your destination; if you use the services of a porter or skycap, tip him for taking your bags to your bus or taxi. "Wait a minute!" you say, "I'm shelling out all these dollars and I haven't even reached the ship yet." Well, that's true. And one way to avoid tipping is to do everything yourself. It's perfectly acceptable to carry (or roll) your own luggage into and out of airports, but if you accept assistance you should extend a tip.

When transfers to and from your ship are a part of your Air & Sea program, gratuities are generally included for luggage handling. In that case, don't worry about the interim tipping. However, if you take a taxi to the pier and hand over your bags to a stevedore, be sure to tip him. He's the person responsible for getting your suitcases onto a pallet and on their way to the ship, but he's not a cruise line employee. Stiff this guy, and hours later you may be filing a missing baggage report. Better to treat him with respect and pass along at least $5 with a handshake and big smile.

You're on board. Now what? Relax. With a couple of exceptions, which are addressed below, cash tips won't be expected until the last night of your cruise.

4

ON BOARD YOUR SHIP

TIPPING PROCEDURES

During your last day of cruising there will be a disembarkation talk, which is usually conducted by the cruise director. One member of each family is encouraged to attend and, in addition to customs and immigration procedures, tipping is discussed. (Don't worry if you miss the meeting, it will be replayed on television all day long.)

With the advent of alternative dining venues and options for open seating for dinner on contemporary ships, most cruise lines now either automatically add gratuities to passengers' onboard charge accounts or offer automatic tipping as an option, usually in the amount of $11 to $12 per passenger, per day (or, in the case of some lines, the amounts may be a few dollars higher if you are accommodated in a suite). If that's your cruise line's policy and the amount suits you, then do nothing. In most cases, you're certainly free to adjust the amounts up or down to more appropriate levels or ask that the charge be removed altogether if you prefer distributing cash gratuities.

If your ship is one of those on which tips are still given in cash, small white tip envelopes will appear in your stateroom during the last day of the cruise, along with luggage tags and written disembarkation instructions. As a general rule of thumb, you can count on the following amounts falling within the tipping guidelines:

- Room Steward: $4.50 per day
- Dining Room Waiter: $4.50 per day
- Dining Room Assistant Waiter: $3 per day

Give the tip envelopes to your dining room waiter and assistant waiter on the last night of the cruise, at dinner. If you see your room steward in the hall, you can deliver the tip envelope personally, or you may leave it in the cabin when you go to dinner on the last night. When your accommodations include the services of a butler, you should also reward his service in a similar manner. Whatever you do, don't skip out on dinner in the dining room on the final night of your cruise just to avoid tipping. If you prefer to dine elsewhere that evening, by all means do so, but stop by the dining room to recognize the service of the waitstaff.

As a rule of thumb, for a seven-day cruise, count on gratuities of at least $80 to $95 per person, or more if you are served by a butler in a suite. In addition, it may be suggested that you tip the headwaiter $5 per person per week. If he's rendered some special service (prepared tableside desserts) or if he's been particularly attentive and kept things moving, by all means give him a tip. If he shows up only that last evening with a smile and his hand out, you needn't feel obliged to tip him.

Some passengers claim that a cash tip offered to their cabin steward at the beginning of a cruise does wonders to produce exceptional service. Although I tried it once, I saw no difference in the level of attention I received.

Of course, some higher-end cruise lines suggest higher gratuity amounts per person, per day, such as Cunard and Oceania. There are also some truly no-tipping-required cruise lines, which include Azamara, Crystal, Paul Gauguin, SeaDream, Seabourn, Silversea, and Regent Seven Seas Cruises. On these cruises, gratuities are considered prepaid. If you feel the service warrants recognition, ask at the Reception Desk if there's a crew appreciation fund to which you can contribute.

Naturally, it would be gauche to offer a tip to an officer or a member of the cruise line's professional staff. However, if an officer or someone on the cruise staff renders out-of-the-ordinary service or is especially helpful, a letter of praise to the cruise line's home office can do wonders for that employee's career.

Finally, remember to have some dollar bills on hand when you disembark the ship. There will still be palms to cross in the cruise terminal and at the airport.

TIPPING FOR YOUR KIDS

Parents often argue the need to tip the entire recommended amount for their children, especially little ones. I wonder if the messes their children leave in the bathroom, cabin, and dining room are invisible to these parents. Not to mention that some tykes run their waiters ragged replacing plates of food that they don't like. Simply because children are smaller than adults doesn't mean they are less trouble to clean up after. Parents have often already gotten a reduced (third or fourth passenger) fare for their children or, in some cases, free passage. Some cruise lines, such as MSC Cruises, suggest you tip the cabin steward half the recommended amount for children under 12 when they are the third or fourth person occupying the stateroom. It is customary to tip the counselors in the children's center, particularly if your children have participated in many activities.

AUTOMATIC GRATUITIES

On virtually all ships, a 15% gratuity will automatically be added to your bar bills. That would include the fruity welcome drink you signed for when the ship pulled away from the dock as well as cappuccinos and lattes from the specialty coffee bar. If you use salon and spa services, a similar percentage might be added to the bill; if it isn't, then a 15% tip is expected.

Past Passengers—an Exclusive Group

Your cruise is over—pat yourself on the back. Your plans and preparation for an out-of-the-ordinary trip have paid off, and you'll now have lasting memories of a great vacation. Before you even have a chance to fill your scrapbook, the cruise line wants you to consider doing it all over again. And why not? You're a seasoned sailor, so take advantage of your experience. To entice you back on a future cruise, you may find you're automatically a member of an exclusive club—Latitudes (Norwegian Cruise Line), Mariner Society (Holland America Line), Captain's Circle (Princess Cruises), Castaway Club (Disney Cruise Line), Venetian Society (Silversea Cruises)—to name but a few. Members receive the cruise line's magazine for past passengers, exclusive offers, shipboard perks such as a repeaters' party hosted by the captain, and even the opportunity to sail on members-only cruises.

4

THE EXCEPTIONS

There are exceptions to every rule. These days there are two major exceptions to the no-extra-tipping rule on most cruise ships. The first exception is for room service. Except for bar items and soft drinks, there's no additional charge for what you order from room service; however, it's customary to tip the steward who delivers it and to tip in cash. In most cases, this will not be your regular steward. Depending on what you have ordered and whether it was delivered in a timely manner, $1 to $3 will suffice. If it's just juice and a pot of coffee, the lesser amount will do; a heavy tray with a full dinner would warrant the larger amount.

The second exception is in the à la carte restaurant. More common on modern cruise ships, these dining venues offer a change from the main dining room—often in a private, more intimate atmosphere, with a special menu and personal service. Although there's sometimes no extra charge for the meal, a one-time gratuity may be suggested. Your ship's daily schedule will contain instructions for making reservations and outline tipping protocol. You can usually add a tip to your bill or, if you prefer, offer it discreetly in cash to your main server.

PLACES YOU SHOULD KNOW

Every cruise ship has a distinct personality, whether it's a one-of-a-kind vessel or one of several identical ships built in a class, whose members are virtually indistinguishable from one another (with the possible exception of interior decor). Despite their differences, nearly all ships have certain common elements and other characteristics that set the cruise experience apart from other kinds of travel.

RECEPTION DESK

Sometimes referred to as the Purser's Desk, Guest Services, or Information Desk, this is the place to ask questions you might have as well as to take care of any financial matters. The Reception Desk is centrally located in the lobby or atrium and is generally open 24 hours a day for passenger convenience. Should you misplace a personal item, check for it at the Reception Desk, which also functions as the ship's Lost & Found.

SHORE EXCURSION DESK

Manned by a knowledgeable staff, the Shore Excursion Desk can offer not only the sale of ship-sponsored tours but may also be the place to learn more about ports of call and gain information to tour independently. Although staff members—and the focus of their positions— vary widely, the least you can expect are basic information and port maps. Happily, some shore excursion staff members possess a wealth of information and share it without reservation. On some ships the port lecturer may emphasize shopping, and the cruise lines' recommended merchants, with little to impart regarding sightseeing or the history and culture of ports.

PHOTO SHOP

Caribbean cruises are a series of photo opportunities, and ship's photographers are on hand to capture boarding, sail-away, port arrivals, and other highlights such as the Captain's Reception. On formal nights there are often several locations where you can have portraits taken in front of your choice of backdrops. Photographers seem to pop up everywhere and take far more pictures than you could ever want; however, they provide a unique remembrance, and there's no obligation to purchase the photos. Prices for the prints, which are put on display, range from $11 to $24, depending on size.

Film, digital media, batteries, single-use cameras, and related merchandise may be available in the photo shop. Some ship's photography staffers are capable of creating a photo CD or prints from your digital media.

THE LIBRARY

Cruise ship libraries run the gamut from a few shelves of relatively uninspiring titles to huge rooms crammed with volumes of travel guides, classic novels, and the latest best sellers. As a rule, the smaller the ship, the more likely you are to find a well-stocked library. The space allotted to the library falls in proportion to the emphasis on glitzy stage shows; on small ships the passengers are more likely to lean toward quiet diversions. On ships with sophisticated entertainment centers in staterooms, you may find DVD movies as well as books in the library.

INTERNET CAFÉ–BUSINESS CENTER

Being out to sea doesn't mean you have to be out of touch. Ship-to-shore telephone calls can cost $6 to $15 per *minute,* so it makes economic sense to use email to remain in contact with your home or office. Most ships have at the least basic computer systems, while some newer vessels offer more high-tech connectivity—even in-cabin high-speed hookups and wireless connections (Wi-Fi) for either your own laptop computer or one you can rent on board. Expect these services to cost between 35¢ and $1 per minute. However, on many ships you can purchase blocks of time or even unlimited access for the length of your cruise; in these cases, you pay more up front, but you'll save substantially on the per-minute connection charges.

There really is such a thing as a working vacation, and cruise ships are an ideal venue (a substantial portion of this book was written while I was at sea). Meeting rooms with audiovisual equipment are available for corporate functions on many ships. As with any group business function, these facilities should be reserved well in advance of sailing.

DINING ON BOARD

All food, all the time? Not quite, but it's possible to literally eat away the day and most of the night on a cruise. A popular cruise director's joke is "You came on as passengers, and you will be leaving as cargo." Although it's meant in fun, it does contain a ring of truth. Food—tasty and plentiful—is available around the clock on most cruise ships, and the dining experience at sea has reached almost mythical proportions. Perhaps it has something to do with legendary midnight buffets, the absence of menu prices, or the vast selection and availability. Whatever the reason, there's a strong emphasis on food aboard cruise ships.

Nearly every cruise passenger can expect numerous opportunities to satisfy hunger pangs: coffee and Danish for early risers, Lido buffet breakfast, sit-down breakfast in the dining room, Lido buffet lunch, sit-down lunch in the dining room, midafternoon ice cream and snacks, afternoon tea, casual buffet dinner, formal dining room dinner, and a midnight buffet or canapés offered by waiters passing through public rooms. Whew! You may also find a pizzeria or a specialty coffee bar on your ship—increasingly popular favorites cropping up on ships old and new. Although pizza is complimentary, expect an additional charge for specialty coffees; cappuccino, espresso, and latte usually cost extra at the coffee bar and, possibly, in the dining room. There may also be a charge for fancy pastries and premium ice cream.

Every ship has at least one main restaurant and a Lido, or casual, buffet alternative, and specialty restaurants are an increasingly important option. Meals in the primary and buffet restaurants are included in the cruise fare, as are round-the-clock room service, midday tea and snacks, and late-night buffets. Most cruise lines levy a surcharge for dining in alternative restaurants, and the extra charge may or may not include a gratuity (if not, you should leave one), although there generally is no additional charge on upscale ships.

Cruise lines make every possible attempt to ensure dining satisfaction. If you have special dietary considerations, such as low-salt, kosher, or food allergies, be sure to indicate them well ahead of time, and check to be certain your needs are known by your waiter once on board. In addition to the usual menu items, spa, low-calorie, low-carbohydrate, or low-fat selections and vegetarian as well as children's menus, are usually available. Requests for dishes not featured on the menu can often be granted if you ask in advance.

Legend has it that a nouveau riche passenger's response to an invitation to dine with the captain during a round-the-world cruise was, "I didn't shell out all those bucks to eat with the help!" Although some cruise passengers decline invitations to dine at the captain's table, there are far more who covet such an experience. You'll know you have been included in that exclusive coterie when an embossed invitation arrives in your stateroom on the day of a formal dinner. RSVP as soon as possible; if you're unable to attend, someone else will be invited in your place.

The evening begins with cocktails, either in a reserved area of a public lounge or the captain's quarters, where the ship's social hostess greets you and makes introductions to the captain and other high-ranking officers. After getting acquainted, you're escorted to the captain's table and you take your place according to prearranged seating; place cards show the way. Then you just sit back and enjoy a sumptuous dinner with exquisite service and fine wines. A photographer will likely appear to preserve the memory, and the picture will be delivered to you the next day, perhaps with a copy of the menu or a note of thanks from your host.

Who is invited? Unfortunately, although there are hundreds of passengers on every cruise who would no doubt enjoy dining with him, there's just one captain. However, some factors can work in your favor when guest lists are drawn up. For instance, if you're a frequent repeater of the cruise line, the occupants of an expensive suite, or if you hail from the captain's hometown and speak his native language you may be considered, but you can't count on an invitation. Honeymooning couples are sometimes selected at random, as are couples celebrating a golden wedding anniversary. Attractive unattached female passengers often round out an uneven number of guests. Requests made by travel agents on behalf of their clients sometimes do the trick.

ENTERTAINMENT

It's hard to imagine, but in the early years of cruise travel, shipboard entertainment consisted of little more than poetry readings and recitals that exhibited the talents of fellow passengers. Those bygone days of sedate amusements in an intimate setting have been replaced by lavish showrooms where sequined and feathered showgirls strut their stuff on stage amid special effects unimagined in the past.

Seven-night Caribbean cruises usually include two original production shows—one often a Las Vegas–style extravaganza and the other a best-of-Broadway show featuring old and new favorites from the Great White Way.

Other shows highlight the talents of individual singers, dancers, magicians, comedians, and even acrobats. Don't be surprised if you're plucked from the audience to take the brunt of a comedian's jokes or act as the magician's temporary assistant. Sit in the front row if appearing onstage appeals to you.

Whether it's relegated to a late-afternoon interlude between bingo and dinner, or a featured evening highlight, a passenger talent show is often a don't-miss production. From pure camp to stylishly slick, what passes for talent is sometimes surprising but seldom boring. Stand-up

Smoking on a Cruise Ship

One of the unhappiest groups of cruisers I've ever met were four World War II veterans back in 1999 aboard a ship belonging to the now-defunct Renaissance Cruises, which was the only no-smoking cruise line in existence at the time. The vets were all cigarette smokers whose wives thought a cruise on a nonsmoking ship would prompt them to abandon their habit. They groused about their wives' deception but managed to take matters into their own hands by holding a "smoker" on the fantail of the ship in the wee hours of every morning while everyone else was fast asleep.

Although such an action isn't necessary on most ships these days, it is getting harder and harder to find a place to light up during a cruise. Ships are catching up to their land-based counterparts, and the smoking lamp has gone out in all restaurants and showrooms at sea, as well as in many of the bars and lounges. Although casinos are one of the last bastions of smokers, some have "smoke-free" sections or entire nights to clear the air.

Only about 20% of American adults are currently smokers, so it's not necessarily a big deal that smoking areas have shrunk. We applaud the cruise lines for their health and safety concerns but also give them high marks for not ostracizing the smoking minority who want to be comfortable.

Smokers realize there are designated places to smoke and places that are entirely smoke-free nearly everywhere they go now, so most are willing to accept the compromise. The first thing they do is check for ashtrays and make friends with other smokers. "We're outcasts, aren't we?" is a common conversation starter between smokers who gather in smoking-designated areas. Cigar aficionados don't suffer the same indignities when they have their own cigar lounge to retreat to. They are accustomed to being banned from most public areas and are happy to find a lounge that accepts them. Otherwise, they are relegated to an outdoor deck, along with pipe smokers.

As a rule of thumb, look for an ashtray; if one is at hand, you can smoke; if there's food served nearby, you can't. *Never* smoke in an elevator, on a stairway, or in a passageway. Nearly all cruise lines restrict smoking in cabins and some lines include private balconies among the no-smoking zones as well. For the most smoke-free environments at sea, consider sailing with Azamara and Oceania—each line limits smoking to a designated outside area of the pool deck.

comedy is generally discouraged. Passengers who want their performance skills to be considered should answer the call for auditions and plan to rehearse the show at least once.

Children are often invited to perform skits they learned during cruise camp, either in passenger talent productions or shows presented for parents and other family members. Not to be outdone, the ship's crew might stage a show featuring the music and culture of their homelands.

If you find the show-lounge stage a bit intimidating and want to perform in a more intimate venue, look for karaoke. Singing along in a lively piano bar is another shipboard favorite for would-be crooners.

Other lounges might feature easy-listening music, jazz, or combos for pre- and postdinner social dancing. Later in the evening, lounges rock with the beat of the 1950s and '60s, and dance clubs with a DJ reign into the late-night hours for the truly energetic.

Dance hosts often address the relative disparity between women and men on a cruise by dancing with unaccompanied female passengers on premium-to-upscale ships. In addition to dancing until the wee hours of the morning, hosts are often called on to greet embarking passengers, give dance lessons, host singles parties and a table in the dining room, and participate in social games, such as bridge, trivia, shuffleboard, and even chess.

Enrichment programs have become a popular pastime at sea. It may come as a surprise that port lecturers on many large contemporary cruise ships offer more information on shore tours and shopping than real insight into the ports of call. If more cerebral presentations are important to you, consider a cruise on a line that features stimulating enrichment programs and seminars at sea. Speakers can include destination-oriented historians, popular authors, business leaders, distinguished government figures, radio or television personalities, and even movie stars.

For a hands-on learning experience, "edutainment" is a popular shipboard pursuit. Pottery and scrapbooking classes are a welcome addition to the old standby napkin-folding and scarf-tying demonstrations. If you never seem to find the time at home, check for the availability of classes for a chance to master new computer software programs, delve into the fine points of digital photography, or take piano lessons. A small fee is usually charged for courses or supplies, but some demonstrations are free.

CASINOS AND GAMBLING

On embarkation day, a sure sign that your ship is in international waters is the opening of the casino. Long gone are the days of brandy, cigars, and shipboard poker in the gentlemen's smoking room. The most notable exceptions are the family-oriented ships of Disney Cruise Line, which shuns gaming in favor of more wholesome pastimes.

On ships that feature them, the rationale for locating casinos where most passengers must pass either through or alongside them is obvious—the unspoken allure of winning. Who can resist the siren song of coins clanging in slot machines or the urge to try one's luck at roulette? Even nongamblers occasionally succumb to the temptation to give it a try. Although most passengers would not qualify for high-roller status in Las Vegas or Atlantic City, dealers often patiently assist first-time players. Novices can have a rewarding session in the casino by attending one of the gambling demonstrations held early on in the cruise where complimentary drinks are sometimes offered and door-prize drawings held.

Drinking and Gambling Ages

Many underage passengers have learned to their chagrin that the rules that apply on land are also adhered to at sea. On most mainstream cruise ships you must be 21 to imbibe alcoholic beverages. There are exceptions—for instance, on cruises departing from countries where the legal drinking age is typically lower than 21. By and large, if you haven't achieved the magic age of 21, your shipboard charge card will be coded as booze-free, and bartenders won't risk their jobs to sell you alcohol.

Gambling is a bit looser, and 18-year-olds can try their luck on cruise lines such as Carnival, Celebrity, Silversea, Norwegian, and Royal Caribbean; most other cruise lines adhere to the age-21 minimum. Casinos are trickier to patrol than bars, though, and minors who look "old enough" may get away with dropping a few coins in an out-of-the-way slot machine before being spotted on a hidden security camera. If you hit a big jackpot, you may have a lot of explaining to do to your parents.

In addition to slot machines in a variety of denominations, cruise ship casinos might feature roulette, craps, and a variety of card games: Caribbean Stud, Let It Ride, Texas Hold 'Em, and blackjack, to name a few. Cruise lines strive to provide fair and professional gambling entertainment and supply gaming guides that set out the rules of play and betting limits for each game. Slot machine and poker tournaments are sometimes scheduled as fast-paced diversions on sea days.

Most casinos are required to close while ships are in port; others may be able to offer 24-hour slot machines and simply close table games. Every casino has a cashier, and you may be able to charge a cash advance to your shipboard account. If you win big—congratulations!—be prepared to complete a W2G form for the Internal Revenue Service. The U.S. Federal Income Tax Act stipulates that all U.S. citizens and permanent residents are required to pay income tax on gambling winnings, even if they were made overseas.

If you don't care for casinos, bingo games and scratch-off lotteries are usually offered.

SHOPPING ON BOARD

You may consider it your duty to shop. Indeed, duty-free shopping is such a popular cruise ship pastime that it's possibly second only to eating. Since shopping in many U.S. territories and Caribbean countries is duty-free, you'll find affordable prices on many goods in your ports of call. But you can also shop right on the ship itself.

Shops on board your cruise ships will carry merchandise ranging from funky to fashionable. Expect reasonable prices on souvenirs and logo items as well as imported perfumes, cosmetics, jewelry, electronics, designer items, clothing, and toys. Additionally, liquor and tobacco products can often be purchased at a substantial savings. At the very least you will not have to pay sales tax and may find rare or difficult-to-find imported brands. Art auctions are another shopping opportunity on many cruise ships.

If you're planning to make any sizable purchase in the Caribbean—whether in duty-free shops or at an art auction—do your homework. Check prices locally and online before you commit a large chunk of money on something that might not live up to its stated value. Although cruise lines offer a value guarantee when purchases are made from certain recommended stores, going through a refund process can be a headache.

Whatever you do, don't fudge the value of your purchases when completing the U.S. Customs form before disembarkation. If you exceed your personal allowance in the ship's duty-free shop, the customs agents will know. It's a murky little secret that cruise lines notify them of big spenders before docking and, at the very least, agents will bust you for the duty and may even confiscate any items you fail to declare. They have seen it all. *For more specific information on customs regulations, see Customs and Duties in Disembarking, below.*

HEALTH AND FITNESS

THE SPA

With all the usual pampering and service in luxurious surroundings, simply being on a cruise can be a stress-reducing experience. Add to that the menu of spa and salon services at your fingertips and you have a recipe for total sensory pleasure.

Most cruise-ship spas are operated by Steiner Leisure, the largest spa and salon operator at sea (the company operates Mandara and the Greenhouse spas aboard cruise ships), with facilities on more than 100 cruise ships worldwide.

In addition to facials, manicures, pedicures, massages, and sensual body treatments, other hallmarks of Steiner Leisure are salon services and products for hair and skin. Founded in 1901 by Henry Steiner of London, by the mid-1990s Steiner Leisure began taking an active role in creating shipboard spas offering a wide variety of wellness therapies and beauty programs for women and men.

Spa services don't usually come cheap, though they are more or less equivalent to what you might pay in any resort spa. Expect to pay $120 for a one-hour Swedish massage ($195 to $265 for a hot stone or specialty massage), $119 to $169 for a facial, and $110 to $120 for an hour of reflexology (therapeutic foot massage). Salon services are also equivalent to what you'd pay in a big-city salon: $35 to $59 for hair styling, $29 to $50 for a manicure, and $45 to $70 for a pedicure. Recently, other kinds of treatments, including teeth whitening, acupuncture, and cosmetic treatments have been on offer aboard some ships. You can brighten your smile for about $200, manage your aching back for $155 to $175 per session, and remove your frown lines with Botox for $350.

CLOSE UP

Spa Tips

Spas have grown in popularity. Here are some useful things to keep in mind to help you enjoy your shipboard spa experience:

■ Salon appointments for formal nights fill up quickly; book yours as soon as possible.

■ Arrive on time or a few minutes early for appointments.

■ Prior to your appointment, shower off any sunscreen lotions or oils.

■ Towels, robes, and slippers are usually provided for your use, but you may wish to wear your own pool or shower flip-flops.

■ Attend the spa orientation—you may win a door prize or be selected for a demonstration (such as a minifacial).

■ Watch for port day specials, packages of discounted spa services.

■ Don't feel pressured to purchase any of the products used during your treatment; if they're recommended but you don't want to buy them, just say no.

■ Check your charge slip before adding a gratuity; most shipboard spas automatically add a tip (however, you may adjust the amount or remove it altogether).

■ While spa and salon services are extras that sometimes come with a hefty price tag, you can still indulge yourself in the complimentary or low-cost facilities that are available on most ships. Saunas, steam rooms, therapy pools, and thermal chambers are relaxing alternatives to expensive body wraps and massages. Depending on the ship, some are free.

4

THE FITNESS CENTER

Cruise vacations can be hazardous to your waistline if you're not careful. Eating "out" for all meals and sampling different cuisines tends to pile on calories. Maintaining a fitness regimen at sea is no problem with a wide assortment of exercise machines such as stationary bikes, treadmills, and stair steppers. As a bonus, shipboard fitness centers with floor-to-ceiling windows have some of the world's most inspiring sea views.

For guests who prefer a more social atmosphere as they burn off sinful chocolate desserts, there are fitness classes for all levels of ability. High-impact energetic aerobics are not for everyone, but any class that raises the heart rate can be toned down and tailored to individual capabilities. In addition, there are stretching classes to warm up for a light jog or brisk walk on deck, and even sit-for-fitness classes for mature passengers or those with delicate joints. Basic aerobics and group exercise classes are most often complimentary, but there's typically a charge of $12 to $30 for specialty classes, such as Pilates, Spinning, yoga, or kickboxing. Perhaps you're just starting a fitness program and require individualized attention. Ask about the services of fitness experts or personal trainers to get you off on the right foot. Their fee is around $85 to $100 per hour.

Even if you don't want to take time out to hit the gym, you can walk on the ship's promenade deck or turn your back on the elevators and use the stairs—they're the ultimate step machines. And you can always control calories by requesting that any sauces be served on the side. Have no fear; it's actually possible to lose weight on a cruise and return home more buff than buffet.

SPORTS ACTIVITIES AND PROGRAMS

Shipboard sports facilities might include a court for basketball, volleyball, or tennis—or all three—a jogging track, or even an in-line skate track. Innovative and unexpected facilities, such as rock-climbing walls, surfing simulators, and bungee trampolines are challenges introduced at sea by Royal Caribbean International. For the less adventurous, more sedate pursuits include table tennis and shuffleboard.

Naturally you'll find at least one swimming pool and possibly several. Just be aware that cruise ship pools are usually on the small side, more appropriate for cooling off than doing laps, and that many contain filtered salt water. Princess Grand-class ships have challenging swim-against-the-current pools filled with freshwater for swimming enthusiasts.

Golf is a perennial seagoing favorite of players who want to log the Caribbean's most beautiful and challenging courses on their scorecards and take their games to the next level. Shipboard programs can include clinics, use of full-motion golf cages, and even individual instruction from resident pros using state-of-the-art computer analysis. Once ashore, escorted excursions include everything needed for a satisfying round of play, including equipment and tips from the pro, and the ability to schedule tee times at exclusive courses.

STAYING HEALTHY

THE MEDICAL CENTER

Accidents can happen to even the most careful people, and an unexpected illness can strike at any time. That's why almost every ship has a medical center staffed by a physician. Savvy travelers carry a first-aid kit that should be adequate for minor scrapes and ailments. For more serious problems, the ship's doctor should be able to treat you as well as any general practitioner or clinic ashore. For really complicated medical conditions, such as a heart attack or appendicitis, the ship's medical team evacuates passengers to the nearest hospital ashore. While at sea, evacuation by helicopter can easily cost thousands of dollars. To cover those expenses, travel insurance is a must.

If you're examined by the ship's doctor, you'll be charged for your office visit. Depending on your illness or injury, fees can run from $90 to several hundred dollars. Any medicines prescribed are extra. Recently, an office visit and medications to treat my simple sinus infection cost me $135. A notable exception is if you're injured in some manner aboard ship or during a shore excursion arranged by the cruise line, in which case your treatment should be free. Unless you carry very comprehensive medical insurance coverage, you may not be covered for treatment aboard a cruise ship, or in any foreign country for that matter. You'll be expected to pay for any treatment you require at the time you visit the medical center; you'll then file your own claim later. If your medical coverage is through Medicare, you certainly will not be covered outside the United States. It's worth noting once again that all ships of foreign registry are considered to be outside the United States by Medicare; however, this point is not explained clearly in Medicare's manual.

A ship's pharmacy is limited in scope, so it may or may not have what you need if you forget or lose the prescription medications that you regularly take. Just be aware that even if a drug you require is in stock, you should not expect the ship's doctor to dispense medication without examining you.

4

COMMON AILMENTS

SEASICKNESS

Many first-time passengers are anxious about whether they'll be stricken by seasickness, but there's no way to tell until you actually sail. Those who are felled by it claim that only dying will relieve their discomfort. If you have a problem with motion sickness in automobiles and airplanes, you may be more prone to seasickness; however, if you get nauseated in a smallish sailboat, that doesn't necessarily mean you'll get seasick on a large cruise ship. Modern vessels are equipped with stabilizers that eliminate much of the motion responsible for seasickness. Unless your cruise includes the open sea and wind-whipped water, you may not even feel the ship's movement, particularly if your ship is a megaliner. For first-time passengers concerned with seasickness, a megaliner is precisely the ship of choice. They're very stable in the calm waters of the Caribbean.

Seasickness is a balance problem generally attributed to overactive nerve fibers in the inner ear. Your sensory perception gets out of sync as these nerve fibers attempt to compensate for the unfamiliar motion of the ship moving through water. This condition often disappears on its own in a few days, once you get your sea legs, but by that time you've seen far too much of the inside of your bathroom and are ready to bolt the ship at any cost. You need not suffer; there are a number of remedies available to help align your gyros. Seasickness medications are available for purchase in the ship's shop and sometimes dispensed at no charge from the Medical Center or at the Reception Desk.

Even hardy sailors who never get seasick have been known to avail themselves of medications on occasion. The most common drugs are Dramamine, Dramamine II, and Bonine. All of these are over-the-counter antihistamines that are available at most pharmacies. Antihistamines make most people drowsy, and Dramamine is almost certain to have that effect. Dramamine II and Bonine are nondrowsy formulas, but they still put some people to sleep for a few hours. Considering the alternative, that's not necessarily a bad side effect. If you want to beat *mal de mer* before it has the chance to sneak up on you, it's better if you take one of these remedies two hours before sailing.

Worn behind the ear, the Transderm Scop patch is a remedy that dispenses a continuous metered dose of medication that's absorbed into the skin and enters the bloodstream. Apply the patch four hours before sailing and it will continue to be effective for three days. You'll need a prescription from your physician for the patch and, while wearing it, you must be vigilant for possible side-effects that include blurred vision, dry mouth, and drowsiness. Unfortunately, you should neither drink alcohol nor drive as long as you are wearing the patch.

If you have a history of motion sickness, do not book an inside cabin. For the terminally seasick, it will begin to resemble a movable coffin in short order.

CONTAGIOUS ILLNESSES

When hundreds of cruise passengers report to the infirmary with similar symptoms that have nothing in common with the motion of the ocean, does that necessarily mean their ship has been attacked by a mysterious disease? Hardly, but you'd never know that from news reports about nasty cruise ship diseases that attack unsuspecting vacationers. Let's face facts—travel by cruise ship often brings together large numbers of people from different regions of North America, as well as other parts of the world. There's no such thing as a cruise ship disease. In confined quarters, certain respiratory and gastrointestinal diseases can quickly spread through person-to-person contact—just as they do in schools, nursing homes, hospitals, and day-care centers. In addition, when ships dock and passengers go ashore, they might be at risk for diseases prevalent in the ports of call they visit. It's even quite possible that some passengers who become ill during a cruise were infected prior to boarding and were actually sick before their symptoms became apparent.

Because respiratory and gastrointestinal diseases can percolate a few days before their symptoms strike with a vengeance, it's highly likely that some passengers bring their bugs on board with them. Although most people are unaware that they have contracted an illness before embarking, others know they are sick but go aboard anyway, not acknowledging their illness for fear of being denied boarding. They might not seek treatment once on board due to the threat of being confined to their staterooms. These alpha passengers can be the beginning of a shipboard epidemic. Two of the most prevalent diseases that spread through cruise ship populations are influenza and noroviruses.

INFLUENZA

In recent studies, influenza infection among travelers has been found to be quite common and may rank right up there with hepatitis A as one of the most common vaccine-preventable diseases infecting travelers. Seasonal epidemics of influenza generally occur during the winter months on an annual or near-annual basis and can cause disease in all age groups. Although rates of infection are highest among infants, children, and adolescents, rates of serious illness and death are highest among people over 65 years of age and people of any age who have

CLOSE UP

Nonmedical Seasickness Remedies

No one wants to be drugged up and drowsy when they should be enjoying a cruise. There are nearly as many remedies for seasickness as there are sufferers, but they aren't all medicinal. If you want to cure seasickness but avoid additional medication, you may wish to explore a few homeopathic and natural cures.

■ **Bitters.** Have the bartender mix up a couple tablespoons of Angostura Bitters in a half glass of water or club soda. Do this right away, and you probably will not need the rest of these remedies.

■ **Food.** You may not have an appetite, but you should try to eat something if you become seasick. The nausea associated with seasickness is magnified by an empty stomach. Crackers, bread sticks, or light broth may help. (Any woman who has lived through morning sickness knows the virtues of Saltine crackers.) Crackers and apples are recommended for those who cannot keep liquids down—the apples replace vital bodily fluids.

■ **Fresh Air.** If nothing else, fresh sea air smells good and is bound to improve your mood. Keeping an eye on the horizon can also help restore your sense of balance.

■ **Ginger.** Ginger ale is a widely used home remedy for an upset stomach, and it cannot hurt if you can keep the liquid down. Ginger capsules and crystallized ginger, available in health food stores and supermarkets, are reportedly even more effective.

■ **Ice.** A hospital trick to prevent vomiting is an ice bag held against the throat just beneath the chin. It really works.

■ **Lying Down.** Spending valuable cruise time in bed is not fun, but a horizontal position may alleviate some of your symptoms.

■ **Sea-Bands.** These wristbands work on the principle of acupressure. Each elastic Sea-Band has a round button on the inside; when positioned to press a particular point on the inside of the wrist, the nausea associated with seasickness disappears. Although they look rather tacky with cocktail dresses, they are effective little gems and can be found in many pharmacies, luggage stores, and even at some travel agencies. Many shipboard sundries shops also have them, but if the ship begins to rock and roll, they'll sell out in a heartbeat.

4

medical conditions that place them at high risk for complications from influenza (e.g., people with chronic cardiopulmonary disease).

When you're traveling, the risk for exposure to influenza depends on the time of year and destination. In the tropics, influenza can occur throughout the year; in the temperate regions of the Southern Hemisphere most activity occurs from April through September. In temperate climates, travelers can also be exposed to influenza in summer, especially when on board a cruise ship with travelers from areas of the world where influenza viruses are circulating. Influenza might be, at best, an inconvenience; however, it can lead to complications, including life-threatening pneumonia, especially among people at increased risk for complications. Annual influenza vaccination is the primary method for preventing influenza and its complications.

NOROVIRUSES

Noroviruses are a group of related viruses that cause acute gastro-enteritis in humans. The incubation period for norovirus-associated gastroenteritis is usually between 24 and 48 hours, but cases can occur within 12 hours of exposure. Symptoms of norovirus infection include vomiting, diarrhea with abdominal cramps, and nausea. Low-grade fever occasionally occurs, and vomiting is more common in children. Dehydration is the most common complication, especially among the young and elderly, and may require medical attention. Symptoms generally last 24 to 60 hours. Recovery is usually complete, and there's no evidence of any serious long-term effect.

Highly contagious noroviruses are transmitted primarily through the fecal-oral route, either by consumption of contaminated food or water or by direct person-to-person spread. During outbreaks of norovirus gastroenteritis, several modes of transmission have been documented. Passengers may be infected initially by contaminated food in a restaurant; they may pass it along to other people directly.

Norovirus is often termed the cruise ship virus, even though the vast majority—some 60% to 80% of outbreaks—occur on land. According to Princess Cruises, "Statistics have shown that the chance of contracting norovirus on land is 1 in 12, and 1 in 4,000 on a cruise ship." However, the virus is harder to miss on a cruise ship because all the sick passengers and crew members are treated by the same physician, who is required to prepare a special report for the CDC if an outbreak affects 2% or more of the passengers or crew. The CDC may launch an investigation if 3% of passengers or crew members become ill. As of this writing, most ship infirmaries treat passengers who exhibit norovirus symptoms at no charge.

HOW TO AVOID ILLNESS

Outbreaks of diseases on cruise ships initially led to the creation of the CDC-operated Vessel Sanitation Program (VSP) in the 1970s. Since that time, twice a year, unannounced inspections have been conducted on all cruise ships calling at or sailing from U.S. ports on foreign itineraries. Inspectors use a checklist to score ships on a 100-point system. A score of 86 or higher is satisfactory. Anything below 86 is not satisfactory, or failing. While VSP standards are not mandated by law, cruise lines voluntarily comply.

In addition to water and food, which are inspected for cleanliness, VSP inspectors scrutinize whirlpool spas, hot tubs, children's facilities, and other areas of cruise ships. Inspection scores are made public and compiled on what VSP calls a green sheet, making it easy to compare all ships. The green sheet for each ship is available on the Internet at the CDC's website. Current scores can be faxed, or an inspection report on an individual ship can even be mailed to you if you request it.

No one wants to get sick during a highly anticipated vacation. The best way to avoid illness is to wash your hands thoroughly and often. A waterless, sanitizing hand cleaner is also recommended by the CDC in conjunction with hand washing or when water is unavailable (hand sanitizers are effective and come in travel-size bottles). You'll see dispensers for hand sanitizer on most ships. Some passengers even go so far as to pack a small aerosol can of a germ-killing spray or packaged disinfectant wipes to treat their stateroom furnishings, bedding, and bathrooms before using them.

If all fails and you get sick, seek medical treatment and observe quarantine procedures as long as you are symptomatic so you don't infect other passengers.

> **WORD OF MOUTH**
>
> "My husband and I discovered we are closet pleasure hounds. He got a massage with warm oils and heated stones and used the Alpha Capsule which involved music, aromatherapy, warmth, and vibration. He said the massage was heavenly, and the Alpha Capsule was pleasant, but over-rated. As for me, I got a deluxe manicure and pedicure, a facial, and a deep conditioning scalp treatment complete with scalp and shoulder massage. I have never felt so relaxed and pampered. It added to an already fabulous vacation experience."
> —Sherry L.

Ship Inspection Reports Vessel Sanitation Program (☎ 800/232–4636 ⊕ www.cdc.gov/nceh/vsp).

DAYS AT SEA

All days at sea are not identical, but they do follow a certain rhythm. Most ships schedule activities, port talks, lectures, games, and fitness programs on a nonstop basis. This is the time to personalize your cruise experience—you can participate in any or all scheduled activities or do nothing more strenuous than lift an umbrella drink while reading a book poolside.

No doubt you noticed the shops and casino were closed when you boarded your ship. Local regulations preclude them from opening while in port; however, once at sea, all the ship's facilities are available during set hours.

Let your daily schedule be your guide. You may want to pack a highlighter to mark the events you don't want to miss. If you want to be active, you can take exercise and fitness classes. If you want to revive and beautify yourself, consider spa and salon services (but remember the caveat about booking these in advance, because the spa is busy on sea days). If you like to gamble, there will usually be casino gaming tournaments and bingo games. Lectures might include port or shopping talks, health and fitness talks, and lifestyle or language classes. Nonstop activities may include bridge lessons and tournaments, pool games, Ping-Pong or shuffleboard, art auctions, dance classes, computer lessons, or even wine tastings and culinary demonstrations. Most activities are complimentary, but some (wine tasting, for example) may carry a

Safety at Sea

Safety begins with you, the passenger. Once settled into your cabin, locate your life vests and review the posted emergency instructions. Make sure the vests are in good condition and learn to secure them properly. Make certain the ship's purser knows if you have a physical infirmity that may hamper a speedy exit from your cabin so that in an emergency he or she can quickly dispatch a crew member to assist you. If you're traveling with children, be sure that child-size life jackets are placed in your cabin.

Before your ship sails you'll be required to attend a mandatory lifeboat drill. Do so and listen carefully. If you're unsure about how to use your vest, now is the time to ask. Only in the most extreme circumstances will

you need to abandon ship—but it has happened. The time you spend learning the procedure may serve you well in a mishap.

In actuality, the greatest danger facing cruise ship passengers is fire. All cruise lines must meet international standards for fire safety, which require sprinkler systems, smoke detectors, and other safety features. Fires on cruise ships are not common, but they do happen, and these rules have made ships much safer. You can do your part by *not* using an iron in your cabin and taking care to properly extinguish smoking materials. Never throw a lit cigarette overboard—it could be blown back into an opening in the ship and start a fire.

---

fee. In addition, the library and card room are available for quiet pursuits, as are many of the ship's lounges.

The swimming pool is one of the most popular spots on board during sunny sea days. Towels are provided, but you shouldn't use them to save deck chairs. A lively band usually plays poolside, and the pool bar is a great spot to meet and greet new acquaintances. Even if you're not a sun worshipper, you can enjoy the festivities from a shaded chair.

Sea days, particularly if they're the second and next-to-the last days of the cruise, are usually capped by formal evenings. During the first formal night, the captain hosts a reception for all passengers. Complimentary beverages and hors d'oeuvres are usually served, and the captain takes the stage to introduce his officers and staff.

PORT CALLS

Port calls add an allure to cruise ship travel that cannot be duplicated by any other type of vacation experience. In a given seven-day cruise, you'll usually have the opportunity to visit at least four unique destinations. Each morning you wake up in a new place, and each afternoon you steam off to the next stop. What you do ashore depends entirely on your interests and comfort level when confronted by a new environment and culture. After your ship is cleared by local immigration officials, you'll either have a chance to walk down the gangway or board a tender and be taken ashore.

SHORE EXCURSIONS

Cruise lines offer shore excursions that appeal to a wide variety of tastes: sightseeing, hiking, biking, sailing, swimming, kayaking, snorkeling, and a host of other activities. These excursions are tried and tested and, as a rule, provide a good experience for the money. If you prefer to do your own touring, you're naturally free to book a private guide or taxi, rent a vehicle, or

CAUTION
The ship's daily program should list the name and telephone number of the port agent. If you have a problem ashore, you can call on the port agent for assistance. Always carry that information with you when going ashore.

use public transportation, and delve into whatever interests you. A cautionary rule of thumb is that it's often better to take a ship's tour if you want to explore an area some distance from where the ship is berthed. In case of any delay, your ship will wait for you if you've booked a ship-sponsored excursion. On the other hand, if you're on your own, well, you're on your own, and the ship will depart without you if you haven't returned by the announced departure time. Give yourself plenty of time to be back at the ship (not on the dock waiting for a tender): at least a half hour before it's scheduled to sail.

To make the most of your hours ashore, research your options ahead of time. Guidebooks are an excellent resource, as are Internet sites devoted to travel—particularly the official tourism sites developed by the countries you're visiting. Friends and fellow passengers who have been there and done that can offer valuable insights into your ports of call.

With the majority of passengers ashore while the vessel is in port, the number of activities on most cruise ships is somewhat curtailed, but programs do not cease entirely. There are still exercise classes, the spa and fitness center remain open, and games and movies are sometimes planned. You can also enjoy the pools in near solitude.

The two activities you won't be able to take part in are gambling and shopping. Customs regulations dictate that both casino and shops close. Also, check your daily schedule for mealtimes and locations, as they may vary on port days.

DISEMBARKING

All cruises come to an end eventually, and it hardly seems fair that you have to leave when it feels as if your vacation has just begun. The debarkation process actually begins the day before you arrive at your ship's home port. During that day your cabin steward delivers special luggage tags to your stateroom, along with customs forms and instructions.

No matter where you live, keep in mind while packing for home that you need to set aside clothing to wear the next morning when you leave the ship. Many people dress in whatever casual outfits they wear for the final dinner on board, or they change into travel clothes after dinner. Be sure to put your passport or other proof of citizenship, airline tickets, and medications in hand luggage.

After packing, remove all the old tags, except for your personal identification, from your suitcases. Then attach the new debarkation tags (they are color- or number-coded according to postcruise transportation plans and flight schedules). Follow the instructions provided, and place the luggage outside your stateroom door for pickup during the hours indicated. (Some ships now offer disembarkation at will and allow you to carry your own bags off the ship; if your ship offers that service and you wish to partake, then you don't have to worry about placing your luggage outside the door.)

A statement itemizing your shipboard charges is delivered before you arise on the morning of debarkation. Plan to get up early enough to check it over for accuracy, finish packing your personal belongings, and vacate your stateroom by the appointed hour. Any discrepancies in your account should be taken care of before leaving the ship, usually at the Reception Desk.

Room service is not available on most ships on debarkation day; however, breakfast is served in the main restaurant as well as the buffet. After breakfast, there's not much to do but wait comfortably in a lounge or on deck for your tag color or number to be called. Some cruise lines make this process more pleasant by allowing passengers to remain in their cabins until it's time to leave the ship. Debarkation procedures can sometimes be drawn out by passengers who are unprepared. This is no time to abandon your patience or sense of humor.

Remember that all passengers must meet with Customs and Immigration officials during the debarkation process, either on the ship or in the terminal. Procedures vary and are outlined in your instructions. In some ports, passengers must meet with the officials at a specified hour (usually very early) in an onboard lounge; in other ports, customs forms are collected in the terminal and passports and identification papers are examined there as well.

Once in the terminal, you'll find the luggage is sorted by color or number. Locate yours and, if desired, flag down a porter for assistance. Then, either proceed to your prearranged transportation, get in the taxi line, or retrieve your vehicle from the parking lot. Your cruise is complete and you're officially a veteran sailor!

CUSTOMS AND DUTIES

You're always allowed to bring goods of a certain value back home without having to pay any duty or import tax. But there's a limit on the amount of tobacco and liquor you can bring back duty-free, and some countries have separate limits for perfumes; for exact figures, check with your customs department. The values of so-called duty-free goods are included in these amounts. When you shop abroad, save all your receipts, as customs inspectors may ask to see them as well as the items you purchased. If the total value of your goods is more than the duty-free limit, you'll have to pay a tax (most often a flat percentage) on the value of everything beyond that limit.

CLOSE UP

Dressing for Disembarkation

On the last night of your cruise, don't shrug off the reminder to set aside clothing to wear ashore before you place your luggage outside your stateroom door. I laughed it off as a corny cruise director's joke. It isn't. On one cruise, a friend accompanying us awoke just in time to report to Immigration that final morning and couldn't find his trousers. Where were they? Oops. Being efficient, he had tucked them into his suitcase the night before! Fortunately, his wife was able to retrieve them, but not before the mandatory 7 am inspection. Wearing a longish golf shirt and navy blue boxers, he reported as instructed and hoped no one would notice that his shorts weren't a bathing suit. Red-faced, he took a lot of good-natured ribbing during a leisurely breakfast.

4

U.S. CUSTOMS

ALLOWANCES

Individuals entering the United States from the Caribbean are allowed to bring in $800 worth of duty-free goods for personal use ($1,600 from the U.S. Virgin Islands), including one liter of alcohol (two liters if one was produced in the Caribbean and five liters from the USVI), one carton of cigarettes (five cartons if four are from the USVI), and 100 non-Cuban cigars. Antiques and original artwork are also duty-free. Remember that any liquids, such as alcohol or perfume, that you buy on your cruise—or anytime before you pass through airport security— will have to be packed into your checked luggage before you board your flight home.

SENDING PACKAGES HOME

Although you probably won't want to spend much of your precious shore time looking for a post office, you can send packages home duty-free, with a limit of one parcel per addressee per day (except alcohol or tobacco products or perfume worth more than $5). You can mail up to $200 worth of goods for personal use; label the package "personal use" and attach a list of the contents and their retail value. If the package contains your used personal belongings, mark it "personal goods returned" to avoid paying duty on your laundry. You may also send up to $100 worth of goods as a gift ($200 from the U.S. Virgin Islands); mark the package "unsolicited gift." Items you mailed do not affect your duty-free allowance on your return.

NONCITIZENS

Non-U.S. citizens who are returning home within hours of docking may be exempt from all U.S. Customs duties. Everything you bring into the United States must leave with you when you return home, though. When you reach your own country, you'll have to pay duties there.

Information **U.S. Customs and Border Protection** (*For inquiries and complaints,* ⊠ *1300 Pennsylvania Ave. NW, Washington, DC* ☎ *877/227–5511 or 202/354–1000* ⊕ *www.cbp.gov*).

How Safe Is Your Cruise Ship?

The Poseidon Adventure probably wasn't the most comforting movie my husband could have viewed the night before embarking on our first cruise. The film stars an ocean liner that goes bottom-up after being swamped by a monster wave, sending the cast scurrying to reach the keel in an upside-down attempt to be rescued. As we ascended the gangway of SS Norway the following morning, my husband grinned wickedly and hummed "There's Got to Be a Morning After."

We encountered no severe weather, no massive wave action, no rocking or swaying that we could even feel. It was almost disappointing to be on a cruise liner and not experience any adventure. Unfortunately that isn't always the case, as we have subsequently learned. Water is a powerful force, and weather conditions exist that can cause a ship to bob and stagger through thundering waves. The worst are rogue waves that appear out of the depths and smash into ships without warning. Such waves are not uncommon; however, it's rare for a cruise ship to encounter one. Most storms are mildly irritating at best, and their importance only increases in dimension if the weather doesn't clear quickly enough for seasick passengers.

The Cruise Lines International Association (CLIA), whose mission is to promote all measures that foster a safe, secure, and healthy cruise ship environment, reminds us: U.S. Coast Guard inspections include reviewing cruise ship plans before construction is begun, inspections during construction, a comprehensive initial examination on delivery, and annual examinations for compliance with federal and international regulations. If the U.S. Coast Guard finds a cruise ship to be in serious violation of any required regulation or considers it unsafe in any way, it has the authority to prevent departure from a U.S. port with passengers onboard until those deficiencies are corrected.

Had Norwegian Dawn passengers known how well their ship was constructed, they might have been less anxious when a 70-foot wall of water smacked into the ship in April 2005. The rogue wave reached as high as Deck 10, and windows were broken in two cabins. As frightful as the situation was, only four people received minor injuries, and 62 staterooms were waterlogged (the ship has more than 1,100). That alone says a lot for the reliability of not only Norwegian Dawn, but for all cruise ships at sea that must meet International Maritime Organization (IMO) regulations for safety and seaworthiness. CLIA agrees the incident was "an excellent example of the high level of structural integrity found on today's cruise ships."

No one at Norwegian Cruise Line could have foreseen how prophetic one of their past marketing campaigns would become. A 1997 brochure suggested, "Out here, the laws of the land do not apply . . . it's different out here." Passengers should never lose sight of one important difference between a cruise and a resort vacation—a cruise ship is not a hotel. Ships move, and the action of the ocean is as unpredictable as the weather.

PROBLEM SOLVING

There's no such thing as a perfect vacation, so it's probably unrealistic to expect that you'll have a flawless cruise. Various things—small and large—can go wrong. The best piece of advice I can give you is to remember that no one—not your travel agent, not the cruise line, not the crew, and most of all not you—wants problems to occur. Every officer and staff member on your ship has the same goal: to meet passenger expectations and provide a safe and satisfying voyage. The more you know as a passenger, the better you'll be prepared for what happens—and what doesn't—during the cruise.

YOUR LUGGAGE IS MISSING

As a rule, the larger the ship, the longer it takes for luggage to be delivered on embarkation day. Being one of the first passengers to board the ship doesn't necessarily mean you'll be the first to get your luggage. Sometimes it will all appear early in the day; however, it may materialize piece by piece during the course of the afternoon or perhaps even later on in the evening. On the largest ships, it's not at all uncommon that you would not receive your checked luggage until after the ship has sailed; this doesn't mean your luggage is not on the ship.

If your luggage hasn't arrived by 8 pm and if it appears that all the luggage has been distributed (i.e., you don't see any more in the passageways or being delivered), check with the Reception Desk. Sometimes the room tag affixed to a suitcase has been damaged. In that case, your bag would be set aside until the name on the luggage identification tag could be matched with the manifest. This illustrates why it's very important to have your name on the outside *and* inside of your suitcases.

In the extreme, luggage has been known to be loaded on the wrong ship or accidentally left behind in the cruise terminal. This very rarely happens, but when it does, the guest services staff will do whatever they can to have misdirected suitcases delivered to the ship in the next port of call. In the meantime, they may offer assistance in the form of a shipboard credit so you can purchase clothing and other personal items in the ship's boutiques.

YOU NEED TO SWITCH STATEROOMS

Congratulations if you received a last-minute complimentary upgrade or were able to purchase an upgrade to better accommodations at the pier. After you board the ship and inspect your superior digs, tell your steward about the change and request that he take care of getting your luggage to the right stateroom. It's a good idea to be proactive as well, so take the time to stop by your original cabin. You might find your luggage there already, as well as anything that was delivered for you (rented tuxedo, bon voyage gifts, messages, etc). If the steward is available, tell him your new cabin number. Then, be patient because stewards are very busy on embarkation day.

What if there's something really wrong with your accommodations? Perhaps the air-conditioning doesn't work or there's a major plumbing problem that can't be fixed after repeated attempts. You may be fortunate enough to be moved to a similar cabin, but when ships sail full

CLOSE UP

Cruise Manners

Most passengers want to have a satisfying vacation—to explore new places, relax, spend time with family and friends, and have some carefree fun. Unfortunately, some people can get carried away with the carefree part and forget to pack the good manners practiced every day at home:

■ **Adhere to the dress code.** The ship's daily program will indicate the appropriate attire for every evening of the cruise, generally beginning at 6 pm. It's inconsiderate to ignore the guidelines and do as you please.

■ **Do not hog the lounge chairs.** Every morning an invisible cadre of passengers piles towels and personal belongings on chaise longues by the pool to save them for later. This is extremely selfish behavior.

■ **Do not save seats.** Do save a seat for your spouse or traveling companion, but do not try to save entire rows of seats in the show lounge or complete tables in the casual dining area.

■ **Control your children.** For their safety—and the safety of others—children shouldn't be allowed to roam freely around the ship, run around the swimming pool, splash water on other passengers, cavort in the hot tubs, or play in the elevators. Do not allow your children to intrude in adults-only spaces. Some parents are in total denial when it comes to the unruly actions of their children (the disruptive kids can't be theirs).

■ **Be a considerate smoker.** Those who smoke should light up their cigarettes, cigars, and pipes only in areas clearly approved for that purpose.

■ **Do not jog before daybreak.** It should be obvious that if there are cabins located below the deck where jogging is permitted, then passengers are probably still asleep in them. Run only during the hours indicated in the daily program.

■ **Be mindful of others in the spa and gym.** Wear appropriate workout attire and wipe down the equipment when you are finished using it. Take your turn in a reasonable amount of time.

■ **Turn down the sound.** Portable electronics are wonderful gadgets, but not everyone has the same musical taste as you. In public areas, music players should be used with headphones. When using two-way radios and cell phones, it's seldom necessary to shout.

■ **Await your turn.** Events and activities are scheduled in a certain way for a purpose, including the orderly filling of shore tenders and the disembarkation procedure at the end of the cruise. Do not be in such a hurry that you compromise safety.

■ **Do not complain while you wait.** No one cares to listen to grumbling and whining. It's a vacation, so lighten up and go with the flow.

■ **Listen and follow instructions.** This is never more important than during the muster drill! Listening can ensure your safety in case of an emergency.

Don't forget that the three Cs at sea—Consideration, Courtesy, and Civility—are your guideposts. And don't forget to bring along a pleasant attitude, your sunniest smile, and good manners.

there often isn't one available. If you're offered a less-expensive category—for instance, your stateroom is outside, but all that is open is an inside—you should expect compensation for the downgrade. The purser may be able to apply a credit for the difference to your shipboard account or advise you that the cruise line will issue a partial refund after the cruise. Permission must be granted by the company's headquarters, so be patient. And get any promise for compensation in writing.

Don't count on moving if you simply don't like your cabin, though. You may notice a small sign on the Reception Desk informing all passengers that the ship is full and change requests cannot be granted. Whether every cabin is occupied or not (the ship may be full to maximum capacity standards), after sailing, the ship's staff is loath to make changes for any reason other than those above.

> **WORD OF MOUTH**
>
> "Remember, whenever you are not happy with an order, tell the waiters and they are more than happy to bring you something more to your liking. We do, and thus have never experienced a bad meal aboard. We actually wish we could order half portions, since invariably the portions are so large that we cannot finish them. The waiters may think we don't like the food, but actually we are saving room for dessert!"
> —Vincent F.

YOUR DINING ARRANGEMENTS ARE UNSATISFACTORY

When you booked your cruise, you requested early seating, but once on board you discover a late dinner-seating assignment (or vice versa). Perhaps you requested a romantic table for two but find that you're assigned to a table that seats eight. Despite what anyone tells you, cruise lines make no guarantees up front—after all, the dining rooms have only so much space. However, they do want to please all their passengers. They recognize that dining is a highlight of the overall cruise experience, so they make it relatively painless to correct any glitches. The maître d' will be available on embarkation day at a time and place specified in the ship's bulletin to iron out any problems. You may be asked to dine at your assigned table that first night until a more acceptable arrangement can be worked out, at which time you'll be informed of your new table-seating assignment.

Even if you get the seating time and table size you prefer, you could encounter another problem. Sometimes you just don't hit it off with your assigned dining partners, or you meet other people you'd like to spend more time with. Go to the maître d' as soon as possible—no later than the morning of your first full day on board—to make your request for a change. Be patient. He will do his best to accommodate all requests but often changes aren't made on the spot.

YOU MISS A PORT OF CALL

Sometimes weather conditions or mechanical problems cause a cruise ship to bypass a particular port of call. If you read the Contract of Carriage on your ticket, you'll see that cruise lines reserve the right to change the itinerary for just cause. They don't make itinerary alterations on a whim. Don't take it personally—they're not trying to ruin your vacation plans. In this case, there's not much you can do.

If you booked a shore excursion on board, your account will automatically be credited for the cancelled tour. Be sure to check your balance for accuracy, though. If you've prebooked your own tour with an independent shore operator and you've paid in advance, the situation may be a bit trickier. Whether you receive a refund depends on the tour company with which you're dealing. Make sure you understand their policy for refunds in the case of a missed port call before finalizing your plans. If you reserved a rental car, the same caveat applies; make sure you understand the car-rental company's cancellation policy.

YOU DON'T KNOW WHAT'S GOING ON

A problem with communication might more accurately be termed lack of communication. In the event of an unusual situation or emergency, the officers and crew of your vessel are usually more concerned with problem solving than keeping passengers informed. In these situations, it helps to be patient rather than complain that you're not being apprised. The captain and his officers will give you the information you need as soon as they can do so.

A case in point is my experience on the maiden voyage of a brand-new ship. Mel and I noticed while dressing for dinner that our cabin seemed to be getting warm, and it soon became apparent that the entire ship's interior was growing hotter as the evening progressed. Plus, the ship was dead in the water. We were soon informed that an electrical panel had failed and that engineers had shut down the air-conditioning and stopped the ship while making repairs. We appreciated not being left in the dark—a real possibility considering the electrical problem. However, before the captain's announcement over the public address system, the Reception Desk was literally overwhelmed with concerned (and irate) passengers. If you're truly frightened by a situation you don't understand, check with Reception.

EFFECTIVE COMPLAINING

Minor quibbles can be brought to the attention of your waiter (your soup is cold), cabin steward (you need extra pillows), or the Reception Desk (there's a mysterious charge on your account). For slightly weightier matters, the headwaiter or chief housekeeper should be able to work things out—your dinner partners have atrocious eating habits and you want to switch tables, or your cabin steward isn't cleaning your room satisfactorily. However, for big problems, go to the top. See the hotel director immediately when a situation occurs that you feel should be addressed. His assistance will most assuredly be needed if a pipe breaks and floods your accommodations. The most important thing to remember is that you should deal with problems on the ship when they occur; there's not much that can be done after the cruise is over.

If you have a major problem, you'll usually get more satisfaction if you tell the hotel director what you want in terms of compensation, but it's important to be reasonable. If your cabin is flooded, you should expect to be moved and you should expect to have sodden clothing cleaned at no cost to you, and if any of your belongings are ruined, you should expect them to be replaced; you should not expect a refund of your entire fare.

Klaus Lugmaier, longtime Norwegian Cruise Lines hotel director, confides that the most common passenger gripes are bad weather, delays caused by Immigration clearances, and long check-in lines. Possibly his most unusual request was an incident when a passenger wanted to leave the ship during a day at sea and commanded him to order a helicopter. Obviously, there are some requests that cannot be granted under any circumstances.

Keep your travel agent in the loop if something major goes wrong and you need postcruise assistance. Travel agents have the inside track on solving problems by using channels not available to their clients. Getting better service after your cruise (as well as before it) is just one reason why it's better to use a travel agent.

COMMENT CARDS

When you receive a comment card to complete, assess your experience honestly, and take the time to make any suggestions you have for improvements. Those comments are taken very seriously. Also, praise crew members by name if you've received particularly good service from them. They could receive a promotion as a result.

CRUISE LINES AND CRUISE SHIPS

One person's "dreadful" cruise vacation can be another person's best cruise ever. You may love every meal; another person may hate the food. Your cabin may feel comfortable and cheery, if not large; the identical accommodations may have resembled a "cave" for someone else. In cruising, one size definitely does not fit all. What's appealing to one passenger may be unacceptable to another. Ultimately, most cruise complaints arise from passengers whose expectations were not met. They were on the wrong ship for them.

Make no mistake about it: cruise ships have distinct personalities. Windstar's sails and lack of formality define their relaxed appeal, while an ethereal sense of peace and tranquillity permeates the more formal Crystal ships. Even those belonging to the same class and nearly indistinguishable from one another have certain traits that make them stand out. The most notable examples are vessels in the Carnival fleet, which are built in classes. Although the layouts of the ships in the same class vary little, each has its own distinctive theme—on Conquest-class ships you might find yourself amid a celebration of color (*Carnival Glory*) or unabashed heroics (*Carnival Valor*).

Cruise ships may appear to be floating resorts, but you can't check out and go someplace else if you don't like your ship. Whichever one you choose will be your home for seven days or more in most cases. The ship will determine the type of accommodations you'll have, what kind of food you'll eat, what style of entertainment you'll see, and even the destinations you'll visit. If you don't enjoy your ship, you probably won't enjoy your cruise.

That is why the most important choice you'll make when booking a cruise is the combined selection of cruise line and cruise ship. Cruise lines set the tone for their fleets, which is why we have classified lines loosely as Mainstream, Premium, and Luxury, plus unique sailing ships. Not all cruise lines in those categories are alike, although they will share many basic similarities. The cruise industry is relatively fluid, meaning that new features introduced on one ship may not be found on all the ships owned by the same cruise line. For instance, you'll find ice-skating rinks only on the biggest Royal Caribbean ships. However, most cruise lines attempt to standardize the overall experience throughout their fleets (for example, you'll find a rock-climbing wall on *every* Royal Caribbean ship).

Just as trends and fashions evolve over time, cruise lines embrace the ebb and flow of change. To keep up with today's diverse lifestyles, some cruise lines strive to include something that will appeal to everyone on their ships. Others focus on narrower, more traditional elements. Today's passengers have higher expectations, and they sail on ships that are far superior to their predecessors. Happily, they often do so at a much lower comparable fare than in the past.

So, which ship is best? To be honest and direct: only you can determine which ship is best *for you*. You won't find ratings by Fodor's—either quality stars or value scores. Why? Think of those people described above whose expectations were unmet. They assuredly would rate their experience differently than you did if everything on board was to your liking. Ratings are personal and heavily weighted to the reviewer's opinion. What we've tried to do in these cruise line and cruise ship profiles is to give you the telling details that help distinguish one cruise line and cruise ship from another. Rather than inundate you with facts and bury you with opinions, we've tried to be brief and to the point. Travel guides should be empowering, not overwhelming. Use these profiles as a guide, but also ask your friends for their opinions, use a good travel agent who knows the intimate details of the ships he or she sells, and, perhaps most important, trust your own instincts. Your responsibility is to select not only the right cruise line but the right ship for you, and no one knows your expectations better than you do yourself. It's your precious time and money that are at stake. No matter how knowledgeable your travel agent is, how sincere your friends are, or how clearly any expert lays the cards on the table, you're the only one who really knows what you like. A short wait for a table at dinner might not bother you because you would prefer a casual atmosphere with open seating, whereas some people want the security of a set time at an assigned table, where they're served by a waiter who gets to know their preferences. You know what you're willing to trade in order to get what you want most.

RATE YOUR CRUISE SHIP

One way to narrow down your choices is to rate the cruise ships that interest you the most and see which come out on top. Gather cruise line brochures and take a look at the ship profiles that follow in this chapter. Then rank the ships you wish to compare by making a side-by-side list of each ship's features, assigning each one a ranking, such as:

4 = Gotta have it!

3 = Not essential but good to have

2 = Can take it or leave it

1 = Don't care; just not important to me

You can create your own list of desired features, which can be as long and specific as you feel it needs to be. It might look something like this:

- Itinerary
- Home port
- Ship size
- Dining options
- Dinner seatings
- Dress code
- Cabin amenities

- Entertainment options
- Activities
- Enrichment programs
- Recreation facilities
- Fitness center
- Spa
- Children's facilities/programs

The cruise line profiles that follow offer a general idea of what you can expect in terms of the overall experience, quality, and service; individual cruise ship reviews identify features that apply to particular ships or classes of ships. You'll want to compare the features of several cruise lines and ships to determine which ones come closest to matching your needs. Then narrow them down further to a few that appeal most to you.

Service is one important characteristic that is difficult to grade. The composition of staff and crew members on any particular ship can change from week to week as employees complete their contracts and are replaced by others returning from their vacations. To get an idea of what level of service you might anticipate, you can use the cruise-industry concept of passenger-to-crew ratio. Basically, it illustrates how many passengers each crew member must serve and, in theory, the lower the number, the higher the service level. Cruise-industry standard is about 2.5 to 1. Luxury lines may have 1 to 1 ratios or better (a few ships have more crew members than passengers). To compute the passenger-to-crew ratios of ships you're considering, simply divide the number of passengers (based on double occupancy) by the number of crew members. You'll find these figures in the ship statistics for each cruise ship.

The overall price you pay for your cruise is always a consideration. Don't think of the bottom line in terms of the fare alone: there are shipboard charges to factor in as well. The ultimate cost isn't computed only in dollars spent; it's in what you get for your money. The real bottom line is value. Many cruise passengers don't mind spending a bit more to get the vacation they really want.

TYPES OF CRUISE LINES

MAINSTREAM CRUISE LINES

These are contemporary cruise lines with big, big ships that have all the bells and whistles. More passengers sail on mainstream ships than any others, and mainstream cruises account for the mass appeal of cruise vacations.

The biggest player in the cruise industry is Carnival Cruise Lines. With the most ships and lavish—some would say extraordinary—interiors chock-full of grand public spaces and sports facilities, these ships offer a great deal of choice within the Carnival fleet. Nipping at their heels are Royal Caribbean and Norwegian Cruise Line, whose ships are also

New for 2014 and Beyond

Caribbean-bound ships scheduled for launch between 2014 and 2016 include some of the largest and most feature-rich vessels ever to float. We offer an advance preview here of brand-new ships coming over the horizon.

CARNIVAL CRUISE LINES

Carnival Cruise Lines will introduce a new class of ships with a 135,000-ton, 4,000-passenger vessel scheduled for delivery in winter 2016. No specific features are available at the time of this writing.

HOLLAND AMERICA LINE

Although details of their new Pinnacle-class of ships are scarce at this time, a 99,000-ton, 2,660-passenger ship for Holland America Line is scheduled for delivery early in 2016.

NORWEGIAN CRUISE LINE

Norwegian Getaway—essentially a twin of *Norwegian Breakaway*, which was introduced in 2013—is set to launch in 2014 at 143,500 tons and with a passenger capacity of 4,000. *Norwegian Getaway* will be the largest ship to home port year-round in Miami and will embody a unique Miami vibe. Tentatively scheduled for introduction in 2015 is a "Breakaway Plus" ship, which will weigh in at 163,000 tons and carry 4,200 passengers. No specific details about that ship class have been revealed at this writing.

PRINCESS CRUISES

Regal Princess is scheduled to launch in 2014 at 141,000 tons and will carry 3,600 passengers in double occupancy. Similar in design to *Royal Princess*, the ship's features are an evolution of the line's style, including expanded signature spaces.

ROYAL CARIBBEAN

Royal Caribbean will introduce an entirely new class of cruise ships with *Quantum of the Seas* in 2014, to be followed in 2015 by *Anthem of the Seas*. At 158,000 tons, each ship will accommodate 4,100 passengers in double occupancy (though less than *Oasis* and *Allure of the Seas*) and build on Royal Caribbean's legacy of innovative ship design and features. A highly anticipated third and—as of this writing—unnamed Oasis-class ship is expected to launch in 2016.

5

big and crammed with features, but neither line is quite as bold as Carnival. Costa Cruises and Disney Cruise Line don't have as many ships in their Caribbean-based fleets, but their mainstream appeal lies in different areas. Can't go to Europe? Let Costa deliver a bit of Italy to you. Plan to bring the family? The Disney ships are universally loved by children of all ages.

Once aboard, you can discover why the mainstream cruise lines are so popular. The furnishings and fittings vary, but all generate their own type of excitement. There's nothing like this in Kansas (or Indiana, Ohio, or Arizona). Glittering and glamorous decor in public areas is the norm. Though it's a bit over-the-top sometimes, the setting is still comfortable and inviting. Accommodations are available in a wide range of sizes and price ranges, from inside cabins with no windows for bargain-basement prices to some of the largest suites at sea that cost a king's ransom.

What you do on a mainstream cruise ship is up to you. Activities are scheduled all day and into the evening. Every evening, the professional entertainment staff goes into high gear, and you can either watch production shows and cabaret or participate in karaoke and passenger games. Try a few hands of blackjack in the casino, even if you're not a gambler (except on Disney ships, which have no casinos).

Lounging in the sun is seemingly the most popular daytime pursuit during Caribbean cruises, but there will be a full-service spa and salon for the pampered set and a fitness center for gym rats. Options ashore are fairly standard—large mainstream ships sail to many of the same Caribbean ports and offer similar, if not exactly the same, excursions.

Food on mainstream ships may be lacking in the gourmet department, but the choices will be vast. You can find something to eat almost 24/7, either in traditional shipboard dining rooms, a casual Lido buffet, or alternative dining restaurants. Norwegian Cruise Line and Disney Cruise Line put innovative spins on mainstream ships; Norwegian offers casual, open seating dining, while Disney has a unique alternating restaurant concept.

Everyone sets sail to have a good time, and the atmosphere on board is exhilarating, even overwhelming to some people. You're sure to find passengers who share your interests among the couples, singles, and families on these popular ships.

PREMIUM CRUISE LINES

Ships in premium fleets have a lot in common with those in mainstream lines. They're just a little more: there's a more refined atmosphere, more gracious surroundings, more attentive service. There are still things like pool games, although not quite the high jinks typical of mainstream ships.

Premium ships are among some of the newest afloat, from medium to very large in size. Holland America Line, Princess Cruises (of *Love Boat* fame), and Celebrity Cruises are among the best-known lines, and they have the largest vessels and fleets. Relative newcomers are Azamara Club Cruises and Oceania Cruises with small, yet growing, fleets. Accommodations usually are a step up in comfort and have refrigerators and other amenities that make them pleasant havens.

Activities tend to be more lifestyle-oriented; computer classes, foreign-language lessons, and enrichment programs are more prevalent. Dress codes range from country-club casual at all times to more traditional, often with two formal nights on a one-week cruise. The overall mix of passengers may be a bit older, but many families sail during summer and peak school vacation periods, so most of the ships have facilities for children, and some premium ships are among the most family-friendly afloat. Exceptions are Azamara and Oceania Cruises, which have no children's programs at all.

The social and entertainment staffs on premium vessels are no less busy keeping passengers happy. Although some activities sound similar to those on mainstream ships, including pool games and bingo, everything tends to be a bit more sedate. Afternoon music at the pool might be a jazz quartet instead of a reggae band. Production shows are just as lavish on the larger premium ships; cabaret acts fill in on their off-nights and are the norm on smaller ships.

Spas and salons are elaborate, and fitness buffs won't be disappointed by the gym facilities. The itineraries, ports of call, and excursions aren't very different than those on mainstream cruises, but premium cruise lines frequently schedule lengthier cruises to more-far-flung destinations.

Premium ships can't boast about true gourmet dining, but they do ramp up the quality and presentation of their food. Oceania Cruises is highly regarded in this segment for imaginative menus and upscale alternative restaurants. Attentive service shines with more polish and professionalism.

With rare exceptions, ships categorized as premium don't spend the entire year in the Caribbean. From about April or May through October, they reposition to Europe, Alaska, Bermuda, and even Asia and South America. Nevertheless, while in the sunny Caribbean, they aren't your grandparents' cruise lines. Although it may not last as long into the night, the camaraderie that develops naturally at sea is still there.

LUXURY CRUISE LINES

Step aboard and enter the exclusive realm of foie gras and caviar on ships that run the gamut from megayachts for only a hundred or so guests to one of the largest ships ever built. The deluxe and ultraplush ships that belong to luxury fleets are as good as it gets at sea. You can expect to be welcomed as a valued guest and treated to all the courtesies you would expect at any five-star resort.

At the top end of the top lines, you won't be bothered with signing drink receipts—all beverages (alcoholic or not) are included on the ships of Regent Seven Seas Cruises, Silversea Cruises, Seabourn Cruise Line, Crystal Cruises and SeaDream Yacht Club. Cunard Line and Windstar Cruises aren't as inclusive, but have other attributes that nudge them into the luxury category. Most important, all luxury ships provide a level of personal service and courtesy that is unmatched. It's unlikely you'll get more than a few steps from the buffet line before a server relieves you of your plate and shows you to a seat.

With the exception of Cunard, Crystal, and Windstar, luxury ships have all-suite accommodations. Most of these upscale cabins have an ocean view or a private balcony and enough space to throw an intimate predinner cocktail party. These are very social ships, and most are small enough that passengers mix easily. They are also quite formal; guests really like to dress up in their finest. Only Windstar and SeaDream are always casual chic.

Dining is the main event of the evening on most luxury ships. Meals are served during a single open seating (exceptions are Cunard and

Crystal), and full dinners from the restaurant menu can be served in your stateroom (served course by course, of course). On the highest of the high-end ships, wine is poured freely during the meals, and no one is rushed to finish dessert and coffee. Main courses are cooked to order, and the food on some lines approaches the level of that in a fine restaurant in any city.

Classical concerts, lectures on the economy and current events, and scaled-back production shows or cabaret are likely diversions. Passengers tend to entertain themselves and need no more stimulation than interesting conversation to have a pleasant time.

No one will hit you with a volleyball at the pool, but you may have to schedule a tee time to use popular golf simulators. Even on the smallest ships, the libraries are stocked with a wide variety of books, and movies are available to watch in the privacy of your stateroom. A call to room service can bring fresh, hot popcorn to your suite. Luxury ships tend to be adult-oriented; only Cunard and Crystal have dedicated facilities and programs for children.

Elegant and serene, luxury ships are stylish without being stuffy. The well-to-do, sophisticated travelers they attract are collectors of destinations. These ships sail to the Caribbean only part-time, usually during the winter season; otherwise, they are sailing less-charted waters around the world.

SAILING SHIPS

Sun, sky, sea, and sails. Just add a brisk wind, and you have a perfect combination. The tall-ship fleet that sails in the Caribbean is truly maritime magic. One of the most magnificent sights at sea is a tall ship under full sail. Star Clippers are superdeluxe sailing vessels that only look as though they've been around for years. In reality, they are modern sailing ships with many of the same comforts and amenities associated with traditional cruise ships.

ABOUT THESE REVIEWS

For each cruise line described, ships that regularly sail in the Caribbean are grouped by class or similar configuration. Keep in mind that not all ships are deployed in the Caribbean year-round; some head for Alaska and Europe during summer months. Some ships owned by the cruise lines listed do not include regularly scheduled Caribbean cruises on their published itineraries as of this writing and are not reviewed in this book. ⇨ *For a complete listing of the ships and the itineraries they are scheduled to follow in the 2014–2015 cruising season, see the Ships by Itinerary and Home Port chart in Chapter 1.*

Because cruise ships can float off to far-flung (and not always tropical) regions, many are designed with an eye to less than perfect weather. For that reason, you're likely to find indoor swimming pools featured on their deck plans. Except in rare cases, such as Norwegian Cruise Line's *Norwegian Dawn,* these are usually dual-purpose pools that can be covered when necessary by a sliding roof or magrodome to create an indoor swimming environment. Our reviews indicate the total number of swimming pools found on each ship, with such permanently and/or temporarily covered pools included in the total and also noted as "# indoors" in parentheses.

When ships belong to the same class—or are basically similar—they're listed together in the subhead under the name of the class; the year each was introduced is also given in the same order in the statistics section. Capacity figures are based on double occupancy, but when maximum capacity numbers are available (the number of passengers a ship holds when all possible berths are filled), those are listed in parentheses. Many larger ships have three- and four-berth cabins that can substantially increase the total number of passengers on board when all berths are booked.

Unlike other cruise guides, we describe not only the features but also list the cabin dimensions for each accommodation category available on the ships reviewed. Dimensions should be considered approximate and used for comparison purposes, because they sometimes vary depending on the actual location of the cabin. For instance, although staterooms are largely prefabricated and consistent in size and configuration, those at the front of some ships may be oddly curved to conform to the shape of the bow.

Demand is high, and cruise ships are sailing at full capacity these days, so someone is satisfied by every ship. When you're armed with all the right information, we're sure you'll be able to find one that not only fits your style but that offers you the service and value you expect.

AZAMARA CLUB CRUISES

In a surprise move parent company Royal Caribbean International announced the formation of an all-new, deluxe cruise line in 2007. Two vessels originally slated for service in the Celebrity Cruises fleet, which were built for now-defunct Renaissance Cruises

Azamara Journey at sea

and acquired with the purchase of the Spanish cruise line Pullmantur, were the basis for the new line, Azamara Club Cruises. Designed to offer exotic destination-driven itineraries, Azamara Club Cruises presents a more intimate onboard experience while allowing access to the less traveled ports of call experienced travelers want to visit.

☎ *877/999–9553*
⊕ *www.azamaraclub-cruises.com*
☞ *Cruise Style: Premium.*

When a cruise line sets a course to break the mold in an industry where the product falls into traditional categories—mainstream, premium, luxury—it's an exciting opportunity for experienced travelers who may want more than what a traditional cruise can deliver. More interested in traveling than cruising, they may still prefer the comfort and convenience that only a cruise ship can deliver in some exotic locales. Azamara Club Cruises gives this underserved group of travelers what they want—a cruise experience that's a bit different. Not quite luxury but more than premium, Azamara offers a deluxe cruise with concierge-style amenities for which you'd have to upgrade to a suite on other cruise lines.

In addition, since its launch Azamara Club Cruises has added a number of more inclusive amenities to passengers' fares, with no charge for a specific brand of bottled water, specialty coffees and teas; shuttle bus service to/from port communities, where available; standard spirits, wines, and international beers throughout the ships during bar hours; and complimentary self-service laundry.

Extensive overhauls of two ships that formerly sailed for the now-defunct Renaissance Cruises have resulted in interiors that are brighter with the addition of light, neutral carpeting throughout, and splashes of bold color in the upholstery and drapes. Areas that once appeared stuffy are now welcoming, with contemporary artwork further enhancing the decor. Each vessel weighs in at 30,277 tons and carries only 694 passengers. Although the size affords a high level of intimacy and makes the ships easy to navigate, there is no skimping on features normally abundant on larger ships, such as private balconies and alternative dining. Cruisers may feel that they've checked into an upscale boutique hotel that just happens to float.

Food

Expect dinner favorites to have an upscale twist, such as gulf shrimp with cognac and garlic, or a filet mignon with black truffle sauce. Azamara chefs bring a fresh approach to contemporary and lighter cuisine—a reflection of what's happening all over the United States. Even though the menus list some trendier items, there will always be classic dishes available. Prime rib and other favorites will continue to be featured on the menu.

Specialty restaurants include the Mediterranean-influenced Aqualina and the stylish steak-and-seafood restaurant Prime C. Passengers in Club suite accommodations may dine in the specialty restaurants every night of the cruise at no charge; all other passengers pay a cover charge. Reservations are offered on a space-available basis.

Entertainment

One distinguishing feature of Azamara is a wide range of enrichment programs to accompany the destination-rich itineraries. Popular programs include guest speakers who are experts on a wide variety of topics, including destinations, technology, cultural explorations, art, music, and design. Lectures might include how to get the best photos from your digital camera or the proper way to pair wine and food, as taught by resident sommeliers. An onboard "excursion expert" can not only help you select shore excursions based on your personal interests but also will serve as a destination guide, offering information about the culture and history of each port of call, not just shopping suggestions. Entertainment, on the other hand, leans toward cabaret-size production shows and variety entertainers in the main lounge. Diverse musical offerings throughout the ships range from upbeat dance bands to intimate piano bar entertainers.

KNOWN FOR

■ **More Time in Port:** Azamara ships often spend longer days and overnights in popular and exotic ports of call and offer a complimentary evening event ashore on each voyage.

■ **No Smoking:** A virtually smoke-free environment; smokers on Azamara ships are restricted to a small section of the pool deck.

■ **Service:** Friendly but not obtrusive service, delivered with attention to detail.

■ **Wine:** Extensive wine cellars that hold limited production, small label, and rare vintage wines, along with knowledgeable sommeliers.

5

AZAMARA CLUB CRUISES

Top: Grand Lobby on *Azamara Journey*
Bottom: Chairs grouped on deck allow for quiet conversation

Fitness and Recreation

In addition to a well-equipped gym and an outdoor jogging track, features of Azamara's fitness program include yoga at sunset, Pilates, and access to an onboard wellness consultant. Both ships offer a full menu of spa treatments, and an aesthetics suite featuring acupuncture, laser hair removal, and microdermabrasion. An outdoor spa relaxation lounge with saltwater therapy pool is complimentary for suite guests and those receiving spa treatments. Passes for other guests are available for $19 per day or $99 per cruise.

Your Shipmates

Azamara is designed to appeal to discerning travelers, primarily American couples of any age who appreciate a high level of service in an unstructured atmosphere.

Dress Code

Although passengers who choose to wear formal attire are certainly welcome to do so, there are no scheduled formal nights. The nightly dress code is simply "sophisticated" casual—a jacket and tie are never required, but you may see that many men who are accustomed to wearing them will do so anyway.

Junior Cruisers

Azamara Club Cruises is adult-oriented and not a good choice for families who depend on the availability of childcare. The ships have no facilities or programs for children; older teenagers, however, might appreciate the diverse itineraries and well-stocked library.

Service

Gracious and polished service throughout the ships is extended to every guest. Suite accommodations are served by a butler, who will assist with unpacking/packing; delivery of room service, plus afternoon tea, evening hors d'oeuvres, and complimentary cappuccino and espresso; shoe-shine service; and booking assistance with spa, shore excursions, and specialty dining. Stateroom attendants work in teams, and routine stateroom cleaning is done by an assistant steward, much as on other cruise lines.

CHOOSE THIS LINE IF ...

Your taste leans toward luxury, but your budget doesn't.

You prefer leisurely open seating dining in casual attire to the stiffness of assigned tablemates and waiters.

The manner in which you "get there" is as important to you as your destination.

Tipping

Housekeeping, dining, and bar staff gratuities are included in the fare.

Past Passengers

Once you've sailed with Azamara Club Cruises for the first time, you will automatically become a member of Azamara's loyalty program, Le Club Voyage, and receive benefits commensurate with the number of cruises you've taken, including such things as onboard bookings savings for future cruises and free Internet minutes. Adventurer members have been on at least one Azamara Club Cruises cruise. Explorer members have sailed five to nine cruises and get more perks, including an invitation to a senior officer's cocktail party, and a complimentary bag of laundry washed, dried, and pressed per week. After 10 cruises, you become a Discoverer member and can take advantage of expanded Internet minutes and other perks. Azamara Club Cruises also offers Reunion Cruises that feature exclusive members-only benefits, activities, and a private, complimentary excursion during the sailings.

HELPFUL HINTS

Azamara doesn't quite hit the luxury mark, but it is a high-end product at a more affordable price.

In addition to complimentary wine and beer served with meals, standard alcoholic beverages are also included in the fare.

The line is beginning to add more short cruises of less than 10 nights, but they are still the minority of sailings.

The best place to relax is the covered patio area near the pool, furnished with comfortable, oversize loungers and other seating.

When Azamara acquired its ships, it converted 48 standard staterooms into spacious Club Continent suites with more amenities for lower fares than those on true luxury lines.

5

AZAMARA CLUB CRUISES

DON'T CHOOSE THIS LINE IF ...

You want glitzy, high-energy evening entertainment.

You require the services of a butler; only suites have them.

You insist on smoking whenever and wherever you want to.

AZAMARA JOURNEY, AZAMARA QUEST

CREW MEMBERS	390
ENTERED SERVICE	2000, 2001
GROSS TONS	30,277
LENGTH	593 feet
NUMBER OF CABINS	347
PASSENGER CAPACITY	694
WIDTH	95 feet

700 ft.

500 ft.

300 ft.

At 30,277 tons, *Azamara Quest* and *Azamara Journey* are medium-size ships and well suited to the somewhat more exotic itineraries for which they are deployed, whether in the Caribbean, Europe, Asia, or South America. The ships initially entered service for Renaissance Cruises and served in Spain under the Pullmantur flag until 2007. With their entry into the Azamara Club Cruises fleet, a new option is available to passengers who prefer the boutique-hotel atmosphere of a smaller ship without the luxury-class price tag.

Each ship has a variety of signature features, including the Martini Bar in Casino Luxe, a casual sidewalk café–style coffee bar, and the distinctive Astral Spa with an acupuncture suite and expansive relaxation deck with therapy pool. Each ship has two specialty restaurants. The exclusive experience includes butler service in suites and concierge-style amenities in all categories of accommodations.

Cabins

Layout: Designed for lengthy cruises, all staterooms have ample closet and storage space, and even standard cabins have at least a small seating area, although bathrooms in lower categories are somewhat tight. Wood cabinetry adds warmth to the decor. In keeping with the trend for more balconies, 73% of all outside cabins and suites have them.

Amenities: Amenities include plush beds and Egyptian-cotton bedding. Bath toiletries, a hair dryer, TV, refrigerator, personal safe, and robes for use during the cruise are all included, but you must move up to a suite to have a bathtub, as lower-category cabins have showers only.

Suites: Club World Owner's and Club Ocean suites are particularly luxurious, with living–dining rooms, entertainment centers, two TVs, separate bedrooms, whirlpool bathtubs, guest powder rooms, and very large balconies overlooking either the bow or stern. Thirty-two Club Continent suites on each ship have a queen-size bed, television, bathtub, personal safe, and hair dryer. All suites have a welcoming bottle of sparkling wine, minibars with two bottles of spirits, and butler service.

Accessibility: Six staterooms are designated as wheelchair accessible.

Top: Open seating dining
Bottom: Balcony stateroom

Restaurants

The formal Discoveries restaurant has a single open seating for breakfast, lunch, and dinner. Evening meals feature classic favorites with a twist, such as filet mignon with black truffle sauce. Supplementing the main restaurant is the casual Windows Café, where you can dine indoors or alfresco with a view over the ship's stern. Two upscale alternative restaurants—Aqualina and Prime C—require reservations and carry a cover charge for most guests. A poolside grill offers hamburgers, salads, pasta, and other favorites for lunch and dinner, a pizzeria dishes up a variety of pies by the slice, and patisseries serve specialty coffee drinks and pastries; 24-hour room service augments dining choices.

Spas

Operated by Steiner Leisure, each ship's spa offers a full menu of massages, facials, and other treatments; and an aesthetics suite featuring acupuncture, laser hair removal, teeth whitening, and microdermabrasion. The relaxation deck with its huge therapy pool is available to guests who book a spa treatment or purchase a day pass.

Bars and Entertainment

Bars tend to be on the quiet side, suitable for socializing and conversation; however, the Looking Glass observation lounge can be lively when the entertainment staff takes over and the band plays dance music. Entertainment is also sedate, with cabaret-style shows by night and enrichment lectures by day.

Pros and Cons

Pros: one staff member for every two passengers ensures unparalleled service; bartenders in the Martini Bar are willing to follow your instructions to mix your favorite variation; the quiet sounds of a grand piano add to the ambience of the Drawing Room.

Cons: aft-facing Club Deluxe Veranda staterooms on decks 6 and 7 are simply standard balcony cabins with larger balconies; there are no children's programs or facilities; upscale amenities don't quite make up for the lack of bathroom space in standard staterooms.

Cabin Type	Size (sq. ft.)
Club World Owner's Suite	560
Club Ocean Suites	440–501
Club Continent Suites	266
Ocean-View Balcony	175
Ocean View	170–175
Inside	158

FAST FACTS

- ■ 9 passenger decks
- ■ 2 specialty restaurants, dining room, buffet, pizzeria
- ■ Wi-Fi, safe, refrigerator, DVD (some)
- ■ 1 pool
- ■ Fitness classes, gym, hot tubs, spa, steam room
- ■ 8 bars, casino, dance club, library, show room
- ■ Dry-cleaning, laundry facilities, laundry service
- ■ Internet terminal
- ■ No-smoking cabins

5

AZAMARA CLUB CRUISES

Casual dining

CARNIVAL CRUISE LINES

The world's largest cruise line originated the Fun Ship concept in 1972 with the relaunch of an aging ocean liner, which got stuck on a sandbar during its maiden voyage. In true entrepreneurial spirit, founder Ted Arison shrugged off an inauspicious

Lobby Bar on board *Carnival Fantasy*

beginning to introduce superliners a decade later. Sporting red-white-and-blue flared funnels, which are easily recognized from afar, new ships are continuously added to the fleet and rarely deviate from a successful pattern. If you find something you like on one vessel, you're likely to find something similar on another.

☎ *305/599–2600 or 800/227–6482*
⊕ *www.carnival.com*
☞ *Cruise Style: Mainstream.*

Each vessel features themed public rooms, ranging from ancient Egypt to futuristic motifs, although many of those elements are being replaced with a more tropical decor as older ships are upgraded and new ones enter service. Carnival is also introducing features either branded by the line itself, such as the poolside Blue Iguana Tequila Bar with an adjacent burrito cantina and the Red Frog Rum Bar that also serves Carnival's own brand of Thirsty Frog Red beer, or in partnership with well known brands, such as EA SPORTS to create EA SPORTS Bars at sea and Guy's Burger Joint, in partnership with Food Network star Guy Fieri. Implementation of the new features is scheduled for completion in 2015.

Food

Carnival ships have both flexible dining options as well as casual alternative restaurants. Although the tradition of two set mealtimes for dinner prevails on Carnival ships, the line's open seating concept—Your Time Dining—is available fleet-wide.

Choices are numerous, and the skill of Carnival's chefs has elevated the line's menus to an unexpected level. Although the waiters still sing and dance, the good-to-excellent dining room food appeals to American tastes.

Upscale steakhouses on certain ships serve cuisine comparable to the best midrange steakhouses ashore.

Carnival serves the best food of the mainstream cruise lines. In addition to the regular menu, vegetarian, low-calorie, low-carbohydrate, low-salt, and no-sugar selections are available. A children's menu includes such favorites as macaroni and cheese, chicken fingers, and peanut-butter-and-jelly sandwiches. If you don't feel like dressing up for dinner, the Lido buffet serves full meals, including sandwiches, a salad bar, rotisserie chicken, Asian stir-fry, and excellent pizza.

Entertainment
More high-energy than cerebral, the entertainment consists of lavish Las Vegas–style revues presented in main show lounges by a company of singers and dancers. Other performers might include magicians, jugglers, acrobats, passengers performing in the talent show, or karaoke. Live bands play a wide range of musical styles for dancing and every ship has a nightclub, piano bar, and a comedy club. Adult activities, particularly the competitive ones, tend to be silly and hilarious and play to full houses. With Carnival's new branding initiative, look for the introduction of Hasbro, The Game Show, and performances created by Playlist Productions.

Fitness and Recreation
Manned by staff members trained to keep passengers in shipshape form, Carnival's trademark spas and fitness centers are some of the largest and best equipped at sea. Spas and salons are operated by Steiner Leisure, and treatments include a variety of massages, body wraps, and facials; salons offer hair and nail services and even tooth whitening. Fitness centers have state-of-the-art cardio and strength-training equipment, a jogging track, and basic exercise classes at no charge. There's a fee for personal training, body composition analysis, and specialized classes such as yoga and Pilates.

Your Shipmates
Carnival's passengers are predominantly active Americans, mostly couples in their mid-thirties to mid-fifties. Many families enjoy Carnival cruises in the Caribbean year-round. Holidays and school vacation periods are very popular with families, and you'll see lots of kids in summer. More than 710,000 children sailed on Carnival ships in 2012—a sixfold increase in just 12 years.

Dress Code
Two "cruise elegant" nights are standard on seven-night cruises; one is the norm on shorter sailings. Although

Top: *Carnival Victory* dining room
Bottom: *Carnival Legend* waterslide

5

CARNIVAL CRUISE LINES

Top: *Carnival Elation* at sea
Middle: *Carnival Triumph*
walking and jogging track
Bottom: Entertainment on
Carnival Victory

men should feel free to wear tuxedos, dark suits (or sport coats) and ties are more prevalent. All other evenings are "cruise casual," with jeans and dress shorts permitted in the dining rooms. All ships request that no short-shorts or cutoffs be worn after 6 pm, but that policy is often ignored.

Junior Cruisers

Camp Carnival, run year-round by professionals, earns high marks for keeping young cruisers busy and content. Dedicated children's areas include great playrooms with separate splash pools. Toddlers from two to five years are treated to puppet shows, sponge painting, face painting, coloring, drawing, and crafts. As long as diapers and supplies are provided, staff will change toddlers. Activities for ages six to eight include arts and crafts, pizza parties, computer time, T-shirt painting, a talent show, and fitness programs. Nine- to 11-year-olds can play Ping-Pong, take dance lessons, play video games, and participate in swim parties, scavenger hunts, and sports. Tweens ages 12 to 14 appreciate the social events, parties, contests, and sports in Circle C. Every night they have access to the ships' discos, followed by late-night movies, karaoke, or pizza.

Club O2 is geared toward teens 15 to 17. Program directors play host at the spacious teen clubs, where kicking back is the order of the day between scheduled activities. The fleet-wide Y-Spa program for older teens offers a high level of pampering. Staff members also accompany teens on shore excursions designed just for them.

Daytime group babysitting for infants two and under allows parents the freedom to explore ports of call without the kids until noon. Parents can also pursue leisurely adults-only evenings from 10 pm to 3 am, when slumber party–style group babysitting is available for children from ages 6 months to 11 years. Babysitting is available for a fee.

Service

Service on Carnival ships is friendly but not polished. Stateroom attendants are not only recognized for their attention to cleanliness but also for their expertise in creating towel animals—cute critters fashioned from

CHOOSE THIS LINE IF ...

You want an action-packed casino with a choice of table games and rows upon rows of clanging slot machines.

You don't mind standing in line—these are big ships with a lot of passengers, and lines are not uncommon.

You don't mind hearing announcements over the public-address system reminding you of what's next on the schedule.

bath towels that appear during nightly turndown service. They've become so popular that Carnival publishes an instruction book on how to create them yourself.

Tipping

A gratuity of $11.50 per passenger per day is automatically added to passenger accounts, and gratuities are distributed to stewards and waitstaff. Passengers may adjust the amount based on the level of service experienced. All beverage tabs at bars get an automatic 15% addition.

Past Passengers

After sailing on one Carnival cruise, you'll receive a complimentary subscription to the company email magazine, and access to your past sailing history on the Carnival website. You are recognized on subsequent cruises with color-coded key cards determined by points or the number of days you've sailed—Red (starting on your second cruise), Gold (when you've accumulated 25–74 points); Platinum (75–199 points); and Diamond (200-plus points)—which serve as your entrée to a by-invitation-only cocktail reception. Platinum and Diamond members are eligible for benefits including priority embarkation and debarkation, priority dining assignments, supper club and spa reservations, a logo item gift, and limited complimentary laundry service.

HELPFUL HINTS

The line's Fun Ship 2.0 improvements are toning down the noisy, brash style in lieu of something more relaxed and tropical.

New features introduced in partnership with recognized brands (Hasbro, The Game Show, a diner crafted by Guy Fieri) have stepped up the complimentary elements of the onboard experience.

Casinos are good, and you can use your onboard charge card for casino play.

Carnival's great online planning tool (⊕ *www.carnivalconnections.com*) offers planning tips, cruise reviews, and a message board.

Most activities for children are free, but fees attached to their late-night party program can add up, in addition to the charges for video games.

5

CARNIVAL CRUISE LINES

DON'T CHOOSE THIS LINE IF ...

You want an intimate, sedate atmosphere. Carnival's ships are big and bold.

You want elaborate accommodations. Carnival suites are spacious but not as feature-filled as the term *suite* may suggest.

You're turned off by men in tank tops. Casual on these ships means casual indeed.

CARNIVAL SUNSHINE

CREW MEMBERS	1,150
ENTERED SERVICE	2013 (originally 1996)
GROSS TONS	102,853
LENGTH	893
NUMBER OF CABINS	1,503
PASSENGER CAPACITY	3,006
WIDTH	116

700 ft.

500 ft.

300 ft.

A $155-million transformation turned *Carnival Destiny,* the first of Carnival's Destiny-class megaships weighing in at more than 100,000 tons, into *Carnival Sunshine.* From stem to stern, no part of the ship was left untouched, and she has reentered service as an essentially unique, new vessel. Along with a fresh Caribbean-inspired decor, new restaurants and bars were added in keeping with Carnival's fleet-wide upgrades.

The variety of indoor and outdoor spaces ranges from relatively intimate lounges with a nightclub atmosphere to a huge show room where lavish production shows are staged. Most public rooms open off wide, indoor promenades that branch fore and aft from the spectacular atrium to the Ocean Plaza where live bands perform for dancing. Expansive pools and sport decks offer plenty of room to spread out for sunning and more active pursuits, including water slides and a ropes course. A triple-deck Serenity area for adults and huge family water park were added in the transformation.

Cabins

Cabins: As on all Carnival ships, cabins are spacious and comfortable. More than half have an ocean view, and of those, 60% have balconies. For suites and ocean-view cabins that have them, private balconies are outfitted with chairs and tables, adding living space. Every cabin has adequate closet and drawer/shelf storage, as well as bathroom shelves. High-thread-count linens and plump pillows and duvets are a luxurious touch. Top suites also have a whirlpool tub and walk-in closet. Numerous ocean-view and inside stateroom categories have connecting doors and are suitable for families. Ninety-five spa staterooms include spa amenities.

Decor: Light-wood cabinetry, soft pastels, mirrored accents, a small refrigerator, a personal safe, a hair dryer, and a seating area with sofa, chair, and table are typical for ocean-view cabins and suites. Some cabins categorized Indoor have a seating area; some have one twin bed and either an upper bunk or sofa bed.

Bathrooms: Shampoo and bath gel dispensers are mounted on shower walls; an array of toiletry samples is stocked, as well as fluffy towels. Bathrobes for use during the cruise are provided for all.

Top: Pool deck, *Carnival Sunshine*
Bottom: The Shake Spot

Accessibility: Twenty-five staterooms are designed for wheelchair accessibility.

Restaurants

Two restaurants serve open seating breakfast and lunch. Dinner is served in two traditional assigned evening seatings with an open seating option. Formal dining is supplemented by a casual Lido buffet offering a variety of food choices (including a deli, salad bar, dessert station, and regional cuisines that change daily) and casual dining at night. The ship has an upscale steakhouse that requires reservations and has a cover charge; Italian and Asian specialty restaurants require reservations for dinner, there is a cover charge, but are complimentary at lunch; and a Sushi restaurant features à la carte pricing. There are also a pizzeria, coffee bar/patisserie, poolside burrito bar and burger joint, a specialty coffee bar/patisserie, ice cream bar, and 24-hour room service with a limited menu of breakfast selections, sandwiches, and snacks.

Spas

Operated by Steiner Leisure, expansive spa facilities offer a full menu of treatments, such as a variety of massages, body wraps, and facials for adults and teens. There is a charge for use of the thermal suite, but complimentary saunas are in men's and women's changing rooms. Hair and nail services and teeth whitening are also on the salon menu.

Bars and Entertainment

A spirited piano bar, nightclubs, and the Ocean Plaza offer music for dancing and listening provided by musicians or a DJ. The Red Frog Pub is a hot spot for music and pub games. Production companies and guest entertainers perform in the show lounge and comedy club. Karaoke, and deck parties are signature nighttime activities.

Pros and Cons

Pros: tiered sunning decks above the Lido pool offer a good view of the jumbo-size LED screen; the expansive triple-deck Serenity area for adults is far from the noisy water park; the library bar is a surprisingly off-the-beaten-path space for a quiet drink.

Cons: private balconies on high decks in the middle of the ship may be noisy when there are activities on the Lido deck above; there is no covered pool if the weather turns bad; lines at the buffet can be seemingly endless at peak meal times.

Cabin Type	Size (sq. ft.)
Captain's Suite	500
Grand Suite	345
Ocean Suite	275
Ocean View with Balcony	185
Scenic Ocean View/Ocean View	220–280/185
Interior	185

FAST FACTS

- 13 passenger decks
- 3 specialty restaurants, 2 dining rooms, buffet, ice cream parlor, pizzeria
- Wi-Fi, safe, refrigerator
- 2 pools, children's pool
- Fitness classes, gym, 3 hot tubs, sauna, spa
- 14 bars, casino, dance club, library, show room, video game room
- Children's programs
- Laundry facilities, laundry service
- Internet terminal
- No-smoking cabins

5

CARNIVAL CRUISE LINES

CONQUEST-CLASS
Carnival Conquest, Glory, Valor, Liberty, Freedom

CREW MEMBERS	1,160
ENTERED SERVICE	2002, 2003, 2004, 2005, 2007
GROSS TONS	110,000
LENGTH	952 feet
NUMBER OF CABINS	1,487
PASSENGER CAPACITY	2,974 (3,700 max)
WIDTH	116 feet

700 ft.

500 ft.

300 ft.

Conquest-class ships are among the largest in the Carnival fleet. They're basically larger and more feature-filled versions of earlier Destiny-class vessels. More space translates into additional decks, an upscale steakhouse, and even more bars and lounges; however, well-proportioned public areas belie the ships' massive size. You'll hardly notice that there's slightly less space per passenger after you take a thrilling trip down the spiral waterslide.

Public rooms flow forward and aft from stunning central atriums. Just off each ship's main boulevard is an array of specialty bars, dance lounges, discos, piano bars, and show lounges, plus seating areas along the indoor promenades. The promenade can get crowded between dinner seatings and show-lounge performances, but with so many different places to spend time, you're sure to find one with plenty of room and an atmosphere to suit your taste.

Cabins

Cabins: As on all Carnival ships, cabins are roomy. More than 60% have an ocean view and, of those, 60% have balconies. For those suites and ocean-view cabins that have them, private balconies outfitted with chairs and tables add additional living space; extended balconies are 50% larger than standard ones. Every cabin has adequate closet and drawer/shelf storage, as well as bathroom shelves. High-thread-count linens and plush pillows and duvets are a luxurious touch in all accommodations. Suites have a whirlpool tub and walk-in closet; two Captain's suites that were added to *Carnival Liberty* in 2008 have two bathrooms. A plus for families are a number of connecting staterooms in a variety of ocean-view and interior categories. Balcony dividers can be unlocked to provide connecting access in upper categories.

Decor: Light-wood cabinetry, pastel colors, mirrored accents, a small refrigerator, a personal safe, a hair dryer in the top vanity-desk drawer, and a seating area with sofa, chair, and table are typical amenities.

Bathrooms: Shampoo and bath gel are provided in shower-mounted dispensers; you also get an array of sample toiletries, as well as fluffy towels and a wall-mounted magnifying mirror. Bathrobes for use during the cruise are provided for all.

Top: *Carnival Glory* at sea
Bottom: Conquest-class
balcony cabin

Accessibility: Twenty-five staterooms are designed for wheelchair accessibility.

Restaurants

Two formal restaurants serve open seating breakfast and lunch, and dinner is served in two traditional assigned seatings or an open seating option. The casual Lido buffet's food stations offer a variety of choices (including a deli, salad bar, dessert station, and different daily regional cuisines). By night the Lido buffet is transformed into the Seaview Bistro for casual dinner. The ship also has an upscale supper club that requires reservations and assesses a cover charge. You'll also find a pizzeria, a poolside burrito bar and burger joint, a specialty coffee bar with pastries, a complimentary sushi bar, and 24-hour room service that offers a limited selection of breakfast items, sandwiches, and snacks.

Spas

Operated by Steiner Leisure, spas and salons are and treatments include a variety of massages, body wraps, and facials for adults and teens. Complimentary steam rooms and saunas in men's and women's changing rooms are glass walled with endless sea vistas. Salons offer hair and nail services and even tooth whitening.

Bars and Entertainment

Conquest-class ships were the first to receive Carnival's newly branded bars and comedy club in 2012. While *Valor* and *Freedom* won't be outfitted with all of them until 2014, they will be the first Conquest-class ships to have Hasbro, The Game Show. All have lively piano bars and nightclubs featuring music for dancing and listening. Deck parties are a staple that are highlighted by new poolside bars and related musical performances.

Pros and Cons

Pros: the lounge chairs on the deck above the aft Lido pool are almost always quiet; steakhouses on these ships are some of the best bargains at sea; the ships have been retrofitted with Carnival's Seaside Theatres—the jumbo-size poolside LED screens.

Cons: cabins and balconies on deck 8 from midship to aft are beneath the Lido and suffer from pool-deck noise overhead; seating at the casino bar can be noisy; likewise, sound from the Seaside Theatre can be annoyingly loud.

Cabin Type	Size (sq. ft.)
Captain's Suite	750 (*Carnival Liberty* only)
Penthouse Suite	345
Suite	230
Ocean View	185
Interior	185

FAST FACTS

- 13 passenger decks
- Specialty restaurant, 2 dining rooms, buffet, ice cream parlor, pizzeria
- Wi-Fi, safe, refrigerator
- 3 pools (1 indoor), children's pool
- Fitness classes, gym, hot tubs, sauna, spa, steam room
- 9 bars, casino, dance club, library, show room, video game room
- Children's programs
- Laundry facilities, laundry service
- Internet terminal
- No-smoking cabins

5

CARNIVAL CRUISE LINES

SPIRIT-CLASS
Carnival Spirit, Pride, Legend, Miracle

CREW MEMBERS	930
ENTERED SERVICE	2001, 2001, 2002, 2004
GROSS TONS	88,500
LENGTH	960 feet
NUMBER OF CABINS	1,062
PASSENGER CAPACITY	2,124 (2,667 max)
WIDTH	105.7 feet

700 ft.
500 ft.
300 ft.

Spirit-class vessels may have seemed to be a throwback in size on their introduction, but these sleek ships have the advantage of fitting through the Panama Canal and, with their additional length, include all the trademark characteristics of their larger fleet mates. They're also racehorses with the speed to reach far-flung destinations. *Carnival Spirit*—for which the class is named—makes its home port in Australia, primarily serving the Australian and New Zealand markets.

A rosy red skylight in the front bulkhead of the funnel—which houses the reservations-only upscale steakhouse—caps a soaring, 11-deck atrium. Lovely chapels are available for weddings, either on embarkation or while in a port of call, and are also used for occasional shipboard religious services.

The upper and lower interior promenade decks are unhampered by a midship restaurant or galley, which means that passenger flow throughout the ships is much improved over earlier, and even subsequent, designs.

Cabins

Cabins: Cabins on Carnival ships are spacious, and these are no exception. Nearly 80% have an ocean view and, of those, more than 80% have balconies. Suites and some ocean-view cabins have private balconies outfitted with chairs and tables; some cabins have balconies at least 50% larger than average. Every cabin has adequate closet and drawer/shelf storage, as well as bathroom shelves. High-thread-count linens and plush pillows and duvets are a luxurious touch in all accommodations. Suites also have a whirlpool tub and walk-in closet. Decks 5, 6, and 7 each have a pair of balcony staterooms that connect to adjoining interior staterooms that are ideal for families because of their close proximity to children and teen areas.

Decor: Light-wood cabinetry, soft pastels, mirrored accents, a small refrigerator, a personal safe, a hair dryer, and a seating area with sofa, chair, and table are typical for ocean-view cabins and suites. Inside cabins have ample room but no seating area.

Bathrooms: Extras include shampoo and bath gel provided in shower-mounted dispensers and an array of sample toiletries, as well as fluffy towels and a wall-

Top: *Carnival Legend* at sea
Bottom: Spirit-class balcony stateroom

mounted magnifying mirror. Bathrobes for use during the cruise are provided for all.

Accessibility: Sixteen staterooms are designed for wheelchair accessibility.

Restaurants

One formal restaurant serves open seating breakfast and lunch; it also serves dinner in two traditional assigned evening seatings or an open seating option. The casual Lido buffet with stations offers a variety of food choices (including a deli, salad bar, dessert station, and different daily regional cuisines); at night it becomes the Seaview Bistro for casual dinners. There's also an upscale steakhouse that requires reservations and an additional charge, a pizzeria, poolside outdoor grills for burgers, hot dogs, and the trimmings, a specialty coffee bar and patisserie, a complimentary sushi bar, and 24-hour room service with a limited menu of breakfast selections, sandwiches, and snacks.

Spas

Steiner Leisure operates the 14,500 square-foot spas that offer an indoor therapy pool as well as such indulgences as a variety of massages, body wraps, and facials for adults and teens. Complimentary steam rooms and saunas in men's and women's changing rooms feature glass walls for sea views. Salons offer tooth whitening in addition to hair and nail services.

Bars and Entertainment

Pride and *Legend* are scheduled to receive newly branded bars and comedy club features in 2013. All have high-energy shows by resident singers and dancers or guest performers in the main show room, spirited piano bars, and nightclubs featuring music for dancing and listening. Comedy clubs, karaoke, and deck parties add to the fun of nighttime activities.

Pros and Cons

Pros: the enclosed space located forward on the promenade deck is quiet and good for reading; for relaxation, his-and-hers saunas and steam rooms have glass walls and sea views; complimentary self-serve ice-cream dispensers are on the Lido deck.

Cons: these are long ships, and some cabins are quite far from elevators; connecting staterooms are relatively scarce; the video arcade is almost hidden at the forward end of the ship.

Cabin Type	Size (sq. ft.)
Penthouse Suites	370 (average)
Suite	275
Ocean View	185
Interior	185

FAST FACTS

- 12 passenger decks
- Specialty restaurant, dining room, buffet, ice cream parlor, pizzeria
- Wi-Fi, safe, refrigerator
- 3 pools (1 indoor), children's pool
- Fitness classes, gym, hot tubs, sauna, spa, steam room
- 7 bars, casino, 2 dance clubs, library, show room, video game room
- Children's programs
- Laundry facilities, laundry service
- Internet terminal
- No-smoking cabins

5

CARNIVAL CRUISE LINES

Carnival Miracle Gatsby's Garden

DESTINY-CLASS
Carnival Triumph, Victory

CREW MEMBERS	1,100
ENTERED SERVICE	1999, 2000
GROSS TONS	102,000
LENGTH	893 feet
NUMBER OF CABINS	1,379
PASSENGER CAPACITY	2,758 (3,470 max)
WIDTH	116 feet

700 ft.

500 ft.

300 ft.

Top: *Carnival Victory* in Miami
Bottom: *Carnival Triumph*
atrium

The first class of Carnival megaships weighing in at more than 100,000 tons, everything on these vessels is in keeping with their size—bold interiors highlighted by nine-deck atriums, 200-foot corkscrew waterslides on the Lido deck, and public areas that often span multiple decks. *Carnival Triumph* and *Carnival Victory* are bigger and have more cabins and crew than the original *Carnival Destiny,* for which the class was named and which was totally rebuilt and renamed *Carnival Sunshine* in 2013.

The variety of indoor and outdoor spaces ranges from relatively small lounges with a nightclub atmosphere to huge show rooms where lavish production shows are staged. Most public rooms open off wide indoor promenades that branch fore and aft from the spectacular atrium.

Expansive pools and sport decks have plenty of room to spread out for sunning and more active pursuits; both ships have been retrofitted with massive poolside 270-square-foot LED screens.

Cabins

Cabins: As on all Carnival ships, cabins are spacious and comfortable. More than half have an ocean view, and of those, 60% have balconies. For suites and ocean-view cabins that have them, private balconies are outfitted with chairs and tables, adding living space. Every cabin has adequate closet and drawer/shelf storage, as well as bathroom shelves. High-thread-count linens and plump pillows and duvets are a luxurious touch. Suites also have whirlpool tubs and walk-in closets. Numerous ocean-view and inside stateroom categories have connecting doors and are suitable for families.

Decor: Light-wood cabinetry, soft pastels, mirrored accents, a small refrigerator, a personal safe, a hair dryer, and a seating area with sofa, chair, and table are typical for ocean-view cabins and suites. Inside cabins do not have a seating area.

Bathrooms: Shampoo and bath gel dispensers are mounted on shower walls; an array of toiletry samples is stocked, as well as fluffy towels. Bathrobes for use during the cruise are provided for all.

Accessibility: Twenty-five staterooms are designed for wheelchair accessibility.

Restaurants

Two restaurants, each spanning two decks, serve open seating breakfast and lunch. Dinner is served in two traditional assigned evening seatings with an open seating option. Formal dining is supplemented by a casual Lido buffet, offering a variety of food choices (including a deli, salad bar, dessert station, and regional cuisines that change daily); the buffet restaurant becomes the Seaview Bistro by night for casual dining in a relaxed atmosphere. There are also a pizzeria, coffee bar/patisserie, poolside outdoor grill for burgers, hot dogs, and the trimmings, a specialty coffee bar/patisserie, a complimentary sushi bar, and 24-hour room service with a limited menu of breakfast selections, sandwiches, and snacks.

Spas

Operated by Steiner Leisure, expansive spa facilities offer a full menu of treatments, such as a variety of massages, body wraps, and facials for adults and teens; complimentary steam rooms and saunas are located in men's and women's changing rooms. Hair and nail services and teeth whitening are also on the salon menu.

Bars and Entertainment

Triumph and *Victory* are scheduled to receive newly branded bars and other features in 2013 and 2014 respectively. Both have lively piano bars and nightclubs featuring music for dancing and listening. High-energy production shows, comedy clubs, karaoke, and deck parties are signature nighttime activities.

Pros and Cons

Pros: tiered sunning decks above the Lido pools offer a good view of the jumbo-size LED screens; the upper-level seating area in the Lido restaurant almost always has tables available; the lobby bar is a surprisingly off-the-beaten-path space with a lot of visual impact.

Cons: there is no steakhouse on either ship; private balconies on high decks in the middle of the ship may be noisy when there are activities on the Lido deck above; lines at the buffet can be seemingly endless at peak meal times.

Cabin Type	Size (sq. ft.)
Penthouse Suite	345
Suite	275
Ocean View	185
Interior	185

FAST FACTS

- 13 passenger decks
- 2 dining rooms, buffet, ice cream parlor, pizzeria
- Wi-Fi, safe, refrigerator
- 3 pools (1 indoor), children's pool
- Fitness classes, gym, hot tubs, sauna, spa, steam room
- 7 bars, casino, 3 dance clubs, library, show room, video game room
- Children's programs
- Laundry facilities, laundry service
- Internet terminal
- No-smoking cabins

5

CARNIVAL CRUISE LINES

Carnival Triumph

FANTASY-CLASS

Carnival Fantasy, Ecstasy, Sensation, Fascination, Imagination, Inspiration, Elation, Paradise

CREW MEMBERS	920
ENTERED SERVICE	1990, 1991, 1993, 1994, 1995, 1996, 1998, 1998
GROSS TONS	70,367
LENGTH	855 feet
NUMBER OF CABINS	1,028
PASSENGER CAPACITY	2,056 (2,610 max)
WIDTH	103 feet

700 ft.

500 ft.

300 ft.

Bathed in fiber-optic light, glitzy Fantasy-class interiors added expansive six-deck atriums and a new dimension to the original superliner concept. To keep the fun going, these ships offer an almost wearying assortment of places to have a good time. As times and tastes have changed, the ships have evolved as well, with new lobby bars, dedicated club spaces for teens and tweens, miniature golf, and Internet centers. Even newer are Carnival's WaterWorks water park and the Serenity Adult-Only Retreat, which increase the appeal of the older Fantasy-class vessels.

Only one level below the Lido deck, the indoor promenade connects major public rooms on a single deck, with only formal dining rooms, shops, and other small spaces one deck below. Large in size and ideal for a short itinerary, these ships have sprawling outdoor pool and sunning areas, but they can feel cramped when sailing at maximum capacity. Cabins provide calm oases from sensory overload. With the exception of *Carnival Sensation, Carnival Fascination,* and *Carnival Ecstasy,* to which balconies were added to existing cabins, you'll have to book a suite if you want the solitude of a private balcony.

Cabins

Cabins: Fantasy-class ships have a higher percentage of inside cabins than the fleet's newer ships, and with the exception of *Carnival Sensation, Carnival Fascination,* and *Carnival Ecstasy,* only the suite categories offer balconies. Every cabin has adequate closet and drawer/shelf storage, as well as bathroom shelves. Light-wood cabinetry and simple decor are the norm for all cabins, while suite embellishments add the convenience of a seating area and small refrigerator. In addition to the extra space, a whirlpool tub is a deluxe appointment in Penthouse suites. Inside cabins have ample room, and their curtained faux windows mimic those in the more expensive standard ocean-view accommodations. High-thread-count linens and plush pillows and duvets add a touch of luxury to all accommodations. Doors have been added to a limited number of adjacent cabins to create connecting accommodations on Fantasy-class ships, and lighting in the vanity/desk area has been improved on some. Bring your own hair dryer.

Top: *Imagination* at sea
Bottom: *Inspiration* Lido pool deck

Bathrooms: Extras include shower-mounted shampoo and bath gel dispensers and an array of sample toiletries, as well as fluffy towels. Bathrobes for use during the cruise are provided for all.

Accessibility: Twenty-two staterooms are designed for wheelchair accessibility.

Restaurants

Two formal restaurants serve open seating breakfast and lunch; dinner is served in two traditional assigned evening seatings or an open seating option. The casual Lido buffet with stations offers a variety of food choices (including a deli, salad bar, dessert station, and different daily regional cuisines); at night it becomes the Seaview Bistro for casual dinners. There's also a pizzeria; rotisserie; poolside outdoor grills for burgers, hot dogs, and the trimmings; a specialty coffee bar and patisserie; a complimentary sushi bar; and 24-hour room service with a limited menu of breakfast selections, sandwiches, and snacks.

Spas

Steiner Leisure operates the well-appointed spas that offer treatments including a variety of massages, body wraps, and facials for adults and teens; there are relaxation rooms where you can chill out before or after your appointment and complimentary steam rooms and saunas in men's and women's changing rooms. Salons offer tooth whitening in addition to hair and nail services.

Bars and Entertainment

Only *Elation* and *Paradise* are scheduled to receive Carnival's new bar features in 2014 and 2015 respectively. All have spirited piano bars and nightclubs offering music for dancing and listening. Production companies and guest entertainers performing in the show lounge, comedy clubs, karaoke, and deck parties are signature nighttime activities.

Pros and Cons

Pros: central atriums are stunning when sunlight streams in through skylights; surprisingly large libraries are ideal retreats for reading or playing board games; freshly made pizza and calzones are available around the clock.

Cons: despite upgrades, the decor is still pretty gaudy; these are ships designed for partying, so quiet spots can be difficult to find; sushi bars earn high marks for their complimentary creations, but sake costs extra.

Cabin Type	Size (sq. ft.)
Penthouse Suite	330
Suite	220
Ocean View	185
Interior	160–185

FAST FACTS

- 10 passenger decks
- 2 dining rooms, buffet, ice cream parlor, pizzeria
- Wi-Fi, safe, refrigerator (some)
- 1 pool, children's pool
- Fitness classes, gym, hot tubs, sauna, spa, steam room
- 5 bars, casino, dance club, library, show room, video game room
- Children's programs
- Laundry facilities, laundry service
- Internet terminal
- No-smoking cabins

Elation Tiffany's Lounge

DREAM-CLASS
Carnival Dream, Magic, Breeze

CREW MEMBERS	1,367, 1,386, 1,386
ENTERED SERVICE	2008, 2011, 2012
GROSS TONS	130,000
LENGTH	1,004 feet
NUMBER OF CABINS	1,823, 1,845, 1,845
PASSENGER CAPACITY	3,646 (4,631 max), 3,690 (4,724 max), 3,690 (4,724 max)
WIDTH	122 feet

700 ft.

500 ft.

300 ft.

Carnival's Dream-class, the line's largest group of ships, is marked by a sleek hull and distinctive profile. The added size has allowed Carnival to create some truly spectacular onboard facilities and amenities. Unique is the Ocean Plaza, an indoor–outdoor café and live music venue with a large, circular dance floor with a massive floor-to-ceiling curved-glass wall separating the room; and in a first for Carnival, there's a half-mile, open-air promenade encircling the ship.

Four "scenic" whirlpools located on the promenade cantilever out over the sea and offer maximum views while you're soaking. Higher up, the Lido deck is the most elaborate open area of any Carnival ship, with a tropical, resort-style main pool complete with a Seaside Theatre LED screen; a two-level adults-only retreat (called Serenity); and a huge Carnival WaterWorks aqua park featuring one of the longest waterslides at sea. Family-friendly amenities include separate, purpose-built facilities for the line's three distinct children's programs, along with a full schedule of activities catering.

Cabins

Cabins: As on all Carnival ships, cabins are roomy and comfortable. About 1/3 have ocean views; almost half have balconies. New "cove" balcony staterooms, located closer to the water line, offer up-close sea views and a bit more interior space. Also new are deluxe ocean-view staterooms offering 5 berths and a 2-bath configuration (one full bath and a second with a combination tub/shower). Every cabin has adequate storage as well as bathroom shelves. High-quality linens and plush pillows and duvets are a luxurious touch. New on *Carnival Breeze* is a more tropical decor. There are connecting staterooms in both ocean-view and interior categories, as well as the spacious new deluxe ocean-view staterooms.

Bathrooms: Shampoo and bath gel are provided in shower-mounted dispensers; you also receive an array of sample toiletries, as well as fluffy towels and a wall-mounted magnifying mirror. Bathrobes for use during the cruise are provided for all.

Accessibility: Thirty-five staterooms are designed for wheelchair accessibility.

Top: RedFrog Pub, *Carnival Magic*
Bottom: Cucina del Capitano, *Carnival Magic*

Restaurants

Two formal restaurants serve open seating breakfast and lunch; dinner is a choice of two assigned seatings or open seating. The casual Lido buffet's food stations offer a variety of choices (including a deli, salad bar, dessert station, and different daily regional cuisines). By night, it is transformed into the Seaview Bistro for casual dinner. The ships also have upscale steakhouses that require reservations and have a cover charge. *Carnival Magic* and *Carnival Breeze* have added an Italian specialty restaurant that requires reservations for dinner, when there is a cover charge, but is complimentary at lunch. *Carnival Breeze* also has an Asian restaurant with à la carte pricing. You'll also find a pizzeria, outdoor poolside grills where burgers and other favorites are prepared, a specialty coffee bar with pastries, a complimentary sushi bar, and 24-hour room service that offers a limited selection of breakfast items, sandwiches, and snacks.

Spas

Dream-class spas cover 23,750 square feet on two decks. Included in that space are flotation and mud treatment rooms, a huge thalassotherapy pool, and thermal suite with tepidarium, laconium, Oriental and aroma steam baths, and a relaxation lounge. Although the thermal areas are only available for a fee, there are complimentary saunas and steam rooms in the men's and women's changing rooms.

Bars and Entertainment

Dream-class ships have spirited piano bars, nightclubs, and the Ocean Plaza offering music for dancing and listening provided by musicians or a DJ. The Red Frog Pub on *Carnival Magic* and *Carnival Breeze* is a hot spot for music and pub games. Production companies and guest entertainers performing in the show lounge, comedy clubs, karaoke, and deck parties are signature nighttime activities.

Pros and Cons

Pros: spa staterooms and suites have exclusive amenities and spa privileges; 2-bathroom staterooms are a boon for families; the atrium has a cantilevered bandstand atop a massive dance floor.

Cons: lines can be a problem everywhere, especially in the buffet; if the weather is bad outside, interior spaces feel overwhelmed; decor is considerably but not completely toned down.

Cabin Type	Size (sq. ft.)
Grand Suite	430
Suite	310
Ocean View with Cove Balcony	230
Ocean View with Balcony	220
Deluxe Ocean View/Ocean View	230/220
Interior	185

FAST FACTS

- 13 passenger decks
- Specialty restaurant (*Dream*), 2 specialty restaurants (*Magic*), 3 specialty restaurants (*Breeze*), 2 dining rooms, buffet, café, ice cream parlor, pizzeria
- Wi-Fi, safe, refrigerator, DVD (some)
- 3 pools, children's pool
- Fitness classes, gym, hot tubs, sauna, spa, steam room
- 10 bars (*Dream*), 12 bars (*Magic*), 13 bars (*Breeze*), casino, 2 dance clubs, library, 2 show rooms, video game room
- Children's programs
- Laundry facilities, laundry service
- Internet terminal, Wi-Fi
- No-smoking cabins

5

CARNIVAL CRUISE LINES

CELEBRITY CRUISES

The Chandris Group, owners of budget Fantasy Cruises, founded Celebrity in 1989. Initially utilizing an unlovely, refurbished former ocean liner from the Fantasy fleet, Celebrity gained a reputation for professional service and fine food despite the shabby-chic

Celebrity Century at anchor

vessel on which it was elegantly served. The cruise line eventually built premium sophisticated cruise ships. Signature amenities followed, including large standard staterooms with generous storage, fully equipped spas, and butler service. Valuable art collections grace the fleet.

☎ *800/647–2251*
⊕ *www.celebritycruises. com*
☞ *Cruise Style: Premium.*

Although spacious accommodations in every category are a Celebrity standard, Concierge-class, an upscale element on all ships, makes certain premium ocean-view and balcony staterooms almost the equivalent of suites in terms of service. A Concierge-class stateroom includes numerous extras, such as chilled champagne, fresh fruit, and flowers upon arrival, exclusive room-service menus, evening canapés, luxury bedding, pillows, and linens, upgraded balcony furnishings, priority boarding and luggage service, and other VIP perks. At the touch of a single telephone button, a Concierge-class desk representative is at hand to offer assistance. Suites are still the ultimate, though, and include the services of a butler to assist with unpacking, booking spa services and dining reservations, shining shoes, and even replacing a popped button.

Food

Aside from the sophisticated ambience of its restaurants, the cuisine has always been a highlight of a Celebrity cruise. Happily, every ship in the fleet has a highly experienced team headed by executive chefs and food and beverage managers who have developed their skills in some of the world's finest restaurants and hotels.

Alternative restaurants throughout the fleet offer fine dining and a variety of international cuisines in splendid surroundings. A less formal evening alternative is offered in Lido restaurants, where you'll find made-to-order sushi, stir-fry, pasta, pizza, and curry stations, as well as a carving station, an array of vegetables, "loaded" baked potatoes, and desserts. The AquaSpa Cafés serve light and healthy cuisine from breakfast until evening. Cafés serve a variety of coffees, teas, and pastries that carry an additional charge. Late-night treats served by white-gloved waiters in public rooms throughout the ships can include mini–beef Wellingtons and crispy tempura.

To further complement the food, Celebrity's extensive wine collection features more than 500 choices, including vintages from every major wine-producing region.

Entertainment

Entertainment has never been a primary focus of Celebrity Cruises, although every ship offers a line-up of lavish production shows. In addition, ships have guest entertainers and music for dancing and listening, and you'll find lectures on every Celebrity cruise. Presentations may range from financial strategies, astronomy, wine appreciation, photography tips, and politics to the food, history, and culture of ports of call. Culinary demonstrations, bingo, and art auctions are additional diversions throughout the fleet. There are plenty of activities outlined in the daily program of events. There are no public address announcements for bingo or hawking of gold-by-the-inch sales. You can still play and buy, but you won't be reminded repeatedly.

Fitness and Recreation

Celebrity's AquaSpa by Elemis and fitness centers are some of the most tranquil and nicely equipped at sea, with complimentary access to thalassotherapy pools on Millennium-class ships. Spa services are operated by Steiner Leisure, and treatments include a variety of massages, body wraps, and facials. Trendy and traditional hair and nail services are offered in the salons.

State-of-the-art exercise equipment, a jogging track, and basic fitness classes are available at no charge. There's a fee for personal training, body composition analysis, and specialized classes such as yoga and Pilates. Golf pros offer hands-on instruction, and game simulators allow passengers to play world-famous courses. Each ship also has an Acupuncture at Sea treatment area staffed by licensed practitioners of Oriental medicine.

KNOWN FOR

■ **AquaSpa:** The AquaSpa facilities on Celebrity ships are considered some of the finest at sea.

■ **Art:** Celebrity's contemporary style is complemented by stunning modern art collections.

■ **Food:** Sophisticated cuisine and menu options make Celebrity's dining experience outstanding at this level of cruising.

■ **Service:** With a high ratio of staff to guests, Celebrity offers personal and intuitive, yet unobtrusive service.

Top: The *Millennium* AquaSpa
Bottom: Millennium-class cinema and conference center

Your Shipmates

Celebrity caters to American cruise passengers, primarily couples from their mid-thirties to mid-fifties. Many families enjoy cruising on Celebrity's fleet during summer months and holiday periods, particularly in the Caribbean. Lengthier cruises and exotic itineraries attract passengers in the over-sixty age group.

Dress Code

Two formal nights are standard on seven-night cruises. Men are encouraged to wear tuxedos, but dark suits or sport coats and ties are more prevalent. Other evenings are designated "smart casual and above." Although jeans are discouraged in formal restaurants, they are appropriate for casual dining venues after 6 pm. The line requests that no shorts be worn in public areas after 6 pm, and most people observe the dress code of the evening, unlike on some other cruise lines.

Junior Cruisers

Each Celebrity vessel has a dedicated playroom and offers a four-tier program of age-appropriate games and activities designed for children ages 3 to 5, 6 to 8, and 9 to 11. Younger children must be toilet trained to participate in the programs and use the facilities; however, families are welcome to borrow toys for their non–toilet-trained kids. A fee may be assessed for participation in children's dinner parties, the Late-Night Slumber Party, and Afternoon Get-Togethers while parents are ashore in ports of call. Evening in-cabin babysitting can be arranged for a fee. All ships have teen centers, where tweens and teenagers (ages 12 to 17) can hang out and attend mock-tail and pizza parties.

Service

Service on Celebrity ships is unobtrusive and polished. Concierge-class adds an unexpected level of service and amenities that are usually reserved for luxury ships or passengers in top-category suites on other premium cruise lines.

Top: *Century* Rendezvous Lounge
Middle: Lunch on deck
Bottom: Lounging on deck

CHOOSE THIS LINE IF ...

You want an upscale atmosphere at a really reasonable fare.	You don't mind paying extra for exceptional specialty dining experiences.	You want to dine amid elegant surroundings in some of the best restaurants at sea.

Tipping

Gratuities are automatically added daily to onboard accounts in the following amounts (which may be adjusted at your discretion): $12 per person per day for passengers in stateroom categories; $12.50 per person per day for Concierge-class and Aqua-class staterooms; and $15.50 per person per day for suites. An automatic gratuity of 15% is added to all beverage tabs, minibar purchases, and salon and spa services.

Past Passengers

Once you've sailed with Celebrity, you become a member of the Captain's Club and receive benefits commensurate with the number of cruises you've taken, including free upgrades, the chance to make dining reservations before sailing, and other benefits. Classic members have been on at least one Celebrity cruise. Select members have sailed at least six cruises and get more perks, including an invitation to a senior officer's cocktail party. After 10 cruises you become an Elite member and can take advantage of a private departure lounge. Royal Caribbean International, the parent company of Celebrity Cruises, also extends the corresponding levels of their Crown & Anchor program to Celebrity Captain's Club members.

DON'T CHOOSE THIS LINE IF ...

You need to be reminded of when activities are scheduled. Announcements are kept to a minimum.

You look forward to boisterous pool games and wacky contests. These cruises are fairly quiet and sophisticated.

You think funky avant-garde art is weird. Abstract modernism abounds in the art collections.

SOLSTICE-CLASS
Solstice, Equinox, Eclipse, Silhouette, Reflection

CREW MEMBERS	
1,253	
ENTERED SERVICE	
2008, 2009, 2010, 2011, 2012	
GROSS TONS	
122,000, 126,000 (*Reflection*)	
LENGTH	
1,033 feet, 1,047 feet (*Reflection*)	
NUMBER OF CABINS	
1,425, 1,515 (*Reflection*)	
PASSENGER CAPACITY	
2,850, 3,046 (*Reflection*)	
WIDTH	
121 feet, 123 feet (*Reflection*)	

700 ft.
500 ft.
300 ft.

Solstice-class ships are the largest in the Celebrity fleet. While the ships are contemporary in design—even a bit edgy for Celebrity—the line included enough spaces with old-world ambience to satisfy traditionalists. The atmosphere is not unlike a hip boutique hotel yet filled with grand spaces, as well as intimate nooks and crannies. *Celebrity Reflection* adds an additional deck for more high-end suite accommodations.

The Lawn Club, a half acre of real grass on deck 15, is where you can play genteel games of croquet, practice golf putting, indulge in lawn games and picnics, or simply take barefoot strolls. In a nearby open-air "theater" on *Solstice, Eclipse,* and *Equinox,* artisans demonstrate glassmaking in the Hot Glass Show. A similar space on *Silhouette* and *Reflection* houses an outdoor grill restaurant, and those ships also have private cabanas in the Lawn Club (for a fee). These ships have a lot to offer families, with a family pool and the most extensive children's facilities in the Celebrity fleet.

Cabins

Layout: Although cabins are larger than those on other Celebrity ships, closet and drawer storage is barely adequate. On the other hand, bathrooms are generous and have plentiful storage space. An impressive 85% of all outside accommodations have balconies. With sofa–trundle beds, many categories are capable of accommodating third and fourth occupants. Connecting staterooms are also available. Family staterooms have a second bedroom with bunk beds.

Amenities: A refrigerator, TV, personal safe, hair dryer, seating area with sofa and table, bathroom toiletries (shampoo, soaps, and lotion), and bathrobes for use during the cruise are standard.

Suites: Most suites have a whirlpool tub, DVD, and walk-in closet, while all have butler service, personalized stationery, and a logo tote bag. Penthouse suites have guest powder rooms; Penthouse and Royal suites have whirlpool tubs on the balconies. *Celebrity Reflection* introduces several additional suite categories.

Accessibility: Thirty staterooms are designed for wheelchair accessibility.

Top: Blu, the AquaClass specialty restaurant
Bottom: Lawn bowling

Restaurants

The main restaurant serves open seating breakfast and lunch; dinner is served in two traditional assigned seatings or an open seating option. A second dining room, reserved for Aqua-class passengers, serves lighter cuisine. There are also a casual Lido buffet, pizza, sushi bar, the AquaSpa Café with healthy selections, a luncheon grill, a café that offers crêpes (cover charge), and specialty coffee, tea, and gelato bar (extra charge). Three upscale alternative restaurants require dinner reservations and charge extra for contemporary French, Asian fusion, and Italian. *Eclipse, Silhouette,* and *Reflection* replaced the Asian restaurant with one serving modern American food. Additionally, *Silhouette* and *Reflection* feature the Lawn Club Grill for evening alfresco dining (cover charge) and the Porch for light breakfast and lunch fare (cover charge). Available 24 hours, room service rounds out the dining choices.

Spas

The AquaSpa by Elemis is one of the most tranquil at sea with spa services operated by Steiner Leisure. In addition to treatments that include a variety of massages, body wraps, and facials, each ship also has an acupuncture treatment area and Medi-Spa Cosmetic services. A relaxation room and thermal suite with dry and aromatherapy steam rooms and a hot Turkish bath are available to Aqua-class passengers and those who have booked a treatment or purchased a pass. Changing rooms for men and women have complimentary saunas.

Bars and Entertainment

Production companies and guest entertainers perform in the show lounges. Bars and lounges are designed as unique destinations on board with drink menus offering not only a selection of classics, but also "signature" and trendier cocktails. Some drinks are a reflection of the regions you are visiting. Live bands or DJs provide music for listening and dancing.

Pros and Cons

Pros: an interactive TV system allows you to book shore excursions and order room service; Aqua-class has its own staircase direct to the spa; a Hospitality Director oversees restaurant reservations.

Cons: closet space is skimpy in standard cabins; there are no self-service laundries; dining choices are plentiful, but pricey.

Cabin Type	Size (sq. ft.)
Penthouse/Reflection Suite	1,291/ 1,636
Royal Suites	590
Celebrity/Signature Suites	394/441
Sky/Aqua-class Suites	300
Family Ocean-View Balcony	575
Ocean-View Balcony	194
Sunset Veranda	194
Ocean View	177
Inside	183–200

FAST FACTS

■ 13 passenger decks (14 *Celebrity Reflection*)

■ 4 specialty restaurants (5 *Celebrity Reflection*), 3 dining rooms, buffet, ice cream parlor, pizzeria

■ Wi-Fi, safe, refrigerator, DVD (some)

■ 3 pools (1 indoor)

■ Fitness classes, gym, hot tubs, sauna, spa

■ 11 bars, casino, dance club, library, show room, video game room

■ Children's programs

■ Dry-cleaning, laundry service

■ Internet terminal

■ No-smoking cabins

The solarium on *Solstice*

MILLENNIUM-CLASS
Millennium, Summit, Infinity, Constellation

CREW MEMBERS	999
ENTERED SERVICE	2000, 2001, 2001, 2002
GROSS TONS	91,000
LENGTH	965 feet
NUMBER OF CABINS	1069, 1079, 1085, 1085
PASSENGER CAPACITY	2,138, 2,158, 2,170, 2,170
WIDTH	105 feet

700 ft.

500 ft.

300 ft.

Millennium-class ships are among the largest and most feature-filled in the Celebrity fleet. The ships include show lounges reminiscent of splendid opera houses, and an alternative restaurant with a classic ocean liner theme. The spas are immense and house a complimentary hydrotherapy pool and café. These ships have a lot to offer families, with some of the most expansive children's facilities in the Celebrity fleet. Recent upgrades have introduced more accommodation categories and dining venues similar to those found on Solstice-class ships.

Rich fabrics in jewel tones mix elegantly with the abundant use of marble and wood accents throughout public areas. The atmosphere is not unlike a luxurious European hotel filled with grand spaces that flow nicely from one to the other.

Cabins

Cabins: As on most Celebrity ships, cabins are thoughtfully designed, with ample closet and drawer/shelf storage, as well as bathroom shelves. Some ocean-view cabins and suites have balconies. Penthouse suites also have guest powder rooms. Most staterooms and suites have convertible sofa beds, and many can accommodate third and fourth occupants. Connecting staterooms are also widely available. Family staterooms have huge balconies, and some have two sofa beds. Aqua-class accommodations with direct spa access are a relatively new addition.

Amenities: A small refrigerator, personal safe, hair dryer, and a seating area with sofa, chair, and table are typical standard amenities. Extras include bathroom toiletries (shampoo, soaps, and lotion) and bathrobes. Suite luxuries vary, but most include a whirlpool tub, a DVD, an Internet-connected computer, and a walk-in closet, while all have butler service, personalized stationery, and a logo tote bag. Penthouse and Royal suites have outdoor whirlpool tubs on the balconies.

Accessibility: Twenty-six staterooms are designed for wheelchair accessibility.

Restaurants

The formal two-deck restaurant serves open seating breakfast and lunch; while dinner is served in two assigned seatings or open seating. The casual Lido buffet

Top: *Millennium* Café al Bacio
Bottom: *Millennium*
Ocean Grill

offers breakfast and lunch; for dinner, it has made-to-order entrées, a carving station, and an array of side dishes. A poolside grill offers fast food, while a spa café serves lighter fare. Each ship has an upscale alternative restaurant that specializes in tableside food preparation; each also has a demonstration kitchen and wine cellar (reservation and cover charge). Each also has a café that offers crêpes and other light items (cover charge), and an extra-charge specialty coffee, tea, and gelato bar. All ships feature a second specialty restaurant serving modern American food except *Constellation,* which serves Italian cuisine. Pizza delivery and 24-hour room service augment dining choices.

Spas
The AquaSpa by Elemis is one of the most nicely equipped at sea with spa services operated by Steiner Leisure. In addition to treatments that include a variety of massages, body wraps, and facials, each ship also has an acupuncture treatment area and offers Medi-Spa Cosmetic services. A relaxation room and thermal suite with a dry sauna, aromatherapy steam room, and a Turkish bath are available to Aqua-class passengers and those who have booked a treatment or purchased a pass. Changing rooms for men and women have complimentary saunas, and a large hydrotherapy pool is available to all adults at no charge.

Bars and Entertainment
Production companies and guest entertainers perform in the show lounges. Bars and lounges are designed as unique destinations on board with drink menus with both classic and also "signature" and trendier cocktails. Some drinks are a reflection of the regions you are visiting. Live bands or DJs provide music for listening and dancing.

Pros and Cons
Pros: stylishly appointed Grand Foyers have sweeping staircases; there's no charge for use of the thalassotherapy pool in the Solarium; the AquaSpa Café serves complimentary light and healthy selections.

Cons: these ships just have too many passengers to offer truly personal service; wines in the specialty restaurants are pricey; there are no self-service laundries.

Cabin Type	Size (sq. ft.)
Penthouse Suite	1,432
Royal Suite	538
Celebrity Suite	467
Sky Suite	251
Family Ocean View	271
Concierge-Class	191
Ocean View/ Interior	170

FAST FACTS

- 11 passenger decks
- 3 specialty restaurants, dining room, buffet, ice cream parlor, pizzeria
- Internet (*Constellation*), Wi-Fi, safe, refrigerator, DVD (some)
- 3 pools (1 indoor), children's pool
- Fitness classes, gym, hot tubs, sauna, spa, steam room
- 7 bars, casino, dance club, library, show room, video game room
- Children's programs
- Dry-cleaning, laundry service
- Internet terminal
- No-smoking cabins

5

CELEBRITY CRUISES

CENTURY-CLASS
Century

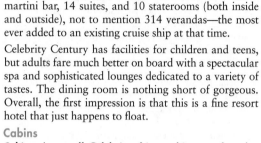

CREW MEMBERS	858
ENTERED SERVICE	1995
GROSS TONS	70,606
LENGTH	815 feet
NUMBER OF CABINS	907
PASSENGER CAPACITY	1,814
WIDTH	105 feet

700 ft.

500 ft.

300 ft.

Although quietly elegant, *Celebrity Century* has an eclectic air, due in part to the fine collections of modern and classical art displayed throughout public rooms. A 2006 refit added a stunning specialty restaurant, an ice-topped martini bar, 14 suites, and 10 staterooms (both inside and outside), not to mention 314 verandas—the most ever added to an existing cruise ship at that time.

Celebrity Century has facilities for children and teens, but adults fare much better on board with a spectacular spa and sophisticated lounges dedicated to a variety of tastes. The dining room is nothing short of gorgeous. Overall, the first impression is that this is a fine resort hotel that just happens to float.

Cabins

Cabins: As on all Celebrity ships, cabins are thoughtfully designed with ample closet and drawer/shelf storage and bathroom shelves. Some ocean-view cabins and suites have balconies with chairs and tables. Penthouse and Royal suites have a whirlpool bathtub and separate shower as well as a walk-in closet; Penthouse suites have a guest powder room. *Century* also has Family Veranda Staterooms.

Amenities: Light-wood cabinetry, mirrored accents, a refrigerator, a personal safe, a hair dryer, and a seating area with sofa, chair, and table are typical standard amenities. Extras include bathroom toiletries (shampoo, soaps, and lotion) and bathrobes for use during the cruise. Penthouse and Royal suites have an elaborate entertainment center with a large TV, while all suites include butler service, personalized stationery, DVD, and a tote bag.

Accessibility: Eight staterooms are designed for wheelchair accessibility.

Restaurants

The formal two-deck restaurant serves open seating breakfast, lunch, and evening meals in two assigned seatings; however, Celebrity Select Dining, an open seating option, allows participants to be seated any time the main restaurant is open. Formal dining is supplemented by a casual Lido restaurant offering buffet-style breakfast and lunch. By night, the Lido restaurant offers made-to-order entrées, a carving station, and an array of side dishes. *Century* has both a complimentary spa café and

Top: Formal dining on *Century*
Bottom: *Century* Shipmates Fun Factory

an upscale, reservations-only restaurant that specializes in tableside preparation and has an extra cover charge. Poolside grills offer burgers and other fast-food favorites and specialty coffees, teas, and pastries are available for an additional charge in the café. Room service is available 24 hours and includes pizza delivered to your door.

Spas

The AquaSpa by Elemis facilities are nicely equipped with services operated by Steiner Leisure. In addition to treatments that include a variety of massages, body wraps, and facials, each ship also has an acupuncture treatment area and offers Medi-Spa cosmetic services. A thermal suite with dry sauna and aromatherapy steam rooms and a hot Turkish bath is available to passengers who have booked a treatment or purchased a pass. Changing rooms for men and women have complimentary saunas.

Bars and Entertainment

Bars and lounges are designed as unique destinations on board with drink menus offering not only a selection of classics, but also "signature" and trendier cocktails. Some drinks are a reflection of the regions you are visiting. Production shows and guest entertainers are a staple in the show lounge and live bands or DJs provide music for listening and dancing.

Pros and Cons

Pros: Michael's Club, once a cigar lounge, is now a smoke-free piano bar; the food and service is more than worth the price; you can descend a fairly grand staircase to dine in the tradition of great ocean liners.

Cons: the trendsetting thalassotherapy pool has been removed; there is no dedicated swimming pool for small children; a downside for smokers is that smoking is not allowed in most indoor spaces or on balconies.

Cabin Type	Size (sq. ft.)
Penthouse Suite	1,101
Royal Suite/Sky Suite	537/246
Century Suite/ Family Stateroom	190/192
Concierge, Veranda/Ocean View	170–175/ 172–175
Interior	171–174

FAST FACTS

- 10 passenger decks
- Specialty restaurant, dining room, buffet, ice cream parlor, pizzeria
- Wi-Fi, safe, refrigerator, DVD (some)
- 2 pools
- Fitness classes, gym, hot tubs, sauna, spa
- 7 bars, casino, dance club, library, show room, video game room
- Children's programs
- Dry-cleaning, laundry service
- Internet terminal
- No-smoking cabins

5

CELEBRITY CRUISES

COMPAGNIE DU PONANT

Compagnie du Ponant operates three designer ships for all-season premium yet unpretentious yacht cruising in places inaccessible to larger cruise ships. At this writing, a fourth ship was expected for delivery in July 2013. With distinctively French flair, the cruise

Le Boréal at sea

company strikes an appealing balance between destination choice and price point on luxuriously refurbished modern sailing vessels that feature French gastronomy, elegant styling, and unique voyages with all-inclusive packages. Travel is privileged yet unpretentious aboard a small majestic three-masted sailing yacht or larger megayacht.

☎ *888/400–1082 toll-free in U.S. and Canada, (033) 4/88–66–64–00 in France* ⊕ *www.ponant.com* ☞ *Cruise Style: Luxury.*

Food

Gastronomy is taken pretty seriously on Compagnie du Ponant ships. Buttery croissants and artisanal baguettes with confiture, fruit, yogurts, coffee, and juices are available for breakfast; eggs and specialty dishes can be ordered à la carte. International buffets for lunch and dinner lay out a high-quality spread of cold and hot appetizers, entrées, salads, and desserts. Fresh ingredients and skilled preparation by resident French chefs and bakers keep culinary standards at an outstanding level for grilled and roasted meat, fish, vegetarian meals, and desserts. In more formal dining areas, most dinner menus offer a choice between two soups, three appetizers/salads, two main courses, a cheese tray, and a couple of sumptuous desserts. Although oenophiles may be disappointed with the free table wine served for lunch and dinner, premium bottles can be ordered for a supplementary cost. Back by popular demand, the Food & Wine Cruise pleases passenger palates with Flavors of the Riviera. All lunches and dinners include complimentary mineral water, tea, coffee, and wines. Twenty-four-hour room service is available.

Entertainment

Special events including the Captain's cocktail party and farewell dinner spice up the rather unimaginative entertainment program that does not promise to be grandiose and theatrical. Instead, most passengers simply relax while watching small groups of performers and dancers. Guest speakers lecture on geography, conservation, and wildlife in the cabaret-style theater on larger ships, which is also used for evening shows. On smaller vessels, piano bars and chic lounges offer opportunities to make new friends from around the world.

Fitness and Recreation

Passengers burn off calories in a fully equipped gym, outdoor heated swimming pool, or spa equipped with sauna and steam rooms. Plenty of lounges, sundecks, panoramic promenades, bars, reading rooms, library, casino, and shops satisfy early birds and night owls. Shore excursions on landing perhaps constitute the most fun activity. Some of these include spectacular terrain hikes and Zodiac cruises across frozen vistas, turquoise horizons, or historic coastlines. Themed cruises offer comprehensive activities, including demonstrations, classes, performances, and well-planned excursions. On larger ships, Wi-Fi stations offer gaming consoles. All vessels have Internet rooms and Wi-Fi—which costs €5 per half hour.

Your Shipmates

Compagnie du Ponant cruisers are a sophisticated group consisting of affluent adventurers and sportive globetrotters. Families with kids are not uncommon on the larger vessels, but the general age ranges between 40 and 70. A multicultural blend of primarily French, Australians, and North Americans comprise the passenger list. The common language heard on board is French, although English is widely spoken and understood by the experienced crew and most of the well-traveled guests.

Dress Code

There is no strict dress code, and ships are relatively informal. During the day, smart leisurewear is recommended. For excursions and shore leaves, bring practical clothes and comfortable shoes. Expeditions to the Arctic and Antarctica using Zodiacs require waterproof parkas (provided on board), flexible trousers, boots, gloves, and fleece hats. Sunglasses are highly advised. Evening attire is at your discretion, but men are required to wear a jacket.

Top: *L'Austral* at sea
Bottom: Cabin aboard *L'Austral*

5

COMPAGNIE DU PONANT

Top: The main lobby aboard
L'Austral
Middle: Dining al fresco aboard
Le Ponant
Bottom: A spacious cabin
aboard *Le Boréal*

Junior Cruisers

Children over the age of eight are allowed on board. The good life begins early for young sailors privileged to tag along on Compagnie du Ponant yachts. Outfitted with facilities and amenities catering to both young and old, the four vessels offer flexible "communicating" cabins, children's menus, tea parties, games, and piano and cooking lessons, Wii game consoles, Internet stations, reading areas, and the Ponant Kid's Club on deck 5 (free for one child, age 8–12, sharing a cabin with two adults) that has a carpeted area with sofas, assorted toys, TV, and play zone. Themed family cruises are sometimes offered, and these provide a more child-friendly atmosphere and babysitting service.

Service

Building a strong reputation for personalized, friendly service, the four cruise ships have multilingual crew and staff that understand the demands and expectations of an international traveler. Attention to detail with food service, cabin maintenance and cleanliness, overall ship hygiene, spa services, and special requests is handled with discretion and satisfactory efficiency. Announcements are made in both French and English.

Tipping

The cruise line changed its tipping policy in 2012. All gratuities are now included for restaurant, hotel, and ship staffs as well as local guides and drivers.

Past Passengers

The Ponant Yacht Club loyalty program has Major, Admiral, and Grand Admiral levels. As members, cruisers benefit from exclusive services and amenities on board. They are also eligible for exclusive offers in the shop, wine cellar, or open-bar package depending on membership level.

Ships of the Line

L'Austral. International dining and destinations stand out on this newer yachting vessel, amenity-wise the identical twin to *Le Boréal*. Child-friendly cabins, a knowledgeable crew, friendly staff, and excellent food and service are hallmarks of this ship. Having earned the international "green ship" label (like *Le Boréal*), *L'Austral*

CHOOSE THIS LINE IF ...

You've always dreamt of sailing on your own private yacht.

Destinations in remote ports of call and inaccessible landscapes are a priority.

You appreciate open-air cruising (large sundecks, terraces, sea-level platforms, and cabins with private balconies) and discreet elegance.

consistently receives rave reviews from demanding, experienced voyagers for its first-class accommodations and service. The majority of the 132 cabins and suites measure a comfortable 200 square feet and have a small, private balcony.

Le Boréal. A unique megayacht carrying 264 passengers, *Le Boréal* boasts a history of fine design by Jean-Philippe Nuel with superb exterior and interior detailing. The ship's sleek silhouette and large arched windows, not to mention the interior, ooze elegance. The ship has 132 spacious staterooms (many have private balconies) with personal safe, hair dryer, and Wi-Fi. Dance floors, live music, library, and large terraces extending toward the sea or overlooking the outdoor heated swimming pool create an upbeat ambience. Leisure facilities include a well-equipped fitness center, full-service salon, hammam and balneo room, and two massage and relaxation rooms.

Le Ponant. In the nautical tradition of the three-masted sailing yacht, *Le Ponant* is the ideal vessel on which to embark for a special, intimate voyage of discovery. Carrying only 64 passengers and a 32-member crew, the 288-foot stylishly designed ship offers a luxurious experience with personalized service and modern amenities. Open-air sophistication is shared and savored on four passenger decks with 32 cabins of approximately 150 square feet. For the ultimate indulgence, rent the entire yacht (crew included) for a private charter.

Le Soléal. The flagship 264-passenger *Le Soléal* debuts in July 2013, duplicating the elegant contours of her sister ships. Designer chic, the 132 staterooms and suites are decorated in shades of grey, white, and brown. Enjoy a spa, theater, and multiple lounges. Original 4- to 22-day itineraries cruise perennially through the Mediterranean, Norway, Iceland, Greenland, Russia, and the Arctic.

■ TIP→ Two older vessels Le Levant and Le Diamant were put out of commission in fall 2012.

HELPFUL HINTS

In summer 2012, Compagnie du Ponant announced a new all-inclusive pricing structure that includes meals, drinks, minibars, tips, and port charges.

Select itineraries offer air-inclusive pricing.

Open dining allows you to eat meals when you want and with whom you want, though you can still expect group settings for special occasions and lunchtime sightseeing excursions.

Select itineraries allow kids 8 to 18 to sail for free when they stay with their parents in a Superior cabin or Prestige suite.

With direct access to the sea from an open deck, ships offer the chance to swim in the surrounding crystalline waters.

5

COMPAGNIE DU PONANT

DON'T CHOOSE THIS LINE IF ...

You seek a no-frills holiday with loud parties and prefer sandwiches for dinner.

You like to dress up in ostentatious glitz and glamorous eveningwear.

Luxury travel with refined French elegance, sophistication, and language just isn't your cup of tea.

COSTA CRUISES

Europe's number-one cruise line combines a Continental experience, enticing itineraries, and Italy's classical design and style with relaxing days and romantic nights at sea. Genoa-based Costa Crociere, parent company of Costa Cruise Lines, had been in the ship-

Dining alfresco

ping business for more than 100 years and in the passenger business for almost 50 years when it was bought by Airtours and Carnival Corporation in 1997. In 2000 Carnival completed a buyout of the Costa line and began expanding the fleet with larger and more dynamic ships.

☎ 954/266–5600 or 800/462–6782
⊕ *www.costacruise.com*
☞ *Cruise Style: Main-stream.*

An ongoing shipbuilding program has brought Costa ships into the 21st century with innovative large-ship designs that reflect their Italian heritage and style without overlooking the amenities expected by modern cruisers. Acknowledging changing habits (even among Europeans), Costa Cruises has eliminated smoking entirely in dining rooms and show lounges. However, smokers are permitted to light up in designated areas in other public rooms, as well as on the pool deck.

Food
Costa is noted for themed dinner menus that convey the evening's mood. Dining features regional Italian cuisines: a variety of pastas, chicken, beef, and seafood dishes, as well as authentic pizza. European chefs and culinary school graduates, who are members of Chaîne des Rôtisseurs, provide a dining experience that's notable for a delicious, properly prepared pasta course, if not exactly living up to gourmet standards. Vegetarian and healthy diet choices are also offered, as are selections for children. Alternative dining is by reservation only in the upscale supper clubs, which serve traditional Italian cuisine.

While specialty restaurants usually have a separate à la carte charge for each menu item, suite passengers receive one complimentary dinner for two.

Costa ships also retain the tradition of lavish nightly midnight buffets, a feature that is beginning to disappear on other mainstream lines. Room service is available 24 hours from a limited menu.

Entertainment

Italian-style cruising is a mixture of Mediterranean flair and American comfort, beginning with a *buon viaggio* celebration. The supercharged social staff works overtime to get everyone in the mood during the line's signature nighttime parties and encourages everyone to be a part of the action.

Shipboard activities include games of bocce, dancing the tarantella, and tossing pizza dough during the Festa Italiana, an Italian street festival at sea. Other nights are themed as well—a welcome-aboard celebration (*Benvenuto A Bordo*), hosted by the captain on the first formal night, and *Notte Tropical,* a tropical deck party with a Mediterranean twist that culminates with the presentation of an alfresco midnight buffet. When it is time to say good-bye, Costa throws a Roman Bacchanal.

There's also a nod to the traditional cruise ship entertainment expected by North American passengers. Pool games, trivia, bingo, and sophisticated production shows blend nicely with classical concerts in lounges, where a wide range of musical styles invite dancing or listening. Italian language, arts and crafts, and cooking classes are extremely popular.

Fitness and Recreation

Taking a cue from the ancient Romans, Costa places continuing emphasis on wellness and sensual pleasures. Spas and salons are operated by Steiner Leisure, and treatments include a variety of massages, body wraps, and facials that can be scheduled à la carte or combined in packages to enjoy during one afternoon or throughout the entire cruise. Hair and nail services are available in the salons.

State-of-the-art exercise equipment in the gym, a jogging track, and basic fitness classes for all levels of ability are available. Costa ships offer a Golf Academy at Sea, with PGA clinics on the ship and golf excursions in some ports.

Your Shipmates

Couples in the 35- to 55-year-old range are attracted to Costa Cruises; on most itineraries, up to 80% of

Top: Showtime on Costa
Bottom: Casino action

Top: Costa chefs
Middle: Jogging on deck
Bottom: Las Vegas–style
entertainment

passengers are European, and many of them are of Italian descent. An international air prevails on board, and announcements are often made in a variety of languages. The vibe on Costa's newest megaships is most likely to appeal to American tastes and expectations.

Dress Code

Two formal nights are standard on seven-night cruises. Men are encouraged to wear tuxedos, but dark suits or sport coats and ties are appropriate and more common than black tie. All other evenings are resort casual, although jeans are discouraged in restaurants. It's requested that no shorts be worn in public areas after 6 pm.

Junior Cruisers

All sailings feature age-specific youth programs that include such daily activities as costume parties, board games, junior aerobics, and even Italian-language lessons for children in four age groups: 3 (toilet trained) to 6; 7 to 11; junior teens 12 to 14; and teens 15 to 17. The actual age groupings may be influenced by the number of children on board. Special counselors oversee activities, and specific rooms are designed for children and teens, depending on the ship. Children under three years old can use the playroom facilities if accompanied and supervised by their parents.

Organized sessions for all children between the ages of 3 and 17 are available every day, even when in port, from 9 to noon and 3 to 6, as well as from 9 to 11:30 in the evening. Parents can enjoy at least a couple of evenings alone by taking advantage of two complimentary Parents Nights Out while their children dine at a supervised buffet or pizza party and take part in evening and nighttime activities. Nighttime group babysitting for children ages 3 to 11 is complimentary in the children's area until 1:30 am. Unfortunately, no late-night babysitting service is offered for children under 3, nor is there in-cabin babysitting.

CHOOSE THIS LINE IF ...

You're a satisfied Carnival past passenger and want a similar experience with an Italian flavor.

You want pizza hot out of the oven whenever you get a craving for it.

You're a joiner: there are many opportunities to be in the center of the action.

Service

Service in dining areas can be spotty and rushed, but is adequate, if not always overly friendly.

Tipping

A standard gratuity of $11 per adult per day is automatically added to shipboard accounts and distributed to cabin stewards and dining-room staff when cruising in the Caribbean; when sailing transatlantic or in Europe, the amount is €7 per day. The applicable charge for children between the ages of 4 and 14 is 50% of the standard amount; there is no charge for children under the age of four. Passengers may adjust the amount based on the level of service experienced. An automatic 15% gratuity is added to all beverage tabs, as well as to checks for spa treatments and salon services.

Past Passengers

The Costa Club has three levels of membership: Aquamarine (2,000 points), Coral (2,001 to 5,000 points), and Pearl (5,001 or more points). Points are assigned for the number of cruising days (100 points per day) and the amount of money spent on board.

Membership privileges vary, and can include discounts on selected cruises, fruit baskets, and bottles of spumante delivered to your cabin, discounts on boutique merchandise and beauty treatments, or a complimentary dinner in a specialty restaurant.

5

COSTA CRUISES

DON'T CHOOSE THIS LINE IF ...

You find announcements in a variety of languages annoying.

You want an authentic Italian cruise. The crew has grown more international than Italian as the line has expanded.

You prefer sedate splendor in a formal atmosphere; many of the ships are almost Fellini-esque in style.

COSTA ATLANTICA, COSTA MEDITERRANEA

CREW MEMBERS	920
ENTERED SERVICE	2000, 2003
GROSS TONS	86,000
LENGTH	960 feet
NUMBER OF CABINS	1,057
PASSENGER CAPACITY	2,114 (2,682 max)
WIDTH	106 feet

700 ft.
500 ft.
300 ft.

The basic layout of these contemporary ships is nearly identical to parent Carnival Cruise Line's Spirit-class vessels. Interiors were designed by Carnival's ship architect Joe Farcus, whose abundant use of marble reflects Costa's Italian heritage. Artwork commissioned specifically for each ship was created by contemporary artists and includes intricate sculptures in silver and glass. Don't overlook the lighting fixtures, which were created especially for the ship, most of them crafted by the artisans in Venice's Murano-glass factories.

The nice flow between public lounges is broken only by piazzas, where you can practice the Italian custom of *passeggiata* (strolling to see and be seen). And there's plenty to see; these are visually stimulating interiors, with vivid colors and decor elements to arouse a sense of discovery. One of the most elegant spaces on board *Costa Atlantica* is Café Florian—inspired by the original in Venice's St. Mark's Square.

Cabins

Cabins: Cabins generally follow the outline of their Carnival counterparts, with the distinctive addition of a Grand suite category. Nearly 80% of the suites and staterooms have an ocean view, and of those more than 80% have balconies. Every cabin has adequate closet and drawer/shelf storage, as well as bathroom shelves; suites have a walk-in closet. Although connecting staterooms are somewhat scarce throughout the ships, balcony dividers can be unlocked to provide connecting access in upper-category staterooms.

Amenities: Light-wood cabinetry, pastel decor, Murano-glass lighting fixtures, mirrored accents, a small refrigerator, a personal safe, a hair dryer, and a seating area with sofa, chair, and table are typical for ocean-view cabins and suites. Inside cabins have somewhat smaller seating areas for lounging. Suites have DVD players.

Bathrooms: Extras include shampoo and bath gel in shower-mounted dispensers; suites have a whirlpool bathtub.

Accessibility: Eight staterooms are designed for wheelchair accessibility.

Top: *Costa Mediterranea* at sea
Bottom: European service

Restaurants

A single two-deck-high formal restaurant serves open seating breakfast and lunch, while the Italian-accented cuisine is served in two traditional assigned dinner seatings. An upscale, reservations-only alternative restaurant features Italian specialties—while there is a charge, it's well worth it for the intimate, candlelit atmosphere and interesting menu selection. Reserved for guests occupying Wellness cabins and suites, a Wellness Restaurant on each ship serves lighter fare at lunch and dinner. Coffee shops serve delightful, authentic Italian specialty coffees and treats. The casual Lido buffet, pizzeria, and 24-hour room service are alternatives to dining room meals. Costa is one of the few cruise lines to continue the seagoing tradition of lavish midnight buffets. Room service is available 24 hours from a limited menu.

Spas

The Ischia spa has a hydrotherapy pool and complimentary saunas and steam rooms in men's and women's changing rooms, but it has no thermal suite. A complete menu of spa treatments includes facials, body wraps, and massages.

Bars and Entertainment

After dinner and a coffee in the coffee bar, on most nights there are performances by the resident production singers and dancers as well as guest entertainers in the main theater. The secondary show lounges feature singers and musicians and are the venues for Costa's signature parties, during which the entertainment staff encourages passenger participation. There is a quieter and intimate piano bar as well as other lounges with music for dancing and listening as well as a disco.

Pros and Cons

Pros: if earlier Costa ships were Armani (cool and serene), then these are Versace (sexy and slightly outrageous); duty-free boutiques offer enough Italian designer items to satisfy most shopaholics; forward on the outdoor promenade decks are serene retreats in the form of enclosed terraces.

Cons: Italians consider cappuccino a breakfast beverage, so ordering it in the dining room following dinner is frowned on; frequent announcements are annoying; coffee is available at numerous bars, but there is a charge.

Cabin Type	Size (sq. ft.)
Grand Suites	650
Suites	360
Ocean View*	185
Interior	160

*Extended balcony cabins have balconies at least 50% larger than average.

FAST FACTS

- 12 passenger decks
- Specialty restaurant, dining room, buffet, pizzeria
- Wi-Fi, safe, refrigerator, DVD (some)
- 3 pools (1 indoor), children's pool
- Fitness classes, gym, hot tubs, sauna, spa, steam room
- 6 bars, casino, 2 dance clubs, 2 show rooms, video game room
- Children's programs
- Laundry facilities, laundry service
- Internet terminal

Workout with a sea view

5

COSTA CRUISES

CRYSTAL CRUISES

Winner of accolades and too many hospitality industry awards to count, Crystal Cruises offers a taste of the grandeur of the past along with all the modern touches discerning passengers demand today. Founded in 1990 and owned by Nippon Yusen Kaisha

Crystal Serenity wraparound promenade

(NYK) in Japan, Crystal ships, unlike other luxury vessels, are large, carrying upward of 900 passengers. What makes them distinctive are superior service, a variety of dining options, spacious accommodations, and some of the highest ratios of space per passenger of any cruise ship.

☎ *888/799–4625 or 310/785–9300*
⊕ *www.crystalcruises. com*
☞ *Cruise Style: Luxury*.

Beginning with ship designs based on the principles of *feng shui*, the Eastern art of arranging your surroundings to attract positive energy, no detail is overlooked to provide passengers with the best imaginable experience. Just mention a preference for a certain food or beverage and your waiter will have it available whenever you request it.

Afternoon tea in the Palm Court is a delightful daily ritual. You're greeted by staff members in 18th-century Viennese brocade and velvet costumes for Mozart Tea; traditional scones and clotted cream are served during English Colonial Tea; and American Tea is a summertime classic created by Crystal culinary artists.

The line's Ambassador Host Program brings cultured gentlemen on each cruise to dine, socialize, and dance with unaccompanied ladies who wish to participate.

Food

The food alone is reason enough to book a Crystal cruise. Dining in the main restaurants is an event starring a Continental-inspired menu of dishes served by European-trained waiters. Off-menu item requests are honored when possible, and special dietary considerations are handled with ease. Full-course vegetarian menus are among the best at sea. Themed to the region you are sailing, lavish luncheon buffets take place on deck on select days at sea. Casual poolside dining beneath the stars is offered on some evenings in a relaxed, no-reservations option. A variety of hot-and-cold hors d'oeuvres are served in bars and lounges every evening before dinner and again during the wee hours in the Bistro.

But the specialty restaurants really shine. Contemporary Asian cuisine is served in Silk Road and the Sushi Bar, featuring the signature dishes of Nobu Matsuhisa. Both ships also have Prego, which serves regional Italian cuisine by Piero Selvaggio, owner of Valentino in Los Angeles and Las Vegas.

Exclusive Wine & Champagne Makers dinners are hosted in the Vintage Room. On select evenings, casual poolside theme dinners are served under the stars.

Crystal has an extensive wine list, including its own proprietary label called C Wines, which are produced in California. Complimentary wines are poured with meals, as is common on other luxury cruise lines. You won't pay extra for any alcoholic beverages, bottled water, soft drinks, and specialty coffees; all are included in your basic fare.

Entertainment

The complete roster of entertainment and activities includes Broadway-style production shows and bingo, but where Crystal really shines is in the variety of enrichment and educational programs. Passengers can participate in the hands-on Computer University@ Sea, interactive Creative Learning Institute classes, or attend lectures featuring top experts in their fields: keyboard lessons with Yamaha, language classes by Berlitz, wellness lectures with the Cleveland Clinic, and an introduction to tai chi with the Tai Chi Cultural Center. Professional ACBL Bridge instructors are on every cruise, and dance instructors offer lessons in contemporary and social dance styles.

Fitness and Recreation

Large spas offer innovative pampering therapies, body wraps, and exotic Asian-inspired treatments by Steiner Leisure. Feng shui principles were scrupulously adhered to in their creation, to assure the spas and salons remain havens of tranquility.

Fitness centers have a range of exercise and weight-training equipment and workout areas for aerobics classes, plus complimentary yoga and Pilates instruction. In addition, golfers enjoy extensive shipboard

KNOWN FOR

■ **Food:** The food is a good enough reason to book a cruise with Crystal—it's that exceptional, and the specialty restaurants are complimentary.

■ **Inclusiveness:** Cruise fares now include gratuities, as well as all alcoholic beverages, soft drinks, and specialty coffees.

■ **Itineraries:** Exotic worldwide itineraries and numerous overnight port calls are signature elements of Crystal's voyages.

■ **Service:** Personalized service is a key component.

■ **Style in a Big Package:** Crystal Cruises are large but notably luxurious and stylish.

Crystal Serenity fitness center

facilities, including a driving range practice cage and putting green. Passengers can leave their bags at home and rent top-quality TaylorMade clubs for use ashore. The line's resident golf pros offer complimentary lessons and group clinics.

Your Shipmates

Affluent, well-traveled couples, from their late-thirties and up, are attracted to Crystal's destination-rich itineraries, shipboard enrichment programs, and elegant ambience. The average age of passengers is noticeably higher on longer itineraries.

Dress Code

Formal attire is required on at least two designated evenings, depending on the length of the cruise. Men are encouraged to wear tuxedos, and many do, although dark suits are also acceptable. Other evenings are informal or resort casual; the number of each is based on the number of sea days. The line requests that dress codes be observed in public areas after 6 pm, and few, if any, passengers disregard the suggestion. Most, in fact, dress up just a notch from guidelines.

Junior Cruisers

Although these ships are decidedly adult-oriented, Crystal welcomes children but limits the number of children under age three on any given cruise. Children under six months are not allowed without a signed waiver by parents.

Dedicated facilities for children and teens ages 3 to 17 are staffed by counselors during holiday periods, select summer sailings, and when warranted by the number of children booked. The program is three-tiered for 3- to 7-year-olds, 8- to 12-year-olds, and 13- to 17-year-olds. Activities—including games, computer time, scavenger hunts, and arts and crafts—usually have an eye toward the educational. Teenagers can play complimentary video games to their hearts' content in Waves, the arcade dedicated for their use. Babysitting can be arranged with staff members for a fee. Baby food, high chairs, and booster seats are available on request.

Top: Spa treatment
Middle: Keyboard lessons
Bottom: *Crystal Symphony*
Crystal Penthouse

CHOOSE THIS LINE IF ...

You crave peace and quiet. Announcements are kept to a bare minimum, and the ambience is sedate.

You prefer to plan ahead. You can make spa, restaurant, shore excursion, and class reservations when you book your cruise.

You love sushi and other Asian delights—Crystal ships serve some of the best at sea.

Service

Crystal's European-trained staff members provide gracious service in an unobtrusive manner.

Tipping

Housekeeping and dining gratuities are included in the fare. A 15% gratuity is suggested for spa and salon services.

Past Passengers

You're automatically enrolled in the Crystal Society on completion of your first Crystal cruise and are entitled to special savings and members-only events. Membership benefits increase with each completed Crystal cruise and include such perks as stateroom upgrades, shipboard spending credits, special events, gifts, air upgrades, and even free cruises. Society members also receive Crystal Cruises' complimentary quarterly magazine, which shares up-to-date information on itineraries, destinations, special offers, and society news.

HELPFUL HINTS

■ Before sailing, each passenger receives a personal email address.

■ Ambassador Hosts on Crystal cruises interact with female passengers.

■ Each ship has complimentary self-service laundry rooms.

■ Specialty restaurants can fill up quickly; make reservations immediately after booking.

■ In more than 24 European ports, Crystal's exclusive Local Insights program brings aboard native experts.

5

CRYSTAL CRUISES

DON'T CHOOSE THIS LINE IF

You don't want to follow the dress code. Everyone does, and you'll stand out—and not in a good way—if you rebel.

You want a smoke-free environment. Smoking is allowed in cabins and in designated areas of public rooms and decks.

You want a less structured cruise. Even with open seating dining, Crystal is a bit more regimented than other luxury lines.

CRYSTAL SERENITY

CREW MEMBERS	655
ENTERED SERVICE	2003
GROSS TONS	68,000
LENGTH	820 feet
NUMBER OF CABINS	544
PASSENGER CAPACITY	1,070
WIDTH	106 feet

700 ft.

500 ft.

300 ft.

Crystal Serenity was introduced in 2003, the line's first new ship since 1995. Although more than a third larger than Crystal's earlier ships, it's similar in layout and follows the successful formula of creating intimate spaces in understated yet sophisticated surroundings. Stylish public rooms, uncrowded and uncluttered, are clubby in the tradition of elegantly proportioned drawing rooms (even the main show lounge is on a single level).

Muted colors and warm woods create a soft atmosphere conducive to socializing in the refined environment. The Palm Court could be mistaken for the kind of British colonial–era lounge you might have seen in Hong Kong or India in the 19th century. A thoughtful touch is an entirely separate room for scrutinizing the art pieces available for auction. The understatement even continues into the casino, although it contains plenty of slot machines and gaming tables.

Cabins

Cabins: *Crystal Serenity* has no inside cabins. Although suites are generous in size, lesser categories are somewhat smaller than industry standard at this level. All accommodations are designed with ample closet and drawer/shelf storage, as well as bathroom shelves and twin sinks. An impressive 85% of all cabins have private balconies furnished with chairs and tables. Most suites and penthouses have walk-in closets. Crystal Penthouse suites have private workout areas, pantries, and guest powder rooms. There are 46 connecting staterooms and 165 staterooms with a third berth for families.

Amenities: All cabins have a refrigerator with complimentary water and soft drinks, a personal safe, hair dryer, Wi-Fi access, a flat-screen TV with a DVD player, MP3 player input, Aveda bath products, slippers, Frette bathrobes, and an umbrella. A seating area with sofa, chair, and table are typical standard features of all cabins. Suites and penthouses have butler service, personalized stationery, and a complimentary fully stocked minibar on embarkation.

Accessibility: Eight staterooms are designed for wheelchair accessibility.

Top: *Crystal Serenity* at sea
Bottom: Sushi bar

Restaurants

The formal restaurant serves open seating breakfast and lunch and offers international cuisine in two traditional early and late assigned dinner seatings; Open Dining by Reservation is also available. There's no additional charge for the intimate Asian- and Italian-specialty restaurants, but reservations are required. Theme luncheons and dinners are sometimes held poolside; special wine dinners are held in the Vintage Room. Tastes, a casual café, serves breakfast, lunch, and dinner; the Lido buffet has breakfast and lunch; a poolside grill serves casual lunch and snacks; The Bistro, a specialty coffee and wine bar also offers snacks; and there's an ice cream bar. Afternoon tea is served in the Palm Court. Room service is available 24 hours, and during dinner hours selections can be delivered from the formal restaurant menu. Suite passengers also have the option of ordering dinner from the specialty restaurants, to be served by their butlers.

Spas

Inspired by the principles of feng shui, the Crystal Spa is a tranquil haven where such services as aroma stone therapy, a Japanese silk booster facial, and well-being massage are offered. A private, canopied relaxation area on the spa's aft deck is available before or after a treatment. Facilities for men and women include saunas and changing areas featuring showers with multiple head and side body jets, fiber optic lighting, and a selection of rain and mist functions.

Bars and Entertainment

With the open-bar policy setting a convivial tone, Crystal's lounges are the ships' social centers. Every lounge has a different atmosphere, ranging from the signature cocktail and piano bar known for its intimate "clubby" feel to the cigar lounge that is ideal for after-dinner drinks and conversation. After a production show or concert in the main show room, dance aficionados can find musical styles that range from big band to contemporary.

Pros and Cons

Pros: alternative restaurants are yours to enjoy at no additional cost; every bathroom has a full-size tub; a wide teak promenade deck encircles the ship.

Cons: few staterooms have a third berth for families; reservations for specialty restaurants can be hard to secure; the "clubiness" of repeat passengers can be off-putting to people new to Crystal.

Cabin Type	Size (sq. ft.)
Crystal Penthouse	1,345
Penthouse Suites	538
Regular Penthouses	403
Deluxe Ocean View (w/balcony)	269
Deluxe Ocean View (regular)	226

All dimensions except for regular Deluxe staterooms (the only category that does not have a balcony) include the balcony square footage.

FAST FACTS

- 9 passenger decks
- 2 specialty restaurants, dining room, buffet, ice cream parlor
- Wi-Fi, safe, refrigerator, DVD
- 2 pools (1 indoor)
- Fitness classes, gym, 2 hot tubs, sauna, spa, steam room
- 6 bars, casino, 2 dance clubs, library, show room, video game room
- Children's programs
- Dry-cleaning, laundry facilities, laundry service
- Internet terminal
- No kids under 6 months

CRYSTAL SYMPHONY

CREW MEMBERS	545
ENTERED SERVICE	1995
GROSS TONS	51,044
LENGTH	781 feet
NUMBER OF CABINS	461
PASSENGER CAPACITY	922 (1,010 max)
WIDTH	99 feet

700 ft.

500 ft.

300 ft.

Although large, *Crystal Symphony* is noteworthy in the luxury market for creating intimate spaces in understated, yet sophisticated, surroundings. Generous per-passenger space ratios have become a Crystal trademark, along with forward-facing observation decks, a Palm Court lounge, and a wide teak promenade encircling the ship. An extensive refurbishment in 2009 transformed the Crystal Penthouses, Lido Café, and Prego Italian restaurant. The most dramatic change was the removal of the indoor swimming pool and hot tub to expand seating for the Trident Grill. The remaining hot tub was expanded and includes a water feature.

Accented by a lovely waterfall, the focal point of the central two-deck atrium is a sculpture of two ballet dancers created especially for the space. Crystal Cove, the lobby lounge, is the spot to meet for cocktails as you make your way to the nearby dining room. Throughout the ship, public rooms shine with low-key contemporary style and flow easily from one to the next.

Cabins

Cabins: There are no inside cabins on *Crystal Symphony,* but staterooms are relatively small, with boutique hotel–style decor. All cabins have ample closet and drawer/shelf storage, as well as bathroom shelves. Many have private balconies furnished with chairs and tables. Most suites and penthouses have a walk-in closet. Crystal Penthouse suites have guest powder rooms. There are 24 connecting staterooms, and nearly a quarter of accommodations have a third berth suitable for families.

Amenities: A small refrigerator with complimentary bottled water and soft drinks, a safe, hair dryer, a flat-screen TV with DVD player, Wi-Fi access, MP3 player input, and a seating area with sofa, chair, and table are typical standard features in all cabins. Suite and penthouse extras vary, but all have a DVD/CD player, butler service, personalized stationery, and fully stocked minibar.

Bathrooms: Every bathroom has oval glass sinks, granite counters, a full-size tub, Aveda toiletries, plush towels, and bathrobes for use during the cruise. Many suites and penthouses have a whirlpool tub and separate shower.

Accessibility: Four staterooms are wheelchair accessible.

Top: Casino gaming
Bottom: University@Sea

Restaurants

The formal restaurant serves open seating breakfast and lunch and dinner in two assigned seatings, or an open seating option. Although there's no additional charge for the intimate Asian- and Italian-specialty restaurants, reservations are required. On select days and evenings, theme luncheons and dinners are held poolside; special wine dinners are held in the Vintage Room. Other dining choices include the Lido buffet for breakfast and lunch; a poolside grill for casual lunch and snacks; the Bistro, a specialty coffee and wine bar offering snacks all day and evening; and an ice cream bar. Afternoon tea is served in the Palm Court. Room service, with an extensive menu, is available 24 hours, and during dinner hours selections can be delivered from the formal restaurant menu. Suite passengers can also order from the specialty restaurants, to be served by their butlers.

Spas

The Crystal Spa is a tranquil haven where such services as aroma stone therapy, Japanese silk booster facial, and well-being massage are offered. A private, canopied relaxation area on the spa's aft deck is available before or after a treatment. Changing areas have elaborate showers with fiber optic lighting and a selection of rain and mist functions as well as saunas.

Bars and Entertainment

With the open bar policy setting a convivial tone, Crystal's lounges are the ship's social hubs. Lounges feature unique styles ranging from the signature cocktail and piano bar known for its intimate "clubby" atmosphere to the clublike cigar lounge, ideal for after-dinner drinks and conversation. After a production show or concert in the main show room, dance aficionados can find musical styles that range from classic to contemporary.

Pros and Cons

Pros: the professionalism of the ships staff sets them apart; the large theater has ample seating and free popcorn; casual dining areas have more than enough seating indoors and outside.

Cons: few staterooms can accommodate families; while large, the solitary pool and hot tub can feel crowded at times; lower-category staterooms can feel cramped for a luxury ship.

Cabin Type	Size (sq. ft.)
Crystal Penthouse	982
Penthouse Suites	491
Regular Penthouses	367
Deluxe Ocean View (w/balcony)	246
Deluxe Ocean View (regular)	202

All dimensions except for regular Deluxe staterooms (the only category that does not have a balcony) include the balcony square footage.

FAST FACTS

- 8 passenger decks
- 2 specialty restaurants, dining room, buffet, ice cream parlor
- Wi-Fi, safe, refrigerator, DVD
- 1 pool
- Fitness classes, gym, hot tub, sauna, spa, steam room
- 5 bars, casino, dance club, library, show room, video game room
- Children's programs
- Dry-cleaning, laundry facilities, laundry service
- Internet terminal
- No kids under 6 months

5

CRYSTAL CRUISES

CUNARD LINE

One of the world's most distinguished names in ocean travel since 1840, the Cunard Line has a long history of deluxe transatlantic crossings and worldwide cruising. The line's ships are legendary for their comfortable accommodations, excellent cuisine, and personal service.

Romantic sunset at sea

After a series of owners tried with little success to revive the company's flagging passenger shipping business, Carnival Corporation offered an infusion of ready cash and the know-how to turn the line around in 1998. Exciting new ships have followed.

☎ 661/753–1000 or
800/728–6273
⊕ www.cunard.com
☞ Cruise Style: Luxury.

Delightful daily events include afternoon tea and the maritime tradition of sounding the ship's bell at noon. The line offers North Atlantic crossings and seasonal shorter cruises, including Northern European and Mediterranean itineraries.

Food

Dining aboard a Cunard ship is by class, so dining-room assignments are made according to the accommodation category booked. You can get as much luxury as you are willing to pay for on Cunard liners, where passengers in Junior suites are assigned to the single-seating Princess Grill; the posh Queen's Grill serves passengers booked in duplex apartments and the most lavish suites. All other passengers are assigned to one of two seatings in the dramatic, multideck-high Britannia Restaurant or Britannia Club Restaurant on *Queen Elizabeth*.

Although fare in Britannia is reasonably traditional and often outstanding, off-menu requests by Grill passengers are commonly granted—provided the galley has the ingredients. Menus also include vegetarian and low-calorie selections.

The most coveted table reservations are those on *Queen Mary 2* and *Queen Victoria* in the restaurants named for

Todd English, the celebrity American chef and restaurateur noted for his innovative Mediterranean cuisine and sumptuous desserts. Both à la carte dinner and lunch are offered in the intimate restaurant.

Aboard *Queen Mary 2,* the Chef's Galley is a small reservations-required restaurant, where diners look on as their food is prepared in an open galley setting; the only charge here is for wine. The King's Court buffet is transformed each evening into three no-charge casual alternative dining spots: the Carvery specializes in carved meats; La Piazza is dedicated to pasta, pizza, and Italian dishes; and Lotus offers Asian regional specialties. All ships feature an alternating casual dinner of either Asian, Mexican, Indian, or South American fare with a nominal cover charge.

Entertainment

Entertainment has a decidedly English flavor, with nightly production shows or cabaret-style performances and even plays. An authentic pub gives the liners an even more British air, while music for dancing and listening is played in other bars and lounges. In *Queen Mary 2*'s first-ever shipboard planetarium, high-tech presentations and virtual-reality shows offer a ride through space.

Cunard's fine enrichment programs include lectures by experts in their fields, including top designers, master chefs, and artists. Even seamanship and navigation courses are offered to novice mariners. Passengers can plan their activities prior to departure by consulting the syllabus of courses available online at Cunard Line's website.

Fitness and Recreation

Swimming pools, golf driving ranges, table tennis, paddle tennis court, shuffleboard, and jogging tracks barely scratch the surface of shipboard facilities dedicated to recreation. Top-quality fitness centers offer high-tech workout equipment, a separate weight room, and classes ranging from aerobics to healthy living workshops.

Queen Mary 2's Canyon Ranch Spa Club is a one-of-a-kind facility at sea offering salon services for women and men, including the famous land-based spa's signature 80-minute Canyon Stone Massage. A huge 30- by 15-foot thalassotherapy pool offers a deluge waterfall, air tub, neck fountains, and massage-jet benches and recliner lounges located in the pool. The thermal suite has an herbal sauna, Finnish sauna, aromatic steam room, and reflexology basins. Use of these spe-

5

CUNARD LINE

Top: Cunard White Star service
Bottom: Illuminations planetarium

cial features is complimentary with a massage or body treatment; otherwise, there's a per-day charge.

The daily SpaClub Passport includes use of the fitness center, thermal suite, aquatherapy center, locker rooms, and a choice of fitness classes. Robes, sandals, and beverages are also available for spa goers and SpaClub Passport holders in the relaxation lounge. Steiner Leisure operates the more pedestrian spas on the rest of the fleet.

Your Shipmates

Discerning, well-traveled American and British couples from their late-thirties to retirees are drawn to Cunard's traditional style and the notion of a cruise aboard an ocean liner. The availability of spacious accommodations and complimentary self-service laundry facilities makes Cunard liners a good option for families, although there may be fewer children on board than on similar size ships.

Dress Code

Glamorous evenings are typical of Cunard cruises, and specified attire includes formal, informal, and casual. Although resort casual clothing prevails throughout the day, Cunard vessels are ocean liners at heart and, as expected, are dressier than most cruise ships at night. To maintain their high standards, the cruise line requests passengers to dress as they would for dining in fine restaurants; however, ties are no longer required with a gentleman's jacket on informal evenings.

Junior Cruisers

The Kid Zone has a dedicated play area and a splash pool for children ages one to six. Separate programs are reserved for older children ages 7 to 12 and teens up to age 17. Toys and activities range from simple games to more educational computer classes. Children can practice their social graces when they're served their own afternoon teatime goodies. Toddlers are supervised by English nannies. Facilities are operated only until midnight; group babysitting is complimentary. Infants under one year are not allowed; children ages one to two sail free (except for government fees).

Top: Fine dining
Middle: Royal Court Theater
Bottom: Junior suite

CHOOSE THIS LINE IF ...

You want to boast that you have sailed on the world's largest ocean liner, though larger cruise ships are already plying the waves.

You enjoy a brisk walk. *Queen Mary 2* is massive, and you'll find yourself walking a great deal.

A posh English pub is your idea of the perfect place to hang out.

Service

Although most crew members are international rather than British, service is formal and sophisticated.

Tipping

Suggested gratuities of $13.50 per person per day (for Grill Restaurant accommodations) or $11.50 per person per day (all other accommodations) are automatically charged to shipboard accounts for distribution to stewards and waitstaff. An automatic 15% gratuity is added to beverage tabs for bar service. Passengers can still tip individual crew members directly in cash for any special services.

Past Passengers

After one sailing aboard a Cunard liner, passengers are automatically enrolled as members of Cunard World Club; they are accorded Silver status on their second cruise. Silver-level members receive discounts of up to 50% off Early Booking Savings on all sailings, access to the shipboard World Club Representative and World Club Desk, and a quarterly newsletter, *The Cunarder.*

After completing two Cunard cruises or 20 days on board, members are accorded Gold status and are additionally invited to shipboard World Club cocktail receptions, two hours of Internet service, and receive a Gold Cunarder pin. Passengers who complete seven sailings or sail for 48 consecutive days or more achieve the Platinum status. Additional benefits to Platinum members include a shipboard World Club cocktail reception, priority check-in and boarding in certain embarkation ports, an invitation to the Senior Officers' party, four hours of Internet service, and a Platinum Cunarder pin.

Diamond membership is for guests who have completed 15 voyages or 150 days on board. In addition to the above, they receive priority luggage delivery, complimentary lunch in Todd English, eight hours of Internet service, and a Diamond Cunarder pin.

HELPFUL HINTS

Weddings can't be performed on the spur of the moment, but captains on board all Cunard Line ships can marry couples at sea.

The currency on board is the United States dollar, even for cruises in Europe.

Seasickness pills are available in the medical center or at the reception desk, but they are not free.

Cunard provides gentlemen hosts to dance with unaccompanied ladies.

Men may wish to pack their little-used tuxedos for this ship; on formal nights they are in wide use.

5

CUNARD LINE

DON'T CHOOSE THIS LINE IF

You prefer informality. Cunard ships are traditional formal liners.

You want real luxury with no add-on costs.

Your sense of direction is really bad. Nearly everyone gets lost on board *QM2* at least once.

QUEEN ELIZABETH

CREW MEMBERS	1,005
ENTERED SERVICE	2010
GROSS TONS	92,000
LENGTH	965 feet
NUMBER OF CABINS	1,034
PASSENGER CAPACITY	2,068
WIDTH	106 feet

700 ft.
500 ft.
300 ft.

Although the deck plans for *Queen Elizabeth* appear to be nearly identical to her fleet mate *Queen Victoria,* make no mistake—this queen bears her own regal trappings. A successor to her namesake, the original *Queen Elizabeth,* which entered service in 1940, Cunard's latest liner boasts touches of art deco that recall a time when the first queen ruled the waves. The newest Cunard ship to bear the name also recalls the *QE2* via artwork and memorabilia and has its own nautically themed Yacht Club, named after the lively aft lounge on *QE2.*

Curved staircases, geometric patterns, and spectacular artwork grace the soaring Grand Lobby, which is overlooked by the two-tier Library—a calm, wood-paneled haven bathed in natural reading light and crowned with a leaded glass ceiling. As on her fleet mates, double- and triple-height spaces play a large part in defining the grand interiors; however, there's still the warmth of an authentic British pub, a clubby cigar room, and lounges with intimate seating areas where you might feel you've stumbled into a high society event of the 1930s or 1940s.

Cabins

Cabins: With more than two-dozen stateroom and suite categories to choose from, cabins really fall into eight basic configurations. At the top are the luxurious Queens Grill suites, which have the most luxurious amenities; next are Princess Grill suites; next are the Britannia Club AA balcony staterooms, standard staterooms (many with a balcony), and inside cabins, all of whose passengers dine in the Britannia Restaurant. The majority of the cabins fall into the standard categories. More than 86% of the staterooms on the ship are outside and 76% have private balconies. All are designed with adequate closet and storage space, and even the least expensive outside categories have a small seating area. Private balconies are furnished with a table and chairs, and some have loungers.

Amenities: All passengers are greeted on embarkation with sparkling wine or champagne and will find a refrigerator, safe, hair dryer, fresh fruit basket, bath toiletries, slippers, and a bathrobe for use during the cruise. Butlers are on hand to attend to Queens Grill occupants, whose bars are stocked with spirits, wine, and soft drinks.

Accessibility: Twenty cabins are wheelchair accessible.

Top: A curved staircase in the Grand Lobby
Bottom: *Queen Elizabeth* in a calm harbor

Restaurants

The Britannia Restaurant serves dinner in two assigned seatings for most passengers, while those in Britannia Club, Princess- and Queens Grill–classes dine in a single open seating at an assigned table. The Verandah, the alternative restaurant (reservations, fee), serves French cuisine. In the evenings, one of three regional cuisines— such as Asian, Mexican, Indian, and South American— is highlighted, and waiter table service becomes available in the Lido restaurant for a small charge. In addition, the Lido buffet and Golden Lion Pub offer relaxed dining options, while specialty teas, coffees, and pastries are featured in Café Carinthia. A proper English tea is served daily and room service is always available.

Spas

Operated by Steiner Leisure, the spa offers a wide range of exotic and contemporary treatments. Chakra rasul and herbal steam chambers are designed for couples to indulge in ancient Eastern rituals. A relaxation room, hydrotherapy pool, and thermal suite with three steam and sauna rooms are available for the use of spa clients who've booked a treatment and others who've purchased a pass. Complimentary saunas are found in men's and women's changing rooms.

Bars and Entertainment

Evening entertainments can include production shows and concerts and Cunard's traditional themed formal balls. Other options are as diverse as the clubby Midships Bar with its pianist, an authentic English Pub, or the Yacht Club, an intimate venue for dancing until the small hours with the resident DJ.

Pros and Cons

Pros: professional dance instructors are on board to help you with your technique; dance hosts are available to women looking for a partner; the library's shelves contain 6,000 books so there's no need to pack your own.

Cons: Though more cruise ship than ocean liner, she still provides a formal and traditional experience; service is certainly white-glove, but it's more international than British; if you aren't an Anglophile, you might not appreciate the Britishness of a Cunard ship.

Cabin Type	Size (sq. ft.)
Grand Suite/Master Suite	1,375–1,493/ 1,100
Penthouse Suite/ Queens Suite/ Princess Suite	551–615/ 484–671/ 335–513
Ocean View with Balcony	242–472
Ocean View/ Interior	180–201/ 152–243

All dimensions include the square footage for balconies.

FAST FACTS

- 12 passenger decks
- Specialty restaurant, 3 dining rooms, buffet, café, ice cream parlor, pizzeria
- Wi-Fi, safe, refrigerator, DVD (some)
- 2 pools
- Fitness classes, gym, hot tubs, sauna, spa, steam room
- 10 bars, casino, 2 dance clubs, library, show room
- Children's programs
- Dry-cleaning, laundry facilities, laundry service
- Internet terminal
- No-smoking cabins

5

CUNARD LINE

Britannia Restaurant

QUEEN MARY 2

CREW MEMBERS	1,253
ENTERED SERVICE	2004
GROSS TONS	151,400
LENGTH	1,132 feet
NUMBER OF CABINS	1,310
PASSENGER CAPACITY	2,620 (3,090 max)
WIDTH	135 feet

700 ft.

500 ft.

300 ft.

With the clever use of design elements, *Queen Mary 2,* one of the largest passenger liners ever built, bears a striking external resemblance to Cunard's former flagship, the smaller, older *Queen Elizabeth 2,* which was retired from service in 2008. The world's grandest and most expensive liner is a transitional ship, incorporating classic ocean-liner features—sweeping staircases, soaring public rooms, a 360-degree promenade deck, and a grand ballroom—all comfortably within a hull that also includes a trendy Canyon Ranch Spa and a full-scale planetarium.

Interior spaces blend the traditional style of early-20th-century liners with all the conveniences 21st-century passengers expect. Public rooms are mainly located on two decks low in the ship—remember, this is a liner designed for North Atlantic crossings. The grand lobby is palatial, and the wide passageways lead to a variety of lounges, shops, a casino, show room, and planetarium. The Queen's Room is especially regal.

Cabins

Cabins: An impressive 78% of accommodations are outside cabins, and more than 86% of these have private balconies. There are fewer than 300 inside cabins, including a few with an atrium view. All are designed with ample closet, drawer/shelf storage, and bathroom shelves. Private balconies are furnished with chairs, loungers, and tables. Duplex apartment and suite luxuries vary, but most have a whirlpool tub, dressing area, entertainment center, and dining area, and all have private balconies. In addition, duplex apartments and most suites feature guest powder rooms and whirlpool tubs; some have his-and-hers dressing rooms.

Amenities: A small refrigerator, personal safe, hair dryer, broadband hookup, interactive TV, and seating area with sofa or chairs and dual-height table are standard amenities. Toiletries, slippers, and bathrobes for use during the cruise are also standard.

Accessibility: Thirty cabins are wheelchair accessible.

Restaurants

Dining is assigned by your accommodation category. The Britannia Restaurant serves open seating breakfast and lunch and dinner in two seatings to most passengers; those in AA Britannia Club Balcony Cabins dine in

Top: Intimate lounges
Bottom: Grand Duplex suite

the single-seating Britannia Club Dining Room; those in Junior suites and above dine in the single-seating Queens and Princess Grill restaurants. The Todd English specialty restaurant serves lunch and dinner (by reservation). The Chef's Galley is a small reservations-required restaurant, where diners watch as their food is prepared in an open galley; the only charge is for wine. The King's Court buffet serves breakfast and lunch, and is transformed each evening into three no-charge casual alternative dining spots: the Carvery specializes in carved meats; La Piazza is dedicated to pizza and Italian food; and Lotus offers Asian cuisine. During the day you can opt for a pub lunch, snacks in Sir Samuel's, afternoon tea, and 24-hour room service.

Spas

The Canyon Ranch Spa Club is a one-of-a-kind facility at sea offering services for women and men, including the famous land-based spa's signature Canyon Stone Massage. A huge thalassotherapy pool offers a deluge waterfall, air tub, neck fountains, and massage-jet benches and recliner lounges located in the pool. The thermal suite has an herbal sauna, Finnish sauna, aromatic steam room, and reflexology basins. Use of these is complimentary with a massage or body treatment; otherwise, there's a per-day charge.

Bars and Entertainment

Evenings boast another of Cunard's finest traditions as guests take to the floor to enjoy elegant ballroom dancing or groove to more contemporary sounds offered up by the resident DJ. After the theater or a concert, the entertainment options range from a rollicking pub to the more sedate bars and lounges where a pianist plays in the background for easy conversation and socializing.

Pros and Cons

Pros: proper afternoon tea suggests that Britannia still rules the waves; the Queen's Room is a true ballroom, where you can waltz the night away; Todd English restaurant is named for the celebrity chef who designed the menu.

Cons: there's no illusion that booking an inside cabin results in the same level of pampering received by occupants of top suites; there is no Lido area buffet; it's very easy to get lost.

Cabin Type	Size (sq. ft.)
Grand Duplex	2,249
Duplex	1,194
Royal Suite	796
Penthouse	758
Suite	506
Junior Suite	381
Deluxe	248
Premium Balcony	249
Standard Ocean View/Inside	194

FAST FACTS

- 14 passenger decks
- 2 specialty restaurants, 3 dining rooms, buffet, ice cream parlor, pizzeria
- Internet, Wi-Fi, safe, refrigerator, DVD (some)
- 5 pools (2 indoor), 2 children's pools
- Fitness classes, gym, hot tubs, sauna, spa, steam room
- 11 bars, casino, cinema, 2 dance clubs, library, show room, video game room
- Children's programs
- Dry-cleaning, laundry facilities, laundry service
- Internet terminal
- No kids under age 1
- No-smoking cabins

5

CUNARD LINE

QUEEN VICTORIA

CREW MEMBERS	981
ENTERED SERVICE	2007
GROSS TONS	90,000
LENGTH	965 feet
NUMBER OF CABINS	985
PASSENGER CAPACITY	1,990
WIDTH	106 feet

700 ft.

500 ft.

300 ft.

Designers drew upon the history of previous Cunard ocean liners to conceive *Queen Victoria*'s elegant interiors. From the ship's double- and triple-height spaces—design features of grand liners of the past—to rooms imbued with an elegant yet understated British charm, the overall effect is contemporary and historically classic. The impact of the Grand Lobby's triple-height ceiling, sweeping staircase, and sculpted balconies is immediate and unmistakable.

Queen Victoria herself might well feel at home on entering the double-height Queens Room, a loggia-style venue designed in the manner of the grand ballrooms found in large English country estates, such as Her Majesty's own Osborne House. The ballroom has cantilevered balconies overlooking an inlaid-wood dance floor; the staircase is detailed with classically ornate, curved railings.

In addition to the intimate dining spaces and a lounge reserved for occupants of Queens and Princess Grill accommodations, an outdoor terrace is devoted to their exclusive use. All other public rooms are accessible to everyone on board.

Cabins

Cabins: Although there are more than two dozen stateroom and suite categories from which to choose, cabins really fall into eight configurations. At the top are the Queens Grill suite categories, which have the most luxurious amenities; next are Princess Grill suites; finally come the standard staterooms (some with a balcony) as well as inside cabins, whose passengers dine in the Britannia Restaurant. The majority of the cabins fall into the standard categories. More than 86% of the staterooms on the ship are outside and 76% have private balconies. All are designed with ample closet and storage space, and even the least expensive outside categories have a small seating area. Private balconies are furnished with a table and chairs and some have loungers.

Amenities: All passengers are greeted upon embarkation with sparkling wine or champagne and will find a refrigerator, safe, hair dryer, fresh fruit basket, bath toiletries, slippers, and a bathrobe for use during the cruise. Butlers are on hand to attend to Queens Grill occupants, whose bars are stocked with spirits, wine, and soft drinks.

Accessibility: Fourteen cabins are wheelchair accessible.

Top: Main pool
Bottom: Queens Grill suite

Restaurants

The Britannia Restaurant serves dinner in two assigned seatings for most passengers, while those in AA Britannia Club Balcony Cabins dine in the single-seating Britannia Club Dining Room, and those in Princess and Queens Grill-classes also dine in a single seating in their respective restaurants. Todd English, the alternative restaurant, requires reservations and has a fee. The Lido buffet and Golden Lion Pub offer relaxed dining options, while specialty teas, coffees, and pastries are featured in Café Carinthia. A proper English tea is served daily, and room service is always available.

Spas

Operated by Steiner Leisure, the spa features a wide range of exotic and contemporary treatments. Chakra rasul and herbal steam chambers are designed for couples to indulge in ancient Eastern rituals. A relaxation room, hydrotherapy pool, and thermal suite have three steam and sauna rooms that are available for the use of spa clients who've booked a treatment and others who've purchased a pass. Complimentary saunas are found in men's and women's changing rooms.

Bars and Entertainment

Evening entertainment can include production shows and concerts and Cunard's traditional themed formal balls in the Queen's Lounge ballroom. Other options are as diverse as the exclusive Champagne bar, an authentic English pub, or Hemispheres, the glass-domed lounge for dancing until the small hours to the beat of a big band or with the resident DJ.

Pros and Cons

Pros: the promenade deck that encircles the ship is ideal for casual strolls or jogging; the shops on board are well-stocked; the Winter Garden with a glass roof that opens is a pleasing spot to relax with a cup of tea.

Cons: the first Cunardia museum exhibit at sea is disappointingly small; standard accommodations don't have enough drawer space; private box seating for shows in the Royal Court Theater requires a reservation and fee.

Cabin Type	Size (sq. ft.)
Grand Suite/Master Suite	1,918–2,131/ 1,100
Penthouse Suite/ Queens Suite/ Princess Suite	520–707/ 508–771/ 335–513
Ocean View with Balcony	242–472
Ocean View/ Interior	180–201/ 152–243

All dimensions include the square footage for balconies.

FAST FACTS

- 12 passenger decks
- Specialty restaurant, 3 dining rooms, buffet, café, ice cream parlor, pizzeria
- Wi-Fi, safe, refrigerator, DVD (some)
- 2 pools
- Fitness classes, gym, hot tubs, sauna, spa, steam room
- 10 bars, casino, 2 dance clubs, library, show room
- Children's programs
- Dry-cleaning, laundry facilities, laundry service
- Internet terminal
- No-smoking cabins

5

CUNARD LINE

Britannia stateroom

DISNEY CRUISE LINE

With the launch of Disney Cruise Line in 1998, families were offered yet another reason to take a cruise. The magic of a Walt Disney resort vacation plus the romance of a sea voyage are a tempting combination, especially for adults who discovered Disney

Disney ships have a classic style

movies and the Mickey Mouse Club as children. Mixed with traditional shipboard activities, who can resist scheduled opportunities for the young and young-at-heart to interact with their favorite Disney characters?

☎ *407/566–3500 or 888/325–2500*
⊕ *www.disneycruise. com*
☞ *Cruise Style: Mainstream.*

Although Disney Cruise Line voyages stuck to tried and true Bahamas and Caribbean itineraries in their formative years, and sailed exclusively from Port Canaveral, Florida, where a terminal was designed especially for Disney ships, the line has branched out to other regions, including Europe.

Food

Don't expect top chefs and gourmet food. This is Disney, and the fare in each ship's casual restaurants is all-American for the most part. A third restaurant is a bit fancier, with French-inspired dishes on the menus. Naturally, all have children's menus with an array of favorite sandwiches and entrées. Vegetarian and healthy selections are also available in all restaurants. A bonus is complimentary soft drinks, lemonade, and iced tea throughout the sailing. A beverage station in the buffet area is always open; however, there is a charge for soft drinks ordered from the bars and room service.

Palo, the adults-only restaurant serving northern Italian cuisine, requires reservations for a romantic evening of fine dining. Although there's a cover charge for dinner, it's a steal and reservations go fast. Brunch also commands a surcharge. More upscale and pricey, Remy on

Disney Dream and *Disney Fantasy* serves French cuisine in an elegant atmosphere.

Entertainment

Shipboard entertainment leans heavily on popular Disney themes and characters. Parents are actively involved in the audience with their children at production shows, movies, live character meetings, deck parties, and dancing in the family nightclub. Teens have a supervised, no-adults-allowed club space in the forward fake funnel, where they gather for activities and parties. For adults, there are traditional no-kids-allowed bars and lounges with live music, dancing, theme parties, and late-night comedy, as well as daytime wine-tasting sessions, game shows, culinary arts and home entertaining demonstrations, and behind-the-scenes lectures on animation and filmmaking. This is Disney, so there are no casinos.

A giant LED screen is affixed to the forward funnels of both the original ships and their newer fleetmates. Passengers can watch movies and special broadcasts while lounging in the family pool area.

Fitness and Recreation

Three swimming pool areas are designated for different groups: children (Mickey's Pool, which has a waterslide and requires a parent to be present); families (Goofy Pool); and adults (Quiet Cove). Young children who aren't potty trained can't swim in the pools but are invited to splash about in the fountain play area near Mickey's Pool. Be sure to bring their swim diapers.

The salon and spa feature a complete menu of hair- and nail-care services as well as facials and massages. The Tropical Rainforest is a soothing coed thermal suite with heated tile lounges. It's complimentary for the day if you book a spa treatment or available on a daily or cruise-long basis for a fee. SpaVillas are indoor–outdoor treatment suites that feature a veranda with a hot tub and an open-air shower. In addition to a nicely equipped fitness center and aerobics studio are a jogging track and basketball court.

Your Shipmates

Disney Cruises appeal to kids of all ages—the young and not-so-young, singles, couples, and families. Multigeneration family groups are the core audience for these ships, and the facilities are ideal for family gatherings. What you might not have expected are the numerous newlywed couples celebrating their honeymoons on board.

KNOWN FOR

■ **Character Interaction:** Disney characters make frequent appearances.

■ **Classic Ships:** Classic ship design: Disney's are the first passenger ships since the 1950s to have two funnels.

■ **Entertainment:** Some of the best entertainment at sea for guests of all ages.

■ **Fireworks:** Among the only ships that are allowed to host fireworks at sea.

■ **Kid Stuff:** Excellent facilities for children and teens.

5

DISNEY CRUISE LINE

Dining in Palo, the adults-only restaurant

Top: A day ashore
Middle: Making a splash in
Mickey's Pool
Bottom: *Disney Magic* and
Disney Wonder at sea

Dress Code

One-week cruises schedule a semiformal evening and a formal night, during which men are encouraged to wear tuxedos, but dark suits or sport coats and ties are acceptable for both. Resort casual is the evening dress code for dinner in the more laid-back dining rooms. A sport coat is appropriate for the restaurants designated as fancier, as well as the adults-only specialty restaurants, where a jacket is required at Remy and suggested for Palo.

Junior Cruisers

As expected, Disney ships have extensive programs for children and teens, including shore excursions designed for families to enjoy together. Parents are issued a pager for peace of mind while their children are participating in onboard activities and to alert them when their offspring need them. Complimentary age-appropriate activities are scheduled from 9 am to midnight in the Oceaneer Club and Oceaneer Lab for ages 3 to 12. While some activities are recommended for certain age groups, participation is based on the child's interest level and maturity. Activities include arts projects, contests, computer games, pool parties, interactive lab stations, and opportunities for individual and group play. The emphasis is on fun over education, but subtle educational themes are certainly there. Coffeehouse-style tween (ages 11–14) and teen (ages 14–17) clubs offer music, a dance floor, big-screen TV, and Internet café for the younger set. Scheduled activities include challenging games, photography lessons, sporting contests, beach events, and parties, but they are also great places to just hang out with new friends in an adult-free zone.

An hourly fee is charged for child care in Flounder's Reef Nursery, which is open during select hours for infants as young as three months through three years. Supply your own diapers, and nursery attendants will change them. Private, in-cabin babysitting is not available.

Service

Friendly service is extended to all passengers, with particular importance placed on treating children with the same courtesy extended to adults.

CHOOSE THIS LINE IF ...

You want to cruise with the entire family—Mom, Dad, the kids, and grandparents.

You enjoy having kids around. (There are adults-only areas to retreat to when the fun wears off.)

Your family enjoys Disney's theme parks and can't get enough wholesome entertainment.

Tipping

Suggested gratuity amounts are calculated on a per-person per-cruise rather than per-night basis and can be added to onboard accounts or offered in cash on the last night of the cruise. Guidelines include gratuities for your dining-room server, assistant server, head server, and stateroom host/hostess on the basis of $12 per night in the following amounts: $36 for three-night cruises, $48 for four-night cruises, and $84 for seven-night cruises. Tips for room-service delivery, spa services, and the dining manager are at the passenger's discretion. An automatic 15% gratuity is added to all bar tabs.

Past Passengers

Castaway Club membership is automatic after completing a Disney cruise. Benefits include a complimentary gift (such as a tote bag or beach towel), communication about special offers, priority check-in, invitations to shipboard cocktail parties during subsequent cruises, and a special toll-free reservation telephone number (☎ 800/449–3380) for convenience.

HELPFUL HINTS

There are hidden Mickeys all over the ships, just as in the theme parks.

Consider buying pins and autograph books at a Disney store before your cruise.

You can reserve many services and make dinner reservations prior to sailing.

Roomier than average standard cabins can easily handle four occupants.

Alcohol may be brought on board but must be hand-carried on embarkation by an adult, age 21 or older.

5

DISNEY CRUISE LINE

DON'T CHOOSE THIS LINE IF ...

You want to spend a lot of quality time bonding with your kids. Your kids may not want to leave the fun activities.

You want to dine in peace and quiet. The dining rooms and buffet can be boisterous.

You want to gamble. There are no casinos, so you'll have to settle for bingo.

DISNEY MAGIC, DISNEY WONDER

CREW MEMBERS	950
ENTERED SERVICE	1998, 1999
GROSS TONS	83,000
LENGTH	964 feet
NUMBER OF CABINS	877
PASSENGER CAPACITY	1,754 (2,400 max)
WIDTH	106 feet

700 ft.
500 ft.
300 ft.

Reminiscent of classic ocean liners, Disney vessels have two funnels (the forward one is nonfunctional) and high-tech interiors behind their art deco and art nouveau styling. Whimsical design accents cleverly incorporate images of Mickey Mouse and his friends without over-powering the warm and elegant decor. Artwork show-cases the creativity of Disney artists and animators. The atmosphere is never stuffy.

More than 15,000 square feet—nearly an entire deck—are devoted to children's activity centers, outdoor activity areas, and swimming pools. Theaters cater to family entertainment with large-scale production shows, movies, dances, lively game shows, and even 3-D movies.

Adults-only hideaways include an avenue of theme bars and lounges tucked into the area just forward of the lobby atrium; the Promenade Lounge, near the aft elevator lobby; and Cove Café, a quiet spot adjacent to the adult pool to relax with coffee or a cocktail, surf the Internet, or read.

Cabins

Cabins: Designed for families, Disney ships have some of the roomiest, most functional staterooms at sea. Natural woods, imported tiles, and a nautical flavor add to the decor, which even includes the touch of Disney-inspired artwork on the walls. Most cabins can accommodate at least three people and have a seating area and unique bath-and-a-half arrangement. Three-quarters of all accommodations are outside cabins, and 44% of those include private balconies with kid-proof door handles and higher-than-usual railings for safety. All cabins have adequate closet and drawer/shelf storage, as well as bathroom shelves.

Suites: Suites are truly expansive, with master bedrooms separated from the living areas for privacy. All suites have walk-in closets, a dining table and chairs, a wet bar, a DVD player, and a large balcony.

Amenities: Though not luxurious, Disney cabins are comfortably furnished. Each has a flat-screen TV, a small refrigerator, a personal safe, and a hair dryer; bathrobes are provided for use during the cruise in the top-category staterooms. All suites have concierge service.

Accessibility: Sixteen cabins are wheelchair accessible.

Top: Friendships are forged on a cruise
Bottom: Dreams come true on a Disney cruise

Restaurants

In a novel approach to dining, passengers (and their waiters) rotate through the three main dining rooms in assigned seatings. Parrot Cay (*Disney Wonder*), Carioca's (*Disney Magic*) and Animator's Palate are casual, while Triton's (*Disney Wonder*) and Lumière's (*Disney Magic*) are a bit fancier. Palo is a beautifully appointed northern Italian restaurant for adults only that requires reservations for brunch, dinner, or tea and carries an extra charge. Breakfast and lunch are open seating in dining rooms. Disney characters make an appearance at a character breakfast on seven-night cruises. Breakfast, lunch, and dinner are also offered in the casual pool-deck buffet, while poolside pizzerias, snack bars, grills, and ice-cream bars serve everything from pizza, burgers, and hot dogs to fresh fruit, wraps, and frozen treats during the day. Specialty coffees are available in the adults-only Cove Café for an extra charge. Room service is available around the clock.

Spas

Spas feature a complete menu of facials and massages. The Tropical Rainforest is a soothing coed thermal suite with heated tile lounges and is complimentary for the day if you book a spa treatment; it's available on a daily or cruise-long basis for a fee. SpaVillas, indoor–outdoor treatment suites, each have a veranda with a hot tub and an open-air shower.

Bars and Entertainment

After the energetic production shows, deck parties, and activities designed for the entire family, adults can slip off to bars and lounges reserved for them after dark, including a sports bar or nightclub where the entertainment staff offers activities such as karaoke or themed dance parties. For quiet conversation and a drink under the stars, there's a cozy bar alongside the adult pool.

Pros and Cons

Pros: there are plenty of connecting cabins that fit three up to seven; soft drinks at meals and beverage stations are complimentary; for adults, each ship has a piano bar.

Cons: the splash play areas are available for youngsters who wear swim diapers; although a Disney cruise isn't all Disney all the time, it can get tiring if you aren't really into the atmosphere; there's no library on board.

Cabin Type	Size (sq. ft.)
Royal Suites	1,029
Two-Bedroom Suite	945
One-Bedroom Suite	614
Deluxe Family Balcony	304
Deluxe Balcony	268
Ocean View	226
Deluxe Inside	214
Standard Inside	184

Dimensions include the square footage for balconies.

FAST FACTS

- 11 passenger decks
- Specialty restaurant, 3 dining rooms, buffet, ice cream parlor, pizzeria
- Wi-Fi, safe, refrigerator, DVD (some)
- 2 pools, children's pool
- Fitness classes, gym, hot tubs, sauna, spa
- 6 bars, dance club, 2 show rooms, video game room
- Children's programs
- Dry-cleaning, laundry facilities, laundry service
- Internet terminal
- No kids under 12 weeks
- No-smoking cabins

5

DISNEY CRUISE LINE

DISNEY DREAM, DISNEY FANTASY

CREW MEMBERS	1,458
ENTERED SERVICE	2011, 2012
GROSS TONS	128,000
LENGTH	1,115 feet
NUMBER OF CABINS	1,250
PASSENGER CAPACITY	2,500 (4,000 max)
WIDTH	125 feet

700 ft.

500 ft.

300 ft.

Disney Cruise Line's largest ships are also their most lavish, distinguished for their classic early-20th-century design and their state-of-the-art technology. Playful design accents cleverly incorporate the images of Disney themes without overpowering the stylish decor. Artwork showcases the creativity of Disney artists and animators. The atmosphere is never stuffy.

As on earlier ships, vast areas are devoted to children's activity centers, outdoor activity areas, and swimming pools. The AquaDuck is a unique 765-foot-long water coaster that travels around four outside decks. Theaters cater to family entertainment with large-scale production shows, movies, dances, lively game shows, and even 3-D movies. Adults-only hideaways include an avenue of bars and lounges tucked into deck four aft; Meridian Lounge, located between the specialty restaurants; and Cove Café, a quiet spot adjacent to the adult pool to relax with coffee or a cocktail.

Cabins

Cabins: Designed specifically for families, these are some of the most functional staterooms at sea. Eighty-eight percent of the staterooms have an ocean view and, of those, 90% have a private balcony. Most can accommodate at least three people; family cabins can sleep four or even five comfortably. To accommodate larger groups, many staterooms connect. All have a seating area and, with the exception of the standard inside category, feature a unique bath-and-a-half arrangement. Suites feature two bathrooms, including one with double sinks and a whirlpool tub. Royal suites have a second whirlpool tub on the balcony.

Amenities: Though not luxurious, Disney cabins are comfortably furnished and have some useful amenities, including a flat-screen TV, small refrigerator, safe, iPod docking station, and hair dryer. All inside staterooms have a real-time view of the outside of the ship on an LCD flat-screen monitor disguised as a "virtual porthole," which can be turned off at night. Shampoo, conditioner, and lotion are provided for all; suites receive upgraded toiletries and bathrobes for use during the cruise. All suites have concierge service and daily deliveries of canapés, fruit, or cookies.

Top: Relaxing in the lounge
Bottom: *A Disney Dream* cabin

Accessibility: Thirty-seven staterooms in a variety of categories are equipped for accessibility.

Restaurants

Passengers (and their waiters) rotate through the three main dining rooms in assigned seatings for dinner; breakfast and lunch are open seating. Palo is a beautifully appointed northern Italian restaurant for adults that requires reservations for brunch, dinner, or tea and carries an extra charge. Also adults-only and requiring reservations and a surcharge is Remy, the ships' upscale French restaurant (dinner only). All meals are also offered in the casual pool-deck buffet, which has table service for dinner. Poolside pizzerias, snack bars, grills, and ice cream bars serve food and snacks all day. Specialty coffees are available in the adults-only Cove Café for an extra charge. Disney characters make an appearance at a character breakfast on seven-night cruises. Room service is available around the clock.

Spas

Treatments such as massages, body wraps, and facials are offered in the Senses Spa, but the Rainforest is a show-stopper. Offering the benefits of steam, heat, and hydrotherapy combined with aromatherapy, the specialized areas include steam baths, sauna, and aromatic showers that simulate everything from a waterfall or tropical rain to a refreshing mist. Heated tile lounges and two hot tubs on the adjacent private teak deck offer sea views. The Chill Spa for teens occupies its own space.

Bars and Entertainment

Shows, deck parties, and other activities are family-friendly, but there are also adults-only areas after dark, including a sports bar, wine and champagne bar, and nightclubs with karaoke or themed dance parties. For quiet conversation and a nightcap under the stars, Meridian is a cozy bar with adjacent outdoor seating.

Pros and Cons

Pros: Mickey's Pool (for young kids) and Donald's Pool (for families) have seating for parents; adults-only Quiet Cove has loungers in the shallow section of the pool; a privacy curtain can be drawn between the sitting and sleeping areas in staterooms.

Cons: the largest suites sleep a maximum of five; toddlers in swim diapers are restricted to Mickey's Pool splash play area; the Disney element can be tiring for passengers who aren't into it.

Cabin Type	Size (sq. ft.)
Concierge Royal Suite/One-Bedroom Suite	1,781/622
Concierge Family Balcony/Deluxe Family Balcony/Deluxe Balcony	306/299/246
Family Ocean View/Ocean View	306/204
Deluxe Interior/Standard Interior	200/169

Dimensions include the square footage for balconies.

FAST FACTS

- 14 passenger decks
- 2 specialty restaurants, 3 dining rooms, buffet, café, ice cream parlor, pizzeria
- Wi-Fi, safe, refrigerator, DVD (some)
- 3 pools, children's pool
- Fitness classes, gym, hot tubs, sauna, spa
- 11 bars, dance club, show room, video game room
- Children's programs
- Dry-cleaning, laundry facilities, laundry service
- Internet terminal
- No kids under 12 weeks
- No-smoking cabins

HOLLAND AMERICA LINE

Holland America Line has enjoyed a distinguished record of traditional cruises, world exploration, and transatlantic crossings since 1873—all facets of its history that are reflected in the fleet's multimillion-dollar shipboard art and antiques collections. Even the

A day on the Lido deck

ships' names follow a pattern set long ago: all end in the suffix *dam* and are either derived from the names of various dams that cross Holland's rivers, important Dutch landmarks, or points of the compass. The names are even recycled when vessels are retired, and some are in their fifth and sixth generation of use.

☎ *206/281–3535 or 800/577–1728*
⊕ *www.hollandameri-ca.com*
☞ *Cruise Style: Premium.*

Noted for focusing on passenger comfort, Holland America Line cruises are classic in design and style, and with an infusion of younger adults and families on board, they remain refined without being stuffy or stodgy. Following a basic design theme, returning passengers feel as at home on the newest Holland America vessels as they do on older ones.

Food

Holland America Line chefs, led by Master Chef Rudi Sodamin, utilize more than 500 different food items on a typical weeklong cruise to create the modern Continental cuisine and traditional favorites served to their passengers. Vegetarian options as well as health-conscious cuisine are available, and special dietary requests can be handled with advance notice. But the food quality, taste, and selection have greatly improved in recent years. A case in point is the reservations-required Pinnacle Grill alternative restaurants, where fresh seafood and premium cuts of Sterling Silver beef are used to prepare creative specialty dishes. The $25-per-person charge for dinner would be worth it for the Dungeness crab cakes starter and dessert alone. Other delicious traditions are afternoon tea, a Dutch

Chocolate Extravaganza, and Holland America Line's signature bread pudding.

Flexible scheduling allows for early or late seatings in the two-deck, formal restaurants. An open-seating option from 5:15 to 9 has been introduced fleetwide.

Entertainment

Entertainment tends to be more Broadway-stylish than Las Vegas–brash. Colorful revues are presented in main show lounges by the ships' companies of singers and dancers. Other performances might include a range of cabaret acts: comedians, magicians, jugglers, and acrobats. Live bands play a wide range of musical styles for dancing and listening in smaller lounges and piano bars. Movies are shown daily in cinemas that double as the Culinary Arts Centers.

Holland America Line may never be considered cutting-edge, but their innovative Signature of Excellence concept sets it apart from other premium cruise lines. An interactive Culinary Arts Center offers cooking demonstrations and wine-tasting sessions; Explorations Café (powered by the *New York Times*) is a coffeehouse, library, and Internet center; the Explorations Guest Speakers Series is supported by in-cabin televised programming on flat-screen TVs in all cabins; the traditional Crow's Nest observation lounge has a nightclub-disco layout, video wall, and sound-and-light systems; and facilities for children and teens have been greatly expanded.

Fitness and Recreation

Well-equipped and fully staffed fitness facilities contain state-of-the-art exercise equipment; basic fitness classes are available at no charge. There's a fee for personal training, body composition analysis, and specialized classes such as yoga and Pilates.

Treatments in the Greenhouse Spa include a variety of massages, body wraps, and facials. Hair styling and nail services are offered in the salons. All ships have a jogging track, multiple swimming pools, and sports courts; some have hydrotherapy pools and soothing thermal suites.

Your Shipmates

No longer just your grandparents' cruise line, today's Holland America sailings attract families and couples, mostly from their late thirties on up. Holidays and summer months are peak periods when you'll find more children in the mix. Retirees are often still in the majority, particularly on longer cruises. Families

5

HOLLAND AMERICA LINE

Top: Casino action
Bottom: Stay fit or stay loose

Top: Wine tasting
Middle: Production Showtime
Bottom: Spa relaxation

cruising together who book five or more cabins receive perks such as a fountain-soda package for each family member, a family photo for each stateroom, and complimentary water toys at Half Moon Cay (for Caribbean itineraries that call at the private island). If the group is larger than 10 cabins, the Head-of-Family is recognized with an upgrade from outside stateroom to a veranda cabin. It's the best family deal at sea, and there's no extra charge.

Dress Code

Evenings on Holland America Line cruises fall into two categories: smart casual and formal. For the two formal nights standard on seven-night cruises, men are encouraged to wear tuxedos, but dark suits or sport coats and ties are acceptable, and you'll certainly see them. On smart-casual nights, expect the type of attire you'd see at a country club or upscale resort. It's requested that no T-shirts, jeans, swimsuits, tank tops, or shorts be worn in public areas after 6 pm.

Junior Cruisers

Club HAL is Holland America Line's professionally staffed youth and teen program. Age-appropriate activities planned for children ages 3 to 7 include storytelling, arts and crafts, ice cream or pizza parties, and games; for children ages 8 to 12 there are arcade games, Sony PlayStations, theme parties, on-deck sports events, and scavenger hunts. Club HAL After Hours offers late-night activities from 10 pm until midnight for an hourly fee. Baby food, diapers, cribs, high chairs, and booster seats may be requested in advance of boarding. Private in-cabin babysitting is sometimes available if a staff member is willing.

Teens ages 13 to 17 have their own lounge, with activities including dance contests, arcade games, sports tournaments, movies, and an exclusive sundeck on some ships. Most Caribbean itineraries offer water park–type facilities and kid-friendly shore excursions to Half Moon Cay, Holland America Line's private island in the Bahamas.

CHOOSE THIS LINE IF ...

You crave relaxation. Grab a padded steamer chair on the teak promenade deck and watch the sea pass by.

You like to go to the movies, especially when the popcorn is free.

You want to bring the kids. Areas designed exclusively for children and teens are hot new features on all ships.

Service

Professional, unobtrusive service by the Indonesian and Filipino staff is a fleet-wide standard on Holland America Line. Crew members are trained in Indonesia at a custom-built facility called the MS *Nieuw Jakarta,* where employees polish their English-language skills and learn housekeeping in mock cabins.

Tipping

Gratuities of $11.50 per passenger per day, or $12 per passenger per day for suite passengers, are automatically added to shipboard accounts, and distributed to stewards and waitstaff. Passengers may adjust the amount based on the level of service experienced. Room-service tips are usually given in cash (it's at the passenger's discretion here). Gratuities for spa and salon services can be added to the bill or offered in cash. An automatic 15% gratuity is added to bar-service tabs.

Past Passengers

All passengers who sail with Holland America Line are automatically enrolled in the Mariner Society and receive special offers on upcoming cruises, as well as insider information concerning new ships and product enhancements. Mariner Society benefits also include preferred pricing on many cruises; Mariner baggage tags and buttons that identify you as a member during embarkation; an invitation to the Mariner Society champagne reception and awards party hosted by the captain; lapel pins and medallions acknowledging your history of Holland America sailings; a special collectible gift delivered to your cabin; and a subscription to *Mariner,* the full-color magazine featuring news and Mariner Society savings.

HELPFUL HINTS

Charges for specialty dining on Holland America Line ships are some of the most reasonable at sea.

All passengers are presented with a complimentary canvas tote bag imprinted with the line's logo.

Narrated iPod art tours of the ships' art collections can be borrowed from the library on each vessel.

A wide variety of shore excursions that fit lifestyles ranging from easygoing to active adventure can be booked before sailing.

A reservation may be cancelled for any reason whatsoever up to 24 hours prior to departure and a refund of 80% to 90% of eligible amounts will be paid.

5

HOLLAND AMERICA LINE

DON'T CHOOSE THIS LINE IF ...

You want to party hard. Most of the action on these ships ends relatively early.

Dressing for dinner isn't your thing. Passengers tend to ramp up the dress code most evenings.

You have an aversion to extending tips. The line's "tipping not required" policy has been dropped.

SIGNATURE-CLASS
Eurodam, Nieuw Amsterdam

CREW MEMBERS	929
ENTERED SERVICE	2008, 2010
GROSS TONS	86,273, 86,700
LENGTH	936 feet
NUMBER OF CABINS	1,052, 1,053
PASSENGER CAPACITY	2,104, 2,106
WIDTH	106 feet

700 ft.
500 ft.
300 ft.

Signature-class vessels were the first ships in the fleet to be launched with all the so-called Signature of Excellence features fully integrated into them. Larger than the other midsize ships in the fleet, they are pure Holland America, with all the traditional amenities and services plus some added bonuses. You'll find familiar public spaces as well as a second specialty restaurant and adjacent lounge, a new bar that anchors the Explorer's Lounge, and an Italian eatery tucked into a corner of the Lido.

No-smoking Spa staterooms near the Greenhouse Spa feature Asian-inspired decor and spa amenities. Poolside are private, draped cabanas, and one deck up the tented Retreat cabanas are filled with amenities that include the use of handheld fans, an Evian spray mister, iPods with music preloaded, and chilled water. You can look forward to icy refreshments and afternoon champagne. Cabanas are reserved by the day or by the cruise (for an extra fee).

Cabins

Cabins: Warm wood tones, burnished nickel fixtures, and punches of color complement the drapery, carpeting, and bedspreads in all categories. Eighty-five percent have an ocean view, and 79% of outside staterooms and suites offer a private veranda with attractive furnishings.

Suites: Penthouse suites are the ultimate in luxury, with separate living-room, dining-room, and bedroom areas. A veranda with hot tub, walk-in closets, bathroom with whirlpool tub, double sinks, separate guest powder room, and butler's pantry complete the features. Offering similar amenities, Deluxe and Superior Verandah suites have large verandas, dressing areas, and generous sitting areas; the bathrooms also have double sinks, a whirlpool tub, and a separate shower. Suite occupants can use the private Neptune Lounge and personal concierge service.

Amenities: All categories are outfitted with plush pillow-top mattresses, bathrobes, Egyptian cotton towels, flat-panel TVs, DVD players, lighted makeup mirrors, hair dryers, massaging showerheads, personal safes, refrigerators, and closets configured for hanging and/or drop-down shelves.

Top: *Eurodam* at sea
Bottom: The Retreat on
Eurodam, the ultimate getaway

Accessibility: Thirty cabins are designed for wheelchair accessibility.

Restaurants

The formal restaurant offers open seating for breakfast and lunch, with dinner in two traditional assigned dinner seatings or open seating. The Pinnacle Grill (reservation, cover charge) serves lunch and dinner. Tamarind (reservation, cover charge) offers Pan-Asian fare, and lunch is free. For casual dining, the Lido restaurant serves buffet breakfast and lunch; for dinner there is waiter service, and a section becomes Canaletto, serving Italian fare (reservation, cover charge). A poolside grill features items ranging from tacos to hamburgers. The extra-charge Explorations Café offers specialty coffees and pastries. Daily afternoon tea service is offered, hors d'oeuvres are served by waiters before dinner, chocolates are offered after dinner, and a chocolate extravaganza buffet is served one night during every cruise. Room service is available 24 hours.

Spas

Treatments in the Greenhouse Spa include a variety of massages, body wraps, and facials, as well as acupuncture services and tooth-whitening treatments. A hydrotherapy pool and thermal suite with heated ceramic loungers for relaxation as well as dry saunas and steam rooms can be used for a fee (one-time or for the cruise); it's complimentary for the day when a spa appointment is booked. Complimentary saunas for men and women are near the entrance to the spa.

Bars and Entertainment

Popular spots before dinner are the Ocean Club and Explorers Lounge, where servers pass through with appetizers. After dinner and a show or concert, those bars are quiet spots for drinks and conversation. For livelier action, there's the Sports Bar, a Piano Bar, or the Crow's Nest for late night dancing.

Pros and Cons

Pros: spa staterooms and suites are completely no-smoking; with sea views and intimate seating alcoves, the Silk Den Lounge is one of the prettiest in the fleet; guests love the state-of-the-art demonstration kitchen.

Cons: shelves are okay, but drawer space is inadequate in standard cabins; some spa staterooms have unusable Juliet balconies; teens are somewhat slighted here compared to other Holland America ships.

Cabin Type	Size (sq. ft.)
Penthouse Suite	1,318
Deluxe Verandah	510–700
Superior Verandah	398
Deluxe Verandah	254
Ocean View	185
Inside	170–200

Dimensions include the square footage for balconies.

FAST FACTS

- 11 passenger decks
- 3 specialty restaurants, dining room, buffet, pizzeria
- Wi-Fi, safe, refrigerator, DVD
- 2 pools
- Fitness classes, gym, hot tubs, spa
- 11 bars, casino, 2 dance clubs, library, show room, video game room
- Children's programs
- Dry-cleaning, laundry service
- Internet terminal
- No-smoking cabins

Eurodam atrium

5

HOLLAND AMERICA LINE

VISTA-CLASS
Zuiderdam, Oosterdam, Westerdam, Noordam

ENTERED SERVICE	2002, 2003, 2004, 2006
PASSENGER CAPACITY	1,916, 1,916, 1,916, 1,924
700 ft. **CREW MEMBERS**	817, 817, 817, 820
NUMBER OF CABINS	958, 958, 958, 959
500 ft. **GROSS TONS**	82,305
LENGTH	936 feet
300 ft. **WIDTH**	106 feet

Ships for the 21st century, Vista-class vessels integrate new, youthful and family-friendly elements into Holland America Line's classic fleet. Exquisite Waterford-crystal sculptures adorn triple-deck atriums and reflect vivid, almost daring color schemes throughout. Although all the public rooms carry the traditional Holland America names (Ocean Bar, Explorer's Lounge, Crow's Nest) and aren't much different in atmosphere, their louder decor (toned down a bit since the introduction of the *Zuiderdam*) may make them unfamiliar to returning passengers.

Veterans of cruises on older Holland America ships will find the layout of public spaces somewhat different; still, everyone's favorite Crow's Nest lounges continue to offer those commanding views.

Cabins

Cabins: Comfortable and roomy, 85% of all Vista-class accommodations have an ocean view, and almost 80% of those also have the luxury of a private balcony furnished with chairs, loungers, and tables. Every cabin has adequate closet and drawer/shelf storage, as well as bathroom shelves. Some suites have a whirlpool tub, powder room, and walk-in closet.

Suites: Suites include duvets on beds and a fully stocked minibar; some also have a whirlpool tub, powder room, and walk-in closet. Penthouse and Deluxe Verandah suites have exclusive use of the private Neptune Lounge, personal concierge service, canapés before dinner, and complimentary laundry, pressing, and dry-cleaning services.

Amenities: All staterooms and suites are appointed with pillow-top mattresses, 250-thread-count cotton bed linens, magnifying halogen-lighted makeup mirrors, hair dryers, a fruit basket, flat-panel TVs, and DVD players. Bathroom extras include Egyptian cotton towels, shampoo, body lotion, and bath gel, plus deluxe bathrobes to use during the cruise.

Accessibility: Twenty-eight staterooms are wheelchair accessible.

Restaurants

The formal dining room offers open-seating breakfast and lunch, with a choice at dinner between two assigned seatings or open seating. The Pinnacle Grill (reservation,

Top: *Oosterdam* Hydropool
Bottom: Vista-class Ocean
View stateroom

cover charge) serves lunch and dinner. A casual Lido restaurant serves buffet breakfast and lunch; at dinner the Lido offers table service with entrées from both the Lido and main dining room menus, and Italian fare is served in the adjacent Canaletto Restaurant (reservation, cover charge). Poolside lunch at the Terrace Grill includes nachos, hamburgers, and hot dogs with all the trimmings to sandwiches and gourmet sausages. The extra-charge Explorations Café offers specialty coffees and pastries. Daily afternoon tea service is elevated to Royal Dutch High Tea once per cruise. Complimentary hors d'oeuvres are served by waiters during cocktail hour, hand-dipped chocolates are offered after dinner in the Explorer's Lounge, and a late-night buffet and chocolate extravaganza is served in the Lido restaurant during every cruise. Room service is available 24 hours.

Spas

The Greenhouse Spa treatments include a variety of massages, body wraps, and facials, as well as acupuncture and tooth-whitening services. A hydrotherapy pool and thermal suite with heated ceramic lounges for relaxation and dry sauna and steam rooms are free to use when a spa appointment is booked and available for a fee to all other passengers.

Bars and Entertainment

Before dinner, the Ocean Club and Explorers Lounge are popular spots where servers pass through with appetizers. After dinner and a show or concert, those bars are quiet spots for drinks and conversation. For livelier action, there's the Sports Bar, a Piano Bar, or the Crow's Nest for late-night dancing.

Pros and Cons

Pros: next to the Crow's Nest, an outdoor seating area is a quiet hideaway; exterior panoramic elevators offer an elevated view of the seascape; you can borrow iPod shipboard art tours.

Cons: Vista-class ships do not have self-service laundry rooms; murals in Pinnacle Grill restaurants look out of place alongside priceless art found throughout the rest of the ships; some chairs in Pinnacle Grill are so heavy that they barely budge without effort.

Cabin Type	Size (sq. ft.)
Penthouse Suites	1,318
Deluxe Verandah Suite	510–700
Superior Verandah Suite	398
Deluxe Ocean View	254
Standard Ocean View	185
Inside	170–200

Dimensions include the square footage for balconies.

FAST FACTS

- 11 passenger decks
- Specialty restaurant, dining room, buffet, pizzeria
- Internet, Wi-Fi, safe, refrigerator, DVD
- 2 pools (1 indoor)
- Fitness classes, gym, hot tubs, spa
- 9 bars, casino, 2 dance clubs, library, show room, video game room
- Children's programs
- Dry-cleaning, laundry service
- Internet terminal
- No-smoking cabins

5

HOLLAND AMERICA LINE

ROTTERDAM, AMSTERDAM

CREW MEMBERS	600, 615
ENTERED SERVICE	1997, 2000
GROSS TONS	61,859, 62,735
LENGTH	780 feet
NUMBER OF CABINS	702, 690
PASSENGER CAPACITY	1,404, 1,380
WIDTH	106 feet

700 ft.

500 ft.

300 ft.

The most traditional ships in the fleet, the interiors of sister ships *Amsterdam* and *Rotterdam* display abundant wood appointments in the public areas on promenade and lower promenade decks and priceless works of art throughout.

The Ocean Bar, Explorer's Lounge, Wajang Theater, and Crow's Nest are familiar lounges to longtime Holland American passengers. Newer additions include the spa's thermal suite, a culinary-arts demonstration center in the theater, Explorations Café, and expansive areas for children and teens. Multimillion-dollar collections of art and artifacts are showcased throughout both vessels. In addition to works commissioned specifically for each ship, Holland America Line celebrates its heritage by featuring antiques and artworks that reflect the theme of worldwide Dutch seafaring history.

Cabins

Cabins: Staterooms are spacious and comfortable, although fewer have private balconies than newer fleetmates. Lanai cabins were added during *Rotterdam*'s latest upgrade. Every cabin has adequate closet and drawer/shelf storage, as well as bathroom shelves. Some suites also have a whirlpool tub, powder room, and walk-in closet. Connecting cabins are available in a range of categories, as well as a number of triple and a few quad cabins.

Suites: Extras include duvets on beds, a fully stocked minibar, and personalized stationery. Penthouse and Deluxe Verandah suites have exclusive use of the Neptune Lounge, concierge service, canapés before dinner, binoculars and umbrellas for use during the cruise, an invitation to a VIP party with the captain, and complimentary laundry, pressing, and dry-cleaning services.

Amenities: All staterooms and suites are appointed with pillow-top mattresses, 250-thread-count cotton bed linens, magnifying halo-lighted mirrors, hair dryers, a fruit basket, flat-panel TVs, and DVD players. Bathrooms have Egyptian cotton towels, nice toiletries, plus deluxe bathrobes to use during the cruise.

Accessibility: Twenty-one staterooms are designed for wheelchair accessibility on *Amsterdam*, 22 on *Rotterdam*.

Top: Pinnacle Grill dining
Bottom: *Rotterdam* at sea

Restaurants

The formal dining room offers open-seating breakfast and lunch, as well as two assigned seatings or open seating for dinner. Pinnacle Grill (reservation, cover charge) serves lunch and dinner. A casual Lido restaurant serves buffet breakfast and lunch; at dinner, the Lido offers waiter service. Italian fare is served in the adjacent Canaletto Restaurant (reservation, cover charge). Poolside lunch at the Terrace Grill includes fast food and sandwiches. The extra-charge Explorations Café offers specialty coffees and pastries. There's daily afternoon tea service. Complimentary hors d'oeuvres are served by waiters during cocktail hour, hand-dipped chocolates are offered after dinner in the Explorer's Lounge, and a late-night buffet and chocolate extravaganza is served in the Lido restaurant during every cruise. Room service is available 24 hours.

Spas

Treatments in the Greenhouse Spa include a variety of massages, body wraps, and facials, as well as acupuncture and tooth-whitening services. A thermal suite with heated ceramic lounges for relaxation and dry sauna and steam rooms is available for a fee or complimentary for use when a spa appointment is booked. Changing rooms for men and women have complimentary saunas.

Bars and Entertainment

Popular spots before dinner are the Ocean Club and Explorers Lounge, where servers pass through with canapés. Later, those bars are quiet spots for drinks and conversation. For livelier action aboard *Amsterdam*, there's a Sports and Piano Bar; on *Rotterdam*, try Mix—where champagne, martinis, ales, and spirits are served near the piano. The late night dance spot on both is the Crow's Nest.

Pros and Cons

Pros: *Rotterdam* has the Retreat, a resort-style pool on the aft Lido deck; as the line's flagships, *Rotterdam* and *Amsterdam* have the fleet's most elegant interior decor; realistic landscapes with surreal touches accent walls in *Amsterdam*'s Pinnacle Grill.

Cons: one-way window glass in outside cabins on lower promenade deck does not offer occupants complete privacy; there is little shipboard nightlife more than an hour after dinner; despite excellent facilities designed for kids and teens, family cabins are limited.

Cabin Type	Size (sq. ft.)
Penthouse Suite	1,159
Deluxe Verandah Suite	556
Verandah Suite	292
Lanai	197 (Rotterdam only)
Ocean View	197
Inside	182

Dimensions include the square footage for balconies.

FAST FACTS

- 9 passenger decks
- Specialty restaurant, dining room, buffet
- Wi-Fi, safe, refrigerator, DVD
- 2 pools (1 indoor), 2 children's pools
- Fitness classes, gym, 2 hot tubs, sauna, spa
- 6 bars, casino, dance club, library, show room, video game room
- Children's programs
- Dry-cleaning, laundry facilities, laundry service
- Internet terminal
- No-smoking cabins

A brisk walk starts the day.

STATENDAM-CLASS
Statendam, Maasdam, Ryndam, Veendam

CREW MEMBERS	
580	
ENTERED SERVICE	
1993, 1993, 1994, 1996	
GROSS TONS	700 ft.
55,819, 55,575, 55,819, 57,092	
LENGTH	
720 feet	
NUMBER OF CABINS	500 ft.
630, 658, 630, 675	
PASSENGER CAPACITY	
1,260, 1,258, 1260, 1,350	
WIDTH	300 ft.
101 feet	

The sister ships included in the S- or Statendam-class retain the most classic and traditional characteristics of Holland America Line vessels. Routinely updated with innovative features, including Signature of Excellence upgrades, they combine all the advantages of intimate, midsize vessels with high-tech and stylish details.

At the heart of the ships, triple-deck atriums graced by suspended glass sculptures open onto three so-called promenade decks; the lowest contains staterooms encircled by a wide, teak outdoor deck furnished with padded steamer chairs, while interior, art-filled passageways flow past lounges and public rooms on the two decks above. Either reach the lower dining room floor via the aft elevator, or enter one deck above and make a grand entrance down the sweeping staircase.

Cabins

Cabins: Staterooms are spacious and comfortable, although fewer of them have private balconies than on newer ships. Lanai cabins, with a door that directly accesses the promenade deck, were added to *Maasdam* and *Veendam* during the ships' latest upgrades. Every cabin has adequate closet and drawer/shelf storage, as well as bathroom shelves. Connecting cabins are featured in a range of categories.

Suites: Suites have duvets on beds, a fully stocked mini-bar, and personalized stationery. Penthouse Verandah and Deluxe Verandah suites have exclusive use of the private Neptune Lounge, personal concierge service, canapés before dinner on request, binoculars and umbrellas for use during the cruise, an invitation to a VIP party with the captain, and complimentary laundry, pressing, and dry-cleaning services.

Amenities: All staterooms and suites are now appointed with pillow-top mattresses, 250-thread-count cotton bed linens, magnifying lighted mirrors, hair dryers, a fruit basket, flat-panel TVs, and DVD players. Bathroom extras include Egyptian cotton towels, shampoo, body lotion, and bath gel, plus deluxe bathrobes to use during the cruise. Accommodations near the spa on *Ryndam, Statendam,* and *Veendam* offer extras such as a yoga mat and iPod docking station.

Accessibility: Nine cabins on each ship are modified with ramps although doors are standard width.

Top: Select from an extensive wine list
Bottom: Deluxe Veranda suite

Spas

Treatments in the Greenhouse Spa include a variety of massages, body wraps, and facials, as well as acupuncture services and tooth-whitening treatments. A thermal suite with heated ceramic loungers for relaxation as well as dry saunas and steam rooms can be used by anyone for a fee or is complimentary when a spa appointment is booked.

Restaurants

The formal dining room offers open-seating breakfast and lunch, as well as both assigned and open-seating dinner. Pinnacle Grill (reservation, cover charge) serves lunch and dinner. A casual Lido restaurant serves buffet breakfast and lunch; at dinner the Lido offers waiter service; Italian fare is served in the adjacent Canaletto Restaurant (reservation, cover charge). Poolside lunch is served at the Terrace Grill; on *Veendam* the pizzeria is in the aft pool Retreat area. The extra-charge Explorations Café offers specialty coffees and pastries. Daily afternoon tea service is elevated to Royal Dutch High Tea once per cruise. Complimentary hors d'oeuvres are served by waiters during cocktail hour, hand-dipped chocolates are offered after dinner in the Explorer's Lounge, and a late-night buffet and chocolate extravaganza is served in the Lido restaurant during every cruise. Room service is available 24 hours.

Bars and Entertainment

Popular before-dinner spots are the Ocean Club and Explorers Lounge, where servers pass through with appetizers. After dinner and a show, a movie, or concert, those bars are quiet spots for drinks and conversation. For livelier action, try Mix—where champagne, martinis, ales, and spirits are served near the piano. The late-night dance spot is still the Crow's Nest.

Pros and Cons

Pros: Statendam-class ships have some of the fleet's most trendy bars; the Ocean Bar hits the right balance for socializing with the after-dinner crowd; movie theaters double as culinary arts centers.

Cons: railings on the balcony level of the main show lounge obstruct the view of the stage; Club HAL can feel empty on some cruises; the addition of Explorations Café means no more free coffee bar.

Cabin Type	Size (sq. ft.)
Penthouse Suite	1,159
Deluxe Verandah Suite	556
Verandah Suite	292
Lanai	197
Ocean View	197
Inside	182

Dimensions include the square footage for balconies.

FAST FACTS

- 10 passenger decks
- Specialty restaurant, dining room, buffet, pizzeria
- Wi-Fi, safe, refrigerator, DVD
- 2 pools (1 indoor), 2 children's pools
- Fitness classes, gym, hot tubs, spa
- 9 bars, casino, dance club, library, show room, video game room
- Children's programs
- Dry-cleaning, laundry facilities, laundry service
- Internet terminal
- No-smoking cabins

5

HOLLAND AMERICA LINE

Share a sunset.

MSC CRUISES

More widely known as one of the world's largest cargo shipping companies, MSC has operated cruises with an eclectic fleet since the late 1980s. When the line introduced two graceful, medium-size ships in 2003 and 2004, it ushered in an era of new ship-

Pool deck after dark

building that has seen the fleet grow faster than any other European cruise line. This line is growing into a major player in both Europe and the Caribbean, where it plans to have a year-round presence.

☎ 800/666–9333
⊕ *www.msccruisesusa.com*
☞ *Cruise Style: Premium.*

MSC blankets the Mediterranean nearly year-round with a dizzying selection of cruise itineraries that allow a lot of time in ports of call and include few if any sea days. In summer months, several ships sail off to northern Europe to ply the Baltic. Itineraries planned for repositioning sailings visit some intriguing, off-the-beaten-track ports of call that other cruise lines bypass.

No glitz, no clutter—just elegant simplicity—is the standard of MSC's seaworthy interior decor. Extensive use of marble, brass, and wood reflects the best of Italian styling and design; clean lines and bold colors set their modern sophisticated tone.

MSC adopts some activities that appeal to American passengers without abandoning those preferred by Europeans; however, regardless of the itinerary, be prepared for an Italian-influenced experience. Also expect to hear announcements in several languages.

Food
Dinner on MSC ships is a traditional multiple-course event centered on authentic Italian fare. Menus list Mediterranean regional specialties and classic favorites prepared from scratch. Some favorites include lamb-and-mushroom quiche (a Tuscan dish) and veal

scaloppini with tomatoes and mozzarella (a recipe from Sorrento in Campania). Although food is still prepared the Italian way, in a nod to American tastes broiled chicken breast, grilled salmon, and Caesar salad are additions to the dinner menu that are always available. Healthy Choice and vegetarian items are offered as well as tempting sugar-free desserts. A highlight is the bread, freshly baked on board daily. Pizza served in the buffet is some of the best at sea. The midnight buffet is a retro food feast missing from most of today's cruises. Room service is always available, though the options are somewhat limited.

Entertainment

In addition to the guest lecturers, computer classes, and cooking lessons featured in the enrichment programs, Italian-language classes are a popular option. Nightly shows accentuate the cruise line's Mediterranean heritage; there might be a flamenco show in the main show room and live music for listening and dancing in the smaller lounges, although the disco is a happening late-night spot.

MSC entertainment staff members shine offstage as well as in front of the spotlight. They seek out passengers traveling solo, who might be looking for activity or dance partners, so that they feel fully included in the cruise.

Fitness and Recreation

Up-to-date exercise equipment, a jogging track, and basic fitness classes for all levels are available in the fitness centers.

Spa treatments include a variety of massages, body wraps, and facials that can be scheduled à la carte or combined in packages to encompass an afternoon or the entire cruise. The hottest hair-styling techniques and nail services are offered in the salons. Unlike most cruise lines, MSC Cruises operates its own spas.

Your Shipmates

Most passengers are couples in the 35- to 55-year-old range, as well as some family groups who prefer the international atmosphere prevalent on board. Although more than half the passengers on Caribbean itineraries are North Americans, expect a more international mix on European cruises, with North Americans in the minority.

Dress Code

Two formal nights are standard on seven-night cruises, and three may be scheduled on longer sailings. Men are

KNOWN FOR

■ **Affordability:** MSC affords a contemporary cruise experience at favorable price points.

Eco-Friendliness: If you're looking for a "green" cruise, MSC Cruises has received many awards for its commitment to safeguarding the environment.

■ **Family-Friendliness:** With a kids-sail-free policy, MSC Cruises' ships are ideally suited for family cruise vacations.

■ **Italian Heritage:** MSC embraces its Italian heritage and style—not to flaunt it, but to share it.

■ **Sophia Loren:** An Italian treasure, the iconic movie actress serves as godmother to MSC's ships.

Top: Miniature golf is family fun
Bottom: *MSC Lirica*

5

MSC CRUISES

encouraged to wear dark suits, but sport coats and ties are appropriate. All other evenings are casual, although jeans are discouraged in restaurants. It's requested that no shorts be worn in public areas after 6 pm.

Junior Cruisers

MSC Cruises is particularly family friendly with its year-round "kids sail free" program for children 11 and younger and reduced rates for children ages 12 to 17 on all ships and all itineraries. Children ages 3 to 17 are welcome to participate in age-appropriate youth programs. The Mini Club is for ages 3 to 8, Junior Club for ages 9 to 12, and Teenage Club for youths 13 years and older. Counselors organize daily group activities such as arts and crafts, painting, treasure hunts, games, a mini-Olympics, and shows. Children under age three may use the playroom if accompanied at all times by an adult. Babysitting can be arranged for a fee once you're on board.

Service

Service can be inconsistent, yet it's more than acceptable, even if it's not overly gracious. The mainly Italian staff can seem befuddled by American habits and expectations. Ongoing training and improved English proficiency for staff are top priorities for MSC, and those weaknesses have shown improvement.

Tipping

Customary gratuities are added to your shipboard account for adults (18 and over) in the amount of €7 when sailing in Europe on cruises of eight nights or less, €6 per night for cruises nine nights or longer; gratuities of US$12 per person per day are charged on Caribbean sailings. Half of those amounts are charged for children age 3 to 17; there is no gratuity charge for children under age three. You can always adjust these amounts at the reception desk but payment in cash is discouraged. Automatic 15% gratuities are incorporated into all bar purchases. You may also reward staff in the spa and casino for exceptional service.

Top: Thermal suite
Middle: Expansive pool deck
Bottom: *MSC Lirica* suite with balcony

CHOOSE THIS LINE IF ...

You appreciate authentic Italian cooking. This is the real thing, not an Olive Garden clone.

You want your ship to look like a ship. MSC's vessels are very nautical in appearance.

You want the Continental flair of a premium cruise at a fair price.

Past Passengers

After sailing on MSC Cruises once, you are eligible to join the MSC Club by completing the registration form found in your cabin or by writing to the club through the line's website. Membership benefits include discounts on your cruise fare for the best itineraries, travel cancellation insurance, shore excursions, and even onboard purchases. You will also receive MSC *Club News* magazine.

Membership levels are achieved on a point system determined by the number of cruises taken. Classic members have up to 21 points; Silver, between 22 and 42 points; Gold, 43 points and over. Silver and Gold members receive pins to commemorate their status.

HELPFUL HINTS

All-inclusive packages for adults and children may be purchased before boarding, and the packages even include stateroom minibar.

For cruises in Europe, as well as transatlantic cruises departing from Europe, the onboard currency is the euro; in the Caribbean it's the U.S. dollar.

To give young passengers under age 18 a taste of independence without overspending their allowance, parents can purchase a prepaid Teen Card for use on board.

You may gamble up to a maximum of €2,000 per day in the casino if you link your key card to a credit card.

Entertainment is designed with the nationality and preferences of the passengers in mind and shows are introduced by a multilingual host in Italian, English, French, German, and Spanish.

5

MSC CRUISES

DON'T CHOOSE THIS LINE IF ...

Announcements in more than one language get on your nerves.

You aren't able to accept things that are not always done the American way.

You prefer myriad dining choices and casual attire. MSC cruises have assigned seating and observe a dress code.

FANTASIA-CLASS
MSC Fantasia, Splendida, Divina, Preziosa

CREW MEMBERS	1,332
ENTERED SERVICE	2008, 2009, 2012, 2013
GROSS TONS	137,936, 137,936, 140,000, 139,400
LENGTH	1,093 feet
NUMBER OF CABINS	1,637, 1,637, 1,739, 1,751
PASSENGER CAPACITY	3,274, 3,274, 3,502, 3,502
WIDTH	124 feet

700 ft.
500 ft.
300 ft.

MSC Cruises' newest ships are also their largest and include the MSC Yachts Club—luxury suites with their own private library, lounge, swimming pool, restaurant, and sundeck. The spa's well-being center has a thermal cave and therapy pool for relaxation. The children's play area includes a swimming pool with water-slide. To test your driving skills, there are Formula 1 simulators. Unusual for a cruise ship, there is also a squash court. The extensive use of various colored marbles adds a luxurious quality to the traditionally styled public lounges and a hint of Italian style as well as art deco and art nouveau touches.

MSC Cruises has always been sensitive to environmental issues, and Fantasia-class ships are on the cutting edge ecologically. They are equipped with the most innovative technological systems to guarantee savings in energy and protection of the environment, such as the water-processing systems. *MSC Divina* has a stunning infinity pool at the back of the ship.

Cabins

Cabins: A whopping 80% of staterooms have an ocean view, and 95% of those have balconies. All accommodations are beautifully decorated and comfortable yet still somewhat smaller than comparable cabins on other lines. All are furnished with two twin beds that can be combined to create a king, a vanity-desk, TV, Ethernet connection for use with laptops, adequate closet and storage space, small refrigerator, and hair dryer.

Suites: Yacht Club Suites have access to a private lounge with complimentary bar and a sundeck with swimming pool, bar, and small buffet. Some suites do not have balconies, but all have access to a concierge and butler service, including laundry, dry-cleaning, and pressing services. Amenities include a Nintendo Wii console, pillow menu, complimentary minibar, Egyptian-cotton sheets, slippers and robe during the cruise, walk-in closets, and marble bathrooms with bathtubs. Standard suites are comparable in size to minisuites on most cruise ships. They feature a combination tub-shower in the bathroom, plenty of storage in a walk-in closet, and a sitting area.

Top: A cabin on *MSC Fantasia*
Bottom: Gambling in the ship's casino

Amenities: Bathrooms are supplied with MSC Cruises' own brand of shampoo, bath gel, and soaps, plus a handy sewing repair kit.

Accessibility: Forty-three cabins are wheelchair accessible (45 on *MSC Preziosa*), including two in the MSC Yacht Club.

Restaurants

The two-deck-high formal restaurant serves an open-seating breakfast and lunch; dinner is in two assigned seatings. Specialty restaurants (reservation, extra charge) serve Italian or Tex-Mex cuisine. The Lido buffet is the casual-dining option for all meals; at night, the buffet restaurant also serves pizza. Coffee bars are a good snack option for times when the buffet is closed, but there is a charge for coffee and pastries. Room service has a limited menu of Continental breakfast and cold sandwiches. Midnight buffets vary nightly, ranging from snacks to a gala affair.

Spas

The Zen-like, Asian-inspired Aurea Spa offers a full menu of treatments, some of them Asian-inspired as well. The large therapy pool and thermal suite, which has a Turkish bath and sauna, are complimentary for occupants of Yacht Club accommodations and available to all for a daily fee.

Bars and Entertainment

After dinner, the coffee bars are the main social gathering spots, as is customary on European ships. Elaborate evening entertainment in the show lounges is designed for multilingual audiences and relies on sight and familiarity with musical selections rather than language. Bars and lounges range from sports bars, piano bars, and cigar lounges to high-energy dance spots, with the entertainment staff on hand to get things going. More sedate bars are also available for a quiet nightcap.

Pros and Cons

Pros: the buffet is huge, with several serving areas and plenty of seating; extra-charge ice cream parlors serve excellent gelato; the ship's atrium is designed as a gorgeous Italian piazza.

Cons: the Yacht Club sundeck can sometimes be uncomfortably windy; although there is an outdoor big-screen cinema, it's most often used for cruise line–related messages; currency on board is the euro when sailing in Europe.

Cabin Type	Size (sq. ft.)
Yacht Club Suites	237–549*
Standard Suite with Balcony	290
Ocean-View Balcony	194
Ocean View	183–218
Inside	172

*Some forward-facing Yacht Club Suites do not have balconies.

FAST FACTS

- 13 passenger decks
- Specialty restaurants, 3 dining rooms, buffet, ice cream parlor, pizzeria
- Internet, Wi-Fi, safe, refrigerator
- 3 pools (1 indoor), children's pool
- Fitness classes, gym, hot tubs, sauna, spa, steam room
- 13 bars, casino, dance club, library, show room, video game room
- Children's programs
- Laundry service
- Internet terminal
- No-smoking cabins

5

MSC CRUISES

Colorful shipboard decor

NORWEGIAN CRUISE LINE

Norwegian Cruise Line (originally known as Norwegian Caribbean Line) set sail in 1966 with
an entirely new concept: regularly
scheduled Caribbean cruises from
the then-obscure port of Miami.
Good food and friendly service
combined with value fares estab-

Cirque du Soleil–style extravaganza on
Norwegian Cruise Line

lished Norwegian as a winner for active adults and families. With the
introduction of the now-retired SS *Norway* in 1979, Norwegian ushered in the era of cruises on megasize ships. Innovative and forward-
looking, Norwegian has been a cruise-industry leader for four
decades, and is as much at home in Europe as it is in the Caribbean.

☎ *305/436–4000 or*
800/327–7030
⊕ *www.ncl.com*
☞ *Cruise Style:*
Mainstream.

Noted for top-quality, high-energy entertainment and
emphasis on fitness facilities and programs, Norwegian combines action, activities, and a variety of dining
options in a casual, free-flowing atmosphere. Freestyle
cruising signaled an end to rigid dining schedules and
dress codes. Norwegian ships now offer a host of flexible dining options that allow passengers to eat in the
main dining rooms or any of a number of à la carte and
specialty restaurants at any time and with whom they
please. Now co-owned by Genting Hong Kong Limited
and Apollo Management, a private equity company,
Norwegian continues to be an industry innovator.

From a distance, most cruise ships look so similar that
it's often difficult to tell them apart, but Norwegian's
largest, modern ships stand out with their distinctive
use of hull art. Each new ship is distinguished by murals
extending from bow to midship.

Food
Main dining rooms serve what is traditionally deemed
Continental fare, although it's about what you would
expect at a really good hotel banquet. Health-conscious
menu selections are nicely prepared, and vegetarian
choices are always available. Where Norwegian really

shines is the specialty restaurants, especially the French-Mediterranean Le Bistro (on all ships), the pan-Asian restaurants, and steakhouses (on the newer ships). As a rule of thumb, the newer the ship, the wider the variety, because new ships were purpose-built with as many as 10 or more places to eat. You may find Spanish tapas, an Italian trattoria, a steakhouse, a pub, and a pan-Asian restaurant complete with a sushi and sashimi bar and teppanyaki room. Most carry a cover charge or are priced à la carte and require reservations. A Norwegian staple, the late-night Chocoholic Buffet continues to be a favorite event.

Entertainment

More high jinks than highbrow, entertainment after dark features extravagant Las Vegas–style revues presented in main show lounges by lavishly costumed singers and dancers. Other performers might include comedians, magicians, jugglers, and acrobats. Passengers can get into the act by taking part in talent shows or step up to the karaoke microphone. Live bands play for dancing and listening in smaller lounges, and each ship has a lively dance club. Some ships include shows by Chicago's world-famous Second City improvisational comedy company. With the launch of *Norwegian Epic* in 2010, the Blue Man Group and Cirque Productions (a U.S.-based company somewhat similar in style to Cirque du Soleil) joined Norwegian's talent lineup.

Casinos, bingo sessions, and art auctions are well attended. Adult games, particularly the competitive ones, are fun to participate in and provide laughs for audience members. Goofy pool games are a Norwegian staple, and the ships' bands crank up the volume during afternoon and evening deck parties.

Fitness and Recreation

Mandara Spa offers exotic spa treatments fleet-wide on Norwegian, although facilities vary widely. Spa treatments include a long menu of massages, body wraps, and facials, and current trends in hair and nail services are offered in the salons. The latest addition on board is a medi-spa physician, who can create individualized treatment plans using nonsurgical treatments such as Botox Cosmetic. State-of-the-art exercise equipment, jogging tracks, and basic fitness classes are available at no charge. There's a fee for personal training, body composition analysis, and specialized classes such as yoga and Pilates.

KNOWN FOR

■ **Casual Atmosphere:** With no dress code, Norwegian's ships have shed the "stuffy" reputation of cruises in the past.

■ **Dining Options:** Norwegian Cruise Line is an industry innovator in onboard dining, from open-seating dining rooms to specialty restaurants.

■ **Entertainment:** Their partnership with widely recognized acts and shows has made Norwegian a leader in entertainment at sea.

■ **Family-Friendliness:** Numerous connecting staterooms and suites on Norwegian's ships can be combined to create multicabin accommodations ideal for families.

■ **Itineraries:** With some exceptions, Norwegian's sailings don't stray far from the tried-and-true one-week length.

5

NORWEGIAN CRUISE LINE

Norwegian Jewel spa relaxation suite

Your Shipmates

Norwegian's mostly American cruise passengers are active couples ranging from their mid-thirties to mid-fifties. Many families enjoy cruising on Norwegian ships during holidays and summer months. Longer cruises and more exotic itineraries attract passengers in the over-55 age group.

Dress Code

Resort casual attire is appropriate at all times; the option of one formal evening is available on all cruises of seven nights and longer. Most passengers actually raise the casual dress code a notch to what could be called casual chic attire.

Junior Cruisers

For children and teens, each Norwegian vessel offers a Splash Academy program of supervised entertainment for young cruisers ages 3 to 17. Younger children are split into three groups, ages 3 to 5, 6 to 9, and 10 to 12; activities range from storytelling, games, and arts and crafts to dinner with counselors, pajama parties, and treasure hunts. The program now also offers activities for kids from six months to three years old. "Guppies" offers their parents the opportunity to engage in a variety of sensory-based programs with them, including baby art, storytelling, and a parent and baby mini-workout. Certain ships feature Nickelodeon programming, and the presence of favorite characters is a highlight for junior cruisers.

Group Port Play is available in the children's area to accommodate parents booked on shore excursions. Evening babysitting services are available for a fee. Parents whose children are not toilet trained are issued a beeper to alert them when diaper changing is necessary. Reduced fares are charged for third and fourth guests in the same stateroom, including all children. Infants under six months of age cannot travel on Norwegian ships.

For teens ages 13 to 17, options in the Entourage program include sports, pool parties, teen disco, movies, and video games. Some ships have their own cool clubs where teens hang out in adult-free zones.

Top: Casino play
Middle: Stay connected to the Internet.
Bottom: *Norwegian Dream* Superior Ocean-View stateroom

CHOOSE THIS LINE IF ...

Doing your own thing is your idea of a real vacation. You could almost remove your watch and just go with the flow.	You want to leave your formal dress-up wardrobe at home.	You're competitive. There's always a pickup game in progress on the sports courts.

Service

Somewhat inconsistent, service is nonetheless congenial. Although crew members tended to be outgoing Caribbean islanders in the past; they have largely been replaced by Asians and Eastern Europeans who are well trained yet are inclined to be more reserved.

Tipping

A fixed service charge of $12 per person per day for passengers three years of age and older is added to shipboard accounts. An automatic 15% gratuity is added to bar tabs. Staff members may also accept cash gratuities. Passengers in suites who have access to concierge and butler services are asked to offer a cash gratuity at their own discretion.

Past Passengers

On completion of your first Norwegian cruise you're automatically enrolled in Latitudes, the club for repeat passengers. Membership benefits accrue based on the number of cruise nights sailed: Bronze (1 through 19), Silver (20 through 47), Gold (48 through 75), and Platinum (75 or more). Everyone receives *Latitudes*, Norwegian's e-magazine, special pricing and check-in at the pier, a ship pin, access to a special customer service desk and liaison on board, and a members-only cocktail party. Higher tiers receive a welcome basket, an invitation to the captain's cocktail party and dinner in Le Bistro, and priority for check-in, tender tickets, and disembarkation. Milestone gifts are awarded at the 250, 500, 700, and 1,000 point levels.

HELPFUL HINTS

Norwegian's Signature Trio dining package saves you 15% if you book three dinners before sailing.

Popular Nickelodeon characters make regular appearances for photo opportunities on certain Norwegian ships and you don't have to pay for pictures if you use your own camera.

Although Norwegian has one of the newest fleets at sea, the oldest ships just don't have quite the panache or as many free-style dining venues as are found on the newer ships.

Children three years old and younger dine free in specialty restaurants, and children ages 4 to 12 can eat from the complimentary kids menu or a specialty kids menu for a reduced cover charge.

While the ships are family-friendly, the line has removed all its self-service laundries to add more inside staterooms.

5

NORWEGIAN CRUISE LINE

DON'T CHOOSE THIS LINE IF ...

You don't like to pay extra for food on a ship. All the best specialty restaurants have extra charges.

You don't want to stand in line. There are lines for nearly everything.

You don't want to hear announcements. They're frequent on these ships—and loud.

BREAKAWAY-CLASS
Norwegian Breakaway, Norwegian Getaway

CREW MEMBERS	1,640
ENTERED SERVICE	2013, 2014
GROSS TONS	146,600
LENGTH	1,062 feet
NUMBER OF CABINS	2,014
PASSENGER CAPACITY	4,028
WIDTH	130

Norwegian's newest class of ships is impressive, slightly smaller than *Norwegian Epic* but with improved flow in the main dining and entertainment district, 678 Ocean Place. A major innovation is the addition of outdoor dining at almost all specialty restaurants. You can check wait times and make reservations on digital screens throughout the ship. As on other Norwegian ships, entertainment is a strong suit and includes not only a Latin ballroom dance show and a full-fledged Broadway show. *Norwegian Breakaway* has a branch of Carlo's Bakery.

Outdoors, there an impressive ropes course on the sports deck, as well as five water slides and an aqua park for smaller kids. The kids and teen clubs are impressively large and offer a wide variety of programs and activities. The adults-only Vibe Beach Club has a cover charge. The ships' electronic screens now make reservations for dining and entertainment as well as giving wait times. Automated wine dispensers in the atrium and buffet let you buy a glass (or taste) whenever you want.

Cabins
Cabins: Cabin decor is more understated and modern, but balconies are small. Storage is merely adequate, with drawer space seriously lacking. Bathrooms are good-size, with small showers, or expansive multijet showers in minisuite categories and above, but few cabins have a tub. Sinks are quite large, and minisuites and above have extra-wide double sinks. All cabins have a safe, hair dryer, minibar, flat-screen TV, and improved lighting. Shower gel and shampoo dispensers (but no conditioner) are attached to shower walls.

Suites: Haven suites include access to an exclusive concierge lounge, restaurant, and shared private courtyard with pool, hot tub, sundeck, and small gym. Spa suites include access to the spa and its thermal suite throughout the cruise.

Studios: These small cabins are strictly for solo cruisers. Although each is tiny, it has a private bath, and occupants have access to the shared Studio Lounge.

Accessibility: Forty-two cabins are wheelchair accessible.

Top: *Breakaway's* Peter Max–designed hull
Bottom: *Norwegian Breakaway's* pool complex

Restaurants

Three main dining rooms serve open-seating breakfast, lunch, and dinner (the Manhattan Room has entertainment on some nights). There are myriad specialty restaurants, including Ocean Blue by Geoffrey Zakarian, which serves seafood (reservations, cover charge for all). Casual choices are the Lido buffet for all meals; O'Sheehan's Pub for sandwiches and snacks; and the poolside grill for lunch. The Atrium Bar serves specialty coffees and cakes for an additional charge; Carlo's Bakery serves specialty cakes as well as gelato for an extra charge (only on *Breakaway*). While the 24-hour room-service menu is limited, made-to-order pizza will be delivered to you anywhere on the ship for a fee.

Spas

The Mandara Spa is huge, with more than 50 treatment rooms offering both beauty and Medi-Spa treatments; a full-service salon; an expansive thermal suite with multiple pools and hot tubs, a heated salt room, sauna, steam room, and more than a dozen heated loungers; and an extensive health club with a wide range of machines and free weights, spinning classes in a dedicated room, and special exercise classes by the Rockettes (on *Norwegian Breakaway*).

Bars and Entertainment

Almost two-dozen bars are throughout the ship. These include an ice bar, Bliss Ultralounge (disappointing here), the outdoor Spice H2O, and the adults-only Vibe Beach Club. Entertainment is a strong suit, with a jazz and blues, dueling piano bar, *Burn the Floor* (a Latin Ballroom production show), Second City on *Breakaway* (to be replaced by a comedy club on *Getaway*), and *Rock of Ages* (on *Breakaway*) and *Legally Blonde* (on *Getaway*). There's a fireworks display one night per cruise. *Cirque Dreams* has a dedicated theater on *Breakaway*; on *Getaway* the space will be occupied by the Illusionarium magic experience. Most shows require free reservations.

Pros and Cons

Pros: you'll now find hand-washing stations outside the buffet; you can make make reservations on screens throughout the ship; there's a branch of Hoboken's Carlo's Bakery of "Cake Boss" fame.

Cons: at $49, Ocean Blue by Geoffrey Zakarian is expensive; most entertainment requires reservations; balcony size has been shrunk dramatically in most cabin categories.

Cabin Type	Size (sq. ft.)
Owner's Suite/ Family Villa	572, 543–545
Penthouse	334–505
Minisuite	236
Ocean View/ Ocean View with balcony	161–226, 204–366
Interior	129–194
Studio	97

Square footage includes balconies.

FAST FACTS

- 18 passenger decks
- Specialty restaurants, 3 dining rooms, buffet, ice cream parlor
- Wi-Fi, safe, refrigerator
- 3 pools, children's pool
- Fitness classes, gym, hot tubs, sauna, spa, steam room
- 22 bars, casino, dance club, library, show room, video game room
- Children's programs
- Dry-cleaning, laundry service
- Internet terminal, Wi-Fi
- No-smoking cabins

5

NORWEGIAN CRUISE LINE

NORWEGIAN EPIC

CREW MEMBERS	1,708
ENTERED SERVICE	2010
GROSS TONS	153,000
LENGTH	1,081 feet
NUMBER OF CABINS	2,114
PASSENGER CAPACITY	4,100
WIDTH	133 feet

700 ft.

500 ft.

300 ft.

NCL's newest and largest ship is all about the entertainment. While *Norwegian Epic* has a unique new cabin design and more than 20 places to dine, entertainment options include Blue Man Group, Howl at the Moon (a dueling-pianos show), the Second City comedy ensemble, Legends in Concert, and a theatrical dining experience with Cirque du Soleil–style performers. For the kids, there are Nickelodeon characters on board and a character breakfast. The only extra entertainment charges are for the Cirque dinner show and the character breakfast.

Also epic are the numerous bars and lounges. For the coolest drinks at sea, *Norwegian Epic* has an ice bar (for an extra charge). Expansive areas are reserved for children and teens and the aft pool is exclusively for adults during the day. The other pool area has three waterslides and a plethora of lounge chairs. For the best view of the sea, there is a rock-climbing wall.

Cabins

Cabins: *Epic*'s New Wave–style staterooms have curved walls and a unique bathroom with toilet and shower in separate compartments and the sink in the main cabin area. All have a sitting area with sofa and table and exceedingly generous storage. All outside staterooms have a balcony. Several spa-accommodations categories have Zen-like appointments and key card access to the spa facilities.

Courtyard Villas and Penthouses: Courtyard Villas and Penthouses and Owner's suites located in the Haven have an exclusive concierge lounge and restaurant in addition to a shared private courtyard with pool, hot tub, sundeck, and small gym.

Studios: These small cabins are strictly for solo cruisers. Although each is tiny, it has a private bath and occupants have access to the Studio Lounge, a shared lounge for hanging out.

Amenities: A small refrigerator, tea/coffeemaker, safe, Wi-Fi, duvets on beds, a wall-mounted hair dryer, and bathrobes are standard. Showers have a shampoo/bathgel dispenser on the wall. Suites have a whirlpool tub, an entertainment center with a CD/DVD player, and concierge and butler service. Spa Staterooms have complimentary access to the spa's thermal suite.

Top: *Norwegian Epic* casino
Bottom: *Norwegian Epic*
Courtyard Penthouse

Accessibility: Some staterooms interconnect in most categories. Forty-two staterooms are wheelchair accessible.

Restaurants

Two main dining rooms serve open-seating breakfast, lunch, and dinner. Specialty restaurants, including Norwegian's signature French restaurant Le Bistro, Cagney's Steakhouse, a Chinese restaurant, sushi bar, teppanyaki room, a South American churrascaria, and an Italian trattoria (reservations, cover charge for all). Screens located throughout the ship display wait times for tables. Casual choices are the Lido buffet for breakfast, lunch, and dinner; O'Sheehan's Pub for soup, sandwiches, and snacks; and the poolside grill for lunch. The Atrium Bar serves specialty coffees for an additional charge. While the 24-hour room-service menu is somewhat limited, made-to-order pizza will be delivered to you anywhere on the ship for a fee.

Spas

Mandara Spa offers unique and exotic spa treatments, including a long menu of massages, body wraps, facials, and teeth whitening. There is also a Medi-Spa physician on hand who can create individualized treatment plans using nonsurgical treatments that include Botox. The spa features a thermal suite with multitreatment therapy pool, wet and dry saunas, and relaxation area with heated lounges for which there is a charge.

Bars and Entertainment

Even though show reservations are required, almost all show options are available for no additional charge (Cirque Dreams & Dinner includes a dining charge). Bars and lounges run the gamut from a blues and jazz club, comedy club, an ice bar, martini bar, a beer and whiskey bar, and lounges with bowling alleys, including a pub. Most feature musicians for listening or dancing, but if you want a quiet getaway, the bar at the adult pool is open late for an alfresco nightcap.

Pros and Cons

Pros: restaurant and show reservations can be made prior to sailing; the ice bar cover charge includes drinks; the Haven offers more private amenities than older fleetmates.

Cons: the odd bathroom layout can be a privacy issue in standard cabins; reservations for dining and headline shows eliminates spontaneity; pools are great for cooling off but small for a ship this size.

Cabin Type	Size (sq. ft.)
Owner's Suite/ Courtyard Villa	852/506
Penthouse	322
Deluxe Balcony	245
Ocean View with Balcony	216
Inside	128
Studio	100

Square footage includes balconies.

FAST FACTS

- 19 passenger decks
- 8 restaurants, 2 dining rooms, buffet, ice cream parlor, pizzeria
- Internet, Wi-Fi, safe, refrigerator, DVD (some)
- 3 pools, children's pool
- Fitness classes, gym, hot tubs, spa
- 10 bars, casino, dance club, library, 3 show rooms, video game room
- Children's programs
- Dry-cleaning, laundry service
- Internet terminal
- No-smoking cabins

5

NORWEGIAN CRUISE LINE

Norwegian Epic at sea

DAWN-CLASS
Norwegian Star, Norwegian Dawn

CREW MEMBERS	1,066, 1,065
ENTERED SERVICE	2001, 2002
GROSS TONS	92,250, 91,740
LENGTH	965 feet
NUMBER OF CABINS	1,112, 1,174
PASSENGER CAPACITY	2,224, 2,348 (2,683 max)
WIDTH	105 feet

700 ft.
500 ft.
300 ft.

Purpose-built for Norwegian's Freestyle cruising concept, *Norwegian Dawn* and *Norwegian Star* each have more than a dozen dining options, a variety of entertainment selections, and expansive facilities for children and teens.

These ships introduced Norwegian's superdeluxe Garden Villa accommodations, English pubs, and 24-hour dining in the Blue Lagoon Restaurant. Interior spaces are bright and cheerful, especially the atrium area adjacent to the outdoor promenade, which is flooded with sunlight through expansive windows. A second smaller garden atrium with a prominent waterfall leads the way to the spa lobby. Near the children's splash pool is a hot tub for parents' enjoyment.

Cabins

Cabins: Norwegian ships are not noted for large staterooms, but all have a small sitting area with sofa, chair, and table. Most bathrooms are compartmentalized with a sink area, shower, and toilet separated by sliding glass doors. Every cabin has adequate closet and drawer/shelf storage, as well as limited bathroom storage. Suites have walk-in closets. Family-friendly staterooms interconnect in most categories, enabling families of nearly any size to find suitable accommodations. Nearly every stateroom has a third or fourth berth, and some can sleep as many as five and six.

Amenities: Cherrywood cabinetry, tropical decor, mirrored accents, a small refrigerator, tea/coffeemaker, personal safe, broadband Internet connection, duvets on beds, a wall-mounted hair dryer over the dressing table, and bathrobes for use during the cruise are standard. Bathrooms have a shampoo/bath-gel dispenser mounted on the shower wall as well as a magnifying mirror. Suites have a whirlpool tub, an entertainment center with a CD/DVD player, and concierge and butler service.

Accessibility: Twenty-four staterooms on *Norwegian Dawn* and 20 staterooms on *Norwegian Star* are designed for wheelchair accessibility.

Restaurants

Two complimentary dining rooms serve open-seating meals for breakfast, lunch, or dinner. Specialty restaurants, including Norwegian's signature French

Top: Cagney's Steakhouse on
Norwegian Dawn
Bottom: Minisuite

restaurant Le Bistro, Cagney's Steakhouse, an Asian restaurant, sushi bar, teppanyaki room, Tex-Mex eatery, and Italian restaurant carry varying cover charges and require reservations. Screens located throughout the ship illustrate the status (full, moderately busy, empty) and waiting time you can expect for each restaurant on board. Casual choices are the Lido buffet for breakfast, lunch, and dinner; Blue Lagoon for soup, sandwiches, and snacks around the clock; and the poolside grill for lunch. Java Café serves specialty coffees and pastries for an extra charge. Although the 24-hour room-service menu is somewhat limited, suite occupants may order from any restaurant on the ship.

Spas

The Mandara Spa treatments include a long menu of massages, body wraps, and facials as well as Medi-Spa treatment plans. With indoor lap pools, the enormous spas have what might be termed a supersize thermal suite on other ships. In addition, the pools are surrounded by lounge chairs, large whirlpools, saunas, and steam rooms; unfortunately, there is an additional charge to use these spa facilities.

Bars and Entertainment

After attending a high-energy production show, Second City comedy performance, or a show by a featured entertainer, options for the rest of the evening range from an elegant champagne bar to an authentic English pub. You'll find music for dancing, signature Norwegian parties, and even a cigar lounge. The Star Bar's pianist and views to sea are the perfect backdrop for a quiet nightcap.

Pros and Cons

Pros: show rooms have full proscenium stages for the lavish shows; you can look forward to performances by the improvisational company Second City; three-bedroom Garden Villas are among the largest suites at sea, with private whirlpools and outdoor patios.

Cons: Freestyle dining doesn't mean you get to eat precisely when you want; overcrowding can be a problem when the ships are fully booked; there is a charge for the most popular restaurants.

Cabin Type	Size (sq. ft.)
Garden Villa	5,350
Owner's Suite	750
Penthouse Suite	366
Romance Suite	288
Minisuite	229
Ocean View with Balcony	166
Ocean View	158
Inside	142

FAST FACTS

- 11 passenger decks
- 7 restaurants, 2 dining rooms, buffet, ice cream parlor, pizzeria
- Internet, Wi-Fi, safe, refrigerator, DVD (some)
- 2 pools (1 indoor), children's pool
- Fitness classes, gym, hot tubs, spa
- 9 bars, casino, 2 dance clubs, library, show room, video game room
- Children's programs
- Dry-cleaning, laundry service
- Internet terminal
- No-smoking cabins

5

NORWEGIAN CRUISE LINE

Norwegian Dawn at sea

JEWEL-CLASS

Norwegian Jewel, Norwegian Jade, Norwegian Pearl, Norwegian Gem

CREW MEMBERS	081, 1,075, 1,084, 1,092
ENTERED SERVICE	05, 2006, 2006, 2007
GROSS TONS	558, 93,530, 93,530
LENGTH	965 feet
NUMBER OF CABINS	1,201, 1,197, 1,197
PASSENGER CAPACITY	2,402, 2,394, 2,394
WIDTH	105 feet

700 ft.

9

500 ft.

300 ft.

Jewel-class ships are the next step in the continuing evolution of Freestyle ship design: the interior location of some public rooms and restaurants has been tweaked since the introduction of Freestyle cruising vessels, and new categories of deluxe accommodations have been added.

These ships have more than a dozen dining alternatives, a variety of entertainment options, and expansive areas reserved for children and teens. Pools have waterslides and a plethora of lounge chairs, although when your ship is full, it can be difficult to find one in a prime location. *Norwegian Pearl* and *Norwegian Gem* introduced the line's first rock-climbing walls, as well as Bliss Lounge, which has trendy South Beach decor, and the first full-size 10-pin bowling alleys on modern cruise ships.

Cabins

Cabins: Norwegian ships are not noted for large staterooms, but all have a small sitting area with sofa, chair, and table. Every cabin has adequate closet and drawer/shelf storage, as well as limited bathroom storage. Suites have walk-in closets. Some staterooms interconnect in most categories.

Garden and Courtyard Villas: Garden Villas, with three bedrooms, a living-dining room, and private deck garden with a spa tub, are among the largest suites at sea. Courtyard Villas—not as large as Garden Villas—have an exclusive concierge lounge and a shared private courtyard with pool, hot tub, sundeck, and small gym.

Amenities: A small refrigerator, tea/coffeemaker, personal safe, broadband Internet connection, duvets on beds, a wall-mounted hair dryer, and bathrobes are standard. Bathrooms have a shampoo/bath-gel dispenser on the shower wall and a magnifying mirror. Suites have a whirlpool tub, an entertainment center with a CD/DVD player, and concierge and butler service.

Accessibility: Twenty-seven staterooms are wheelchair accessible.

Restaurants

Two main complimentary dining rooms serve open-seating breakfast, lunch, and dinner. Specialty restaurants, including Norwegian's signature French restaurant Le Bistro, Cagney's Steakhouse, an Asian

Top: *Norwegian Jewel's* Azura restaurant
Bottom: Hydropool in the spa

restaurant, sushi bar, teppanyaki room, tapas and salsa eatery, and an Italian trattoria–style restaurant carry varying cover charges and require reservations. Screens located throughout the ship illustrate the status (full, moderately busy, empty) and waiting time you can expect for each restaurant on board. Casual choices are the Lido buffet for breakfast, lunch, and dinner; Blue Lagoon for soup, sandwiches, and snacks around the clock; and the poolside grill for lunch. Java Café serves specialty coffees and pastries for an additional charge. Although the 24-hour room-service menu is somewhat limited, suite occupants may order from any restaurant on the ship.

Spas

The Mandara Spa's treatments include a long menu of massages, body wraps, and facials and include the services of a Medi-Spa physician. Spa facilities include an enormous thermal suite with hydrotherapy pool, heated lounges, steam rooms, and saunas for which there is a charge.

Bars and Entertainment

Your evening might start with a high-energy production show, Second City comedy performance, or a show by a featured entertainer, then continue in the bar complex that includes a beer and whiskey bar, martini bar, and a champagne bar. You'll find music for dancing, signature Norwegian parties, and even a cigar lounge. The perfect spot to end the night is the Star Bar with its pianist and views of the pool deck and the sea.

Pros and Cons

Pros: there are both main-stage and nightclub performances by Second City; the ship's tranquil library offers a quiet escape with a sea view; Courtyard Villa accommodations are like a ship within a ship and have a private pool area.

Cons: there is a fee for use of the thermal suites in the spa; Freestyle dining doesn't mean you can get to eat precisely when you want to; for such a large ship, the Internet center is tiny.

Cabin Type	Size (sq. ft.)
Garden Villa	4,390
Courtyard Villa	574
Owner's Suites	823
Deluxe Owner's Suites*	928
Penthouse Suite	575
Minisuite	284
Ocean View with Balcony	205–243
Ocean View	161
Inside	143

*Deluxe Owner's Suites on *Norwegian Pearl* and *Norwegian Gem* only.

FAST FACTS

■ 15 passenger decks

■ 7 restaurants, 2 dining rooms, buffet, ice cream parlor, pizzeria

■ Internet, Wi-Fi, safe, refrigerator, DVD (some)

■ 2 pools, children's pool

■ Fitness classes, gym, hot tubs, spa

■ 9 bars, casino, dance club, library, show room, video game room

■ Children's programs

■ Dry-cleaning, laundry service

■ Internet terminal

■ No-smoking cabins

The sports deck

5

NORWEGIAN CRUISE LINE

NORWEGIAN SKY, NORWEGIAN SUN

CREW MEMBERS	917, 916
ENTERED SERVICE	1999, 2001
GROSS TONS	77,104, 78,309
LENGTH	853 feet
NUMBER OF CABINS	1,002, 968
PASSENGER CAPACITY	2,004, 1,936
WIDTH	105 feet

700 ft.
500 ft.
300 ft.

Norwegian Cruise Line hadn't introduced many new ships in awhile at the time *Norwegian Sky* was launched and *Norwegian Sun* was on the drawing board, but it didn't take long before they got the hang of it. With Freestyle cruising growing in popularity, the vessels moved into the forefront of the fleet with multiple restaurant choices, expansive casino, trendy spas, and more family- and kid-friendly facilities.

Rich wood tones and fabric colors prevail throughout. The Observation Lounge is a subdued spot for afternoon tea in a light, tropical setting with nothing to distract attention from the expansive views beyond the floor-to-ceiling windows.

The Internet café is large, and the nearby coffee bar is a delight. Sunshine pours into the atrium through an overhead skylight by day; at night it's the ship's glamorous hub of activity.

Cabins

Cabins: Staterooms are a bit more generous in size than on the previous vessels in the Norwegian fleet and contain adequate closet and drawer space for a one-week cruise. More than two-thirds have an ocean view, and nearly two-thirds of those have a private balcony. All have a sitting area with sofa, chair, and table. Clever use of primary colors and strategically placed mirrors achieve an open feeling. Connecting staterooms are available in several categories, including those with balconies. Oddly sandwiched in between decks 6 and 7 forward is deck 6A, which has no direct elevator access.

Suites: Suites have walk-in closets as well as whirlpool tubs and entertainment centers. Butlers and a concierge are at the service of suite occupants.

Amenities: Light-wood cabinetry, mirrored accents, a small refrigerator, a tea/coffeemaker, a personal safe, broadband Internet connections, duvets on beds, a wall-mounted hair dryer over the dressing table, and bathrobes for use during the cruise are typical standard amenities. Bathrooms have shampoo and bath gel in shower-mounted dispensers, as well as limited storage.

Accessibility: Sixteen cabins are wheelchair accessible.

Top: Las Ramblas Tapas Bar &
Restaurant
Bottom: *Norwegian Sun* at sea

Restaurants

Two complimentary dining rooms serve open-seating breakfast, lunch, and dinner. Specialty restaurants on both ships that carry varying cover charges and require reservations include Norwegian's signature French restaurant Le Bistro, steakhouses, and Italian eateries; *Norwegian Sun* also has an extra-charge Japanese restaurant, sushi bar, and teppanyaki room, and complimentary tapas bar. Screens located throughout the ship illustrate the status (full to empty) and waiting time you can expect for each restaurant. Casual choices are the Lido buffet for breakfast, lunch, and dinner; the poolside grill for lunch; a pizzeria; and an ice cream bar. A coffee bar serves specialty coffees and pastries priced by item. Room service is available 24 hours from a somewhat limited menu.

Spas

Although the facilities aren't as extensive as on newer ships, Mandara Spa offers a lengthy menu of massages, body wraps, and facials. A Medi-Spa physician is on hand to create individualized therapies. Each ship has saunas and steam rooms that are available to all at no extra charge.

Bars and Entertainment

You'll find a nice selection of bars and lounges where musicians or DJs provide dance tunes; the entertainment staff hosts Norwegian's signature late-night parties after performances by the production company; other nights, comedians or other entertainers perform in the main theater. Each ship has a top-deck lounge ideal for an intimate nightcap (*Norwegian Sky*) or complimentary tapas (*Norwegian Sun*).

Pros and Cons

Pros: many of the elements found in newer fleetmates have been added to these older ships; there is a hot tub exclusively for kids; *Norwegian Sun* has separate steam rooms and saunas for men and women.

Cons: the main restaurant is not on a direct route from the main atrium; these are sister ships but not twins, and dining facilities vary; standard accommodations are somewhat tight for more than two people.

Cabin Type	Size (sq. ft.)
Owner's Suite	828
Penthouse and Romance Suite	504
Minisuite	332
Ocean View with Balcony	221
Ocean View	145
Deluxe Interior	172
Interior	145

FAST FACTS

- 11 passenger decks
- 4 specialty restaurants, 2 dining rooms, buffet, ice cream parlor, pizzeria
- Wi-Fi, safe, refrigerator (some), DVD (some)
- 2 pools, children's pool
- Fitness classes, gym, hot tubs, sauna, spa, steam room
- 8 bars, casino, dance club, library, show room, video game room
- Children's programs
- Dry-cleaning, laundry service
- Internet terminal
- No-smoking cabins

Balcony stateroom

OCEANIA CRUISES

This distinctive cruise line was founded by Frank Del Rio and Joe Watters, cruise-industry veterans with the know-how to satisfy the wants of inquisitive passengers. By offering itineraries to interesting ports of call and upscale touches—all for fares much lower

Oceania's *Regatta*

than you would expect—they are succeeding quite nicely. Oceania Cruises set sail in 2003 to carve a unique, almost boutique niche in the cruise industry by obtaining midsize R-class ships that formerly made up the popular Renaissance Cruises fleet. The line is now owned by Prestige Cruise Holdings.

☎ 305/514–2300 or 800/531–5658
⊕ www.oceaniacruises. com
☞ Cruise Style: Premium.

Intimate and cozy public spaces reflect the importance of socializing on Oceania ships. Indoor lounges feature numerous conversation areas, and even the pool deck is a social center. The Patio is a shaded slice of deck adjacent to the pool and hot tubs. Defined by billowing drapes and carpeting underfoot, it is furnished with plush sofas and chairs ideal for relaxation.

Thickly padded single and double loungers are arranged around the pool, but if more privacy appeals to you, private cabanas are available for rent. Each one has a double chaise longue with a view of the sea; overhead drapery can be drawn back for sunbathing, and the side panels can be left open or closed. Waiters are on standby to offer chilled towels or serve occupants with beverages or snacks. In addition, you can request a spa service in your cabana.

Varied, destination-rich itineraries are an important characteristic of Oceania Cruises, and most sailings are in the 10- to 12-night range.

Food
Several top cruise-industry chefs were lured away from other cruise lines to ensure that the artistry of world-renowned master chef Jacques Pépin, who crafted

five-star menus for Oceania, is properly carried out. The results are sure to please the most discriminating palate. Oceania simply serves some of the best food at sea, particularly impressive for a cruise line that charges far less than luxury rates. The main restaurant offers trendy, French-Continental cuisine with an always-on-the-menu steak, seafood, or poultry choice and a vegetarian option.

Intimate specialty restaurants require reservations, but there's no additional charge for Toscana, the Italian restaurant, or Polo Grill, the steakhouse. On *Marina* and *Riviera,* passengers have those and more restaurants from which to choose—Jacques, the first restaurants to bear Jacques Pépin's name, serves French cuisine; Red Ginger features contemporary interpretations of Asian classics; Privée hosts private, seven-course menu degustation dinners for a single party of up to 10; and La Reserve serves exclusive wine and food pairings.

A casual dinner option is alfresco dining at the Terrace Café (the daytime Lido deck buffet). Although service is from the buffet, outdoor seating on the aft deck is transformed into a charming Mediterranean courtyard with candleholders and starched linens.

The Terrace Café also serves breakfast and lunch buffet-style, and has a small pizzeria window that operates during the day. At an outdoor poolside grill you can order up burgers, hot dogs, and sandwiches for lunch and then take a seat; waiters are at hand to serve you either at a nearby table or your lounge chair by the pool. Afternoon tea is a decadent spread of finger foods and includes a rolling dessert cart, which has to be seen to be believed.

Entertainment

Culinary demonstrations by guest presenters and Oceania's own executive chefs are extremely popular. Lectures on varied topics, computer courses, hands-on arts and crafts classes, and wine or champagne seminars round out the popular enrichment series on board. Before arrival in ports of call, lectures are presented on the historical background, culture, and traditions of the destinations.

Evening entertainment leans toward light cabaret, solo artists, music for dancing, and conversation with fellow passengers; however, you'll find lively karaoke sessions on the schedule as well. The sophisticated, adult atmosphere on days at sea is enhanced by a combo performing jazz or easy-listening melodies poolside. Enrichment programs feature guest lecturers who are experts in such

KNOWN FOR

■ **Cuisine:** Oceania Cruises' chefs are serious about food and serve noteworthy cuisine in all restaurants on board.

■ **Great Destinations:** Oceania itineraries are destination-oriented and offer overnights in many top ports.

■ **Midsize Ships:** Oceania's deluxe ships are quite manageable in size: three have fewer than 850 passengers, the largest fewer than 1,300 passengers.

■ **No Smoking:** Oceania ships are almost entirely smoke-free, with small, designated areas set aside for smokers.

■ **Surprisingly Affordable:** Cruises on Oceania approach true luxury in style, but not when it comes to fares—they are quite affordable.

Top: Penthouse suite
Bottom: Toscana Restaurant

5

OCEANIA CRUISES

topics as wine appreciation, culinary arts, history, and world events.

Fitness and Recreation

The Canyon Ranch SpaClub spas and salons and well-equipped fitness centers are adequate for the number of passengers on board. In addition to individual body-toning machines and complimentary exercise classes, there's a walking-jogging track circling the top of the ship. A personal trainer is available for individual instruction for an additional charge.

Your Shipmates

Oceania Cruises appeal to singles and couples from their late-thirties to well-traveled retirees who have the time for and prefer longer cruises. Most are American couples attracted to the casually sophisticated atmosphere, creative cuisine, and high level of service. Many are past passengers of the now-defunct Renaissance Cruises who are loyal to their favorite ships, which now offer a variety of in-depth destination-rich itineraries.

Dress Code

Leave the formal wear at home—attire on Oceania ships is country-club casual every evening, although some guests can't help dressing up to dine in the beautifully appointed restaurants. A jacket and tie are never required for dinner, but many men wear sport jackets, as they would to dine in an upscale restaurant ashore. Jeans, shorts, T-shirts, and tennis shoes are discouraged after 6 pm in public rooms.

Junior Cruisers

Oceania Cruises are adult-oriented and not a good choice for families, particularly those traveling with infants and toddlers. No dedicated children's facilities are available, and parents are completely responsible for their behavior and entertainment. Teenagers with sophisticated tastes (and who don't mind the absence of a video arcade) might enjoy the intriguing ports of call.

Top: Cocktails before dinner
Middle: Veranda stateroom
Bottom: Martini bar

CHOOSE THIS LINE IF ...

Socializing plays a more important role in your life-style than boogying the night away.

You love to read. These ships have extensive libraries that are ideal for curling up with a good book.

You have a bad back. You're sure to love the Tranquility Beds.

Service

Highly personalized service by a mostly European staff is crisp and efficient without being intrusive. Butlers are on hand to fulfill the requests of suite guests and will even assist with packing and unpacking when asked.

Tipping

Gratuities of $15 per person per day are added to shipboard accounts for distribution to stewards and waitstaff; an additional $7 per person per day is added for occupants of suites with butler service. Passengers may adjust the amount based on the level of service experienced. An automatic 18% gratuity is added to all bar tabs for bartenders and drink servers and to all bills for salon and spa services.

Past Passengers

After you take one Oceania cruise, you'll receive several benefits along with a free subscription to the *Oceania Club Journal*. Shipboard Club parties hosted by the captain and senior officers, complimentary amenities or exclusive privileges on select sailings, an Oceania Club membership recognition pin after 5, 10, 15, and 20 cruises, and special pricing and mailings about upcoming promotions are some of the benefits. Members further qualify for elite-level status based on the number of sailings aboard Oceania Cruises. Starting with your fifth cruise, you begin to accrue credit on every cruise you take, beginning with a $200 shipboard credit per stateroom on cruises five through nine. On your 10th cruise, you receive a $400 shipboard credit per stateroom plus complimentary gratuities on cruises 10 through 14. On your 15th cruise, you receive a $500 shipboard credit per stateroom, plus two complimentary spa treatments and complimentary gratuities on cruises 15 through 19. Once you take your 20th cruise, you get a free cruise as well as complimentary spa treatments, a shore excursion, and gratuities on all future cruises.

HELPFUL HINTS

Many Oceania voyages include airfare in the fare pricing.

Pre- or postcruise Hotel Collection Packages are available and include private group transfers.

There is never a dining charge on Oceania ships, but cocktail and wine prices are relatively high.

You may bring up to three bottles of wine per stateroom on board from ports of call, but there's a corkage fee of $25 per bottle if you bring wine to the dining room.

Oceania Cruises offers two shore excursion collections that must be reserved prior to sailing and can save a lot of money.

Oceania was the first cruise line to upgrade their bedding to the highest standard, so you can count on a good night's sleep on one of these ships.

5

OCEANIA CRUISES

DON'T CHOOSE THIS LINE IF ...

You like the action in a huge casino. Oceania casinos are small, and seats at a poker table can be difficult to get.

You want to bring your children. Most passengers book with Oceania anticipating a kid-free atmosphere.

Glitzy production shows are your thing. Oceania's show rooms are decidedly low-key.

MARINA, RIVIERA

CREW MEMBERS	800
ENTERED SERVICE	2011, 2012
GROSS TONS	65,000
LENGTH	774 feet
NUMBER OF CABINS	629
PASSENGER CAPACITY	1,258
WIDTH	105 feet

700 ft.

500 ft.

300 ft.

Marina and *Riviera* are the first brand-new ships built for Oceania Cruises and, although they are an all new design in a larger ship, they include the basic deluxe features found on the smaller fleetmates—specialty dining in intimate restaurants, country-club casual ambience, and enrichment programs. The emphasis is on destination cruising in style and the decor is classic and comfortable. With a larger ship, designers expanded some of the elements, such as the staircase in the grand foyer, which has a landing with two sweeping sets of steps.

Attention to detail is an Oceania hallmark that can be found in Privée—the private dining room that can be reserved for dinner parties—where a custom-made one-of-a-kind Lalique-crystal table is illuminated by a white Venini-glass chandelier, and fanciful Murano-glass chandeliers glitter in the buffet restaurant. A classical string quartet plays softly in the background at afternoon tea in Horizons, the observation lounge with dramatic floor-to-ceiling windows.

Cabins

Cabins: All accommodations have a vanity-desk and a seating area with sofa or chair and a table, generous closet and drawer/shelf storage, marble- and granite-clad bathrooms, hair dryer, robes for use during the cruise, safe, and refrigerator. Inside staterooms have a shower only; all other categories have a separate shower and bathtub. Oceania's Tranquility Beds are dressed in high thread-count linens. Concierge-level stateroom occupants are greeted with a bottle of champagne on ice and have access to a private concierge lounge, a laptop to use during the cruise, complimentary shoeshine and pressing services, priority dining reservations, designer toiletries, and a tote bag.

Suites: In addition to the concierge amenities, suites have an entertainment center with a DVD and CD player, a refrigerator, walk-in closet, an iPad for use during the cruise, and marble- and granite-bathrooms with a bathtub and designer toiletries. The top three suite categories have whirlpool tubs and separate showers and a guest powder room. Oceania Suites also have a media room, while Vista and Owner's suites have private workout rooms and iPod docking stations. Butlers are on hand to coordinate reservations and serve evening canapés and dinner ordered from the ship's restaurants.

Top: Balcony suite
Bottom: Barista's Coffee Bar

Accessibility: Six staterooms are designed to be wheelchair-accessible.

Restaurants

The Grand Dining Room serves open-seating breakfast, lunch, and dinner. Specialty restaurants require reservations, but there's no additional charge for Toscana, the Italian restaurant; Polo Grill, the steakhouse; the French cuisine served in Jacques, the first restaurant to bear Jacques Pépin's name; or Red Ginger, featuring contemporary interpretations of Asian classics. Also requiring reservations are the exclusive Privée, which hosts private seven-course-menu degustation dinners for a single party of up to 10; and La Reserve, where wine and food pairings are featured. The casual buffet restaurant is open for breakfast, lunch, and dinner. In addition, a poolside grill serves hamburgers and a variety of sandwiches and salads at lunchtime, and a pizzeria is in the buffet area. Room service is available 24 hours.

Spas

Canyon Ranch SpaClub offers a long menu of body wraps, massages with an Eastern influence, conditioning body scrubs, skin care and tanning treatments and acupuncture. Thermal suites include single-sex aromatic steam rooms. A highlight of the tranquil open-air Spa Terrace is a therapy whirlpool. All Concierge-level and suite guests have unlimited complimentary access to the private Spa Terrace; all other guests can purchase passes.

Bars and Entertainment

Bars and lounges have an intimate quality, from the martini bar where piano music is a played, to the show lounge offers small-scale entertainment ranging from headline acts and concerts to comedians and magicians. The observation lounge is a late night hot spot with dance music and even karaoke on tap.

Pros and Cons

Pros: Baristas coffee bar is adjacent to the library; the library is well stocked with more than 2,000 books and periodicals; artists share their expertise during hands-on classes in the enrichment center.

Cons: self-serve laundry rooms can be crowded on sea days; there is a fee to use the hot tub adjacent to the spa; there is no charge for food and service in Le Reserve, but wine is a pricey addition.

Cabin Type	Size (sq. ft.)
Owner's Suite/ Vista Suite	2,000/ 1,200– 1,500
Oceania Suite/ Penthouse Suite	1,000/420
Ocean View with Balcony	282
Ocean View/ Interior	242/174

FAST FACTS

- 11 passenger decks
- 6 specialty restaurants, 1 dining room, buffet, café, pizzeria
- Wi-Fi, safe, refrigerator, DVD (some)
- 1 pool
- Fitness classes, gym, hot tubs, sauna, spa, steam room
- 7 bars, casino, dance club, library
- Dry-cleaning, laundry facilities, laundry service
- Internet terminal, Wi-Fi
- No-smoking cabins

5

OCEANIA CRUISES

Martinis, *Marina*

INSIGNIA, REGATTA, NAUTICA

CREW MEMBERS	400
ENTERED SERVICE	1998, 1998, 2000
GROSS TONS	30,277
LENGTH	594 feet
NUMBER OF CABINS	342
PASSENGER CAPACITY	684 (824 max)
WIDTH	84 feet

Carefully furnished to impart the atmosphere of a private English country manor, these midsize ships are casual yet elegant, with sweeping central staircases and abundant flower arrangements. Brocade and toile fabrics window coverings, overstuffed sofas, and wing chairs create a warm and intimate feeling throughout. The entire effect is that of a weekend retreat in the English countryside.

Authentic-looking faux fireplaces are adjacent to cozy seating areas in the Grand Bar, near the martini bar's grand piano, and in the beautiful libraries—some of the best at sea, with an enormous selection of bestsellers, nonfiction, and travel books. The casinos are quite small and can feel cramped, and smoking is prohibited. Though there may be a wait for a seat at a poker table, there are enough slot machines to go around.

Other than decorative trompe-l'oeil paintings in several public areas, the artwork is unremarkable.

Cabins

Cabins: Private balconies outfitted with chairs and tables add additional living space to nearly 75% of all outside accommodations. All cabins have a vanity-desk and a seating area with sofa, chair, and table. Every cabin has generous closet and drawer/shelf storage and bathroom shelves. Owner's and Vista suites have a separate living-dining room, as well as a separate powder room. Concierge-level accommodations and above include an iPad for use during the cruise. Several cabins accommodate third and fourth passengers, but few have connecting doors.

Suites: Owner's and Vista suites have an entertainment center with a DVD and CD player, a small refrigerator, and a second TV in the bedroom; the main bathroom has a combination shower-whirlpool tub. Penthouse suites also have refrigerators and bathtubs. Butlers are on hand to coordinate reservations and serve evening canapés and dinner ordered from any of the ship's restaurants.

Amenities: Dark-wood cabinetry, soothing blue decor, mirrored accents, safe, Tranquility Beds, 350-thread-count linens, goose-down pillows, and silk-cut duvets are typical stateroom features. Bathrooms have a hair dryer, shampoo, lotion, and bath gel, plus robes.

Accessibility: Three staterooms are designed for wheelchair accessibility.

Top: Teatime in Horizons
Bottom: Breakfast in bed

Restaurants

Oceania passengers enjoy the flexibility of four open-seating restaurants. The Grand Dining Room, open for breakfast, lunch, and dinner, serves Continental cuisine. Alternative, reservations-required dinner options are Toscana, which serves gourmet Italian dishes, and Polo Grill, the steakhouse. Terraces, the buffet restaurant, serves breakfast, lunch, and dinner and is transformed into Tapas on the Terrace after dark for a relaxed atmosphere and alfresco dining. All dining venues have nearby bars, and there's no additional cover charge for dining. In addition, a poolside grill serves hamburgers and a variety of sandwiches and salads at lunchtime, and there is a pizzeria in the buffet area. Afternoon tea is an elaborate affair served in Horizons, the observation lounge. Room service is available 24 hours.

Spas

The Canyon Ranch SpaClub offers a long menu of body wraps, massages, conditioning body scrubs, skin care and tanning treatments, and acupuncture. Thermal suites include complimentary single-sex aromatic steam rooms. A highlight of the tranquil open-air Spa Terrace is a therapy whirlpool, to which all Concierge-level and suite guests have unlimited complimentary access; all other guests must purchase passes.

Bars and Entertainment

Bars and lounges have an intimate quality, from the martini bar, where piano music is played, to the show lounge that offers small-scale cabaret-style entertainment ranging from headline acts and concerts to comedians and magicians. The observation lounge is a late-night hot spot with music for dancing and even karaoke led by the entertainment staff.

Pros and Cons

Pros: a relaxed, social atmosphere pervades all areas on board; the lobby staircase is a must-see—it's practically identical to the one in the movie *Titanic*; on board, you'll find some of the most lavish afternoon teas at sea.

Cons: shipboard charges can add up fast, because drink prices and even Internet services are on the high side; there is only one self-serve laundry room; the absence of a sauna in the spa is an unfortunate oversight.

Cabin Type	Size (sq. ft.)
Owner's	962
Vista Suite	786
Penthouse Suite	322
Concierge/Ocean View with Balcony	216
Deluxe Ocean View	165
Standard Ocean View	150–165
Inside	160

FAST FACTS

- 9 passenger decks
- 2 specialty restaurants, dining room, buffet, pizzeria
- Wi-Fi, safe, refrigerator, DVD (some)
- 1 pool
- Fitness classes, gym, hot tubs, spa, steam room
- 4 bars, casino, dance club, library, show room
- Dry-cleaning, laundry facilities, laundry service
- Internet terminal
- No-smoking cabins

5

OCEANIA CRUISES

Regatta at sea

PAUL GAUGUIN CRUISES

With one ship built specifically to sail the waters of Tahiti, French Polynesia, and the South Pacific and synonymous with luxury and exotic destinations, Paul Gauguin Cruises remains a top choice for discerning travelers and honeymooners. The MS *Paul Gauguin*

Tere Moana cruising

has been in service since 1998 and lays claim to being the only luxury ship in history to have offered a single-destination focus and high level of expertise on a year-round basis for such an extended period of time. The line now has a second ship that will sail in Europe and the Caribbean.

☎ *800/848–6172*
⊕ *www.pgcruises.com*
☞ *Cruise Style: Luxury.*

The well-loved ship sailed for more than a dozen years under the flag of Radisson (later Regent) Seven Seas Cruises until the ship was sold. Paul Gauguin Cruises began in 2010 with the single ship when the *Paul Gauguin* was acquired by Pacific Beachcomber SC, the largest luxury hotel and cruise operator in French Polynesia. To offer similarly luxurious cruises in other regions—Europe in summer months and the Caribbean during the winter season—the line introduced a second vessel, MV *Tere Moana* in 2012.

Intimate and luxurious, Paul Gauguin ships offer a cruise experience tailored to the regions in which they sail. On board you can enjoy a dip in the swimming pool or simply relax poolside in a deck chair, with a good book and a beverage from the nearby bar. You won't want to miss the Fare Tahiti art exhibit in front of La Veranda restaurant on *Paul Gauguin*, although you may want to bring your own reading material as the library has only a few shelves of mostly English-language books. Passengers aboard *Tere Moana* fare a bit better with a larger library. A relaxed atmosphere prevails throughout both vessels, but the cruise line definitely has a split personality, with voyages on MS *Paul Gauguin* limited to the

South Pacific and those of MV *Tere Moana* as varied as the Caribbean and Europe.

Food

On each ship, the main dining room, L'Etoile, serves French food with Polynesian flair and is open only for dinner. For breakfast and lunch, you either order off the menu or make your selections from the extensive buffet in La Veranda, which often features fare with an international theme. In the evening, La Veranda is transformed into an elegant, reservation-only dining venue featuring gourmet cuisine. In 2013, the culinary creations of Jean-Pierre Vigato, chef and owner of the Michelin two-star Restaurant Apicius in Paris, made their appearance on Paul Gauguin Cruises vessels—in L'Etoile aboard *Tere Moana* and in La Veranda on the *Paul Gauguin*. The latter also has Le Grill for a more casual dining experience for all meals; breakfast is a buffet, and lunch includes a choice of grilled favorites, salads, and fresh tropical fruits, while dinner features Polynesian specialties in a relaxed atmosphere.

All beverages, including soft drinks, spirits, beer, wine, and bottled water are included in the fare, and wines chosen to complement the menu are served at lunch and dinner. There is a separate charge for premium wines by the bottle and some other premium alcohol. For those on special diets, three options—vegetarian, light and healthy, and no salt—are available.

Entertainment

Excellent musicians with extensive play lists perform for listening and dancing from the sail-away party through the last farewell. *Paul Gauguin* features Les Gauguines, a group of talented young Tahitian women, who travel with the ship to teach passengers about French Polynesia, as well as to sing, dance, and share the lore of their homeland. These young ladies add a dimension to the cruise that is not available anywhere else. Entertainment aboard *Tere Moana* is as varied as the destinations she visits, but always reflects the spirit of the region through which she is sailing. Nevertheless, entertainment aboard *Moana* is on a smaller scale, befitting a ship with only 90 passengers. Guest lecturers are popular on both ships. The small casino on *Paul Gauguin* offers gaming tables and slot machines; *Tere Moana* has no casino.

Fitness and Recreation

The line's spas and fitness centers are on the small side, as would be expected on ships carrying fewer than 350 guests. Each ship features the high-end Deep Nature Spa by Algotherm, noted for combining the art of gentle

5

PAUL GAUGUIN CRUISES

Ocean View stateroom

Top: La Veranda
Bottom: The sun deck on *Tere Moana*

pampering with services that are tailored to each individual. Fitness centers are equipped with Lifecycles, treadmills, elliptical trainers, and weight machines. From the onboard water-sports marina, you can go kayaking, windsurfing, or paddle boarding. *Paul Gauguin* features an exclusive, optional PADI scuba-diving program.

Your Shipmates

Paul Gauguin Cruises attracts passengers of all ages, and on *Paul Gauguin* especially you'll see young honeymooners mingling with mature well-traveled couples. Most enjoy the relaxed atmosphere on board in addition to the exotic ports and unique experiences ashore.

Dress Code

Elegant resort casual attire is appropriate at all times. Slacks and a golf or sport shirt for men and sporty dresses or skirts or pants with a sweater or blouse for women are suggested for evening. Jackets are not required, but many men bring along a sport coat for the Captain's Welcome Reception.

Junior Cruisers

There are no dedicated children's facilities or youth programs on board either ship. However, on the MS *Paul Gauguin,* the Ambassadors of the Environment Youth program, created in collaboration with Jean-Michel Cousteau's Ocean Futures Society, is offered on select sailings. The program introduces participants ages 9 to 17 to the ecological wonders of Tahiti and French Polynesia by exploring coral reefs, hiking rain forest trails, and visiting ancient Polynesian temples. Otherwise, not many kids travel on these ships, and there is nothing comparable on the *Moana*.

Service

Service is attentive, but not intrusive. Top accommodations categories have butlers to provide an additional level of attention.

Tipping

Tipping is neither required nor expected, though passengers can contribute to the crew welfare fund.

CHOOSE THIS LINE IF ...

You have a taste for exploring exotic regions and ports; these ships go to places large cruise ships cannot go.

You enjoy a social atmosphere with low-key entertainment; these are not traditional cruises with lots of nightly options.

You love water sports; both ships have excellent water sports offerings.

Past Passengers

Guests become members of the Paul Gauguin Society on completion of their first cruise and receive savings of 5% when reserving subsequent voyages.

HELPFUL HINTS

Some premium liquors, specialty wines, and certain cognacs incur an additional charge.

Groups of 10 or more travelers get an additional 5% discount off the applicable cruise fares.

Tips are included, but passengers can make a donation at the purser's office to the Crew Welfare Fund, which is used for crew parties and events.

The itinerary can be changed if you charter the full ship, provided that embarkation and debarkation ports remain as published.

With Paul Gauguin Personalized Services (PGPS), as a guest of *Tere Moana*, you can book private tours and service arranged and customized for you.

5

PAUL GAUGUIN CRUISES

DON'T CHOOSE THIS LINE IF ...

You never set sail without a tuxedo; these cruises offer a luxurious atmosphere but with very little formality.

Your preference is for a full schedule of high-energy activities; the focus on these cruises is off the ship.

You use a scooter for mobility. These ships are older and smaller and just can't accommodate them.

TERE MOANA

CREW MEMBERS	57
ENTERED SERVICE	1999
GROSS TONS	3,504
LENGTH	330 feet
NUMBER OF CABINS	45
PASSENGER CAPACITY	90
WIDTH	46 feet

700 ft.

500 ft.

300 ft.

The second vessel acquired by Paul Gauguin Cruises originally entered service in 1999 for French cruise line Compagnie du Ponant Cruises as *Le Levant*. After an extensive multimillion-dollar, multifaceted renovation, the boutique ship debuted as *Tere Moana* with a luxurious new look—chic and stylish with Polynesian touches similar to her fleetmate *Paul Gauguin*—in late 2012. The extreme makeover of *Tere Moana* included new furniture, upholstery, art, lighting, wall coverings, carpeting, ceiling finishes, window treatments, flooring, floor coverings, and a soft color palette throughout.

More megayacht than cruise ship, *Tere Moana*'s public spaces are small but include a high-end spa, a small fitness center equipped with the latest cardio and weightlifting equipment, and water-sports marina from where kayaking and paddle boarding are available in select ports. Although there are two restaurants, there is only one lounge for daytime lectures and nightly entertainment. You will find a generous library space on board but no casino. Deck space, with its pool, bar, chaise longues, and Balinese sun beds, is adequate for the small passenger complement.

Cabins
Cabins: All accommodations are luxuriously appointed with tasteful furnishings and decor in soothing tropical colors. Only eight staterooms have balconies, but all have an ocean view and contain amenities such as bathrobes for use during the cruise, slippers, hair dryer, flat-screen TV, CD/DVD player, safe, and a refrigerator stocked with soft drinks, beer, and bottled water. Queen-size beds dressed with fine linens and feather-down duvets are convertible to twin-bed configurations.

Bathrooms: Bathrooms are stocked with toiletries including shampoo, conditioner, moisturizer, and bath gel.

Accessibility: None of the accommodations is designed for wheelchair accessibility.

Restaurants
Open seating dinners in the formal restaurant L'Etoile are French-inspired and regionally infused by the destinations on the ship's itinerary, often featuring fresh ingredients from local markets. Open only for dinner, L'Etoile showcases culinary creations by Jean-Pierre Vigato, Chef of Apicius restaurant in Paris. For breakfast and lunch,

Top: *Tere Moana*
Bottom: Balcony stateroom, *Tere Moana*

you either order off the menu or make your selections from the extensive internationally themed buffet in La Veranda. Tea is also served in La Veranda, where seating is available indoors or on the adjacent deck. In the evening, La Veranda is transformed into an elegant, reservation-only dining venue featuring gourmet cuisine for which there is no charge. Complimentary wines chosen to complement the menu are freely poured at lunch and dinner. Room service is available around the clock, and select items from the L'Etoile menu can be ordered during dinner hours.

Spas

The luxurious Deep Nature Spa by Algotherm is noted for combining the art of gentle pampering with services that are uniquely tailored to each individual. A full menu of treatments includes facials utilizing an AlgoDerm machine, skin care therapies and exfoliation, massage, reflexology, aromatherapy, and body wraps. Unique treatments are the supreme "gold massage," inspired by traditional Russian massage methods, and AlgoSilhouette contouring, toning, and firming techniques. Use of the steam room is complimentary.

Bars and Entertainment

With only one lounge and a pool bar, organized evening entertainment aboard *Tere Moana* is limited. Le Salon is well suited as a venue for cabaret-size shows, either performed by the Paul Gauguin staff or a guest troupe from ashore. Live music is featured nightly for listening and dancing.

Pros and Cons

Pros: ship's small size means you'll get to know other passengers; dining is elegant, but the ambience is casual; the water-sports marina offers complimentary use of kayaks and paddleboards.

Cons: with a limited number of stateroom balconies, you'll have to plan ahead to get one; there are no facilities for children; the ship is not suitable for passengers requiring accessible accommodations.

Cabin Type	Size (sq. ft.)
Ocean View with Balcony	298*
Ocean View	161–194

*Square footage includes balcony.

FAST FACTS

- 5 passenger decks
- Specialty restaurant, dining room, buffet
- Wi-Fi, safe, DVD
- 1 pool
- Fitness classes, gym, spa, steam room
- 2 bars, show room
- Dry-cleaning, laundry service
- Internet terminal
- No-smoking cabins

5

PAUL GAUGUIN CRUISES

PRINCESS CRUISES

Princess Cruises may be best known for introducing cruise travel to millions of viewers, when its flagship became the setting for *The Love Boat* television series in 1977. Since that heady time of small-screen stardom, the Princess fleet has grown both in the num-

Splash around in the family pool.

ber and size of ships. Although most are large in scale, Princess vessels manage to create the illusion of intimacy through the use of color and decor in understated yet lovely public rooms graced by multimillion-dollar art collections.

☎ *661/753–0000 or 800/774–6237*
⊕ *www.princess.com*
☞ *Cruise Style: Premium.*

Princess has also become more flexible; Personal Choice Cruising offers alternatives for open seating dining (when you wish and with whom you please) and entertainment options as diverse as those found in resorts ashore.

Lovely chapels or the wide-open decks are equally romantic settings for weddings at sea with the captain officiating.

Food

Personal choices regarding where and what to eat abound, but because of the number of passengers, unless you opt for traditional assigned seating, you might have to wait for a table in one of the open seating dining rooms. Menus are varied and extensive in the main dining rooms, and the results are good to excellent, considering how much work is going on in the galleys. Vegetarian and healthy lifestyle options are always on the menu, as well as steak, fish, or chicken. A special menu is designed for children.

Alternative restaurants are a staple throughout the fleet but vary by ship class. Grand-class ships have upscale steakhouses and Sabatini's, an Italian restaurant; both require reservations and carry an extra cover charge. Sun-class ships offer complimentary sit-down dining in the pizzeria and a similar steak-house option, although it's in a sectioned-off area of the buffet restaurant. On *Caribbean, Crown, Emerald,* and *Ruby Princess,* a casual evening alternative to the dining rooms and usual buffet is Café Caribe—adjacent to the Lido buffet restaurant, it serves cuisine with a Caribbean flair. With a few breaks in service, Lido buffets on all ships are almost always open, and a pizzeria and grill offer casual daytime snack choices. The fleet's patisseries and ice cream bars charge for specialty coffee, some pastries, and premium ice cream. A daily British-style pub lunch served in the ships' Wheelhouse Bar has been introduced fleet-wide, with the exception of the Sun-class and smaller ships.

Ultimate Balcony Dining—either a champagne breakfast or full-course dinner—is a full-service meal served on your cabin's balcony. The Chef's Table allows guests (for a fee) to dine on a special menu with wine pairings. After a meeting with the executive chef in the galley (and some champagne and appetizers), guests sit at a special table in the dining room. The chef joins them for dessert.

Entertainment

The roster of adult activities still includes standbys like bingo and art auctions, but you'll also find guest lecturers, cooking classes, wine-tasting seminars, pottery workshops, and computer and digital photography classes. Nighttime production shows tend toward Broadway-style revues presented in the main show lounge, and performers might include comedians, magicians, jugglers, and acrobats. Live bands play a wide range of musical styles for dancing and listening, and each ship has a dance club. The cruise director's staff leads lively evenings of fun with passenger participation. At the conclusion of the second formal night, champagne trickles down in a waterfall, painstakingly created by the arrangement of glasses in a pyramid shape. Ladies are invited to join the maître d' to assist in the pouring for a great photo op.

Fitness and Recreation

Spa rituals include a variety of massages, body wraps, and facials; numerous hair and nail services are offered in the salons. Both the salons and spa are operated by Steiner Leisure, and the menu of spa services includes special pampering treatments designed specifically for men and teens as well as couples. For a half-day fee, escape to the Sanctuary—the adults-only haven—which offers a relaxing outdoor spa-inspired setting with signa-

Disco into the night.

ture beverages, light meals, massages, attentive service, and relaxing personal entertainment.

Modern exercise equipment, a jogging track, and basic fitness classes are available at no charge. There's a fee for personal training, body composition analysis, and specialized classes such as yoga and Pilates. Grand-class ships have a resistance pool so you can get your laps in effortlessly.

Your Shipmates

Princess Cruises attract mostly American passengers, ranging from their mid-thirties to mid-fifties. Families enjoy cruising together on the Princess fleet, particularly during holiday seasons and in summer months, when many children are on board. Longer cruises appeal to well-traveled retirees and couples who have the time.

Dress Code

Two formal nights are standard on seven-night cruises; an additional formal night may be scheduled on longer sailings. Men are encouraged to wear tuxedos, but dark suits are appropriate. All other evenings are casual, although jeans are discouraged, and it's requested that no shorts be worn in public areas after 6 pm.

Junior Cruisers

For young passengers ages 3 to 17, each Princess vessel (except *Ocean Princess* and *Pacific Princess*) has a playroom, teen center, and programs of supervised activities designed for different age groups: ages 3 to 7, 8 to 12, and 13 to 17. Activities to engage youngsters include arts and crafts, pool games, scavenger hunts, deck parties, backstage and galley tours, games, and videos. Events such as dance parties in their own disco, theme parties, athletic contests, karaoke, pizza parties, and movie fests occupy teenage passengers. With a nod toward science and educational entertainment, children also participate in learning programs focused on the environment and wildlife in areas where the ships sail.

Top: Sunset at sea
Middle: Morning stretch
Bottom: Freshwater Jacuzzi

To allow parents independent time ashore, youth centers operate as usual during port days, including lunch with counselors. For an additional charge, group babysitting is available nightly from 10 pm until 1 am. Family-friendly conveniences include self-service

CHOOSE THIS LINE IF ...

You're a traveler with a disability. Princess ships are some of the most accessible at sea.

You like to gamble but hate a smoke-filled casino. Princess casinos are well ventilated and spacious.

You want a balcony. Princess ships feature them in abundance at affordable rates.

laundry facilities. Infants under six months are not permitted; private in-cabin babysitting is not available on any Princess vessel. Children under age three are welcome in the playrooms if supervised by a parent.

Service

Professional service by an international staff is efficient and friendly. It's not uncommon to be greeted in passageways by smiling stewards who know your name.

Tipping

A gratuity of $11.50 per person per day ($12 for passengers in suites and minisuites) is added to shipboard accounts for distribution to stewards and waitstaff. Passengers may adjust the amount based on the level of service experienced. An automatic 15% is added to all bar tabs for bartenders and drink servers; gratuities to other staff members may be extended at passengers' discretion.

Past Passengers

Membership in the Captain's Circle is automatic following your first Princess cruise. All members receive a free subscription to *Captain's Circle News,* a quarterly newsletter, as well as discounts on selected cruises.

Perks are determined by the number of cruises completed: Gold (2 and 3), Medallion (4 and 5), Platinum (6 through 15), and Elite (16 and above). Although Gold members receive only the magazine, an invitation to an onboard event, and the services of the Circle Host on the ship, benefits really begin to accrue once you've completed five cruises. Platinum members receive upgraded insurance (when purchasing the standard policy), expedited check-in, a debarkation lounge to wait in on the ship, and, best of all, limited free Internet access during the cruise. Elite benefits are even more lavish, with many complimentary services.

HELPFUL HINTS

Princess Cruises pioneered the concept of affordable balcony accommodations and continues to lead the industry in that regard.

If you're unsure, select Traditional dining when you reserve your cruise; it can be impossible to change from Anytime Dining to Traditional onboard, but it's easy to go the other way.

Princess Cruises is the only contemporary cruise line that offers deluxe Ultimate Balcony Dining—either an intimate breakfast or romantic dinner served by your own dedicated waiters on your stateroom balcony.

A Princess cruise can be enhanced by adding a Cruisetour, a five- to eight-day in-depth land tour, to your voyage to create a land and sea vacation.

5

PRINCESS CRUISES

DON'T CHOOSE THIS LINE IF ...

You have a poor sense of direction. Most ships, especially the Grand-class ships, are very large.

You think Princess is still as depicted in *The Love Boat.* That was just a TV show, and it was more than three decades ago.

You're too impatient to stand in line or wait. Debarkation from the large ships can be lengthy.

ROYAL PRINCESS, REGAL PRINCESS

CREW MEMBERS	1,346
ENTERED SERVICE	2013, 2014
GROSS TONS	141,000
LENGTH	1,083 feet
NUMBER OF CABINS	1,780
PASSENGER CAPACITY	3,600
WIDTH	155 feet

700 ft.
500 ft.
300 ft.

The largest ships in the fleet introduce some exciting new innovations—including a SeaWalk that extends from the side of the ship on the line's largest pool deck with views 128 feet straight down—and signature features that have been expanded from other ships, including an even larger atrium with more entertainment and casual dining options. The top-deck pool features a water and light show, a 30% larger Movies Under the Stars screen, and poolside cabanas that appear to float on the water.

While the adults-only Serenity Deck has its own pool, families will find more amenities designed especially for children and teens that include expanded space for youth centers with dedicated outdoor areas, including a new teen lounge. Toddlers can also join the fun with a special play area just for kids under age three.

Cabins

Cabins: On these ships, all outside staterooms have balconies. The standard balcony stateroom has a seating area with a chair and table and ample storage; the new Deluxe Balcony Cabin is larger, with a sofa in the sitting area. Minisuites have a separate seating area with sofa bed, a walk-in closet, a combination shower-tub, and a balcony, as well as two TVs. Suites have separate sitting rooms, some with sofa beds, walk-in closets, two 42-inch flat-screen TVs, a CD/DVD player, separate bathtub and shower, access to a private concierge lounge, breakfast in Sabatini's daily, and complimentary laundry and dry cleaning service. Connecting cabins are available, but some have two twin lower berths that cannot be combined, or a queen that cannot be separated. The fourth person in some staterooms will be proved with a rollaway bed.

Amenities: Decorated in attractive pastel hues, all accommodations have a refrigerator, a hair dryer, a safe, and bathrobes to use during the cruise. Bathrooms have shampoo, lotion, and bath gel.

Accessibility: Thirty-six staterooms are wheelchair accessible.

Restaurants

Passengers choose between two assigned dinner seatings or open seating; breakfast and lunch are always open seating. Dinner options include reservations-only Sabatini's and Crown Grill (both with a cover) and the

Top: *Royal Princess* at sea
Bottom: An aerobics studio in the fitness center

complimentary casual Horizon Court buffet and Alfredo's Pizzeria. The Lido buffets are almost always early and late. A pub lunch is served in the Wheelhouse Bar, and a pool deck pizzeria and grill offer casual daytime snack choices. The wine bars, patisseries, and gelato bars charge for artisan cheeses, specialty coffee and tea, some pastries, and premium ice cream. New is an à la carte seafood bar in the atrium. There's an afternoon tea and 24-hour room service.

Spas

Spas operated by Steiner Leisure offer the standard treatments, including a variety of massages, body wraps, and facials, as well as some designed specifically for men, teens, and couples. Medi-Spa treatments are also available. The expansive spas feature Couples Villas and the Enclave—thermal suites that have a relaxing hydrotherapy pool, aromatic wet and dry saunas, and heated loungers that are complimentary for those in suites, but a fee is charged for everyone else.

Bars and Entertainment

Nighttime production shows tend toward Broadway-style revues; other performers might include comedians, magicians, jugglers, and acrobats. Live bands play a wide range of musical styles for dancing and listening in the lounges. New is "Princess Live," a TV studio that presents events including interactive culinary shows, live concerts, late night comedy, and game shows. Movies Under the Stars with popcorn and other movie fare are popular.

Pros and Cons

Pros: the poolside screen is larger than on other ships; alcoves at the buffet restaurant entrances feature convenient sinks for hand washing; the adults-only Sanctuary is a private deck enclave with posh loungers and private cabanas for a fee.

Cons: To fully transit the Promenade Deck, you have to go inside the ship; there is an extra charge for gelato and ice cream in the gelateria; the over-the-water SkyWalk is unnerving for those with a fear of heights.

Cabin Type	Size (sq. ft.)
Premium Suite	471
Penthouse/Owner's Suite	357/344
Minisuite	258
Deluxe Balcony Cabin	192
Balcony Cabin	181
Interior	161–172

FAST FACTS

- 15 passenger decks
- 2 specialty restaurants, 3 dining rooms, buffet, ice cream parlor, 2 pizzerias
- Wi-Fi, safe, refrigerator
- 3 pools
- Fitness classes, gym, hot tubs, sauna, spa, steam room
- 8 bars, casino, 2 dance clubs, library, show room, video game room
- Children's programs
- Dry cleaning, laundry facilities, laundry service
- Internet terminal
- No-smoking cabins

5

PRINCESS CRUISES

CARIBBEAN, CROWN, EMERALD, RUBY PRINCESS

CREW MEMBERS	?00, 1,200, 1,200, 1,225
ENTERED SERVICE	)4, 2006, 2007, 2008
GROSS TONS	113,000
LENGTH	951 feet
NUMBER OF CABINS	, 1,538, 1,532, 1540
PASSENGER CAPACITY	3,080, 3,080, 3,080
WIDTH	118 feet

700 ft.
500 ft.
300 ft.

With dramatic atriums and Skywalker's Nightclub (the spoiler hovering 150 feet above the stern), *Caribbean Princess* is a supersize version of the older Grand-class vessels with an extra deck of passenger accommodations. Not quite identical to *Caribbean Princess*, the younger ships in the class, *Crown, Emerald,* and *Ruby Princess* have introduced more dining options. Several signature public spaces have been redesigned or relocated on these ships as well—the atrium on *Crown, Emerald,* and *Ruby Princess* resembles an open piazza and sidewalk café; Sabatini's Italian Trattoria is found on a top deck with views on three sides and alfresco dining; and Skywalker's Disco is forward near the funnel (where it's topped with a sports court). Inside spaces on all three vessels are quietly neutral, with touches of glamour in the sweeping staircases and marble-floor atriums. Surprising intimacy is achieved by the number of public rooms and restaurants that swallow up passengers.

Cabins

Cabins: On these ships 80% of the outside staterooms have balconies. The typical stateroom has a seating area with a chair and table; all have ample storage. Minisuites have a separate seating area, a walk-in closet, a combination shower-tub, and a balcony, as well as two TVs. Larger deluxe suites have separate sitting rooms and walk-in closets, some with sofa beds. Two family suites have interconnecting staterooms with a balcony and sleep up to eight (D105/D101 and D106/D102). Some staterooms can accommodate three and four, and some adjacent cabins can be connected through interior doors or balcony dividers.

Amenities: Decorated in attractive pastel hues, all cabins have a refrigerator, a hair dryer, a safe, and bathrobes to use during the cruise. Bathrooms have shampoo, lotion, and bath gel.

Accessibility: Twenty-five staterooms are wheelchair accessible on *Caribbean* and *Crown Princess; Emerald* and *Ruby Princess* have 31.

Restaurants

Passengers choose between two assigned dinner seatings or open seating; breakfast and lunch are always open seating. Dinner options include reservations-only

Top: Movies Under the Stars
Bottom: Broadway-style revue

Sabatini's and Crown Grill (both with cover) and the complimentary Café Caribe, a casual Caribbean buffet with linen-dressed tables and limited waiter service. Lido buffets on all ships are almost always open. A pub lunch is served in the Wheelhouse Bar, and a pizzeria and grill offer casual daytime snack choices. The wine bars, patisseries, and ice cream bars charge for artisan cheeses, specialty coffee, some pastries, and premium ice cream. Ultimate Balcony Dining and Chef's Table options are available, as are afternoon tea and 24-hour room service.

Spas

Spas operated by Steiner Leisure offer the standard treatments, including a variety of massages, body wraps, and facials, as well as some designed specifically for men, teens, and couples. Medi-Spa treatments are also available. The spas' thermal suites have relaxing aromatic wet and dry saunas and heated loungers that are complimentary for those in suites, but a fee is charged for everyone else. Complimentary to all are saunas and steam rooms adjacent to men's and women's changing rooms.

Bars and Entertainment

Nighttime production shows tend toward Broadway-style revues presented in the main show lounge, and performers might include comedians, magicians, jugglers, and acrobats. Live bands play a wide range of musical styles for dancing and listening in the lounges and each ship has a dance club. The cruise director's staff leads lively evenings of fun with passenger participation. Movies Under the Stars with popcorn and other movie fare are a popular option.

Pros and Cons

Pros: Movies Under the Stars on the huge poolside screen have proven to be a big hit; the Wheelhouse Bar serves complimentary pub lunch at noon; the adults-only Sanctuary is a private deck with posh loungers for a fee.

Cons: priority dining reservations are extended only to Elite Captain's Circle members; the terrace overlooking the aft pool is a quiet spot after dark, but the nearest bar often closes early; opt for Anytime dining and you may encounter a wait for a table.

Cabin Type	Size (sq. ft)
Grand Suite	1,279
Other Suites	461–689
Family Suite	607
Minisuite	324
Ocean View with Balcony	233–285
Ocean View	158–182
Inside	163

All dimensions include the square footage for balconies.

FAST FACTS

- 15 passenger decks
- 2 specialty restaurants, 3 dining rooms, buffet, ice cream parlor, pizzeria
- Wi-Fi, safe, refrigerator, DVD (some)
- 4 pools (1 indoor), children's pool
- Fitness classes, gym, hot tubs, sauna, spa, steam room
- 9 bars, casino, 2 dance clubs, library, 2 show rooms, video game room
- Children's programs
- Dry-cleaning, laundry facilities, laundry service
- Internet terminal
- No kids under 6 months
- No-smoking cabins

Sailing at sunset

PRINCESS CRUISES

5

CORAL-CLASS
Coral Princess, Island Princess

CREW MEMBERS	900
ENTERED SERVICE	2003, 2003
GROSS TONS	92,000
LENGTH	964 feet
NUMBER OF CABINS	987
PASSENGER CAPACITY	1,970
WIDTH	106 feet

700 ft.

500 ft.

300 ft.

Princess includes *Coral Princess* and *Island Princess* in their Sun-class category. However, they are larger ships (albeit with a similar capacity to *Sun Princess* and her two sisters), which means much more space per passenger; we feel this necessitates a separate category. All the Personal Choice features attributed to the larger Grand-class ships were incorporated into this design as well as a few unique additions, such as a demonstration kitchen and ceramics lab complete with kiln where ScholarShip@ Sea programs are presented. The four-story atrium is similar to that on Sun-class ships, but public rooms are mainly spread fore and aft on two lower decks.

Although signature rooms such as the Wheelhouse Bar are more traditional, the casinos have subtle London- or Paris-like atmospheres with themed slot machines; Crooner's Bar is a retro 1960s Vegas-style martini and piano bar. In addition to the stately Princess Theater show room, the Universe Lounge has three stages for shows and flexible seating on two levels, making it a multipurpose space.

Cabins
Cabins: Stepped out in wedding-cake fashion, more than 83% of ocean-view staterooms include Princess Cruises' trademark private balconies. Even the least expensive inside categories have plentiful storage and a small seating area with a chair and table. Suites have two TVs, a seating area, a wet bar, a large walk-in closet, and a separate bathtub and shower. Minisuites have a separate seating area, two TVs, a walk-in closet, and a combination bathtub/shower.

Suites: Occupants of 16 suites receive complimentary Internet access, dry cleaning, and shoe polishing, afternoon tea and evening canapés delivered to their suites, and priority embarkation, disembarkation, and tendering privileges. An extended room service menu is also available for them, as are priority reservations for dining and shore excursions.

Amenities: Decorated in pastels and light-wood tones, typical staterooms have a safe, hair dryer, refrigerator, and bathrobes for use during the cruise. Bathrooms have shampoo, lotion, and bath gel.

Top: Fast-paced shows
Bottom: Aqua biking

Accessibility: Twenty staterooms are designed for wheelchair accessibility and range in size from 217 to 374 square feet, depending on category.

Restaurants

Passengers may choose between traditional dinner seating times in one assigned dining room or open seating in the other formal dining room; breakfast and lunch are open seating. Alternative dinner options include reservations-only Sabatini's Italian trattoria and Bayou Café & Steakhouse (both with an extra charge). With a few breaks in service, Lido buffets are almost always open. A pub lunch is served in the Wheelhouse Bar, and a pizzeria and grill offer casual daytime snack choices. The patisseries and ice cream bars charge for specialty coffee, some pastries, and premium ice cream. Ultimate Balcony Dining and Chef's Table options are available, as is afternoon tea, and 24-hour room service.

Spas

The spa, which is operated by Steiner Leisure, offers a menu of massages, body wraps, and facials, including treatments specifically designed for men, teens, and couples. Acupuncture is also available. Thermal suites have relaxing aromatic wet and dry saunas and heated loungers and are complimentary for those in suites, but there is a fee for everyone else. Adults can escape to the Sanctuary, a relaxing outdoor spa-inspired setting for which there is also a fee. Complimentary to all are saunas adjacent to men's and women's changing rooms.

Bars and Entertainment

Nighttime production shows tend toward Broadway-style revues presented in the main show lounge; other performers might include comedians, magicians, jugglers, and acrobats. Live bands play a wide range of musical styles for dancing and listening in the lounges and each ship has a dance club. The cruise director's staff leads lively evenings of fun with passenger participation. Movies Under the Stars with popcorn and other movie fare are a popular option.

Pros and Cons

Pros: as many as 20 courses in the ScholarShip@Sea program are offered on each cruise; cabins that sleep third and fourth passengers are numerous; the Fine Art Gallery is a dedicated area, so displays don't clutter other public spaces.

Cons: the library and card room often become noisy passageways; there are only 16 suites on each ship; engine pods on the funnel give the ships a futuristic space-age appearance but are mainly decorative.

Cabin Type	Size (sq. ft.)
Suite	470
Minisuite	285–302
Ocean View Balcony	217–232
Ocean View Stand	162
Deluxe	212
Inside	156–166

All dimensions include the square footage for balconies.

FAST FACTS

- 11 passenger decks
- 2 specialty restaurants, 2 dining rooms, buffet, ice cream parlor, pizzeria
- Wi-Fi, safe, refrigerator, DVD (some)
- 3 pools (1 indoor), children's pool
- Fitness classes, gym, hot tubs, sauna, spa
- 7 bars, casino, 2 dance clubs, library, 2 show rooms, video game room
- Children's programs
- Dry-cleaning, laundry facilities, laundry service
- Internet terminal
- No kids under 6 months
- No-smoking cabins

Lavish buffets in Horizon Court

GRAND-CLASS
Grand Princess, Golden Princess, Star Princess

CREW MEMBERS	1,100, 1,100, 1,200
ENTERED SERVICE	1998, 2001, 2002
GROSS TONS	109,000
LENGTH	951 feet
NUMBER OF CABINS	1,300
PASSENGER CAPACITY	2,590
WIDTH	118 feet

700 ft.
500 ft.
300 ft.

When *Grand Princess* was introduced as the world's largest cruise ship in 1998, futuristic Skywalker's Disco hovered approximately 150 feet above the waterline, but in a dramatic—and fuel saving—transformation, it was removed from *Grand Princess* in 2011 and replaced with a more conventional nightclub in the heart of the ship. Subsequent ships did not have the same design problem, so there are no plans on the drawing board to remove Skywalker's.

All Grand-class vessels have more than 700 staterooms that include private balconies. Like their predecessors, the interiors of Grand-class ships have splashy glamour in the sweeping staircases and marble-floor atriums. Surprisingly intimate for such large ships, human scale in public lounges is achieved by judicious placement of furniture as unobtrusive room dividers. The 300-square-foot Times Square–style LED screens that hover over the pools show up to seven movies or events daily.

Cabins
Cabins: On these ships, 80% of the outside staterooms have balconies. The typical stateroom has a seating area with a chair and table; even the cheapest categories have ample storage. Minisuites have a separate seating area, a walk-in closet, a combination shower-tub, and a balcony, as well as two TVs. More deluxe suites have even more room, some with sofa beds. Two family suites have interconnecting staterooms with a balcony that can sleep up to eight people (D105/D101 and D106/D102). Staterooms in a variety of categories will accommodate three and four people, and some adjacent cabins can be interconnected through interior doors or by unlocking doors in the balcony dividers.

Amenities: Decorated in attractive pastel hues, all cabins have a refrigerator, hair dryer, safe, and bathrobes to use during the cruise. Bathrooms have shampoo, lotion, and bath gel.

Accessibility: Twenty-eight staterooms are wheelchair accessible.

Restaurants
Passengers choose between two assigned dinner seatings or open seating; breakfast and lunch are open seating. Alternative dinner options include the reservations-only

Top: *Star Princess* at sea
Bottom: *Golden Princess* grand plaza atrium

Crown Grill and Sabatini's Italian restaurants (both with cover). Lido buffets on all ships are open around the clock. A pub lunch is served in the Wheelhouse Bar, and a pizzeria and grill offer casual daytime snack choices. The patisseries and ice cream bars charge for specialty coffee, some pastries, and premium ice cream. A wine bar serves extra-charge evening snacks and artisan cheeses. Ultimate Balcony Dining and Chef's Table options are available, as is afternoon tea and 24-hour room service.

Spas

Spas operated by Steiner Leisure offer a menu of massages, body wraps, and facials, as well as treatments specifically designed for men, teens, and couples. Acupuncture is also available. Only Star Princess has a thermal suite (complimentary for those in suites but open to others for a fee), but saunas and steam rooms adjacent to men's and women's changing rooms are complimentary on all three ships. Adults can escape to the Sanctuary, a relaxing outdoor spa-inspired setting for which there is a fee.

Bars and Entertainment

Nighttime production shows presented in the main show lounge lean toward Broadway-style revues; guest performers might include comedians, magicians, jugglers, and acrobats. Live bands play a wide range of musical styles for dancing and listening in the lounges, and each ship has a dance club. The cruise director's staff leads lively evenings of fun with passenger participation. Movies Under the Stars, where popcorn is free, is a popular evening option.

Pros and Cons

Pros: Skywalker's Nightclub on *Golden Princess* and *Star Princess* is virtually deserted during the day, when it's the ideal quiet spot to watch the sea; self-service passenger laundry rooms have ironing stations; the nautical Wheelhouse Bar is a Princess tradition for predinner cocktails and dancing.

Cons: sports bars get jam-packed—and stuffy—when big games are on; accommodations aft and above the Vista lounge are noisy when bands crank up the volume; minisuites don't include the perks offered to full suites.

Cabin Type	Size (sq. ft.)
Grand Suite	730/ 1,314*
Other Suites	468–591
Family Suite	607
Minisuite	323
Ocean View Balcony	232–274
Standard	168
Inside	160

All dimensions include the square footage for balconies. *Grand Princess* dimensions followed by *Golden* and *Star Princess*.

FAST FACTS

- 14 passenger decks
- 2 specialty restaurants, 3 dining rooms, buffet, ice cream parlor, pizzeria
- Wi-Fi, safe, refrigerator
- 4 pools (1 indoor), children's pool
- Fitness classes, gym, hot tubs, sauna, spa, steam room
- 9 bars, casino, 2 dance clubs, library, 2 show rooms, video game room
- Children's programs
- Dry-cleaning, laundry facilities, laundry service
- Internet terminal
- No kids under 6 months
- No-smoking cabins

SUN-CLASS
Sun Princess, Dawn Princess, Sea Princess

CREW MEMBERS	900
ENTERED SERVICE	1995, 1997, 1998
GROSS TONS	77,000
LENGTH	856 feet
NUMBER OF CABINS	975
PASSENGER CAPACITY	1,950
WIDTH	106 feet

Refined and graceful, Sun-class ships offer many of the choices attributed to larger Grand-class ships without sacrificing the smaller-ship atmosphere for which they're noted. The four-story atrium with a circular marble floor, stained-glass dome, and magnificent floating staircase are ideal settings for relaxation, people-watching, and making a grand entrance. *Sea, Sun,* and *Dawn Princess* are deployed in the South Pacific.

Onboard decor is a combination of neutrals and pastels, which are easy on the eyes after a sunny day ashore. The main public rooms are in a vertical arrangement on four lower decks, and, with the exception of promenade deck, cabins are forward and aft. In a nice design twist, the casino is somewhat isolated, and passengers aren't forced to use it as a passageway to reach dining rooms or the art deco main show lounge. *Sea Princess* also has an outdoor Movies Under the Stars LED screen.

Cabins

Cabins: Princess Cruises' trademark is an abundance of staterooms with private balconies, and even the least expensive inside categories have ample storage and a small seating area with a chair and table. Suites have two TVs, a separate seating area, a dining-height table with chairs, a walk-in closet, double-sink vanities, and a separate shower and whirlpool tub. Minisuites have a separate seating area, two TVs, a walk-in closet, and a separate shower and whirlpool tub. Cabins that sleep third and fourth passengers aren't as numerous as on other Princess ships, and no staterooms have interconnecting interior doors, although adjacent cabins with balconies can be connected by unlocking balcony divider doors.

Amenities: Decorated in pastel tones, staterooms typically have mirrored accents, a safe, a refrigerator, a hair dryer, and bathrobes for use during the cruise. Bathrooms have shampoo, lotion, and bath gel.

Accessibility: Nineteen staterooms are designed for wheelchair accessibility and range in size from 213 to 305 square feet, depending on category.

Restaurants

Sun-class ships have one dining room with two traditional assigned dinner seatings and one open seating

Top: *Sea Princess* at sea
Bottom: Sun-class ocean-view stateroom

dining room for Personal Choice cruisers; breakfast and lunch are open seating. Alternative dinner options are the reservations-only Sterling Steakhouse (a section of the buffet that's dressed up for the evening and for which there's a charge) and complimentary traditional Italian dishes in a trattoria-style setting in the pizzeria. With a few breaks in service, Lido buffets on all ships are almost always open. The pizzeria and a grill near the main pool offer casual daytime snack choices. The patisseries and ice cream bars charge for specialty coffee, some pastries, and premium ice cream. Ultimate Balcony Dining is available, as is afternoon tea and 24-hour room service.

Spas

Spas operated by Steiner Leisure offer a menu of massages, body wraps, and facials, including some designed specifically for men and teens as well as couples. Acupuncture is also available. Adults can escape to the Sanctuary, a relaxing outdoor spa-inspired setting for which there is also a fee. There are no thermal suites, but complimentary saunas are available adjacent to men's and women's changing rooms.

Bars and Entertainment

Nighttime production shows tend to be Broadway-style revues presented in the main show lounge, and guest performers might include comedians, magicians, jugglers, and acrobats. Live bands play a wide range of musical styles for dancing and listening in the lounges and on each ship even the atrium has a dance floor. The entertainment staff leads lively evenings of fun with passenger participation. Movies Under the Stars with free popcorn is a popular option.

Pros and Cons

Pros: you can always escape the crowds by ducking into the cozy reading room; no matter what flavor is on the menu, dessert soufflés can't be beat; on Riviera Deck a dramatic, partially shaded pool with two hot tubs appears suspended between two decks.

Cons: Horizon Court Lido buffet restaurants occupy the far forward space, meaning there is no observatory lounge; there's nothing about the interior decor that'll knock your socks off; these are large ships but not large enough to overcome the invasive art auctions.

Cabin Type	Size (sq. ft.)
Suite	538–695
Minisuite	370–536
Ocean View Balcony	179
Deluxe	173
Ocean View Standard	135–155
Interior	135–148

All dimensions include the square footage for balconies.

FAST FACTS

- 10 passenger decks
- 2 dining rooms, buffet, ice cream parlor, pizzeria
- Wi-Fi, safe, refrigerator
- 3 pools (1 indoor), children's pool
- Fitness classes, gym, hot tubs, sauna, spa
- 7 bars, casino, 2 dance clubs, library, 2 show rooms, video game room
- Children's programs
- Dry-cleaning, laundry facilities, laundry service
- Internet terminal
- No kids under 6 months
- No-smoking cabins

Riviera pool

5

PRINCESS CRUISES

REGENT SEVEN SEAS

The 1994 merger of Radisson Diamond Cruises and Seven Seas Cruise Line launched Radisson Seven Seas Cruises with an eclectic fleet of vessels that offers a nearly all-inclusive cruise experience in sumptuous, contemporary surroundings. The line was

rebranded as Regent Seven Seas Cruises in 2006, and ownership passed to Prestige Cruise Holdings (which also owns Oceania Cruises) in 2008.

☎ 877/505–5370
⊕ *www.rssc.com*
☞ *Cruise Style: Luxury.*

Even more inclusive than in the past, the line has maintained its traditional tried-and-true formula—delightful ships offering exquisite service, generous staterooms with abundant amenities, a variety of dining options, and superior lecture and enrichment programs. Guests are greeted with champagne upon boarding and find an all-inclusive beverage policy that offers not only soft drinks and bottled water, but also cocktails and select wines at all bars and restaurants throughout the ships. Round-trip air, ground transfers, and shore excursions in every port are included in the cruise fare.

On board, casinos are more akin to Monaco than Las Vegas. All ships display tasteful and varied art collections, including pieces that are for sale.

Food

Menus may appear to include the usual beef Wellington and Maine lobster, but in the hands of Regent Seven Seas chefs the results are some of the most outstanding meals at sea. Specialty dining varies within the fleet, but *Seven Seas Voyager* and *Seven Seas Mariner,* have the edge with the sophisticated Signatures, featuring the most authentic French cuisine to be found outside of Paris. Prime 7, on all three ships, is a contemporary adaptation of the classic American steakhouse offering fresh, distinctive decor and an innovative menu of the finest prime-aged steaks and chops, along with fresh seafood and poultry specialties. In addition, Mediterranean-influenced bistro dinners that need no reservations are served in Sette Mari at La Veranda, the venue that is the daytime casual Lido buffet restaurant.

Wine Connoisseurs Dinners are offered occasionally on longer cruises to bring together people with an interest in wine and food. Each course on the degustation menu is complemented by a wine pairing. The cost varies according to the special vintage wines that are included.

Room-service menus are fairly extensive, and you can also order directly from the restaurant menus during regular serving hours.

Although special dietary requirements should be relayed to the cruise line before sailing, general considerations such as vegetarian, low-salt, or low-cholesterol food requests can be satisfied on board the ships simply by speaking with the dining room staff. Wines chosen to complement dinner menus are freely poured each evening.

Entertainment

Most sailings host guest lecturers, including historians, anthropologists, naturalists, and diplomats, and there are often discussions and workshops. Spotlight cruises center around popular pastimes and themes, such as food and wine, photography, history, archaeology, literature, performing arts, design and cultures, active exploration and wellness, antiques, jewelry and shopping, the environment, and marine life. All passengers have access to these unique experiences on board and on shore.

Activities and entertainment are tailored for each of the line's distinctive ships with the tastes of sophisticated passengers in mind. Don't expect napkin-folding demonstrations or nonstop action. Production revues, cabaret acts, concert-style piano performances, solo performers, and comedians may be featured in show lounges, with combos playing for listening and dancing in lounges and bars throughout the ships.

Fitness and Recreation

Although gyms and exercise areas are well equipped, these are not large ships, so the facilities also tend to be limited in size. Each ship has a jogging track, and the larger ones feature a variety of sports courts. The spas and salons aboard Regent Seven Seas ships are operated

KNOWN FOR

■ **All-Inclusive:** Regent Seven Seas Cruises offers the longest list of inclusive features for the money.

■ **Destination Focused:** Regent even includes select shore excursions in the fare—a real bonus when the ships reach ports of call.

■ **Fine Cuisine:** Ships in the Regent fleet have some of the finest specialty restaurants afloat and there is no charge for dining in them.

■ **Great Service:** Exemplary service is a signature feature of Regent's voyages.

■ **Luxurious but Informal:** Socializing is easygoing on Regent's less formal ships.

Top: Sunrise jog
Bottom: *Seven Seas Navigator*

5

REGENT SEVEN SEAS CRUISES

Top: Fitness center
Middle: Pool decks are
never crowded.
Bottom: Pampering in
the Carita of Paris spa

by Canyon Ranch SpaClub, which offers an array of customizable treatments and services.

Your Shipmates

Regent Seven Seas Cruises are inviting to active, affluent, well-traveled couples ranging from their late-thirties to retirees who enjoy the ship's chic ambience and destination-rich itineraries. Longer cruises attract veteran passengers in the over-sixty age group.

Dress Code

Elegant casual is the dress code for most nights; formal and semiformal attire is optional on sailings of 16 nights or longer, but it's no longer required. It's requested that dress codes be observed in public areas after 6 pm.

Junior Cruisers

Regent Seven Seas' vessels are adult-oriented and do not have dedicated children's facilities. However, a Club Mariner youth program for children ages 5 to 8, 9 to 12, and 13 to 17 is offered on select sailings, both during summer months and during school holiday periods. Supervised by counselors, the organized, educational activities focus on nature and the heritage of the ship's destinations. Activities, including games, craft projects, movies, and food fun, are organized to ensure that every child has a memorable experience. Teens are encouraged to help counselors select the activities they prefer. Only infants that are one year of age before the first day of the cruise may sail.

Service

The efforts of a polished, unobtrusive staff go almost unnoticed, yet special requests are handled with ease. Butlers provide an additional layer of personal service to guests in the top-category suites.

Tipping

Gratuities are included in the fare, and none are expected. To show their appreciation, passengers may elect to make a contribution to a crew welfare fund that benefits the ship's staff.

Past Passengers

Membership in the Seven Seas Society is automatic on completion of a Regent Seven Seas cruise. Members

---

CHOOSE THIS LINE IF ...

You want to learn the secrets of cooking like a Cordon Bleu chef (for a fee, of course).

You don't want the hassle of signing bar tabs or the extra expense of shore excursions.

A really high-end spa experience is on your agenda.

receive discounted cruise fare savings on select sailings, exclusive shipboard and shore-side special events on select sailings, a Seven Seas Society recognition cocktail party on every sailing, and *Inspirations* newsletter highlighting special events, sailings, and destination- and travel-related information. The tiered program offers rewards based on the number of nights you have sailed with RSSC. The more you sail, the more you accrue. Bronze benefits are offered to members with 4 to 20 nights. From 21 through 74 nights, Silver members also receive complimentary Internet access on board, free pressing, and an hour of free phone time. From 75 through 199 nights, Gold members are awarded priority disembarkation at some ports, an additional two hours of complimentary phone time, more complimentary pressing, an exclusive Gold & Platinum activity aboard or ashore on every sailing, and priority reservations at restaurants and spas. From 200 through 399, Platinum members can add complimentary air deviation services (one time per sailing), nine hours of complimentary phone use, and unlimited free pressing and laundry services. Titanium members who have sailed 400 or more nights also get free dry-cleaning and free transfers.

HELPFUL HINTS

Other luxury lines don't always include round-trip air, ground transfers, and unlimited shore excursions in every port of call.

Regent Seven Seas ships offer all-suite accommodations.

Regent Choice Shore Excursions carry a supplement, but they delve much deeper into a region's culture and history.

Multinight pre- and post-cruise land programs are available to extend your cruise vacation.

Regent Seven Seas ships are luxurious but not stuffy, and there's a "block party" on every cruise where passengers are invited to meet their neighbors in adjacent suites.

5

REGENT SEVEN SEAS CRUISES

DON'T CHOOSE THIS LINE IF ...

Connecting cabins are a must. Very few are available, and only the priciest cabins connect.

You can't imagine a cruise without the hoopla of games in the pool; these ships are much more discreet.

You don't want to dress up for dinner. Most passengers still dress more formally than on other lines.

SEVEN SEAS NAVIGATOR

CREW MEMBERS	340
ENTERED SERVICE	1999
GROSS TONS	33,000
LENGTH	560 feet
NUMBER OF CABINS	245
PASSENGER CAPACITY	490
WIDTH	81 feet

700 ft.

500 ft.

300 ft.

The first ship outfitted uniquely to Regent Seven Seas' specifications, the *Seven Seas Navigator* is a particular favorite of returning passengers for its small-ship intimacy, big-ship features, and comfortable, well-designed accommodations, which are all considered suites.

The generous use of wood and the addition of deep-tone accents to the predominantly blue color palette give even the larger lounges an inviting feel. Artwork and elaborate flower arrangements add a bit of sparkle and interest to the somewhat angular modern decor.

Due to the aft location of the two-deck-high main show room, the only lounges that afford sweeping seascapes are Galileo's—typically the most popular public space, with nightly entertainment—and the Vista Lounge. Although views from the Vista Lounge are spectacular, there's no permanent bar, and it's primarily a quiet spot for reading when there are no lectures or activities scheduled there.

Cabins

Cabins: Attractive textured fabrics and honeyed wood finishes add a touch of coziness to the larger-than-usual suites in all categories, 90% of which have balconies. All have a vanity-desk, walk-in closet, and seating area with a sofa, chairs, and table. Marble bathrooms have a separate tub and shower. Master suites have a separate sitting–dining room, a separate bedroom, and a powder room; only Grand suites also have a powder room. Master suites have a second TV in the bedroom, butler service, and whirlpool tub in the master bathroom. Grand and Navigator suites are similarly outfitted. The top three suite categories feature Bose music systems, an iPad, and an iPod docking station. Penthouse suites, which include butler service, are only distinguished from Deluxe suites by location and do not have a whirlpool bathtub. Few suites have the capacity to accommodate three people, and only 10 far-forward suites adjoin with those adjacent to them.

Amenities: Every suite has an entertainment center with CD/DVD player, stocked refrigerator, stocked bar, safe, hair dryer, and beds dressed with fine linens and duvets. Bath toiletries include shampoo, lotion, and bath gel. Passengers in Concierge suites and higher receive 15 min-

Top: Casino
Bottom: *Navigator* suite

utes of free ship-to-shore phone time and 60 minutes of free Internet access.

Accessibility: Four suites are wheelchair accessible.

Restaurants

Compass Rose restaurant, the main dining room, functions on an open seating basis for breakfast, lunch, and dinner, so there are no set dining assignments. La Veranda, the daytime buffet, which serves breakfast and lunch, is transformed into an evening bistro serving Mediterranean cuisine. Prime 7, the specialty steakhouse, requires reservations for dinner, but there is no charge. At least once during each cruise, dinner is served alfresco on the pool deck. In addition to the buffet, a choice for casual lunch and snacks is the poolside grill. Afternoon tea is served daily, and room service is available 24 hours a day. Dinner can be ordered from the main dining room menu during restaurant hours and served en suite, course by course.

Spas

Canyon Ranch SpaClub offers an array of treatments, such as massages, facials, and body wraps utilizing organic and natural materials that can be individually customized. Guests can also enjoy complimentary aromatic steam rooms infused with pure plant essences or Finnish-style saunas.

Bars and Entertainment

Socializing over dinner is a major evening pursuit, and there's music for dancing before and after dining, including deck parties when the weather permits. Dance Hosts are on hand to partner unaccompanied ladies on the dance floor. The main show lounge features small-scale production shows, and guest entertainers range from classical to modern vocalists and musicians.

Pros and Cons

Pros: library is excellent and includes a wide selection of both books and DVDs; fellow passengers might be as wealthy as Midas, but most are unpretentious; when nothing on the menu appeals to you, just ask for what you'd really like to have.

Cons: computer room is next to the library and can cause noise and congestion when Internet use is heavy; if you book a suite in the far-aft section of the ship, be prepared for an annoying vibration; unless you pre-book tables in specialty restaurants online, you could find them unavailable after boarding.

Cabin Type	Size (sq. ft.)
Master Suite	1,067
Grand Suite	539
Navigator Suite	448
Penthouse/Balcony Suite	301
Window Suite	301*

*Except for Suite 600, which measures 516 square feet.

FAST FACTS

- 8 passenger decks
- Specialty restaurant, dining room, buffet
- Wi-Fi, safe, refrigerator, DVD
- Pool
- Fitness classes, gym, hot tub, sauna, spa, steam room
- 4 bars, casino, dance club, show room
- Children's programs
- Dry-cleaning, laundry facilities, laundry service
- Internet terminal
- No-smoking cabins

Casual poolside dining

5

REGENT SEVEN SEAS CRUISES

ROYAL CARIBBEAN

Big, bigger, biggest! In the early 1990s, Royal Caribbean launched Sovereign-class ships, the first of the modern megacruise liners, which continue to be the all-around favorite of passengers who enjoy traditional cruising ambience with a touch of daring

Adventure of the Seas solarium

and whimsy. Plunging into the 21st century, each ship in the current fleet carries more passengers than the entire Royal Caribbean fleet of the 1970s, and has amenities—such as new surfing pools—that were unheard of in the past.

☎ *305/539–6000 or 800/327–6700*
⊕ *www.royalcaribbean. com*
☞ *Cruise Style: Main-stream.*

All Royal Caribbean ships are topped by the company's signature Viking Crown Lounge, a place to watch the seascape by day and dance at night. Expansive multideck atriums and promenades, as well as the generous use of brass and floor-to-ceiling glass windows, give each vessel a sense of spaciousness and style. The action is nonstop in casinos and dance clubs after dark, while daytime hours are filled with poolside games and traditional cruise activities. Port talks tend to lean heavily on shopping recommendations and the sale of shore excursions.

Food

Dining is an international experience, with nightly changing themes and cuisines from around the world. Passenger preference for casual attire and a resortlike atmosphere has prompted the cruise line to add laid-back alternatives to the formal dining rooms: the Windjammer Café and, on certain ships, Johnny Rockets Diner; Seaview Café evokes the ambience of an island beachside stand. Royal Caribbean offers you the choice of early or late dinner seating and has introduced an open seating program fleet-wide.

Room service is available 24 hours, but for orders between midnight and 5 am there's a $3.95 service charge. There's a limited menu.

Royal Caribbean doesn't place emphasis on celebrity chefs or specialty alternative restaurants, although they have introduced a more upscale and intimate dinner experience in the form of an Italian specialty restaurant and/or a steakhouse on all ships.

Entertainment

A variety of lounges and high-energy stage shows draw passengers of all ages out to mingle and dance the night away. Production extravaganzas showcase singers and dancers in lavish costumes. Comedians, acrobats, magicians, jugglers, and solo entertainers fill show lounges on nights when the ships' companies aren't performing. Professional ice shows are a highlight of cruises on Voyager-, Freedom-, and Oasis-class ships—the only ships at sea with ice-skating rinks.

Fitness and Recreation

Royal Caribbean has pioneered such new and previously unheard-of features as rock-climbing walls, ice-skating rinks, bungee trampolines, and even the first self-leveling pool tables on a cruise ship. Interactive water parks, boxing rings, surfing simulators, and cantilevered whirlpools suspended 112 feet above the ocean made their debuts on the Freedom-class ships.

Facilities vary by ship class, but all Royal Caribbean ships have state-of-the-art exercise equipment, jogging tracks, and rock-climbing walls; passengers can work out independently or in classes guaranteed to sweat off extra calories. Most exercise classes are included in the fare, but there's a fee for specialized spin, yoga, and Pilates classes, as well as the services of a personal trainer. Spas and salons are top-notch, with full menus of day spa–style treatments and services for pampering and relaxation for adults and teens.

Your Shipmates

Royal Caribbean cruises have a broad appeal for active couples and singles, mostly in their thirties to fifties. Families are partial to the newer vessels that have larger staterooms, huge facilities for children and teens, and seemingly endless choices of activities and dining options.

Dress Code

Two formal nights are standard on seven-night cruises; one formal night is the norm on shorter sailings. Men are encouraged to wear tuxedos, but dark suits or sport

KNOWN FOR

■ **A Step Above:** Offering the same value as other mainstream lines, Royal Caribbean's ships are more sophisticated than its competitors'.

■ **Big Ships:** The Royal Caribbean fleet boasts the world's largest cruise ships.

■ **Extra Charges:** You will have to break out your wallet quite often once on board, as the cruise fare is far from inclusive.

■ **Recreation:** Gym rats and sports and fitness buffs find multiple facilities available to satisfy their active lifestyles while at sea.

■ **Something for Everyone:** With activities that appeal to a broad demographic, Royal Caribbean is a top choice for multigenerational cruise vacations.

Top: Adventure Beach for kids
Bottom: Voyager-class interior stateroom

Top: Miniature golf
Middle: *Adventure of the Seas*
Bottom: *Serenade of the Seas*
rock-climbing wall

coats and ties are more prevalent. All other evenings are casual, although jeans are discouraged in restaurants. It's requested that no shorts be worn in public areas after 6 pm, although there are passengers who can't wait to change into them after dinner.

Junior Cruisers

Supervised age-appropriate activities are designed for children ages 3 through 17; babysitting services are available as well. Children are assigned to the Adventure Ocean youth program by age. They must be at least three years old and toilet trained to participate (children who are in diapers and pull-ups or who are not toilet trained are not allowed in swimming pools or whirlpools; however, they may use the Baby Splash Zone designated for them on the *Freedom, Liberty, Independence, Oasis,* and *Allure of the Seas*). Youngsters who wish to join a different age group must participate in one daytime and one night activity session with their proper age group first; the manager will then make the decision based on their maturity level.

In partnership with toymaker Fisher-Price, Royal Caribbean offers interactive 45-minute Aqua Babies and Aqua Tots play sessions for children ages 6 months to 36 months. The playgroup classes, which are hosted by youth staff members, were designed by early childhood development experts for parents and their babies and toddlers, and teach life skills through playtime activities. Nurseries have been added for babies 6 to 36 months old, with drop-off options during the day and evening— and if parents supply diapers, attendants will change them. There is an hourly fee, and only eight babies and toddlers can be accommodated at a time.

A teen center with a disco is an adult-free gathering spot that will satisfy even the pickiest teenagers.

Service

Service on Royal Caribbean ships is friendly but inconsistent. Assigned meal seatings assure that most passengers get to know the waiters and their assistants, who in turn get to know the passengers' likes and dislikes; however, that can lead to a level of familiarity that is uncomfortable for some people. Most ships have a concierge

CHOOSE THIS LINE IF ...

You want to see the sea from atop a rock wall—it's one of the few activities on these ships that's free.

You're active and adventurous. Even if your traveling companion isn't, there's an energetic staff on board to cheer you on.

You want your space. There's plenty of room to roam; quiet nooks and crannies are there if you look.

lounge for the use of suite occupants and top-level past passengers.

Tipping

Tips that are not prepaid when the cruise is booked are automatically added to shipboard accounts in the amount of $12 per person per day ($14.25 for suites), to be shared by dining and housekeeping staff. A 15% gratuity is automatically added to all bar tabs and spa and salon services.

Past Passengers

After one cruise, you can enroll in the Crown & Anchor Society. Tiered membership levels are achieved according to a point system. All members receive the *Crown & Anchor* magazine and have access to the member section on the Royal Caribbean website. All members receive an Ultimate Value Booklet and an invitation to a welcome-back party. Platinum members also have the use of a private departure lounge and receive priority check-in (where available), the onboard use of robes during the cruise, an invitation to an exclusive onboard event, and complimentary custom air arrangements. As points are added to your status, the benefits increase to Emerald, Diamond, Diamond Plus, and Pinnacle Club. For instance, Diamond and above receive such perks as access to a private lounge, behind-the-scenes tours, and priority seating for certain events.

HELPFUL HINTS

Reservations can be made online precruise for specialty restaurants, shore excursions, and spa treatments on all ships, as well as the shows on *Oasis of the Seas, Allure of the Seas, Freedom of the Seas,* and *Liberty of the Seas.*

The signature Viking Crown Lounge found on every Royal Caribbean ship is a daytime observation lounge and a nightclub after dark.

Popular with children of all ages, the DreamWorks Experience on certain ships offers character meals, meet-and-greet gatherings, and photo ops.

With a multibottle package you can save up to 25% off regular list prices on wine.

A complimentary Coca-Cola souvenir cup is included with the fountain soft drink package.

Bottled water and bottled juice packages of varying quantities can be delivered to your stateroom and will save you up to 25%.

5

ROYAL CARIBBEAN INTERNATIONAL

DON'T CHOOSE THIS LINE IF ...

Patience is not one of your virtues. Lines are not uncommon.

You want to do your own laundry. There are no self-service facilities on any Royal Caribbean ships.

You don't want to hear announcements. There are a lot on Royal Caribbean ships.

OASIS-CLASS
Oasis, Allure of the Seas

	CREW MEMBERS
	2,394
	ENTERED SERVICE
	2009, 2010
700 ft.	GROSS TONS
	225,282
	LENGTH
	1,187 feet
500 ft.	NUMBER OF CABINS
	2,706
	PASSENGER CAPACITY
	5,400
300 ft.	WIDTH
	208 feet

The world's largest cruise ships are so massive that each is divided into seven neighborhoods—distinguished by purpose (spa and fitness, pool and sports), age (youth zone), design (Central Park and the Boardwalk), or function (entertainment). At the heart of the ships are the indoor Royal Promenade, lined with café-style eateries and lounges. Central Park's pathways are tranquil and peaceful during the day and a gathering space for alfresco dining and entertainment in the evening. Connecting the two is an open-air elevator that doubles as a bar where patrons can order drinks during the ride.

Royal Caribbean hits all the marks with nearly two-dozen bars and lounges and a wide variety of restaurants to choose from. There are many open spaces to play in—including two surfing simulators, two rock-climbing walls, and the first zip line on a cruise ship that stretches across the Boardwalk neighborhood. The Boardwalk itself features a carousel in a setting that evokes the nostalgia of seaside piers of yesteryear. The centerpiece of the AquaTheater is the largest and deepest freshwater pool found on a ship where you can swim by day and watch a water show after the sun goes down.

Cabins

Cabins: Three-dozen accommodation categories may seem confusing when making a selection, but they really boil down to variety of suites, outside cabins with balconies that face either the sea or overlook open-air interiors, ocean-view cabins, and interior cabins, some of which overlook the inside promenade. All standard accommodations include a small seating area, TV, desk-vanity, hair dryer, refrigerator, and safe. Fares and even size are determined more by location.

Suites: Suite and junior-suite guests get several special amenities, including bathrobes, nicer bath amenities, coffee and tea service, and a suite attendant to fulfill special requests.

Accessibility: Forty-six staterooms are wheelchair accessible.

Restaurants

A huge, triple-deck dining room serves open seating breakfast and lunch; dinner is served in either assigned or open seating. Several specialty restaurants—Giovanni's Table (Italian), Chops Grille (steakhouse), and the

Top: *Allure of the Seas* sailing
Bottom: A romantic moment on a stateroom balcony

gourmet 150 Central Park—charge a supplement and require reservations. Either the casual Windjammer or Wipe Out Café offer buffet service nearly around the clock for breakfast, lunch, dinner, and snacks. Other venues for which there is a charge are Izumi (Asian); Johnny Rockets Diner (burgers); Vintages (tapas); and the Seafood Shack (on *Oasis*) and Rita's Cantina (on *Allure*). The Solarium Bistro serves spa cuisine and is complimentary at breakfast and lunch, but there is a charge for dinner. There's also a pizzeria, coffee bar, and doughnut shop. The ice cream parlor and cupcake bakery charge for frozen and sweet treats. Room service is available 24 hours; however, there is a delivery charge after midnight.

Spas

The full-service spa operated by Steiner Leisure offers an extensive treatment menu including facials, teeth whitening, body wraps and scrubs, massages, rasul, acupuncture, and FDA-approved Medi-Spa treatments performed by trained physicians. Spa rituals also include treatments designed especially for men and teens. The thermal suite has heated lounging beds and a collection of exotic steam vapors throughout.

Bars and Entertainment

Nightlife on these ships runs the gamut from Broadway shows (*Hairspray* on *Oasis*, *Chicago* on *Allure*) and comedy clubs to aquatic extravaganzas and ice-skating performances. Bar and lounges from a piano bar to a disco come to life after dark with a wide range of music for dancing and listening. You can end the evening with a stroll down the indoor promenade or by meandering through the Central Park beneath a starry sky.

Pros and Cons

Pros: reservations for specialty dining and most shows can be made prior to sailing; the adults-only solarium has cabanas for rent; you can rent a "Wow Phone," essentially an iPhone that only works on board.

Cons: the sprawling Central Park is open to the elements; on ships this large, lines are inevitable; hold onto your wallet—there are extra charges at every turn, even for cupcakes.

Cabin Type	Size (sq. ft.)
Royal, Sky, Crown Loft Suites	1,524, 722, 545
Royal, Owner's, Grand Suites	1,275, 556, 371
Presidential, Royal Family Suites	1,142, 580
AquaTheater Suites	673–823
Junior Suite, Family Balcony	287, 271
Outside/Balcony, Family Outside	179–199, 260
Interior/Balcony, Family Interior	149–194, 260

FAST FACTS

- 16 passenger decks
- 5 specialty restaurants, dining room, 2 buffets, 3 cafés, ice cream parlor, pizzeria
- Wi-Fi, safe, refrigerator, DVD (some)
- 4 pools, children's pool
- Fitness classes, gym, hot tubs, spa
- 18 bars, casino, dance club, library
- Children's programs
- Dry-cleaning, laundry service
- Internet terminal
- No-smoking cabins

5

ROYAL CARIBBEAN INTERNATIONAL

FREEDOM-CLASS
Freedom, Liberty, Independence of the Seas

CREW MEMBERS	1,360
ENTERED SERVICE	2006, 2007, 2008
GROSS TONS	160,000
LENGTH	1,112 feet
NUMBER OF CABINS	1,817
PASSENGER CAPACITY	3,634
WIDTH	185 feet

700 ft.
500 ft.
300 ft.

Although they are no longer the world's largest cruise ships, the Freedom-class vessels live up to Royal Caribbean's reputation for creative thinking that results in features to stir the imagination and provide a resortlike atmosphere at sea. Whether you are hanging ten in the surf simulator, going a few rounds in the boxing ring, or strolling the Royal Promenade entertainment boulevard, there's almost no reason to go ashore. The layout is more intuitive than you might expect on such a gigantic ship. A mall-like promenade is lined with shops and bistros, an ice-skating rink/theater, numerous lounges, and dining options, but these are not simply enlarged Voyager-class ships. With plenty of room, even the most intimate spaces feel uncrowded. A good fit for extended families, these ships have expansive areas devoted to children and teens and enough adults-only spaces to satisfy everyone.

Cabins

Cabins: Although 60% are outside cabins—and 78% of those have balconies—bargain inside cabins, including some with a bowed window overlooking the promenade, are plentiful. Cabins in every category have adequate closet and drawer/shelf storage, as well as bathroom shelves. Family ocean-view cabins with a window sleep up to six people with two twin beds (convertible to queen size), bunk beds in a separate area, a sitting room with a sofa bed, a vanity area, and a shower-only bathroom. At 1,215 square feet, the Presidential suite sleeps 14 people and has an 810-square-foot veranda with a hot tub and bar.

Amenities: Wood cabinetry, a small refrigerator-minibar, broadband Internet connection, a vanity-desk, a flat-panel TV and DVD player, a safe, a hair dryer, and a seating area with sofa, chair, and table are typical features in all categories. Bathrooms have shampoo and bath gel. Premium beds and bedding complete the package.

Accessibility: Thirty-two staterooms are wheelchair accessible.

Restaurants

Triple-deck-high dining rooms serve open-seating breakfast and lunch; dinner is served in two assigned seatings or open seating. Two specialty restaurants—Portofino, serving Italian, and Chops Grille, a steakhouse—both charge a supplement and require reservations. The casual

Top: Dining is fun at Johnny Rockets.
Bottom: Hang 10 on the surf simulator.

Lido buffet offers service nearly around the clock for breakfast, lunch, dinner, and snacks. Jade, a section in the buffet, serves Asian food. Johnny Rockets (cover charge) is a popular option for casual meals. In the promenade are a complimentary pizzeria and a coffee bar serving regular and specialty coffees (also complimentary, unlike on other lines). There's also a Cupcake Cupboard and Ben & Jerry's ice cream, but they charge a fee. A complimentary ice cream bar is poolside, as is a juice bar, which charges by the item. Room service is available 24 hours; however, there is a delivery charge after midnight.

Spas

The full-service spa operated by Steiner Leisure offers an extensive treatment menu including facials, teeth whitening, body wraps and scrubs, massages, rasul, acupuncture, and FDA-approved Medi-Spa treatments performed by trained physicians. Spa rituals also include treatments designed especially for men and teens. While there are no thermal suites, complimentary saunas and steam rooms are in men's and women's changing rooms.

Bars and Entertainment

Nightlife runs the gamut from Broadway-style production shows to ice-skating extravaganzas on all three and a real Broadway show—*Saturday Night Fever*—on *Liberty of the Seas*. Lounges range from a piano bar and a pub to a wine bar, a Latin-themed dance club, and even a disco. You can end the evening with a movie on the outdoor screen overlooking the pool on all three ships or in the 3-D cinema on *Freedom* and *Liberty*.

Pros and Cons

Pros: FlowRider surfing simulator is exciting, even for observers; the H2O Zone is a fun place to beat the heat beneath a waterfall, in the fountain sprays, and along a lazy river; a sports pool accommodates water volleyball, basketball, and golf.

Cons: the location of a self-serve frozen-yogurt bar near the kids' pool means that it often ends up messy; hang on to your wallet—the malts in Johnny Rockets diner aren't included in the price; on a ship this large, lines are inevitable, particularly at disembarkation.

Cabin Type	Size (sq. ft.)
Royal Suite	1,406
Presidential Suite	1,215
Owner's Suite	614
Grand Suite	387
Junior Suite	287
Family Stateroom	293
Balcony Stateroom	177–189
Ocean View	161–214
Inside	149–152

FAST FACTS

- 15 passenger decks
- 2 specialty restaurants, dining room, buffet, ice cream parlor, pizzeria
- Internet, Wi-Fi, safe, refrigerator, DVD (some)
- 3 pools, children's pool
- Fitness classes, gym, hot tubs, sauna, spa, steam room
- 14 bars, casino, cinema, 2 dance clubs, library, 3 show rooms, video game room
- Children's programs (ages 3–17)
- Dry-cleaning, laundry service
- Internet terminal
- No-smoking cabins

Climb the wall.

ROYAL CARIBBEAN INTERNATIONAL

2

VOYAGER-CLASS
Voyager, Explorer, Adventure, Navigator, Mariner of the Seas

CREW MEMBERS	1,185
ENTERED SERVICE	1999, 2000, 2001, 2002, 2003
GROSS TONS	142,000
LENGTH	1,020 feet
NUMBER OF CABINS	1,557
PASSENGER CAPACITY	3,114 (3,835 max)
WIDTH	158 feet

700 ft.
500 ft.
300 ft.

A truly impressive building program introduced one of these gigantic Voyager-class ships per year over a five-year period. With their rock-climbing walls, ice-skating rinks, in-line skating tracks, miniature golf, and multiple dining venues, they are destinations in their own right. Sports enthusiasts will be thrilled with nonstop daytime action.

The unusual horizontal, multiple-deck promenade-atriums on Voyager-class vessels can stage some of the pageantry for which Royal Caribbean is noted. Fringed with boutiques, bars, and even coffee shops, the mall-like expanses set the stage for evening parades and events, as well as spots to simply kick back for some people-watching.

Other public rooms are equally dramatic. Though it's considered to be three separate dining rooms, the triple-deck height of the single space is stunning. These ships not only carry a lot of people, but carry them well. Space is abundant, and crowding is seldom an issue.

Cabins

Cabins: As on other Royal Caribbean ships, cabins are bright and cheerful. Although more than 60% are outside—and a hefty 75% of those have private verandas—there are still plenty of bargain inside cabins, some with a bowed window for a view overlooking the action-packed promenade. Cabins in every category have adequate closet and drawer/shelf storage and bathroom shelves. Junior suites have a seating area, vanity area, and bathroom with bathtub. Family ocean-view cabins with a window sleep up to six people and can accommodate a roll-away bed and/or crib, have two twin beds (convertible to a queen), and additional bunk beds in a separate area, a separate seating area with a sofa bed, a vanity area, and a private bathroom with shower.

Amenities: Wood cabinetry, a small refrigerator-minibar, broadband Internet connection, a vanity-desk, a TV, a safe, a hair dryer, and a seating area with sofa, chair, and table are typical Voyager-class features in all categories. Bathrooms have shampoo and bath gel.

Accessibility: Twenty-six staterooms are designed for wheelchair accessibility.

Top: Rock-climbing wall
Bottom: Fitness class

Restaurants

Triple-deck-high formal dining rooms serve open-seating breakfast and lunch; dinner is served in two evening assigned seatings or open-seating My Time Dining. For a more upscale dinner, each ship has an Italian specialty restaurant; *Mariner* and *Navigator* also have a steakhouse. Both specialty restaurants charge a supplement and require reservations. The casual Lido buffet offers service nearly around the clock for meals and snacks, including dinner; *Mariner* and *Navigator* also serve Asian fare in their Jade section. Johnny Rockets is a popular option for casual meals, though it also has a separate charge. In the promenade are a pizzeria, coffee bar, and Ben & Jerry's ice cream, which charges for frozen treats. All but *Mariner* have Park Café, which serves casual fare. Room service is available 24 hours; however, there is a delivery charge after midnight.

Spas

The full-service spa operated by Steiner Leisure offers an extensive treatment menu including facials, teeth whitening, body wraps and scrubs, massages, acupuncture, and FDA-approved Medi-Spa treatments performed by trained physicians. Spa rituals also include treatments designed especially for men and teens. While there are no thermal suites, complimentary saunas and steam rooms are in men's and women's changing rooms.

Bars and Entertainment

Nightlife runs the gamut from Broadway-style production shows to bars and lounges that include a piano bar, pub, wine bar, and disco, and on *Mariner* and *Navigator*, a Latin-themed bar. Music abounds for dancing or listening, or you can choose to end the evening with a movie on the outdoor screen overlooking the pool.

Pros and Cons

Pros: Royal Promenade may elicit the biggest "Wow!" on board when a parade is center stage; professional ice-skating performances are staged twice during each cruise; equipment to participate in sports activities is provided at no additional charge.

Cons: with the exception of the gym and some fitness classes, nearly everything else on board carries a price tag; although there is no charge to attend, you must get tickets for the ice-skating shows; smokers may be frustrated to find that smoking is prohibited in cabins and in most indoor areas.

Cabin Type	Size (sq. ft.)
Royal Suite	1,188–1,325
Other Suites*	277–610
Superior/Deluxe/Family Ocean View**	173–328
Large Ocean View	211
Standard Ocean View	161–180
Interior	153–167

*Owner's (506–618 sq. ft.), Grand (381–390 sq. ft.), Royal family (512–610 sq. ft.), Junior (277–299 sq. ft). **Superior (202–206 sq. ft.), Deluxe (173–184 sq. ft.), Family (265–328 sq. ft.).

FAST FACTS

- 14 passenger decks
- 1 specialty restaurant (2 on *Mariner* and *Navigator*), dining room, buffet, ice cream parlor, pizzeria
- Internet, Wi-Fi, safe, refrigerator, DVD (some)
- 3 pools, children's pool (only *Voyager*, *Explorer*, and *Adventure*)
- Fitness classes, gym, hot tubs, sauna, spa, steam room
- 12 bars, casino, 2 dance clubs, library, 3 show rooms, video game room
- Children's programs
- Dry-cleaning, laundry service
- Internet terminal
- No-smoking cabins

RADIANCE-CLASS
Radiance, Brilliance, Serenade, Jewel of the Seas

CREW MEMBERS	857
ENTERED SERVICE	2001, 2002, 2003, 2004
GROSS TONS	90,090
LENGTH	962 feet
NUMBER OF CABINS	1,056
PASSENGER CAPACITY	2,112 (2,501 max)
WIDTH	106 feet

700 ft.

500 ft.

300 ft.

Considered by many people to be the most beautiful vessels in the Royal Caribbean fleet, Radiance-class ships are large but sleek and swift, with sun-filled interiors and panoramic elevators that span 10 decks along the ships' exteriors.

High-energy and glamorous spaces are abundant throughout these sister ships. From the rock-climbing wall, children's pool with waterslide, and golf area to the columned dining room, sweeping staircases, and the tropical garden of the solarium, these ships hold appeal for a wide cross section of interests and tastes.

The ships are packed with multiple dining venues, including the casual Windjammer, with its indoor and outdoor seating, and the Latte-Tudes patisserie, offering specialty coffees, pastries, and ice cream treats.

Cabins
Cabins: With the line's highest percentage of outside cabins, standard staterooms are bright and cheery as well as roomy. Nearly three-quarters of the outside cabins have private balconies. Every cabin has adequate closet and drawer/shelf storage, as well as bathroom shelves.

Suites: All full suites and family suites have private balconies and include concierge service. Top-category suites have wet bars, separate living–dining areas, multiple bathrooms, entertainment centers with flat-screen TVs, DVD players, and stereos. Some bathrooms have twin sinks, steam showers, and whirlpool tubs. Junior suites have a seating area, vanity area, and bathroom with a tub.

Amenities: Light-wood cabinetry, a small refrigerator-minibar, broadband Internet connection, a vanity-desk, a TV, a safe, a hair dryer, and a seating area with sofa, chair, and table are typical Radiance-class features in all categories. Bathroom extras include shampoo and bath gel.

Accessibility: Fifteen staterooms are designed for wheelchair accessibility on *Radiance* and *Brilliance*; 19 on *Serenade* and *Jewel*.

Restaurants
The double-deck-high formal dining room serves open-seating breakfast and lunch; dinner is served in two

Top: Pool deck
Bottom: Shared moments on your personal balcony

assigned seatings, but open seating is an option. For a more upscale dinner, each ship has an Italian restaurant and a steakhouse. In addition, *Radiance of the Seas* has a Brazilian-style steakhouse. All but *Jewel* have an Asian restaurant; *Brilliance, Serenade,* and *Radiance* have Mexican restaurants. There is a supplement charged for specialty dining, and reservations are required. The casual Lido buffet serves nearly around the clock for breakfast, lunch, dinner, and snacks. Seaview Café is open for quick lunches and dinners on *Jewel of the Seas.* A pizzeria in *Serenade*'s Solarium serves slices; the other ships have Park Café for casual fare in that space, and *Radiance* also serves custom hot dogs at Boardwalk Doghouse. The coffee bar features specialty coffees and pastries, for which there is a charge. Room service is available 24 hours; however there is a charge after midnight.

Spas

The full-service spa operated by Steiner Leisure offers an extensive treatment menu including facials, teeth whitening, body wraps and scrubs. Spa rituals also include treatments designed especially for men and teens. There are thermal suites for a fee as well as complimentary saunas, and steam rooms are located in men's and women's changing rooms.

Bars and Entertainment

Nightlife options range from Broadway-style productions in the main show lounge to movies in the cinema or on the outdoor screen overlooking the pool. Bars and lounges include a piano bar and wine bar, and most have music for dancing or listening. There's also a pub or sports bar and a lounge for billiards. Look high above for aerial performances in the central atriums on *Serenade, Brilliance,* and *Jewel of the Seas.*

Pros and Cons

Pros: aft on deck 6, four distinct lounges and a billiard room form a clubby adult entertainment center; spacious family ocean-view cabins sleep up to six people; ships offer a wide range of family-friendly activities and games.

Cons: upgraded features of the fleet are not consistent throughout this ship class, so check before booking; dining options that charge have replaced some that were previously complimentary; libraries are tiny and poorly stocked for ships this size.

Cabin Type	Size (sq. ft.)
Royal Suite	1,001
Owner's Suite	512
Grand Suite	358–384
Royal Family Suite	533–586
Junior Suites	293
Superior Ocean View	204
Deluxe Ocean View	179
Large Ocean View	170
Family Ocean View	319
Interior	165

FAST FACTS

- 12 passenger decks
- 2 specialty restaurants on *Jewel;* 4 on *Serenade* and *Brilliance;* 5 on *Radiance,* dining room, buffet, pizzeria
- Internet, Wi-Fi, safe, refrigerator, DVD (some)
- 2 pools (1 indoor), children's pool
- Fitness classes, gym, hot tubs, sauna, spa, steam room
- 11 bars, casino, dance club, library, show room, video game room
- Children's programs
- Dry-cleaning, laundry service
- Internet terminal
- No-smoking cabins

Sports courts

ENCHANTMENT OF THE SEAS

CREW MEMBERS	840
ENTERED SERVICE	1997
GROSS TONS	81,500
LENGTH	989 feet
NUMBER OF CABINS	1,126
PASSENGER CAPACITY	2,252 (2,730 max)
WIDTH	106 feet

700 ft.

500 ft.

300 ft.

In 2005 *Enchantment of the Seas* (originally a Vision-class ship identical to *Grandeur of the Seas*) was the third Royal Caribbean ship to be lengthened to increase her capacity and facilities. After she was cut in half, a new, 73-foot middle section containing 151 staterooms and suspension bridges that span the pool area and over-hang the sea were added. Not only was the pool area expanded by almost 50%, but four bungee trampolines were installed—for real thrills you can soar high above the bow while safely tethered to the trampoline.

For a buzz of a different sort, a pool bar juts out over the water where peekaboo windows set into the deck afford views of the sea below. Nearby floor-mounted water jets create a splash deck for children that transforms into a lighted fountain after dark. Recreational facilities and the spa were also expanded during the renovation. Not to be overlooked, interiors now include the South Beach–style Bolero's lounge as well as a coffee and ice cream bar, a steakhouse, and an enlarged Windjammer Café.

Cabins

Cabins: Cabins are light and comfortable, although the smallest can be a tight squeeze for more than two adults. Every cabin has adequate closet and drawer/shelf storage, as well as bathroom shelves.

Suites: All full suites and family suites have private balconies and a small refrigerator-minibar; full suites include concierge service. Royal suites have a living room, wet bar, separate dining area, TV, stereo, DVD player, separate bedroom, bathroom (with twin sinks, a whirlpool tub, steam shower, and bidet), and separate powder room. Owner's suites have separate living area, mini-bar, TV, stereo, DVD player, dinette area, and bathroom with twin sinks, bathtub, separate shower, and bidet. Grand suites have a seating area, stereo and DVD player, bathroom with combination bathtub-shower, and double sink.

Amenities: A vanity-desk, a TV, a safe, a hair dryer, and a seating area with sofa, chair, and table are typical features in all categories. Bathrooms have shampoo and bath gel.

Accessibility: Fourteen staterooms are designed for wheelchair accessibility.

Top: Formal dining
Bottom: Ocean-view
stateroom

Restaurants

The double-deck-high formal dining room serves open-seating breakfast and lunch; dinner is served in two evening assigned seatings or open-seating My Time Dining. For a more upscale dinner, there is the specialty steakhouse, Chops Grille, which charges a supplement and requires reservations. The casual Lido buffet offers service nearly around the clock for breakfast, lunch, dinner, and snacks, and the café in the adults-only Solarium serves light fare. The coffee bar features specialty coffees and pastries and Ben & Jerry's ice cream, for which there is a charge. Room service is available 24 hours; however, there is a delivery charge after midnight.

Spas

The full-service spa operated by Steiner Leisure offers an extensive treatment menu including facials, teeth whitening, body wraps and scrubs, and massages. Spa rituals also include treatments designed especially for men and teens. Although there is no thermal suite, complimentary saunas are in men's and women's changing rooms.

Bars and Entertainment

After a Broadway-style production show, performances by guest entertainers, or a movie on the outdoor screen overlooking the pool, look high above the central atrium for dazzling aerial performances, or head to Bolero's, the Latin dance club. You'll find lounges with music for listening and dancing when the entertainment staff ramps up the fun with themed parties. The Viking Crown Lounge is a great spot for late-night dancing or a nightcap.

Pros and Cons

Pros: transformation of an underutilized lounge into Bolero's Latin nightclub was a brilliant move; the glass canopy over the solarium can be opened or closed as the weather dictates; bungee trampolines offer some serious fun for thrill seekers.

Cons: when the ship is full, public areas can suffer overload; the tranquil library suffers from an underabundance of books; the poolside Island Bar is only steps away from the kids-oriented splash deck.

Cabin Type	Size (sq. ft.)
Royal Suites	1,119
Owner's Suites	511
Grand Suites	349
Royal Family Suites	532
Junior Suites	245
Superior Ocean View	190
Large Ocean View	154
Family Ocean View	449
Family Interior	230
Large Interior	146
Standard Interior	140

FAST FACTS

- 11 passenger decks
- Specialty restaurant, dining room, buffet, ice cream parlor, pizzeria
- Wi-Fi, safe, refrigerator, DVD (some)
- 3 pools (1 indoor), children's pool
- Fitness classes, gym, hot tubs, sauna, spa
- 6 bars, casino, dance club, library, show room, video game room
- Children's programs
- Dry-cleaning, laundry service
- Internet terminal
- No-smoking cabins

5

ROYAL CARIBBEAN INTERNATIONAL

Enchantment of the Seas at sea

VISION-CLASS
Legend, Splendour, Grandeur, Rhapsody, Vision of the Seas

CREW MEMBERS	726, 762, 760, 765, 742
ENTERED SERVICE	1995, 1996, 1996, 1997, 1998
GROSS TONS	69, 130–178, 491
LENGTH	867, 867, 916, 915, 915 feet
NUMBER OF CABINS	902, 915, 996, 1,020, 999
PASSENGER CAPACITY	1,800–2,000 (2,076–2,435)
WIDTH	106 feet

700 ft.
500 ft.
300 ft.

The first Royal Caribbean ships to offer balconies in a number of categories, these Vision-class vessels, named for sister ship *Vision of the Seas,* have acres of glass skylights that allow sunlight to flood in and windows that offer wide sea vistas. The soaring central atrium at the heart of each ship is anchored by a chic bar that fills with music after dark and is the ideal spot for watching the daring aerial performances overhead.

Built in pairs, the ships follow the same general layout but are different in overall size and the total number of passengers on board. Cabin sizes also vary somewhat; as the total size of the ships increased from *Legend* and *Splendour* at 69,130 tons (1,800 passengers) to *Grandeur* at 74,140 tons (1,992 passengers), and finally, *Rhapsody* and *Vision* at 78,491 tons (2,000 passengers), so did the size of the accommodations. In some categories, it's only a matter of a few feet, so don't look for huge—or even noticeable—differences.

Cabins

Cabins: Cabins are airy and comfortable, but the smaller categories are a tight squeeze for more than two adults. Every cabin has adequate closet and drawer/shelf storage.

Suites: All full suites and family suites have private balconies and a small minibar; full suites also include concierge service. Royal suites have a living room; wet bar; separate dining area; entertainment center with TV, stereo, and DVD player; separate bedroom; bathroom (twin sinks, whirlpool tub, separate steam shower, bidet); and separate powder room. Owner's suites have a separate living area; minibar; entertainment center with TV, stereo, and DVD player; dinette area; and one bathroom (twin sinks, bathtub, separate shower, bidet). Grand suites have similar amenities on a smaller scale.

Amenities: A vanity-desk, a TV, a safe, a hair dryer, and a seating area with sofa, chair, and table are typical Vision-class features in all categories. Bathrooms have shampoo and bath gel.

Accessibility: On *Legend* and *Splendour,* 17 cabins are wheelchair accessible; on *Grandeur, Vision,* and *Rhapsody,* 14 cabins are wheelchair accessible.

Top: Viking Crown lounge overlooks the pool deck.
Bottom: *Splendour of the Seas*

Restaurants

The two-deck formal dining room serves evening meals in two assigned seatings or an open seating; breakfast and lunch in the dining room are always open seating. Windjammer, the casual Lido buffet, serves three meals a day, including a laid-back dinner. As was the norm when these ships were built, dining selections on board are pretty basic; however, specialty-dining options have been added. All ships now have restaurants serving Asian cuisine, and steakhouses, while *Rhapsody* and *Grandeur* also have Italian restaurants. Depending on the ship, Park Café or Solarium Café serves light fare and snacks in the solarium. *Splendour* also has Boardwalk Doghouse serving custom hot dogs. A coffee bar and ice cream bar offer specialty coffees and frozen treats for an additional fee. Room service is available 24 hours a day; however, there is a delivery charge after midnight.

Spas

The full-service spa operated by Steiner Leisure offers an extensive treatment menu including facials, teeth whitening, body wraps and scrubs, massages, and acupuncture. Spa rituals also include treatments designed especially for men and teens. Although there is no thermal suite, complimentary saunas and steam rooms are in men's and women's changing rooms.

Bars and Entertainment

Enjoy a Broadway-style production show, performances by guest entertainers, or a movie on the outdoor screen overlooking the pool, but don't forget to look high above the central atrium for dazzling aerial performances. You'll find lounges with music for listening and dancing when the entertainment staff ramps up the fun with themed parties. The Viking Crown Lounge is a great spot for late-night dancing or a nightcap.

Pros and Cons

Pros: open, light-filled public areas offer sea views from almost every angle; each vessel now offers numerous dining options, both free and for a fee; daring aerialists offer a new wow-factor high above the central atrium.

Cons: some lounges serve as a thoroughfare and suffer from continuous traffic flow; except for premium suites, accommodations lean toward the small side; there are no self-service laundry rooms.

Cabin Type	Size (sq. ft.)
Royal Suite	1,074
Owner's Suite	523
Grand Suite	355
Royal Family Suite	512
Junior Suite	240
Superior Ocean View	193
Large Ocean View*	154
Interior	135–174

All cabin sizes are averages of the five ships since cabins vary somewhat in size among the Vision-class ships (all *Legend* and *Splendour* cabins are the same size). *Rhapsody* has family Ocean View cabins at 237 sq. ft.

FAST FACTS

- 11 passenger decks
- 2 specialty restaurants (3 on *Grandeur* and *Rhapsody*), dining room, buffet, ice cream parlor, pizzeria
- Wi-Fi, safe, refrigerator (some), DVD (some)
- 2 pools (1 indoor)
- Fitness classes, gym, hot tubs, sauna, spa, steam room
- 6 bars, casino, dance club, library, show room, video game room
- Children's programs
- Dry-cleaning, laundry service
- Internet terminal
- No-smoking cabins

5

ROYAL CARIBBEAN INTERNATIONAL

SOVEREIGN-CLASS
Majesty of the Seas

CREW MEMBERS	912
ENTERED SERVICE	1992
GROSS TONS	74,077
LENGTH	880 feet
NUMBER OF CABINS	1,829
PASSENGER CAPACITY	2,350 (2,767 max)
WIDTH	106 feet

700 ft.
500 ft.
300 ft.

Precursor of vessels to come, *Sovereign of the Seas,* which no longer sails in the Royal Caribbean fleet, was the largest cruise ship afloat when it was introduced in 1988. Two sister ships followed, but only *Majesty of the Seas* remains. *Majesty* has received major refurbishments, with the addition of a Miami Beach–style Latin club and a Johnny Rockets diner. Other improvements include an expanded spa and enlarged areas for children and teens. Balconies were also added to Junior suites.

The futuristic atrium, combined with the abundant use of marble and gleaming metal, virtually assured the Sovereign-class ships design longevity. The addition of rock-climbing walls and other features found on subsequent Royal Caribbean vessels, plus sparkling new interior colors, belie *Majesty of the Seas'* age.

Cabins

Cabins: Cabins are comfortable, but standard ocean-view and inside categories are a tight squeeze for more than two occupants. When this ship was conceived, staterooms were viewed as primarily for sleeping and changing clothes, so even the suites are on the small size by current standards. Every cabin has adequate closet and drawer/shelf storage. The added personal space provided by the balconies in higher-end accommodations is a real plus. Third and fourth Pullman beds are found in a variety of stateroom categories, as are connecting staterooms—a plus for families that require more room to spread out.

Suites: All suites and junior suites have a minibar, balcony, and bathtub. Royal family suites have a seating area, dining area, two bedrooms (one with two twin beds and an upper bunk, one with queen-size bed), and two bathrooms.

Amenities: A vanity-desk, TV, safe, and hair dryer are typical Sovereign-class features in all categories. Bathrooms have shampoo and bath gel.

Accessibility: Six staterooms are designed for wheelchair accessibility.

Restaurants

As was the norm when this ship was built, dining selections on board are pretty basic. Although there are no upscale specialty restaurants, casual dining options are a bit more tempting. Two formal dining rooms serve

Majesty of the Seas:
The Centrum

breakfast and lunch in open seatings and dinner in two assigned seatings with an open-seating option. The Windjammer casual Lido buffet serves three meals a day, including a casual dinner option. In addition, *Majesty* has Sorrento's Pizza restaurant, Johnny Rockets Diner, and a deli in the Windjammer, as well as Latte-Tudes, a patisserie serving specialty coffees and pastries. Some options carry an extra charge. Room service is available 24 hours; however, there is a delivery charge after midnight.

Spas
The full-service spa operated by Steiner Leisure offers an extensive treatment menu including facials, teeth whitening, body wraps and scrubs, and massages. Spa rituals also include treatments designed especially for men and teens. Although there are no thermal suites, complimentary saunas and steam rooms are in men's and women's changing rooms.

Bars and Entertainment
After a Broadway-style production show or performances by guest entertainers, head to Bolero's, the Latin dance club. If that's not your style, you'll find other lounges with music for listening and dancing when the entertainment staff ramps up the fun with themed parties. The Viking Crown Lounge is a great spot for late-night dancing or a nightcap.

Pros and Cons
Pros: Wi-Fi is available in public rooms; the Schooner Bar is Royal Caribbean's popular signature piano bar with seagoing flair; the multideck atrium—a cruise ship first in this class—is still stunning.

Cons: some remnants of late-1980s design are difficult to overcome, including few balconies and low ceilings in the dining rooms; the rock-climbing wall is impressive, but looks like an afterthought; standard accommodations are really tight for more than two people.

Cabin Type	Size (sq. ft.)
Royal Suite	670
Owner's Suite	446
Grand Suite	382
Royal Family Suite*	371
Junior Suite	264
Superior Ocean View	157
Standard Ocean View	122
Inside	119

*Only on *Majesty of the Seas*

FAST FACTS

- 11 passenger decks
- 2 dining rooms, buffet, pizzeria
- Wi-Fi, safe (some), refrigerator (some), DVD (some)
- 2 pools
- Fitness classes, gym, hot tubs, sauna, spa, steam room
- 7 bars, casino, 2 dance clubs, library, show room, video game room
- Children's programs
- Dry-cleaning, laundry service
- Internet terminal
- No-smoking cabins

Formal dining room

SEABOURN CRUISE LINE

Seabourn was founded on the principle that dedication to personal service in elegant surroundings would appeal to sophisticated, independent-minded passengers whose lifestyles demand the best. Lovingly maintained since their introduction in 1987—and rou-

Make memories to last a lifetime.

tinely updated with new features—the original megayachts of Seabourn and their new fleetmates have proved to be a smashing success over the years. They remain favorites with people who can take care of themselves but would rather do so aboard a ship that caters to their individual preferences.

☎ 800/929–9391
⊕ www.seabourn.com
☞ Cruise Style: Luxury.

Recognized as a leader in small-ship, luxury cruising, Seabourn delivers all the expected extras—complimentary wines and spirits, a stocked minibar in all suites, and elegant amenities. Expect the unexpected as well—from exclusive travel-document portfolios and luggage tags to the pleasure of a complimentary minimassage while lounging at the pool. If you don't want to lift a finger, Seabourn will even arrange to have your luggage picked up at home and delivered directly to your suite—for a price.

Peace and tranquility reign on these ships, so the daily roster of events is somewhat thin. Wine tastings, lectures, and other quiet pursuits might be scheduled, but most passengers are satisfied to simply do what pleases them. One don't-miss activity is the daily team trivia contest. Prizes are unimportant: it's the bragging rights that most guests seek.

Although the trio of original Seabourn ships has been upgraded over the years, the line launched a newer set of larger, even more luxurious triplets that were introduced in 2009 (*Seabourn Odyssey*), 2010 (*Seabourn Sojourn*), and 2011 (*Seabourn Quest*). The smaller megayachts were sold to Windstar Cruises in 2013 and will leave the Seabourn fleet in 2014 (*Seabourn Pride*) and 2015 (*Seabourn Spirit* and *Seabourn Legend*).

Food

As expected from a member of Chaîne des Rôtisseurs, Seabourn offers exceptional cuisine prepared à la minute and served in open-seating dining rooms. Upscale menu offerings include foie gras, quail, fresh seafood, and jasmine crème brûlée. Dishes low in cholesterol, salt, and fat, as well as vegetarian selections, are prepared with the same artful presentation and attention to detail. Wines are chosen to complement each day's luncheon and dinner menus, and caviar is always available. A background of classical music sets the tone for afternoon tea. The weekly Gala Tea features such items as crêpes suzette.

A casual dinner alternative on the original ships is Restaurant 2, serving innovative cuisine in multiple courses nightly in the Veranda Café, where outdoor tables enhance the romantic atmosphere. Evening attire in the Veranda Café is specified as casual or elegant casual—when men are asked to wear a jacket but no tie. A second and even more laid-back dinner alternative is offered on select occasions in the open-air Sky Bar, where grilled seafood and steaks are served. Sky Grill dinners are scheduled on a couple of nights during each cruise, weather permitting. Both Restaurant 2 and Sky Grill require reservations, but happily there is no additional charge for either. Aboard the new ships, Restaurant 2 has a dedicated space, and the Colonnade indoor-outdoor restaurant is centered on an open kitchen where you can watch chefs prepare your breakfast, lunch, or dinner order. Each evening has a different theme, offering an ever-changing culinary experience.

Room service is always available. Dinner can even be served course by course in your suite during restaurant hours.

Entertainment

Dining and evening socializing are generally more stimulating to Seabourn passengers than splashy song-and-dance revues. Still, proportionately scaled production shows and cabarets are presented in the main show room and smaller lounges. Movies are shown on the wind-protected sundeck at least one evening on virtually all cruises as long as the weather permits. The library stocks not only books but also DVDs for those who prefer to watch movies in the privacy of their suites—popcorn will naturally be delivered with a call to room service.

KNOWN FOR

- **Ever-Changing Itineraries:** Seabourn ships seldom repeat port calls from one voyage to the next, nor do ships sail from a single home port.

- **Formality:** Seabourn cruises are a bit more formal than most other luxury lines, but never stuffy.

- **Intimacy:** The line's luxury ships can sail into the heart of landmark cities as well as visit smaller ports where larger ships cannot venture.

- **Older Clientele:** Fellow passengers on Seabourn's cruises are generally older and more well-traveled than on most cruise lines.

- **Service:** Service is a premiere element of all Seabourn voyages.

Make memories to last a lifetime.

Top: A good book and breakfast in bed
Bottom: The Club

Top: French balcony
Middle: Dining by candlelight
in the Restaurant
Bottom: Relax on deck.

The inspiring enrichment program features guest appearances by luminaries in the arts, literature, politics, and world affairs; during certain culinary-focused sailings you can learn the secrets of the world's most innovative chefs. Due to the size of Seabourn ships, passengers have the opportunity to mingle with presenters and interact one-on-one.

Fitness and Recreation

A full array of exercise equipment, free weights, and basic fitness classes is available in the small gym, while some specialized fitness sessions are offered for a fee.

Many passengers are drawn to the pampering spa treatments, including a variety of massages, body wraps, and facials. Hair and nail services are offered in the salon. Both spa and salon are operated by Steiner Leisure.

Your Shipmates

Seabourn's yachtlike vessels appeal to well-traveled, affluent couples of all ages who enjoy destination-intense itineraries, a subdued atmosphere, and exclusive service. Passengers tend to be 50-plus and retired couples who are accustomed to evening formality.

Dress Code

At least one formal night is standard on seven-night cruises and three to four nights, depending on the itinerary, on two- to three-week cruises. Men are required to wear tuxedos or dark suits after 6 pm, and the majority prefer black tie. All other evenings are elegant casual, and slacks with a jacket over a sweater or shirt for men and a sundress or skirt or pants with a sweater or blouse for women are suggested.

Junior Cruisers

Seabourn Cruise Line is adult-oriented and does not accommodate children under six months (or under one year for trans-ocean sailings and voyages of 15 days or longer). A limited number of suites are available for triple occupancy. No dedicated children's facilities are present on these ships, so parents are responsible for the behavior and entertainment of their children.

CHOOSE THIS LINE IF ...

You consider fine dining the highlight of your vacation.

You own your own tuxedo. These ships are dressy, and most men wear them on formal evenings.

You feel it's annoying to sign drink tabs; everything is included on these ships.

Service

Personal service and attention by the professional staff are the orders of the day. Your preferences are noted and fulfilled without the necessity of reminders. It's a mystery how nearly every staff member knows your name within hours, if not minutes, after you board.

Tipping

Tipping is neither required nor expected.

Past Passengers

Once you have completed your first Seabourn cruise, you are automatically enrolled in the Seabourn Club for past guests. Benefits include discounts on selected cruises (not combinable with Early Booking Savings); the Seabourn Club newsletters and periodic mailings featuring destinations, special programs, and exclusive savings; and an exclusive online email contact point to the club desk through the membership page on the Seabourn website.

On the ships, club members receive a 5% discount on future bookings, special recognition for frequent cruising, and a club party hosted by the captain. As members reach Silver, Gold, Platinum, and Diamond Club levels, the benefits increase. Milestone Awards offer a complimentary cruise of up to seven days when 140 days sailed have been completed, or a complimentary cruise of up to 14 days when 250 days sailed is reached.

HELPFUL HINTS

Seabourn's shore excursions often include privileged access to historic and cultural sites when they are not open to the general public.

Most warm-weather cruises include a beach picnic (albeit one with champagne and caviar); on itineraries where a beach isn't available, a similar party is held on the ships' water-sports marina.

A Vintage Seabourn prepurchase wine option offers access to a varied selection of premium wines from the ships' well-stocked cellars at advantageous prices.

Every passenger gets a complimentary canvas logo tote bag.

Ground transfers are included in air and sea packages purchased through Seabourn, but passengers traveling independently are responsible for their own transfer to the ship.

5

SEABOURN CRUISE LINE

DON'T CHOOSE THIS LINE IF ...

Dressing down is on your agenda.

You absolutely must have a spacious private balcony. They are limited in number and book fast.

You need to be stimulated by constant activity.

SEABOURN ODYSSEY, SOJOURN, QUEST

CREW MEMBERS	330
ENTERED SERVICE	2009, 2010, 2011
GROSS TONS	32,000
LENGTH	650 feet
NUMBER OF CABINS	225, 225, 229
PASSENGER CAPACITY	450, 450, 458
WIDTH	84 feet

700 ft.

500 ft.

300 ft.

As the first new class of ultraluxurious ships to be introduced in nearly a decade, *Seabourn Odyssey* and her sister ships promise to continue the line's tradition of understated elegance and signature features in a larger setting. With more space, there are more pools, more hot tubs, and a two-deck spa. The specialty dining room gets its own dedicated space, and there's more room to spread out on deck and in gracious public lounges indoors. As on the trio of smaller Seabourn vessels, there is a Club bar for predinner cocktails and an observation lounge affording expansive sea views. New for the larger ships is a spacious show lounge with a proper stage for entertainment. When the water-sports marina is extended, there's even a third swimming option—an enclosed in-sea "pool" with teak deck.

Cabins

Cabins: All suites, 90% with balconies, are midship to forward; none are aft. Eight categories of roomier accommodations are true suites, with separate bedrooms in all but the least expensive. Even the most modest suites have walk-in closets, a seating area with coffee table that converts to a dining table for meals, a dressing table–desk, and a granite-topped bathroom with double-sink vanities and a separate shower and tub (some with whirlpool tubs).

Amenities: Amenities include flat-screen TV with DVD player, safe, hair dryer, fully stocked minibar, fresh fruit and flowers, world atlas, personalized stationery, shampoo, conditioner, designer soap and lotion, Egyptian-cotton towels and robes, slippers, umbrellas, and beds dressed with silky, high-thread-count linens. Top-category suites have a butler's pantry and guest powder room. Wintergarden and Signature suites can be configured with two bedrooms. Four Penthouse Spa Suites with spa-style amenities, unlimited access to the spa's Serene Area, and the services of a Spa Concierge, were added to *Seabourn Quest* in 2013 and similar suites will be added to *Odyssey* in May 2014 and *Sojourn* in November 2014.

Accessibility: Seven suites are designed for wheelchair accessibility.

Restaurants

The formal Restaurant serves breakfast, lunch, and dinner in open seating. In Restaurant 2 (reservations), dishes

Top: *Seabourn Odyssey* at sea
Bottom: *Seabourn Odyssey* penthouse

are prepared individually by the chef in tasting portions. For casual indoor-outdoor dining, The Colonnade serves breakfast, lunch, and dinner from an open kitchen, with à la minute preparation. Breakfast, lunch, and dinner are also offered poolside at the Patio Grill. Espresso and cappuccino are available at the coffee bar. Meals and snacks can be ordered from an extensive room-service menu around the clock. During restaurant hours, dinner can be served course by course en suite.

Spas

Treatments in the spa operated by Steiner Leisure include massages, facials, and body wraps that incorporate natural ingredients. Along with a treatment, you receive use of the thermal suite, with a large hydrotherapy pool (on *Seabourn Odyssey*) or the Kneipp Walk, a walking pool with hot water on one side and cold water on the other, utilized to stimulate circulation (on *Sojourn* and *Quest*). Heated loungers surround the pools, and a variety of steam and thermal rooms are included. Day passes (for a fee) are available for just the thermal suite, or you can opt for the free sauna in changing rooms.

Bars and Entertainment

Proportionately scaled production shows, performances by guest artists, and cabarets are presented in the Grand Salon and smaller Club lounge, where dancing is held most nights. A pianist entertains in the Observation Bar. Movies and a deck party with dancing are scheduled on the wind-protected pool deck on most cruises as long as the weather permits.

Pros and Cons

Pros: kayaks, waterskiing, and other complimentary water toys are available at the fold-down marina when the ships are at anchor; the fully equipped gym has a Kinesis Wall, an innovative method of exercise utilizing a pulley-and-cable system; there is never a cover charge for specialty dining.

Cons: choose your suite location carefully—not all balconies are equal, even within the same category; although the spa is opulent, it's still operated by Steiner, which operates spas on most cruise ships; past passengers take a proprietary interest in the ships and may seem cliquish to newcomers.

Cabin Type	Size (sq. ft.)
Grand Wintergarden	1,182
Wintergarden Suites	914
Grand Signature	1,135
Signature Suites	819
Owner's Suites	611–675
Penthouse Suites/ Spa Suites	436–611/ 516–538
Veranda Suite	269–302
Ocean View Suite	295

FAST FACTS

- ■ 8 passenger decks
- ■ Specialty restaurant, dining room, buffet
- ■ Wi-Fi, safe, refrigerator, DVD
- ■ 2 pools
- ■ Fitness classes, gym, hot tubs, sauna, spa
- ■ 5 bars, casino, dance club, library, show room
- ■ Dry-cleaning, laundry facilities, laundry service
- ■ Internet terminal

5

SEABOURN CRUISE LINE

Standard suite

SEABOURN LEGEND, PRIDE, SPIRIT

CREW MEMBERS	160
ENTERED SERVICE	1992, 1988, 1989
GROSS TONS	10,000
LENGTH	439 feet
NUMBER OF CABINS	104
PASSENGER CAPACITY	208
WIDTH	63 feet

700 ft.

500 ft.

300 ft.

The height of absolute luxury, Seabourn's megayachts surround passengers in comfort and understated style punctuated by polished brass accents and etched-glass panels. Public rooms are intimate but not cramped, although predinner cocktail gatherings tend to strain the available room in the popular Club bar.

The relative amount of shipwide space devoted to passengers is among the highest in the cruise industry, and the public areas and deck spaces were designed so that no one aboard feels crowded. Fresh flower arrangements add a gracious touch to the classic decor of every public room.

After ambitious programs of extensive refurbishment, each of Seabourn's yachtlike vessels emerged from dry dock in shipshape.

Cabins

Cabins: All suites are on three midlevel decks and none are aft, which can be noisy on a ship with a water-sports marina. The roomy accommodations are truly of suite proportions, with large walk-in closets, a spacious seating area with coffee table that converts to a dining table for meals, a vanity-desk, and a marble bathroom with a separate shower and tub (in most suites). Owner's, Classic, and Double suites have an actual dining table and chairs; Owner's suites have a guest bathroom. Both Owner's and Classic suites have fully furnished balconies.

Amenities: Amenities are also befitting a true luxury suite: a flat-screen TV with DVD player, a Bose Wave CD stereo, a safe, and a hair dryer. Other amenities include a stocked minibar, fresh fruit and flowers, a world atlas, personalized stationery, shampoo, conditioner, designer soap and lotion, Egyptian-cotton towels and robes, slippers, umbrellas, and beds dressed with silky, high-thread-count linens. The only apparent difference between the sister ships is that *Seabourn Spirit* and *Seabourn Pride* have twin sinks in the bathrooms, while *Seabourn Legend* bathrooms have but one.

Accessibility: Four suites are designed for wheelchair accessibility.

Restaurants

The formal restaurant offers open-seating breakfast, lunch, and dinner during scheduled hours. For a more laid-back setting, the Veranda Café has indoor and

Top: Sky Bar
Bottom: Balcony suite

outdoor seating for breakfast and lunch, plus reservations-required Restaurant 2 serves tasting dinners in a smart-casual atmosphere every evening, including formal nights. The grill serves outdoors when weather permits for lunch and when Sky Grill dinners are scheduled on a couple of nights during each cruise. Tea is served every afternoon, and room service is available 24 hours. While you can order just about anything you want at any time, during scheduled lunch and dinner hours in the formal restaurant, room service is available from the restaurant menu.

Spas
Treatments that range from massages and facials to body treatments and wraps that incorporate natural ingredients are offered in the Steiner Leisure–operated spa. There is no thermal suite, but complimentary steam rooms and saunas are in men's and women's changing rooms.

Bars and Entertainment
Proportionately scaled cabaret shows and performances by guest artists are presented in the Show Lounge and smaller Club Lounge, where the options might be a pianist or a dance party. Movies or dancing are scheduled on the pool deck on most cruises as long as the weather permits. There's little late-night action—most socializing takes place early and is subdued.

Pros and Cons
Pros: as the high crew-to-guest ratio suggests, service is nonstop and the staff seems to anticipate your wishes; for pure indulgence, make a selection from the aromatherapy bath menu before a soak in the tub; complimentary Massage Moments on deck are soothing tension tamers.

Cons: a few minibalconies are available in standard suites, but they're simply for fresh air because there's no room to stand outside on them; a single outdoor swimming pool is deep but not long enough for serious laps; art, or the absence of it, is noteworthy on a ship of this style.

Cabin Type	Size (sq. ft.)
Owner's Suite	530–575
Classic Suite	400
Double Suite	554
Balcony Suite*	277
Ocean-View Suite	277

*The balcony isn't functional.

FAST FACTS

- 6 passenger decks
- Specialty restaurant, dining room, buffet
- Wi-Fi, safe, refrigerator, DVD
- Pool
- Fitness classes, gym, hot tubs, sauna, spa, steam room
- 3 bars, casino, dance club, library, show room
- Dry-cleaning, laundry facilities, laundry service
- Internet terminal

5

SEABOURN CRUISE LINE

Water-sports marina

SEADREAM YACHT CLUB

SeaDream yachts began sailing in 1984 beneath the Sea Goddess banner, and after a couple of changes of ownership and total renovations, they have evolved into the ultimate boutique ships. A voyage on one of these sleek megayachts is all about personal

SeaDream I at sea

choice. Passengers enjoy an unstructured holiday at sea doing what they please, making it easy to imagine the diminutive vessel really is a private yacht. The ambience is refined and elegantly casual.

☎ *305/631–6100 or 800/707–4911*
⊕ *www.seadream.com*
☞ *Cruise Style: Luxury.*

Fine dining and socializing with fellow passengers and the ships' captains and officers are preferred yachting pastimes.

A well-stocked library has books and movies for those who prefer quiet pursuits in the privacy of their staterooms. In addition, MP3 players stocked with all types of music—enough to play for a complete sailing without repeating a selection—are available for personal use at no charge.

The weekly picnic on a private beach is considered by many passengers as their most memorable experience ashore during a SeaDream cruise. It begins with refreshing drinks served during a wet landing from Zodiacs and is followed by SeaDream's signature champagne-and-caviar splash served to passengers from a surfboard bar in the crystal clear water. On voyages where it isn't possible to host the champagne-and-caviar splash ashore, it is celebrated poolside.

SeaDream yachts are often chartered by families, corporations, and other affinity groups, but the company does not charter both ships at the same time. If your chosen sailing is closed to you because of a charter, the other yacht will be available.

Food

Every meal is prepared to order using the freshest seafood and U.S. prime cuts of beef and often incorporate the flavors of the ships' sailing regions with locally sourced fresh, high-quality ingredients. Menus include vegetarian alternatives and Asian wellness cuisine for the health-conscious, as well as a Raw Food Menu option, created with the renowned Hippocrates Health Institute in West Palm Beach, Florida. Cheeses, petits fours, and chocolate truffles are offered after dinner with coffee, and the Grand Marnier soufflé is to die for. A weekly dining event, Le Menu de Degustation, features an interesting medley of dishes planned by the executive chef for their variety and flavor; portions are sensibly sized, enabling diners to enjoy each course.

Weather permitting, daily breakfast, lunch, and special dinners are served alfresco in the canopied Topsider Restaurant. Wines are chosen to complement each luncheon and dinner menu from shipboard cellars that stock 3,500 bottles on each ship. Sommeliers are more than happy to discuss the attributes of each vintage and steam off the labels if you want to search for them at home. Snacks, from caviar to popcorn, are always available and delivered wherever you might be when hunger strikes, although there is a charge for caviar.

Room service is always available, and not just in your suite; you can dine anywhere you wish on deck.

Entertainment

One of the most important daily events takes place before dinner, either in the Main Salon or poolside for cocktails and a review of the next day's activities. Other than a pianist in the tiny piano bar, a small casino, and movies in the main lounge, there's no roster of activities. The late-night place to be is the Top of the Yacht Bar, where passengers gather to socialize and dance on the teak deck. The captain hosts welcome-aboard and farewell cocktail receptions in the Main Salon each cruise. Otherwise, you're on your own to do as you please.

Fitness and Recreation

Small gyms on each ship are equipped with treadmills, elliptical machines, recumbent bikes, and free weights. A personal trainer is available for consultation, and tai chi, yoga and aerobics classes are offered on deck as requested by passengers.

The yachts' unique SeaDream Spa facilities are also on the small side, yet offer a full menu of individualized, gentle European and Thai pampering therapies including massages, facials, and body wraps utilizing

5

SEADREAM YACHT CLUB

Top: Relax on a Balinese "dream bed."
Bottom: Fitness classes

Top: Dining at Topside
Restaurant
Middle: *SeaDream* Spa
Bottom: The Top of the
Yacht Bar

gentle techniques. Hair- and nail services are offered in the salon. SeaDream Spa is a member of the Thai Spa Association; products utilized for spa and salon services are among the best available from around the world. Massages are also available in cabanas ashore during the private beach party. Although the spa has regularly scheduled hours, treatments can be arranged outside those hours by special request. It's recommended that passengers schedule time for use of the sauna and steam room, as their size limits the number of people who can comfortably use them at once.

Your Shipmates

SeaDream yachts attract energetic, affluent travelers of all ages, as well as groups. Passengers tend to be couples in their mid-40s up to retirees who enjoy the unstructured informality, subdued ambience, and utterly exclusive service.

These ships are not recommended for passengers who use wheelchairs. Although there's one accessible stateroom, public facilities have thresholds and the elevator doesn't reach the uppermost deck. Tide conditions can cause the gangway to be steep when docked, and negotiating shore tenders would be impossible.

Dress Code

Leave the formal duds at home—every night is yacht casual on SeaDream. Men wear open-collar shirts and slacks; sport coats are preferred but not required. A tie is never necessary. For women, sundresses, dressy casual skirts and sweaters, or pants and tops are the norm.

Junior Cruisers

SeaDream yachts are adult-oriented. Children under the age of one are not allowed. High chairs and booster seats are available for the youngsters occasionally on board, but no children's facilities or organized activities are available. Parents are responsible for the behavior and entertainment of their children.

Service

Personal service and attention to detail are amazing; everyone will greet you by name within minutes of boarding. Passenger preferences are shared among staff

CHOOSE THIS LINE IF ...

You enjoy dining as an event; courses are presented with a flourish, and wine flows freely.

You don't like to hear the word no.

You have good sea legs. In rough seas, the SeaDream yachts tend to bob up and down.

members, who all work hard to assist one another. You seldom, if ever, have to repeat a request. Waiting in line for anything is unthinkable.

Tipping

Tipping is neither required nor expected.

Past Passengers

The SeaDream Club was designed to extend appreciation to past passengers, who are automatically enrolled in the club upon completion of one sailing. Members receive the *SeaDreamer* newsletter, which is published three times a year and features news and photos from the SeaDream yachts, profiles of the yachts' captains and other onboard personalities, profiles of various ports of call, news of special sailings, and other information of interest.

Other SeaDream Club benefits include advance notice of new itineraries, an annual club-members cruise, perks for introducing new passengers to SeaDream, a priority wait list on sold-out cruises, the ability to reserve spa appointments and shore excursions online, 5% to 15% savings when booking a future cruise while on board, an onboard club member cocktail party, and 15% onboard savings vouchers, which will be in your stateroom upon embarkation, for use towards onboard wine cellar purchases and treatments in the Asian Spa.

HELPFUL HINTS

SeaDream Yacht Clubs can be chartered, but the line never charters both ships at once.

If you skip the evening cocktail hour, you may miss hearing about a last-minute decision by the captain to extend a port call or even change the order of ports if there's something of interest going on ashore.

SeaDream gives you the "pillow gift" of logo pajamas, which come in handy if you decide to sleep under the stars on a Balinese dream bed.

Special parties can be arranged on board by the club and activities director.

Even if there is no dinner scheduled on deck, just let the maître d' know at breakfast and your meal will be served outside that evening.

5

SEADREAM YACHT CLUB

DON'T CHOOSE THIS LINE IF ...

You like to dress up. Although you could wear a sport coat to dinner, no one ever wears a tie on these ships.

You must have a balcony. There are none on any of Seadream's yachtlike vessels.

You need structured activities. You'll have to plan your own.

SEADREAM I, SEADREAM II

CREW MEMBERS	95
ENTERED SERVICE	1984, 1985
GROSS TONS	4,300
LENGTH	344 feet
NUMBER OF CABINS	56
PASSENGER CAPACITY	112
WIDTH	47 feet

700 ft.

500 ft.

300 ft.

Although these vessels are not huge, the public rooms are quite spacious; the Main Salon and Dining Salon are large enough to comfortably seat all passengers at once. Decor is elegant in its simplicity and is surprisingly non-nautical. Instead, it's modern and sleek, utilizing the hues of the sea, sky, and sandy beaches. Oriental rugs cover polished teak floors in the reception area and in the large, sun-splashed library, where you'll find more than 1,000 books from which to choose, as well as computers to access the Internet. The library also lends movies to watch on the flat-screen TV/DVD player in your suite.

Balinese sun beds are the ideal spot to relax by day, either for sunbathing or reading beneath an umbrella. A telescope mounted at each ship's stern is handy for spotting land and other vessels at sea.

Cabins

Cabins: Although none has a balcony, every stateroom has an ocean view, a seating area, and plenty of drawer space for storage. Bathrooms are marble-clad and have large, glass-enclosed showers with multijet shower massage that make up for the tiny bathrooms. The single Owner's suite has a living room, a dining area, a separate bedroom, a bathroom with a sea view (as well as a separate tub and shower), and a guest bathroom. Each ship has an Admiral's suite, which features an open-plan living-dining area, a separate master bedroom, three panoramic windows, a marble bathroom with separate tub and shower, and a guest half-bath. Commodore Club staterooms are basically double staterooms with one side configured as a sitting-dining area room and feature two identical bathrooms with showers.

Amenities: All cabins have a large flat-screen TV, CD, and DVD system; iPod docking station; broadband Internet connection; personalized stationery; and a wet bar stocked with complimentary beer, soft drinks, and bottled water. A lighted magnifying mirror and hair dryer are at a vanity table. Beds are dressed with Belgian linens, a down duvet or woolen blanket, and your choice of synthetic or down pillows. Bathrooms are stocked with deluxe Bulgari shampoo, shower gel, soap, and lotion. Turkish cotton bathrobes and slippers are provided for use during the cruise.

Top: Outdoor table at the Top of the Yacht Bar
Bottom: Casino play

Accessibility: One stateroom is designed for wheelchair accessibility.

Restaurants
The formal dining room serves open-seating breakfast, lunch, and dinner during scheduled hours. For a more casual setting, the Topside restaurant has outdoor seating for breakfast and lunch—either with table service or from a small buffet—plus scheduled dinners alfresco (the indoor restaurant is also open for those who do not wish to dine outside). Snacks are available at the Top of the Yacht Bar, and you only have to ask to receive anything from popcorn to caviar, although the caviar is no longer complimentary. A beach barbecue is scheduled once during every cruise. Room service is always available, and servers will bring your order to you on deck or in your suite.

Spas
The Asian-inspired SeaDream Spa features Thai therapies in an extensive menu that includes such treatments as an Asian Blend massage, Javanese Lulur body treatment, and Traditional Thai Massage either in the tiny spa facility or in the open air private massage area (weather permitting). The sauna and steam room are complimentary, but appointments are recommended due to their small size.

Bars and Entertainment
Passengers gather nightly before dinner for cocktails and a review of the next day's activities. On two evenings during each cruise, the captain hosts welcome-aboard and farewell cocktail receptions in the Main Salon. Other than a pianist in the tiny piano bar and perhaps a movie or "disco night" in the Main Salon, there's no formal entertainment. The Top of the Yacht Bar is where most passengers gather to socialize and dance on the teak deck after dinner.

Pros and Cons
Pros: the barbecue held on a deserted stretch of beach would be a highlight even without champagne and caviar; the Top of the Yacht Bar is the sociable choice; no smoking is allowed indoors.

Cons: these ships are not wheelchair-accessible, and the elevator doesn't reach the uppermost deck; there's a charge for wines and spirits ordered to your suite; you might miss schedule changes if you skip cocktails before dinner.

Cabin Type	Size (sq. ft.)
Owner's Suite	447
Admiral Suite	375
Commodore Club	390
Yacht Club*	195

*Sixteen of the Yacht Club staterooms are convertible to eight Commodore staterooms, giving a variable passenger capacity.

FAST FACTS

- 5 passenger decks
- Dining room, buffet
- Internet, safe, refrigerator, DVD
- Pool
- Fitness classes, gym, hot tub, sauna, spa, steam room
- 3 bars, casino, library, show room
- Dry-cleaning, laundry service
- Internet terminal
- No-smoking cabins

5

SEADREAM YACHT CLUB

Pool deck

SILVERSEA CRUISES

Silversea Cruises was launched in 1994 by the former owners of Sitmar Cruises, the Lefebvre family of Rome, whose concept for the new cruise line was to build and sail the highest-quality luxury ships at sea. Intimate ships, paired with exclusive amenities and unparal-

The most captivating view on board

leled hospitality, are the hallmarks of Silversea cruises. All-inclusive air-and-sea fares can be customized to include not just round-trip airfare but all transfers, porterage, and deluxe precruise accommodations as well.

☎ *954/522–2299 or*
877/276–6816
⊕ *www.silversea.com*
☞ *Cruise Style: Luxury.*

Personalization is a Silversea maxim. Their ships offer more activities than other comparably sized luxury vessels. Take part in those that interest you, or opt instead for a good book and any number of quiet spots to read or snooze in the shade. Silversea's third generation of ships introduced even more luxurious features when the 36,000-ton *Silver Spirit* launched late in 2009. Silversea's *Silver Explorer* is the top choice for luxurious soft adventure expedition cruising, and in 2013 Silversea will add a second exploration ship, *Silver Galapagos,* that will sail exclusively in the Galápagos Islands.

Food

Dishes from the galleys of Silversea's master chefs are complemented by those of La Collection du Monde, created by Silversea's culinary partner, the world-class chefs of Relais & Châteaux. Menus include hot and cold appetizers, at least four entrée selections, a vegetarian alternative, and Cruiselite cuisine (low in cholesterol, sodium, and fat). Special off-menu orders are prepared whenever possible, provided that the ingredients are available on board. In the event that they aren't, you may find after a day in port that a trip to the market was made in order to fulfill your request.

Chef Marco Betti, the owner of Antica Pasta restaurants in Florence, Italy, and Atlanta, Georgia, has designed a new menu for La Terrazza that focuses on one of the most luxurious food trends: the Slow Food movement. The goal of the movement is to preserve the gastronomic traditions of Italy through the use of fresh, traditional foods, and it has spread throughout the world. At La Terrazza (by day, a casual buffet) the menu showcases the finest in Italian cooking, from classic favorites to Tuscan fare. The restaurant carries no surcharge. Seating is limited, so reservations are a must to ensure a table—it's one reservation you'll be glad you took the time to book.

An intimate dining experience aboard each vessel is the wine restaurant by Relais & Châteaux—Le Champagne. Adding a dimension to dining, the exquisite cuisine is designed to celebrate the wines served—a different celebrated vintage is served with each course. Menus and wines are chosen by Relais & Châteaux sommeliers to reflect regions of the world noted for their rich wine heritage.

An evening poolside barbecue is a weekly dinner event, weather permitting. A highlight of every cruise is the Galley Brunch, when passengers are invited into the galley to select from a feast decorated with imaginative ice and vegetable sculptures. Even when meals are served buffet style in La Terrazza, you will seldom have to carry your own plate, as waiters are at hand to assist you to your table. Wines are chosen to complement each day's luncheon and dinner menus.

Grilled foods, sandwiches, and an array of fruits and salads are served daily for lunch at the Poolside Grill. After dark, the venue is transformed into the Grill featuring "hot rock" dining under the stars. Always available are extensive selections from the room-service menu. The full restaurant menu may be ordered from room service and can be served course by course in your suite during regular dining hours.

Entertainment

Guest lecturers are featured on nearly every cruise; language, dance, and culinary lessons and excellent wine-appreciation sessions are always on the schedule of events. Silversea also schedules culinary arts cruises and a series of wine-focused voyages that feature award-winning authors, international wine experts, winemakers, and acclaimed chefs from the world's top restaurants. During afternoon tea the ranks of highly competitive trivia teams increase every successive day.

KNOWN FOR

■ **All Suites:** All accommodations on Silversea ships are suites and all come with the service of butlers.

■ **Friendly Crowd:** Unlike on some luxury lines, the well-traveled and well-heeled, sophisticated Silversea passengers are anything but stodgy.

■ **International Clientele:** An international mix of passengers are often found on the luxury line's voyages.

■ **Luxury Chic:** The style of Silversea ships is chic, but not stuffy.

■ **Varied Destinations:** Silversea's destination-intensive fleet roams the globe, seldom repeating ports from one voyage to the next.

5

SILVERSEA CRUISES

Top: Stylish entertainment
Bottom: La Terrazza alfresco dining

Top: Table tennis
Middle: Caring personal service
Bottom: Veranda suite

After dark, the Bar is a predinner gathering spot and the late-night place for dancing to a live band. A multi-tiered show lounge is the setting for talented singers and musicians, classical concerts, magic shows, big-screen movies, and folkloric entertainers from ashore. A small casino offers slot machines and gaming tables.

Fitness and Recreation

The rather small gyms are equipped with cardiovascular and weight-training equipment, and fitness classes on *Silver Whisper* and *Silver Shadow* are held in the mirror-lined, but somewhat confining, exercise room. *Silver Spirit* introduced an expansive 8,300-square-foot spa and more spacious fitness center.

South Pacific–inspired Mandara Spa offers numerous treatments including exotic-sounding massages, facials, and body wraps. Hair and nail services are available in the busy salon. A plus is that appointments for spa and beauty salon treatments can be made online from 60 days until 48 hours prior to sailing.

Golfers can sign up with the pro on board for individual lessons utilizing a high-tech swing analyzer and attend complimentary golf clinics or participate in a putting contest.

Your Shipmates

Silversea Cruises appeal to sophisticated, affluent couples who enjoy the country-club-like atmosphere, exquisite cuisine, and polished service on board, not to mention the exotic ports and unique experiences ashore.

Dress Code

Two formal nights are standard on seven-night cruises and three to four nights, depending on the itinerary, on longer sailings. Men are required to wear tuxedos or dark suits after 6 pm. All other evenings are either informal, when a jacket is called for (a tie is optional, but most men wear them), or casual, when slacks with a jacket over an open-collar shirt for men and sporty dresses or skirts or pants with a sweater or blouse for women are suggested.

CHOOSE THIS LINE IF ...

Your taste leans toward learning and exploration.

You enjoy socializing as well as the option of live entertainment, just not too much of it.

You like to plan ahead. You can reserve shore tours, salon services, and spa treatments online.

Junior Cruisers

Adult-oriented Silversea Cruises does not accommodate children less than six months of age, and the cruise line limits the number of children under the age of three on board. The availability of suites for a third passenger is capacity controlled. A youth program staffed by counselors is available on holiday and select sailings. No dedicated children's facilities are available, so parents are responsible for the behavior and entertainment of their children.

Service

Personalized service is exacting and hospitable yet discreet. The staff strives for perfection and often achieves it. The attitude is decidedly European and begins with a welcome-aboard flute of champagne, then continues throughout as personal preferences are remembered and satisfied. The word *no* doesn't seem to be in the staff vocabulary in any language. Guests in all suites are pampered by butlers.

Tipping

Tipping is neither required nor expected.

Past Passengers

Membership in the Venetian Society is automatic on completion of one Silversea cruise, and members begin accruing benefits: Venetian Society cruise days and eligibility for discounts on select voyages, onboard recognition and private parties, milestone rewards; exclusive gifts, the *Venetian Society Newsletter,* ship visitation privileges, and complimentary early embarkation or late debarkation at certain milestones. After reaching the 500-day milestone, the Venetian Society member will receive a complimentary seven-day voyage for each additional 150 days sailed.

HELPFUL HINTS

Every Silversea voyage includes an exclusive Silversea Experience—a complimentary shoreside event, such as private access to museums after hours.

Silversea offers a customized collection of pre- and postcruise land programs linking some of Relais & Châteaux's worldwide properties together with Silversea's global itineraries.

For a fee, Silversea will pick up your bags at home and deliver them to the ship, or vice versa.

If adults travel with minors under the age of 18 who are not their children, a signed parental consent guardianship form is required.

Requests must be made in writing no later than 14 days prior to departure if you want to arrange a Bon Voyage Party or have visitors board the ship at your embarkation port.

DON'T CHOOSE THIS LINE IF ...

You want to dress informally at all times on your cruise. Passengers on these cruises tend to dress up.

You need highly structured activities and have to be reminded of them.

You prefer the glitter and stimulation of Las Vegas to the understated glamour of Monte Carlo.

SILVER SPIRIT

CREW MEMBERS	376
ENTERED SERVICE	2010
GROSS TONS	36,000
LENGTH	642 feet
NUMBER OF CABINS	270
PASSENGER CAPACITY	540
WIDTH	86 feet

700 ft.   500 ft.   300 ft.

The stylish interiors of *Silver Spirit*'s public rooms reflect a 1930s art deco flavor. Although the decor is warmer and more inviting than previous Silversea ships, you'll still find signature spaces like the Connoisseur's Corner cigar lounge, the Bar, and the indoor–outdoor La Terrazza restaurant.

With one of the most generous space-to-guest ratios in the cruise industry, *Silver Spirit* features an expansive 8,300-square-foot spa with a thermal suite and outdoor whirlpool; a state-of-the-art fitness complex with two aerobics studios; six places to dine; three high-end, duty-free boutiques; and the largest suites in the Silversea fleet. In addition, deck space is expansive, with plenty of teak chaise longues, two whirlpools, and a poolside bar. The resort-style pool is even heated for cooler weather.

Cabins

Cabins: Every suite has an ocean view, and 95% have a private teak-floor balcony. Standard suites have a seating area that can be curtained off from the bed. Marble bathrooms have double sinks and a separate glass-enclosed shower as well as a tub. All suites have generous walk-in closets. Sixteen suites have connecting doors.

Top Suites: In addition to much more space, top-category suites have all the standard amenities plus dining areas, separate bedrooms, and CD players. Silver suites and above have whirlpool tubs. All categories have butler service.

Amenities: Standard suites have a flat-screen TV and DVD, personalized stationery, cocktail cabinet, safe, and fully stocked refrigerator. A hair dryer is provided at a vanity table. Beds are dressed with high-quality linens, duvets, or blankets, and your choice of synthetic or down pillows. Bathrooms have huge towels and plush terry bathrobes for use during the cruise as well as a choice of designer shampoos, soaps, and lotions.

Accessibility: Four suites are designed for wheelchair accessibility.

Restaurants

The formal restaurant offers open-seating breakfast, lunch, and dinner. Le Champagne (reservation, cover charge) offers a gourmet meal and wine pairings; Sieshin Restaurant serves Kobe beef, sushi, and Asian seafood (some items with surcharge). Stars Supper Club offers

Top: *Silver Spirit* at sea
Bottom: Standard suite

trendsetting menus, and La Terrazza serves Italian cuisine. For casual meals, La Terrazza has indoor and outdoor seating for buffet-style breakfast and lunch. The outdoor Grill offers a laid-back lunch option poolside as well as an alfresco dinner, when it is called Black Rock Grill, which allows you to cook meats and seafood to your liking on preheated volcanic stones at your table. Afternoon tea is served daily. Room service arrives with crystal, china, and linens. You may order at any time from the extensive room-service menu, or the full restaurant menu during dining hours.

Spas

Mandara Spa, a division of Steiner Leisure, offers treatments including exotic massages, facials, and body wraps, teeth whitening, acupuncture, and Medi-Spa cosmetic treatments. Also available are indoor-outdoor relaxation areas, an outdoor whirlpool, and a thermal suite furnished with heated lounge chairs and a Turkish bath. There's a fee to use the spa's thermal areas, but the men's and ladies' locker rooms have complimentary saunas and steam rooms.

Bars and Entertainment

A multitiered show lounge is the setting for talented singers and musicians, classical concerts, magic shows, big-screen movies, and folkloric entertainers from ashore. The Bar is a predinner gathering spot and a late-night place for dancing to a live band. A pianist or other entertainers perform in the Panorama Lounge for listening and dancing. When the weather permits, concerts or movies are presented on deck.

Pros and Cons

Pros: onboard atmosphere is sophisticated yet relaxed; chilled champagne welcomes every passenger to his suite; Silver Suites are the most popular accommodations on Silversea ships, and *Silver Spirit* has twice as many as her fleetmates.

Cons: one accommodations deck doesn't have a passenger laundry room; the addition of a limited children's program could mean more youngsters on board than normal; you could get so spoiled aboard *Silver Spirit* that you'll never want to go home.

Cabin Type	Size (sq. ft.)
Grand Suite	1,425–1,532
Owner's Suite	1,292
Royal Suite	990
Silver Suite	742
Veranda Suite	376
Vista Suite	312

FAST FACTS

- 8 passenger decks
- 4 specialty restaurants, dining room, buffet
- Wi-Fi, safe, refrigerator, DVD
- Pool
- Fitness classes, gym, hot tubs, sauna, spa, steam room
- 3 bars, casino, dance club, library, show room
- Children's program
- Dry-cleaning, laundry facilities, laundry service
- Internet terminal
- No-smoking cabins

The spa at Silversea

SILVER SHADOW, SILVER WHISPER

CREW MEMBERS	295
ENTERED SERVICE	2000, 2001
GROSS TONS	28,258
LENGTH	610 feet
NUMBER OF CABINS	191
PASSENGER CAPACITY	382
WIDTH	82 feet

700 ft.

500 ft.

300 ft.

The logical layout of these sister ships, with suites in the forward two-thirds of the ship and public rooms aft, makes orientation simple. The clean, modern decor that defines public areas and lounges might seem almost stark, but it places the main emphasis on large expanses of glass for sunshine and sea views as well as passenger comfort.

Silversea ships boast unbeatable libraries stocked with bestsellers, travel books, classics, and movies for en suite viewing. Extremely wide passageways in public areas are lined with glass-front display cabinets full of interesting and unusual artifacts from the places the ships visit. The Connoisseur's Corner is a clubby cigar smoking room with overstuffed leather seating and a ventilation system that makes it possible for even nonsmokers to appreciate.

Cabins

Cabins: Every suite has an ocean view, and more than 80% have a private teak-floor balcony. Standard suites have a seating area that can be curtained off from the bed. Marble bathrooms have double sinks and a separate glass-enclosed shower as well as a tub. All suites have generous walk-in closets.

Top Suites: In addition to much more space, top-category suites have all the standard amenities plus dining areas, separate bedrooms, and CD players. Silver Suites and above have whirlpool tubs. The top three categories have espresso makers and separate powder rooms. All are served by butlers.

Amenities: Standard suites have a TV and DVD, personalized stationery, cocktail cabinet, safe, and stocked refrigerator. A hair dryer is provided at a vanity table, and you can request a magnifying mirror. Beds are dressed with high-quality linens and your choice of synthetic or down pillows. Bathrooms have huge towels and terry robes for use during the cruise as well as designer shampoo, soaps, and lotion.

Accessibility: Two suites are designed for wheelchair accessibility.

Top: The casino
Bottom: *Silver Shadow* at sea

Restaurants

The Restaurant offers open-seating breakfast, lunch, and dinner. Le Champagne (reservation, cover charge) offers a gourmet meal and wine pairings; La Terrazza serves Italian cuisine. For casual meals, La Terrazza has indoor and outdoor seating for buffet-style breakfast and lunch. The outdoor Grill offers a laid-back lunch option with poolside table service. The do-it-yourself Black Rock Grill allows you to cook meats and seafood to your liking on preheated volcanic stones tableside. Elaborate afternoon tea is served daily. An evening poolside barbecue is a weekly dinner event as a galley brunch. Room service is available anytime and arrives with crystal, china, and a linen tablecloth; if desired, service can be course by course.

Spas

South Pacific–inspired Mandara Spa, a division of Steiner Leisure, offers treatments including exotic-sounding massages, facials, and body wraps, teeth whitening, acupuncture, and Medi-Spa cosmetic treatments. There is no thermal suite, but complimentary saunas and steam rooms are in the men's and ladies' locker rooms.

Bars and Entertainment

The show lounge is the setting for singers and musicians, classical concerts, magic shows, big-screen movies, and folkloric entertainers from ashore. The Bar is the most popular predinner gathering spot and a late-night place for dancing to a live band. A pianist or other entertainers perform in the Panorama Lounge for listening and dancing. Concerts or movies are presented on deck, weather permitting.

Pros and Cons

Pros: champagne flows freely throughout your cruise; sailing on a Silversea ship is like spending time as a guest at a home in the Hamptons where everything is at your fingertips; Silversea is so all-inclusive that you'll seldom use your room card for anything but opening your suite door.

Cons: lines can form to use a washing machine in the smallish (yet totally free) laundry rooms; in an odd contrast to the contents of display cases and lovely flower arrangements, artwork on the walls is fairly ho-hum; the spa's complimentary saunas and steam rooms are quite small.

Cabin Type	Size (sq. ft.)
Grand Suite	1,286–1,435
Royal Suite	1,312–1,352
Owner's Suite	1,208
Silver Suite	701
Medallion Suite	521
Verandah Suite	345
Terrace Suite	287
Vista Suite	287

FAST FACTS

- 7 passenger decks
- 2 specialty restaurants, dining room, buffet
- Wi-Fi, safe, refrigerator, DVD
- Pool
- Fitness classes, gym, hot tubs, sauna, spa, steam room
- 3 bars, casino, dance club, library, show room
- Dry-cleaning, laundry facilities, laundry service
- Internet terminal
- No-smoking cabins

5

SILVERSEA CRUISES

The Poolside Grill serves lunch and light snacks.

SILVER CLOUD, SILVER WIND

CREW MEMBERS	212
ENTERED SERVICE	1994, 1995
GROSS TONS	17,400
LENGTH	514 feet
NUMBER OF CABINS	148
PASSENGER CAPACITY	298
WIDTH	71 feet

700 ft.

500 ft.

300 ft.

These two yachtlike gems are all about style, understatement, and personal choice, so if you want to snuggle into a book in the well-stocked library, no one will lift an eyebrow. Although there simply isn't enough square footage on these ships for huge rooms, the public spaces are more than adequate and designed to function well. These ships served as the models for their larger sisters, *Silver Shadow* and *Silver Whisper,* which expanded on the smaller ships' concept of locating all passenger accommodations forward and public rooms aft.

The Restaurant is one of the loveliest dining rooms at sea, with a domed ceiling and musicians to provide dance music between courses. Both the Bar and Panorama Lounge are comfortable spots to socialize, dance, or enjoy cocktails before or after the evening entertainment, which might include a classical concert or smallish production show in the show room or Moonlight Movies, feature films shown outside on the pool deck.

Cabins

Cabins: All accommodations are considered suites; all are outside and have at least an ocean view; 80% also have private balconies. Suite interiors are enhanced with appealing artwork, flowers, seating areas, and bedding topped with plush duvets and choice of pillow style. A writing desk, refrigerator, TV with DVD player, dressing table with lighted mirror and hair dryer, walk-in closet, and safe are all standard. The marble and stone bathrooms have full-size bathtubs. Teak-floor balconies have patio furniture and floor-to-ceiling glass doors. All suites have butler service.

Amenities: Champagne on ice awaits the arrival of all passengers, and it is replenished as desired; the beverage cabinet is stocked daily on request with individual selections of wines, spirits, and beverages. A fruit basket is replenished daily. Bathrooms are stocked with plush towels and European toiletries, and slippers and bathrobes are provided for use during the cruise.

Accessibility: Two suites are wheelchair accessible.

Restaurants

The formal restaurant offers open-seating breakfast, lunch, and dinner during scheduled hours. Specialty dining is offered by reservation in Le Champagne, where an extra charge applies for the gourmet meal and wine

Top: The Bar
Bottom: Royal suite

pairings, and La Terrazza, which is complimentary and serves Italian cuisine. For casual meals, La Terrazza has indoor and outdoor seating for buffet-style breakfast and lunch. The outdoor Grill offers a laid-back lunch option with poolside table service. An alfresco dinner option is the Black Rock Grill, which allows you to cook meats and seafood to your liking on preheated volcanic stones right at your table. Elaborate afternoon tea is served daily. An evening poolside barbecue is a weekly dinner event, as is the Galley Brunch, when passengers are invited into the galley to make their selections. Room service arrives with crystal, china, and a linen tablecloth for a complete dining room–style setup en suite. You may order at any time from the extensive room-service menu or the full restaurant menu, which can be served course by course in your suite during regular dining hours.

Spas

Mandara Spa, operated by Steiner Leisure, offers treatments including exotic massages, facials, and body wraps, teeth whitening, acupuncture, and Medi-Spa cosmetic treatments. There is no thermal suite, but complimentary saunas and steam rooms are in the men's and ladies' locker rooms.

Bars and Entertainment

The show lounge is the setting for singers and musicians, classical concerts, magic shows, big-screen movies, and folkloric entertainers from ashore. The Bar is a predinner gathering spot and a late-night place for dancing to a live band. A pianist or other entertainers perform in the Panorama Lounge for listening and dancing. When the weather permits, concerts or movies are presented on deck.

Pros and Cons

Pros: ambience on board is comfortably upscale, and you never have to sign a bar ticket; wine is poured freely at lunch and dinner; every cruise features regionally specific expert lectures.

Cons: minimalist modern decor could be improved; the sophisticated, all-adult atmosphere is sometimes disrupted by bored children who have nothing to do; the slow pace of evening entertainment isn't satisfying if you prefer splashy production revues and Vegas-type shows.

Cabin Type	Size (sq. ft.)
Grand Suite	1,019–1,314
Royal Suite	736–1,031
Owner's Suite	587–827
Silver Suite	541
Medallion Suite	470–678
Veranda Suite	295
Vista Suite	240

Grand, Royal, and Owner's suites available with one or two bedrooms; Medallion suite on deck 7 has no balcony.

FAST FACTS

- 6 passenger decks
- 2 specialty restaurants, dining room, buffet
- Wi-Fi, safe, refrigerator, DVD
- 1 pool
- Fitness classes, gym, hot tub, sauna, spa, steam room
- 3 bars, casino, dance club, library, show room
- Dry-cleaning, laundry facilities, laundry service
- Internet terminal
- No-smoking cabins

The pool deck

STAR CLIPPERS

In 1991, Star Clippers unveiled a new tall-ship alternative to sophisticated travelers whose desires include having an adventure at sea but not on board a conventional cruise ship. Star Clippers vessels are four- and five-masted sailing beauties—the world's

Sun yourself on the bow netting.

largest barkentine and full-rigged sailing ships. Filled with modern, high-tech equipment as well as the amenities of private yachts, the ships rely on sail power while at sea unless conditions require the assistance of the engines. Minimal heeling, usually less than 6%, is achieved through judicious control of the sails.

☎ *305/442–0550 or 800/442–0551*
⊕ *www.starclippers. com*
☞ *Cruise Style: Small ship.*

A boyhood dream became a cruise-line reality when Swedish entrepreneur Mikael Krafft launched his fleet of authentic recreations of classic 19th-century clipper ships. The day officially begins when the captain holds an informative daily briefing on deck with a bit of storytelling tossed in.

The lack of rigid scheduling is one of Star Clippers' most appealing attractions. The bridge is always open, and passengers are welcome to peer over the captain's shoulder as he plots the ship's course. Crew members are happy to demonstrate how to splice a line, reef a sail, or tie a proper knot.

As attractive as the ships' interiors are, the focal point of Star Clippers cruises is the outdoors. Plan to spend a lot of time on deck soaking in the sun, sea, and sky. It doesn't get any better than that. Consider also that each ship has at least two swimming pools. Granted, they are tiny, but they are a refreshing feature uncommon on true sailing ships and all but the most lavish yachts.

Although the Star Clippers ships are motorized, their engines are shut down whenever crews unfurl the sails (36,000 square feet on *Star Clipper* and *Star Flyer,* and 56,000 square feet on *Royal Clipper*) to capture the wind. On a typical cruise, the ships rely exclusively on sail power any time favorable conditions prevail.

As the haunting strains of Vangelis's symphony "1492: Conquest of Paradise" are piped over the PA system and the first of the sails is unfurled, the only thing you'll hear on deck is the sound of the music and the calls of the line handlers until every sail is in place. While the feeling of the wind powering large ships through the water is spine-tingling, you will miss the wondrous sight of your ship under sail unless the captain can schedule a photo opportunity utilizing one of the tenders. It's one of the most memorable sights you'll see if this opportunity avails itself. However, when necessary, the ships will cruise under motor power to meet the requirements of their itineraries.

Food

Not noted for gourmet fare, the international cuisine is what you would expect from a trendy shoreside bistro, albeit an elegant one. All meals are open seating in the formal dining room during scheduled hours; breakfast and lunch—an impressive spread of seafood, salads, and grilled items—are served buffet-style, while dinners are leisurely affairs served in the European manner. Hint: If you want your salad *before* your main course, just ask; the French style is to serve it after the main course. Menus include appetizers, soups, pasta, a sorbet course, at least three choices of entrées, salad, cheese, and, of course, dessert. Mediterranean-inspired entrées, vegetarian, and light dishes are featured. A maître d' is present at the more formal evening meals to seat passengers, but it isn't uncommon on these small ships for passengers to arrange their own groups of dinner company.

Early risers on each ship find a continental breakfast offered at the Tropical Bar, and coffee and fresh fruit are always available in the Piano Bar. Should you want to remain in your swimsuit, casual buffets are set up adjacent to the Tropical Bar at noon (the Deck Snack Buffet) and at 5 pm (the Afternoon Snack). Some of the snacks are themed and quite popular—a Neptune seafood luncheon, snacks with waffles or crepes, or a midday taco bar. On select itineraries, an outdoor barbecue is served on shore.

With the exception of occupants of Owner's suites and Deluxe suites on *Royal Clipper*, there is no room service unless you are sick and can't make it to the dining room for meals.

KNOWN FOR

- **Casual:** Totally casual, Star Clipper voyages are unstructured.

- **Comfort:** Appointments are nautical and cabins a bit small, yet as elegant as a millionaire's yacht.

- **Sailing:** Star Clippers are real sailing vessels that only use their engines to augment the wind and stay on schedule.

- **Soft Adventure:** Itineraries offer the opportunity to experience adventurous activities ashore and in the water, and most include beach breaks.

- **Unique Destinations:** Star Clippers sailing ships can visit ports where large ships cannot go.

Sun yourself on the bow netting.

Top: Cooling off in one of the pools
Bottom: *Royal Clipper* Deluxe suite

Entertainment

Star Clippers are not cruise ships in the ordinary sense with strict agendas and pages of activities. You're free to do what you please day and night, but many passengers join the crew members topside when the sails are raised or for some of the lighthearted events like crab-racing contests, scavenger hunts, and a talent night. The informality of singing around a piano bar typifies an evening on one of these ships, although in certain ports local performers come aboard to spice up the action with an authentic taste of the local music and arts.

Fitness and Recreation

Formal exercise sessions take a backseat to water sports, although aerobics classes and swimming are featured on all ships. Only *Royal Clipper* has a marina platform that can be lowered in calm waters to access water sports and diving; however, the smaller ships replicate the experience by using motorized launches to reach reefs for snorkeling. A gym-spa with an array of exercise equipment, free weights, spa treatments, and unisex hair services are also found only on *Royal Clipper*. Despite the lack of a formal fitness center on *Star Flyer* and *Star Clipper,* morning aerobics or yoga classes are usually held on deck for active passengers. Massages, manicures, and pedicures can be arranged as well.

Your Shipmates

Star Clippers cruises draw active, upscale American and European couples in their thirties and up, who enjoy sailing but in a casually sophisticated atmosphere with modern conveniences. Many sailings are equally divided between North Americans and Europeans, so announcements are made in several languages accordingly.

Top: View from the bow
Middle: *Royal Clipper* piano bar
Bottom: *Royal Clipper* spa

This is not a cruise line for the physically challenged: There are no elevators or ramps, nor are staterooms or bathrooms wheelchair accessible. Gangways and shore launches can also be difficult to negotiate.

Dress Code

All evenings are elegant casual, so slacks and open-collar shirts are fine for men, and sundresses, skirts, or pants with a sweater or blouse are suggested for women. Coats

---

CHOOSE THIS LINE IF ...

You wouldn't consider a vacation on a traditional cruise ship but are a sailing enthusiast.	You love water sports, particularly snorkeling and scuba diving.	You want to anchor in secluded coves and visit islands that are off the beaten path.

and ties are never required. Shorts and T-shirts are not allowed in the dining room at dinner.

Junior Cruisers

Star Clippers ships are adult-oriented. Although children are welcome and may participate in shipboard activities suited to their ability, there are no dedicated youth facilities. Parents are responsible for the behavior and entertainment of their children. Mature teens who can live without video games and the company of other teens are the best young sailors.

Service

Service is friendly and gracious, similar to what you would find in a boutique hotel or restaurant. You may find that you have to flag down a waiter for a second cup of coffee, though.

Tipping

Gratuities are not included in the cruise fare and are extended at the sole discretion of passengers. The recommended amount is €8 per person per day. Tips are pooled and shared; individual tipping is discouraged. You can either put cash in the tip envelope provided, and drop it at the Purser's Office, or charge gratuities to your shipboard account. An automatic 15% gratuity is added to each passenger's bar bill.

Past Passengers

Top Gallant is the loyalty club for past passengers. No specific fare discount is offered to members; however, they receive a newsletter and special offers on fare reductions from time to time. Nearly 60% of all passengers choose to make a repeat voyage on Star Clippers ships.

HELPFUL HINTS

The currency for all onboard charges is the euro regardless of where you are sailing.

A guaranteed single fare is available at a specific rate depending on the travel season and length of sailing, but passengers sailing as guaranteed singles may not choose their cabin.

Passengers cannot bring alcoholic beverages onboard for consumption on the ship (duty-free liquor is held until the end of the cruise).

Star Clippers aren't handicap accessible. They have no elevators or ramps and access to land is often via the ships' launches.

For precruise planning, detailed port information and shore excursion descriptions are available online at the Star Clippers website.

5

STAR CLIPPERS

DON'T CHOOSE THIS LINE IF ...

You have a preexisting or potentially serious medical condition. There's no physician on board.

You must have a private balcony—there are a few, but only in top accommodation categories.

You can't live without room service. Only *Royal Clipper* has it, and only in a few high-end suites.

ROYAL CLIPPER

CREW MEMBERS	106
ENTERED SERVICE	2000
GROSS TONS	5,000
LENGTH	439 feet
NUMBER OF CABINS	114
PASSENGER CAPACITY	227
WIDTH	54 feet

700 ft.
500 ft.
300 ft.

Royal Clipper is the first five-masted, full-rigged sailing ship built since 1902. As the largest true sailing clipper ship in the world today, she carries 42 sails with a total area of 56,000 square feet.

Unusual for a sailing ship, a three-deck atrium graces the heart of the vessel.

Her interior is decorated in Edwardian-era style with abundant gleaming wood, brass fixtures, and nautical touches. Light filters into the piano bar, three-deck-high atrium, and dining room through the glass bottom and portholes of the main swimming pool located overhead.

The rarely used Observation Lounge is forward of the Deluxe suites and affords great sea views. It is also the location of the computer station for all Internet access.

Cabins

Cabins: Think yacht, and the cabin sizes make sense. Although efficiently laid out with tasteful, seagoing appointments and prints of clipper ships and sailing yachts on the walls, cabins are small in comparison to those on most cruise ships. All have a TV, safe, vanity-desk, small settee, hair dryer, and marble bathroom with standard toiletries. Closet space is compact, and bureau drawers are narrow, but an under-the-bed drawer is a useful nautical touch for extra storage. Cabins have 220-volt electrical outlets and a 110-volt outlet suitable only for electric shavers. For 110-volt appliances, you'll need to bring a transformer; for dual-voltage appliances, pack a plug converter.

Suites: Owner's suites, Deluxe suites, and Category 1 cabins have a seating area, minibar, whirlpool tub-shower combination, and bathrobes to use during the cruise. Deluxe suites also feature a private veranda. Category 1 cabins have doors that open onto a semiprivate area on the outside deck. Only the two Owner's suites have connecting doors.

Accessibility: None of the staterooms are designed for wheelchair accessibility, nor are there any elevators.

Restaurants

The multilevel dining room serves a single open-seating buffet-style breakfast and lunch. Dinner in the dining room is seated and served European style. For early risers, a continental breakfast with coffee, fruit, and

Top: *Royal Clipper* dining room
Bottom: Sighting land

pastries is set up in the piano bar; specialty coffees are available at the bar for a charge. A buffet lunch is offered most days on deck in the Tropical Bar, as are late-afternoon snacks and predinner canapés. On select itineraries an outdoor luncheon barbecue is prepared one day ashore. Room service is available only to occupants of the Owner's and Deluxe suites and passengers who are ill and unable to make it to the dining room.

Spas

The tiny spa offers an array of reasonably priced, nononsense massages and body treatments, but a large steam room is an unexpected bonus.

Bars and Entertainment

There is no lavish entertainment, but there are entertaining ways to pass the evenings, starting with the raising of the sails. Performers come aboard in certain ports to provide an authentic taste of local music and arts, but with the exception of live music in the piano bar and for dancing on deck, fun largely takes place outside at the Tropical Bar. Expect crab races, wacky games, and a Talent Night starring crew members and passengers.

Pros and Cons

Pros: the feeling of the wind moving this large vessel through the water is spine-tingling; you won't miss the glorious sight of *Royal Clipper* underway when the captain schedules a photo op via the tenders; the library is a cozy place to read and offers a good selection of books.

Cons: in Category 3 cabins near the bow, you'll notice a definite slant to the floor; you may also feel a bit more motion forward than aft, and be aware that creaking sounds are common on sailing ships; tall passengers will find it difficult to use the treadmills in the low-ceilinged gym.

Cabin Type	Size (sq. ft.)
Owner's Suite	355
Deluxe Suite and Category 1 Ocean View	204
Standard Ocean View	150
Category 5 Ocean View	118
Inside	107

FAST FACTS

- 5 passenger decks
- Dining room
- Safe, refrigerator, DVD (some)
- 3 pools
- Fitness classes, gym, spa, steam room
- 3 bars, library
- Dry-cleaning, laundry service
- Internet terminal
- No-smoking cabins

5

STAR CLIPPERS

Royal Clipper under sail

STAR CLIPPER, STAR FLYER

CREW MEMBERS	72
ENTERED SERVICE	1992
GROSS TONS	3,000
LENGTH	360 feet
NUMBER OF CABINS	85
PASSENGER CAPACITY	170
WIDTH	50 feet

700 ft.
500 ft.
300 ft.

With its bright brass fixtures, teak-and-mahogany paneling and rails, and antique prints and paintings of famous sailing vessels, the interior decor of these ships reflects the heritage of grand sailing vessels.

Porthole-shape skylights create an atrium-like effect in the Piano Bar, which leads to a graceful staircase and the dining room one deck below. The centerpiece of the vaguely Edwardian-style library is a belle époque–period fireplace.

The Piano Bar is intimate and cozy. The Tropical Bar, one of the most popular areas on board, is the center of social activity for predinner cocktails and late-night dancing. It's the covered outdoor lounge adjacent to the open deck space, where local entertainers often perform.

Cabins

Cabins: Traditional, yachtlike, and efficiently designed, cabins are adequate but far from spacious by modern standards. All cabins have a safe, vanity-desk, small settee, hair dryer, TV (except Category 6 Inside), and marble bathroom with standard toiletries. As would normally be expected on a sailing vessel, staterooms forward and aft are more susceptible to motion than those midship. There is also a noticeable slant to the floor in cabins near the bow. Unless you are particularly agile, you will want to avoid the inside cabins on Commodore Deck, where beds are strictly upper and lower berths. Some cabins are outfitted with a third pull-down berth, but most passengers will find the space too cramped for three occupants. All cabins are equipped with regular 110-volt electrical outlets and one 110-volt outlet in the bathroom that is suitable for electric shavers only.

Top-Category Cabins: The Owner'sSuite and Category 1 cabins have a minibar, whirlpool tub-shower combination, and the use of bathrobes during the cruise. Category 1 cabin doors open onto the outside deck, and the Owner'sSuite has a sitting room.

Accessibility: None of the staterooms are designed for wheelchair accessibility, nor do any staterooms have connecting doors.

Top: Dining on *Star Clipper*
Bottom: Friendly, efficient service

Restaurants

The mahogany-panel dining room serves a single open-seating buffet-style breakfast and lunch. Dinner in the dining room is seated and served European-style. For early risers, a continental breakfast with coffee, fruit, and pastries is set up in the Piano Bar; specialty coffees are available at the bar for a charge. A buffet lunch is offered most days on deck in the Tropical Bar, as are late-afternoon snacks and predinner canapés. On select itineraries an outdoor luncheon barbecue is prepared one day ashore. Late-night canapés are offered in the Piano Bar. There's no room service unless you're sick and can't make it out to meals.

Spas

Neither ship has a spa facility.

Bars and Entertainment

The most entertaining way to start the evening is topside with the raising of the sails. Performers come aboard in certain ports to provide an authentic taste of local music and arts, but with the exception of music in the piano bar and musicians providing accompaniment for dancing on deck, fun takes place outside at the Tropical Bar. Expect crab races, wacky games, and a Talent Night starring crew members and passengers.

Pros and Cons

Pros: the sheer beauty of real sailing combined with the luxury of creature comforts; coffee and tea available around the clock at the piano bar; seating for six to eight in the dining room is designed to maximize socializing.

Cons: there are no tables for two in the dining room; designed to conserve water, bathroom taps can be frustrating until you are accustomed to the regulated water flow; on a ship this size there aren't too many spots to get away from fellow passengers.

Cabin Type	Size (sq. ft.)
Owner's Suite	266
Category 1 Ocean View	150
Category 2 Ocean View	129
Standard Ocean View	118
Inside	97

FAST FACTS

- 4 passenger decks
- Dining room
- Safe, no TV (some)
- 2 pools
- Fitness classes
- 2 bars, library, laundry service
- Internet terminal
- No-smoking cabins

5

STAR CLIPPERS

Star Clipper under sail

WINDSTAR CRUISES

Are they cruise ships with sails or sailing ships designed for cruises? Since 1986, these masted sailing yachts have filled an upscale niche. They often visit ports of call inaccessible to huge, traditional cruise ships and offer a unique perspective of any cruis-

Your Windstar ship at anchor

ing region. Though Windstar ships seldom depend on wind alone to sail, if you're fortunate and conditions are perfect, as they sometimes are, the complete silence of pure sailing is heavenly. Stabilizers and computer-controlled ballast systems ensure no more than a mere few degrees of lean.

☎ 206/292–9606 or 800/258–7245
⊕ *www.windstarcruises. com*
☞ *Cruise Style: Luxury.*

When you can tear yourself away from the sight of thousands of yards of Dacron sail overhead, it doesn't take long to read the daily schedule of activities on a typical Windstar cruise. Simply put, there are few scheduled activities. Diversions are for the most part social, laid-back, and impromptu. There's never pressure to join in or participate if you simply prefer relaxing with a fully loaded iPod, which you can check out on board.

Multimillion-dollar upgrades in 2012 enhanced each ship from stern to stern with chic new decor that mimics the colors of the sky and sandy beaches. The Yacht Club, which replaced the library on *Wind Surf*, is designed to be the social hub of the ship, with computer stations, a coffee bar, and a more expansive feel than the room it replaced. You will be able to join other passengers in comfortable seating around a large flat-screen TV to cheer on your favorite team during sporting events. In addition, all accommodations and bathrooms have been remodeled with updated materials; new weights and televisions were added to the gym; a couples massage room enhances the *Wind Surf* spa; the casual Veranda was expanded; the decks now have Balinese sun beds; and cooling mist sprayers are near the pools.

Acquired by Xanterra Parks & Resorts in 2011, the line has announced the purchase of Seabourn Cruises' trio of small vessels. *Seabourn Pride* will be christened as *Star Pride* and enter the fleet in 2014; *Seabourn Spirit* and *Seabourn Legend* will be transferred to Windstar in 2015. At this writing, details on changes planned by Windstar were not yet available.

Food

Dining on Windstar ships is as casually elegant as the dress code. There's seldom a wait for a table in open-seating dining rooms where tables for two are plentiful. Whether meals are taken in the open and airy top-deck buffet, with its floor-to-ceiling windows and adjacent tables outside, or in the formal dining room, dishes are as creative as the surroundings. Expect traditional entrées but also items that incorporate regional ingredients, such as plantains, for added interest. Save room for petits fours with coffee and a taste of the fine cheeses from the after-dinner cheese cart.

In a nod to healthy dining, low-calorie and low-fat spa cuisine alternatives for breakfast, lunch, and dinner are prepared to American Heart Association guidelines. Additional choices are offered from the vegetarian menu.

A midcruise deck barbecue featuring grilled seafood and other favorites is fine dining in an elegantly casual alfresco setting. Desserts are uniformly delightful, and you'll want to try the bread pudding, a Windstar tradition available at the luncheon buffet. With daily tea and hot and cold hors d'oeuvres served several times during the afternoon and evening, no one goes hungry. Room service is always available, and you can place your order for dinner from the restaurant's menu during scheduled dining hours.

Entertainment

Evening entertainment is informal, with a small dance combo playing in the main lounges. Compact casinos offer games of chance and slot machines, but don't look for bingo or other organized games. A weekly show by the crew is delightful; attired in the traditional costumes of their homelands, they present music and dance highlighting their cultures. You may find occasional movies in the main lounges, which are outfitted with state-of-the-art video and sound equipment. Most passengers prefer socializing, either in the main lounge or an outdoor bar where Cigars Under the Stars attracts not only cigar aficionados but stargazers as well.

Welcome-aboard and farewell parties are hosted by the captain, and most passengers attend those as well as

KNOWN FOR

■ **Fine Dining:** Windstar combines fine cuisine and superb service with a single open seating at dinner.

■ **Just the Right Size:** The graceful sailing ships are large enough to offer a few big-ship features, yet small enough to give the feel of a private yacht.

■ **Not All-Inclusive:** Windstar cruises are luxurious but far less inclusive than other luxury cruise lines.

■ **The Romance of the Sea:** With their sails billowing overhead, Windstar ships are among the most romantic at sea.

■ **Smaller Ports:** The size of Windstar's motor-sailing ships allows them to call at ports that large ships simply cannot visit.

Top: Dining well on board
Bottom: Compass Rose Bar on *Wind Surf*

5

WINDSTAR CRUISES

Top: Backgammon on deck
Middle: Scuba with the dive masters
Bottom: *Wind Surf* stateroom

the nightly informational sessions regarding ports of call and activities that are presented by the staff during predinner cocktails.

Fitness and Recreation

Most of the line's massage and exercise facilities are quite small, as would be expected on a ship that carries fewer than 150 passengers; however, *Wind Surf*'s WindSpa and fitness areas are unexpectedly huge. An array of exercise equipment, free weights, and basic fitness classes are available in the gym and Nautilus room. There is an extra charge for Pilates and yoga classes. A wide variety of massages, body wraps, and facial treatments are offered in the spa, while hair- and nail services are available for women and men in the salon. Both spa and salon are operated by Steiner Leisure.

Stern-mounted water-sports marinas are popular with active passengers who want to kayak, windsurf, and water-ski. Watery activities are free, including the use of snorkel gear that can be checked out for the entire cruise. The only charge is for diving; PADI-certified instructors offer a two-hour course for noncertified divers who want to try it, and are also available to lead experienced certified divers on underwater expeditions. The dive teams take care of everything, even prepping and washing down the gear. If you prefer exploring on solid ground, sports coordinators are often at hand to lead an early-morning guided walk in port.

Your Shipmates

Windstar Cruises appeal to upscale professional couples in their late-thirties to sixties who enjoy the unpretentious, yet casually sophisticated atmosphere, creative cuisine, and refined service. Windstar's ships were not designed for accessibility, and are not a good choice for the physically challenged. *Wind Surf* has only two staterooms, and the smaller ships have none. There are no staterooms or bathrooms with wheelchair accessibility, and gangways can be difficult to navigate, depending on the tide and angle of ascent. Service animals are permitted to sail if arrangements are made at the time of booking.

CHOOSE THIS LINE IF ...

You want a high-end experience yet prefer to dress casually every night of your vacation.

You love water sports, particularly scuba diving, kayaking, and windsurfing.

You're a romantic: tables for two are plentiful in the dining rooms.

Dress Code

All evenings are country-club casual, and slacks with a jacket over a sweater or shirt for men, and sundresses, skirts, or pants with a sweater or blouse for women are suggested. Coats and ties for men are not necessary, but some male passengers prefer to wear a jacket with open-collar shirt to dinner.

Junior Cruisers

Windstar Cruises' unregimented atmosphere is adult-oriented, and children are not encouraged. Children less than two years of age are not allowed at all; older children traveling as the third passenger in a stateroom with their parents incur the applicable third-person fare. No dedicated children's facilities are available.

Service

Personal service and attention by the professional staff is the order of the day. Your preferences are noted and fulfilled without the necessity of reminders. Expect to be addressed by name within a short time of embarking.

Tipping

A service charge of $12 per guest per day (including children) is added to each shipboard account. A 15% service charge is added to all bar bills. All these proceeds are paid directly to the crew.

Past Passengers

Windstar guests who cruise once with the line are automatically enrolled in the complimentary Foremast Club. Member benefits include savings on many sailings in addition to the Advance Savings Advantage Program discounts, Internet specials, and a free subscription to the *Foremast Club* magazine.

HELPFUL HINTS

Windstar's luxury sailing ships were completely transformed in late 2012 in a major stem-to-stern renovation.

Expansive white sails are hoisted on the ships, but they are mostly for show; most sailing is done under engine power.

All nonalcoholic beverages are included in the fare, but there is a charge for beer, wine, and other alcoholic drinks.

Each Windstar ship has a water-sports platform with complimentary water sports, including snorkeling, windsailing, paddleboating and even water skiing.

Hotel or hotel and tour packages are available to extend your trip pre- or postcruise.

5

WINDSTAR CRUISES

DON'T CHOOSE THIS LINE IF ...

You must have a spacious private balcony. There are none.

You're bored unless surrounded by constant stimulation. Activities are purposefully low-key.

You have mobility problems. These ships are simply not good for passengers in wheelchairs.

WIND SURF

CREW MEMBERS	190
ENTERED SERVICE	1990
GROSS TONS	14,745
LENGTH	617 feet
NUMBER OF CABINS	156
PASSENGER CAPACITY	312
WIDTH	66 feet

700 ft.   500 ft.   300 ft.

Wind Surf's public areas are designed for comfort and feature wood finishes with sand and marine colors for a casual elegant look and feel. Fresh flower arrangements and sailing-related artwork are lovely touches shipwide. To make finding your way around simple, remember that all dining and entertainment areas are on the top three decks, with restaurants located forward and indoor-outdoor bars facing aft. The main lounge and casino are midship on Main Deck, as is the Yacht Club, which functions as library/Internet café/coffee bar. The fitness center is one deck higher. Most public areas have expansive sea views, although an exception is the spa, which is tucked away aft on deck 2. Stairways are rather steep, but forward and aft elevators assure that moving about is relatively easy.

Cabins

Cabins: Ocean-view staterooms are a study in efficiency and design. Closets are generous and have a safe; there's also a flat-screen TV, DVD, and Bose SoundDock speakers for an iPod. The combination vanity-desk and bedside table has drawers for ample storage. A few standard cabins have upper fold-down Pullman berths. Special touches are fresh flowers, terry robes and slippers, and toiletries. Teak-floor bathrooms are sensibly laid out and spacious enough for two people to share. All staterooms and suites are equipped with barware, minibar, and hair dryer. All voltage is 220, not 110.

Suites: Double the size of standard staterooms, suites were created from two standard cabins and have two bathrooms and a seating area with a sofa bed. A privacy curtain separates the bedroom from the sitting room. New spa suites include plush spa robes, tea service, and credits for certified organic spa services and fitness classes in WindSpa. Two supersize bridge suites have living and dining areas, a bedroom, a walk-in closet, and a bathroom with a whirlpool tub and separate shower.

Accessibility: No cabins are wheelchair accessible.

Restaurants

The formal AmphorA Restaurant serves open-seating dinner. For a casual setting, the buffet-style Veranda Café has indoor and outdoor seating for breakfast and lunch. An adjacent grill whips up cooked-to-order breakfast items and serves barbecue selections outdoors. A

Top: Sea views at the rail
Bottom: *Wind Surf* at sea

continental breakfast spread is offered in the Compass Rose bar. The Yacht Club Sandwich Bar offers a selection of sandwiches and an espresso bar. Stella Bistro, serving cuisine with a French flair, is the reservations-only, casual alternative for dinner. Other evening choices are Le Marché, an alfresco seafood bar serving fish and shellfish, and Candles, the poolside grill with a steak-and-skewers menu for which there is no charge (although reservations are suggested). Dining service in outdoor areas is subject to weather conditions. Afternoon tea with finger sandwiches and sweets is served daily. Room service is always available, and will serve selections from the dining-room menu during restaurant hours.

Spas

The Wind Spa, operated by Steiner Leisure, is surprisingly large for a ship this size, with an extensive menu of massages, facials, body wraps, and even teeth whitening. There is a couples massage room, but no thermal suite. However, a coed sauna is complimentary.

Bars and Entertainment

Nightly informational sessions regarding ports of call and activities are presented by the staff before dinner. Evening entertainment is informal and social, with a small dance combo playing in the main lounge and a duo in the Compass Rose. A crew show during each cruise is a delight, showcasing their homeland cultures. You may find occasional movies in the main lounge, which is outfitted with state-of-the-art video and sound equipment.

Pros and Cons

Pros: service is delivered with a smile by staff members who greet you by name virtually from the moment you board; all cabins are outside, and none have obstructed views; teatime, when sweets are served in addition to the finger foods, is an afternoon highlight.

Cons: when the caviar spread is served one day during the cruise, you might have to fight fellow passengers to get near it; there are no private balconies on these ships; there are no tables in the standard staterooms, which makes dining from room service trays inelegant at best.

Cabin Type	Size (sq. ft.)
Suite	376
Ocean View	188
Bridge Suite	500

FAST FACTS

- 6 passenger decks
- Specialty restaurant, dining room, buffet
- Wi-Fi, safe, refrigerator, DVD
- 2 pools
- Fitness classes, gym, hot tubs, sauna, spa
- 4 bars, casino, dance club, library
- Laundry service
- Internet terminal
- No-smoking cabins

5

WINDSTAR CRUISES

Unwind with a soothing massage.

WIND SPIRIT, WIND STAR

CREW MEMBERS	90
ENTERED SERVICE	1988
GROSS TONS	5,350
LENGTH	440 feet
NUMBER OF CABINS	74
PASSENGER CAPACITY	148
WIDTH	52 feet

700 ft.

500 ft.

300 ft.

Comfort is the element that ties these ships' interiors together. Blue-green and cream, echoing hues of the sea and sandy beaches, predominate in the cozy main lounge, where you'll find a tiny casino tucked into a corner. With its large windows and a skylight, the lounge is flooded with natural light during daytime hours.

Public spaces are proportionally small on such a diminutive vessel and feature yachtlike touches of polished wood shipwide, as well as abundant fresh flower arrangements. The library contains books, movies to play in your cabin, and a computer center.

Passenger accommodations and public areas are all found in the aft two-thirds of the ship, with dining and entertainment located on the top two decks.

Cabins

Cabins: The ocean-view staterooms are ingeniously designed for efficiency. Hanging lockers (closets) are generous, and contain shoe racks and shelves for gear. A small, enclosed cabinet conceals a safe, and an entertainment center includes a flat-screen TV, DVD, and Bose SoundDock speaker for an iPod, which you can borrow from reception fully loaded with music. The combination vanity-desk and bedside table has drawers for ample storage. A countertop lifts up to reveal a lighted makeup mirror, a locking security compartment, and a shallow cubby. Special touches in each stateroom are fresh flowers, terry robes and slippers for use during the voyage, and bath toiletries. The teak-floor bathrooms are big enough for two. All staterooms and suites are equipped with a minibar, barware, and hair dryer (voltage is standard 110 AC); portholes have deadheads, which can be closed in high seas. Ten staterooms have adjoining doors on *Wind Spirit* and 12 on *Wind Star,* and a limited number of standard cabins have upper fold-down Pullman berths for a third passenger.

Suites: A single Owner's suite, the only premium accommodation on board, has a seating area with a sofa bed to offer a berth for a third passenger.

Accessibility: There are no cabins configured for wheelchair accessibility.

Top: Elegant dining in a casual atmosphere
Bottom: A sunny day at the pool

Restaurants

The formal AmphorA Restaurant offers open-seating dinner during scheduled hours and is large enough to serve all passengers at once, so there is seldom a wait for a table. In a more casual setting, the buffet-style Veranda Café has indoor and outdoor seating for breakfast and lunch. A grill whips up cooked-to-order breakfast and lunch choices. Dinner under the stars is available at Candles, the poolside grill with a steak-and-skewers menu (no extra charge, but reservations are suggested). The pool bar has a permanent food station for continental breakfast, afternoon tea, desserts, and evening canapés. Afternoon tea with finger sandwiches and sweets is served daily. Room service is always available, and will serve selections from the dining-room menu during restaurant hours.

Spas

The tiny spa consists of only two treatment rooms, but it offers a nice menu of massages and facials. There is a complimentary coed sauna.

Bars and Entertainment

The captain hosts a reception at least one evening during each cruise, and nightly informational sessions regarding ports of call and activities are presented before dinner. Other evening entertainment is informal and social, perhaps a pianist playing in the main lounge. A crew show, showcasing their homeland cultures, is a delight.

Pros and Cons

Pros: ships have an extensive DVD collection; socializing is effortless on these intimate ships; mist sprayers near the pool offer a refreshing way to keep cool.

Cons: the aft pool and hot tub are popular and apt to feel crowded; the water-sports marina can open only when the ship is at anchor; ways to entertain yourself are sparse—the gym and library are tiny, and the casino is small.

Cabin Type	Size (sq. ft.)
Suite	220
Ocean View	188

FAST FACTS

- 5 passenger decks
- Dining room, buffet
- Wi-Fi, safe, refrigerator, DVD
- Pool
- Fitness classes, gym, hot tub, sauna
- 2 bars, casino, dance club, library
- Laundry service
- Internet terminal
- No-smoking cabins

5

WINDSTAR CRUISES

Wind Spirit at sea

PORTS OF
EMBARKATION

Miami is the world's cruise capital, and more cruise ships are based year-round there than anywhere else. Caribbean cruises depart for their itineraries from several ports on either of Florida's coasts, as well as from cities on the Gulf Coast and East Coast of the United States.

Generally, if your cruise is on an Eastern Caribbean itinerary, you'll likely depart from Miami, Fort Lauderdale, Jacksonville, or Port Canaveral; short three- and four-day cruises to the Bahamas also depart from these ports. Most cruises on Western Caribbean itineraries depart from Tampa, New Orleans, Houston, or Galveston, though some depart from Miami as well. Cruises from farther up the East Coast of the United States, including such ports as Baltimore, Maryland; Charleston, South Carolina; and even New York City, usually go to the Bahamas or sometimes Key West and often include a private-island stop or a stop elsewhere in Florida. Cruises to the Southern Caribbean might depart from Miami if they are 10 days or longer, but more likely they will depart from San Juan, Puerto Rico, or some other port deeper in the Caribbean, often Barbados.

Regardless of which port you depart from, air connections may prevent you from leaving home on the morning of your cruise or going home the day you return to port. Or you may wish to arrive early simply to give yourself a bit more peace of mind, or you may just want to spend more time in one of these interesting port cities. Many people choose to depart from New Orleans or Galveston just to have an excuse to spend a couple of days in the city before or after their cruise.

PORT ESSENTIALS

CAR RENTAL
Major Agencies Alamo ☎ *877/222–9075* ⊕ *www.alamo.com.* **Avis**
☎ *800/331–1212 U.S. reservations, 800/331–1084 international reservations*
⊕ *www.avis.com.* **Budget** ☎ *800/527–0700 U.S. reservations, 800/472–3325*
international reservations ⊕ *www.budget.com.* **Hertz** ☎ *800/654–3131 U.S. and*
Canada reservations, 800/654–3001 international reservations ⊕ *www.hertz.*
com. **National Car Rental** ☎ *877/222–9058* ⊕ *www.nationalcar.com.*

SURCHARGES
To avoid a hefty refueling fee, fill the tank just before you turn in the car, but be aware that gas stations near rental outlets and airports may charge more than those farther away. This is a particular problem in Orlando, but it can be true in other Florida cities. If you plan to do a lot of driving (and if you can get a good price), it can sometimes be a better deal to buy a full tank of gas when you rent so you can return the car with an empty tank. However, it's never a good deal to pay the huge surcharge for not returning a tank full unless you simply have no other choice. Other surcharges may apply if you are under 25 or over 75, if

you want to add an additional driver to the contract, or if you want to drive over state borders or out of a specific radius from your point of rental. You'll also pay extra for child seats, which are compulsory for children under 5, and for a GPS navigation system or electronic toll pass. You can sometimes avoid the charge for insurance if you have your own, either from your own policy or from a credit card, but know what you are covered for, and read the fine print before making this decision.

HOTELS

Whether you are driving or flying into your port of embarkation, it is often more convenient to arrive the day before or to stay for a day after your cruise. For this reason we offer lodging suggestions near each port of embarkation.

RESTAURANTS

For each port of embarkation, we offer some restaurant suggestions that are convenient to the cruise port and the other hotels we recommend. Unless otherwise noted, the restaurants we recommend accept major credit cards and are open for both lunch and dinner.

HOTEL AND RESTAURANT PRICES

Restaurant prices are based on the average main course price at dinner, excluding gratuity. Hotel prices are for two people in a standard double room in high season, excluding any taxes, service charges, and resort fees.

BALTIMORE, MARYLAND

Laura Rodini

Baltimore's charm lies in its neighborhoods. Although stellar downtown attractions such as the National Aquarium and Camden Yards draw torrents of tourists each year, much of the city's character can be found outside the Inner Harbor. Scores of Baltimore's trademark narrow red-brick row houses with white marble steps line the city's east and west sides. Some neighborhood streets are still made of cobblestone, and grand churches and museums and towering, glassy high-rises fill out the growing skyline. Now the city's blue-collar past mixes with present urban-professional revitalization. Industrial waterfront properties are giving way to high-end condos, and corner bars formerly dominated by National Bohemian beer—once made in the city—are adding microbrews to their beverage lists. And with more and more retail stores replacing old, run-down buildings and parking lots, Baltimore is one of the nation's up-and-coming cities.

ESSENTIALS

HOURS

During the summer tourist season, most of Baltimore's stores and attractions usually open around 9 am and close around 9 pm.

VISITOR INFORMATION

Contacts Baltimore Visitor Center ✉ *401 Light St., Inner Harbor* ☎ *877/225-8466* ⊕ *www.baltimore.org.*

Security

All cruise lines have instituted stricter security procedures in recent years; however, you may not even be aware of all the changes.

Some of the changes will be more obvious to you. For example, only visitors who have been authorized well in advance are allowed onboard. Proper identification (a government-issued photo ID) is required in all instances to board the ship, whether you are a visitor or passenger. Ship security personnel are stationed at all points of entry to the ship. All hand-carried items are searched by hand in every port (this applies to both crew and passengers).

Some of the changes are more behind the scenes. All luggage is scanned, whether you carry it aboard with you or not, and all packages and provisions brought onboard are scanned.

In addition, every ship has added professionally trained security officers and taken many other measures to ensure the safety of all passengers. Many cruise-line security personnel are former navy or marine officers with extensive maritime experience. Some cruise lines recruit shipboard security personnel from the ranks of former British Gurkha regiments. From Nepal, the Gurkhas are renowned as soldiers of the highest caliber.

THE CRUISE PORT

Well marked and easily accessible by major highways, the South Locust Point Cruise Terminal is about a mile from center city. Several cruise lines offer seasonal cruises from the port; *Grandeur of the Seas* is based here year-round. Ships dock near the main cruise building, which itself is little more than a hub for arrivals and departures. There are few facilities for passengers in the immediate port area, which is out of walking distance to Baltimore's attractions.

During cruise season, taxis are the best transportation to the downtown area. They cost about $5 one-way and frequent the port. Taxis to Baltimore–Washington International Airport charge a flat rate of $30. Rental cars are generally not necessary; if you fly into Baltimore, you can see the majority of Baltimore by taxi. Guided tours of the city range from $20 to $60.

Airport Baltimore–Washington International Airport (*BWI*). ⊠ *Exit 2 off Baltimore-Washington Pkwy., Hanover* ☏ *410/859-7111* ⊕ *www.bwiairport.com.*

Airport Transfers Airport Taxis ☏ *410/859-1100* ⊕ *www.bwiairporttaxi. com.* **Arrow Taxicab** ☏ *443/575-4111* ⊕ *www.arrowcabmd.com.* **BWI Airport rail station** ☏ *410/672-6167* ⊕ *www.bwiairport.com.* **BWI SuperShuttle** ☏ *800/258-3826* ⊕ *www.supershuttle.com.* **Carey Limousines** ☏ *410/880-0999, 800/336-4646* ⊕ *www.carey.com.* **Maryland Area Rail Commuter** (*MARC*). ☏ *800/325-7245, 410/539-5000* ⊕ *www.mtamaryland.gov.* **Penn Station** ⊠ *1515 N. Charles St., Mount Vernon* ☏ *800/523-8720.* **Private Car/RMA Worldwide Chauffeured Transportation** ☏ *410/519-0000, 800/878-7743* ⊕ *www.rmalimo.com.*

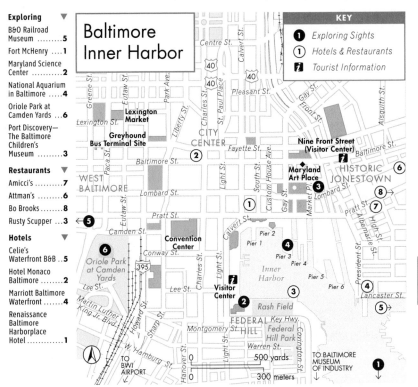

Baltimore Inner Harbor

Exploring ▼
B&O Railroad Museum **5**
Fort McHenry **1**
Maryland Science Center **2**
National Aquarium in Baltimore **4**
Oriole Park at Camden Yards ...**6**
Port Discovery— The Baltimore Children's Museum **3**

Restaurants ▼
Amicci's **7**
Attman's **6**
Bo Brooks **8**
Rusty Scupper ...**3**

Hotels ▼
Celie's Waterfront B&B ..**5**
Hotel Monaco Baltimore **2**
Marriott Baltimore Waterfront **4**
Renaissance Baltimore Harborplace Hotel **1**

KEY
❶ Exploring Sights
① Hotels & Restaurants
🛈 Tourist Information

Information Port of Baltimore ✉ 2001 E. McComas St. ☎ 866/427–8963 ⊕ www.cruisemaryland.com.

PARKING
There's a secure parking lot next to the cruise terminal, where parking costs $15 per day. Drop off your luggage before parking.

EXPLORING BALTIMORE

B&O Railroad Museum. The famous Baltimore & Ohio Railroad was founded on the site that now houses this museum, which contains more than 120 full-size locomotives and a great collection of railroad memorabilia, from dining-car china and artwork to lanterns and signals. The 1884 roundhouse (240 feet in diameter and 120 feet high) adjoins one of the nation's first railroad stations. Train rides are available Wednesday through Sunday (weekends only in January). TraxSide Snax serves food and drinks. ✉ 901 W. Pratt St., West Baltimore ☎ 410/752–2490 ⊕ www.borail.org ☑ $14, $3 for train rides ☉ Mon.–Sat. 10–4, Sun. 11–4.

Fort McHenry. This star-shaped brick fort is forever associated with Francis Scott Key and "The Star-Spangled Banner," which Key penned while watching the British bombardment of Baltimore during the War of 1812. Key had been detained onboard a truce ship, where he had been negotiating the release of one Dr. William Beanes, when the bombardment began; Key knew too much about the attack plan to be released. Through the next day and night, as the battle raged, Key strained to be sure, through the smoke and haze, that the flag still flew above Fort McHenry—indicating that Baltimore's defenders held firm. "By the dawn's early light" of September 14, 1814, he saw the 30-by 42-foot "Star-Spangled Banner" still aloft and was inspired to pen the words to a poem (set to the tune of an old English drinking song).

The flag that flew above Fort McHenry that day had 15 stars and 15 stripes, and was hand-sewn for the fort. A visit to the fort includes a 15-minute history film, guided tour, and frequent living-history displays on summer weekends. To see how the formidable fortifications might have appeared to the bombarding British, catch a water taxi from the Inner Harbor to the fort instead of driving. ⊠ *E. Fort Ave., Locust Point* ✛ *From Light St., take Key Hwy. for 1½ miles and follow signs* ☎ *410/962–4290* ⊕ *www.nps.gov/fomc* ⊠ *$7* ☉ *Memorial Day–Labor Day, daily 8–8; Labor Day–Memorial Day, daily 8–5.*

FAMILY **Maryland Science Center.** Originally known as the Maryland Academy of Sciences, this 200-year-old scientific institution is one of the oldest in the United States. Now housed in a contemporary building, the three floors of exhibits on the Chesapeake Bay, Earth science, physics, the body, dinosaurs, and outer space are an invitation to engage, experiment, and explore. The center has a planetarium, a simulated archaeological dinosaur dig, an IMAX movie theater with a screen five stories high, and a playroom especially designed for young children. ⊠ *601 Light St., Inner Harbor* ☎ *410/685–5225* ⊕ *www.mdsci.org* ⊠ *$16.95* ☉ *May–Aug., Sun.–Thurs. 10–6, Fri.–Sat. 10–8; Sept., Sat. 10–6, Sun. 11–5; Oct.–Apr., Tues.–Fri. 10–5, Sat. 10–6, Sun. 11–5.*

National Aquarium in Baltimore. The most-visited attraction in Maryland has more than 16,000 fish, sharks, dolphins, and amphibians dwelling in 2 million gallons of water. The Animal Planet Australia: Wild Extremes exhibit mimics a river running through a gorge. It features lizards, crocodiles, turtles, bats, and a black-headed python, among other animals from Down Under. The aquarium also features reptiles, birds, plants, and mammals in its rain-forest environment, inside a glass pyramid 64 feet high. The rain-forest ecosystem harbors two-toed sloths in calabash trees, parrots in the palms, iguanas on the ground, and red-bellied piranhas in a pool (a sign next to it reads, "Do not put hands in pool"). Each day in the Marine Mammal Pavilion, Atlantic bottlenose dolphins are part of several entertaining presentations that highlight their agility and intelligence. The aquarium's famed shark tank and Atlantic coral reef exhibits are spectacular; you can wind through an enormous glass enclosure on a spiral ramp while hammerheads and brightly hued tropical fish glide by. Hands-on exhibits include such docile sea creatures as horseshoe crabs and starfish. ■ TIP➔ **Arrive early to ensure admission, which is by timed intervals; by noon, the wait is often two to three hours, especially on weekends and holidays.** ⊠ *Pier 3, Inner Harbor* ☎ *410/576–3800* ⊕ *www.aqua.org* ✉ *$34.95* ☉ *Nov.–Feb., Sat.–Thurs. 10–5, Fri. 10–8; Mar.–June, Sept., and Oct., Sat.–Thurs. 9–5, Fri. 9–8; July–Aug. 19, daily 9–8; Aug. 20–31, Sat.–Thurs. 9–6, Fri. 9–8. Visitors may tour for up to 1½ hrs after closing.*

FAMILY **Oriole Park at Camden Yards.** Home of the Baltimore Orioles, Camden Yards and the nearby area bustle on game days. Since it opened in 1992, this nostalgically designed baseball stadium has inspired other cities to emulate its neotraditional architecture and amenities. The Eutaw Street promenade, between the warehouse and the field, has a view of the stadium; look for the brass baseballs embedded in the sidewalk that mark where home runs have cleared the fence, or visit the Orioles Hall of Fame display and the monuments to retired Orioles. Daily 90-minute tours take you to nearly every section of the ballpark, from the massive, JumboTron scoreboard to the dugout to the state-of-the-art beer-delivery system. ⊠ *333 W. Camden St., Downtown* ☎ *410/685–9800 for general information, 410/547–6234 for tour times, 888/848–2473 for tickets* ⊕ *www.theorioles.com* ✉ *Eutaw St. promenade free; tour $9* ☉ *Eutaw St. promenade daily 10–3, otherwise during games and tours. Tours Apr.–Oct., Mon.–Sat. at 10, 11, noon, and 1, Sun. at noon, 1, 2, and 3.*

FAMILY **Port Discovery—The Baltimore Children's Museum.** At this interactive museum, adults are encouraged to play every bit as much as children. A favorite attraction is the three-story KidWorks, a futuristic jungle gym on which the adventurous can climb, crawl, slide, and swing their way through stairs, slides, ropes, zip lines, and tunnels, and even cross a narrow footbridge three stories up. In Miss Perception's Mystery House, youngsters help solve a mystery surrounding the disappearance of the Baffeld family by sifting through clues; some are written or visual, and others are gleaned by touching and listening. Changing interactive exhibits allow for even more play. ⊠ *35 Market Pl., Inner Harbor* ☎ *410/727–8120* ⊕ *www.portdiscovery.com* ✉ *$13.95* ☉ *Memorial Day–Labor Day, Mon.–Sat. 10–5, Sun. noon–5; Sept., Fri. 9:30–4:30, Sat. 10–5, Sun. noon–5; Oct.–May, Tues.–Fri. 9:30–4:30, Sat. 10–5, Sun. noon–5.*

SHOPPING

Baltimore isn't the biggest shopping town, but it does have some malls and good stores here and there. Hampden (the "p" is silent), a neighborhood west of Johns Hopkins University, has funky shops selling everything from housewares to housedresses along its main drag, 36th Street (better known as "The Avenue"). Some interesting shops can be found along Charles Street in Mount Vernon and along Thames Street in Fells Point. Federal Hill has a few fun shops, particularly for furnishings and vintage items.

Harborplace and the Gallery. At the Inner Harbor, the Pratt Street and Light Street pavilions of Harborplace and the Gallery contain almost 200 specialty shops that sell everything from business attire to children's toys. The Gallery has Forever 21, Banana Republic, and the Gap, among others. ⊠ *201 E. Pratt St.* ☎ *410/332–4191* ⊕ *www.harborplace. com.*

NIGHTLIFE

Fells Point, just east of the Inner Harbor; Federal Hill, due south; and Canton, due east, have hosts of bars, restaurants, and clubs that draw a rowdy, largely collegiate crowd. If you're seeking quieter surroundings, head for the upscale comforts of downtown or Mount Vernon clubs and watering holes.

BARS AND LOUNGES

$$

EUROPEAN

Fodor'sChoice

★

✕ **The Brewer's Art.** Part brewpub, part restaurant, and part lounge, this spot in a redone mansion feels young but urbane, with an ambitious menu, a clever wine list, and the Belgian-style beers it brews itself. Try the potent, delicious Resurrection ale. The upstairs dining room serves seasonal dishes with high-quality, locally available ingredients to create European-style country fare that is both hearty and sophisticated. In the dungeonlike downstairs bar, the menu and decor are more casual. Made with rosemary and garlic, the classic steak frites are a best bet. $ *Average main: $26* ⊠ *1106 N. Charles St., Mount Vernon* ☎ *410/547–6925* ⊕ *www.thebrewersart.com.*

Club Charles. With its stylized art deco surroundings, the funky Club Charles is a favorite hangout for an artsy crowd, moviegoers coming from the Charles Theater across the street, and, reputation has it, John Waters. ⊠ *1724 N. Charles St., Station North Arts District* ☎ *410/727–8815.*

Club Hippo. This club is Baltimore's longest-reigning gay bar. ⊠ *1 W. Eager St., Mount Vernon* ☎ *410/547–0069* ⊕ *www.clubhippo.com.*

Grand Central. A dance club, martini bar, and pub have all helped make Grand Central into a hip gay hotspot. ⊠ *1003 N. Charles St., Mount Vernon* ☎ *410/752–7133.*

Max's Taphouse. Beer lovers should visit Max's Taphouse, which has more than 140 brews on tap and about 1,200 more in bottles. ⊠ *737 S. Broadway, Fells Point* ☎ *410/675–6297* ⊕ *www.maxs.com.*

Red Maple. Red Maple is one of the city's most stylish spots for drinks and tapas. ⊠ *930 N. Charles St., Mount Vernon* ☎ *410/547–0149* ⊕ *www.930redmaple.com.*

13th Floor. At the top of The Belvedere, the 13th Floor offers a great view, a long martini list, and live jazz. Recent renovations restored the space to Gatsbyesque glory, with exposed wrought-iron beams, stained glass windows and sexy decor. ⊠ *1 E. Chase St., Mount Vernon* ☎ *410/347–0880* ⊕ *www.13floorbelvedere.com.*

WHERE TO EAT

Baltimore loves crabs. Soft- or hardshell crabs, crab cakes, crab dip—the city's passion for clawed crustaceans seems to have no end. Flag down a Baltimore native and ask them where the best crab joint is, and you'll get a list of options. In addition to crabs and seafood, Baltimore's restaurant landscape also includes Italian, Afghan, Greek, American, tapas, and other cuisines. The city's dining choices may not compare with those of New York, or even Washington, but it does have some real standouts. Note that places generally stop serving by 10 pm.

$ ✕**Amicci's.** At this self-proclaimed "very casual eatery," you don't have
ITALIAN to spend a fortune to get a satisfying taste of Little Italy. Bluejean-clad diners and walls hung with movie posters make for a fun atmosphere. Service is friendly and usually speedy, and the food comes in large portions. Try the chicken Lorenzo: breaded chicken breast covered in a marsala wine sauce, red peppers, prosciutto, and provolone. Ⓢ *Average main: $15* ✉ *231 S. High St., Little Italy* ☎ *410/528–1096* ⊕ *www.amiccis.com.*

$ ✕**Attman's.** Open since 1915, this authentic New York–style deli near
DELI the Jewish Museum is the king of Baltimore's "Corned Beef Row." Of the three delis on the row, Attman's has the longest waits and steepest prices, but delivers the highest-quality dishes. Don't be put off by the long lines—they move fairly quickly, and the outstanding corned beef sandwiches are worth the wait, as are the pastrami, homemade chopped liver, and other oversized creations. Attman's closes at 6:30 pm Monday through Saturday and at 5 pm Sunday. Ⓢ *Average main: $9* ✉ *1019 Lombard St., Historic Jonestown* ☎ *410/563–2666* ⊕ *www.attmansdeli.com.*

$$ ✕**Bo Brooks.** Picking steamed crabs on Bo Brooks's waterfront deck as
SEAFOOD sailboats and tugs ply the harbor is a quintessential Baltimore pleasure. Locals spend hot summer days cracking into warm, spicy crabs and enjoying a refreshing pitcher of beer while a cool breeze blows in from the harbor. Brooks serves its famous crustaceans year-round, along with a menu of Chesapeake seafood classics. Locals know to stick to the Maryland crab soup, crab dip, jumbo lump crab cakes, and fried oysters. Ⓢ *Average main: $22* ✉ *2780 Boston St., Canton* ☎ *410/558–0202* ⊕ *www.bobrooks.com.*

$$ ✕**Rusty Scupper.** A tourist favorite, the Rusty Scupper undoubtedly has
SEAFOOD the best view along the waterfront; sunset here is magical, with the sun sinking slowly into the harbor as lights twinkle on the city's skyscrapers. The interior is decorated with light wood and windows from floor to ceiling; the house specialty is seafood, particularly the jumbo lump crab cake, but the menu also includes beef, chicken, and pasta. Reservations are essential on Friday and Saturday and for the popular Sunday Jazz brunch. Ⓢ *Average main: $28* ✉ *402 Key Hwy., Inner Harbor* ☎ *410/727–3678* ⊕ *www.selectrestaurants.com/rusty.*

6

WHERE TO STAY

When booking a hotel or bed-and-breakfast in Baltimore, focus on the Inner Harbor, where you're likely to spend a good deal of time. The downside to staying in hotels downtown is the noise level, which can rise early in the morning and stay up late into the night—especially if there's a baseball or football game. For quieter options, head to neighborhoods like Fells Point and Canton.

For expanded reviews, facilities, and current deals, visit Fodors.com.

$$
B&B/INN
⌂ **Celie's Waterfront Bed & Breakfast.** Proprietors Nancy and Kevin Kupec oversee every detail of this small inn in the heart of Fells Point. **Pros:** intimate accommodations; situated next to an entertainment district. **Cons:** it can get noisy late at night. ⑤ *Rooms from: $149* ⊠ *1714 Thames St., Fells Point* ☎ *410/522–2323, 800/432–0184* ⊕ *www.celiesinn.com* ⇱ *7 rooms, 2 suites* ⑩ *Breakfast.*

$$
HOTEL
FAMILY
Fodor's Choice
★
⌂ **Hotel Monaco Baltimore.** This boutique hotel is located in the historic headquarters of the B&O Railroad, just 2½ blocks from the Inner Harbor and within easy walking distances of First Mariner Arena, Everyman Theatre, and Oriole Park at Camden Yards. **Pros:** daily wine hour; no extra charge for pets; friendly service. **Cons:** reception is on the second floor; there can be street noise in lower-floor rooms; not all rooms have bathtubs. ⑤ *Rooms from: $159* ⊠ *2 N. Charles St., Inner Harbor* ☎ *443/692–6170, 866/974–1904* ⊕ *www.monaco-baltimore. com* ⇱ *202 rooms, 27 suites* ⑩ *No meals.*

$$$
⌂ **Marriott Baltimore Waterfront.** The city's tallest hotel and the only one directly on the Inner Harbor itself, this upscale 31-story Marriott has a neoclassical interior that uses multihue marbles, rich jewel-tone walls, and photographs of Baltimore architectural landmarks. **Pros:** nice amenities; great location and view. **Cons:** pricey compared to nearby hotels. ⑤ *Rooms from: $239* ⊠ *700 Aliceanna St., Inner Harbor East* ☎ *410/385–3000* ⊕ *www.marriott.com* ⇱ *751 rooms* ⑩ *No meals.*

$$$
⌂ **Renaissance Baltimore Harborplace Hotel.** The most conveniently located of the Inner Harbor hotels—across the street from the shopping pavilions—the Renaissance Harborplace meets the needs of tourists, business travelers, and conventioneers. **Pros:** snappy service. **Cons:** some rooms are a bit threadbare. ⑤ *Rooms from: $189* ⊠ *202 E. Pratt St., Inner Harbor* ☎ *410/547–1200, 800/468–3571* ⊕ *www.marriott.com* ⇱ *562 rooms, 60 suites* ⑩ *No meals.*

CHARLESTON, SOUTH CAROLINA

Anna Evans,
Kinsey Gidick,
Rob Young

Charleston looks like a movie set, an 18th-century etching brought to life. The spires and steeples of more than 180 churches punctuate her low skyline, and tourists ride in horse-drawn carriages that pass grandiose, centuries-old mansions and gardens brimming with heirloom plants. Preserved through the poverty following the Civil War and natural disasters like fires, earthquakes, and hurricanes, much of Charleston's earliest public and private architecture still stands. And thanks to a rigorous preservation movement and strict Board of Architectural Review, the city's new structures blend with the old ones. If you're boarding your cruise ship here, it's worth coming a few days early to explore the historic downtown and to eat in one of the many superb restaurants. In late spring, plan in advance for the Spoleto U.S.A. Festival. For more than 30 memorable years, arts patrons have gathered to enjoy the international dance, opera, theater, and other performances at venues citywide. Piccolo Spoleto showcases local and regional concerts, dance, theater, and comedy shows.

ESSENTIALS

HOURS

Most shops are open from 9 or 10 am to at least 6 pm, but some are open later. A new city ordinance requires bars to close by 2 am.

VISITOR INFORMATION

Contact **Charleston Visitor Center** ⊠ *375 Meeting St., Upper King* ☎ *843/853–8000, 800/868–8118* ⊕ *www.charlestoncvb.com.*

THE CRUISE PORT

Cruise ships sailing from Charleston depart from the Union Pier Terminal, which is in Charleston's historic district. If you are driving, however, and need to leave your car for the duration of your cruise, take the East Bay Street exit off the new, majestic Ravenel Bridge on I–17 and follow the "Cruise Ship" signs. On ship embarkation days police officers will direct you to the ship terminal from the intersection of East Bay and Chapel streets. Cruise parking is adjacent to Union Pier.

Information **Port of Charleston** ⊠ *Union Pier, 280 Concord St., Market area* ☎ *843/958–8298 for cruise information* ⊕ *www.port-of-charleston.com.*

AIRPORT TRANSFERS

Several cab companies service the airport; expect to pay between $25 and $35 for a trip downtown. Airport Ground Transportation arranges shuttles, which cost $12 to $15 per person to the downtown area, double for a return trip to the airport. CARTA's Bus No. 11, a public bus, now goes to the airport for a mere $1.75; it leaves downtown from the Meeting/Mary St. parking garage every 50 minutes, from 5:45 am until 11:09 pm.

PARKING

Parking costs $17 per day ($119 per week) for regular vehicles, $40 per day ($280 per week) for RVs or other vehicles more than 20 feet in length. You pay in advance by cash, check, or credit card. A free shuttle bus takes you to the cruise-passenger terminal. Be sure to drop your large luggage off at Union Pier *before* you park your car; only carry-on size luggage is allowed on the shuttle bus, so if you have any bags larger than 22 inches by 14 inches, they will have to be checked before you park. Also, you'll need your cruise tickets to board the shuttle bus.

EXPLORING CHARLESTON

The heart of the city is on a peninsula, sometimes just called "downtown" by the nearly 60,000 residents who populate the area. Walking Charleston's peninsula is the best way to get to know the city. The

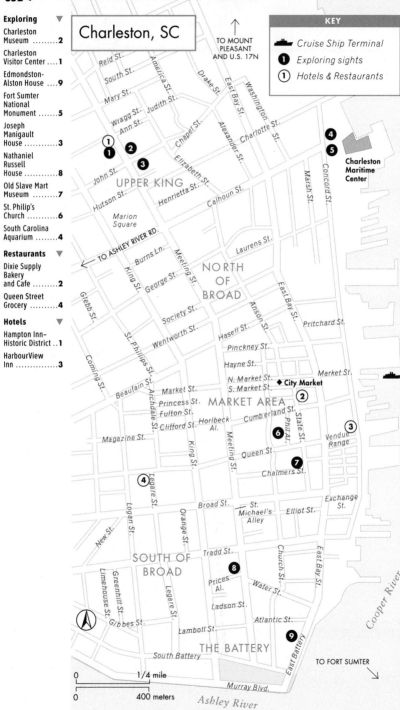

Charleston, SC

KEY

🚢 Cruise Ship Terminal

1 Exploring sights

① Hotels & Restaurants

TO MOUNT
PLEASANT
AND U.S. 17N

Charleston
Maritime
Center

UPPER KING

Marion
Square

TO ASHLEY RIVER RD.

NORTH
OF
BROAD

◆ City Market

MARKET AREA

Vendue
Range

Exchange
St.

SOUTH OF
BROAD

St.
Michael's
Alley

THE BATTERY

Cooper River

TO FORT SUMTER

South Battery

Murray Blvd.

Ashley River

Reid St., South St., Mary St., Wragg St., Ann St., John St., Hutson St., Henrietta St., Calhoun St., Laurens St., Burns Ln., George St., Society St., Wentworth St., Hasell St., Pinckney St., Hayne St., N. Market St., S. Market St., Princess St., Fulton St., Clifford St., Magazine St., Horlbeck Al., Cumberland St., Queen St., Chalmers St., Broad St., Elliot St., Tradd St., Prices Al., Water St., Ladson St., Atlantic St., Lamboll St., Gibbes St.

America St., Drake St., East Bay St., Washington St., Charlotte St., Alexander St., Judith St., Chapel St., Elizabeth St., Marsh St., Concord St., Anson St., Pritchard St., East Bay St., Market St., State St., Phil Al., Church St., East Bay St., East Battery

King St., Meeting St., St. Phillips St., Archdale St., Logan St., Legare St., Orange St., New St., Beaufain St., Coming St., Glebb St., Greenhill St., Limehouse St.

0 — 1/4 mile

0 — 400 meters

main downtown historic district is roughly bounded by Lockwood Boulevard to the west, Calhoun Street to the north, the Cooper River to the east, and the Battery to the south. Nearly 2,000 historic homes and buildings occupy this fairly compact area divided into South of Broad (Street) and North of Broad. King Street, the main shopping street in town, cuts through Broad Street, and the most trafficked tourist area ends a few blocks south of the Crosstown, where U.S. 17 cuts across Upper King. If you don't wish to walk, there are bikes, pedicabs, and trolleys. Street parking is irksome, as meter readers are among the city's most efficient public servants. Parking garages, both privately and publicly owned, charge around $1.50 an hour.

> ## CHARLESTON BEST BETS
>
> ■ **Viewing Art.** The city is home to some 120 galleries, exhibiting art from Charleston, the South, and around the world. The Gibbes Museum of Art and a half-dozen other museums add to the cultural mix.
>
> ■ **The Battery.** The views from the point—both natural and man-made—are the loveliest in the city. Look west to see the harbor; to the east you'll find elegant Charleston mansions.
>
> ■ **Historic Homes.** Charleston's preserved, centuries-old, stately homes, including the Nathaniel Russell House, are highlights.

FAMILY **Charleston Museum.** Although housed in a modern-day brick complex, this institution was founded in 1773 and is the country's oldest museum. To the delight of fans of *Antiques Roadshow,* the collection is especially strong in South Carolina decorative arts, from silver to snuffboxes. There's also a large gallery devoted to natural history (don't miss the giant polar bear). Children love the permanent Civil War exhibition, with plenty of Confederate uniforms, and the interactive "Kidstory" area, where they can try on reproduction clothing in a miniature historic house. A recent addition is the Historic Textiles Gallery, featuring changing displays that showcase everything from couture gowns to antique quilts. Combination tickets that give you admission to the Joseph Manigault House and the Heyward-Washington House are a bargain at $22. ✉ *360 Meeting St., Upper King* ☎ *843/722–2996* ⊕ *www.charlestonmuseum.org* 🎫 *$10* ⊗ *Mon.–Sat. 9–5, Sun. 1–5.*

Charleston Visitor Center The center's 20-minute film *Forever Charleston* is a fine introduction to the city. ■**TIP**➜ **The first 30 minutes are free at the parking lot, making it a real bargain.** ✉ *375 Meeting St., Upper King* ☎ *843/853–8000, 800/868–8118* ⊕ *www.charlestoncvb.com* 🎫 *Free* ⊗ *Apr.–Oct., daily 8:30–5:30; Nov.–Mar., daily 8:30–5.*

Edmondston-Alston House. In 1825, Charles Edmondston built this house in the Federal style, with Charles Alston transforming it into the imposing Greek Revival structure you see today beginning in 1838. Tours of the home—furnished with antiques, portraits, silver, and fine china—are informative. ✉ *21 E. Battery, South of Broad* ☎ *843/722–7171* ⊕ *www.edmondstonalston.com* 🎫 *$12; $44 with combination ticket for Middleton Place* ⊗ *Tues.–Sat. 10–4:30, Sun. 1–4:30.*

6

FAMILY
Fodor's Choice
★
Fort Sumter National Monument. Set on a man-made island in Charleston's harbor, this is the hallowed spot where the Civil War began. On April 12, 1861, the first shot of the war was fired from Fort Johnson (now defunct) across the way. After a 34-hour battle, Union forces surrendered and Confederate troops occupied Sumter, which became a symbol of Southern resistance. The Confederacy managed to hold it, despite almost continual bombardment, from August 1863 to February of 1865. When it was finally evacuated, the fort was a heap of rubble. Today, the National Park Service oversees it, and rangers give interpretive talks and conduct guided tours. To reach the fort, you have to take a ferry or a private boat; ferries depart from the Fort Sumter Visitor Education Center, downtown, and from Patriots Point in Mount Pleasant. There are six trips daily between mid-March and mid-August. The schedule is abbreviated the rest of the year, so call ahead for details. For those using a GPS to find the boat departure points for Fort Sumter, remember to use the address for Patriots Point and the Visitor Education Center, not the mailing address for the fort. ☎ *843/883–3123* ⊕ *www.nps.gov/fosu* ✉ *Fort free; ferry $17* ☉ *Mid-Mar.–early Sept., daily 10–5:30; early Sept.–Dec. and early Mar., daily 10–4; Dec.–Feb., daily 11:30–4.*

Fodor's Choice
★
Joseph Manigault House. Considered by many to be the finest example of Federal-style architecture in the South, this 1803 home was built for a rich rice-planting family of Huguenot heritage. Having toured Europe as a gentleman architect, Gabriel Manigault returned to design this residence for his brother Joseph as the city's first essay in neoclassicism. The house glows in red brick and is adorned with a two-story piazza balcony. Inside, marvels await: a fantastic "flying" staircase in the central hall; a gigantic Venetian window; elegant plasterwork and mantels; notable Charleston-made furniture; and a bevy of French, English, and American antiques, including some celebrated tricolor Wedgwood pieces. Outside, note the garden "folly." ✉ *350 Meeting St., Upper King* ☎ *843/723–2926* ⊕ *www.charlestonmuseum.org* ✉ *$10* ☉ *Mon.–Sat. 10–5, Sun. 1–5.*

Fodor's Choice
★
Nathaniel Russell House. One of the nation's finest examples of Federal-style architecture, the Nathaniel Russell House was built in 1808, when Russell was 70 years old. Its grand beauty is proof of the immense wealth he accumulated as one of the city's leading merchants. In addition to the famous "free-flying" staircase that spirals up three stories with no visible support, the ornate interior is distinguished by fine, Charleston-made furniture as well as paintings and works on paper by well-known American and European artists, including Henry Benbridge, Samuel F. B. Morse, and George Romney. The extensive formal garden is worth a leisurely stroll. ✉ *51 Meeting St., South of Broad* ☎ *843/724–8481* ⊕ *www.historiccharleston.org* ✉ *$10; $16 with admission to Aiken-Rhett House Museum* ☉ *Mon.–Sat. 10–5, Sun. 2–5.*

Fodor's Choice
★
Old Slave Mart Museum. This is likely the only building still in existence in South Carolina that was used for slave auctioning, a practice that ended here in 1863. It was once part of a complex called Ryan's Mart, which also contained a slave jail, kitchen, and morgue. It is now a museum that recounts the history of Charleston's role in the slave trade,

an unpleasant story but one that is vital to understand. Charleston once served as the center of commercial activity for the South's plantation economy, and slaves were the primary source of labor both within the city and on the surrounding plantations. Galleries are outfitted with some interactive exhibits, including push buttons that allow you to hear voices relating stories from the age of slavery. The museum is on one of the few remaining cobblestone streets in town. ⊠ *6 Chalmers St., Market area* ☎ *843/958–6467* ⊕ *www.charlestoncity.info* ⊠ *$7* ⊙ *Mon.–Sat. 9–5.*

Fodor'sChoice ★ **St. Philip's Church.** One of the three churches that gave Church Street its name, this graceful Corinthian-style building is the second one to rise on its site: the first one burned down in 1835 and was rebuilt in 1838. A shell that exploded in the churchyard while services were being held one Sunday during the Civil War didn't deter the minister from finishing his sermon (the congregation gathered elsewhere for the remainder of the war). Notable Charlestonians such as John C. Calhoun are buried in the eastern and western churchyards. If you want to tour the church, call ahead, as open hours depend upon volunteer availability. ⊠ *142 Church St., Market area* ☎ *843/722–7734* ⊕ *www.stphilipschurchsc.org* ⊙ *Churchyard weekdays 9–4.*

FAMILY **Fodor'sChoice** ★ **South Carolina Aquarium.** The 385,000-gallon Great Ocean Tank houses the tallest aquarium window in North America. Along with sharks, moray eels, and sea turtles, exhibits include more than 7,000 creatures, representing 350-plus species. In 2011, the 2,500-square-foot Saltmarsh Aviary opened, offering views of Charleston Harbor and allowing you to catch sight of herons, diamondback terrapins, puffer fish, and stingrays. The latest exhibit is Madagascar Journey, filled with exotic animals including ring-tailed lemurs—a favorite among visitors, who can step inside an observation bubble within the primates' habitat. The 4-D theater shows popular family films complete with special effects such as wind gusts and splashes of water. ⊠ *100 Aquarium Wharf, Upper King* ☎ *800/722–6455, 843/720–1990* ⊕ *www.scaquarium.org* ⊠ *$29.95* ⊙ *Mar.–Aug., daily 9–5; Sept.–Feb., daily 9–4.*

SHOPPING

City Market. The Market area is a cluster of shops and restaurants centered around the City Market. Sweetgrass basket weavers work here, and you can buy the resulting wares, although these artisan-crafts have become expensive. There are T-shirts and souvenir stores here as well as upscale boutiques. In the covered, open-air market, shops are open daily and vendors have stalls with everything from jewelry to dresses and purses. And, thanks to a beautiful 2011 remodel, you can peruse the middle section of the market in enclosed, air-conditioned comfort. ⊠ *E. Bay and Market sts., Market area* ⊕ *www.thecharlestoncitymarket.com.*

Fodor'sChoice ★ **King Street.** King Street is Charleston's main street and the major shopping corridor downtown. The latest lines of demarcation divide the street into districts: Lower King (from Broad Street to Market Street) is the Antiques District, lined with high-end antiques dealers; Middle King (from Market Street to Calhoun Street) is now called the Fashion District and is a mix of national chains like Banana Republic and Pottery Barn, alternative shops, and locally owned landmark stores and boutiques; and Upper King (from Calhoun Street to Spring Street) has been dubbed the Design District, an up-and-coming area becoming known for its furniture and interior-design stores selling home fashion. Check out Second Sundays on King, when the street closes for pedestrian use from Calhoun Street to Queen Street, and visit the Farmers' Market in Marion Square throughout the summer months. ⊕ *www. kingstreetantiquedistrict.com, www.kingstreetfashiondistrict.com, or littleworksofheart.typepad.com/upperkingcharleston.*

> **CHARLESTON CRUISE PACKAGES**
>
> For a listing of all hotel package discounts you can book along with your cruise, not to mention discounted tours (including the popular plantation tours), attractions, and shopping and dining coupons, visit ⊕ *www. charlestoncruisepackages.com.*

NIGHTLIFE

Charleston Grill. The elegant Charleston Grill has live jazz from 7 to 10 on Friday and 8 to midnight on Saturday. Shows range from the internationally acclaimed, Brazilian-influenced Quentin Baxter Ensemble to the Bob Williams Duo, a father and son who play classical guitar and violin. It draws a mature, upscale clientele, hotel guests, well-known locals, and more recently an urbane thirtysomething crowd. ⊠ *Charleston Place Hotel, 224 King St., Market area* ☎ *843/577–4522* ⊕ *www. charlestongrill.com.*

WHERE TO EAT

$

SOUTHERN

✕ **Dixie Supply Bakery and Cafe.** It might be a lil' eatery buttressed by a Lil' Cricket convenience store, but don't be fooled by its size. Dixie Supply Bakery and Cafe belongs to an old Charlestonian family (and by old, we mean they arrived here in 1698 or so) that seeks to honor its roots through food. It's here you'll find Lowcountry and Southern classics: shrimp and creamy stone-ground grits, fried chicken, and a mighty fine tomato pie. Daily alternating blue-plate specials abound, including fried green tomatoes, shrimp from nearby Wadmalaw Island, summer-squash-and-ricotta-cheese ravioli, and a steady assortment of locally plucked vegetables. $ *Average main: $7* ⊠ *62 State St., Market area* ☎ *843/722–5650* ⊕ *www.dixiecafecharleston.com.*

$

AMERICAN

✕ **Queen Street Grocery.** For crêpes and cold-pressed coffee, most folks turn to a venerable Charleston institution: Queen Street Grocery. Established in 1922, the corner shop has endured several guises through the years: butchery, candy shop, and late-night convenience store. Back in 2008, new owners returned the store to its roots as a neighborhood grocery store, sourcing much of the produce and other goods from local growers. It's a great preservation act, improved upon by QSG's newest offerings: sweet and savory crepes named for the islands surrounding Charleston. $ *Average main: $9* ✉ *133 Queen St., Market area* ☎ *843/723–4121* ⊕ *www.qsg29401.com.*

WHERE TO STAY

While the city's best hotels and B&Bs are in the historic district, most of them do not have free parking. If you stay outside of downtown in a chain hotel, you will give up much in charm and convenience but pay significantly less, not to mention park for free. High-season rates are traditionally in effect from March through May and September through November.

For expanded reviews, facilities, and current deals, visit Fodors.com.

$$
HOTEL
Hampton Inn–Historic District. Hardwood floors, a fireplace, and cozy new furnishings in the lobby of what was once an 1800s warehouse help elevate this chain hotel a bit above the rest. **Pros:** hot breakfast; located near the business and retail district of Upper King and near a couple of really good restaurants. **Cons:** a long walk to the Market area; rooms are smallish; no views. $ *Rooms from: $199* ✉ *373 Meeting St., Upper King* ☎ *843/723–4000, 800/426–7866* ⊕ *www.hamptoninn.com* ⤶ *170 rooms* ❦ *Breakfast.*

$$$$
B&B/INN
HarbourView Inn. This is the only hotel on the harbor, and if you ask for a room facing the harbor, you can gaze out onto the kid-friendly fountain and 8 acres of Waterfront Park. **Pros:** Continental breakfast can be delivered to the room or the rooftop; service is notable. **Cons:** rooms are off long, modern halls; rooms are not particularly spacious. $ *Rooms from: $279* ✉ *2 Vendue Range, Market area* ☎ *843/853–8439, 888/853–8439* ⊕ *www.harbourviewcharleston.com* ⤶ *52 rooms* ❦ *Breakfast.*

FORT LAUDERDALE, FLORIDA

Paul Rubio

In the 1960s Fort Lauderdale's beachfront was lined with T-shirt shops interspersed with quickie-food outlets, and downtown consisted of a lone office tower, some dilapidated government buildings, and motley other structures waiting to be razed. Today the beach is home to upscale shops and restaurants, while downtown has exploded with new office and luxury residential development. The entertainment and shopping areas—Las Olas Boulevard, Las Olas Riverfront, and Himmarshee Village—are thriving. And Port Everglades is giving Miami a run for its money in passenger cruising, with a dozen cruise-ship terminals, including the world's largest, hosting more than 20 cruise ships with some 3,000 departures annually. A captivating shoreline with wide ribbons of sand for beachcombing and sunbathing makes Fort Lauderdale and Broward County a major draw for visitors, and often tempts cruise-ship passengers to spend an extra day or two in the sun. Fort Lauderdale's 2-mile (3-km) stretch of unobstructed beachfront has been further enhanced with a sparkling promenade designed more for the pleasure of pedestrians than vehicles.

ESSENTIALS

HOURS

Many museums close on Monday.

BOAT TOURS

A water taxi provides service along the intracoastal waterway in Fort Lauderdale between the 17th Street Causeway and Oakland Park Boulevard, and west into downtown along New River daily from 10 am until midnight. A day pass costs $20.

Water Taxi. A great way to experience the multimillion-dollar homes, hotels, and seafood restaurants along Fort Lauderdale's waterways is via the public Water Taxi, which runs every 30 minutes beginning at 10 am and ending at midnight. An unlimited day pass serves as both a tour and a means of transportation between Fort Lauderdale's hotels and hot spots, though Water Taxi is most useful when viewed as a tour. It's possible to cruise all afternoon while taking in the waterfront sights. Captains and helpers indulge guests in fun factoids about Fort Lauderdale, white lies about the city's history, and bizarre tales about the celebrity homes along the Intracoastal. A day pass is $20. There are 10 regularly scheduled pickup stations in Fort Lauderdale. Water Taxi also connects Fort Lauderdale to Hollywood, where there are seven scheduled stops. ⊠ *Fort Lauderdale* ⊕ *www.watertaxi.com.*

VISITOR INFORMATION
Contact **Greater Fort Lauderdale Convention and Visitors Bureau**
☎ 954/765–4466 ⊕ www.sunny.org.

THE CRUISE PORT

Port Everglades, Fort Lauderdale's cruise port (nowhere near the Everglades, but happily near the beach and less than 2 miles [3 km] from the airport), is among the world's largest, busiest ports. It's also the straightest, deepest port in the southeastern United States, meaning you'll be out to sea in no time flat once your ship sets sail. At a cost of $75 million, Cruise Terminal 18 has been tripled in size to accommodate Royal Caribbean's Oasis-class ships, the 5,400-passenger *Oasis of the Seas* and sister *Allure of the Seas*. The terminal's megasize (240,000 square feet) accommodates both arriving and departing passengers and their luggage, simultaneously going through processing procedures. The port is south of downtown Fort Lauderdale, spread out over a huge area extending into Dania Beach, Hollywood, and a patch of unincorporated Broward County. A few words of caution: Schedule plenty of time to navigate the short distance from the airport, your hotel, or wherever else you might be staying, especially if you like to be among the first to embark for your sailing. Increased security (sometimes you'll be asked for a driver's license and/or other identification, and on occasion for boarding documentation on entering the port; other times not) combined with increased traffic, larger parking facilities, construction projects, roadway improvements, and other obstacles mean the old days of popping over to Port Everglades and running up a gangplank in the blink of an eye are history.

If you are driving, there are two entrances to the port. One is from 17th Street, west of the 17th Street Causeway Bridge, turning south at the traffic light onto Eisenhower Boulevard. Or to get to the main entrance, take either State Road 84, running east–west, to the intersection of Federal Highway and cross into the port, or take I–595 east straight into the Port (I–595 becomes Eller Drive once inside the Port). I–595 runs east–west with connections to the Fort Lauderdale–Hollywood International Airport, U.S. 1 (Federal Highway), I–95, State Road 7 (U.S. 441), Florida's Turnpike, Sawgrass Expressway, and I–75.

Contact **Port Everglades** ✉ 1850 Eller Dr., Fort Lauderdale ☎ 954/523–3404 ⊕ www.porteverglades.org.

AIRPORT TRANSFERS
Fort Lauderdale–Hollywood International Airport is 4 miles (6 km) south of downtown and 2 miles (3 km [about 5 to 10 minutes]) from the docks. If you haven't arranged an airport transfer with your cruise line, you can take a taxi to the cruise-ship terminals. The ride in a metered taxi costs about $15 to $18, depending on your departure terminal. Taxi fares for up to four passengers, regulated by the county, are $4.50 for the first mile and $2.40 for each additional mile, 40¢ per minute for waiting time, plus a $2 surcharge for cabs departing from the airport. Yellow Cab is a major presence, and Go Airport Shuttle provides limousine or shared-ride service to and from Port Everglades to all

parts of Broward County; fares to most Fort Lauderdale beach hotels are in the $25 to $30 range. Fort Lauderdale Shuttle offers one-way transportation from FLL Airport or surrounding hotels to Port Everglades Cruise Ships. For two people it's a total of $22, three people $25, and four people $32.

Contacts Go Airport Shuttle ☎ 954/561-8888, 800/244-8252 ⊕ goairportshuttle.com. **Fort Lauderdale Shuttle** ☎ 954/525-7796, 866/386-7433 ⊕ fortlauderdaleshuttle. com. **Yellow Cab** ☎ 954/777-7777.

PARKING

Two covered parking facilities close to the terminals are Northport (expanded to 4,250 spaces) and Midport (for 2,000 vehicles). Use the Northport garage if your cruise leaves from Terminal 1, 2, or 4; use Midport if your cruise leaves from Terminal 19, 21, 22/24, 25, 26, 27, or 29. The Midport Surface Lot at Terminal 18 has 600 spaces. The cost is $15 per day for either garage or surface lot ($19 for oversize vehicles up to 20 feet); you pay by cash or credit card when you leave. To save a few bucks on your parking tab, two separate companies, Park 'N Fly ($12 per day) and Park 'N Go ($12 per day) provide remote parking just outside Port Everglades, at the exit off I–595, with shuttles to all cruise terminals. Book ahead online for even deeper discounts.

Contacts Park 'N Fly ⊠ 2200 N.E. 7th Ave., Dania Beach ⊕ At the Port Everglades exit off I–595 ☎ 954/779-1776 ⊕ www.pnf.com. **Park 'N Go** ⊠ 1101 Eller Dr., Fort Lauderdale ⊕ At the Port Everglades exit off I–595 ☎ 954/760-4525, 888/764-7275 ⊕ www.bookparkngo.com.

FORT LAUDERDALE BEST BETS

The Beach. With more than 20 miles of ocean shoreline, the scene at Greater Fort Lauderdale's best beaches, especially between Bahia Mar and Sunrise Boulevard, is not to be missed.

The Everglades. Take in the wild reaches in or near the Everglades with an airboat ride. Mosquitoes are friendly, so arm yourself accordingly.

Las Olas Boulevard and the Riverwalk. This is a great place to stroll before and after performances, dinner, libations, and other entertainment.

EXPLORING FORT LAUDERDALE

Like its southeast Florida neighbors, Fort Lauderdale has been busily revitalizing for several years. In a state where gaudy tourist zones often stand aloof from workaday downtowns, Fort Lauderdale is unusual in that the city exhibits consistency at both ends of the 2-mile (3-km) Las Olas corridor. The sparkling look results from efforts to thoroughly improve both beachfront and downtown. Matching the downtown's innovative arts district, cafés, and boutiques is an equally inventive beach area with its own share of cafés and shops facing an undeveloped shoreline.

FAMILY **Ah-Tah-Thi-Ki Museum.** A couple of miles from Billie Swamp Safari is Ah-Tah-Thi-Ki Museum, whose name means "a place to learn, a place to remember." This museum documents the traditions and culture of the Seminole Tribe of Florida through artifacts, exhibits, and reenactments of rituals and ceremonies. The 60-acre site includes a living-history Seminole village, nature trails, and a wheelchair-accessible boardwalk through a cypress swamp. Guided tours are available daily at 2:30; self-guided audio tours are available anytime. There are also children's programs. ⊠ *34725 W. Boundary Rd., Western Suburbs and Beyond, Clewiston* ☎ *877/902–1113* ⊕ *www.ahtahthiki.com* ✉ *$9* ⊗ *Wed.–Sun. 9–5.*

> **IT'S A GIRL**
>
> Even as far back as ancient times, mariners have traditionally referred to their ships as "she." To a seaman, a ship is as beautiful and comforting as his mother or sweetheart. You could say a good ship holds a special place in his heart.

FAMILY **Billie Swamp Safari.** At the Billie Swamp Safari, experience the majesty of the Everglades firsthand. Daily tours of wildlife-filled wetlands and hammocks yield sightings of deer, water buffalo, raccoons, wild hogs, hawks, eagles, and alligators. Animal and reptile shows entertain audiences. Ecotours are conducted aboard motorized swamp buggies, and airboat rides are available, too. The on-site Swamp Water Café serves gator nuggets, frogs' legs, catfish, and Indian fry bread with honey. ⊠ *Big Cypress Seminole Indian Reservation, 30000 Gator Tail Trail, Western Suburbs and Beyond, Clewiston* ☎ *863/983–6101, 800/949–6101* ⊕ *www.swampsafari.com* ✉ *Swamp Safari Day Package $49.95 (ecotour, shows, exhibits, and airboat ride)* ⊗ *Daily 9–6.*

Bonnet House Museum & Gardens. A 35-acre oasis in the heart of the beach area, this subtropical estate on the National Register of Historic Places stands as a tribute to the history of Old South Florida. This charming home, built in the 1920s, was the winter residence of the late Frederic and Evelyn Bartlett, artists whose personal touches and small surprises are evident throughout. If you're interested in architecture, artwork, or the natural environment, this place is worth a visit. After admiring the fabulous gardens, be on the lookout for playful monkeys swinging from trees. ⊠ *900 N. Birch Rd., along the beach, Fort Lauderdale* ☎ *954/563–5393* ⊕ *www.bonnethouse.org* ✉ *$20 for house tours, $10 gardens only* ⊗ *Tues.–Sun. 9–4; tours hrly 9:30–3:30.*

FAMILY **Butterfly World.** As many as 80 butterfly species from South and Central America, the Philippines, Malaysia, Taiwan, and other Asian nations are typically found within the serene 3-acre site inside Tradewinds Park in the northwest reaches of Broward County. A screened aviary called North American Butterflies is reserved for native species. The Tropical Rain Forest Aviary is a 30-foot-high construction, with observation decks, waterfalls, ponds, and tunnels filled with thousands of colorful butterflies. There are lots of birds, too; and kids love going in the lorikeet aviary, where the colorful birds land on every limb! ⊠ *3600 W. Sample Rd., Western Suburbs and Beyond, Coconut Creek* ☎ *954/977–4400* ⊕ *www.butterflyworld.com* ✉ *$24.95* ⊗ *Mon.–Sat. 9–5, Sun. 11–5.*

6

FAMILY **Museum of Discovery & Science/AutoNation IMAX Theater.** With more than
Fodor's Choice 200 interactive exhibits, the aim here is to entertain children *and* adults
★ with the wonders of science and the wonders of Florida. In 2012, the
museum doubled in size—meaning twice the fun! Exhibits include the
Ecodiscovery Center with an Everglades Airboat Adventure ride, resident otters, and an interactive Florida storm center. Florida Ecoscapes
has a living coral reef, plus sharks, rays, and eels. Runways to Rockets
offers stimulating trips to Mars and the moon while nine different cock-
pit simulators let you try out your pilot skills. The AutoNation IMAX
theater, part of the complex, shows films, some in 3-D, on an 80-foot by
60-foot screen with 15,000 watts of digital surround sound broadcast
from 42 speakers. ⊠ *401 S.W. 2nd St., Downtown and Las Olas, Fort
Lauderdale* ☎ *954/467–6637 museum, 954/463–4629 IMAX* ⊕ *www.
mods.org* ⊠ *Museum $14, $19 with one IMAX show* ☉ *Mon.–Sat.
10–5, Sun. noon–6.*

Riverwalk. Lovely views prevail on this paved promenade on the New
River's north bank. On the first Sunday of every month a free jazz
festival attracts visitors. From west to east, the Riverwalk begins at
the residential New River Sound, passes through the Arts and Science
District, then the historic center of Fort Lauderdale, and wraps around
the New River until it meets with Las Olas Boulevard's shopping district. ⊠ *Fort Lauderdale.*

BEACHES

Fort Lauderdale's **beachfront** offers the best of all possible worlds, with
easy access not only to a wide band of beige sand but also to restaurants
and shops. For 2 miles (3 km) heading north, beginning at the Bahia
Mar yacht basin, along Route A1A you'll have clear views, typically
across rows of colorful beach umbrellas, of the sea, and of ships passing into and out of nearby Port Everglades. If you're on the beach, gaze
back on an exceptionally graceful promenade.

Pedestrians rank above vehicles in Fort Lauderdale. Broad walkways
line both sides of the beach road, and traffic has been trimmed to two
gently curving northbound lanes, where in-line skaters skim past slow-
moving cars. On the beach side, a low masonry wall doubles as an
extended bench, separating sand from the promenade. At night the
wall is accented with ribbons of fiber-optic color, quite pretty when
working, although outages are frequent. The most crowded portion
of beach is between Las Olas and Sunrise boulevards. Tackier aspects
of this onetime strip—famous for the springtime madness spawned by
the film *Where the Boys Are*—are now but a fading memory, with the
possible exception of the icon Elbo Room, an ever-popular bar at the
corner of Las Olas and A1A.

North of the redesigned beachfront are another 2 miles (3 km) of open
and natural coastal landscape. Much of the way parallels the **Hugh
Taylor Birch State Recreation Area,** preserving a patch of primeval Florida.

SHOPPING

Galleria Fort Lauderdale. Fort Lauderdale's most upscale mall is just west of the Intracoastal Waterway. The split-level emporium entices with Neiman Marcus, Dillard's, Macy's, an Apple Store plus 150 specialty shops for anything from cookware to exquisite jewelry. Upgrades in 2010 included marble floors and fine dining options. Chow down at Capital Grille, Truluck's, Blue Martini, P. F. Chang's, or Seasons 52, or head for the food court, which will defy expectations with its international food-market feel. Galleria is open 10–9 Monday through Saturday, noon–5:30 Sunday. ⊠ *2414 E. Sunrise Blvd., Intracoastal and Inland, Fort Lauderdale* ☎ *954/564–1015* ⊕ *www.galleriamall-fl.com.*

The Gallery at Beach Place. Just north of Las Olas Boulevard on Route A1A, this shopping gallery is attached to the mammoth Marriot Beach Place timeshare. Spaces are occupied by touristy shops that sell everything from sarongs to alligator heads, chain restaurants like Hooter's, bars serving frozen drinks, and a super sized CVS pharmacy, which sells everything you need for the beach. ■TIP→ **Beach Place has covered parking, and usually has plenty of spaces, but you can pinch pennies by using a nearby municipal lot that's metered.** ⊠ *17 S. Fort Lauderdale Beach Blvd., along the beach, Fort Lauderdale* ⊕ *www.galleryatbeachplace.com.*

Las Olas Boulevard. Las Olas Boulevard is the heart and soul of Fort Lauderdale. Not only are the city's best boutiques, top restaurants, and art galleries found along this beautifully landscaped street, but Las Olas links Fort Lauderdale's growing downtown with its superlative beaches. Though you'll find a Cheesecake Factory on the boulevard, the thoroughfare tends to shun chains and welcomes one-of-a-kind clothing boutiques, chocolatiers, and ethnic eateries. Window shopping allowed. ⊠ *East Las Olas Boulevard, Downtown and Las Olas, Fort Lauderdale* ⊕ *www.lasolasboulevard.com.*

NIGHTLIFE

O Lounge. This lounge and two adjacent establishments, **Yolo** and **Vibe**, on Las Olas and under the same ownership, cater to Fort Lauderdale's sexy yuppies, business men, desperate housewives, and hungry cougars letting loose during happy hour and on the weekends. Crowds alternate between Yolo's outdoor fire pit, O Lounge's chilled atmosphere and lounge music, and Vibe's more intense beats. Expect flashy cars in the driveway and a bit of plastic surgery. ⊠ *333 E. Las Olas Blvd., Downtown and Las Olas, Fort Lauderdale* ☎ *954/523–1000* ⊕ *www.yolorestaurant.com.*

Tarpon Bend. This casual two-story restaurant transforms into a jovial resto-bar in the early evening, ideal for enjoying a few beers, mojitos, and some great bar food. It's consistently busy, day, night, and late night with young professionals, couples, and large groups of friends. It's one place that has survived all the ups and downs of downtown Fort Lauderdale. ⊠ *200 S.W. 2nd St., Downtown and Las Olas, Fort Lauderdale* ☎ *954/523–3233* ⊕ *www.tarponbend.com.*

6

WHERE TO EAT

$$ ✕ **Southport Raw Bar.** You can't go wrong at this unpretentious spot
SEAFOOD   where the motto, on bumper stickers for miles around, proclaims, "eat
fish, live longer, eat oysters, love longer, eat clams, last longer." Raw
or steamed clams, raw oysters, and peel-and-eat shrimp are market
priced. Sides range from Bimini bread to key lime pie, with conch frit-
ters, beer-battered onion rings, and corn on the cob in between. Order
wine by the bottle or glass, and beer by the pitcher, bottle, or can.
Eat outside overlooking a canal, or inside at booths, tables, or in the
front or back bars. Limited parking is free, and a grocery-store park-
ing lot is across the street. $ *Average main: $18* ⊠ *1536 Cordova Rd.,
Intracoastal and Inland, Fort Lauderdale* ☎ *954/525–2526* ⊕ *www.
southportrawbar.com.*

$$$$ ✕ **Steak 954.** It's not just the steaks that impress at Stephen Starr's super-
STEAKHOUSE   star restaurant. The lobster and crab-coconut ceviche and the red snap-
Fodor's Choice   per tiradito are divine; the butter-poached Maine lobster is perfection;
★   and the raw bar showcases only the best and freshest seafood on the
market. Located on the first floor of the swanky W Fort Lauderdale,
Steak 954 offers spectacular views of the ocean for those choosing
outdoor seating. Inside, there's a sexy, sophisticated ambience for those
choosing to dine in the main dining room, with bright tropical colors
balanced with dark wood and an enormous jellyfish tank spanning the
width of the restaurant. Sunday brunch is very popular, so arrive early
for the best views. $ *Average main: $35* ⊠ *W Fort Lauderdale, 401
N. Fort Lauderdale Beach Blvd., along the beach, Fort Lauderdale*
☎ *954/414–8333* ⊕ *www.steak954.com.*

WHERE TO STAY

Fort Lauderdale has a growing and varied roster of lodging options, from
beachfront luxury suites to intimate B&Bs to chain hotels along the Intra-
coastal Waterway. If you want to be on the beach, be sure to mention this
when booking your room, because many hotels advertise "waterfront"
accommodations that are actually on inland waterways, not the beach.

For expanded reviews, facilities, and current deals, visit Fodors.com.

$$ ⬚ **Hyatt Regency Pier Sixty-Six Resort & Spa.** Don't let the 1970s exterior
RESORT   of the iconic 17-story tower fool you; this lovely 22-acre resort teems
with contemporary interior-design sophistication and remains one of
Florida's few hotels where a rental car isn't necessary. **Pros:** great views;
plenty of activities; free shuttle to beach; easy Water Taxi access. **Cons:**
tower rooms are far less stylish than Lanai rooms; totally retro rotating rooftop is used exclusively for private events. $ *Rooms from: $189*
⊠ *2301 S.E. 17th St. Causeway, Intracoastal and Inland, Fort Lauderdale* ☎ *954/525–6666* ⊕ *www.pier66.com* ⇆ *384 rooms* ⦿ *No meals.*

$$$ ⬚ **Pelican Grand Beach Resort.** Smack on Fort Lauderdale beach, this yel-
RESORT   low spired, Key West–style property maintains its heritage of Old Flor-
FAMILY   ida seaside charm with rooms adorned in florals, pastels, and wicker;
an old-fashioned emporium; and a small circulating lazy-river pool that
allows kids to float 'round and 'round. **Pros:** free popcorn in the Post-
card Lounge; directly on the beach; Ocean 2000 restaurant. **Cons:** high

tide can swallow most of beach area; decor appeals to older generations. ⑤ *Rooms from: $224* ✉ *2000 N. Atlantic Blvd., Along the beach, Fort Lauderdale* ☎ *954/568–9431, 800/525–6232* ⊕ *www.pelicanbeach. com* ☛ *135 rooms* ❍ *No meals.*

GALVESTON, TEXAS

Kristin Finan

A thin strip of an island in the Gulf of Mexico, Galveston is big-sister Houston's beach playground—a year-round coastal destination just 50 miles away. Many of the first public buildings in Texas, including a post office, bank, and hotel, were built here, but most were destroyed in the Great Storm of 1900. Those that endured have been well preserved, and the Victorian character of the Historic Downtown Strand shopping district and the neighborhood surrounding Broadway is still evident. On the Galveston Bay side of the island (northeast), quaint shops and cafés in old buildings are near the Seaport Museum, harborfront eateries, and the cruise-ship terminal. On the Gulf of Mexico side (southwest), resorts and restaurants line coastal Seawall Boulevard. The 17-foot-high seawall abuts a long ribbon of sand and provides a place for rollerblading, bicycling, and going on the occasional surrey ride. The city was badly damaged from flooding during Hurricane Ike in 2008, but businesses are now up and running, with few remnants of the storm.

Galveston is a port of embarkation for cruises on Western Caribbean itineraries. It's an especially popular port of embarkation for people living in the southeastern states who don't wish to fly to their cruise. Carnival and Royal Caribbean have ships based in Galveston, offering four-, five-, six-, and seven-day cruises along the Mexican coast and to Jamaica, Grand Cayman, Belize, Bahamas, Key West, and Honduras, plus a 14-night cruise to the Azores and Spain.

ESSENTIALS

HOURS

Shops in the historic district are usually open until at least 7. During peak season some stay open later; the rest of the time they close at 6. This is also the city's nightlife district, and is hopping until late.

VISITOR INFORMATION

Contact Galveston Visitors Center ✉ *Ashton Villa, 2328 Broadway* ☎ *888/425–4753* ⊕ *www.galveston.com.*

THE CRUISE PORT

The relatively sheltered waters of Galveston Bay are home to the Texas Cruise Ship Terminal. It's only 30 minutes to open water from here. Driving south from Houston on I–45, you cross a long causeway before reaching the island. Take the first exit, Harborside Drive, left after you've crossed the causeway onto Galveston Island. Follow that for a few miles to the port. Turn left on 22nd Street (also called Kempner Street); there is a security checkpoint before you continue down a driveway. The drop-off point is set up much like an airport terminal, with pull-through lanes and curbside check-in.

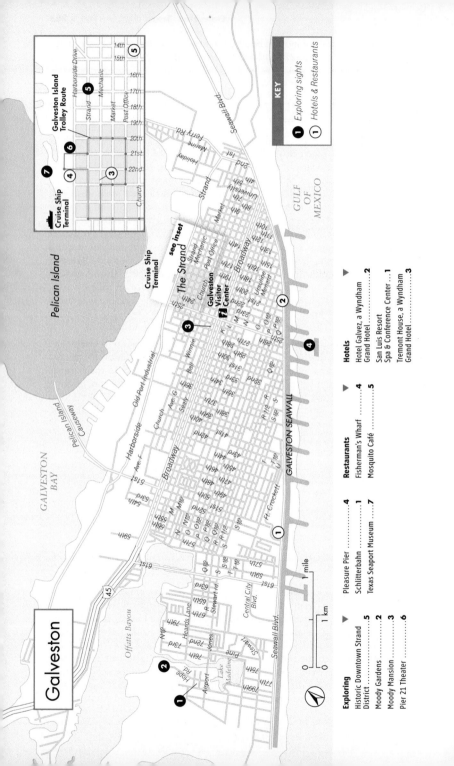

Galveston

GALVESTON BAY

Pelican Island

GULF OF MEXICO

GALVESTON SEAWALL

The Strand

see inset

Cruise Ship Terminal

Galveston Visitor Center

Galveston Island Trolley Route

Cruise Ship Terminal

0 — 1 km
0 — 1 mile

▶ **Exploring**

Historic Downtown Strand District	**5**
Moody Gardens	**2**
Moody Mansion	**3**
Pier 21 Theater	**6**
Pleasure Pier	**4**
Schlitterbahn	**1**
Texas Seaport Museum	**7**

▶ **Restaurants**

Fisherman's Wharf	**4**
Mosquito Café	**5**

▶ **Hotels**

Hotel Galvez, a Wyndham Grand Hotel	**2**
San Luis Resort Spa & Conference Center	**1**
Tremont House, a Wyndham Grand Hotel	**3**

KEY

1 *Exploring sights*

① *Hotels & Restaurants*

Port Contact Port of Galveston ✉ *Harborside Dr. and 22nd St.* ☎ *409/765–9321* ⊕ *www.portofgalveston.com.*

AIRPORT TRANSFERS

The closest airports are in Houston, 50 miles from Galveston. Houston has two major airports: Hobby Airport, 9 miles (15 km) southeast of downtown, and George Bush Intercontinental, 15 miles (24 km) northeast of the city. Traffic into Galveston can be delayed because of ongoing construction.

Unless you have arranged airport transfers through your cruise line, you'll have to make arrangements to navigate the miles between the

Houston airport at which you land and the cruise-ship terminal. Galveston Limousine Service provides scheduled transportation (return reservations required) between either airport and Galveston hotels or the cruise-ship terminal. Hobby is a shorter ride (1 hour; $45 one-way, $80 round-trip), but Intercontinental (2 hours; $55 one-way, $100 round-trip) is served by more airlines, including international carriers. Taking a taxi allows you to set your own schedule, but can cost twice as much (it's also important to note that there aren't always enough taxis to handle the demands of disembarking passengers, so you might have to wait after you leave your ship). Negotiate the price before you get in.

Contact Galveston Limousine Service ☎ *800/640–4826* ⊕ *www.galvestonlimousineservice.com.*

PARKING

Parking is coordinated by the Port Authority. After you drop off your checked luggage and passengers at the terminal, you receive a color-coded parking pass from the attendant, with directions to a parking lot for your cruise departure. The lots are approximately ½ mile (1 km) from the terminal. Check-in, parking, and boarding are generally allowed four hours prior to departure. A shuttle bus (carry-on luggage only) runs back and forth between the lots and the terminal every 7 to 12 minutes on cruise arrival and departure days (be sure to drop off your luggage *before* you park the car). The lot is closed other days. Port Authority security checks the well-lighted, fenced-in lots every two hours; there is also a limited amount of covered parking. Parking for a 5-day cruise is $50, 7-day is $70 ($80 covered). Cash, traveler's checks, and credit cards (Visa and MasterCard only) are accepted for payment.

EXPLORING GALVESTON

Historic Downtown Strand District. This shopping area is defined by the architecture of its 19th- and early-20th-century buildings, many of which survived the storm of 1900 and are on the National Register of Historic Places. When Galveston was still a powerful port city—before the Houston Ship Channel was dug, diverting most boat traffic inland—this stretch, formerly the site of stores, offices, and warehouses, was known as the Wall Street of the South. As you stroll up the Strand, you'll pass dozens of shops and cafés. ⊠ *Between Strand and Postoffice sts., and 25th and 19th sts.* ⊕ *www.thestrand.com.*

FAMILY **Moody Gardens.** Moody Gardens is a multifaceted entertainment and educational complex inside pastel-colored glass pyramids. Attractions include the 13-story Discovery Pyramid, showcasing marine life from four oceans in tanks and touch pools; Rainforest Pyramid, a 40,000-square-foot tropical habitat for exotic flora and fauna; Discovery Pyramid, a joint venture with NASA featuring more than 40 interactive exhibits; and two theaters, one of which has a space adventure ride. Outside, Palm Beach has white-sand beach, landscaped grounds, man-made lagoons, a kid-size waterslide and games, and beach chairs. ⊠ *1 Hope Blvd.* ☎ *800/582–4673* ⊕ *www.moodygardens.com* ⊠ *$9.95–$23.95 per venue, $49.95 day pass or $64.94 two-day pass* ☉ *Memorial Day–Labor Day, daily 10–9; Labor Day–Memorial Day, weekdays 10–6, weekends 10–8.*

Moody Mansion. Moody Mansion, the residence of generations of one of Texas's most powerful families, was completed in 1895. Tour its interiors of exotic woods and gilded trim filled with family heirlooms and personal effects. ⊠ *2618 Broadway* ☎ *409/762–7668* ⊕ *www. moodymansion.org* ⊠ *$10* ☉ *Daily 11–4; tours hrly.*

Pier 21 Theater. At this Harborside Drive theater, watch the Great Storm of 1900 come back to life in a multimedia presentation that includes video clips of archival drawings, still photos, and narrated accounts from survivors' diaries. Also playing is a film about the exploits of pirate Jean Lafitte, who used the island as a base. ⊠ *Pier 21, Harborside Dr. and 21st St.* ☎ *409/763–8808* ⊕ *www.galveston.com/pier21theatre* ⊠ *Great Storm $6, Pirate Island $6* ☉ *Daily 11–6.*

Pleasure Pier. Owned by the ubiquitous Landry's Inc., this amusement park and entertainment district built on a historic pier over the Gulf of Mexico has a little something for everyone. Like thrills? Look danger in the face on the Iron Shark roller coaster, which reaches speeds of 52 miles an hour and includes a 100-foot vertical lift. Into games? Try your luck along the midway. Feeling hungry? Texas's first Bubba Gump Shrimp Co. is among your options. The attractions here can be expensive and parking can be difficult, but overall it offers an enjoyable time for visitors to Galveston. Hours vary quite a bit seasonally, but the park is open year-round with restricted hours and days from fall through spring. ⊠ *2501 Seawall Blvd.* ☎ *855/789–7437* ⊕ *www. pleasurepier.com* ⊠ *$26.99 all-day pass; individual rides begin at $4 each* ☉ *June–Labor Day, weekdays 10–10, weekends 10–11 or midnight; off-season hrs vary, so call or check the website.*

Schlitterbahn. The entire family will have a fun time at this water park, located on the bay side of the island. Schlitterbahn features speed slides, lazy river rides, uphill water coasters, a wave pool (with surfing), and water playgrounds for the little ones. There's even a heated indoor water park for chilly winter months. During summer, less expensive afternoon-only rates are in effect, and ticket prices drop in the off-season. Actually closing times do vary by the season, so outside of the busiest months of June through August, verify closing times on the park's website, or call for exact hours. ⊠ *2026 Lockheed St.* ☎ *409/770–9283* ⊕ *www.schlitterbahn.com* ⊠ *$43.99* ⊙ *Mid-May–late Aug., daily 10–8; Mar.–mid-May and Oct.–Dec., weekends 10–5.*

Texas Seaport Museum. Aboard the restored 1877 tall ship *Elissa*, detailed interpretive signs provide information about the shipping trade in the 1800s, including the routes and cargoes this ship carried into Galveston. Inside the museum building is a replica of the historic wharf and a one-of-a-kind computer database containing the names of more than 133,000 immigrants who entered the United States through Galveston after 1837 ⊠ *Pier 21, Number 8* ☎ *409/763–1877* ⊕ *www. galvestonhistory.org/Texas_Seaport_Museum.asp* ⊠ *$8* ⊙ *Weather permitting 10–5 daily.*

6

BEACHES

Galveston Island State Park. On the western, unpopulated end of the island, this state park is a 2,000-acre natural beach habitat ideal for birding, walking, and renewing your spirit. It's open daily from 8 am to 10 pm. ⊠ *14901 FM 3005, 10 miles (16 km) southwest on Seawall Blvd.* ☎ *409/737–1222* ⊕ *www.galvestonislandstatepark.org* ⊠ *$5.*

Seawall. The seawall on the Gulfside waterfront attracts runners, cyclists, and rollerbladers. Just below it is a long, free beach near many big hotels and resorts. ⊠ *Seawall Blvd., from 61st St. to 25th St.*

Stewart Beach Park. This park has a bathhouse, amusement park, bumper boats, miniature-golf course, and a water coaster in addition to saltwater and sand. It's open weekdays 9 to 5, weekends 8 to 6 from March through May; weekdays 8 to 6 and weekends 8 to 7 from June through September; and weekends 9 to 5 during the first two weekends of October. ⊠ *6th St. and Seawall Blvd.* ☎ *409/765–5023* ⊠ *$5 per vehicle.*

SHOPPING

The Emporium at Eibands. More than 50 antiques dealers are represented at The Emporium at Eibands, an upscale showroom filled with custom upholstery, bedding and draperies, antique furniture, and interesting architectural finds. ⊠ *2201 Postoffice St.* ☎ *409/750–9536.*

Head to Footsies. Head to Footsies offers footwear for men and women along with trendy women's accessories and fashions from sportswear to eveningwear. ⊠ *2211 Strand St.* ☎ *409/762–2727.*

Old Strand Emporium. Old Strand Emporium is a charming deli and grocery reminiscent of an old-fashioned ice-cream parlor and sandwich shop, with candy bins, packaged nuts, and more. ⊠ *2112 Strand St.* ☎ *409/515–0715.*

Strand. The Strand is the best place to shop in Galveston. Old storefronts are filled with gift shops, antiques stores, and one-of-a-kind boutiques. ⊠ *Bounded by Strand and Postoffice sts. (east–west), and 25th and 19th sts. (north–south)* ⊕ *www.thestrand.com.*

NIGHTLIFE

For a relaxing evening, choose any of the harborside restaurant-bars on piers 21 and 22 to sip a glass of wine or a frozen Hurricane as you watch the boats go by.

The Grand 1894 Opera House. This venue stages musicals and hosts concerts year-round. It's worth visiting for the ornate architecture alone. Sarah Bernhardt and Anna Pavlova both performed on this storied stage. ⊠ *2020 Postoffice St.* ☎ *409/765–1894, 800/821–1894* ⊕ *www. thegrand.com.*

WHERE TO EAT

$$$ ✕ **Fisherman's Wharf.** Even though Landry's has taken over this harbor-
SEAFOOD   side institution, locals keep coming here for the reliably fresh seafood and reasonable prices. Dine indoors or watch the boat traffic (and waiting cruise ships) from the patio. Start with a cold combo, like boiled shrimp and grilled rare tuna. For entrées, the fried fish, shrimp, and oysters are hard to beat. $ *Average main: $24* ⊠ *Pier 22, 2200 Harborside Dr.* ☎ *409/765–5708* ⊕ *www.fishermanswharfgalveston.com.*

$ ✕ **Mosquito Café.** This popular eatery in Galveston's historic East End
AMERICAN   serves fresh, contemporary food—including some vegetarian dishes—in a hip, high-ceilinged dining room and on an outdoor patio. Wake up to a fluffy egg frittata or a homemade scone topped with whipped cream, or try a large gourmet salad for lunch. The grilled snapper with Parmesan grits is a hit in the evening. $ *Average main: $10* ⊠ *628 14th St.* ☎ *409/763–1010* ⊕ *www.mosquitocafe.com* ☯ *Closed Mon. No dinner Sun.*

WHERE TO STAY

For expanded reviews, facilities, and current deals, visit Fodors.com.

$$$$ ⌂ **Hotel Galvez, a Wyndham Grand Hotel.** This renovated six-story Span-
HOTEL   ish colonial hotel, built in 1911, was once called "Queen of the Gulf." **Pros:** directly on beach; incredible pool area; beautiful grounds; recently renovated rooms. **Cons:** rooms can be small (especially the bathrooms) $ *Rooms from: $269* ⊠ *2024 Seawall Blvd.* ☎ *409/765–7721* ⊕ *www. wyndham.com* ⇆ *231 rooms* ❢⊘❢ *No meals.*

$$$$ ⌂ **San Luis Resort, Spa & Conference Center.** A long marble staircase along-
RESORT   side a slender fountain with sculpted dolphins welcomes you to the beachfront elegance of this resort. **Pros:** great Gulf views; nice pool area. **Cons:** public parking (nonvalet) is not convenient. $ *Rooms from: $329* ⊠ *5222 Seawall Blvd.* ☎ *409/744–1500, 800/445–0090* ⊕ *www. sanluisresort.com* ⇆ *244 rooms* ❢⊘❢ *No meals.*

$$ HOTEL$$ ⚟ **Tremont House, a Wyndham Grand Hotel.** A four-story atrium lobby, with ironwork balconies and full-size palm trees, showcases an 1872 hand-carved rosewood bar in what was once a busy dry-goods warehouse. **Pros:** beautiful, historic environment; great location; free Wi-Fi. **Cons:** not a fun scene for young single travelers. $⑤ Rooms from: $139 ✉ 2300 Ship's Mechanic Row ☎ 409/763–0300 ⊕ www.wyndham.com ⇆ 119 rooms ❚◎❙ No meals._

BOARDING PASSES

Modern ID cards and scanning equipment record passenger comings and goings on the majority of cruise ships these days. With a swipe through a machine—it looks much like a credit-card swipe at the supermarket—security personnel know who is on board the vessel at all times. On almost all ships passengers' pictures are recorded digitally at check-in.

HOUSTON, TEXAS

Jessica Dupuy

Unbridled energy has always been Houston's trademark. Once a swamp near the junction of the Buffalo and White Oak bayous, Houston is now the nation's fourth-largest city and the energy capital of the United States. Excellent museums, galleries, and performance halls affirm the city's commitment to the arts, and its many ethnic restaurants add to the cosmopolitan flavor. Just a few hours' sailing time from the Gulf of Mexico, the Port of Houston—a vibrant component to the regional economy—is comprised of the Port Authority and the 150-plus private industrial companies along the Houston Ship Channel. At this writing, both Norwegian Cruise Line and Princess will be sailing out of Houston's single cruise terminal. This cruise terminal is convenient for Houstonians and residents of the smaller cities in the bay area.

ESSENTIALS

HOURS

Some museums are closed on Monday. Stores in malls tend to be open later, often until 9 pm.

VISITOR INFORMATION

Contact **Greater Houston Convention and Visitors Bureau** ☎ 713/437–5200 ⊕ www.visithoustontexas.org.

THE PORT OF HOUSTON

The Port of Houston is a 25-mile-long complex of diversified public and private industrial terminal facilities designed to handle general cargo. The facilities of this massive port cover several municipal jurisdictions, including the cities of Houston, Pasadena, Galena Park, LaPorte, Baytown, Deer Park, and Morgan's Point. Adjacent to the Port's Bayport Container Terminal is the Bayport Cruise Terminal, a new construction that is set to open at the end of 2013 with both Princess Cruises and Norwegian Cruise Line beginning cruises in 2014. The new terminal features modern amenities in a state-of-the-art facility that combines streamlined passenger convenience and innovative security for international travel. Passenger access from parking and drop-off areas is directly in front of the terminal. Covered walkways connect the building to bus and private passenger drop-offs and taxi stands. The terminal is a little more than 30 miles from downtown Houston with proximity to restaurants and hotels as well as access to both regional airports. To reach the port by car from downtown Houston, take I–45 south to 610 N, then continue to 225 E. Merge onto 146 S and exit onto Port Road. Follow Port Road to the end, and the cruise terminal will be on the left.

> **HOUSTON BEST BETS**
>
> ■ **Kemah Boardwalk**. This bayside entertainment and dining center is a good family destination.
>
> ■ **Menil Collection**. Art lovers will appreciate this eclectic collection—and it's all free.
>
> ■ **NASA Space Center Houston**. Though not as extensive in its visitor facilities (or as expensive) as the Kennedy Space Center in Florida, this is still worth a trip.

Contact **Port of Houston** ⊠ *Bayport Cruise Terminal, 4700 Cruise Rd., Pasadena* ⊕ *www.portofhouston.com.*

AIRPORT TRANSFERS

There are two major airports in Houston. Bush Intercontinental Airport, northeast of downtown Houston, is 45 miles (72 km) and approximately 50 minutes from the Port of Houston. William P. Hobby Airport, southeast of downtown, is closer, at 20 miles (32 km) and approximately 30 minutes. You may purchase a transfer option from the cruise line when you book your cruise, or you can arrange for your own transfers. A private car transfer from Airport Taxi & Town Car will cost $70 to $75 from Houston Hobby and $90 to $95 from Bush Intercontinental. Super Shuttle offers both shared van service (much cheaper than a private transfer) or private van service (which a good option if you have a large group).

Contacts **Airport Taxi & Town Car** ☎ *281/630–1137* ⊕ *www.24hrairporttaxi. com.* **Super Shuttle** ☎ *800/258–3826* ⊕ *www.supershuttle.com.*

PARKING

Parking is available at the terminal for weekly rates of $80 per week for 7-day cruises. Twenty-four hour security is provided, and the facility is secured for the duration of the cruise with $5 discount for prepaid parking. Passenger access from parking and drop-off areas is immediately adjacent to the front of the terminal.

EXPLORING HOUSTON

Houston can be divided neatly into three major areas. One is its very modern downtown (including the theater district), which spurred one architecture critic to declare the city "America's future." Another is the area a couple of miles south of downtown, the museum district, where some of the Southwest's leading museums are found along with Rice University and the internationally renowned Texas Medical Center. There is the thriving shopping and business center west of downtown,

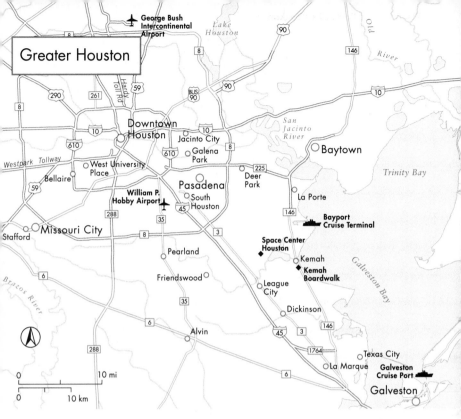

known as both the Galleria and Uptown. Finally, there are neighborhoods south of downtown Houston that are convenient to the cruise port and ripe for exploring.

DOWNTOWN

Texas Avenue, downtown's main street, is 100 feet wide, precisely the width needed to accommodate 14 Texas longhorns tip to tip in the days when cattle were driven to market along this route.

JPMorgan Chase Tower. Get a quick overview of Houston by taking in the entire urban panorama from the 60th-floor observation deck of the Texas's tallest building (weekdays 8–5). Architect I. M. Pei designed this 75-story structure, built in 1981. ☒ *600 Travis St., Downtown* ☎ *713/223–0441* ⊕ *www.chasetower.com* ☒ *Free.*

Minute Maid Park. The Houston Astros play in Minute Maid Park, a modern-but-retro baseball stadium, which has a retractable roof and a monster a/c system to defy Houston's frequently changing weather. Upper-deck seats on the first base side have great views of the downtown skyline—even when the roof is closed, due to a very cool retractable glass wall. The stadium incorporates Houston's 1911 Union Station (designed by Warren and Wetmore of New York's Grand Central Station fame), which houses the ball club offices, retail stores, and eateries. Heavy hitters can rent out Union Station's rooftop, which has views into the stadium from above. There are no tours on afternoon gamedays during the season (roughly April through September). ✉ *501 Crawford St., at Prairie St., Downtown* ☎ *713/259–8000* ⊕ *www.astros. mlb.com* 📷 *Tours $11* ⊘ *Apr.– Sept., weekdays 10, noon, and 2, Sat. 10 and noon; Oct.–Mar., Mon.–Sat. 10 and noon.*

> **CAUTION**
>
> An endlessly ringing telephone is a hint that you are not home. Before leaving the house, either turn off the telephone ringers or set the answering machine to pick up after two rings.

Sam Houston Park. Houston's first and oldest municipal park, contains nine historic structures and a museum gallery. The Kellum-Noble House is Houston's oldest standing brick structure still on its original foundation. If you're visiting around the holidays, try to catch the annual Candlelight Tour in the Park, when costumed actors give tours of the park's homes. ✉ *1100 Bagby St., Downtown* ☎ *713/655–1912* ⊕ *www. heritagesociety.org* 📷 *Park free; $6 to tour historic structures.*

Tranquility Park. This cool oasis of fountains and walkways was built to commemorate the first landing on the moon by the Apollo 11 mission. The terrain of mounds and depressions throughout the two-block park evokes the cratered surface of the moon, and the fountain's stainless-steel cylinders are designed to resemble rocket boosters. ✉ *Bordered by Walker, Smith, Rusk, and Bagby sts., Downtown.*

THE MUSEUM DISTRICT

Most museums are clustered within an area bordering the verdant campus of Rice University, one of Texas's finest educational institutions, and Hermann Park, the city's playground. Walking from one institution to the other is possible, but the expanse can be taxing; it's best to segment your visit.

Menil Collection. This is one of the city's premier cultural treasures. Italian architect Renzo Piano designed the spacious building, with its airy galleries. John and Dominique de Menil collected the eclectic art, which ranges from tribal African sculptures to Andy Warhol's paintings of Campbell's soup cans. A separate gallery across the street houses the paintings of American artist Cy Twombly; Richmond Hall, a few blocks away, houses one of only two permanent Dan Flavin installations in America. ✉ *1515 Sul Ross St., Museum District* ☎ *713/525–9400* ⊕ *www.menil.org* 📷 *Free* ⊘ *Wed.–Sun. 11–7.*

Museum of Fine Arts, Houston. Remarkable for the completeness of its enormous collection, the Museum of Fine Arts, Houston is housed in a complicated series of wings and galleries, many designed by Ludwig Mies van der Rohe. When the Audrey Jones Beck Building, the work of famed Spanish architect Rafael Maneo, opened in 2000 it doubled the museum's size. Renaissance and 18th-century art is particularly well represented, and there's a fine selection of impressionist and post-impressionist works. You'll also find an ample survey of Asian, Pre-Columbian, Oceanic, and African art, and an impressive collection of modernist paintings, prints, and sculpture. Across the street, the museum's **Lillie and Hugh Roy Cullen Sculpture Garden** displays 19th- and

20th-century sculptures by Rodin, Matisse, Giacometti, and Stella in an outdoor space designed by Isamu Noguchi. ✉ *1001 Bissonnet St., north of Rice University, between Montrose Blvd. and Main St., Museum District* ☎ *713/639–7300* ⊕ *www.mfah.org* ✎ *Museum $13 (free Thurs.); sculpture garden free* ☉ *Tues. and Wed. 10–5, Thurs. 10–9, Fri. and Sat. 10–7, Sun. 12:15–7.*

OTHER NEIGHBORHOODS

Space Center Houston. Remember Apollo 13's "Houston, we have a problem?" Space Center Houston is the "Houston" that Jim Lovell and his crew were talking to—and the home of the Mission Control that NASA astronauts communicate with today when they're in space. Visitors to the center can learn about the history and science of space exploration at the Living in Space exhibit, which simulates what life is like aboard the space station—and how even "simple" tasks like showering and eating get complicated in zero-gravity. In the Kids Space Place, children can ride on a lunar rover and try out tasks in an Apollo command module. Want to know exactly how it feels to be launched into space? Then check out the Blast Off Theater, where you'll experience the rocket boosters and billowing exhaust of liftoff. You'll then dock at the International Space Station to get started on your mission. The adjacent Johnson Space Center tour includes a visit to (the real) Mission Control and laboratories that simulate weightlessness and other space-related concepts. You can also see a real Saturn V, the launch vehicle for the Apollo moon missions, in Rocket Park. Be sure to allow several hours for your visit. ✉ *1601 NASA Parkway, off I–45, 25 miles south of downtown, South Houston* ☎ *281/244–2100* ⊕ *www.spacecenter.org* ✎ *$22.95 at door, $17.95 prepaid online* ☉ *Weekdays 10–5, weekends 10–6.*

Kemah Boardwalk. OK, we'll cut to the chase—the Kemah Boardwalk is a commercial, touristy development run by Landry's Restaurants (the folks who brought you Joe's Crab Shack and Saltgrass Steakhouse)—but most people love it. Just off I–45 between Houston and Galveston, this cluster of moderately priced restaurants, amusement-park rides, game arcades, and inns is set on a bustling ship channel. It's a family-oriented destination where you can catch a Gulf breeze, eat seafood, shop, or just watch the ships sail by. Kids can get up close to some of nature's most misunderstood creatures at Stingray Reef—they can even feed them. A 96-foot-tall wooden coaster called the Boardwalk Bullet was recently added to the mix. It reaches speeds of 51 mph—5 feet from the water's edge. Don't eat first! ✉ *215 Kipp Ave., off 2nd St., Keman* ☎ *877/285–3624* ⊕ *www.kemahboardwalk.com* ✎ *Rides $3.50–$17; all-day pass $21.99* ☉ *Rides Sun.–Thurs. 10:30–10; Fri. and Sat. 10:30 am–midnight.*

SHOPPING

Houston's premier shopping area is the Galleria/Uptown area, which is barely outside the loop, literally on the other side of 610 at Westheimer Road, 15 minutes from downtown. The business, office towers, and shopping complexes here have made the neighborhood one of the most important business districts in the city. Many of Houston's best restaurants are here, and the River Oaks neighborhood, with its multimillion-dollar mansions and garden parkways, is nearby.

Galleria. Not to be confused with the neighborhood, this is the actual Galleria, the region's anchor shopping complex. It's famous for high-quality stores like Neiman Marcus, Cartier, Yves Saint Laurent, Chanel, and Saks Fifth Avenue. But don't be scared off by all these big-ticket names—also here are establishments like Urban Outfitters, Macy's, Banana Republic, and the man-friendly Fox Sports Grill. Kids (and adults) will enjoy the year-round indoor ice rink; during the holidays you can skate around the giant Christmas tree. ⊠ *Westheimer Rd. at Post Oak Blvd.* ☎ *713/966–3500* ⊕ *www.galleriahouston.com.*

Highland Village. Chic national retailers like Anthropologie, Williams-Sonoma, and Crate & Barrel grace Highland Village, an elegant 50-year-old shopping plaza where you also find scene-y restaurants Smith & Wollensky and RA Sushi. ⊠ *4055 Westheimer Rd.* ☎ *713/850–3100* ⊕ *www.shophighlandvillage.com.*

Uptown Park. A charming European-style outdoor shopping center, Uptown Park gladly accepts plastic—and you'll need plenty of it—at its cafés, upscale restaurants, designer-clothing boutiques, fine jewelry shops and day spas. ⊠ *Uptown Park Blvd. at Post Oak Blvd.* ☎ *713/850–1400* ⊕ *www.uptownparkhouston.com.*

NIGHTLIFE

Houston's nightlife scene seems to be constantly on the move. Right now most of the action is centered in Midtown—between the Pierce Elevated and West Alabama on the north and south, respectively, and stretching from San Jacinto Street on the East to Brazos on the West. Healthy outposts can also be found downtown, in Montrose, and along Washington Avenue (stretching from downtown to Memorial Park). There are popular places in the Uptown/Galleria area, too, but you'll find more international tourists and an older crowd than hard-partying twenty- and thirtysomethings.

Anvil Bar & Refuge. Perhaps one of the most touted craft cocktail bars in Texas, Anvil is the inspiration behind the craft cocktail scene in the entire state. It was opened under the direction of young bartender Bobby Heugel, whose vision for Houston's evolving bar and restaurant scene extended far beyond cocktails. On any given evening, this Montrose bar is packed late into the night with a steady flow of both new and loyal customers clamoring for the latest in the bar's inventive mixed drinks. ⊠ *1424 Westheimer Rd., Montrose* ☎ *713/523–1622* ⊕ *www.anvilhouston.com.*

Continental Club. This is a sister of the legendary Austin original (which has been open since the 1950s). This Houston branch brings more loud, live music to an even bigger dance floor. ⊠ *3700 Main St., Midtown* ☎ *713/529–9899* ⊕ *www.continentalclub.com/Houston.html.*

OKRA Charity Saloon. An acronym for an "Organized Kollaboration on Restaurant Affairs," OKRA opened in 2013 as bar concept collaboration from many of Houston's community-focused bar and restaurant owners. All of the bar's proceeds are donated to different Houston-based organizations and social causes each month. Patrons are able to select which charity is chosen as a beneficiary by voting from among four nominations each month. For each drink purchased, guests will receive one vote that they may cast before leaving the bar for the evening. OKRA is downtown, which has grown in popularity in recent years for its thriving restaurant and bar scene. It's open daily 4 pm–2 am. ⊠ *924 Congress St., Downtown* ☎ *713/237–8828* ⊕ *www. friedokra.org.*

WHERE TO EAT

In the U.S.'s fourth-largest city, the average resident eats out four times per week. There are thousands of choices—from Pan-Asian to Italian, barbecue to nouvelle Southwestern, and burgers to bistros to Bolivian and beyond. You can even find fusion cuisines like Chinese and hamburgers. And, of course, Tex-Mex rules. It can all be a bit overwhelming, but it's a nice problem to have: dining in Houston spoils you completely.

About 20 miles (32 km) south of downtown Houston you can experience the Kemah Boardwalk, a waterfront dining park and shopping center that is near Clear Lake, just south of the Port of Houston cruise terminal.

$$

BARBECUE

✕ **Goode Company Texas Bar-B-Q.** Down-home Texas barbecue is prepared ranch-style—mesquite-smoked and served with tasty red sauce. Patrons young and old line up on the sidewalk to eat at picnic tables on the covered patio. A standard order is the chopped-beef brisket sandwich on jalapeño-cheese bread. Don't skip the celebrated pecan pie for dessert. Goode Company Hamburgers and Taqueria across the street serves—no surprise here—hamburgers and tacos, as well as great weekend breakfasts. And for some honky-tonk atmosphere, shuffleboard, dominoes, pool, and lots of cold beer, check out Goode's Armadillo Palace next door. You can't miss the place: it's the building with the giant stainless-steel armadillo standing guard out front. ⑤ *Average main: $13* ⊠ *5109 Kirby Dr., West University* ☎ *713/522–2530* ⊕ *www. goodecompany.com.*

$$

JAPANESE

✕ **Uchi.** Sister restaurant to the Austin original, Uchi extends its mastery of Japanese-inspired sushi and cuisine through visionary chef and owner Tyson Cole. A James Beard Award–winner, Cole uses a blend of global ingredients with traditional Japanese flavors to deliver innovative dishes. Though the daily menu changes regularly, permanent menu items, including "macho cure" (smoked yellowtail with Asian pear, Marcona almond, and yucca root crisp), "uchiviche" (salmon and striped bass sashimi with bell pepper, grape tomato, and cilantro), and the restaurant's famous "shag roll" (tempura-fried salmon, avocado, and sundried tomato roll), are among the top dishes. ⑤ *Average main: $17* ⊠ *904 Westheimer Rd., Montrose* ☎ *713/522–4808* ⊕ *www. uchirestaurants.com/houston* ⬥ *Reservations essential* ⊗ *Closed Mon.*

6

$$$$ ✕ **Underbelly.** A recent addition to the Montrose scene, Underbelly is
ECLECTIC   chef Chris Shepherd's vision of telling the rich and layered story of
Houston and its diverse culture through the medium of food. Using the
best of the area's local farm produce as well as line-caught Gulf Coast
seafood and locally sourced meats and poultry, Underbelly's menu varies daily but includes everything from Wagyu pot roast with market vegetables and bacon marmalade to crispy whole fish with masala-scented
vegetables, or Korean braised goat and dumplings. All meat is butchered
and processed on-site. $ *Average main: $35* ✉ *1100 Westheimer Rd.,
Montrose* ☎ *713/528–9800* ⊕ *www.underbellyhouston.com* 🍴 *Reservations essential* ⊙ *Closed Sun.*

WHERE TO STAY

Sprawling Houston has a seemingly endless variety of respectable hotels
that are convenient to the Port of Houston cruise terminal. However,
the revitalized downtown offers both a central location and quick access
to I–45 S and the port. Downtown Houston offers world-class hotels,
a vibrant nightlife, and varied, if trendy, restaurants. Moderate hotels
are even closer to the Port of Houston in LaPorte, which is a mostly
industrial area, so do not expect the same urban scene. Although rack
rates for many Houston hotels seem high, they drop dramatically on
weekends or if you make your reservation online or in advance.

$ 🏨 **Best Western NASA–Space Center.** Near NASA and the Johnson Space
HOTEL   Center, the Kemah Boardwalk, Baybrook Mall, and Clear Lake Area
marinas, this basic, reliable property is a good value in the Clear
Lake area. **Pros:** proximity to water activities; low price; proximity to
cruise port. **Cons:** far from downtown Houston; cookie-cutter design
and decor. $ *Rooms from: $59* ✉ *889 W. Bay Area Blvd., Webster*
☎ *281/338–6000* ⊕ *www.bestwestern.com* 🛏 *80 rooms* ⊙|*Breakfast.*

$$ 🏨 **Hilton Houston NASA Clear Lake.** On the shores of Clear Lake, Hilton
HOTEL   Houston NASA Clear Lake is a suburban resort hotel with a number of
water sports—including jet-skiing and waterskiing—and easy access to
NASA/Johnson Space Center and Space Center Houston, which are just
across the street. **Pros:** right on the water; close to NASA, Galveston,
and Kemah; close to cruise port. **Cons:** far from Houston's cultural,
sports, fine dining, and shopping attractions. $ *Rooms from: $135*
✉ *3000 NASA Pkwy., Nassau Bay* ☎ *281/333–9300* ⊕ *www.hilton.
com* 🛏 *243 rooms* ⊙|*Breakfast.*

JACKSONVILLE, FLORIDA

Sharon
Hoffmann

One of Florida's oldest cities and at 758 square miles (1,926 square
km) the largest city in the continental United States in terms of land
area, Jacksonville is underrated, and makes a worthwhile vacation spot
for an extra day or two before or after your cruise. It offers appeal-
ing downtown riverside areas, handsome residential neighborhoods,
the region's only skyscrapers, a thriving arts scene, and, for football
fans, the NFL Jaguars and the NCAA Gator Bowl. Remnants of the
Old South flavor the city, especially in the Riverside/Avondale historic

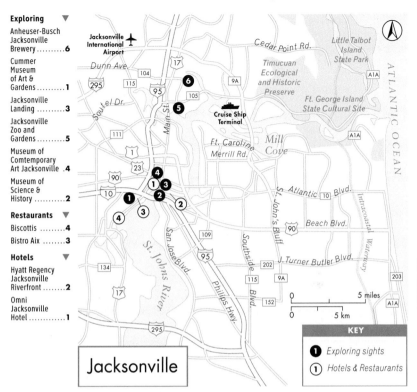

district, where moss-draped oak trees frame prairie-style bungalows and Tudor Revival mansions, and palm trees, Spanish bayonet, and azaleas populate Jacksonville's landscape. Northeast of the city, Amelia Island and Fernandina Beach offer some of the nicest coastline in Florida.

ESSENTIALS
HOURS
Many museums close on Monday.

VISITOR INFORMATION
Contact **Visit Jacksonville** ✉ 208 N. Laura St., Ste. 102, Downtown ☎ 904/798–9111, 800/733–2668 ⊕ www.visitjacksonville.com.

THE CRUISE PORT

Limited in the sizes of ships it can berth, JAXPORT currently serves as home port to the *Carnival Fascination,* which departs weekly on four- and five-night cruises to Key West and the Bahamas during the fall and winter cruising seasons, with occasional week-long sailings to Grand Turk, Half Moon Cay, and Nassau. The facility is fairly sparse, consisting basically of some vending machines and restrooms, but the embarkation staff receives high marks. The terminal itself is a temporary structure; a permanent cruise terminal has been under consideration for some time, but its fate is uncertain at this writing.

JAXPORT is about 15 minutes from Jacksonville International Airport. Take I–95 South to S.R. 9-A East. Follow 9-A to Heckscher Drive (S.R. 105) west until you reach August Drive. Head south on August Drive, and follow the signs to the cruise terminal.

Port Contact Jacksonville Port Authority ⊠ *9810 August Dr.* ☎ *904/357–3006* ⊕ *www.jaxport.com.*

AIRPORT TRANSFERS

The transfer from Jacksonville airport takes about 15 minutes and costs $30 for up to three passengers by taxi, not including tip.

Contact Yellow Cab–Jacksonville ☎ *904/999–9999.*

PARKING

There is a fenced and guarded parking lot next to the cruise terminal, within walking distance. Parking costs $15 per day for regular vehicles, $25 for RVs. You must pay in advance by cash or major credit card.

> ## JACKSONVILLE BEST BETS
>
> ■ **Budweiser Brewery Tour.** Behind the scenes on the making of one of the country's most popular beers.
>
> ■ **Jacksonville Zoo.** One of the best midsize zoos you'll visit.
>
> ■ **Museum of Contemporary Art Jacksonville.** Though small, this excellent museum is an unexpected treat in northeast Florida.

EXPLORING JACKSONVILLE

Because Jacksonville was settled along both sides of the twisting St. Johns River, a number of attractions are on or near a riverbank. Both sides of the river, which is spanned by myriad bridges, have downtown areas and waterfront complexes of shops, restaurants, parks, and museums; some attractions can be reached by water taxi or the Skyway Express monorail system—scenic alternatives to driving back and forth across the bridges—but a car is generally necessary.

Anheuser-Busch Jacksonville Brewery Tour. Guided tours give a behind-the-scenes look at how barley, malt, rice, hops, and water form the King of Beers. Or you can hightail it through the self-guided tour and head straight to the free beer tastings—if you're 21 years or older, that is. ⊠ *111 Busch Dr.* ☎ *904/696–8373* ⊕ *www.budweisertours.com* ✆ *Free* ⊗ *Mon.–Sat. 10–4; guided tours, call for availability.*

Cummer Museum of Art & Gardens. The Wark Collection of early-18th-century Meissen porcelain is just one reason to visit this former riverfront estate, which includes 13 permanent galleries with more than 5,500 items spanning more than 8,000 years, and 3 acres of riverfront gardens reflecting northeast Florida's blooming seasons and indigenous varieties. Art Connections allows kids to experience art through hands-on, interactive exhibits. The Thomas H. Jacobsen Gallery of American Art focuses on works by American artists, including Max Weber, N.C. Wyeth, and Paul Manship. ⊠ *829 Riverside Ave., Riverside*

☎ *904/356–6857* ⊕ *www.cummer.org* ⊠ *$10, free Tues. 4–9* ⊙ *Tues. 10–9, Wed.–Fri. 10–4, Sat. 10–5, Sun. noon–5.*

Jacksonville Landing. During the week, this riverfront market caters to locals and tourists alike, with specialty shops, full-service restaurants—including a sushi bar, Italian bistro, and a steakhouse—and an internationally flavored food court. The Landing hosts more than 250 weekend events each year, ranging from the good clean fun of the Lighted Boat Parade and Christmas Tree Lighting to the just plain obnoxious Florida/Georgia game after-party, as well as live music (usually of the local cover-band variety) in the courtyard. ⊠ *2 W. Independent Dr., Downtown* ☎ *904/353–1188* ⊕ *www.jacksonvillelanding. com* ⊠ *Free* ⊙ *Mon.–Thurs. 10–8, Fri.–Sat. 10–9, Sun. noon–5:30; restaurant hrs vary.*

FAMILY
Fodor'sChoice
★
Jacksonville Zoo and Gardens. What's new at the zoo? Plenty. Not only has it seen the births of a rare Amur leopard and a greater kudu calf, but it now offers Tuxedo Coast, a controlled environment for a group of Magellanic penguins. Among the other highlights are rare waterfowl and the African Reptile Building, which showcases some of the world's most venomous snakes. Wild Florida is a 2½-acre area with black bears, bald eagles, white-tailed deer, and other animals native to Florida. The African Loop has elephants, white rhinos, and two highly endangered leopards, among other species of African birds and mammals. The Range of the Jaguar, winner of the Association of Zoos and Aquarium's Exhibit of the Year, includes 4 acres of exotic big cats as well as 20 other species of animals. Play Park contains a Splash Ground, forest play area, two mazes, and discovery building; Stingray Bay has a 17,000-gallon pool where visitors can pet and feed the mysterious creatures; and Butterfly Hollow is a flower-filled "fairy world" open seasonally. Parking is free. ⊠ *370 Zoo Pkwy., off Heckscher Dr. E* ☎ *904/757–4463* ⊕ *www.jaxzoo.org* ⊠ *$14.95* ⊙ *Daily 9–5.*

Fodor'sChoice
★
Museum of Contemporary Art Jacksonville. In this loftlike downtown building, the former headquarters of the Western Union Telegraph Company, a permanent collection of 20th-century art shares space with traveling exhibitions. The museum encompasses five galleries and ArtExplorium, a highly interactive educational exhibit for kids, as well as a funky gift shop and Café Nola, open for lunch on weekdays and for dinner on Thursday. MOCA Jacksonville also hosts film series and workshops throughout the year, and packs a big art-wallop into a relatively small 14,000 square feet. Sunday is free for families; a once-a-month Art Walk is free to all. ⊠ *Hemming Plaza, 333 N. Laura St.* ☎ *904/366–6911* ⊕ *www.mocajacksonville.org* ⊠ *$8* ⊙ *Tues., Wed., Fri., and Sat. 11–5, Thurs. 11–9, Sun. noon–5; Art Walk 1st Wed. of month 5–9.*

FAMILY
Museum of Science & History. Also known locally as MOSH, this museum is home to the Bryan-Gooding Planetarium. As a next-generation planetarium, it can project 3-D laser shows that accompany the ever-popular weekend Cosmic Concerts. For those taking in the planetarium shows, the resolution is significantly sharper than that of the biggest 1080p HDTV currently on the market. Whether you're a kid taking in the awe of the new *Dinosaurs at Dusk,* or an adult falling into darkness during

Black Holes: The Other Side of Infinity, the experience is awesome. MOSH also has a wide variety of interactive exhibits and programs that include JEA Science Theater, where you can participate in live science experiments; JEA Power-Play: Understanding our Energy Choices, where you can energize the future city of MOSHtopia as you learn about alternative energy resources and the science of energy; the Florida Naturalist's Center, where you can interact with northeast Florida wildlife; and the Currents of Time, where you'll navigate 12,000 years of Northeast Florida history, from the region's earliest Native American settlers to modern day events. Nationally acclaimed traveling exhibits are featured along with signature exhibits on regional history. ⊠ *1025 Museum Circle* ☎ *904/396–6674* ⊕ *www.themosh.org* ✉ *Museum $10, museum and planetarium $15, Cosmic Concerts $5; Fri. $5 all admissions* ☉ *Mon.– Thurs. 10–5, Fri. 10–8, Sat. 10–6, Sun. 12–5.*

> **BRING GEORGE**
>
> Whenever you leave for a cruise, bring a supply of one-dollar bills. They will come in handy for tipping both airport and port personnel.

SHOPPING

Five Points. This small but funky shopping district less than a mile southwest of downtown has new and vintage-clothing boutiques, shoe stores, and antiques shops. It also has a handful of eateries and bars, not to mention some of the city's most colorful characters. ⊠ *Intersection of Park, Margaret, and Lomax sts., Riverside* ⊕ *www.5pointsjax.com.*

San Marco Square. Dozens of interesting apparel, home, and jewelry stores and restaurants are in 1920s Mediterranean revival–style buildings. ⊠ *San Marco and Atlantic blvds., San Marco* ⊕ *www.mysanmarco. com.*

The Shoppes of Avondale. The highlights here include upscale clothing and accessories boutiques, art galleries, home-furnishings shops, a chocolatier, and trendy restaurants. ⊠ *St. Johns Ave., between Talbot Ave. and Dancy St., Avondale* ⊕ *www.shoppesofavondale.com.*

WHERE TO EAT

JAXPORT's location on Jacksonville's Westside means there aren't too many nearby restaurants. But by taking a 10- to 15-minute drive south, you'll find a wealth of restaurants for all tastes and price categories.

$$
AMERICAN

✕ **Biscottis.** The local artwork on the redbrick walls is a mild distraction from the jovial yuppies, soccer moms, and metrosexuals—all of whom are among the crowd jockeying for tables in this midsize restaurant. Elbows almost touch, but no one seems to mind. The menu offers the unexpected: wild mushroom ravioli with a broth of corn, leek, and dried apricot; or curry-grilled swordfish with cucumber-fig bordelaise sauce. Be sure to sample from Biscottis's decadent desserts (courtesy of "b the bakery"). Brunch, a local favorite, is served until 3 on weekends.

⑤ *Average main: $21* ✉ *3556 St. Johns Ave.* ☎ *904/387–2060* ⊕ *www. biscottis.net* ⚠ *Reservations not accepted.*

$$$ ✕ **Bistro Aix.** When a Jacksonville restaurant can make Angelinos feel
ECLECTIC like they haven't left home, that's saying a lot. With its slick leather
booths, 1940s brickwork, olive drapes, and intricate marbled globes,
Bistro Aix (pronounced "X") is just that place. Regulars can't get
enough of the creamy onion soup or escargot appetizers, prosciutto
and goat cheese salad, or entrées like oak-grilled fish Aixoise, steak
frites, or mushroom and fontina wood-fired pizza. Most items (salads
included) come in full or lighter-appetite portions, and you'll definitely
want to save room for dessert. Aix's in-house pastry team ensures no
sweet tooth leaves unsatisfied, with offerings such as profiteroles (mini
cream puffs filled with vanilla ice cream and topped with chocolate and
caramel sauce) and warm chocolate banana walnut bread pudding.
Call for preferred seating. ⑤ *Average main: $24* ✉ *1440 San Marco
Blvd., San Marco* ☎ *904/398–1949* ⊕ *www.bistrox.com* ⚠ *Reservations essential* ⊗ *No lunch weekends.*

WHERE TO STAY

Hotels near the cruise terminals are few and far between, so most cruisers needing a room make the drive to Downtown (15 minutes) or to Southbank or Riverside (20 minutes).

For expanded reviews, facilities, and current deals, visit Fodors.com.

$$$ 🏨 **Hyatt Regency Jacksonville Riverfront.** It doesn't get much more con-
HOTEL venient than this 19-story, downtown, waterfront hotel within walk-
ing distance of Jacksonville Landing, EverBank Field, Florida Theatre,
Times-Union Center, corporate office towers, and the county courthouse. **Pros:** riverfront location; rooftop pool and hot tub; free Wi-Fi
in public areas; 24-hour gym and business center. **Cons:** not all rooms
are riverfront; slow valet service; no minibars; fee for in-room Wi-Fi.
⑤ *Rooms from: $159* ✉ *225 E. Coastline Dr., Downtown* ☎ *904/588–
1234* ⊕ *www.jacksonville.hyatt.com* 🛏 *963 rooms, 21 suites* ⦿ *No
meals.*

$$ 🏨 **Omni Jacksonville Hotel.** Jacksonville's most luxurious and glamorous
HOTEL hotel last underwent a major update in 2011—right down to new flat-
FAMILY screen HD TVs in its chic, spacious guest rooms—with more work in
2012. **Pros:** four-diamond onsite restaurant; downtown location; large
rooms; rooftop pool; great kids' offerings. **Cons:** congested valet area;
restaurant pricey; can be chaotic when there's a show at the Times-
Union Center across the street. ⑤ *Rooms from: $119* ✉ *245 Water St.*
☎ *904/355–6664, 800/843–6664* ⊕ *www.omnijacksonville.com* 🛏 *354
rooms, 4 two-bedroom suites* ⦿ *No meals.*

MIAMI, FLORIDA

Paul Rubio
Miami is the busiest of Florida's very busy cruise ports. Because there's
so much going on here, you might want to schedule an extra day or two
before and/or after your cruise to explore North America's most Latin
city. Downtown is a convenient place to stay if you are meeting up with

6

a cruise ship, but South Beach is still the crown jewel of Miami. Miami Beach, particularly the Art Deco District in South Beach—the square-mile section between 6th and 23rd streets—is the heart of Miami's vibrant nightlife and restaurant scene. But you may also want to explore beyond the beach, including the Little Havana, Coral Gables, and Coconut Grove sections of the city.

ESSENTIALS

HOURS

Most of the area's attractions are open every day.

VISITOR INFORMATION

Contacts Greater Miami Convention & Visitors Bureau ⊠ *701 Brickell Ave., Suite 2700* ☎ *305/539–3000, 800/933–8448 in U.S.* ⊕ *www.miamiandbeaches. com.* **Visit Miami Beach–Visitors Center** ⊠ *1901 Convention Center Dr., Hall C, Miami Beach* ☎ *786/276-2763, 305/673-7400 Miami Beach Tourist Hotline* ⊕ *www.miamibeachguest.com.*

THE CRUISE PORT

The Port of Miami, in downtown Miami near Bayside Marketplace and the MacArthur Causeway, justifiably bills itself as the Cruise Capital of the World. Home to 12 cruise lines and the largest year-round cruise fleet in the world, the port accommodates more than 4 million passengers a year for sailings from 3 to 14 days and sometimes longer duration. Seven air-conditioned terminals are decorated with dramatic public art installations reflecting sun-drenched waters off the Florida coastline and the Everglades ecosystems. There's duty-free shopping and limousine service. You can get taxis at all the terminals, and car-rental agencies offer shuttles to off-site lots.

If you are driving, take I–95 north or south to I–395. Follow the directional signs to the Biscayne Boulevard exit. When you get to Biscayne Boulevard, make a right. Go to 5th Street, which becomes Port Boulevard (look for the American Airlines Arena); then make a left and go over the Port Bridge. Follow the directional signs to your terminal.

Contact Port of Miami ⊠ *1015 North American Way* ☎ *305/347–4800* ⊕ *www. miamidade.gov/portofmiami.*

AIRPORT TRANSFERS

If you have not arranged an airport transfer through your cruise line, you have a couple of options for getting to the cruise port. The first is a taxi, and fares are regulated by the county, with a flat fare of $24 from Miami International Airport (MIA). This fare is per trip, not per passenger, and includes tolls and $1 airport surcharge but not a tip. Super Shuttle vans transport passengers between MIA and local hotels, as well as the Port of Miami. At MIA the vans pick up at the ground level of each concourse (look for clerks with yellow shirts, who will flag one down). Super Shuttle service from MIA is available on demand; for the return it's best to make reservations 24 hours in advance. The cost from MIA to the cruise port is $15 per person, or $50 if you want the entire van to yourselves.

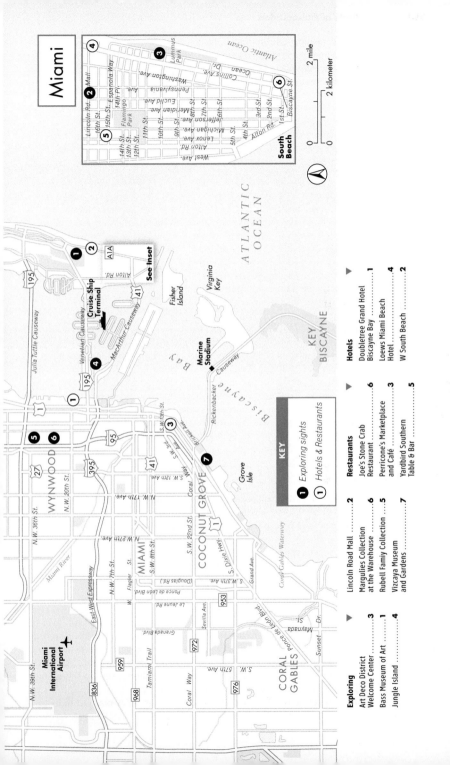

Miami

South Beach

Atlantic Ocean

0 — 2 mile
0 — 2 kilometer

ATLANTIC OCEAN

KEY BISCAYNE

KEY

1 Exploring sights

1 Hotels & Restaurants

Exploring

Art Deco District Welcome Center	**3**
Bass Museum of Art	**1**
Jungle Island	**4**
Lincoln Road Mall	**2**
Margulies Collection at the Warehouse	**6**
Rubell Family Collection	**5**
Vizcaya Museum and Gardens	**7**

Restaurants

Joe's Stone Crab Restaurant	**6**
Perricone's Marketplace and Café	**3**
Yardbird Southern Table & Bar	**5**

Hotels

Doubletree Grand Hotel Biscayne Bay	**1**
Loews Miami Beach Hotel	**4**
W South Beach	**2**

Contacts **Super Shuttle.** This 24-hour service runs air-conditioned vans between MIA and the Homestead-Florida City area; pickup is outside baggage claim and costs around $61 per person depending on your destination. For a return to MIA, reserve 24 hours in advance and know your pickup zip code for a price quote. ✉ *Florida City* 📞 *305/871–2000* 🌐 *www.supershuttle. com.*

PARKING

Street-level lots are right in front of each of the cruise terminals. In 2010 the $15-million Parking Garage D (with 873 spaces on four levels) opened near two recently constructed terminals serving Carnival Cruise Lines. Altogether the port's three parking garages (each with an open-air top floor) accommodate 5,871 vehicles, with 56 spaces designated for handicapped guests and another half-dozen or so for passengers with infants. The cost for all, payable in advance, is $20 per day ($40 for RVs, which can be parked in Lot 2, across from Terminal E) and $7 for short-term parking of less than 4 hours for drop-off/pick-up. You can pay with cash, credit card, or traveler's checks but not with a debit card. There is no valet parking, but a shuttle for cruise passengers (one is wheelchair-accessible) can pick you up at the parking garage/lot, take you to the appropriate terminal, and return you to your vehicle after your cruise.

> ### MIAMI BEST BETS
>
> ■ **South Beach.** Take a 10- to 15-minute cab to South Beach for great people-watching, an art deco tour, or a bit of sun.
>
> ■ **Bayside Marketplace.** If you want to stay close to the port, grab some outdoor drinks and eclectic eats at touristy Bayside Marketplace.
>
> ■ **Bill Baggs Cape Florida State Park.** Unleash your outdoor enthusiasm at Key Biscayne's Bill Baggs Cape Florida State Park.
>
> ■ **Vizcaya Museum.** One of south Florida's largest historic homes is one of the city's best museums.

EXPLORING MIAMI

In the 1950s Miami was best known for alligator wrestlers and you-pick strawberry fields or citrus groves. Well, things have changed. Miami on the mainland is South Florida's commercial hub, while its sultry sister Miami Beach (America's Riviera) encompasses 17 islands in Biscayne Bay. Seducing winter refugees with its sunshine, beaches, palms, and nightlife, this is what most people envision when planning a trip to what they think of as Miami. If you want to do any exploring, you'll have to drive.

Art Deco District Welcome Center. Run by the Miami Design Preservation League, the center provides information about the buildings in the district. An improved gift shop sells 1930s–50s art deco memorabilia, posters, and books on Miami's history. Several tours—covering Lincoln Road, Española Way, North Beach, and the entire Art Deco District, among others—start here. You can choose from a self-guided iPod audio tour or join one of the regular morning walking tours at 10:30 every day. On Thursday a second tour takes place at 6:30 pm.

Arrive at the center 15 minutes beforehand and prepurchase tickets online. All of the options provide detailed histories of the art deco hotels as well as an introduction to the art deco, Mediterranean revival, and Miami Modern (MiMo) styles found within the Miami Beach Architectural Historic District. Don't miss the special boat tours

> **CAUTION**
>
> Airline carry-on restrictions are updated continuously. Check with your airline before packing, and be aware that large purses will sometimes be counted as a carry-on item!

during Art Deco Weekend, in early January. ⊠ *1001 Ocean Dr., South Beach, Miami Beach* ☎ *305/672–2014* ⊕ *www.mdpl.org* ☜ *Tours $20* ⊘ *Daily 9:30–7.*

Bass Museum of Art. Special exhibitions join a diverse collection of European art at this museum whose original building is constructed of keystone and has unique Maya-inspired carvings. An expansion designed by Japanese architect Arata Isozaki houses another wing and an outdoor sculpture garden. Works on permanent display include *The Holy Family,* a painting by Peter Paul Rubens; *The Tournament,* one of several 16th-century Flemish tapestries; and works by Albrecht Dürer and Henri de Toulouse-Lautrec. Docent tours are by appointment but free with entry. ⊠ *2100 Collins Ave., South Beach, Miami Beach* ☎ *305/673–7530* ⊕ *www.bassmuseum.org* ☜ *$8* ⊘ *Wed.–Sun. noon–5.*

FAMILY **Jungle Island.** Originally located deep in south Miami and known as Parrot Jungle, South Florida's original tourist attraction opened in 1936 and moved closer to Miami Beach in 2003. Located on Watson Island, a small stretch of land off of I–395 between Downtown Miami and South Beach, Jungle Island is far more than a park where cockatoos ride tricycles; this interactive zoological park is home to just about every unusual and endangered species you would want to see, including a rare albino alligator, a liger (lion and tiger mix), and myriad exotic birds. The most intriguing offerings are the VIP animal tours, including the Lemur Experience ($79.95), in which the highly social primates make themselves at home on your lap or shoulders. Jungle Island offers complimentary shuttle service to most Downtown Miami and South Beach hotels. ⊠ *1111 Parrot Jungle Trail, off MacArthur Causeway (I–395), Downtown* ☎ *305/400–7000* ⊕ *www.jungleisland.com* ☜ *$34.95, plus $8 parking* ⊘ *Weekdays 10–5, weekends 10–6.*

FAMILY
Fodor's Choice
★

Lincoln Road Mall. This open-air pedestrian mall flaunts some of Miami's best people-watching. The eclectic interiors of myriad fabulous restaurants, colorful boutiques, art galleries, lounges, and cafés are often upstaged by the bustling outdoor scene. It's here among the prolific alfresco dining enclaves that you can pass the hours easily beholding the beautiful people. Indeed, outdoor restaurant and café seating take center stage along this wide pedestrian road adorned with towering date palms, linear pools, and colorful broken-tile mosaics. Some of the shops on Lincoln Road are owner-operated boutiques carrying a smart variety of clothing, furnishings, jewelry, and decorative elements. You'll also find typical upscale chain stores: H & M, Banana Republic, and

6

so on. Lincoln Road is fun, lively, and friendly for people—old, young, gay, and straight—and their dogs.

Two landmarks worth checking out at the eastern end of Lincoln Road are the massive 1940s keystone building at 420 Lincoln Road, which has a 1945 Leo Birchanky mural in the lobby, and the 1921 Mission-style Miami Beach Community Church, at Drexel Avenue. The Lincoln Theatre (No. 541–545), at Pennsylvania Avenue, is a classical four-story art deco gem with friezes. At Euclid Avenue there's a monument to Morris Lapidus, the brains behind Lincoln Road Mall, who in his 90s watched the renaissance of his whimsical South Beach creation. At Lenox Avenue, a black-and-white art deco movie house with a Mediterranean barrel-tile roof is now the Colony Theater (No. 1040), where live theater and experimental films are presented. ⊠ *Lincoln Rd. between Washington Ave. and Alton Rd., South Beach, Miami Beach* ⊕ *www.lincolnroad.org.*

Margulies Collection at the Warehouse. Make sure a visit to Wynwood includes a stop at the Margulies Collection at the Warehouse. Martin Margulies's collection of vintage and contemporary photography, videos, and installation art in a 45,000-square-foot space makes for eye-popping viewing. Admission proceeds go to the Lotus House, a local homeless shelter for women and children. ⊠ *591 N.W. 27th St., between N.W. 5th and 6th aves., Wynwood* ☎ *305/576–1051* ⊕ *www. margulieswarehouse.com* ▣ *$10* ☽ *Oct.–Apr., Wed.–Sat. 11–4.*

Rubell Family Collection. Fans of edgy art will appreciate the Rubell Family Collection. Mera and Don Rubell have accumulated work by artists from the 1970s to the present, including Jeff Koons, Cindy Sherman, Damien Hirst, and Keith Haring. Admission includes a complimentary audio tour. ⊠ *95 N.W. 29th St., between N. Miami and N.W. 1st aves., Wynwood* ☎ *305/573–6090* ⊕ *www.rfc.museum* ▣ *$10* ☽ *Wed.–Sat. 10–6.*

Fodor'sChoice **Vizcaya Museum and Gardens.** Of the 10,000 people living in Miami ★ between 1912 and 1916, about 1,000 of them were gainfully employed by Chicago industrialist James Deering to build this European-inspired residence. Once comprising 180 acres, this National Historic Landmark now occupies a 30-acre tract that includes a rockland hammock (native forest) and more than 10 acres of formal gardens with fountains overlooking Biscayne Bay. The house, open to the public, contains 70 rooms, 34 of which are filled with paintings, sculpture, antique furniture, and other fine and decorative arts. The collection spans 2,000 years and represents the Renaissance, baroque, rococo, and neoclassical periods. The 90-minute self-guided Discover Vizcaya Audio Tour is available in multiple languages for an additional $5. Moonlight tours, offered on evenings that are nearest the full moon, provide a magical look at the gardens; call for reservations. ⊠ *3251 S. Miami Ave., Coconut Grove* ☎ *305/250–9133* ⊕ *www.vizcayamuseum.org* ▣ *$15* ☽ *Wed.–Mon. 9:30–4:30.*

BEACHES

Fodor's Choice
★

Bill Baggs Cape Florida State Park. Thanks to inviting beaches, sunsets, and a tranquil lighthouse, this park at Key Biscayne's southern tip is worth the drive. In fact, the 1-mile stretch of pure beachfront has been named several times in Dr. Beach's revered America's Top 10 Beaches list. It has 18 picnic pavilions available as daily rentals, two cafés that serve light lunches (Lighthouse Café, overlooking the Atlantic Ocean, and the Boater's Grill, on Biscayne Bay) , and plenty of space to enjoy the umbrella and chair rentals. A stroll or ride along walking and bicycle paths provides wonderful views of Miami's dramatic skyline. From the southern end of the park you can see a handful of houses rising over the bay on wooden stilts, the remnants of Stiltsville, built in the 1940s and now protected by the Stiltsville Trust. The nonprofit group was established in 2003 to preserve the structures, because they showcase the park's rich history. Bill Baggs has bicycle rentals, a playground, fishing piers, and guided tours of the **Cape Florida Lighthouse,** South Florida's oldest structure. The lighthouse was erected in 1845 to replace an earlier one damaged in an 1836 Seminole attack, in which the keeper's helper was killed. Free tours are offered at the restored cottage and lighthouse at 10 am and 1 pm Thursday to Monday. Be there a half hour beforehand. **Amenities:** food and drink, lifeguards, parking, showers, toilets. **Best for:** solitude, sunsets, walking. ✉ *1200 S. Crandon Blvd., Key Biscayne* ☎ *305/361–5811* ⊕ *www.floridastateparks.org/capeflorida* 🚗 *$8 per vehicle; $2 per person on bicycle, bus, motorcycle, or foot* ☉ *Daily 8–sunset.*

Fodor's Choice
★

South Beach. A 10-block stretch of white sandy beach hugging the turquoise waters along Ocean Drive—from 5th to 15th streets—is one of the most popular in America, known for drawing unabashedly modelesque sunbathers and posers. With the influx of new luxe hotels and hotspots from 1st to 5th and 16th to 25th streets, the South Beach stand-and-pose scene is now bigger than ever and stretches yet another dozen plus blocks. The beaches crowd quickly on the weekends with a blend of European tourists, young hipsters, and sun-drenched locals offering Latin flavor. Separating the sand from the traffic of Ocean Drive is palm-fringed **Lummus Park,** with its volleyball nets and chickee huts (huts made of palmetto thatch over a cypress frame) for shade. The beach at **12th Street** is popular with gays, in a section often marked with rainbow flags. Locals hang out on 3rd Street beach, in an area called **SoFi** (South of Fifth) where they watch fit Brazilians play foot volley, a variation of volleyball that uses everything but the hands. Because much of South Beach leans toward skimpy sunning—women are often in G-strings and casually topless—many families prefer the tamer sections of Mid- and North Beach. Metered parking spots next to the ocean are a rare find. Instead, opt for a public garage a few blocks away and enjoy the people-watching as you walk to find your perfect spot on the sand. **Amenities:** food and drink; lifeguards; parking (fee); showers; toilets. **Best for:** partiers; sunrise; swimming; walking. ✉ *Ocean Dr., from 5th to 15th St., then Collins Ave. to 25th St., South Beach, Miami Beach.*

6

SHOPPING

In Greater Miami you're never more than 15 minutes from a major commercial area that serves as both a shopping and entertainment venue for tourists and locals. The shopping is great on a two-block stretch of **Collins Avenue** between 6th and 8th streets. The busy **Lincoln Road Mall** is a few blocks from the

beach and convention center, making it popular with locals and tourists. There's an energy here, especially on weekends, when the pedestrian mall is filled with locals. Creative merchandise, galleries, and a Sunday-morning antiques market can be found among the art galleries and cool cafés. An 18-screen movie theater anchors the west end of the street.

NIGHTLIFE

Miami's pulse pounds with nonstop nightlife that reflects the area's potent cultural mix. On sultry, humid nights with the huge full moon rising out of the ocean and fragrant night-blooming jasmine intoxicating the senses, who can resist Cuban salsa, Jamaican reggae, and Dominican merengue, with some disco and hip-hop thrown in for good measure? When this place throws a party, hips shake, fingers snap, bodies touch. It's no wonder many clubs are still rocking at 5 am.

WHERE TO EAT

At many of the hottest spots you'll need a reservation to avoid a long wait for a table. And when you get your check, note whether a gratuity is included; most restaurants add 15% (ostensibly for the convenience of—and protection from—Latin-American and European tourists who are used to this practice in their homelands and would not normally tip), but you can reduce or supplement it depending on your opinion of the service. One of Greater Miami's most popular pursuits is bar-hopping. Bars range from intimate enclaves to showy see-and-be-seen lounges to loud, raucous frat parties. There's a New York–style flair to some of the newer lounges, which are increasingly catering to the Manhattan party crowd who escape to South Beach for long weekends. If you're looking for a relatively nonfrenetic evening, your best bet is one of the chic hotel bars on Collins Avenue.

$$$$
SEAFOOD
Fodor's Choice
★

✕ **Joe's Stone Crab Restaurant.** In South Beach's decidedly new-money scene, the stately Joe's Stone Crab is an old-school testament to good food and good service. South Beach's most storied restaurant started as a turn-of-the-century eating-house when Joseph Weiss discovered succulent stone crabs off the Florida coast. Almost a century later, the restaurant stretches a city block and serves 2,000 dinners a day to local politicians and moneyed patriarchs. Stone crabs, served with legendary mustard sauce, crispy hash browns, and creamed spinach, remain the staple. Though stone-crab season runs from October 15 to May 15, Joe's remains open year-round (albeit with a limited schedule) serving other phenomenal seafood dishes. Finish your meal with tart key lime pie, baked fresh daily. ■TIP➔ **Joe's famously refuses reservations, and weekend waits can be three hours long—yes, you read that correctly—so come early or order from Joe's Take Away next door.** ⑤ *Average main: $42* ⊠ *11 Washington Ave., South Beach, Miami Beach* ☎ *305/673–0365, 305/673–4611 for takeout* ⊕ *www.joesstonecrab.com* ⚓ *Reservations not accepted* ⊘ *No lunch Sun. and Mon. and mid-May–mid-Oct.*

$$
ITALIAN

✕ **Perricone's Marketplace and Café.** Brickell Avenue south of the Miami River is a haven for Italian restaurants, and this lunch place for local bigwigs is the biggest and most popular among them. It's housed partially outdoors and partially indoors in an 1880s Vermont barn. Recipes were handed down from generation to generation, and the cooking is simple and good. Buy your wine from the on-premises deli, and enjoy it (for a small corking fee) with homemade minestrone; a generous antipasto; linguine with a sauté of jumbo shrimp, scallops, and calamari; or gnocchi with four cheeses. The homemade tiramisu and cannoli are top-notch. ⑤ *Average main: $22* ⊠ *Mary Brickell Village, 15 S.E. 10th St., Downtown* ☎ *305/374–9449* ⊕ *www.perricones.com.*

$$
SOUTHERN
Fodor's Choice
★

✕ **Yardbird Southern Table & Bar.** *Top Chef* contestant Jeff McInnis brings a helluva lot of Southern lovin' (from the Lowcountry to South Beach) to this lively and funky spot. Miami's A-list puts calorie-counting aside for decadent nights filled with comfort foods and innovative drinks. The family-style menu is divided between "small shares" and "big shares," but let's not kid ourselves—all the portions are huge (and surprisingly affordable). You'll rave about Mama's chicken biscuits, the Atlantic fried oysters, the fried-green-tomato BLT, the grilled-mango salad, the 27-hour-fried chicken, and the shrimp and grits. Oh, and then there are the sides, like "caviar"-topped deviled eggs, house-cut fries with a buttermilk dipping sauce and bacon salt, and the super-creamy macaroni-and-cheese. Don't plan on hitting the beach in a bikini the next day. ⑤ *Average main: $18* ⊠ *1600 Lenox Ave., South Beach, Miami Beach* ☎ *305/538–5220* ⊕ *www.runchickenrun.com.*

WHERE TO STAY

Staying in downtown Miami will put you close to the cruise terminals, but there is little to do at night. South Beach is the center of the action in Miami Beach, but it's fairly distant from the port. Staying in Miami Beach, but north of South Beach's Art Deco District, will put you on the beach but nominally closer to the port.

For expanded reviews, facilities, and current deals, visit Fodors.com.

$
HOTEL

🏨 **Doubletree Grand Hotel Biscayne Bay.** Near the Port of Miami at the north end of downtown, this waterfront hotel offers relatively basic, spacious rooms and convenient access to and from the cruise ships and downtown, making it a good crash pad for budget-conscious cruise passengers. **Pros:** marina; proximity to port. **Cons:** still need a cab to get around; dark lobby and neighboring arcade of shops; worn rooms.

Rooms from: $171 ⊠ *1717 N. Bayshore Dr., Downtown* ☎ *305/372–0313, 800/222-8733* ⊕ *www.doubletree.com* ⤳ *152 rooms, 56 suites* ⏀ *No meals.*

$$$ **Loews Miami Beach Hotel.** Loews Miami Beach, a two-tower 800-room
HOTEL   megahotel with top-tier amenities, a massive spa, a great pool, and direct beachfront access, is good for families, businesspeople, groups, and pet-lovers. **Pros:** top-notch amenities; immense spa; pets welcome. **Cons:** insanely large size; constantly crowded. *Rooms from: $399* ⊠ *1601 Collins Ave., South Beach, Miami Beach* ☎ *305/604–1601, 800/235-6397* ⊕ *www.loewshotels.com/miamibeach* ⤳ *733 rooms, 57 suites* ⏀ *No meals.*

$$$$ **W South Beach.** Fun, fresh, and funky, the W South Beach is also the
HOTEL   flagship for the brand's evolution towards young sophistication, which
Fodor's Choice   means less club music in the lobby, more lighting, and more attention to
★   the multimillion dollar art collection lining the lobby's expansive walls. **Pros:** pool scene; masterful design; ocean-view balconies in each room. **Cons:** not a classic art deco building; hit-or-miss service. *Rooms from: $450* ⊠ *2201 Collins Ave., South Beach, Miami Beach* ☎ *305/938–3000* ⊕ *www.whotels.com/southbeach* ⤳ *312 rooms* ⏀ *No meals.*

NEW ORLEANS, LOUISIANA

Todd Price   The spiritual and cultural heart of New Orleans is the French Quarter, where the city was settled by the French in 1718. You could easily spend several days visiting museums, shops, and eateries in this area, but you can get a small sense of the place quickly. If you have time, the rest of the city's neighborhoods, radiating out from this focal point, also make for rewarding rambling. The mansion-lined streets of the Garden District and Uptown, the aboveground cemeteries that dot the city, and the open air along Lake Pontchartrain provide a nice balance to the commercialization of the Quarter. Despite its sprawling size, New Orleans has a small-town vibe, perhaps due to locals' shared cultural habits and history.

ESSENTIALS

HOURS

Shops in the French Quarter tend to be open late, but stores in most of the malls close by 9. Restaurants tend to be open late as well, and many bars never close their doors.

VISITOR INFORMATION

Contacts **New Orleans Convention & Visitors Bureau** ☎ *800/672–6124, 504/566–5011* ⊕ *www.neworleanscvb.com.* **New Orleans Multicultural Tourism Network** ⊕ *www.soulofneworleans.com.*

THE CRUISE PORT

The Julia Street Cruise Terminal is at the end of Julia Street on the Mississippi River; the Erato Street Terminal is just to the north. Both terminals are behind the Ernest N. Morial Convention Center. You can walk to the French Quarter from here in about 10 minutes; it's a short

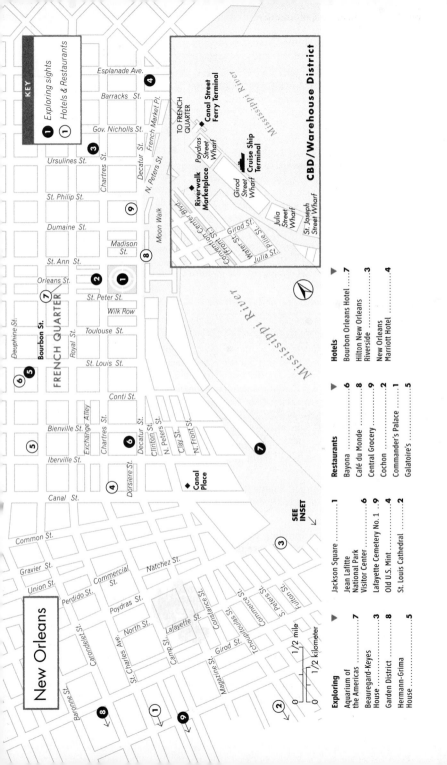

New Orleans

KEY
- **1** Exploring sights
- **①** Hotels & Restaurants

FRENCH QUARTER

CBD/Warehouse District

Mississippi River

Canal Street Ferry Terminal
TO FRENCH QUARTER
Poydras Street Wharf
Cruise Ship Terminal
Riverwalk Marketplace
Girod Street Wharf
Julia Street Wharf
St. Joseph Street Wharf

Esplanade Ave.
Barracks St.
Gov. Nicholls St.
Ursulines St.
St. Philip St.
Dumaine St.
St. Ann St.
Orleans St.
St. Peter St.
Wilk Row
Toulouse St.
St. Louis St.
Conti St.
Bienville St.
Iberville St.
Canal St.
Common St.
Gravier St.
Union St.
Perdido St.
Poydras St.

French Market Pl.
Decatur St.
Chartres St.
N. Peters St.
Madison St.
Dauphine St.
Bourbon St.
Royal St.
Exchange Alley
Chartres St.
Decatur St.
Clinton St.
N. Peters St.
Clay St.
N. Front St.
Dorsiere St.
Canal Place

Moon Walk
Convention Center Blvd.
Front St.
Girod St.
Water St.
Julia St.
Julia St.

Natchez St.
Commercial St.
Lafayette St.
North St.
Carondelet St.
Baronne St.
St. Charles Ave.
Camp St.
Magazine St.
Girod St.
Tchoupitoulas St.
Commerce St.
S. Peters St.
Fulton St.
Constance St.

SEE INSET

0   1/2 mile
0   1/2 kilometer

Exploring
- Aquarium of the Americas **7**
- Beauregard-Keyes House **3**
- Garden District **8**
- Hermann-Grima House **5**
- Jackson Square **1**
- Jean Lafitte National Park Visitor Center **6**
- Lafayette Cemetery No. 1 ... **9**
- Old U.S. Mint **4**
- St. Louis Cathedral **2**

Restaurants
- Bayona **6**
- Café du Monde **8**
- Central Grocery **9**
- Cochon **2**
- Commander's Palace **1**
- Galatoire's **5**

Hotels
- Bourbon Orleans Hotel **7**
- Hilton New Orleans Riverside **3**
- New Orleans Marriott Hotel **4**

taxi ride to the Quarter or nearby hotels. Carnival and Norwegian base ships here year round.

If you are driving, you'll probably approach New Orleans on I–10. Take the Business 90 West/Westbank exit, locally known as Pontchartrain Expressway, and proceed to the Tchoupitoulas Street/South Peters Street exit. Continue to Convention Center Boulevard, where you will take a right turn. Continue to Henderson Street, where you will turn left, and then continue to Port of New Orleans Place. Take a left on Port of New Orleans Place to Julia Street Terminals 1 and 2, or take a right to get to the Robin Street Wharf.

NEW ORLEANS BEST BETS

■ **Audubon Aquarium of the Americas.** Especially good for families is this fantastic aquarium on the edge of French Quarter.

■ **Eating Well.** A highlight in New Orleans is dining. If you ever wanted to splurge on a great restaurant meal, this is the place to do it. At the very least, have a beignet at Café du Mond.

■ **Hermann-Grima House.** This is one of the best-preserved historic homes in the French Quarter.

Port Contact Port of New Orleans ⊠ *Port of New Orleans Pl., at foot of Julia St.* ☏ *504/522–2551* ⊕ *www.portno.com.*

AIRPORT TRANSFERS

Shuttle-bus service to and from the airport and the cruise port is available through Airport Shuttle New Orleans. Buses leave regularly from the ground level near the baggage claim. Return trips to the airport need to be booked in advance. A one-way ticket is $20 per person and a round-trip ticket $38. The trip takes about 30 minutes.

A cab ride to or from the airport from uptown or downtown New Orleans costs a flat $33 for the first two passengers and $14 for each additional passenger. At the airport, pick-up is on the lower level, outside the baggage claim area. There may be an additional charge for extra baggage.

Contact Airport Shuttle New Orleans ☏ *504/522–3500, 866/596–2699* ⊕ *www.airportshuttleneworleans.com.*

PARKING

If you are spending some time in the city before or after your cruise, finding a parking space is fairly easy in most of the city, except for the French Quarter, where meter maids are plentiful and tow trucks eager. If in doubt about a space, pass it up and pay to use a parking lot. Avoid parking spaces at corners and curbs: less than 15 feet between your car and the corner will result in a ticket. Watch for temporary "No Parking" signs, which pop up along parade routes and film shoots. Long-term and overnight parking are extremely expensive at hotels and garages. Parking for the duration of your cruise is available for $16 per night and is on Erato Street; if you want, SeaCaps will take your bags directly to the ship so you just have to deal with your hand luggage. RVs can park in a lot on Poydras Street next to Terminal 2 at the Julia Street dock for $32 per night.

EXPLORING NEW ORLEANS

The **French Quarter,** the oldest part of the city, lives up to all you've heard: it's alive with the sights, sounds, odors, and experiences of a major entertainment hub. At some point, ignore your better judgment and take a stroll down **Bourbon Street,** past the bars, restaurants, music clubs, and novelty shops that have given this strip its reputation as the playground of the South. Be sure to find time to stop at Café du Monde for chicory-laced coffee and beignets. With its beautifully landscaped gardens surrounding elegant antebellum homes, the **Garden District** is mostly residential, but most home owners do not mind your enjoying the sights from outside the cast-iron fences surrounding their magnificent properties.

FAMILY

Fodor'sChoice

★

Aquarium of the Americas. Power failures during Katrina resulted in the major loss of the aquarium's collection of more than 7,000 aquatic creatures. In a dramatic gesture of solidarity, aquariums around the country joined together with the Aquarium of the Americas in an effort to repopulate its stock. The museum, now fully reopened, has four major exhibit areas—the Amazon Rain Forest, the Caribbean Reef, the Mississippi River, and the Gulf Coast—all of which have fish and animals native to that environment. A special treat is Parakeet Pointe, where you can get up close to hundreds of parakeets and even feed them by hand. The aquarium's spectacular design allows you to feel part of the watery worlds by providing close-up encounters with the inhabitants. A gift shop and café are on the premises. **Woldenberg Riverfront Park,** which surrounds the aquarium, is a tranquil spot with a view of the Mississippi. ■**TIP→** You can combine tickets for the aquarium and the Entergy IMAX Theater ($29), but the best deal is the "Audubon Experience": aquarium, IMAX, Audubon Insectarium, and Audubon Zoo for $44.50 (tickets are good for 14 days). ⊠ *1 Canal St., French Quarter* ☎ *504/581–4629, 800/774–7394* ⊕ *www.auduboninstitute.org* ⊡ *$22.50* ☉ *Tues.–Sun. 10–5.*

6

Beauregard-Keyes House. The Confederate general and Louisiana native P. G. T. Beauregard briefly made his home at this stately 19th-century mansion. A more long-term resident, however, was the novelist Frances Parkinson Keyes, who found the place in a sad state when she arrived in the 1940s. Keyes restored the home, today filled with period furnishings. Her studio at the back of the large courtyard remains intact, complete with family photos, original manuscripts, and her doll, fan, and teapot collections. Keyes wrote 40 novels there, all in longhand, among them the local favorite *Dinner at Antoine's.* Even if you don't have time to tour the house, take a peek through the gates at the beautiful walled garden at the corner of Chartres and Ursulines streets. Landscaped in the same sun pattern as Jackson Square, it blooms throughout the year. ⊠ *1113 Chartres St., French Quarter* ☎ *504/523–7257* ⊕ *www.bkhouse.org* ⊡ *$10* ☉ *Mon.–Sat. 10–3, tours on the hr.*

Garden District. The Garden District is divided into two sections by Jackson Avenue. Upriver from Jackson is the wealthy **Upper Garden District,** where the homes are meticulously kept. Below Jackson, the **Lower Garden District** is considerably rougher. Though the homes here are often just as structurally beautiful, most of them lack the recent restorations of those of the Upper Garden District. The streets are also less well patrolled; wander cautiously. **Magazine Street,** lined with antiques shops and coffeehouses (ritzier along the Upper Garden District, hipper along the Lower Garden District), serves as a southern border to the Garden District, and St. Charles Avenue forms the northern border.

Hermann-Grima House. One of the largest and best-preserved examples of American architecture in the Quarter, this Georgian-style house has the only restored private stable and the only working 1830s Creole kitchen in the Quarter. American architect William Brand built the house in 1831. Cooking demonstrations on the open hearth are held here every other Thursday from October through May. You'll want to check the gift shop, which has many local crafts and books. ⊠ *820 St. Louis St., French Quarter* ☎ *504/525–5661* ⊕ *www.hgghh.org* ✉ *$12, combination ticket with Gallier House $20* ☉ *Mon., Tues., Thurs., and Fri. 10–2, Sat. noon–3; tours on the hr.*

FAMILY

Fodor'sChoice
★

Jackson Square. Surrounded by historic buildings and plenty of the city's atmospheric street life, the heart of the French Quarter is this beautifully landscaped park. Among the notable buildings around the square are **St. Louis Cathedral** and **Faulkner House.** Two Spanish colonial–style buildings, the **Cabildo** and the **Presbytère,** flank the cathedral. The handsome rows of brick apartments on each side of the square are the **Pontalba Buildings.** The park is landscaped in a sun pattern, with walkways set like rays streaming out from the center, a popular garden design in the royal court of King Louis XIV, the Sun King. In the daytime, dozens of artists hang their paintings on the park fence and set up outdoor studios where they work on canvases or offer to draw portraits of passersby. A **statue of Andrew Jackson,** victorious leader of the Battle of New Orleans in the War of 1812, commands the center of the square; the park was renamed for him in the 1850s. The words carved in the base on the cathedral side of the statue—"The Union must and shall be preserved"—are a lasting reminder of the Federal troops who occupied New Orleans during the Civil War and who inscribed them. ⊠ *French Quarter* ☉ *Park daily 8 am–dusk; paths on park's periphery open 24 hrs.*

Jean Lafitte National Park Visitor Center. Visitors who want to explore the areas around New Orleans should stop here first. The office supervises and provides information on Jean Lafitte National Park Barataria Unit, a nature preserve complete with alligators across the river from New Orleans, along with the Chalmette Battlefield, where the Battle of New Orleans was fought in the War of 1812. Each year in January, near the anniversary of the battle, a reenactment is staged at the Chalmette site. This center has free visual and sound exhibits on the customs of various communities throughout the state, as well as information-rich daily riverfront tours called "history strolls." The one-hour daily tour leaves at 9:30 am; tickets are handed out one per person (you must be present to get a ticket), beginning at 9 am, for that day's tour only. Arrive at least 15 minutes before tour time to be sure of a spot. You'll need a car to visit the preserve or the battlefield. ⊠ *419 Decatur St., French Quarter* ☎ *504/589–2636* ⊕ *www.nps.gov/jela* ☉ *Daily 9–5.*

Fodor'sChoice **Lafayette Cemetery No. 1.** Built in 1833, Lafayette Cemetery No. 1
★ remains a testament to the city's history. The cemetery was built when
the area was seeing a large influx of Italian, German, Irish, and American immigrants from the North. Many who fought or played a role
in the Civil War have plots here, indicated by plaques and headstones
that detail the site of their death. Several tombs also reflect the toll the
yellow fever epidemic took on the city during the 19th century, which
affected mostly children and newcomers to New Orleans; 2,000 yellow fever victims were buried here in 1852. Movies such as *Interview
with the Vampire* and *Double Jeopardy* have used this walled cemetery
for its eerie beauty. Open to the public daily, the magnolia tree–lined
cemetery is a short walk from the streetcar and a beautiful spot to learn
about New Orleans's history. Save Our Cemeteries, a nonprofit, offers
hourlong, volunteer-led tours at 10:30 Monday through Saturday. All
proceeds benefit the organization's cemetery restoration and advocacy
efforts. ⊠ *1400 block of Washington Ave., Garden District* ⊙ *Weekdays
7:30–3, weekends 9–6.*

Old U.S. Mint. Minting began in 1838 in this ambitious Ionic structure,
a project of President Andrew Jackson. The New Orleans mint was to
provide currency for the South and the West, which it did until Louisiana
seceded from the Union in 1861. Both the short-lived Republic of Louisiana and the Confederacy minted coins here. When supplies ran out, the
building served as a barracks for Confederate soldiers, then a prison. The
production of U.S. coins recommenced only in 1879; it stopped again,
for good, in 1909. After years of neglect, the federal government handed
the Old Mint over to Louisiana in 1966. The state now uses the quarters
to exhibit collections of the Louisiana State Museum, although the feds
have returned with the third-floor music hall. At the main Barracks Street
entrance, which is set back from the main surrounding gates and not well
marked, notice the one remaining sample of the mint's old walls—it'll give
you an idea of the building's deterioration before its restoration. ⊠ *400
Esplanade Ave., French Quarter* ☎ *504/568–6993* ⊕ *www.crt.state.la.us,
www.nps.gov/jazz* 🎟 *Free* ⊙ *Tue.–Sun. 10–4:30.*

St. Louis Cathedral. The oldest active cathedral in the United States, this
iconic church and basilica at the heart of the Old City is named for the
13th-century French king who led two crusades. The current building, which replaced two structures destroyed by fire, dates from 1794
(although it was remodeled and enlarged in 1851). The austere interior
is brightened by murals covering the ceiling and stained-glass windows
along the first floor. Pope John Paul II held a prayer service for clergy
here during his New Orleans visit in 1987; to honor the occasion,
the pedestrian mall in front of the cathedral was renamed Place Jean
Paul Deux. Of special interest is his portrait in a Jackson Square setting, which hangs on the cathedral inner side wall. Pick up a brochure
($1) for a self-guided tour; books about the cathedral are available
in the gift shop. Docents often give free tours. The garden has been
redesigned by famed French landscape architect Louis Benech, who
also redesigned the Tuileries gardens in Paris, and impressively restored
in 2011. ⊠ *615 Père Antoine Alley, French Quarter* ☎ *504/525–9585*
⊕ *www.stlouiscathedral.org* 🎟 *Free* ⊙ *Daily 8–4.*

6

SHOPPING

The fun of shopping in New Orleans is in the regional items available throughout the city, in the smallest shops or the biggest department stores. You can take home some of the flavor of the city: its pralines (pecan candies), seafood (packaged to go), Louisiana red beans and rice, coffee (pure or with chicory), and creole and Cajun spices (cayenne pepper, chili, and garlic). There are even packaged mixes of such local favorites as jambalaya, gumbo, beignets, and the sweet red local cocktail called the Hurricane.

> ### CALLING CARDS
>
> Print cards with your name, address, phone number, and email address to share with new friends. Stiff, business card–style paper can be purchased at nearly any office supply store, and you can make the cards on your computer at home. Having your cards handy sure beats hunting for pens and scribbling on scraps of paper to swap addresses.

Cookbooks also share the secrets of preparing distinctive New Orleans dishes. The French Quarter is well known for its fine antiques shops, located mainly on Royal and Chartres streets. The main shopping areas in the city are the French Quarter, with narrow, picturesque streets lined with specialty, gift, fashion, and antiques shops and art galleries; the Central Business District (CBD), populated mostly with jewelry, specialty, and department stores; the Warehouse District, best known for contemporary arts galleries and cultural museums; Magazine Street, home to antiques shops, art galleries, home-furnishing stores, dining venues, fashion boutiques, and specialty shops; and the Riverbend/Maple Street area, filled with clothing stores and some specialty shops.

Canal Place. This high-end shopping center focuses on national chains, including Saks Fifth Avenue, Michael Kors, Anthropologie, Banana Republic, Coach, J. Crew, Lululemon, and BCBG Max Azria. But the mall also includes quality local shops, such as the artists co-op RHINO ("Right Here in New Orleans"), Jean Therapy denim boutique, Wehmeier's Belt Shop, and Saint Germain shoes. A highlight is the Mignon Faget jewelry store, which carries the local designer's full line of upscale, Louisiana-inspired creations. ⊠ *333 Canal St., CBD* ☎ *504/522–9200* ⊕ *www.theshopsatcanalplace.com.*

Jax Brewery. A historic building that once was a factory for Jax beer now holds a mall filled with local shops and a few national chain stores, such as Chico's, along with a food court and balcony overlooking the Mississippi River. Shops carry souvenirs, clothing, books, and more, with an emphasis on New Orleans–themed items. The mall is open daily, and during summer days serves as an air-conditioned refuge. ⊠ *600 Decatur St., French Quarter* ☎ *504/566–7245* ⊕ *www.jacksonbrewery.com.*

NIGHTLIFE

No American city places such a premium on pleasure as New Orleans. From swank hotel lounges to sweaty dance clubs, refined jazz clubs and raucous Bourbon Street bars, this city is serious about frivolity. And famous for it. Partying is more than an occasional indulgence in this city—it's a lifestyle. Bars tend to open in the early afternoon and stay open into the morning hours; live music, though, follows a more restrained schedule. Some jazz spots and clubs in the French Quarter stage evening sets around 6 or 9 pm; at a few clubs, such as the Palm Court, the bands actually finish by 11 pm. But this is the exception: for the most part, gigs begin between 10 and 11 pm, and locals rarely emerge for an evening out before 10. Keep in mind that the lack of legal closing time means that shows advertised for 11 may not start until after midnight.

Harrah's New Orleans. The only land-based casino in the New Orleans area, Harrah's contains 115,000 square feet of gaming space divided into five areas, each with a New Orleans theme: Jazz Court, Court of Good Fortune, Smugglers Court, Mardi Gras Court, and Court of the Mansion. There are also 100 table games, 2,100-plus slots, and live entertainment at Masquerade, which includes an ice bar, lounge, video tower, and dancing show. Check the website for seasonal productions, including music, theater, and comedy. Dining and libation choices include the extensive Harrah's buffet, Cafés on Canal food court, Besh Steak House, Gordon Biersch, Grand Isle, Manning's, and Ruth's Chris Steak House. The last four are part of Harrah's newly developed Fulton Street Mall, a pedestrian promenade that attracts casual strollers, club goers, and diners. ⊠ *8 Canal St., CBD* 🕾 *504/533–6000, 800/427–7247* ⊕ *www.harrahs.com* ☉ *Daily 24 hrs.*

Mulate's. Across the street from the Convention Center, this large venue seats 400, and the dance floor quickly fills with couples twirling and two-stepping to authentic Cajun bands from the countryside. Regulars love to drag first-timers to the floor for impromptu lessons. The home-style Cajun cuisine is acceptable, but what matters is nightly music. ⊠ *201 Julia St., Warehouse District* 🕾 *504/522–1492* ⊕ *www.mulates.com.*

Pat O'Brien's. Sure, it's touristy, but there are reasons Pat O's has been a must-stop on the New Orleans drinking trail since Prohibition. There's plenty of room to spread out, from the elegant side bar and piano bar that flank the carriageway entrance to the lush (and in winter, heated) patio. Friendly staff, an easy camaraderie among patrons, and a signature drink—the pink, fruity, and extremely potent Hurricane, which comes with a souvenir glass—make this French Quarter stalwart a pleasant afternoon diversion. Expect a line on weekend nights, and if you don't want your glass, return it for the deposit. ⊠ *718 St. Peter St., French Quarter* 🕾 *504/525–4823* ⊕ *www.patobriens.com.*

FAMILY
Fodor's Choice
★
Preservation Hall. At this cultural landmark founded in 1961, a cadre of distinguished New Orleans musicians, most of whom were schooled by an ever-dwindling group of elder statesmen, nurture the jazz tradition that flowered in the 1920s. There is limited seating on benches—many patrons end up squatting on the floor or standing in back—and no beverages are served, although you can bring your own drink in a plastic cup. Nonetheless, legions of satisfied music lovers regard an evening at this all-ages venue as an essential New Orleans experience. Cover charge is $15 (cash only). The price can be a bit higher for special

6

appearances. A limited number of $30 VIP tickets let you skip the line. ⊠ *726 St. Peter St., French Quarter* ☎ *504/522–2841* ⊕ *www. preservationhall.com.*

Fodor'sChoice **The Spotted Cat.** Jazz, old time, and
★ swing bands perform nightly at this rustic club right in the thick of the Frenchmen Street action. Sets start at 4 pm on weekdays and 3 pm on the weekends. Drinks cost a little more at this cash-only destination, but there's never a cover charge and the entertainment is great—from

the popular bands to the cadres of young, rock-step swing dancers. ⊠ *623 Frenchmen St., Faubourg Marigny* ⊕ *www.spottedcatmusicclub. com.*

Tipitina's. Rub the bust of legendary New Orleans pianist Professor Longhair, or "Fess," inside this Uptown landmark named for one of the late musician's popular songs. The old concert posters on the walls read like an honor roll of musical legends, both local and national. The mid-sized venue still boasts an eclectic and well-curated calendar, particular during the weeks of Jazz Fest. The long-running Sunday afternoon Cajun dance party still packs the floor. Although the neighborhood isn't dangerous, it's enough out of the way to require a cab trip. ⊠ *501 Napoleon Ave., Uptown* ☎ *504/895–8477* ⊕ *www.tipitinas.com.*

SIGHTSEEING TOURS

Several local tour companies give two- to four-hour city tours by bus that include the French Quarter, the Garden District, uptown New Orleans, and the lakefront. Prices range from $25 to $125 per person, depending on the kind of experience. Both Gray Line and New Orleans Tours offer a longer tour that combines a two-hour city tour by bus with a two-hour steamboat ride on the Mississippi River. Gray Line and Tours by Isabelle both offer tours of Hurricane Katrina devastation as well.

Tour Contacts New Orleans Tours ☎ *504/592–1991* ⊕ *www.notours.com.*

WHERE TO EAT

Regardless of where you decide to eat, don't miss the beignets at Café du Monde.

$$$ ✕ **Bayona.** "New World" is the label Louisiana native Susan Spicer
MODERN applies to her cooking style, and resulting delicious dishes include the
AMERICAN goat cheese crouton with mushrooms, a Bayona specialty, or the Carib-
Fodor'sChoice bean pumpkin soup with coconut. A legendary favorite at lunch is
★ the sandwich of smoked duck, cashew peanut butter, and pepper jelly.
■ **TIP➔ A three-course small-plates lunch is available on Saturday for $25.**
The imaginative dishes on the constantly changing menu are served in

an early-19th-century Creole cottage that glows with flower arrangements, elegant photographs, and trompe l'oeil murals suggesting Mediterranean landscapes. Don't skip the sweets, like a maple-semolina cake with golden-raisin compote and pomegranate sauce. $ *Average main: $28* ⊠ *430 Dauphine St., French Quarter* ☎ *504/525–4455* ⊕ *www. bayona.com* ☺ *Closed Sun. No lunch Mon. and Tues.*

$ ✗ **Café du Monde.** No visit to New Orleans is complete without a chicory-laced café au lait paired with the addictive, sugar-dusted beignets at this venerable institution. The tables under the green-and-white-striped awning are jammed with locals and tourists at almost every hour. ■ TIP➡ **If there's a wait, head around back to the takeout window, get your coffee and beignets to go, and enjoy them overlooking the river right next door or in Jackson Square.** The most magical time to go is just before dawn, before the bustle begins. You can hear the birds in the crepe myrtles across the way. The metro-area satellites (there's one in the CBD at the Port of New Orleans) lack the character of the original. $ *Average main: $3* ⊠ *800 Decatur St., French Quarter* ☎ *504/525–4544* ⊕ *www. cafedumonde.com* ⚐ *Reservations not accepted* ▬ *No credit cards.*

CAFÉ
FAMILY
Fodor'sChoice
★

$ ✗ **Central Grocery.** This old-fashioned grocery store creates authentic muffulettas, a gastronomic gift from the city's Italian immigrants. Made by filling nearly 10-inch round loaves of seeded bread with ham, salami, provolone, Emmentaler cheese, and olive salad, the muffuletta is nearly as popular locally as the po'boy. Central Grocery also sells a vegetarian version. The sandwiches are available in wholes and halves (they're huge—unless you're starving, you'll do fine with a half). Eat at one of the counters or get your sandwich to go and dine on a bench in Jackson Square or the Moon Walk along the Mississippi riverfront. The Grocery closes at 5 pm. $ *Average main: $8* ⊠ *923 Decatur St., French Quarter* ☎ *504/523–1620* ☺ *Closed Sun. and Mon. No dinner.*

DELI
FAMILY

$$ ✗ **Cochon.** Chef-owned restaurants are common in New Orleans, but this one builds on owner Donald Link's family heritage as he, working with co-owner Stephen Stryjewski (who received a James Beard Award for his work here), prepares Cajun dishes he learned to cook at his grandfather's knee. The interior may be a bit too hip and noisy for some patrons, but the food makes up for it. The fried boudin with pickled peppers is a must—trust us on this one—then move on to black-eyed pea–and-pork gumbo, and a hearty Louisiana *cochon* (pork) with turnips, cracklings, and cabbage. Despite the pork-centric reputation, all the vegetable sides are excellent. $ *Average main: $20* ⊠ *930 Tchoupitoulas St., Warehouse District* ☎ *504/588–2123* ⊕ *www. cochonrestaurant.com* ⚐ *Reservations essential* ☺ *Closed Sun.*

CAJUN
Fodor'sChoice
★

$$$$ ✗ **Commander's Palace.** No restaurant captures New Orleans's gastronomic heritage and celebratory spirit as well as this grande dame of New Orleans fine dining. Upstairs, the Garden Room's glass walls have marvelous views of the giant oak trees on the patio below. The menu's classics include a spicy and meaty turtle soup; shrimp and tasso Henican (shrimp stuffed with ham, with pickled okra); and a wonderful pecan-crusted Gulf fish. The bread-pudding soufflé might ruin you for other bread puddings. The weekend brunch is a not-to-be-missed New Orleans tradition. Jackets are preferred at dinner. Shorts and T-shirts

CREOLE

6

are forbidden, and men must wear closed-toe shoes. $ *Average main: $35* ✉ *1403 Washington Ave., Garden District* ☎ *504/899–8221* ⊕ *www.commanderspalace.com* ⌂ *Reservations essential.*

$$$

CREOLE

Fodor's Choice

★

✕ **Galatoire's.** With many of its recipes dating to 1905, Galatoire's epitomizes the old-style French-Creole bistro. Fried oysters and bacon en brochette are worth every calorie, and the brick-red rémoulade sauce sets a high standard. Other winners include veal chops with optional béarnaise sauce, and seafood-stuffed eggplant. Downstairs in the white-tableclothed, narrow dining room, lit with gleaming brass chandeliers, is where boisterous regulars congregate and make for excellent entertainment; you can only reserve a table in the renovated upstairs rooms. Friday lunch starts early and continues well into the evening. Shorts and T-shirts are never allowed; a jacket is required for dinner and all day Sunday. $ *Average main: $30* ✉ *209 Bourbon St., French Quarter* ☎ *504/525–2021* ⊕ *www.galatoires.com* ⊘ *Closed Mon.*

WHERE TO STAY

You can stay in a large hotel near the cruise-ship terminal or in more intimate places in the French Quarter. Hotel rates in New Orleans tend to be on the high end, though deals abound.

For expanded reviews, facilities, and current deals, visit Fodors.com.

$$

HOTEL

Bourbon Orleans Hotel. With a location that's about as central as it gets, plus upgraded, spacious guest rooms, this lodging remains one of the most popular options on Bourbon Street. **Pros:** a 2011 renovation delivered upgraded bedding and furnishings; free Wi-Fi; welcome cocktail and gym; beautiful courtyard and pool. **Cons:** lobby level is often crowded and noisy due to curious passersby; hotel is steps from loud, 24-hour Bourbon Street action. $ *Rooms from: $173* ✉ *717 Orleans St., French Quarter* ☎ *504/523–2222* ⊕ *www.bourbonorleans.com* ⇔ *218 rooms, 28 suites* ⦿ *No meals.*

$$$$

HOTEL

FAMILY

Hilton New Orleans Riverside. The superb river views are hard to beat at this sprawling multilevel Hilton complex sitting right on the Mississippi. **Pros:** well-maintained facilities; hotel runs like a well-oiled machine; great security. **Cons:** the city's biggest hotel; typical chain service and surroundings; groups can overwhelm lobby. $ *Rooms from: $279* ✉ *2 Poydras St., CBD* ☎ *504/561–0500, 800/445–8667* ⊕ *www3.hilton. com/en/hotels/louisiana/hilton-new-orleans-riverside-MSYNHHH/ index.html* ⇔ *1,600 rooms, 60 suites* ⦿ *No meals.*

$$$

HOTEL

New Orleans Marriott Hotel. This centrally located skyscraper Marriott boasts fabulous views of the Quarter, the CBD, and the river. **Pros:** excellent chef-driven restaurant; good location; stunning city and river views. **Cons:** typical chain hotel; inconsistent service; lacks charm; daily charge for Wi-Fi and phone calls. $ *Rooms from: $249* ✉ *555*

Canal St., French Quarter ☎ *504/581–1000, 800/228–9290* ⊕ *www. neworleansmarriott.com* 🛏 *1,274 rooms, 55 suites* ⦿ *No meals.*

NEW YORK, NEW YORK

A few cruise lines now base Caribbean-bound ships in New York City year-round; other ships do seasonal cruises to New England and Bermuda or trans-Atlantic crossings. If you're coming to the city from outside the immediate area, you can easily arrive the day before and do a bit of sightseeing and perhaps take in a Broadway show. The cruise port in Manhattan is fairly close to Times Square and Midtown hotels and theaters. But the New York City region now has three major cruise ports. You can also leave from Cape Liberty Terminal in Bayonne, New Jersey, on both Celebrity and Royal Caribbean ships. There's also a cruise terminal in Red Hook, Brooklyn, and this terminal serves Princess ships as well as Cunard's *Queen Mary 2*.

ESSENTIALS

HOURS

They say that New York never sleeps, and that's particularly true around Times Square, where some stores are open until 11 pm or later even during the week. But most stores outside of the immediate Times Square area are open from 9 or 10 until 6 or 7. Many museums close on Monday.

VISITOR INFORMATION

Contacts NYC & Company Convention & Visitors Bureau ✉ *Midtown Information Center, 810 7th Ave., between W. 52nd and W. 53rd sts., Midtown West* ☎ *212/484-1222* ⊕ *www.nycgo.com.* **Times Square Information Center** ✉ *1560 Broadway, between 46th and 47th sts., Midtown West* ☎ *212/730-7555* ⊕ *www.timessquarenyc.org* Ⓜ *1, 2, 3, 7, N, Q, R, S to Times Square–42nd St.*

THE CRUISE PORT

The New York Passenger Ship Terminal is on the far west side of Manhattan, five very long blocks from the Times Square area, between 48th and 52nd streets; the vehicle entrance is at 55th Street. Traffic can be backed up in the area on days that cruise ships arrive and depart, so allow yourself enough time to check in and go through security. There are no nearby subway stops, though city buses do cross Midtown at 50th and 42nd streets. If you don't have too much luggage, it is usually faster and more convenient to have a taxi drop you off at the intersection of 50th Street and the West Side Highway, directly across the street from the entrance to the lower level of the terminal; then you can walk right in and take the escalator or elevator up to the embarkation level.

Cape Liberty Terminal in Bayonne is off Route 440. From the New Jersey Turnpike, take Exit 14A, then follow the signs for 440 South, and make a left turn into the Cape Liberty Terminal area (on Port Terminal Boulevard). If you are coming from Long Island, you cross Staten Island, and after crossing the Bayonne Bridge take 440 North, making a right into the terminal area. If you are coming from Manhattan,

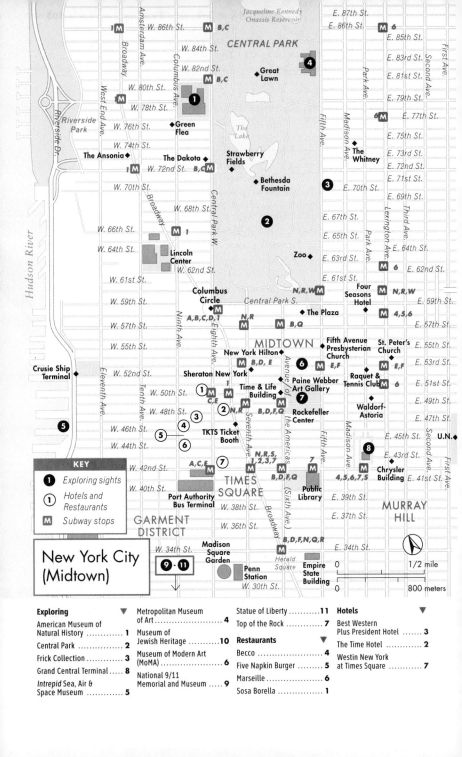

New York City (Midtown)

KEY

- ❶ Exploring sights
- ① Hotels and Restaurants
- Ⓜ Subway stops

you can also reach the terminal by public transit. Take the New Jersey Transit light rail from the PATH station in Hoboken; get off at the 34th Street stop in Bayonne, and from there you can call for a taxi to the terminal (about 2 miles [3 km] away); there may be a free shuttle bus on cruise sailing dates, but confirm that with your cruise line.

The Brooklyn cruise terminal at Pier 12 in Red Hook, which opened in April 2006, is not convenient to public transportation, so you should plan to take a taxi, drive, or take the bus transfers offered by the cruise lines (the cost for this is about $45 per person from either LaGuardia or JFK). There is a secure, 500-car outdoor parking lot on site. To reach the terminal from LaGuardia Airport, take I–278 W (the Brooklyn–Queens Expressway), Exit 26, Hamilton Avenue; the terminal entrance is actually off Browne Street. From JFK, take I–278 E (again, the Brooklyn–Queens Expressway), and then the same exit. If you arrive early, there's not much in the neighborhood, but there are a few neighborhood delis and restaurants about 15 minutes away on foot; the area is a safe place to walk around during daylight hours, though it's very industrial and unattractive. Red Hook is the home of ships from the Princess and Cunard cruise lines.

> ### NEW YORK BEST BETS
>
> ■ **An Art Museum.** Take your pick: the Met, MOMA, or the Frick, but museum-going is a true highlight of New York.
>
> ■ **A Broadway Show.** The theater experience in New York is better than almost anywhere else in the world.
>
> ■ **Central Park.** Even if you have time for just a stroll, come if the weather is good; it's about 30 minutes from the cruise terminal by foot.

Conatacts Cape Liberty Cruise Port ✉ *14 Port Terminal Blvd., Bayonne, New Jersey* ☎ *201/823–3737* ⊕ *www.cruiseliberty.com.* **New York Passenger Ship Terminal** ✉ *711 12th Ave., vehicle entry at 55th St., Midtown West* ☎ *212/246–5450* ⊕ *www.nycruise.com* ✉ *Pier 12, Bldg. 112, 72 Browne St., at Imlay St., Red Hook, Brooklyn* ☎ *718/246–2794.*

AIRPORT TRANSFERS

A cab to or from JFK to the passenger-ship terminal in **Manhattan** will cost $52 (a flat fare) plus toll and tip; expect to pay at least $35 on the meter if you are coming from LaGuardia and at least $60 or $70 (not including tolls of about $10 and the tip) from Newark in a car service (from Newark airport, it's usually more cost-effective to call for a car service to pick you up; regular taxis can be considerably more expensive; if possible, reserve a car in advance, and call when you pick up your bags to find out where to meet it).

From Newark Airport it's approximately $30 to **Cape Liberty,** $90 from JFK (plus tolls and tip, so count on at least $120 and be aware that taxis are not obligated to take this route from JFK), and $90 from LaGuardia (plus tolls and tip; count on paying more than $110). Royal Caribbean offers bus service from several Mid-Atlantic and Northeast cities on sailing dates, but confirm that with the cruise line.

6

If your cruise is leaving from **Red Hook,** the taxi fare will be much cheaper if you fly into either La Guardia (about $35) or JFK (about $45); you'll pay at least $80 for a car service from Newark Airport (not including tolls and tip, and perhaps more in a regular taxi). Cruise lines provide bus transfers from all three of the area's airports, but it may be cheaper to take a taxi if you are traveling with more than one other person. Note that all these taxi fares do not include tolls and tips. From Newark, the tolls to Brooklyn can be substantial, adding almost $20 to the fare.

PARKING

You can park at the New York Passenger Ship Terminal for a staggering $35 a day; the fee is payable in advance in cash or credit card (no Amex).

Parking at Cape Liberty Terminal in Bayonne is $19 per day, payable in cash, traveler's checks, and major credit cards.

Parking at Red Hook, Brooklyn, costs $23 for the first 24 hours and then $20 per day.

TOP ATTRACTIONS

There's no way to do justice to even the most popular tourist stops in New York. *Below is information about several top attractions.* If you have only a day in the city, choose one or two attractions and buy a Metro card to facilitate easy transfers between the subway and bus (put on as much money as you think you'll use in a day but no less than $5, which is good for two rides at $2.50 each plus $1 for the card, which may be shared). There's a moving series of panels about the World Trade Center at the so-called "Ground Zero" site across from the Millennium Hotel (take the 1 train to Cortlandt Street or the E to World Trade Center); there's another series of memorial panels underneath at the World Trade Center PATH station, which is accessible from the main, streetside memorial area. Times Square is approximately 20 minutes by foot from the cruise terminal; just walk straight out of the gate and east along 48th Street.

Fodor's Choice ★   **American Museum of Natural History.** The largest natural history museum in the world is also one of the most impressive sights in New York. Four city blocks make up its 45 exhibition halls, which hold more than 30 million artifacts and wonders from the land, the sea, and outer space. With all those wonders, you won't be able to see everything on a single visit, but you can easily hit the highlights in half a day. The **Rose Center for Earth and Space** should not be missed. *Journey to the Stars,* narrated by actress Whoopi Goldberg, launches viewers through space and time; you'll never see the night sky in the same way again.* ⊠ Central Park W at 79th St., Upper West Side* ☎ *212/769–5100* ⊕ *www.amnh.org* ☜ *$19 suggested donation, includes admission to Rose Center for Earth and Space* ☉ *Daily 10–5:45* Ⓜ *B, C to 81st St.–Museum of Natural History.*

FAMILY
Fodor's Choice ★   **Central Park.** Central Park's creators had a simple goal: design a place where city dwellers can go to forget the city. And even though New York eventually grew far taller than the trees planted to hide it, this goal

never falters. A combination escape hatch and exercise yard, Central Park is an urbanized Eden that offers residents and visitors alike a bite of the apple. And indeed, without the Central Park's 843 acres of meandering paths, tranquil lakes, ponds, and open meadows, New Yorkers (especially Manhattanites) might be a lot less sane. The busy southern section of Central Park, from 59th to 72nd Street, is where most visitors get their first impression. But no matter how many people congregate around here, you can always find a spot to picnic, ponder, or just take in the greenery, especially on a sunny day. Playgrounds, lawns, jogging and biking paths, and striking buildings populate the midsection of the park, from 72nd Street to the Reservoir. You can soak up the sun, have a picnic, have your photo taken at Bethesda Fountain, visit the penguins at the Central Park Zoo, or join the runners huffing counterclockwise on the dirt track that surrounds the reservoir. 🕾 *212/794–6564 Dairy visitor center, 646/310–6600 Central Park Conservancy ⊕ www. centralparknyc.org* Ⓜ *1, A, B, C, D to 59th St.–Columbus Circle; N, Q, R to 5th Ave.–59th St.*

Fodor's Choice
★ **Frick Collection.** Henry Clay Frick made his fortune amid the soot and smoke of Pittsburgh, where he was a coke (a coal fuel derivative) and steel baron, but this lovely museum, once Frick's private New York residence, is decidedly removed from soot. With an exceptional collection of works from the Renaissance through the late 19th century that includes Édouard Manet's *The Bullfight* (1864), a Chinard portrait bust (1809), three Vermeers, three Rembrandts, works by El Greco, Goya, van Dyck, Hogarth, Degas, and Turner, as well as sculpture, decorative arts, and 18th century French furniture, everything here is a highlight. The Portico Gallery, an enclosed portico along the building's 5th Avenue garden, houses the museum's growing collection of sculpture. An audio guide, available in several languages, is included with admission, as are the year-round temporary exhibits. The tranquil indoor garden court is a magical spot for a rest. Children under 10 are not admitted, and those age 10–16 with adult only. ⊠ *1 E. 70th St., at 5th Ave., Upper East Side* 🕾 *212/288–0700 ⊕ www.frick.org* ⊠ *$18* ☉ *Tues.–Sat. 10–6, Sun. 11–5* Ⓜ *6 to 68th St.–Hunter College.*

Fodor's Choice
★ **Grand Central Terminal.** Grand Central is not only the world's largest (76 acres) and the nation's busiest (nearly 700,000 commuters and subway riders use it daily) railway station, but also one of the world's most magnificent, majestic public spaces. Past the glimmering chandeliers of the waiting room is the jaw-dropping **main concourse**, 200 feet long, 120 feet wide, and 120 feet (roughly 12 stories) high, modeled after an ancient Roman public bath. In spite of it being completely cavernous, Grand Central manages to evoke a certain sense of warmth rarely found in buildings its size. Overhead, a twinkling fiber-optic map of the constellations covers the robin's egg–blue ceiling. The **Municipal Art Society** (*212/935–3960 ⊕ www.mas.org/tours*) leads an official daily walking tour to explore the 100-year-old terminal's architecture, history, and hidden secrets. Tours begin in the main concourse at 12:30 and last for 75 minutes. Tickets ($20) can be purchased in advance online or from the ticket booth in the main concourse. ⊠ *Main entrance,*

6

E. 42nd St. at Park Ave., Midtown East ☎*212/935–3960* ⊕ *www. grandcentralterminal.com* Ⓜ *4, 5, 6, 7, S to Grand Central–42nd St..*

FAMILY **Intrepid Sea, Air & Space Museum.** The centerpiece of the *Intrepid* Sea, Air & Space Museum complex is the 900-foot *Intrepid* aircraft carrier, Manhattan's only floating museum, which is next to the main cruise terminal. The museum has a renovated welcome center and a reinforced home for the space shuttle *Enterprise,* NASA's first prototype orbiter, which joined the Intrepid in July 2012. You can skip the worst of the lines by buying tickets online. ⊠ *Pier 86, 46th St. and 12th Ave., Midtown West* ☎ *212/245–0072, 877/957–7447* ⊕ *www.intrepidmuseum. org* ⊠ *$24* ☉ *Apr.–Oct., weekdays 10–5, weekends 10–6; Nov.–Mar., Tues.–Sun. 10–5; last admission 1 hr before closing* Ⓜ *A, C, E to 42nd St.–Port Authority Bus Terminal; M42 bus to pier.*

Fodor'sChoice **The Metropolitan Museum of Art.** If Manhattan held no other museum
★ than the colossal Metropolitan Museum of Art, you could still occupy yourself for days roaming its labyrinthine corridors. The Metropolitan Museum has more than 2 million works of art representing 5,000 years of history, so it's a good idea to plan ahead; looking at everything here could take a week. Before you begin exploring the museum, check the museum's floor plan, available at all entrances, for location of the major wings and collections. Pick up the "Today's Events" flier at the desk where you buy your ticket. The museum offers gallery talks on a range of subjects; taking a tour with a staff curator can show you some of the collection's hidden secrets. In late 2012, the Met commenced its two-year, $60 million renovation of the museum's plaza. The staircase and museum entrances will remain open while the plaza is being upgraded with public seating, a fountain, new lighting, landscaping, and improved museum access. ⊠ *1000 5th Ave., at 82nd St., Upper East Side* ☎ *212/535–7710* ⊕ *www.metmuseum.org* ⊠ *$25 suggested donation; $7 for audio guide* ☉ *Sun.–Thurs. 10–5:30, Fri.–Sat. 10–9* Ⓜ *4, 5, 6 to 86th St.*

Museum of Jewish Heritage—A Living Memorial to the Holocaust. In a granite 85-foot hexagon at the southern end of Battery Park City, this museum pays tribute to the 6 million Jews who perished in the Holocaust. Architects Kevin Roche and John Dinkeloo built the museum in the shape of a Star of David, with three floors of exhibits demonstrating the dynamism of 20th-century Jewish culture. Visitors enter through a gallery that provides a context for the early-20th-century artifacts on the first floor: an elaborate screen hand-painted for the fall harvest festival of Sukkoth, wedding invitations, and tools used by Jewish tradesmen. Original documentary films play throughout the museum. The second floor details the rise of Nazism and anti-Semitism, and the ravages of the Holocaust. A gallery covers the doomed voyage of the SS *St. Louis,* a ship of German Jewish refugees that crossed the Atlantic twice in 1939 in search of a safe haven. Signs of hope are also on display, including a trumpet that Louis Bannet (the "Dutch Louis Armstrong") played for three years in the Auschwitz-Birkenau inmate orchestra. The third floor covers postwar Jewish life. New exhibits added in early 2013 explore American Jews who tried to rescue European Jews leading up to and during the Holocaust, as well as the rich Jewish history of Oswiecim, the town the Germans called Auschwitz. The museum's east wing has a theater, a memorial garden, a library, more galleries, and a café. An audio guide, with narration by Meryl Streep and Itzhak Perlman, is available at the admissions desk for $5. ☒ *36 Battery Pl., Battery Park City, Financial District* ☎ *646/437–4202* ⊕ *www.mjhnyc.org* ✉ *$12, free Wed. 4–8* ☉ *Thurs. and Sun.–Tues. 10–5:45, Wed. 10–8, Fri. and eve of Jewish holidays 10–3* Ⓜ *4, 5 to Bowling Green.*

Fodor's Choice
★

The Museum of Modern Art (MoMA). Art enthusiasts and novices alike are often awestruck by the masterpieces before them here, including Monet's *Water Lilies,* Picasso's *Les Demoiselles d'Avignon,* and van Gogh's *Starry Night.* In 2004, the museum's $425 million face-lift by Yoshio Taniguchi increased exhibition space by nearly 50%, including space to accommodate large-scale contemporary installations. The museum continues to collect: most recently it obtained important works by Willem de Kooning, Valie Export, Christian Marclay, David Wojnarowicz, and Kara Walker. One of the top research facilities in modern and contemporary art is housed inside the museum's eight-story Education and Research building. Tickets are available online at a reduced price. Free Wi-Fi service within the museum allows you to listen to audio tours as you wander through the museum (log on to ⊕ *www.moma.org/wifi* with your smartphone). ☒ *11 W. 53rd St., between 5th and 6th aves., Midtown West* ☎ *212/708–9400* ⊕ *www.moma.org* ✉ *$25* ☉ *Sat.–Thurs. 10:30–5:30, Fri. 10:30–8.* Ⓜ *E, M to 5th Ave./53rd St.; B, D, F, M to 47th–50th Sts./Rockefeller Center.*

National 9/11 Memorial and Museum. Finished just in time for the 10th anniversary of 9/11, this somber work, designed by Michael Arad and Peter Walker, reflects none of the setbacks and complications to the building process that have arisen in the years since the tragedy. Central to the memorial and museum are recessed, 30-foot waterfalls that sit on the footprint where the Twin Towers once stood. Every minute, some 60,000 gallons of water cascades down the sides and then down into smaller square holes in the center of the pools. The pools are each nearly an acre in size, and they are said to be the largest manmade waterfalls in North America. There's also a single Callery pear tree in the plaza that is known as the "survivor tree," which was revived and replanted here after being damaged during the 9/11 attacks. Until the construction going on throughout the rest of the World Trade Center site is finished, a visit to the memorial requires dealing with strict security, including a trip through airport-like scanners. No large bags are allowed; there's no bag storage, and no public restrooms, either. ■ TIP➔ **It's best to book a free, timed ticket online before your visit, but at low-traffic times stand-by tickets may also be available, both at the site and from the Preview Site (90 Vesey Street) and the Visitor Center (90 West Street).** ☒ *Entry at northeast corner of Albany and Greenwich sts., Financial District* ☎ *212/266–5211 for reservation help* ⊕ *www.911memorial.org* ✉ *Free (with timed ticket obtained in advance)* ☉ *Memorial: early Mar.–early Oct., daily 10–8; early Oct.–early Mar., daily 10–6 (daily 10–8 for wks around Thanksgiving and Christmas); last entry 1 hr before closing. Visitor center: early Mar.–early Oct., daily 10–8:30; early Oct.–early Mar., daily 10–7 (daily 10–8:30 for wks around Thanksgiving and Christmas)*

6

Ⓜ *1 to Rector St.; R to Rector St.; 2, 3, 4, 5, A, C, J, Z to Fulton St.; E to World Trade Center*

The Statue of Liberty. For millions of immigrants, the first glimpse of America was the Statue of Liberty, growing from a vaguely defined figure on the horizon into a towering, stately colossus. Visitors approaching Liberty Island on the ferry from Battery Park may experience a similar sense of wonder as they approach. There is no admission fee for either the Statue of Liberty or Ellis Island, but the ferry ride (which goes round trip from Battery Park to Liberty Island to Ellis Island) has a fee. Ferries leave from Battery Park every 30 to 40 minutes depending on the time of year (buy your tickets online at ⊕ *www.statuecruises. com*). There are often long lines, so arrive early, especially if you have a reserved-time ticket. There is a pleasant indoor/outdoor café on Liberty Island. ⊠ *Liberty Island, Ste. 210, New York Harbor* ☎ *212/363–3200, 877/523–9849 ticket reservations* ⊕ *www.statueofliberty.org* 🎟 *Free; ferry $13 round-trip (includes Ellis Island), $21 with audio guide, crown tickets $3* ⊙ *Daily 9:30–5; last ferry at 3:30, extended hrs in summer.*

Fodor's Choice
★

Top of the Rock. Rockefeller Center's multifloor observation deck, the Top of the Rock, on the 69th–70th floors of the building provides views that rival those from the Empire State Building—some would say they're even better because the views include the Empire State Building. Arriving just before sunset affords a view of the city that morphs before your eyes into a dazzling wash of colors, with a bird's-eye view of the tops of the Empire State Building, the Citicorp Building, and the Chrysler Building, and sweeping views northward to Central Park and south to the Statue of Liberty. Reserved-time ticketing eliminates long lines. Indoor exhibits include films of Rockefeller Center's history and a model of the building. Especially interesting is a Plexiglas screen on the floor with footage showing Rock Center construction workers dangling on beams high above the streets; the brave can even "walk" across a beam to get a sense of what it might have been like to erect this skyscraper. A Sun & Stars ticket ($38) allows you to see the city as the sun rises and sets in the same day. ⊠ *Entrance on 50th St., between 5th and 6th aves., 30 Rockefeller Plaza, Midtown West* ☎ *212/698–2000, 212/698–2000* ⊕ *www.topoftherocknyc.com* 🎟 *$25 adult; children under 6 not admitted* ⊙ *Daily 8–midnight; last elevator at 11 pm* Ⓜ *B, D, F, M to 47th–50th Sts./Rockefeller Center.*

SHOPPING

You can find almost any major store from virtually any designer or chain in Manhattan. High-end designers tend to be along **Madison Avenue,** between 55th and 86th streets. Some are along **57th Street,** between Madison and 7th avenues. **Fifth Avenue,** starting at Saks Fifth Avenue (at 50th Street) and going up to 59th Street, is a hodgepodge of high-end stores and more accessible options, including the high-end department store Bergdorf-Goodman, at 58th Street. More interesting and individual stores can be found in **SoHo** (between Houston and Canal, West Broadway and Lafayette), and the **East Village** (between 14th Street and

Houston, Broadway and Avenue A). **Chinatown** is chock-full of designer knockoffs, crowded streets, and dim sum palaces; though frenetic during the day, it's a fun stop. The newest group of stores in Manhattan is at the **Time-Warner Center,** at Columbus Circle (at 8th Avenue and 59th Street); the high-rise mall has upscale stores and some of the city's best-reviewed and most expensive new restaurants.

> **CAUTION**
>
> Store any irreplaceable valuables in the ship purser's safe rather than the one in your cabin. Some insurance policies will not cover the loss of items left in your cabin.

BROADWAY SHOWS

Scoring tickets to Broadway shows is fairly easy except for the very top draws. For the most part, the top ticket price for Broadway musicals is now around $145; the best seats for Broadway plays can run as high as $130.

Telecharge ☎ *212/239–6200* ⊕ *www.telecharge.com.*

Ticketmaster ☎ *212/307–4100* ⊕ *www.ticketmaster.com.*

TKTS ✉ *Duffy Sq., W. 47th St. and Broadway, Times Square, Midtown West* ⊕ *www.tdf.org* Ⓜ *1, 2, 3, 7, N, Q, R, S, to Times Sq.–42nd St.; N, Q, R, to 49th St.; 1 to 50th St..*

WHERE TO EAT

The restaurants we recommend below are all in Midtown West, near Broadway theaters and hotels. Make reservations at all but the most casual places or face a numbing wait.

$$
ITALIAN
✕ **Becco.** An ingenious concept makes Becco a prime Restaurant Row choice for time-constrained theatergoers. There are two pricing scenarios: one includes an all-you-can-eat selection of antipasti and three pastas served hot out of pans that waiters circulate around the dining room; the other adds a generous entrée to the mix. The pasta selection changes daily, but often includes gnocchi, fresh ravioli, and fettuccine in a cream sauce. The entrées include braised veal shank, grilled double-cut pork chop, and rack of lamb, among other selections. $ *Average main: $23* ✉ *355 W. 46th St., between 8th and 9th aves., Midtown West* ☎ *212/397–7597* ⊕ *www.becco-nyc.com* Ⓜ *A, C, E to 42nd St.–Port Authority Bus Terminal*

$
AMERICAN
✕ **Five Napkin Burger.** This perennially packed Hell's Kitchen burger joint/brasserie has been a magnet for burger lovers since day one. Bottles of Maker's Mark line the sleek, alluringly lighted bar in the back, a collection of antique butcher's scales hangs on a tile wall near the kitchen, and meat hooks dangle from the ceiling between the light fixtures. Though there are many menu distractions—deep-fried pickles, warm artichoke dip, to name a few—the main attractions are the juicy burgers, like the original 10-ounce chuck with a tangle of onions, Gruyère cheese, and rosemary aioli. There's a patty variety for everyone, including a ground lamb *kofta* and an onion ring–topped ahi tuna

burger. For dessert, have an überthick black-and-white malted milk-shake. $ *Average main: $16* ✉ *630 9th Ave., at 45th St., Midtown West* ☎ *212/757–2277* ⊕ *www.5napkinburger.com* Ⓜ *A, C, E to 42nd St.–Port Authority Bus Terminal.*

$$ ✕ **Marseille.** With great food and a convenient location near several

MEDITERRANEAN Broadway theaters, Marseille is perpetually packed. The Mediterranean creations are continually impressive, including the bouillabaisse, the signature dish of the region for which the restaurant is named—a mélange of mussels, shrimp, and white fish in a fragrant broth, topped with a garlicky crouton and served with rouille on the side. Leave room for the spongy beignets with chocolate and raspberry dipping sauces. $ *Average main: $22* ✉ *630 9th Ave., at 44th St., Midtown West* ☎ *212/333–2323* ⊕ *www.marseillenyc.com* ⌛ *Reservations essential* Ⓜ *A, C, E to 42nd St.–Port Authority Bus Terminal.*

$$ ✕ **Sosa Borella.** This is one of the Theater District's top spots for reliable

ITALIAN food at a reasonable cost. The bi-level, casual Argentinian-Italian eatery is an inviting and friendly space where diners choose from a wide range of options. The lunch menu features staples like warm sandwiches and entrée-size salads, whereas the dinner menu is slightly gussied up with meat, fish, and pasta dishes (the rich agnolotti with lamb Bolognese sauce, topped with a wedge of grilled pecorino cheese, is a must-try). The freshly baked bread served at the beginning of the meal with pesto dipping sauce is a nice touch as you wait for your meal. The service can be slow at times, so leave yourself plenty of time before the show. $ *Average main: $25* ✉ *832 8th Ave., between 50th and 51st sts., Midtown West* ☎ *212/262–8282* ⊕ *www.sosaborella.com* Ⓜ *C, E to 50th St.; 1 to 50th St.*

WHERE TO STAY

There are no real bargains in the Manhattan hotel world, and you'll find it difficult to get a decent room for under $250 during much of the year. However, occasional weekend deals can be found. All the hotels we recommend for cruise passengers are on the West Side, in relatively easy proximity to the cruise ship terminal.

For expanded reviews, facilities, and current deals, visit Fodors.com.

$ 🖼 **Best Western Plus President Hotel.** The President is the only politically

HOTEL themed hotel in the city, starting with the purple color scheme, a combination of Republican red and Democratic blue. **Pros:** sleek rooms for the price; convenient location; unique theme. **Cons:** cramped lobby; dark bathrooms; poor views. $ *Rooms from: $249* ✉ *234 W. 48th St., between 8th Ave. and Broadway, Times Square* ☎ *212/246–8800, 800/828–4667* ⊕ *www.bestwestern.com* ↩ *334 rooms* ⦿ *No meals* Ⓜ *C, E to 50th St.*

$ 🖼 **The Time Hotel.** One of the neighborhood's first boutique hotels, this

HOTEL spot half a block from the din of Times Square tempers trendiness with a touch of humor. **Pros:** acclaimed and popular Serafina restaurant downstairs; surprisingly quiet for Times Square location; good turndown service. **Cons:** decor makes the rooms a little dated; service is inconsistent; water pressure is lacking. $ *Rooms from: $275* ✉ *224 W. 49th*

St., between Broadway and 8th Ave., Midtown West ☏ *212/246–5252, 877/846–3692* ⊕ *www.thetimeny.com* ⇄ *164 rooms, 29 suites* ⦿ *No meals* Ⓜ *1 to 50th St.; C, E to 50th St.*

$$ 🏨 **Westin New York at Times Square.** This giant Midtown hotel has all
HOTEL the amenities and service you would expect from a reliable brand, at fairly reasonable prices, though without much style. **Pros:** central for Midtown attractions; big rooms; great gym. **Cons:** congested area near the Port Authority; small bathroom sinks; some rooms need to be refreshed. Ⓢ *Rooms from: $319* ✉ *270 W. 43rd St., at 8th Ave., Midtown West* ☏ *212/201–2700, 866/837–4183* ⊕ *www.westinny. com* ⇄ *834 rooms, 29 suites* ⦿ *No meals* Ⓜ *A, C, E to 42nd St.–Port Authority Bus Terminal.*

PORT CANAVERAL, FLORIDA

Steve Master This once-bustling commercial fishing area is still home to a small shrimping fleet, charter boats, and party fishing boats, but its main business these days is as a cruise-ship port. Cocoa Beach itself isn't the spiffiest place around, but what *is* becoming quite clean and neat is the north end of the port, where the Carnival, Disney, and Royal Caribbean cruise lines set sail, as well as Sun Cruz and Sterling casino boats. Port Canaveral is now Florida's second-busiest cruise port. Because of Port Canaveral's proximity to Orlando theme parks (about an hour away), many cruisers combine a short cruise with a stay in the area. The port is also convenient to popular Space Coast attractions such as the Kennedy Space Center and United States Astronaut Hall of Fame in Titusville.

6

ESSENTIALS
HOURS
Most of the area's attractions are open every day.

VISITOR INFORMATION
Contact Space Coast Office of Tourism ✉ *430 Brevard Ave., Ste. 150, Cocoa* ☏ *877/572–3224, 321/433–4470* ⊕ *www.visitspacecoast.com.*

THE CRUISE PORT

Port Canaveral sees about 3.8 million passengers passing through its terminals annually, about equal to Miami.

The port has six cruise terminals and is home to ships from Carnival Cruise Lines, Disney Cruise Line, and Royal Caribbean International. Other cruise lines operate seasonally. The port serves as the embarkation point for three-, four-, and seven-day cruises to the Bahamas, Key West, Mexico, Jamaica, and the Virgin Islands.

In Brevard County, Port Canaveral is on State Road (S.R.) 528, also known as the Beeline Expressway, which runs straight to Orlando, which has the nearest airport. To drive to Port Canaveral from there, take the north exit out of the airport, staying to the right, to S.R. 528 (Beeline Expressway) East. Take S.R. 528 directly to Port Canaveral; it's about a 45-minute drive.

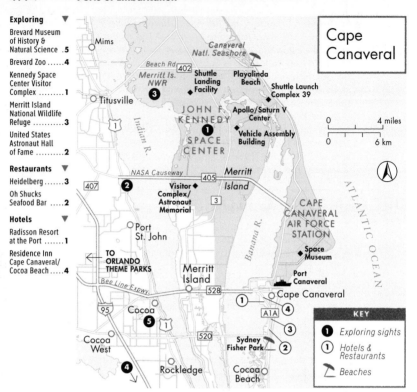

Port Contact Canaveral Port Authority ✉ *445 Challenger Rd., Ste. 301, Cape Canaveral* ☎ *321/783–7831, 888/767–8226* ⊕ *www.portcanaveral.org.*

AIRPORT TRANSFERS

If you are flying into the area, the Orlando airport is 45 minutes away from the docks. If you have not arranged airport transfers with your cruise line, you will need to make your own arrangements. Taxis are expensive, but many companies offer shared minivan and bus shuttles to Port Canaveral. They are all listed on the Canaveral Port Authority website. Some shuttles charge for the entire van, which is a good deal for groups but not for individuals or couples; some will charge a per-person rate. Expect to pay at least $38 per person round-trip, and check the Internet for coupons and special offers.

You will need to make a reservation in advance regardless of which service you use. Some cruisers who want to do some exploring before the cruise rent a car at the airport and drop it off at the port, which houses several major rental-car agencies.

Contacts AAA Cruise Line Connection ☎ *407/908–5566* ⊕ *www. aaasuperride.com.* **Busy Traveler Transport Service** ☎ *321/453–5278, 800/496–7433* ⊕ *www.abusytraveler.com.*

PARKING

Outdoor gated lots and a six-story parking garage are near the terminals and cost $120 per week for vehicles up to 20 feet in length and $208 per week for vehicles over 20 feet, which must be paid in advance, either in cash, traveler's checks, or by major credit card (MasterCard and Visa only).

EXPLORING THE CAPE CANAVERAL AREA

With the Kennedy Space Center 20 minutes away, there is plenty to do in and around Cape Canaveral, though many folks opt to travel the extra hour into Orlando to visit the popular theme parks.

FAMILY **Brevard Museum of History & Natural Science.** This is the place to come to see what the lay of the local land looked like in other eras. Hands-on activities draw children, who especially migrate toward the Imagination Center, where they can act out history or reenact a space shuttle flight. Not to be missed is the Windover Archaeological Exhibit of 7,000-year-old artifacts indigenous to the region. In 1984, a shallow pond revealed the burial ground of more than 200 American Indians who lived in the area about 7,000 years ago. Preserved in the muck were bones and, to the archeologists' surprise, the brains of these ancient people. Nature lovers appreciate the museum's butterfly garden and the nature center with 22 acres of trails encompassing three distinct ecosystems—sand pine hills, lake lands, and marshlands. ✉ *2201 Michigan Ave., Cocoa* ☎ *321/632–1830* ⊕ *www. brevardmuseum.org* ▱ *$6* ☉ *Thurs.–Sat. 10–4.*

FAMILY **Brevard Zoo.** At the only Association of Zoo and Aquariums–accredited Fodor'sChoice zoo built by a community, you can stroll along the shaded boardwalks ★ and get a close-up look at rhinos, giraffes, cheetahs, alligators, crocodiles, giant anteaters, marmosets, jaguars, eagles, river otters, kangaroos, exotic birds, and kookaburras. Alligator, crocodile, and river-otter feedings are held on alternate afternoons—and no, the alligators don't dine on the otters. Stop by Paws-On, an interactive learning playground with a petting zoo, wildlife detective training academy, and the Indian River Play Lagoon. Hand-feed a giraffe in Expedition Africa or a lorikeet in the Australian Free Flight Aviary, and step up to the Wetlands Outpost, an elevated pavilion that's a gateway to 22 acres of wetlands through which you can paddle kayaks and keep an eye open for the 4,000 species of wildlife that live in these waters and woods. Adventurers seeking a chimp's-eye view can zipline through the zoo on Treetop Trek. ✉ *8225 N. Wickham Rd., Melbourne* ☎ *321/254–9453* ⊕ *www.*

PORT CANAVERAL BEST BETS

■ **Kennedy Space Center.** Kennedy Space Center in Titusville is the region's biggest attraction.

■ **Merritt Island.** If you want to get out and commune with nature, this is the place, especially for bird-watchers.

■ **Orlando Theme Parks.** With Orlando just an hour away, many cruisers combine a theme-park visit with their cruise.

6

brevardzoo.org 🖾 *$15, $19.50 including train and giraffe and lorikeet food; Treetop Trek $22–$54* ☉ *Daily 9:30–5, last admission 4:15.*

FAMILY
Fodor's Choice
★

Kennedy Space Center Visitor Complex. This must-see attraction, just southeast of Titusville, is one of Central Florida's most popular sights. Located on a 140,000-acre island 45 minutes outside Orlando, Kennedy Space Center is NASA's launch headquarters. The Visitor Complex gives guests a unique opportunity to learn about—and experience—the past, present, and future of America's space program.

Interactive programs make for the best experiences here, but if you want a low-key overview of the facility (and if the weather is foul) take the bus tour, included with admission. Buses depart every 15 minutes, and you can get on and off any bus whenever you like. Stops include the Launch Complex 39 Observation Gantry, which has an unparalleled view of the launchpads and Apollo/Saturn V Center, with a don't-miss presentation at the Firing Room Theater, where the launch of America's first lunar mission, 1968's *Apollo VIII,* is re-created with a ground-shaking, window-rattling liftoff. The Apollo/Saturn V center also features one of three remaining Saturn V moon rockets. Other exhibits near the center's entrance include the Early Space Exploration display, which highlights the rudimentary yet influential *Mercury* and *Gemini* space programs. The most moving exhibit is the Astronaut Memorial. The 70,400-pound black-granite tribute to astronauts who lost their lives in the name of space exploration stands 42½ feet high by 50 feet wide.

More befitting Walt Disney World or Universal Studios (complete with the health warnings), the Shuttle Launch Experience is the center's most spectacular attraction. Designed by a team of astronauts, NASA experts, and renowned attraction engineers, the 44,000-square-foot structure uses a sophisticated motion-based platform, special-effects seats, and high-fidelity visual and audio components to simulate the sensations experienced in an actual space-shuttle launch, including MaxQ, Solid Rocker Booster separation, main engine cutoff, and External Tank separation. The journey culminates with a breathtaking view of Earth from space. The only back-to-back twin IMAX theater in the world is in the complex, too. 🖾 *Rte. 405, Kennedy Space Center, Titusville* 🖾 *877/313–2610* ⊕ *www.kennedyspacecenter.com* 🖾 *$50, includes bus tour, IMAX space movies, Visitor Complex shows and exhibits, and Astronaut Hall of Fame* ☉ *Daily 9–5; last regular tour 2½ hrs before closing. Call ahead if visiting on a launch day.*

Fodor's Choice
★

Merritt Island National Wildlife Refuge. Owned by the National Aeronautics and Space Administration (NASA), this 140,000-acre refuge, which adjoins the Canaveral National Seashore, acts as a buffer around Kennedy Space Center while protecting 1,000 species of plants and 500 species of wildlife, including 15 considered federally threatened or endangered. It's an immense area dotted by brackish estuaries and marshes and patches of land consisting of coastal dunes, scrub oaks, pine forests and flatwoods, and palm and oak hammocks. You can borrow field guides and binoculars at the visitor center (5 miles east of U.S. 1 in Titusville on State Road 402) to track down falcons, ospreys, eagles, turkeys, doves, cuckoos, owls, and woodpeckers, as well as log-gerhead turtles, alligators, and otters. A 20-minute video about refuge wildlife and accessibility—only 10,000 acres are developed—can help orient you.

You might take a self-guided tour along the 7-mile Black Point Wildlife Drive. On the Oak Hammock Foot Trail you can see wintering migratory waterfowl and learn about the plants of a hammock community. If you exit the north end of the refuge, look for the Manatee Observation Area just north of the Haulover Canal (maps are at the visitor center). They usually show up in spring and fall. There are also fishing camps, fishing boat ramps, and six hiking trails scattered throughout the area. Most of the refuge is closed 24 hours prior to a launch. ⊠ *Rte. 402, across Titusville Causeway, Titusville* ☎ *321/861–0667, 321/861–0669 visitor center* ⊕ *www.fws.gov/merrittisland* ⊠ *Free* ☽ *Daily sunrise-sunset; visitor center weekdays 8–4:30, weekends 9–5.*

United States Astronaut Hall of Fame. The original *Mercury 7* team and the later *Gemini, Apollo, Skylab,* and shuttle astronauts contributed to make the hall of fame the world's premium archive of astronauts' personal stories. Authentic memorabilia and equipment from their collections tell the story of human space exploration. You can watch videotapes of historic moments in the space program and see one-of-a-kind items like Wally Schirra's relatively archaic *Sigma 7* Mercury space capsule, Gus Grissom's space suit (colored silver only because NASA thought silver looked more "spacey"), and a flag that made it to the moon. The exhibit First on the Moon focuses on crew selection for *Apollo 11* and the Soviet Union's role in the space race. Don't miss Simulation Station, a hands-on discovery center with interactive exhibits that help you learn about space travel. One of the more challenging activities is a space-shuttle simulator that lets you try your hand at landing the craft—and afterward replays a side view of your rolling and pitching descent. ⊠ *6225 Vectorspace Blvd., Titusville* ☎ *877/313–2610* ⊕ *www.kennedyspacecenter.com* ⊠ *$27 Hall of Fame only; included in KSC Visitor Complex admission ($50)* ☽ *Opens daily at noon, closing times vary by season (call for details).*

ORLANDO THEME PARKS

FAMILY **SeaWorld Orlando.** In the world's largest marine adventure park, every attraction is devoted to demonstrating the ways that humans can protect the mammals, birds, fish, and reptiles that live in the ocean and its tributaries. The presentations are gentle reminders of our responsibility to safeguard the environment, and you'll find that SeaWorld's use of humor plays a major role in this education. The park is small enough that, armed with a map that lists show times, you can plan a chronological approach that flows easily from one attraction to the next. Near the intersection of I–4 and the Beeline Expressway; take I–4 to Exit 71 or 72 and follow signs. ⊠ *7007 Sea Harbor Dr., International Drive Area, Orlando* ☎ *888/800–5447* ⊕ *www.seaworld.com* ⊠ *$81.99 for a 1-day ticket ($10 cheaper if bought online in advance)* ☽ *Daily 9–6* *or 7, until as late as 10 summer and holidays; educational programs daily, some beginning as early as 6:30 am.*

FAMILY **Universal Orlando.** The resort consists of **Universal Studios** (the original movie theme park), **Islands of Adventure** (the second theme park, which includes The Wizarding World of Harry Potter), and **CityWalk** (the dining-shopping-nightclub complex). Although it's bordered by residential neighborhoods and thickly trafficked International Drive, Universal Orlando is surprisingly expansive yet intimate and accessible, with two massive parking complexes, easy walks to all attractions, and a motor launch that cruises to the hotels. Universal Orlando emphasizes "two parks, two days, one great adventure," but you may find the presentation, creativity, and cutting-edge technology bring you back for more. ⊠ *1000 Universal Studios Plaza, Orlando* ☎ *407/363–8000* ⊕ *www. universalorlando.com* 🖾 *1-day, 1-park ticket $88* ⊘ *Daily 9–7, but hrs vary seasonally; CityWalk restaurants and bars have individual hrs.*

FAMILY **Walt Disney World.** Walt Disney World is a huge complex of theme parks and attractions, each of which is worth a visit. Parks include the **Magic Kingdom,** a family favorite and the original here; **Epcot,** Disney's international, educational park; **Disney Hollywood Studios,** a movie-oriented theme park; and **Disney's Animal Kingdom,** which is much more than a zoo. Beyond these, there are water parks, elaborate minigolf courses, a sports center, resorts, restaurants, and nightlife. If you have only one day, you'll have to concentrate on a single park; Disney–MGM Studios or Animal Kingdom are easiest to do in a day, but arrive early and expect to stay until park closing, which might be as early as 5 pm for Animal Kingdom or as late as 11 pm during busy seasons at the Magic Kingdom. The most direct route to the Disney Parks from Port Canaveral is S.R. 528 (the Beeline Expressway) to I–4; when you get through Orlando, follow the signs to Disney and expect traffic. ⊠ *Lake Buena Vista* ☎ *407/824–4321* ⊕ *disneyworld.disney. go.com* 🖾 *1-day, 1-park pass $99* ⊘ *Most parks open by 9 am; closing hrs vary, but usually 5 pm for Animal Kingdom and 6–11 pm for other parks, depending on season.*

BEACHES

Playalinda Beach. The southern access for the Canaveral National Seashore, remote Playalinda Beach has pristine sands and is the longest stretch of undeveloped coast on Florida's Atlantic seaboard. Hundreds of giant sea turtles come ashore here from May through August to lay their eggs. Fourteen parking lots anchor the beach at 1-mile intervals. From Interstate 95, take Exit 249 and head east. Bring bug repellent in case of horseflies, and note that you may see some unauthorized clothing-optional activity. **Amenities:** lifeguards (seasonal); parking (fee); toilets. **Best for:** solitude; swimming; walking. ⊠ *Northern end of Rte. 402 (Beach Rd.), Titusville* ☎ *321/867–4077* ⊕ *www.nps.gov/ cana* 🖾 *$5 per vehicle for national seashore.*

SHOPPING

Cocoa Beach Surf Company. The world's largest surf complex has three floors of boards, apparel, sunglasses, and anything else a surfer, wannabe-surfer, or souvenir-seeker could need. Also on-site are a 5,600-gallon fish and shark tank and the Shark Pit Bar & Grill. Here you can also rent surfboards, bodyboards, and wet suits, as well as umbrellas, chairs, and bikes. And

> **WRITE EASY**
>
> Preaddress a page of stick-on labels before you leave home; use them for postcards to the folks back home and you will not have to carry along a bulky address book.

staffers teach grommets (dudes) and gidgets (chicks)—from kids to seniors—how to surf. There are group, semi-private, and private lessons available in one-, two-, and three-hour sessions. Prices range from $40 (for a one-hour group lesson) to $120 (three-hour private). All gear is provided. ⊠ *4001 N. Atlantic Ave., Cocoa Beach* ☎ *321/799–9930.*

Fodor'sChoice ★ **Ron Jon Surf Shop.** It's impossible to miss Ron Jon: it takes up nearly two blocks along Route A1A and has a giant surfboard and an art-deco facade painted orange, blue, yellow, and turquoise. What started in 1963 as a small T-shirt and bathing-suit shop has evolved into a 52,000-square-foot superstore that's open every day 'round the clock. The shop rents water-sports gear as well as chairs and umbrellas, and it sells every kind of beachwear, surf wax, plus the requisite T-shirts and flip-flops. ⊠ *4151 N. Atlantic Ave., Rte. A1A, Cocoa Beach* ☎ *321/799–8820* ⊕ *www.ronjonsurfshop.com.*

WHERE TO EAT

The Cove at Port Canaveral has several restaurants if you are looking for a place to eat right at the port.

$$$
GERMAN

✕ **Heidelberg.** As the name suggests, the cuisine here is definitely German, from the sauerbraten served with potato dumplings and red cabbage to the beef Stroganoff and spaetzle to the classically prepared Wiener schnitzel. All the soups and desserts are homemade; try the Viennese-style apple strudel and the rum-zapped almond-cream tortes. Elegant interior touches include crisp linens and fresh flowers. There's live music Wednesday through Saturday evenings. You can also dine inside the jazz club, Heidi's, next door. ⓢ *Average main: $27* ⊠ *7 N. Orlando Ave., opposite City Hall, Cocoa Beach* ☎ *321/783–6806* ⊕ *www.heidisjazzclub.com* ☉ *Closed Mon. and Tues. No lunch.*

$
SEAFOOD

✕ **Oh Shucks Seafood Bar.** At the only open-air seafood bar on the beach, at the entrance of the Cocoa Beach Pier, the main item is oysters, served on the half shell. You can also grab a burger here, crab legs by the pound, or Oh Shucks's most popular item, coconut beer shrimp. Some diners complain that the prices don't jibe with the ultracasual atmosphere (e.g., plastic chairs), but they're also paying for the "ex-Pier-ience." During high season, there's live entertainment on Wednesday, Friday, Saturday, and Sunday. ⓢ *Average main: $12* ⊠ *401*

6

Meade Ave., Cocoa Beach Pier, Cocoa Beach ☎ *321/783–7549* ⊕ *www. cocoabeachpier.com.*

WHERE TO STAY

Many local hotels offer cruise packages that include one night's lodging, parking for the duration of your cruise, and transportation to the cruise port.

For expanded reviews, facilities, and current deals, visit Fodors.com.

EXTRA BATTERIES
Even if you don't think you'll need them, bring along extra camera batteries and change them before you think the old ones are dead.

$$ 🛏 **Radisson Resort at the Port.** For cruise-ship passengers who can't wait to get under way, this splashy resort, done up in pink and turquoise, already feels like the Caribbean. **Pros:** cruise-ship convenience; pool area; free shuttle. **Cons:** rooms around the pool can be noisy; loud air-conditioning in some rooms; no complimentary breakfast. $ *Rooms from: $120* ⊠ *8701 Astronaut Blvd., Cape Canaveral* ☎ *321/784–0000, 888/201–1718* ⊕ *www. radisson.com/capecanaveralfl* ⇆ *284 rooms, 72 suites* ⦿ *No meals.*

$$$ 🛏 **Residence Inn Cape Canaveral/Cocoa Beach.** Billing itself as the closest all-suites hotel to the Kennedy Space Center, this four-story Residence Inn, painted cheery yellow, is also convenient to other area attractions such as Port Canaveral, the Cocoa Beach Pier, the Brevard Zoo, and Cocoa Village, and is only an hour from the Magic Kingdom. **Pros:** helpful staff; free breakfast buffet; pet-friendly. **Cons:** less than picturesque views; street noise in some rooms. $ *Rooms from: $179* ⊠ *8959 Astronaut Blvd., Cape Canaveral* ☎ *321/323–1100, 800/331–3131* ⊕ *www.marriott.com* ⇆ *150 suites* ⦿ *Breakfast.*

SAN JUAN, PUERTO RICO

Heather
Rodino

In addition to being a major port of call, San Juan is also a common port of embarkation for cruises on Southern Caribbean itineraries.

⇨ *For information on dining, shopping, nightlife, and sightseeing see San Juan, Puerto Rico in Chapter 7.*

THE CRUISE PORT

Most cruise ships dock within a couple of blocks of Old San Juan; however, there is a second cruise pier across the bay, and if your ship docks there you'll need to take a taxi to get anywhere on the island. The Paseo de la Princesa, a tree-lined promenade beneath the city wall, is a nice place for a stroll—you can admire the local crafts and stop at the refreshment kiosks. Major sights in the Old San Juan area are mere blocks from the piers, but be aware that the streets are narrow and steeply inclined in places.

AIRPORT TRANSFERS

If you are embarking or disembarking in San Juan, the ride to or from the Luis Muñoz Marín International Airport, east of downtown San Juan, to the docks in Old San Juan takes about 20 minutes, depending on traffic. The white "Taxi Turistico" cabs, marked by a logo on the door, have a fixed rate of $19 to and from the cruise-ship piers; there is a $1 charge for each piece of luggage. Other taxi companies charge by the mile, which can cost a little more. Be sure the driver starts the meter, or agree on a fare beforehand.

Visitor Information Puerto Rico Tourism Company ⊠ *Rafael Hernández Airport, Hwy. 2, Km 148.7, Aguadilla* ☎ *787/890–3315* ⊕ *www.seepuertorico.com.*

WHERE TO STAY

If you are planning to spend one night in San Juan before your cruise departs, you'll probably find it easier to stay in Old San Juan, where the cruise-ship terminals are. But if you want to spend a few extra days in the city, there are other possibilities near good beaches a bit farther out. We make some nightlife suggestions in the San Juan port of call section (⌫ *See San Juan in Chapter 7*).

For expanded reviews, facilities, and current deals, visit Fodors.com.

$$ 🏨 **The Gallery Inn.** Nothing like this rambling, eclectic inn exists anywhere else in San Juan—or Puerto Rico, for that matter. **Pros:** one-of-a-kind lodging; ocean views; wonderful classical music concerts. **Cons:** several narrow, winding staircases; an uphill walk from rest of Old San Juan; sometimes raucous pet macaws and cockatoos. ⑤ *Rooms from: $160* ⊠ *204–206 Calle Norzagaray, Old San Juan* ☎ *787/722–1808* ⊕ *www.thegalleryinn.com* ➳ *20 rooms, 5 suites* ⧀ *Breakfast.*

B&B/INN

$$$ 🏨 **Hotel El Convento.** There's no longer anything austere about this 350-year-old former convent. **Pros:** lovely building; atmosphere to spare; plenty of nearby dining options. **Cons:** near some noisy bars; small pool and small bathrooms. ⑤ *Rooms from: $325* ⊠ *100 Calle Cristo, Old San Juan* ☎ *787/723–9020* ⊕ *www.elconvento.com* ➳ *53 rooms, 5 suites* ⧀ *No meals.*

HOTEL

Fodors Choice

★

$$ 🏨 **Sheraton Old San Juan Hotel & Casino.** This hotel's triangular shape subtly echoes the cruise ships docked nearby. **Pros:** harbor views; near many dining options; good array of room types. **Cons:** chain-hotel feel; noise from casino overwhelms lobby and restaurants; uphill walk to the rest of Old San Juan. ⑤ *Rooms from: $229* ⊠ *100 Calle Brumbaugh, Old San Juan* ☎ *787/721–5100, 866/376–7577* ⊕ *www.sheratonoldsanjuan. com* ➳ *200 rooms, 40 suites* ⧀ *No meals.*

HOTEL

TAMPA, FLORIDA

Kate
Bradshaw

Although glitzy Miami seems to hold the trendiness trump card and Orlando is the place your kids want to visit annually until they hit middle school, the Tampa Bay area has that elusive quality that many attribute to the "real Florida." The state's second-largest metro area is less fast-lane than its biggest (Miami), or even Orlando, but its strengths are just as varied, from broad cultural diversity to a sun-worshipping

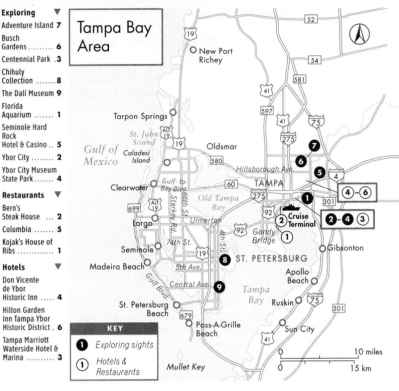

beach culture. Florida's third-busiest airport, a vibrant business community, world-class beaches, and superior hotels and resorts—many of them historic—make this an excellent place to spend a week or a lifetime. Several ships are based here year-round and seasonally, most doing Western Caribbean itineraries.

ESSENTIALS

HOURS

Some museums are closed on Monday.

VISITOR INFORMATION

Contacts Tampa Bay & Company ⊠ *401 E. Jackson St., Ste. 2100* ☎ *800/448–2672, 813/223–1111* ⊕ *www.visittampabay.com.* **Ybor City Chamber Visitor Bureau** ⊠ *1600 E. 8th Ave., Ste. B104* ☎ *813/241–8838* ⊕ *www.ybor.org.*

THE CRUISE PORT

Tampa is the largest shipping port in the state of Florida, and it's becoming ever more important to the cruise industry, now with three passenger terminals. In Tampa's downtown area, the port is linked to nearby Ybor City and the rest of the Tampa Bay Area by the TECO streetcar line.

To reach the port by car, take I–4 West to Exit 1 (Ybor City), and go south on 21st Street. To get to terminals 2 and 6, turn right on Adamo

Drive (Highway 60), then left on Channelside Drive.

Contact Tampa Port Authority ✉ *1101 Channelside Dr.* ☎ *813/905–7678, 800/741–2297* ⊕ *www.tampaport.com.*

AIRPORT TRANSFERS

Both Bay Shuttle and SuperShuttle provide shared van service to and from the airport and the cruise terminal. Expect to pay about $13 to $14 per person.

Information Blue One Transportation ☎ *813/282-7351* ⊕ *www.blueonetransportation.com.* **SuperShuttle** ☎ *800/258-3826* ⊕ *www.supershuttle.com.*

PARKING

Parking is available at the port directly across from the terminals. For Terminal 2 (Carnival Cruise Lines), parking is in a garage across the street. For Terminal 3 (Royal Caribbean and Norwegian Cruise Line), parking is also in a garage across the street. For Terminal 6 (Holland America Line), parking is outdoors in a guarded, enclosed lot. The cost is $15 a day, payable by credit card (MasterCard or Visa) or in cash in advance; valet parking is available for the same rate but with the addition of a $20 "convenience fee."

> ## TAMPA BEST BETS
>
> ■ **Busch Gardens.** The area's best theme park is a good family destination.
>
> ■ **Florida Aquarium.** The aquarium is next to the cruise port, so you can just walk, making it a good option even if you have a couple of hours to kill before boarding (they'll even store your luggage if you want to visit after disembarking).
>
> ■ **The Dalí Museum.** One of the finest and most interesting museums in the United States.
>
> ■ **Ybor City.** For nightlife and restaurants, this historic district is Tampa's hot spot.

EXPLORING THE TAMPA BAY AREA

Florida's west-coast crown jewel as well as its business and commercial hub, Tampa has high-rises and heavy traffic. Amid the bustle is the region's greatest concentration of restaurants, nightlife, stores, and cultural events.

FAMILY **Adventure Island.** From spring until fall, rides named Calypso Coaster, Gulf Scream, and Key West Rapids promise heat relief at Busch Gardens' water park. Tampa's most popular "wet" park features waterslides and artificial wave pools, along with tranquil "beaches" in a 30-acre package. One of the attraction's headliners, Riptide, challenges you to race three other riders on a sliding mat through twisting tubes and hairpin turns. Planners of this park also took the younger kids into account, with offerings such as Fabian's Funport, which has a scaled-down pool and interactive water gym. Along with a volleyball complex and a rambling river, there are cafés, snack bars, picnic and sunbathing areas, changing rooms, and private cabanas. ✉ *10001 N. McKinley Dr., less than 1 mile north of Busch Gardens, Central Tampa* ☎ *813/987–5660, 888/800–5447* ⊕ *www.adventureisland.com* 🖙 *$46; parking $12* ⊘ *Mid-Mar.–Aug., daily 10–5; Sept.–Oct., weekends only 10–5.*

FAMILY
Fodor's Choice
★

Busch Gardens. The Jungala exhibit at Busch Gardens brings Bengal tigers to center stage and puts them at eye level—allowing you to view them from underground caves and underwater windows. The big cats are just one of the reasons the theme park attracts some 4½ million visitors each year. This is a world-class zoo, with more than 2,000 animals, and a live entertainment venue that provides a full day (or more) of fun for the whole family. If you want to beat the crowds, start in the back of the park and work your way around clockwise. The 335-acre adventure park's habitats offer views of some of the world's most endangered and exotic animals. For the best animal sightings, go to their habitats early, when it's cooler. You can experience up-close animal encounters on the Serengeti Plain, a 65-acre free-roaming habitat, home to reticulated giraffes, Grevy's zebras, white rhinos, bongos, impalas, and more. Myombe Reserve allows you to view lowland gorillas and chimpanzees in a lush, tropical-rain-forest environment. Down Under–themed Walkabout Way offers those ages five and up an opportunity to hand-feed kangaroos and wallabies (a cup of vittles is $5). But this is also a theme park, so there ar also plenty of rides and roller coasters to enjoy. ⊠ *3000 E. Busch Blvd., 8 miles northeast of downtown Tampa and 2 miles east of I–275 Exit 50, Central Tampa* ☎ *813/987–5000, 888/800–5447* ⊕ *www.buschgardens.com* ⊠ *$85; parking $13* ☉ *Daily 9:30–6.*

Centennial Park. You can step back into the past at Centennial Park, which re-creates a period streetscape and hosts a farmer's market called the "Fresh Market" every Saturday. ⊠ *8th Ave. and 19th St., Ybor City.*

Fodor's Choice
★

Chihuly Collection. For the uninitiated, those passing this collection's polished exterior may think it's a gallery like any other. Yet what's contained inside is an experience akin to *Alice in Wonderland*. This, the first permanent collection of world-renowned glass sculptor Dale Chihuly's work, has such impossibly vibrant, larger-than-life pieces as "Float Boat" and "Ruby Red Icicle." You can tour the museum independently or with one of its volunteer docents (no added cost; tours are given hourly on the half-hour during the week). Each display is perfectly lit, which adds to the drama of Chihuly's designs. After passing under a hallway with a semi-transparent ceiling through which a brilliant array of smaller glass pieces shine, you'll wind up at the breathtaking finale, "Mille Fiore" ("Thousand Flowers"), a spectacular, whimsical glass montage mimicking a wildflower patch, critters and all. Check out the gift shop at the end if you'd like to take some of the magic home with you. A combination ticket gets you a glimpse into Morean Arts Center's off-site glass-blowing studio, where you can watch resident artisans create a unique glass piece before your eyes. ⊠ *400 Beach Dr., Downtown, St. Petersburg* ☎ *727/822–7872* ⊕ *www.moreanartscenter.com.* ⊠ *$15* ☉ *Mon.–Sat. 10–5, Sun. 12–5.*

Fodor's Choice
★

The Dalí Museum. Inside and out, the waterfront Dalí Museum, which opened on 1/11/11 (Dali is said to have been into numerology), is almost as remarkable as the Spanish surrealist's work. The state-of-the-art building has a surreal geodesic-like glass structure called the Dalí Enigma, as well as an outdoor labyrinth and a DNA-inspired spiral staircase leading up to the collection. All this, before you've even seen the collection, which is one of the most comprehensive of its kind—courtesy of Ohio magnate A. Reynolds Morse, a friend of Dalí's. The mind-expanding paintings in this downtown headliner include *Eggs on a Plate Without a Plate, The Hallucinogenic Toreador,* and more than 90 other oils. You'll also discover more than 2,000 additional works including watercolors, drawings, sculptures, photographs, and objets d'art. Free hour-long tours are led by well-informed docents. ⊠ *1 Dali Blvd., St. Petersburg* ☎ *727/823–3767* ⊕ *www.thedali.org* ⌨ *$21* ⊙ *Mon.–Wed. and Fri.–Sat. 10–5:30, Thurs. 10–8, Sun. noon–5:30.*

FAMILY **Florida Aquarium.** Although eels, sharks, and stingrays are the headliners, the Florida Aquarium is much more than a giant fishbowl. This architectural landmark features an 83-foot-high, multitier, glass dome; 250,000 square feet of air-conditioned exhibit space; and more than 20,000 aquatic plants and animals representing species native to Florida and the rest of the world—from black-tip sharks to leafy sea dragons. Floor-to-ceiling interactive displays, behind-the-scenes tours, and in-water adventures allow kids to really get hands-on—and even get their feet wet. Adventurous types (certified divers age 15 and up) can dive with mild-mannered sharks and sea turtles, participate in shark-feeding programs (age 12 and up), or shallow-water swim with reef fish such as eels and grouper (age 6 and up).

However, you don't have to get wet to have an interactive experience: the Ocean Commotion exhibit offers virtual dolphins and whales and multimedia displays and presentations, and even allows kids to upload video to become part of the exhibit. The Coral Reef Gallery is a 500,000-gallon tank with viewing windows, an awesome 43-foot-wide panoramic opening, and a walk-through tunnel that gives the illusion of venturing into underwater depths. There you see a thicket of elkhorn coral teeming with tropical fish, and a dark cave reveals sea life you would normally see only on night dives. ⊠ *701 Channelside Dr., Downtown* ☎ *813/273–4000* ⊕ *www.flaquarium.org* ⌨ *Aquarium $21.95; Aquarium/Adventure Cruise combo $37.95; Penguins: Backstage Pass combo $48.95; Behind the Scenes Combo $29.95; Dive with the Sharks $175; Swim with the Fishes $75; parking $6* ⊙ *Daily 9:30–5.*

Seminole Hard Rock Hotel & Casino. In addition to playing one of the hundreds of Vegas-style slot machines, gamers can get their kicks at the casino's poker tables and video-gaming machines. The lounge serves drinks 24 hours a day. Hard Rock Cafe, of course, has live music, dinner, and nightlife. There is a heavy smell of cigarette smoke here, as with most casinos. ⊠ *5223 N. Orient Rd., off I–4 at N. Orient Rd. exit, East Tampa* ☎ *813/627–7625, 866/502–7529* ⊕ *www.seminolehardrock. com* ⌨ *Free* ⊙ *Daily 24 hrs.*

Fodor's Choice ★ **Ybor City.** Tampa's lively Latin quarter is one of only a few National Historic Landmark districts in Florida. Bordered by I–4 to the north, 22nd Street to the east, Adamo Drive to the south, and Nebraska Avenue to the West, it has antique-brick streets and wrought-iron balconies. Cubans brought their cigar-making industry to Ybor (pronounced *ee-bore*) City in 1886, and the smell of cigars—hand-rolled by Cuban immigrants—still wafts through the heart of this east Tampa area, along with the strong aroma of roasting coffee. These days the neighborhood is one of Tampa's hot spots, if at times a rowdy one, as empty cigar factories and historic social clubs have been transformed into trendy boutiques, art galleries, restaurants, and nightclubs. ⊠ *Ybor City.*

Ybor City Museum State Park. This park provides a look at the history of the cigar industry. Admission includes a tour of La Casita, one of the shotgun houses occupied by cigar workers and their families in the late 1890s, held every half-hour between 10 and 3. ⊠ *1818 E. 9th Ave., between Nuccio Pkwy. and 22nd St. from 7th to 9th aves., Ybor City* ☎ *813/247–6323* ⊕ *www.ybormuseum.org* ⌨ *$4* ☉ *Daily 9–5.*

BEACHES

FAMILY **Fort De Soto Park.** Spread over five small islands, 1,136-acre Fort De Soto Park lies at the mouth of Tampa Bay. It has 7 miles of waterfront (much of it beach), two fishing piers, a 4-mile hiking and skating trail, picnic-and-camping grounds, and a historic fort that kids of any age can explore. The fort for which it's named was built on the southern end of Mullet Key to protect sea lanes in the gulf during the Spanish-American War. Roam the fort or wander the beaches of any of the islands within the park. Kayaks and beach cruisers are available for rental. ⊠ *3500 Pinellas Bayway St., Tierra Verde* ☎ *727/582–2267* ⊕ *www.pinellascounty.org/park/05_ft_desoto.htm* ⌨ *$5* ☉ *Beaches, daily sunrise–sunset; fishing and boat ramp, 24 hrs.*

FAMILY

Fodor's Choice

★

Pass-a-Grille Beach. At the southern tip of St. Pete Beach (past the Don Cesar), this is the epitome of Old Florida. One of the most popular beaches in the area, it skirts the west end of charming, historic Pass-a-Grille, a neighborhood that draws tourists and locals alike with its stylish yet low-key mom-and-pop motels and restaurants. On weekends, check out the Art Mart, an open-air market off the boulevard between 9th and 10th avenues that showcases the work of local artisans. **Amenities:** food and drink; parking; showers; toilets. **Best for:** sunset; windsurfing. ⊠ *1000 Pass-a-Grille Way, St. Pete Beach.*

SHOPPING

Centro Ybor. Ybor City's destination within a destination is this dining-and-entertainment palace. It has shops, trendy bars and restaurants, and a 20-screen movie theater. ⊠ *1600 E. 8th Ave., Ybor City* ⊕ *www.centroybor.com.*

International Plaza. If you want to grab something at Neiman Marcus or Nordstrom, this is the place. You'll also find Juicy Couture, J. Crew, LUSH, Louis Vuitton, Tiffany & Co., and many other upscale shops. Stick around after hours, when watering holes in the mall's courtyard become a high-end club scene. ⊠ *2223 N. West Shore Blvd., Airport Area* ⊕ *www.shopinternationalplaza.com.*

Old Hyde Park Village. It's a typical upscale shopping district in a quiet, shaded neighborhood near the water. Williams-Sonoma and Brooks Brothers are mixed in with bistros and sidewalk cafés. ⊠ *1602 W. Swann Ave., Hyde Park* ⊕ *www.hydeparkvillage.net.*

NIGHTLIFE

Although there are more boarded storefronts than in the past, the biggest concentration of nightclubs, as well as the widest variety, is found along 7th Avenue in Ybor City. It becomes a little like Bourbon Street in New Orleans on weekend evenings.

Centro Cantina. There are lots of draws here: a balcony overlooking the crowds on Seventh Avenue, live music Thursday through Sunday nights, a large selection of margaritas, and more than 30 brands of tequila. Food is served until 2 am. ⊠ *1600 E. 8th Ave., Ybor City* ☎ *813/241–8588.*

Hub. Considered something of a dive—but a lovable one—by a loyal and young local following that ranges from esteemed jurists to nose-ring-wearing night owls, the Hub is known for strong drinks and a jukebox that goes well beyond the usual. ⊠ *719 N. Franklin St., Downtown* ☎ *813/229–1553.*

WHERE TO EAT

$$$$
STEAKHOUSE
Fodor's Choice
★

✕ **Bern's Steak House.** With the air of an exclusive club, this is one of Florida's finest steakhouses. Rich mahogany paneling and ornate chandeliers define the legendary Bern's, where the chef ages his own beef, grows his own organic vegetables, and roasts his own coffee. There's also a Cave Du Fromage, housing a discriminating selection of artisanal cheeses from around the world. Cuts of topmost beef are sold by weight and thickness. There's a 60-ounce strip steak that's big enough to feed your pride (of lions), but for most appetites the veal loin chop or 8-ounce chateaubriand is more than enough. The wine list includes approximately 7,000 selections (with 1,000 dessert wines). After dinner, tour the kitchen and wine cellar before having dessert upstairs in a cozy booth. The dessert room is a hit. For a real jolt, try the Turkish coffee with an order of Mississippi mud pie. Business casual attire is recommended. ⑤ *Average main: $32* ⊠ *1208 S. Howard Ave., Hyde Park* ☎ *813/251–2421* ⊕ *www.bernssteakhouse.com* ⌸ *Reservations essential* ⌸ *Jacket and tie.*

$$
SPANISH
Fodor's Choice
★

✕ **Columbia.** Make a date for some of the best Latin cuisine in Tampa. A fixture since 1905, this magnificent structure with an old-world air and spacious dining rooms takes up an entire city block and seems to feed the entire city—locals as well as visitors—throughout the week, but especially on weekends. The paella, bursting with seafood, chicken, and pork, is arguably the best in Florida, and the 1905 salad—with ham, olives, cheese, and garlic—is legendary. The menu has Cuban classics such as *boliche criollo* (tender eye of round stuffed with chorizo sausage), *ropa vieja* (shredded beef with onions, peppers, and tomatoes), and *arroz con pollo* (chicken with yellow rice). Don't miss the flamenco show every night but Sunday. This place is also known for its sangria. If you can, walk around the building and check out the elaborate, antique decor along every inch of the interior. ⑤ *Average main: $19* ⊠ *2117 E. 7th Ave., Ybor City* ☎ *813/248–4961* ⊕ *www.columbiarestaurant.com.*

6

$$ ✕ **Kojak's House of Ribs.** Few barbecue joints can boast the staying power
SOUTHERN of this family-owned and -operated pit stop. Located along a shaded
stretch in South Tampa, it debuted in 1978 and has since earned a fol-
lowing of sticky-fingered regulars who have turned it into one of the
most popular barbecue stops in central Florida. It's located in a 1927
house complete with veranda, pillars supporting the overhanging roof,
and brick steps. Day and night, three indoor dining rooms and an out-
door dining porch have a steady stream of hungry patrons digging into
tender pork spareribs that are dry-rubbed and tanned overnight before
visiting the smoker for a couple of hours. Then they're bathed in the
sauce of your choice. Kojak's also has a nice selection of sandwiches,
including chopped barbecue chicken and country-style sausage. This is
definitely not the kind of place you'd want to bring a vegan. $ *Aver-
age main: $14 ⊠ 2808 Gandy Blvd., South Tampa ☎ 813/837–3774
⊕ www.kojaksbbq.net ⊘ Closed Mon.*

WHERE TO STAY

If you want to be close to the cruise-ship terminal, then you'll have
to stay in Tampa, but if you want to spend more time in the area and
perhaps stay on the beach, St. Petersburg and the beaches are close by.

For expanded reviews, facilities, and current deals, visit Fodors.com.

$$$ ▦ **Don Vicente de Ybor Historic Inn.** Built as a home in 1895 by town
B&B/INN founder Don Vicente de Ybor, this inn shows that the working-class
cigar city had an elegant side, too. **Pros:** elegant rooms; rich in history;
walking distance to nightlife. **Cons:** rowdy neighborhood on weekend
nights. $ *Rooms from: $150 ⊠ 1915 Republica de Cuba, Ybor City
☎ 813/241–4545, 866/206–4545 ⊕ www.donvicenteinn.com ⇆ 13
rooms, 3 suites* ⦿ *Breakfast.*

$$$ ▦ **Hilton Garden Inn Tampa Ybor Historic District.** Although its modern
HOTEL architecture makes it seem out of place in this historic district, this
chain hotel's location across from Centro Ybor is a plus. **Pros:** good
location for business travelers; reasonable rates. **Cons:** chain-hotel feel;
far from downtown. $ *Rooms from: $179 ⊠ 1700 E. 9th Ave., Ybor
City ☎ 813/769–9267 ⊕ www.hiltongardeninn.com ⇆ 84 rooms, 11
suites* ⦿ *No meals.*

$$$ ▦ **Tampa Marriott Waterside Hotel & Marina.** Across from the Tampa Con-
HOTEL vention Center, this downtown hotel was built for conventioneers but is
also convenient to tourist spots such as the Florida Aquarium and the
Ybor City and Hyde Park shopping and nightlife districts. **Pros:** great
downtown location; near shopping. **Cons:** gridlock during rush hour;
streets tough to maneuver; area sketchy after dark. $ *Rooms from:
$190 ⊠ 700 S. Florida Ave., Downtown ☎ 888/268–1616 ⊕ www.
marriott.com ⇆ 683 rooms, 36 suites* ⦿ *No meals.*

PORTS OF CALL

Nowhere in the world are conditions better suited to cruising than in the Caribbean Sea. Tiny island nations, within easy sailing distance of one another, form a chain of tropical enchantment that curves from Cuba in the north all the way down to the coast of Venezuela. There's far more to life here than sand and coconuts, however. The islands are vastly different, with a variety of cultures, topographies, and languages represented. Colonialism has left its mark, and the presence of the Spanish, French, Dutch, Danish, and British is still felt. Slavery, too, has left its cultural legacy, blending African overtones into the colonial-Indian amalgam. The one constant, however, is the weather. Despite the islands' southerly latitude, the climate is surprisingly gentle, due in large part to the cooling influence of the trade winds.

The Caribbean is made up of the Greater Antilles and the Lesser Antilles. The former consist of those islands closest to the United States: Cuba, Jamaica, Hispaniola (Haiti and the Dominican Republic), and Puerto Rico. (The Cayman Islands lie south of Cuba.) The Lesser Antilles, including the Virgin, Windward, and Leeward islands and others, are greater in number but smaller in size, and constitute the southern half of the Caribbean chain.

GOING ASHORE

Traveling by cruise ship presents an opportunity to visit many places in a short time. The flip side is that your stay in each port of call will be brief. For this reason cruise lines offer shore excursions, which maximize passengers' time. There are a number of advantages to shore excursions arranged by your ship: in some destinations, transportation may be unreliable, and a ship-packaged tour is the best way to see distant sights. Also, you don't have to worry about missing the ship. The disadvantage of a shore excursion is the cost—you usually pay more for the convenience of having the ship do the legwork for you, but it's not always a lot more. Of course, you can always book a tour independently, hire a taxi, or use foot power to explore on your own. For each port of call included in this guide we've provided some suggestions for the best ship-sponsored excursions—in terms of both quality of experience and price—as well as some suggestions for what to do if you want to explore on your own.

ARRIVING IN PORT

When your ship arrives in a port, it will tie up alongside a dock or anchor out in a harbor. If the ship is docked, passengers walk down the gangway to go ashore. Docking makes it easy to move between the shore and the ship.

TENDERING

If your ship anchors in the harbor, you will have to take a small boat—called a launch or tender—to get ashore. Tendering is a nuisance, but participants in shore excursions are given priority. Passengers wishing to disembark independently may be required to gather in a public room, get sequenced tendering passes, and wait until their numbers are called. The ride to shore may take as long as 20 minutes. If you don't like waiting, plan to go ashore an hour or so after the ship drops its anchor. On a very large ship, the wait for a tender can be quite long and frustrating.

Because tenders can be difficult to board, passengers with mobility problems may not be able to visit certain ports. Larger ships are more likely to use tenders. It is usually possible to learn before booking a cruise whether the ship will dock or anchor at its ports of call.

Before anyone is allowed to walk down the gangway or board a tender, the ship must be cleared for landing. Immigration and customs officials board the vessel to examine the ship's manifest or possibly passports and sort through red tape. It may be more than an hour before you're allowed ashore. You will be issued a boarding pass, which you'll need to get back on board.

7

RETURNING TO THE SHIP

Cruise lines are strict about sailing times, which are posted at the gangway and elsewhere and announced in the daily schedule of activities. Be sure to be back on board (not on the dock waiting to get a tender back to the ship) at least an hour before the announced sailing time or you may be stranded. If you are on a shore excursion that was sold by the cruise line, however, the captain will wait for your group before casting off. That is one reason many passengers prefer ship-packaged tours.

If you're not on one of the ship's tours and the ship sails without you, immediately contact the cruise line's port representative, whose phone number is often listed on the daily schedule of activities. You may be able to hitch a ride on a pilot boat, although that is unlikely. Passengers who miss the boat must pay their own way to the next port.

CARIBBEAN ESSENTIALS

CURRENCY

The U.S. dollar is the official currency on Puerto Rico, the U.S. Virgin Islands, the Turks and Caicos, Bonaire, and the British Virgin Islands. On Grand Cayman you will usually have a choice of Cayman or U.S. dollars when you take money out of an ATM, and you may even be able to get change in U.S. dollars. In Cozumel, Calica, Costa Maya, and Progreso, the Mexican peso is the official currency. The euro is

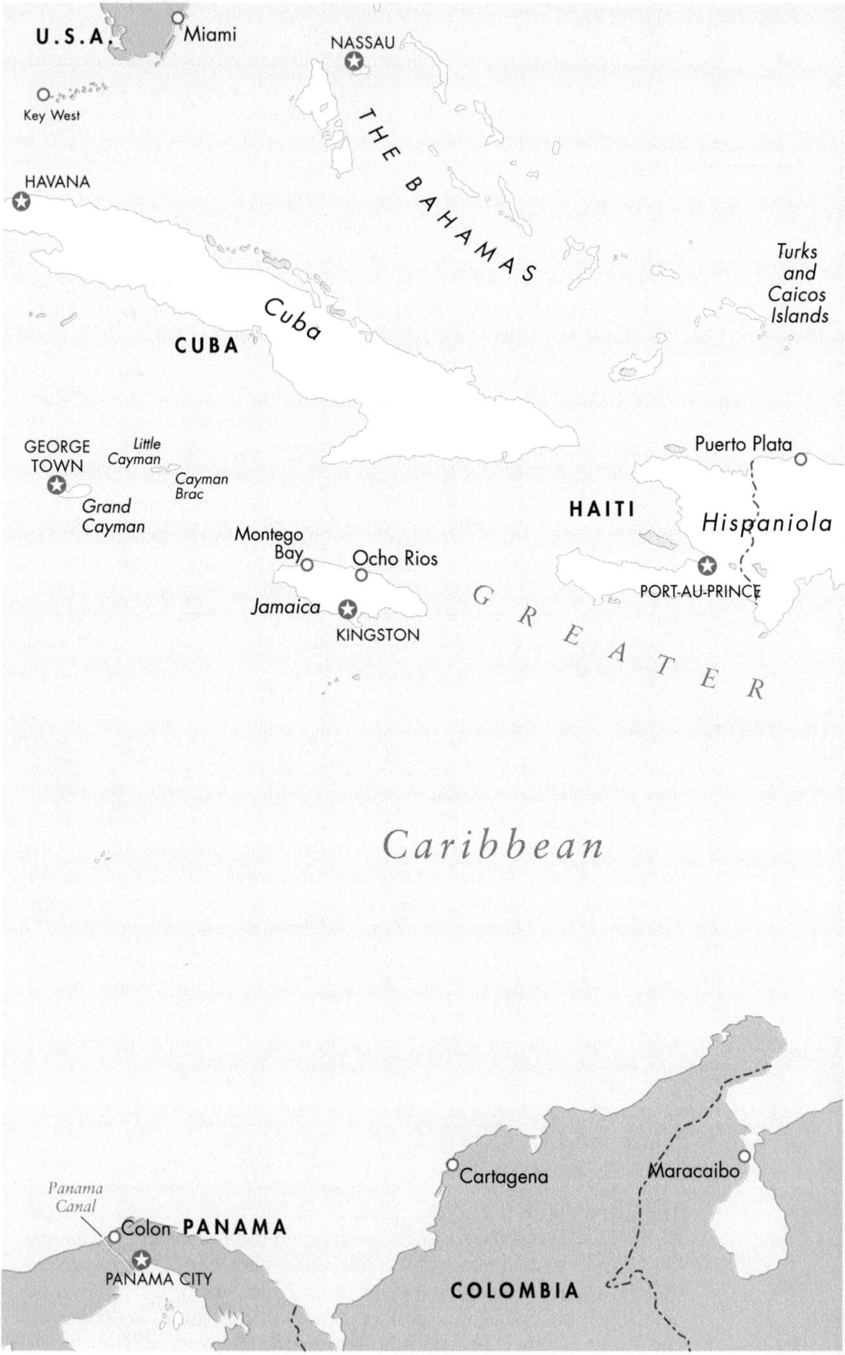

U.S.A. Miami

Key West

NASSAU

THE BAHAMAS

Turks
and
Caicos
Islands

HAVANA

Cuba

CUBA

GEORGE
TOWN   Little
Cayman

Cayman
Brac

Grand
Cayman

Montego
Bay

Ocho Rios

Jamaica

KINGSTON

Puerto Plata

HAITI   Hispaniola

PORT-AU-PRINCE

G R E A T E R

Caribbean

Panama
Canal

Colon PANAMA

PANAMA CITY

Cartagena

Maracaibo

COLOMBIA

Caribbean

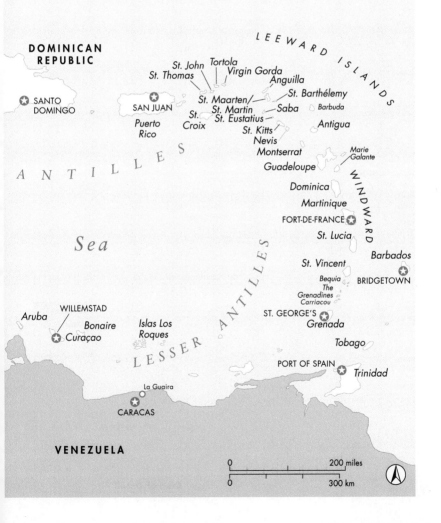

ATLANTIC OCEAN

LEEWARD ISLANDS

DOMINICAN REPUBLIC

SANTO DOMINGO

St. John Tortola
St. Thomas Virgin Gorda
Anguilla
St. Barthélemy
SAN JUAN St. Maarten/
St. Martin Saba Barbuda
St. Eustatius
St. St. Kitts Antigua
Croix Nevis
Puerto Rico
Montserrat Marie Galante
Guadeloupe

ANTILLES

Dominica

Martinique
FORT-DE-FRANCE

St. Lucia

Sea

Barbados

St. Vincent

Bequia BRIDGETOWN
The Grenadines
Carriacou

WILLEMSTAD ST. GEORGE'S
Aruba Islas Los Roques Grenada
Bonaire
Curaçao

Tobago

LESSER ANTILLES

PORT OF SPAIN Trinidad

La Guaira

CARACAS

VENEZUELA

WINDWARD

| 0 | | 200 miles |
| 0 | | 300 km |

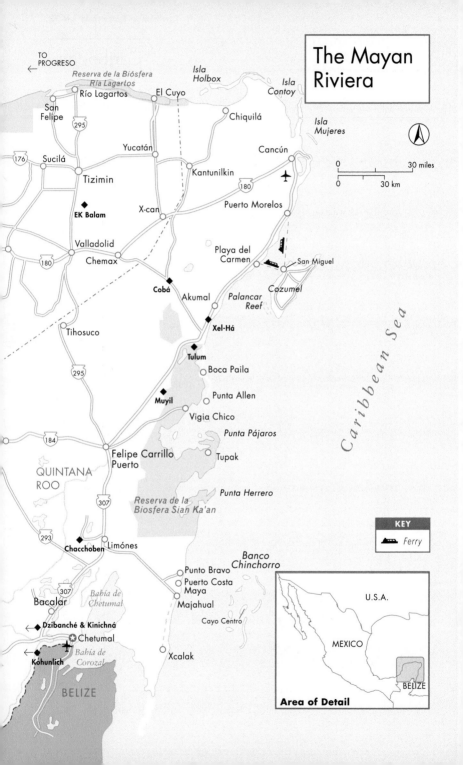

used in a handful of French islands (St. Barth, St. Martin, Martinique, Guadeloupe). In most Caribbean ports U.S. paper currency (not coins) is accepted readily. When you pay in dollars you'll almost always get change in local currency, so it's best to carry bills in small denominations. If you need local currency (say, for a trip to one of the French islands that uses the euro), change money at a local bank or use an ATM for the best rate. Most major credit cards are accepted all over the Caribbean, except at local market stalls and small establishments.

> **BUYING LIQUOR AND PERFUME**
>
> If you buy duty-free liquor or perfume while in a Caribbean port, don't forget that you may not bring it aboard your flight home. You will have to put it in your checked bags. Many liquor stores will pack your bottles in bubble wrap and a good cardboard box. Take advantage of this service.

KEEPING IN TOUCH

Internet cafés are now fairly common on many islands, and you'll sometimes find Internet cafés in the cruise-ship terminal itself—or perhaps in an attached or nearby shopping center. If you want to call home, most cruise-ship terminal facilities have phones that accept credit cards or local phone cards (local phone cards are almost always the cheapest option). And on most islands GSM multiband mobile phones will work, though roaming charges may be steep (some plans include Puerto Rico and the U.S. Virgin Islands in their nationwide calling regions).

WHERE TO EAT

Cuisine on the Caribbean's islands is as varied as the islands themselves. The region's history as a colonial battleground and ethnic melting pot creates plenty of variety and adds lots of unusual tropical fruit and spices. In fact, the one quality that defines most Caribbean cooking is its spiciness, acquired from nutmeg, mace, allspice, peppers, saffron, and many other seasonings grown in the islands. Dress is generally casual, although throughout the islands beachwear is inappropriate most anywhere except on the beach. Unless otherwise noted, prices are given in U.S. dollars.

SHORE EXCURSIONS

Typical excursions include an island or town bus tour, a visit to a beach or rum factory, a boat trip, a snorkeling or diving trip, and charter fishing. In recent years, however, shore excursions have gotten more adventurous, with mild river-rafting, parasailing, jet-skiing, hiking, and biking added to the mix. It's often easier to take a ship-arranged excursion, but it's almost never the cheapest option.

If you prefer to break away from the pack, find a knowledgeable taxi driver or tour operator—they're usually within a stone's throw of the pier—or wander around on your own. A group of four to six people will usually find this option more economical and practical than will a single person or a couple.

Renting a car is also a good option on many islands—again, the more people, the better the deal. But get a good island map before you set off, and be sure to find out how long it will take you to get around.

Conditions are ideal for water sports of all kinds—scuba diving, snorkeling, windsurfing, sailing, waterskiing, and fishing excursions abound. Your shore-excursion director can usually arrange these activities for you if the ship offers no formal excursion.

PRIVATE ISLANDS

Linda Coffman

When evaluating the "best" Caribbean ports of call, many repeat cruise passengers often add the cruise lines' own private islands to their lists of preferred destinations.

The cruise lines established "private" islands to provide a beach break on an island (or part of one) reserved for their exclusive use. Although most passengers don't select an itinerary based solely on calling at a private island, they usually consider them a highlight of their cruise vacation. The very least you can expect of your private island is lush foliage and a wide swath of beach surrounded by azure water. Facilities vary, but a beach barbecue, water-sports equipment rental, lounge chairs, hammocks, and restrooms are standard. Youth counselors come ashore to conduct sand-castle building competitions and lead junior pirates on swashbuckling island treasure hunts.

The use of strollers and wheelchairs equipped with all-terrain wheels may be offered on a complimentary first-come, first-served basis. However, with the exception of some participation sports on the beach, plan to pay for most water toys and activities. Costs associated with private-island fun and recreation can range from $9 for use of a snorkel vest (you may use your own snorkel equipment; however, in the event a floatation vest is required for safety, you must rent one) to $25 to $30 for rental of an entire snorkeling outfit for the day (mask, fins, snorkel vest, a mesh bag, fish identification card, and fish food). You can often take a banana-boat ride for $19 (15-minute ride), sail a small boat or catamaran for $30 to $50 (one hour), paddle a kayak for $29 to $64 (half-hour to three hours-and-a-half), ride Jet Skis for $59 to $99 (45 minutes to one hour), parasail for a hefty $79 to $119 (10 minutes or less), or fly through the treetops on a zip line for $93. Floating mats or inner tubes are a relative bargain at $6 to $12 for all-day lounging in the water. You might also find open-air massage cabanas with pricing comparable to the spa charges onboard.

There is generally no charge for food or basic beverages such as those served onboard ship. Although soft drinks and tropical cocktails can usually be charged to your shipboard account, as can paid activities like motorized water sports, stingray encounters, private cabanas, and other options that vary by cruise line.

You might want to bring a small amount of cash ashore for souvenir shopping, which is almost always possible from vendors set up on or near the beach. You will also want to bring beach towels ashore and return them to the ship at the end of the day, because, as Princess Cruises reminds passengers, "Although the locals may offer to do this for you, unfortunately we seldom see the towels again!"

Even if you do nothing more than lie in a shaded hammock and sip fruity tropical concoctions, the day can be one of the most fun and relaxing of your entire cruise.

ISLANDS BY CRUISE LINE

Carnival Cruise Lines is currently the only major cruise line without an extensive private island experience available to the entire fleet. However, select Carnival itineraries include calls at Half Moon Cay, Holland America Line's private paradise, where "Fun Ship" passengers can use all the facilities and participate in organized activities. Similarly, certain Regent Seven Seas cruises include beach days at Cayo Levantado, located off the Samaná Peninsula on the northeast coast of the Dominican Republic.

Although they do not stop at "private islands" in the strictest sense, the smaller ships of Seabourn and SeaDream offer passengers a day ashore on secluded private beaches where they can enjoy lavish barbecues and take a break from swimming and snorkeling to indulge in champagne and caviar served in the surf.

COSTA CRUISES

Catalina Island. An unspoiled island paradise, Costa's Catalina Island is just off the coast of the Dominican Republic. Passengers can participate in Costa's "Beach Olympics," schedule a seaside massage, or just kick back on a chaise longue or a complimentary water float. Water-toy rentals, banana-boat rides, and sailing tours are available from independent concessionaires. Local vendors set up souvenir shops offering crafts and T-shirts. The ship provides the food for a lunch barbecue and tropical beverages at the beach bar.

Activities: Snorkeling, sailing, jet-skiing, waterskiing, hiking, volleyball, organized games, massages, shopping. ⊠ *Parc Nacional Isla Catalina, Catalina Island, Dominican Republic* ⊕ *www.costacruise.com.*

DISNEY CRUISE LINE

Castaway Cay. Disney's Castaway Cay has a dock, so passengers simply step ashore (rather than tendering, as is required to reach most cruise lines' private islands). Like everything associated with Disney, the line's private island is almost too good to be true. Located in the Abacos, a chain in the Bahamas, only 10% of Castaway Cay is developed, leaving plenty of unspoiled area to explore in Robinson Crusoe fashion. Trams are provided to reach separate beaches designated for children, teens, families, and adults, and areas where Disney offers age-specific activities and extensive, well-planned children's activities. Biking and hiking are so popular that two nature trails—one of them with an observation tower—are mapped out. Passengers can swim to a water platform complete with two slides or cool off in a 2,400-square-foot water-play area equipped with water jets and a splash pad. A 1,200-square-foot soft wet deck area provides freshwater fun for children with an array of pop jets, geysers, and bubblers. There is no charge for the water-play facilities.

Excursions range from as passive as a glass-bottom-boat tour to the soaring excitement of parasailing. An interactive experience with sting-rays is educational and safe—the gentle creatures' barbs are blunted for safety. In addition to barbecue fare served in two buffet areas with covered seating and several beverage stations, beach games, island-style music, and a shaded game pavilion, there are shops, massage cabanas by the sea, and even a post office. Popular with couples as well as families, 20 private rental cabanas provide the luxury of a deluxe beach retreat with an option to add the personalized service of a cabana host. Teens have their own private retreat just steps from the beach.

Activities: Snorkeling, kayaking, parasailing, sailing, jet-skiing, pad-dleboats, water cycles, fishing, bicycles, basketball, billiards, hiking, Ping-Pong, shuffleboard, soccer, volleyball, organized games, massages, shopping. ⊠ *Castaway Cay, Bahamas* ⊕ *disneycruise.disney.go.com.*

HOLLAND AMERICA LINE

Half Moon Cay. Little San Salvador, one of the Bahamian out-islands, was renamed Half Moon Cay by Holland America Line to honor Henry Hudson's ship (depicted on the cruise line's logo) as well as to reflect the beach's crescent shape. Even after development, the island is still so unspoiled that it has been named a Wild Bird Preserve by the Bahamian National Trust. Passengers, who are welcomed ashore at a West Indies Village complete with shops and straw market, find Half Moon Cay eas-ily accessible—all facilities are connected by hard-surfaced and packed-sand pathways and meet or exceed ADA requirements. An accessible tram also connects the welcome center with the food pavilion and bars; wheelchairs with balloon tires are available. In addition to the beach area for lazing in the sun or in the shade of a rented clamshell, the island has a post office, Bahamian-style chapel, a lagoon where you can interact with stingrays, and the Captain Morgan on the Rocks Island Bar in a "beached" pirate ship. For family fun, you'll find a beachfront water park with waterslides and fanciful sea creatures tethered to the sandy bottom of the shallow water. Massage services are available, as are fitness activities. Air-conditioned Cabanas, two-story Beach Villas with hot tubs on the second floor, and a Grand Cabana that features an 8-person hot tub and a slide from the cabana deck straight into the ocean can be rented for the day, with or without the services of your own butler.

Activities: Scuba diving, snorkeling, windsurfing, kayaking, parasail-ing, sailing, jet-skiing, Aqua Bikes, fishing, bicycles, basketball, hiking, horseback riding, shuffleboard, volleyball, massages, shopping. ⊠ *Half Moon Cay, Bahamas* ⊕ *www.hollandamerica.com.*

NORWEGIAN CRUISE LINE

Great Stirrup Cay. Only 120 miles east of Fort Lauderdale in the Berry Island chain of the Bahamas, much of Great Stirrup Cay looks as it did when it was acquired by Norwegian Cruise Line in 1977, with bou-gainvillea, sea grape, and coconut palms as abundant as the colorful tropical fish that inhabit the reef. The first uninhabited island purchased to offer cruise-ship passengers a private beach day, Great Stirrup Cay's white-sand beaches are fringed by coral and ideal for swimming and snorkeling. Permanent facilities have been added to and improved in the intervening years and a seawall was erected to reduce beach erosion and preserve the environment. A straw market, water-sports centers, bars, volleyball courts, beachside massage stations, a food pavilion, and a 40-feet high and 175-feet long Hippo inflatable waterslide round out the facilities. Sand wheelchairs are available on the island, but the only paved pathway is along the seawall. Extensive island improvements began in 2010 with the excavation of a new entrance channel for tenders and construction of tender docking facilities and a welcome pavilion that is now the site for landings. As a result, the beachfront has been expanded significantly to alleviate crowding. Private beachfront rental cabanas, two dining facilities, a kid's play area, wave runners, a floating Aqua Park with a variety of water toys, kayak tours through man-made rivers within the island, an ecocruise, and a stingray encounter experience are additional amenities.

Activities: Snorkeling, kayaking, parasailing, sailing, paddleboats, Ping-Pong, hiking, volleyball, organized games, massages, shopping. ⊠ *Great Stirrup Cay, Berry Islands, Bahamas* ⊕ *www.ncl.com.*

PRINCESS CRUISES

Princess Cays. Princess Cays is a 40-acre haven on the southern tip of Eleuthera Island in the Bahamas. Not quite an uninhabited island, it nevertheless offers a wide ribbon of beach, long enough for passengers to splash in the surf, relax in a hammock, or limbo to the beat of local music and never feel crowded. In a similar fashion to booking shore excursions, snorkeling equipment, sea boards, floats, kayaks, paddle wheelers, banana boat rides, aqua chairs, beach clamshells, and bungalows can be pre-reserved on Princess Cruises' website. All other equipment and activities must be booked onboard. Nestled in a picturesque palm grove, private bungalows with air-conditioning and ceiling fans and a deck for lounging can be rented for parties of up to six. The Sanctuary at Princess Cays, complete with bungalows for parties of four (two additional guests may be added at an additional charge), is an adults-only haven. A pirate-theme play area for children is supervised. In addition to three tropical bars and the area where a Bahamian barbecue is served, permanent facilities include small shops that sell island crafts and trinkets, but if you head around the back and through the fence, independent vendors sell similar goods for lower prices.

Activities: Snorkeling, kayaking, banana boat rides, sailing, paddleboats, Aqua Bikes, windsurfing, surf fishing, deep sea fishing, hiking, organized games, shopping. ⊠ *Princess Cays, Eleuthera Island, Bahamas* ⊕ *www.princess.com.*

ROYAL CARIBBEAN, CELEBRITY CRUISES, AND AZAMARA CLUB CRUISES

Royal Caribbean, Azamara Club Cruises, and Celebrity Cruises passengers have twice as many opportunities to visit a private island. The lines share two, and many Caribbean itineraries include one or the other.

Coco Cay. Coco Cay is a 140-acre island in the Berry Island chain between Nassau and Freeport. Originally known as Little Stirrup Cay, it's within view of Great Stirrup Cay (NCL's private island) and the snorkeling is just as good, especially around a sunken airplane and a replica of Blackbeard's flagship, *Queen Anne's Revenge*. In addition to activities and games ashore, Coco Cay has one of the largest Aqua Parks in the Caribbean, where children and adults alike can jump on an in-water trampoline or climb a floating sand castle before they dig into a beach barbecue or explore a nature trail. Attractions also include an inflatable 40-foot waterslide (fun for adults and kids alike) and a Power Wheels track, where youngsters age 3 to 8 can take a miniature car for a spin at a sedate 3 mph. Rounding out the facilities are a Bahamian marketplace, several beach bars, and numerous hammocks for relaxation in the sun or shade.

Activities: Scuba diving, snorkeling, jet-skiing, kayaking, parasailing, hiking, volleyball, organized games, shopping. ⊠ *Coco Cay, Berry Islands, Bahamas* ⊕ *www.royalcaribbean.com.*

Labadee. Labadee is a 260-acre peninsula approximately 6 miles (10 km) from Cap Haitien on the secluded north coast of Haiti (the port of call is occasionally called "Hispaniola"). Passengers can step ashore on the dock, from which water taxis and five different walking paths, trails, and avenues lead to many areas throughout the peninsula, including the Labadee Town Square and Dragon's Plaza, where a welcome center and central tram station are located. In addition to swimming, water sports, an Aqua Park with floating trampolines and waterslides, and nature trails to explore, bonuses on Labadee are an authentic folkloric show presented by island performers and a market featuring work of local artists and crafters, where you might find an interesting painting or unique wood carving. Only cash is accepted, and bargaining is expected in the market. More adventurous activities include an Alpine Coaster, a thrilling roller coaster experience, and one of the most exciting—and at 2,600 feet in length the longest—zip-line experiences in the Caribbean, which takes place 500 feet above the beaches of Labadee, where riders can reach speeds of 40 to 50 mph over the water. The use of beach chairs is complimentary; however, tipping the beach attendants for their service is always appreciated. The Barefoot Beach Club & Cabanas is reserved for top suite guests and those who rent one of the 20 cabanas, which can accommodate 4 to 5 guests. Only the nine Palm Cabanas are wheelchair-accessible, but even they have two steps to climb.

Activities: Snorkeling, jet-skiing, kayaking, parasailing, zip-lining, hiking, volleyball, organized games, shopping. ⊠ *Labadee* ⊕ *www.royalcaribbean.com.*

ANTIGUA (ST. JOHN'S)

Jordan Simon

Some say Antigua has so many beaches that you could visit a different one every day for a year. Most have snow-white sand, and many are backed by lavish resorts that offer sailing, diving, windsurfing, and snorkeling. The largest of the British Leeward Islands, Antigua was the headquarters from which Lord Horatio Nelson (then a mere captain) made his forays against the French and pirates in the late 18th century. You may wish to explore English Harbour and its carefully restored

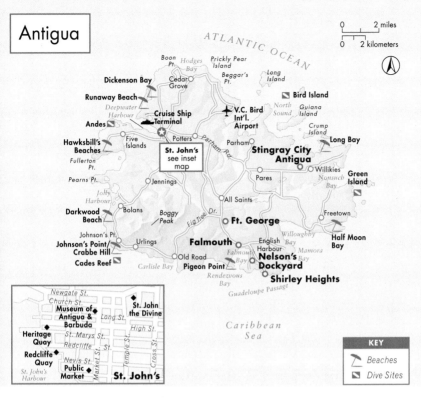

Antigua

ATLANTIC OCEAN

Boon Pt.
Hodges Bay
Prickly Pear Island
Beggar's Pt.
Long Island

Dickenson Bay
Cedar Grove

Runaway Beach

Bird Island

Deepwater Harbour

Cruise Ship Terminal

V.C. Bird Int'l. Airport

North Sound

Guiana Island

Andes

Hawksbill's Beaches

Five Islands

Potters

Parham

Crump Island

Long Bay

St. John's
see inset map

Stingray City Antigua

Fullerton Pt.

Willikies

Green Island

Pearns Pt.

Jennings

Pares

Nonsuch Bay

Jolly Harbour

All Saints

Darkwood Beach

Bolans

Boggy Peak

Fig Tree Dr.

Ft. George

Freetown

Willoughby

Johnson's Pt.

Johnson's Point/ Crabbe Hill

Urlings

Falmouth

English Harbour

Bay

Half Moon Bay

Cades Reef

Carlisle Bay

Old Road

Pigeon Point

Falmouth Bay

Mamora Bay

Nelson's Dockyard

Shirley Heights

Rendezvous Bay

Guadeloupe Passage

Caribbean Sea

Newgate St.
Church St.
Museum of Antigua & Barbuda
St. John the Divine
Long St.
High St.
Heritage Quay
St. Marys St.
Redcliffe St.
Redcliffe Quay
Nevis St.
St. John's Harbour
Public Market
St. John's

Market St.
Temple St.
Cross St.

KEY

Beaches

Dive Sites

0   2 miles
0   2 kilometers

Nelson's Dockyard, as well as tour old forts, historic churches, and tiny villages. Appealing aspects of the island's interior include a small tropical rain forest ideal for hiking and zip-lining, ancient Native American archaeological digs, and restored sugar mills. Due to time constraints, it's best to make trips this far from port with an experienced tour operator, but you can easily take a taxi to any number of fine beaches on your own and escape from the hordes descending from the ship.

ESSENTIALS
CURRENCY
Eastern Caribbean (EC) dollar. U.S. dollars are generally accepted.

TELEPHONES
GSM tri-band mobile phones from the United States and United Kingdom usually work on Antigua; you can also rent one from LIME (formerly Cable & Wireless) and APUA (Antigua Public Utilities Authority). Basic rental costs range between EC$25 and EC$50 per day. You can use the LIME Phone Card (available in $5, $10, and $20 denominations in most hotels and post offices) for local and long-distance calls.

COMING ASHORE

Though some ships dock at the deepwater harbor in downtown St. John's, most use Heritage Quay, a multimillion-dollar complex with shops, condominiums, a casino, and restaurants. Most St. John's attractions are an easy walk from Heritage Quay; the older part of the city is eight blocks away. A tourist information booth is in the main docking building.

If you intend to explore beyond St. John's, consider hiring a taxi driver–guide. Taxis meet every cruise ship. They're unmetered; fares are fixed, and drivers are required to carry a rate card. Agree on the fare before setting off (make sure you know whether the price quoted is one-way or round-trip), and plan to tip drivers 10%. Some cabbies may take you from St. John's to English Harbour and wait for a "reasonable" amount of time (about a half hour) while you look around, for about $50; you can usually arrange an island tour for around $25 per hour. Renting your own car isn't usually practical, because you must purchase a $20 temporary driving permit in addition to the car-rental fee, which is usually about $50 per day in the high season.

> **BEST BETS FOR CRUISERS**
>
> ■ **Dickenson Bay Beach.** One of Antigua's best beaches.
>
> ■ **Ecotourism.** Explore the island's forested interior on foot or surrounding coves by kayak.
>
> ■ **Jolly Harbour.** A cheap day pass at the Jolly Harbour Resort is a great day at the beach.
>
> ■ **Nelson's Dockyard.** This is one of the Caribbean's best historic sights, with many stores, restaurants, and bars.
>
> ■ **St. John's.** There's excellent duty-free shopping, especially in Heritage Quay and Redcliffe Quay.

EXPLORING ANTIGUA

ST. JOHN'S

Antigua's capital, with some 45,000 inhabitants (approximately half the island's population), lies at sea level at the inland end of a sheltered northwestern bay. Although it has seen better days, a couple of notable historic sights and some good waterfront shopping areas make it worth a visit.

At the far south end of town, where Market Street forks into Valley and All Saints roads, haggling goes on every Friday and Saturday, when locals jam the **Public Market** to buy and sell fruits, vegetables, fish, and spices. Ask before you aim a camera; your subject may expect a tip. This is old-time Caribbean shopping, a jambalaya of sights, sounds, and smells.

Anglican Cathedral of St. John the Divine. At the south gate of the Anglican Cathedral of St. John the Divine are figures of St. John the Baptist and St. John the Divine, said to have been taken from one of Napoléon's ships and brought to Antigua. The original church was built in 1681, replaced by a stone building in 1745, and destroyed by an earthquake in 1843. The present neo-baroque building dates from 1845; the parishioners had the interior completely encased in pitch pine, hoping to forestall future earthquake damage. Tombstones bear eerily eloquent testament to the colonial days. ⊠ *Between Long and Newgate sts.* ☏ *268/461–0082.*

Heritage Quay. Shopaholics head directly for Heritage Quay, an ugly multimillion-dollar complex. The two-story buildings contain stores that sell duty-free goods, sportswear, down-island imports (paintings, T-shirts, straw baskets), and local crafts. There are also restaurants, a bandstand, and a casino. Cruise-ship passengers disembark here from the 500-foot-long pier. Expect heavy shilling. ⊠ *High and Thames sts.*

Museum of Antigua and Barbuda. Signs at the Museum of Antigua and Barbuda say "Please touch," encouraging you to explore Antigua's past. Try your hand at the educational video games or squeeze a cassava through a *matapi* (grass sieve). Exhibits interpret the nation's history, from its geological birth to its political independence in 1981. There are fossil and coral remains from some 34 million years ago; models of a sugar plantation and a wattle-and-daub house; an Arawak canoe; and a wildly eclectic assortment of objects from cannonballs to 1920s telephone exchanges. The museum occupies the former courthouse, which dates from 1750. The superlative museum gift shop carries such unusual items as calabash purses, seed earrings, warri boards (warri being an African game brought to the Caribbean), and lignum vitae pipes, as well as historic maps and local books (including engrossing monographs on varied subjects by the late Desmond Nicholson, a longtime resident). ⊠ *Long and Market sts.* ☏ *268/462–1469* ⊕ *www. antiguamuseum.org* ☞ *$3; children under 12 free* ☉ *Weekdays 8:30–4, Sat. 10–2. Closed Sun.*

Fodor's Choice
★ **Redcliffe Quay.** Redcliffe Quay, at the water's edge just south of Heritage Quay, is the most appealing part of St. John's. Attractively restored (and superbly re-created) 19th-century buildings in a riot of cotton-candy colors house shops, restaurants, galleries, and boutiques and are linked by courtyards and landscaped walkways.

ELSEWHERE ON ANTIGUA

Falmouth. This town sits on a lovely bay backed by former sugar plantations and sugar mills. The most important historic site here is St. Paul's Church, which was rebuilt on the site of a church once used by troops during the Horatio Nelson period.

Ft. George. East of Liberta—one of the first settlements founded by freed slaves—on Monk's Hill, this fort was built from 1689 to 1720. Among the ruins are the sites for 32 cannons, water cisterns, the base of the old flagstaff, and some of the original buildings.

Fodor's Choice
★ **Nelson's Dockyard.** Antigua's most famous attraction is the world's only Georgian-era dockyard still in use, a treasure trove for history buffs and nautical nuts alike. In 1671 the governor of the Leeward Islands wrote to the Council for Foreign Plantations in London, pointing out the advantages of this landlocked harbor. By 1704 English Harbour was in regular use as a garrisoned station.

In 1784, 26-year-old Horatio Nelson sailed in on the HMS *Boreas* to serve as captain and second-in-command of the Leeward Island Station. Under him was the captain of the HMS *Pegasus,* Prince William Henry, duke of Clarence, who was later crowned King William IV. The prince acted as best man when Nelson married Fannie Nisbet on Nevis in 1787.

When the Royal Navy abandoned the station at English Harbour in 1889, it fell into a state of decay, though adventuresome yachties still lived there in near-primitive conditions. The Society of the Friends of English Harbour began restoring it in 1951; it reopened with great fanfare as Nelson's Dockyard on November 14, 1961. Within the compound are crafts shops, restaurants, and two splendidly restored 18th-century hotels, the Admiral's Inn and the Copper & Lumber Store Hotel, worth peeking into. (The latter, occupying a supply store for Nelson's Caribbean fleet, is a particularly fine example of Georgian architecture, its interior courtyard evoking Old England.) The Dockyard is a hub for oceangoing yachts and serves as headquarters for the annual Boat Show in early December and the Sailing Week Regatta in late April and early May. Water taxis will ferry you between points for EC$5. The Dockyard National Park also includes serene nature trails accessing beaches, rock pools, and crumbling plantation ruins and hilltop forts.

The **Dockyard Museum,** in the original Naval Officer's House, presents ship models, mock-ups of English Harbour, displays on the people who worked there and typical ships that docked, silver regatta trophies, maps, prints, antique navigational instruments, and Nelson's very own telescope and tea caddy. ⊠ *English Harbour* ☎ *268/481–5027 or 268/460–1379 for Dockyard Museum, 268/481–5028 for National Parks Authority* ⊕ *www.nationalparksantigua.com, www. dockyardmuseum.org* 🖃 *$2 suggested donation* ☉ *Daily 9–5.*

Shirley Heights. This bluff affords a spectacular view of English Harbour and Falmouth Harbour. The heights are named for Sir Thomas Shirley, the governor who fortified the harbor in 1781. At the top is Shirley Heights Lookout, a restaurant built into the remnants of the 18th-century fortifications. Most notable for its boisterous Sunday barbecues that continue into the night with live music and dancing, it serves dependable burgers, pumpkin soup, grilled meats, and rum punches. ☎ *268/481–5021* ⊕ *www.nationalparksantigua.com.*

Dows Hill Interpretation Centre. Not far from Shirley Heights is the Dows Hill Interpretation Centre, where observation platforms provide still more sensational vistas of the English Harbour area. A multimedia sound-and-light presentation on island history and culture, spotlighting lifelike figures and colorful tableaux accompanied by running commentary and music, results in a cheery, if bland, portrait of Antiguan life from Amerindian times to the present. ☎ *268/481–5045* ⊕ *www. nationalparksantigua.com* 🖃 *EC$15* ☉ *Daily 9–5*

FAMILY **Stingray City Antigua.** Stingray City Antigua is a carefully reproduced "natural" environment nicknamed by staffers the "retirement home," though the 30-plus stingrays, ranging from infants to seniors, are frisky.

You can stroke, feed, even hold the striking gliders ("they're like puppy dogs," one guide swears), as well as snorkel in deeper, protected waters. The tour guides do a marvelous job of explaining the animals' habits, from feeding to breeding, and their predators (including man). ⊠ *Seaton's Village* ☎ *268/562–7297* ⊕ *www.stingraycityantigua.com.*

BEACHES

Dickenson Bay. Along a lengthy stretch of powder-soft white sand and exceptionally calm water you can find small and large hotels (including Siboney Beach Club, Sandals and Rex Halcyon Cove), water sports, concessions, and beachfront restaurants. There's decent snorkeling at either point. **Amenities:** food and drink, water sports. **Best for:** partiers, snorkeling, swimming, walking. ⊠ *2 miles (3 km) northeast of St. John's, along main coast road.*

Johnson's Point/Crabbe Hill. This series of connected, deserted beaches on the southwest coast looks out toward Montserrat, Guadeloupe, and St. Kitts. Notable beach bar–restaurants include OJ's, Jacqui O's Beach House, and Turner's. The water is generally placid, though not good for snorkeling. **Amenities:** food and drink. **Best for:** swimming, sunset, walking. ⊠ *3 miles (5 km) south of Jolly Harbour complex, on main west-coast road.*

Pigeon Point. Near Falmouth Harbour lie two fine white-sand beaches. The leeward side is calmer, the windward side is rockier, and there are sensational views and snorkeling around the point. Several restaurants and bars are nearby, though Bumpkin's (and its potent banana coladas) satisfies most on-site needs. **Amenities:** food and drink. **Best for:** snorkeling, swimming, walking. ⊠ *Off main south-coast road, southwest of Falmouth.*

SHOPPING

Redcliffe Quay, on the waterfront at the south edge of St. John's, is by far the most appealing shopping area. Several restaurants and more than 30 boutiques, many with one-of-a-kind wares, are set around landscaped courtyards shaded by colorful trees. **Heritage Quay,** in St. John's, has 35 shops—including many that are duty-free—that cater to the cruise-ship crowd, which docks almost at its doorstep. Outlets here include Benetton, the Body Shop, Sunglass Hut, Dolce & Gabbana, and Oshkosh B'Gosh. There are also shops along **St. John's, St. Mary's, High,** and **Long** streets. The tangerine-and-lilac-hue four-story **Vendor's Mall** at the intersection of Redcliffe and Thames streets gathers the pushy, pesky vendors that once clogged the narrow streets. It's jammed with stalls; air-conditioned indoor shops sell some higher-price, if not higher-quality, merchandise. On the west coast the Mediterranean-style, arcaded **Jolly Harbour Marina** holds some interesting galleries and shops, as do the marinas and Main Road snaking around English and Falmouth Harbours.

ACTIVITIES

ADVENTURE TOURS

Adventure Antigua. The enthusiastic Eli Fuller, who is knowledgeable not only about the ecosystem and geography of Antigua but also about its history and politics (his grandfather was the American consul), runs Adventure Antigua. His thorough seven-hour excursion (Eli dubs it "re-creating my childhood explorations") includes stops at Guiana Island (for lunch and guided snorkeling; turtles, barracuda, and stingrays are common sightings), Pelican Island (more snorkeling), Bird Island (hiking to vantage points to admire the soaring ospreys and frigate and red-billed tropic birds), and Hell's Gate (a striking limestone rock formation where the more intrepid may hike and swim through sunken caves and tide pools painted with pink and maroon algae). The company also offers a fun "Xtreme Circumnavigation" variation on a racing boat catering to adrenaline junkies who "feel the need for speed" that also visits Stingray City and Nelson's Dockyard, as well as a more sedate Antigua Classic Yacht sail-and-snorkel experience that explains the rich West Indian history of boatbuilding. ☎ 268/727–3261, 268/726–6355 ⊕ www.adventureantigua.com.

Antigua Rainforest Canopy Tours. Release your inner Tarzan at Antigua Rainforest Canopy Tours. You should be in fairly good condition for the ropes challenges, which require upper-body strength and stamina; there are height and weight restrictions. But anyone (vertigo or acrophobia sufferers, beware) can navigate the intentionally rickety "Indiana Jones–inspired" suspension bridges, then fly (in secure harnesses) over a rain-forest-filled valley from one towering turpentine tree to the next on lines with names like "Screamer" and "Leap of Faith." There are 21 stations, as well as a bar–café and interpretive signposting. First-timers, fear not: the "rangers" are affable, amusing, and accomplished. Admission varies slightly, but is usually $85. It's open Monday–Saturday from 8 to 6, with two scheduled tours at 9 and 11 (other times by appointment). ✉ Fig Dr., Wallings ☎ 268/562–6363 ⊕ www.antiguarainforest.com.

DIVING

Antigua is an unsung diving destination, with plentiful undersea sights to explore, from coral canyons to sea caves. Barbuda alone features roughly 200 wrecks on its treacherous reefs. The most accessible wreck is the 1890s bark *Andes,* not far out in Deep Bay, off Five Islands Peninsula. Among the favorite sites are **Green Island, Cades Reef,** and **Bird Island** (a national park). Memorable sightings include turtles, stingrays, and barracuda darting amid basalt walls, hulking boulders, and stray 17th-century anchors and cannon. One advantage is accessibility in many spots for shore divers and snorkelers. Double-tank dives run about $90.

Dockyard Divers. Owned by British ex-merchant seaman Captain A.G. "Tony" Fincham, Dockyard Divers is one of the island's most established outfits and offers diving and snorkeling trips, PADI courses, and dive packages with accommodations. They're geared to seasoned divers, but staff work patiently with novices. Tony is a wonderful source of information on the island; ask him about the "Fincham's Follies" musical extravaganza he produces for charity. ✉ Nelson's Dockyard,

English Harbour ☎ 268/460–1178
⊕ *www.dockyard-divers.com.*

KAYAKING

"Paddles" Kayak Eco Adventure.
"Paddles" Kayak Eco Adventure
takes you on a 3½-hour tour of
serene mangroves and inlets with
informative narrative about the

fragile ecosystem of the swamp and reefs and the rich diversity of flora
and fauna. The tour ends with a hike to sunken caves and snorkeling
in the North Sound Marine Park, capped by a rum punch at the fun
Creole-style clubhouse. Experienced guides double as kayaking and
snorkeling instructors, making this an excellent opportunity for novices. Conrad and Jennie's brainchild is one of Antigua's better bargains.
⊠ *Seaton's Village* ☎ *268/463–1944* ⊕ *www.antiguapaddles.com.*

WHERE TO EAT

$$
PIZZA

✕ **Big Banana—Pizzas in Paradise.** This tiny, often crowded spot is tucked
into one side of a restored 18th-century rum warehouse with broad
plank floors, wood-beam ceiling, and stone archways. Cool, Benetton-style photos of locals and musicians jamming adorn the brick walls.
Big Banana serves some of the island's best pizza—try the lobster or the
seafood variety—as well as fresh fruit crushes, classic pastas, wraps,
burgers, and sub sandwiches bursting at the seams. There's live entertainment some nights, and a large-screen TV for sports fans. ⑤ *Average main: $16* ⊠ *Redcliffe Quay, St. John's* ☎ *268/480–6985* ⊕ *www.
bigbanana-antigua.com* ⊘ *Closed Sun.*

$$$$
ECLECTIC

✕ **Coconut Grove.** Coconut palms grow through the roof of this open-air thatched restaurant, flickering candlelight illuminates colorful local
murals, waves lap the white sand, and the waitstaff provides just the
right level of service. Jean-François Bellanger's artfully presented dishes
fuse French culinary preparations with island ingredients. Top choices
include pan-seared mahimahi served over cauliflower puree with fingerling potatoes and mango-pineapple chutney; and sautéed shrimp
with roasted plantain and hickory bacon finished with Champagne-parmesan sauce. The kitchen can be uneven, the wine list is unimaginative and overpriced, and the buzzing happy-hour bar crowd lingering
well into dinnertime can detract from the otherwise romantic atmosphere. Nonetheless, Coconut Grove straddles the line between casual
beachfront boîte and elegant eatery with aplomb. ⑤ *Average main:
$30* ⊠ *Siboney Beach Club, Dickenson Bay* ☎ *268/462–1538* ⊕ *www.
coconutgroveantigua.net* ⚞ *Reservations essential.*

ARUBA (ORANJESTAD)

Vernon
O'Reilly
Ramesar

Few islands can boast the overt dedication to tourism and the quality
of service that Aruba offers. The arid landscape is full of attractions to
keep visitors occupied, and the island offers some of the most dazzling
beaches in the Caribbean. Casinos and novelty nightclubs abound in

Oranjestad, giving the capital an almost Las Vegas appeal. To keep tourists coming back year after year, the island boasts a tremendous variety of restaurants ranging from upscale French eateries to toes-in-the-sand casual dining. Aruba may not be an unexplored paradise, but hundreds of thousands of tourists make it a point to beat a path here every year. Because it's not a very large island, cruise-ship visitors can expect to see a large part of the island on their day ashore. Or they can simply see several of the beautiful beaches. Whether you're planning to be active or to simply relax, this is an ideal cruise port.

ESSENTIALS

CURRENCY

The Aruban florin. The florin is pegged to the U.S. dollar, and Arubans accept U.S. dollars readily. Note that the Netherlands Antilles florin used on Curaçao is not accepted on Aruba.

TELEPHONE

You can dial international calls directly or call from the SETAR office in Oranjestad. Simply dial the seven-digit number in Aruba. AT&T customers can dial 800–8000 from special phones at the cruise dock and in the airport's arrival and departure halls. From other phones, dial 121 to contact the SETAR international operator to place a collect or calling-card call.

COMING ASHORE

The Port of Oranjestad is a busy place and is generally full of eager tourists looking for souvenirs or a bite to eat. The port can accommodate up to five ships at a time (and frequently does). The Renaissance Marketplace is right on the port, as are a number of souvenir shops and some decent and inexpensive restaurants. The main shopping areas of Oranjestad are all within 10 minutes' walk of the port.

Taxis can be flagged down on the street that runs alongside the port (look for license plates with a "TX" tag). Rates are fixed (i.e., there are no meters; the rates are set by the government and displayed on a chart), though you and the driver should agree on the fare before your ride begins. Rides to Eagle Beach run about $10; to Palm Beach, about $11. If you want to rent a car, you can do so for a reasonable price; driving is on the right, just as in the United States, and it's pretty easy to get around, though a four-wheel-drive vehicle does help in reaching some of the more out-of-the-way places.

EXPLORING ARUBA

ORANJESTAD

Aruba's charming capital is best explored on foot. L. G. Smith Boulevard, the palm-lined thoroughfare in the center of town, runs between pastel-painted buildings, old and new, of typical Dutch design. You'll find many malls with boutiques and shops here.

FAMILY **Archaeological Museum of Aruba.** This small museum has two rooms chock-full of fascinating artifacts from the indigenous Arawak people, including farm and domestic utensils dating back hundreds of

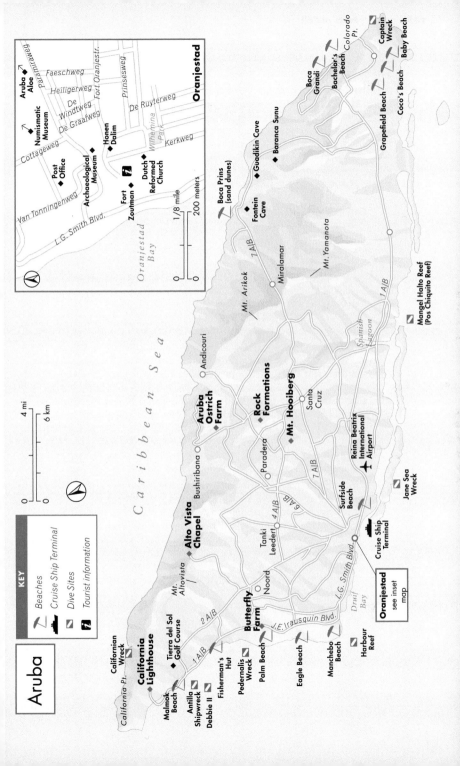

years. ✉ *J. E. Irausquin Blvd. 2A* ☎ *297/582–8979* 🖃 *Free* ⊘ *Tues.– Sun. 10–5.*

Aruba Aloe. Learn all about aloe—its cultivation, processing, and production—at this farm and factory. Guided tours lasting about a half hour will show you how the gel—revered for its skin-soothing properties—is extracted from the aloe vera plant and used in a variety of products, including after-sun creams, soaps, and shampoos. Though not the most exciting tour on the island—and unlikely to keeps kids entertained—it is free and might be a good option on a rainy day. You can purchase the finished goods in the gift shop where the tour ends. ✉ *Pitastraat 115* ☎ *297/588–3222* 🖃 *Free* ⊘ *Weekdays 8:30–4, Sat. 9–noon.*

Ft. Zoutman. One of the island's oldest edifices, Aruba's historic fort was built in 1796 and played an important role in skirmishes between British and Curaçao troops in 1803. The Willem III Tower, named for the Dutch monarch of that time, was added in 1868 to serve as a lighthouse. Over time the fort has been a government office building, a police station, and a prison; now its historical museum displays Aruban artifacts in an 18th-century house. ✉ *Zoutmanstraat, Oranjestad* ☎ *297/582–6099* 🖃 *Free* ⊘ *Weekdays 8–noon and 1–4.*

WESTERN ARUBA

Alto Vista Chapel. Alone near the island's northwest corner sits this scenic little chapel. The wind whistles through the simple mustard-color walls, eerie boulders, and looming cacti. Along the side of the road back to civilization are miniature crosses with depictions of the stations of the cross and hand-lettered signs with "Pray for us Sinners" and other heartfelt evocations of faith. ✉ *Alto Vista Rd., Oranjestad* ⊹ *Follow the rough, winding dirt road that loops around the island's northern tip, or from the hotel strip, take Palm Beach Road through three intersections and watch for the asphalt road to the left just past the Alto Vista Rum Shop.*

Aruba Ostrich Farm. Everything you ever wanted to know about the world's largest living birds can be found at this farm. A large *palapa* (palm-thatched roof) houses a gift shop and restaurant that draws large bus tours, and tours of the farm are available every half hour. This operation is virtually identical to the facility in Curaçao; it's owned by the same company. ✉ *Makividiri Rd., Paradera* ☎ *297/585–9630* ⊕ *www.arubaostrichfarm.com* 🖃 *$12* ⊘ *Daily 9–4.*

FAMILY **Butterfly Farm.** Hundreds of butterflies from around the world flutter about this spectacular garden. Guided 30- to 45-minute tours (included in the price of admission) provide an entertaining look into the life cycle of these insects, from egg to caterpillar to chrysalis to butterfly. After your initial visit, you can return as often as you like for free during your vacation. ⊠ *J.E. Irausquin Blvd., Palm Beach* ☎ *297/586–3656* ⊕ *www.thebutterflyfarm.com* 🖾 *$15* ⊙ *Daily 9–4:30; last tour at 4.*

California Lighthouse. The lighthouse, built by a French architect in 1910, stands at the island's far northern end. Although you can't go inside, you can climb the hill to the lighthouse base for some great views. It's surrounded by huge boulders and sand dunes; in this stark landscape you might feel as though you've just landed on the moon. ⊠ *Arashi, Oranjestad.*

Mt. Hooiberg. Named for its shape (*hooiberg* means "haystack" in Dutch), this 541-foot peak lies inland just past the airport. If you have the energy, you can climb the 562 steps to the top for an impressive view of Oranjestad (and Venezuela on clear days). ⊠ *Oranjestad.*

Rock Formations. The massive boulders at Ayo and Casibari are a mystery, as they don't match the island's geological makeup. You can climb to the top for fine views of the arid countryside. On the way you'll doubtless pass Aruba whiptail lizards—the males are cobalt blue, and the females are blue-gray with light-blue dots. The main path to Casibari has steps and handrails, and you must move through tunnels and along narrow steps and ledges to reach the top. At Ayo you can find ancient pictographs in a small cave (the entrance has iron bars to protect the drawings from vandalism). You may also encounter boulder climbers, who are increasingly drawn to Ayo's smooth surfaces. ⊠ *Paradera* ✛ *Access the rock formations at Casibari via Tanki Hwy. 4A; you can reach Ayo via Rte. 6A. Watch carefully for the turnoff signs near the center of the island on the way to the windward side.*

BEACHES

The beaches on Aruba are beautiful, clean, and easily reached from the cruise-ship terminal in Oranjestad.

Fodor's Choice ★ **Eagle Beach.** On the southwestern coast, across the highway from what is quickly becoming known as Time-Share Lane, is one of the Caribbean's—if not the world's—best beaches. With all the resorts here, this mile-plus-long beach is always hopping. The white sand is literally dazzling, and sunglasses are essential. Many of the hotels have facilities on or near the beach, and refreshments are never far away. **Amenities:** food and drink; toilets. **Best for:** swimming; walking; sunset. ⊠ *J. E. Irausquin Blvd., north of Manchebo Beach.*

Manchebo Beach (*Punta Brabo*). Impressively wide, the white sand shoreline in front of the Manchebo Beach Resort is where officials turn a blind eye to the occasional topless sunbather. This beach merges with Druif Beach, and most locals use the name Manchebo to refer to both. **Amenities:** food and drink; toilets. **Best for:** swimming. ⊠ *J. E. Irausquin Blvd., at Manchebo Beach Resort.*

Palm Beach. This stretch runs from the Westin Aruba Resort, Spa & Casino to the Marriott's Aruba Ocean Club. It's the center of Aruban tourism, offering good swimming, sailing, and other water sports. In some spots you might find a variety of shells that are great to collect, but not as much fun to

> **CAUTION**
>
> Pack and wear a hat to protect your scalp, ears, and face from sun damage and premature aging. Excessive sun exposure contributes to wrinkles and dark spots.

step on barefoot—bring sandals. **Amenities:** food and drink; toilets; water sports. **Best for:** swimming; walking. ⊠ *J. E. Irausquin Blvd., between Westin Aruba Resort and Marriott's Aruba Ocean Club.*

SHOPPING

Caya G. F. Betico Croes. Aruba's chief shopping street, Caya G. F. Betico Croes is a busy thoroughfare and is lined with several shops advertising "duty-free prices" (again, these are not truly duty-free), boutiques, and jewelry stores noted for the aggressiveness of their vendors on cruise-ship days. ⊠ *Oranjestad.*

Renaissance Marketplace. Five minutes from the cruise-ship terminal, the Renaissance Marketplace, also known as Seaport Mall, has more than 120 stores selling merchandise to meet every taste and budget; the Seaport Casino is also here. ⊠ *L.G. Smith Blvd. 82, Oranjestad.*

Royal Plaza Mall. Across from the cruise-ship terminal, the Royal Plaza Mall's pink, gabled building has cafés, a post office (open weekdays 8 to 3:30), and such stores as Nautica, Benetton, and Tommy Hilfiger. There's also a cybercafé. ⊠ *L.G. Smith Blvd. 94, Oranjestad.*

ACTIVITIES

BICYCLING

Pedal pushing is a great way to get around the island; the climate is perfect, and the trade winds help to keep you cool.

Rancho Notorious. Exciting mountain-biking tours are available here. The 2½-hour tour to the Alto Vista Chapel and the California Lighthouse are $50 ($75 with bike rental). ⊠ *Boroncana, Noord* ☎ *297/586–0508* ⊕ *www.ranchonotorious.com.*

DIVING AND SNORKELING

With visibility of up to 90 feet, the waters around Aruba are excellent for snorkeling and diving. Advanced and novice divers alike will find plenty to occupy their time, as many of the most popular sites—including some interesting shipwrecks—are found in shallow waters ranging from 30 to 60 feet.

De Palm Watersports. This is one of the best choices for your undersea experience; the options go beyond basic diving. You can don a helmet and walk along the ocean floor near De Palm Island, home of huge blue parrotfish. You can even do Snuba—which is like scuba diving but without the heavy air tanks—a one-hour snuba adventure costs

$41. ⊠ *De Palm Island, Oranjestad* ☎ *297/582–4400, 800/766–6016* ⊕ *www.depalm.com.*

GOLF

Fodor's Choice
★

Tierra del Sol. Designed by Robert Trent Jones Jr., this 18-hole championship course combines Aruba's native beauty—cacti and rock formations—with the lush greens of the world's best courses. This stunning course is on the northwest coast near the California Lighthouse. The greens fees vary depending on the time of day (from December to March it is $159 in the morning, $131 for early afternoon, and $100 from 3 pm). The fee includes a golf cart equipped with a communications system that allows you to order drinks for your return to the clubhouse. Half-day golf clinics, a bargain at $55, are available Monday, Tuesday, and Thursday. The pro shop is one of the Caribbean's most elegant, with an extremely attentive staff. ⊠ *Malmokweg* ☎ *297/586–0978.*

WHERE TO EAT

$$$
CUBAN

✕ **Cuba's Cookin'.** Nightly entertainment, great authentic Cuban food, and a lively crowd are the draws here. The empanadas are excellent, as is the chicken stuffed with plantains. Don't leave without trying the roast pork, which is pretty close to perfection. The signature dish is the *ropa vieja*, a sautéed flank steak served with a rich sauce (the name literally translates as "old clothes"). Service can be a bit spotty at times, depending on how busy it gets. There's often live music and dancing is encouraged. ⑤ *Average main: $28* ⊠ *Renaissance Marketplace, L. G. Smith Blvd. 82, Oranjestad* ☎ *297/588–0627* ⊕ *www.cubascookin. com.*

$$
CARIBBEAN
Fodor's Choice
★

✕ **Gostoso.** Locals adore the magical mixture of Portuguese, Aruban, and international dishes on offer at this consistently excellent establishment. The decor walks a fine line between kitschy and cozy, but the atmosphere is relaxed and informal and outdoor seating is available. The *bacalhau* vinaigrette (dressed salt cod) is a delightful Portuguese appetizer and pairs nicely with most of the Aruban dishes on the menu. Meat lovers are sure to enjoy the Venezuelan mixed grill, which includes a 14-ounce steak and chorizo accompanied by local sides like fried plantain. ⑤ *Average main: $23* ⊠ *Caya Ing Roland H. Lacle 12, Oranjestad* ☎ *297/588–0053* ⊕ *www.gostosoaruba.com* ⚞ *Reservations essential* ⊗ *Closed Mon.*

BARBADOS (BRIDGETOWN)

Jane E. Zarem

Barbadians (Bajans) are a warm, friendly, and hospitable people, who are genuinely proud of their country and culture. Although tourism is the island's number one industry, the island has a sophisticated business community and stable government, so life here doesn't skip a beat after passengers return to the ship. Barbados is the most "British" island in the Caribbean. Afternoon tea is a ritual, and cricket is the national sport. The atmosphere, though, is hardly stuffy. This is still the Caribbean, after all. Beaches along the island's south and west coasts are picture-perfect, and all are available to cruise passengers. On the rugged east coast, the Atlantic Ocean attracts world-class surfers. The northeast is dominated by rolling hills and valleys, while the interior of the island is covered by acres of sugarcane and dotted with small villages. Historic plantations, a stalactite-studded cave, a wildlife preserve, rum distilleries, and tropical gardens are among the island's attractions. Bridgetown is the capital city, and its downtown shops and historic sites are a short walk or taxi ride from the pier.

ESSENTIALS

CURRENCY

The Barbados dollar (BDS$) is pegged to the U.S. dollar at the rate of BDS$1.98 to US$1. U.S. dollars (but not coins) are accepted universally across the island.

TELEPHONE

Most U.S. cell phones will work in Barbados, though roaming charges can be expensive. Renting a cell phone or buying a local SIM card for your own unlocked phone may be a less expensive alternative if you're planning an extended stay or expect to make a lot of local calls. Top-off services are available at several locations throughout the island.

COMING ASHORE

Up to eight ships at a time can dock at Bridgetown's Deep Water Harbour, on the northwest side of Carlisle Bay near Bridgetown. The cruise-ship terminal has duty-free shops, handicraft vendors, a post office, a telephone station, a tourist information desk, and a taxi stand. To get downtown, follow the shoreline to the Careenage. It's a 15-minute walk or a $4 taxi ride.

Taxis await ships at the pier. Drivers accept U.S. dollars and appreciate a 10% tip. Taxis are unmetered and operate at an hourly rate of $35 to $40 per carload (up to three passengers). Most drivers will cheerfully narrate an island tour. You can rent a car with a valid driver's license, but rates are steep—$60 to $85 per day during the high season—and some agencies require a two-day rental at that time. Note, too, that driving is on the left, British-style.

EXPLORING BARBADOS

BRIDGETOWN

This bustling capital city is a major duty-free port with a compact shopping area. The principal thoroughfare is Broad Street, which leads west from National Heroes Square.

Nidhe Israel Synagogue. Providing for the spiritual needs of one of the oldest Jewish congregations in the Western Hemisphere, this synagogue was formed by Jews who left Brazil in the 1620s and introduced sugarcane to Barbados. The adjoining cemetery has tombstones dating from the 1630s. The original house of worship, built in 1654, was destroyed in an 1831 hurricane, rebuilt in 1833, and restored with the assistance of the Barbados National Trust in 1987. Friday-night services are held during the winter months, but the building is open to the public year-round. Shorts are not acceptable during services but may be worn at other times. ⌧ *Synagogue La.* ☏ *246/436–6869* ⬛ *Donation requested* ⊙ *Weekdays 9–4.*

CENTRAL AND WEST

FAMILY
Fodor'sChoice
★
Gun Hill Signal Station. The 360-degree view from Gun Hill, 700 feet above sea level, gave this location strategic importance to the 18th-century British army. Using lanterns and semaphore, soldiers based here could communicate with their counterparts at the Garrison on the south coast and at Grenade Hill in the north. Time moved slowly in 1868, and Captain Henry Wilkinson whiled away his off-duty hours by carving a huge lion from a single rock—which is on the hillside just below the tower. Come for a short history lesson but mainly for the view; it's so gorgeous, military invalids were once sent here to convalesce. ⌧ *Gun Hill, St. George* ☏ *246/429–1358* ⬛ *$5* ⊙ *Weekdays 9–5.*

FAMILY
Fodor'sChoice
★
Harrison's Cave. This limestone cavern, complete with stalactites, stalagmites, subterranean streams, and a 40-foot waterfall, is a rare find in the Caribbean—and one of Barbados's most popular attractions. Tours include a nine-minute video presentation and a 40-minute underground journey through the cavern via electric tram. The visitor center has interactive displays, life-size models and sculptures, a souvenir shop, restaurant facilities, and elevator access to the tram for people with disabilities. Tours fill up fast, so book a reservation. ⌧ *Hwy. 2, Welchman Hall, St. Thomas* ☏ *246/417–3700* ⊕ *www.harrisonscave.com* ⬛ *$30* ⊙ *Daily 8:30–4:30 (last tour 3:45).*

Mount Gay Rum Visitors Centre. On this popular tour, you learn the colorful story behind the world's oldest rum—made in Barbados since 1703. Although the modern distillery is in the far north, in St. Lucy Parish, tour guides at the Visitors Centre here in St. Michael explain the rum-making procedure. Equipment, both historic and modern, is on display, and rows and rows of barrels are stored in this location. The 45-minute tour runs hourly (last tour begins at 3:30 weekdays, 2:30 on Saturday) and concludes with a tasting and an opportunity to buy bottles of rum and gift items—and even have lunch or cocktails, depending on the time of day. ⌧ *Spring Garden Hwy., Brandons* ☏ *246/425–8757* ⊕ *www.mountgayrum.com* ⬛ *$7, $50 with lunch, $35 with cocktails* ⊙ *Weekdays 9–5, Saturday 10–4.*

NORTH AND EAST

Fodor'sChoice
★
Andromeda Botanic Gardens. More than 600 beautiful and unusual plant specimens from around the world are cultivated in 6 acres of gardens nestled among streams, ponds, and rocky outcroppings overlooking the sea above the Bathsheba coastline. The gardens were created in 1954 with flowering plants collected by the late horticulturist Iris Bannochie. They're now administered by the Barbados National Trust. The Hibiscus Café serves snacks and drinks. ⌧ *Bathsheba, St. Joseph* ☏ *246/433–9384* ⬛ *$10* ⊙ *Daily 9–5.*

Fodor'sChoice
★
St. Nicholas Abbey. The island's oldest great house (circa 1650) was named after the original British owner's hometown, St. Nicholas Parish near Bristol, and Bath Abbey nearby. Its stone-and-wood architecture makes it one of only three original Jacobean-style houses still standing in the Western Hemisphere. It has Dutch gables, finials of coral

7

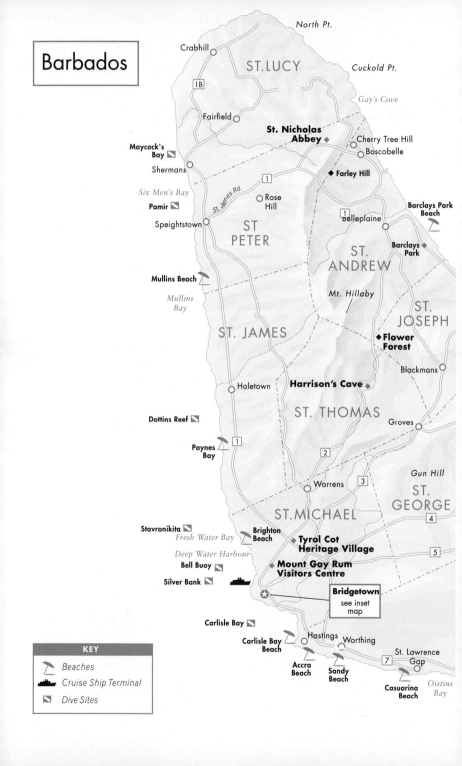

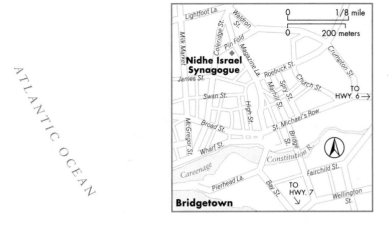

ATLANTIC OCEAN

Lightfoot La.
Waldron St.
Milk Market
Coleridge St.
Pin Fold
Magazine La.

**Nidhe Israel
Synagogue**

James St.
Roebuck St.
Church St.
Crumpton St.

TO
HWY. 6 →

Swan St.
Marhill St.
Spry St.

McGregor St.
High St.
St. Michael's Row

Broad St.
Bridge St.

Wharf St.
Constitution R.

Careenage
Fairchild St.

Pierhead La.
Bay St.
Wellington St.

TO
HWY. 7

0   1/8 mile
0   200 meters

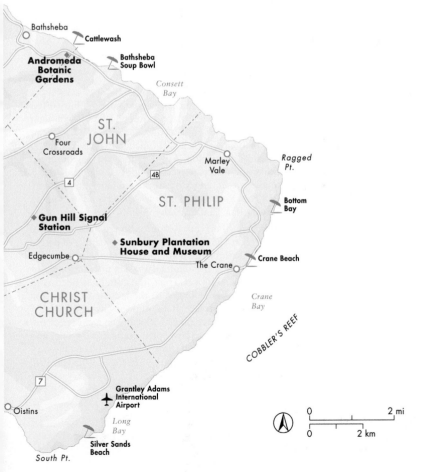

Bathsheba

Cattlewash

**Andromeda
Botanic
Gardens**

Bathsheba
Soup Bowl

Consett
Bay

**ST.
JOHN**

Four
Crossroads

Marley
Vale

Ragged
Pt.

4   4B

ST. PHILIP

Bottom
Bay

**Gun Hill Signal
Station**

**Sunbury Plantation
House and Museum**

Edgecumbe

The Crane

Crane Beach

**CHRIST
CHURCH**

Crane
Bay

COBBLER'S REEF

7

**Grantley Adams
International
Airport**

Oistins

Long
Bay

**Silver Sands
Beach**

South Pt.

0   2 mi
0   2 km

stone, and beautiful grounds that include an "avenue" of mahogany trees, a "gully" filled with tropical trees and plantings, formal gardens, and an old sugar mill. The first floor, fully furnished with period furniture and portraits of family members, is open to the public. A fascinating home movie, shot by a previous owner's father, records Bajan life in the 1930s. Behind the greathouse is a rum distillery with a 19th-century steam press. Visitors can purchase artisanal plantation rum produced nearby (the Abbey's production will become fully aged about 2018), browse the gift shop, and enjoy light refreshments at the Terrace Café. ⊠ *Cherry Tree Hill, St. Peter* ☏ *246/422–5357* ⊕ *www. stnicholasabbey.com* ✉ *$17.50* ☽ *Sun.–Fri. 10–3:30.*

> **BARBADOS BEST BETS**
>
> ■ **The East Coast.** The island's windward coast, with its crashing surf, is a "don't-miss" sight.
>
> ■ **Harrison's Cave.** This extensive limestone cave system is deep beneath Barbados.
>
> ■ **Mount Gay Rum Visitors Centre.** Take a tour and a tasting.
>
> ■ **Flower Gardens.** Andromeda Botanic Gardens, Flower Forest, and Orchid World are all scenic and fragrant.
>
> ■ **St. Nicholas Abbey.** Not an abbey at all, this is one of the oldest Jacobean-style houses in the Western Hemisphere.

SOUTH

Fodor's Choice
★

Sunbury Plantation House and Museum. Lovingly rebuilt after a 1995 fire destroyed everything but the thick flint-and-stone walls, Sunbury offers an elegant glimpse of the 18th and 19th centuries on a Barbadian sugar estate. Period furniture, old prints, and a collection of horse-drawn carriages lend an air of authenticity. A buffet luncheon is served daily in the courtyard for $32.50 per person. A five-course candlelight dinner is served ($100 per person, reservations required) two nights a week at the 200-year-old mahogany dining table in the Sunbury dining room. ⊠ *Off Hwy. 5, Six Cross Roads, St. Philip* ☏ *246/423–6270* ⊕ *www. barbadosgreathouse.com* ✉ *$7.50* ☽ *Daily 9–4:30.*

Tyrol Cot Heritage Village. This coral-stone cottage just south of Bridgetown, constructed in 1854, is preserved as an example of period architecture. In 1929, it became the home of Sir Grantley Adams, the first premier of Barbados and the namesake of its international airport. Part of the Barbados National Trust, the cottage is filled with antiques and memorabilia that belonged to the late Sir Grantley and Lady Adams. It's also the centerpiece of an outdoor "living museum," where artisans and craftsmen have their workshops in a cluster of traditional chattel houses. Workshops are open, crafts are for sale, and refreshments are available at the "rum shop" primarily during the winter season and when cruise ships are in port. ⊠ *Rte. 2, Codrington Hill* ☏ *246/424–2074* ✉ *$5.75* ☽ *Weekdays 9–5.*

BEACHES

All beaches on Barbados are open to cruise-ship passengers. The west coast has the stunning coves and white-sand beaches dear to the hearts of postcard publishers, plus calm, clear water for snorkeling and swimming. Waterskiing and parasailing are also available on most beaches along the south and west coasts. Windsurfing is best on the south coast.

> **TIME TIP**
>
> If you don't want to rely on shipboard wake-up calls, be sure to bring your own travel alarm clock; most staterooms do not have clocks.

FAMILY **Accra Beach.** This popular beach, also known as Rockley Beach, is next to the Accra Beach Hotel. You'll find a broad swath of white sand with gentle surf and a lifeguard, plenty of nearby restaurants for refreshments, a children's playground, and beach stalls for renting chairs and equipment for snorkeling and other water sports. **Amenities:** food and drink; lifeguards; parking (free); water sports. **Best for:** snorkeling; swimming. ⊠ *Hwy. 7, Rockley, Christ Church.*

Fodor'sChoice **Mullins Beach.** This lovely beach just south of Speightstown is a perfect ★ place to spend the day. The water is safe for swimming and snorkeling, there's easy parking on the main road, and Mullins Restaurant serves snacks, meals, and drinks—and rents chairs and umbrellas. **Amenities:** food and drink; parking (free); toilets. **Best for:** sunset; swimming; walking. ⊠ *Hwy. 1, Mullins Bay, St. Peter.*

Fodor'sChoice **Pebbles Beach.** On the southern side of Carlisle Bay, just south of ★ Bridgetown, this broad half circle of white sand is one of the island's best beaches—but it can become crowded on weekends and holidays. The southern end of the beach wraps around the Hilton Barbados; the northern end is a block away from Island Inn. Park at Harbour Lights or at the Boatyard Bar and Bayshore Complex, both on Bay Street, where you can also rent umbrellas and beach chairs and buy refreshments. **Amenities:** food and drink. **Best for:** swimming; walking. ⊠ *Off Bay St., south of Bridgetown, Needham's Point.*

SHOPPING

Duty-free shopping is found in Bridgetown's Broad Street stores and their branches in Holetown and at the cruise-ship terminal. Stores are generally open weekdays 8:30–4:30, Saturday 8:30–1. ■**TIP➔ To purchase items duty-free, you must show your passport and cabin key card.**

Best of Barbados. Best of Barbados was the brainchild of architect Jimmy Walker as a place to showcase the works of his artist wife. Now with five locations, the shops offer products that range from Jill Walker's frameable prints, housewares, and textiles to arts and crafts in both "native" style and modern designs. Everything is made or designed on Barbados. Branch shops are located at Chattel Village in Holetown and in the airport departure lounge mall. ⊠ *Quayside Centre, Main Rd., Rockley, Christ Church* ☎ *246/435–6820* ⊕ *www.best-of-barbados. com.*

7

Pelican Village Craft Centre. Pelican Village is a cluster of workshops located halfway between the cruise-ship terminal and downtown Bridgetown where craftspeople create and sell locally made leather goods, batik, basketry, carvings, jewelry, glass art, paintings, pottery, and other items. It's open weekdays 9 to 5 and Saturday 9 to 2; things here are most active when cruise ships are in port. ⊠ *Princess Alice Hwy.* ☎ *246/427–5350.*

ACTIVITIES

FISHING

Billfisher II. A 40-foot Pacemaker, *Billfisher II* accommodates up to six passengers with three fishing chairs and five rods. Captain Winston ("The Colonel") White has been fishing these waters since 1975. His full-day charters include a full lunch and guaranteed fish (or a 25% refund); all trips include drinks and transportation to and from the boat. ⊠ *Bridge House Wharf, The Careenage* ☎ *246/431–0741.*

GOLF

Barbados Golf Club. The first public golf course on Barbados, Barbados Golf Club is an 18-hole championship course (6,805 yards, par 72) redesigned in 2000 by golf course architect Ron Kirby. Greens fees with a pull trolley are $114 for 18 holes, $71 for 9 holes. Unlimited three-day and seven-day golf passes are available. Several hotels offer preferential tee-time reservations and reduced rates. Club and shoe rentals are available. ⊠ *Hwy. 7, Durants, Christ Church* ☎ *246/428–8463* ⊕ *www.barbadosgolfclub.com.*

Fodor's Choice ★ **Country Club at Sandy Lane.** At the prestigious Country Club at Sandy Lane, golfers can play on the Old Nine or on either of two 18-hole championship courses: the Tom Fazio–designed Country Club Course or the spectacular Green Monkey Course, which is reserved for hotel guests and club members only. Golfers have complimentary use of the club's driving range. The Country Club Restaurant and Bar, which overlooks the 18th hole, is open to the public. Greens fees in high season are $155 for 9 holes ($135 for hotel guests) or $240 for 18 holes ($205 for hotel guests). Golf carts, caddies, or trolleys are available for hire, as are clubs and shoes. Carts are equipped with GPS, which alerts you to upcoming traps and hazards, provides tips on how to play the hole, and allows you to order refreshments! ⊠ *Sandy Lane, Hwy. 1, Paynes Bay, St. James* ☎ *246/444–2500* ⊕ *www.sandylane.com/golf.*

WHERE TO EAT

$$$

CARIBBEAN

Fodor's Choice ★ ✕ **The Atlantis.** For decades, an alfresco lunch on the Atlantis deck overlooking the ocean has been a favorite of visitors and of Bajans alike. Totally renovated and reopened in 2009, the revived restaurant effectively combines the atmosphere and good food that have always been the draw with an up-to-date, elegant dining room and a top-notch menu that focuses on local produce, seafood, and meats. The Bajan buffet lunch on Wednesday and Sunday is particularly popular. At dinner, entreés include fresh fish, lobster (seasonal), roasted black-belly lamb or free-range chicken, fricassee of rabbit, and more. Or choose more traditional pepper pot, saltfish, or chicken stew with peas and rice, cou-cou, yam pie, or breadfruit mash, all of which are available at the Bajan buffet. $ *Average main: $25* ⊠ *The Atlantis Hotel, Tent Bay, St. Joseph* ☎ *246/433–9445* ⊕ *www.atlantishotelbarbados.com* ⌕ *Reservations essential* ⊘ *No dinner Sun.*

$$$
CARIBBEAN

✕ **Waterfront Café.** This friendly bistro alongside the Careenage is the perfect place to enjoy a drink, snack, or meal—and to people-watch. Locals and tourists alike gather for alfresco all-day dining on sand-wiches, salads, fish, pasta, pepper-pot stew, and tasty Bajan snacks such as buljol, fish cakes, or plantation pork (plantains stuffed with spicy minced pork). The panfried flying-fish sandwich is an especially popular lunchtime treat. $ *Average main: $25* ⊠ *The Careenage* ☎ *246/427–0093* ⊕ *www.waterfrontcafe.com.bb* ⊘ *Closed Sun. No dinner.*

BELIZE CITY, BELIZE

Lan Sluder

Belize probably has the greatest variety of flora and fauna of any country of its size in the world. Here you'll often find more iguanas or howler monkeys than humans. A few miles off the mainland is the Belize Barrier Reef, a great wall of coral stretching the entire 200-mile (333-km) length of the coast. Over 200 cayes (pronounced keys) dot the reef like punctuation marks, and three coral atolls lie farther out to sea. All are superb for diving and snorkeling. Many, like Ambergris Caye (pronounced *Am*-bur-griss Key) and Caye Caulker, are cheery resort islands with ample bars and restaurants, easily reachable on day trips from Belize City. The main choice you'll have to make is whether to stay in Belize City for a little stroll and shopping, and perhaps a dram at one of the Fort George hotels or restaurants, or alternatively to head out by boat, rental car, taxi, or tour on a more active adventure.

ESSENTIALS

CURRENCY

U.S. currency is universally accepted, so there's no need to acquire the Belize dollar (BZ$2 to US$1).

FLIGHTS

Especially if you are going to Ambergris Caye, you may prefer to fly, or you can water-taxi over and fly back to maximize your time. There are hourly flights on two airlines. The flight to Caulker takes about 10 minutes and that to San Pedro about 25 minutes. The cost is about BZ$250 round-trip to either island. Be sure you fly out of Belize City's Municipal, not out of the international airport north of the city.

Contacts **Maya Island Airways** ☎ *223/1140, 223/0734* ⊕ *www.mayaregional. com.* **Tropic Air** ☎ *226/2012, 800/422–3435 in U.S. or Canada* ⊕ *www.tropicair. com.*

TELEPHONE

Calling locally or internationally is easy, but rates are high; around BZ$1.50 a minute for calls to the United States. To call the United States, dial 001 or 10–10–199 plus the area code and number. Pay phones, which are located in the Fort Street Tourism Village where you

Belize

MEXICO

Buena Vista

SHIPSTERN WILDLIFE RESERVE

COROZAL DISTRICT

Orange Walk

Bahía de Chetumal

Ambergris Caye

August Pine Ridge

Shipyard

San Pedro

San Felipe

Blue Creek Village

Crooked Tree Wildlife Sanctuary

HOL CHAN MARINE RESERVE

Caye Caulker

ORANGE WALK DISTRICT

Crooked Tree

Community Baboon Sanctuary

Altun Ha

Caye Chapel

New River

Burrell Boom

Belize City see inset map

Belize Zoo

Ladyville

St. George's Caye

BELIZE DISTRICT

Belize City

GUANACASTE PARK

Hattieville

Turneffe Islands

Spanish Lookout

Northern Lagoon

Roaring Creek

Western Hwy.

Southern Lagoon

Gales Point

BELMOPAN

Manatee Road

St. Herman's Blue Hole

Hummingbird Hwy.

Dangriga

Hummingbird Highway

0 15 miles

0 15 km

Museum of Belize

Orange St.

Fort George Lighthouse

Belize Harbour

St. John's Cathedral

House of Culture

Belize City

are tendered, and elsewhere downtown, accept only prepaid Belize Telecommunications Ltd. (BTL) phone cards, available in shops in denominations from $5 to $50. Special "USA Connect" prepaid cards, for sale at some stores in Belize City, in denominations of $5 to $20, claim discounts of as much as 57% for calls to the United States only. Your U.S.-based GSM phone will probably work on Belize's GSM 1900 system, but you will pay a high surcharge to use it abroad. Foreign calling cards are generally blocked in Belize. Call 113 for local directory assistance, and 115 for an operator.

VISITOR INFORMATION
Contacts Belize Tourism Board ⊠ 64 Regent St. ☎ 227/2420 ⊕ www.travelbelize.org.

COMING ASHORE

Because Belize City's harbor is shallow, passengers are tendered in. If you're going the independent route, try to get in line early for the tenders, as it sometimes takes 90 minutes or more for all passengers to be brought ashore. You arrive at the Fort Street Tourism Village complex. It has a collection of gift shops, restaurants, and tour operators nicely situated along the harbor. Bathrooms are spick-and-span, too. At this writing, construction is sputtering on a much-delayed $50-million cruise terminal south of the city center; when it will finally open is anyone's guess.

Taxis, tour guides, and car-rental desks are readily available. Cabs cost BZ$7–BZ$10 for one person between any two points in the city, plus BZ$1 for each additional person. Taxi fares at night are slightly higher. Outside the city, and from downtown to the suburbs, you're charged by the distance you travel. Hourly rates are negotiable, but expect to pay around $30, or $150 for the day. Drivers are required to display a Taxi Federation rate card. There's no need to tip them. You can also rent a car at the Tourism Village, but rates can be high (at least $75 per day), and gas is also expensive. Green directional signs point you to nearby destinations such as the Belize Zoo. The Wet Lizard, next to the Tourism Village, also organizes tours for cruise-ship passengers.

BELIZE CITY BEST BETS

■ **Belize Zoo.** Though small, this collection of native Belize wildlife is excellent.

■ **Cave Tubing.** If you are not claustrophobic, this is an unforgettable excursion.

■ **Diving.** Belize is becoming known as one of the world's best dive destinations. For the certified, this is a must.

■ **Snorkeling in Hol Chan.** The water is teeming with fish, and you don't need to be certified to enjoy the underwater world here.

EXPLORING BELIZE

Many Belize hands will tell you that the best way to see Belize City is through a rearview window. But, with an open mind to its peculiarities, and with a little caution (the city has a crime problem, but the tourist police keep a close watch on cruise-ship passengers), you may decide Belize City has a raffish, atmospheric charm rarely found in other Caribbean ports of call. You might even see the ghost of Graham Greene, who visited Belize in 1978 as a guest of General Torrijos.

BELIZE CITY

A 5- to 10-minute stroll from the colorful Fort Street Tourism Village brings you into the other worlds of Belize City. On the north side of Haulover Creek is the colonial-style Fort George, where large old homes, stately but sometimes down at the heels, take the breezes off the sea and share their space with hotels and restaurants. On the south side is bustling Albert Street, the main commercial thoroughfare. But don't stroll too far since parts of Belize City are unsafe. During the daylight hours, as long as you stay within the main commercial district and the Fort George area—and ignore the street hustlers—you should have no problem.

Fort George Lighthouse and Bliss Memorial. Towering over the entrance to Belize Harbor, the lighthouse stands guard on the tip of Fort George Point. It was designed and funded by one of the country's greatest benefactors, Baron Henry Edward Ernest Victor Bliss. The English nobleman never actually set foot on the Belizean mainland, though in his yacht he visited the waters offshore. In his will he bequeathed most of his fortune to the people of Belize, and the date of his death, March 9, is celebrated as a national holiday, now officially called National Heroes and Bene-factors Day. Bliss is buried here, in a small, low mausoleum perched on the seawall, up a short run of limestone stairs. The lighthouse and mausoleum are for photo ops only—you can't enter. ✉ *Marine Parade, near Radisson Fort George Hotel, Fort George* ☎ *Free* ☉ *Daily 24 hrs.*

House of Culture. Formerly called Government House, the city's finest colonial structure is said to have a design inspired by the illustrious British architect Sir Christopher Wren. Built in 1814, it was once the residence of the governor-general, the queen's representative in Belize. Following Hurricane Hattie in 1961, the governor and the rest of the government moved to Belmopan, and the house became a venue for social functions and a guesthouse for visiting VIPs. (Queen Elizabeth stayed here in 1985, Prince Philip in 1988.) Now it's open to the public. You can peruse its archival records, art, photographs, silver, glassware, and furniture collections, or mingle with the tropical birds that frequent the gardens. ⚠ **If going here after dark, take a cab, because it's close to some of the city's most crime-ridden areas.** ✉ *Regent St. at Southern Fore-shore, opposite St. John's Cathedral, Commercial District* ☎ *227/3050* ⊕ *www.nichbelize.org* ✉ *BZ$10* ☉ *Weekdays 8:30–5.*

Museum of Belize. This small but fascinating museum was the Belize City jail from 1857 to 1993. Permanent displays include ancient jade and other Mayan artifacts; medicinal, ink, and alcoholic-beverage bot-tles dating from the 1670s; Belize coins and colorful postage stamps; and an actual prison cell. Temporary exhibitions change periodically. ✉ *8 Gabourel La., Belize Central Bank Compound, Fort George* ☎ *223/4524* ⊕ *www.nichbelize.org* ✉ *BZ$20* ☉ *Mon.–Sat. 8–4:30.*

St. John's Cathedral. On Albert Street's south end is the oldest Anglican church in Central America and the only one outside England where kings were crowned. From 1815 to 1845, four kings of the Mosquito Coast (a British protectorate along the coast of Honduras and Nicara-gua) were crowned here. The cathedral, built of brick brought to Brit-ish Honduras as ballast on English ships, is thought to be the oldest building in Belize, other than Mayan structures. Its foundation stone was laid in 1812. Inside, it has whitewashed walls and mahogany pews. The roof is constructed of local sapodilla wood, with mahogany beams. ■ TIP→ **You can combine a visit to St. John's Cathedral with a visit to the House of Culture, as they are just cross the street from each other.** ⚠ **Safe to visit during day; at night take a cab.** ✉ *Albert St. at Regent St., Oppo-site the House of Culture, Commercial District* ☎ *227/3029* ⊕ *www. belizeanglican.org* ✉ *Free* ☉ *Daily 8:30–5; Sunday hrs vary.*

INLAND FROM BELIZE CITY

FAMILY   **Altun Ha.** If you've never experienced an ancient Mayan city, make a trip to Altun Ha, which is a modern translation in Mayan of the name "Rockstone Pond," a nearby village. It's not Belize's most dramatic site—Caracol and Lamanai vie for that award—but it's one of the most accessible and most thoroughly excavated. The first inhabitants settled before 300 BC, and their descendants finally abandoned the site after

AD 1000. At its height during the Classic period the city was home to 10,000 people. Tours from Belize City, Orange Walk, and Crooked Tree also are options. Altun Ha is a regular stop on cruise ship excursions. Several tour operators in San Pedro and Caye Caulker also offer day trips to Altun Ha, often combined with lunch at the nearby Maruba Resort Jungle Spa. Most of these tours from the cayes are by boat, landing at Bomba Village. From here, a van makes the short ride to Altun Ha. If traveling independently or on a tour that includes it, you can stop at Maruba Resort Jungle Spa for a drink, lunch, or a spa treatment. ⊠ *Rockstone Pond Rd., off Old Northern Hwy., Maskall Village* ✛ *From Belize City, take Northern Hwy. north to mile 18.9. Turn right (east) on Old Northern Hwy., which is only partly paved, and go 14 miles (23 km) to signed entrance road at Rockstone Pond Rd. to Altun Ha on left. Follow this paved road 2 miles (3 km) to visitor center.* ☎ *822/2106 NICH/Belize Institute of Archeology* ⊕ *www. nich.org* ⊠ *BZ$10* ☉ *Daily 8–5.*

Belize Zoo. One of the smallest, but arguably one of the best, zoos in the Americas, the Belize Zoo packs a lot into 29 acres. Containing more than 150 animals and 45 different species, all native to Belize, the zoo has self-guided tours through several Belizean ecosystems—rain forest, lagoons, and riverine forest. Plan for about 2 hours to see the zoo. Along with jaguars you'll see the country's four other wild cats: the puma, margay, ocelot, and jaguarundi. Perhaps the zoo's most famous resident is April, a Baird's tapir that is more than a quarter-century old. This relative of the horse and rhino is known to locals as the mountain cow, and is also Belize's national animal. At the zoo you'll also see jabiru storks, a harpy eagle, scarlet macaws, howler monkeys, crocodiles, and many snakes, including the fer-de-lance. The zoo owes its existence to the dedication and drive of one gutsy woman, Sharon Matola. An American who came to Belize as part of a film crew, Matola stayed on to care for some of the semi-tame animals used in the production. She opened the zoo in 1983, and in 1991 it moved to its present location. ⊠ *Mile 29, George Price Hwy. (formerly Western Hwy.)* ☎ *220/8004* ⊕ *www.belizezoo.org* ⊠ *BZ$30* ☉ *Daily 8:30–5:30 (last admission 4:30).*

FAMILY **Community Baboon Sanctuary.** One of Belize's most fascinating wildlife conservation projects is the Community Baboon Sanctuary, which is actually a haven for black howler monkeys (baboon is Kriol for the howler). Spanning a 20-mile (32-km) stretch of the Belize River, the reserve was established in 1985 by a group of local farmers. The howler monkey—an agile bundle of black fur with a disturbing roar—was then zealously hunted throughout Central America and was facing extinction. Today the sanctuary is home, on some 200 private properties, to more than 2,000 black howler monkeys, as well as numerous species of birds and mammals. Thanks to ongoing conservation efforts countrywide, you can see the howler monkeys in a number of other areas, including at Lamanai in northern Belize, along the Macal, Mopan, and Belize rivers in western Belize, near Monkey River and around Punta Gorda in southern Belize. Exploring the Community Baboon Sanctuary is easy, thanks to about 3 miles (5 km) of trails that start

7

near a small museum and visitor center. The admission fee includes a 45-minute guided nature tour during which you definitely will see howlers. ✉ *Community Baboon Sanctuary, 31 miles (50 km) northwest of Belize City, Bermudian Village* ☎ *249/2009* ⊕ *www.howlermonkeys.org* 🎟 *BZ$14 per person (includes admission to visitor center and a guided monkey-spotting tour); night hike BZ$24 per person* ⊙ *Daily 8–5.*

Crooked Tree Wildlife Sanctuary. Crooked Tree Wildlife Sanctuary is one of Belize's top birding spots. The 16,400-acre sanctuary includes more than 3,000 acres of lagoons, swamp, and marsh, surrounding what is essentially an inland island. Traveling by canoe, you're likely to see iguanas, crocodiles, coatis, and turtles. The sanctuary's most prestigious visitors, however, are the jabiru storks, which usually visit between November and May. With a wingspan up to 12 feet, the jabiru is the largest flying bird in the Americas. ■ **TIP→ For birders the best time to come is in the dry season, roughly from February to late May, when lowered water levels cause birds to group together to find water and food, making them easy to spot.** Birding is good year-round, however, and the area is more scenic when the lagoons are full. ✉ *Crooked Tree* ✛ *Turn west off Philip Goldson Hwy. (formerly Northern Hwy.) at mile 30.8, then drive 2 miles (3 km)* ☎ *223/4987 for Belize Audubon Society* ⊕ *www. belizeaudubon.org* 🎟 *BZ$8* ⊙ *Daily 8–4:30.*

Hummingbird Highway. Hands down, Hummingbird Highway is the most scenic roadway in Belize. The Hummingbird, a paved two-lane road, runs 54½ miles (91 km) from the junction of the Western Highway at Belmopan to Dangriga. Technically, only the first 32 miles (53 km) is the Hummingbird—the rest is the Stann Creek District Highway, but most people ignore that distinction. As measured from Belmopan at the junction of the Western Highway—the road has a few mileposts running from Dangriga north, but we'll ignore them—the Hummingbird first winds through limestone hill country, passing St. Herman's Cave (mile 12.2) and the inland Blue Hole (mile 13.1). It then starts rising steeply, with the Maya Mountains on the west or right side, past Five Blue Lake (mile 23). The views, of green mountains studded with cohune palms and tropical hardwoods, are incredible. At the Hummingbird Gap (mile 26, elevation near 1,000 feet, with mountains nearby over 3,000 feet), you're at the crest of the highway and now begin to drop down toward the Caribbean Sea. At Middlesex village (mile 32), technically the road becomes the Stann Creek District Highway. Now you're in citrus country, with groves of grapefruit and Valencia oranges. At mile 48.7 you pass the turn-off to the Southern Highway and at mile 54.5 you enter Dangriga, with the sea just ahead. ✉ *Belmopan to Dangriga, Hummingbird Hwy., Belmopan.*

FAMILY **St. Herman's Blue Hole National Park.** Less than a half hour south of Belmopan, the 575-acre St. Herman's Blue Hole National Park has a natural turquoise pool surrounded by mosses and lush vegetation, wonderful for a cool dip. The "inland Blue Hole" is actually part of an underground river system. On the other side of the hill is St. Herman's Cave, once inhabited by the Maya. There's a separate entrance to St. Herman's. A path leads up from the highway, but it's quite steep and difficult to climb unless the ground is dry. To explore St. Herman's cave beyond the first 300 yards or so, you must be accompanied by a guide (available at the park), and no more than five people can enter the cave at one time. With a guide, you also can explore part of another cave system here, the Crystal Cave (sometimes called the Crystalline Cave), which stretches for miles; the additional cost is BZ$20 per person for a two-hour guided tour. The main park visitor center is 12½ miles (20½ km) from Belmopan. St. Herman's Blue Hole National Park is managed by the Belize Audubon Society. ⊠ *Mile 42.5, Hummingbird Hwy., Belmopan* ☎ *223/5004 Belize Audubon Society* ⊕ *www.belizeaudubon. org* ☞ *BZ$10* ☉ *Daily 8–4:30.*

THE CAYES

Ambergris Caye. Ambergris is the queen of the cayes. With a population of around 9,000, the island's only town, San Pedro, remains a small, friendly, and prosperous village. It has one of the highest literacy rates in the country and an admirable level of awareness about the fragility of the reef. The large number of substantial private houses being built on the edges of town is proof of how much tourism has enriched San Pedro. A water taxi from the Marine Terminal takes about 75 minutes and costs BZ$20 each way. You can also fly.

Fodor's Choice
★

Hol Chan Marine Reserve. The reef's focal point for diving and snorkeling near Ambergris Caye and Caye Caulker is the spectacular Hol Chan Marine Reserve (Maya for "little channel"). It's a 20-minute boat ride from San Pedro, and about 30 minutes from Caye Caulker. Hol Chan is a break in the reef about 100 feet wide and 20 to 35 feet deep, through which tremendous volumes of water pass with the tides. Shark-Ray Alley, now a part of Hol Chan, is famous as a place to swim, snorkel, and dive with sharks (nearly all are nurse sharks) and Southern sting rays.

Because fishing generally is off-limits here, divers and snorkelers can see abundant marine life, including spotted eagle rays and sharks. There are throngs of squirrelfish, butterfly fish, parrotfish, and queen angelfish, as well as Nassau groupers, barracuda, and large shoals of yellowtail snappers. Unfortunately, also here are lionfish, an invasive Indo-Pacific species that is eating its way—destroying small native fish—from Venezuela to the North Carolina coast. Altogether, more than 160 species of fish have been identified in the marine reserve, along with 40 species of coral, and five kinds of sponges. Hawksbill, loggerhead, and green turtles have also been found here, along with spotted and common dolphins, West Indian manatees, sting rays and several species of sharks. ⊠ *Off southern tip of Ambergris Caye* ☎ *526/2247 Hol Chan office in San Pedro* ⊕ *www.holchanbelize.org* ☞ *BZ$20, normally included in snorkel or dive tour charge.*

Caye Caulker. On Caye Caulker, where its one village is home to around 2,000 people, brightly painted houses on stilts line the coral-sand streets. Although the island is being developed more each year, flowers still outnumber cars 10 to 1 (golf carts, bicycles, and bare feet are the preferred means of transportation). The living is easy, as you might guess from all the *no shirt, no shoes, no problem* signs at the bars. This is the kind of place where most of the listings in the telephone directory

7

give addresses like "near football field." A water taxi from the Marine Terminal costs about BZ$20 each way and takes about 45 minutes.

BEACHES

Although the barrier reef limits the wave action and brings seagrass to the shore floor, the wide sandy beaches of Ambergris Caye are among the best in Belize. All beaches in Belize are public. **Mar de Tumbo,** 1½ miles (3 km) south of town near the Tropica Hotel, is the best beach on the south end of the island. **North Ambergris,** accessible by water taxi from San Pedro or by golf cart over the bridge to the north, has miles of narrow beaches and fewer people. **Ramon's Village's beach,** across from the airstrip, is the best in the town area. The beaches on Caulker are not as good as those on Ambergris. Along the front side of the island is a narrow strip of sand, but the water is shallow and swimming conditions are poor. The **Split,** on the north end of the village (turn to your right from the main public pier), is the best place on Caye Caulker for swimming.

SHOPPING

Belize does not have the crafts tradition of its neighbors, Guatemala and Mexico, and imported goods are expensive due to high duties, but hand-carved items of ziricote or other local woods make good souvenirs. Near the Swing Bridge at Market Square is the **Commercial Center,** which has some food and craft vendors on the first floor and a restaurant and shops on the second. The **Fort Street Tourism Village,** where the ship tenders come in, is a collection of bright and clean gift shops selling T-shirts and Belizean and Guatemalan crafts. Beside the Tourism Village is an informal **Street Vendor Market,** with funkier goods and performances by a "Brukdown" band or a group of Garifuna drummers.

Belizean Handicraft Market Place. Belizean Handicraft Market Place (formerly National Handicraft Center) has Belizean souvenir items, including hand-carved figurines, handmade furniture, pottery, and woven baskets. The prices are about as good as you'll find anywhere in Belize, and the sales clerks are friendly. It faces the small Memorial Park, which commemorates the Battle of St. George's Caye and is just a short stroll from the harbor front, the Tourism Village, and many of the hotels in the Fort George area, including the Radisson, Chateau Caribbean, and The Great House. ⌧ *2 S. Park St., in Fort George area across from Memorial Park* ☎ *223/3627.*

ACTIVITIES

CANOPY TOURS
You may feel a little like Tarzan as you dangle 80 feet above the jungle floor, suspended by a harness, moving from one treetop platform to another.

Jaguar Paw/Chukka Caribbean. Formerly a jungle lodge and now a tour operation and part of the Chukka Caribbean tours empire, off mile 37 of the Western Highway, Jaguar Paw has eight zip line platforms set

100 to 250 feet apart. At the last platform you have to rappel to the ground. There's a 240-pound weight limit. Zip line tours often are combined with cave tubing in the Caves Branch River. The cost is around BZ$120–BZ$180, depending on the tour and whether lunch and transportation are included. ☎ *223/4438* ⊕ *www.chukkacaribbean.com.*

CAVE TUBING

Very popular with cruise passengers are river-tubing trips that go through a cave, where you'll turn off your headlamp for a minute of absolute darkness, but these are not for the claustrophobic or those afraid of the dark.

Cave-Tubing in Belize ☎ *605/1575* ⊕ *www.cave-tubing.com.*

DIVING AND SNORKELING

Most companies on Ambergris Caye offer morning and afternoon single-tank dives; snorkel trips begin mid-morning or early afternoon. Dive and snorkeling trips that originate in Caye Caulker are a bit cheaper.

Amigos del Mar. Established in 1991, Amigos del Mar is perhaps the island's most consistently recommended dive operation. The PADI facility offers a range of local dives as well as trips to Turneffe Atoll and Lighthouse Reef in a fast 48-foot dive boat. Amigos charges BZ$150 per person for a local two-tank dive, not including equipment rental, and BZ$500 for a 12-hour trip to the Blue Hole, including park fee and lunch but not equipment rental. ⊠ *On water off Barrier Reef Dr., near Mayan Princess Hotel, Ambergris Caye* ☎ *226/2706* ⊕ *www. amigosdive.com.*

Raggamuffin Tours. Go out for a snorkel on a sailboat with Raggamuffin Tours, which goes to Hol Chan for BZ$100, including the park entrance fee, lunch, and cocktails. ⊠ *Front St., Caye Caulker* ☎ *226/0348* ⊕ *www.raggamuffintours.com.*

INDEPENDENT TOURS

Several Belize City–based tour guides and operators offer custom trips for ship passengers; companies will usually meet you at the Fort Street Tourism Village.

Belize Trips ☎ *223/0376, 561/210–7015 U.S. number* ⊕ *www.belize-trips.com.*

Ecological Tours & Services ⊠ *Tourism Village, Fort St.* ☎ *223/4874* ⊕ *www.ecotoursbelize.com.*

WHERE TO EAT

$ ✕ **Nerie's.** Always packed with locals, Nerie's is the vox populi of dining
LATIN AMERICAN in Belize City. The many traditional dishes on the menu include fry jacks for breakfast and cow-foot soup for lunch. At dinner stewed chicken with rice and beans and a soft drink will set you back only BZ$11. $ *Average main: BZ$12* ⊠ *Queen and Daly sts., Commercial District* ☎ *223/4028* ▬ *No credit cards* $ *Average main: BZ$12* ⊠ *Douglas Jones St., Commercial District* ☎ *224/5199* ▬ *No credit cards.*

$$ ✕ **Riverside Tavern.** Owned and managed by the Bowen (Belikin beer)
AMERICAN family, Riverside Tavern opened in 2006 and immediately became one
Fodor'sChoice of the city's most popular restaurants. The huge signature hamburgers
★ are arguably the best in Belize. (The 6-ounce burger is BZ$16.) The
Riverside has added new steak and prime rib dishes, from cattle from
the Bowen farm at Gallon Jug. Sit inside in air-conditioned comfort, at
tables set around a huge bar, or on the outside covered patio overlook-
ing Haulover Creek. This is one of the few restaurants in Belize with a
dress code—shorts aren't allowed at night. The fenced, guarded parking
lot right in front of the restaurant makes it easy and safe to park for
free. $ *Average main: BZ$24* ✉ *2 Mapp St., off Freetown Rd., Com-
mercial District* ☎ *223/5640.*

BERMUDA

Robyn
Bardgett, Amy
Peniston

Basking in the Atlantic, 508 miles (817 km) due east of Cape Hatteras,
North Carolina, restrained and polite Bermuda is a departure from
other sunny, beach-strewn isles. You won't find laid-back locals wan-
dering around barefoot proffering piña coladas. Bermuda is somewhat
formal, and despite the gorgeous weather, residents wearing stockings
and heels or jackets, ties, Bermuda shorts, and knee socks are a com-
mon sight, whether on the street by day or in restaurants at night.
On Bermuda's 22 square miles (57 square km) you will discover that
pastel cottages, quaint shops, and manicured gardens betray a more
staid, suburban way of life. A self-governing British colony since 1968,
Bermuda has maintained some of its English character even as it is
increasingly influenced by American culture. Most cruise ships make
seven-night loops from U.S. embarkation ports, with four nights at sea
and three tied up in port. Increasingly popular are round-trip itinerar-
ies originating in northeastern embarkation ports that include a single
day or overnight port call in Bermuda before continuing south to the
Bahamas or the Caribbean.

ESSENTIALS

CURRENCY

The Bermuda dollar (B$) is on par with the U.S. dollar. You can use
American money anywhere.

TELEPHONE

To make a local call, simply dial the seven-digit number. You can find
specially marked AT&T USADirect phones at the airport, the cruise-
ship dock in Hamilton, and King's Square and Ordnance Island in St.
George's. You can also make international calls with a calling card from
the main post office. You can make prepaid international calls from
the Cable & Wireless Office, which also has international fax services,
weekdays from 9 to 4:45.

COMING ASHORE

Three Bermuda harbors serve cruise ships: Hamilton (the capital), St.
George's, and King's Wharf at the Royal Naval Dockyard.

In Hamilton, cruise ships tie up right on the city's main street, Front Street. A Visitors Service Bureau is next to the ferry terminal, also on Front Street and nearby; maps and brochures are displayed in the cruise terminal itself.

St. George's actually has two piers that accommodate cruise ships. One is on Ordnance Island, which is in the heart of the city; another pier is nearby at Penno's Wharf. A Visitors Service Bureau is at the World Heritage Centre, 19 Penno's Wharf.

King's Wharf, in the Royal Naval Dockyard at the westernmost end of the island, is the most isolated of the three cruise-ship berthing areas, and it is where the largest vessels dock. But it is well connected to the rest of the island by taxi, bus, and ferry. A Visitors Service Bureau is adjacent to bus stops and the ferry pier.

Taxis are the fastest and easiest way to get around the island, but they are also quite expensive. Four-seater taxis charge $6.40 for the first mile and $2.80 for each subsequent mile. For a personalized taxi tour of the island, the minimum duration is three hours, at $40 per hour for one to four people and $55.50 an hour for five or six, excluding tip. If you can round up a group of people, this is often cheaper than an island tour offered by your ship. Tip drivers 15%. Rental cars are prohibited, but the island has a good bus and ferry system. You can also rent scooters, but this can be dangerous for the uninitiated and is not recommended.

7

EXPLORING BERMUDA

HAMILTON

Bermuda's capital since 1815, the city of Hamilton is a small, bustling harbor town. It's the economic and social center of Bermuda, with busy streets lined with shops and offices. International influences, from both business and tourism, have brought a degree of sophistication unusual in so small a city. There are several museums and galleries to explore, but the favorite pastimes are shopping in Hamilton's numerous boutiques and dining in its many upscale restaurants.

FAMILY **Bermuda Underwater Exploration Institute (BUEI).** The 40,000-square-foot Ocean Discovery Centre showcases local contributions to oceanographic research and undersea discovery. Guests can ogle the world-class shell collection amassed by resident Jack Lightbourne (three of the 1,000 species were identified by and named for Lightbourne himself); or visit a gallery honoring native-born archaeologist Teddy Tucker to see booty retrieved from Bermudian shipwrecks. The types of gizmos that made such discoveries possible are also displayed: including a replica of the bathysphere William Beebe and Otis Barton used in their record-smashing 1934 dive. ⊠ *40 Crow La., off E. Broadway* ☎ *441/292–7219* ⊕ *www.buei.org* ✆ *$15* ☾ *Weekdays 9–5, weekends 10–5; last admission at 4.*

City Hall & Arts Centre. Set back from the street, City Hall contains Hamilton's administrative offices as well as two art galleries and a performance hall. Instead of a clock, its tower is topped with a bronze wind vane—a prudent choice in a land where the weather is as important

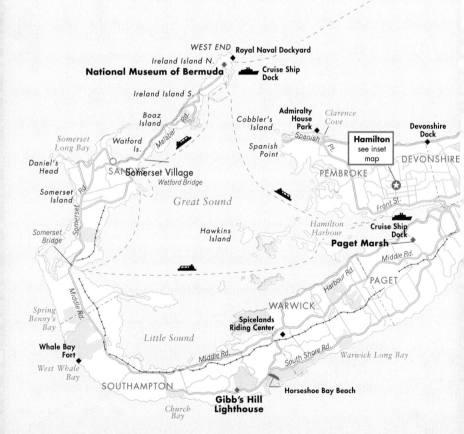

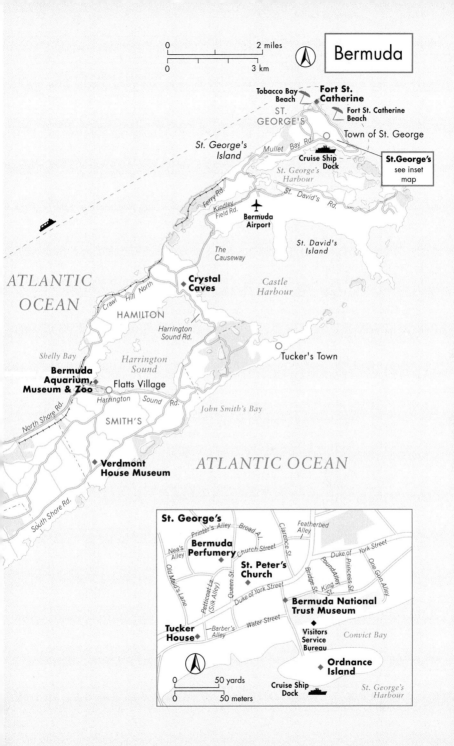

as the time. The building itself was designed in 1960 by Bermudian architect Wilfred Onions, a champion of balanced simplicity. Massive cedar doors open onto an impressive lobby notable for its beautiful chandeliers and portraits of mayors past and present. To the left is City Hall Theatre, a major venue for concerts, plays, and dance performances. To the right are the civic offices, where you can find souvenirs such as pens, T-shirts, and paperweights showing the Corporation of Hamilton's logo. A handsome cedar staircase leads upstairs to two upper-floor art galleries. (An elevator gets you there, too.) ⊠ 17 Church St. ☎ 441/292–1234 ⊗ City Hall weekdays 9–5; National Gallery and Society of the Arts weekdays 10–4, Sat. 10–2.

> **BERMUDA BEST BETS**
>
> ■ **Gibbs Hill Lighthouse.** Make the climb to the top, where the reward is an expansive view of the inlets and harbors.
>
> ■ **National Museum of Bermuda.** Absorb Bermuda's nautical and military history in this Royal Navy Dockyard museum.
>
> ■ **St. George's.** Attend the pier-side show hosted by the town crier, where gossips and nagging wives are drenched in a dunk tank.

FAMILY **Fort Hamilton.** This imposing moat-ringed fortress has underground passageways that were cut through solid rock by Royal Engineers in the 1860s. Built to defend the West End's Royal Naval Dockyard from land attacks, it was outdated even before its completion, but remains a fine example of a polygonal Victorian fort. Even if you're not a big fan of military history, the hilltop site's stellar views and stunning gardens make the trip worthwhile. ⊠ Happy Valley Rd. ☎ 441/292–1234 ⊠ Free ⊗ Daily 8–sunset.

Museum of the Bermuda Historical Society/Bermuda National Library. Mark Twain admired the giant rubber tree that stands on Queen Street in the front yard of this Georgian house, formerly owned by Postmaster William Bennet Perot and his family. Though charmed by the tree, which had been imported from what is now Guyana in the mid-19th century, Twain lamented that it didn't bear rubbery fruit in the form of overshoes and hot-water bottles. The library, about which he made no tongue-in-cheek comment, was established in 1839, and its reference section has virtually every book ever written about Bermuda, as well as a microfilm collection of Bermudian newspapers dating back to 1784. To the left of the library entrance is the Historical Society's museum. The collection is eclectic, chronicling the island's past through interesting—and in some cases downright quirky—artifacts. One display, for instance, is full of Bermudian silver dating from the 1600s; another focuses on tools and trinkets made by Boer War prisoners who were exiled here in 1901 and 1902. Check out the portraits of Sir George Somers and his wife, painted around 1605, and of William Perot and his wife that hang in the entrance hall. The newest exhibit is a selection of portraits of prominent Bermudians painted in the 1970s. ⊠ 13 Queen St., opposite Reid St ☎ 441/295–2905 library, 441/295–2487 museum ⊕ www.bnl.bm ⊠ Library free; museum donations accepted ⊗ Library

Mon.–Thur. 8:30–6, Fri. 10–5, Sat. 9–5. Museum Apr.–Nov., weekdays 10–2; Dec.–Mar., weekdays 10–1. Tours by appointment.

ST. GEORGE'S

The settlement of Bermuda began in what is now the town of St. George's nearly 400 years ago, when the *Sea Venture* was shipwrecked on Bermuda's treacherous reefs on its way to the colony of Jamestown, Virginia. No trip to Bermuda is complete without a visit to this historic town and UNESCO World Heritage Site.

Bermuda National Trust Museum at the Globe Hotel. Erected as a governor's mansion around 1700, this building became a hotbed of activity during the American Civil War. From here, Confederate Major Norman Walker coordinated the surreptitious flow of guns, ammunition, and war supplies from England, through Union blockades, into American ports. It saw service as the Globe Hotel during the mid-19th century and became a National Trust property in 1951. A short video, *Bermuda, Centre of the Atlantic,* recounts the history of Bermuda, and a memorabilia-filled exhibit entitled "Rogues & Runners: Bermuda and the American Civil War" describes St. George's when it was a port for Confederate blockade runners. ✉ *32 Duke of York St.* ☎ *441/297–1423* ⊕ *www.bnt.bm* 🖃 *$5; $10 combination ticket includes admission to Tucker House and Verdmont* ⊙ *Apr.–Nov., Wed.–Sat. 10–4; limited winter hrs.*

Bermuda Perfumery & Gardens. In 2005 this perfumery moved from Bailey's Bay in Hamilton Parish, where it had been based since 1928, to historic Stewart Hall. Although the location changed, the techniques it uses did not: the perfumery still manufactures and bottles all its island-inspired scents on-site using more than 3,000 essential oils extracted from frangipani, jasmine, oleander, and passionflower. Guides are available to explain the entire process, and there's a small museum that outlines the company's history. You can also wander around the gardens and stock up on your favorite fragrances in the showroom. ✉ *Stewart Hall, 5 Queen St.* ☎ *441/293–0627* ⊕ *www.lilibermuda.com* 🖃 *Free* ⊙ *Mon.–Sat. 9–5.*

FAMILY **Ordnance Island.** Ordnance Island, directly across from King's Square, is dominated by a splendid bronze statue of Sir George Somers, commander of the *Sea Venture.* Somers looks surprised that he made it safely to shore—and you may be surprised that he ever chose to set sail again when you spy the nearby *Deliverance II.* It's a full-scale replica of one of two ships—the other was the *Patience*—built under Somers's supervision to carry survivors from the 1609 wreck onward to Jamestown. But considering her size (just 57 feet from bow to stern) *Deliverance II* hardly seems ocean-worthy by modern standards. ✉ *Across from King's Sq..*

Fodor's Choice ★ **St. Peter's Church.** Because parts of this whitewashed stone church date back to 1620, it holds the distinction of being the oldest continuously operating Anglican church in the Western Hemisphere. It was not, however, the first house of worship to stand on this site. It replaced a 1612 structure made of wooden posts and palmetto leaves that was destroyed in a storm. The present church was extended in 1713 (the oldest part is the area around the triple-tier pulpit), with the tower and wings being added in the 19th century. ✉ *33 Duke of York St.* ☎ *441/297–2459* ⊕ *www.anglican.bm* ✉ *Donations appreciated* ☉ *Mon.–Sat. 10–4, Sun. service at 11:15.*

Tucker House. Tucker House is owned and lovingly maintained as a museum by the Bermuda National Trust. It was built in the 1750s for a merchant who stored his wares in the cellar (a space that now holds an archaeological exhibit). But it's been associated with the Tucker family ever since Henry Tucker, president of the Governor's Council and a key participant in the Bermuda Gunpowder Plot, purchased it in 1775. His descendents lived here until 1809, and much of the fine silver and heirloom furniture—which dates primarily from the mid-18th and early-19th centuries—was donated by them. As a result, the house is essentially a tribute to this well-connected clan whose members included a Bermudian governor, a U.S. treasurer, a Confederate navy captain, and an Episcopal bishop. The kitchen, however, is dedicated to another notable—Joseph Haine Rainey—who is thought to have operated a barber's shop in it during the Civil War. (Barber's Alley, around the corner, is also named in his honor.) As a freed slave from South Carolina, Rainey fled to Bermuda at the outbreak of the war. Afterward he returned to the United States and, in 1870, became the first black man to be elected to the House of Representatives. A short flight of stairs leads down to the kitchen, originally a separate building, and to an enclosed kitchen garden. ✉ *5 Water St.* ☎ *441/297–0545* ⊕ *www. bnt.bm* ✉ *$5; $10 combination ticket includes admission to National Trust Museum in Globe Hotel and Verdmont* ☉ *Apr.–Oct., Wed.–Sat. 11–3; winter hrs limited.*

ELSEWHERE ON THE ISLAND

FAMILY
Fodor's Choice
★

Bermuda Aquarium, Museum & Zoo (*BAMZ*). Established in 1926, the BAMZ has always been a pleasant diversion. But following an ambitious decade-long expansion program, it rates as one of Bermuda's premier attractions. In the aquarium the big draw is the North Rock Exhibit, a 140,000-gallon tank that gives you a diver's-eye view of the area's living coral reefs and the colorful marine life it sustains. The museum section has multimedia and interactive displays focusing on native habitats and the impact humans have had on them. The island-theme zoo, meanwhile, displays more than 300 birds, reptiles, and mammals. Don't miss the "Islands of Australasia" exhibit with its lemurs, wallabies, and tree kangaroos or "Islands of the Caribbean," a huge walk-through enclosure that gets you within arm's length of ibises and golden lion tamarins. Other popular areas include an outdoor seal pool, tidal touch tank, and cool kid-friendly Discovery Room. ■ TIP➔ Take a break at the AZU Beastro on the grounds of the zoo. The food is great but it also has one of the best views. ✉ *40 N. Shore Rd., Flatts Village, Hamilton Parish* ☎ *441/293–2727* ⊕ *www.bamz.org* ✉ *$10* ☉ *Daily 9–5, last admission at 4; seal feeding daily at 9, 1:30 and 4.*

FAMILY
Fodor's Choice
★

Crystal Caves. Bermuda's limestone caves have been attracting attention since the island was first settled. Inside, tour guides will lead you across a pontoon bridge that spans a 55-foot-deep subterranean lake. Look up to see stalactites dripping from the ceiling or down through the perfectly clear water to see stalagmites rising from the cave floor.

Amateur spelunkers can also journey through geologic time at Crystal's smaller sister cave, Fantasy. After being closed to the public for decades, it reopened in 2001. Set aside 30 minutes to see one cave; 75 minutes if you plan to take in both. ⊠ *8 Crystal Caves Rd., off Wilkinson Ave., Bailey's Bay, Hamilton Parish* ☎ *441/293–0640* ⊕ *www.caves. bm* ⊠ *One cave $22; combination ticket $30* ⊗ *Daily 9:30–5, last combination tour at 4:30.*

FAMILY **Fort St. Catherine.** This restored hilltop fort is arguably the most formidable looking one on the island. Surrounded by a dry moat and accessed by a drawbridge, it has enough tunnels, towers, redoubts, and ramparts to satisfy even the most avid military historian—or adrenaline-fueled child. The original fort was built around 1614 by Bermuda's first governor, Richard Moore, but it was remodeled and enlarged at least five times. In fact, work continued on it until late in the 19th century. ⊠ *15 Coot Pond Rd., St. George's Parish* ☎ *441/297–1920* ⊠ *$7* ⊗ *Weekdays 10–4.*

FAMILY **Gibb's Hill Lighthouse.** This cast-iron lighthouse soars above Southampton Parish. Designed in London and opened in 1846, the tower stands 117 feet high and 362 feet above the sea. The light was originally produced by a concentrated burner of four large, circular wicks. Today the beam from the 1,000-watt bulb can be seen by ships 40 miles out to sea and by planes 120 miles away at 10,000 feet. The haul up the 185 spiral stairs is an arduous one—particularly if you dislike heights or tight spaces. But en route to the top you can stop to catch your breath on eight landings, where photographs and drawings of the lighthouse help divert attention from your aching appendages. ⊠ *68 St. Anne's Rd., Southampton Parish* ☎ *441/238–8069* ⊕ *www.bermudalighthouse.com* ⊠ *$2.50* ⊗ *Daily 9–5. Closed Feb.*

FAMILY
Fodor's Choice
★

National Museum of Bermuda. The Maritime Museum, ensconced in Bermuda's largest fort, displays its collections in a series of old munitions warehouses that surround the parade grounds and Keep Pond. Insulated from the rest of the Dockyard by a moat and massive stone ramparts, it is entered by way of a drawbridge. At the Shifting House, right inside the entrance, you can wander through rooms filled with relics from some of the 350-odd ships wrecked on the island's reefs. Other buildings are devoted to seafaring pursuits such as whaling, shipbuilding, and yacht racing. More displays are in the 19th-century Commissioner's House, on the museum's upper grounds. Built as both home and headquarters for the Dockyard commissioner, the house later served as a barracks during World War I and was used for military intelligence during World War II. Today, after an award-winning restoration, it contains exhibits on Bermuda's social and military history. A must-see is the Hall of History, a mural of Bermuda's history covering 1,000 square feet. It took local artist Graham Foster more than 3½ years to paint. You'll also likely want to snap some photos of the goats that graze outside the building: their job is to keep the grass well mowed. ⊠ *Old Royal Naval Dockyard, Dockyard* ☎ *441/234–1418* ⊕ *www.bmm.bm* ⊠ *$10.*

Paget Marsh. Take a walk on the wild side at Paget Marsh: a 25-acre tract of land that's remained virtually untouched since presettlement times. Along with some of the last remaining stands of native Bermuda palmetto and cedar, this reserve—jointly owned and preserved by the Bermuda National Trust and the Bermuda Audubon Society—contains a mangrove forest and grassy savanna. These unspoiled habitats can be explored via a boardwalk that features interpretive signs describing the endemic flora and fauna. When listening to the cries of the native and migratory birds that frequent this natural wetland, you can quickly forget that bustling Hamilton is just minutes away. ⊠ *Lovers La., Paget Parish* ☎ *441/236–6483* ⊕ *www.bnt.bm* ✉ *Free* ☉ *Daily sunrise–sunset.*

FAMILY **Verdmont House Museum.** Even if you think you've had your fill of old houses, Verdmont deserves a look. The National Trust property, which opened as a museum in 1956, is notable for its Georgian architecture. Yet what really sets this place apart is its pristine condition. Though used as a residence until the mid-20th century, virtually no structural changes were made to Verdmont since it was erected around 1710. Former owners never even added electricity or plumbing (so the "powder room" was strictly used for powdering wigs). ⊠ *6 Verdmont La., off Collector's Hill, Smith's Parish* ☎ *441/236–7369* ⊕ *www.bnt.bm* ✉ *$5; $10 combination ticket with Bermuda National Trust Museum in Globe Hotel and Tucker House* ☉ *Apr.–Oct., Wed.–Fri 10–4; winter hrs limited.*

BEACHES

FAMILY **Elbow Beach.** Swimming and bodysurfing are great at this beach, which is bordered by the prime strand of sand reserved for guests of the Elbow Beach Hotel on the left, and the ultra-exclusive Coral Beach Club beach area on the right. It's a pleasant setting for a late-evening stroll, with the lights from nearby hotels dancing on the water, but the romance dissipates in daylight, when the beach is noisy and crowded. Groups also gather here to play football and volleyball. Protective coral reefs make the waters the safest on the island, and a good choice for families. A lunch wagon sometimes sells fast food and cold drinks during the day, and Mickey's Beach Bar (part of the Elbow Beach Hotel) is open for lunch and dinner, though it may be difficult to get a table. **Pros:** beautiful stretch of beach; safest waters on the island, snorkel rental shop. **Cons:** busy; parking fills up quickly; need to watch out for stray footballs and volleyballs. ⊠ *Off South Rd., Paget Parish* Ⓜ *Bus No. 2 or No. 7 from Hamilton.*

FAMILY **Horseshoe Bay.** When locals say they're going to "the beach," they're
Fodor's Choice generally referring to Horseshoe Bay, the island's most popular. With
★ clear water, a 0.3-mile crescent of pink sand, a vibrant social scene, and the uncluttered backdrop of South Shore Park, Horseshoe Bay has everything you could ask of a Bermudian beach. A snack bar, changing rooms, beach-rental facilities, and lifeguards add to its appeal. The Good Friday Annual Kite Festival also takes place here. The undertow can be strong, especially on the main beach. A better place for children is **Horseshoe Baby Beach.** Before 2003's Hurricane Fabian, this beach was reached by climbing a trail over the dunes at the western end

of Horseshoe Bay. Fabian's storm surge ploughed right through those dunes, creating a wide walkway for eager little beachgoers. Sheltered from the ocean by a ring of rocks, this cove is shallow and almost perfectly calm. In summer, toddlers can find lots of playmates. **Pros:** adjoining beach is perfect for small children; snack bar with outdoor seating. **Cons:** the bus stop is a long walk up a huge hill; gets very crowded; busiest beach on the island. ⊠ *Off South Rd., Southampton Parish* ☎ *441/238–2651* Ⓜ *Bus No. 7 from Hamilton.*

Tobacco Bay. The most popular beach near St. George's—about 15 minutes northwest of the town on foot—this small north-shore strand is huddled in a coral cove. Its beach house has a snack bar, equipment rentals, toilets, showers, changing rooms, and ample parking. It's a 10-minute hike from the bus stop in the town of St. George's, or you can flag down a St. George's Minibus Service van and ask for a lift ($2 per person). In high season the beach is busy, especially midweek, when the cruise ships are docked. **Pros:** beautiful rock formations in the water; great snorkeling. **Cons:** so popular it becomes overcrowded; no bus stops nearby. ⊠ *Coot Pond Rd., St. George's Parish* ☎ *441/297–2756* Ⓜ *Bus No. 10 or No. 11 from Hamilton.*

SHOPPING

Hamilton has the greatest concentration of shops in Bermuda, and Front Street is its pièce de résistance. Lined with small, pastel-color buildings, this most fashionable of Bermuda's streets houses sedate department stores and snazzy boutiques, with several small arcades and shopping alleys leading off it. A smart canopy shades the entrance to the 55 Front Street Group, which houses Crisson Jewelers. Modern Butterfield Place has galleries and boutiques selling, among other things, Louis Vuitton leather goods. The Emporium, a renovated building with an atrium, has a range of shops, from antiques to souvenirs.

St. George's Water Street, Duke of York Street, Hunters Wharf, Penno's Wharf, and Somers Wharf are the sites of numerous renovated buildings that house branches of Front Street stores, as well as artisans' studios. Historic King's Square offers little more than a couple of T-shirt and souvenir shops.

In the West End, **Somerset Village** has a few shops, but they hardly merit a special shopping trip. However, the **Clocktower Mall,** in a historic building at the Royal Naval Dockyard, has a few more shopping opportunities, including branches of Front Street shops and specialty boutiques. The Dockyard is also home to the Craft Market, the Bermuda Arts Centre, and Bermuda Clayworks.

ACTIVITIES

BICYCLING

The best and sometimes only way to explore Bermuda's nooks and crannies—its little hidden coves and 18th-century tribe roads—is by bicycle or motor scooter. A popular option for biking in Bermuda is the **Railway Trail,** a dedicated cycle path blissfully free of cars. Running intermittently the length of the old Bermuda Railway (old "Rattle 'n' Shake"), this trail is scenic and restricted to pedestrian and bicycle traffic. You can ask the staff at any bike-rental shop for advice on where to access the trail.

Eve Cycle. With three convenient locations around the island, Eve's office in Dockyard is just a short walk from the cruise terminal– perfect if you're arriving by boat. This cycle shop also rents out adult mountain bikes, as well as motor scooters, including your mandatory helmet. The staff readily supplies advice on where to ride and detailed maps of the island. Be prepared to pay an extra $20 for mandatory third-party insurance. Other branches are in St. George's and Paget, and if these are a bit of a walk from your accommodation, a shuttle service is offered. ✉ *10 Dockyard Terr., Dockyard* ☎ *441/236–6247* ⊕ *www. evecycles.com.*

GOLF

Golf courses make up nearly 17% of the island's 21.6 square miles. The scenery on the courses is usually spectacular, with flowering trees and shrubs decked out in multicolor blossoms against a backdrop of brilliant blue sea and sky. The layouts are remarkably challenging, thanks to capricious ocean breezes, daunting natural terrain, and the clever work of world-class golf architects.

Fairmont Southampton Golf Club. Spreading across the hillside below the high-rise Fairmont Southampton, this executive golf course is known for its steep terrain, giving players who opt to walk (for sunset tee times only) an excellent workout. ✉ *Fairmont Southampton Resort, 101 South Rd., Southampton Parish* ☎ *441/239–6952* ⊕ *www.fairmont. com* ⛳ *Greens fees $89 before 2:30 with cart (mandatory), $67 after 2:30 with cart or $45 walking. Pull-cart rental $7.50. Shoe rentals $10. Titleist club rentals $40. Lessons $75 for half-hour, $120 per hour* 🏌 *18 holes. 2,684 yards. Par 54. Rating: 53.7.*

Mid Ocean Club. The elite Mid Ocean Club is a 1921 Charles Blair Macdonald design revamped in 1953 by Robert Trent Jones Sr. *Golf Digest* ranked it 56th in the top 100 courses outside the United States. ✉ *1 Mid Ocean Dr., off S. Shore Rd., Tucker's Town* ☎ *441/293–1215* ⊕ *www.themidoceanclubbermuda.com* ⛳ *Greens fees $250 ($100 when playing with a member). Non-members must be sponsored by a club member (your hotelier can arrange this); non-member starting times available Mon., Wed., and Fri. except holidays. Caddies $55 for double or $65 for single per bag (tip not included). Cart rental $32 per person. Shoe rentals $12. Club rentals $50. Lessons available.* 🏌 *18 holes. 6,548 yards. Par 71. Rating: blue tees 73.0; white tees 71.3; red tees 75.0.*

SNORKELING

Snorkeling cruises are generally offered from April through September. Smaller boats, which limit capacity to 10 to 16 passengers, offer more personal attention and focus more on the beautiful snorkeling areas themselves. Guides on such tours often relate interesting historical and ecological information about the island. Some larger boats take up to 40 passengers.

Jessie James Cruises. Prepare for three memorable hours with Jessie James Cruises. You'll sail between two different shipwrecks and pass over a third, peering through a glass-bottom on the 31-foot *Pisces*. Snorkeling equipment, masks, and vests are provided. *Pisces,* which holds up to 17 people, typically departs from Hamilton, although a complimentary pick-up from Dockyard is available upon request. ⊠ *11 Clarence St., St. George's* ☏ *441/236–4804* ⊕ *www.jessiejames.bm* ✉ *Half-day trips $65.*

WHERE TO EAT

$

BRITISH

✕ **Docksider.** Locals come to mingle at this sprawling Front Street sports bar. It's generally more popular as a drinking venue, as it can get quite overcrowded and rowdy. But if you want to catch the game on the big screen with everyone else, an all-day menu of standard pub fare is available, as well as local fish. Go for the English beef pie, fish-and-chips, or a fish sandwich, and sip your dessert—a Dark 'n Stormy—out on the porch as you watch Bermuda stroll by. Or if you can't make up your mind, you can always rely on the hearty full English breakfast to fill you up. Food is served until 10. The pub has a good jukebox and there's often a DJ or a band on summer weekends. $ *Average main: $15* ⊠ *121 Front St., Hamilton* ☏ *441/296–3333* ⊕ *www.dockies.com.*

$

CARIBBEAN

✕ **Spring Garden Restaurant & Bar.** If you've never had Barbadian, or as Barbados natives like to call it, "Bajan" food, come sit under the indoor palm tree and try panfried flying fish—a delicacy in Barbados. Another good choice is the broiled mahimahi served in creole sauce, with peas and rice. During lobster season, an additional menu appears, featuring steamed, broiled, or curried lobster ($38.50 for the complete dinner). For dessert, try coconut cream pie or raspberry-mango cheesecake. Or eat with the locals at the Friday lunchtime bargain buffet; help yourself to as many starters, mains, and desserts you can eat for $22. $ *Average main: $18* ⊠ *19 Washington Lane, off Reid St., Hamilton* ☏ *441/295–7416* ⊗ *Closed Sun.*

7

BONAIRE (KRALENDIJK)

Vernon
O'Reilly
Ramesar

Starkly beautiful Bonaire is the consummate desert island. Surrounded by pristine waters, it is a haven for divers and snorkelers, who flock here from around the world to take advantage of the excellent visibility, easily accessed reefs, and bountiful marine life. Bonaire is the most rustic of the three ABC islands, and despite its dependence on tourism it manages to maintain its identity and simple way of life. There are many good restaurants, most of which are within walking distance of the port. Most of the island's 14,000-some inhabitants live in and around Kralendijk, which must certainly qualify as one of the cutest and most compact capitals in the Caribbean. The best shopping is to be found along the very short stretch of road that constitutes "downtown." Bonaire's beaches tend to be small and rocky, but there is a nice stretch of sandy beach at Lac Bay. It is entirely possible to see almost

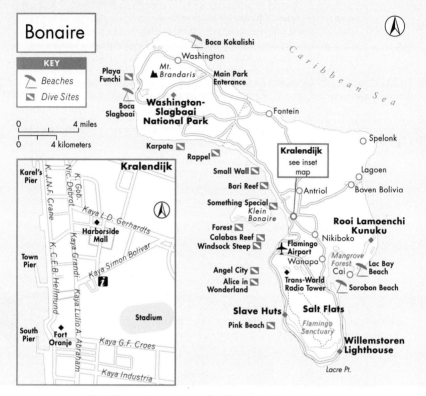

Bonaire

KEY

⚐ Beaches

◪ Dive Sites

0 —— 4 miles
0 —— 4 kilometers

Boca Kokalishi

Washington

Mt. Brandaris

Main Park Enterance

Playa Funchi

Boca Slagbaai

Washington-Slagbaai National Park

Karpata

Rappel

Fontein

Spelonk

Kralendijk see inset map

Lagoen

Small Wall

Bari Reef

Antriol

Boven Bolivia

Something Special

Klein Bonaire

Forest

Calabas Reef

Windsock Steep

Flamingo Airport

Nikiboko

Wanapa

Rooi Lamoenchi Kunuku

Mangrove Forest

Cai

Lac Bay Beach

Angel City

Alice in Wonderland

Trans-World Radio Tower

Sorobon Beach

Slave Huts

Pink Beach

Salt Flats

Flamingo Sanctuary

Willemstoren Lighthouse

Lacre Pt.

Caribbean Sea

Kralendijk

Karel's Pier

Town Pier

South Pier

Fort Oranje

K. Gob. Nic. Debrot

K.J.N.F. Crane

Kaya L.D. Gerhardts

Harborside Mall

Kaya Grandi

Kaya Simon Bolivar

Kaya Lulio A. Abraham

K.C.E.B. Hellmund

Stadium

Kaya G.F. Croes

Kaya Industria

all of the sights and sounds of the island in one day by taking one of the island tours on offer.

ESSENTIALS

CURRENCY

U.S. dollar.

TELEPHONE

The country code for Bonaire is 599; 717 is the exchange for every four-digit number on the island. Phone cards from home rarely work on Bonaire. You can try AT&T by dialing 001–800/872–2881 from public phones. To call Bonaire from the United States, dial 011–599/717 plus the local four-digit number.

COMING ASHORE

One of the great benefits of Bonaire to cruise passengers is that the port is right in downtown Kralendijk. Ships usually tender passengers ashore. A four-minute walk takes you to most of the best shopping and restaurants on the island.

Bonaire lives for tourism; on the arrival of a cruise ship, the locals are ready, and an impromptu crafts market springs up in the park across from the port entrance. Taxis wait right at the port and operate on fixed government rates. All the sights of Kralendijk are within easy walking distance, and a taxi ride to one of the larger resorts on the island will run between $10 and $17. A half-day island tour by taxi costs about $25 per hour for up to two passengers and will allow you to see most of the major sights. Fares increase by 50% between midnight and 6 am.

EXPLORING BONAIRE

Two routes, north and south from Kralendijk, the island's small capital, are possible on the 24-mile-long (39-km-long) island; either route will take from a few hours to a full day, depending on whether you stop to snorkel, swim, dive, or lounge. Those pressed for time will find that it's easy to explore the entire island in a day if stops are kept to a minimum.

KRALENDIJK

Bonaire's small, tidy capital city (population 3,000) is five minutes from the airport. The main drag, J. A. Abraham Boulevard, turns into **Kaya Grandi** in the center of town. Along it are most of the island's major stores, boutiques, and restaurants. Across Kaya Grandi, opposite the Littman jewelry store, is Kaya L. D. Gerharts, with several small supermarkets, a handful of snack shops, and some of the better restaurants. Walk down the narrow waterfront avenue called Kaya C. E. B. Hellmund, which leads straight to the **North and South piers.** In the center of town, the Harbourside Mall has chic boutiques. Along this route is **Ft. Oranje,** with its cannons. From December through April, cruise ships dock in the harbor once or twice a week. The diminutive ocher-and-white structure that looks like a tiny Greek temple is the **fish market**; local anglers no longer bring their catches here (they sell out of their homes these days), but you can find plenty of fresh produce brought over from Colombia and Venezuela. Pick up the brochure *Walking and Shopping in Kralendijk* from the tourist office to get a map and full listing of all the monuments and sights in the town.

> ### BONAIRE BEST BETS
>
> ■ **Diving.** Bonaire is one of the world's top diving destinations. Shore diving is especially good.
>
> ■ **Snorkeling.** With reefs close to shore, snorkeling is good right off the beach.
>
> ■ **Flamingo spotting.** These shy, graceful birds are one of Bonaire's scenic delights.
>
> ■ **Kralendijk.** The accessible town has a nice assortment of restaurants and stores.
>
> ■ **Washington–Slagbaai National Park.** Bonaire's best land-based sight is this well-preserved national park.

ELSEWHERE ON BONAIRE

FAMILY **Rooi Lamoenchi Kunuku.** Owner Ellen Herrera restored her family's homestead north of Lac Bay, in the Bonairean *kadushi* (cactus) wilderness, to educate tourists and residents about the history and tradition of authentic kunuku living and show unspoiled terrain in two daily tours. You must make an appointment in advance and expect to spend a couple of hours. ⊠ *Kaya Suiza 23, Playa Baribe* ☎ *599/717–8489* ✉ *$21* ⊗ *By appointment only.*

Salt Flats. You can't miss the salt flats—voluptuous white drifts that look like mountains of snow. Harvested once a year, the "ponds" are owned by Cargill, Inc., which has reactivated the 19th-century salt industry with great success (one reason for that success is that the ocean on this part of the island is higher than the land—which makes irrigation a snap). Keep a lookout for the three 30-foot obelisks—white, blue, and red—that were used to guide the trade boats coming to pick up the salt. Look also in the distance across the pans to the abandoned solar salt-works that's now a designated **flamingo sanctuary.** With the naked eye you might be able to make out a pink-orange haze just on the horizon; with binoculars you will see a sea of bobbing pink bodies. The sanctuary is completely protected, and no entrance is allowed (flamingos are extremely sensitive to disturbances of any kind).

FAMILY **Slave Huts.** The salt industry's gritty history is revealed in Rode Pan, the site of two groups of tiny slave huts. The white grouping is on the right side of the road, opposite the salt flats; the second grouping, called the red slave huts (though they appear yellow), stretches across the road toward the island's southern tip. During the 19th century, slaves working the salt pans by day crawled into these huts to rest. Each Friday afternoon they walked seven hours to Rincon to weekend with their families, returning each Sunday. Only very small people will be able to enter, but walk around and poke your head in for a look.

FAMILY **Washington–Slagbaai National Park.** Once a plantation producing divi-divi trees (the pods were used for tanning animal skins), aloe (used for medicinal lotions), charcoal, and goats, the park is now a model of conservation. It's easy to tour the 13,500-acre tropical desert terrain on the dirt roads. As befits a wilderness sanctuary, the well-marked, rugged routes force you to drive slowly enough to appreciate the animal life and the terrain. (Think twice about coming here if it has rained recently—the mud you may encounter will be more than inconvenient.) If you're planning to hike, bring a picnic lunch, camera, sunscreen, and plenty of water. There are two routes: the long one (22 miles [35½ km]) is marked by yellow arrows, the short one (15 miles [24 km]) by green arrows. Goats and donkeys may dart across the road, and if you keep your eyes peeled, you may catch sight of large iguanas camouflaged in the shrubbery.

Bird-watchers are really in their element here. Right inside the park's gate, flamingos roost on the salt pad known as **Salina Mathijs,** and exotic parakeets dot the foot of **Mt. Brandaris,** Bonaire's highest peak, at 784 feet. Some 130 species of birds fly in and out of the shrubbery in the park. Keep your eyes open and your binoculars at hand. Swimming, snorkeling, and scuba diving are permitted, but you're asked not to frighten the animals or remove anything from the grounds. Absolutely no hunting, fishing, or camping is allowed. A useful guide to the park is available at the entrance for about $6. To get here, take the secondary road north from the town of Rincon. The Nature Fee for swimming and snorkeling also grants you free admission to this park—simply present proof of payment and some form of photo ID. ☎ *599/717–8444* ⊕ *www.washingtonparkbonaire.org* ▭ *Free with payment of scuba diving Nature Fee ($25) or $15 with non-scuba Nature*

Fee ($10). Otherwise $25 for one calendar year of entry. ☉ *Daily 8–5; last entry at 3.*

Willemstoren Lighthouse. Bonaire's first lighthouse was built in 1837 and is now automated (but closed to visitors). Take some time to explore the beach and notice how the waves, driven by the trade winds, play a crashing symphony against the rocks. Locals stop here to collect pieces of driftwood in spectacular shapes and to build fanciful pyramids from objects that have washed ashore.

BEACHES

Don't expect long stretches of glorious powdery sand. Bonaire's beaches are small, and though the water is blue (several shades of it, in fact), the sand isn't always white. Bonaire's National Parks Foundation requires all nondivers to pay a $10 annual Nature Fee in order to enter the water anywhere around the island (divers pay $25). The fee can be paid at most dive shops.

Klein Bonaire. Just a water-taxi hop across from Kralendijk, this little island offers picture-perfect white-sand beaches. The area is protected, so absolutely no development has been allowed. Make sure to pack everything before heading to the island, including water and an umbrella to hide under, because there are no refreshment stands or changing facilities, and there's almost no shade to be found. Boats leave from the Town Pier, across from the City Café, and the round-trip water-taxi ride costs roughly $20 per person. **Amenities:** none. **Best for:** solitude; snorkeling; swimming; walking.

Lac Bay Beach. Known for its festive music on Sunday nights, this open bay area with pink-tinted sand is equally dazzling by day. It's a bumpy drive (10 to 15 minutes on a dirt road) to get here, but you'll be glad when you arrive. It's a good spot for diving, snorkeling, and kayaking (as long as you bring your own), and there are public restrooms and a restaurant for your convenience. **Amenities:** food and drink; parking; showers; toilets. **Best for:** partiers; surfing; swimming; windsurfing. ⊠ *Off Kaminda Sorobon, Lac Cai.*

Windsock Beach (*aka Mangrove Beach*). This pretty little spot looks out toward the north side of the island and has about 200 yards of white sand along a rocky shoreline. It's a popular dive site, and swimming conditions are good. **Amenities:** none. **Best for:** snorkeling; swimming. ⊠ *Off E. E. G. Blvd., near Flamingo Airport.*

SHOPPING

Although it is a relatively small town, Kralendijk offers a good range of high-end items like watches and jewelry at attractive prices. There are a number of souvenir shops offering T-shirts and trinkets lining the main street of Kaya Grandi.

Atlantis. This shop carries a large range of precious and semiprecious gems; the tanzanite collection is especially beautiful. You will also find Sector, Raymond Weil, and Citizen watches, among others, all at great savings. Since gold jewelry is sold by weight here, it's an especially good buy. ⊠ *Kaya Grandi 32B* ☎ *599/717–7730.*

JanArt Gallery. On the outskirts of town, JanArt Gallery sells unique paintings, prints, and art supplies; artist Janice Huckaby also hosts art classes. ⊠ *Kaya Gloria 7* ☎ *599/717–5246.*

Littman's. Owner Steven Littman handpicks many of the items available in this upscale jewelry and gift shop during his regular trips to Europe. Look for Rolex, Omega, Cartier, and Tag Heuer watches; fine gold jewelry; antique coins; nautical sculptures; resort clothing; and accessories. ⊠ *Kaya Grandi 33* ☎ *599/717–8160.*

Yenny's Art. Every visitor should make a point of visiting Yenny's Art. Roam around her house, which is a replica of a traditional Bonaire town complete with her handmade life-size dolls and the skeletons of all her dead pets. Fun (and sometimes kitschy) souvenirs made out of driftwood, clay, and shells are all handmade by Jenny Rijna. ⊠ *Kaya Betico Croes 6, near post office* ☎ *599/717–5004.*

ACTIVITIES

BICYCLING

Bonaire is generally flat, so bicycles are an easy way to get around. Because of the heat it's essential to carry water if you're planning to cycle for any distance, and especially if your plans involve exploring the deserted interior. There are more than 180 miles (290 km) of unpaved routes (as well as the many paved roads) on the island.

Tropical Travel. This tour operator offers bikes for $14 per day or $60 per week (a $300 deposit is required). ⊠ *Plaza Resort Bonaire, 80 J. A. Abraham Blvd.* ☎ *599/701–1232* ⊕ *www.tropicaltravelbonaire.com.*

DIVING AND SNORKELING

Diving and snorkeling are almost a religion on Bonaire, and are by far the most popular activities for cruise passengers. Bonaire has some of the best reef diving this side of Australia's Great Barrier Reef. It takes only 5 to 25 minutes to reach many sites, the current is usually mild, and although some reefs have sudden, steep drops, most begin just offshore and slope gently downward at a 45-degree angle. General visibility runs 60 to 100 feet, except during surges in October and November. You can see several varieties of coral: knobby-brain, giant-brain, elkhorn, staghorn, mountainous star, gorgonian, and black.

Mushi Mushi. The *Mushi Mushi* is a catamaran offering a variety of two- and three-hour cruises starting at $55 per person. It departs from the Bonaire Nautico Marina in downtown Kralendijk (opposite the restaurant It Rains Fishes). ☎ *599/790–5399.*

WHERE TO EAT

$$ ✕ **Appetite.** This delightful establishment is an oasis of chic. The historic
EUROPEAN   house offers cozy private rooms and a large courtyard, which always seems to be buzzing. The menu encourages diners to forget the main course and order a series of starters, but such items as stewed veal cheek

with crispy sweetbreads are worth the splurge. A four course chef's menu is available as well. The restaurant is just a few steps away from the Tourism Corporation Bonaire office. ⑤ *Average main: $28* ⊠ *Kaya Grandi 12* ☎ *599/717–3595* ⊘ *Closed Sun.*

$$
ECLECTIC
Fodor's Choice
★

✗ **City Café/City Restaurant.** This busy waterfront eatery is also one of the most reliable nightspots on the island, so it's always hopping day or night. Breakfast, lunch, and dinner are served daily at reasonable prices. Seafood is always featured, as are a variety of sandwiches and salads. The pita sandwich platters are a good lunchtime choice for the budget challenged. Weekends, there's always live entertainment and dancing. This is the place to people-watch on Bonaire, as it seems everyone ends up at City Café eventually. ⑤ *Average main: $15* ⊠ *Hotel Rochaline, Kaya Grandi 7* ☎ *599/717–6050* ⊕ *www.citybonaire.com.*

CALICA (PLAYA DEL CARMEN), MEXICO

Marie Elena
Martinez

Just minutes away from Calica, Playa del Carmen has become one of Latin America's fastest-growing communities, with a pace almost as hectic as Cancún's. Hotels, restaurants, and shops multiply here faster than you can say "Kukulcán." Some are branches of Cancún establishments whose owners have taken up permanent residence in Playa, while others are owned by American and European expats (predominately Italians) who came here years ago. It makes for a varied, international community. Avenida 5, the first street in town parallel to the beach, is a long pedestrian walkway with shops, cafés, and street performers; small hotels and stores stretch north from this avenue. Avenida Juárez, running east–west from the highway to the beach, is the main commercial zone for the Riviera Maya corridor. Here locals visit the food shops, pharmacies, hardware stores, and banks that line the curbs. People traveling the coast by car usually stop here to stock up on supplies—its banks, grocery stores, and gas stations are the last ones until Tulum.

ESSENTIALS

CURRENCY

The Mexican peso. U.S. dollars and credit cards are widely accepted in the area, from the port to Playa del Carmen, but it's best to have pesos—and small bills—when you visit ruins, where cashiers often run out of change.

TELEPHONE

Most pay phones accept prepaid Ladatel cards, sold in 30-, 50-, or 100-peso denominations. To use the card, insert it in the pay phone's slot, dial 001 (for calls to the United States) or 01 (for calls within Mexico), followed by the area code and number. Credit is deleted from the card as you use it, and the balance is displayed on the small screen on the phone. Most tri-band mobile phones from the U.S. work in Mexico, though you must pay roaming charges.

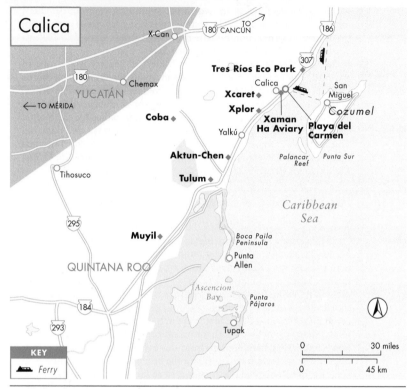

COMING ASHORE

The port at Calica, about 3 miles south of the town of Playa del Carmen (between Playa del Carmen and Xcarat), is small. Sometimes ships actually dock, and other times passengers are tendered to shore. There is a makeshift market at the port, where locals sell crafts. Beyond that, there is not much to do, and you'll need to head into Playa del Carmen proper to find restaurants and even tour operators. If you really want to shop, skip the vendors at the port and head to Playa del Carmen's Avenida 5, where you can easily spend an afternoon browsing shops and enjoying restaurants.

Taxis and tour buses are available at the port to take you to Playa del Carmen and other destinations, but lines often form as passengers wait for taxis, so plan accordingly if you really want to pack a lot of activity into your day. Your taxi will have you in Playa del Carmen or in Xcaret in under 10 minutes, but you'll pay a whopping $10 for the short trip.

EXPLORING CALICA

FAMILY
Fodor's Choice
★

Aktun-Chen (*Indiana Joes*). Aktun-Chen is Mayan for "the cave with cenotes inside," and these amazing underground caves, estimated to be about 5 million years old, are the area's largest. You walk through the underground passages, past stalactites and stalagmites, until you reach the cenote with its various shades of deep green. There's also a canopy tour and one cenote where you can swim. This is a top family attraction, and one that's not as crowded or touristy as Xplor, Xel-Há, or Xcaret. ✉ *Carretera 307, km 107, opposite Bahia Principe resort, between Akumal and Xel-Ha.* ☎ *998/881–9400* ⊕ *www.indiana-joes.com* ✉ *$30 cave tour, $40 canopy tour, $30 cenote tour* ⊗ *Mon.–Sat. 9–5.*

Muyil (*Chunyaxché*). This photogenic archaeological site just 15 km (9 miles) down the 307 from Tulum, at the northern end of the

Sian Ka'an biosphere reserve, is underrated. Once known as Chunyaxché, it's now called by its ancient name, Muyil (pronounced moo-*hill*). It dates from the late preclassic era, when it was connected by road to the sea and served as a port between Cobá and the Mayan centers in Belize and Guatemala. The most notable site at Muyil today is the remains of the 56-foot **Castillo**—one of the tallest on the Quintana Roo coast—at the center of a large acropolis. During excavations of the Castillo, jade figurines representing the moon and fertility goddess Ixchel were found. Recent excavations at Muyil have uncovered some smaller structures. The ruins stand near the edge of a deep-blue lagoon and are surrounded by almost impenetrable jungle—so be sure to bring insect repellent. You can drive down a dirt road on the side of the ruins to swim or fish in the lagoon. ✉ *Carretera 307, 15 km south of Tulum, Sian Ka'an* ⊕ *muyil.smv.org* ✉ *$3* ⊗ *Daily 8–5.*

PLAYA DEL CARMEN

Once upon a time, Playa del Carmen was a fishing village with a ravishing deserted beach. The villagers fished and raised coconut palms to produce copra, and the only foreigners who ventured here were beach bums and travelers catching ferries to Cozumel. That was a long time ago, however. These days the beach is far from deserted, although it is still delightful, with its alabaster-white sand and turquoise-blue waters. In fact Playa has become one of Latin America's fastest-growing communities, with a population of more than 135,000 and a pace almost as hectic as Cancún's. The ferry pier, where the hourly boats arrive from and depart for Cozumel, is another busy part of town. The streets leading from the dock have shops, restaurants, cafés, a hotel, and food stands. If you take a stroll north from the pier along the beach, you'll find the serious sun worshippers. On the pier's south side is the sprawling Playacar complex. The development is a labyrinth of residences and all-inclusive resorts bordered by an 18-hole championship golf course. ✛ *3 miles (5 km) north of Calica.*

Fodor's Choice ★ **Tulum.** Tulum is one of the few Mayan cities known to have been inhabited when the conquistadores arrived in 1518. In the 16th century it was a trade center, a safe harbor for trade goods from rival Mayan factions who considered the city neutral territory. The city reached its height when its merchants, made wealthy through trading, for the first time outranked Maya priests in authority and power. Although you can see the ruins thoroughly in two hours, you might want to allow extra time for a swim or a stroll on the beach. The largest and most-photographed structure, the **Castillo** (Castle), looms at the edge of a 40-foot limestone cliff just past the Temple of the Frescoes. The front wall of the Castillo has faint carvings of the Descending God and columns depicting the plumed serpent god, Kukulcán, who was introduced to the Maya by the Toltecs. A few small altars sit atop a hill at the north side of the cove, with a good view of the Castillo and the sea. ■**TIP**→ **To avoid the longest lines, be sure to arrive before 11 am.** ⊠ *Carretera 307, km 133, Tulum* ☎ *983/837–2411* 🖾 *$5 entrance, $3 parking, $4 video fee, $1.50 shuttle from parking to ruins* ⊙ *Daily 8–4:30.*

FAMILY **Xcaret.** Among the most popular attractions are the Paradise River raft tour that takes you on a winding, watery journey through the jungle; the Butterfly Pavilion, where thousands of butterflies float dreamily through a botanical garden while New Age music plays in the background; and an ocean-fed aquarium where you can see local sea life drifting through coral heads and sea fans. The entrance fee covers only access to the grounds and the exhibits; all other activities and equipment—from sea treks and dolphin tours to lockers and swim gear—are extra. The $109 Plus Pass includes park entrance, lockers, snorkel equipment, food, and drinks. You can buy tickets from any travel agency or major hotel along the coast. ⊠ *Carretera 307, km 282, Xcaret* ☎ *800/292–2738 in Mexico, 888/922–7381 in U.S.* ⊕ *www.xcaret.com* 🖾 *$79 Basic Pass; $109 Plus Pass* ⊙ *Daily 8:30 am–9:30 pm.*

FAMILY **Xplor.** Designed for thrill-seekers, this 125-acre park features underground rafting in stalactite-studded water caves and cenotes. Swim in a stalactite river, ride in an amphibian vehicle, or soar across the park on 13 of the longest zip-lines in Mexico. The price includes all food, drink, and equipment. ⊠ *Carretera 307, km 282* ☎ *984/147–6560, 888/922–7381 in U.S.* ⊕ *www.xplor.travel* 🖾 *$109* ⊙ *Mon.–Sat. 8:30–5.*

SHOPPING

Playa del Carmen's Avenida 5 between calles 4 and 10 is the best place to shop along the coast. Boutiques sell folk art and textiles from around Mexico, and clothing stores carry lots of sarongs and beachwear made from Indonesian batiks. A shopping area called Calle Corazon, between calles 12 and 14, has a pedestrian street, art galleries, restaurants, and boutiques.

Hacienda Tequila. Hacienda Tequila sells 480 different types of tequila and kitschy Mexican crafts and souvenirs. Free tastings are available, and there's an exhibit that walks you through the world of agave booze. ⊠ *Av. 5 and Calle 14* ☎ *984/803–0821.*

La Hierbabuena Artesanía. At La Hierbabuena Artesanía, owner Melinda Burns offers a collection of fine Mexican clothing and crafts. ✉ *Av. 5, between Calles 8 and 10* ☎ *984/873–1741.*

ACTIVITIES

DIVING

Abyss. The PADI and SSI-affiliated Abyss offers introductory courses and dive trips ($50 for one tank, $70 for two tanks). They also run dives in Tulum, as Cenote Dive Center. ✉ *Av. 1, between Calles 10 and 12* ☎ *984/873–2164* ⊕ *www.abyssdiveshop.com.*

Tank-Ha Dive Center. Playa's original dive outfit, Tank-Ha Dive Center has PADI-certified teachers and runs diving and snorkeling trips to the reefs and caverns. A one-tank dive costs $45; for a two-tank trip it's $65. Dive packages are also available, as well as trips to Cozumel. ✉ *Calle 10, between Avs. 5 and 10* ☎ *984/873–0302* ⊕ *www.tankha.com.*

GOLF

Casa Club de Golf. Playa del Carmen's golf course is an 18-hole, par-71 championship course designed by Nick Price. The greens fee is $165; there's also a special twilight fee of $120. ✉ *Grand Coral Riviera Maya Resort, Carretera 307, km 294* ☎ *984/109–6020* ⊕ *www. grandcoralrivieramaya.com.mx.*

WHERE TO EAT

$$ ✗ **Babe's Noodles & Bar.** Photos and paintings of old Hollywood pin-up
THAI models share decor space with a large stone Buddha at this Swedish-owned Thai restaurant, known for its fresh and interesting fare cooked to order. Try the spring rolls with peanut sauce, or the Korean sesame noodles, made with chicken or pork, veggies, chile, sesame and peanut cream, and wash it all down with a refreshing lemonade, blended with ice and mint. $ *Average main: $10* ✉ *Calle 10, between avs. 5 and 10* ☎ *984/879–3569* ⊕ *www.babesnoodlesandbar.com* ☉ *Closed Mon.*

$ ✗ **Hot Baking Company.** This cheap streetside breakfast café opens at
CAFÉ 7 am, and it's one of the few places where you can get breakfast before early-morning sightseeing. Known for Mexican egg dishes like the chili-and-cheese omelet, which will get your day off to a spicy start, Hot also serves more pedestrian packaged muffins and pastries. Salads and sandwiches are available at lunch and dinner. If vacation funds are running low, you can grab a light dinner here since the kitchen stays open until 10:30. $ *Average main: $7* ✉ *Calle 14 Norte, between avs. 5 and 10* ☎ *984/879–4520* ⊕ *www.hotbakingcompany.com.*

CARTAGENA, COLOMBIA

Jeffrey Van Fleet

Ever wondered what the "Spanish Main" refers to? This is it. Colombia's Caribbean coast invokes ghosts of conquistadors, pirates, and missionaries journeying to the New World in search of wealth, whether material or spiritual. Anchoring this shore is the magnificent colonial city of Cartagena—officially *Cartagena de Indias* (Cartagena of the

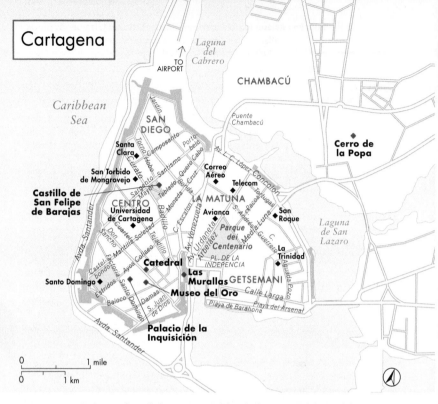

Cartagena

Caribbean Sea

TO AIRPORT

Laguna del Cabrero

CHAMBACÚ

SAN DIEGO

Puente Chambacú

Cerro de la Popa

Santa Clara

San Torbido de Mongrovejo

Correo Aéreo

Telecom

Castillo de San Felipe de Barajas

CENTRO

Universidad de Cartagena

LA MATUNA

Avianca

San Roque

Laguna de San Lazaro

Parque del Centenario

La Trinidad

PL. DE LA INDEPENCIA

Catedral

Las Murallas

GETSEMANI

Santo Domingo

Museo del Oro

Calle Larga

Playa del Arsenal

Playa de Barahona

Palacio de la Inquisición

Avda. Santander

0   1 mile
0   1 km

Indies)—founded in 1533. Gold and silver passed through here en route to Spain, making the city an obvious target for pirates, hence the construction of Cartagena's trademark walls and fortresses. Outside the *Ciudad Amurallada* (walled city) lie less historic beaches and water excursions. If Colombia conjures up images of drug lords and paramilitary guerillas, think again: security is quite visible (without being oppressive) here in the country's top tourist destination. Take the same precautions you would visiting any city of one million people, and you should have a grand time.

ESSENTIALS

CURRENCY
The Colombian peso. In Colombia, peso prices are denoted with the "$" sign too. If they carry a lot of zeros, they likely are not dollar prices, but always ask.

SAFETY
Security is tighter in Cartagena than elsewhere in Colombia, so you certainly can navigate the city on your own. (Knowing some Spanish helps.) However, the scarcity of English speakers and English signposting at the city's tourist attractions and the persistence of vendors, street touts, and the periodic con artist mean that many cruise passengers opt for the reassurance of an organized shore excursion. If you set out on

your own, under no circumstances should you deal with anyone who approaches you on the street offering to change money; rip-offs are guaranteed.

TELEPHONE

The Terminal de Cruceros has ample phones for your use. Local numbers in Cartagena have seven digits. For international calls, dial 009 followed by country and area codes and local number. AT&T offers roaming options in this region of Colombia for calls back to the United States; if you have a tri-band GSM phone it should work.

COMING ASHORE

Cruise ships dock at the modern Terminal de Cruceros (cruise terminal) on Isla de Manga, an island connected by a bridge to the historic city center, about 2 miles (3 km) northwest of the docks. You'll find telephones, Internet cafés, and a duty-free shop in the terminal.

A small army of taxis waits in front of the terminal. Expect to pay 15,000 pesos for the 10-minute drive to the walled city; the same fare will get you to the nearby beaches at Bocagrande. Drivers are all too happy to take you on your own do-it-yourself guided tour. Most charge around 20,000 pesos for an hour of waiting time. There's little need to rent a car here. Cartagena, at least the area of tourist interest, is so compact, and walking the labyrinth of cobblestone streets in the Old City is far more enjoyable—and a lot less hassle—than driving.

CARTAGENA BEST BETS

■ **Cruise the Harbor.** A boat trip around the city's inner bay allows to you appreciate the city's formidable walls and fortresses.

■ **Islas del Rosario.** The beaches of nearby Islas del Rosario are an hour away by boat.

■ **Ride a Coche.** Take the quintessential horse-and-buggy ride through the streets.

■ **Walk Las Murallas.** Walking the city's massive stone walls is a favorite tourist pastime.

■ **Visit Palacio de la Inquisición.** Cartagena's most-visited sight is this historic—and creepy—center for the Spanish Inquisition.

EXPLORING CARTAGENA

Nothing says Cartagena quite like a ride in a horse-drawn carriage, or *coche*, as it is known locally. Drivers are a wealth of information about Cartagena, and many do speak English. The downside for you is that most rides begin near dusk—it's a far cooler time of the day, after all—and your need to be back on ship may not coincide with that schedule. Do check. You can pick up carriages at many places, including the Plaza de los Coches, near the Puerta del Reloj in the walled city, or the Hotel Caribe in Bocagrande. Expect to pay around $200 (in U.S. dollars) for a two-hour tour, or around $60 for a half-hour (this kind of excursion is best when the cost is split among a group).

Castillo de San Felipe de Barajas. Designed by Antonio de Arévalo in 1639, the Fort of St. Philip's steep-angled brick and concrete battlements were arranged so that if part of the castle were conquered the rest could still be defended. A maze of tunnels, minimally lit today to allow for spooky exploration, still connects vital points of the fort. Notice the near-perfect acoustics in the tunnels here: Occupants could hear the footsteps of the approaching enemy. The climb is strenuous, but you'll be rewarded with some of the best views in Cartagena. Plan to get here by taxi—and expect to pay about 12,000 pesos one-way. ⊠ *Av. Pedro de Heredia at Carrera 17* ☎ *5/666–4790* 🖥 *18,000 pesos* ☉ *Daily 8–6.*

Catedral Metropolitana. Any Latin American city centers on its cathedral and main square. Plaza de Bolívar—a statue of South American liberator Simón Bolívar stands watch over the square—is a shady place from which to admire Cartagena's 16th-century cathedral. (It's officially the "Catedral Basílica Metropolitana de Santa Catalina de Alejandria.") Construction lasted from 1577–1612. British pirates attacked and pillaged the site about halfway through the process, a fate that befell many buildings in Cartagena in those early days. The colorful bell tower and dome date from the early 20th-century. Inside is a massive gilded altar. ⊠ *Plaza de Bolívar* ☎ *5/664–5308* ⊕ *www.arquicartagenadeindias.org.*

Fodor's Choice **Cerro de la Popa.** For spectacular views of Cartagena, ascend this hill
★ around sunset. Because of its strategic location, the 17th-century monastery here intermittently served as a fortress during the colonial era. It now houses a museum and a chapel dedicated to the Virgen de la Candelaria, Cartagena's patron saint. Taxis charge around 10,000 pesos one way to bring you here—have them wait—and the sight can be included on one of Cartagena's popular *chiva* (horsedrawn carriage) tours. ⚠ **Under no circumstances should you walk between the city center and the hill; occasional muggings of tourists have been reported along the route.** ⊠ *3 km (2 miles) southeast of Ciudad Amurallada* ☎ *5/666–2331* 🖥 *8,000 pesos* ☉ *Daily 8:30–5.*

Las Murallas. Cartagena survived only because of its walls, and its *murallas* remain today the city's most distinctive feature. Repeated sacking by pirates and foreign invaders convinced the Spaniards of the need to enlcose the region's most important port. Construction began in 1600 and finished in 1796. The Puerta del Reloj is the principal gate to the innermost sector of the walled city. Its four-sided clock tower was a relatively late addition (1888), and has become the symbol of the city. Walking along the thick walls is still today one of Cartagena's time honored pastimes, especially late in the afternoon when you can watch the setting sun redden the Caribbean. ⊠ *Area bounded by Bahía de las Ánimas, Laguna de San Lázaro, and Caribbean Sea.*

Museo del Oro y Arqueología. The Gold and Archaeological Museum, an institution funded and operated by Colombia's Central Bank, displays an assortment of artifacts culled from the Sinús, an indigenous group that lived in this region 2,000 years ago. ⊠ *Carrera 4 No. 33–26* ☎ *5/660–0778* 🖥 *Free* ☉ *Tues.–Fri. 10–1 and 3–7, Sat. 10–1 and 2–5, Sun. 11–4.*

Fodor's Choice
★ **Palacio de la Inquisición.** Arguably Cartagena's most visited tourist site documents the darkest period in the city's history. A baroque limestone doorway marks the entrance to the 1770 Palace of the Inquisition, the headquarters of the repressive arbiters of political and spiritual orthodoxy who once exercised jurisdiction over Colombia, Ecuador, and Venezuela. Although the museum displays benign colonial and pre-Columbian artifacts, everyone congregates on the ground floor to "Eeewww!" over the implements of torture—racks and thumbscrews, to name but two. We recommend you hire an English-speaking guide since many of the displays need explanations and all signs are in Spanish. ⊠ *Carrera 4 No. 33–26* ☎ *5/665–4229* 🎫 *15,000 pesos* ⊗ *Mon.–Sat. 9–6, Sun. 10–4.*

BEACHES

For white sand and palm trees, your best bet is **Playa Blanca,** about 15 minutes away by boat. Many people opt for a visit to the **Islas del Rosario,** a verdant archipelago surrounded by aquamarine waters and coral reefs. Tour boats leave from the Muelle de los Pegasos, the pier flanked by statues of two flying horses that is just outside the city walls. Plenty of men with boats will also offer to take you on the one-hour journey. A final option is **Bocagrande,** the resort area on a 3-mile-long (5-km-long) peninsula south of the walled city. High-rise hotels and condos front the gray-sand beach. It gets quite crowded and is very lively, but Bocagrande is probably not the Caribbean beach of which you've always dreamed.

SHOPPING

Think "Juan Valdez" if you're looking for something to take the folks back home. Small bags of fine Colombian coffee, the country's signature souvenir, are available in most tourist-oriented shops. Colombia also means emeralds, and you'll find plenty in the jewelry shops on or near Calle Pantaleón, beside the cathedral. Don't forget the duty-free shop in the Terminal de Cruceros for those last-minute purchases.

Las Bóvedas, a series of arched, one-time munitions storerooms in the Ciudad Amurallada's northern corner now houses about two-dozen shops with the best selection of local and national crafts.

ACTIVITIES

DIVING

Coral reefs line the coast south of Cartagena, although warm-water currents have begun to erode them in recent years. There is still good diving to be had in the Islas del Rosario, an archipelago of 27 coral islands about 21 miles (35 km) southwest of the city.

Buzos de Barú. Buzos de Barú at the Hotel Caribe organizes snorkeling trips to the Islas del Rosario, scuba diving at underwater-wreck sites, and dive instruction. ⊠ *Hotel Caribe, Local 9, Bocagrande* ☎ *5/665–7061* ⊕ *www.buzosdebaru.com.*

WHERE TO EAT

$$ ✕ **Café San Pedro.** Although it serves Colombian fare, this restaurant's
ECLECTIC   eclectic menu also includes dishes from Thailand, Italy, and Japan. You
can also drop by to have a drink and to watch the activity on the plaza
from one of the outdoor tables. $ *Average main: 23,000 pesos* ✉ *Plaza
San Pedro Claver No. 30–11* ☎ *5/664–5121.*

$$ ✕ **Paco's.** Heavy beams, rough terra-cotta walls, wooden benches, and
LATIN AMERICAN   tunes from an aging Cuban band are the hallmarks of this downtown
eatery. Drop by for a drink and some tapas, or try the more substantial
langostinos a la sifú (lobsters fried in batter). You can sit in the dining
room or outside on the Plaza Santo Domingo. $ *Average main: 25,000
pesos* ✉ *Plaza Santo Domingo, Calle 35 No. 3–02* ☎ *5/660–1638.*

COLÓN, PANAMA

David Duden-
hoefer and Jef-
frey Van Fleet

When you consider the decades it took to build the canal, not to mention the lives lost and government failures and triumphs involved during its construction, it comes as no surprise that the Panama Canal is
often called the Eighth Wonder of the Modern World. Best described
as an aquatic bridge, the Panama Canal connects the Caribbean Sea
with the Pacific Ocean by raising ships up and over Central America,
through artificially created Gatún Lake, the highest point at 85 feet
above sea level, and then lowering them back to sea level by using a
series of locks, or water steps. A masterful engineering feat, three pairs
of locks—Gatún, Pedro Miguel, and Miraflores—utilize gravity to fill
and drain as ships pass through chambers 1,000 feet long by 110 feet
wide that are "locked" by doors weighing 80 tons apiece, yet actually
float into position. Most cruise ships pass through the canal seasonally,
when repositioning from one coast to the other; however, partial transits
have become an increasingly popular "destination" on regularly scheduled 10- and 11-night Caribbean itineraries. These loop cruises enter
the canal from the Caribbean Sea and sail into Gatún Lake, where they
remain for a few hours as passengers are tendered ashore for excursions.
Ships then pass back through the locks, returning to the Caribbean and
stopping at either Cristobal Pier or Colón 2000 Pier to retrieve passengers at the conclusion of their tours.

A day transiting the canal's Gatún Locks begins before dawn as your
passenger ship passes through *Bahia Limon* and lines up with dozens
of other vessels to await its turn to enter. Before your ship can proceed,
two pilots and a narrator will board. The sight of a massive cruise ship
being raised dozens of feet into the air by water is so mesmerizing that
passengers eagerly crowd to all forward decks at the first lock. If you
don't find a good viewing spot, head for the rear decks, where there
is usually more room and the view is just as intriguing. If you remain
aboard, as many passengers do, you'll find plenty of room up front later
in the day as your ship retraces its path down to the sea. Due to the
tight scheduling of the day's activities—it takes at least 90 minutes for
a ship to pass through Gatún Locks—passengers who wish to go ashore

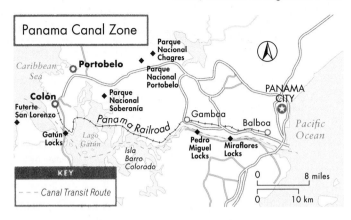

early in the day are advised to sign up for one of the many available shore excursions.

ESSENTIALS
CURRENCY
The U.S. dollar.

TELEPHONE
You'll find telephones inside Colón's cruise terminal where you can purchase phone cards, a handy and inexpensive way to make calls.

COMING ASHORE

Colón, Panama's second-largest city, has little to offer of historic interest, and is simply a jumping-off point to the rain forest and a wide variety of organized tours. Infrequent cruise itineraries may include a day docked in Colón, rather than a partial canal transit. However, no matter how much time your ship spends in Colón, it is usually easier (and recommended) to take an organized shore excursion. If you don't want to go on a ship-sponsored shore excursion, taxi drivers also await ship arrivals, and some can be acceptable private guides for $100 to $120 per day if you just want to explore Portabelo or San Lorenzo. However, as in any foreign port, before setting out with any unofficial car and driver, you should set a firm price and agree upon an itinerary as well as look over the vehicle carefully. It's also possible to rent a car from either Budget or Hertz, both of which have desks at the Colón 2000 terminal.

Although entry time into the canal is always approximate, passenger ships have priority, and most pass through Gatún Locks early in the morning. Passengers booked on shore excursions begin the tendering process soon after the ship sets anchor, which can be as early as 8:30 am. Alternatives to excursions offered by your cruise ship are available from independent tour operators that can be arranged in advance through websites or travel agents. You will likely be informed that Panamanian regulations restrict passengers going ashore in Gatún Lake to only those who have booked the cruise line's excursions; however, anyone who has a shore-excursion reservation with a local company should be able to leave the vessel. Before making independent tour arrangements, confirm with your cruise line that you will be allowed to go ashore after presenting your private tour confirmation to the shore-excursion staff on board the ship.

Colón 2000. Two blocks from the Zona Libre is the city's cruise-ship port, Colón 2000, which is basically a two-story strip mall next to the dock where ships tie up and passengers load onto buses for day trips. It has a supermarket, restaurants, two rental-car offices, and English-speaking taxi drivers who can take you on sightseeing excursions ($70–$100 for a full day). A second terminal opened in 2008 and became the home port for Royal Caribbean's *Enchantment of the Seas,* with the Panamanian government aggressively courting other cruise companies to set up shop here too. ✉ *Calle El Paseo Gorgas* ☎ *507/447–3197* ⊕ *www.colon2000.com.*

> ## COLÓN BEST BETS
>
> ■ **Explore an Embera Village.** You'll travel by dugout canoe through Chagres National Park.
>
> ■ **Kayak on Gatún Lake.** You can paddle among the many islands and mangrove forests.
>
> ■ **Panama Railway.** Take a train trip to Panama City for a quick sightseeing tour (you can come back by taxi to save some time).
>
> ■ **Portobelo.** Visit historic Panamanian forts.
>
> ■ **Rain Forest Aerial Tram.** Travel to Gamboa Rainforest Resort and see the rain forest canopy from above.

EXPLORING THE PANAMA CANAL ZONE

The provincial capital of **Colón,** beside the canal's Atlantic entrance, has clearly seen better days, as the architecture of its older buildings attests. Its predominantly Afro-Caribbean population has long had a vibrant musical scene, and in the late 19th and early 20th centuries Colón was a relatively prosperous town. But it spent the second half of the 20th century in steady decay, and things have only gotten worse in the 21st century. For the most part, the city is a giant slum, with unemployment at 30% to 40% and crime on the rise. ⚠ **Travelers who explore Colón on foot are simply asking to be mugged, and the route between the train station and the bus terminal is especially notorious; do all your traveling in a taxi or rental car. If you do the Panama Railway trip on your own without a tour company, take one of the shuttle vans or hire a taxi to the train station.**

Esclusas de Gatún (*Gatún Locks*). Twelve kilometers (7 miles) south of Colón are the Esclusas de Gatún (Gatún Locks), a triple-lock complex that's nearly a mile long and raises and lowers ships the 85 feet between sea level and Gatún Lake. There's a small visitor center with a viewing platform and information about the boats passing through is broadcast over speakers. The visitor's center doesn't compare to the one at Miraflores Locks, but given the sheer magnitude of the Gatún Locks—three sets of locks, as opposed to two at Miraflores—it is an impressive sight, especially when packed with ships. You have to cross the locks on a swinging bridge to get to San Lorenzo and the **Represa Gatún** (Gatún Dam), which holds the water in Gatún Lake. At 1½ miles long, it was the largest dam in the world when it was built, a title it held for several decades. Get there by taking the first left after crossing the locks. ⊠ *12 km (7 miles) south of Colón* ⊑ *$5* ⊘ *Daily 8–4.*

Fuerte San Lorenzo (*San Lorenzo Fort*). Perched on a cliff overlooking the mouth of the Chagres River are the ruins of the ancient Spanish Fuerte San Lorenzo, destroyed by pirate Henry Morgan in 1671 and rebuilt shortly after, then bombarded a century later. The Spaniards built Fort San Lorenzo in 1595 in an effort to protect the South American gold they were shipping down the Chagres River, which was first carried along the Camino de Cruces from Panamá Viejo. The gold was then shipped up the coast to the fortified city of Portobelo, where it was stored until the Spanish armada arrived to carry it to Spain. The fortress's commanding position and abundant cannons weren't enough of a deterrent for Morgan, whose men managed to shoot flaming arrows into the fort, causing a fire that set off stored gunpowder and forced the Spanish troops to surrender. Morgan then led his men up the river and across the isthmus to sack Panamá Viejo.

In the 1980s UNESCO restored the fort to its current condition, which is pretty sparse—it hardly compares to the extensive colonial ruins of Portobelo. Nevertheless, the setting is gorgeous, and the view from that promontory of the blue-green Caribbean, the coast, and the vast jungle behind it is breathtaking. ⚠ **Be careful walking around the edge outside the fort; there are some treacherous precipices, and guardrails are almost nonexistent. One visitor did have a fatal fall several years ago.** ⊠ *23 km (14 miles) northwest of Gatún Locks* ⊑ *Free* ⊘ *Daily 8–4.*

LAGO GATÚN (*GATÚN LAKE*)

Covering about 163 square miles, an area about the size of the island nation Barbados, Gatún Lake extends northwest from Parque Nacional Soberanía to the locks of Gatún, just south of Colón. The lake was created when the U.S. government dammed the Chagres River, between 1907 and 1910, so that boats could cross the isthmus at 85 feet above sea level. By creating the lake, the United States saved decades of digging that a sea-level canal would have required. It took several years for the rain to fill the convoluted valleys, turning hilltops into islands and killing much forest (some trunks still tower over the water nearly a century later). When it was completed, Gatún Lake was the largest man-made lake in the world. The canal route winds through its northern half, past several forest-covered islands (the largest is Barro Colorado, one of the world's first biological reserves). To the north of Barro Colorado are the Islas Brujas and Islas Tigres, which together hold a primate refuge—visitors aren't allowed. The lake itself is home to crocodiles—forego swimming here—manatees, and peacock bass, a species introduced from South America and popular with fishermen.

PORTOBELO

Portobelo is an odd mix of colonial fortresses, clear waters, lushly forested hills, and an ugly little town of cement-block houses crowded amid the ancient walls. It holds some of Panama's most interesting colonial ruins, with rusty cannons still lying in wait for an enemy assault, and is a UNESCO World Heritage Site, together with San Lorenzo.

Iglesia de San Felipe. One block east of the Real Aduana is the Iglesia de San Felipe, a large white church dating from 1814 that's home to the country's most venerated religious figure: the **Cristo Negro** (Black Christ). According to legend, that statue of a dark-skinned Jesus carrying a cross arrived in Portobelo in the 17th century on a Spanish ship bound for Cartagena, Colombia. Each time the ship tried to leave, it encountered storms and had to return to port, convincing the captain to leave the statue in Portobelo. Another legend has it that in the midst of a cholera epidemic in 1821 parishioners prayed to the Cristo Negro, and the community was spared. The statue spends most of the year to the left of the church's altar, but once a year it's paraded through town in the Festival del Cristo Negro. Each year the Cristo Negro is clothed in a new purple robe, donated by somebody who's earned the honor. Many of the robes that have been created for the statue over the past century are on display in the Museo del Cristo Negro (Black Christ Museum) in the Iglesia de San Juan, a smaller, 17th-century church next to the Iglesia de San Felipe. ⊠ *Calle Principal* ▤ *$1* ⊗ *Daily 8–4.*

Parque Nacional Portobelo (*Portobelo National Park*). Parque Nacional Portobelo is a vast marine and rain-forest reserve contiguous with Chagres National Park that protects both natural and cultural treasures. It extends from the cloud forest atop 3,212-foot Cerro Brujo down to offshore islands and coral reefs, and comprises the bay and fortresses of Portobelo. It holds an array of ecosystems and a wealth of biodiversity that ranges from nurse sharks and sea turtles along the coast to toucans and spider monkeys in the mountains. There is no proper park entrance, but you can explore the rain forest and mangrove estuaries along the coast on hiking or boat trips from Portobelo.

You can't miss the remains of the three Spanish fortresses that once guarded Portobelo Bay. The first is **Fuerte Santiago de la Gloria,** which is on the left as you arrive at the bay. It has about a dozen cannons and sturdy battlements that were built out of blocks of coral, which were cut from the platform reefs that line the coast. Coral was more abundant and easier to cut than the igneous rock found inland, so the Spaniards used it for most construction in Portobelo.

Portobelo's largest and most impressive fort is **Fuerte San Jerónimo,** at the end of the bay. Surrounded by the "modern" town, it was built in the 1600s but was destroyed by Vernon and rebuilt to its current state in 1758. Its large interior courtyard was once a parade ground, but it's now the venue for annual celebrations such as New Year's, Carnaval, the Festival de Diablos y Congos (shortly after Carnaval), and the town's patron saint's day (March 20).

Fuerte San Fernando, across the bay from Fuerte Santiago, consists of two battlements—one near the water and one on the hill above. The upper fortress affords a great view of the bay and is a good place to see birds because of the surrounding forest.

■**TIP→** Local boatmen who dock their boats next to Fuerte Santiago or Fuerte San Jerónimo can take you across the bay to explore **Fuerte San Fernando** for a few dollars. They also offer tours to local beaches, or a trip into the estuary at the end of the bay, which is a good place to see birds. ⊠ *Surrounding Portobelo* ☎ *507/448–2599 park office* ⊡ *Free* ⊙ *Daily 24 hrs.*

Real Aduana (*Royal Customs House*). Near the entrance to Fuerte San Jerónimo is the Real Aduana, where servants of the Spanish crown made sure that the king and queen got their cut from every ingot that rolled through town. Built in 1630, the Real Aduana was damaged during pirate attacks and then destroyed by an earthquake in 1882, only to be rebuilt in 1998. It is an interesting example of colonial architecture—note the carved coral columns on the ground floor—and it houses a simple museum with some old coins, cannonballs, and displays on Panamanian folklore. ⊠ *Calle de la Aduana* ⊡ *$1* ⊙ *Daily 8–4.*

SHOPPING

Both Cristobal Pier and Colón 2000 Pier have large shopping malls, where you will find Internet access, telephones, refreshments, and duty-free souvenir shops in relatively secure environments. Stores in both locations feature local crafts such as baskets, wood carvings, and toys, as well as liquor, jewelry, and the ubiquitous souvenir T-shirts. In addition to shops and cafés, Cristobal Pier features an open-air arts and craft market; Colón 2000 Pier has a well-stocked supermarket. Portobelo has a wide-ranging artisan market next to Iglesia de San Felipe.

The most unique locally made souvenirs are colorful appliquéd *molas,* the whimsical textile artwork created by native Kuna women, who come from the San Blas Islands; they are likely to be hand stitching new designs while they sell the ones they just completed. If you take an excursion to Portobelo, the best selection can be found in the artisan market next to Iglesia de San Felipe, where there are other locally made souvenirs that are well worth bargaining for.

WHERE TO EAT

$ ✕**Restaurante Los Cañones.** This rambling restaurant with tables among SEAFOOD palm trees and Caribbean views is one of Panama's most attractive lunch spots. The food and service fall a little short of the setting, but not so far that you'd want to scratch it from your list. In good weather, dine at tables edging the sea surrounded by dark boulders and lush foliage. The other option is the open-air restaurant, decorated with shells, buoys, and driftwood, with a decent view of the bay and forested hills. House specialties include *pescado entero* (whole fried snapper), *langosta al ajillo* (lobster scampi), and *centolla al jengibre* (king crab in a ginger sauce). ⑤ *Average main: $12* ⊠ *2 km (1 mile) before Portobelo on left* ☎ *507/448–2980* ▭ *No credit cards* ⊙ *Closes at 7 pm.*

COSTA MAYA, MEXICO

Marie Elena Martinez

Puerto Costa Maya is an anomaly. Unlike other tourist attractions in the area (the island of Cozumel being the primary Yucatán cruise port), this port of call near Mahahual has been created exclusively for cruise-ship passengers. The port added a second berth in July 2008. This latest addition known as "New Mahahual" comprises theme restaurants like Hard Rock Cafe and Señor Frog's, as well as boutique shops and chain stores such as Lapis Jewelry.

At first glance, the port complex itself may seem to be little more than an outdoor mall. The docking pier (which can accommodate three ships at once) leads to a 70,000-square-foot bazaar-type compound where shops selling local crafts—jewelry, pottery, woven straw hats and bags, and embroidered dresses—are interspersed with duty-free stores and souvenir shops. There are two alfresco restaurants, which serve seafood, American-friendly Mexican dishes like tacos and quesadillas, and cocktails at shaded tables. An outdoor amphitheater stages eight daily performances of traditional music and dance.

> ## COSTA MAYA BEST BETS
>
> ■ **Chacchoben.** This archaeological site is near the Belize border.
>
> ■ **Kohunlich.** This ruined city is best known for its great temples with sculpted masks.
>
> ■ **Mahahual.** This small fishing village (pronounced *Ma-ha-wal*) near the cruise pier has plenty of fine sand and glassy waters for a cushy afternoon in the sun.
>
> ■ **Snorkeling at Banco Chinchorro.** Excellent catamaran snorkeling trips go here.
>
> ■ **Xcalak.** This national reserve offers excellent saltwater fly-fishing and deserted beaches.

The strip of beach edging the complex has been outfitted with colorful lounge chairs and *hamacas* (hammocks), and may tempt you to linger and sunbathe. If you want to have a truly authentic Mexican experience, though, you'll take advantage of the day tours offered to outlying areas. These give you a chance to see some of the really spectacular sights in this part of Mexico, many of which are rarely visited. This is one port where the shore excursion is the point, and there are no options except to purchase what your ship offers. You can preview what excursions may be offered on the Puerto Costa Maya's own website.

Among the best tours are those that let you explore the gorgeous (and usually deserted) Mayan ruin sites of Kohunlich, Dzibanché, and Chacchoben. The ancient pyramids and temples at these sites, surrounded by jungle that's protected them for centuries, are still dazzling to behold. Because the sites are some distance from the port complex—and require some road travel in one of the port's air-conditioned vans—these tours are all-day affairs. One of the most popular activities with cruise passengers is the three-hour ATV excursion along jungle roads and the Mahahual coastline. Although an adventure, the ATVs tend to be a nuisance to residents and business owners, not to mention wildlife.

Prior to a devastating 2007 hurricane, there was no real reason to go into the small, nearby fishing village of Mahahual (pronounced

Ma-ha-*wal*). Though there are still about 300 residents, posthurricane renovations have put the village on the map; it now has its own pier as well as a smattering of hotels, restaurants, and shops. Be sure to venture beyond "New Mahahual," which lacks the charm of the nearby beachfront area. Its cement boardwalk along the beach has made Mahahual an ideal spot for a sunset stroll. The crystal-clear waters and unspoiled beaches are delightful for snorkeling, diving, and fishing.

ESSENTIALS

CURRENCY
The Mexican peso. U.S. dollars and credit cards are widely accepted in the area.

TELEPHONE
Most pay phones accept prepaid Ladatel cards, sold in 30-, 50-, or 100-peso denominations. To use the card, insert it in the pay phone's slot, dial 001 (for calls to the United States) or 01 (for calls within Mexico), followed by the area code and number. Credit is deleted from the card as you use it, and the balance is displayed on the small screen on the phone. Most tri-band mobile phones from the U.S. work in Mexico, though you must pay roaming charges.

BEACHES

Fodor's Choice ★ **Nacional Beach Club.** Many travelers stumble on this colorful beach club and end up staying past sunset. For just $10, you get a beach chair, umbrella, and access to the pool, showers, and changing facilities. Margaritas can be delivered to you beachside, or you can escape the heat by grabbing a bite in the enclosed patio. By day you can munch on tacos, enchiladas, and sandwiches; by night the menu expands to include delicious smoked fish or grilled shrimp (there's also an impressive vegetarian menu), but reservations are required at the restaurant. The $3 Coronas and free Wi-Fi make this a popular spot to while away the day. There's decent snorkeling right out front, and equipment available next door at Gypsea Divers. Movies are shown under the stars on Wednesday at 6. There are also three bungalows for rent if you feel like staying the night. **Amenities:** food and drink; showers; toilets. **Best for:** partiers; snorkeling; swimming. ✉ *Av. Mahahual, SN Lote 4, Manzana 14, Mahahual, Quintana Roo* ☎ *983/834–5719* ⊕ *www. nacionalbeachclub.com* 🍴 *$10* ☉ *Daily 8–5.*

WHERE TO EAT

$ | MEXICAN — ✗ **100% Agave.** Fernando's beloved *palapa* (thatch-roofed) shack is a Mahahual institution, with a friendly, homey atmosphere that's made the restaurant a sort of ersatz visitor bureau. The affordable menu features Mexican and Yucatecan specialties with a generous splash of gringo—great food that's an even better bang for your buck. Should you be in the market for a margarita, don't be shy—this is the place for expert guidance on all things agave, as suggested by the name, and the man-size tequila bottle out front. You can even buy a bottle of Fernando's homemade tequila to go. If the indoor party scene isn't lively enough for you, head to the beachfront tables, where a DJ spins beats on the sandy dance floor. $ *Average main: $8* ⊠ *Calle Huachinango, between Coronado and Martillo; north of the soccer field, Mahahual, Quintana Roo* ☎ *983/834–5609.*

$ ✕ **Nacional Beach Club.** Many travelers stumble on this colorful beach
MEXICAN   club and end up staying past sunset. For just $10, you get a beach chair, umbrella, and access to the pool, shower, and changing facilities. Margaritas can be delivered to you beachside or you can escape the heat by grabbing a bite in the enclosed patio. By day you can munch on tacos, enchiladas, and sandwiches and by night enjoy the delicious smoked fish or grilled shrimp (reservations are required for dinner). The $3 Coronas and free Wi-Fi make this a popular spot to wile away the day. There are also three bungalows for rent if you feel like staying the night. $ *Average main: $8* ⊠ *Av. Mahahual, Mahahual* ☎ *983/834–5719* ⊕ *www. nacionalbeachclub.com* ☺ *Open daily 8–5.*

COZUMEL, MEXICO

Marie Elena
Martinez

Cozumel, with its sun-drenched ivory beaches fringed with coral reefs, fulfills the tourist's vision of a tropical Caribbean island. It's a heady mix of the natural and the commercial. Despite a miniconstruction boom in the island's sole city, San Miguel, there are still wild pockets scattered throughout the island where flora and fauna flourish. Smaller than Cancún, Cozumel surpasses its fancier neighbor in many ways. It has more history and ruins, superior diving and snorkeling, more authentic cuisine, and a greater diversity of handicrafts at better prices. The numerous coral reefs, particularly the world-renowned Palancar Reef, attract divers from around the world. On a busy cruise-ship day the island can seem completely overrun, but it's still possible to get away, and some good Mayan sights are within reach on long (and expensive) shore excursions.

ESSENTIALS

CURRENCY

The Mexican peso, but U.S. dollars and credit cards are widely accepted in the area.

TELEPHONE

Most pay phones accept prepaid Ladatel cards, sold in 30-, 50-, or 100-peso denominations. To use the card, insert it in the pay phone's slot, dial 001 (for calls to the United States) or 01 (for calls within Mexico), followed by the area code and number. Credit is deleted from the card as you use it, and the balance is displayed on the small screen on the phone. Most tri-band mobile phones from the U.S. work in Mexico, though you must pay roaming charges.

COMING ASHORE

As many as six ships call at Cozumel on a busy day, tendering passengers to the downtown pier in the center of San Miguel or docking at the two international piers 4 miles (6 km) away. From the downtown pier you can walk into town or catch the ferry to Playa del Carmen.

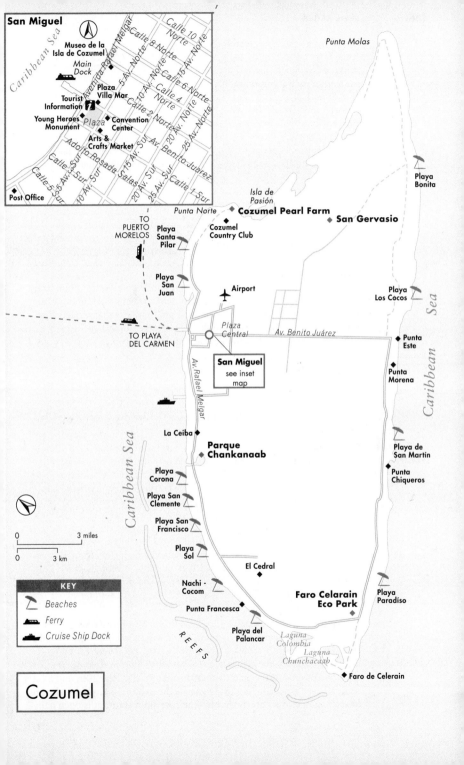

San Miguel

Caribbean Sea

Museo de la
Isla de Cozumel

Main
Dock

Tourist
Information

Young Heroes
Monument

Plaza
Villa Mar

Plaza

Arts &
Crafts Market

Convention
Center

Calle 10
Norte

Calle 8 Norte

Calle 6 Norte

Calle 4
Norte

Calle 2 Norte

Avenida Rafael Melgar

5 Av. Norte

10 Av. Norte

15 Av. Norte

20 Av. Norte

25 Av. Norte

Av. Benito Juárez

Adolfo Rosada Salas

Calle 1 Sur

Calle 3 Sur

Calle 5 Sur

5 Av. Sur

10 Av. Sur

15 Av. Sur

20 Av. Sur

25 Av. Sur

Post Office

Punta Molas

Playa
Bonita

Isla de
Pasión

Punta Norte

Cozumel Pearl Farm

San Gervasio

Cozumel
Country Club

TO
PUERTO
MORELOS

Playa
Santa
Pilar

Playa
San
Juan

Airport

Playa
Los Cocos

TO PLAYA
DEL CARMEN

Plaza
Central

Av. Benito Juárez

Punta
Este

San Miguel
see inset
map

Punta
Morena

Av. Rafael Melgar

La Ceiba

Parque
Chankanaab

Playa de
San Martín

Playa
Corona

Punta
Chiqueros

Playa San
Clemente

Playa San
Francisco

Playa
Sol

El Cedral

Nachi -
Cocom

Faro Celarain
Eco Park

Playa
Paradiso

Punta Francesca

Playa del
Palancar

R E E F S

Laguna
Colombia

Laguna
Chunchacaab

Faro de Celerain

Caribbean Sea

Caribbean Sea

Caribbean Sea

0   3 miles

0   3 km

KEY

Beaches

Ferry

Cruise Ship Dock

Cozumel

Taxi tours are also available. A four-hour island tour (4 people maximum), including the ruins and other sights, costs about $70 to $100, but negotiate the price before you get in the cab. The international pier is close to many beaches, but you'll need a taxi to get into town. There's rarely a wait for a taxi, but prices are high, and drivers are often aggressive, asking double or triple the reasonable fare. When in doubt, ask to see the rate card required of all taxi drivers. Expect to pay $10 for the ride into San Miguel from the pier. Tipping is not necessary.

COZUMEL BEST BETS

■ **Diving and Snorkeling.** Excellent reefs close to shore make either diving or snorkeling a must-do activity.

■ **Mayan Ruins.** Some of the most famous and dazzling ruins are reachable from Cozumel, and if you have never seen a Mayan pyramid, this is your chance.

■ **People-Watching.** You can spend hours just sitting in the main plaza (or at a sidewalk café) watching island life pass by.

Passenger ferries to Playa del Carmen leave Cozumel's main pier approximately every other hour from 5 am to 10 pm. They also leave Playa del Carmen's dock about every other hour on the hour, from 6 am to 11 pm (but note that service sometimes varies according to demand). The trip takes 45 minutes. Verify the times: bad weather and changing schedules can prompt cancellations.

EXPLORING COZUMEL

San Miguel is not tiny, but you can easily explore the waterfront and plaza area on foot. The main attractions are the small eateries and shops that line the streets and the main square, where the locals congregate in the evening.

FAMILY **Cozumel Pearl Farm.** Currently the only pearl farm operating in the Carib-
Fodor's Choice bean, the Cozumel Pearl Farm is located on a beautiful private beach of
★ white sand surrounded by turquoise waters and grows Caribbean pearl oysters over a period of eight years. Conceived as a project of research and development, this spectacular place opened its doors to visitors in early 2012. Small groups of up to 12 people a day can visit to discover how to grow a pearl, as well as snorkel and relax on the beach. Accessible only by boat, the farm will make you feel like a castaway on a desert island during the six-hour experience, which runs from 10 to 4. Transportation (from San Miguel Pier or other meeting point), gear, lunch, beer, and soft drinks are included in the price. ☒ *Punta Norte, Cozumel, Quintana Roo* ☎ *987/119–9417, 984/114–9604 From the U.S.* ⊕ *www.cozumelpearlfarm.com* ☒ *$110.*

FAMILY **Museo de la Isla de Cozumel.** Filling two floors of a former hotel, Cozumel's island museum has displays on natural history—the island's origins, endangered species, topography, and coral-reef ecology—as well as human history during the pre-Columbian and colonial periods. The photos of the island's transformation over the 20th and 21st centuries are especially fascinating, as is the exhibit of a typical Mayan home. Guided tours are available. The rooftop restaurant is open daily from 7 am to 11 pm. ⊠ *Av. Rafael E. Melgar, between calles 4 and 6 Norte* ☎ *987/872–1475* ≈ *$4* ⊙ *Mon.–Sat. 9–5, Sun 9–4.*

FAMILY **Parque Chankanaab.** The National Park of Chankanaab, translated as "small sea," consists of a saltwater lagoon, an archaeological park, and a botanical garden, with reproductions of a Mayan village and Olmec, Toltec, Aztec, and Mayan stone carvings scattered throughout. You can swim, scuba dive, or snorkel at the beach; the park also offers dolphin encounters, which are a highlight for kids. There's plenty to see beneath the surface: underwater caverns, a sunken ship, crusty old cannons and anchors, and a sculpture of la Virgen del Mar (Virgin of the Sea), all populated by parrotfish and sergeant majors galore. To preserve the ecosystem, park rules forbid touching the reef or feeding the fish. You'll also find dive shops, restaurants, gift shops, a snack stand, and dressing rooms with lockers and showers right on the sand. ⊠ *Carretera Sur, km 9* ☎ *987/872–4014* ⊕ *www. cozumelparks.com* ≈ *$21* ⊙ *Daily 8–4.*

San Gervasio. Surrounded by a forest, these temples make up Cozumel's largest remaining Mayan and Toltec site. San Gervasio was the island's capital and ceremonial center, dedicated to the fertility goddess Ixchel. The classic- and postclassic-style buildings and temples were continuously occupied from AD 300 to 1500. Typical architectural features include limestone plazas and arches atop stepped platforms, as well as stelae and bas-reliefs. Be sure to see the temple "Las Manitas," with red handprints all over its altar. Plaques in Mayan, Spanish, and English clearly describe each structure. ⊠ *Off Carretera Transversal* ⊹ *From San Miguel, take cross-island road (follow signs to the airport) east to San Gervasio access road; turn left and follow road 7 km (4½ mile)* ☎ *987/872–0093* ≈ *$8* ⊙ *Daily 8–4.*

BEACHES

Cozumel's beaches vary from sandy treeless stretches to isolated coves to rocky shores. Most of the development is on the leeward (western) side. Beach clubs have sprung up on the southwest coast; admission, however, is usually free, as long as you buy food and drinks. Clubs offer typical tourist fare: souvenir shops, palapa restaurants, kayaks, and cold beer. A cab ride from San Miguel to most clubs costs about $15 each way. Reaching beaches on the windward (eastern) side is more difficult, but the solitude is worth it.

Playa Palancar. South of the resorts, down a rutted and potholed road and way off the beaten path lies the serene Playa Palancar. The on-site dive shop can outfit you for trips to the famous Palancar Reef just offshore. There's also a water-sports center, a bar-café, and a long beach with hammocks hanging under coconut palms. **Amenities:** food and drink; showers; restrooms; parking (free); water sports. **Best For:** snorkeling; swimming. ⊠ *Carretera Sur, km 19* ≈ *Free.*

Playa San Francisco. Playa San Francisco was one of the first beach clubs on the coast. The inviting 5-km (3-mile) stretch of sandy beach, which extends along Carretera Sur south of Parque Chankanaab at about Km 14, is among the longest and finest on Cozumel. Encompassing the beaches Playa Maya and Santa Rosa, it's typically packed with cruise-ship passengers in high season. On Sunday locals flock here to eat fresh fish. Amenities include two outdoor restaurants, a bar, dressing rooms, gift shops, beach chairs, restrooms, massage treatments, and water-sports equipment rentals. Divers use the beach as a jumping-off point for the San Francisco reef. In lieu of a fee, there's a $10 minimum purchase of food or drinks for adults. **Amenities:** food and drink; lifeguards; parking (free); showers; toilets. **Best For:** walking; swimming. ⊠ *Carretera Costera Sur, km 14* 🖼 *Free ($10 minimum for food and drink).*

FAMILY **Punta Chiqueros.** Punta Chiqueros, a half moon-shaped cove sheltered by an offshore reef, is the first popular swimming area as you drive north on the coastal road. (It's about 12 km [8 miles] north of Faro Celarain Park.) Part of a longer beach that some locals call Playa Bonita, it has fine sand, clear water, and moderate waves. This is a great place to swim, watch the sunset, and eat fresh fish at the restaurant, also called Playa Bonita. **Amenities:** food and drink; toilets; parking (free). **Best For:** walking; sunseta; swimming. ⊠ *Carretera C–1, km 38.*

SHOPPING

Cozumel's main souvenir-shopping area is downtown along Avenida Rafael E. Melgar and on some side streets around the plaza. There are also clusters of shops at **Plaza del Sol** (east side of the main plaza) and **Vista del Mar** (⊠ *Av. Rafael E. Melgar 45*). As a general rule, the newer, trendier shops line the waterfront, and the better craft shops can be found around Avenida 5a. Malls at the cruise-ship piers aim to please passengers seeking jewelry, perfume, sportswear, and low-end souvenirs at high-end prices.

Most downtown shops accept U.S. dollars; many goods are priced in dollars. To get better prices, pay with cash—some shops tack a hefty surcharge on credit-card purchases. Shops, restaurants, and streets are always crowded between 10 am and 2 pm, but get calmer in the evening. Traditionally, stores are open from 9 to 1 (except Sunday) and 5 to 9, but those nearest the pier tend to stay open all day, particularly during high season. Most shops are closed Sunday morning.

ACTIVITIES

DIVING AND SNORKELING

Cozumel is famous for its reefs. In addition to Chankanaab Nature Park, a great dive site is La Ceiba Reef, in the waters off La Ceiba and Sol Caribe hotels. Here lies the wreckage of a sunken airplane blown up for a Mexican disaster movie. Cozumel has plenty of dive shops to choose from.

Aqua Safari. One of the island's oldest and most professional shops, Aqua Safari provides beginning and advanced PADI certification and daily introductory scuba courses. Owner Bill Horn has long been involved in efforts to protect the reefs and stays on top of local environmental issues. ⊠ *Av. Rafael E. Melgar 429, between calles 5 and 7 Sur* ☎ *987/872–0101* ⊕ *aquasafari.com.*

Blue Angel. Blue Angel offers combo dive and snorkel trips so families who don't all scuba can still have fun together. Along with dive trips to local reefs, they offer PADI courses. Two-tank dives run $79 plus tax. ⊠ *Carretera Sur, km 2.2* ☎ *987/872–1631* ⊕ *www.blueangelresort.com.*

Eagle Ray Divers. Eagle Ray Divers offers snorkeling trips and dive instruction. (The three-reef snorkel trip lets non-divers explore beyond the shore.) As befits their name, the company keeps track of the eagle rays that appear off Cozumel from December to February and runs trips for advanced divers to walls where the rays congregate. Beginners can also see rays around some of the reefs. ⊠ *La Caleta Marina, near the Presidente InterContinental hotel* ☎ *987/872–5735, 866/465–1616 in U.S.* ⊕ *www.eagleraydivers.com.*

FISHING

You can charter high-speed fishing boats for about $420 per half-day or $600 per day (with a maximum of six people). Your hotel can help arrange daily charters—some offer special deals, with boats leaving from their own docks.

Albatros Deep Sea Fishing. Albatros Deep Sea Fishing offers half- and full-day trips that include boat and crew, tackle and bait, and lunch (quesadillas or your own fresh catch) with beer and soda starting at $420 for up to six people. ⊠ *Puerto Abrigo Marina* ☎ *987/872–7904, 888/333–4643 toll-free in the U.S. and Canada* ⊕ *www.albatroscharters.com.*

3 Hermanos. This outfit specializes in deep-sea and fly-fishing trips, with rates for a half-day deep-sea fishing trip starting at $350 (a full day runs $450). The company also offers scuba-diving trips, and their boats are available for group charters—a great way to snorkel and cruise at your own pace—for $400 for up to six passengers. ⊠ *Puerto Abrigo Marina* ☎ *987/107–0655* ⊕ *www.cozumelfishing.com.*

WHERE TO EAT

$$$ ✕ **Guido's.** Chef Yvonne Villiger works wonders with fresh fish—if the
ITALIAN   wahoo with capers and black olives is on the menu, don't miss it. But Guido's is best known for its pizzas baked in a wood-burning oven, which tends to make sections of the indoor dining room rather warm. Instead, enjoy a pitcher of sangria in the pleasant, roomy courtyard. ⑤ *Average main: $19* ⊠ *Av. Rafael E. Melgar 23, between calles 6 and 8 Norte* ☎ *987/872–0946* ⊕ *www.guidoscozumel.com* ☾ *No lunch Sun.*

$$$ ✕ **Pancho's Backyard.** Marimbas play beside a bubbling fountain in
MEXICAN   the charming courtyard behind one of Cozumel's best folk-art shops. Though Pancho's is always busy, the waitstaff is patient and helpful. Cruise-ship passengers seeking a taste of Mexico pack the place at lunch; dinner is a bit more serene. The American-style, English menu is geared toward tourists, but regional ingredients like smoky chipotle chile make even the standard steak stand out. Other stars include the

cilantro cream soup and shrimp flambéed with tequila. ⑤ *Average main: $16* ⊠ *Av. Rafael Melgar between calles 8 and 10 Norte* ☎ *987/872–2141* ⊕ *www.panchosbackyard.com* ⊘ *No lunch Sun.*

CURAÇAO (WILLEMSTAD)

Vernon
O'Reilly-
Ramesar

Try to be on deck as your ship sails into Curaçao. The tiny Queen Emma floating bridge swings aside to allow ships to pass through the narrow channel. Pastel gingerbread buildings on shore look like dollhouses, especially from a large cruise ship. Although the gabled roofs and red tiles show a Dutch influence, the gleeful colors of the facades are peculiar to Curaçao. It's said that an early governor of the island suffered from migraines that were aggravated by the color white, so all the houses were painted in hues from magenta to mauve. Thirty-five miles (56 km) north of Venezuela and 42 miles (68 km) east of Aruba, Curaçao is, at 38 miles (61 km) long and 3 to 7.5 miles (5 to 12 km) wide, the largest of the Netherlands Antilles. Although always sunny, it's never stiflingly hot here because of the constant trade winds. Water sports attract enthusiasts from all over the world, and the reef diving is excellent.

ESSENTIALS
CURRENCY
Currency in Curaçao is the florin (also called the guilder) and is indicated by *fl* or *NAf* on price tags, but U.S. dollars are accepted almost everywhere.

TELEPHONE
To call Curaçao direct from the United States, dial 011–5999 plus the number in Curaçao. International roaming for most GSM mobile phones is available in Curaçao. Local companies are UTS (United Telecommunication Services) and Digicel. You can also rent a mobile phone or buy a prepaid SIM card for your own phone.

COMING ASHORE

Ships dock at the terminal just beyond the Queen Emma Bridge, which leads to the floating market, cafés, and the shopping district. The walk to downtown takes less than 10 minutes. Easy-to-read maps are posted dockside and in the shopping area. The terminal has a duty-free shop, telephones, and a taxi stand.

Taxis, which meet every ship, have meters, although rates are still fixed from point to point of your journey. The government-approved rates, which do not include waiting time, can be found in a brochure called "Taxi Tariff Guide," available at the cruise-ship terminal and at the tourist board. Rates are for up to four passengers. There's a 25% surcharge after 11 pm. It's easy to see the sights on Curaçao without going on an organized shore excursion. Downtown can be done on foot, and a taxi for up to four people will cost about $45 an hour. Taxi fares to places in and around the city range from $8 to $20. Car rentals are available but are not cheap (about $40 per day, plus $10 compulsory insurance).

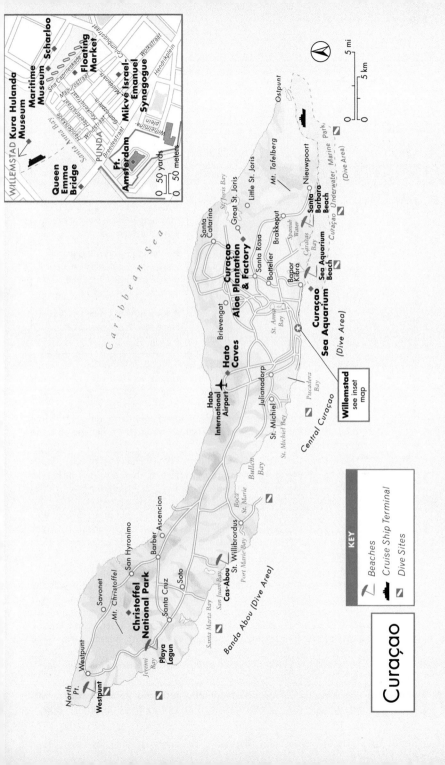

WILLEMSTAD

Kura Hulanda Museum

Maritime Museum

Scharloo

Floating Market

Mikvé Israel-Emanuel Synagogue

PUNDA

Ft. Amsterdam

Queen Emma Bridge

Santa Anna Bay

Columbusstraat
Sha Caprileskade
Madurostraat
Wilhelminaplein
Breedestraat
Keukenstraat
Handelskade
Heerenstraat
Hendrikplein
Wolkstraat

0   50 yards
0   50 meters

Caribbean Sea

Ostpunt

Mt. Tafelberg

Nieuwpoort

Curaçao Underwater Marine Park

Santa Barbara Beach

Brakkeput

Spanish Water

Caracas Bay

Sea Aquarium Beach

Bapor Kibra

Santa Rosa

Botelier

St. Joris Bay

Santa Catarina

Great St. Joris

Little St. Joris

Curaçao Aloe Plantation & Factory

Brievengat

Hato Caves

Hato International Airport

Julianadorp

St. Michiel

St. Michiel Bay

Bullen Bay

Boca St. Marie

St. Marie

Port Marie Bay

St. Willibrordus

Cas-Abou

San Juan Bay

Santa Marta Bay

Banda Abou (Dive Area)

Soto

Santa Cruz

Ascencion

Barber

San Hyronimo

Savonet

Mt. Christoffel

Christoffel National Park

Westpunt

North Pt.

Westpunt

Playa Lagun

Jeremi Bay

St. Anna Bay

Piscadera Bay

Central Curaçao

Curaçao Sea Aquarium (Dive Area)

Willemstad see inset map

KEY

Beaches

Cruise Ship Terminal

Dive Sites

Curaçao

5 mi

5 km

EXPLORING CURAÇAO

WILLEMSTAD

Willemstad is small and navigable on foot. You needn't spend more than two or three hours wandering around here, although the narrow alleys and various architectural styles are enchanting. English, Spanish, and Dutch are widely spoken. Narrow Santa Anna Bay divides the city into two sides: Punda, where you'll find the main shopping district, and Otrabanda (literally, the "other side"), where the cruise ships dock. Punda is crammed with shops, restaurants, monuments, and markets. Otrabanda has narrow, winding streets full of colonial homes notable for their gables and Dutch-influenced designs.

> ### CURAÇAO BEST BETS
>
> ■ **Diving.** After Bonaire, Curaçao has probably the best diving in the region.
>
> ■ **Punda.** Willemstad's chic and beautiful shopping area is a joy to explore on foot.
>
> ■ **Curaçao Sea Aquarium.** Explore the wonders of the ocean without getting wet.
>
> ■ **Floating Market.** This unique market is a fun destination, even though it's mostly fruits and vegetables.
>
> ■ **Kurá Hulanda Museum.** This is the island's best historical museum.

You can cross from Otrabanda to Punda in one of three ways: walk over the Queen Emma Bridge; ride the free ferry, which runs when the bridge swings open to let seagoing vessels pass; or take a cab across the Juliana Bridge (about $9). On the Punda side of the city, Handelskade is where you'll find Willemstad's most famous sights—the colorful colonial buildings that line the waterfront. The original red roof tiles came from Europe on trade ships as ballast.

Floating Market. Each morning dozens of Venezuelan schooners laden with tropical fruits and vegetables arrive at this bustling market on the Punda side of the city. Mangoes, papayas, and exotic vegetables vie for space with freshly caught fish and herbs and spices. The buying is best at 6:30 am—too early for many people on vacation—but there's plenty of action throughout the afternoon. Any produce bought here should be thoroughly washed or peeled before being eaten. ⊠ *Sha Caprileskade, Punda.*

Ft. Amsterdam. Step through the archway of this fort and enter another century. The entire structure dates from the 1700s, when it was the center of the city and the island's most important fortification. Now it houses the governor's residence, a church (which has a small museum), and government offices. Outside the entrance, a series of majestic gnarled wayaka trees are fancifully carved with human forms—the work of local artist Mac Alberto. ⊠ *Foot of Queen Emma Bridge, Punda* ☎ *5999/461–1139* ⊠ *Fort free, church museum $2* ☉ *Weekdays 9:30–1, Sun. service at 10.*

Fodor's Choice ★ **Kura Hulanda Museum.** This fascinating anthropological museum reveals the island's diverse roots. Housed in a restored 18th-century village, the museum is built around a former mercantile square (Kura Hulanda means "Holland courtyard"), where the Dutch once sold slaves. An exhibit on the transatlantic slave trade includes a gut-wrenching replica of a slave-ship hold. Other sections feature relics from West African empires, examples of pre-Columbian gold, and Antillean art. The complex is the brainchild of Dutch philanthropist Jacob Gelt Dekker, and the museum grew from his personal collection of artifacts. ⊠ *Klipstraat 9, Otrobanda* ☎ *5999/434–7765* ⊕ *www.kurahulanda.com* ▧ *$10* ◉ *Thurs.–Sat. 10–5.*

Maritime Museum. The museum—designed to resemble the interior of a ship—gives you a sense of Curaçao's maritime history, using model ships, historic maps, nautical charts, navigational equipment, and audiovisual displays. Topics explored in the exhibits include the development of Willemstad as a trading city, Curaçao's role as a contraband hub, the remains of *De Alphen* (a Dutch marine freighter that exploded and sank in St. Anna Bay in 1778 and was excavated in 1984), the slave trade, the development of steam navigation, and the role of the Dutch navy on the island. The museum also offers a two-hour guided tour (Wednesday and Saturday, 2 pm) on its "water bus" through Curaçao's harbor—a route familiar to traders, smugglers, and pirates. The museum is wheelchair accessible. ⊠ *Van der Brandhofstraat 7, Scharloo* ☎ *5999/465–2327* ⊕ *www.curacaomaritime.com* ▧ *Museum $6.50, museum and harbor tour $15* ◉ *Tues.–Sat. 9–4.*

Mikvé Israel-Emanuel Synagogue. The temple, the oldest in continuous use in the Western Hemisphere, is one of Curaçao's most important sights and draws thousands of visitors a year. The synagogue was dedicated in 1732 by the Jewish community, which had already grown from the original 12 families who came from Amsterdam in 1651. They were later joined by Jews from Portugal and Spain fleeing persecution from the Inquisition. White sand covers the synagogue floor for two symbolic reasons: a remembrance of the 40 years Jews spent wandering the desert, and a re-creation of the sand used by secret Jews, or *conversos,* to muffle sounds from their houses of worship during the Inquisition. English and Hebrew services are held Friday at 6:30 pm and Saturday at 10 am. Men who attend should wear a jacket and tie. Yarmulkes are provided to men for services and tours. ⊠ *Hanchi Snoa 29, Punda* ☎ *5999/461–1067* ⊕ *www.snoa.com* ▧ *$10; donations also accepted* ◉ *Weekdays 9–4:30.*

Queen Emma Bridge. Affectionately called the Swinging Old Lady by the locals, this bridge connects the two sides of Willemstad—Punda and Otrobanda—across the Santa Anna Bay. The bridge swings open at least 30 times a day to allow passage of ships to and from the sea. The original bridge, built in 1888, was the brainchild of the American consul Leonard Burlington Smith, who made a mint off the tolls he charged for using it: 2¢ per person for those wearing shoes, free to those crossing barefoot. Today it's free to everyone. The bridge was dismantled and completely repaired and restored in 2005.

Scharloo. The Wilhelmina Drawbridge connects Punda with the once-flourishing district of Scharloo, where the early Jewish merchants built stately homes. The architecture along Scharlooweg (much of it from the 17th century) is magnificent, and, happily, many of the colonial mansions that had become dilapidated have been meticulously renovated. The area closest to Kleine Werf is a red-light district and fairly run-down, but the rest is well worth a visit.

ELSEWHERE ON THE ISLAND

Christoffel National Park. The 1,239-foot Mt. Christoffel, Curaçao's highest peak, is at the center of this 4,450-acre garden and wildlife preserve. The exhilarating climb up—a challenge to anyone who hasn't grown up scaling the Alps—takes about two hours for a reasonably fit person. On a clear day, the panoramic view from the peak stretches to the mountain ranges of Venezuela.

Throughout the park are eight hiking trails and a 20-mile (32-km) network of driving trails (use heavy-treaded tires if you wish to explore the unpaved stretches). All these routes traverse hilly fields full of prickly pear cacti, divi-divi trees, bushy-haired palms, and exotic flowers. Guided nature walks, horseback rides, and jeep tours can be arranged through the main park office. If you're going without a guide, first study the *Excursion Guide to Christoffel Park,* sold at the visitor center. It outlines the various routes and identifies the indigenous flora and fauna. Start out early, as by 10 am the park starts to feel like a sauna. Most island sports outfitters offer some kind of activity in the park, such as kayaking, specialized hiking tours, and drive-through tours (⇨ *See Sports and Activities, below).* ⊠ *Savonet* ☎ *5999/864–0363 for information and tour reservations, 5999/462–6262 for jeep tours* 🖃 *$12* 🕙 *Mon.–Sat. 8–4, Sun. 6–3; last admission 90 mins before closing.*

Curaçao Aloe Plantation & Factory. Drop in for a fascinating tour that takes you through the various stages of production of aloe vera, renowned for its healing powers. You'll get a look at everything from the fields to the final products. At the gift shop, you can buy CurAloe products, including homemade goodies like soap, pure aloe gel, and pure aloe juice, as well as sunscreen and other skin-care products. The plantation is on the way to the Ostrich Farm and run by the same owner. Tours are offered throughout the day. ⊠ *Weg Naar Groot St. Joris z/n, Groot St. Joris* ☎ *5999/767–5577* ⊕ *www.aloecuracao.com* 🖃 *$7* 🕙 *Mon.–Sat. 9–4; last tour at 3.*

FAMILY **Curaçao Sea Aquarium.** You don't have to get your feet wet to see the island's underwater treasures. The aquarium has about 40 saltwater tanks filled with more than 400 varieties of marine life. A restaurant, a snack bar, two photo centers, and souvenir shops are on-site. ⊠ *Seaquarium Beach, Bapor Kibra z/n* ☎ *5999/461–6666* ⊕ *www.curacao-sea-aquarium.com* 🖃 *$20* 🕙 *Daily 8:30–5:30.*

Hato Caves. Stalactites and stalagmites form striking shapes in these 200,000-year-old caves. Hidden lighting adds to the dramatic effect. Indians who used the caves for shelter left petroglyphs about 1,500 years ago. More recently, slaves who escaped from nearby plantations used the caves as a hideaway. Hour-long guided tours wind down to the pools in various chambers. Keep in mind that there are 49 steps to climb up to the entrance and the occasional bat might not be to everyone's taste. To reach the caves, head northwest toward the airport, take a right onto Gosieweg, follow the loop right onto Schottegatweg, take another right onto Jan Norduynweg and a final right onto Roosevelt-weg, and follow signs. ⊠ *Rooseveltweg z/n, Hato* ☎ *5999/868–0379* 🖅 *$8* ☉ *Daily 10–4.*

BEACHES

FAMILY **Cas Abao.** This white-sand gem has the brightest blue water in Curaçao, a treat for swimmers, snorkelers, and sunbathers alike. You can take respite beneath the hut-shaded snack bar. The restrooms and showers are immaculate. The only drawback is the weekend crowds, especially Sunday, when local families descend in droves; come on a weekday for more privacy. You can rent beach chairs, paddleboats, and snorkeling and diving gear. The entry fee is $3, and the beach is open from 8 to 6. Turn off Westpunt Highway at the junction onto Weg Naar Santa Cruz; follow until the turnoff for Cas Abao, and then drive along the winding country road for about 10 minutes to the beach. **Amenities:** food and drink; lifeguards; parking; showers; toilets; water sports. **Best for:** partiers; snorkeling; swimming. ⊠ *West of St. Willibrordus, about 3 miles (5 km) off Weg Naar Santa Cruz.*

FAMILY **Playa Knip.** Two protected coves offer crystal clear turquoise waters. Big (Groot) Knip is an expanse of alluring white sand, perfect for swimming and snorkeling. You can rent beach chairs and hang out under the palapas or cool off with ice cream at the snack bar. There are restrooms here but no showers. It's particularly crowded on Sunday and school holidays. Just up the road, also in a protected cove, Little (Kleine) Knip is a charmer, too, with picnic tables and palapas. Steer clear of the poisonous manchineel trees. There's no fee for these beaches. **Amenities:** food and drink; lifeguards; parking; toilets; water sports. **Best for:** snorkeling; sunrise; sunset; surfing; swimming. ⊠ *Just east of Westpunt, Banda Abou.*

FAMILY **Seaquarium Beach.** This 1,600-foot stretch of sandy beach is divided into separate sections, each uniquely defined by a seaside resort or restaurant as its central draw. By day, no matter where you choose to enter the palm-shaded beach, you can find lounge chairs in the sand, thatched shelters, and restrooms. The sections at Mambo and Kontiki beaches also have showers. The island's largest water-sports center (Ocean Encounters at Lions Dive) caters to nearby hotel guests and walk-ins. Mambo Beach is always a hot spot and quite a scene on weekends, especially during the much-touted Sunday-night fiesta that's become a fixture of the island's nightlife. The ubiquitous beach mattress is also the preferred method of seating for the Tuesday-night movies at Mambo Beach (check the *K-Pasa* guide for listings—typically B-films or old classics—and reserve your spot with a shirt or a towel). At Kontiki Beach, you can find a spa, a hair braider, and a restaurant that serves refreshing piña colada ice cream. Unless you're a guest of a resort on the beach, the entrance fee to any section is $3. **Amenities:** food and drink; lifeguards; parking; showers; toilets. **Best for:** partiers; snorkeling; walking. ⊠ *About 1 mile (1½ km) east of downtown Willemstad, Bapor Kibra z/n.*

SHOPPING

From Dutch classics like embroidered linens, delft earthenware, cheeses, and clogs to local artwork and handicrafts, shopping in Curaçao can turn up some fun finds. But don't expect major bargains on watches, jewelry, or electronics; Willemstad is not a duty-free port (the few establishments that claim to be "duty-free" are simply absorbing the cost of some or all of the tax rather than passing it on to consumers); however, if you come prepared with some comparison prices, you might still dig up some good deals. Hours are usually Monday through Saturday, from 8 to noon and 2 to 6. Most shops are within the six-block area of Willemstad *described above*. The main shopping streets are Heerenstraat, Breedestraat, and Madurostraat.

Boolchand's. Head here for electronics, jewelry, Swarovski crystal, Swiss watches, cameras, and more, sold behind a façade of red-and-white checkered tiles. ⊠ *Breedstraat 50, Punda* ☏ *5999/461–6233.*

Cigar Emporium. A sweet aroma permeates Cigar Emporium, where you can find the largest selection of Cuban cigars on the island, including H. Upmann, Romeo y Julieta, and Montecristo. Visit the climate-controlled cedar cigar room. However, remember that Cuban cigars cannot be taken back to the United States legally. ⊠ *Gomezplein, Punda* ☏ *5999/465–3955.*

New Amsterdam. Hand-embroidered tablecloths, napkins, and pillowcases, as well as blue delft, are available at New Amsterdam. ⊠ *Gomezplein 14, Punda* ☏ *5999/461–2437.*

ACTIVITIES

BICYCLING

Wanna Bike Curaçao. So you wanna bike Curaçao? This shop has the fix: kick into gear and head out for a guided mountain-bike tour through the Caracas Bay peninsula and the salt ponds at the Jan Thiel Lagoon. Although you should be fit to take on the challenge, mountain-bike experience is not required. Tour prices vary, depending on skill level and duration, and cover the bike, helmet, water, refreshments, park entrance fee, and guide—but don't forget to bring a camera. ⊠ *Jan Thiel Beach z/n, Jan Thiel* ☏ *5999/527–3720* ⊕ *www.wannabike.com.*

DIVING AND SNORKELING

FAMILY **Ocean Encounters.** This is the largest dive operator on the island. Its operations cover the popular east-coast dive sites, including the *Superior Producer* wreck, where barracudas hang out, and a tugboat wreck. West-end hot spots—including the renowned Mushroom Forest and Watamula dive sites—are accessible from the company's outlet at Westpunt. Ocean Encounters offers a vast menu of scheduled shore and boat dives and packages, as well as certified PADI instruction. In July, the dive center sponsors a kids' sea camp in conjunction with the Sea Aquarium. ⊠ *Lions Dive & Beach Resort, Seaquarium Beach, Bapor Kibra z/n* ☏ *5999/461–8131* ⊕ *www.oceanencounters.com.*

WHERE TO EAT

$ ✕ **Awa di Playa.** Formerly a fisherman's hangout, this ramshackle shed-
CAFÉ like structure located on an ocean inlet gives way to an equally ram-
shackle interior and some of the best local lunches anywhere on the
island. There's no menu—the waiter will tell you what's available, and
you can watch it being cooked in the tiny kitchen. The presentation isn't
fancy, and the occasional fly makes an appearance, but the food is honest and delicious. ⑤ *Average main: $8* ⊠ *Behind Hook's Hut and Hil-
ton, Piscadera Bay* ☎ *5999/462–6939* ▭ *No credit cards* ◎ *No dinner.*

$$ ✕ **Gouverneur de Rouville Restaurant & Café.** Dine on the verandah of a
ECLECTIC restored 19th-century Dutch mansion overlooking the Santa Anna Bay
and the resplendent Punda skyline. Though often busy and popular with
tourists, the ambience makes it worth a visit. Intriguing soup options
include Cuban banana soup and Curaçao-style fish soup. *Keshi yena*
(seasoned meat wrapped in cheese and then baked) and spareribs are
among the savory entrées. After dinner, you can stick around for live
music at the bar, which stays open until 1 am. The restaurant is also
popular for lunch and attracts crowds when cruise ships dock. Reserve
ahead if you would like a balcony table. ⑤ *Average main: $22* ⊠ *De
Rouvilleweg 9, Otrabanda* ☎ *5999/462–5999* ⊕ *www.de-gouverneur.
com.*

DOMINICA (ROSEAU)

7

Roberta
Sotonoff

In the center of the Caribbean archipelago, wedged between the two
French islands of Guadeloupe, to the north, and Martinique, to the
south, Dominica is a wild place. So unyielding is the terrain that colo-
nists surrendered efforts at colonization, and the last survivors of the
Caribbean's original people, the Carib Indians, have made her rug-
ged northeast their home. Dominica—29 miles (47 km) long and 16
miles (26 km) wide—is an English-speaking island, though family and
place names are a mélange of French, English, and Carib. The capital is
Roseau (pronounced rose-*oh*). If you've had enough of casinos, crowds,
and swim-up bars and want to take leave of everyday life—to hike, bike,
trek, and spot birds and butterflies in the rain forest; explore waterfalls;
discover a boiling lake; kayak, dive, snorkel, or sail in marine reserves;
or go out in search of the many resident whale and dolphin species—
this is the place to do it.

ESSENTIALS
CURRENCY
The Eastern Caribbean dollar (EC$), but U.S. dollars are widely
accepted.

TELEPHONES
To call Dominica from the United States, dial the area code (767) and
the local access code (44), followed by the five-digit local number. On
the island, dial only the seven-digit number that follows the area code.

Dominica

Roseau (inset map)

Independence St.
Great George St.
King George V St.
Roseau River
Old St.
Bath Rd.
Bay St.

Botanical Gardens ◆

Dominica Museum ◆

Dominica Passage

Capucin Pt.

Toucari Beach and Reef

Morne Aux Diables

Vieille Case

Hampstead

Hodges

L'Anse Tortue

Woodford Hill Bay

ATLANTIC OCEAN

Douglas Bay

Cabrits Drop-Off

Purple Beach

Portsmouth

Calibishie

Bense

Melville Hall Airport ✈

Marigot

Fort Shirley ◆

Indian Rd.

Indian R.

Prince Rupert Bay

Picard Beach

Picard R.

Londonderry Bay

Pt. Ronde

Morne Diablotin

Dublanc

Colihaut

Carib Indian Territory ◆

Nose Reef

Castle Bruce

Brain Coral Garden

Salisbury Falls

Salisbury

Mero

Layou River

Emerald Pool

Petit Soufrière Bay

Castaways

Macoucherie River

Rosalie

Rodney's Rock

Mahaut

Pont Casse

Bout Sable Bay

Pringles Bay

Cochrane

Laudat

Morne Trois Pitons National Park

Pt. Giraud

Canefield Airport ✈

Trafalgar

La Plaine

Woodbridge Bay

Wotten Waven Rd.

Roseau
see inset map

Petite Savanne Delices Rd.

Caribbean Sea

Pointe Michel

Champagne

Soufrière Bay

Grand Bay

Soufrière Marine Reserve

Scotts Head Village

Scotts Head

Martinique Passage

KEY

⚲ Beaches
⛴ Cruise Ship Terminal
◣ Dive Sites

0 — 4 miles
0 — 6 km

COMING ASHORE

In Roseau most ships dock along the bay front. Across the street from the pier, in the old post office, is a visitor information center. Taxis, minibuses, and tour operators are available at the berths. If you do decide to tour with one of them, choose one who is certified, and be explicit when discussing where you will go and how much you will pay—don't be afraid to ask questions. The drivers usually quote a fixed fare, which is regulated by the Division of Tourism and the Transportation Board, and also offer their services for tours anywhere on the island beginning at $30 an hour for up to four people; a four- to five-hour island tour for up to four people will cost approximately $200. You can rent a car in Roseau for about $35–$70, not including insurance and a mandatory EC$30 ($12) driving permit, but it can be difficult to find things, so you might do better on a guided tour here.

> **DOMINICA BEST BETS**
>
> ■ **Kalinago Barana Autê.** This reserve is a great place to learn about the fierce Caribs.
>
> ■ **Rain-Forest Trips.** Hiking in Dominica's rain forest is the best way to experience its natural beauty.
>
> ■ **Snorkeling in Champagne.** A bubbling volcanic vent makes you feel as if you are snorkeling in champagne.
>
> ■ **Whale-Watching.** November through February offers the best whale-watching in the Caribbean.
>
> ■ **Indian River.** A rowboat ride on the river is relaxing and peaceful.

EXPLORING DOMINICA

Most of Dominica's roads are narrow and winding, so you'll need a few hours to take in the sights. Be adventurous, whether you prefer sightseeing or hiking—you'll be amply rewarded.

ROSEAU

Although it's one of the smallest capitals in the Caribbean, Roseau has the highest concentration of inhabitants of any town in the eastern Caribbean. Caribbean vernacular architecture and a bustling marketplace transport visitors back in time. Although you can walk the entire town in about an hour, you'll get a much better feel for the place on a leisurely stroll.

FAMILY **Botanical Gardens.** The 40-acre Botanical Gardens, founded in 1891 as an annex of London's Kew Gardens, is a great place to relax, stroll, or watch a cricket match. In addition to the extensive collection of tropical plants and trees, there's also a parrot aviary. At the Forestry Division office, which is also on the garden grounds, you can find numerous publications on the island's flora, fauna, and national parks. The forestry officers are particularly knowledgeable on these subjects and can also recommend good hiking guides. ⊠ *Valley Rd.* ☎ *767/266–3807, 767/266–3812* ⊕ *www.da-academy.org/dagardens.html* 🎟 *Free* ⊙ *Daily 8–4.*

Dominica Museum. The old post office now houses the Dominica Museum. This labor of love by local writer and historian Dr. Lennox Honychurch contains furnishings, documents, prints, and maps that date back hundreds of years; you can also find an entire Carib hut as well as Carib canoes, baskets, and other artifacts. ⊠ *Dame M. E. Charles Blvd., opposite cruise-ship berth* ☎ *767/448–2401* ✉ *$3* ⊘ *Weekdays 9–4, Sat. 9–noon; closed Sun. except when a cruise ship is in port.*

ELSEWHERE ON DOMINICA

FAMILY **Carib Indian Territory.** In 1903, after centuries of conflict, the Caribbean's first settlers, the Kalinago (more popularly known as the Caribs), were granted approximately 3,700 acres of land on the island's northeast coast. Here a hardened lava formation, **L'Escalier Tête Chien** (Snake's Staircase), runs down into the Atlantic. The name is derived from a snake whose head resembles that of a dog. The ocean alongside Carib Territory is particularly fierce, and the shore is full of countless coves and inlets. According to Carib legend, every night the nearby Londonderry Islets transform into grand canoes to take the spirits of the dead out to sea.

A chief administers the Carib Territory, where about 3,000 natives reside. The reservation's Catholic church in Salybia has a canoe as its altar, which was designed by Dr. Lennox Honychurch, a local historian, author, and artist.

   Kalinago Barana Autê. You might catch canoe builders at work at Kalinago Barana Autê, the Carib Territory's place to learn about Kalinago customs, history, and culture. A guided, 45-minute tour explores the village, stopping along the way to see some traditional dances and to learn about plants, dugout canoes, basket weaving, and cassava bread making. The path offers wonderful viewpoints of the Atlantic and a chance to glimpse Isukulati Falls. There's also a good souvenir shop. ⊠ *Crayfish River, Salybia* ☎ *767/445–7979* ⊕ *www.kalinagobaranaaute.com* ✉ *Basic package is about $10* ⊘ *Daily 9–5.*

FAMILY **Emerald Pool.** Quite possibly the most visited nature attraction on the island, this emerald-green pool fed by a 50-foot waterfall is an easy trip to make. To reach this spot in the vast Morne Trois Pitons National Park, you follow a trail that starts at the side of the road near the reception center (it's an easy 20-minute walk). Along the way, there are lookout points with views of the windward (Atlantic) coast and the forested interior. If you don't want a crowd, check whether there are cruise ships in port before going out, as this spot is popular with cruise-ship tour groups. ✉ *$3 for pre-organized tours; $5 for private and stay-over visitors; $12 weekly site pass covers all parks.*

Morne Trois Pitons National Park. A UNESCO World Heritage Site, this 17,000-acre swath of lush, mountainous land in the south-central interior (covering 9% of Dominica) is the island's crown jewel. Named after one of the highest (4,600 feet) mountains on the island, it contains the island's famous "boiling lake," majestic waterfalls, and cool mountain lakes. There are four types of vegetation zones here. Ferns grow 30 feet tall, wild orchids sprout from trees, sunlight leaks through green canopies, and a gentle mist rises over the jungle floor. A system of trails has been developed in the park, and the Division of Forestry and Wildlife works hard to maintain them—with no help from the excessive rainfall and the profusion of vegetation that seems to grow right before your eyes. Access to the park is possible from most points, though the easiest approaches are via the small mountaintop villages of Laudat (pronounced lau-*dah*) and Cochrane.

On your way to Boiling Lake you pass through the **Valley of Desolation,** a sight that definitely lives up to its name. Harsh sulfuric fumes have destroyed virtually all the vegetation in what must once have been a lush forested area. Small hot and cold streams with water of various colors—black, purple, red, orange—web the valley. Stay on the trail to avoid breaking through the crust that covers the hot lava. During this hike you'll pass rivers where you can refresh yourself with a dip (a particular treat is a soak in a hot-water stream on the way back). At the beginning of the Valley of Desolation trail is the **TiTou Gorge,** where you can swim in the pool or relax in the hot-water springs along one side. If you're a strong swimmer, you can head up the gorge to a cave (it's about a five-minute swim) that has a magnificent waterfall; a crack in the cave about 50 feet above permits a stream of sunlight to penetrate the cavern.

Also in the national park are some of the island's most spectacular waterfalls. The 45-minute hike to **Sari Sari Falls,** accessible through the east-coast village of La Plaine, can be hair-raising. But the sight of water cascading some 150 feet into a large pool is awesome. So large are these falls that you feel the spray from hundreds of yards away. Just beyond the village of Trafalgar and up a short hill is the reception facility, where you can purchase passes to the national park and find guides to take you on a rain-forest trek to the twin **Trafalgar Falls;** the 125-foot-high waterfall is called the Father, and the wider, 95-foot-high one, the Mother. If you like a little challenge, let your guide take you to the riverbed and the cool pools at the base of the falls (this trip is popular with cruise passengers). Guides for these hikes are available at the trailheads; still, it's best to arrange a tour before setting out. ✉ *$3 for pre-organized tours; $5 for private and stay-over visitors; $12 weekly site pass covers all parks.*

Boiling Lake. The undisputed highlight of the park is the Boiling Lake. Reputedly one of the world's largest such lakes, it's a cauldron of gurgling gray-blue water, 70 yards wide and of unknown depth, with water temperatures from 180°F to 197°F. Although generally believed to be a volcanic crater, the lake is actually a flooded fumarole—a crack through which gases escape from the molten lava below. The two- to four-hour (one way) hike up to the lake is challenging (on a very rainy day, be prepared to slip and slide the whole way up and back). You'll need clothes appropriate for a strenuous hike. Most guided trips start early (no later than 8:30 am) for this all-day, 7-mile (11-km) round-trip trek. Do not attempt this trek without a trained guide.

BEACHES

FAMILY **Champagne.** On the west coast, just south of the village of Pointe Michel, this stony beach is hailed as one of the best spots for swimming, diving, and (especially) snorkeling. Forget the sunning, though, because the beach is strewn with rocks. Champagne gets its name from volcanic vents that constantly puff steam into the sea, which makes you feel as if you are swimming in warm champagne. A boardwalk leads to the beach from Soufrière/Scotts Head Marine Reserve. **Amenities:** none. **Best for:** snorkeling; swimming. ⊠ *1 mile (1½ km) south of Pointe Michel, Soufrière.*

SHOPPING

Dominicans produce distinctive handicrafts, with various communities specializing in their specific products. The crafts of the Carib Indians include traditional baskets made of dyed *larouma* reeds and waterproofed with tightly woven *balizier* leaves. These are sold in the Carib Indian Territory and Kalinago Barana Auté as well as in Roseau's shops. Vertivert straw rugs, screw-pine tableware, *fwije* (the trunk of the forest tree fern), and wood carvings are just some examples. Also notable are local herbs, spices, condiments, and herb teas.

One of the easiest places to pick up a souvenir is the Old Market Plaza, just behind the Dominica Museum, in Roseau. Slaves were once sold here, but today handcrafted jewelry, T-shirts, spices, souvenirs, batik, and lacquered and woven bamboo boxes and trays are available from a group of vendors in open-air booths set up on the cobblestones. These are usually busiest when there's a cruise ship berthed across the street. On these days you can also find a vast number of vendors along the bay front.

Baroon International. Baroon International sells unusual jewelry from Asia, the United States, and other Caribbean islands. It also features pieces that are assembled in the store, as well as personal accessories, souvenirs, and special gifts. ⊠ *Castle St.* ☎ *767/449–2888.*

Kalinago Barana Auté. Kalinago Barana Auté sells carvings, pottery, and lovely handwoven baskets, which you can watch the women weave. ⊠ *Salybia, Carib Territory* ☎ *767/445–7979* ⊕ *www.kalinagobaranaaute.com* ☉ *Daily 9–5.*

ACTIVITIES

ADVENTURE PARKS

FAMILY **Wacky Rollers.** Wacky Rollers will make you feel as if you are training for the marines as you swing on a Tarzan-style rope and grab onto a vertical rope ladder, rappel across zip lines, and traverse suspended log bridges, a net bridge, and four monkey bridges (rope loops). It costs $65 for the adult course and should take from 1½ to 3½ hours to conquer the 28 "games." There is also an abbreviated kids' course for $25 (kids 10 and under). Wacky Rollers also organizes adventure tours around the island plus kayak and tubing trips. Although the office is in Roseau, the park itself is in Hillsborough Estate, about 20 to 25 minutes north of Roseau. ⊠ *Front St.* ☎ *767/440–4386* ⊕ *www.wackyrollers.com.*

DIVING AND WHALE-WATCHING

Fodor's Choice ★ Dominica has been voted one of the top 10 dive destinations in the world by *Skin Diver* and *Rodale's Scuba Diving* magazines—and has won many other awards for its underwater sites. They are truly memorable. There are numerous highlights all along the west coast

of the island, but the best are those in the southwest—within and around **Soufrière/Scotts Head Marine Reserve.** There is a $2 fee per person to dive, snorkel, or kayak in the reserve. The conditions for underwater photography, particularly macrophotography, are unparalleled. Rates start at about $55 for a single-tank dive and about $90 for a two-tank dive or from about $75 for a resort course with one open-water dive. All scuba-diving operators also offer snorkeling. Equipment rents for $10 to $25 a day; trips with gear range from $15 to $35. A 10% tax is not included.

Anchorage Dive & Whale Watch Center. The Anchorage Dive & Whale Watch Center has two dive boats that can take you out day or night. It also offers PADI instruction (all skill levels), snorkeling and whale-watching trips, and shore diving. It has many of the same trips as Dive Dominica. ⊠ *Anchorage Hotel, Castle Comfort* ☎ *767/448–2638, 888/790–5264 in U.S.* ⊕ *www.anchoragehotel.dm.*

Dive Dominica. Dive Dominica, one of the island's dive pioneers, conducts NAUI, PADI, and SSI courses as well as Nitrox certification courses. With four boats, it offers diving, snorkeling, and whale-watching trips and packages, including accommodation at the Castle Comfort Lodge. Its trips are similar to Anchorage's. ⊠ *Castle Comfort Lodge, Castle Comfort* ☎ *767/448–2188, 646/502–6800 in U.S.* ⊕ *www. divedominica.com.*

HIKING

Dominica's majestic mountains, clear rivers, and lush vegetation conspire to create adventurous hiking trails. The island is crisscrossed by ancient footpaths of the Arawak and Carib Indians and the Nègres Maroons, escaped slaves who established camps in the mountains. Existing trails range from easygoing to arduous. To make the most of your excursion, you'll need sturdy hiking boots, insect repellent, a change of clothes (kept dry), and a guide. Hikes and tours run $25 to $80 per person, depending on destinations and duration. A poncho or light raincoat is recommended. Some of the natural attractions within the island's national parks require visitors to purchase a site pass. These are sold for varying numbers of visits. A single-entry site pass costs $5, and a weekly pass $12.

Bertrand Jno Baptiste. Local bird and forestry expert Bertrand Jno Baptiste leads hikes up Morne Diablotin and along the Syndicate Nature Trail; if he's not available, ask him to recommend another guide. ☎ 767/245–4768.

WHERE TO EAT

$ ✗ **Cocorico.** It's hard to miss the umbrella-shaded chairs and tables at
ECLECTIC this Parisian-style café on a prominent bay-front corner in Roseau.
FAMILY Breakfast crepes, croissants, baguette sandwiches, and piping-hot café au lait are available beginning at 8:30 am. Throughout the day you can relax indoors or out and enjoy any of the extensive menu selections with the perfect glass of wine. You can also surf the Internet on its computers. In the cellar downstairs, the Cocorico wine store has a reasonably priced selection from more than eight countries, plus a wide assortment of pâtés and cheeses, crepes, sausages, cigars, French bread, and chocolates. ⑤ *Average main: $10* ✉ *Bay Front at Kennedy Ave.* ☎ 767/449–8686 ⊕ *www.natureisle.com/cocorico* ☯ *Closed Sun. unless ship is in port, then 10–4. No dinner.*

$ ✗ **Pearl's Cuisine.** In a Creole town house in central Roseau, chef Pearl,
CARIBBEAN with her robust and infectious character, prepares some of the island's best local cuisine, such as callaloo soup, fresh fish, and rabbit. Her menu changes daily, but she offers such local delicacies as souse (pickled pigs' feet), blood pudding, and rotis. When sitting down, ask for a table on the open-air gallery that overlooks Roseau. Servings are large here, but make sure you leave space for dessert. If you're on the go, enjoy a quick meal from the daily, varied menu in the ground-floor snack bar. You're spoiled for choice when it comes to the fresh fruit juices. ⑤ *Average main: $12* ✉ *Sutton Place Hotel, 25 Old St.* ☎ 767/448–8707 ☯ *Closed Sun. No dinner.*

FALMOUTH, JAMAICA

Catherine
MacGillivray

Midway between Ocho Rios and Montego Bay, Falmouth, founded in 1790, prospered from Jamaica's status as the world's leading sugar producer. From the late 18th to the early 19th century, it was the was the wealthiest port in the Caribbean. With more than 80 sugar estates nearby, the town was meticulously mapped out in the colonial tradition, with streets named after British royalty and heroes. The richness of the town's historic Georgian structures, many of which are still occupied and maintained, is reflected in its heritage. The city has long been heralded for its forward-thinking hygiene policies (the first piped water supply system in the Western Hemisphere—established here in 1799—continues to be a source of pride) and progressive politics (Falmouth was the birthplace of Jamaica's abolitionist movement in the early 19th century). The site of many slave revolts, Falmouth had several safe houses for escaped slaves until the practice of slavery was outlawed in the British Empire in 1833 and came into effect the following year. Although the town is seeing a revival with the opening of a purpose-built cruise port in 2011 (a joint venture between the government and Royal Caribbean Cruises Limited), buildings that may seem unimpressive as they undergo restoration are still rich in history. Indeed, in 1996 the historic areas were declared a national monument. Plans are underway to erect a statue of star sprinter Usain Bolt on the pier. The six-time Olympian grew up only a few miles from Falmouth, and his family still lives nearby.

ESSENTIALS
CURRENCY
The Jamaican dollar, but the U.S. dollar is accepted virtually everywhere.

TELEPHONE
Public telephones are by the bus stop at the Falmouth Cruise Terminal. Some U.S. phone companies won't permit credit-card calls to be placed from Jamaica because of problems with fraud, so collect calls are often the top option. GSM cell phones equipped with tri-band or world-roaming service will find coverage throughout the Falmouth area.

COMING ASHORE

Cruise ships, including the world's largest, are able to dock at the Falmouth Cruise Port's two berths. A visitor information facility is in the pier area. The town is right outside the port gates, and places of interest are easily within walking distance. The Falmouth tourist trolley offers a one-hour tour of the town with regular departures from inside the port. Tickets and trolley schedules are available at the trolley kiosk outside the arrivals hall. You can also take a horse and carriage to explore the town in genteel fashion.

For travel out of town, buses and taxis are available inside the port gates. The bus fare to Red Stripe Beach, a seven-minute drive, is US$20 round-trip and includes the entrance fee. Facilities include restrooms and there are craft vendors on-site. Taxis to other attractions are priced according to the destination. For example, a round-trip to Montego Bay costs US$20 per person (a 20-minute drive), or US$150 to Ocho Rios (a 90-minute drive) for up to four persons and an extra US$35 for each additional passenger. Cruise passengers are welcomed by a reggae band as they disembark from the ship and are entertained by steel pan players in the main cruise terminal. While the ship is in, the pier is bustling with souvenir shops and craft market vendors to keep you occupied all day. However, there is so much to see in the lush countryside outside of Falmouth that many passengers may opt to take an organized tour.

Falmouth's location, almost equidistant to both Montego Bay and Ocho Rios, makes most tours offered at those ports available from Falmouth as well. Many of the most popular and adventurous tours are operated by Chukka Caribbean and can only be booked by cruise passengers directly with the cruise lines, as space is presold to ships for their arrival dates. Coaches for prebooked tours pick up passengers inside the cruise port, but authorized independent tour operators are also available there to arrange tours on the spot. Car rental isn't recommended in Jamaica because of the aggressive drivers.

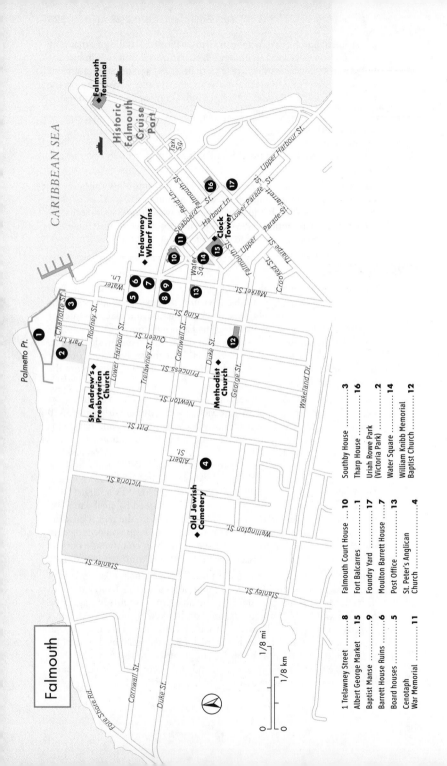

Falmouth

CARIBBEAN SEA

Palmetto Pt.

Historic Falmouth Cruise Port

Falmouth Terminal

Taxi Sq.

St. Andrew's Presbyterian Church

Trelawney Wharf ruins

Clock Tower

Water Sq.

Methodist Church

Old Jewish Cemetery

Fort Shore Rd.

0   1/8 mi
0   1/8 km

1 Trelawney Street **8**
Albert George Market **15**
Baptist Manse **9**
Barrett House Ruins **6**
Board houses **5**
Cenotaph
War Memorial **11**

Falmouth Court House ...**10**
Fort Balcarres **1**
Foundry Yard **17**
Moulton Barrett House ...**7**
Post Office **13**
St. Peter's Anglican
Church **4**

Southby House **3**
Tharp House **16**
Uriah Rowe Park
(Victoria Park) **2**
Water Square **14**
William Knibb Memorial
Baptist Church **12**

EXPLORING FALMOUTH

Falmouth's streets, which were laid out in a grid plan in the mid-1700s, are easily explored on your own. However, even with a map, finding your way around can be confusing due to a lack of street signs. If you become disoriented or require directions, look for a member of the Falmouth Tourism Courtesy Corps wearing official white shirts and hats, who are on hand to assist visitors. The one-hour trolley tour, which leaves from inside the cruise port, is an excellent way to see the historic sites and buildings and help you avoid getting lost.

Points of interest include the Falmouth Courthouse and the adjacent Cenotaph War Memorial; Water Square, where Falmouth residents got running water before New York City; Fort Balcarres, built to guard Falmouth Harbour; and Barrett House ruins, the remains of the town home of planter Edward Barrett (grandfather of Elizabeth Barrett Browning), who founded Falmouth. Also of interest is the William Knibb Baptist Church, which dates back to 1832 and was rebuilt in 1837 by Baptist missionary William Knibb, a pro-emancipation activist. St. Peter's Anglican Church is the oldest public building in Falmouth still in use.

Other sights include fine examples of Falmouth's Georgian-era architecture. These buildings are recognizable by their double-hung sash windows, keystones, columns, symmetry of facade, and full-length verandas. Constructed of a native limestone over brick, and remarkably preserved, most structures are occupied as either private residences or commercial buildings.

Jamaica Swamp Safari Village. With a large sign declaring that "Trespassers Will be Eaten," this attraction on the outskirts of Falmouth will most fascinate reptile enthusiasts. The village was started as a crocodile farm in the 1970s by American Ross Kananga, who was a stunt man in the James Bond film *Live and Let Die*. Scenes from the film *Papillon*, starring Steve McQueen and Dustin Hoffman, were also shot here. Although Ross passed away some years ago and the attraction fell into disrepair, it has recently reopened. It now houses a number of Jamaican crocodiles as well as the Jamaican yellow boa snake. There are other exotic animals from South America and colorful tropical birds in the aviary. ⌧ *Foreshore Rd.* ☎ *876/617–2798* ⊕ *www.jamaicaswampsafari. com.*

FALMOUTH BEST BETS

■ **Good Hope Great House.** The expansive view of the plantation grounds and surrounding countryside from the front garden includes the Martha Brae River.

■ **Historic Trolley Tour.** Absorb Falmouth's Colonial-era history and discover the town's landmarks and Georgian architectural treasures.

■ **Martha Brae River.** A trip to Falmouth would not be complete without a rafting trip on the nearby Martha Brae River.

■ **Rose Hall Great House.** The historic home is one of the region's top sights.

7

WHAT TO SEE OUTSIDE OF FALMOUTH

Good Hope Great House. A visit to Good Hope Great House, about a 20-minute drive inland from Falmouth, will give you a real sense of Jamaica's rich history as a sugar-estate island. The house, built in 1755, is now a museum where a guide leads you through opulently furnished rooms. John Tharp, who acquired the house in the mid-18th century, was one of the few planters to educate his slaves, and he also built a hospital for them. After your tour, you can have tea on the terrace. ☎ *876/356–8502, 876/276–2082* ⊕ *www.chukkacaribbean.com/ tour_info.php?Good-Hope-Great-House-30&lang=eng* ✉ *US$15 for entrance to the house only, additional fee for high tea* ☉ *By reservation only.*

SHOPPING

Coming ashore, you will find more than four dozen shops along the cruise port's pedestrian thoroughfares housing well-known international and established Jamaican merchants. Also in the port is a covered open-air craft market, where many vendors offer their wares, including hand-carvings, and items such as T-shirts, caps, and local seasonings. In town, souvenir vendors set up on Seaboard Street near the Courthouse. Water Square is the location of the Albert George market, where artisans offer local craftwork that showcases the history and culture of the area. The upscale Shops at Rose Hall are within easy reach by taxi between Falmouth and Montego Bay.

ACTIVITIES

Most adventure activities offered to cruise-ship passengers in Montego Bay and Ocho Rios, including water sports, trips to nearby beaches, golf, river-rafting, scuba diving, and sightseeing, are also available to cruise passengers in Falmouth. See both Montego Bay and Ocho Rios for more information. Chukka at Good Hope offers the majority of activities aimed at cruise passengers out of Good Hope Plantation.

Chukka at Good Hope. This adventure facility at the lush Good Hope Estate includes an ATV safari, river-tubing safari, zip lining, dune buggies, and a horse-and-carriage ride. Aside from the adventures, points of interest around the former sugar estate include the ruins of a waterwheel and kiln, former trading house, countinghouse, sugar-boiling house, and the hut in which slaves were born. ✉ *Good Hope* ☎ *876/619–1441 Digicel in Jamaica, 876/656–8026 Lime in Jamaica, 877/424–8552 in the U.S.* ⊕ *www.chukkacaribbean.com* ✉ *US$53–$124.*

Falmouth Heritage Walks. This leisurely paced walk takes you through Falmouth's commercial and residential streets while your guide shares the little-known history of the town and what made it a rich and significant port in the late 18th and early 19th centuries. Your guide will also explain how the movement to abolish slavery was essentially founded in Falmouth when you visit the former home and grave of the famous abolitionist William Knibb. The full tour takes about 2 hours 15 minutes.

876/407–2245 ⊕ *www.falmouthheritagewalks.com* ✉ *$25* ⊙ *Times vary throughout the day when ships are in port.*

Historic Trolley Tour. The easiest way to see the historic sites of Falmouth is on this covered trolley with a guide who offers a lively commentary about the town and its many historical buildings. The majority of these are Georgian in style and date to the 18th century. The one-hour tours leave regularly from inside the cruise port and include attractions such as Falmouth Court House, the market, Water Square, and several churches. Trams—though not motorized ones—were the mode of transport in Jamaica 300 years ago when Falmouth was in its heyday as a busy sugar port. ✉ *Falmouth cruise port* ☎ *876/509–0454* ✎ *info@ falmouthtoursbytrolley.com.*

WHERE TO EAT

Visitors planning to shop at the Half Moon shopping village can eat at Seagrape Terrace. Good Hope Great House also offers afternoon tea.

$$
AMERICAN

✕ **Margaritaville.** The latest outpost of Jimmy Buffet's bar and restaurant chain to open in Jamaica is in the Falmouth cruise port in 2013. Like its counterparts in Montego Bay, Ocho Rios, and Negril, this branch offers plenty of fun, along with American-Caribbean fare on the menu. The menu includes staples such as a "Cheeseburger in Paradise," and jerk pork or chicken. Cocktails such as 5 o'clock Somewhere are sure to keep things lively while Jimmy Buffet's hit songs are played on rotation. There's a party atmosphere here that some parents may feel is not suitable for younger kids (shots poured directly into patrons' mouths, for instance). ⑤ *Average main: $20* ✉ *At cruise pier* ☎ *876/979–8149* ⊕ *www.margaritaville.com* ⊙ *Closed when no ship is in port.*

FREEPORT-LUCAYA, BAHAMAS

Jamie Werner

Grand Bahama Island, the fourth-largest island in the Bahamas, lies 52 miles (84 km) off Palm Beach, Florida. In 1492, when Columbus first set foot in the Bahamas, Grand Bahama was already populated. Skulls found in caves attest to the existence of the peaceable Lucayans, who were constantly fleeing the more bellicose Caribs. But it was not until the 1950s, when the harvesting of Caribbean yellow pine trees (now protected by Bahamian environmental law) was the island's major industry, that American financier Wallace Groves envisioned Grand Bahama's grandiose future as a tax-free port for the shipment of goods to the United States. It was in that era that the city of Freeport and later Lucaya evolved. They are separated by a 4-mile (6-km) stretch of East Sunrise Highway, although few can tell you where one community ends and the other begins. Most of Grand Bahama's commercial activity is concentrated in Freeport, the Bahamas' second-largest city. Lucaya, with its sprawling shopping complex and water-sports reputation, stepped up to the role of island tourism capital. Resorts, beaches, a casino, and golf courses make both cities popular with visitors.

ESSENTIALS

CURRENCY

The Bahamian dollar (which trades one-to-one with the U.S. dollar), but the latter is universally accepted.

TELEPHONE

Pay phones accept Bahamas Direct Prepaid cards purchased from BTC at vending machines, stores, and BTC offices. You can use these cards to call within the country or to the United States. Although most U.S. cell phones work in the Bahamas, the roaming cost can be very high, so check with your provider in advance.

CRUISE TRAVEL

Cruise-ship passengers arrive at Lucayan Harbour, which has a Bahamian-style look, extensive cruise-passenger terminal facilities, and an entertainment-shopping village. The harbor lies about 10 minutes west of Freeport. Taxis and limos meet all cruise ships. Two passengers are charged $20 and $27 for trips to Freeport and Lucaya, respectively. Fare to Xanadu Beach is $21; it's $30 to Taïno Beach. The price per person drops $5 for larger groups. It's customary to tip taxi drivers 15%. A three-hour sightseeing tour of the Freeport-Lucaya area costs $25 to $35. Four-hour East or West End trips cost about $40. At this writing, an additional two-berth cruise-ship port in William's Town is undergoing the approval process, but no opening date is set yet.

Grand Bahama's flat terrain and straight, well-paved roads make for good scooter riding. Rentals run $35 a day (about $15 an hour). Helmets are required and provided. Look for small rental stands in parking lots and along the road in Freeport and Lucaya and at the larger resorts. It's usually cheaper to rent a car than to hire a taxi. Automobiles, jeeps, and vans can be rented at the Grand Bahama International Airport. Some agencies provide free pickup and delivery service to the cruise-ship port and Freeport and Lucaya, but prices are still not cheap; cars begin at $65 per day.

EXPLORING FREEPORT-LUCAYA

Grand Bahama is the only planned island in the Bahamas. Its towns, villages, and sights are well laid out but far apart. Downtown Freeport and Lucaya are both best appreciated on foot. Buses and taxis can transport you the 4-mile (6-km) distance between the two. In Freeport shopping is the main attraction. Bolstered by the Our Lucaya Resort complex, Lucaya has its beautiful beach and water-sports scene, plus more shopping and a big, beautiful new casino. Outside of town, isolated fishing villages, beaches, natural attractions, and the once-rowdy town of West End make it worthwhile to hire a tour or rent a car. The island stretches 96 miles (154 km) from one end to the other.

FREEPORT

The Bahamian Brewery. One hundred percent Bahamian owned, this 20-acre brewery opened in 2007, bringing to the Bahamian islands five new beers including Sands, High Rock Lager, Bush Crack, and Strong Back Stout. The brewery even makes a signature red ale served

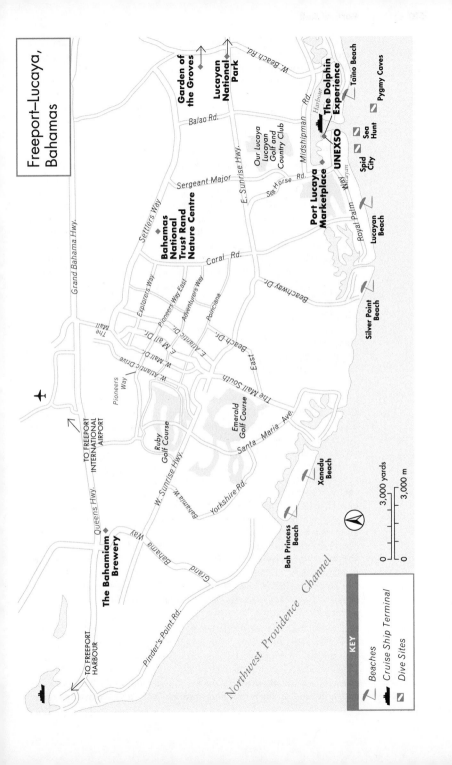

Freeport–Lucaya, Bahamas

Garden of the Groves
Lucayan National Park
W. Beach Rd.
Taino Beach
Pygmy Caves
The Dolphin Experience
Balao Rd.
Sea Hunt
Our Lucaya Lucayan Golf and Country Club
Midshipman Rd.
UNEXSO
Sergeant Major
Spid City
E. Sunrise Hwy.
Sea Horse Rd.
Port Lucaya Marketplace
Harbour
Settlers' Way
Royal Palm Way
Bahamas National Trust Rand Nature Centre
Lucayan Beach
Coral Rd.
Explorers' Way
Pioneers Way East
Adventurers' Way
Poinciana
Beach Dr.
Beachway Dr.
The Mall
E. Mall Dr.
E. Atlantic Dr.
W. Mall Dr.
Silver Point Beach
Pioneers Way
W. Atlantic Drive
East Beach Dr.
The Mall South
TO FREEPORT INTERNATIONAL AIRPORT
Ruby Golf Course
Emerald Golf Course
Santa Maria Ave.
W. Sunrise Hwy.
Bahamia W.
Yorkshire Rd.
Xandu Beach
Queens Hwy.
The Bahamian Brewery
Bahamia Way
Grand
Bah Princess Beach
TO FREEPORT HARBOUR
Pinder's Point Rd.
Grand Bahama Hwy.

Northwest Providence Channel

3,000 yards
0
3,000 m
0

KEY

Beaches
Cruise Ship Terminal
Dive Sites

exclusively at the Atlantis Resort on Paradise Island. The brewery does everything on-site including bottling and labeling, and offers 15- to 20-minute tours that take you along each step in the brewing process. The tour ends in the tasting room where you can belly up to the bar or cocktail tables to sample each beer. Tours are $5 and walk-ins are accepted. Beer and liquor can be purchased in the retail store; Bahamian Brewery souvenirs are available in the gift shop. ⊠ *Just off Queen's Hwy., east of the turn to West End* ☎ *242/352–4070* ⊕ *www. bahamianbrewery.com.*

Bahamas National Trust Rand Nature Centre. On 100 acres just minutes from downtown Freeport, a half mile of self-guided botanical trails shows off 130 types of native plants, including many orchid species. The center is the island's birding hot spot, where you might spy a red-tailed hawk or a Cuban emerald hummingbird. Visit the caged one-eyed Bahama parrot the center has adopted, and a Bahama boa, a species that inhabits most Bahamian islands, but not Grand Bahama. On Tuesday and Thursday free (with admission) guided tours depart at 10:30 am. The visitor center hosts changing local art exhibits. ⊠ *E. Settlers Way* ☎ *242/352–5438* ⊕ *www.bnt.bs* 🖃 *$5* ⊙ *Weekdays 9–4, Sat. 9–1; guided nature walk by advance resv.*

LUCAYA

Lucaya, on Grand Bahama's southern coast and just east of Freeport, was developed as the island's resort center. These days it's booming with the megaresort complex called the Our Lucaya Resort, a fine sandy beach, championship golf courses, a casino, a first-class dive operation, and Port Lucaya's shopping and marina facilities. Most cruise ships offer excursions that include a day at Our Lucaya.

FAMILY   **The Dolphin Experience.** Encounter Atlantic bottlenose dolphins in Sanctuary Bay at one of the world's first and largest dolphin facilities, about 2 miles east of Port Lucaya. A ferry takes you from Port Lucaya to the bay to observe and photograph the animals. If you don't mind getting wet, you can sit on a partially submerged dock or stand waist deep in the water and one of these friendly creatures will swim up to you. You can also engage in one of two swim-with-the-dolphins programs, but participants must be 55 inches or taller. The Dolphin Experience began in 1987, when it trained five dolphins to interact with people. Later, the animals learned to head out to sea and swim with scuba divers on the open reef. A two-hour dive program is available. You can buy tickets for the Dolphin Experience at UNEXSO in Port Lucaya, but be sure to make reservations as early as possible. ⊠ *Port Lucaya, next to Pelican Bay Hotel* ☎ *242/373–1244, 800/992–3483* ⊕ *www.unexso.com* 🖃 *Close Encounter $85, Swim with the Dolphins $179, Open-Ocean Swim $219* ⊙ *Daily 8–6.*

Fodor's Choice   **Underwater Explorers Society (UNEXSO).** One of the world's most respected
★   diving facilities, UNEXSO welcomes more than 50,000 individuals each year and trains hundreds of them in scuba diving. Facilities include a 17-foot-deep training pool with windows that look out on the harbor, changing rooms and showers, docks, equipment rental, an outdoor bar and grill, and an air-tank filling station. Daily dive excursions range

from one-day discovery courses and dives to specialty shark, dolphin, and cave diving. ☒ *Port Lucaya, next to Pelican Bay Hotel* ☏ *242/373–1244, 800/992–3483* ⊕ *www.unexso.com* ☒ *One-tank reef dives $59, Discover Scuba course $109, night dives $79, dolphin dives $219, shark dives $109, equipment included.* ☉ *Daily 8–6.*

BEYOND FREEPORT-LUCAYA

Grand Bahama Island narrows at picturesque West End, once Grand Bahama's capital and still home to descendants of the island's first settlers. Seaside villages, with concrete-block houses painted in bright blue and pastel yellow, fill in the landscape between Freeport and West End. The East End is Grand Bahama's "back-to-nature" side. The road east from Lucaya is long,

flat, and mostly straight. It cuts through a vast pine forest to reach McLean's Town, the end of the road.

Garden of the Groves. This vibrant 12-acre garden, featuring a trademark chapel and waterfalls, is filled with native Bahamian flora, butterflies, birds, and turtles. Interpretative signposting identifies plant and animal species. First opened in 1973, the park was renovated and reopened in 2008; additions include a labyrinth modeled after the one at France's Chartres Cathedral, colorful shops and galleries with local arts and crafts, a playground, and a multideck outdoor café. Explore on your own or take a guided tour. Enjoy the garden under twinkling lights on Friday nights only, with dinner specials and live music. ☒ *Midshipman Rd. and Magellan Dr.* ☏ *242/374–7778* ⊕ *www.thegardenofthegroves. com* ☒ *$15* ☉ *Daily 9–5; guided tours Mon.–Sat. at 10.*

Lucayan National Park. In this extraordinary 40-acre seaside land preserve, trails and elevated walkways wind through a natural forest of wild tamarind and gumbo-limbo trees, past an observation platform, a mangrove swamp, sheltered pools, and one of the largest explored underwater cave systems in the world (more than 6 miles long). You can enter the caves at two access points; one is closed in June and July, the bat-nursing season. Twenty-six miles east of Lucaya, the park contains examples of the island's five ecosystems: beach, hardwood forest, mangroves, rocky coppice, and pine forest. Across the road from the caves, two trails form a loop. Creek Trail's boardwalk showcases impressive interpretive signposting, and crosses a mangrove-clotted tidal creek to Gold Rock Beach, a great place for a swim or picnic at low tide, and edged by some of the island's highest dunes and jewel-tone sea. At high tide the beach all but disappears. ☒ *Grand Bahama Hwy.* ☏ *242/353–4149, 242/352–5438* ⊕ *www.bnt.bs* ☒ *$5* ☉ *Daily 9–4.*

7

BEACHES

Some 60 miles of magnificent, pristine stretches of sand extend between Freeport-Lucaya and the island's eastern end. Most are used only by people who live in adjacent settlements. The beaches have no public facilities, so beachgoers often headquarter at one of the local beach bars, which provide free transportation. **Lucayan Beach**

> **HANGERS**
>
> Folding or inflatable travel hangers are useful if you need to dry out hand laundry or a bathing suit in your cabin. The ones in your cabin's closet may not be removable.

is readily accessible from the town's main drag and is always lively and lovely. **Taïno Beach,** near Freeport, is fun for families, water-sports enthusiasts, and partyers. Near Freeport, **Xanadu Beach** provides a mile of white sand. **Gold Rock Beach** is about 45 minutes from the cruise port, but it's one of the most widely photographed beaches in the Bahamas; at low tide, unique sandbars and ridges form.

SHOPPING

In the stores, shops, and boutiques on Grand Bahama you can find duty-free goods costing up to 40% less than what you might pay back home. At the numerous perfume shops fragrances are often sold at a sweet-smelling 25% below U.S. prices. Be sure to limit your haggling to the straw markets.

Port Lucaya Marketplace. Lucaya's capacious and lively shopping complex is on the waterfront across the street from the Grand Lucayan Resort and Treasure Bay Casino. The shopping center, whose walkways are lined with hibiscus, bougainvillea, and croton, has about 100 well-kept establishments, among them waterfront restaurants and bars, water-sports operators, and shops that sell clothes, crystal and china, jewelry, perfumes, and local arts and crafts. The marketplace's centerpiece is **Count Basie Square,** where live entertainment featuring Bahamian bands appeals to joyful nighttime crowds every Thursday through Monday. Lively outdoor watering holes line the square, which is also *the* place to celebrate the holidays: a tree-lighting ceremony takes place in the festively decorated spot at the beginning of December and fireworks highlight New Year's Eve, the Fourth of July, and Bahamian Independence Day, July 10th. ⊠ *Sea Horse Rd., Lucaya* ☎ *242/373–8446, 242/373–2387* ⊗ *Daily 10–6. Restaurants and bars remain open at night.*

ACTIVITIES

FISHING

Private boat charters for up to four people cost $100 per person and up for a half day. Bahamian law limits the catching of game fish to six each of dolphinfish, kingfish, tuna, or wahoo per vessel.

Reef Tours Ltd. This company offers deep-sea fishing for four to six people on custom boats. Equipment and bait are provided free. All vessels are licensed, inspected, and insured. Trips run from 8:30 to 12:15 and from 1 to 4:45, weather permitting ($130 per angler, $60 per spectator). Full-day trips are also available, as are paddle board and kayak rentals, bottom-fishing excursions, glass-bottom boat tours, snorkeling trips, sailing–snorkeling cruises, and guided Segway tours. Reservations are essential. ⊠ *Port Lucaya Marketplace* ☏ *242/373–5880, 242/373-5891* ⊕ *www.bahamasvacationguide.com/reeftours.*

GOLF

Grand Lucayan Reef Course. The Grand Lucayan Reef Course is a par-72, 6,930-yard links-style course. Designed by Robert Trent Jones Jr., it features lots of water (on 13 of the holes), wide fairways flanked by strategically placed bunkers, and a tricky dogleg left on the 18th. While it is the most expensive and nicest of the three golf courses on the island, budget constraints have left it comparable to an average municipal course in the states. ⊠ *Grand Lucayan Beach & Golf Resort, Lucaya* ☏ *242/373–2002, 800/870–7148* ⊕ *www.grandlucayan.com* ⊠ *Resort guests $120, nonguests $130* ⊙ *Daily 10–6.*

Ruby Golf Course. This course reopened in 2008 with renovated landscaping but basically the same 18-hole, par-72 Jim Fazio design. It features a lot of sand traps and challenges on holes 7, 9, 10, and 18—especially playing from the blue tees. Hole 10 requires a tee shot onto a dogleg right fairway around a pond. Popular with locals, there is also a small restaurant-bar and pro shop. ⊠ *West Sunrise Hwy. and Wentworth Ave., Freeport* ☏ *242/352–1851* ⊕ *www.rubygolfcoursebahamas.com* ⊙ *Daily 7:30–5.*

7

WHERE TO EAT

$ ╳ **Billy Joe's on the Beach.** Eating fresh conch salad and drinking a cold beer, island music in the background and your toes in the sand: it doesn't get any better or more Bahamian. Billy Joe's has been a fixture on Lucaya beach for almost 40 years, selling his freshly made-on-the-spot (watch it being prepared!) conch salad, cracked conch, roast conch, and grilled conch (minced and cooked with tomatoes, onions, and bell peppers in an aluminum packet on the barbecue). Fried lobster and ribs are also favorites, and there's even a special menu for kids. ⑤ *Average main: $12* ⊠ *Lucaya Beach, behind the police station, Lucaya* ☏ *242/373–1333* ▭ *No credit cards* ⊙ *No dinner.*

BAHAMIAN

$$ ╳ **East Sushi at Pier One.** Pier One has one of the most unique settings of any restaurant in Grand Bahama. Built on stilts above the ocean near the Harbour, it offers one-of-a-kind views of magnificent sunsets, larger than life cruise ships departing, and sharks swimming for chum. Pier one has two levels and two menus, the best one being East's. Their menu is both creative and extensive including Japanese favorites such as miso soup, seaweed salads, tempura, and a variety of rolls—try the Bahama Mama with tempura conch, avocado, mango, and chili-lime mayo for a tropical twist. Diners can eat inside either upstairs or downstairs, but the large tables on the balcony offer the best views of the shark feedings, done every hour on the hour starting at 7 pm. For those who prefer their fish cooked or Continental fare, the other menu includes grilled

SUSHI
Fodor's Choice
★

fish, vegetable pasta, steaks, and chicken. $ *Average main: $25* ⊠ *Free-port Harbour, Freeport* ☎ *242/352–6674* ⊕ *www.pieroneandeast.com* ☺ *No lunch Sun.*

GRAND CAYMAN, CAYMAN ISLANDS

Jordan Simon

The largest and most populous of the Cayman Islands, Grand Cayman is also one of the most popular cruise destinations in the Western Caribbean, largely because it doesn't suffer from the ailments afflicting many larger ports: panhandlers, hasslers, and crime. Instead, the Cayman economy is a study in stability, and the environment is healthy and prosperous. Though the island is rather featureless, Grand Cayman is a diver's paradise, with pristine waters and a colorful variety of marine life. Compared with other Caribbean ports, there are fewer things to see on land here; instead, the island's most impressive sights are underwater. Snorkeling, diving, and glass-bottom-boat and submarine rides top every ship's shore-excursion list, and can also be arranged at major aquatic shops if you don't go on a ship-sponsored excursion. Grand Cayman is also famous for the nearly 600 offshore banks in George Town; not surprisingly, the standard of living is high, and nothing is cheap.

ESSENTIALS

CURRENCY

The Cayman Island dollar (CI$1 to US$1.25). The U.S. dollar is accepted everywhere, and most ATMs dispense cash in either currency.

TELEPHONE

To dial the United States, dial 1 followed by the area code and telephone number. To place a credit-card call, dial 800/744–7777; credit-card and calling-card calls can be made from any public phone.

COMING ASHORE

Ships anchor in George Town Harbour and tender passengers onto Harbour Drive, the center of the shopping district. If you just want to walk around town and shop or visit Seven Mile Beach, you're probably better off on your own, but the Stingray City Sandbar snorkeling trip is a highlight of many Caribbean vacations and fills up quickly on cruise-ship days, so it's often better to order that excursion from your ship, even though it will be more crowded and expensive than if you took an independent trip.

A tourist information booth is on the pier, and taxis queue for disembarking passengers. Although taxi fares may seem high, cabbies rarely try to rip off tourists. All taxis are required by law to install meters letting passengers know how much the trip costs. Taxi drivers won't usually do hourly rates for small-group tours; you must arrange a sightseeing tour with a company. Car rentals range in price from $40 to $95 per day (plus a $7.50 driving permit), so they are a good option if you want to do some independent exploring. You can easily see the entire island and have time to stop at a beach in a single day. △ **Driving in the Cayman Islands is on the left (as in the United Kingdom), though the steering wheel may be on the left (as in the United States).**

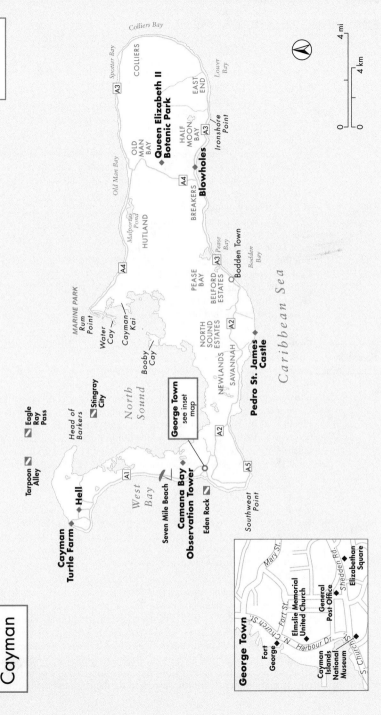

Grand Cayman

KEY

Dive Sites

Colliers Bay

Spotter Bay

COLLIERS

A3

Queen Elizabeth II
Botanic Park

OLD
MAN
BAY

Old Man Bay

Lower
Bay

EAST
END

HALF
MOON
BAY

A3

A4

Blowholes

Ironshore
Point

Malportas
Pond

HUTLAND

BREAKERS

A4

MARINE PARK
Rum
Point

Water
Cay

Cayman
Kai

Booby Cay

PEASE
BAY

Pease
Bay

A3

Bodden Town

Bodden
Bay

BELFORD
ESTATES

Eagle
Ray
Pass

Head of
Barkers

Stingray
City

North
Sound

NORTH
SOUND
ESTATES

A2

Caribbean Sea

Tarpoon
Alley

George Town
see inset
map

NEWLANDS

SAVANNAH

Pedro St. James
Castle

Cayman
Turtle Farm

Hell

West
Bay

Seven Mile Beach

A1

Camana Bay
Observation Tower

Eden Rock

A2

A5

Southwest
Point

N

0   4 km

0   4 mi

George Town

Mary St.

N. Fort St.

Elmslie Memorial
United Church

General
Post Office

Shedden Rd.

Elizabethan
Square

Fort
George

N. Church St.

Harbour Dr.

Cayman
Islands National
Museum

S. Church St.

EXPLORING GRAND CAYMAN

GEORGE TOWN

Begin exploring the capital by strolling along the waterfront Harbour Drive to **Elmslie Memorial United Church,** named after the first Presbyterian missionary to serve in Cayman. Its vaulted ceiling, wooden arches, and sedate nave reflect the religious nature of island residents. In front of the court building, in the center of town, names of influential Caymanians are inscribed on the **Wall of History,** which commemorates the islands' quincentennial in 2003. Across the street is the **Cayman Islands Legislative Assembly Building,** next door to the **1919 Peace Memorial Building.** In the middle of the financial district is the **General Post Office,** built in 1939. Let the kids pet the big blue iguana statues.

> **GRAND CAYMAN BEST BETS**
>
> ■ **Diving.** If you're a diver, you'll find several good sites close to shore.
>
> ■ **Queen Elizabeth II Botanic Garden.** A beautiful garden has native plants and rare blue iguanas.
>
> ■ **Seven Mile Beach.** One of the Caribbean's best beaches is a short ride from the cruise pier.
>
> ■ **Shopping.** George Town has a wide range of shops near the cruise-ship pier.
>
> ■ **Stingray City.** This is one of the most fun adventures the Caribbean has to offer.

FAMILY
Fodor's Choice
★
Cayman Islands National Museum. Built in 1833, the historically significant clapboard home of the national museum has had several different incarnations over the years, serving as courthouse, jail, post office, and dance hall. It features an ongoing archaeological excavation of the Old Gaol and excellent 3-D bathymetric displays, murals, dioramas, and videos that illustrate local geology, flora and fauna, and island history. There are also temporary exhibits focusing on aspects of Caymanian culture, a local art collection, and interactive displays for kids. ✉ *Harbour Dr.* ☎ *345/949–8368* ⊕ *www.museum.ky* ✉ *$8, $5.60 Saturday* ⊗ *Weekdays 9–5, Sat. 9–1.*

ELSEWHERE ON THE ISLAND

FAMILY
Blowholes. When the easterly trade winds blow hard, crashing waves force water into caverns and send impressive geysers shooting up as much as 20 feet through the ironshore. The blowholes were partially filled during Hurricane Ivan in 2004, so the water must be rough to recapture their former elemental drama. ✉ *Frank Sound Rd., roughly 10 miles (16 km) east of Bodden Town, near East End.*

FAMILY
Camana Bay Observation Tower. This 75-foot structure provides striking 360-degree panoramas of otherwise flat Grand Cayman, sweeping from George Town and Seven Mile Beach to the North Sound. The double-helix staircase is impressive in its own right. Running alongside the steps (though an elevator is also available), a floor-to-ceiling mosaic replicates the look and feel of a dive from seabed to surface. Constructed of countless tiles in 114 different colors, it's one of the world's largest marine-themed mosaic installations. Benches and lookout points

encourage you to take your time and take in the views as you ascend. Afterward you can enjoy 500-acre Camana Bay's gardens, waterfront boardwalk, and pedestrian paths lined with shops and restaurants, or frequent live entertainment. ⊠ *Extending between Seven Mile Beach and North Sound, 2 miles (3 km) north of George Town, Camana Bay* ☎ *345/640–3500* ⊕ *www.camanabay.com* ⊠ *Free* ☉ *Sunrise–10 pm.*

FAMILY

Fodor's Choice

★

Cayman Turtle Farm. Cayman's premier attraction, the Turtle Farm, has been transformed into a marine theme park. The expanded complex now has several souvenir shops and restaurants. Still, the turtles remain a central attraction, and you can tour ponds in the original research–breeding facility with thousands in various stages of growth, some up to 600 pounds and more than 70 years old. Turtles can be picked up from the tanks, a real treat for children and adults as the little creatures flap their fins and splash the water. Four areas—three aquatic and one dry—cover 23 acres; different-color bracelets determine access (the steep full-pass admission includes snorkeling gear). The park helps promote conservation, encouraging interaction (a tidal pool houses invertebrates such as starfish and crabs) and observation. Animal Program events include Keeper Talks, where you might feed birds or iguanas, and biologists speaking about conservation and their importance to the ecosystem. The freshwater **Breaker's Lagoon,** replete with cascades plunging over moss-carpeted rocks evoking Cayman Brac, is the islands' largest pool. The saltwater **Boatswain's Lagoon,** replicating all the Cayman Islands and the Trench, teems with 14,000 denizens of the deep milling about a cannily designed synthetic reef. You can snorkel here (lessons and guided tours are available). Both lagoons have underwater 4-inch-thick acrylic panels that look directly into **Predator Reef,** home to six brown sharks, four nurse sharks, and other predatory fish such as tarpons, eels, and jacks. These predators can also be viewed from terra (or terror, as one guide jokes) firma. Make sure you check out feeding times! The free-flight **Aviary,** designed by consultants from Disney's Animal Kingdom, is a riot of color and noise as feathered friends represent the entire Caribbean basin, doubling as a rehabilitation center for Cayman Wildlife and Rescue. A winding interpretive **nature trail** culminates in the Blue Hole, a collapsed cave once filled with water. Audio tours are available with different focuses, from butterflies to bush medicine. The last stop is the living museum, **Cayman Street,** complete with facades duplicating different types of vernacular architecture; an herb and fruit garden; porch-side artisans, musicians, and storytellers; model catboats; live cooking on an old-fashioned caboose (outside kitchen) oven; and interactive craft demonstrations from painting mahogany to thatch weaving. ⊠ *825 Northwest Point Rd., Box 812, West Bay* ☎ *345/949–3894* ⊕ *www.turtle.ky, www.caymanturtlefarm.ky, www. boatswainsbeach.ky* ⊠ *Comprehensive ticket $45 ($25 children under 12); Turtle Farm only, $30* ☉ *Mon.–Sat. 8–5, Sun. varies according to season. Lagoons close 1 hr early.*

Hell. Quite literally the tourist trap from Hell, this attraction does offer free admission, fun photo ops, and sublime surrealism. Its name refers to the quarter-acre of menacing shards of charred brimstone thrusting up like vengeful spirits (actually blackened and "sculpted" by

7

acid-secreting algae and fungi over millennia). Ivan Farrington, the owner of the Devil's Hang-Out store, cavorts in a devil's costume (horn, cape, and tails), regaling you with demonically bad jokes. ⊠ *Hell Rd., West Bay* ☎ *345/949–3358* ⊠ *Free* ⊙ *Daily 9–6.*

Fodor's Choice
★

Pedro St. James Castle. Built in 1780, the greathouse is Cayman's oldest stone structure and the only remaining late-18th-century residence on the island. In its capacity as courthouse and jail, it was the birthplace of Caymanian democracy, where in December 1831 the first elected parliament was organized and in 1835 the Slavery Abolition Act signed. The structure still has original or historically accurate replicas of sweeping verandahs, mahogany floors, rough-hewn wide-beam ceilings, outside louvers, stone and oxblood- or mustard-color limewash-painted walls, brass fixtures, and Georgian furnishings (from tea caddies to canopy beds to commodes). Paying obsessive attention to detail, the curators even fill glasses with faux wine. The mini-museum also includes a hodgepodge of displays from slave emancipation to old stamps. The buildings are surrounded by 8 acres of natural parks and woodlands. You can stroll through landscaping of native Caymanian flora and experience one of the most spectacular views on the island from atop the dramatic Great Pedro Bluff. First watch the impressive multimedia theater show, complete with smoking pots, misting rains, and two film screens where the story of Pedro's Castle is presented on the hour. The poignant Hurricane Ivan Memorial outside uses text, images, and symbols to represent important aspects of that horrific 2004 natural disaster. ⊠ *Pedro Castle Rd., Savannah* ☎ *345/947–3329* ⊕ *www.pedrostjames.ky* ⊠ *$10* ⊙ *Daily 9–5.*

Fodor's Choice
★

Queen Elizabeth II Botanic Park. This 65-acre wilderness preserve showcases a wide range of indigenous and nonindigenous tropical vegetation, approximately 2,000 species in total. Splendid sections include numerous water features from limpid lily ponds to cascades; a Heritage Garden with a traditional cottage and "caboose" (outside kitchen) that includes crops that might have been planted on Cayman a century ago; and a Floral Colour Garden arranged by color, the walkway wandering through sections of pink, red, orange, yellow, white, blue, mauve, lavender, and purple. The nearly mile-long Woodland Trail encompasses every Cayman ecosystem from wetland to cactus thicket, buttonwood swamp to lofty woodland with imposing mahogany trees. You'll encounter birds, lizards, turtles, agoutis, and more, but the park's star residents are the protected endemic blue iguanas, found only in Grand Cayman. The world's most endangered iguana, they're the focus of the National Trust's Blue Iguana Recovery Program, a captive breeding and reintroduction facility. The Trust conducts 90-minute behind-the-scenes safaris Monday–Saturday at 11 am for $30. ⊠ *367 Botanic Rd.* ☎ *345/947–9462* ⊕ *www.botanic-park.ky* ⊠ *$10* ⊙ *Apr.–Sept., daily 9–6:30; Oct.–Mar., daily 9–5:30; last admission 1 hr before closing.*

BEACHES

Fodor's Choice
★

Seven Mile Beach. Grand Cayman's west coast is dominated by the famous Seven Mile Beach—actually a 6½-mile-long (10-km-long) expanse of powdery white sand overseeing lapis water stippled with a rainbow of parasails and kayaks. Free of litter and pesky peddlers, it's an unspoiled (though often crowded) environment. Most of the island's resorts, restaurants, and shopping centers sit along this strip. The public beach toward the north end offers chairs for rent ($10 for the day, including a beverage), a playground, water toys aplenty, beach bars, restrooms, and showers. The best snorkeling is at either end, by the Marriott and Treasure Island or off the northern section called Cemetery Reef Beach. **Amenities:** food and drink, parking, showers, toilets, water sports. **Best for:** partiers, snorkeling. ⊠ *West Bay Rd..*

> ### STROLLERS
>
> Parents should bring along an umbrella stroller for walks around the ship as well as the ports of call; people often underestimate how big ships are. It also comes in handy at the airport. Wheel baby right to the departure gate—the stroller is gate checked and will be waiting for you when you arrive at your port of embarkation.

SHOPPING

Cathy Church's Underwater Photo Centre and Gallery. Come see a collection of the acclaimed underwater shutterbug's spectacular color and limited-edition black-and-white underwater photos. The store also carries the latest marine camera equipment. ⊠ *S. Church St., George Town* ☎ *345/949–7415* ⊕ *www.cathychurch.com.*

Guy Harvey's Gallery and Shoppe. This is where world-renowned marine biologist, conservationist, and artist Guy Harvey showcases his aquatic-inspired action-packed art in nearly every conceivable medium, branded tableware, and sportswear (even logo soccer balls and Zippos). The soaring, two-story 4,000-square-foot space is almost more theme park than store. ⊠ *49 S. Church St., George Town* ☎ *345/943–4891* ⊕ *www.guyharvey.com.*

Kirk Freeport Plaza. This downtown shopping center, home to the Kirk Freeport flagship department store, is ground zero for couture; it's also known for its boutiques selling fine watches and jewelry, china, crystal, leather, perfumes, and cosmetics, from Baccarat to Bulgari, Raymond Weil to Waterford and Wedgwood (the last two share their own autonomous boutique). Just keep walking—there's plenty of eye-catching, mind-boggling consumerism in all directions: Boucheron, Cartier (with its own miniboutique), Chanel, Clinique, Christian Dior, Clarins, Estée Lauder, Fendi, Guerlain, Lancôme, Yves Saint Laurent, Issey Miyake, Jean Paul Gaultier, Nina Ricci, Rolex, Roberto Coin, Rosenthal and Royal Doulton china, and more. ⊠ *Cardinall Ave., George Town.*

Landmark. Stores in the Landmark sell perfumes, treasure coins, and upscale beachwear; Breezes by the Bay restaurant is upstairs. ⊠ *Harbour Dr., George Town.*

Tortuga Rum Company. This company bakes, then vacuum-seals, more than 10,000 of its world-famous rum cakes daily, adhering to the original "secret" century-old recipe. There are seven flavors, from banana to Blue Mountain coffee. The 12-year-old rum, blended from private stock though actually distilled in Guyana, is a connoisseur's delight for after-dinner sipping. You can buy a fresh rum cake at the airport on the way home at the same prices as at the factory store. ⊠ *N. Sound Rd., Industrial Park, George Town* ☎ *345/949–7701* ⊕ *www.tortugarumcakes.com.*

ACTIVITIES

DIVING AND SNORKELING

Pristine water (visibility often exceeding 100 feet [30 meters]), breathtaking coral formations, and plentiful and exotic marine life mark the **Great Wall**—a world-renowned dive site just off the north side of Grand Cayman. A must-see for adventurous souls is **Stingray City** in the North Sound, noted as the best 12-foot (3½-meter) dive in the world, where dozens of stingrays congregate, tame enough to suction squid from your outstretched palm. Nondivers gravitate to **Stingray Sandbar,** a shallower part of the North Sound, which has become a popular snorkeling spot; it is also a hangout for the stingrays. If someone tells you that the minnows are in at **Eden Rock,** drop everything and dive here (on South Church Street, south of George Town). The schools swarm around you as you glide through the grottoes, forming quivering curtains of liquid silver as shafts of sunlight pierce the sandy bottom.

FAMILY

Fodor's Choice

★

DiveTech. DiveTech has opportunities for shore diving at its two north-coast locations, which provide loads of interesting creatures, a mini-wall, and the North Wall. With quick access to West Bay, the boats are quite comfortable. ⊠ *Cobalt Coast Resort & Suites, 18-A Sea Fan Dr., West Bay* ☎ *345/946–5658, 888/946–5656* ⊕ *www.divetech.com.*

FAMILY

Red Sail Sports. Red Sail Sports offers daily trips from most of the major hotels. Dives are often run as guided tours, a perfect option for beginners. If you're experienced and your air lasts a long time, consult the boat captain to see if he requires that you come up with the group (determined by the first person who runs low on air). There is a full range of kids' dive options for ages 5 to 15, including SASY and Bubblemakers. The company also operates Stingray City tours, dinner and sunset sails, and just about every major water sport from Wave Runners to windsurfing. ⊠ *Grand Cayman* ☎ *345/949–8745, 345/623–5965, 877/506–6368* ⊕ *www.redsailcayman.com.*

FISHING

Cayman waters are abundant with blue and white marlin, yellowfin tuna, sailfish, dolphinfish, bonefish, and wahoo. Two-dozen boats are available for charter.

Sea Star Charters. Sea Star Charters, aka Clinton's Watersports, is run by Clinton Ebanks, a fine and very friendly Caymanian who will do whatever it takes to make sure that you have a wonderful time on his two 27- and 28-foot cabin cruisers (and from the 35-foot trimaran used primarily for snorkeling cruises), enjoying light-tackle, bone-, and bottom-fishing.

He's a good choice for beginners and offers a nice cultural experience as well as sailing charters and snorkeling with complimentary transportation and equipment. Only cash and traveler's checks are accepted. ⊠ *Grand Cayman* ☎ *345/949–1016 evenings, 345/916–5234.*

HIKING

Mastic Trail. The National Trust's internationally significant Mastic Trail, used in the 1800s as the only direct path to and from the North Side, is a rugged 2-mile (3-km) slash through 776 dense acres of woodlands, black mangrove swamps, savannah, agricultural remnants, and ancient rock formations. It embraces more than 700 species, including Cayman's largest remaining contiguous ancient forest (one of the heavily deforested Caribbean's last examples). Call the National Trust to determine suitability and to book a guide for $30; tours are run daily from 9 to 5 by appointment only, and regularly on Wednesday at 9 am (sometimes earlier in summer). Or walk on the wild side with a $5 guidebook that provides information on the ecosystems you traverse, the endemic wildlife you might encounter, seasonal changes, poisonous plants to avoid, and folkloric uses of various flora. The trip takes about three hours. ⊠ *Frank Sound Rd., entrance by fire station at botanic park, Breakers, East End* ☎ *345/749–1121, 345/749–1124 for guide reservations* ⊕ *www.nationaltrust.org.ky.*

WHERE TO EAT

$$ ✕**Breezes by the Bay.** There isn't a bad seat in the house at this nonstop
CARIBBEAN fiesta festooned with tiny paper lanterns, Christmas lights, ship murals, model boats, and Mardi Gras beads (you're "lei'd" upon entering). Wraparound balconies take in a dazzling panorama from South Sound to Seven Mile Beach. It's happy hour all day every day, especially during Countdown to Sunset. Signs promise "the good kind of hurricanes," referring to the 23-ounce signature "category 15" cocktails with fresh garnishes; rum aficionados will find 30-plus varieties (flights available). Equally fresh food at bargain prices, including homemade baked goods and ice creams, isn't an afterthought. Chunky, velvety conch chowder served in a bread bowl or conch fritters are meals in themselves. Hefty sandwiches are slathered with yummy jerk mayo or garlic aioli. Signature standouts include meltingly moist whole fish escoveitch, popcorn shrimp, and any pie from the pizza station. ⑤ *Average main: $18* ⊠ *Harbor Dr., George Town* ☎ *345/943–8439* ⊕ *www.breezesbythebay.com.*

$$ ✕**Sunshine Grill.** This cheerful, cherished locals' secret serves haute com-
CARIBBEAN fort food at bargain-basement prices. Even the chattel-style poolside
FAMILY building, painted a delectable lemon with lime shutters, whets the appetite. Sunshine ranks high in the island's greatest burger debate, while the jerk chicken egg rolls and fabulous fish and Cuban chicken tacos elevate pub grub to an art form. Wash it down with one of the many signature libations, like the Painkiller. Take advantage of affordably priced nightly dinner specials such as Thai chili salmon, red snapper amandine, and Cuban pork loin with *sofrito* (a dip of cilantro, garlic, onions, tomatoes, and oregano). ⑤ *Average main: $18* ⊠ *Sunshine Suites, 1465 Esterley Tibbetts Hwy., Seven Mile Beach* ☎ *345/949–3000, 345/946–5848.*

7

GRAND TURK, TURKS AND CAICOS ISLANDS

Ramona Settle   Just 7 miles (11 km) long and a little over 1 mile (1½ km) wide, Grand Turk, the political capital of the Turks and Caicos Islands, has been a longtime favorite destination for divers eager to explore the 7,000-foot-deep pristine coral walls that drop down only 300 yards out to sea. On shore, the tiny, quiet island is home to white-sand beaches, the National Museum, and a small population of wild horses and donkeys, which leisurely meander past the white-walled courtyards, pretty churches, and bougainvillea-covered colonial inns on their daily commute into town. The main settlement on the island is tranquil Cockburn Town, and that's where most of the small hotels, not to mention Pillory Beach, can be found. Although it has the second-largest number of inhabitants of all the Turks and Caicos Island, Grand Turk's permanent population has still not reached 4,000.

ESSENTIALS

CURRENCY

The official currency on the islands is the U.S. dollar.

TELEPHONE

To make local calls, dial the seven-digit number. To make calls from the Turks and Caicos, dial 0, then 1, the area code, and the number. All telephone service is provided by LIME (formerly Cable & Wireless), and your U.S. cell phone may work on Grand Turk, but you will pay international roaming charges. Calling cards are available, or you can make a call using AT&T's USADirect by dialing 800/872–2881 to charge the call to your credit card or an AT&T prepaid calling card.

COMING ASHORE

Cruise ships dock at the southern end of the island, near the former U.S. Air Force base south of the airport. The $40 million cruise center is about 3 miles (5 km) from tranquil Cockburn Town, Pillory Beach, and the Ridge, and far from most of the western shore dive sites. The center has many facilities, including shopping, a large, free-form pool, car-rental booths, and even a dock from which many sea-bound excursions depart. Governor's Beach is adjacent to the cruise-ship complex and one of the island's best beaches, but others are right in and around Cockburn Town.

If you want to come into Cockburn Town, it's reachable by taxi. Rates are per person and by "zone"; you'll find a rate card outside the cruise terminal. You can also rent a car to explore the island on your own terms and schedule.

Grace Bay Car Rentals. Grace Bay Car Rentals can meet at the port, so you can see the sights on your own time. Remember, driving is on the left. ⊠ *Providenciales* ☎ *649/231–8500* ⊕ *www.gracebaycarrentals.com.*

Grand Turk Cruise Terminal. Head to the Web site for cruise schedules, a list of the shops at the terminal, and options for excursions and transportation. There's even a live webcam so you can check the actual weather

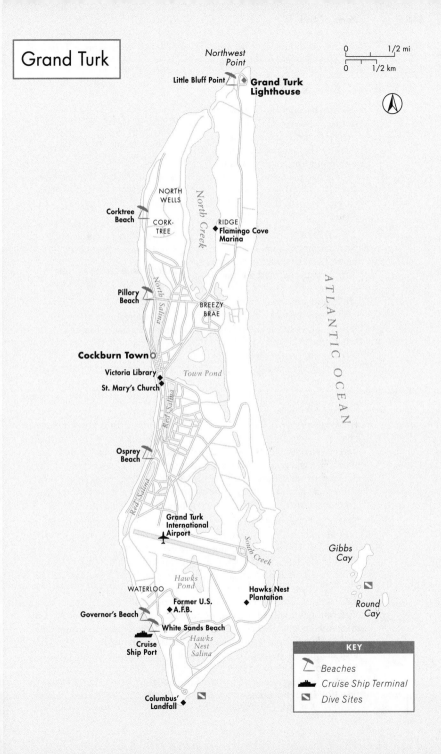

at any given moment. ⊠ *South Base, Grand Turk Cruise Terminal* ☎ *649/946–1040* ⊕ *www.grandturkcc.com.*

EXPLORING GRAND TURK

Pristine beaches with vistas of turquoise waters, small local settlements, historic ruins, and native flora and fauna are among the sights on Grand Turk. Fewer than 4,000 people live on this 7½-square-mile (19-square-km) island, and it's hard to get lost, as there aren't many roads.

COCKBURN TOWN

The buildings in the colony's capital and seat of government reflect a 19th-century Bermudian style. Narrow streets are lined with low stone walls and old street lamps, which are now powered by electricity. The once-vital *salinas* (natural salt pans, where the sea leaves a film of salt) have been restored, and covered benches along the sluices offer shady spots for observing wading birds, including flamingos that frequent the shallows. Be sure to pick up a copy of the tourist board's *Heritage Walk* guide to discover Grand Turk's rich architecture.

> ### GRAND TURK BEST BETS
>
> ■ **Beaches.** The sand is powdery soft, the water azure blue.
>
> ■ **Diving.** If you're certified, there are several world-class dive sights within each reach.
>
> ■ **Gibb's Cay.** To swim with stingrays, take a ship-sponsored trip here; it's an excellent beach.
>
> ■ **Front Street.** Colorful Front Street will give you the feeling you've stepped back in time.
>
> ■ **Turks and Caicos National Museum.** Small but worthy.

Her Majesty's Prison. This prison was built in the 19th century to house runaway slaves and slaves who survived the wreck of the *Trouvadore* in 1841. After the slaves were granted freedom, the prison housed criminals and even modern-day drug runners until it closed in the 1990s. The last hanging here was in 1960. Now you can see the cells, solitary-confinement area, and exercise patio. The prison is open only when there is a cruise ship at the port. ⊠ *Pond St..*

FAMILY **Turks and Caicos National Museum.** In one of the oldest stone buildings on the islands, the national museum houses the Molasses Reef wreck, the earliest shipwreck—dating to the early 1500s—discovered in the Americas. The natural-history exhibits include artifacts left by Taíno, African, North American, Bermudian, French, and Latin American settlers. The museum has a 3-D coral reef exhibit, a walk-in Lucayan cave with wooden artifacts, and a gallery dedicated to Grand Turk's little-known involvement in the Space Race (John Glenn made landfall here after being the first American to orbit the Earth). An interactive children's gallery keeps knee-high visitors "edutained." The museum also claims that Grand Turk was where Columbus first landed in the New World. The most original display is a collection of messages in bottles that have washed ashore from all over the world. ⊠ *Duke St.* ☎ *649/946–2160* ⊕ *www.tcmuseum.org* 🖃 *$5* ☉ *Mon., Tues., Thurs., and Fri. 9–4, Wed. 9–5, Sat. 9–1.*

ELSEWHERE ON THE ISLAND

Grand Turk Lighthouse. More than 150 years ago, the lighthouse, built in the United Kingdom and transported piece by piece to the island, protected ships from wrecking on the northern reefs. Use this panoramic landmark as a starting point for a breezy cliff-top walk by following the donkey trails to the deserted eastern beach. ⊠ *Lighthouse Rd., North Ridge.*

BEACHES

Grand Turk is spoiled for choices when it comes to beach options: sunset strolls along miles of deserted beaches, picnics in secluded coves, beachcombing on the coralline sands, snorkeling around shallow coral heads close to shore, and admiring the impossibly turquoise-blue waters.

Governor's Beach. A beautiful crescent of powder-soft sand and shallow, calm turquoise waters front the official British governor's residence, called Waterloo, framed by tall casuarina trees that provide plenty of natural shade. To have it all to yourself, go on a day when cruise ships are not in port (but bring your own water). On days when ships are in port, the beach is lined with lounge chairs, and bars and restaurants are open. **Amenties:** parking (free), toilets. **Best for:** swimming, walking. ⊠ *Cockburn Harbour, Grand Turk.*

Pillory Beach. With sparkling neon turquoise water, this is the prettiest beach on Grand Turk; it also has great off-the-beach snorkeling. **Amenities:** food and drink; parking (free); toilets. **Best for:** snorkeling; swimming; walking. ⊠ *Pillory Beach, Grand Turk.*

SHOPPING

There's not much to buy in Grand Turk, and shopping isn't a major activity here. However, there is a duty-free mall right at the cruise-ship center, where you'll find the usual array of upscale shops, including Ron Jon's Surf Shop, the largest Margaritaville in the world, and Piranha Joe's. There are also shops in Cockburn Town itself.

ACTIVITIES

Most of the activities offered to cruise-ship passengers can be booked only on your ship. These include a horseback ride and swim, dune-buggy safaris, and 4x4 safaris.

BICYCLING

If you love to ride a bike, then out of all of the islands in Turks and Caicos, Grand Turk is your island because it's both small enough and flat enough that it's possible to tour it by bike. You will find biking the perfect (and for some preferred) mode of transportation for people living here. The island's mostly flat terrain isn't very taxing, and most roads have hard surfaces. Take water with you: there are few places to stop for refreshments. Most hotels have bicycles available, but you can also rent them for $10 to $15 a day from Oasis Divers (⇨ *See Diving and Snorkeling*), which also offers fun Segway tours.

DIVING AND SNORKELING

In these waters you can find undersea cathedrals, coral gardens, and countless tunnels, but note that you must carry and present a valid certificate card before you'll be allowed to dive. As its name suggests, the **Black Forest** offers staggering black-coral formations as well as the occasional black-tip shark. In the **Library** you can study fish galore, including large numbers of yellowtail snapper. At the Columbus Passage separating South Caicos from Grand Turk, each side of a 22-mile-wide (35-km-wide) channel drops more than 7,000 feet. From January through March thousands of Atlantic humpback whales swim through en route to their winter breeding grounds. **Gibb's Cay,** a small cay a couple of miles off Grand Turk, where you can swim with stingrays, makes for a great excursion.

> ### WATER
>
> Tap water on your ship is perfectly safe to drink; purchasing bottled water is only necessary if you prefer the taste.

Blue Water Divers. In operation on Grand Turk since 1983, Blue Water Divers is the only PADI Gold Palm five-star dive center on the island. The owner, Mitch, may put some of your underwater adventures to music in the evenings when he plays at the Osprey Beach Hotel or Salt Raker Inn. ⊠ *Duke St., Cockburn Town* ☎ *649/946–2432* ⊕ *www. grandturkscuba.com.*

Oasis Divers. Oasis Divers provides complete gear handling and pampering treatment. It also supplies Nitrox and rebreathers. The company also offers a wide variety of other tours, as well as renting bicycles and operating Segway tours. ⊠ *Duke St., Cockburn Town* ☎ *649/946–1128* ⊕ *www.oasisdivers.com.*

WHERE TO EAT

$
AMERICAN
✕ **Jack's Shack.** Walk 500 meters down the beach from the cruise terminal and you'll find this local beach bar. It gets busy with volleyball players, and offers chair rentals and tropical drinks. Casual food such as burgers and hot dogs satisfy your hunger. Print a coupon from the website for a free shot of T&C's local rum, Bamberra. ⑤ *Average main: $12* ⊠ *North of the pier, Grand Turk Cruise Terminal* ☎ *649/232–0099* ⊘ *Closed when no ship is in port.*

$$
AMERICAN
✕ **Jimmy Buffet's Margaritaville.** When you're at this branch of the party-loving chain restaurant, you can engage in cruise activities even though you're on land. One of the largest Margaritavilles in the world opens its doors when a cruise ship is parked at the dock. Tables are scattered around a large winding pool; there's even a DJ and a FlowRider (a wave pool where you can surf on land—for a fee). You can enjoy 52 flavors of margaritas or the restaurant's own beer, Landshark, while you eat casual bar food such as wings, quesadillas, and burgers. The food is good, the people-watching is great. ⑤ *Average main: $15* ⊠ *Grand Turk Cruise Terminal* ☎ *649/946–1880* ⊕ *www.margaritavillecaribbean.com* ⊘ *Closed when no ship is in port.*

GRENADA (ST. GEORGE'S)

Jane E. Zarem

Nutmeg, cinnamon, cloves, cocoa . . . those heady aromas fill the air in Grenada (pronounced gruh-*nay*-da). Only 21 miles (33½ km) long and 12 miles (19½ km) wide, the Isle of Spice is a tropical gem of lush rain forests, white-sand beaches, secluded coves, exotic flowers, and enough locally grown spices to fill anyone's kitchen cabinet. St. George's is one of the most picturesque capital cities in the Caribbean, St. George's Harbour is one of the most picturesque harbors, and Grenada's Grand Anse Beach is one of the region's finest beaches. The island has friendly, hospitable people and enough good shopping, restaurants, historic sites, and natural wonders to make it a popular port of call. About one-third of Grenada's visitors arrive by cruise ship, and that number continues to grow each year.

ESSENTIALS

CURRENCY

Eastern Caribbean (E.C.) dollar, but U.S. dollars are generally accepted.

TELEPHONE

The area code is 473. Prepaid phone cards, which can be used for local or international calls from special card phones located throughout the Caribbean, are sold in denominations of EC$20 ($7.50), EC$30 ($12), EC$50 ($20), and EC$75 ($28) at shops, attractions, transportation centers, and other convenient outlets. For international calls using a major credit card, dial 111; to place a collect call or use a calling card, dial 800/225–5872 from any telephone. Most cell phones will work in Grenada, but international roaming charges can be high.

COMING ASHORE

The Cruise Ship Terminal, on the north side of St. George's, accommodates two large ships; up to four can anchor in the outer harbor. A full range of passenger facilities is available at the terminal, which opens directly into the Esplanade Mall and the minibus terminus; it is also a block from Market Square. You can easily tour the capital on foot, but be prepared to negotiate steep hills. If you don't want to walk up and down through town, you can find a taxi ($3 or $4 each way) or a water taxi right at the terminal to take you around to the Carenage ($4 each way). To explore areas beyond St. George's, hiring a taxi or arranging a guided tour is more sensible than renting a car. Taxis are plentiful, and fixed rates to popular island destinations are posted at the terminal's welcome center.

A taxi ride from the terminal to Grand Anse Beach will cost $15, but water taxis are a less expensive and more picturesque way to get there; the one-way fare is about $8 per person, depending on the number of passengers. Minibuses are the least expensive way to travel between St. George's and Grand Anse; pay EC$1.50 (55¢), but hold on to your hat. They're crowded with local people getting from here to there and often make quick stops and take turns at quite a clip. Still, it's an inexpensive, fun, and safe way to travel around the island. If you want to rent a car and explore on your own, be prepared to pay $12 for a temporary driving permit (arranged by the car-rental agency) and about $55 to $75 for a day's car rental.

EXPLORING GRENADA

ST. GEORGE'S

Grenada's capital is a bustling West Indian city, much of which remains unchanged from colonial days. Narrow streets lined with shops wind up, down, and across steep hills. Brick warehouses cling to the waterfront, and pastel-painted homes rise from the waterfront and disappear into steep green hills.

The horseshoe-shape **St. George's Harbour,** a submerged volcanic crater, is arguably the prettiest harbor in the Caribbean. Schooners, ferries, and tour boats tie up along the seawall or at the small dinghy dock. **The Carenage** (pronounced car-a-*nahzh*), which surrounds the harbor, is the capital's center. Warehouses, shops, and restaurants line the waterfront. The *Christ of the Deep* statue that

> ### GRENADA BEST BETS
>
> ■ **The Beach.** Grand Anse Beach is one of the Caribbean's most beautiful.
>
> ■ **Diving and Snorkeling.** Explore dozens of fish-filled sites off Grenada's southwest coast.
>
> ■ **Market Square.** Market Square is a bustling produce and spice market.
>
> ■ **Nutmeg.** Don't miss a visit to a nutmeg cooperative (and get a pocketful to take home).
>
> ■ **Waterfalls.** Concord Falls, just south of Gouyave, and Annandale Falls are among the island's most spectacular.

sits on the pedestrian plaza at the center of the Carenage was presented to Grenada by Costa Cruise Line in remembrance of its ship *Bianca C,* which burned and sank in the harbor in 1961 and is now a favorite dive site.

An engineering feat for its time, the 340-foot-long **Sendall Tunnel** was built in 1895 and named for Walter Sendall, an early governor. The narrow tunnel, used by both pedestrians and vehicles, separates the harbor side of St. George's from the Esplanade on the bay side of town, where you can find the markets (produce, meat, and fish), the Cruise Ship Terminal, the Esplanade Mall, and the public bus station.

Ft. Frederick. Overlooking the city of St. George's and the inland side of the harbor, historic Ft. Frederick provides a panoramic view of about one-fourth of Grenada. The fort was started by the French and completed in 1791 by the British; it was also the headquarters of the People's Revolutionary Government before and during the 1983 coup. Today, it's simply a peaceful spot with a bird's-eye view of much of Grenada. ⊠ *Richmond Hill.*

FAMILY

Fodor's Choice ★

Ft. George. Ft. George is high on the hill at the entrance to St. George's Harbour. Grenada's oldest fort, it was built by the French in 1705 to protect the harbor. No shots were ever fired here until October 1983, when Prime Minister Maurice Bishop and several of his followers were assassinated in the courtyard. The fort now houses police headquarters

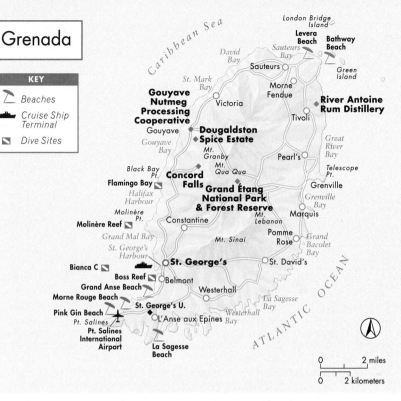

Grenada

KEY

⚓ Beaches

🚢 Cruise Ship Terminal

◣ Dive Sites

Caribbean Sea

London Bridge Island

Levera Beach

Bathway Beach

Sauteurs Bay

Sauteurs

Green Island

David Bay

St. Mark Bay

Morne Fendue

Gouyave Nutmeg Processing Cooperative

Victoria

River Antoine Rum Distillery

Gouyave

Tivoli

Gouyave Bay

Dougaldston ◆Spice Estate

Mt. Granby

Pearl's

Great River Bay

Black Bay Pt.

Concord Falls

Mt. Qua Qua

Telescope Pt.

Flamingo Bay ◣

Grand Étang National Park & Forest Reserve

Grenville

Halifax Harbour

Grenville Bay

Molinère Pt.

Constantine

Mt. Lebanon

Marquis

Molinère Reef ◣

Grand Mal Bay

Mt. Sinai

Pomme Rose

Grand Bacolet Bay

St. George's Harbour

Bianca C ◣

St. George's

St. David's

Boss Reef ◣

Belmont

Grand Anse Beach ⚓

Westerhall

Morne Rouge Beach ⚓

St. George's U.

La Sagesse Bay

Pink Gin Beach ⚓

L'Anse aux Epines

Westerhall Bay

Pt. Salines

Pt. Salines International Airport

La Sagesse Beach

ATLANTIC OCEAN

0   2 miles

0   2 kilometers

but is open to the public daily. The 360-degree view of the capital city, St. George's Harbour, and the open sea is spectacular. ⊠ *Church St.* 💷 *$2*.

Market Square. Plan to visit St. George's Market Square, a block from the Cruise Ship Terminal and Esplanade Mall in downtown St. George's. This is the place to buy fresh spices, bottled sauces, and handcrafted gifts and souvenirs to take home. In addition to local spices and heaps of fresh produce, vendors sell baskets, brooms, clothing, knickknacks, coconut water, and more. The market is open every weekday morning but really comes alive on Saturday from 8 to noon. Historically, Market Square is where parades begin and political rallies take place. ⊠ *Granby St.*.

ELSEWHERE ON GRENADA

FodorsChoice ★ **Concord Falls.** About 8 miles (13 km) north of St. George's, a turnoff from the West Coast Road leads to Concord Falls—actually three separate waterfalls. The first is at the end of the road; when the currents aren't too strong, you can take a dip under the 35-foot cascade. Reaching the two other waterfalls requires an hour's hike into the forest reserve. The third and most spectacular waterfall, at Fountainbleu, thunders 65 feet over huge boulders and creates a small pool. It's smart to hire a guide for that trek. The path is clear, but slippery boulders toward the end can be treacherous without assistance. ⊠ *Off West Coast Rd., Concord, St. John* 🖀 *Changing room $2* ⊙ *Daily 9–5.*

FAMILY **Dougaldston Spice Estate.** Just south of Gouyave, this historic plantation, now primarily a museum, still grows and processes spices the old-fashioned way. You can see cocoa, nutmeg, mace, cloves, and other spices laid out on giant racks to dry in the sun. A worker will be glad to explain the process (and will appreciate a small donation). You can buy spices for about $5 a bag. ⊠ *Gouyave, St. John* 🖀 *Free* ⊙ *Weekdays 9–4.*

FAMILY **Gouyave Nutmeg Processing Station.** Touring the nutmeg-processing co-op,
Fodor'sChoice in the center of the west-coast fishing village of Gouyave (pronounced
★ *gwahv*), is a fragrant, fascinating way to spend a half-hour. You can learn all about nutmeg and its uses, see the nutmegs laid out in bins, and watch the workers sort them by hand and pack them into burlap bags for shipping worldwide. The three-story plant turned out 3 million pounds of Grenada's most famous export each year before Hurricane Ivan's devastating effect on the crop in 2004, when most of the nutmeg trees were destroyed. By 2013, production finally began to reach pre-hurricane levels. ⊠ *Main Rd., Gouyave, St. John* 🖀 *473/444–8337* 🖀 *$1* ⊙ *Weekdays 10–1 and 2–4.*

FAMILY **Grand Étang National Park & Forest Reserve.** A rain forest and wildlife
Fodor'sChoice sanctuary deep in the mountainous interior of Grenada, Grand Étang
★ has miles of hiking trails for all levels of ability. There are also lookouts to observe the lush flora and many species of birds and other fauna (including the Mona monkey), and a number of streams for fishing. **Grand Étang Lake** is a 36-acre expanse of cobalt-blue water that fills the crater of an extinct volcano 1,740 feet above sea level. Although legend has it the lake is bottomless, maximum soundings have been recorded at 18 feet. The informative **Grand Étang Forest Center** has displays on the local wildlife and vegetation. A forest ranger is on hand to answer questions; a small snack bar and souvenir stands are nearby. ⊠ *Main interior road, between Grenville and St. George's, St. Andrew* 🖀 *473/440–6160* 🖀 *$1* ⊙ *Daily 8:30–4.*

River Antoine Rum Distillery. At this rustic operation, kept open primarily as a museum, a limited quantity of Rivers rum is produced by the same methods used since the distillery opened in 1785. River Antoine (pronounced An-*twyne*) is the oldest functioning water-propelled distillery in the Caribbean. The process begins with the crushing of sugarcane from adjacent fields; the discarded canes are used as fuel to fire the boilers. The end result is a potent overproof rum, sold only in Grenada, that will knock your socks off. (A less strong version is also available.) ⊠ *River Antoine Estate, St. Patrick* 🖀 *473/442–7109* 🖀 *$2* ⊙ *Guided tours daily 9–4.*

BEACHES

Bathway Beach. This broad strip of white sand on the northeastern tip of Grenada is part of Levera National Park. A natural coral reef protects swimmers and snorkelers from the rough Atlantic surf; swimming beyond the reef is dangerous. A magnet for local folks on national holidays, the beach is almost deserted at other times. Changing rooms are located at the park headquarters. A vendor or two sometimes sets up shop near the beach, but you're smart to bring your own refreshments. **Amenities:** parking (no fee); toilets. **Best for:** solitude; snorkeling; swimming; walking. ⊠ *Levera National Park, Levera, St. Patrick.*

Fodor's Choice ★ **Grand Anse Beach.** Grenada's loveliest and most popular beach is Grand Anse: a gleaming 2-mile (3-km) semicircle of white sand, lapped by gentle surf, and punctuated by sea grape trees and coconut palms that provide shady escapes from the sun. Brilliant rainbows frequently spill into the sea from the high green mountains that frame St. George's Harbour to the north. Several resorts are on the beach here, from Flamboyant and Mount Cinnamon at the southern end of the beach to Spice Island Beach Resort, Coyaba Beach Resort, Grenada Grand Beach Resort, and Allamanda Beach Resort as you head north. Several of these hotels have dive shops for arranging dive trips or renting snorkeling equipment. At the beach's midpoint are a water-taxi dock and the Grand Anse Craft & Spice Market, where vendors also rent beach chairs and umbrellas. Restrooms and changing facilities are available at Camerhogne Park, which is the public entrance and parking lot. Hotel guests, cruise-ship passengers, and other island visitors love this beach, as do local people who come to swim and play on weekends. There's plenty of room for everyone. **Amenities:** food and drink; parking (no fee); toilets; water sports. **Best for:** sunset; swimming; walking. ⊠ *3 miles (5 km) south of St. George's.*

> ### ID CASES
>
> You can keep track of your boarding pass, shipboard charge/key card, and picture ID when you go ashore by slipping them into a bi-fold business-card carrying case. Cases with a sueded finish are less likely to fall out of your pocket. With security as tight as it is these days, you don't want to lose your ID.

SHOPPING

Grenada's best souvenirs or gifts for friends back home are spice baskets filled with cinnamon, nutmeg, mace, bay leaves, cloves, turmeric, and ginger. You can buy them for as little as $4 in practically every shop, at the open-air produce market at **Market Square** in St. George's, at the vendor stalls near the pier, and at the **Vendor's Craft and Spice Market** on Grand Anse Beach. Vendors also sell handmade fabric dolls, coral jewelry, seashells, and hats and baskets handwoven from green palm fronds. Bargaining is not appropriate in the shops, and it isn't customary with vendors—although most will offer you "a good price."

Art Fabrik. At Art Fabrik, you'll find batik fabric created by hand by as many as 45 home workers. It's sold by the yard or fashioned into pareos, dresses, shirts, shorts, hats, scarves, and bags. Part of the boutique is dedicated to demonstrating the batik process. ⊠ *Young St.* ☎ *473/440–0568* ⊕ *www.artfabrikgrenada.com.*

Tikal. Regional artwork, carvings, jewelry, home goods, batik items, and a few fashions are the specialties at Tikal, established in 1959 as one of the first arts and crafts shops in Grenada. ⊠ *Young St.* ☎ *473/440–2310.*

ACTIVITIES

DIVING AND SNORKELING

You can see hundreds of varieties of fish and some 40 species of coral at more than a dozen sites off Grenada's southwest coast—only 15 to 20 minutes by boat—and another couple of dozen sites around Carriacou's reefs and neighboring islets. Depths vary from 20 to 120 feet, and visibility varies from 30 to 100 feet.

A spectacular dive is *Bianca C*, a 600-foot cruise ship that caught fire in 1961, sank to 100 feet, and is now encrusted with coral and serves as a habitat for giant turtles, spotted eagle rays, barracuda, and jacks. **Boss Reef** extends 5 miles (8 km) from St. George's Harbour to Point Salines, with a depth ranging from 20 to 90 feet. **Flamingo Bay** has a wall that drops to 90 feet and is teeming with fish, sponges, sea horses, sea fans, and coral. **Molinère Reef** slopes from about 20 feet below the surface to a wall that drops to 65 feet. It's a good dive for beginners, and advanced divers can continue farther out to view the wreck of the *Buccaneer,* a 42-foot sloop.

Aquanauts Grenada. Every morning Aquanauts Grenada heads out on two-tank dive trips, each accommodating no more than eight divers, to both the Caribbean and Atlantic sides of Grenada. Also available: guided snorkel trips; beach snorkeling; and special activities, courses, and equipment for children. ⊠ *Spice Island Beach Resort, Grand Anse Beach, Grand Anse, St. George* ☎ *473/444–1126, 800/513–5257 in U.S.* ⊕ *www.aquanautsgrenada.com.*

EcoDive. This full-service PADI dive shop offers two trips daily, both drift and wreck dives, as well as weekly trips to dive Isle de Rhonde and a full range of diving courses. EcoDive employs two full-time marine biologists who run Grenada's marine-conservation and education center and conduct coral-reef monitoring and restoration efforts. ⊠ *Coyaba Beach Resort, Grand Anse Beach, Grand Anse, St. George* ☎ *473/444–7777* ⊕ *www.ecodiveandtrek.com.*

FISHING

Deep-sea fishing around Grenada is excellent, with marlin, sailfish, yellowfin tuna, and dolphinfish topping the list of good catches. You can arrange sportfishing trips that accommodate up to five people starting at $475 for a half day and $700 for a full day.

True Blue Sportfishing. British-born Captain Gary Clifford, who has been fishing since the age of six, has run True Blue Sportfishing since 1998. He offers big-game charters for up to six passengers on the 31-foot *Yes Aye.* The boat has an enclosed cabin, a fighting chair, and professional tackle. Refreshments and transportation to the marina are included. ⊠ *True Blue Bay Marina, True Blue, St. George* ☎ *473/444–2048* ⊕ *www.yesaye.com.*

WHERE TO EAT

Restaurants add an 8% government tax to your bill and usually add a 10% service charge; if not, tip 10% to 15% for a job well done.

$$ ✕**Belmont Estate.** If you're visiting the northern reaches of Grenada, plan
CARIBBEAN   to stop at Belmont Estate, a 400-year-old working nutmeg and cocoa
FAMILY   plantation. Settle into the breezy open-air dining room, which overlooks enormous trays of nutmeg, cocoa, and mace drying in the sunshine. A waiter will offer some refreshing local juice and a choice of callaloo or pumpkin soup. Then head to the buffet and help yourself to the buffet: salad, rice, stewed chicken, beef curry, stewed fish, and vegetables. Dessert may be homemade ice cream, ginger cake, or another delicious confection. Afterward, feel free to take a tour of the museum, cocoa fermentary, sugarcane garden, and old cemetery. Farm animals (and a couple of monkeys) roam the property, and there's often folk music and dancing on the lawn. ⑤ *Average main: $17* ⊠ *Belmont, St. Patrick* ☎ *473/442–9524* ⊕ *www.belmontestate.net* ⊘ *Closed Sat. No dinner.*

$$ ✕**The New Nutmeg.** West Indian specialties, fresh seafood, great ham-
CARIBBEAN   burgers, and a waterfront view make the New Nutmeg a favorite with locals and visitors alike. It's on the Carenage (upstairs from the Sea Change bookstore), with large, open windows from which you can view the harbor activity and catch a cool breeze as you eat. Try the callaloo soup, curried lamb, fresh seafood, or a steak—or just stop by for a roti and a cold beer or a rum punch with grated nutmeg on top, of course. ⑤ *Average main: $18* ⊠ *The Carenage* ☎ *473/435–9525.*

GUADELOUPE (POINTE-À-PITRE)

Eileen Robinson Smith   On a map, Guadeloupe looks like a giant butterfly resting on the sea between Antigua and Dominica. Its two wings—Basse-Terre and Grande-Terre—are the two largest islands in the 659-square-mile (1,706-square-km) Guadeloupe archipelago. The Rivière Salée, a 4-mile (6-km) channel between the Caribbean and the Atlantic, forms the "spine" of the butterfly. A drawbridge near Pointe-à-Pitre, the main city, connects the two islands. Gorgeous scenery awaits, as Guadeloupe is one of the most physically attractive islands in the Caribbean. If you're seeking a resort atmosphere, casinos, and nearly white sandy beaches, your target is Grande-Terre. On the other hand, Basse-Terre's Parc National de la Guadeloupe, laced with trails and washed by waterfalls and rivers, is a 74,100-acre haven for hikers, nature lovers, and anyone brave enough to peer into the steaming crater of an active volcano. The tropical beauty suggests the mythical Garden of Eden.

ESSENTIALS

CURRENCY

The euro. You must exchange currency at a *bureau de change,* but ATMs are your best bet if you need euros.

TELEPHONE

To make on-island calls, dial 0590 (0690 if it is a cellular phone) and then the six-digit phone number. To call Guadeloupe from the United States, dial 00–590–590, then the local number. For cell phone numbers,

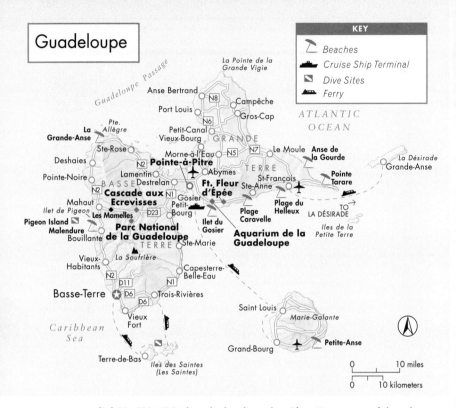

Guadeloupe

KEY

- Beaches
- Cruise Ship Terminal
- Dive Sites
- Ferry

Guadeloupe Passage

La Pointe de la Grande Vigie

Anse Bertrand
N8
Campêche
Port Louis
N6
Gros-Cap

ATLANTIC
OCEAN

Pte. Allègre
La Grande-Anse
Petit-Canal
Vieux-Bourg
GRANDE

Ste-Rose
Morne-à-l'Eau
N5
N7
Le Moule
Anse de la Gourde

Deshaies
N2
Pointe-à-Pitre
TERRE
La Désirade
Grande-Anse

Pointe-Noire
Lamentin
Abymes
St-François
Pointe Tarare

BASSE
Destrelan
Ft. Fleur d'Épée
Ste-Anne

Mahaut
Cascade aux Ecrevisses
N1
Petit-
Gosier
Plage du Helleux
TO
LA DÉSIRADE

Ilet de Pigeon
Les Mamelles
D23
Bourg
Plage Caravelle
Iles de la Petite Terre

Pigeon Island
Parc National
Ilet du Gosier

Malendure
de la Guadeloupe
Aquarium de la

Bouillante
TERRE
Ste-Marie
Guadeloupe

Vieux-Habitants
La Soufrière

N2
Capesterre-Belle-Eau

Basse-Terre
D11
N1

D6
Trois-Rivières

Saint Louis
Marie-Galante

Caribbean Sea
Vieux Fort

Grand-Bourg
Petite-Anse

Terre-de-Bas
Iles des Saintes (Les Saintes)

0 ____ 10 miles
0 ____ 10 kilometers

dial 00–590–690, then the local number. If you're on one of the other islands in the French West Indies, dial 0590 and then the local number.

COMING ASHORE

Ships now dock at a cruise terminal in downtown Pointe-à-Pitre, at Pier 5/6. It houses an Internet café, a duty-free shop, and the colorful Karuland Village, where cruisers can browse and buy spices, pareos, and souvenirs or just sit and listen to the local music while having coconut ice cream. It's about a five-minute walk from the shopping district. Passengers are greeted by local musicians and hostesses, usually dressed in the traditional madras costumes—and often dispensing samplings of local rum and creole specialties. These multilingual staffers operate the information booth and can pair you up with an English-speaking taxi driver for a customized island tour. To get to the main tourist office, walk along the quay to the Place de la Victoire; it is a large white Victorian building with wraparound verandah.

Taxis are metered and expensive; during rush hour, they can be *very* expensive. Renting a car is a good way to see Guadeloupe, but it is expensive and best booked in advance. Be aware that traffic around Pointe-à-Pitre can be horrible during rush hour, so allow plenty of time to drop off your car rental and get back to the ship. There are many rental agencies at the airport, but it will be at least a €35 taxi ride from the city.

EXPLORING GUADELOUPE

POINTE-À-PITRE

Although not the capital, this is the island's largest city, a commercial and industrial hub in the southwest of Grande-Terre. The Isles of Guadeloupe have 450,000 inhabitants, 99.6% of whom live in the cities. Pointe-à-Pitre is bustling, noisy, and hot—a place of honking horns and traffic jams and cars on sidewalks for want of a parking place. By day its pulse is fast, but at night, when its streets are almost deserted, you don't want to be there.

The heart of the old city is Place de la Victoire; surrounded by wooden buildings with balconies and shutters (including the tourism office) and by sidewalk cafés, it was named in honor of Victor Hugues's 1794 victory over the British. During the French Revolution Hugues ordered the guillotine set up here so that the public could witness the bloody end of 300 recalcitrant royalists.

> ### GUADELOUPE BEST BETS
>
> ■ **Beaches.** The southern coast of Grand-Terre has stretches of soft, nearly white sand.
>
> ■ **Diving.** Jacques Cousteau called the reef off Pigeon Island one of the world's top dive sites.
>
> ■ **Hiking.** The Parc National de la Guadeloupe is one of the Caribbean's most spectacular scenic destinations.
>
> ■ **Shopping.** Though Point-à-Pitre itself can be frenetic, it does have a good choice of French goods.

Even more colorful is the bustling marketplace, between rues St-John Perse, Frébault, Schoelcher, and Peynier. It's a cacophonous place, where housewives bargain for spices, herbs (and herbal remedies), and a bright assortment of papayas, breadfruits, christophenes, and tomatoes.

Cathédrale de St-Pierre et St-Paul. If you like churches, then make a pilgrimage to the imposing Cathédrale de St-Pierre et St-Paul, built in 1807. Although battered by hurricanes, it has fine stained-glass windows and Creole-style balconies. Still under renovation, it's reinforced with pillars and ribs that look like leftovers from the Eiffel Tower. ⊠ *Rue Alexandre Isaac at rue de l'Eglise.*

Musée Schoelcher. Musée Schoelcher celebrates Victor Schoelcher, a high-minded abolitionist from Alsace who fought against slavery in the French West Indies in the 19th century. The museum contains many of his personal effects, and exhibits trace his life and work. ⊠ *24 rue Peynier* ☎ *0590/82–08–04* ☎ *€2* ⊙ *Weekdays 9–5.*

Musée St-John Perse. Those with a strong interest in French literature and culture (not your average sightseer) will want to see the Musée St-John Perse, which is dedicated to the poet Alexis Léger, Guadeloupe's most famous son. Better known as Saint-John Perse, he was the winner of the Nobel Prize for literature in 1960. Some of his finest poems are inspired by the history and landscape—particularly the sea—of his

7

beloved Guadeloupe. The museum, in a restored colonial house, contains a collection of his poetry and some of his personal belongings. Before you go, look for his birthplace at 54 rue Achille René-Boisneuf. ⊠ *9 rue Nozières* ☎ *0590/90–01–92* 🖃 *€2.50* ⊙ *Weekdays 9–5, Sat. 8:30–12:30.*

ELSEWHERE ON GUADELOUPE

FAMILY **Aquarium de la Guadeloupe.** Unique in the Antilles, this aquarium in the marina near Pointe-à-Pitre is a good place to spend an hour. The well-planned facility has an assortment of tropical fish, crabs, lobsters, moray eels, coffer fish, and some live coral. It's also a turtle rescue center, and the shark tank is spectacular. The aquarium also offers a half-day ecotour, in which small boats travel through the mangroves, reefs, and a lagoon, with a biologist guide and a diving instructor on board. Leaving daily at 8:30 am and 1 pm, the tours are €59. Snorkeling gear is included, and kids are more than welcome. A full-day ecotour includes lunch and a visit to the aquarium (€95). ⊠ *Place Créole, off Rte. N4, La Marina, Pointe-à-Pitre, Grande-Terre* ☎ *0590/90–92–38* ⊕ *www. aquariumdelaguadeloupe.com* 🖃 *€11* ⊙ *Daily 9–6:30.*

Ft. Fleur d'Épée. The main attraction in Bas-du-Fort is this fortress, built between 1759 and 1763. It hunkers down on a hillside behind a deep moat. The fort was the scene of hard-fought battles between the French and the English in 1794. You can explore its well-preserved dungeons and battlements and take in a sweeping view of Iles des Saintes and Marie-Galante. The free guided tour here explores the fort's history and architecture and helps explain the living conditions of the soldiers who lived here. Included on the tour is an exploration of its underground galleries, now decorated with graffiti. If a bilingual person is on duty, she will explain it all in English. Call ahead to make certain of that day's hours. Registered as an historic monument since 1979, the fort also provides superb views for walkers. ⊠ *Bas-du-Fort, Grande-Terre* ☎ *0590/90–94–61* 🖃 *Free* ⊙ *Mon.–Sun. 9–5.*

Parc National de la Guadeloupe. This 74,100-acre park has been recognized by UNESCO as a Biosphere Reserve. Before going, pick up a *Guide to the National Park* from the tourist office; it rates the hiking trails according to difficulty, and most are quite difficult indeed. Most mountain trails are in the southern half. The park is bisected by the route de la Traversée, a 16-mile (26-km) paved road lined with masses of tree ferns, shrubs, flowers, tall trees, and green plantains. It's the ideal point of entry. Wear rubber-soled shoes and take along a swimsuit, a sweater, water, and perhaps food for a picnic. Try to get an early start to stay ahead of the hordes of cruise-ship passengers making a day of it. Check on the weather; if Basse-Terre has had a lot of rain, give it up. In the past, after intense rainfall, rockslides have closed the road for months. ⊠ *Administrative Headquarters, rte. de la Traversée, St-Claude, Basse-Terre* ☎ *0590/80–86–00* ⊕ *www.guadeloupe-parcnational.com* 🖃 *Free* ⊙ *Weekdays 8–5:30.*

Cascade aux Ecrevisses. Within the Parc National de la Guadeloupe, Crayfish Falls is one of the island's loveliest (and most popular) spots. There's a marked trail (walk carefully—the rocks can be slippery) leading to this splendid waterfall, which dashes down into the Corossol River—a good place for a dip. Come early, though; otherwise you definitely won't have it to yourself. ⊠ *St-Claude, Basse-Terre* ⊕ *www. guadeloupe-parcnational.com*

BEACHES

Plage de la Grande-Anse. One of Guadeloupe's widest beaches has soft beige sand sheltered by palms. To the west it's a round verdant mountain. It has a large parking area and some food stands, but no other facilities. The beach can be overrun on Sunday, not to mention littered, due to the food carts. Right after the parking lot, you can see signposting for the creole restaurant Le Karacoli; if you have lunch there (it's not cheap), you can *sieste* on the chaise longues. At the far end of the beach, which is more rough-and-ready, is Tainos Cottages, which has a restaurant. **Amenities:** food and drink; parking (no fee). **Best for:** partiers; solitude; swimming; walking. ⊠ *Rte. N6, north of Deshaies, Deshaies, Basse-Terre.*

Plage Caravelle. Just southwest of Ste-Anne is one of Grande-Terre's longest and prettiest stretches of sand, the occasional dilapidated shack notwithstanding. Protected by reefs, it's also a fine snorkeling spot. Club Med occupies one end of this beach, and nonguests can enjoy its beach and water sports, as well as lunch and drinks, by buying a day pass. You can also have lunch on the terrace of La Toubana Hotel & Spa, then descend the stairs to the beach or enjoy lunch at its beach restaurant, wildly popular on Sunday. **Amenities:** food and drink; parking (no fee); toilets; water sports. **Best for:** partiers; snorkeling; sunset; swimming; walking; windsurfing. ⊠ *Rte. N4, southwest of Ste-Anne, Ste-Anne, Grande-Terre.*

Plage de Malendure. Across from Pigeon Island and the Jacques Cousteau Underwater Park, this long, gray, volcanic beach on the Caribbean's calm waters has restrooms, a few beach shacks offering cold drinks and snacks, and a huge parking lot. There might be some litter, but the beach is cleaned regularly. Don't come here for solitude, as the beach is a launch point for many dive boats. The snorkeling's good. Le Rocher de Malendure, a fine seafood restaurant, is perched on a cliff over the bay. Food carts work the parking lot. **Amenities:** food and drink; parking (no fee); toilets. **Best for:** partiers; snorkeling; swimming. ⊠ *Rte. N6, Bouillante, Basse-Terre.*

SHOPPING

For serious shopping in Pointe-à-Pitre, browse the boutiques and stores along rue Schoelcher, rue Frébault, and rue Noizières. The multicolor market square and stalls of La Darse are filled mostly with vegetables, fruits, delicious homemade rum liqueurs, and housewares. The air is filled with the fragrance of spices, and they have lovely gift baskets of spices and vanilla lined with madras fabric.

Dody. Across from the market, Dody is the place to go if you want white eyelet lace (blouses, skirts, dresses, even bustiers). A single place costs from €100 to €300. There's lots of madras, too, which is especially cute in children's clothing. ⊠ *31 rue Frébault, Pointe-à-Pitre, Grande-Terre* ☎ *0590/82–18–59* ⊕ *www.dodyshop.com.*

ACTIVITIES

DIVING

The main diving area at the **Cousteau Underwater Park,** just off Basse-Terre near Pigeon Island, offers routine dives to 60 feet. The numerous glass-bottom boats and other crafts make the site feel like a marine parking lot; however, the underwater sights are spectacular. Guides and instructors are certified under the French CMAS (some also have PADI, but none have NAUI). Most operators offer two-hour dives three times per day for about €45 to €50 per dive; three-dive packages are €120 to €145. Hotels and dive operators usually rent snorkeling gear.

FAMILY **Les Heures Saines.** Les Heures Saines is the premier operator for dives in the Cousteau Underwater Park. Trips to Les Saintes offer one or two dives for average and advanced divers, with plenty of time for lunch and sightseeing. Wreck, night, and Nitrox diving are also available. The instructors, many of them English speakers, are excellent with children. The company also offers winter whale- and dolphin-watching trips with marine biologists as guides. These tours, aboard a 60-foot catamaran, cost €55 (less for children). ⊠ *Le Rocher de Malendure, Plage de Malendure, Bouillante, Basse-Terre* ☎ *0590/98–86–63* ⊕ *www. heures-saines.gp.*

HIKING

Fodor's Choice With hundreds of trails and countless rivers and waterfalls, the **Parc**
★ **National de la Guadeloupe** on Basse-Terre is the main draw for hikers. Some of the trails should be attempted only with an experienced guide. All tend to be muddy, so wear a good pair of boots. Know that even the young and fit can find these outings arduous; the unfit may find them painful.

Vert Intense. Vert Intense organizes hikes in the national park and to the volcano. You move from steaming hot springs to an icy waterfall in the same hike. Guides are patient and safety-conscious, and can bring you to heights that you never thought you could reach, including the top of Le Soufrière. The volcano hike costs €30 and must be booked four days in advance. Note that when you are under the fumaroles you can smell the sulfur (like rotten eggs) and you, your hair and clothes will smell like sulfur until you take a shower. A mixed-adventure package spanning three days costs €225. The two-day bivouac and other adventures can be extreme, so before you decide to play Indiana Jones, know what is expected. The French-speaking guides, who also know some English and Spanish, can take you to other tropical forests and rivers for canyoning (climbing and scrambling on outcrops, usually along and above the water). If you are just one or two people, the company can team you up with a group. Vert Intense now has a guesthouse where you can combine a stay with trekking and other activities. ⊠ *Rte. de la Soufrière, Mourne Houel, Basse-Terre* ☎ *0590/99–34–73, 0690/55–40–47* ⊕ *www.vert-intense.com.*

WHERE TO EAT

$$$ ✕ **Le Rocher de Malendure.** Guests first climb the worn yellow stairs
FRENCH because of the panoramic sea views, but they return again and again
for the food. If you arrive before noon, when the divers pull in, you
might snag one of the primo tables in a gazebo that literally hangs over
the Caribbean. Begin with a perfectly executed mojito. With fish just off
the boat, don't hesitate to try the sushi *antillaise* or grilled crayfish and
lobster from the pool. ⑤ *Average main: €25* ✉ *Bord de Mer, Malendure
de Pigeon, Bouillante, Basse-Terre* ☎ *0590/98–70–84* ⊗ *Closed Tues.
and Sept.–early Oct.*

KEY WEST, FLORIDA

Jill Martin   Along with the rest of Florida, Key West—the southernmost city in the
continental United States—became part of American territory in 1821.
In the late 19th century it was Florida's wealthiest city per capita. The
locals made their fortunes from "wrecking"—rescuing people and sal-
vaging cargo from ships that foundered on nearby reefs. Cigar making,
fishing, shrimping, and sponge gathering also became important indus-
tries. Locally dubbed the "Conch Republic," Key West today makes for
a unique port of call. A genuinely American town, it nevertheless exudes
the relaxed atmosphere and pace of a typical Caribbean island. Major
attractions include the home of the Conch Republic's most famous
residents, Ernest Hemingway and Harry Truman; the imposing Key
West Museum of Art and History, a former U.S. Customs House and
site of the military inquest of the USS *Maine*; and the island's renowned
sunset celebrations.

ESSENTIALS
CURRENCY
The U.S. dollar.

TELEPHONE
You'll be able to find plenty of public phones around Mallory Square.
They're also along the major tourist thoroughfares.

COMING ASHORE
Cruise ships dock at three different locations in Key West. Mallory
Square and Pier B are within walking distance of Duval and Whitehead
streets, the two main tourist thoroughfares. Passengers on ships that
dock at Outer Mole Pier (aka Navy Mole) are shuttled via Conch Train
or Old Town Trolley to Mallory Square. Because Key West is so eas-
ily explored on foot, there's rarely a need to hire a taxi. If you plan to
venture beyond the main tourist district, a fun way to get around is by
bicycle or scooter (bike rentals begin at about $12 per day). Key West
is a cycling town. In fact, there are so many bikes around that cyclists
must watch out for one another as much as for cars. You can get tour-
ist information from the Greater Key West Chamber of Commerce,
which is located one block off Duval Street, at 510 Greene Street, in
the old "city hall."

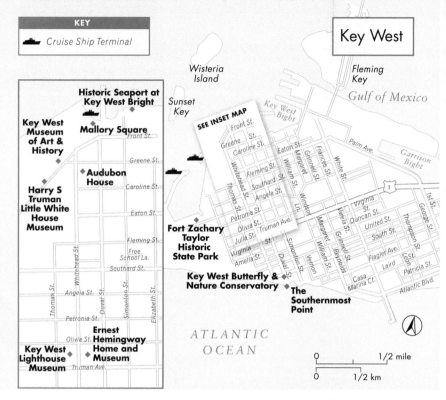

Key West

Wisteria Island

Fleming Key

Gulf of Mexico

Historic Seaport at Key West Bright

Sunset Key

Key West Bight

SEE INSET MAP

Key West Museum of Art & History

Mallory Square

Front St.

Palm Ave.

Garrison Bight

Front St.

Greene St.

Caroline St.

Eaton St.

Frances St.

Grinnell St.

White St.

Greene St.

Audubon House

Caroline St.

Whitehead St.

Fleming St.

Southard St.

William St.

Windsor Ln.

Virginia St.

Duncan St.

1st St.

George St.

Harry S Truman Little White House Museum

Eaton St.

Angela St.

United St.

Fleming St.

Thomas St.

Petronia St.

Margaret St.

Varela St.

Grinnell St.

South St.

Thompson St.

Free School La.

Olivia St.

Truman Ave.

Reynolds St.

Flagler Ave.

Leon St.

Southard St.

Fort Zachary Taylor Historic State Park

Julia St.

Virginia

Amelia St.

Simonton St.

Duval St.

Vernon St.

Margaret St.

William St.

Casa Marina Ct.

Laird

Patricia St.

Atlantic Blvd.

Whitehead St.

Angela St.

Duval St.

Simonton St.

Elizabeth St.

Key West Butterfly & Nature Conservatory

The Southernmost Point

ATLANTIC OCEAN

Petronia St.

Ernest Hemingway Home and Museum

Key West Lighthouse Museum

Olivia St.

Truman Ave.

0 _____ 1/2 mile

0 _____ 1/2 km

The Conch Tour Train can be boarded at Mallory Square or Flagler Station every half-hour; it costs $29 per adult for the 90-minute tour. The Old Town Trolley operates trolley-style buses starting from Mallory Square every 30 minutes for the same price, and these smaller trolleys go places the train won't fit. The Old Town Trolley also has pick up and drop off locations at numerous points around the island.

EXPLORING KEY WEST

Audubon House and Tropical Gardens. If you've ever seen an engraving by ornithologist John James Audubon, you'll understand why his name is synonymous with birds. See his works in this three-story house, which was built in the 1840s for Captain John Geiger and filled with period furniture. It now commemorates Audubon's 1832 stop in Key West while he was traveling through Florida to study birds. After an introduction by a docent, you can do a self-guided tour of the house and gardens (or just the gardens). An art gallery sells lithographs of the artist's famed portraits. ⌧ *205 Whitehead St.* ☎ *305/294–2116, 877/294–2470* ⊕ *www.audubonhouse.com* ⌸ *$12 house and gardens, $7.50 gardens only* ⊙ *Daily 9:30–5, last tour at 4:30.*

Ernest Hemingway Home and Museum. Amusing anecdotes spice up the guided tours of Ernest Hemingway's home, built in 1801 by the town's most successful wrecker. While living here between 1931 and 1942, Hemingway wrote about 70% of his life's work, including classics like *For Whom the Bell Tolls*. Few of his belongings remain aside from some books, and there's little about his actual work, but photographs help you visualize his day-to-day life. The famous six-toed descendants of Hemingway's cats—many named for actors, artists, authors, and even a hurricane—have free rein of the property. Tours begin every 10 minutes and take 30 minutes; then you're free to explore on your own. ✉ *907 Whitehead St.* ☏ *305/294–1136* ⊕ *www. hemingwayhome.com* 💳 *$13.00* ⊙ *Daily 9–5.*

KEY WEST BEST BETS

■ **Boat Cruise.** Being out on the water is what Key West is all about.

■ **Conch Train.** Hop aboard for a narrated tour of the town's tawdry past and rare architectural treasures.

■ **Hemingway.** Visit Ernest Hemingway's historic home for a literary treat.

■ **Duval Crawl.** Shop, eat, drink, repeat.

■ **Sunset in Mallory Square.** The nightly street party is the quintessential Key West experience.

Fort Zachary Taylor Historic State Park.
Construction of the fort began in 1845 but was halted during the Civil War. Even though Florida seceded from the Union, Yankee forces used the fort as a base to block Confederate shipping. More than 1,500 Confederate vessels were detained in Key West's harbor. The fort, finally completed in 1866, was also used in the Spanish-American War. Take a 30-minute guided walking tour of the redbrick fort, a National Historic Landmark, at noon and 2, or self-tour anytime between 8 and 5. In February a celebration called Civil War Heritage Days includes costumed reenactments and demonstrations. From mid-January to mid-April the park serves as an open-air gallery for pieces created for Sculpture Key West. One of its most popular features is its man-made beach, a rest stop for migrating birds in the spring and fall; there are also picnic areas, hiking and biking trails and a kayak launch. ✉ *Box 6565, end of Southard St., through Truman Annex* ☏ *305/292–6713* ⊕ *www. floridastateparks.org/forttaylor* 💳 *$4 for single occupant vehicles, $6 for 2–8 people in a vehicle, plus a 50¢ per person county surcharge.* ⊙ *Daily 8–sunset.*

Harry S. Truman Little White House Museum. Renovations to this circa-1890 landmark have restored the home and gardens to the Truman era, down to the wallpaper pattern. A free photographic review of visiting dignitaries and presidents—John F. Kennedy, Jimmy Carter, and Bill Clinton are among the chief executives who passed through here—is on display in the back of the gift shop. Engaging 45-minute tours begin every 20 minutes until 4:30. They start with an excellent 10-minute video on the history of the property and Truman's visits. On the grounds of **Truman Annex**, a 103-acre former military parade grounds and barracks, the home served as a winter White House for presidents Truman, Eisenhower, and Kennedy. ■**TIP→** The house tour does require climbing steps. Visitors can do a free self-guided botanical tour of the grounds with a brochure from the museum store. ✉ *111 Front St.* ☎ *305/294–9911* ⊕ *www.trumanlittlewhitehouse.com* 🖾 *$16.13* ⊙ *Daily 9–5, grounds 7–6.*

Historic Seaport at Key West Bight. What was once a funky—in some places even seedy—part of town is now an 8½-acre historic restoration of 100 businesses, including waterfront restaurants, open-air bars, museums, clothing stores, bait shops, dive shops, docks, a marina, and watersports concessions. It's all linked by the 2-mile waterfront **Harborwalk,** which runs between Front and Grinnell streets, passing big ships, schooners, sunset cruises, fishing charters, and glass-bottom boats. ✉ *100 Grinnell St.* ☎ *305/293–8309* ⊕ *www.keywestseaport.com.*

FAMILY **Key West Butterfly & Nature Conservatory.** This air-conditioned refuge for butterflies, birds, and the human spirit gladdens the soul with hundreds of colorful wings—more than 45 species of butterflies alone—in a lovely glass-encased bubble. Waterfalls, artistic benches, paved pathways, birds, and lush, flowering vegetation elevate this above most butterfly attractions. The gift shop and gallery are worth a visit on their own. ✉ *1316 Duval St.* ☎ *305/296–2988, 800/839–4647* ⊕ *www. keywestbutterfly.com* 🖾 *$12* ⊙ *Daily 9–5, gallery and shop until 5:30.*

Key West Lighthouse Museum & Keeper's Quarters Museum. For the best view in town, climb the 88 steps to the top of this 1847 lighthouse. The 92-foot structure has a Fresnel lens, which was installed in the 1860s at a cost of $1 million. The keeper lived in the adjacent 1887 clapboard house, which now exhibits vintage photographs, ship models, nautical charts, and lighthouse artifacts from all along the Key reefs. A kids' room is stocked with books and toys. ✉ *938 Whitehead St.* ☎ *305/295–6616* ⊕ *www.kwahs.com* 🖾 *$10* ⊙ *Daily 9:30–4:30.*

Fodor'sChoice **Key West Museum of Art & History in the Custom House.** When Key West ★ was designated a U.S. port of entry in the early 1820s, a customhouse was established. Salvaged cargoes from ships wrecked on the reefs were brought here, setting the stage for Key West to become—for a time—the richest city in Florida. The imposing redbrick-and-terra-cotta Richardsonian Romanesque–style building reopened as a museum and art gallery in 1999. Smaller galleries have long-term and changing exhibits about the history of Key West, including a Hemingway room and a fine collection of folk artist Mario Sanchez's wood paintings. In 2011, to commemorate the 100th anniversary of the railroad's arrival to Key West in 1912, a new permanent Flagler exhibit opened. ✉ *281 Front St.* ☎ *305/295–6616* ⊕ *www.kwahs.com* 🖾 *$7* ⊙ *Daily 9:30–4:30.*

Mallory Square and Pier. For cruise-ship passengers, this is the disembarkation point for an attack on Key West. For practically every visitor, it's the requisite venue for a nightly sunset celebration that includes street performers—human statues, sword swallowers, tightrope walkers, musicians, and more—plus craft vendors, conch fritter fryers, and other regulars who defy classification ("Wanna picture with my pet iguana?"). With all the activity, don't forget to watch the main show: a dazzling tropical sunset. ✉ *Mallory Sq.*

The Southernmost Point. Possibly the most photographed site in Key West (even though the actual geographic southernmost point in the continental United States lies across the bay on a naval base, where you see a satellite dish), this is a must-see. Who wouldn't want his picture taken next to the big striped buoy that marks the southernmost point in the continental United States? A plaque next to it honors Cubans who lost their lives trying to escape to America and other signs tell Key West history. ⊠ *Whitehead and South sts.*

BEACHES

FAMILY **Fort Zachary Taylor Beach.** The park's beach is the best and safest place to swim in Key West. There's an adjoining picnic area with barbecue grills and shade trees, a snack bar, and rental equipment, including snorkeling gear. A café serves sandwiches and other munchies. **Amenities:** food and drink, showers, toilets, water sports. **Best for:** swimming, snorkeling. ⊠ *Box 6565, end of Southard St., through Truman Annex* ☎ *305/292–6713* ⊕ *www.floridastateparks.org/forttaylor* ☜ *$4 for one-occupant vehicles, $6 for 2–8 people in a vehicle, plus 50¢ per person county surcharge* ☉ *Daily 8–sunset, tours at noon and 2.*

7

SHOPPING

On these streets you'll find colorful local art of widely varying quality, key limes made into everything imaginable, and the raunchiest T-shirts in the civilized world. Browsing the boutiques—with frequent pub stops along the way—makes for an entertaining stroll down Duval Street. Key West is filled with art galleries, and the variety is truly amazing. Much is locally produced by the town's large artist community, but many galleries carry international artists from as close as Haiti and as far away as France. Local artists do a great job of preserving the island's architecture and spirit.

Bahama Village. Where to start your shopping adventure? This cluster of spruced-up shops, restaurants, and vendors is responsible for the restoration of the colorful historic district where Bahamians settled in the 19th century. The village lies roughly between Whitehead and Fort streets and Angela and Catherine streets. Hemingway frequented the bars, restaurants, and boxing rings in this part of town. ⊠ *Between Whitehead and Fort sts. and Angela and Catherine sts..*

ACTIVITIES

BOAT TOURS

Lazy Dog Kayak Guides. Take a two- or four-hour guided sea kayak–snorkel tour around the mangrove islands just east of Key West. The $40 or $60 charge, respectively, covers transportation, bottled water, a snack, and supplies, including snorkeling gear. Paddleboard tours are

$40. Rentals for self-touring are also available. ⊠ *5114 Overseas Hwy.* ☎ *305/295–9898* ⊕ *www.lazydog.com.*

White Knuckle Thrill Boat Ride. For something with an adrenaline boost, book with this specially designed jet boat. It holds up to 10 people and does amazing maneuvers like 360s, fishtails, and other water stunts. The cost is $59 per person, and includes pickup shuttle. Another unique experience is their Sea Spi Eco Tour. These individual glass bottom boats are electric powered so they glide quietly, giving you a peek below the sea without getting in the water. Tours are 90 minutes for $69 plus tax. ⊠ *Sunset Marina, 555 College Rd.* ☎ *305/797–0459* ⊕ *www. whiteknucklethrillboatride.com.*

DIVING AND SNORKELING

The Florida Keys National Marine Sanctuary extends along Key West and beyond to the Dry Tortugas. Key West National Wildlife Refuge further protects the pristine waters. Most divers don't make it this far out in the Keys, but if you're looking for a day of diving as a break from the nonstop party in Old Town, expect to pay about $65 and upward for a two-tank dive. Serious divers can book dive trips to the Dry Tortugas.

Captain's Corner. This PADI-certified dive shop has classes in several languages and twice-daily snorkel and dive trips ($40–$65) to reefs and wrecks aboard the 60-foot dive boat *Sea Eagle.* Use of weights, belts, masks, and fins is included. ⊠ *125 Ann St.* ☎ *305/296–8865* ⊕ *www. captainscorner.com.*

Snuba of Key West. Safely dive the coral reefs without getting a scuba certification. Ride out to the reef on a catamaran, then follow your guide underwater for a one-hour tour of the coral reefs. You wear a regulator with a breathing hose that is attached to a floating air tank on the surface. No prior diving or snorkeling experience is necessary, but you must know how to swim. The $99 price includes beverages. ⊠ *Garrison Bight Marina, Palm Ave. between Eaton St. and N. Roosevelt Blvd.* ☎ *305/292–4616* ⊕ *www.snubakeywest.com.*

FISHING

Any number of local fishing guides can take you to where the big ones are biting, either in the backcountry for snapper and snook or to the deep water for the marlins and shark that brought Hemingway here in the first place.

Key West Bait & Tackle. Prepare to catch a big one with the live bait, frozen bait, and fishing equipment provided here. They even offer rod and reel rentals (starting at $15 for 24 hours). Stop by their onsite Live Bait Lounge where you can sip ice-cold beer while telling fish tales. ⊠ *241 Margaret St.* ☎ *305/292–1961* ⊕ *www.keywestbaitandtackle.com.*

Key West Pro Guides. Trips include flats and backcountry fishing ($400–$450 for a half day) and reef and offshore fishing (starting at $550 for a half day). ⊠ *G-31 Miriam St.* ☎ *866/259–4205* ⊕ *www. keywestproguides.com.*

WHERE TO EAT

$$ ✕ **El Meson de Pepe.** If you want to get a taste of the island's Cuban CUBAN heritage, this is the place. Perfect for after watching a Mallory Square sunset, you can dine alfresco or in the dining room on refined versions of Cuban classics. Begin with a megasized mojito while you enjoy the basket of bread and savory sauces. The expansive menu offers *tostones rellenos* (green plantains with different traditional fillings), *ceviche* (raw fish "cooked" in lemon juice), and more. Choose from Cuban specialties such as roasted pork in a cumin mojo sauce and ropa vieja. At lunch, the local Cuban population and cruise-ship passengers enjoy Cuban sandwiches and smaller versions of dinner's most popular entrées. A Latin band performs outside at the bar during sunset celebration. ⑤ *Average main: $19* ✉ *Mallory Sq., 410 Wall St.* ☎ *305/295–2620* ⊕ *www. elmesondepepe.com.*

$ ✕ **Lobo's Mixed Grill.** Famous for its selection of wrap sandwiches, Lobo's AMERICAN has a reputation among locals for its 8-ounce, charcoal-grilled ground FAMILY chuck burger—thick and juicy and served with lettuce, tomato, and pickle on a toasted bun. Mix it up with toppings like Brie, blue cheese, or portobello mushroom. The menu of 30 wraps includes rib eye, oyster, grouper, Cuban, and chicken Caesar. The menu includes salads and quesadillas, as well as a fried-shrimp-and-oyster combo. Beer and wine are served. This courtyard food stand closes around 5, so eat early. Most of Lobo's business is takeout (it has a half-dozen outdoor picnic tables), and it offers free delivery within Old Town. ⑤ *Average main: $9* ✉ *5 Key Lime Sq., east of intersection of Southard and Duval sts.* ☎ *305/296–5303* ⊕ *www.lobosmixedgrill.com* ⌦ *Reservations not accepted* ⊗ *Closed Sun. Apr.–early Dec.*

NIGHTLIFE

Three spots stand out for first-timers among the saloons frequented by Key West denizens. All are within easy walking distance of the cruise-ship piers.

Capt. Tony's Saloon. When it was the original Sloppy Joe's in the mid-1930s, Hemingway was a regular. Later, a young Jimmy Buffett sang here and made this watering hole famous in his song "Last Mango in Paris." Captain Tony was even voted mayor of Key West. Yes, this place is a beloved landmark. Stop in and take a look at the "hanging tree" that grows through the roof, listen to live music seven nights a week, and play some pool. ✉ *428 Greene St.* ☎ *305/294–1838* ⊕ *www. capttonyssaloon.com.*

Schooner Wharf Bar. This open-air waterfront bar and grill in the historic seaport district retains its funky Key West charm and hosts live entertainment daily. Its margaritas rank among Key West's best, as does the bar itself, voted Best Local's Bar six years in a row. For great views, head up to the second floor and be sure to order up some fresh seafood and fritters. ✉ *202 William St.* ☎ *305/292–3302* ⊕ *www.schoonerwharf. com.*

Sloppy Joe's. There's history and good times at the successor to a famous 1937 speakeasy named for its founder, Captain Joe Russell. Decorated with Hemingway memorabilia and marine flags, the bar is popular with travelers and is full and noisy all the time. A Sloppy Joe's T-shirt is a de rigueur Key West souvenir, and the gift shop sells them like crazy. Grab a seat (if you can) and be entertained by the bands and by the parade of people in constant motion. ✉ *201 Duval St.* ☎ *305/294–5717* ⊕ *www.sloppyjoes.com.*

LA ROMANA, DOMINICAN REPUBLIC

Eileen Robinson Smith

The Dominican Republic is a beautiful island bathed by the Atlantic Ocean to the north and the Caribbean Sea to the south, and some of its most beautiful beaches are in the area surrounding La Romana, notably Bayahibe Bay. The famed Casa de Campo resort and Marina will be the destination for most cruise passengers who land at La Romana's International Tourist Pier. A port call here will allow you to explore the immediate region—even take a day-trip into Santo Domingo—or simply stay and enjoy some nice (but expensive) restaurants and shops. There is also a host of activities cruise passengers can take part in on organized shore excursions.

ESSENTIALS

CURRENCY

The Dominican peso, but you can almost always use U.S. dollars.

TELEPHONE

Telephones are available at the dock, as soon as passengers disembark, and telephone cards can be purchased there as well. Tele-cards can also be bought at the supermarket at Casa de Campo Marina. To call the United States or Canada from the D.R., just punch in 1 plus the area code and number. To make calls on the island, you must tap in the area code (809), plus the seven-digit number; if you are calling a Dominican cell phone, you must first punch in 1 then 809 or 829.

COMING ASHORE

Ships enter the Casa de Campo International Tourist Port (Muelle Turístico Internacional Casa de Campo). A group of folkloric dancers and local musicians, playing merengue, greets passengers as they come down the gangway. An information booth with English-speaking staffers is there to assist cruise-ship passengers; the desk is open the entire time the ship is in port.

It is a 15-minute walk into the town of La Romana, or you can jump into a waiting taxi. It's safe to stroll around town, but it's not particularly beautiful, quaint, or even historic; however, it is a real slice of Dominican life. Most people just board the complimentary shuttle and head for the Casa de Campo Marina and/or Altos de Chavón, both of which are at the Casa de Campo resort. Shuttles run all day long.

Taxis line up at the port's docks, and some, but not all, drivers speak English. Staff members from the information kiosk will help to make

taxi arrangements. Most rates are fixed and spelled out on a board: $15 to Casa de Campo Marina, $20 to Altos de Chavón. You may be able to negotiate a somewhat lower rate if a group books a taxi for a tour. You can also rent a car at Casa de Campo from National Car Rental; rates are expensive, usually more than $70 a day. Driving into Santo Domingo can be a hair-raising experience and isn't for the faint of heart, so we don't recommend it.

EXPLORING LA ROMANA

Fodor's Choice ★ **Altos de Chavón.** This re-creation of a 16th-century Mediterranean village sits on a bluff overlooking the Río Chavón, on the grounds of Casa de Campo but about 3 miles (5 km) east of the main facilities. There are cobblestone streets lined with lanterns, wrought-iron balconies, wooden shutters, courtyards swathed with bougainvillea, and **Iglesia St. Stanislaus,** the romantic setting for many a Casa de Campo wedding. More than a museum piece, this village is a place where artists live, work, and play. Dominican and international painters, sculptors, and artisans come here to teach sculpture, pottery, silk-screen printing, weaving, dance, and music at the school, which is affiliated with New York's Parsons School of Design. The artists work in their studios and crafts shops selling their finished wares. The village also has an amber museum, an archaeological museum, a handful of restaurants, and a number of unique shops. ⊠ *Casa de Campo* ⊕ *www.casadecampo. com.do.*

Isla Saona. Off the east coast of Hispaniola and part of Parque Nacional del Este lies this island, inhabited by sea turtles, pigeons, and other wildlife. Indigenous people once used the caves here. The beaches are beautiful, and legend has it that Columbus once stopped over. However, the island is not nearly as pristine as one might expect for a national park Getting here, on catamarans and other excursion boats, is half the fun, but it can be a crowd scene once you arrive. Vendors are allowed to sell to visitors, and there are a number of beach shacks serving lunch and drinks. Most boats traveling here leave out of the beach at Bayahibe

Village. ✉ *20 mins. from Bayahibe harbor by boat.*

Santo Domingo. Spanish civilization in the New World began in the 12-block Zona Colonial of Santo Domingo. Strolling its narrow streets, it's easy to imagine this old city as it was when the likes of Columbus, Cortés, and Ponce de León walked the cobblestones, pirates sailed in and out, and colonists were settling themselves. Tourist brochures tout that "history comes alive here"—a surprisingly truthful statement. A fun horse-and-carriage ride throughout the Zone costs $25 for an hour. The steeds are no thoroughbreds, but they clip right along, though any commentary will be in Spanish. The drivers usually hang out in front of the Hostal Nicolas de Ovando. History buffs will want to spend a day exploring the many "firsts" of our continent, which will be included in any cruise-ship excursion. Do wear comfortable shoes.

LA ROMANA BEST BETS

■ **Altos de Chavón.** You'll find shopping and dining as well as great views.

■ **Golf.** The Teeth of the Dog is one of the Caribbean's best courses despite the cost.

■ **Horseback Riding.** Casa de Campo has an excellent equestrian center.

■ **Isla Saona.** The powder-soft beach and beautiful water are excellent.

■ **Kandela.** The tropical, Las Vegas–style review is a highlight if your ship stays late in port on a night it is performed.

BEACHES

Cruise passengers can buy a day-pass to use the beach and facilities at Casa de Campo ($75 for adults, $45 for children 4–12 years); with that, you get a place in the sun at **Minitas Beach**, towels, nonmotorized water sports, lunch in the Beach Club, and entrance to Altos de Chavón. Otherwise, excursions (sometimes cheaper) are available to several area beaches.

Catalina Island is a diminutive, picture-postcard Caribbean island off the coast of the mainland. Catalina is about a half-hour away by catamaran, and most excursions offer the use of snorkeling equipment as well as a beach barbecue. **Playa Bayahibe** is a beautiful stretch of beach. Shore excursions are organized by the cruise lines to the beach, which is about 30 minutes away from the cruise port by bus. You can also book your own taxi here, and the trip may be cheaper than the cost of a shore excursion if you come with a group. **Saona Island** was once a pristine, idyllic isle. Now, on a busy cruise-ship day there may be as many as 1,000 swimmers there. However, the beach is beautiful. Excursions here usually include a powerboat ride from Casa de Campo Marina; otherwise, you are bused to Bayahibe and board a boat there.

SHOPPING

Altos de Chavón. Altos de Chavón is a re-creation of a 16th-century Mediterranean village on the grounds of the Casa de Campo resort, where you can find a church, art galleries, boutiques,restaurants and souvenir shops, and a 5,000-seat amphitheater for concerts grouped around a cobbled square. At the Altos de Chavón Art Studios you can find ceramics, weaving, and screen prints made by local artists. Extra special is Casa Montecristo, a chic cigar lounge, which also offers a tour with cigar history and trivia. The mini-market sells sundries and some food items. ⊠ *Casa de Campo.*

The Casa de Campo Marina. Casa de Campo's top-ranked marina is home to shops and international boutiques, galleries, and jewelers scattered amid restaurants, an ice-cream parlor, bars, banks, beauty salons, and a yacht club. It's a great place to spend some time shopping, sightseeing, and staring at the extravagant yachts. The chic shopping scene at the marina includes Bleu Marine (cosmetics) and Everett Designs (high-end larimar and amber jewelry). Art Arena sells local artisan jewelry and gifts. Dominican designer Jenny Polanco sells clothes, purses, and jewelry. The Bibi Leon boutique, is known for its tropical-themed home accessories. There's also a marvelous Italian antiques shop, Nuovo Rinascimento, and the Club de Cigarro (Fumo). By the way, the supermercado Nacional at the marina has not only groceries but sundries, postcards, and snacks. ⊠ *Casa de Campo Marina, Calle Barlovento.*

ACTIVITIES

Most activities available at Casa de Campo are open to cruise-ship passengers. You'll need to make reservations on the ship, particularly for golf.

FISHING

Blue and white marlin, wahoo, sailfish, dorado, and mahimahi are among the most common catches in these waters.

Casa de Campo Marina. Casa de Campo Marina is the best charter option in the La Romana area. Yachts (22 to 60 footers) are available for deep-sea fishing charters for half or full days. Prices go from $708 to $1,591. They can come equipped with rods, bait, dinghies, drinks and experienced guides. Going out for the big billfish that swim the depths of the Caribbean is a major adrenaline rush. ⊠ *Casa de Campo, Calle Barlovento 3* ☎ *809/523–3333 ext. 3165, 809/523–3333 ext. 3166.*

GOLF

Fodor's Choice
★
Casa de Campo Golf. The famed 18-hole **Teeth of the Dog** course at Casa de Campo, with seven holes on the sea, is ranked as the number-one course in the Caribbean and is among the top courses in the world (coming in 47th in the Top 100 Courses of the World rankings released in late 2011). Greens fees in high season for nonhotel guests are $325 per round per golfer, $185 per round per player for guests. The Teeth of the Dog also requires a caddy for each round, an additional $25 (plus tip). Pete Dye has designed this and two other globally acclaimed courses here. **Dye Fore,** now with a total of 27 holes, is close to Altos de Chavón, hugging a cliff that looks over the sea, a river, Dominican mountains, and the marina (in high season: $250 for nonguests, $185 for guests). **The Links** is an 18-hole inland course (in high season: $175 for nonguests; $155 for hotel guests). Resort guests must reserve tee times for all courses at least one day in advance; nonguests should make reservations earlier. Jim McLean operates a golf school at Casa de Campo; an instructor is on site year-round. Half- and full-day lessons are available to individuals and groups; one-hour private lessons for adults are priced at $150. ☎ *809/523–3333 resort, 809/523–8115 golf director* ⊕ *www.casadecampo.com.do.*

HORSEBACK RIDING

Equestrian Center at Casa de Campo. The 250-acre Equestrian Center at Casa de Campo has something for both Western and English riders—a dude ranch, a rodeo arena (where Casa's trademark "Donkey Polo" is played), guided trail rides, and jumping and riding lessons. Guided rides run about $56 an hour, $88 for two hours; lessons cost $65 an hour, and jumping lessons are $88 an hour or $55 a half-hour. There are early morning and sunset trail rides, too. Handsome, old-fashioned carriages are available for hire as well. Unlimited horseback riding is included if you are a hotel guest staying on the all-inclusive plan. Great for families, trail rides are offered through the property's private cattle ranch, including a catered lunch. ☎ *809/523–3333 resort* ⊕ *www. casadecampo.com.do.*

WHERE TO EAT

$$$
ECLECTIC
Fodor's Choice
★
✕ **Peperoni.** Although the name may sound as Italian as *amore,* this restaurant's menu is much more eclectic than Italian. It has a classy, contemporary, white-dominated decor in a dreamy, waterfront setting. Strolling musicians perpetuate the mood. Astounding appetizers are found under the Asian section, like the sweet plantain roll or the Peperoni roll. Pasta dishes and risottos with rock shrimp or porcinis taste authentic, and the more inventive items such as house-made pear-and-goat-cheese ravioli with pine nuts and a key-lime emulsion are delectable. *Pulpo* (octopus) with fava beans stewed in limoncello vinaigrette is highly recommended. You can also opt for stylishly simple charcoal-grilled steaks (sauce or no), burgers, gourmet wood-oven pizzas, sandwiches, or even sushi and sashimi. Desserts are worthy here. Ⓢ *Average main: $21* ✉ *Casa de Campo, Plaza Portafino 16, Casa de Campo Marina* ☎ *809/523–2227, 809/523–3333 resort.*

MARTINIQUE (FORT-DE-FRANCE)

Eileen Robinson Smith

The largest of the Windward Islands, Martinique is 4,261 miles (6,817 km) from Paris, but its spirit and language are decidedly French, with more than a soupçon of West Indian spice. Tangible, edible evidence of the fact is the island's cuisine, a superb blend of French and Creole. Martinique is lushly landscaped with tropical flowers. Trees bend under the weight of fruits such as mangoes, papayas, lemons, limes, and bright-red West Indian cherries. Acres of banana plantations, pineapple fields, and waving sugarcane stretch to the horizon. The towering mountains and verdant rain forest in the north lure hikers, while underwater sights and sunken treasures attract snorkelers and scuba divers. Martinique is also wonderful if your idea of exercise is turning over every 10 minutes to get an even tan and your taste in adventure runs to duty-free shopping. A popular excursion goes to St-Pierre, which was buried by ash when Mount Pelée erupted in 1902.

ESSENTIALS

CURRENCY
The euro. Change currency at a bureau de change, but you'll get the best rate from any ATM.

TELEPHONE
Public phones use a télécarte, which you can buy at post offices, café-tabacs, hotels, and bureaux de change. To call the United States from Martinique, dial 00+1, the area code, and the local seven-digit number. To call locally, you now have to dial 0596 before the six-digit number. You can get the AT&T or MCI operators from blue, special-service phones at the cruise ports and in town.

COMING ASHORE

Most cruise ships call either at Tourelles (in the old port, about 1½ miles [2 km] from Fort-de-France) or at Pointe Simon, right in downtown Fort-de-France. (It is rare to have a ship anchor in the Baie des Flamands and tender passengers ashore.) Tourist information offices are at each cruise terminal. Uniformed dispatchers assist passengers in finding English-speaking taxi drivers. Passengers who do not wish to walk 20 minutes into Fort-de-France from Tourelles can take a taxi (set rate of €8 for up to four passengers in a van, or €2 for each additional passenger). Expect to pay about €50 per hour for touring; in larger vans the price is usually €10 per person per hour. Independent cruisers can explore the capital and the nearby open-air market on their own. Beaming and knowledgeable hostesses in Creole dress greet cruise passengers. Civilian auxiliary police (in blue-and-orange uniforms) supplement the regular police.

Know that traffic in Fort-de-France can be nightmarish. If you want to go to the beach, a much cheaper option is to take a ferry from Fort-de-France. *Vedettes* (ferries) operate daily between the waterfront pier next to the public land-transport terminal and the marina in Pointe du Bout, Anse-Mitan, and Anse-à-l'Ane. Any of the three trips takes about 15 minutes, and the ferries operate about every 30 minutes on weekdays.

Renting a car in Fort-de-France is possible, but the heavy traffic can be forbidding. Rates are about €70 per day (high season) for a car with manual transmission; automatics are substantially more expensive and seldom available without reservations.

EXPLORING MARTINIQUE

If you want to see the lush island interior and St-Pierre on your own, take the N3, which snakes through dense rain forests, north through the mountains to Le Morne Rouge, then take the coastal N2 back to Fort-de-France via St-Pierre. You can do the 40-mile (64-km) round-trip in half a day, but your best option is to hire an English-speaking driver.

FORT-DE-FRANCE

With its historic fort and superb location beneath the towering Pitons du Carbet on the Baie des Flamands, Martinique's capital—home to about one-quarter of the island's 400,000 inhabitants—should be a grand place. It hasn't been for decades but it's now coming up fast. An ambitious redevel-

> ### MARTINIQUE BEST BETS
>
> ■ **Beaches.** If you want to relax, the most beautiful beach is Les Salines.
>
> ■ **French Culture.** Excellent French food and music make this a *paradis* for Francophiles.
>
> ■ **La Route des Rhums.** Visit a distillery and become a rum connoisseur.
>
> ■ **Shopping.** Browse Fort-de-France's many upscale boutiques and department stores for French wares.
>
> ■ **St-Pierre.** Wander the narrow, winding streets of this hill town.

opment project, still under way, hopes to make it one of the most attractive cities in the Caribbean. The most pleasant districts, such as Didier, Bellevue, and Schoelcher, are on the hillside, reachable only by car or taxi; there are some good shops with Parisian wares and lively street markets. Near the harbor is a marketplace where local crafts and souvenirs are sold. The urban beach between the waterfront and the fort, La Française, has been cleaned up; white sand was brought in, and many cruise-ship passengers frequent it. The new Stewards Urbaine, easily recognized by their red caps and uniforms, are able to answer most visitor questions and give directions.

Bibliothèque Schoelcher. This wildly elaborate Romanesque public library was named after Victor Schoelcher, who led the fight to free the slaves in the French West Indies in the 19th century. The eye-popping structure was built for the 1889 Paris Exposition, after which it was dismantled, shipped to Martinique, and reassembled piece by piece. ⊠ *At rue de la Liberté, which runs along west side of La Savane* ☎ *0596/55–68–30* ✉ *Free* ☼ *Mon. 1:00–5:30, Tues.–Thurs. 8:30–5:30, Fri. 8:30–5:00, Sat. 8:30–noon.*

La Savane. The heart of Fort-de-France, La Savane is a 12½-acre park filled with trees, fountains, and benches. A massive revitalization, completed in 2010, made it the focal point of the city again, with entertainment, shopping, and a pedestrian mall. Attractive wooden stands

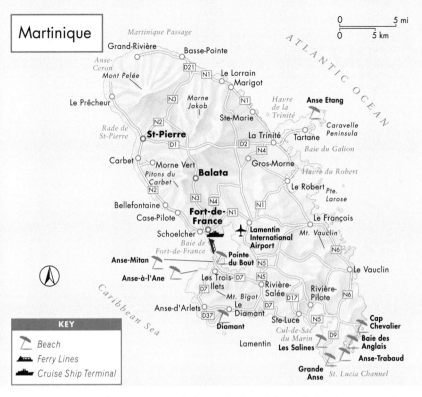

Martinique

KEY

⛱ *Beach*

🚢 *Ferry Lines*

🚢 *Cruise Ship Terminal*

have been constructed along the edge of the park that house a tourism information office, public restrooms, arts-and-crafts vendors, a crêpe stand, an ice-cream stand, and numerous other eateries. There are some homeless types around, but everyone considers them harmless.

The Hotel L'Imperatrice, directly across from the park, has become a real gathering place—particularly for its café, which opens to the sidewalk. The hotel also has one of the best kiosks in the area for lunch and snacks.

Diagonally across from La Savane, you can catch the ferries for the 20-minute run across the bay to Pointe du Bout and the beaches at Anse-Mitan and Anse-à-l'Ane. It's relatively cheap as well as stress-free—much safer, more pleasant, and faster than by car.

The most imposing historic site in Fort-de-France is **Ft. St-Louis**, which runs along the east side of La Savane. Now a military installation, it's closed to the public.

Le Musée Régional d'Histoire et d'Ethnographie. This museum is best undertaken at the beginning of your vacation, so you can better understand the history, background, and people of the island. Housed in an elaborate former residence (circa 1888) with balconies and fretwork, the museum displays some of the garish gold jewelry that prostitutes wore after emancipation as well as the sorts of rooms that a proper, middle-class Martinican would have lived in. Oil paintings, engravings, and old historical documents also help sketch out the island's culture. ✉ *10 bd. Général de Gaulle* ☎ *0596/72–81–87* 💷 *€3* 🕙 *Mon. and Wed.–Fri. 8:30–5, Tues. 2–5, Sat. 8:30–noon.*

Rue Victor Schoelcher. Stores sell Paris fashions and French perfume, china, crystal, and liqueurs, as well as local handicrafts along this street running through the center of the capital's primary shopping district, a six-block area bounded by rue de la République, rue de la Liberté, rue Victor Severe, and rue Victor Hugo.

St-Louis Cathedral. This Romanesque cathedral with lovely stained-glass windows was built in 1878, the sixth church on this site (the others were destroyed by fires, hurricanes, and earthquakes). ✉ *Rue Victor Schoelcher, Schoelcher* 🕙 *Dawn to dusk.*

ELSEWHERE ON MARTINIQUE
BALATA

This quiet little town has two sights worth visiting. Built in 1923 to commemorate those Martinicans who fought and died in World War I, **Balata Church** is an exact replica of Paris's Sacré-Coeur Basilica. The gardens, **Jardin de Balata,** are lovely.

Jardin de Balata (*Balata Gardens*). The Jardin de Balata has thousands of varieties of tropical flowers and plants; its owner is a dedicated horticulturist. There are shaded benches from which to take in the mountain views and a plantation-style house furnished with period furniture. An aerial path gives visitors an astounding, bird's-eye view of the gardens and surrounding hills, from wooden walkways suspended 50 feet in the air. There is no restaurant, though beverages are for sale. This worthy site shows why Martinique is called the Island of Flowers. It's 15 minutes from Fort-de-France, in the direction of St-Pierre. You can order anthuriums and other tropical flowers to be delivered to the airport from the mesmerizing flower boutique here. ■TIP➔ **The gardens close at 6, but the ticket office will not admit anyone after 4:30.** ✉ *Km 10, Rte. de Balata* ☎ *0596/64–48–73* ⊕ *www.jardindebalata.fr* 💷 *€12.50* 🕙 *Daily 9–6.*

ST-PIERRE

The rise and fall of St-Pierre is one of the most remarkable stories in the Caribbean. Martinique's modern history began here in 1635. By the turn of the 20th century St-Pierre was a flourishing city of 30,000, known as the Paris of the West Indies. As many as 30 ships at a time stood at anchor. By 1902 it was the most modern town in the Caribbean, with electricity, phones, and a tram. On May 8, 1902, two thunderous explosions rent the air. As Mont Pelée erupted, it split in half, belching forth a cloud of burning ash, poisonous gas, and lava that raced down the mountain at 250 mph. At 3,600°F, the flow instantly vaporized everything in its path; 30,000 people were killed in two minutes.

The **Cyparis Express,** a small tourist train, will take you around to the main sights with running narrative (in French) for a half hour on Saturday, an hour on weekdays, for €10 (€5 for children).

An Office du Tourisme is on the seafront promenade. Stroll the main streets and check the blackboards at the sidewalk cafés before deciding where to lunch. At night some places have live music. Like stage sets for a dramatic opera, there are the ruins of the island's first church (built in 1640), the imposing theater, and the toppled statues. This city, situated on its naturally beautiful harbor and with its narrow, winding streets, has the feel of a European seaside hill town, and many of the historic buildings need work. With every footstep you touch a page of history. There is now a recommendable small hotel on the Bay as well as new ferry service between the town and Guadeloupe. As much potential as it has, this is one place in Martinique where real estate is cheap—for obvious reasons.

Fodor'sChoice
★ **Depaz Distillery.** An excursion to Depaz Distillery is one of the best things to do on the island. Established in 1651, it sits at the foot of the volcano. After a devastating eruption in 1902, the fields of blue cane were replanted, and in time, the rum-making began all over again. A self-guided tour includes the workers' gingerbread cottages. The tasting room sells its rums, including golden and aged rum, and liqueurs made from orange, ginger, and basil, among other flavors, that can enhance your cooking. Unfortunately, the plantation's great house, or château, is currently closed, and there's no projected date for completion. The restaurant **Le Moulin a Canne** (☏ 0596/69–80–44), open only for lunch, has both Creole specialties and some French classics on the menu, plus—you guessed it—Depaz rum to wash it down. ■**TIP**➔ **Shutters are drawn at the tasting room and the staff leaves at exactly 5 pm (or 4 on Saturday), so plan to be there at least an hour before.** ✉ *Mont Pelée Plantation* ☏ *0596/78–13–14* ⊕ *www.depazrhum.com* 🎫 *Distillery free* ⏱ *Weekdays 10–5, Sat. 9–4.*

Le Centre de Découverte des Sciences de la Terre. If you want to know more about volcanoes, earthquakes, and hurricanes, check out Le Centre de Découverte des Sciences de la Terre. Housed in a sleek building that looks like a dramatic white box, this earth-science museum has high-tech exhibits and interesting films. Watch the documentary on the volcanoes in the Antilles, highlighting the eruption of the nearby Mont Pelée. This site has fascinating summer programs on Wednesday on dance, food, and ecotourism. ■**TIP**➔ **The Depaz Distillery is nearby, and it's easy to visit both on the same day.** ✉ *Habitation Perinelle* ☏ *0596/52–82–42* ⊕ *cdst.e-monsite.com* 🎫 *€5* ⏱ *Sept.–June, Tues.–Sun. 9–5; July and Aug., Tues.–Sun. 10–6.*

FAMILY Musée Vulcanologique Frank Perret. For those interested in Mont Pelée's eruption of 1902, the Musée Vulcanologique Frank Perret is a must. It was established in 1933 by Frank Perret, a noted American volcanologist. The museum houses photographs of the old town, documents, and a number of relics—some gruesome—excavated from the ruins, including molten glass, melted iron, and contorted clocks stopped at 8 am. An English-speaking guide is often available. ✉ *Rue Victor Hugo* ☏ *0596/78–15–16* 🎫 *€3* ⏱ *Daily 9–5.*

BEACHES

Anse-Mitan. There are often yachts moored offshore in these calm waters. This long stretch of beach can be particularly fun on Sunday. Small, family-owned seaside restaurants are half-hidden among palm trees and are footsteps from the lapping waves. Nearly all offer grilled lobster and some form of music on weekends, perhaps a zouk band. Inexpensive waterfront hotels line the clean, golden beach, which has excellent snorkeling just offshore. Chaise longues are available for rent from hotels for about €7, and there are also usually vendors on weekends. When you get to Pointe du Bout, take a left at the yellow office of Budget Rent-A-Car, then the next left up a hill, and park near the little white church. **Amenities:** food and drink. **Best for:** partiers; snorkeling; swimming; walking. ⊠ *Pointe du Bout, Les Trois-Ilets.*

FAMILY **Les Salines.** A short drive south of Ste-Anne brings you to a mile-long (1.5-km-long) cove lined with soft white sand and coconut palms. The beach is awash with families and children during holidays and on weekends, but quiet during the week. The far end—away from the makeshift souvenir shops—is most appealing. The calm waters are safe for swimming, even for the kids. You can snorkel, but it's not that memorable. Food vendors roam the sand, and there are also pizza stands and simple seafood restaurants. From Le Marin, take the coastal road toward Ste-Anne. You will see signs for Les Salines. If you see the sign for Pointe du Marin, you have gone too far. **Amenities:** food and drink; parking; showers; toilets. **Best for:** partiers; swimming; walking. ⊠ *Ste-Anne.*

FAMILY **Pointe du Bout.** The beaches here are small, man-made, and lined with resorts. Each little strip is associated with its resident hotel, and security guards and closed gates make access difficult. However, if you take a left across from the main pedestrian entrance to the marina—after the taxi stand—then go left again, you will reach the beach for Hotel Bakoua, which has especially nice facilities and several options for lunch and drinks. If things are quiet—particularly during the week—one of the beach boys may rent you a chaise; otherwise, just plop your beach towel down, face forward, and enjoy the delightful view of the Fort-de-France skyline. The water is dead calm and quite shallow, but it eventually drops off if you swim out a bit. **Amenities:** food and drink; showers. **Best for:** snorkeling; sunset; swimming. ⊠ *Pointe du Bout, Les Trois-Ilets.*

SHOPPING

French fragrances, designer scarves and sunglasses, fine china and crystal, leather goods, wine (amazingly inexpensive at supermarkets), and liquor are all good buys in Fort-de-France. Purchases are further sweetened by the 20% discount on luxury items when paid for with certain credit cards. Among the items produced on the island, look for *bijoux creole* (local jewelry, such as hoop earrings and heavy bead necklaces), white and dark rum, and handcrafted straw goods, pottery, and tapestries.

The area around the cathedral in Fort-de-France has a number of small shops that carry luxury goods. Of particular note are the shops on rue Victor Hugo, rue Moreau de Jones, rue Antoine Siger, and rue Lamartine. The **Galleries Lafayette** department store on rue Schoelcher in downtown Fort-de-France sells everything from perfume to pâté.

ACTIVITIES

FISHING

Deep-sea fishing expeditions in these waters hunt down tuna, barracuda, dolphin fish, kingfish, and bonito, and the big ones—white and blue marlins. You can hire boats from the bigger marinas, particularly in Pointe du Bout, Le Marin, and Le François; most hotels arrange these Hemingway-esque trysts, but will often charge a premium. If you call several days in advance, companies can also put you together with other anglers to keep costs down.

Centre de Peche. This fully loaded Davis 47-foot fishing boat has become a legend in the Caribbean. In recent years, she has won many of the sportfishing competitions, from Trinidad and Tobago to the B.V.I. Her skipper, Captain Yves Pelisson, has been fishing out of Martinique since 1982; he knows how to find the billfish, including the prized blue marlin. Depending on the season, a catch might include tuna, dolphinfish, and sailfish. Yves speaks English fluently and is one fun guy, too. The boat goes out with a minimum of five anglers for a half day or full day, which includes lunch. Non-anglers can come for the ride for about half the price. ⊠ *Port de Plaisance, bd. Allègre, Le Marin* ☎ *0596/76–24–20, 0696/28–80–58* ⊕ *www.sailfish-marlin.com.*

GOLF

Golf de l'Impératrice Josephine. The 18-hole Le Golf de l'Impératrice Josephine is named in honor of Empress Joséphine Napoléon, whose birthplace, La Pagerie, adjoins this 150-acre track of rolling hills. Completely American in design, the par-71 Robert Trent Jones course comes with an English-speaking pro, a pro shop, a bar, and an especially good restaurant. (You can finish your visit here with foie gras or a full meal, being mesmerized by the turquoise waters all the while.)

The club offers special greens fees to cruise-ship passengers. Public greens fees are €30 for 9 holes and €45 for 18; a cart costs another €25 for 9, €40 for 18. Ask about weekly rates. For those who don't mind walking while admiring the Caribbean view between the palm trees, club trolleys (called "chariots") are €6 for 18 holes, €4 for nine. There are no caddies. ⊠ *Les Trois-Ilets* ☎ *0596/52–04–13.*

HIKING

Parc Naturel Régional de la Martinique. Two-thirds of Martinique is designated as protected land. Trails, all 31 of them, are well marked and maintained. At the beginning of each, a notice is posted advising on the level of difficulty, the duration of a hike, and any interesting facts. The Parc Naturel Régional de la Martinique organizes inexpensive guided excursions year-round. If there have been heavy rains, though, give it up. The tangle of ferns, bamboo trees, and vines is dramatic, but during rainy season, the wet, muddy trails will temper your enthusiasm. ⊠ *9 bd. Général de Gaulle, Fort-de-France* ☎ *0596/64–42–59 Secretary, 0596/64–45–64 Communication Department.*

HORSEBACK RIDING

Horseback-riding excursions can traverse scenic beaches, palm-shaded forests, sugarcane fields, and a variety of other tropical landscapes. Trained guides often include running commentaries on the history, flora, and fauna of the island.

Ranch de Caps. Some guides are English-speaking at Ranch de Caps, where you can take a half-day ride (Western saddle) on the wild southern beaches and across the countryside for €45. These beautiful, deserted beaches can't be reached by car. Guides will allow those who are capable to gallop. Rides go out in the morning (8:30 to noon) and afternoon (1:30 to 5) every day but Monday. If you can manage a full day in the saddle, it costs €75 and includes lunch. Seasoned riders may even want to attempt the two-day trip (€160).

A real treat is the full-moon ride, but it needs to accrue a group of 10. Most of the 20 mounts are Anglo-Arabs. Riders are encouraged to help cool and wash their horses at day's end. Reserve in advance. Riders of all levels are welcomed. ⊠ *Cap Macré, Le Marin* ☎ *0596/74–70–65, 0696/23–18–18* ⊕ *www.ranchdescaps.com.*

Ranch Jack. Ranch Jack has a large stable of some 30 horses. Its trail rides (English-style) cross some beautiful country for €36 for two hours; half-day excursions for €54 (€62 with transfers from nearby hotels) go through the fields and forests to the beach. Short rides can range from €16 to €25. They also have a wonderful program to introduce kids ages 3–7 to horses. ⊠ *Morne habitué, Trois-Ilets* ☎ *0596/68–37–69, 0696/92–26–58* ✎ *ranch.jack@wanadoo.fr.*

WHERE TO EAT

$$ ✕ **Mille & Une Brindilles.** At this trendy salon you can order anything from CAFÉ a glass of wine to an aromatic pot of tea in flavors like vanilla or mango. You'll find a litany of tapenades, olive cakes, and flans on the prix-fixe menu. Fred, the bubbly Parisian who is both chef and proprietress, is the queen of terrines, and she can make a delicious tart (like Roquefort and pear) or pâté out of any vegetable or fish. The Saturday brunch (€22) is a very social occasion. The best-ever desserts, such as the Amadéus—as appealing as the classical music that plays—and *moelleux au chocolat,* are what you would want served at your last meal on Earth. Look for the sign on the left side, since this place is easy to miss. ⑤ *Average main: €18* ⊠ *27 rte. de Didier, Didier, Fort-de-France* ☎ *0596/71–75–61* ⊟ *No credit cards* ⊘ *Closed Sun. and Wed. No dinner.*

MONTEGO BAY, JAMAICA

Catherine
MacGillivray

Today many explorations of MoBay are conducted from a reclining chair—frothy drink in hand—on Doctor's Cave Beach. As home of Jamaica's busiest cruise pier and the north-shore airport, Montego

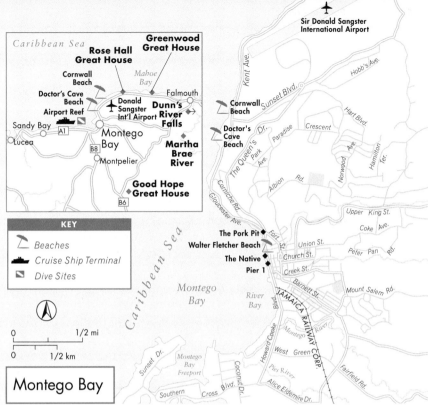

Montego Bay

Bay—or MoBay—is the first taste most visitors have of the island. Travelers from around the world come and go in this bustling community, which ranks as Jamaica's second-largest city. The name Montego is derived from *manteca* (lard in Spanish). The Spanish first named this Bahía de Manteca, or Lard Bay. Why? The Spanish once shipped hogs from this port city. Jamaican tourism began here in 1924, when the first resort opened at Doctor's Cave Beach so that health-seekers could "take the waters." If you can pull yourself away from the water's edge and brush the sand off your toes, you can find some interesting colonial sights in the surrounding area.

ESSENTIALS

CURRENCY
The Jamaican dollar, but U.S. dollars are widely accepted.

TELEPHONE
Public telephones (and faxes) are at the communications center at the Montego Bay Cruise Terminal. Travelers also find public phones in major Montego Bay malls, such as the City Centre Shopping Mall. Some U.S. phone companies won't permit credit-card calls to be placed from Jamaica because they've been victims of fraud, so collect calls are often the top option. GSM cell phones equipped with tri-band or world-roaming service will find coverage throughout the Montego Bay region.

COMING ASHORE

Ships dock at the Montego Cruise Terminal, operated by the Port Authority of Jamaica. West of Montego Bay, the cruise terminal has five berths and accommodates both cruise and cargo shipping. The terminal has shops, a communications center, a visitor information booth, and a taxi stand supervised by the Port Authority of Jamaica. The cruise port in Montego Bay is not within walking distance of the heart of town; however, there's one shopping center (the Freeport Shopping Centre) within walking distance of the docks. If you just want to visit a beach, then Doctor's Cave or the Cornwall Bathing Beach, both public beaches, are good nearby alternatives, and they are right in town.

From the Montego Cruise Terminal both taxis and shuttle buses take passengers downtown. Taxi service is about $5 each way to downtown. Expect to pay $5 per person each way by shuttle bus to the two crafts markets, the City Centre Shopping Mall, Margaritaville, or Doctor's Cave Beach. A day pass for the shuttle bus is $15 and allows passengers to get on and off as they wish. Jamaica is one place in the Caribbean where it's usually to your advantage to take an organized shore excursion offered by your ship unless you just want to do a bit of shopping in town. Private taxis and other transportation providers aren't particularly cheap, and a full-day tour for a small group will run $150 to $180; however, road conditions and travel time have improved significantly with the completion of the North Coast Highway.

If you take a private taxi, you should know that rates are per car, not per passenger. You can flag cabs on the street. All licensed and properly insured taxis display red Public Passenger Vehicle (PPV) license plates. Licensed minivans also bear the red PPV plates. If you hire a taxi driver as a tour guide, be sure to agree on a price before the vehicle is put into gear. Car-rental fees in Jamaica include the cost of insurance. It is not difficult to rent a car, but driving in Jamaica is done on the left side of the road, and it can take a little getting used to.

EXPLORING MONTEGO BAY

Fodor's Choice
★
Dunn's River Falls. One of Jamaica's most popular attractions is an eye-catching sight: 600 feet of cold, clear mountain water splashing over a series of stone steps to the warm Caribbean. The best way to enjoy the falls is to climb the slippery steps: don a swimsuit, take the hand of the person ahead of you, and trust that the chain of hands and bodies leads to an experienced guide. The leaders of the climbs are personable fellows who reel off bits of local lore while telling you where to step; you can hire a guide's service for a few dollars' tip. After the climb, you exit through a crowded market, another reminder that this is one of Jamaica's top tourist attractions. If you can, try to schedule a visit on a day when no cruise ships are in port. ■ TIP➔ Always climb with a licensed guide at Dunn's River Falls. Freelance guides might be a little cheaper, but the experienced guides can tell you just where to plant each footstep—helping you prevent a fall. ⊠ Off Rte. A1, between St. Ann's Bay and Ocho Rios, Ocho Rios ☎ 876/974–4767 ⊕ www.dunnsriverfallsja.com ⊠ $20 ⊘ Daily 8:30–5 (last entry at 4).

Greenwood Great House. Unlike Rose Hall, Greenwood has no spooky legend to titillate, but it's much better than Rose Hall at evoking life on a sugar plantation. The Barrett family, from whom the English poet Elizabeth Barrett Browning descended, once owned all the land from Rose Hall to Falmouth; on their vast holdings they built this and several other great houses. (The poet's father, Edward Moulton Barrett, "the Tyrant of Wimpole Street," was born at nearby Cinnamon Hill, later the estate of country singer Johnny Cash.) Highlights of Greenwood include oil paintings of the Barretts, china made for the family by Wedgwood, a library filled with rare books from as early as 1697, fine antique furniture, and a collection of exotic musical instruments. There's a pub on-site as well. It's 15 miles (24 km) east of Montego Bay. ✉ *Greenwood* ☎ *876/953–1077* ⊕ *www.greenwoodgreathouse.com* ✈ *$20* ⊙ *Daily 9–6 (last tour at 5).*

Martha Brae River. This gentle waterway about 25 miles (40 km) southeast of Montego Bay takes its name from an Arawak woman who killed herself because she refused to reveal the whereabouts of a local gold mine. According to legend, she agreed to take her Spanish interrogators there and, on reaching the river, used magic to change its course, drowning herself and the greedy Spaniards with her. Her *duppy* (ghost) is said to guard the mine's entrance. Rafting on this river is a very popular activity—many operators are on hand to take you for a glide downstream.

Fodor's Choice ★ Rose Hall. In the 1700s it may well have been one of the greatest great houses in the West Indies. Today it's popular less for its architecture than for the legend surrounding its second mistress, Annie Palmer. As the story goes, Annie was born in 1802 in England to an English mother and Irish father. When she was 10, her family moved to Haiti, and soon her parents died of yellow fever. Annie was adopted by a Haitian voodoo priestess and soon became skilled in the practice of witchcraft. Annie moved to Jamaica, married, and became mistress of Rose Hall, an enormous plantation spanning 6,600 acres with more than 2,000 slaves. You can take a spooky nighttime tour of the property and then have a drink at the White Witch pub, located in the great house's cellar. ✉ *North Coast Hwy., St. James* ✛ *15 miles (24 km) east of Montego Bay* ☎ *876/953–2323* ⊕ *www.rosehall.com* ✈ *$20* ⊙ *Sat.–Thurs. 9:15–5:15 and 6–10, Fri. 9:15–5:15 and 8:30 pm–10:30 pm.*

MONTEGO BAY BEST BETS

■ **Doctor's Cave Beach.** This public beach club is right in the heart of Montego Bay.

■ **Dunn's River Falls.** A visit to the falls is touristy but still exhilarating.

■ **Martha Brae Rafting.** A slow rafting trip down the river is relaxing and very enjoyable.

■ **Shopping.** MoBay has several good shopping centers, as well as bustling craft markets.

■ **Rose Hall Greathouse.** The island's most visited greathouse offers a peek back into the days of the plantations.

7

BEACHES

FAMILY **Doctor's Cave Bathing Club.** Montego Bay's tourist scene has its roots right on the "Hip Strip," the bustling entertainment district along Gloucester Avenue. Here, a sea cave whose waters were said to have healing powers drew travelers from around the world. Although the cave was destroyed by a hurricane long ago, the beach is always busy and has a perpetual spring-break feel. The clubhouse has changing rooms, showers, a gift shop, a restaurant, and free Wi-Fi. You can rent beach chairs and umbrellas. Its location within the Montego Bay Marine Park—with protected coral reefs and plenty of marine life—makes it a good spot for snorkeling. Glass-bottom boat rides are offered at the beach. **Amenities:** food and drink; lifeguards; parking (fee); showers; toilets; water sports. **Best for:** partiers; snorkeling; swimming; sunsets. ✉ *Gloucester Ave.* ☎ *876/952–2566* 🌐 *www.doctorscavebathingclub.com* 🎟 *$6.*

FAMILY **Walter Fletcher Beach.** Although it's not as pretty as Doctor's Cave Beach, Walter Fletcher Beach is home to Aquasol Theme Park, which offers a large beach (with lifeguards and security personnel), glass-bottom boats, snorkeling, go-kart racing, a skating rink at night, and a bar and restaurant. Near the center of town, the beach has unusually fine swimming; the calm waters make it a good bet for children. **Amenities:** food and drink; lifeguards; parking; showers; toilets; water sports; **Best for:** partiers; snorkeling; sunset; swimming. ✉ *Gloucester Ave.* ☎ *876/979–9447* 🎟 *J$350* 🕒 *Daily 9–6.*

SHOPPING

Jamaican artisans express themselves in silk-screening, wood carvings, resort wear, hand-loomed fabrics, and paintings. Jamaican rum makes a great gift, as do Tia Maria (the famous coffee liqueur) and Blue Mountain coffee. Wood carvings are one of the top purchases; the finest carvings are made from the Jamaican national tree, lignum vitae, or tree of life, a dense wood that talented carvers transform into dolphins, heads, or fish. Bargaining is expected with crafts vendors.

ACTIVITIES

GOLF

Golfers appreciate both the beauty and the challenges offered by Jamaica's courses. Caddies are almost always mandatory throughout the island, and rates are $15 to $45 per round of golf. Cart rentals are available at most courses; costs are $20 to $40. Some of the best courses in the country are found near MoBay.

Half Moon Golf Course. This Robert Trent Jones–designed 18-hole course is the home of the Jamaica Open. The nonguest cost is $181, which includes greens fees, cart, and caddy for 18 holes, and $118.20 for 9 holes. The course is also the home of the Half Moon Golf Academy, which offers one-day sessions, multiday retreats, and hour-long private sessions. ✉ *Half Moon, North Coast Hwy., 7 miles (11 km) east of Montego Bay* ☎ *876/953–2560* 🌐 *www.halfmoon.com.*

Hilton Rose Hall Resort & Spa. Four miles (6 km) east of the airport, Hilton Rose Hall Resort & Spa hosts several invitational tournaments. Green fees run $149 for guests, $169 for nonguests, and $109 for a twilight round of nine holes at the 18-hole championship **Cinnamon Hill Golf Course.** The course was designed by Robert von Hagge and Rick Baril (the designers of the White Witch course at the Ritz-Carlton) and is adjacent to historic Cinnamon Hill. ⊠ *North Coast Hwy., 15 miles (24 km) east of Montego Bay, St. James* ☎ *876/953–2650* ⊕ *www.cinnamonhilljamaica.com.*

> **BINOCULARS**
>
> Binoculars are as useful indoors as they are outside. You might think they are only for bringing far-off wildlife and sights within view, but take them into museums, churches, and other buildings to examine the details of artwork, sculptures, and architectural elements.

RIVER RAFTING

Jamaica's many rivers mean a multitude of freshwater experiences, from mild to wild. Jamaica's first tourist activity off the beaches was relaxing rafting trips aboard bamboo rafts poled by local boatmen. Recently, soft-adventure enthusiasts have also been able to opt for white-water action as well with guided tours through several operators.

Fodor's Choice ★ Bamboo rafting in Jamaica originated on the **Rio Grande,** a river in the Port Antonio area. Jamaicans had long used the bamboo rafts to transport bananas downriver; decades ago actor and Port Antonio resident Errol Flynn saw the rafts and thought they'd make a good tourist attraction, and local entrepreneurs quickly rose to the occasion. Today the slow rides are a favorite with romantic travelers and anyone looking to get off the beach for a few hours. The popularity of the Rio Grande's trips spawned similar trips down the **Martha Brae River,** about 25 miles (40 km) from MoBay. Near Ocho Rios, the **Great River** has lazy river rafting as well as energetic kayaking.

Jamaica Tours Limited. This big tour company conducts raft trips down at Martha Brae, approximately 12 miles (19 km) east of MoBay; the excursion can include lunch if requested. Bookings can be made through hotel tour desks. Price depends on the number of people on the trip and your pickup location. ⊠ *Providence Dr.* ☎ *876/953–3700* ⊕ *www.jamaicatoursltd.com.*

River Raft Ltd. This company leads trips down the Martha Brae River, about 25 miles (40 km) from most hotels in Mo'Bay. The cost is $60 per person for the 1½-hour river run. ⊠ *Martha Brae* ☎ *876/940–6398* ⊕ *www.jamaicarafting.com.*

WHERE TO EAT

$$ ✕ **Margaritaville Montego Bay.** Along Montego Bay's Hip Strip, this colorful restaurant is a favorite spot thanks to its 110-foot waterslide into the sea, two water trampolines, and a sunset deck. When it's time to settle down for lunch, the menu offers some Caribbean-influenced items such as jerk burgers and conch fritters, along with lots of all-American fare. ⑤ *Average main: $20* ⊠ *Gloucester Ave.* ☎ *876/952–4777.*

ECLECTIC

$ JAMAICAN   Fodor's Choice   ★

$ ✕ **Pork Pit.** A favorite with many Mo'Bay locals, this no-frills eatery serves Jamaican specialties including some fiery jerk—note that it's spiced to local tastes, not watered down for tourists. Many people get their food to go, but you can also eat at picnic tables. ⑤ *Average main: $10* ⊠ *27 Gloucester Ave.* ☎ *876/940–3008.*

NASSAU, BAHAMAS

Jessica
Robertson

Nassau, the capital of the Bahamas, has witnessed Spanish invasions and hosted pirates, who made it their headquarters for raids along the Spanish Main. The heritage of old Nassau blends the Southern charm of British loyalists from the Carolinas, the African tribal traditions of freed slaves, and a bawdy history of blockade-running during the Civil War and rum-running in the Roaring 1920s. The sheltered harbor bustles with cruise-ship hubbub, while a block away, broad, shop-lined Bay Street is alive with commercial activity. Over it all is a subtle layer of civility and sophistication, derived from three centuries of British rule. Nassau's charm, however, is often lost in its commercialism. There's excellent shopping, but if you look past the duty-free shops you'll also find sights of historical significance that are worth seeing.

ESSENTIALS

CURRENCY

The Bahamian dollar, which is on par with U.S. dollar, but U.S. dollars are widely accepted.

TELEPHONE

Pay phones accept Bahamas Direct Prepaid cards purchased from BTC at vending machines, stores, and BTC offices. You can use these cards to call within the country or to the United States. Although most U.S. cell phones work in the Bahamas, the roaming coast can be very high, so check with your provider in advance.

COMING ASHORE

Cruise ships dock at one of three piers on Prince George Wharf. Taxi drivers who meet the ships may offer you a $2 "ride into town," but the historic government buildings and duty-free shops lie just steps from the dock area. As you leave the pier, look for a tall pink tower—diagonally across from here is the tourist information office. Stop in for maps of the island and downtown Nassau. On most days you can join a one-hour walking tour ($10 per person) conducted by a well-trained guide. Tours generally start every hour on the hour from 10 am to 4 pm; confirm the day's schedule in the office. Just outside, an ATM dispenses U.S. dollars.

As you disembark from your ship, you will find a row of taxis and air-conditioned limousines. Fares are fixed by the government by zones. Unless you plan to jump all over the island, taxis are the most convenient way to get around. The fare is $9 plus $1 bridge toll between downtown Nassau and Paradise Island, $20 from Cable Beach to Paradise Island (plus $1 toll), and $18 from Cable Beach to Nassau. Fares are for two passengers; each additional passenger is $3. It's customary to tip taxi drivers 15%.

Nassau, Bahamas

KEY	
⌐	Beach
▰▰	Ferry Lines
▐	Cruise Ship Terminal

300 yards
300 meters

Silver Cay

Lighthouse

Paradise Island

Paradise Beach

Nassau Harbour

Paradise Lake

Atlantis Paradise Island Resort

Casuarina Dr.

Paradise Beach Dr.

Casino Dr.

Comfort Suites Paradise Island

Paradise Is. Dr.

Harbor Dr.

TO PARADISE ISLAND

GOLF COURSE

Cabbage Beach

Paradise Island Bridge

Potter's Cay

Fort Montagu

Lake Waterloo

East Bay St.

John Evans

Sutton St.

Kemp Rd

St. James Rd.

Church St.

Mackey St.

Mount Royal Ave.

Montrose Ave.

Madeira St.

Rosetta St.

Collins Ave.

North St.

Queen's Staircase

East St.

Shirley St.

Dowdeswell St.

Bay St.

Sands Rd.

Elizabeth Ave.

Parliament Square

Parliament St.

Frederick St.

Woodes Rogers Walk

Prince George Wharf

Union Dock

John Alfred Wharf

East Hill St.

Duke St.

King St.

George St.

Cumberland Rd.

Marlborough St.

West Hill St.

Delancy St.

National Art Gallery of the Bahamas

Nassau St.

Junkaroo Beach

Paradise Beach

Meeting St.

Hospital Lane

Blue Hill Rd

King St.

Market St.

West St.

Infant View Rd.

West Bay St.

Ardastra Gardens

Fort Charlotte

Arawak Cay

TO CABLE BEACH

Water taxis travel between Prince George Wharf and Paradise Island during daylight hours at half-hour intervals. The one-way cost is $3 per person, and the trip takes 12 minutes.

EXPLORING NASSAU

Shops angle for tourist dollars with fine imported goods at duty-free prices, yet you will find a handful of stores overflowing with authentic Bahamian crafts, foods, and other delights. Most of Nassau's historic sites are centered on downtown.

With its thoroughly revitalized downtown—the revamped British Colonial Hilton lead the way—Nassau is recapturing some of its glamour. Nevertheless, modern influence is apparent: fancy restaurants, suave clubs, and trendy coffeehouses have popped up everywhere. This trend comes partly in response to the burgeoning uppercrust crowds that now supplement the spring-breakers and cruise passengers who have traditionally flocked to Nassau.

> **NASSAU BEST BETS**
>
> ■ **Ardastra Gardens.** Flocks of flamingos, the country's national bird, "march" in three shows daily (you can mingle with the flamboyant pink stars afterward).
>
> ■ **Atlantis.** Though very costly, the water park here is a must for families.
>
> ■ **Shopping.** To many, shopping is one of Nassau's great delights.
>
> ■ **Junkanoo Beach.** Head to this beach (aka Long Wharf Beach) and sit in the shade of a coconut palm (it's a 10-minute walk from the duty-free shops on Bay Street).

Today the seedy air of the town's not-so-distant past is almost unrecognizable. Petty crime is no greater than in other towns of this size, and the streets not only look cleaner but feel safer. You can still find a wild club or a rowdy bar, but you can also sip cappuccino while viewing contemporary Bahamian art or dine by candlelight beneath prints of old Nassau, serenaded by soft, island-inspired calypso music.

Arawak Cay. Known to Nassau residents as "The Fish Fry," Arawak Cay is one of the best places to knock back a Kalik beer, chat with locals, watch or join in a fast-paced game of dominoes, or sample traditional Bahamian fare. You can get small dishes such as conch fritters or full meals at one of the pastel-color waterside shacks. Order a fried snapper served up with a sweet homemade roll, or fresh conch salad (a spicy mixture of chopped conch—just watching the expert chopping is a show as good as any in town—mixed with diced onions, cucumbers, tomatoes, and hot peppers in a lime marinade). The two-story Twin Brothers and Goldie's Enterprises are two of the most popular places. Try their fried "cracked conch" and Goldie's famous Sky Juice (a sweet but potent gin, coconut-water, and sweet-milk concoction sprinkled with nutmeg). Local fairs and craft shows are often held in the adjacent field. ⊠ *W. Bay St. and Chippingham Rd., Paradise Island.*

FAMILY **Ardastra Gardens, Zoo, and Conservation Centre.** Marching flamingos? These national birds give a parading performance at Ardastra daily at 10:30, 2:10, and 4:10. The brilliant pink birds are a delight—especially

CLOSE UP

Saving on Atlantis

Frugal cruisers have long known about **Comfort Suites Paradise Island** (⊕ www.comfortsuitespi.com), which is right across the street from the Atlantis Resort. They use it to avoid paying for expensive and limited ship-sponsored day-passes to the resort, which cost well over $150 per person. Book a room here, and everyone in the room (up to four people, regardless of age) is entitled to a free day-pass to the Atlantis Resort's water park. In addition to the base rate (often more than $300 for two adults and two children depending on the season), you will also have to pay (at check-in) an additional energy surcharge of $15.95 per *adult* and a housekeeper gratuity of $5 per *adult* on top of the quoted rate, even if you prepay for the room; the third and fourth person cost $40 each *plus* all the service charges (sometimes kids

are free, sometimes not). Frankly, this isn't as good a deal as it used to be, but families or groups of four can still save money by going this route, and then you will have a room in which to shower and change before returning to the ship. Of course, it's a better deal if you can get a discounted rate. (Be aware that you may not have more than four people on a single reservation regardless of their age, and you may not get access to the room in the morning, but it will be ready when you get back from your day of fun at the water park, and the room rate includes free Wi-Fi.) When it's time for lunch, you'll find cheaper restaurants within walking distance of Atlantis. You can also book your room and day-pass through the Barbados-based travel agency that operates ⊕ CaribbeanDaypass.com.

7

for children, who can walk among the flamingos after the show. The zoo, with more than 5 acres of tropical greenery and ponds, also has an aviary of rare tropical birds including the bright green Bahama parrot, native Bahamian creatures such as rock iguanas and the little (and harmless) Bahamian boa constrictors, and a global collection of small animals. ⊠ *Chippingham Rd. south of W. Bay St., Paradise Island* ☎ *242/323–5806* ⊕ *www.ardastra.com* ✉ *$16* ☾ *Daily 9–5.*

FAMILY **Fort Charlotte.** Built in 1788, this imposing fort comes complete with a waterless moat, drawbridge, ramparts, and a dungeon, where children love to see the torture device where prisoners were "stretched." Young local guides bring the fort to life. (Tips are expected.) Lord Dunmore, who built it, named the massive structure in honor of George III's wife. At the time, some called it Dunmore's Folly because of the staggering expense of its construction. It cost eight times more than was originally planned. (Dunmore's superiors in London were less than ecstatic with the high costs, but he managed to survive unscathed.) Ironically, no shots were ever fired in battle from the fort. The fort and its surrounding 100 acres offer a wonderful view of the cricket grounds, the beach, and the ocean beyond. ⊠ *W. Bay St. at Chippingham Rd., Paradise Island* ✉ *$5* ☾ *Tours daily 8–4.*

Fodor's Choice **National Art Gallery of the Bahamas.** Opened in July 2003, the museum
★ houses the works of esteemed Bahamian artists such as Max Taylor,

Amos Ferguson, Brent Malone, John Cox, and Antonius Roberts. The glorious Italianate-colonial mansion, built in 1860 and restored in the 1990s, has double-tiered verandas with elegant columns. It was the residence of Sir William Doyle, the first chief justice of the Bahamas. Don't miss the museum's gift shop, where you'll find books about the Bahamas as well as Bahamian quilts, prints, ceramics, jewelry, and crafts. ⊠ *West and W. Hill sts., across from St. Francis Xavier Cathedral, Nassau* ☎ *242/328–5800* ⊕ *www.nagb.org.bs* ☒ *$5* ☉ *Tues.–Sat. 10–4, Sun. 12–4.*

Parliament Square. Nassau is the seat of the national government. The Bahamian Parliament comprises two houses—a 16-member Senate (Upper House) and a 38-member House of Assembly (Lower House)—and a ministerial cabinet headed by a prime minister. If the House is in session, sit in to watch lawmakers debate. Parliament Square's pink, colonnaded government buildings were constructed in the late 1700s and early 1800s by Loyalists who came to the Bahamas from North Carolina. The square is dominated by a statue of a slim young Queen Victoria that was erected on her birthday, May 24, in 1905. In the immediate area are a handful of magistrates' courts. Behind the House of Assembly is the **Supreme Court.** Its four-times-a-year opening ceremonies (held the first weeks of January, April, July, and October) recall the wigs and mace-bearing pageantry of the Houses of Parliament in London. The Royal Bahamas Police Force Band is usually on hand for the event. ⊠ *Bay St., Nassau* ☎ *242/322–2041* ☒ *Free* ☉ *Weekdays 10–4.*

Queen's Staircase. A popular early-morning exercise regime for locals, the "66 Steps" (as Bahamians call them) are thought to have been carved out of a solid limestone cliff by slaves in the 1790s. The staircase was later named to honor Queen Victoria's reign. Pick up some souvenirs at the ad hoc straw market along the narrow road that leads to the site. ⊠ *Top of Elizabeth Ave. hill, south of Shirley St., Nassau.*

BEACHES

New Providence is blessed with stretches of white sand studded with palm and sea grape trees. Some of the beaches are small and crescent-shape; others stretch for miles.

FAMILY

Fodor's Choice
★

Cabbage Beach. At this beach you'll find 3 miles of white sand lined with shady casuarina trees, sand dunes, and sun worshippers. This is the place to go to rent Jet Skis or get a bird's-eye view of Paradise Island while parasailing. Hair braiders and T-shirt vendors stroll the beach, and hotel guests crowd the areas surrounding the resorts, including Atlantis. For peace and quiet, stroll east. **Amenities:** food and drink; lifeguards; parking (fee); water sports. **Best For:** solitude; partiers; swimming; walking. ⊠ *Paradise Island.*

Cable Beach. Hotels dot the length of this 3-mile beach, so don't expect isolation. Music from the hotel pool decks wafts out onto the sand, Jet Skis race up and down the waves, and vendors sell everything from shell jewelry to coconut drinks right from the shell. If you get tired of lounging around, join a game of beach volleyball. Access via new hotels may be limited, but join the locals and park at Goodman's Bay park on the eastern end of the beach. **Amenities:** parking (no fee); water sports. **Best for:** partiers; sunset; swimming; walking. ⊠ *Cable Beach*.

Junkanoo Beach. Right in downtown Nassau, this beach is spring-break central from late February through April. The man-made beach isn't the prettiest on the island, but it's conveniently located if you only have a few quick hours to catch a tan. Music is provided by bands, DJs, and guys with boom boxes; a few bars keep the drinks flowing. **Amenities:** food and drink; parking (no fee); toilets; water sports. **Best for:** partiers; swimming. ⊠ *Immediately west of the British Colonial Hilton, Nassau*.

SHOPPING

Most of Nassau's shops are on Bay Street between Rawson Square and the British Colonial Hotel, and on the side streets leading off Bay Street. Some stores are popping up on the main shopping thoroughfare's eastern end and just west of the Cable Beach strip. Bargains abound between Bay Street and the waterfront. Upscale stores can also be found in Marina Village and the Crystal Court at Atlantis and in the arcade joining the Sheraton Nassau Beach and the Wyndham on Cable Beach. You'll find duty-free prices—generally 25%–50% less than U.S. prices—on imported items such as crystal, linens, watches, cameras, jewelry, leather goods, and perfumes.

ACTIVITIES

FISHING

The waters here are generally smooth and alive with many species of game fish, which is one of the reasons why the Bahamas has more than 20 fishing tournaments open to visitors every year. A favorite spot just west of Nassau is the Tongue of the Ocean, so called because it looks like that part of the body when viewed from the air. The channel stretches for 100 miles. For boat rental, parties of two to six will pay $600 or so for a half-day, $1,600 for a full day.

Born Free Charters. This charter company has three boats and guarantees a catch on full-day charters—if you don't get a fish, you don't pay. ☎ 242/393–4144 ⊕ *www.bornfreefishing.com*.

Charter Boat Association. The Charter Boat Association has 15 boats available for fishing charters. ☎ *242/393–3739*.

GOLF

One & Only Ocean Club Golf Course. Designed by Tom Weiskopf, One & Only Ocean Club Golf Course (6,805 yards, par 72) is a championship course surrounded by the ocean on three sides, which means that winds can get stiff. Call to check on current availability and up-to-date prices (those not staying at Atlantis or the One & Only Ocean Club can play at management's discretion, and at a higher rate). ⊠ *Paradise Island Dr. next to airport, Paradise Island, New Providence Island* ☎ *242/363–3925, 800/321–3000 in U.S.* ⛳ *18 holes: $270; $180 after 1. Club rentals: $70* ⊙ *Daily 6 am–sundown*.

WHERE TO EAT

$ ✕ **The Green Parrot.** Two locations—

AMERICAN Green Parrot Harbourfront and Green Parrot Hurricane Hole— mean you get incomparable views of Nassau Harbour and a fresh breeze, whichever way the wind is blowing. The large Works Burger is a favorite at these casual, all-outdoor restaurants and bars. The menu includes burgers, wraps, quesadillas, and other simple but tasty dishes. The conch po'boy is a new favorite. The weekday happy hour from 5–9 and a DJ on Friday nights draw a lively local crowd. $ *Average main: $20* ⊠ *E. Bay St., west of the bridges to Paradise Island, Nassau* ☎ *242/322–9248, 242/363–3633* ⊕ *www.greenparrotbar.com.*

> **CAUTION**
>
> Mail overflowing your mailbox is a neon sign to thieves that you aren't home. Have someone pick it up, or better yet, have the post office hold all your mail for you.

NEVIS (CHARLESTOWN)

Jordan Simon   In 1493, when Columbus spied a cloud-crowned volcanic isle during his second voyage to the New World, he named it Nieves—the Spanish word for "snows"—because it reminded him of the peaks of the Pyrenees. Nevis rises from the water in an almost perfect cone, the tip of its 3,232-foot central mountain hidden by clouds. Even less developed than sister island St. Kitts—2 miles (3 km) away at their closest point, Nevis is known for its long beaches with white and black sand, its lush greenery, the charming if slightly dilapidated Georgian capital of Charlestown, mountain hikes, and its restored sugar plantations that now house charming inns. Even on a day trip Nevis feels relaxed and quietly upscale. You might run into celebrities at the Four Seasons or lunching at the beach bars on Pinney's, the showcase strand. Yet Nevisians (not to mention the significant expat American and British presence) never put on airs, offering warm hospitality to all visitors.

ESSENTIALS

CURRENCY

The Eastern Caribbean dollar (EC$), but U.S. dollars are readily accepted.

TELEPHONE

Phone cards, which you can buy in denominations of $5, $10, and $20, are handy for making local phone calls, calling other islands, and accessing U.S. direct lines. To make a local call, dial the seven-digit number. To call Nevis from the United States, dial the area code 869, then access code 465, 466, 468, or 469 and the local four-digit number.

COMING ASHORE

Cruise ships dock in Charlestown harbor; all but the smallest ships bring passengers in by tender to the central downtown ferry dock. The pier leads smack onto Main Street, with shops and restaurants steps away. Taxi drivers often greet tenders, and there's also a stand a block

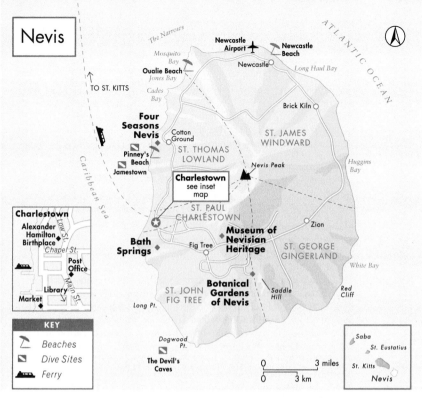

Nevis

TO ST. KITTS

The Narrows

Mosquito Bay
Jones Bay
Oualie Beach
Cades Bay

Newcastle Airport
Newcastle Beach
Newcastle
Long Haul Bay

ATLANTIC OCEAN

Brick Kiln

Four Seasons Nevis
Cotton Ground
ST. THOMAS LOWLAND

Pinney's Beach
Jamestown

ST. JAMES WINDWARD

Nevis Peak

Huggins Bay

Caribbean Sea

Charlestown
see inset map

ST. PAUL
CHARLESTOWN

Zion

Bath Springs
Fig Tree

Museum of Nevisian Heritage

ST. GEORGE GINGERLAND

White Bay

ST. JOHN
FIG TREE

Botanical Gardens of Nevis

Saddle Hill

Red Cliff

Long Pt.

Charlestown

Alexander Hamilton Birthplace
Chapel St.
Low St.
Post Office
Library
Main St.
Market

Dogwood Pt.

The Devil's Caves

0   3 miles
0   3 km

Saba
St. Eustatius
St. Kitts
Nevis

KEY	
∠	*Beaches*
◥	*Dive Sites*
⛴	*Ferry*

away. Fares are fairly expensive, but a three-hour driving tour of Nevis costs about $80 for up to four people. Several restored greathouse plantation inns are known for their lunches; your driver can provide information and arrange drop-off and pickup. Before setting off in a taxi, be sure to clarify whether the rate quoted is in EC or U.S. dollars.

If your ship docks in St. Kitts, Nevis is a 30- to 45-minute ferry ride from Basseterre. You can tour Charlestown, the capital, in a half hour or so, but you'll need three to four hours to explore the entire island. Most cruise ships arrive in port around 8 am, and the ferry schedule (figure $18 round-trip) can be irregular, so many passengers sign up for a cruise-line-run shore excursion. If you travel independently, confirm departure times with the tourist office to be sure you'll make it back to your ship on time.

EXPLORING NEVIS

CHARLESTOWN

About 1,200 of Nevis's 10,000 inhabitants live in the capital. If you arrive by ferry, as most people do, you'll walk smack onto Main Street from the pier. It's easy to imagine how tiny Charlestown, founded in 1660, must have looked in its heyday. The weathered buildings still have fanciful galleries, elaborate gingerbread fretwork, wooden shutters, and hanging plants. The stone building with the clock tower (1825, but mostly rebuilt after a devastating 1873 fire) houses the courthouse and second-floor library (a cool respite on sultry days). The little park next to the library is Memorial Square, dedicated to the fallen of World Wars I and II. Down the street from the square, archaeologists have discovered the remains of a Jewish cemetery and synagogue (Nevis reputedly had the Caribbean's second-oldest congregation), but there's little to see.

Alexander Hamilton Birthplace. The Alexander Hamilton Birthplace, which contains the Hamilton Museum, sits on the waterfront. This bougainvillea-draped Georgian-style house is a reconstruction of what is believed to have been the American patriot's original home, built in 1680 and likely destroyed during a mid-19th earthquake. Born here in 1755, Hamilton moved to St. Croix when he was about 12. He moved to the American colonies to continue his education at 17; he became George Washington's Secretary of the Treasury and died in a duel with political rival Aaron Burr in 1804. The Nevis House of Assembly occupies the second floor; the museum downstairs contains Hamilton memorabilia, documents pertaining to the island's history, and displays on island geology, politics, architecture, culture, and cuisine. The gift shop is a wonderful source for historic maps, crafts, and books on Nevis. ⊠ *Low St.* ☎ *869/469–5786* ⊕ *www.nevis-nhcs.org* ▤ *$5, $7 with admission to Museum of Nevisian History* ☉ *Weekdays 9–4, Sat. 9–noon.*

> **NEVIS BEST BETS**
>
> ■ **Charlestown.** The well-preserved little capital is worth a quick stroll.
>
> ■ **Golf.** The stunner at the Four Seasons provides challenge aplenty.
>
> ■ **Hiking.** Getting out in the countryside on foot is one of the best ways to experience Nevis.
>
> ■ **Pinney's Beach.** This long sensuous strand has several beach bars where you can "lime" with locals.

ELSEWHERE ON NEVIS

Bath Springs. The Caribbean's first hotel, the Bath Hotel, built by businessman John Huggins in 1778, was so popular in the 19th century that visitors, including such dignitaries as Samuel Taylor Coleridge and Prince William Henry, traveled two months by ship to "take the waters" in the property's thermal springs. Local volunteers have cleaned up the spring and built a stone pool and steps to enter the waters; now residents and visitors enjoy the springs, which range from 104°F to 108°F, though signs still caution that you bathe at your own risk, especially if you have heart problems. ⊠ *Charlestown outskirts.*

Botanical Gardens of Nevis. In addition to terraced gardens and arbors, this remarkable 7.8-acre site in the glowering shadow of Mt. Nevis has natural lagoons, streams, and waterfalls, superlative bronze mermaids, Buddhas, egrets and herons, and extravagant fountains. A splendid re-creation of a plantation-style greathouse contains the appealing Oasis in the Gardens Thai restaurant with sweeping sea views, and the upscale World Art & Antiques Gallery selling artworks, textiles, jewelry, and

Indonesian teak furnishings sourced during the owners' world travels. ✉ *Montpelier Estate* ☎ *869/469–3509* ⊕ *www.botanicalgardennevis. com* 🎫 *$13* ⊗ *Mon.–Sat. 9–4.*

Museum of Nevisian History. Purportedly this is the Western Hemisphere's largest collection of Lord Horatio Nelson memorabilia, including letters, documents, paintings, and even furniture from his flagship. Nelson was based in Antigua but came on military patrol to Nevis, where he met and eventually married Frances Nisbet, who lived on a 64-acre plantation here. Half the space is devoted to often-provocative displays on island life, from leading families to vernacular architecture to the adaptation of traditional African customs, from cuisine to Carnival. The shop is an excellent source for gifts, from homemade soaps to historical guides. ✉ *Bath Rd., Charlestown* ☎ *869/469–0408* ⊕ *www.nevis-nhcs. org* 🎫 *$5, $7 with Hamilton Museum* ⊗ *Weekdays 8:30–4, Sat. 10–1.*

BEACHES

All beaches are free to the public (the plantation inns cordon off "private" areas on Pinney's Beach for guests), but there are no changing facilities, so wear a swimsuit under your clothes.

Oualie Beach. South of Mosquito Bay and north of Cades and Jones Bays, this beige-sand beach lined with palms and sea grapes is where the folks at Oualie Beach Hotel can mix you a drink and fix you up with water-sports equipment. There's excellent snorkeling amid calm water and fantastic sunset views with St. Kitts silhouetted in the background. Several beach chairs and hammocks (free with lunch, $3 rental without) line the sand and the grassy "lawn" behind it. Oualie is at the island's northwest tip, approximately 3 miles (5 km) west of the airport. **Amenities:** food and drink, water sports. **Best for:** snorkeling, sunset. ✉ *Oualie Beach, St. Kitts.*

Pinney's Beach. The island's showpiece has soft, golden sand on the calm Caribbean, lined with a magnificent grove of palm trees. The Four Seasons Resort is here, as are the plantation inns' beach clubs and casual beach bars such as Sunshine's, Chevy's, and the Lime. Beach chairs are gratis when you purchase a drink or lunch. Regrettably, the waters can be murky and filled with kelp if the weather has been inclement anywhere within a hundred miles, depending on the currents. **Amenities:** food and drink, water sports. **Best for:** swimming, walking. ✉ *Pinney's Beach, St. Kitts.*

SHOPPING

Nevis is certainly not the place for a shopping spree, but there are some wonderful surprises, notably the island's stamps, fragrant honey, ceramics, and batik and hand-embroidered clothing. Other than a few hotel boutiques and isolated galleries, virtually all shopping is concentrated on or just off Main Street in Charlestown. The lovely old stonework and wood floors of the waterfront Cotton Ginnery Complex make an appropriate setting for shops of local artisans.

CraftHouse. This marvelous source for local specialties, from vetiver mats to leather moccasins, also has a smaller branch in the Cotton Ginnery. ⊠ *Pinney's Rd., Charlestown* ☎ *869/469–5505.*

Nevis Handicraft Co-op Society. This shop across from the tourist office offers works by local artisans (clothing, ceramic ware, woven goods) and locally produced honey, hot sauces, and jellies (try the guava and soursop). ⊠ *Main St., Charlestown* ☎ *869/469–1746.*

Philatelic Bureau. St. Kitts and Nevis are famous for their decorative, and sometimes valuable, stamps. Collectors will find real beauties here including the butterfly, hummingbird, and marine-life series. ⊠ *Cotton Ginnery, opposite the tourist office, Charlestown* ☎ *869/469–0617.*

ACTIVITIES

GOLF

Fodor'sChoice **Four Seasons Golf Course.** The Robert Trent Jones Jr.–designed Four Sea-
★ sons Golf Course is beautiful and impeccably maintained. The front nine holes are fairly flat until Hole 8, which climbs uphill after your tee shot. Most of the truly stunning views are along the back nine. The signature hole is the 15th, a 660-yard monster that encompasses a deep ravine; other holes include bridges, steep drops, rolling pitches, extremely tight and unforgiving fairways, sugar-mill ruins, and fierce doglegs. Attentive attendants canvas the course with beverage buggies, handing out chilled, peppermint-scented towels and preordered Cubanos that help test the wind. Greens fees per 18 holes are $195 for hotel guests, $205 for nonguests. ⊠ *Four Seasons Resort Nevis, Pinney's Beach* ☎ *869/469–1111* ⛳ *18 holes, par 72, 6,766 yd.*

HIKING

The center of the island is Nevis Peak—also known as Mt. Nevis—which soars 3,232 feet and is flanked by Hurricane Hill on the north and Saddle Hill on the south. If you plan to scale Nevis Peak, a daylong affair, it's highly recommended that you go with a guide. The **Upper Round Road Trail** is a 9-mile (14.5-km) road constructed in the late 1600s that was cleared and restored by the Nevis Historical and Conservation Society. It connects the Golden Rock Plantation Inn, on the east side of the island, with Nisbet Plantation Beach Club, on the northern tip. The trail encompasses numerous vegetation zones, including pristine rain forest, and impressive plantation ruins. The original cobblestones, walls, and ruins are still evident in many places.

Peak Heaven at Herbert Heights. This tour company is run by the Herbert family, who lead four-hour nature hikes up through the rain forest to panoramic Herbert Heights, where you drink in fresh local juices and views of Montserrat; the powerful telescope, donated by Greenpeace, makes you feel as if you're staring right into that island's simmering volcano (or staring down migratory whales). The solar-powered Coal Pot restaurant offers heaping helpings of affordable island fare (try any soup, the thyme-seared snapper, and scrumptious homemade ice creams) alongside the splendid vistas. Hike prices start at $25. ⊠ *Nevis* ☎ *869/469–2856, 869/665–6926* ⊕ *www.peakheavennevis.com.*

Sunrise Tours. Run by Lynell and Earla Liburd, Sunrise Tours offers a range of hiking trips, but their most popular is Devil's Copper, a rock configuration full of ghostly legends. Local people gave it its name because at one time the water was hot—a volcanic thermal stream. The area features pristine waterfalls and splendid bird-watching. They also do a Nevis village walk, a Hamilton Estate Walk, a Charlestown tour, an Amerindian walk along the wild southeast Atlantic coast, and trips to the rain forest and Nevis Peak. They love highlighting Nevisian heritage, explaining time-honored cooking techniques, the many uses of dried grasses, and medicinal plants. Hikes range from $25 to $40 per person, and you receive a certificate of achievement. ⊠ *Nevis* ☎ *869/469–2758* ⊕ *www.nevisnaturetours.com.*

WINDSURFING

Windsurfing Nevis. Waters are generally calm and northeasterly winds steady yet gentle, making Nevis an excellent spot for beginners and intermediates. Windsurfing Nevis offers top-notch instructors (Winston Crooke is one of the best in the islands) and equipment for $30 per hour. Beginners get equipment and two-hour instruction for $60. Groups are kept small (eight maximum), and the equipment is state-of-the-art from Mistral, North, and Tushingham. It also offers kayak rentals and tours along the coast, stopping at otherwise inaccessible beaches. ⊠ *Oualie Beach* ☎ *869/469–9682.*

WHERE TO EAT

$$
SEAFOOD

✕ **Double Deuce.** Mark Roberts, the former chef at Montpelier, decided to chuck the "five-star lifestyle" and now co-owns this jammed, jamming bar just off Pinney's, which lures locals with fine, fairly priced fare and creative cocktails. The overgrown shack is plastered with sailing and fishing pictures, as well as Balinese masks, fish nets, license plates, and wind chimes. Behind the cool mauve bar is a gleaming modern kitchen where Mark (and fun-loving firebrand partner Lyndeta) prepare sublime seafood he often catches himself, as well as organic beef burgers, velvety pumpkin soup, inventive pastas, and lip-smacking ribs. The "DD" is as cool and mellow as it gets. Stop by for free Wi-Fi and proper espresso, a game of pool, or just to hang out with a Double Deuce Stinger (Lyndy's answer to Sunshine's Killer Bee punch). Kids have their own trampoline. Dinner can be arranged for parties of 6 to 10. $ *Average main: $20* ⊠ *Pinney's Beach* ☎ *869/469–2222* ⊕ *www.doubledeucenevis.com* ⚐ *Reservations essential* ▤ *No credit cards* ⊘ *Closed Mon.*

$$
CARIBBEAN

✕ **Sunshine's.** Everything about this shack overlooking (and spilling onto) the beach is larger than life, including the Rasta man Llewelyn "Sunshine" Caines himself. Flags and license plates from around the world complement the international patrons (including an occasional movie or sports star wandering down from the Four Seasons). Picnic tables are splashed with bright sunrise-to-sunset colors; even the palm trees are painted, though "it gone upscaled," as locals say, with VIP cabanas. Fishermen cruise up with their catch—you might savor lobster rolls or snapper creole. Don't miss the lethal house specialty, Killer Bee rum punch. As Sunshine boasts, "One and you're stung, two, you're stunned, three, it's a knockout." $ *Average main: $20* ⊠ *Pinney's Beach* ☎ *869/469–5817* ⊕ *www.sunshinesnevis.com.*

OCHO RIOS, JAMAICA

Catherine
MacGillivray

About two hours east of Montego Bay lies Ocho Rios (often just "Ochi"), a lush destination that's favored by honeymooners for its tropical beauty. Often called the garden center of Jamaica, this community is perfumed by flowering hibiscus, bird of paradise, bougainvillea, and other tropical blooms year-round. Ocho Rios is a popular cruise port and the destination where you'll find one of the island's most recognizable attractions: the stairstep Dunn's River Falls, which invites travelers to climb in daisy-chain fashion, hand-in-hand behind a sure-footed guide. This spectacular waterfall is actually a series of falls that cascades from the mountains to the sea. That combination of hills, rivers, and sea also means many activities in the area, from seaside horseback rides to mountain biking and lazy river rafting.

ESSENTIALS

CURRENCY
The Jamaican dollar, but the U.S. dollar is widely accepted.

TELEPHONE
Public telephones are found at the communications center at the Ocho Rios Cruise Pier. Travelers also find public phones in major Ocho Rios malls. Some U.S. phone companies won't permit credit-card calls to be placed from Jamaica because they've been victims of fraud, so collect calls are often the top option. GSM cell phones equipped with tri-band or world-roaming service will find coverage throughout the Ocho Rios region.

COMING ASHORE

Most cruise ships are able to dock at this port on Jamaica's North Coast, near Dunn's River Falls (a $10 taxi ride from the pier). Also less than 1 mile (2 km) from the Ocho Rios pier are Island Village (within walking distance), Taj Mahal Duty-Free Shopping Center, and the Ocean Village Shopping Center. If you're going anywhere else beyond Island Village, a taxi is recommended; expect to pay $10 for a taxi ride downtown. The pier, which includes a cruise terminal with the basic services and transportation, is also within easy walking distance of Turtle Beach.

Licensed taxis are available at the pier; expect to pay about $35 per hour for a guided taxi tour. Jamaica is one place in the Caribbean where it's usually to your advantage to take an organized shore excursion offered by your ship unless you just want to go to the beach or do a bit of shopping in town. Car rental isn't recommended off the main highways in Jamaica because of high prices, bad roads, and aggressive drivers.

EXPLORING OCHO RIOS

Fodor's Choice
★

Dunn's River Falls. One of Jamaica's most popular attractions is an eye-catching sight: 600 feet of cold, clear mountain water splashing over a series of stone steps to the warm Caribbean. The best way to enjoy the falls is to climb the slippery steps: don a swimsuit, take the hand of the person ahead of you, and trust that the chain of hands and bodies leads to an experienced guide. The leaders of the climbs are personable fellows who reel off bits of local lore while telling you where to step; you can hire a guide's service for a tip of a few dollars. After the climb, you exit through a crowded market, another reminder that this is one of Jamaica's top tourist attractions. If you can, try to schedule a visit on a day when no cruise ships are in port. ■TIP→ Always climb with a licensed guide at Dunn's River Falls. Freelance guides might be a little cheaper, but the experienced guides can tell you just where to plant each footstep—helping you prevent a fall. ⊠ *Off Rte. A1, between St. Ann's Bay and Ocho Rios* ☎ *876/974–4767* ⊕ *www.dunnsriverfallsja.com* ⊠ *$20* ☉ *Daily 8:30–5 (last entry at 4).*

> ## OCHO RIOS BEST BETS
>
> ■ **Chukka Caribbean.** Any of the great adventure tours here is sure to please.
>
> ■ **Dunn's River Falls.** A visit to the falls is touristy, yet it's still exhilarating.
>
> ■ **Mystic Mountain.** Live out your *Cool Runnings* fantasies on the bobsled ride.
>
> ■ **Dolphin Cove at Treasure Reef.** Swim with a dolphin, stingray, or shark at this popular stop.
>
> ■ **Firefly.** The former home of playwright Noël Coward can be seen on a guided tour.

Mystic Mountain. This attraction covers 100 acres of mountainside rain forest near Dunn's River Falls. Visitors board the Rainforest Sky Explorer, a chairlift that soars through and over the pristine rain forest to the apex of Mystic Mountain. On top, there is a restaurant with spectacular views of Ocho Rios, arts-and-crafts shops, and the attraction's signature tours, the Rainforest Bobsled Jamaica ride and the Rainforest Zipline Canopy ride. Custom-designed bobsleds, inspired by Jamaica's Olympic bobsled team, run downhill on steel rails with speed controlled by the driver, using simple push-pull levers. Couples can run their bobsleds in tandem. The zipline tours streak through lush rain forest under the care of an expert guide who points out items of interest. The entire facility was built using environmentally friendly techniques and materials in order to leave the native rain forest undisturbed. ⊠ *North Coast Hwy.* ☎ *876/974–3990* ⊕ *www.rainforestbobsledjamaica.com* ⊠ *$47–$137* ☉ *Daily 9–5 (activities from 9–3:30).*

Prospect Plantation. To learn about Jamaica's agricultural heritage, a trip to this working plantation, just east of town, is a must. It's not just a place for history lovers, however. Everyone enjoys the views over the White River Gorge and the tour in a tractor-pulled cart. The grounds are full of exotic flowers and tropical trees, some planted over the years by such celebrities as Winston Churchill and Charlie Chaplin.

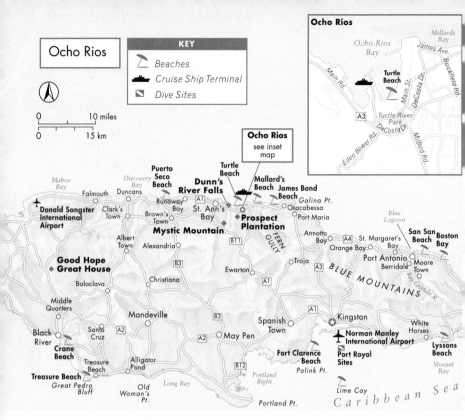

The estate includes a small aviary with free-flying butterflies. You can also saddle up for horseback rides and camel safaris on the plantation's 900 acres, but the actual tour times are usually geared toward the cruise-ship schedule, so call ahead. Prices vary depending on the tour. ✉ *Rte. A1, 4 miles (3.2 km) east of Ocho Rios* ☎ *876/994–1058* ⊕ *www.prospectplantationtours.com.*

BEACHES

Dunn's River Falls Beach. You'll find a crowd (especially if there's a cruise ship in town) at the small beach at the foot of the falls. Although tiny—especially considering the crowds that pack the falls—it's got a great view. Look up from the sands for a spectacular vista of the cascading water, the roar from which drowns out the sea as you approach. All-day access to the beach is included in the entrance fee to Dunn's River Falls. **Amenities:** lifeguards; parking; toilets. **Best for:** swimming. ✉ *Rte. A1, between St. Ann's Bay and Ocho Rios* ☎ *876/974–4767* ⊕ *www. dunnsriverfallsja.com* ✉ *$20* ⊙ *Daily 8:30–5 (last entry at 4).*

FAMILY **Turtle Beach.** One of the busiest beaches in Ocho Rios, Turtle Beach has a mix of residents and visitors. It's next to the Sunset Jamaica Grande hotel and looks out over the cruise port. **Amenities:** food and drink; lifeguards; parking; toilets; water sports. **Best for:** swimming. ✉ *Main St.* ✉ *J$200.*

SHOPPING

Ocho Rios has several malls, and they are less hectic than the one in MoBay. Shopping centers include **Pineapple Place, Ocean Village, Taj Mahal,** and **Coconut Grove.** A fun mall that also serves as an entertainment center is **Island Village,** the place nearest to the cruise port. This open-air mall includes shops selling Jamaican handicrafts, duty-free goods and clothing, a Margaritaville restaurant, and a small beach area with a water trampoline and water sports.

ACTIVITIES

DOLPHIN-SWIM PROGRAMS

FAMILY **Dolphin Cove Ocho Rios.** This company offers dolphin swims as well as lower-price dolphin encounters for ages eight and up; dolphin touch programs for ages six and over; or simple admission to the grounds, which also includes a short nature walk. Programs cost between $49 and $214, depending on your involvement with the dolphins. Advance reservations are advised. ⊠ *Box 21, North Coast Hwy., adjacent to Dunn's River Falls* ☎ *876/974–5335* ⊕ *www.dolphincovejamaica.com.*

GOLF

Ocho Rios courses don't have the prestige of those around Montego Bay, but duffers will find challenges at a few lesser-known courses.

Sandals Golf and Country Club. The golf course in Ocho Rios is 700 feet above sea level (green fees are $65 for non guests; free for guests). ⊠ *5 miles (8 km) southeast of Ocho Rios, turn south at White River and continue 4 miles (6 km)* ☎ *876/975–0119* ⊕ *www.sandals.com/main/ochorios/or-golf.cfm.*

HORSEBACK RIDING

With its combination of hills and beaches, Ocho Rios is a natural for horseback excursions. Most are guided tours taken at a slow pace and perfect for those with no previous equestrian experience. Many travelers opt to pack long pants for horseback rides, especially those away from the beach.

Fodor's Choice ★ **Chukka Caribbean Adventures.** Ocho Rios has excellent horseback riding, and a great option is Chukka Caribbean's two-hour ride-and-swim tour, which takes you along Papillion Cove (where the 1973 movie *Papillion* was filmed), as well as locations used in *Return to Treasure Island* (1985) and *Passion and Paradise* (1988). The trail continues along the coastline to Chukka beach and a bareback ride in the sea. The tour costs $74 for adults, $52 for children. Note that Chukka also has another location west of Montego Bay at Sandy Bay, and that the outfitter handles many other activities and tours beyond just horseback riding. ☎ *876/619–1441 Digicel in Jamaica, 876/656–8026 Lime in Jamaica, 877/424–8552 from U.S.* ⊕ *www.chukkacaribbean.com.*

Prospect Plantation. The plantation offers a horseback rides for ages eight and older. The price ($64) includes use of helmets; advance reservations are required. For the adventurous, Prospect Plantation also offers guided camel rides. ⊠ *Rte. A1, about 3 miles (5 km) east of Ocho Rios* ☎ *876/974–5335* ⊕ *www.prospectplantationtours.com.*

7

WHITE-WATER RAFTING

White-water rafting is increasingly popular in the Ocho Rios area.

Chukka Caribbean Adventures. The big activity outfitter offers the Chukka River Tubing Safari on the White River, an easy trip that doesn't require any previous tubing experience. This tour allows you to travel in your very own tube through gentle rapids. This tour lasts for three hours and costs $64 for adults and $45 for children. ☎ *876/619–1441 Digicel in Jamaica, 876/656–8026 Lime in Jamaica, 877/424–8552 from U.S.* ⊕ *www.chukkacaribbean.com.*

WHERE TO EAT

$ ✕ **Island Grill.** With 16 locations across the island, this eat-in or take-out

JAMAICAN   restaurant about a block from the main tourist area serves a Jamaican version of fast food. Jerk chicken, rice and peas, and Jamaican stew combo meals (called "Yabbas," an African-Jamaican term for bowl) are all on the menu. Many meals are served with festival (fried cornbread) and are spiced for the local palate. ⑤ *Average main: J$400* ⊠ *59 Main St.* ☎ *876/974–3160.*

$ ✕ **Ocho Rios Jerk Centre.** This canopied, open-air eatery is a good place

JAMAICAN   to park yourself for frosty Red Stripe beers and fiery jerk pork, chicken, or seafood such as fish and conch. Milder barbecued meats, also sold by weight (typically, a quarter or half pound makes a good serving), turn up on the fresh-daily chalkboard menu posted on the wall. It's busy at lunch, especially when passengers from cruise ships swamp the place. ⑤ *Average main: J$960* ⊠ *Da Costa Dr.* ☎ *876/974–2549.*

PROGRESO, MEXICO

Marlist
Kast-Myers

The waterfront town closest to Mérida, Progreso, is not particularly historic. It's also not terribly picturesque; still, it provokes a certain sentimental fondness for those who know it well. On weekdays during most of the year the beaches are deserted, but when school is out (Easter week, July, and August) and on summer weekends it's bustling with families from Mérida. Progreso's charm—or lack of charm—seems to hinge on the weather. When the sun is shining, the water looks translucent green and feels bathtub-warm, and the fine sand makes for lovely long walks. When the wind blows during one of Yucatán's winter *nortes,* the water churns with whitecaps and looks gray and unappealing. Whether the weather is good or bad, however, everyone ends up eventually at one of the restaurants lining the main street, Calle 19. Across the street from the oceanfront malecón, restaurants serve cold beer, seafood cocktails, and freshly grilled fish. Most cruise passengers head immediately for Mérida or for one of the nearby archaeological sites.

ESSENTIALS
CURRENCY
The Mexican peso, but U.S. dollars are widely accepted in the area.

TELEPHONE

Most pay phones accept prepaid Ladatel cards, sold in 30-, 50-, or 100-peso denominations. To use the card, insert it in the pay phone's slot, dial 001 (for calls to the United States) or 01 (for calls within Mexico), followed by the area code and number. Credit is deleted from the card as you use it, and the balance is displayed on the small screen on the phone. Most tri-band mobile phones from the U.S. work in Mexico, though you must pay roaming charges.

COMING ASHORE

The pier in Progreso is long, and cruise ships dock at its end, so passengers are shuttled to the foot of the pier, where the Progreso Cruise Terminal offers visitors their first stop. The terminal houses small restaurants and shops selling locally produced crafts. These are some of the best shops in sleepy Progreso (a much wider selection is available in nearby Mérida). The beach lies just east of the pier and can easily be reached on foot. If you want to enjoy the sun and a peaceful afternoon, a drink at one of the small palapa-roof restaurants that line the beach is a good option.

If you are looking to explore, there are plenty of taxis around the pier. A trip around town should not cost more than $5, but ask the taxi driver to quote you a price. If you want to see more of Progresso, a cab can also take you to the local sightseeing tour bus (which departs about every 10 minutes from the Casa de Cultura), a bright blue, open-air, double-decker bus that travels through town and costs only $2. A taxi ride from Progreso to Mérida runs about $30, and most drivers charge around $15 per hour to show you around. If you plan on renting the cab for a good part of the day, talk about the number of hours and the cost with the driver before you take off. It's difficult to rent a car, so most people just band together in a taxi.

EXPLORING MÉRIDA

Just south of Progreso (about 20 or 30 minutes by taxi), Mérida, the cultural and intellectual hub of the Yucatán, offers a great deal to explore. Mérida is rich in art, history, and tradition. Most streets are numbered, not named, and most run one-way. North–south streets have even numbers, which descend from west to east; east–west streets have odd numbers, which ascend from north to south. One of the best ways to see the city is to hire a *calesa*, a horse-drawn carriage. They congregate on the main square or at the Palacio Cantón, near the anthropology museum. Drivers charge about $20 for an hour-long circuit around downtown and up Paseo de Montejo, pointing out notable buildings and providing a little historic background along the way. An extended tour costs $30.

Casa de Montejo. Two Franciscos de Montejo—father and son—conquered the peninsula and founded Mérida in January of 1542, and they built their stately "casa" 10 years later. In the late 1970s it was restored by banker Agustín Legorreta, converted to a branch of Banamex bank, and now sits on the south side of the plaza. It's the city's finest—and oldest—example of colonial plateresque architecture, a

Mérida

Palacio Cantón
Paseo Montejo
Teatro Peón Contreras
Catedral de San Ildefonso
Zócalo
Casa de Montejo
Parque Zoologico El Centenario

Calle 55
Calle 57
Calle 58
Calle 59
Calle 61
Calle 62
Calle 63
Calle 64
Calle 65
Calle 66
Calle 68

100 yards
100 meters
0

Progreso

Golfo de México

San Felipe Parque Nacional
Santa Clara
Dzilam de Bravo
Dzilam González
Temax
Telchac Puerto
Motul
Tixkokob
Kantunil
Dzidós
Pisté
Chichén Itzá

YUCATAN

Progreso
Sisal
Mérida
Umán
Mama
Oxcutzcab
Tzucacab
Mayapán
Muna
Uxmal
Uxmal Ruins
Kabah
Sayil
Labná

Punta Baz
Parque Natural Ría Celestún
Celestún
Maxcanú

CAMPECHE

176
281
261
180
180
80
18
184
261
180

4 miles
4 kilometers
0

Spanish architectural style popular in the 16th century and typified by the kind of elaborate ornamentation you'll see here. A bas-relief on the doorway—the facade is all that remains of the original house—depicts Francisco de Montejo the younger, his wife, and daughter, as well as Spanish soldiers standing on the heads of the vanquished Maya. ⊠ *Calle 63, No. 506, Centro* ☎ *999/923–0633* ⊕ *www.museocasamontejo.com* ☉ *Tues.–Sat. 10–7, Sun. 10–2.*

Catedral de San Ildefonso. Begun in 1561 and completed 38 years later, St. Ildefonso is the oldest cathedral on the American continent (though an older one can be found in the Dominican Republic). It took several hundred Maya laborers, working with stones from the pyramids of the ravaged Mayan city, 36 years to complete it. Designed in the somber Renaissance style by an architect who had worked on the Escorial in Madrid, its facade is stark and unadorned, with gunnery slits instead of windows, and faintly Moorish spires. You can hear the pipe organ play at the 11 am Sunday Mass. ⊠ *Calles 60 and 61, Centro* ☉ *Daily 7–11:30 and 4:30–8.*

Palacio Cantón. The most compelling of the mansions on **Paseo Montejo**, this stately palacio was built as the residence for a general between 1909 and 1911. Designed by Enrique Deserti, who also did the blueprints for the Teatro Peón Contreras, the building has a grandiose air that seems more characteristic of a mausoleum than a home: there's marble everywhere, as well as Doric and Ionic columns and other Italianate beaux arts flourishes. The building also houses the air-conditioned **Museo Regional de Antropología,** which introduces visitors to ancient Mayan culture. Temporary exhibits sometimes brighten the standard collection. ⊠ *Paseo Montejo No. 485, at Calle 43, Paseo Montejo* ☎ *999/928–6719, 999/923–0557* ⊕ *www.inah.gob.mx* 🖙 *$4* ☉ *Tues.–Sun. 8–5.*

Paseo Montejo. North of downtown, this 10-block-long street was *the* place to reside in the late 19th century, when wealthy plantation owners sought to outdo each other with the opulence of their elegant mansions. Mansion owners typically opted for the decorative styles popular in New Orleans, Cuba, and Paris—imported Carrara marble, European antiques—rather than any style from Mexico. The broad boulevard, lined with tamarind and laurel trees, has lost much of its former panache; some of the mansions have fallen into disrepair. Many are now used as office buildings, while others have been or are being restored as part of a citywide, privately funded beautification program. The street is a lovely place to explore on foot or in a horse-drawn carriage.

PROGRESO BEST BETS

■ **Chichén Itzá.** The famous Maya city is an easy day trip from Progreso and is home to the enormous and oft-photographed El Castillo pyramid.

■ **Mérida.** This delightful, though busy, town is full of life as people take to the streets for music, dance, food, and culture.

■ **Uxmal.** One of the most beautiful Mayan cities is reachable on a day trip from Progreso. If you've seen Chichén Itzá already, go here.

Teatro Peón Contreras. This 1908 Italianate theater was built along the same lines as grand turn-of-the-20th-century European theaters and opera houses. In the early 1980s, the marble staircase, dome, and frescoes were restored. Today, in addition to performing arts, the theater houses the **Centro de Información Turística** (Tourist Information Center), which provides maps, brochures, and details about attractions in the city and state. The theater's most popular attraction, however, is the café-bar spilling out into the street facing Parque de la Madre. It's crowded every night with people enjoying the balladeers singing romantic and politically inspired songs. ⊠ *Calle 60 between Calles 57 and 59, Centro* ☎ *999/923–7354 Tourist Information Center, 999/924–9290, 999/923–7354 theater* ⊕ *www.culturayucatan.com* ♡ *Tourist Information Center daily 9–9.*

Zócalo. Méridians traditionally refer to this main square as the Plaza de la Independencia, or the Plaza Principal. Whichever name you prefer, it's a good spot to start a tour of the city, watch dance performances, listen to music, or chill in the shade of a laurel tree when the day gets too hot. The plaza was laid out in 1542 on the ruins of T'hó, the Mayan city demolished to make way for Mérida, and is still the focal point around which the most important public buildings cluster. *Confidenciales* (S-shape benches) invite intimate tête-à-têtes, and lampposts keep the park beautifully illuminated at night. ⊠ *Bordered by calles 60, 62, 61, and 63, Centro.*

FARTHER AFIELD

Fodor'sChoice **Chichén Itzá.** One of the most dramatically beautiful of the ancient Maya
★ cities, Chichén Itzá draws some 3,000 visitors a day from all over the world. Since the remains of this once-thriving kingdom were discovered by Europeans in the mid-1800s, many of the travelers who make the pilgrimage here have been archaeologists and scholars, who study the structures and glyphs and try to piece together the mysteries surrounding them. While the artifacts here give fascinating insight into Mayan civilization, they also raise many, many unanswered questions.

Of course, most of the visitors that converge on Chichén Itzá come to marvel at its beauty, not ponder its significance. Even among laypeople, this ancient metropolis, which encompasses 6 square km (2.25 square miles), is known around the world as one of the most stunning and well-preserved Mayan sites in existence.

The sight of the immense **El Castillo pyramid**, rising imposingly yet gracefully from the surrounding plain, has been known to produce goose pimples on sight. El Castillo (The Castle) dominates the site both in size and in the symmetry of its perfect proportions. Open-jawed serpent statues adorn the corners of each of the pyramid's four stairways, honoring the legendary priest-king Kukulcán (also known as Quetzalcóatl), an incarnation of the feathered serpent god. More serpents appear at the top of the building as sculpted columns. At the spring and fall equinoxes, the afternoon light strikes the trapezoidal structure so that the shadow of the snake-god appears to undulate down the side of the pyramid to bless the fertile earth. Thousands of people travel to the site each year to see this phenomenon.

On the other side of El Castillo, just before a small temple dedicated to the planet Venus, a ruined *sacbé,* or white road, leads to the **Cenote Sagrado** (Holy Well, or Sinkhole), also probably used for ritualistic purposes. Jacques Cousteau and his companions recovered about 80 skeletons from this deep, straight-sided, subsurface pond, as well as thousands of pieces of jewelry and figures of jade, obsidian, wood, bone, and turquoise. In direct alignment with Cenote Sagrado, on the other side of El Castillo, the **Xtaloc Sinkhole** was kept pristine, undoubtedly for bathing and drinking. Adjacent to this water source is a steam bath, its interior lined with benches along the wall like those you'd see in any steam room today. Outside, a tiny pool was used for cooling down during the ritual. ⊠ *Off Hwy. 180, Chichén Itzá* ⊕ *www.chichenitza.com* ⌨ *$10; parking $1* ☉ *Daily 8–4:30.*

Fodor'sChoice
★
Uxmal Ruins. Although much of Uxmal hasn't been restored, the following buildings in particular merit attention:

At 125 feet high, the **Pirámide del Adivino** is the tallest and most prominent structure at the site. Unlike most other Mayan pyramids, which are stepped and angular, the Temple of the Magician has a softer and more-refined round-corner design. This structure was rebuilt five times over hundreds of years, each time on the same foundation, so artifacts found here represent several different kingdoms. The pyramid has a stairway on its western side that leads through a giant open-mouthed mask to two temples at the summit. During restoration work in 2002 the grave of a high-ranking Maya official, a ceramic mask, and a jade necklace were discovered within the pyramid. Continuing excavations have revealed exciting new finds that are still being studied.

West of the pyramid lies the **Cuadrángulo de las Monjas**, considered by some to be the finest part of Uxmal. The name was given to it by the conquistadores, because it reminded them of a convent building in Old Spain (*monjas* means nuns). You may enter the four buildings, each comprising of a series of low, gracefully repetitive chambers that look onto a central patio. Elaborate and symbolic decorations—masks, geometric patterns, coiling snakes, and some phallic figures—blanket the upper facades.

Heading south, you'll pass a small ball court before reaching the **Palacio del Gobernador**, which archaeologist Victor von Hagen considered the most magnificent building ever erected in the Americas. Interestingly, the palace faces east, while the rest of Uxmal faces west. Archaeologists believe this is because the palace was built to allow observation of the planet Venus. Covering 5 acres and rising over an immense acropolis, it lies at the heart of what may have been Uxmal's administrative center. ■**TIP➔ In the summer months, tarantulas are a common sight at the ruins and around the hotels that surround the ruins.** ⌨ *Site, museum, and sound-and-light show $19.50; show only $5; parking $2; use of video camera $4.50 (keep this receipt if visiting other archaeological sites along the Ruta Puuc on the same day)* ☉ *Daily 8–5; sound-and-light show 7 pm in winter, 8 pm in summer.*

SHOPPING

In Progreso between Calle 80 and Calle 81, there is also a small downtown area that is a better place to walk than to shop. There you will find banks, supermarkets, and shops with everyday goods for locals as well as several restaurants that serve simple Mexican fare like *tortas* and tacos.

Mérida offers more places to shop, including colorful Mexican markets selling local goods.

Mercado Municipal. The Mercado Municipal has lots of things you won't need, but which are fascinating to look at: songbirds in cane cages, mountains of mysterious fruits and vegetables, ladles made of hollow gourds (the same way they've been made here for a thousand years). There are also lots of crafts for sale, including hammocks, sturdy leather huaraches, and piñatas in every imaginable shape and color. ■ TIP→ Guides often approach tourists near this market. They expect a tip and won't necessarily bring you to the best deals. You're better off visiting some specialty stores first to learn about the quality and types of hammocks, hats, and other crafts. Then you'll have an idea of what you're buying—and what it's worth—if you want to bargain in the market. Also be wary of pickpockets within the markets. ⊠ *Calles 56 and 67, Centro, Mérida.*

WHERE TO EAT

$ ✕ **Eladio's.** This bar and restaurant is a branch of the classic and popu-
MEXICAN lar Mérida joint by the same name. Under a tall palapa on the beach you can enjoy the view and the breeze through tall windows facing the water. Live music in the afternoons (except Tuesday) adds to the party atmosphere. This place is extremely popular with cruise ship passengers who disembark in Progreso. Tasty appetizers are free with your drinks, and there are plenty to choose from. This is a good place to try different Yucatecan dishes such as *longaniza asada* and *pollo pibil*. Fresh seafood dishes are also on the menu, but these don't come with the drinks. ⑤ *Average main: $7* ⊠ *Av. Malecón s/n, at Calle 80, Centro, Progreso* ☎ *969/935–5670* ⊕ *www.eladios.com.mx.*

PUERTO LIMÓN, COSTA RICA

Jeffrey Van Fleet

Christopher Columbus became Costa Rica's first tourist when he landed on this stretch of coast in 1502 during his fourth and final voyage to the New World. Expecting to find vast mineral wealth, he named the region "Costa Rica" (rich coast). Imagine the Spaniards' surprise eventually to find there was none. Save for a brief skirmish some six decades ago, the country *did* prove itself rich in a long tradition of peace and democracy. No other country in Latin America can make that claim. Costa Rica is also abundantly rich in natural beauty, managing to pack beaches, volcanoes, rain forests, and diverse animal life into an area the size of Vermont and New Hampshire combined. It has successfully parlayed those qualities into its role as one the world's great ecotourism destinations. A day visit is short, but time enough for a quick sample.

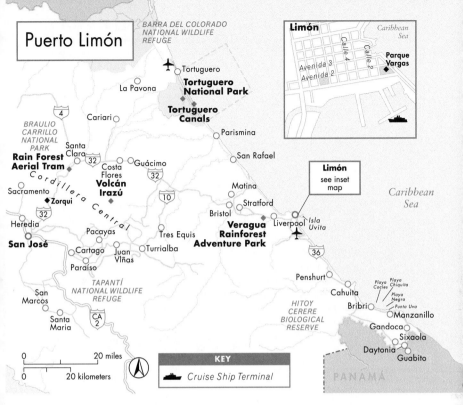

Puerto Limón

BARRA DEL COLORADO
NATIONAL WILDLIFE
REFUGE

Tortuguero

**Tortuguero
National Park**

La Pavona

**Tortuguero
Canals**

Cariari

Parismina

San Rafael

BRAULIO
CARRILLO
NATIONAL
PARK

Santa
Clara

**Rain Forest
Aerial Tram**

Costa
Flores

Guácimo

Matina

Cordillera

Sacramento

◆ **Zorqui**

**Volcán
Irazú**

Stratford

Bristol

Cordillera Central

Heredia

Pacayas

Tres Equis

**Veragua
Rainforest
Adventure Park**

Liverpool

Isla
Uvita

Limón
see inset
map

Caribbean
Sea

San José

Cartago

Juan
Viñas

Turrialba

Penshurt

Limón

Limón

Caribbean
Sea

Avenida 3
Avenida 2

Calle 4

Calle 2

Parque
Vargas

Paraíso

San
Marcos

TAPANTÍ
NATIONAL WILDLIFE
REFUGE

Cahuita

Playa
Cocles

Playa
Chiquita

Playa
Negra

Santa
Maria

HITOY
CERERE
BIOLOGICAL
RESERVE

Bribri

Punta Uva

Manzanillo

Gandoca

Sixaola

Daytonia

Guabito

PANAMÁ

0 ___ 20 miles
0 ___ 20 kilometers

KEY

🚢 Cruise Ship Terminal

ESSENTIALS
CURRENCY
The colón, but U.S. dollars are widely accepted.

TELEPHONE
Telephone numbers have eight digits. Merely dial the number. There are
no area codes. You'll find ample phones for use in the cruise terminal.
Public phones accept locally purchased calling cards.

COMING ASHORE

Ships dock at Limón's spacious, spiffy Terminal de Cruceros (cruise terminal), one block south of the city's downtown. You'll find telephones,
Internet computers, a craft market, tourist information, and tour operators' desks inside the terminal, as well as a small army of manicurists
who do a brisk business. Step outside and walk straight ahead one block
to reach Limón's downtown.

A fleet of red taxis waits on the street in front of the terminal. Drivers
are happy to help you put together a do-it-yourself tour. Most charge
$100 to $150 per carload for a day of touring. There is no place to rent
a car here, but you're better off leaving the driving to someone else.
Cruise lines offer dozens of shore excursions in Costa Rica, and if you

want to go any farther afield than Limón or the coast south, we suggest you take an organized tour. The country looks disarmingly small on a map—it is—but hills give rise to mountains the farther inland you go, and road conditions range from "okay" to "abysmal." Distances are short as the toucan flies, but travel times are longer than you'd expect.

EXPLORING PUERTO LIMÓN

LIMÓN

"Sultry and sweltering" describes this port community of 105,000. The country's most ethnically diverse city mixes the Latino flavor of the rest of Costa Rica with Afro-Caribbean and Asian populations, descendants of laborers brought to do construction and farming in the 19th century.

Parque Vargas. The aquamarine wooden port building faces the cruise terminal, and just to the east lies the city's palm-lined central park, Parque Vargas. From the promenade facing the ocean you can see the raised dead coral left stranded by the 1991 earthquake. Nine or so Hoffman's two-toed sloths live in the trees of Parque Vargas; ask a passerby to point them out, as spotting them requires a trained eye.

> **PUERTO LIMÓN BEST BETS**
>
> ■ **The Rain Forest Tram.** This attraction takes you up into the canopy of the rain forest to see it from a unique angle.
>
> ■ **Tortuguero Canals.** Whether you go on a ship-sponsored tour or arrange it on your own, you see a wild part of Costa Rica that isn't reachable by anything but boat.
>
> ■ **Zip-Line Tours.** If you have never done one of these thrilling tours, flying from tree to tree, Costa Rica is the original place to do it.

Rain Forest Aerial Tram. This 2½-square-mile (4-square-km) preserve houses a privately owned and operated engineering marvel: a series of gondolas strung together in a modified ski-lift pulley system. (To lessen the impact on the jungle, the support pylons were lowered into place by helicopter.) The tram gives you a way of seeing the rain-forest canopy and its spectacular array of epiphyte plant life and birds from just above, a feat you could otherwise accomplish only by climbing the trees yourself. If you book online in advance directly with the company, you save 10% off published rates and can get a full refund if your plans change (say your ship can't dock at Limón for some reason). ⊠ *76 miles (120 km) west of Limón, Braulio Carrillo National Park* ☎ *506/2257–5961, 866/759–8726 in North America* ⊕ *www.rainforestadventure. com* ⊠ *$55 tram only; $82.50 tram, lunch, and hike* ⊙ *Daily 7–4.*

BEYOND LIMÓN

FAMILY
Fodor'sChoice
★

Tortuguero National Park (*Parque Nacional Tortuguero*). In 1975 the Costa Rican government established Tortuguero National Park to protect the sea turtle population, which had been decimated after centuries of being aggressively hunted for its eggs and carapaces. This is the best place in Costa Rica to observe these magnificent creatures nesting, hatching, and scurrying to the ocean. The July-through-October nesting season for the green turtle is Tortuguero's most popular time to visit. Toss in the hawksbill, loggerhead, and leatherback—the three other species of sea turtle who nest here, although to a lesser extent—and you can expand the season from February through October. You can undertake night tours only with an authorized guide, who will be the only person in your party with a light, and that will be a light with a red covering. Photography, flash or otherwise, is strictly prohibited. The sight of a mother turtle furiously digging in the sand to bury her eggs is amazing, even from several yards away, and the spectacle of a wave of hatchlings scurrying out to sea is simply magnificent. ⊠ *Tortuguero* ☎ *2710–2929* ⊠ *$10* ⊘ *Daily 6–6.*

FAMILY **Veragua Rainforest Adventure Park.** Limón's newest attraction is a 4,000-acre nature theme park, about 30 minutes west of the city. It's popular with cruise-ship passengers in port for the day and is well worth a stop if you're in the area. Veragua's great strength is its small army of enthusiastic, super-informed guides who take you through a network of nature trails and exhibits of hummingbirds, snakes, frogs, and butterflies and other insects. A gondola ride overlooks the complex and transports you through the rain-forest canopy. A branch of the Original Canopy Tour, with nine platforms rising 46 meters (150 feet) above the forest floor, is here. The zip-line tour is not included in the basic admission to the park but is priced as an add-on. ⊠ *Veragua de Liverpool, 15 km (9 miles) west of Limón* ☎ *2296–5056 in San José* ⊕ *www.veraguarainforest. com* ⊠ *Full-day tour $66; full-day tour with canopy tour $99; full-day tour (does not include canopy) with transportation from San José $149, from Puerto Viejo de Talamanca $119* ⊘ *Tues.–Sun. 8–3.*

Volcán Irazú. Costa Rica's highest volcano, at 3,422 meters (11,260 feet), is one of the most popular with visitors since you can walk right down into the crater. Its presence is a mixed blessing: The ash fertilizes the Central Valley soil, but the volcano has caused considerable destruction through the centuries. ⚠ **Do not leave anything of value in your car while you visit the volcano. There have been a lot of thefts in the parking lot here, even though it is supposed to be guarded.** Most San José and area tour operators include the volcano among its excursions. ⊠ *Volcán Irazú National Park* ☎ *2200–5025* ⊠ *$10* ⊘ *Daily 8–3:30.*

SAN JOSÉ

Costa Rica's sprawling, congested capital sits in the middle of the country about three hours inland from the coast. Despite the distance, San José figures as a shore excursion—a long one to be sure—on most ships' itineraries. (The vertical distance is substantial, too; the capital sits on a plateau just under a mile above sea level. You'll appreciate a jacket here after so many days at sea level.) Although the city dates from the mid-18th century, little from the colonial era remains. The northeastern San José suburb of **Moravia** is chock-full of souvenir stores lining a couple of blocks behind the city's church.

Museo Nacional. In the mango-color Bellavista Fortress, which dates from 1870, the National Museum gives you a quick and insightful lesson in English and Spanish on Costa Rican culture from pre-Columbian

7

times to the present. Cases display pre-Columbian artifacts, period dress, colonial furniture, religious art, and photographs. Some of the country's foremost ethnographers and anthropologists are on the museum's staff. Outside are a veranda and a pleasant, manicured courtyard garden. A former army headquarters, this now-tranquil building saw fierce fighting during a 1931 army mutiny and the 1948 revolution, as the bullet holes pocking its turrets attest. But it was also here that three-time president José "Don Pepe" Figueres abolished the country's military in 1949. ⊠ *Eastern end of Plaza de la Democracia, Barrio La Soledad* ☎ *2257–1433* ⊕ *www.museocostarica.go.cr* ⊠ *$8* ⊙ *Tues.–Sat. 8:30–4:30, Sun. 9–4:30.*

Fodor'sChoice ★ **Teatro Nacional.** The National Theater is Costa Rica at its most enchanting. Chagrined that touring prima donna Adelina Patti bypassed San José in 1890 for lack of a suitable venue, wealthy coffee merchants raised import taxes and hired Belgian architects to design this building, lavish with cast iron and Italian marble. The theater was inaugurated in 1897 with a performance of Gounod's *Faust,* featuring an international cast. The sandstone exterior is marked by Italianate arched windows, marble columns with bronze capitals, and statues of strange bedfellows Ludwig van Beethoven (1770–1827) and 17th-century Spanish Golden Age playwright Pedro Calderón de la Barca (1600–81). The Muses of Dance, Music, and Fame are silhouetted in front of an iron cupola. The sumptuous neo-baroque interior sparkles, too. Given the provenance of the building funds, it's not surprising that frescoes on the stairway inside depict coffee and banana production. For a nominal admission fee you can also move beyond the lobby for a self-guided visit during the day. Call a day in advance if you'd like a guided tour in English; it's included in your admission price. (The theater is sometimes closed for rehearsals, so call before you go.) ⊠ *Plaza de la Cultura, Barrio La Soledad* ☎ *2221–5341* ⊕ *www.teatronacional.go.cr* ⊠ *$7* ⊙ *Daily 9–4.*

BEACHES

The dark-sand beaches on this sector of the coast are pleasant enough, but won't dazzle you if you've made previous stops at Caribbean islands with their white-sand strands. Nicer beaches than Limón's Playa Bonita lie farther south along the coast and can be reached by taxi or organized shore excursion. Strong undertows make for ideal surfing conditions on these shores, but risky swimming. Exercise caution.

Playa Blanca. Playa Blanca, one of the coast's only white-sand beaches, lies within the boundaries of Cahuita National Park, right at the southern entrance of the pleasant little town of Cahuita. The park's rain forest extends right to the edge of the beach, and the waters here offer good snorkeling. ⊠ *26 miles [44 km] southeast of Limón, Cahuita.*

Playa Bonita. Playa Bonita, the name of Limón's own strand, translates as "pretty beach," but it's your typical urban beach, a bit on the cluttered side. ⊠ *1 mile [2 km] north of Limón.*

Playa Cocles. Playa Cocles, the region's most popular strand of sand, lies just outside Puerto Viejo de Talamanca, one of Costa Rica's archetypal beach towns, with its attendant cafés and bars and all-around good times to be had. ⊠ *38 miles [63 km] southeast of Limón, Puerto Viejo de Talamanca.*

SHOPPING

The cruise-ship terminal contains an orderly maze of souvenir stands. Vendors are friendly; there's no pressure to buy. Many shops populate the restored port building across the street as well.

ACTIVITIES

WHITE-WATER RAFTING

You can experience some of the world's premier white-water rafting in Costa Rica.

Ríos Tropicales. Old standby Ríos Tropicales has tours on a Class III to IV section of the Pacuare River between Siquirres and San Martín, as well as the equally difficult section between Tres Equis and Siquirres. Not quite so wild, but still with Class III rapids, is the nearby Florida section of the Reventazón. Day excursions normally begin in San José, but if you're out in this part of the country, you can kick off your excursion here at the company's operations center in Siquirres. ⊠ *On the hwy in Siquirres* ☎ *2233–6455, 866/722–8273 in North America* ⊕ *www.riostropicales.com.*

ZIP-LINE TOURS

Costa Rica gave birth to the so-called canopy tour, a system of zip lines that transports you from platform to platform in the rain-forest treetops courtesy of a very secure harness. Though billed as a way to get up close with nature, your Tarzan-like yells will probably scare any wildlife away. Think of it more as an outdoor amusement-park ride. The nearest zip-line tour is at **Veragua Rainforest Adventure Park** (⇨ *See listing, above*).

WHERE TO EAT

If you are looking for a bite to eat while off the ship, your best bet is one of the simple "sodas," small restaurants serving local food. There are several in the vicinity of the Mercado Municipal, but Limón isn't a particularly pleasant place to stroll around, so if you aren't on a more far-flung tour you may be happier returning to your ship for lunch. Most tours will include lunch.

ROATÁN, HONDURAS

Jeffrey Van Fleet

You'll swear you hear Jimmy Buffett singing as you step off the ship onto Roatán. The flavor is decidedly Margaritaville, but with all there is to do on this island off the north coast of Honduras, you'll never waste away here. Roatán is the largest and most important of the Bay Islands, though at a mere 40 miles (65 km) from tip to tip, and no more than 3 miles (5 km) at its widest; "large" is relative here. As happened

Roatán, Honduras

Half Moon Bay
West End
West Bay
Gumbalimba Park
Flower Bay
Maya Key

♦ **Carambola Botanical Gardens**
♦ **Roatán Institute for Marine Sciences**
♦ **Roatán Museum**
Sandy Bay

Caribbean Sea

Roatán Airport
Coxen Hole
Brick Bay
Crawfish Rock
French Harbour
Politilli Bight
Punta Gorda
Oak Ridge

Paya Bay

Camp Bay
Port Royal

Bahía de Honduras

Helene Island

To Copán

KEY
⊿ Beaches
🚢 Cruise Ship Terminal

0 ——— 6 mi
0 ——— 6 km

elsewhere on Central America's Caribbean coast, the British got here first—the Bay Islands didn't become part of Honduras until the mid-1800s—and left an indelible imprint in the form of place names such as Coxen Hole, French Harbour, and West End, and, of course, their language, albeit a Caribbean-accented English. The eyes of underwater enthusiasts mist over at the mention of Roatán, one of the world's premier diving destinations, but plenty of topside activity will keep you busy, too.

ESSENTIALS

CURRENCY
The Honduran leimpira.

TELEPHONE
All phone numbers in Honduras have eight digits. There are no area codes, so just dial the number. Public phones are hard to find, but some hotels and businesses will offer phone services to walk-up users for a small fee.

COMING ASHORE

Roatán has two cruise terminals. Carnival and its affiliated lines own and operate an $80-million installation called Mahogany Bay, at Dixon Cove, halfway between the towns of Coxen Hole and French Harbour. The facility is designed to be entirely self-contained, with shops, restaurants, and attractions. A chairlift—$12 for a day pass—transports you to a private beach. You can partake of an entire slate of shore excursions if you wish to see more of the island, though. Other lines use the original Terminal de Cruceros (cruise terminal) in the village of Coxen Hole, the island's administrative center. You'll find telephones, Internet computers, and stands with tour information inside the terminal, as well as a flea market of crafts just outside the gate.

ROATÁN BEST BETS

■ **Diving and Snorkeling.** Roatán is one of the world's great diving destinations. There's snorkeling, too, most of it easily accessible from shore.

■ **Explore Garífuna Culture.** You'd never know it wandering West End, but the island has an original culture that predated the arrival of tourism, and which still dominates Roatán's eastern half.

■ **Hands-On Animal Adventures.** Macaws and monkeys scurry around you at the Gumbalimba Nature Park; dolphin encounters are available at Anthony's Key Resort.

Not to be outdone, Coxen Hole's facility is undergoing a major facelift at this writing. Periodically, schedules and weather mean cruise lines use the opposite terminal.

Taxis are readily available outside the cruise-ship docks, but be prepared to pay a premium for services there. Trips to the major tourism centers like West End and West Bay beach will cost around $20 per person, round-trip. Negotiate the price before you go, and be sure to clarify if the fare is per person and round-trip. If you would like to save money on your taxi fares, you can walk to the main highway (or into the town of Coxen Hole if you dock near there) and look for taxis marked "Colectivo." These taxis charge a flat rate of L20–L150, depending on the distance. They also pick up as many passengers as they can hold, so plan on riding with other locals or tourists. The local public-transport system consists of blue minivans that leave from Main Street in Coxen Hole to various points on the island until 6 pm. Simply wave if you want a minivan to stop. Expect to pay L30 to French Harbour and L50 to Sandy Bay or West End.

Look for the cadre of tourist police if you need help with anything. They wear tan shirts and dark-green trousers and are evident on cruise days. You certainly can rent a car here, but the island's compact size makes it unnecessary. Taxis will happily take you anywhere; expect to pay $80 to $120 for a day's private tour, depending on how far you wish to travel.

7

EXPLORING ROATÁN

Carambola Botanical Gardens. With one of the country's most extensive orchid collections, the Carambola Botanical Gardens is home to many different varieties of tropical plants. It is also a breeding area for iguanas. There are several trails to follow, and many of the trees and plants are identified by small signs. The longest trail leads up to the top of the hill, where you find an amazing view of the West End of the island. Guides can be hired at the visitor center. ⊠ *Across from Anthony's Key Resort, Sandy Bay* ☏ *2445–3117* ⊕ *www.carambolagardens.com* ✉ *$10, guided tour $15* ☉ *Mon.–Sat. 7–5, Sun. 7–noon.*

Gumbalimba Park. This park is part nature reserve, part tourism fun. Macaws, parrots, and monkeys will land on your shoulders as iguanas scuttle around more than 200 tropical tree and plant species. Paved paths lined with boulders lead to sandy beaches and a 91-meter (300-foott) high hanging bridge that crosses a lagoon. The park's zip-line tour is its main attraction, with 13 lines traversing the rain-forest canopy. There is also snorkeling, diving, horseback riding, and kayaking. Coxen's Cave is reminiscent of a theme park ride: recreated cave drawings line the walls, and dotting the interior are life-size pirate statues and replicas of maps, weapons, and treasure. Grab a bite at the poolside grill and take a refreshing shower in the outdoor stalls. Park admission includes the pirate cave, animal preserve, botanical gardens and pool access. All other activities cost extra. ⊠ *West Bay* ⊕ *www. gumbalimbapark.com* ✉ *$25* ☉ *Daily 8–4.*

FAMILY **Maya Key.** One of the premier day excursion—it's a great place for children—for cruisers visiting Roatán is this small, private island near Coxen Hole. The park offers a wide variety of amenities and activities, including sandy beaches, tropical gardens, a museum with cultural displays, and an animal rescue center, where you can meet the animals. The 10-acre island also offers spectacular snorkeling. Most cruise lines offer the island as a shore excursion, the only way it can be visited; the park takes no independent bookings. It's a 3-minute water shuttle ride from the shuttle pier 50 yards east of the Terminal de Cruceros in Coxen Hole ⊠ *Maya Cay, Coxen Hole* ☏ *9995–9589* ⊕ *www.mayakeyroatan. com* ☉ *Mon.–Sat. 7–4.*

FAMILY **Roatán Institute for Marine Sciences.** One of the attractions at Anthony's Key Resort, the Roatán Institute for Marine Sciences is an educational center that researches bottlenose dolphins and other marine animals. A dolphin show takes place every day at 4. For an additional fee you can participate in a "dolphin encounter," which allows you to interact with the dolphins either swimming or snorkeling. There are also programs for children ages 5 to 14, including snorkeling experiences, and the "Dolphin Trainer for a Day" program. (Cruise-ship passengers must make reservations for dolphin encounters through their ship's shore excursion desk.) ⊠ *Anthony's Key Resort, Sandy Bay* ☏ *2445–1327* ⊕ *www.anthonyskey.com* ✉ *$5* ☉ *Daily 8:30–5.*

Roatán Museum. Well worth a visit is the tiny Roatán Museum, named one of the best small museums in Central America. The facility, at Anthony's Key Resort, displays archaeological discoveries from Roatán and the rest of the Bay Islands. ⊠ *Anthony's Key Resort, Sandy Bay* ☎ *2445–1327* ⊕ *www.anthonyskey.com* ✆ *$5, included in admission price to Roatan Institute for Marine Sciences* ☉ *Daily 8:30–5.*

BEACHES

You really can't go wrong with any of Roatán's white-sand beaches. Even those adjacent to populated areas manage to stay clean and uncluttered, thanks to efforts of residents. Water is rougher for swimming on the less-protected north side of the island.

Half Moon Bay. Roatán's most popular beach, Half Moon Bay is also one of its prettiest. Coconut palms and foliage come up to the crescent shoreline. The beach lies just outside the tourist-friendly West End. Crystal-clear waters offer abundant visibility for snorkeling. ⊠ *West End.*

West Bay Beach. Roatán is famous for the picturesque West Bay Beach. It's a de rigueur listing on every shore-excursions list. Once there, you can lounge on the beach or snorkel. ⊠ *West Bay.*

SHOPPING

At the cruise ship dock in Coxen Hole you can find craft vendors, who set up shop outside the cruise-terminal gates; a small number of souvenir shops are scattered around the center of Coxen Hole, a short walk from the docks. Few of the souvenirs for sale here—or anywhere else on the island for that matter—were actually made in Roatán; most come from mainland Honduras. The terminal at Mahogany Bay has 22 shops as well. If you get as far as West End, there are a variety of souvenir and craft sellers in small shops lining the main sand road that runs parallel to the beach.

ACTIVITIES

DIVING AND SNORKELING

Most of the activity on Roatán centers on scuba diving and snorkeling, as well as the newest sensation, snuba, a cross between the two, whereby your mask is connected by a hose to an air source that remains above the water, allowing you to dive for several feet without carrying an air tank on your back. Warm water, great visibility, and thousands of colorful fish make the island a popular destination. Add to this a good chance of seeing a whale shark, and you'll realize why so many people head here each year. Dive sites cluster off the island's western and southern coasts.

One of the most popular destinations—particularly for budget travelers—is West End, offering idyllic beaches stretching as far as the eye can see. One of the loveliest spots is Half Moon Bay, a crescent of brilliant white sand. A huge number of dive shops offer incredibly low-price diving courses.

Competition among the dive shops is fierce in West End, so check out a few. West Bay has great dive sites, but few actual centers. When shopping around, ask about class size (eight is the maximum), the condition of the diving equipment, and the safety equipment on the dive boat.

FAMILY **Mayan Divers.** Mayan Divers is run inside the Mayan Princess resort. The five-star PADI dive center has a Bubblemaker program for children eight and up, plus discovery courses for all fanatics. ⊠ *Mayan Princess Resort, West Bay* ☎ *2445–5050* ⊕ *www.mayandivers.com.*

Native Sons. Native Sons is one of the most popular dive shops on the island. It's run by a native of Roatán who really knows the area. ⊠ *West End* ☎ *2445–4003* ⊕ *www.nativesonsroatan.com.*

West End Divers. This company has four dive boats and is committed to protecting the fragile marine ecology. They offer trips to over 40 dive sites in the area, and have special packages for cruise-ship passengers. ⊠ *West End* ☎ *2445–4289* ⊕ *www.westendivers.com.*

FISHING

Early Bird Fishing Charters. Early Bird Fishing Charters is a great charter fishing company operated by a Roatán native. In addition to deepsea and flats fishing, you'll have a great opportunity to see the island. Roatán has traditionally had a sea-based economy, and many of the small towns and villages look better from the vantage point of a boat. ⊠ *Sandy Bay* ☎ *2445–3019* ⊕ *www.earlybirdfishingcharters.com.*

WHERE TO EAT

$$ **✕ Bite on the Beach.** On a beautiful deck overlooking the beach, the res-
SEAFOOD   taurant serves up a wide selection of seafood, including conch, crab, and lobster. The menu changes often, but you'll almost always find favorites like Thai shrimp with peanut sauce and yellow coconut curry dishes. The restaurant is easily accessible by water taxi from West End, and the restaurant has Wi-Fi for guests. $ *Average main: L230* ⊠ *West Bay* ☎ *9663–6317* ⊕ *www.biteonthebeach.net* ⊘ *Closed Sun. and Mon.*

$$ **✕ The Beach Grill.** Tucked back off the road, just west of Anthony's Key
AMERICAN   in Sandy Bay, The Beach Grill is a popular lunch and dinner destination. Specialties include barbecue from their smoker and delicious seafood. Everything is made from scratch, including the dressings and sauces. The best part is that every table has an ocean view. $ *Average main: L230* ⊠ *Blue Bahia Resort, km 9, Sandy Bay* ☎ *2445–3385* ⊕ *www.bluebahiaresort.com* ⊘ *Closed Mon.*

SAMANÁ (CAYO LEVANTADO), DOMINICAN REPUBLIC

Eileen Robinson Smith

Samaná, the name of both a peninsula in the Dominican Republic as well as the largest town on Samaná Bay, is one of the least-known regions of the country, but the international airport that opened in nearby El Catey in 2006, and the new highway from Santo Domingo that has cut drive-time to two hours, are changing that perception quickly. (Still, only charters fly into El Catey.) Much development is planned, so a visit now will be to a place that is not yet geared to a great deal of mainstream, mass tourism. But with the use of the port by some mega-ships, that, too, is changing rapidly. Samaná is one of the Dominican Republic's newest cruise-ship destinations, with one of the island's greatest varieties of shore excursions. You can explore caves and see an amazing waterfall. And because many humpback whales come here each year to mate and give birth, it's a top whale-watching destination from January through March. Although some cruise lines still use Cayo Levantado as a private-island type of experience, for other lines it is just one of several options.

ESSENTIALS

CURRENCY
The Dominican peso, but U.S. dollars are widely accepted.

TELEPHONE
You can call U.S. or Canadian numbers easily; just dial 1 plus the area code and number.

COMING ASHORE

Cruise ships anchor at a point equidistant between the town of Samaná and Cayo Levantado, an island at the mouth of Samaná Bay with a great beach and facilities to receive 1,500 cruise-ship passengers. Tenders will take you to one of three docks, on the Malecón, referred to as the Samaná Bay Piers. The farthest is a five-minute walk from the town center.

Renting a car, although possible, isn't a good option. Driving in the D.R. can be a hectic and even harrowing experience; if you are in port one only day, don't risk it. You'll do better if you combine your resources with friends from the ship and share a taxi to do some independent exploring. Negotiate prices, and settle before getting in the taxi. To give you an idea of what to expect, a minivan that can take eight people will normally charge $90 for the round-trip to Las Terranas, including a two-hour wait while you explore or enjoy the beach. Similarly, you'll pay $80 to travel to Las Galeras round-trip. Many of the drivers speak some English. Within Samaná, rickshaws are far less costly and are also fun. Called *motoconchos de carretas,* they are not unlike larger versions of the Thai *tuk-tuk,* but can hold up to six people. The least you will pay is RD$10. They're fine for getting around town, but don't even think about going the distance with them.

EXPLORING SAMANÁ

SANTA BARBARA DE SAMANÁ
The official name of the city is Santa Barbara de Samaná; alas, that saint's name is falling into disuse, and you'll more often hear simply "Samaná" these days. An authentic port town, not just a touristic zone, it has a typical *malecón* (seaside promenade) with gazebos and park benches, ideal for strolling and watching the boats in the harbor. The main avenue that borders this zone is lined with restaurants, shops, and small businesses. A small but bustling town, Samaná is filled with

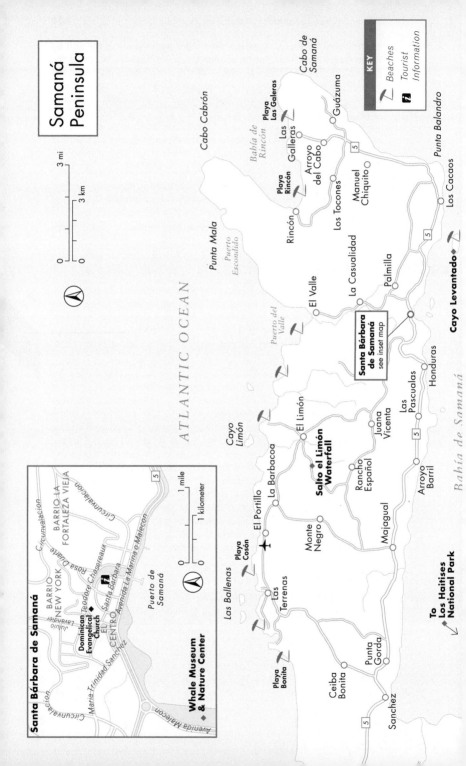

Samaná Peninsula

Santa Bárbara de Samaná

Circunvalación

BARRIO LA FORTALEZA VIEJA

Rosa Duarte

BARRIO NEW YORK

Julio Lavandier

Teodore Chasereaux

Dominican Evangelical Church

EL CENTRO

Santa Bárbara

María-Trinidad Sánchez

Avenida La Marina o Malecón

Puerto de Samaná

Avenida Malecón

Circunvalación

5

Whale Museum & Nature Center

0 — 1 mile
0 — 1 kilometer

ATLANTIC OCEAN

Cabo Cabrón

Punta Mala

Puerto Escondido

Bahía de Rincón

Cabo de Samaná

3 mi
3 km

Las Ballenas

Cayo Limón

Puerto del Valle

Playa Cosón

El Portillo

Las Terrenas

El Limón

Salto el Limón Waterfall

La Barbacoa

El Valle

Guázuma

Playa Las Galeras

Playa Rincón

Rincón

Las Galeras

Arroyo del Cabo

La Casualidad

Los Tocones

Manuel Chiquito

Palmilla

Los Cacaos

5

Punta Balandro

Monte Negro

Rancho Español

Juana Vicenta

Las Pascualas

Honduras

Santa Bárbara de Samaná see inset map

Majagual

5

Arroyo Barril

Bahía de Samaná

Cayo Levantado

Playa Bonita

Ceiba Bonita

Punta Gorda

Sánchez

5

To Los Haitises National Park

KEY

⚲ *Beaches*

🛈 *Tourist Information*

friendly residents, skilled local craftsmen selling their wares, and many outdoor cafés.

Dominican Evangelical Church. Back in 1824, a sailing vessel called the *Turtle Dove,* carrying several hundred slaves that had escaped from Philadelphia, was blown ashore in Samaná. The historic Dominican Evangelical Church is the oldest original building left in Samaná. The structure actually came across the ocean from England in 1881 in a hundred pieces and was reassembled here, serving the spiritual needs of the African-American freedman here. In 1946 a citywide fire wiped out most of Samaná's wooden buildings and Victorian architecture; this church was miraculously saved. ⊠ *Calle Chaseurox, in front of Catholic church, two blocks north of the cruise ship pier.* ☎ *809/538–2579* ✉ *Donations appreciated* ⊘ *Daily dawn–dusk.*

> ## SAMANÁ BEST BETS
>
> ■ **Cayo Levantado.** This resort island puts on an excellent show for day-trippers.
>
> ■ **El Limón Waterfall.** A horseback ride into the forest culminates in dazzling falls cascading into a natural pool.
>
> ■ **Los Haitises National Park.** The caves are filled with Taíno drawings; the mangroves are magnificent.
>
> ■ **Playa Rincón.** This rarely accessed beach offers a river, unspoiled mountainside, perfect beach, and privacy.
>
> ■ **Whale-watching.** In season, this is the top activity on the Samaná Peninsula.

Whale Museum & Nature Center (Centro de Naturaleza). Turn left from the main section of the malecón, en route to the hotel Bahia Principe Cayacoa, to find the tiny Whale Museum & Nature Center (Centro de Naturaleza), dedicated to the mighty mammals of the sea. Samaná Bay is part of one of the largest marine mammal sanctuaries in the world and is a center for whale-watching during the winter migration of humpback whales. The C.E.B.S.E. (Center for Conservation and Ecodevelopment of Samaná Bay and Its Environment) manages this facility, which features a 40-foot female humpback skeleton. Allow 15 to 45 minutes for a visit, depending on your fascination with the subject and your ability to read Spanish. Information in English is available at the entrance. ⊠ *Av. La Marina, Tiro al Blanco* ☎ *809/538–2042* ⊕ *www.Samana.org.do* ✉ *RD$75* ⊘ *Mid-Jan.–mid-Mar., daily 8–5; mid-Mar.–mid-Jan., weekdays 8–3.*

ELSEWHERE IN THE SAMANÁ PENINSULA

Cayo Levantado. There are no public beaches in Samaná town, but you can hire a boat to take you to Cayo Levantado, which has a wonderful white-sand beach on an island in Samaná Bay. Today the small island has largely been turned into a commercial enterprise to accommodate the 1,500 cruise-ship passengers who dock here; it has dining facilities, bars, restrooms, and lounge chairs on the beautiful beach. Unfortunately, it can also be extremely crowded and boisterous when there's a ship in port. The beach, however, is undeniably beautiful. The Bahía Príncipe Cayo Levantado, an upscale, all-inclusive resort, claims the eastern two-thirds of the island for its private use and sells one-day passes for $125. Day trips to Los Haitises often stop here for some beach time before returning to Santa Bárbara de Samaná. ⊠ *Samaná Bay* 🏖 *Public beach free* ⊘ *Daily dawn–dusk.*

Fodor'sChoice
★ **Los Haitises National Park.** One of the highlights of a trip to the Dominican Republic—and probably the most extraordinary part of a visit to the Samaná Peninsula—is a chance to explore Los Haitises National Park. Los Haitises (pronounced High-*tee*-sis), which is across Samaná Bay from the peninsula, is famous for its karst limestone formations, caves, and grottoes filled with pictographs and petroglyphs left by the indigenous Taíno who inhabited this area before Columbus's arrival.

The park is accessible only by boat, and a professionally guided kayaking tour is highly recommended—especially so you can kayak along the shoreline (there's no place to rent a kayak without a guide); regardless, a guide from a licensed tour company or the government is mandatory. On a trip you'll sail around dozens of the dramatic rock islands and spectacular cliff faces and perhaps visit some of the many caverns. Swirling around are hundreds of beautiful coastal birds that represent 121 different species, including Magnificent Frigatebirds, brown pelicans, brown booby, and varieties of egrets and herons. The sight of dozens of different birds continually gliding past the boat at any time is enough to make a bird-watcher out of anyone. ⊠ *Samaná Bay* 🕾 *809/472–4204* 🏖 *$3, not including manadatory use of licensed guide* ⊘ *Daily dawn–dusk.*

Salto el Limón Waterfall. Provided that you're fit and willing to deal with a long and slippery path, an adventurous guided trip to the spectacular Salto el Limón Waterfall is a delight. The journey is done mostly on horseback, but includes some walking down rocky, sometimes muddy trails. You'll have to cross two rivers en route. Horse paths are slippery, and the trek is strenuous. The well-mannered horses take you across rivers and up mountains to El Limón, where you can find the 165-foot waterfall amid luxuriant vegetation. Some snacks and drinks are usually included in the guided trip, but a grilled chicken lunch is only a few more pesos. The outpost for the trek, a local guide service called Santi Rancho, is relatively difficult to find; it's best to ask your hotel for detailed directions or arrange a tour from an operator like Flora Tours in Las Terrenas. The trip to the waterfall by horseback takes 40 minutes each way; the entire excursion lasts about three hours. ⊠ *Santi Rancho, El Limón.*

BEACHES

There are no recommendable beaches in Samaná de Santa Barbara itself. You will have to travel to one of the beautiful ones elsewhere on the peninsula, another reason why the Cayo Levantado excursion is popular on most ships.

Fodor'sChoice
★ **Playa Cosón.** This is a long, wonderful stretch of white sand and the best beach close to the town of Las Terrenas. Previously undeveloped, it's now reachable by a new highway, Carretera Cosón, and there are a dozen condo developments under construction (so the current sense of solitude probably won't last). One excellent restaurant, The Beach,

serves the entire 15-mile shore, and there's the European-owned boutique hotel, Casa Cosón and its restaurant and bar. If beachgoers buy lunch and/or drinks at either, then they can use the restrooms. **Amenities:** food and drink; parking; toilets. **Best for:** swimming; sunset; walking; windsurfing. ⊠ *Las Terrenas.*

Playa Las Galeras. Playa Las Galeras is within this tiny coastal town, a 30-minute drive northeast from Samaná town. It's a lovely, long, and uncluttered beach (except for the wild dogs, some local litter, and the boat hawkers and shell vendors around El Kiosko). The sand is nearly white, the Atlantic waters generally calm. It has been designated a "Blue Flag" beach, which means that it's crystal-clean with no pollution, though there are several small hotels here. This is a good snorkeling spot, too. That said, this is really just a departure point for the nearby virgin beaches closer to the cape to the west. Hire a boat and get to them! **Amenities:** food and drink. **Best For:** partiers; sunset; walking. ⊠ *Las Galeras.*

SHOPPING

Rum, coffee, and cigars are popular local products. You may also find good coconut handicrafts, including coconut-shell candles. Whale-oriented gift items are particularly popular. Most of the souvenir shops are on Samaná's malecón or in the market plaza; you will find more on the major downtown streets in town, all within easy walking distance of the tender piers.

ACTIVITIES

DIVING AND SNORKELING

In 1979 three atolls disappeared after a seaquake off Las Terrenas, providing an opportunity for truly memorable dives. Also just offshore from Las Terrenas are the Islas Las Ballenas (the Whale Islands), a cluster of four little islands with good snorkeling. A coral reef is off Playa Jackson, a beach accessible only by boat.

Las Terrenas Divers. Las Terrenas Divers rents surf and Boogie boards and gives surfing lessons and has other water-sport adventures, as well. ⊠ *Hotel Bahía Las Ballenas, Playa Punta Bonita, Las Terrenas* ☎ *809/889–2422* ⊕ *www.lt-divers.com.*

WHALE-WATCHING

Humpback whales come to Samaná Bay to mate and give birth each year, from approximately January 15 through March 30. Samaná Bay is considered one of the top destinations in the world for watching whales. If you're here in season, this can be the experience of a lifetime.

Whale Samaná. Whale Samaná is owned by Kim Beddall, a Canadian who is incredibly knowledgeable about whales and Samaná in general, having lived here for decades. Her operation is far and away the region's best, most professional, and environmentally sensitive. On board a 55-foot motor vessel, a marine mammal specialist narrates and answers questions in several languages. Kim herself conducts almost all the English-speaking trips. The $50 price does not include the RD$100

Marine Mammal Sanctuary entrance fee (price is subject to change). Normal departure times are 9 for the morning trip and 1:30 for the afternoon trip, but she is flexible whenever possible for cruise ship passengers, yet does require advance reservations. ✉ *Across street from town dock, beside park, Calle Sra. Morellia Kelly, Santa Bárbara de Samaná* ☎ *809/538–2042* ✎ *kim.beddall@whalesamana.com* ⊕ *www. whaleSamana.com.*

WHERE TO EAT

$ ✕ **La Mata Rosada.** The French chef/owner of La Mata, Yvonne Bastian,
SEAFOOD has been luring local expats and foodies since the late 1990s. She sets tables with white linens in an all-white interior that includes an array of ceiling fans to keep you cool; breezes sneak in from the bay across the street. There are plenty of excellent choices, like mahimahi in coconut sauce with a mango chutney or a mix of grilled lobster and other shellfish; the grouper has a potato crust, with tomatoes and eggplant. Begin with the ceviche, a specialty of this port town, made with *dorado* (mahimahi) and conch. Whether you go local or international, order the creole shrimp or a substantial salad, and you should leave satisfied. The desserts, like the chocolate terrine, are also presented with pride. ⑤ *Average main: $13* ✉ *Av. Malecón 5B* ☎ *809/538–2388* ☽ *Closed Wed. June–Nov.*

SAN JUAN, PUERTO RICO

Heather Rodino

Although Puerto Rico is a commonwealth of the United States, few cities in the Caribbean are as steeped in Spanish tradition as San Juan. Within a seven-square-block area in Old San Juan are restored 16th-century buildings, museums, art galleries, bookstores, and 200-year-old houses with balustraded balconies overlooking narrow, cobblestone streets. In contrast, San Juan's sophisticated Condado and Isla Verde areas have glittering hotels, fancy boutiques, casinos, and discos. Out in the countryside is 28,000-acre El Yunque National Forest, a rain forest with more than 240 species of trees growing at least 100 feet high. You can stretch your sea legs on dramatic mountain ranges, numerous trails, in vast caves, at coffee plantations, old sugar mills, and hundreds of beaches. No wonder San Juan is one of the busiest ports of call in the Caribbean. Like any other big city, San Juan has its share of petty crime, so guard your wallet or purse, especially in crowded markets and squares.

ESSENTIALS
CURRENCY
The U.S. dollar.

TELEPHONE
Calling the United States from Puerto Rico is the same as calling within the United States, and virtually all U.S. cell phone plans work here just as they do at home. You can use the long-distance telephone service office in the cruise-ship terminal, or you can use your calling card by

Old San Juan

dialing the toll-free access number of your long-distance provider from any pay phone. You'll find a phone center by the Paseo de la Princesa.

COMING ASHORE

Most cruise ships dock within a couple of blocks of Old San Juan; however, there is a second cruise pier across the bay, and if your ship docks there you'll need to take a taxi to get anywhere on the island. The Paseo de la Princesa, a tree-lined promenade beneath the city wall, is a nice place for a stroll—you can admire the local crafts and stop at the refreshment kiosks. Major sights in the Old San Juan area are mere blocks from the piers, but be aware that the streets are narrow and steeply inclined in places.

It's particularly easy to get to Cataño and the Bacardí Rum Plant on your own; take the ferry (50¢) that leaves from the cruise piers every half hour and then a taxi from the other side. Taxis, which line up to meet ships, are the best option if you want to explore beyond Old San Juan. White taxis labeled "Taxi Turistico" charge set fares of $10 to $19. Less common are metered cabs authorized by the Public Service Commission that charge an initial $1; after that, it's about 10¢ for each additional 1/13 mile. If you take a metered taxi, insist that the meter be turned on, and pay only what is shown, plus a tip of 15% to 20%.

You can negotiate with taxi drivers for specific trips, and you can hire a taxi for as little as $30 per hour for sightseeing tours. If you want to see more of the island but don't want to drive, you may want to consider a shore excursion, though almost all trips can be booked more cheaply with local tour operators

If you are embarking or disembarking in San Juan, the ride to or from the Luis Muñoz Marín International Airport, east of downtown San Juan, to the docks in Old San Juan takes about 20 minutes, depending on traffic. The white "Taxi Turistico" cabs, marked by a logo on the door, have a fixed rate of $19 to and from the cruise-ship piers; there is a $1 charge for each piece of luggage. Other taxi companies charge by the mile, which can cost a little more. Be sure the driver starts the meter, or agree on a fare beforehand.

> ### SAN JUAN BEST BETS
>
> ■ **El Morro.** Explore the giant labyrinthine fort.
>
> ■ **El Yunque National Forest.** This rain forest east of San Juan is a great half-day excursion.
>
> ■ **Casa Bacardí.** Rum lovers can jump on the public ferry and then taxi over to the factory.
>
> ■ **Old San Juan.** Walk the cobblestone streets of Old San Juan.
>
> ■ **Shopping.** Within a few blocks of the port there are plenty of factory outlets and boutiques.

EXPLORING SAN JUAN

Old San Juan, the original city founded in 1521, contains carefully preserved examples of 16th- and 17th-century Spanish-colonial architecture. More than 400 buildings have been beautifully restored. Graceful wrought-iron balconies with lush hanging plants extend over narrow streets paved with *adoquines* (blue-gray stones originally used as ballast on Spanish ships). The Old City is partially enclosed by walls that date from 1633 and once completely surrounded it. Designated a U.S. National Historic Zone in 1950, Old San Juan is chockablock with shops, open-air cafés, homes, tree-shaded squares, monuments, and people. You can get an overview on a morning's stroll (bear in mind that this "stroll" includes some steep climbs). However, if you plan to immerse yourself in history or to shop, you'll need a couple of days.

OLD SAN JUAN

Alcaldía. San Juan's city hall was built between 1602 and 1789. In 1841, extensive alterations were made so that it would resemble the city hall in Madrid, with arcades, towers, balconies, and an inner courtyard. Renovations have refreshed the facade of the building and some interior rooms, but the architecture remains true to its colonial style. Only the patios are open to public viewings. A municipal tourist information center and an art gallery with rotating exhibits are in the lobby. ⊠ *153 Calle San Francisco, Plaza de Armas* ☎ *787/480–2548* ✉ *Free* ⊙ *Weekdays 8–4.*

FAMILY

Fodor's Choice

★

Castillo San Cristóbal. This huge stone fortress, built between 1634 and 1790, guarded the city from land attacks from the east. The largest Spanish fortification in the New World, San Cristóbal was known in the 17th and 18th centuries as the Gibraltar of the West Indies. Five freestanding structures divided by dry moats are connected by tunnels. You're free to explore the gun turrets (with cannon in situ), officers' quarters, re-created 18th-century barracks, and gloomy passageways. Along with El Morro, San Cristóbal is a National Historic Site administered by the U.S. Park Service; it's a World Heritage Site as well. Rangers conduct tours in Spanish and English. ⊠ *Calle Norzagaray at Av. Muñoz Rivera* ☎ *787/729–6777* ⊕ *www.nps.gov/saju* ✉ *$3; $5 includes admission to El Morro* ☉ *Daily 9–6.*

FAMILY

Fodor's Choice

★

Castillo San Felipe del Morro (*El Morro*). At the northwestern tip of the Old City is El Morro ("the promontory"), a fortress built by the Spaniards between 1539 and 1786. Rising 140 feet above the sea, the massive six-level fortress was built to protect the harbor entrance. It is a labyrinth of cannon batteries, ramps, barracks, turrets, towers, and tunnels. Built to protect the port, El Morro has a commanding view of the harbor. You're free to wander throughout. The cannon emplacement walls and the dank secret passageways are a wonder of engineering. The fort's small but enlightening museum displays ancient Spanish guns and other armaments, military uniforms, and blueprints for Spanish forts in the Americas, although Castillo San Cristóbal has more extensive and impressive exhibits. There's also a gift shop. The fort is a National Historic Site administered by the U.S. Park Service; it's a World Heritage Site as well. Various tours and a video are available in English. ⊠ *Calle del Morro* ☎ *787/729–6960* ⊕ *www.nps.gov/saju* ✉ *$3; $5 includes admission to Castillo San Cristóbal* ☉ *Daily 9–6.*

Catedral de San Juan Bautista. The Catholic shrine of Puerto Rico had humble beginnings in the early 1520s as a thatch-roofed, wooden structure. After a hurricane destroyed the church, it was rebuilt in 1540, when it was given a graceful circular staircase and vaulted Gothic ceilings. Most of the work on the present cathedral, however, was done in the 19th century. The remains of Ponce de León are behind a marble tomb in the wall near the transept, on the north side. The trompe l'oeil work on the inside of the dome is breathtaking. Unfortunately, many of the other frescoes suffer from water damage. ⊠ *151 Calle Cristo* ☎ *787/722–0861* ⊕ *www.catedralsanjuan.com* ✉ *$1 donation suggested* ☉ *Mon.–Sat. 8–5, Sun. 8–2:30.*

Galería Nacional. Built by Dominican friars in 1523, this convent—the oldest in Puerto Rico—once served as a shelter during Carib Indian attacks and, more recently, as headquarters for the Antilles command of the U.S. Army. The beautifully restored building contains the Galería Nacional, which showcases the collection of the Institute of Puerto Rican Culture. Arranged chronologically, the museum traces the development of Puerto Rican art over the centuries, from José Campeche and Francisco Oller to Rafael Tufiño and Myrna Báez. You'll also find a good collection of *santos,* traditional wood carvings of saints. ⊠ *98 Calle Norzagaray* ☎ *787/725–2670* ⊕ *www.icp.gobierno.pr* ✉ *$3* ☉ *Tues.–Sat. 9:30–noon and 1–5.*

La Fortaleza. Sitting atop the fortified city walls overlooking the harbor, the Fortaleza was built between 1533 and 1540 as a fortress, but it wasn't a very good one. It was attacked numerous times and was occupied twice, by the British in 1598 and the Dutch in 1625. When El Morro and the city's other fortifications were finished, the Fortaleza became the governor's palace. Numerous changes have been made to the original primitive structure over the past four centuries, resulting in the current eclectic yet eye-pleasing collection of marble and mahogany, medieval towers, and stained-glass galleries. It is still the official residence of the island's governor, and is the Western Hemisphere's oldest executive mansion in continual use. Guided tours of the gardens and the building's exterior are conducted several times a day in English and Spanish. Call ahead, as the schedule changes daily. Proper attire is required: no sleeveless shirts or very short shorts. The tours begin near the main gate in a yellow building called the Real Audiencia, housing the Oficina Estatal de Preservación Histórica. ⊠ *Western end of Calle Fortaleza* ☎ *787/721–7000* ⊕ *www.fortaleza.gobierno.pr* ☞ *Free* ⊙ *Weekdays 9–4:30.*

Museo de las Américas. On the second floor of the imposing former military barracks, Cuartel de Ballajá, this museum houses four permanent exhibits: Popular Arts, African Heritage, the Indian in America, and Conquest and Colonization. You'll also find a number of temporary exhibitions of works by regional artists. A wide range of handicrafts is available in the gift shop. ⊠ *Calle Norzagaray and Calle del Morro* ☎ *787/724–5052* ⊕ *www.museolasamericas.org* ☞ *$3* ⊙ *Tues.–Sat. 9–noon and 1–4; Sun. noon–5.*

ELSEWHERE IN SAN JUAN

Casa Bacardí Visitor Center. Exiled from Cuba, the Bacardí family built a small rum distillery here in the 1950s. Today it's the world's largest, with the capacity to produce 100,000 gallons of spirits a day and 21 million cases a year. You can hop on a little tram to take an approximately 45-minute tour of the visitor center, though you don't visit the distillery itself. Yes, you'll be offered a sample. If you don't want to drive, you can reach the factory by taking the ferry from Pier 2 for 50¢ each way and then a *público* (public van service) from the ferry pier to the factory for about $2 or $3 per person. ⊠ *Bay View Industrial Park, Rte. 165, km 2.6, at Rte. 888, Cataño* ☎ *787/788–1500* ⊕ *www.casabacardi.org* ☞ *Free* ⊙ *Mon.–Sat. 8:30–5:30, last tour at 4:15; Sun. 10–5, last tour at 3:45.*

Fodor's Choice
★

Museo de Arte de Puerto Rico. One of the biggest museums in the Caribbean, this beautiful neoclassical building was once the San Juan Municipal Hospital. The collection of Puerto Rican art starts with works from the colonial era, most of them commissioned for churches. Here you'll find works by José Campeche, the island's first great painter. His *Immaculate Conception,* finished in 1794, is a masterpiece. Also well represented is Francisco Oller y Cestero, who was the first to move beyond religious subjects to paint local scenes. Another gallery room is filled with works by artists inspired by Oller. The original building, built in the 1920s, proved to be too small to house the museum's collection: the newer east wing is dominated by a five-story-tall stained-glass window, the work of local artist Eric Tabales. ⊠ *299 Av. José de*

Diego, Santurce ☎ 787/977–6277 ⊕ www.mapr.org ☑ $6 ⊙ Tues. and Thurs.–Sat. 10–5, Wed. 10–8, Sun. 11–6.

BEACHES

San Juan does not have the island's best beaches, but anyone can rent a chair for the day at one of the public entry points.

FAMILY **Balneario de Carolina.** When people discuss a "beautiful Isla Verde beach," this is the one they're talking about. East of Isla Verde, this Blue Flag beach is so close to the airport that the leaves rustle when planes take off. Thanks to an offshore reef, the surf is not as strong as other nearby beaches, so it's especially good for children and families. There's plenty of room to spread out underneath the palm and almond trees. For meals there are picnic tables and barbecue grills. Although there's a charge for parking, there's not always someone there to take the money. **Amenities:** lifeguards; showers; toilets. **Best for:** swimming; walking. ⊠ *Av. Los Gobernadores, Carolina* ☎ *787/791–2410* ⊕ *www. municipiocarolina.com* ☑ *$3 parking* ⊙ *Tues.–Sun. 8–5.*

FAMILY **Playa del Condado.** East of Old San Juan and west of Ocean Park, this long, wide beach is overshadowed by an unbroken string of hotels and apartment buildings. Beach bars, water-sports outfitters, and chair-rental places abound. You can access the beach from several roads off Avenida Ashford, including Calles Cervantes, Condado, and Candina. The protected water at the small stretch of beach west of the Conrad San Juan Condado Plaza hotel is particularly calm and popular with families; surf elsewhere in Condado can be a bit strong. The stretch of sand near Calle Vendig (behind the Atlantic Beach Hotel) is especially popular with the gay community. If you're driving, on-street parking is your only option. **Best for:** partiers. ⊠ *Condado* ⊙ *Daily dawn–dusk.*

SHOPPING

San Juan is not a duty-free port, so you won't find bargains on electronics and perfumes. However, shopping for native crafts can be fun. Popular souvenirs and gifts include *santos* (small, hand-carved figures of saints or religious scenes), hand-rolled cigars, local coffee, handmade lace, and carnival masks.

In Old San Juan, especially on Calles Fortaleza and Cristo, you can find everything from T-shirt emporiums to selective crafts stores, bookshops, art galleries, jewelry boutiques, and even shops that specialize in made-to-order Panama hats. Calle Cristo is lined with factory-outlet stores, including Coach and Ralph Lauren.

ACTIVITIES

GOLF

Río Mar Country Club. The Río Mar Country Club has a clubhouse with a pro shop, two restaurants between two 18-hole courses, to grab a sit-down lunch or a quick beverage and a bite. The River Course, designed by Greg Norman, has challenging fairways that skirt the Mameyes

River. The Ocean Course, designed by Tom and George Fazio, has slightly wider fairways than its sister; iguanas can usually be spotted sunning themselves near its fourth hole. ■TIP➔ **If you're not a resort guest, be sure to reserve tee times at least 24 hours in advance.** ✉ *Rio Mar Beach Resort & Spa, 6000 Río Mar Blvd., Río Grande* ☎ *787/888–7060* ⊕ *www.wyndhamriomar.com.*

WHERE TO EAT

$$$
SPANISH

✕ **El Picoteo.** You could make a meal of the small dishes that dominate the menu at this tapas restaurant on a mezzanine balcony at the Hotel El Convento. You won't go wrong ordering the grilled cuttlefish or the pistachio-crusted salmon with a Manchego-cheese sauce and passing them around the table. If you're into sharing, there are several kinds of paella that arrive on huge plates. There's a long, lively bar inside; one dining area overlooks a pleasant courtyard, and the other looks out onto Calle Cristo. Even if you have dinner plans elsewhere, consider stopping here for a nightcap or a midday pick-me-up. ⑤ *Average main: $30* ✉ *Hotel El Convento, 100 Calle Cristo, Old San Juan* ☎ *787/723–9202* ⊕ *www.elconvento.com* ⊙ *Closed Mon.*

$$
PUERTO RICAN
Fodor's Choice
★

✕ **La Fonda del Jibarito.** The menus are handwritten and the tables wobble, but *sanjuaneros* have favored this casual, no-frills, family-run restaurant—tucked away on a quiet cobbled street—for years. The conch ceviche, goat fricassee, and shredded beef stew are among the specialties on the menu of typical Puerto Rican *comida criolla* dishes. The tiny back porch is filled with plants, and the dining room is filled with fanciful depictions of life on the street outside. Troubadors serenade patrons, which include plenty of cruise-ship passengers when ships are in dock. ⑤ *Average main: $14* ✉ *280 Calle Sol, Old San Juan* ☎ *787/725–8375.*

NIGHTLIFE

Almost every ship stays in San Juan late or even overnight to give passengers an opportunity to revel in the nightlife—the most sophisticated in the Caribbean.

CASINOS

By law, all casinos are in hotels. The atmosphere is refined, and many patrons dress to the nines, but informal attire (no shorts or tank tops) is usually fine. Casinos set their own hours, which change seasonally, but generally operate from noon to 4 am, although the casino in the Conrad Condado Plaza Hotel is open 24 hours. Other hotels with casinos include the InterContinental San Juan Resort and Casino, the Ritz-Carlton San Juan Hotel, Spa and Casino, and the Sheraton Old San Juan Hotel and Casino.

BARS AND DANCE CLUBS

El Batey. This legendary hole-in-the-wall bar won't win any prizes for decor, but even still, it has an irresistibly artsy and welcoming vibe. Add your own message to the graffiti-covered walls (they have a B.Y.O.S, or Bring Your Own Sharpie policy), or put your business card alongside the hundreds that cover the lighting fixtures. The ceiling may leak, but the jukebox has the best selection of oldies in town. Join locals in a game of pool. ⊠ *101 Calle Cristo, Old San Juan* ☎ *No phone.*

Krash. A balcony bar overlooks all the drama on the dance floor at this popular club. Most of the time DJs spin house, hip-hop, salsa, and reggaetón, but occasionally disco nights send you back to the music of the 1970s and '80s. It's open Wednesday through Saturday. ⊠ *1257 Av. Ponce de León, Santurce* ☎ *787/722–1131.*

SANTO DOMINGO, DOMINICAN REPUBLIC

Eileen Robinson Smith

Spanish civilization in the New World began in Santo Domingo's 12-block Zona Colonial (Colonial Zone). As you stroll its narrow streets, it's easy to imagine this old city as it was when the likes of Cortés and Ponce de León walked the cobblestones, when pirates sailed in and out of the harbor, and when colonists first started building the New World's largest city. Tourist brochures tout that "history comes alive here"—a surprisingly truthful statement. However, many tourists bypass the large, sprawling, and noisy city; it's their loss. The Dominican Republic's seaside capital—despite such detractions as poverty and sprawl, not to mention a population of some 2 million people—has some of the country's best hotels, restaurants, and nightlife (as well as great casinos). Many of these are right on or near the Malecón and within the historic Zona Colonial area, which is separated from the rest of the city by Parque Independencia. If your ship calls or even embarks here, you'll be treated to a vibrant Latin cultural center unlike any other in the Caribbean.

7

ESSENTIALS

CURRENCY
The Dominican peso, but U.S. dollars are widely accepted.

TELEPHONE
From the D.R. you need only dial 1 plus the area code and number to call the United States. To make a local call, you must now dial 809 plus the seven-digit number. Phone cards, which are sold at gift shops and grocery stores, can give you considerable savings on your calls home. If you have a tri-band GSM phone, it should work on the island.

COMING ASHORE

Santo Domingo has two stellar cruise-ship terminals, and has become a growing port for cruise passengers. Despite the sluggish economy, the final tally of cruise-ship passengers for 2010 throughout the country was close to 600,000.

The **Port of Don Diego** is on the Ozuma River, facing the Avenida del Puerto, and across the street are steps that lead up to the main pedestrian shopping street of the Zona Colonial, Calle El Conde. A lovely yellow-and-white building, with stained-glass windows and faux gaslights, it has a small cafeteria, and potted palms soften the cordoned-off lines where passengers wait to have their tickets checked and go through immigration. The reception area has telephones, Internet access, and a

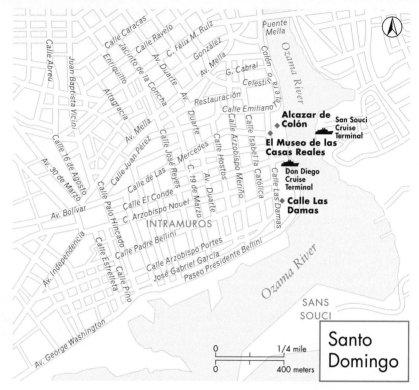

Santo
Domingo

currency exchange. Just down the dock is an ATM; in front of that is a counter where you can get cold drinks and snacks.

The **Sans Souci Terminal** complex, diagonally across the Ozama River from Don Diego Terminal, on Avenida España, has been operational since early 2010, but this long-term redevelopment project is still a work in progress. Its mezzanine level accommodates immigration and customs, duty-free shops, and both Internet and information centers. Like the Port of Don Diego, it has stunning lighting systems that cover the exterior and perimeter areas for greater security and visibility for visitors. When completed, the complex will have finished its marina, and have a full complement of stores, a 122-acre real-estate development, a new sports arena, and more. This major project is aimed at integrating the port area and the Zona Colonial to create an appealing destination for cruisers, yachtsmen, and high-end tourists.

AIRPORT TRANSFERS

If you are embarking in Santo Domingo, you should fly into Las Américas International Airport (SDQ), about 15 miles (24 km) east of downtown. On arrival you will have to pay $10 in cash for a tourist tax. Transportation into the city is usually by taxi; figure on $40 to or from hotels on the Malecón or in the Zona Colonial. You'll be greeted by a melee of hawking taxi drivers and sometimes their English-speaking solicitors (who expect to be tipped, as do the freelance porters who will undoubtedly scoop up your luggage). If you are spending a night or two in Santo Domingo before a cruise, you can probably arrange a driver through your hotel, so you'll be met with someone holding a sign with your name (it's worth the extra $10 or so to avoid the hassle). If you're going straight to your cruise ship, consider taking the cruise line's prearranged transfer. When you disembark from your ship, expect long lines at check-in, and be sure to give yourself a full two hours for check-in and security. The government departure tax should be included in your airline ticket.

EXPLORING SANTO DOMINGO

History buffs will want to spend a day exploring the many "firsts" of our continent. A horse-and-carriage ride throughout the Colonial Zone costs $25 an hour. The steeds are no thoroughbreds, but they clip right along, though any commentary will be in Spanish. You can also negotiate to use them as a taxi, say, down to the Malecón. The drivers hang out in front of the Hostal Nicolas de Ovando hotel.

Alcazar de Colón. The castle of Don Diego Colón, built in 1517, has 40-inch-thick coral-limestone walls. The Renaissance-style structure, with its balustrade and double row of arches, has strong Moorish, Gothic, and Isabelline influences. The 22 rooms are furnished in a style to which the viceroy of the island would have been accustomed—right down to the dishes and the viceregal shaving mug. Costumed "docents" appear on Saturday morning. ⊠ *Plaza de España, off Calle Emiliano Tejera, Zona Colonial* ☎ *809/682–4750* ⊠ *RD$100* ⊙ *Mon.–Sat. 9–5, Sun. 9–4. Closed if no cruise ship in port.*

Calle Las Damas. "Ladies Street" was named after the elegant ladies of the court: in the Spanish tradition, they promenaded in the evening. Here you can see a sundial dating from 1753 and the Casa de los Jesuitas, which houses a fine research library for colonial history as well as the **Institute for Hispanic Culture**; admission is free, and it's open weekdays from 8 to 4:30. If you follow the street going toward the malecón, you will pass a picturesque alley, fronted by a wrought-iron gate, where there are perfectly maintained colonial structures owned by the Catholic Church. ⊠ *Calle las Damas, Zona Colonial.*

El Museo de las Casas Reales. This is a remarkable museum that will help you comprehend the discovery of the New World by Christopher

---

SANTO DOMINGO BEST BETS

■ **Zona Colonial.** Santo Domingo's Colonial Zone is a World Heritage Site and a great place to stroll. It is a trip to the Old World; it is Spain in the 16th century.

■ **Dining.** Some of the D.R.'s best restaurants can be found in the capital. Take advantage of them if you have any extra time to spend here.

■ **Shopping.** The country's best shopping can be found in Santo Domingo. You can go souvenir shopping right on Calle Conde, a pedestrian street that is the main drag of the Zona Colonial.

7

Columbus and the entire 16th-century epic. Housing Taino finds, colonial artifacts, coins salvaged from wrecks of Spanish galleons, authentic colonial furnishings, as well as a collection of weapons, the museum also has one of the handsomest colonial edifices in the Zone. Built in the Renaissance style, it was the seat of Spanish government, housing the governor's office and the Royal Court. It has beautiful windows, for example, done in the plateresque style. A frequent wedding venue, it also functions as an art gallery, with rotating shows. When candlelit at night, it's truly magical. ⊠ *Calle Las Damas, Zona Colonial* ☎ *809/682-4202* ⊕ *www.zonacolonial.com/thingstosee/casasreales* ⊠ *RD$100* ☉ *Tues.–Sat. 9–5, Sun. 9–4.*

BEACHES

If you are just in port for a day, you'll have a better time if you skip the beach and spend some time in the Zona Colonial and on the Malecón.

Playa Boca Chica. You can walk far out into warm, calm, clear waters protected by coral reefs here. On weekends, the strip with the rest of the midrise resorts is busy, drawing mainly Dominican families and some Europeans. But midweek is better, when the beaches are less crowded. Sadly, on the public beach you will be pestered and hounded by a parade of roving sellers of cheap jewelry and sunglasses, hair braiders, seafood cookers, ice-cream men, and masseuses (who are usually peddling more than a simple beach massage). Young male prostitutes also roam the beach and often hook up with older European and Cuban men. The best section of the public beach is in front of Don Emilio's (the blue hotel), which has a restaurant, bar, decent bathrooms, and parking. Better, go to one of the nicer waterfront restaurants—Boca Marina Restaurat & Lounge, El Pelicano, Neptuno's Club,—and skip the public beach altogether. **Amenities:** food and drink; toilets; parking. **Best For:** partiers; sunset; swimming; walking. ⊠ *Autopista Las Américas, 21 miles (34 km) east of Santo Domingo, Boca Chica.*

SHOPPING

Exquisitely hand-wrapped cigars continue to be the hottest commodity coming out of the D.R. Only reputable cigar shops sell the real thing. Dominican rum and coffee are also good buys. *Mamajuana,* an herbal liqueur, is said to be the Dominican answer to Viagra. Look also for the delicate, faceless ceramic figurines that symbolize Dominican culture. Though locally crafted products are often affordable, expect to pay for designer jewelry made of amber and larimar, an indigenous semiprecious stone the color of the Caribbean. Amber, a fossilization of resin from a prehistoric pine tree, often encasing ancient animal and plant life, from leaves to spiders to tiny lizards, is mined extensively. (Beware of fakes, which are especially prevalent in street stalls.)

One of the main shopping streets in the Zone is **Calle El Conde,** a pedestrian thoroughfare. With the advent of so many restorations, the dull and dusty stores with dated merchandise are giving way to some hip new shops. However, many of the offerings, including local designer shops, are still of a caliber and cost that the Dominicans can afford. Some of the best shops are on **Calle Duarte,** north of the Colonial Zone, between Calle Mella and Avenida de Las Américas. **El Mercado Modelo,** a covered market, borders Calle Mella in the Colonial Zone; vendors here sell a dizzying selection of Dominican crafts.

The **Malecón Center,** the latest complex, adjacent to the classy Hilton Santo Domingo, will eventually house 170 shops, boutiques, and services plus several movie theaters. In the tower above are luxury apartments and Sammy Sosa, in one of the penthouses.

WHERE TO EAT

$$$
FRENCH
Fodor$Choice
★

✕ **La Residence.** This fine-dining enclave has always had the setting—Spanish-colonial architecture, with pillars and archways overlooking a courtyard—but only with Chef Denis Schetrit, who serves classically grounded yet innovative cuisine, has it really grown into a destination. He cleverly utilizes local produce and offers many moderately priced choices. An amuse-bouche arrives before your meal, and there is an excellent bread service. The three-course daily *menu de chef* is less than $28, including tax. It could be brochettes of spit-roasted duck, chicken au poivre, or vegetable risotto. You could start with a salad of pan-fried young squid and leave room for a luscious French pastry. Veer from the daily specials menu, and prices can go higher, but they remain fair; even the grilled Angus fillet and braised oxtail with foie-gras sauce and wild mushrooms is reasonable. Often, musicians romantically serenade diners. $ *Average main: $21* ⊠ *Hostal Nicolas de Ovando, Calle Las Damas, Zona Colonial* ☎ *809/685–9955* ⊕ *www.accorhotels. com* ⬧ *Reservations essential.*

WHERE TO STAY

Since Santo Domingo is a port of embarkation for some ships, we list these hotel recommendations for those who want or need to stay overnight.

For expanded reviews, facilities, and current deals, visit Fodors.com.

$$
HOTEL

Hilton Santo Domingo. This has become *the* address on the Malecón for businesspeople, convention attendees, and leisure travelers. **Pros:** Sunday brunch is one of the city's top tickets; luxe bedding; totally soundproof rooms; the executive-level lounge. **Cons:** little about the property is authentically Dominican; Vista Bar in lobby is closed on weekends. $ *Rooms from: $189* ⊠ *Av. George Washington 500, Gazcue* ☎ *809/685–0000* ⊕ *hiltoncaribbean.com/santodomingo* ⬧ *260 rooms* ⊙∣ *No meals.*

$$
HOTEL
Fodor$Choice
★

Hostal Nicolas de Ovando–M Gallery Collection. This historic boutique hotel, which is owned by the Accor group, was sculpted from the residence of the first governor of the Americas, and it just might be the best thing to happen in the Zona since Diego Columbus's palace was finished in 1517. **Pros:** lavish breakfast buffet; beautifully restored historic section. **Cons:** breakfast is no longer included in rates; pricey; rooms could be larger. $ *Rooms from: $220* ⊠ *Calle Las Damas, Zona Colonial*

☎ *809/685–9955, 800/763–4835* ⊕ *www.mgallery.com* ⇌ *104 rooms* ⊙ *No meals.*

NIGHTLIFE

Santo Domingo's nightlife is vast and ever changing. Check with the concierges and hip *capitaleños*. Get a copy of the free newspapers *Touring, Flow,* and *Aqui o Guía de Bares Restaurantes*—available at the tourist office and at hotels—to find out what's happening. At this writing, there is still a curfew for clubs and bars; they must close at midnight during the week, and at 2 am on Friday and Saturday nights. There are some exceptions to the latter, primarily those clubs and casinos located in hotels. Sadly, the curfew has put some clubs out of business, but it has cut down on crime and late-night noise, particularly in the Zona.

SANTO TOMÁS DE CASTILLA, GUATEMALA

Jeffrey Van Fleet

Guatemala's short Caribbean shoreline doesn't generate the buzz of those of neighboring Belize and Mexico. The coast weighs in at a scant 74 miles (123 km), and this mostly highland country wears its indigenous culture on its sleeve and has historically looked inland rather than to the sea. You'll be drawn inland, too, with a variety of shore excursions. This is the land of the Maya, after all. But there's plenty to keep you occupied here in the lowlands. Tourist brochures tout the Caribbean coast as "The Other Guatemala." The predominantly indigenous and Spanish cultures of the highlands give way to an Afro-Caribbean tradition that listens more closely to the rhythms of far-off Jamaica rather than taking its cue from Guatemala City. Think of it as mixing a little reggae with your salsa.

ESSENTIALS

CURRENCY

The Guatemalan quetzal; make sure you get money from the ATM in the cruise terminal in Santo Tomás de Castilla.

TELEPHONE

Guatemalan phone numbers have eight digits. There are no city or area codes. Simply dial the number for any in-country call. Most towns have offices of Telgua, the national telephone company, where you can place both national and international calls. Avoid the ubiquitous public phones with signs promising "Free calls to the USA." The number back home being called gets socked with a hefty bill.

COMING ASHORE

Cruise ships dock at the modern, spacious Terminal de Cruceros, where you'll find a bank, post office, money exchange, telephones, Internet access, a lively craft market, and an office of INGUAT, Guatemala's national tourist office. A marimba band serenades you with its clinking xylophone-like music; a Caribbean ensemble dances for you (and may even pull you in to take part).

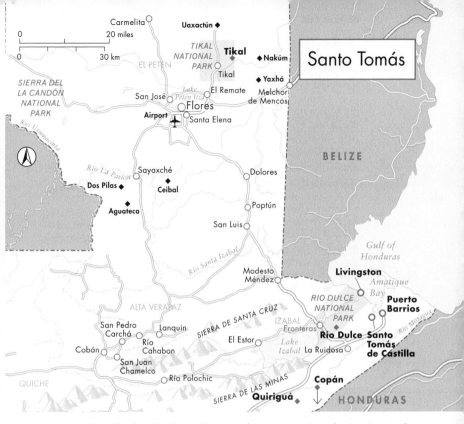

Taxis, both vehicular and water, take you to various destinations in the area. Plan on paying $3 to Santo Tomás de Castilla proper, and $5 to Puerto Barrios. Boats transport cruise visitors to Livingston, charging about $6 for the 20-minute trip. The Amatique Bay Resort provides water taxis from port to resort of $10 per person. Vehicular taxis charge $35 per head to travel by land to the resort.

EXPLORING SANTO TOMÁS DE CASTILLA

SANTO TOMÁS DE CASTILLA

Belgian immigrants settled Santo Tomás in the 19th century, but little remains of their heritage today, save for the preponderance of French and Flemish names in the local cemetery. Most visitors move on. Santo Tomás has experienced a small renaissance as the country's most important port, receiving growing numbers of cruise and cargo ships, and serving as the headquarters of the Guatemalan navy.

PUERTO BARRIOS

3 miles (5 km) north of Santo Tomás de Castilla.

Puerto Barrios maintains the atmosphere of an old banana town, humid and a tad down at the heels, perhaps longing for better days. Santo Tomás has replaced it as the country's largest port, and you'll likely zip through the Caribbean coast's biggest city on your way to somewhere else, but the cathedral and municipal market are worth a look if you find yourself here. Water taxis depart from the municipal docks for Livingston, across the bay, where you start your trip up the Río Dulce.

"Bahía de Amatique" denotes the large bay that washes the Caribbean coast of Guatemala and southern Belize just north of Puerto Barrios, but for most travelers the name is inexorably linked with the **Amatique Bay Resort and Marina,** the region's only five-star hotel. The 61-room resort opens itself up for day visitors, and many cruise passengers stop by for a drink, a meal, or an entire day of swimming, watersliding, kayaking, horseback riding, or bicycling. ✉ *6 miles (10 km) north of Santo Tomás; 14 Calle Final, Finca Pichilingo, Puerto Barrios* ☎ *7931–0000.*

> **SANTO TOMÁS BEST BETS**
>
> ■ **Quiriguá.** If you want to see Mayan ruins but don't want to spend an entire day on the bus, nearby Quiriguá can be impressive.
>
> ■ **Copán.** In neighboring Honduras, this Mayan site is a worthwhile day trip from Santo Tomás.
>
> ■ **Riding on the Río Dulce.** The ride on this river is one of Guatemala's most beautiful boat trips.

LIVINGSTON

15 miles (25 km) by water northwest of Santo Tomás.

Visitors compare Livingston with Puerto Barrios across the bay, and the former wins hands down, for its sultry, seductive Caribbean flavor. Wooden houses, some on stilts, congregate in this old fishing town, once an important railroad hub, but today inaccessible by land from the outside world. Livingston proudly trumpets its Garífuna heritage, a culture unique to Central America's eastern coast and descended from the intermarriage of African slaves with Caribbean indigenous people. Music and dance traditions and a Caribbean-accented English remain, even if old-timers lament the creeping outside influences, namely Spanish rap and reggae.

RÍO DULCE

30 miles (48 km) southwest of Santo Tomás.

The natural crown jewel of this region is the 13,000-hectare (32,000-acre) national park that protects the river leading inland from Livingston to Lago de Izabal, Guatemala's largest lake. Pelicans, herons, egrets, and terns nest and fly along the Río Dulce, which cuts through a heavily forested limestone canyon. Excursions often approach the park by land, but we recommend making the trip upriver from Livingston to immerse yourself in the entire Indiana Jones experience. Some cruise ships offer a trip to Hacienda Tijax for the day for their activities; these trips usually include lunch.

Castillo de San Felipe de Lara. Once an important Mayan trade route, the Río Dulce later became the route over which the conquistadors sent the gold and silver they plundered back to Spain. All this wealth attracted Dutch and English pirates, who attacked both the ships and the warehouses on shore. Spanish colonists constructed this fortress in 1595 to guard the inland waterway from pirate incursions. A 1999 earthquake in this region destroyed the river pier, as well as damaging portions of the fort. If you wish to visit, rather than simply see the structure from the water, you'll need to approach the park overland rather than upriver, all best accomplished on an organized shore excursion. ⊠ *Southwest of Fronteras* 🗐 *$3* ⊙ *Daily 8–5.*

QUIRIGUÁ
60 miles (96 km) southwest of Puerto Barrios.

Fodor's Choice ★ **Quiriguá.** A Mayan city that dates from the Classic period, Quiriguá is famous for the amazingly well-preserved stelae, or carved pillars, which are the largest yet discovered, and dwarf those of Copán, Honduras, some 50 km (30 miles) south. The stelae depict Quiriguá's ruling dynasty, especially the powerful Cauac Chan (Jade Sky), whose visage appears on nine of the structures circling the Great Plaza. Stela E, the largest of these, towers 10 meters (33 feet) high and weighs 65 tons. Several monuments, covered with interesting zoomorphic figures, still stand. The most interesting of these depicts Cauac Chan's conquest of Copán and the subsequent beheading of its then-ruler, 18 Rabbit. The remains of an acropolis and other structures have been partially restored. The ruins are surrounded by a strand of rain forest—an untouched wilderness in the heart of banana country. A small museum here gives insight into Quiriguá's history. ⊠ *54 miles (90 km) southwest of Santo Tomás de Castilla, Los Amates* 🗐 *$10* ⊙ *Daily 8–4:30.*

COPÁN
122 miles (203 km) southeast of Santo Tomás.

Copán. Just across the border in Honduras lie the famed ruins of Copán, the center of a kingdom that rose to prominence in the Classic period (5th to 9th centuries AD). The artistic structures here have led historians to dub the city "the Paris of the Mayan world."

As you stroll past towering cieba trees on your way in from the gate, you'll find the Great Plaza to your left. The ornate stelae standing around the plaza were monuments erected to glorify rulers. Some stelae on the periphery are dedicated to King Smoke Jaguar, but the most impressive—located in the middle of the plaza—depict King 18 Rabbit. Besides stroking the egos of the kings, these monuments had apparent religious significance since vaults for ritual offerings have been found beneath them.

The city's most important ball court lies south of the Great Plaza. Players had to keep a hard rubber ball from touching the ground, perhaps symbolizing the sun's battle to stay aloft. The game was more spiritual than sportslike in nature: the losers—or the winners in some cases—were killed as a sacrifice to Mayan gods.

Near the ball court lies the Hieroglyphic Stairway, containing the largest single collection of hieroglyphs in the world. The 63 steps immortalize the battles won by Copán's kings, especially those of the much revered King Smoke Jaguar.

7

Below the Acropolis here wind tunnels leading to some of the most fascinating discoveries at Copán. Underneath Structure 16 are the near-perfect remains of an older structure, called the Rosalila Temple, dating from AD 571. Uncovered in 1989, the Rosalila was notable in part because of the paint remains on its surface—rose and lilac—for which it was named. Another tunnel called Los Jaguares takes you past tombs, a system of aqueducts, and even an ancient bathroom.

East of the main entrance to Copán, the marvelous Museo de Escultura Maya provides a closer look at the best of Mayan artistry. All the sculptures and replicas are accompanied by informative signs in English as well as Spanish. Here you'll find a full-scale replica of the Rosalila Temple.

The complex employs à la carte pricing, but all should be included if you're on an organized shore excursion. It's a good idea to hire a guide if you're on your own, as they are very knowledgeable about the site, and signposting is sparse among the ruins themselves. English-speakers charge about $30 for a two-hour tour, while Spanish-speaking guides charge about half that. A small cafeteria and gift shop are near the entrance. ✉ *1 km (½ mile) east of Copán Ruinas, Honduras* ☎ *504/2651–4018* 🔗 *Ruins $15 or L300; museum $7 or L140; tunnels $12 or L240* ⊙ *Daily 8–4.*

TIKAL
1 hour by air northwest of Santo Tomás.

Some cruise lines offer excursions to Tikal, but it's not cheap getting there, because you'll travel by plane from the airstrip outside Santo Tomás to the small airport in Santa Elena, near the ruins.

Fodor'sChoice **Tikal.** The high point of any trip to Guatemala is a visit to Central
★ America's most impressive ruins. There's nothing quite like the sight of the towering temples, ringed on all sides by miles of virgin forest, but you need a lot of quetzales to get here. Although this region was home to Mayan communities as early as 600 BC, Tikal wasn't established until around 200 BC. By AD 500 it's estimated that the city covered more than 18 square miles (47 square km) and had a population of close to 100,000. For almost 1,000 years Tikal remained engulfed by the jungle. Excavation began in earnest in the mid-1800s. Today, after more than 150 years of digging, researchers say that Tikal includes some 3,000 buildings. Countless more are still covered by the jungle. Temple IV, the tallest-known structure built by the Maya, offers an unforgettable view from the top. ✉ *Parque Nacional Tikal* ☎ *No phone* 🔗 *$22, museum $2* ⊙ *Daily 6–6.*

SHOPPING

The rest of Guatemala overflows with indigenous crafts and art, but the famous market towns of the highlands are nowhere to be found in Caribbean region. Quite honestly, your best bet for shopping is the Terminal de Cruceros at Santo Tomás de Castilla, and you'll have plenty of opportunity to buy before you board your ship. What you'll find here comes from Guatemala's highlands—the coast does not have a strong artisan tradition—with a good selection of fabrics, weavings, woodwork, and basketry. Markets in Puerto Barrios and Livingston, the only real urban areas you'll encounter in this region, are more geared toward the workaday needs of residents rather than visitors.

ACTIVITIES

BEACHES AND WATER SPORTS

A beach culture has just never developed in this region of Guatemala the way it has in neighboring Belize and Mexico. The only real beach in the region is found within the confines of the **Amatique Bay Resort & Marina** (✉ *6 miles [10 km] north of Santo Tomás* ☎ *502/7931–0000* ⊕ *www.amatiquebay.net*), which is the only place here that has a resort atmosphere to it. Day visitors partake in swimming, waterslides, and kayaking. The resort's launch will bring you over from the cruise-ship terminal in Santo Tomás.

HIKING AND KAYAKING

Hacienda Tijax (✉ *Northeast of Fronteras, near bridge that crosses over Rio Dulce* ☎ *502/7930–5505* ⊕ *www.tijax.com*), which is pronounced tee-*hahsh,* is inland, near the point where the Río Dulce meets Lake Izabal. The staff oversee kayaking and hiking for day visitors.

ST. BARTHÉLEMY (GUSTAVIA)

Elise Meyer

Hilly St. Barthélemy, popularly known as St. Barth (or St. Barts) is 8 square miles (21 square km), but the island has at least 20 good beaches. What draws visitors is its sophisticated but unstudied approach to relaxation: the finest food, excellent wine, high-end shopping, and lack of large-scale commercial development. A favorite among upscale cruise-ship passengers, who also appreciate the shopping opportunities and fine dining, St. Barth isn't really equipped for megaship visits, which is why most ships calling here are from smaller premium lines. This is one place where you don't need to take the ship's shore excursions to have a good time. Just hail a cab or rent a car and go to one of the many wonderful beaches, where you will find some of the best lunchtime restaurants, or wander around Gustavia, shopping and eating. It's the best way to relax on this most relaxing of islands.

ESSENTIALS

CURRENCY

The euro; however, U.S. dollars are accepted in almost all shops and in many restaurants.

TELEPHONE

Public telephones accept télécartes, prepaid calling cards that you can buy at the gas station next to the airport and at post offices in Lorient, St-Jean, and Gustavia. Making an international call using a télécarte is the best way to go.

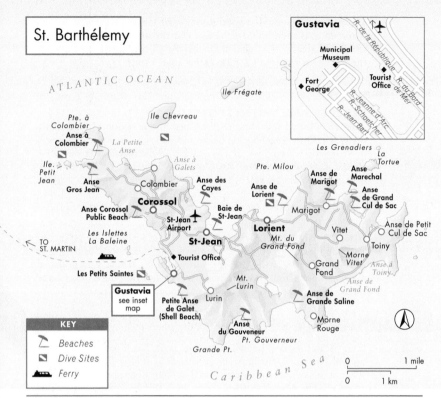

St. Barthélemy

ATLANTIC OCEAN

Ile Frégate

Pte. à Colombier
Anse à Colombier

Ile Chevreau

La Petite Anse

Ile. Petit Jean

Anse Gros Jean

Colombier

Anse à Galets

Corossol

Anse Corossol Public Beach

St-Jean Airport

Les Islettes La Baleine

St-Jean

← TO ST. MARTIN

Les Petits Saintes

Gustavia see inset map

Petite Anse de Galet (Shell Beach)

Lurin

Anse des Cayes

Baie de St-Jean

Pte. Milou

Anse de Lorient

Anse de Marigot

Lorient

Marigot

Mt. du Grand Fond

Mt. Lurin

Anse du Gouveneur
Pt. Gouverneur

Grande Pt.

Les Grenadiers

Anse Marechal

La Tortue

Anse de Grand Cul de Sac

Vitet

Anse de Petit Cul de Sac

Toiny

Grand Fond

Morne Vitet

Anse à Toiny

Anse de Grand Fond

Anse de Grande Saline

Morne Rouge

Caribbean Sea

Gustavia

Municipal Museum

Fort George

Tourist Office

R. de la République
R. du Bord de Mer
R. Jeanne d'Arc
R. Schoelcher
R. Jean Bart

KEY

Beaches

Dive Sites

Ferry

0   1 mile
0   1 km

COMING ASHORE

Even medium-size ships must anchor in Gustavia Harbor and bring passengers ashore on tenders. The tiny harbor area is right in Gustavia, which is easily explored on foot. Taxis, which meet all cruise ships, can be expensive. Technically, there's a flat rate for rides up to five minutes long. Each additional three minutes is an additional amount. In reality, however, cabbies usually name a fixed rate—and will not budge. Fares are 50% higher on Sunday and holidays. St. Barth is one port where it's really worth it to arrange a car rental for a full-day exploration of the island, including the island's out-of-the-way beaches. But be aware that during high season there is often a three-day minimum, so this may not be possible except through your ship (and then you'll pay premium rates indeed). Most car-rental firms operate at the airport; however, renting on your own is usually cheaper than what you'll get if you go with one of the ship's car rentals (you may be able to find a car for €50 per day).

EXPLORING ST. BARTH

With a little practice, negotiating St. Barth's narrow, steep roads soon becomes fun. Free maps are everywhere, roads are well marked, and painted signs will point you where you want to be. Take along a towel, sandals, and a bottle of water, and you will surely find a beach upon which to linger.

GUSTAVIA

You can easily explore all of Gustavia during a two-hour stroll. Most shops close from noon to 3 or 4, so plan lunch accordingly, but stores stay open past 7 in the evening.

FAMILY **Le Musée Territorial de Saint Barthélemy.** On the far side of the harbor known as La Pointe is the charming Municipal Museum, where you can find watercolors, portraits, photographs, and historic documents detailing the island's history, as well as displays of the island's flowers, plants, and marine life. ⊠ *La Pointe* ☎ *590/29–71–55* ⊡ *€2* ⊗ *Mon.– Tues. 8:30–1 and 2:30–5:30, Wed. 9–1, Thurs.–Fri. 8:30–1 and 2:30–5, Sat. 9–1. Call for summer hrs.*

Tourist Office. A good spot to park your car is rue de la République, alongside the catamarans, yachts, and sailboats. The tourist office on the pier can provide maps and a wealth of information. During busier holiday periods, the office may be open all day. ⊠ *Rue de la République* ☎ *0590/27–87–27* ⊕ *www.saintbarth-tourisme.com* ⊗ *Mon. 8:30–12:30, Tues.–Fri. 8–noon and 2–5, Sat. 9–noon.*

COROSSOL

FAMILY Traces of the island's French provincial origins are evident in this two-street fishing village with a little rocky beach.

LORIENT

Site of the first French settlement, Lorient is one of the island's two parishes; a restored church, a school, and a post office mark the spot. Note the gaily decorated graves in the cemetery.

St-Jean. There is a monument at the crest of the hill that divides St-Jean from Gustavia. Called *The Arawak,* it symbolizes the soul of St. Barth. A warrior, one of the earliest inhabitants of the area (AD 800–1,800), holds a lance in his right hand and stands on a rock shaped like the island; in his left hand he holds a conch shell, which sounds the cry of nature; perched beside him are a pelican (which symbolizes the air and survival by fishing) and an iguana (which represents the earth). The half-mile-long crescent of sand at St-Jean is the island's most popular beach. A popular activity is watching and photographing the hair-raising airplane landings (though you should note that it is extremely dangerous to stand in the area at the beach end of the runway). You'll also find some of the best shopping on the island here, as well as several restaurants.

ST. BARTHÉLEMY BEST BETS

■ **Soaking up the Atmosphere.** It's the French Riviera transported to the Caribbean.

■ **Beautiful Beaches.** Pick any of the lovely, uncrowded beaches.

■ **French Food.** St. Barth has some of the best restaurants in the Caribbean.

■ **Shopping.** There is no better fashion shopping in the Caribbean, especially if you are young and slim.

7

BEACHES

There are many *anses* (coves) and nearly 20 *plages* (beaches) scattered around the island, each with a distinctive personality and each open to the general public. Even in season you can find a nearly empty beach. Topless sunbathing is common, but nudism is forbidden—although both Grande Saline and Gouverneur are de facto nude beaches.

Anse de Grand Cul de Sac. The shallow, reef-protected beach is nice for small children, fly-fishermen, kayakers, and windsurfers—and for the amusing pelicanlike frigate birds that dive-bomb the water fishing for their lunch. There is a good dive shop. You needn't do your own fishing; you can have a wonderful lunch at one of the excellent restaurants, and use their lounge chairs for the afternoon. **Amenities:** food and drink; parking (no fee); toilets; water sports. **Best for:** swimming; walking. ⊠ *Grand Cul de Sac.*

FAMILY **Anse de Grande Saline.** With its peaceful seclusion and sandy ocean bot-
Fodor'sChoice tom, this is just about everyone's favorite beach and is great for swim-
★ ming, too. Without any major development (although there is some talk of developing a resort here), it's an ideal Caribbean strand, though there can be a bit of wind at times. In spite of the prohibition, young and old alike go nude. The beach is a 10-minute walk up a rocky dune trail, so be sure to wear sneakers or water shoes, and bring a blanket, umbrella, and beach towels. Although there are several good restaurants for lunch near the parking area, once you get here, the beach is just sand, sea, and sky. The big salt ponds here are no longer in use, and the place looks a little desolate when you approach, but don't despair. **Amenities:** park-ing (no fee). **Best for:** nudists; swimming; walking. ⊠ *Grande Saline.*

FAMILY **Baie de St-Jean.** Like a mini–Côte d'Azur—beachside bistros, terrific shopping, bungalow hotels, bronzed bodies, windsurfing, and day-trippers who tend to arrive on BIG yachts—the reef-protected strip is divided by Eden Rock promontory. Except when the hotels are filled to capacity you can rent chaises and umbrellas at La Plage restaurant or at Eden Rock, where you can lounge for hours over lunch. **Amenities:** food and drink; toilets. **Best for:** partiers, walking. ⊠ *Baie de St-Jean.*

SHOPPING

St. Barth is a duty-free port, and with its sophisticated crowd of visi-tors, shopping in the island's 200-plus boutiques is a definite delight. In Gustavia boutiques line the three major shopping streets. Quai de la République, which is right on the harbor, rivals New York's Madison Avenue or Paris's avenue Montaigne for high-end designer retail, includ-ing shops for **Louis Vuitton, Bulgari, Cartier, Chopard,** and **Hermès.** These shops often carry items that are not available in the United States. The Carré d'Or plaza is great fun to explore. Shops are also clustered in **La Savane Commercial Center** (across from the airport), **La Villa Créole** (in St-Jean), and **Espace Neptune** (on the road to Lorient). It's worth working your way from one end to the other at these shopping complexes—just to see or, perhaps, be seen. Boutiques in all three areas carry the latest in French and Italian sportswear and some haute couture. Bargains may be tough to come by, but you might be able to snag that *pochette* that is sold out stateside, and in any case, you'll have a lot of fun hunting around.

ACTIVITIES

BOATING AND SAILING

St. Barth is a popular yachting and sailing center, thanks to its location midway between Antigua and St. Thomas. Gustavia's harbor, 13 to 16 feet deep, has mooring and docking facilities for 40 yachts. There are also good anchorages available at Public, Corossol, and Colombier. You can charter sailing and motorboats in Gustavia Harbor for as little as a half day. Stop at the tourist office in Gustavia for an up-to-the minute list of recommended charter companies.

Jicky Marine Service. This company offers full-day outings, either on a variety of motorboats, or 42- or 46-foot catamarans, to the uninhabited Île Fourchue for swimming, snorkeling, cocktails, and lunch. The cost starts at about $100 per person; an unskippered motor rental runs about $260 a day. ⊠ *Ferry dock* ☎ *0590/27–70–34* ⊕ *www.jickymarine. com.*

DIVING AND SNORKELING

Several dive shops arrange scuba excursions to local sites. Depending on weather conditions, you may dive at **Pain de Sucre, Coco Island,** or toward nearby **Saba.** There's also an underwater shipwreck to explore, plus sharks, rays, sea tortoises, coral, and the usual varieties of colorful fish. The waters on the island's leeward side are the calmest. For the uncertified who still want to see what the island's waters hold, there's an accessible shallow reef right off the beach at Anse de Cayes that you can explore if you have your own mask and fins.

FAMILY **Plongée Caraïbe.** This company is recommended for its up-to-the-minute equipment and dive boat. They also run two-hour group snorkeling trips on the *Blue Cat Catamaran*; a half-day is €40. ☎ *0590/27–55–94* ⊕ *www.plongee-caraibes.com.*

WHERE TO EAT

A service charge is always added by law, but you should leave the server 5% to 10% extra in cash. It is generally advisable to charge restaurant meals on a credit card, as the issuer will offer a better exchange rate than the restaurant.

$$ ╳ **Le Repaire.** This friendly classic French brasserie overlooks Gustavia's BRASSERIE harbor, and is a popular spot from its early morning opening to its late-FAMILY night closing. The flexible hours are great if you arrive on the island midafternoon and need a substantial snack before dinner. Grab a cappuccino, pull a captain's chair up to the streetside rail, and watch the pretty people go by. The menu ranges from cheeseburgers, which are served only at lunch along with the island's best fries, to simply grilled fish and meat, pastas, and risottos. The mixed salads always please. Wonderful ice cream sundaes round out the menu. ⑤ *Average main: €19* ⊠ *Quai de la République* ☎ *0590/27–72–48* ☉ *Closed Sun. in June.*

$$ ✕ **L'Isoletta.** New in 2012, this Roman-style pizzeria run by the popular
PIZZA   L'Isola restaurant is a chic lounge-style gastropub serving delicious thin-
crust pizzas by the slice or by the meter. Lasagnas and sandwiches are
also available to eat in or take out. Stop in anytime as they are open
from lunch straight through until 11 pm. Don't miss the dessert pizzas.
⑤ *Average main: €10* ✉ *Rue du Roi Oscar II* ☎ *590/52–02–02* ⊕ *www.*
lisolettastbarth.com ⚅ *Reservations not accepted.*

ST. CROIX (FREDERIKSTED)

Lynda Lohr   St. Croix is the largest of the three U.S. Virgin Islands (USVI) that form
the northern hook of the Lesser Antilles; it's 40 miles (64 km) south
of its sister islands, St. Thomas and St. John. Christopher Columbus
landed here in 1493, skirmishing briefly with the native Carib Indians.
Since then, the USVI have played a colorful, if painful, role as pawns
in the game of European colonialism. Theirs is a history of pirates
and privateers, sugar plantations, slave trading, and slave revolt and
liberation. Through it all, Denmark had staying power. From the 17th
to the 19th century, Danes oversaw a plantation slave economy that
produced molasses, rum, cotton, and tobacco. Many of the stones you
tread on in the streets were once used as ballast on sailing ships, and
the yellow fort of Christiansted is a reminder of the value once placed
on this island treasure. Never a major cruise destination, it is still a stop
for several ships each year.

ESSENTIALS
CURRENCY
The U.S. dollar.

TELEPHONE
Calling the United States from St. Croix works the same way as calling
within the United States. Local calls from a public phone cost up to 35¢
for every five minutes. You can use your regular toll-free connections
for long-distance services. Most U.S. cell phone plans include the Virgin
Islands for no additional cost.

COMING ASHORE

Cruise ships dock in Frederiksted, on the island's west end. You'll find
an information center at the pier, and the town is easy to explore on
foot. Beaches are nearby. The only difficulty is that you are far from
the island's main town, Christiansted. Some cruise lines offer bus trans-
portation there; otherwise, you are probably better off renting a car to
explore the island, since both car-rental rates and gasoline prices are
reasonable; just remember to drive on the left.

Taxis of all shapes and sizes are available at the cruise-ship pier and at
various shopping and resort areas. Remember, too, that you can hail a
taxi that's already occupied. Drivers take multiple fares and sometimes
even trade passengers at midpoints. Taxis don't have meters, so you
should check the list of official rates (available at the visitor centers or
from drivers) and agree on a fare before you start, but there are standard

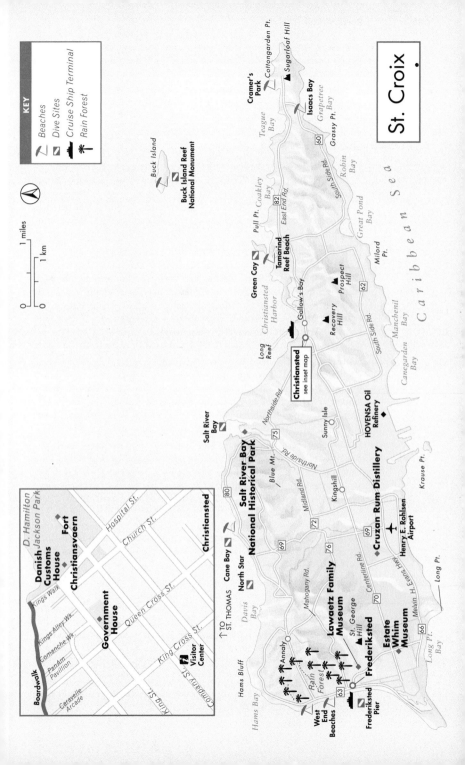

rates for most trips. A taxi to Christiansted will cost about $25 for two people for transportation only; an island tour including Christiansted will cost $110 for four people.

Car Rentals Midwest. This company is outside Frederiksted, but will pick you up at the pier. ☎ *340/772–0438, 877/772–0438* ⊕ *www. midwestautorental.com.*

EXPLORING ST. CROIX

Frederiksted speaks to history buffs with its quaint Victorian architecture and historic fort. There's very little traffic, so this is the perfect place for strolling and shopping. Christiansted is a historic Danish-style town that served as St. Croix's commercial center. Your best bet is to see the historic sights in the morning, when it's still cool. This two-hour endeavor won't tax your walking shoes and will leave you with energy to poke around the town's eclectic shops.

CHRISTIANSTED

In the 1700s and 1800s Christiansted was a trading center for sugar, rum, and molasses. Today there are law offices, tourist shops, and restaurants, but many of the buildings, which start at the harbor and go up the gently sloped hillsides, still date from the 18th century. You can't get lost. All streets lead back downhill to the water.

Danish Customs House. Built in 1830 on foundations that date from a century earlier, the historic building, which is near Ft. Christiansvaern, originally served as both a customshouse and a post office. In 1926 it became the Christiansted Library, and it's been a national park facility since 1972. It's closed to the public, but the sweeping front steps make a nice place to take a break. ⊠ *King St.* ☎ *340/773–1460* ⊕ *www.nps. gov/chri.*

FAMILY **Ft. Christiansvaern.** The large yellow fortress dominates the waterfront.
Fodor's Choice Because it's so easy to spot, it makes a good place to begin a walking
★ tour. In 1749 the Danish built the fort to protect the harbor, but the structure was repeatedly damaged by hurricane-force winds and had to be partially rebuilt in 1771. It's now a national historic site, the best preserved of the few remaining Danish-built forts in the Virgin Islands. The park's visitor center is here. Rangers are on hand to answer questions. ■ TIP➜ Your paid admission also includes the Steeple Building. ⊠ *Hospital St.* ☎ *340/773–1460* ⊕ *www.nps.gov/chri* ☒ *$3* ⊘ *Weekdays 8–4:30, weekends 9–4:30.*

Government House. One of the town's most elegant structures was built as a home for a Danish merchant in 1747. Today it houses offices. If you're here weekdays from 8 to 4:30, slip into the peaceful inner courtyard to admire the still pools and gardens. A sweeping staircase leads you to a second-story ballroom, still used for official government functions. ⊠ *King St.* ☎ *340/773–1404.*

MID ISLAND

Cruzan Rum Distillery. A tour of the company's factory, which was established in 1760, culminates in a tasting of its products, all sold here at good prices. It's worth a stop to look at the distillery's charming old buildings even if you're not a rum connoisseur. ✉ *West Airport Rd., Estate Diamond* ☎ *340/692–2280* ⊕ *www.cruzanrum.com* ✉ *$5* ⊙ *Weekdays 9–4.*

FAMILY

Fodor's Choice

★

Estate Whim Museum. The lovingly restored estate, with a windmill, cook house, and other buildings, gives a sense of what life was like on St. Croix's sugar plantations in the 1800s. The oval-shape great house has high ceilings and antique furniture and utensils. Notice its fresh, airy atmosphere—the water-less stone moat around the great house was used not for defense but for gathering cooling air. If you have kids, the grounds are the perfect place for them to run around, perhaps while you browse in the museum gift shop. It's just outside of Frederiksted. ✉ *Rte. 70, Estate Whim* ☎ *340/772–0598* ⊕ *www.stcroixlandmarks.com* ✉ *$10* ⊙ *Wed.–Sat. 10–4 and cruise ship days.*

> ## ST. CROIX BEST BETS
>
> ■ **Buck Island.** The snorkel-ing trail here is fun, but go by catamaran.
>
> ■ **Christiansted.** The best shop-ping on the island as well as interesting historical sights are here.
>
> ■ **Cruzan Rum Distillery.** This West End rum distillery gives you a tour and samples.
>
> ■ **Kayaking.** The Salt River, with few currents, is a great place to take a guided kayak trip.
>
> ■ **West End Beaches.** The island's best beaches are on the west end, and are just a short hop from the cruise pier.

FREDERIKSTED AND ENVIRONS

This town is noted less for its Danish than for its Victorian architecture, which dates from after the slave rebellion and great fire of July 1848.

Caribbean Museum Center for the Arts. Sitting across from the waterfront in a historic building, this small museum hosts an always-changing roster of exhibits. Many are cutting-edge multimedia efforts that you might be surprised to find in such an out-of-the-way location. The openings are popular events. ✉ *10 Strand St., Frederiksted* ☎ *340/772–2622* ⊕ *www.cmcarts.org* ✉ *Free* ⊙ *Thurs.–Sun. (and cruise-ship days) 10–4.*

Frederiksted Visitor Center. Head here for brochures from numerous St. Croix businesses, as well as a few exhibits about the island. ✉ *Pier, Frederiksted* ☎ *340/773-0495* ⊙ *Weekdays 8–5.*

FAMILY

Fort Frederik. On July 3, 1848, 8,000 slaves marched on this fort to demand their freedom. Danish governor Peter von Scholten, fearing they would burn the town to the ground, stood up in his carriage parked in front of the fort and granted their wish. The fort, completed in 1760, houses an art gallery and a number of interesting historical exhibits, including some focusing on the 1848 Emancipation and the 1917 trans-fer of the Virgin Islands from Denmark to the United States. It's within earshot of the Frederiksted Visitor Center. ✉ *Waterfront, Frederiksted* ☎ *340/772–2021* ✉ *$5* ⊙ *Weekdays (and cruise-ship days) 8:30–4.*

Fodor's Choice

★

Lawaetz Family Museum. For a trip back in time, tour this circa-1750 farm, in a valley at La Grange. It's been owned by the prominent Lawaetz family since 1896, which is just after Carl Lawaetz arrived from Denmark. A Lawaetz family member shows you around the lovely two-story house and the farm, noting the four-poster mahogany bed Carl shared with his wife, Marie, the china Marie painted, the family portraits, and the fruit trees that fed the family for several generations. Initially a sugar plantation, the farm was subsequently used to raise cattle and grow produce. ⊠ *Rte. 76 (Mahogany Rd.), Estate Little La Grange* ☎ *340/772–1539* ⊕ *www.stcroixlandmarks.com* ✉ *$10* ⊙ *Wed., Thurs., and Sat. 10–4.*

NORTH SHORE

Salt River Bay National Historical Park and Ecological Preserve. This joint national and local park commemorates the area where Christopher Columbus's men skirmished with the Carib Indians in 1493 on his second visit to the New World. The peninsula on the bay's east side is named for the event: Cabo de las Flechas (Cape of the Arrows). Although the park is still developing, it has several sights with cultural significance. A ball court, used by the Caribs in religious ceremonies, was discovered at the spot where the taxis park. Take a short hike up the dirt road to the ruins of an old earthen fort for great views of Salt River Bay. The area also encompasses a coastal estuary with the region's largest remaining mangrove forest, a submarine canyon, and several endangered species, including the hawksbill turtle and the roseate tern. A visitor center, open winter only, sits just uphill to the west. The water at the beach can be on the rough side, but it's a nice place for sunning. ⊠ *Rte. 75 to Rte. 80, Salt River* ☎ *340/773–1460* ⊕ *www.nps.gov/sari* ⊙ *Nov.–June, Tues.–Thurs. 9–4.*

BEACHES

West End beaches. There are several unnamed beaches along the coast road north of Frederiksted, but it's best if you don't stray too far from civilization. For safety's sake, most vacationers plop down their towel near one of the casual restaurants spread out along Route 63. The beach at the Rainbow Beach Club, a five-minute drive outside Frederiksted, has a bar, a casual restaurant, water sports, and volleyball. If you want to be close to the cruise-ship pier, just stroll on over to the adjacent sandy beach in front of Ft. Frederik. On the way south out of Frederiksted, the stretch near Sandcastle on the Beach hotel is also lovely. **Amenities:** food and drink; water sports. **Best for:** snorkeling, swimming, walking. ⊠ *Rte. 63, north and south of Frederiksted.*

SHOPPING

The selection of duty-free goods on St. Croix is fairly good. The best shopping is in Christiansted, where most stores are in the historic district near the harbor. King Street, Strand Street, and the arcades that lead off them compose the main shopping district and where you'll find **Sonya's,** the jewelry store that first sold the locally popular hook bracelet. The longest arcade is **Caravelle Arcade,** adjacent to the hotel of the same name. In Frederiksted a handful of shops face the cruise-ship pier.

Sonya's. This store is owned and operated by Sonya Hough, who invented the popular hook bracelet. She has added an interesting decoration to these bracelets: the swirling symbol used in weather forecasts to indicate hurricanes. ⊠ *1 Company St.* ☎ *340/778–8605* ⊕ *www.sonyaltd.com.*

ACTIVITIES

BOAT TOURS

Many people take a day trip to Buck Island aboard a charter boat. Most leave from the Christiansted waterfront or from Green Cay Marina and stop for a snorkel at the island's eastern end before dropping anchor off a gorgeous sandy beach for a swim, a hike, and lunch. Sailboats can often stop right at the beach; a larger boat might have to anchor a bit farther offshore. A full-day sail runs about $100, with lunch included on most trips. A half-day sail costs about $68.

Big Beard's Adventure Tours. From catamarans that depart from the Christiansted waterfront you'll head to Buck Island for snorkeling before dropping anchor at a private beach for a barbecue lunch. ⊠ *Waterfront* ☎ *340/773–4482* ⊕ *www.bigbeards.com.*

DIVING AND SNORKELING

N2 the Blue. N2 takes divers right off the beach near Coconuts restaurant, on night dives off the Frederiksted Pier, or on boat trips to wrecks and reefs. ⊠ *Rte. 631, Frederiksted* ☎ *340/772–3483, 877/579–0572* ⊕ *www.n2theblue.com.*

GOLF

Carambola Golf Club. This spectacular 18-hole course in the northwest valley was designed by Robert Trent Jones, Sr. The greens fees, $125 for 18 holes, include the use of a golf cart. ⊠ *Rte. 69, River* ☎ *340/778–5638* ⊕ *www.golfcarambola.com.*

HORSEBACK RIDING

Paul and Jill's Equestrian Stables. From Sprat Hall, just north of Frederiksted, co-owner Jill Hurd will take you through the rain forest, across the pastures, along the beaches, and through valleys—explaining the flora, fauna, and ruins on the way. A 1½-hour ride costs $100. ⊠ *Rte. 58, Frederiksted* ☎ *340/772–2880, 340/772–2627* ⊕ *www.paulandjills. com.*

KAYAKING

Caribbean Adventure Tours. These kayak tours take you on trips through Salt River Bay National Historical Park and Ecological Preserve, one of the island's most pristine areas. All tours run $45. ⊠ *Salt River Marina, Rte. 80, Salt River* ☎ *340/778–1522* ⊕ *www.stcroixkayak.com.*

WHERE TO EAT

$$$

AMERICAN

Fodor's Choice

★

✕ **Blue Moon.** This terrific little bistro, which has a loyal local following, offers a changing menu that draws on Cajun and Caribbean flavors. Try the spicy gumbo with andouille sausage or crab cakes with a spicy aioli for your appetizer. A grilled chicken breast served with spinach and artichoke hearts and topped with Parmesan and cheddar cheeses makes a good entrée. The Almond Joy sundae should be your choice for dessert. There's live jazz on Wednesday and Friday. $ *Average main: $25* ✉ *7 Strand St., Frederiksted* ☎ *340/772–2222* ⊘ *Closed Mon.*

$$$

ECLECTIC

FAMILY

Fodor's Choice

★

✕ **Rum Runners.** The view is as stellar as the food at this highly popular local standby. Sitting right on the Christiansted boardwalk, Rum Runners serves a little bit of everything, including a to-die-for salad of crispy romaine lettuce and tender grilled lobster drizzled with lemongrass vinaigrette. More hearty fare includes baby back ribs cooked with the restaurant's special spice blend and Guinness stout. $ *Average main: $23* ✉ *Hotel Caravelle, 44A Queen Cross St.* ☎ *340/773–6585* ⊕ *www.rumrunnersstcroix.com.*

ST. JOHN (CRUZ BAY)

Lynda Lohr

St. John's heart is Virgin Islands National Park, a treasure that takes up a full two-thirds of St. John's 20 square miles (53 square km). The park helps keep the island's interior in its pristine and undisturbed state, but if you go at midday you'll probably have to share your stretch of beach with others, particularly at Trunk Bay. The island is booming, and although it can get a tad crowded at the ever-popular Trunk Bay Beach during the busy winter season, you won't find traffic jams or pollution. It's easy to escape from the fray, however: just head off on a hike. St. John doesn't have a grand agrarian past like her sister island, St. Croix, but if you're hiking in the dry season, you can probably stumble upon the stone ruins of old plantations. The less adventuresome can visit the repaired ruins at the park's Annaberg Plantation and Caneel Bay resort. Of the three U.S. Virgin Islands, St. John, which has 5,000 residents, has the strongest sense of community, which is primarily rooted in a desire to protect the island's natural beauty.

ESSENTIALS

CURRENCY

The U.S. dollar.

TELEPHONE

Both Sprint and AT&T phones work in most of St. John (take care that you're not roaming on the Tortola cell network on the island's north coast, though). It's as easy to call home from St. John as from any city in the United States. On St. John, public phones are near telephone poles midway along the Cruz Bay waterfront.

COMING ASHORE

Although a few smaller ships drop anchor at St. John, most people taking a cruise aboard a larger ship visit St. Thomas's sister island on a shore excursion or on an independent day trip from St. Thomas. If you prefer to not take a tour, ferries leave St. Thomas from the Charlotte Amalie waterfront and Red Hook. You'll have to take a taxi to reach the ferry dock.

If you're aboard a smaller ship that calls in St. John, your ship may simply pause outside Cruz Bay Harbor to drop you off or drop anchor if it's spending the day. You'll be tendered to shore at the main town of Cruz

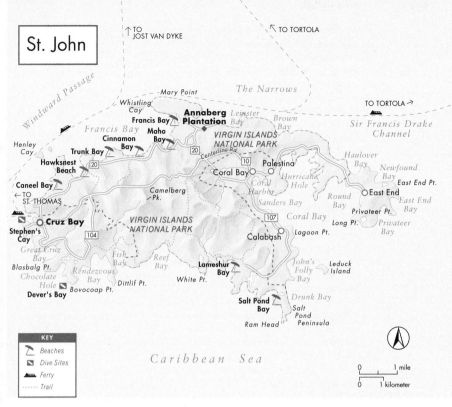

Bay. The shopping district starts just across the street from the tender landing. You'll find an eclectic collection of shops, cozy restaurants, and places where you can just sit and take it all in. The island has few sights to see. Your best bet is to take a tour of the Virgin Islands National Park. (If your ship doesn't offer such a tour, arrange one with one of the taxi drivers who will meet your tender.) The drive takes you past luscious beaches to a restored sugar plantation. With only a single day in port, you're better off just using the island's shared taxi vans rather than renting a car, but if you want to do some independent exploring, you can rent a car in Cruz Bay.

EXPLORING ST. JOHN

CRUZ BAY

St. John's main town may be compact (it consists of only several blocks), but it's definitely a hub: the ferries from St. Thomas and the British Virgin Islands pull in here, and it's where you can get a taxi or rent a car to travel around the island. There are plenty of shops in which to browse, a number of watering holes where you can stop for a breather, many restaurants, and a grassy square with benches where you can sit back and take everything in. Look for the current edition of the handy, amusing *Road Map: St. Thomas–St. John* featuring Max the Mongoose.

V.I. National Park Visitors Center. To pick up a useful guide to St. John's hiking trails, see various large maps of the island, and find out about current Park Service programs, including guided walks and cultural demonstrations, stop by the park visitor center. ⊠ *North Shore Rd., near Creek, Cruz Bay* ☎ *340/776–6201* ⊕ *www.nps.gov/viis* ☉ *Daily 8–4:30.*

ELSEWHERE ON THE ISLAND

Fodor's Choice ★ **Annaberg Plantation.** In the 18th century, sugar plantations dotted the steep hills of this island. Slaves and free Danes and Dutchmen toiled to harvest the cane that was used to create sugar, molasses, and rum for export. Built in the 1780s, the partially restored plantation at Leinster Bay was once an important sugar mill. Although there are no official visiting hours, the National Park Service has regular tours, and some well-informed taxi drivers will show you around. Occasionally you may see a living-history demonstration—someone making johnnycake or weaving baskets. For information on tours and cultural events, contact the V.I. National Park Visitors Center. ⊠ *Leinster Bay Rd., Annaberg* ☎ *340/776–6201* ⊕ *www.nps.gov/viis* ⊠ *Free* ☉ *Daily dawn–dusk.*

> ### ST. JOHN BEST BETS
>
> ■ **Hiking in the National Park.** Hiking trails that crisscross the terrain are easy enough for beginners and offer breathtaking scenery.
>
> ■ **Snorkeling Cruises.** The best snorkeling sites are reachable only by boat.
>
> ■ **Trunk Bay Beach.** St. John's national park beach is beautiful and has an underwater snorkeling trail.

BEACHES

Cinnamon Bay Beach. This long, sandy beach faces beautiful cays and abuts the national park campground. You can rent water-sports equipment here—a good thing, because there's excellent snorkeling off the point to the right; look for the big angelfish and large schools of purple triggerfish. Afternoons on Cinnamon Bay can be windy—a boon for windsurfers but an annoyance for sunbathers—so arrive early to beat the gusts. The Cinnamon Bay hiking trail begins across the road from the beach parking lot; ruins mark the trailhead. There are actually two paths here: a level nature trail (signs along it identify the flora) that loops through the woods and passes an old Danish cemetery, and a steep trail that starts where the road bends past the ruins and heads straight up to Route 10. Restrooms are on the main path from the commissary to the beach and scattered around the campground. **Amenities:** food and drink; parking; showers; toilets; water sports. **Best for:** snorkeling; swimming; walking; windsurfing. ⊠ *North Shore Rd., Rte. 20, about 4 miles (6 km) east of Cruz Bay, Cinnamon Bay* ⊕ *www.nps.gov/viis.*

Fodor's Choice ★ **Trunk Bay Beach.** St. John's most-photographed beach is also the preferred spot for beginning snorkelers because of its underwater trail. (Cruise-ship passengers interested in snorkeling for a day flock here, so if you're looking for seclusion, arrive early or later in the day.) Crowded or not, this stunning beach is one of the island's most beautiful. There are changing rooms with showers, bathrooms, a snack bar, picnic tables, a gift shop, phones, lockers, and snorkeling-equipment rentals. The parking lot often overflows, but you can park along the road as long as the tires are off the pavement. **Amenities:** food and drink; lifeguards; parking; toilets; water sports. **Best for:** snorkeling; swimming, windsurfing ⊠ *North Shore Rd., Rte. 20, about 2½ miles (4 km) east of Cruz Bay, Trunk Bay* ⊕ *www.nps.gov/viis* ✑ *$4.*

SHOPPING

Luxury goods and handicrafts can be found on St. John. Most shops carry a little of this and a bit of that, so it pays to poke around. The Cruz Bay shopping district runs from **Wharfside Village,** just around the corner from the ferry dock, to **Mongoose Junction,** an inviting shopping center on North Shore Road. (The name of this upscale shopping mall, by the way, is a holdover from a time when those furry island creatures gathered at a nearby garbage bin.) Out on Route 104 stop in at the **Marketplace** to explore its gift and crafts shops. At the island's other end, there are a few stores—selling clothes, jewelry, and artwork—here and there from the village of **Coral Bay** to the small complex at **Shipwreck Landing.**

On St. John, store hours run from 9 or 10 to 5 or 6. Wharfside Village and Mongoose Junction shops in Cruz Bay are often open into the evening.

ACTIVITIES

DIVING AND SNORKELING

Cruz Bay Watersports. The owners of Cruz Bay, Marcus and Patty Johnston, offer regular reef, wreck, and night dives and USVI and BVI snorkel tours. The company holds both PADI Five Star and NAUI-Dream-Resort status. ⊠ *Lumberyard Shopping Complex, Boulon Center Rd., Cruz Bay* ☎ *340/776–6234* ⊕ *www.divestjohn.com.*

Low Key Watersports. Low Key Watersports offers two-tank dives and specialty courses. It's certified as a PADI Five Star training facility. ⊠ *1 Bay St., Cruz Bay* ☎ *340/693–8999, 800/835–7718* ⊕ *www.divelowkey.com.*

FISHING

Well-kept charter boats—approved by the U.S. Coast Guard—head out to the north and south drops or troll along the inshore reefs, depending on the season and what's biting. The captains usually provide bait, drinks, and lunch, but you need to bring your own hat and sunscreen. Half-day fishing charters run between about $750 for the boat.

FAMILY **Offshore Adventures.** An excellent choice for fishing charters, Captain Rob Richards is patient with beginners—especially kids—but also enjoys going out with more experienced anglers. He runs the 40-foot center console *Mixed Bag I* and 32-foot *Mixed Bag II.* Although he's based in St. John, he will pick up parties in St. Thomas. ⊠ *Westin St. John, 3008 Chocolate Hole Rd., Great Cruz Bay* ☎ *340/513–0389* ⊕ *www.sportfishingstjohn.com.*

7

HIKING

Although it's fun to go hiking with a Virgin Islands National Park guide, don't be afraid to head out on your own. To find a hike that suits your ability, stop by the park's visitor center in Cruz Bay and pick up the free trail guide; it details points of interest, trail lengths, and estimated hiking times, as well as any dangers you might encounter. Although the park staff recommends long pants to protect against thorns and insects, most people hike in shorts because it can get very hot. Wear sturdy shoes or hiking boots even if you're hiking to the beach. Don't forget to bring water and insect repellent.

Fodor's Choice **Virgin Islands National Park.** Head to the park for more than 20 trails on
★ the north and south shores, with guided hikes along the most popular routes. A full-day trip to Reef Bay is a must; it's an easy hike through lush and dry forest, past the ruins of an old plantation, and to a sugar factory adjacent to the beach. It can be a bit arduous for young kids, however. The park runs a $30 guided tour to Reef Bay that includes a safari bus ride to the trailhead and a boat ride back to the Visitors Center. The schedule changes from season to season; call for times and to make reservations, which are essential. ⊠ *North Shore Rd. near the Creek, Cruz Bay* ☎ *340/776–6201* ⊕ *www.nps.gov/viis.*

WHERE TO EAT

$ ✕ **Deli Grotto.** At this air-conditioned (but no-frills) sandwich shop you
ECLECTIC place your order at the counter and wait for it to be delivered to your table or for takeout. The portobello panino with savory sautéed onions is a favorite, but the other sandwiches, such as the smoked turkey and artichoke, also get rave reviews. Order a brownie or cookie for dessert. ⑤ *Average main: $9* ⊠ *Mongoose Junction Shopping Center, North Shore Rd., Cruz Bay* ☎ *340/777–3061* ▭ *No credit cards* ⊘ *No dinner.*

$$ ✕ **Lime Inn.** The vacationers and mainland transplants who call St. John
ECLECTIC home like to flock to this alfresco spot for the congenial hospitality and good food, including all-you-can-eat shrimp on Wednesday night. Fresh lobster is the specialty, and the menu also includes shrimp-and-steak dishes and rotating chicken and pasta specials. ⑤ *Average main: $26* ⊠ *Lemon Tree Mall, King St., Cruz Bay* ☎ *340/776–6425* ⊕ *www. limeinn.com* ⊘ *Closed Sun. No lunch Sat.*

ST. KITTS (BASSETERRE)

Jordan Simon   Mountainous St. Kitts, the first English settlement in the Leeward Islands, crams some stunning scenery into its 65 square miles (168 square km). Vast, brilliant green fields of sugarcane (the former cash crop, now slowly being replanted) run to the shore. The fertile, lush island has some fascinating natural and historical attractions: a rain forest replete with waterfalls, thick vines, and secret trails; a central mountain range dominated by the 3,792-foot Mt. Liamuiga, whose crater has long been dormant; and Brimstone Hill, known in the 18th century as the Gibraltar of the West Indies. St. Kitts and Nevis, along with Anguilla, achieved self-government as an associated state of Great

Britain in 1967. In 1983 St. Kitts and Nevis became an independent nation. English with a strong West Indian lilt is spoken here. People are friendly but shy; always ask before you take photographs. Also, be sure to wear wraps or shorts over beach attire when you're in public places.

ESSENTIALS

CURRENCY
Eastern Caribbean (EC) dollar, but U.S. dollars are widely accepted.

TELEPHONE
Phone cards, which you can buy in denominations of $5, $10, and $20, are handy for making local phone calls, calling other islands, and accessing U.S. direct lines. To make a local call, dial the seven-digit number. To call St. Kitts from the United States, dial the area code 869, then access code 465, 466, 468, or 469 and the local four-digit number.

COMING ASHORE

Cruise ships calling at St. Kitts dock at Port Zante, which is a deepwater port directly in Basseterre, the capital of St. Kitts. The cruise-ship terminal is right in the downtown area, two minutes' walk from sights and shops. Taxi rates on St. Kitts are fixed, and should be posted right at the dock. If you'd like to go to Nevis, several daily ferries (30 to 45 minutes, $8–$10 one-way) can take you to Charlestown in Nevis; the Byzantine schedule is subject to change, so double-check times.

Taxi rates on St. Kitts are fairly expensive, and you may have to pay $32 for a ride to Brimstone Hill (for one to four passengers). A four-hour tour of St. Kitts runs about $80. It's often cheaper to arrange an island tour with one of the local companies than to hire a taxi driver to take your group around. Several restored plantation greathouses are known for their lunches; your driver can provide information and arrange drop-off and pickup. Before setting off in a cab, be sure to clarify whether the rate quoted is in EC or U.S. dollars.

EXPLORING ST. KITTS

BASSETERRE
On the south coast, St. Kitts's walkable capital is graced with tall palms and flagstone sidewalks; although many of the buildings appear rundown, there are interesting shops, excellent art galleries, and some beautifully maintained houses. Duty-free shops and boutiques line the streets and courtyards radiating from the octagonal **Circus,** built in the style of London's famous Piccadilly Circus.

Independence Square. There are lovely gardens and a fountain on the site of a former slave market at Independence Square. The square is surrounded on three sides by 18th-century Georgian buildings. ✉ *Off Bank St.*

National Museum. In the restored former Treasury Building, the National Museum presents an eclectic collection of artifacts reflecting the history and culture of the island. ✉ *Bay Rd.* ☎ *869/465–5584* 💲 *$3* ⊙ *Weekdays 9:15–5, Sat. 9:15–1.*

Port Zante. Port Zante is an ambitious, ever-growing 27-acre cruise-ship pier and marina in an area that has been reclaimed from the sea. The domed welcome center is an imposing neoclassical hodgepodge, with columns and stone arches, shops, walkways, fountains, and West Indian–style buildings housing luxury shops, galleries, restaurants, and a small casino. A second pier, 1,434 feet long, has a draft that accommodates even leviathan cruise ships. The selection of shops and restaurants (Twist serves global fusion cuisine) is expanding as well. ⊠ *Waterfront, behind Circus* ⊕ *www.portzante.com.*

St. George's Anglican Church. St. George's Anglican Church is a handsome stone building with a crenellated tower originally built by the French in 1670 and called Nôtre-Dame. The British burned it down in 1706 and rebuilt it four years later, naming it after the patron saint of England. Since then it has suffered a fire, an earthquake, and hurricanes and was once again rebuilt in 1869. ⊠ *Cayon St.*

> ## ST. KITTS BEST BETS
>
> ■ **Brimstone Hill Fortress.** Stop here for some of the best views on St. Kitts and historic ambience.
>
> ■ **Nevis.** A trip to Nevis is a worthwhile way to spend the day.
>
> ■ **Plantation Greathouses.** Stop for a lunch at Ottley's or Rawlins Plantation.
>
> ■ **Rain-forest Hikes.** Several operators on the island lead day-long hikes through the rain forest.
>
> ■ **Romney Manor.** This partially restored manor house is enhanced by the chance to shop at Caribelle Batik and watch the elaborate wax-and-dye process.

Brimstone Hill. This 38-acre fortress, a UNESCO World Heritage Site, is part of a national park dedicated by Queen Elizabeth in 1985. After routing the French in 1690, the English erected a battery here; by 1736 the fortress held 49 guns, earning it the moniker Gibraltar of the West Indies. In 1782, 8,000 French troops laid siege to the stronghold, which was defended by 350 militia and 600 regular troops of the Royal Scots and East Yorkshires. When the English finally surrendered, they were allowed to march from the fort in full formation out of respect for their bravery (the English afforded the French the same honor when they surrendered the fort a mere year later). A hurricane severely damaged the fortress in 1834, and in 1852 it was evacuated and dismantled. The beautiful stones were carted away to build houses. The citadel has been partially reconstructed and its guns remounted. It's a steep walk up the hill from the parking lot. The spectacular view includes Montserrat and Nevis to the southeast; Saba and St. Eustatius to the northwest; and St. Barth and St. Maarten to the north. ⊠ *Main Rd., Brimstone Hill* ☎ 869/465–2609 ⊕ *www.brimstonehillfortress.org* ⊠ *$8* ☉ *Daily 9:30–5:30.*

Romney Manor. The ruins of this somewhat restored house (reputedly once the property of Thomas Jefferson) and surrounding replicas of chattel-house cottages are set in 6 acres of glorious gardens, with exotic flowers, an old bell tower, and an enormous, gnarled 350-year-old saman tree (sometimes called a rain tree). Inside, at **Caribelle Batik,** you can watch artisans hand-printing fabrics by the 2,500-year-old Indonesian

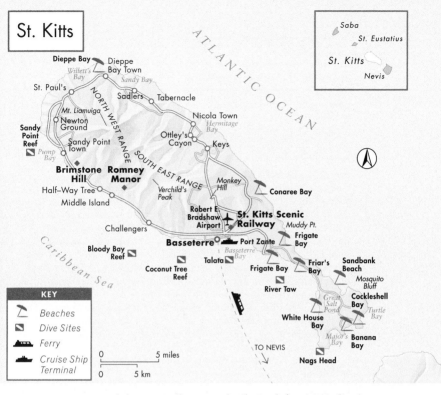

St. Kitts

KEY

⚐ Beaches

◥ Dive Sites

⛴ Ferry

🚢 Cruise Ship
Terminal

0   5 miles

0   5 km

wax-and-dye process known as batik. Look for signs indicating a turn-off for Romney Manor near Old Road. ⊠ *Old Rd.* ☎ *869/465–6253* ⊕ *www.caribellebatikstkitts.com* ⊠ *Free* ⊙ *Daily 9–5.*

St. Kitts Scenic Railway. The old narrow-gauge train that had transported sugarcane to the central sugar factory since 1912 is all that remains of the island's once-thriving sugar industry. Two-story cars bedecked in bright Kittitian colors circle the island in just under four hours (a new Rail and Sail option takes guests going or on the return via catamaran). Each passenger gets a comfortable, downstairs air-conditioned seat fronting vaulted picture windows and an upstairs open-air observation spot. The conductor's running discourse embraces not only the history of sugar cultivation but also the railway's construction, local folklore, island geography, even other agricultural mainstays from papayas to pigs. You can drink in complimentary tropical beverages (including luscious guava daiquiris) along with the sweeping rain-forest and ocean vistas, accompanied by an a cappella choir's renditions of hymns, spirituals, and predictable standards like "I've Been Workin' on the Railroad." ⊠ *Needsmust* ☎ *869/465–7263* ⊕ *www.stkittsscenicrailway.com* ⊠ *$89* ⊙ *Departures vary according to cruise-ship schedules (call ahead, but at least once daily Dec.–Apr., usually 8:30 am).*

BEACHES

The powdery white-sand beaches of St. Kitts, free and open to the public (even those occupied by hotels), are in the Frigate Bay area or on the lower peninsula. Chair rentals cost around $3, though if you order lunch you can negotiate a freebie. Caution: The Atlantic waters are rougher than those on the Caribbean side of the island.

Banana/Cockleshell Bays. These twin connected eyebrows of glittering champagne-color sand—stretching

nearly 2 miles (3 km) total at the southeastern tip of the island—feature majestic views of Nevis and are backed by lush vegetation and coconut palms. The first-rate restaurant-bar Spice Mill (next to Rasta-hue Lion Rock Beach Bar—order the knockout Lion Punch) and Reggae Beach Bar & Grill bracket either end of Cockleshell. At this writing, plans for a 125-room mixed-use Park Hyatt (with additional residential condos and villas) are tentatively back on schedule for development by early 2015. The water is generally placid, ideal for swimming. The downside is irregular maintenance, with seaweed (particularly after rough weather) and occasional litter, especially on Banana Bay. Follow Simmonds Highway to the end and bear right, ignoring the turnoff for Turtle Beach. **Amenities:** food and drink, parking. **Best for:** partiers, snorkeling, swimming, walking. ⊠ *Banana Bay.*

Friar's Bay. Locals consider Friar's Bay, on the Caribbean (southern) side, the island's finest beach. It's a long, tawny scimitar where the water always seems warmer and clearer. The upscale Carambola Beach Club has co-opted roughly one third of the strand. Still, several happening bars, including ShipWreck and Mongoose, serve terrific, inexpensive local food and cheap, frosty drinks. Chair rentals cost around $3, though if you order lunch, you can negotiate a freebie. Friar's is the first major beach along Southeast Peninsula Drive (aka Simmonds Highway), approximately a mile (1½ km) southeast of Frigate Bay. **Amenities:** food and drink. **Best for:** snorkeling, swimming, walking. ⊠ *Friar's Bay.*

Frigate Bay. The Caribbean side offers talcum-powder-fine beige sand framed by coconut palms and sea grapes, and the Atlantic side (a 15-minute stroll)—sometimes called North Frigate Bay—is a favorite with horseback riders. South Frigate Bay is bookended by the Timothy Beach Club's Sunset Café and the popular, pulsating Buddies Beach Hut. In between are several other lively beach spots, including Cathy's (fabulous jerk ribs), Chinchilla's, Vibes, Elvis Love Shack, and Mr. X Shiggidy Shack. Most charge $3 to $5 to rent a chair, though they'll often waive the fee if you ask politely and buy lunch. Locals barhop late into Friday and Saturday nights. Waters are generally calm for swimming; the rockier eastern end offers fine snorkeling. The incomparably scenic Atlantic side is—regrettably—dominated by the Marriott (plentiful dining options), attracting occasional pesky vendors. The surf is choppier and the undertow stronger here. On cruise-ship days, groups stampede both sides. **Amenities:** food and drink, water sports. **Best for:** partiers, snorkeling, swimming, walking. ⊠ *Frigate Bay* ⚓ *Less than 3 miles (5 km) from downtown Basseterre.*

> **CAUTION**
>
> Pack a small flashlight just in case there's an emergency. You don't want to be stumbling around in the dark.

SHOPPING

St. Kitts has limited shopping, but there are several small duty-free shops with good deals on jewelry, perfume, china, and crystal. Numerous galleries sell excellent paintings and sculptures. The batik fabrics, scarves, caftans, and wall hangings of Caribelle Batik are well known. British expat Kate Spencer is an artist who has lived on the island for years, reproducing its vibrant colors on everything from silk pareus (beach wraps) to note cards to place mats. Other good island buys include crafts, jams, and herbal teas. Don't forget to pick up some CSR (Cane Spirit Rothschild), which is distilled from fresh wild sugarcane right on St. Kitts. The Brinley Gold company has made a splash among spirits connoisseurs for its coffee, mango, coconut, lime, and vanilla rums (there is a tasting room at Port Zante). Most shopping plazas are in downtown Basseterre, on the streets radiating from the Circus.

ACTIVITIES

DIVING AND SNORKELING

Though unheralded as a dive destination, St. Kitts has more than a dozen excellent sites, protected by several new marine parks. The surrounding waters feature shoals, hot vents, shallows, canyons, steep walls, and caverns at depths from 40 to nearly 200 feet.

Dive St. Kitts. This PADI–NAUI facility, offers competitive prices, computers to maximize time below, wide range of courses from refresher to technical, and friendly, laid-back dive masters. The Bird Rock location features superb shore diving (unlimited when you book packages): common sightings 20 to 30 feet out include octopuses, nurse sharks, manta and spotted eagle rays, sea horses, even barracudas George and Georgianna. It also offers kayak and snorkeling tours. ⊠ *2 miles (3 km) east of Basseterre, Frigate Bay* ☎ *869/465–1189, 869/465–8914* ⊕ *www.divestkitts.com.*

GOLF

Royal St. Kitts Golf Club. This 18-hole, par-71 links-style championship course underwent a complete redesign by Thomas McBroom to maximize Caribbean and Atlantic views and increase the challenge (there are 12 lakes and 83 bunkers). Holes 15 through 17 (the latter patterned after Pebble Beach No. 18) skirt the Atlantic in their entirety, lending new meaning to the term *sand trap*. The sudden gusts, wide but twisting fairways, and extremely hilly terrain demand pinpoint accuracy and finesse, yet holes such as 18 require pure power. Greens fees are $150 for Marriott guests in high season, $180 for nonguests, with twilight and super-twilight discounts. The development includes practice bunkers, a putting green, a short-game chipping area, and the fairly high-tech Royal Golf Academy. ⊠ *St. Kitts Marriott Resort, Frigate Bay* ☎ *869/466–2700, 866/785–4653* ⊕ *www.royalstkittsgolfclub.com.*

HIKING

Trails in the central mountains vary from easy to don't-try-it-by-yourself. Monkey Hill and Verchild's Peak aren't difficult, although the Verchild's climb will take the better part of a day. Don't attempt Mt. Liamuiga without a guide. You'll start at Belmont Estate—at the west end of the island—on horseback, then proceed on foot to the lip of the crater, at 2,600 feet. You can go down into the crater—1,000 feet deep and 1 mile (1.5 km) wide, with a small freshwater lake—clinging to vines and roots and scaling rocks, even trees. Expect to get muddy. There are several fine operators (each hotel recommends its favorite); tour rates range from $50 for a rain-forest walk to $95 for a volcano expedition, and usually include round-trip transportation from your hotel and picnic lunch.

Duke of Earl's Adventures. Owner Earl "The Duke of Earl" Vanlow is as entertaining as his nickname suggests—and his prices are slightly cheaper ($45 for a rain-forest tour includes refreshments, $70 volcano expeditions add lunch; hotel pickup and drop-off is complimentary). He genuinely loves his island and conveys that enthusiasm, encouraging hikers to swing on vines or sample unusual-looking fruits during his rain-forest trip. He also conducts a thorough volcano tour to the crater's rim and a drive-through ecosafari tour ($50 with lunch). ☎ *869/465–1899, 869/663–0994.*

Greg's Safaris. Greg Pereira of Greg's Safaris, whose family has lived on St. Kitts since the early 19th century, takes groups on half-day trips into the rain forest and on full-day hikes up the volcano and through the grounds of a private 18th-century greathouse. The rain-forest trips include visits to sacred Carib sites, abandoned sugar mills, and an excursion down a 100-foot coastal canyon containing a wealth of Amerindian petroglyphs. The Off the Beaten Track 4x4 Plantation Tour provides a thorough explanation of the role sugar and rum played in the Caribbean economy and colonial wars. He and his staff relate fascinating historical, folkloric, and botanical information. ☎ *869/465–4121* ⊕ *www.gregsafaris.com.*

HORSEBACK RIDING

Trinity Stables. Guides from Trinity Stables offer beach rides ($50) and trips into the rain forest ($60), both including hotel pickup. The latter is intriguing, as guides discuss plants' medicinal properties along the way (such as sugarcane to stanch bleeding) and pick oranges right off a tree to squeeze fresh juice. Otherwise, the staffers are cordial but shy; this isn't a place for beginners' instruction. ☎ *869/465–3226.*

ZIP-LINING

FAMILY **Sky Safari Tours.** On these popular tours, would-be Tarzans and Janes whisk through the "Valley of the Giants" (so dubbed for the towering trees) at speeds up to 50 mph (80 kph along five cable lines); the longest (nicknamed "The Boss") stretches 1,350 feet through towering turpentine and mahogany trees draped thickly with bromeliads, suspended 250 feet above the ground. Following the Canadian-based company's mantra of "faster, higher, safer," it uses a specially designed trolley with secure harnesses attached. Many of the routes afford unobstructed views of Brimstone Hill and the sea beyond. The outfit emphasizes environmental and historic aspects. Guides provide nature interpretation and commentary, and the office incorporates Wingfield Estate's old sugar plantation, distillery, and church ruins, which visitors can explore. Admission is usually $65–$75, depending on the tour chosen. It's open daily 9–6, with the first and last tours departing at 10 and 3. ⊠ *Wingfield Estate* ☎ *869/466–4259, 869/465–4347* ⊕ *www. skysafaristkitts.com.*

WHERE TO EAT

$$ ✕ **Reggae Beach Bar & Grill.** Treats at this popular daytime watering
ECLECTIC hole include honey-mustard ribs, coconut shrimp, grilled lobster, decadent banana bread pudding with rum sauce, and an array of tempting tropical libations. Business cards and pennants from around the world plaster the bar, and the open-air space is decorated with nautical accoutrements, from fishnets and turtle shells to painted wooden crustaceans. You can snorkel here, spot hawksbill turtles and the occasional monkey, visit the enormous house pig Wilbur (who once "ate" beer cans whole, then moved to "lite" beers—but feeding is no longer encouraged), laze in a palm-shaded hammock, or rent a kayak, Hobie Cat or snorkeling gear. Beach chairs are free. Locals come Friday nights for bonfire dinners and Sunday afternoons for dancing to live bands. ⑤ *Average main: $26* ⊠ *S.E. Peninsula Rd., Cockleshell Beach* ☎ *869/762–5050* ⊕ *www. reggaebeachbar.com* ⊗ *No dinner.*

ST. LUCIA (CASTRIES)

Jane E. Zarem   Magnificent St. Lucia—with its towering mountains, dense rain forest, fertile green valleys, and acres of banana plantations—lies in the middle of the Windward Islands. Nicknamed "Helen of the West Indies" because of its natural beauty, St. Lucia is distinguished from its neighbors by its unusual geological landmarks, the Pitons—the twin peaks on the southwest coast that soar nearly ½ mile (1 km) above the ocean floor. Named a World Heritage Site by UNESCO in 2004, the Pitons are the symbol of this island. Nearby, in the former French colonial capital of Soufrière, are a "drive-in" volcano, its neighboring sulfur springs that have rejuvenated bathers for nearly three centuries, and one of the most beautiful botanical gardens in the Caribbean. A century and a half of battles between the French and English resulted in St. Lucia's changing hands 14 times before 1814, when England established possession. In

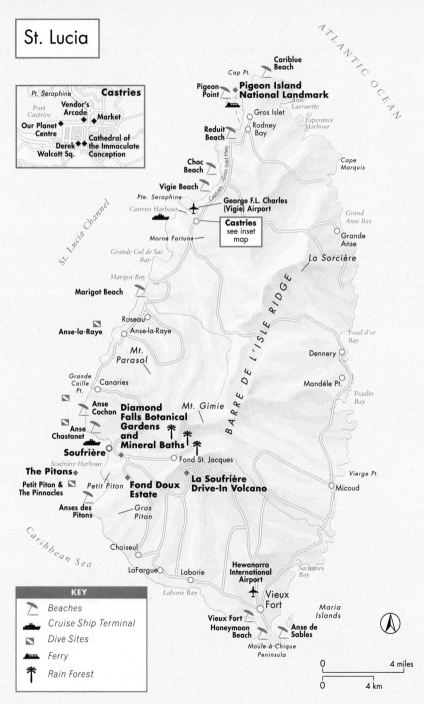

St. Lucia

ATLANTIC OCEAN

Castries

Pt. Seraphine
Port Castries
Vendor's Arcade
Our Planet Centre
Market
Derek Walcott Sq.
Cathedral of the Immaculate Conception

Cap Pt.
Cariblue Beach
Pigeon Point
Pigeon Island National Landmark
Gros Islet
Anse Lavouette
Esperance Harbour
Reduit Beach
Rodney Bay
Cape Marquis
Choc Beach
Vigie Beach
Pte. Seraphine
Castries Harbour
George F.L. Charles (Vigie) Airport
Castries see inset map
Grand Anse Bay
Grande Anse
Morne Fortune
Grande Cul de Sac Bay
La Sorcière
Marigot Bay
Marigot Beach
Roseau
Anse-la-Raye
Anse-la-Raye
Fond d'or Bay
Mt. Parasol
Dennery
Grande Caille Pt.
Canaries
Mandéle Pt.
Praslin Bay
Anse Cochon
Diamond Falls Botanical Gardens and Mineral Baths
Mt. Gimie
Anse Chastanet
Soufrière
Soufrière Harbour
Fond St. Jacques
The Pitons
Petit Piton & The Pinnacles
Petit Piton
Fond Doux Estate
La Soufrière Drive-In Volcano
Vierge Pt.
Micoud
Anses des Pitons
Gros Piton
Caribbean Sea
Choiseul
Savannes Bay
LaFargue
Laborie
Hewanorra International Airport
Laborie Bay
Vieux Fort
Maria Islands
Vieux Fort Honeymoon Beach
Anse de Sables
Moule à Chique Peninsula

KEY
Beaches
Cruise Ship Terminal
Dive Sites
Ferry
Rain Forest

0   4 miles
0   4 km

1979 the island became an independent state within the British Commonwealth of Nations. The official language is English, although most people also speak a French Creole patois.

ESSENTIALS
CURRENCY
Eastern Caribbean (E.C.) dollar, but U.S. dollars are widely accepted.

TELEPHONE
You can make direct-dial overseas and inter-island calls from St. Lucia, and the connections are excellent. You can charge an overseas call to a major credit card with no surcharge by dialing 811. Phone cards can be purchased at many retail outlets.

COMING ASHORE

Most cruise ships dock at the capital city of Castries, on the island's northwestern coast, at either of two docking areas: Pointe Seraphine, a port of entry and duty-free shopping complex, or Port Castries (Place Carenage), a commercial wharf across the harbor. Ferry service connects the two piers. Smaller vessels occasionally call at Soufrière, on the island's southwestern coast. Ships calling at Soufrière must anchor offshore and bring passengers ashore via tender. Tourist information booths are at Pointe Seraphine, at Place Carenage, and along the waterfront on Bay Street in Soufrière. Downtown Castries is within walking distance of the pier, and the produce market and adjacent crafts and vendors' markets are the main attractions. Soufrière is a sleepy West Indian town, but it's worth a short walk around the central square to view the French colonial architecture; many of the island's interesting natural sights are in or near Soufrière.

Taxis are available at the docks in Castries. Although they are unmetered, the standard fares are posted at the entrance to Pointe Seraphine. Taxi drivers are well informed and can give you a full tour—often an excellent one—thanks to government-sponsored training programs. From the Castries area, full-day island tours for up to four people cost $40 to $75 per person, depending on the route and whether entrance fees and lunch are included; a private sightseeing trip, including lunch, costs around $190 for two people. If you plan your own day, expect to pay the driver at least $40 per hour plus a 10% tip. Whatever your destination, negotiate the price with the driver before you depart—and be sure that you both understand whether the rate is quoted in EC or U.S. dollars.

EXPLORING ST. LUCIA

CASTRIES AND THE NORTH
CASTRIES
The capital, a busy commercial city of about 65,000 people, wraps around a sheltered bay. Morne Fortune rises sharply to the south of town, creating a dramatic green backdrop. The charm of Castries lies in its liveliness rather than its architecture, because four fires that occurred between 1796 and 1948 destroyed most of the colonial buildings.

Freighters (exporting bananas, coconut, cocoa, mace, nutmeg, and citrus fruits) and cruise ships come and go frequently, making Castries Harbour one of the Caribbean's busiest ports. **Pointe Seraphine** is a duty-free shopping complex on the north side of the harbor, about a 20-minute walk or two-minute cab ride from the city center; a launch ferries passengers across the harbor when cruise ships are in port. Pointe Seraphine's attractive Spanish-style architecture houses more than 20 upscale duty-free shops, a tourist information kiosk, a taxi stand, and car-rental agencies. **La Place Carenage,** on the south side of the harbor near the pier and markets, is another duty-free shopping complex with a dozen or more shops and a café. **Derek Walcott Square** (formerly Columbus Square), a green oasis bordered by Brazil, Laborie, Micoud, and Bourbon streets, was renamed to honor the hometown poet who won the 1992 Nobel Prize in Literature—one of two Nobel laureates from St. Lucia (the late Sir W. Arthur Lewis won the 1979 Nobel in economic science). Directly across Laborie Street from Derek Walcott Square is the Roman Catholic **Cathedral of the Immaculate Conception,** which was built in 1897. Though it's rather somber on the outside, its interior walls are decorated with colorful murals reworked in 1985, just before Pope John Paul II's visit, by St. Lucian artist Dunstan St. Omer. This church has an active parish and is open daily for both public viewing and religious services.

FAMILY
FodorsChoice
★

Our Planet Centre. The only such attraction of its kind in the world, at least to date, Our Planet Centre is devoted to the many facets of the Earth's environment. It's a fascinating, educational stop for the entire family and an especially good option on a rainy day. The exhibits include an Immersion Tunnel, where you can see how the planet was created and grew into its current state; Hurricane Island, where touch screens allow you to manipulate weather patterns to create a hurricane; Mirrorsphere, which gives a kaleidoscopic view of Earth's plants and animals; Science on a Sphere, installed by NOAA/NASA, which views the Earth from space complete with hurricanes, earthquakes, volcanoes, and tsunamis; and—the best part—a laser show in the Special Effects Theatre, where the lighting, shaking seats, wind, and mist mimic extreme weather events. The personalized guided tour takes about 90 minutes, but you'll probably want to linger longer at some of the exhibits and interactive games—which is fine. A gift shop features locally made recycled, reused, and natural products. ⊠ *La Place Carenage, Jeremie St.* ☎ *758/453–0107* ⊕ *www.ourplanetcentre.org* 🎟 *$38* ⊙ *Mon.–Sat. 9–4:30 (last booking at 3:30), Sun. by reservation or when a cruise ship is in port.*

ELSEWHERE IN THE NORTH

FAMILY
Pigeon Island National Landmark. Jutting out from the northwest coast, Pigeon Island is connected to the mainland via a causeway. Tales are told of the pirate Jambe de Bois (Wooden Leg), who once hid out on this 44-acre hilltop islet—a strategic point during the French and British struggles for control of St. Lucia. Now Pigeon Island is a national park and a venue for concerts, festivals, and family gatherings. In the Museum and Interpretative Centre, housed in the restored British officers' mess, a multimedia display explains the island's ecological and historical

significance. Pigeon Island National Landmark is administered by the St. Lucia National Trust. ✉ *Pigeon Island, Gros Islet* ☎ *758/452–5005* ⊕ *www.slunatrust.org* 🎫 *$5* ⊙ *Daily 9–5.*

Rodney Bay. Hotels, popular restaurants, a huge mall, and the island's only casino surround a natural bay and an 80-acre man-made lagoon named for Admiral George Rodney, who sailed the British Navy out of Gros Islet Bay in 1780 to attack and ultimately destroy the French fleet. With 232 slips, Rodney Bay Marina is one of the Caribbean's premier yachting centers: each December, it's the destination of the Atlantic Rally for Cruisers (a transatlantic yacht crossing). Yacht charters and sightseeing day trips can be arranged at the marina. Rodney Bay is about 15 minutes north of Castries; the Rodney Bay Ferry makes hourly crossings between the marina and the mall, as well as daily excursions to Pigeon Island. ✉ *Rodney Bay Village, Gros Islet.*

ST. LUCIA BEST BETS
■ **The Pitons.** You must see the Pitons, St. Lucia's unique twin peaks.
■ **The Rain Forest.** St. Lucia's lush rain forest is striking.
■ **Diamond Botanical Garden.** Stroll through this tropical paradise to Diamond Waterfall.
■ **Reduit Beach.** St. Lucia's nicest white-sand beach is north of Castries.
■ **Pigeon Island.** This national park is both a historic site and a natural playground.

SOUFRIÈRE AND THE SOUTH
SOUFRIÈRE

The oldest town in St. Lucia and the former French colonial capital, Soufrière was founded by the French in 1746 and named for its proximity to the volcano of the same name. The wharf is the center of activity in this sleepy town (which currently has a population of about 9,000), particularly when a cruise ship anchors in pretty Soufrière Bay. French colonial influences are evident in the second-story verandahs, gingerbread trim, and other appointments of the wooden buildings that surround the market square. The market building itself is decorated with colorful murals.

Soufrière, the site of much of St. Lucia's renowned natural beauty, is the destination of most sightseeing trips. This is where you can get up close to the iconic Pitons and explore the French colonial capital of St. Lucia, with its "drive-in" volcano, botanical gardens, working plantations, waterfalls, and countless other examples of the natural beauty for which St. Lucia is deservedly famous.

Fodor'sChoice
★
Diamond Falls Botanical Gardens and Mineral Baths. These splendid gardens are part of Soufrière Estate, a 2,000-acre land grant presented by King Louis XIV in 1713 to three Devaux brothers from Normandy in recognition of their services to France. The estate is still owned by their descendants; Joan DuBouley Devaux maintains the gardens. Water bubbling to the surface from underground sulfur springs streams downhill in rivulets to become Diamond Waterfall, deep within the botanical gardens. Through the centuries, the rocks over which the cascade

spills have become encrusted with minerals and tinted yellow, green, and purple. Near the falls, mineral baths are fed by the underground springs. It's claimed that the future Joséphine Bonaparte bathed here as a young girl while visiting her father's plantation nearby. In 1930 André DuBoulay had the site excavated, and two of the original stone baths were restored for his use. Outside baths were added later. For a small fee, you can slip into your swimsuit and soak for 30 minutes in one of the outside pools; a private bath costs slightly more. ⊠ *Soufrière Estate, Diamond Rd.* ☎ *758/459–7155* ⊕ *www.diamondstlucia.com* ▨ *$8, public bath $5, private bath $8* ⊙ *Mon.–Sat. 10–5, Sun. 10–3.*

ELSEWHERE IN THE SOUTH

FAMILY **Fond Doux Estate.** One of the earliest French estates established by land grants (1745 and 1763), this plantation still produces cocoa, citrus, bananas, coconut, and vegetables on 135 hilly acres. The restored 1864 plantation house is still in use, as well. A 30-minute walking tour begins at the cocoa fermentary, where you can see the drying process under way. You then follow a trail through the lush cultivated area, where a guide points out various fruit- or spice-bearing trees and tropical flowers. Additional trails lead to old military ruins, a religious shrine, and another vantage point for viewing the spectacular Pitons. Cool drinks and a Creole buffet lunch are served at the Jardin Cacao restaurant. Souvenirs, including just-made chocolate sticks, are sold at the boutique. ⊠ *Chateaubelair* ☎ *758/459–7545* ⊕ *www.fonddouxestate.com* ▨ *$30, includes lunch* ⊙ *Daily 11–2.*

FAMILY **La Soufrière Drive-In Volcano.** As you approach, your nose will pick up the strong scent of the sulfur springs—more than 20 belching pools of muddy water, multicolor sulfur deposits, and other assorted minerals baking and steaming on the surface. Despite the name, you don't actually drive all the way in. Instead, you drive within a few hundred feet of the gurgling, steaming mass and then walk behind your guide—whose service is included in the admission price—around a fault in the substratum rock. It's a fascinating, educational half hour, though it can also be pretty stinky on a hot day. ☎ *758/459–5500* ▨ *$2* ⊙ *Daily 9–5.*

Fodor's Choice **The Pitons.** Rising precipitously from the cobalt-blue Caribbean Sea just
★ south of Soufrière Bay, these two unusual mountains are the symbol of St. Lucia and also a UNESCO World Heritage Site. Covered with thick tropical vegetation, the massive outcroppings were formed by lava from a volcanic eruption 30 to 40 million years ago. They are not identical twins since—confusingly, 2,619-foot Petit Piton is taller than 2,461-foot Gros Piton; Gros Piton is, as the word translates, broader. It's possible to climb the Pitons, but it's a strenuous trip. Gros Piton is the easier climb, though the trail up even this one is still very tough. Either climb requires the permission of the Forest & Lands Department and the use of a knowledgeable guide. ☎ *758/450–2231, 758/450–2078 for St. Lucia Forest & Lands Department* ▨ *Guide services $45* ⊙ *Daily by appointment only.*

BEACHES

All of St. Lucia's beaches are open to the public, but beaches in the north are particularly accessible to cruise-ship passengers.

Fodor'sChoice ★ **Reduit Beach.** Many feel that Reduit (pronounced red-wee) is the island's finest beach. The long stretch of golden sand that frames Rodney Bay is within walking distance of many hotels and restaurants in Rodney Bay Village. Bay Gardens Beach Resort, Royal by Rex Resorts, and St. Lucian by Rex Resorts all face the beachfront; Harmony Suites and Ginger Lily hotels are across the road. The Royal has a water-sports center, where you can rent sports equipment and beach chairs and take windsurfing or waterskiing lessons. **Amenities:** food and drink; toilets; water sports. **Best for:** snorkeling; sunset; swimming; walking; windsurfing. ⊠ *Rodney Bay Village, Gros Islet.*

Vigie/Malabar Beach. This 2-mile (3-km) stretch of lovely white sand runs parallel to the George F. L. Charles Airport runway in Castries and continues on past the Rendezvous resort, where it becomes Malabar Beach. In the area opposite the airport departure lounge, a few vendors sell refreshments. **Amenities:** food and drink. **Best for:** swimming. ⊠ *Adjacent to Vigie Airport, Castries.*

> **BAG IT**
>
> A mesh laundry bag or a "pop-up" mesh clothes hamper are two fairly light items that pack flat in your suitcase. The bag can hang from the closet, but either will keep your closet neat, allow damp clothing to dry out, and help you tote dirty clothes to the self-service laundry room so you can avoid high cleaning charges.

SHOPPING

The island's best-known products are artwork and woodcarvings; clothing and household articles made from batik and silk-screen fabrics, designed and printed in island workshops; and clay pottery. You can also take home straw hats and baskets and locally grown cocoa, coffee, and spices. Duty-free shopping is at **Pointe Seraphine** or **La Place Carenage**, on opposite sides of the harbor. You must show your passport and cabin key card to get duty-free prices. You'll want to experience the **Castries Market** and scour the adjacent **Vendor's Arcade** and **Craft Market** for handicrafts and souvenirs at bargain prices.

ACTIVITIES

DIVING AND SNORKELING

Fodor'sChoice ★ The coral reefs at Anse Cochon and Anse Chastanet, on the southwest coast, are popular beach-entry dive sites. In the north, Pigeon Island is the most convenient site.

Scuba St. Lucia. Daily beach and boat dives and resort and certification courses are available from this PADI Five Star facility on Anse Chastanet Beach, and so is underwater photography and snorkeling equipment. Day trips from the north of the island include round-trip speedboat transportation. ⊠ *Anse Chastanet Resort, Anse Chastanet Rd.* ☎ *758/459–7755, 888/465–8242 in the U.S.* ⊕ *www.scubastlucia.com.*

FISHING

Sportfishing is generally done on a catch-and-release basis. Neither spearfishing nor collecting live fish in coastal waters is permitted. Half- and full-day deep-sea fishing excursions can be arranged at either Vigie Marina or Rodney Bay Marina. A half day of fishing on a scheduled trip runs about $85 per person to join a scheduled party for a half day or $500 to $1,000 for a private charter for up to six or eight people, depending on the size of the boat and the length of time. Beginners are welcome.

Captain Mike's. Named for Captain Mike Hackshaw and run by his family, this operation's fleet of Bertram powerboats (31 to 38 feet) accommodate as many as eight passengers for half-day or full-day sport-fishing charters; tackle and cold drinks are supplied. Customized sight-seeing or whale-watching trips ($45 per person) can also be arranged for small groups (four to six people). ⊠ *Vigie Marina, Ganthers Bay, Castries* ☎ *758/452–7044* ⊕ *www.captmikes.com.*

HORSEBACK RIDING

Creole horses, a breed indigenous to South America and popular on the island, are fairly small, fast, sturdy, and even-tempered animals suitable for beginners. Established stables can accommodate all skill levels and offer countryside trail rides, beach rides with picnic lunches, plantation tours, carriage rides, and lengthy treks. Prices run about $60 for one hour, $70 for two hours, and $85 for a three-hour beach ride and barbecue.

International Pony Club. The beach-picnic ride from the International Pony Club includes time for a swim—with or without your horse. Both English- and Western-style riding are available. ⊠ *East of Rodney Bay, Beauséjour, Gros Islet* ☎ *758/452–8139, 758/450–8665* ⊕ *www. internationalponyclub.net.*

Trim's National Riding Stable. At the island's oldest riding stable there are four sessions per day, plus beach tours, trail rides, and carriage tours to Pigeon Island. ⊠ *Cas en Bas, Gros Islet* ☎ *758/450–8273* ⊕ *horserideslu.50megs.com.*

WHERE TO EAT

$$$

CARIBBEAN

Fodor's Choice

★

✕ **Dasheene Restaurant and Bar.** The terrace restaurant at Ladera resort has breathtakingly close-up views of the Pitons and the sea between them, especially beautiful at sunset. The ambience is casual by day and magical at night. Appetizers may include grilled crab claws with a choice of dips or silky pumpkin soup with ginger. Typical entrées are "fisherman's catch" with a choice of flavored butters or sauces, shrimp Dasheene (panfried with local herbs), grilled rack of lamb with coco-nut risotto and curry sauce, or pan-seared fillet of beef marinated in a lime-and-pepper seasoning. Light dishes, pasta dishes, and fresh salads are also served at lunch—along with the view. $ *Average main: $30*

✉ *Ladera, 2 miles (3 km) south of Soufrière* ☎ *758/459–7323* ⊕ *www. ladera.com.*

$$$$ ✕ **Jacques Waterfront Dining.** Chef-owner Jacky Rioux creates magical

FRENCH dishes in his waterfront restaurant overlooking Rodney Bay. The cooking is decidedly French, as is Rioux, but fresh produce and local spices create a fusion cuisine that's memorable at either lunch or dinner. You might start with a bowl of creamy tomato-basil or pumpkin soup, a grilled portobello mushroom, or octopus and conch in curried coconut sauce. Choose among main dishes such as fresh seafood, perhaps oven-baked kingfish with a white wine–and–sweet pepper sauce, or breast of chicken stuffed with smoked salmon in a citrus-butter sauce. The wine list is impressive. Coming by boat? You can tie up at the dinghy dock. ⑤ *Average main: $32* ✉ *Reduit Beach Ave., at the end of the road, Rodney Bay Village, Gros Islet* ☎ *758/458–1900* ⊕ *www.jacquesrestaurant. com* ⌔ *Reservations essential* ⊙ *Closed Sun.*

ST. MAARTEN (PHILIPSBURG)

Elise Meyer · St. Martin/St. Maarten: one tiny island, just 37 square miles (96 square km), with two different accents and ruled by two sovereign nations. Here French and Dutch have lived side by side for hundreds of years, and when you cross from one country to the next there are no border patrols, no customs agents. In fact, the only indication that you have crossed a border at all is a small sign and a change in road surface. St. Martin/St. Maarten epitomizes tourist islands in the sun, where services are well developed but there's still some Caribbean flavor. The Dutch side is ideal for people who like plenty to do. The French side has a more genteel ambience, more fashionable shopping, and a Continental flair. The combination makes an almost ideal port. On the negative side, the island has been completely developed. It can be fun to shop, and you'll find an occasional bargain, but many goods are cheaper in the United States.

ESSENTIALS

CURRENCY

On the Dutch side, the NAf guilder. On the French side, the euro. However, U.S. currency is accepted almost everywhere on the island.

TELEPHONE

Most U.S. multiband cell phones work in both St. Maarten and St. Martin, but the roaming charges will be steep. Calling from one side of the island to another is an international call. To phone from the Dutch side to the French, you first must dial 00–590–590 for local numbers, or 00–590–690 for cell phones, then the number. To call from the French side to the Dutch, dial 00–721, then the local number. To call a local number on the French side, dial 0590 plus the six-digit number. On the Dutch side, just dial the seven-digit number with no prefix.

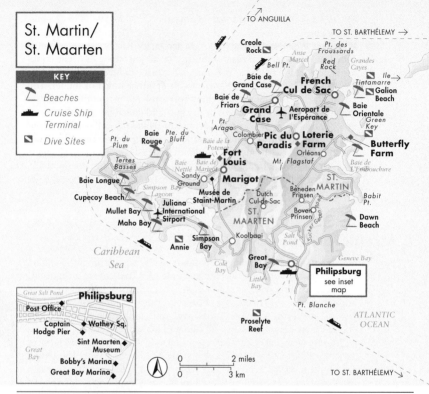

St. Martin/St. Maarten

KEY

- Beaches
- Cruise Ship Terminal
- Dive Sites

TO ANGUILLA

TO ST. BARTHÉLEMY →

Creole Rock

Pt. des Froussards

Anse Marcel

Bell Pt.

Red Rock

Grandes Cayes

Ile Tintamarre

Galion Beach

Baie de Grand Case

French Cul de Sac

Baie de Friars

Grand Case

Aeroport de l'Espérance

Baie Orientale

Green Key

Pt. Arago

Colombier

Pic du Paradis

Loterie Farm

Orléans

Butterfly Farm

Baie de L'Embouchure

Pt. du Plum

Baie Rouge

Pte. du Bluff

Baie de la Potence

Fort Louis

Mt. Flagstaf

Terres Basses

Baie Nettlé

Baie de Marigot

Sandy Ground

Marigot

ST. MARTIN

Baie Longue

Simpson Bay Lagoon

Musée de Staint-Martin

Dutch Cul-de-Sac

Bénéden Prinsen

Babit Pt.

Cupecoy Beach

Juliana International Sirport

ST. MAARTEN

Boven Prinsen

Dawn Beach

Mullet Bay

Maho Bay

Koolbaai

Salt Pond

Sucker Garen

Caribbean Sea

Annie

Simpson Bay

Cole Bay

Great Bay

Geneve Bay

Philipsburg
see inset map

Little Bay

Pt. Blanche

Proselyte Reef

ATLANTIC OCEAN

Philipsburg

Great Salt Pond

Post Office

Captain Hodge Pier

Wathey Sq.

Sint Maarten Museum

Great Bay

Bobby's Marina

Great Bay Marina

0 — 2 miles
0 — 3 km

TO ST. BARTHÉLEMY

COMING ASHORE

Most cruise ships drop anchor off the Dutch capital of Philipsburg or dock in the marina at the southern tip of the Philipsburg harbor; a few small or medium-size ships drop anchor in Marigot Bay and tender passengers ashore in the French capital. If your ship anchors, tenders will ferry you to the town pier in the middle of town, where taxis await passengers. If your ship docks at the marina, downtown is a 15-minute taxi ride away. The walk is not recommended. The island is small, and most spots aren't more than a 30-minute drive from Marigot or Philipsburg.

Doing your own thing will be much less expensive here than a ship-sponsored tour, and because rental cars are cheap (starting at $30 per day for a local car rental), you can easily strike out as soon as your ship docks. This is the best thing to do if you just want to see the island and spend a little time at a beach. Taxis are government-regulated and fairly costly, so they aren't really an option if you want to do much exploring. Authorized taxis display stickers of the St. Maarten Taxi Association. Taxis are also available at Marigot. You may be able to negotiate a favorable deal with a taxi driver for a two- to three-hour island tour for as little as $70 for two passengers or $30 per person for more than two.

EXPLORING ST. MAARTEN/ST. MARTIN

PHILIPSBURG

The capital of Dutch St. Maarten stretches about a mile (1½ km) along an isthmus between Great Bay and the Salt Pond and has five parallel streets. Most of the village's dozens of shops and restaurants are on Front Street, narrow and cobblestone, closest to Great Bay. It's generally congested when cruise ships are in port, because of its many duty-free shops and several casinos. Little lanes called *steegjes* connect Front Street with Back Street, which has fewer shops and considerably less congestion. Along the beach is a ½-mile-long (1-km-long) boardwalk with restaurants and several Wi-Fi hot spots.

Wathey Square (pronounced watty) is in the heart of the village. Directly across from the square are the town hall and the courthouse, in the striking white building with the cupola. The structure was built in 1793 and has served as the commander's home, a fire station, a jail, and a post office. The streets surrounding the square are lined with hotels, duty-free shops, fine restaurants, and cafés. The **Captain Hodge Pier,** just off the square, is a good spot to view Great Bay and the beach that stretches alongside.

St. Maarten Museum. The Sint Maarten Museum hosts rotating cultural exhibits addressing the history, industry, geology, and archaeololgy of the island. Artifacts range from Arawak pottery shards to objects salvaged from the wreck of the HMS *Proselyte.* ⊠ *7 Front St.* ☎ *721/542–4917* ⊕ *www.museumsintmaarten.org* ➾ *$1* ⊗ *Weekdays 10–4.*

ELSEWHERE ON ST. MAARTEN/ST. MARTIN

FAMILY

Fodor'sChoice

★

Butterfly Farm. If you arrive early in the morning when the butterflies first break out of their chrysalis, you'll be able to marvel at the absolute wonder of dozens of butterflies and moths from around the world and the particular host plants with which each evolved. At any given time, some 40 species of butterflies—numbering as many as 600 individual insects—flutter inside the lush screened garden and hatch on the plants housed there. Butterfly art and knickknacks are for sale in the gift shop. In case you want to come back, your ticket, which includes a guided tour, is good for your entire stay. ⊠ *Le Galion Beach Rd., Quartier d'Orléans* ☎ *590/87–31–21* ⊕ *www.thebutterflyfarm.com* ➾ *$12* ⊗ *Daily 9–3:30.*

Fort Louis. Though not much remains of the structure itself, Fort Louis, which was completed by the French in 1789, is great fun if you want to climb the 92 steps to the top for the wonderful views of the island and neighboring Anguilla. On Wednesday and Saturday there is a market in the square at the bottom. ⊠ *Marigot.*

French Cul de Sac. North of Orient Bay Beach, the French colonial mansion of St. Martin's mayor is nestled in the hills. Little, red-roof houses look like open umbrellas tumbling down the green hillside. The area is peaceful and good for hiking. From the beach here, shuttle boats make the five-minute trip to **Ilet Pinel,** an uninhabited island that's fine for picnicking, sunning, and swimming. There are full-service beach clubs there, so just pack the sunscreen and head over.

Grand Case. The Caribbean's own Restaurant Row is the heart of this French side town, a 10-minute drive from either Orient Bay or Marigot, stretching along a narrow beach overlooking Anguilla. You'll find a first-rate restaurant for every palate, mood, and wallet. At lunchtime, or with kids, head to the casual *lolos* (open-air barbecue stands) and feet-in-the-sand beach bars. Twilight drinks and tapas are fun. At night, stroll the strip and preview the sophisticated offerings on the menus posted outside before you settle in for a long and sumptuous meal. If you still have the energy, there are lounges with music (usually a DJ) that get going after 11 pm.

> ## ST. MAARTEN BEST BETS
>
> ■ **Beaches.** The island has 37 beautiful beaches, all open to the public.
>
> ■ **Butterfly Farm.** The terrarium-like Butterfly Farm is a treat for all ages.
>
> ■ **The 12-Metre Challenge.** Help sail an America's Cup yacht.
>
> ■ **Loterie Farm.** On the slopes of Pic du Paradis, an amazing ecofriendly preserve with fun activities.
>
> ■ **Shopping.** Both sides of the island are a shopper's paradise.

Fodor'sChoice
★
Loterie Farm. Halfway up the road to Pic du Paradis is Loterie Farm, a peaceful 150-acre private nature preserve opened to the public in 1999 by American expat B. J. Welch. There are hiking trails and maps, so you can go on your own (€5) or arrange a guide for a group (€25 for six people). Along the marked trails you will see native forest with tamarind, gum, mango, and mahogany trees, and wildlife including greenback monkeys if you are lucky. In 2011 Loterie opened a lovely spring-fed pool and jacuzzi area with lounge chairs, great music, and chic tented cabanas called L'Eau Lounge; if you're with a group, consider the VIP package there. Don't miss a treetop lunch or dinner at **Hidden Forest Café** (⇨ *Where to Eat, below*), Loterie Farm's restaurant, where Julie Perkis cooks delicious, healthy meals and snacks. If you are brave—and over 4 feet 5 inches tall—try soaring over trees on one of the longest zip lines in the Western Hemisphere. ⊠ *Rte. de Pic du Paradis 103, Rambaud* ☎ *590/87–86–16, 590/57–28–55* ⊕ *www.loteriefarm.com* ☎ *€35–€55* ⊘ *Tues.–Sun. 9–4.*

Marigot. It is great fun to spend a few hours exploring the bustling harbor, shopping stalls, open-air cafés, and boutiques of St. Martin's biggest town, especially on Wednesday and Saturday, when the daily open-air craft markets expand to include fresh fruits and veggies, spices, and all manner of seafood. The market might remind you of Provence, especially when aromas of delicious cooking waft by. Be sure to climb up to the fort for the panoramic view, stopping at the museum for an overview of the island. Marina Port La Royale is the shopping–lunchspot central to the port, but rue de la République and rue de la Liberté, which border the bay, have duty-free shops, boutiques, and bistros. The West Indies Mall offers a deluxe (and air-conditioned) shopping experience, with such shops as Lacoste. There's less bustle here than in Philipsburg, but the open-air cafés are still tempting places to sit and people-watch. Marigot is fun into the night, so you might wish to linger through dinnertime. From the harborfront you can catch ferries for Anguilla and St. Barth. Parking can be a real challenge during the business day, and even at night during the high season.

Fodor's Choice

★

Pic du Paradis. Between Marigot and Grand Case, "Paradise Peak," at 1,492 feet, is the island's highest

> **HAND SANTIZER**
>
> Liquid hand sanitizer is a must-have for adventure excursions or where water might be at a premium. Bring a small bottle you can carry along with you.

point. There are two observation areas. From them, the tropical forest unfolds below, and the vistas are breathtaking. The road is quite isolated and steep, best suited to a four-wheel-drive vehicle, so don't head up here unless you are prepared for the climb. There have also been some problems with crime in this area, so it might be best to go with an experienced local guide. ⊠ *Rte. de Pic du Paradis.*

BEACHES

The island's 10 miles (16 km) of beaches are all open to cruise-ship passengers. You can rent chairs and umbrellas at most of the beaches, primarily from beachside restaurants. The best beaches are on the French side. Topless bathing is common on the French side. If you take a cab to a remote beach, be sure to arrange a specific time for the driver to return for you. Don't leave valuables unattended on the beach or in a rental car, even in the trunk.

FAMILY

Baie des Pères (*Friars' Bay*). This quiet cove close to Marigot has beach grills and bars, with chaises and umbrellas, calm waters, and a lovely view of Anguilla. Kali's Beach Bar, open daily for lunch and (weather permitting) dinner, has a Rasta vibe and color scheme—it's the best place to be on the full moon, with music, dancing, and a huge bonfire, but you can get lunch, beach chairs, and umbrellas any time. Friar's Bay Beach Café is a French Bistro on the sand, open from breakfast to sunset. To get to the beach, take National Road 7 from Marigot, go toward Grand Case to the Morne Valois hill, and turn left on the dead-end road at the sign. **Amenities:** food and drink; toilets. **Best for:** partiers; swimming; walking. ⊠ *Friars' Bay.*

Fodor's Choice

★

Baie Orientale (*Orient Bay*). Many consider this the island's most beautiful beach, but its 2 miles (3 km) of satiny white sand, underwater marine reserve, variety of water sports, beach clubs, and hotels also make it one of the most crowded. Lots of "naturists" take advantage of the clothing-optional policy, so don't be shocked. Early-morning nude beach walking is de rigueur for the guests at Club Orient, at the southeastern end of the beach. Plan to spend the day at one of the clubs; each bar has different color umbrellas, and all boast terrific restaurants and lively bars. You can have an open-air massage, try any sea toy you fancy, and stay until dark. To get to Baie Orientale from Marigot, take National Road 7 past Grand Case, past the Aéroport de L'Espérance, and watch for the left turn. **Amenities:** food and drink; parking; toilets; water sports. **Best for:** partiers; nudists; swimming; walking; windsurfing. ⊠ *Baie Orientale.*

Ilet Pinel. A protected nature reserve, this kid-friendly island is a five-minute ferry ride from French Cul de Sac ($7 per person round-trip). The ferry runs every half hour from midmorning until dusk. The water is clear and shallow, and the shore is sheltered. If you like snorkeling, don your gear and paddle along both coasts of this pencil-shaped speck in the ocean. You can rent equipment on the island or in the parking lot before you board the ferry for about $10. Plan for lunch any day of the week at a palm-shaded beach hut, Karibuni (except in September, when it's closed) for the freshest fish, great salads, tapas, and drinks—try the frozen mojito for a treat. **Amenities:** food and drink; parking. **Best for:** swimming, snorkeling. ⊠ *Ilet Pinel.*

SHOPPING

It's true that the island sparkles with its myriad outdoor activities—diving, snorkeling, sailing, swimming, and sunning—but shopaholics are drawn to the sparkle within the jewelry stores. The huge array of such stores is almost unrivaled in the Caribbean. In addition, duty-free shops offer substantial savings—about 15% to 30% below U.S. and Canadian prices—on cameras, watches, liquor, cigars, and designer clothing. It's no wonder that each year 500 cruise ships make Philipsburg a port of call. On both sides of the island, be alert for idlers. They can snatch unwatched purses. Prices are in dollars on the Dutch side, in euros on the French side. As for bargains, there are more to be had on the Dutch side.

Philipsburg's **Front Street** has reinvented itself. Now it's mall-like, with a redbrick walk and streets, palm trees lining the sleek boutiques, jewelry stores, souvenir shops, outdoor restaurants, and the old reliables, like McDonald's and Burger King. Here and there a school or a church appears to remind visitors there's more to the island than shopping. Back Street is where you'll find the **Philipsburg Market Place,** a daily open-air market where you can haggle for bargains on such goods as handicrafts, souvenirs, and beachwear. **Old Street,** near the end of Front Street, has stores, boutiques, and open-air cafés offering French crêpes, rich chocolates, and island mementos.

On the French side, wrought-iron balconies, colorful awnings, and gingerbread trim decorate Marigot's smart shops, tiny boutiques, and bistros in the **Marina Royale** complex and on the main streets, **rue de la Liberté** and **rue de la République.** Also in Marigot are the pricey **West Indies Mall** and the **Plaza Caraïbes,** which house designer shops, although some shops are closing in the economic downturn.

ACTIVITIES

For a wide range of water sports, including parasailing and waterskiing, head to Orient Beach, where a variety of operators have their headquarters.

DIVING AND SNORKELING

Although St. Maarten is not generally known as a dive destination, the water temperature here is rarely below 70°F (21°C). Visibility is often excellent, averaging about 100 feet to 120 feet. The island has more than 40 good dive sites, from wrecks to rocky labyrinths. For snorkelers, the area around Orient Bay, Caye Verte (Green Key), Ilêt Pinel, and Flat Island is especially lovely, and is officially classified, and protected, as a regional underwater nature reserve. On average, one-tank dives start at $55; two-tank dives are about $100. The average cost of an afternoon snorkeling trip is about $45 to $55 per person.

Dive Safaris. Dive Safaris has a shark-awareness dive on Friday where participants can watch professional feeders give reef sharks a little nosh. The company also offers a full PADI training program and can tailor dive excursions to any level. ⊠ *16 Airport Blvd., Simpson Bay* ☎ *721/545–2401* ⊕ *www.divestmaarten.com.*

Ocean Explorers Dive Shop. Ocean Explorers Dive Shop is St. Maarten's oldest dive shop, and offers different types of certification courses. ⊠ *113 Welfare Rd., Simpson Bay* ☎ *721/544–5252* ⊕ *www.stmaartendiving. com.*

FISHING

You can angle for yellowtail snapper, grouper, marlin, tuna, and wahoo on deep-sea excursions. Costs range from $150 per person for a half day to $250 for a full day. Prices usually include bait and tackle, instruction for novices, and refreshments. Ask about licensing and insurance.

Lee's Deepsea Fishing. Lee's Deepsea Fishing organizes excursions, and when you return, Lee's Roadside Grill will cook your tuna, wahoo, or whatever else you catch and keep. Rates start at $200 per person for a half-day. ⊠ *82 Welfare Rd., Cole Bay* ☎ *721/544–4233* ⊕ *www. leesfish.com.*

Rudy's Deep Sea Fishing. Rudy's Deep Sea Fishing has been around for years, and is one of the more experienced sport-angling outfits. A private charter trip for four people starts at $525 for a half-day excursion. ⊠ *14 Airport Rd., Simpson Bay* ☎ *721/545–2177* ⊕ *www. rudysdeepseafishing.com.*

WHERE TO EAT

$$ × **Enoch's Place.** The blue-and-white-striped awning on a corner of the
CARIBBEAN   Marigot Market makes this place hard to miss. But Enoch's cooking is what draws the crowds. Specialties include garlic shrimp, fresh lobster, and rice and beans (like your St. Martin mother used to make). Try the saltfish and fried johnnycake—a great breakfast option. The food more than makes up for the lack of decor, and chances are you'll be counting the days until you can return. ⑤ *Average main: €13* ⊠ *Marigot Market, Front de Mer, Marigot* ☎ *590/29–29–88* ⊕ *www.enochsplace. com* ⌕ *Reservations not accepted* ▭ *No credit cards* ⊘ *Closed Sun. No dinner.*

$$ × **Taloula Mango's.** Ribs are the specialty at this casual beachfront res-
ECLECTIC   taurant, but the jerk chicken and thin-crust pizza, not to mention a
FAMILY   few vegetarian options like the tasty falafel, are not to be ignored. On weekdays lunch is accompanied by (warning: loud) live music; every Friday during happy hour a DJ spins tunes. In case you're wondering, the restaurant got its name from the owner's golden retriever. ⑤ *Average*

main: $17 ⊠ *Sint Rose Shopping Mall, off Front St. on beach boardwalk*
☏ *721/542–1645* ⊕ *www.taloulamango.com.*

ST. THOMAS (CHARLOTTE AMALIE)

Carol
Bareuther

St. Thomas is the busiest cruise port of call in the world. Up to eight mega ships may visit in a single day. Don't expect an exotic island experience: one of the three U.S. Virgin Islands (with St. Croix and St. John), St. Thomas is as American as any place on the mainland, complete with McDonald's and HBO. The positive side of all this development is that there are more tours here than anywhere else in the Caribbean, and every year the excursions get better. Of course, shopping is the big draw in Charlotte Amalie, but experienced travelers remember the days of "real" bargains. Today so many passengers fill the stores that it's a seller's market. On some days there are so many cruise passengers on St. Thomas that you must book a ship-sponsored shore excursion if you want to do more than just take a taxi to the beach or stroll around Charlotte Amalie.

ESSENTIALS

CURRENCY

The U.S. dollar.

TELEPHONE

Both GSM and Sprint phones work in St. Thomas (and the USVI are normally included in most U.S. cell phone plans). It's as easy to call home from St. Thomas and St. John as from any city in the United States. On St. Thomas, public phones are easily found, and AT&T has a telecommunications center across from the Havensight Mall.

COMING ASHORE

Depending on how many ships are in port, cruise ships drop anchor in the harbor at Charlotte Amalie and tender passengers directly to the waterfront duty-free shops, dock at the Havensight Mall at the eastern end of the crescent bay, or dock at Crown Bay Marina a few miles west of town (Holland America almost always docks at Crown Bay).

The distance from Havensight to the duty-free shops is 1½ miles (3 km), which can be walked in less than half an hour; a taxi ride there costs $6 per person ($5 for each additional person). Tourist information offices are at the Havensight Mall (across from Building No. 1) for docking passengers and downtown near Fort Christian (at the eastern end of the waterfront shopping area) for those coming ashore by tender. Both offices distribute free maps. From Crown Bay it's also a half-hour walk or a $5-per-person cab ride ($4 for each additional person). V.I. Taxi Association drivers offer a basic two-hour island tour for $25 per person for two or more people. You can rent a car in St. Thomas, but with all the tour options it's often easier and cheaper to take an organized excursion or just hop in a cab.

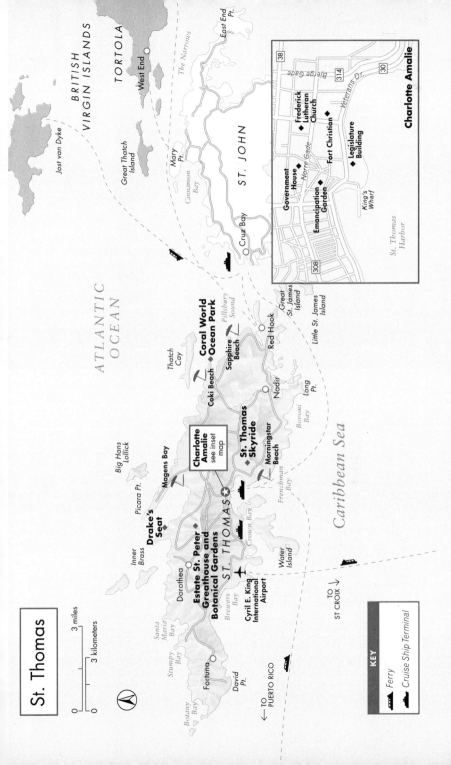

EXPLORING ST. THOMAS

CHARLOTTE AMALIE

St. Thomas's major burg is a hilly shopping town. There are also plenty of interesting historic sights—so take the time to see at least a few.

FAMILY **Emancipation Garden.** A bronze bust of a freed slave blowing a conch shell commemorates slavery's end, in 1848—the garden was built to mark emancipation's 150th anniversary, in 1998. The gazebo here is used for official ceremonies. Two other monuments show the island's Danish-American connection—a bust of Denmark's King Christian and a scaled-down model of the U.S. Liberty Bell. ⊠ *Between Tolbod Gade and Ft. Christian, next to Vendor's Plaza.*

FAMILY **Ft. Christian.** St. Thomas's oldest standing structure, this remarkable building was built between 1672 and 1680 and now has U.S. National Landmark status. Over the years, it was used as a jail, governor's residence, town hall, courthouse, and church. In 2005, a multimillion-dollar renovation project started to stabilize the structure and halt centuries of deterioration. The fort reopened for public tours in 2013. Inside you can visit the inner courtyard and rooms, and from the outside, you can see the four renovated faces of the famous 19th-century clock tower. ⊠ *Waterfront Hwy., east of shopping district* ☎ *340/774–5541* ⊕ *stthomashistoricaltrust.org.*

Frederick Lutheran Church. This historic church has a massive mahogany altar, and its pews—each with its own door—were once rented to families of the congregation. Lutheranism is the state religion of Denmark, and when the territory was without a minister, the governor—who had his own elevated pew—filled in. ⊠ *7 Norre Gade, across from Emancipation Garden and the Grand Hotel* ☎ *340/776–1315* ⊕ *www.felc1666.org* ⊗ *Mon.–Sat. 9–4.*

Government House. Built in 1867, this neoclassical white brick-and-wood structure houses the offices of the governor of the Virgin Islands. Inside, the staircases are of native mahogany, as are the plaques, hand-lettered in gold with the names of the governors appointed and, since 1970, elected. Brochures detailing the history of the building are available, but you may have to ask for them. ⊠ *Government Hill, 21–22 Kongens Gade, across from the Emancipation Garden U.S. Post Office* ☎ *340/774–0001* ⊠ *Free* ⊗ *Weekdays 8–5.*

Legislature Building. Its pastoral-looking lime-green exterior conceals the vociferous political wrangling of the Virgin Islands Senate. Constructed

---

ST. THOMAS BEST BETS

■ **Coral World Ocean Park.** This aquarium attraction is a great bet for families, and it's on one of best snorkeling beaches.

■ **Magen's Bay Beach.** St. Thomas has one of the most picture-postcard perfect beaches you'll ever see. It's great for swimming.

■ **St. John.** It's easy to hop on the ferry to St. John for a day of hiking, then relax for an hour or two on the beach afterward.

■ **Shopping.** Charlotte Amalie is one of the best places in the Caribbean to shop.

originally by the Danish as a police barracks, the building was later used to billet U.S. Marines, and much later it housed a public school. ■**TIP**➔ **You're welcome to sit in on sessions in the upstairs chambers.** ✉ *Waterfront Hwy. (Rte. 30), across from Ft. Christian* ☎ *340/774–0880* ⊕ *www.legvi.org* ⊙ *Daily 8–5.*

ELSEWHERE ON ST. THOMAS

FAMILY

Fodor'sChoice
★

Coral World Ocean Park. This interactive aquarium and water-sports center lets you experience a variety of sea life and other animals. There's a new 2-acre dolphin habitat, as well as several outdoor pools where you can pet baby sharks, feed stingrays, touch starfish, and view endangered sea turtles. During the Sea Trek Helmet Dive, you walk along an underwater trail wearing a helmet that provides a continuous supply of air. You can try "snuba," a cross between snorkeling and scuba diving. Swim with a sea lion and have a chance at playing ball or getting a big, wet, whiskered kiss. You can also buy a cup of nectar and let the cheerful lorikeets perch on your hand and drink. The park also has an offshore underwater observatory, an 80,000-gallon coral reef exhibit (one of the largest in the world), and a nature trail with native ducks and tortoises. Daily feedings take place at most exhibits. ✉ *Coki Point north of Rte. 38, 6450 Estate Smith Bay, Estate Frydendal* ☎ *340/775–1555* ⊕ *www.coralworldvi.com* 🎫 *$19, Sea Lion Swim $105, Sea Lion Encounter $65, Sea Trek $58, Snuba $52, Shark and Turtle Encounters $32, Nautilus $20* ⊙ *Daily 9–4. Off-season (May–Oct.) hrs may vary, so call to confirm.*

Drake's Seat. Sir Francis Drake was supposed to have kept watch over his fleet and looked for enemy ships from this vantage point. The panorama is especially breathtaking (and romantic) at dusk, and if you arrive late in the day, you can miss the hordes of day-trippers on taxi tours who stop here to take a picture. ✉ *Rte. 40, ¼ mile west of the intersection of Rtes. 40 and 35, Estate Zufriedenheit.*

Estate St. Peter Greathouse and Botanical Gardens. This unusual spot is perched on a mountainside 1,000 feet above sea level, with views of more than 20 islands and islets. You can wander through a gallery displaying local art, sip a complimentary rum punch while looking out at the view, or follow a nature trail that leads you past nearly 70 varieties of tropical plants, including 17 varieties of orchids. ✉ *Rte. 40, directly across from Tree Limin' Extreme Zipline, Estate St. Peter* ☎ *340/774–4999* ⊕ *www.greathousevi.com* 🎫 *$10.*

FAMILY

St. Thomas Skyride. Fly skyward in a gondola to Paradise Point, an overlook with breathtaking views of Charlotte Amalie and the harbor. You'll find several shops, a bar, a restaurant, a wedding gazebo, and a Ferris wheel. A ¼-mile (½-km) hiking trail leads to spectacular views of St. Croix. Wear sturdy shoes, as the trail is steep and rocky. You can also skip the $21 gondola ride and taxi to the top for $4 per person from the Havensight Dock. ✉ *Rte. 30, across from Havensight Mall, Havensight* ☎ *340/774–9809* 🎫 *$21* ⊙ *Thurs.–Tues. 9–5, Wed. 9–9.*

BEACHES

FAMILY
Fodor's Choice
★

Coki Beach. Funky beach huts selling local foods such as pâtés (fried turnovers with a spicy ground-beef filling), quaint vendor kiosks, and a brigade of hair braiders and taxi men make this beach overlooking picturesque Thatch Cay feel like an amusement park. But this is the best place on the island to snorkel and scuba dive. Fish, including grunts, snappers, and wrasses, are like an effervescent cloud you can wave your hand through. Major renovations in late 2011 added a new bathhouse and boardwalk. **Amenities:** food and drink; lifeguards; parking; showers; restrooms; watersports. **Best for:** partiers; snorkeling. ⊠ *Rte. 388, next to Coral World Ocean Park, Estate Smith Bay.*

FAMILY
Fodor's Choice
★

Magens Bay. Deeded to the island as a public park, this heart-shape stretch of white sand is considered one of the most beautiful in the world. The bottom of the bay is flat and sandy, so this is a place for sunning and swimming rather than snorkeling. On weekends and holidays the sounds of music from groups partying under the sheds fill the air. There's a bar, snack shack, and beachwear boutique; bathhouses with restrooms, changing rooms, and saltwater showers are close by. Sunfish, paddleboats and paddleboards are the most popular rentals at the water-sports kiosk. East of the beach is Udder Delight, a one-room shop that serves a Virgin Islands tradition—a milk shake with a splash of Cruzan rum. (Kids can enjoy virgin versions, which have a touch of soursop, mango, or banana flavoring). If you arrive between 8 am and 5 pm, you pay an entrance fee of $4 per person, $2 per vehicle; it's free for children under 12. **Amenities:** food and drink; lifeguards; parking (fee); showers; restrooms; water sports. **Best for:** partiers; swimming; walking. ⊠ *Magens Bay, Rte. 35, at end of road on north side of island* ☎ *340/777–6300.*

SHOPPING

The prime shopping area in **Charlotte Amalie** is between Post Office and Market squares; it consists of two parallel streets that run east–west (Waterfront Highway and Main Street) and the alleyways that connect them. Particularly attractive are the historic **A. H. Riise Alley, Royal Dane Mall, Palm Passage,** and pastel-painted **International Plaza.**

Havensight Mall, next to the cruise-ship dock, may not be as charming as downtown Charlotte Amalie, but it does have more than 60 shops. It also has an excellent bookstore, a bank, a pharmacy, a gourmet grocery, and smaller branches of many downtown stores. The shops at **Port of $ale,** adjoining Havensight Mall (its buildings are pink instead of brown), sell discount goods. Next door to Port of $ale is the **Yacht Haven Grande** complex, with many upscale shops. At the Crown Bay cruise-ship pier, the **Crown Bay Center,** off the Harwood Highway in Sub Base about ½ mile (¾ km), has quite a few shops.

East of Charlotte Amalie on Route 38, **Tillett Gardens** is an oasis of artistic endeavor across from the Tutu Park Shopping Mall. The late Jim and Rhoda Tillett converted this Danish farm into an artists' retreat in 1959. Today you can watch artisans produce silk-screen fabrics, candles, pottery, and other handicrafts. Something special is often happening in the gardens as well: the Classics in the Gardens program is a classical music series presented under the stars, Arts Alive is an annual arts-and-crafts fair held in November, and the Pistarckle Theater holds its performances here.

FAMILY **Vendors Plaza.** Here merchants sell everything from T-shirts to African attire to leather goods. Look for local art among the ever-changing selections at this busy market. There are even a group of hair-braiders here too. ⊠ *Waterfront, west of Ft. Christian, Charlotte Amalie* ⊙ *Weekdays 8–6, weekends 9–1.*

ACTIVITIES

DIVING AND SNORKELING

FAMILY **Coki Dive Center.** Snorkeling and dive tours in the fish-filled reefs off Coki Beach are available from this PADI Five Star outfit, as are classes, including one on underwater photography. It's run by the avid diver Peter Jackson. ⊠ *Rte. 388, at Coki Point, Estate Frydendal* ☎ *340/775–4220* ⊕ *www.cokidive.com.*

Snuba of St. Thomas. In snuba, a snorkeling and scuba-diving hybrid, a 20-foot air hose connects you to the surface. The cost is $74. Children must be eight or older to participate. ⊠ *Rte. 388, at Coki Point, Estate Smith Bay* ☎ *340/693–8063* ⊕ *www.visnuba.com.*

FISHING

Charter Boat Center. This is a major source for sail and powerboat as well as sportfishing charters. Sportfishing charters offered include full-day trips for marlin as well as full, three-quarter, and half days for offshore and inshore species such as tuna, wahoo, dolphin (mahimahi), snapper, and kingfish. ⊠ *American Yacht Harbor, 6300 Smith Bay 16-3, Red Hook* ☎ *340/775–7990* ⊕ *www.charterboat.vi.*

GOLF

Mahogany Run Golf Course. The Mahogany Run Golf Course attracts golfers, who are drawn by its spectacular view of the British Virgin Islands and the challenging three-hole Devil's Triangle. At this Tom and George Fazio–designed, par-70, 18-hole course, there's a fully stocked pro shop, snack bar, and open-air clubhouse. Greens fees and half-cart fees for 18 holes are $165 in the winter season. The course is open daily, and there are frequently informal weekend tournaments. It's the only course on St. Thomas. ⊠ *Rte. 42, Estate Lovenlund* ☎ *340/777–6006, 800/253–7103* ⊕ *www.mahoganyrungolf.com.*

WHERE TO EAT

$$ ╳ **Cuzzin's Caribbean Restaurant and Bar.** In a 19th-century livery stable
CARIBBEAN on Back Street, this restaurant is hard to find but well worth it if you want to sample bona fide Virgin Islands cuisine. For lunch, order tender slivers of conch stewed in a rich onion-and-butter sauce, savory braised oxtail, or curried chicken. At dinner the island-style mutton, served in thick gravy and seasoned with locally grown herbs, offers a tasty treat that's deliciously different. Side dishes include peas and

rice, boiled green bananas, fried plantains, and potato stuffing. ⑤ *Average main: $18* ⊠ *7 Wimmelskafts Gade (Back St.), Charlotte Amalie* ☎ *340/777–4711.*

$$ ✗ **Gladys' Cafe.** Even if the local specialties—conch in butter sauce, salt
CARIBBEAN   fish and dumplings, hearty red bean soup—didn't make this a recom-
Fodor's Choice   mended café, it would be worth coming for Gladys's smile. Her cozy
★   alleyway restaurant is rich in atmosphere with its mahogany bar and
native stone walls, making dining a double delight. While you're here,
pick up a $5 or $10 bottle of her special hot sauce. There are mustard-,
oil-and-vinegar-, and tomato-based versions; the tomato-based sauce is
the hottest. ■ **TIP→ Only Amex is accepted.** ⑤ *Average main: $14* ⊠ *Waterfront, 28A Dronningens Gade, west side of Royal Dane Mall, Charlotte Amalie* ☎ *340/774–6604* ⊕ *www.gladyscafe.com* ☾ *No dinner.*

ST. VINCENT (KINGSTOWN)

Jane E. Zarem   You won't find glitzy resorts or flashy discos in St. Vincent. Rather,
you'll be fascinated by its busy capital, mountainous beauty, and fine
sailing waters. St. Vincent is the largest and northernmost island in the
Grenadines archipelago; Kingstown, the capital city of St. Vincent and
the Grenadines, is the government and business center and major port.
Except for one barren area on the island's northeast coast—remnants
of the 1979 eruption of La Soufrière, one of the last active volcanoes
in the Caribbean—the countryside is mountainous, lush, and green. St.
Vincent's topography thwarted European settlement for many years. As
colonization advanced elsewhere in the Caribbean, in fact, the island
became a refuge for Carib Indians—descendants of whom still live in
northeastern St. Vincent. After years of fighting and back-and-forth
territorial claims, British troops prevailed by overpowering the French
and banishing Carib warriors to Central America. Independent since
1979, St. Vincent and the Grenadines remains a member of the British
Commonwealth.

ESSENTIALS
CURRENCY
Eastern Caribbean (EC) dollar, but U.S. dollars are widely accepted.

TELEPHONE
Your cell phone should operate in St. Vincent, but roaming charges can
be hefty. Pay phones are readily available and best operated with the
prepaid phone cards that are sold at many stores. Telephone services
are available at the Cruise Ship Complex in Kingstown. For an interna-
tional operator, dial 115; to charge your call to a credit card, call 117.

COMING ASHORE

The Cruise Ship Complex at Kingstown, St. Vincent's capital city,
accommodates two cruise ships; additional vessels anchor offshore
and transport passengers to the jetty by launch. The facility has about
two-dozen shops that sell duty-free items and handicrafts. There's a
communications center, post office, tourist information desk, restau-
rant, and food court.

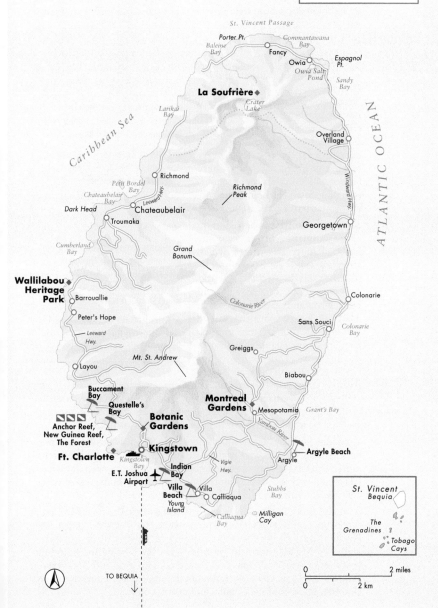

St. Vincent

KEY
- Beaches
- Cruise Ship Terminal
- Dive Sites
- Ferry

St. Vincent Passage

Porter Pt.
Commantawana Bay
Baleine Bay
Fancy
Espagnol Pt.
Owia
Owia Salt Pond
Sandy Bay

La Soufrière
Crater Lake

Larikai Bay

Caribbean Sea

Overland Village

Richmond

Richmond Peak

Pétit Bordel Bay
Chateaubelair Bay
Dark Head
Chateaubelair
Troumaka

Georgetown

ATLANTIC OCEAN

Windward Hwy.

Cumberland Bay

Grand Bonum

Wallilabou Heritage Park

Barrouallie

Peter's Hope

Colonarie River

Colonarie

Sans Souci
Colonarie Bay

Leeward Hwy.

Greiggs

Layou

Mt. St. Andrew

Biabou

Buccament Bay

Questelle's Bay

Montreal Gardens

Mesopotamia

Grant's Bay

Botanic Gardens

Anchor Reef, New Guinea Reef, The Forest

Yambou River

Kingstown

Ft. Charlotte
Kingstown Bay

Indian Bay

Vigie Hwy.

Argyle Beach

E.T. Joshua Airport

Villa Beach
Villa
Calliaqua

Argyle

Young Island

Stubbs Bay

Calliaqua Bay

Milligan Cay

St. Vincent
Bequia

The Grenadines

Tobago Cays

N

TO BEQUIA

0   2 miles
0   2 km

Buses and taxis are available at the wharf. Taxi drivers are well equipped to take you on an island tour; expect to pay $30 per hour for up to four passengers. The ferry to Bequia (one hour each way) is at the adjacent pier. Renting a car for just one day isn't advisable, since car rentals are expensive (at least $55 per day) and require a $24 temporary driving permit on top of that. It's almost always a better deal to take a tour, though you don't have to limit yourself to those offered by your ship.

EXPLORING ST. VINCENT

KINGSTOWN

The capital of St. Vincent and the Grenadines, a city of 13,500 residents, wraps around Kingstown Bay on the island's southwestern coast; a ring of green hills and ridges studded with houses forms a backdrop for the city. This is very much a working city, with a busy harbor and few concessions to tourists. Kingstown Harbour is the only deepwater port on the island.

A few gift shops can be found on and around **Bay Street,** near the harbor. Upper Bay Street, which stretches along the bayfront, bustles with daytime activity—workers going about their business and housewives doing their shopping. Many of Kingstown's downtown buildings are built of stone or brick brought to the island as ballast in the holds of 18th-century ships (and replaced with sugar and spices for the return trip to Europe). The Georgian-style stone arches and second-floor overhangs on former warehouses—which provide shelter from midday sun and the brief, cooling showers common to the tropics—have earned Kingstown the nickname "City of Arches."

> ### ST. VINCENT BEST BETS
>
> ■ **Island Tour.** Tour the greater Kingstown area, then travel up the leeward coast to Wallilabou.
>
> ■ **Falls of Baleine.** An all-day boat trip to the 60-foot falls is a beautiful way to spend a day.
>
> ■ **Ferry to Bequia.** Laid-back Bequia is one hour by ferry from St. Vincent.
>
> ■ **Hiking.** Whether you hike in the rain forest or do the more difficult climb of La Soufrière, it's worth exploring some of the island's rugged terrain.
>
> ■ **Tobago Cays.** These uninhabited islands in the Grenadines are the top destination for snorkeling.

Grenadines Wharf, at the south end of Bay Street, is busy with schooners loading supplies and ferries loading people bound for the Grenadines. The **Cruise-Ship Complex,** just south of the commercial wharf, has a mall with a dozen or more shops, plus restaurants, a post office, communications facilities, and a taxi-minibus stand.

A huge selection of produce fills the **Kingstown Produce Market,** a three-story building that takes up a whole city block on Upper Bay, Hillsboro, and Bedford streets in the center of town. It's noisy, colorful, and open Monday through Saturday—but the busiest times (and the best times to go) are Friday and Saturday mornings. In the courtyard, vendors sell local arts and crafts. On the upper floors, merchants sell clothing, household items, gifts, and other products.

Little Tokyo, so called because funding for the project was a gift from Japan, is a waterfront shopping area with a bustling indoor fish market and dozens of stalls where you can buy inexpensive homemade meals, drinks, ice cream, bread and cookies, clothing, trinkets, and even get a haircut.

St. George's Cathedral, on Grenville Street, is a pristine, creamy-yellow Anglican church built in 1820. The dignified Georgian architecture includes simple wooden pews, an ornate chandelier, and beautiful stained-glass windows; one was a gift from Queen Victoria, who actually commissioned it for London's St. Paul's Cathedral in honor of her first grandson. When the artist created an angel with a red robe, she was horrified by the color and sent the window abroad. The markers in the cathedral's graveyard recount the history of the island. Across the street is **St. Mary's Roman Catholic Cathedral of the Assumption,** built in stages beginning in 1823. The strangely appealing design is a blend of Moorish, Georgian, and Romanesque styles applied to black brick. Nearby, freed slaves built the **Kingstown Methodist Church** in 1841. The exterior is brick, simply decorated with quoins (solid blocks that form the corners), and the roof is held together by metal straps, bolts, and wooden pins. **Scots Kirk** was built from 1839 to 1880 by and for Scottish settlers but became a Seventh-Day Adventist church in 1952.

ELSEWHERE ON ST. VINCENT

FAMILY

Fodor'sChoice

★

Botanic Gardens. The oldest botanical garden in the Western Hemisphere is just north of downtown Kingstown—a few minutes by taxi. The garden was founded in 1765 after Captain Bligh—of *Bounty* fame—brought the first breadfruit tree to this island for landowners to propagate. The prolific bounty of the breadfruit trees was used to feed the slaves. You can see a direct descendant of the original tree among the specimen mahogany, rubber, teak, and other tropical trees and shrubs in the 20 acres of gardens. Two dozen rare St. Vincent parrots, confiscated from illegal collections, live in the small aviary. Guides explain all the medicinal and ornamental trees and shrubs; they also appreciate a tip (about $5 per person) at the end of the tour. ⊠ *Off Leeward Hwy., northeast of town, Montrose, Kingstown* ☎ *784/457–1003* ☒ *Free* ⊙ *Daily 6–6.*

FAMILY

Fodor'sChoice

★

Ft. Charlotte. Started by the French in 1786 and completed by the British in 1806, the fort was ultimately named for Britain's Queen Charlotte, wife of King George III. It sits on Berkshire Hill, a dramatic promontory 2 miles (3 km) north of Kingstown and 636 feet above sea level, affording a stunning view of the capital city and the Grenadines. Interestingly, cannons face inward—the fear of attack by the French and their Carib allies was far greater than any threat approaching from the sea. In any case, the fort saw no action. Nowadays, it serves as a signal station for ships; the ancient cells house historical paintings of the island by Lindsay Prescott. ⊠ *Berkshire Hill, 2 miles north of town, Kingstown.*

La Soufrière. This towering volcano, which last erupted in 1979, is 4,048 feet high and so huge in area that its surrounding mountainside covers virtually the entire northern third of the island. The eastern trail to the rim of the crater, a two-hour ascent, begins at Rabacca Dry River. ⊠ *Rabacca Dry River, Rabacca.*

Fodor'sChoice **Montreal Gardens.** Welsh-born landscape designer Timothy Vaughn reno-
★ vated 7½ acres of neglected commercial flower beds and a falling-down plantation house into a stunning, yet informal, garden spot. Anthurium, ginger lilies, bird-of-paradises, and other tropical flowers are planted in raised beds; tree ferns create a canopy of shade along the walkways. The gardens are in the shadow of majestic Grand Bonhomme Mountain, deep in the Mesopotamia Valley, about 12 miles (19 km) from Kingstown. ⊠ *Montreal St., Mesopotamia* ☎ *784/458–1198* ⊠ *$2* ⊙ *Dec.–Aug., weekdays 9–5.*

FAMILY **Wallilabou Heritage Park.** The Wallilabou Estate, halfway up the island's leeward coast, once produced cocoa, cotton, and arrowroot. Today, it is a recreational site with a river and small waterfall, which creates a small pool where you can take a freshwater plunge. You can also sunbathe, swim, picnic, or buy your lunch at Wallilabou Anchorage—a favorite stop for boaters staying overnight. The *Pirates of the Caribbean* movies left their mark on Wallilabou (pronounced wally-la-*boo*), a location used for filming the opening scenes of *The Curse of the Black Pearl* in 2003. Many of the buildings and docks built as stage sets remain, giving Wallilabou Bay (a port of entry for visiting yachts) an intriguingly historic (but ersatz) appearance. ⊠ *Wallilabou.*

BEACHES

St. Vincent's origin is volcanic, so its beaches range in color from golden-brown to black. Swimming is recommended only in the lagoons and bays along the leeward coast. By contrast, beaches on Bequia and the rest of the Grenadines have pure white sand, palm trees, and crystal-clear aquamarine water; some are even within walking distance of the jetty.

Indian Bay Beach. South of Kingstown and separated from Villa Beach by a rocky hill, Indian Bay has golden sand but is slightly rocky; it's very good for snorkeling. Grand View Hotel, high on a cliff overlooking Indian Bay Beach, operates a beach bar and grill. **Amenities:** food and drink. **Best for:** snorkeling; swimming. ⊠ *Villa.*

Villa Beach. The long stretch of sand in front of the row of hotels facing the Young Island Channel (Mariners, Paradise Beach, Sunset Shores, and Beachcombers hotels on the "mainland" and Young Island Resort across the channel) varies from 20 to 25 feet wide to practically nonexistent. The broadest, sandiest part is in front of Beachcombers Hotel, which is also the perfect spot for sunbathers to get lunch and liquid refreshments. It's a popular beach destination for cruise-ship passengers when a ship is in port. **Amenities:** food and drink; water sports. **Best for:** swimming. ⊠ *Villa.*

SHOPPING

The 12 small blocks that hug the waterfront in **downtown Kingstown** compose St. Vincent's main shopping district. Among the shops that sell goods to fulfill household needs are a few that sell local crafts, gifts, and souvenirs. Bargaining is neither expected nor appreciated. The **cruise-ship complex,** on the waterfront in Kingstown, has a collection of a dozen or so boutiques, shops, and restaurants that cater to cruise-ship passengers.

St. Vincent Craftsmen's Centre. Locally made grass floor mats, place mats, and other straw articles, as well as batik cloth, handmade West Indian dolls, hand-painted calabashes, and framed artwork are all available at this store that's three blocks from the wharf. No credit cards are accepted. ✉ *Frenches St., Kingstown* ☎ *784/457–2516.*

ACTIVITIES

DIVING AND SNORKELING

Novices and advanced divers alike will be impressed by the marine life in the waters surrounding St. Vincent and the Grenadines—brilliant sponges, huge deepwater coral trees, and shallow reefs teeming with colorful fish. The best dive spots on St. Vincent are in the small bays along the coast between Kingstown and Layou; many are within 20 yards of shore and only 20 feet to 30 feet down.

Anchor Reef has excellent visibility for viewing a deep-black coral garden, schools of squid, seahorses, and maybe a small octopus. The **Forest,** a shallow dive, is still dramatic, with soft corals in pastel colors and schools of small fish. **New Guinea Reef** slopes to 90 feet (28 meters) and can't be matched for its quantity of corals and sponges. The pristine waters surrounding the **Tobago Cays,** in the Southern Grenadines, will give you a world-class diving experience.

Dive Fantasea. Earl Habich takes guests on dive and snorkeling trips along the St. Vincent coast and to the Tobago Cays on his custom-built 42-foot snorkel/dive boat. ✉ *Villa Beach, Villa* ☎ *784/457–4477* ⊕ *www.fantaseatours.com.*

Dive St. Vincent. Two PADI-certified dive masters offer beginner and certification courses for ages eight and up, advanced water excursions along the St. Vincent coast and to the southern Grenadines for diving connoisseurs, and an introductory scuba lesson for novices. ✉ *Young Island Dock, Villa Beach, Villa* ☎ *784/457–4714, 784/457–4948* ⊕ *www.divestvincent.com.*

FISHING

From Villa Beach or Indian Bay on St. Vincent, you can go on a half-day or full-day fishing trip for $400–$600 for up to four people, including all equipment and lunch.

Crystal Blue Sportfishing Charters. These sportfishing charters are on a 34-foot pirogue and are for both casual and serious fishermen. ✉ *Villa* ☎ *784/457–4532.*

WHERE TO EAT

$$$ ✕ **Basil's Bar and Restaurant.** It's not just the air-conditioning that makes
CARIBBEAN this restaurant cool. Basil's, at street level at the Cobblestone Inn, is
owned by Basil Charles, whose Basil's Beach Bar on Mustique is a
hangout for the vacationing rich and famous. This is the Kingstown
power-lunch venue. Local businesspeople gather for the daily buffet
(weekdays) or full menu of salads, sandwiches, barbecued chicken,
or fresh seafood platters. Dinner entrées of pasta, local seafood, and
chicken are served at candlelit tables. ⑤ *Average main: $24* ⊠ *Upper
Bay St., below Cobblestone Inn, Kingstown* ☎ *784/457–2713* ⊕ *www.
basilsbar.com* ☉ *Closed Sun.*

$$ ✕ **Cobblestone Roof-Top Bar & Restaurant.** To reach what is perhaps the
CARIBBEAN most pleasant, the breeziest, and the most satisfying breakfast and lunch
spot in downtown Kingstown, diners must climb the equivalent of three
flights of interior stone steps within the historic Cobblestone Inn. But
getting to the open-air rooftop restaurant is half the fun, as en route diners get an up-close view of a 19th-century sugar (and later arrowroot)
Georgian warehouse that's now a very appealing boutique inn. A full
breakfast menu is available to hotel guests and the public alike. The luncheon menu ranges from homemade soups, salads (tuna, chicken, fruit,
or tossed), sandwiches, or burgers and fries to full meals of roast beef,
stewed chicken, or grilled fish served with rice, plantains, macaroni pie,
and fresh local vegetables. ⑤ *Average main: $15* ⊠ *Cobblestone Inn,
Upper Bay St., Kingstown* ☎ *784/456–1937* ☉ *No dinner.*

TORTOLA (ROAD TOWN)

Lynda Lohr   Once a sleepy backwater, Tortola is definitely busy these days, particularly when several cruise ships tie up at the Road Town dock. Passengers
crowd the streets and shops, and open-air jitneys filled with cruise-
ship passengers create bottlenecks on the island's byways. That said, most
folks visit Tortola to relax on its deserted sands or linger over lunch at
one of its many delightful restaurants. Beaches are never more than a
few miles away, and the steep green hills that form Tortola's spine are
fanned by gentle trade winds. The neighboring islands glimmer like
emeralds in a sea of sapphire. Tortola doesn't have many historic sights,
but it does have abundant natural beauty. Beware of the roads, which
are extraordinarily steep and twisting, making driving demanding. The
best beaches are on the north shore.

ESSENTIALS

CURRENCY
The U.S. dollar.

TELEPHONE
To call anywhere in the BVI once you've arrived, dial all seven digits. A
local call from a pay phone costs 25¢, but such phones are sometimes
on the blink. An alternative is a Caribbean phone card, available in
$5, $10, and $20 denominations. They're sold at most major hotels
and many stores, and can be used to call within the BVI as well as all
over the Caribbean, and to access USADirect from special phone-card

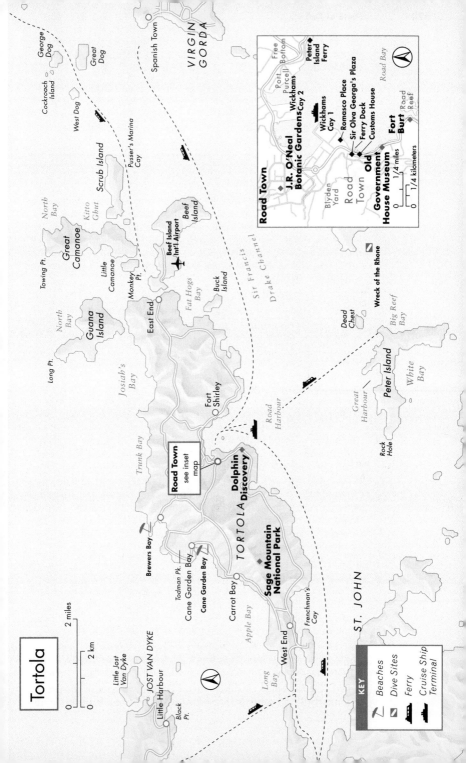

phones. If you're coming ashore at the cruise-ship dock, you'll find pay phones right on the dock. If a tender drops you right in Road Town at the ferry dock, phones are located in the terminal.

AT&T has service in nearby St. John, USVI, so it's possible to get service from there in some spots in Road Town and along the waterfront highway that leads to the West End. You may not have to pay international roaming charges on some U.S. cell-phone plans if you can connect with this network.

COMING ASHORE

Large cruise ships usually anchor in Road Town Harbor and bring passengers ashore by tender. Small ships can sometimes tie up at Wickham's Cay dock. Either way, it's a short stroll to Road Town. If your ship isn't going to Virgin Gorda, you can make the 12-mile (19-km) trip by ferry from the dock in Road Town in about 30 minutes for about $30 round-trip, but you'll still have to take a taxi to get to the Baths for swimming and snorkeling, so it's not necessarily a bad deal to go on your ship's shore excursion.

There are taxi stands at Wickham's Cay and in Road Town. Taxis are unmetered, and there are minimums for travel throughout the island, so it's usually cheaper to travel in groups. Negotiate to get the best fares, as there is no set fee schedule. If you are in the islands for just a day, it's usually more cost-effective to share a taxi with a small group than to rent a car, since you'd have to pay an agency at Wickham's Cay or in Road Town car-rental charges of at least $50 a day. You must be at least age 25 to rent a car.

EXPLORING TORTOLA

The bustling capital of the BVI looks out over Road Harbour. It takes only an hour or so to stroll down Main Street and along the waterfront, checking out the traditional West Indian buildings painted in pastel colors and with corrugated-tin roofs, bright shutters, and delicate fretwork trim. For sightseeing brochures and the latest information on everything from taxi rates to ferry schedules, stop in at the BVI Tourist Board office. Or just choose a seat on one of the benches in Sir Olva Georges Square, on Waterfront Drive, and watch the people come and go from the ferry dock and customs office across the street.

ROAD TOWN

FAMILY **Dolphin Discovery.** Get up close and personal with dolphins as they swim in a spacious seaside pen. There are three different programs. In the Royal Swim, dolphins tow participants around the pen. The less expensive Adventure and Discovery programs allow you to touch the dolphins. ⊠ *Waterfront Dr.* ☎ *284/494–7675, 888/393–5158* ⊕ *www. dolphindiscovery.com* ☞ *Royal Swim $149, Adventure $99, Discovery $79* ☉ *Royal Swim daily at 10, noon, 2, and 4. Adventure and Discovery daily at 11 and 1.*

Ft. Burt. The most intact historic ruin on Tortola was built by the Dutch in the early 17th century to safeguard Road Harbour. It sits on a hill at the western edge of Road Town and is now the site of a small hotel and restaurant. The foundations and magazine remain, and the structure offers a commanding view of the harbor. ⊠ *Waterfront Dr.* 🎫 *Free* ☉ *Daily dawn–dusk.*

J. R. O'Neal Botanic Gardens. Take a walk through this 4-acre showcase of lush plant life. There are sections devoted to prickly cacti and succulents, hothouses for ferns and orchids, gardens of medicinal herbs, and plants and trees indigenous to the seashore. From the tourist office in Road Town, cross Waterfront Drive and walk one block over to Main Street and turn right. Keep walking until you see the high school. The gardens are on your left. ⊠ *Botanic Station* 🕾 *284/494–3650* ⊕ *www. bvinationalparkstrust.org* 🎫 *$3* ☉ *Mon.–Sat. 8:30–4:30.*

Fodor'sChoice **Old Government House Museum.** The official government residence until
★ 1997, this gracious building now displays a nice collection of artifacts from Tortola's past. The rooms are filled with period furniture, hand-painted china, books signed by Queen Elizabeth II on her 1966 and 1977 visits, and numerous items reflecting Tortola's seafaring legacy. ⊠ *Waterfront Dr.* 🕾 *284/494–4091* ⊕ *www.oghm.org* 🎫 *$3* ☉ *Weekdays 9–3.*

ELSEWHERE ON TORTOLA

Sage Mountain National Park. At 1,716 feet, Sage Mountain is the highest peak in the BVI. From the parking area, a trail leads you in a loop not only to the peak itself (and extraordinary views) but also to a small rain forest that is sometimes shrouded in mist. Most of the forest was cut down over the centuries for timber, to create pastureland, or for growing sugarcane, cotton, and other crops. In 1964 this park was established to preserve what remained. Up here you can see mahogany trees, white cedars, mountain guavas, elephant-ear vines, mamey trees, and giant bullet woods, to say nothing of such birds as mountain doves and thrushes. Take a taxi from Road Town or drive up Joe's Hill Road and make a left onto Ridge Road toward Chalwell and Doty villages. The road dead-ends at the park. ⊠ *Ridge Rd., Sage Mountain* 🕾 *284/852–3650* ⊕ *www.bvinationalparkstrust.org* 🎫 *$3* ☉ *Daily dawn–dusk.*

TORTOLA BEST BETS

■ **The** *Rhone.* For certified divers, this is one of the best wreck dives in the Caribbean.

■ **Sage Mountain.** The highest peak in the Virgin Islands has breathtaking views and is a great hiking destination.

■ **Sailing Trips.** Because of its proximity to small islets and good snorkeling sights, Tortola is the sailing capital of the Caribbean.

■ **Virgin Gorda.** Ferries link Tortola and Virgin Gorda, making a half-day trip to the Baths quite possible (just be sure to check the ferry schedules before heading out).

7

BEACHES

Tortola's north side has several perfect palm-fringed white-sand beaches that curl around turquoise bays and coves. Nearly all are accessible by car (preferably one with four-wheel drive), albeit down bumpy roads that corkscrew precipitously. Facilities run the gamut from absolutely none to a number of beachside bars and restaurants as well as places to rent water-sports equipment.

Brewers Bay Beach. This beach is easy to find, but the steep, twisting paved roads leading down the hill to it can be a bit daunting. An old sugar mill and ruins of a rum distillery are off the beach along the road. You can actually reach the beach from either Brewers Bay Road East or Brewers Bay Road West. **Amenities:** none. **Best for:** snorkeling, swimming. ⊠ *Brewers Bay Rd. E, off Cane Garden Bay Rd., Brewers Bay.*

Cane Garden Bay Beach. A silky stretch of sand, Cane Garden Bay has exceptionally calm, crystalline waters—except when storms at sea turn the water murky. Snorkeling is good along the edges. Casual guesthouses, restaurants, bars, and shops are steps from the beach in the growing village of the same name. The beach is a laid-back, even somewhat funky place to put down your towel. It's the closest beach to Road Town—one steep uphill and downhill drive—and one of the BVI's best-known anchorages (unfortunately, it can be very crowded). Watersports shops rent equipment. **Amenities:** food and drink; toilets; water sports. **Best for:** snorkeling; swimming. ⊠ *Cane Garden Bay Rd., off Ridge Rd., Cane Garden Bay.*

SHOPPING

Many shops and boutiques are clustered along and just off Road Town's **Main Street.** You can shop in Road Town's **Wickham's Cay I** adjacent to the marina. The **Crafts Alive Market** on the Road Town waterfront is a collection of colorful West Indian–style buildings with shops that carry items made in the BVI. You might find pretty baskets or interesting pottery or perhaps a bottle of home-brewed hot sauce. An ever-growing number of art and clothing stores are opening at **Soper's Hole** in West End.

ACTIVITIES

DIVING AND SNORKELING

The *Chikuzen,* sunk northwest of Brewers Bay in 1981, is a 246-foot vessel in 75 feet of water; it's home to thousands of fish, colorful corals, and big rays. In 1867 the **RMS *Rhone,*** a 310-foot royal mail steamer, split in two when it sank in a devastating hurricane. It's so well preserved that it was used as an underwater prop in the movie *The Deep.* You can see the crow's nest and bowsprit, the cargo hold in the bow, and the engine and enormous propeller shaft in the stern. Its four parts are at various depths from 30 to 80 feet. Get yourself some snorkeling gear and hop aboard a dive boat to this wreck near Salt Island (across the channel from Road Town). Every dive outfit in the BVI runs scuba and snorkel tours to this part of the BVI National Parks Trust; if you have time for only one trip, make it this one. Rates start at around $75 for a one-tank dive and $100 for a two-tank dive.

Blue Waters Divers. If you're chartering a sailboat, Blue Waters Divers' boat will meet yours at Peter, Salt, Norman, or Cooper Island for a rendezvous dive. The company teaches resort, open-water, rescue, and advanced diving courses, and also makes daily dive trips. Rates include all equipment as well as instruction. Reserve two days in advance. ⊠ *Nanny Cay Marina, Nanny Cay* ☎ *284/494–2847* ⊕ *www. bluewaterdiversbvi.com.*

FISHING

Most of the boats that take you deep-sea fishing for bluefish, wahoo, swordfish, and shark leave from nearby St. Thomas, but local anglers like to fish the shallower water for bonefish. A half day runs about $480, a full day around $850.

Caribbean Fly Fishing ⊠ *Nanny Cay Marina, Nanny Cay* ☎ *284/494–4797* ⊕ *www.caribflyfishing.com.*

SAILING

FAMILY

Fodor'sChoice

★

The BVI are among the world's most popular sailing destinations. They're close together and surrounded by calm waters, so it's fairly easy to sail from one anchorage to the next.

Aristocat Charters. This company's 48-foot catamaran sets sail daily to Jost Van Dyke, Norman Island, and other small islands. ⊠ *West End* ☎ *284/499–1249* ⊕ *www.aristocatcharters.com.*

White Squall II. This 80-foot schooner has regularly scheduled day sails to The Baths at Virgin Gorda, Cooper, the Indians, and the Caves at Norman Island. ⊠ *Village Cay Marina, Road Town* ☎ *284/541–2222* ⊕ *www.whitesquall2.com.*

WHERE TO EAT

$$

ITALIAN

Fodor'sChoice

★

✕ **Capriccio di Mare.** Stop by this casual, authentic Italian outdoor café for an espresso, a fresh pastry, a bowl of perfectly cooked penne, or a crispy tomato-and-mozzarella pizza. Drink specialties include a mango Bellini, an adaptation of the famous cocktail served at Harry's Bar in Venice. $ *Average main: $19* ⊠ *Waterfront Dr., Road Town* ☎ *284/494–5369* ⌖ *Reservations not accepted* ☽ *Closed Sun.*

$$$$

ECLECTIC

✕ **Village Cay Restaurant.** Docked sailboats stretch nearly as far as the eye can see at this busy Road Town restaurant. Its alfresco dining and convivial atmosphere make it popular with both locals and visitors. For lunch, try the grouper club sandwich with an ancho chili mayonnaise. Dinner offerings run to fish served a variety of ways, including West Indian–style with okra, onions, and peppers, as well as a seafood jambalaya with lobster, crayfish, shrimp, mussels, crab, and fish in a mango-passion-fruit sauce. $ *Average main: $32* ⊠ *Wickhams Cay I, Road Town* ☎ *284/494–2771.*

VIRGIN GORDA (THE VALLEY)

Lynda Lohr

Virgin Gorda, or "Fat Virgin," received its name from Christopher Columbus. The explorer envisioned the island as a pregnant woman in languid recline with Gorda Peak being her big belly and the boulders of the Baths her toes. Different in topography from Tortola, with its arid landscape covered with scrub brush and cactus, Virgin Gorda has a slower pace of life, too. Goats and cattle have the right of way, and the unpretentious friendliness of the people is winning. The top sight (and beach for that matter) is the Baths, which draws scores of cruise-ship passengers and day-trippers to its giant boulders and grottoes that form a perfect snorkeling environment. While ships used to stop only in Tortola, saving Virgin Gorda for shore excursions, smaller ships are coming increasingly to Virgin Gorda directly.

ESSENTIALS
CURRENCY
The U.S. dollar.

TELEPHONE
To call anywhere in the BVI once you've arrived, dial all seven digits. There are no longer any pay phones on Virgin Gorda. Instead, get a Caribbean phone card, available in $5, $10, and $20 denominations. They're sold at most major hotels and many stores, and can be used to call within the BVI, as well as all over the Caribbean. Your own cell phone may work in the BVI, but you'll probably pay a hefty roaming fee.

COMING ASHORE

Ships often dock off Spanish Town, Leverick Bay, or in North Sound and tender passengers to the ferry dock. A few taxis will be available at Leverick Bay and at Gun Creek in North Sound—you can set up an island tour for about $45 for two people—but Leverick Bay and North Sound are far away from the Baths, the island's must-see beach, so a shore excursion is often the best choice. If you are tendered to Spanish Town, then it's possible to take a shuttle taxi to the Baths for as little as $4 per person each way. If you are on Virgin Gorda for just a day, it's usually more cost-effective to share a taxi with a small group than to rent a car, since you'd have to pay car-rental charges of at least $50 a day. You must be at least age 25 to rent a car.

EXPLORING VIRGIN GORDA

There are few roads, and most byways don't follow the scalloped shore-line. The main route sticks resolutely to the center of the island, link-ing the Baths on the southern tip with Gun Creek and Leverick Bay at North Sound. The craggy coast, scissored with grottoes and fringed by palms and boulders, has a primitive beauty. If you drive, you can hit all the sights in one day. Stop to climb Gorda Peak, which is in the island's center. Signposting is erratic, so come prepared with a map.

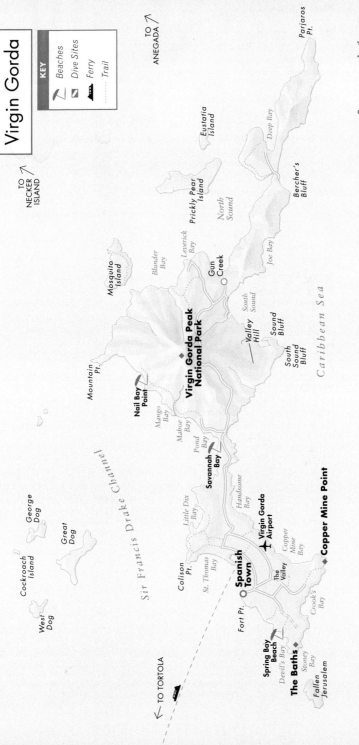

Virgin Gorda

KEY

- Beaches
- Dive Sites
- Ferry
- Trail

TO NECKER ISLAND

TO ANEGADA

Parjaros Pt.

Eustatia Island

Deep Bay

Prickly Pear Island

Bercher's Bluff

Mosquito Island

Blunder Bay

Leverick Bay

North Sound

Gun Creek

Joe Bay

Caribbean Sea

Mountain Pt.

Nail Bay Point

Virgin Gorda Peak National Park

Valley Hill

South Sound

Sound Bluff

South Sound Bluff

Mango Bay

Mahoe Bay

Pond Bay

Savannah Bay

Handsome Bay

Little Dix Bay

Colison Pt.

St. Thomas Bay

Virgin Gorda Airport

The Valley

Copper Mine Bay

Copper Mine Point

Sir Francis Drake Channel

Cockroach Island

George Dog

Great Dog

West Dog

Fort Pt.

Spanish Town

Crook's Bay

Spring Bay Beach

Devil's Bay

Stoney Bay

The Baths

Fallen Jerusalem

TO TORTOLA

1 miles

1 kilometers

0

FAMILY
Fodor's Choice
★

The Baths National Park. At Virgin Gorda's most celebrated sight, giant boulders are scattered about the beach and in the water. Some are almost as large as houses and form remarkable grottoes. Climb between these rocks to swim in the many placid pools. Early morning and late afternoon are the best times to visit if you want to avoid crowds. If it's privacy you crave, follow the shore northward to quieter bays— Spring Bay, the Crawl, Little Trunk, and Valley Trunk—or head south to Devil's Bay. ⊠ *Off Tower Rd., The Valley* ☎ *284/852–3650* ⊕ *www. bvinationalparkstrust.org* 🎫 *$3* ☉ *Daily dawn–dusk.*

Copper Mine Point. A tall stone shaft silhouetted against the sky and a small stone structure that overlooks the sea are part of what was once a copper mine, now in ruins. Established 400 years ago, it was worked first by the Spanish, then by the English, until the early 20th century. The route is not well marked, so turn inland near LSL Restaurant and look for the hard-to-see sign pointing the way. ⊠ *Copper Mine Rd., The Valley* ⊕ *www.bvinationalparkstrust.org* 🎫 *Free.*

Spanish Town. Virgin Gorda's peaceful main settlement, on the island's southern wing, is so tiny that it barely qualifies as a town at all. Also known as the Valley, Spanish Town has a marina, some shops, and a couple of car-rental agencies. Just north of town is the ferry slip. At the Virgin Gorda Yacht Harbour you can stroll along the dock and do a little shopping. ⊠ *Spanish Town.*

Virgin Gorda Peak National Park. There are two trails at this 265-acre park, which contains the island's highest point, at 1,359 feet. Signs on North Sound Road mark both entrances. It's about a 15-minute hike from either entrance up to a small clearing, where you can climb a ladder to the platform of a wooden observation tower and a spectacular 360-degree view. ⊠ *North Sound Rd., Gorda Peak* ⊕ *www. bvinationalparkstrust.org* 🎫 *Free.*

BEACHES

The best beaches are easily reached by water, although they're also accessible on foot, usually after a moderately strenuous 10- to 15-minute hike. Anybody going to Virgin Gorda should experience swimming or snorkeling among its unique boulder formations, which can be visited at several beaches along Lee Road. The most popular of these spots is the Baths, but there are several others nearby that are easily reached.

The Baths Beach. This stunning maze of huge granite boulders extending into the sea is usually crowded midday with day-trippers. The snorkeling is good, and you're likely to see a wide variety of fish, but watch out for dinghies coming ashore from the numerous sailboats anchored offshore. Public bathrooms and a handful of bars and shops are close to the water and at the start of the path that leads to the beach. Lockers are available to keep belongings safe. **Amenities:** food and drink; parking; toilets. **Best for:** snorkeling; swimming. ⊠ *About 1 mile (1½ km) west of Spanish Town ferry dock on Tower Rd., The Valley* ☎ *284/852–3650* ⊕ *www.bvinationalparkstrust.org* ☜ *$3* ☉ *Daily dawn–dusk.*

Savannah Bay Beach. This is a wonderfully private beach close to Spanish Town. It may not always be completely deserted, but you can find a spot to yourself on this long stretch of soft, white sand. Bring your own mask, fins, and snorkel, as there are no facilities. The view from above is a photographer's delight. **Amenities:** none. **Best for:** solitude; snorkeling; swimming. ⊠ *Off N. Sound Rd., ¾ miles (1¼ km) east of Spanish Town ferry dock, Savannah Bay* ☜ *Free* ☉ *Daily dawn–dusk.*

Spring Bay Beach. This national-park beach that gets much less traffic than the nearby Baths, and has the similarly large, imposing boulders that create interesting grottoes for swimming. It also has no admission fee, unlike the more popular Baths. The snorkeling is excellent, and the grounds include swings and picnic tables. **Amenities:** none. **Best for:** snorkeling; swimming. ⊠ *Off Tower Rd., 1 mile (1½ km) west of Spanish Town ferry dock, The Valley* ☎ *284/852–3650* ⊕ *www. bvinationalparkstrust.org* ☜ *Free* ☉ *Daily dawn–dusk.*

SHOPPING

Most boutiques are within hotel complexes or at Virgin Gorda Yacht Harbour. Two of the best are at Biras Creek and Little Dix Bay. Other properties—the Bitter End and Leverick Bay—have small but equally select boutiques.

ACTIVITIES

DIVING AND SNORKELING

The dive companies on Virgin Gorda are all certified by PADI. Costs vary, but count on paying about $100 for a one-tank dive and $130 for a two-tank dive. All dive operators offer introductory courses as well as certification and advanced courses. Should you get an attack of the bends, which can happen when you ascend too rapidly, the nearest decompression chamber is at Roy L. Schneider Regional Medical Center in St. Thomas.

Dive BVI. In addition to day trips, Dive BVI also offers expert instruction and certification. ⊠ *Virgin Gorda Yacht Harbour, Lee Rd., Spanish Town* ☎ *284/495–5513, 800/848–7078* ⊕ *www.divebvi.com.*

Sunchaser Scuba. Resort, advanced, and rescue courses are all available here. ⊠ *Bitter End Yacht Club, North Sound* ☎ *284/495–9638, 800/932–4286* ⊕ *www.sunchaserscuba.com.*

SAILING AND BOATING

The BVI waters are calm, and terrific places to learn to sail. You can also rent sea kayaks, waterskiing equipment, dinghies, and powerboats, or take a parasailing trip.

Double "D" Charters. If you just want to sit back, relax, and let the captain take the helm, choose a sailing or power yacht from Double "D"

> **CAUTION: OBSTRUCTED VIEWS**
>
> If you pick an outside cabin, check to make sure your view of the sea is not obstructed by a lifeboat. The ship's deck plan will help you figure it out.

Charters. Rates are $75 for a half-day trip and $125 for a full-day island-hopping excursion. Private full-day cruises or sails for up to eight people run from $950. ⊠ *Virgin Gorda Yacht Harbour, Lee Rd., Spanish Town* ☎ *284/499–2479* ⊕ *www.doubledbvi.com.*

WHERE TO EAT

$$
ECLECTIC

✕ **Bath and Turtle.** You can sit back and relax at this informal tavern with a friendly staff—although the noise from the television can sometimes be a bit much. Well-stuffed sandwiches, homemade pizzas, pasta dishes, and daily specials such as conch soup round out the casual menu. Local musicians perform many Wednesday and Sunday nights. ⑤ *Average main: $19* ⊠ *Virgin Gorda Yacht Harbour, Lee Rd., Spanish Town* ☎ *284/495–5239* ⊕ *www.bathandturtle.com.*

$$$$
ECLECTIC
FAMILY

✕ **Top of the Baths.** At the entrance to The Baths, this popular restaurant has tables on an outdoor terrace or in an open-air pavilion; all have stunning views of the Sir Francis Drake Channel. The restaurant starts serving at 8 am. For lunch, hamburgers, coconut chicken sandwiches, and fish-and-chips are among the offerings. For dessert, the key lime pie is excellent. The Sunday barbecue, served from noon until 3 pm, is an island event. ⑤ *Average main: $23* ⊠ *The Valley* ☎ *284/495–5497* ⊕ *www.topofthebaths.com* ⊘ *No dinner Mon.*

INDEX

PHOTO CREDITS

Chapter 1: Cruising: The Basics: 15, Andy Newman/Carnival Cruise Lines. 32-33 (diagrams and photos), Celebrity Cruises. Chapter 2: Planning Your Cruise: 45, Radisson Seven Seas Cruises. Chapter 3: Getting Ready: 83, Holland America Line. Chapter 4: Enjoying Your Cruise: 103, Holland America Line. Chapter 5: Cruise Lines & Cruise Ships: 139, Radisson Seven Seas Cruises. 148 (top), Michel Verdure/Azamara Cruises. 148 (bottom) and 150 (both), Azamara Cruises. 152 (top), Fernando Diez/Celebrity Cruises. 152 (bottom), Celebrity Cruises. 153, Nick Garcia/Celebrity Cruises. 154 (top), Andy Newman/Carnival Cruise Lines. 154 (bottom), Carnival Cruise Lines. 155-68, Andy Newman/Carnival Cruise Lines. 170-72, Celebrity Cruises. 174 (top and bottom), and 175, Stephen Beaudet/Celebrity Cruises. 176 (top and bottom), Celebrity Cruises. 178 (top and bottom), Celebrity Cruises. 180 (top), Philip Plisson. 180 (bottom), Mike Louagie. 181 (top), Philip Plisson. 181 (bottom), Francois Lefebvre. 182 (top and center) Francois Lefebvre. 182 (bottom), Eric Laignel. 184-89, Costa Cruises. 190 (top and bottom), Johansen Krause/Crystal Cruises. 191 and 192 (top and center), Crystal Cruises. 192 (bottom), Corey Weiner/Red Square/Crystal Cruises. 194 (top and bottom), Crystal Cruises. 196 (top), Crystal Cruises. 196 (bottom), Corey Weiner/Red Square/Crystal Cruises. 198-99, 200 (top), and 202-203, Cunard Line (center and bottom) and 204, Michel Verdure/Cunard Line. 206-07 Cunard Images. 208-212, © Disney. 214 (top), Disney Dream Inaugural Cruise 178 by Samantha Chapnick http//www.flickr.com/photos/sierraandi/5425983156/Attribution-ShareAlike License. 214 (bottom), Disney Dream Inaugural Cruise 98 by Samantha Capnick http//www.fl ickr.com/photos/sierraandi/5425782064/Attribution-ShareAlikeLicense. 216-18, Holland America Line. 220 (top), Andy Newman/Holland America Line. 220 (bottom) and 221, Michel Verdure/Holland America Line. 222 (top), Andy Newman/Holland America Line. 222 (bottom), Holland America Line. 224-27, Holland America Line. 228-33, MSC Cruises. 234-36, Norwegian Cruise Line. 238 (top and bottom), © NCL. 240 (top and bottom), Rick Diaz/Norwegian Cruise Line, 241-43, Norwegian Cruise Line, 244-45, Michel Verdure/Norwegian Cruise Line. 246-47, Norwegian Cruise Line. 248-55, Oceania Cruises. 256 (top), Pacific Beachcombers/Paul Gaugin Cruises. 256 (bottom) & 257, Paul Gaugin Cruises. 258 (top), Tim McKenna/Paul Gaugin Cruises. 258 (bottom) & 260, Paul Gaigin Cruises. 262-64, Princess Cruises. 266 (top), Phill Jackson Photography. 266 (bottom), Phill Jackson & Steve Dunlop. 268, Princess Cruises. 269, Andy Newman/Princess Cruises. 270-75, Princess Cruises. 276-81, Regent Seven Seas Cruises. 282-84, Royal Caribbean. 286 (top), Michel Verdure/Royal Caribbean, 286 (bottom), Katherine Wessel/Royal Caribbean. 288 (top and bottom), and 289, Hugh Stewart/Royal Caribbean International. 290 (both) Johansen Krause/Royal Caribbean International. 292-99, Royal Caribbean International. 300 (top) and 301 (top), Johansen Krause/ The Yachts of Seabourn. 300 (bottom) and 301 (bottom), The Yachts of Seabourn. 302 (top), Johansen Krause/The Yachts of Seabourn. 302 (center and bottom) and 304-07, The Yachts of Seabourn. 308-13, SeaDream Yacht Club. 314-23, Silversea Cruises. 324-31, Star Clippers. 332-39, Windstar Cruises. Chapter 6: Ports of Embarkation: 341, Royal Caribbean International. Chapter 7: Ports of Call: 429, Celebrity Cruises. Front cover: Danny Lehman/Corbis [Description: Ocho Rios, Jamaica](exp. after 5th ed.). From left to right: onfilm/iStockphoto; Mark Yarchoan/Shutterstock; Yaromir/Shutterstock. Spine: moomsabuy/Shutterstock.